Political Science

Political Science

A Comprehensive Study

Rajesh Mishra

Sangam Books

POLITICAL SCIENCE: A COMPREHENSIVE STUDY

SANGAM BOOKS
(An imprint of The Agricultural Development Commercial Credit and Industrial Investment Company Private Limited)

Registered Office
3-6-747/1/A & 3-6-754/1 Himayatnagar, Hyderabad 500 029, Telangana, India
Email: info@sangambooks.com

First published 2024

ISBN 978-93-95308-29-8

Distributed by
Orient Blackswan Private Limited
3-6-752 Himayatnagar, Hyderabad 500 029, Telangana, India
Email: centraloffice@orientblackswan.com

Other Offices
Bengaluru, Chennai, Guwahati, Hyderabad, Kolkata, Mumbai, New Delhi, Noida, Patna, Visakhapatnam

Typeset in Adobe Garamond Pro 11/12.75
by Shine Graphics, Delhi 110 094

Printed at
Akash Press, Delhi 110 020

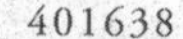

Published by
Sangam Books
(An imprint of The Agricultural Development Commercial Credit And Industrial Investment Company Private Limited)
3-6-747/1/A & 3-6-754/1 Himayatnagar, Hyderabad 500 029, Telangana, India
Email: info@sangambooks.com

CONTENTS

Unit II: Political Thought

Unit III: Indian Political Thought

Unit VI: India's Foreign Policy

Unit 8: Governance and Public Policy in India

LIST OF TABLES

LIST OF FIGURES

PREFACE

In contemporary times, one is surrounded with different competitions and examinations, each having its own significance. Amongst all of them, the UGC-NET examination has emerged as a game-changing one due to its status as a qualifying test.

The syllabus of UGC-NET is vast and multidimensional. It covers different subjects and themes such as political theory, public administration, Indian polity, international relations, and others. Covering all these topics in one book and in a manner that is both comprehensive and succinct was quite a challenging task. The changing trend from fact-centric to concept-centric understanding has also been taken into account while writing the book. This book caters to all the needs of the student community, as per these changing trends, and to prepare them for future trends too. Synthesising fact with concept and theory with praxis has been the main motive behind writing this book.

It would be wrong to claim that this is the first book ever written for political science UGC-NET. However, it would not be wrong to claim that this book is unique, as it encompasses all required subject matter comprehensively within one volume. The primary vision guiding this book was to ensure that after reading this book, students do not feel the need to search for any supplementary material.

Finally, I would like to say that though this book is written mainly for the UGC-NET student community, it can serve very well as an insightful book for all individuals who have the urge to understand politics—at the local, national or international levels. After all, there is no such thing as being apolitical. So one may as well become an informed political citizen.

ACKNOWLEDGEMENTS

As per the fundamental beliefs of Indian thought and philosophy, one is born with a multitude of debts. This is why the work done by any one person involves the contribution of infinite people. Of these, some are worth mentioning here. I am grateful to Professors Nalini Panth and Rajni Ranjan Jha, who inspired me to study the most incredible and fascinating books on political science. I am grateful that they helped me develop an investigation-based and reflective approach to studying the subject.

It would not be an exaggeration to say that nothing would have been possible without the blessings of my parents. Apart from that, the contribution of Rakesh ji, manager of the Saraswati IAS Institute, New Delhi, and Miss Anjali's assistance is noteworthy. They kept me free from managerial work so that I could focus on writing this book. I was able to give my hundred per cent to this book, thanks to my wife Sunita, who kept me disengaged from domestic preoccupations. Thanks to my children, Aditi and Nandita, whose love made the work seem easier. The contribution of my friend Vineet Varma is also commendable. He always inspired me to have original and innovative thoughts. I would like to extend my deepest and sincere gratitude to all the students who have helped me in always being able to develop new and fresh ideas through classroom discussions. Special thanks to one of my students, Prabhat Patel. I would like to extend my thanks to Mohd. Abdullah ji, who played a significant part in giving shape to this book.

With steady support from the publishers, Sangam Books, I have tried to maintain a good standard of writing. This work would not have been possible without their efforts.

ACKNOWLEDGEMENTS

UNIT I

POLITICAL THEORY

Part 1: Political Concepts

KEY CONCEPTS

Liberty; Equality; Justice; Rights; Democracy; Power; Citizenship

1

LIBERTY

KEY CONCEPTS

Conceptions of liberty; liberty and the law; liberty and the state; negative and positive liberty; liberal egalitarianism; liberty as Marxist emancipation; feminist conception of liberty

Liberty is a central moral and political idea in modern societies. The conception of liberty has always been highly contentious and debatable due to its multiple dimensions and its often conflicting individualistic and communitarian interpretations. The word liberty originates from the Latin word *liber* meaning to be free. Liberty in philosophy involves the idea of free will and human agency as opposed to the idea of determinism. The modern idea of liberty, as something natural, inalienable and universal as it is generally understood today, is said to have come into existence only with the arrival of individualism and the Age of Enlightenment. The idea of political liberty however draws its roots from the ancient Greeks, for whom being free meant not being a slave and not having a master, and was closely linked to the Greek ideal of democracy.

Benjamin Constant distinguishes between two types of liberty as understood by ancient and modern societies in a lecture delivered in 1816 titled 'The Liberty of Ancients Compared with That of Moderns' and asserts that confusion between the two has been the 'cause of many an evil'. He defines the two kinds of liberty as follows:

> ***Liberty of the ancients*:** A form of collective social liberty wherein sovereignty was directly exercised, for example, in the ancient Greek Republic of Athens. The collective always took precedence over the individual. The Greeks understood freedom to mean the right of the free citizen to participate in the political affairs of the city: public speaking, debating, voting. But once these were over and a vote was taken, the individual citizen was a slave to the majority decisions of his fellow citizens. Constant says, 'Thus, among the ancients, the individual, almost always sovereign in public affairs, was a slave in all his private relations'. Liberty for them meant political power and autonomy shared as a society, not individual freedom or agency.
>
> ***Liberty of the moderns*:** The conception of man as a free, autonomous agent who chooses his own ends, his own means to achieve his desired ends and lives on his own terms is a modern idea according to Constant. This ideal of individual liberty exercised through representative sovereignty is based on the Charter of Fundamental Rights, the emergence of universal adult franchise and a representative government, which he calls 'a discovery of the moderns'.

CONCEPTIONS OF LIBERTY

John Robert Seeley: 'liberty is the opposite of over-government'.

G. D. H. Cole: 'liberty is the freedom of the individual to express, without external hindrances, his personality'.

Joseph Raz: conceives of liberty as an ideal of self-created, self-authored and self-willed autonomy.

Paul McKechnie: 'freedom means not the absence of all restraints, but rather the substitution of rational ones for the irrational'.

David Miller in his work *The Liberty Reader* enumerates three traditions of liberty.

1. ***Republican liberty*:** This tradition existed in the ancient Greek republics wherein citizens were entitled to participate in day-to-day administrative decision-making. It involved the exercise of direct sovereignty and could therefore only exist in direct democracies. Thinkers like Niccolo Machiavelli, Jean-Jacques Rousseau and Hannah Arendt have also recognised republican liberty**. Quentin Skinner** in discussing *republican liberty* argues that the most important republican value is political liberty or non-domination and freedom from arbitrary power.
2. ***Individual rights*:** The original proponent of this tradition was John Locke, who asserted that all humans are born with natural rights to life, liberty, and property, and that therefore, no one can legitimately interfere with the person or property of others. However, our greatest entitlement is to our own body and mind.
3. ***Self-realisation*:** Thinkers like Rousseau and John Stuart Mill contend that mere possession of one's person and property is not enough—liberty is also about the realisation of one's full potential and capabilities.

Thomas Hobbes: Liberty is the 'absence of external impediments' to act. People are free when no external obstacle prevents them from doing what they wish to do. For Hobbes, laws are artificial external chains that curtail liberty, which can truly exist only when law is silent.

John Locke: Locke believed that all individuals are born with natural and inalienable rights to life, liberty and property, and the freedom to exercise these rights. He also believed that the law protects, facilitates and expands individual liberty.

John Stuart Mill: A great advocate of individual liberty like Locke, Mill stresses on the importance of distinguishing between two spheres in an individual's life: one which concerns the self, and one concerning others. About the *self-regarding sphere*, he says, 'over himself, his body and mind, the individual is sovereign'. About the *other-regarding sphere*, he says for 'that which concerns others there should be constraints.... My liberty to swing my arms ends where the other's nose begins'. For Mill, 'every restraint, qua restraint, is an evil': liberty is doing what one wills. But at the very beginning of his famous essay 'On Liberty', he also says that, 'The subject of this essay is not the so called liberty of the will...but civil or social liberty'.

LIBERTY AND THE LAW/THE STATE

Hobbes said that liberty is not possible in a state of nature, or in other words, that there is a difference between liberty and license. The presence of the state signifies the presence of law. Law and liberty are generally understood to be both mutually complementary as well as mutually antagonistic. Paradoxically, Hobbes supported absolute government and authority of the sovereign/king/state for the protection of civil liberty and the security of the commonwealth and polity. However, he also leaves scope for the exercise of individual liberty when he says: 'Man is free where the Law is silent'. The silence of law here does not mean the absence of law: it means that the law will not act until and unless an individual or group of individuals harms the life or wellbeing of others.

Locke held that liberty can neither be exercised nor enjoyed in the absence of state and government. He famously said that the state not only protects but also enhances liberty. However, liberty demands the presence of a limited, constitutional and democratic state. Further, every state does not support liberty and an absolute authoritarian state denies and destroys civil liberty completely. Therefore, while accepting that liberty is not possible without the law and state, Locke also advocated minimal powers to the state. He modified the ideas of Hobbes and said that laws made by a limited and democratic government are complementary to liberty. According to Locke, the government that governs the least is the best.

LIBERTY AND DEMOCRACY

John Stuart Mill and **Alexis de Tocqueville** held rightly that a democratic and representative government alone does not guarantee the presence of liberty for all its citizens because even in a democracy, liberty may be compromised due to the tyranny of the majority over the minority. Mill recognised that a majoritarian and exclusive society can be as dangerous for liberty as an autocratic government. Liberty must be available and accessible for each and everyone in a polity including the minority, that is, the dissent and disagreement of the few. Mill therefore argued that even in a democracy, liberty had to also be about the safeguarding of individuals from the tyranny of the majority, and that it was essential to consider the spheres in an individual's life which concerned the individual him/herself and those that concerned others. On the importance of the protection and preservation of minority rights, Mill said: 'If entire mankind minus one is of one opinion, the entire mankind is justified in silencing him, as he is in silencing them.'

Mill also talks about three primary dimensions of liberty and their importance:

1. Liberty of thought and discussion
2. Liberty of tastes and pursuits
3. Liberty to form common associations with others

NEGATIVE LIBERTY AND POSITIVE LIBERTY

We are free if no one and nothing is stopping us from doing whatever it is that we want to do. Freedom from external restraint and absence of external obstacles to one's actions and choices is called *negative liberty*. But in order to be free, we must also be able to control our life, determine our choices ourselves and take decisions in our own interests, and not be dictated upon by others or circumstances; *positive liberty* is thus the ability to act on one's free will.

Isaiah Berlin, in his famous lecture and essay 'Two Concepts of Liberty' (1958), called them 'negative' and 'positive' liberty respectively because in the first case, liberty seems to be the *absence* of something (obstacles, interference from others), while in the second it requires the *presence* of something (agency, control, self-realisation, self-mastery).

Berlin thus defined *negative liberty* as the freedom from coercive interference by others in relation to some domain of personal conduct, and *positive liberty* as the freedom to be one's own master and the 'wish to be an instrument of one's own, not of other men's acts of will and to have a voice in laws and practices of society'. Berlin's distinction can hence also be understood as '*freedom from*' and '*freedom to*'.

Isaiah Berlin's Idea of Negative Liberty

Negative liberty, which Berlin emphasises is a precondition of self-creation, is central to his conceptualisation of liberty. It is neither meant for attaining autonomy nor is it linked with democracy or self-government. The 'Individual is free to fly like an eagle or swim like a whale', Berlin asserts. According to Berlin, negative liberty is chiefly associated with:

1. Freedom from interference or absence of restraints
2. Freedom to choose among options
3. ***Value pluralism*** or the idea that there exist multiple different values which may contradict and be in conflict with each other, but are each correct and essential

Isaiah Berlin's Idea of Positive Liberty

According to Berlin, positive liberty is chiefly associated with:

1. The idea of control over the self
2. Within the self/individual, identification of the separate selves: (a) one that controls, and (b) one that is controlled
3. Within society, identification of: (a) the group or part of the group that controls, and of which the individual is a member, and (b) the individual who is being controlled
4. The claim that society as a whole or its representatives may know better as to what the individual needs
5. The idea that what the individual truly wants may often be the opposite of what he or she is conscious of wanting

Although much contested and ultimately unpersuasive, Berlin's distinction between negative and positive liberty has been influential in shaping other schools of thought and therefore it is widely recognised.

The Tradition of Negative Liberty

Philosophers and thinkers associated with the tradition of negative liberty are: **Jeremy Bentham, John Stuart Mill, Alexis de Tocqueville, Herbert Spencer, Lord John Dalberg-Acton, Friedrich A. Hayek, Karl Popper, Milton Friedman, Michael Oakeshott** and **Robert Nozick** to name a few. The proponents of negative liberty conceptualised the ideal of liberty as freedom from constraints and from the coercive exercise of power or forceful interference, which could mainly come either from society and other individuals, or from the state/government.

Friedrich Hayek in his work *The Constitution of Liberty* (1960) contends that liberty is the absence of constraints and that condition wherein the individual is not subjected to coercion by the arbitrary will of others. In his book *The Road to Serfdom* (1944), Hayek insists that the unchecked growth of the state will inevitably lead to totalitarianism. He sees socialism, planning and collectivism as tools to curtail individual freedom, and supports a free market economy. Liberty for Hayek also implies:

1. Equality before law
2. Freedom from arbitrary arrest
3. Freedom of choice
4. Freedom of movement
5. Freedom to own property

Karl Popper argued that liberty is about non-interference. It is a more individualistic interpretation of the ideal of liberty as an intrinsic value of human nature that is necessary for self-realisation and self-mastery and for the independent pursuit of wants.

Lord Acton, and other thinkers like him, despite recognising rightly that 'power tends to corrupt' and that individuals must be freed from the coercive interference of state power, do nevertheless acknowledge that 'The State is a necessary evil'. Acton also famously and controversially asserted that the 'Aspiration for equality destroys liberty'.

Milton Friedman in his book *Capitalism and Freedom* (1962) said, like Hayek, that freedom refers to the freedom from the coercive will of others.

The Tradition of Positive Liberty

Thinkers associated with and in favour of the tradition of positive liberty are: **Jean Jacques Rousseau, Georg W. F. Hegel, Immanuel Kant, Thomas H. Green, Ernest Barker, Bernard Bosanquet, Harold Laski, Franklin D. Roosevelt, Leo Strauss, L. T. Hobhouse** and **C. B. Macpherson**. The conception of positive liberty as '*freedom to*' can be traced back to **Plato** and **Aristotle** when they talk about the discovery and development of aptitudes particular to all individuals and the customisation of the education system to support this process of self-realisation for all members of the polity.

Jean Rousseau, the founder philosopher of democracy, talks at great length about the realisation and creation of a political system based on these principles. He talks about three wills:

1. *Actual will* or the self-interest of individuals
2. *Real will* or the interest of individuals concerning the collective development and attainment of collective social goals
3. *General will* which is formed by a combination of actual and real will (not merely an aggregation) and which causes people to enter into a social contract for the creation of a popular sovereign

Thus Rousseau, for the first time, talks about *individual existence within a collectivity* and an inclusive conception of development through popular participation, and famously asserts that: 'People will be forced to be free.'

T. H. Green held that liberty is action. For Green, freedom lies in the positive power of doing or enjoying something that is worth doing and enjoying, and something that we do or enjoy with others. He defines liberty as self-realisation, which means moral action as real freedom. Green also talks about the preconditions for such self-realisation, and supports a *welfare state* that would provide basic social goods for its citizens. Therefore positive liberty for Green also includes *social* and *economic liberty* apart from the moral dimension.

Georg W. Hegel said that obeying the order of the state is real freedom because for Hegel the state is the highest manifestation of morality.

Harold Laski in *A Grammar of Politics* (1925) said liberty is the maintenance of that atmosphere in which human beings have the opportunity to be their best selves. Laski describes three types of liberty: *individual liberty*, *political liberty*, and *economic liberty*.

Charles Taylor said negative liberty is an *opportunity concept* where 'being free is a matter of what we can do' regardless of whether we actually choose to do it or not, while positive liberty is an *exercise concept* where we do exercise the liberty to determine our self and to shape our life. Taylor said the exercise of positive liberty was essential for democracies, while the idea of negative liberty was inadequate at best and flawed. Taylor supported a *purposive liberty*.

C. B. Macpherson advocates *developmental liberty* and says that the individual has two capabilities: a *developmental* and an *exploitative capability*. He argues that capitalism promotes the exploitative tendency of the individualist and suppresses the developmental ability, while true liberty entails the exercise and enjoyment of the developmental capability, which is not possible under a capitalist economy.

Franklin D. Roosevelt in the draft of the Atlantic Charter enlists four freedoms:

1. The freedom of speech
2. The freedom of worship
3. The freedom from want
4. The freedom from fear

Immanuel Kant is an important name when we talk about individualistic interpretations of liberty. Kant said: 'individuals are the kingdoms of ends and means' and therefore they must be free to define and pursue their own ends rather than having others' ends imposed upon them. Kant compellingly argued that the only way to act freely and exercise complete autonomy is to act upon *categorical imperatives*, or in other words, to act morally. He laid great emphasis on human beings acting not only on material and rational impulses and desires but also on ethical and moral ones and thereby engaging in acts which must also qualify as universal laws. For Kant, *moral laws* are categorical imperatives that apply to everyone unconditionally and universally and therefore they are *universal laws*. Kant's understanding of individual liberty, autonomy and agency is thus inseparably wedded to his idea of morality and universal moral laws.

Criticism of Positive Liberty

1. Berlin himself is critical of the ideas of Locke and Kant as he believed that they fail to recognise that all universal laws are ultimately fictitious or fallible. He calls them *monists* who focus on formulating universal laws, which he believed is a utopian and unattainable objective. Berlin asserts that there is no one perfect or ideal way of living life, collectively or individually, as projected by the Marxists or the Fascists, because no single value is inherently superior to other values.
2. Berlin also criticised the Marxists and Fascists as they sought to justify a single social order and a perfect society and state, which he said would eventually lead to the suppression of liberty.
3. In contrast, Berlin believed that a free civil society must necessarily be based on *value pluralism* or the existence of multiple values, like liberty, equality and justice. He further said that any kind of rationality and morality must emerge from the citizens themselves.
4. Berlin also vehemently argued in support of *methodological pluralism* and said that there are multiple methods to enquire about society and state. He also opposed Karl Popper's positivistic and scientific orientation towards liberty, and instead emphasised upon a diversity of methods and modes of research to acquire a holistic understanding of freedom and its various aspects.
5. According to Berlin, however, despite value pluralism and multiple equal values which may conflict, there must nevertheless be a sacred core of basic inalienable human rights which must be guaranteed. Berlin also held that there is only one universal rational law: *civil liberty*, which is the greatest value that brings about coordination and synthesis with other values.
6. In sum, in Berlin's conception, *freedom from* or negative liberty is about non-interference and the preservation of natural rights, while the idea of *freedom to* or positive liberty consists of the principles of self-mastery, agency and entitlement.

REJECTION OF BERLIN'S DIVISION BETWEEN NEGATIVE AND POSITIVE LIBERTY

Liberty is an integrated concept, and therefore many thinkers felt that the division between positive and negative liberty was not justified, either partially or completely, or that it was inadequate or problematic for various reasons.

1. According to **Dudley Knowles**, Berlin's understanding of self-control and self-realisation is problematic because he feels that these can be manipulated by others.
2. Berlin's idea of ***paternalism***—broadly, an ideology and action that limits the liberty and autonomy of an individual or group for their own supposed good and protection—was also critiqued as faulty because it was argued that Berlin does not make a clear distinction between the kinds of paternalism which may be acceptable or justified and those which need to be rejected outright. **Mill**, for example, categorically opposes state paternalism on the grounds that individuals know their own good better than the state, and that moral equality demands respect for others' liberty, which paternalism violates.
3. **Gerald C. MacCallum** completely rejects Berlin's dual categorisation of liberty as negative and positive, and instead proposes the idea of liberty as a *triadic* relationship: 'X is free (or un-free) from Y to do or become Z.' Here, X is the agent, Y is the constraint or the opportunity, and Z is the end or goal. According to MacCallum, conceptualising liberty as a binary of positive and negative liberties limits and contradicts the idea of individual freedom and agency.

4. Another serious critique of Berlin is that his conception of moral or value pluralism is indistinguishable from *relativism*, or the view that things have value only *relative* to specific contexts and perspectives and that, therefore, nothing is intrinsically valuable or good in and of/for itself. However, in defence of Berlin's pluralism, he does believe that there are at least some core human values that are inherently good and universally valid, even if these are few.

Table 1.1.1: Negative versus Positive Liberty at a Glance

Negative Liberty	*Positive Liberty*
1. The main proponents are classical liberals, libertarians and neo-liberals.	The main proponents are modern liberals, socialists and welfarists.
2. The proponents focus on ensuring the provision and guarantee of civil and political liberties.	The proponents emphasise upon the linkages between morality and freedom.
3. They focus on the absence of external restraints to individual freedom.	They emphasise upon individual self-attainment and self-realisation.
4. They argue for a limited government.	They focus on the importance of the welfare state in ensuring a level playing field for all individuals.
5. It is based on a conceptualisation of 'freedom from'.	It is based on a conceptualisation of 'freedom to'.
6. It is focused on the individual who is conceptualised as the 'isolated, individuated self'.	It focuses on the importance of the 'situated self' within the community and society as quintessential to ensuring greater individual freedom.

LIBERAL EGALITARIANISM

John Rawls in his book *A Theory of Justice* (1971) proposed a theory of *liberal egalitarianism* or liberty compatible to equality to bring about the establishment of a just society where individuals could be free to realise their full potential. The two principles of liberty as propounded by Rawls are self-explanatory in outlining his objective of promoting equality and the redistribution of power and resources as necessary for achieving liberty.

1. ***Liberty principle*:** Ensuring the maximum possible liberty for each individual compatible with similar liberty for all.
2. ***Equality principle*:** Public offices should be open to everyone and maximum benefit should be gained by the most disadvantaged.

Rawls also supported *affirmative action*, subsidies and the establishment of a *welfare state* as necessary conditions for achieving true and full liberty.

MARXIST IDEAL OF LIBERTY AS EMANCIPATION

One of the earliest uses of the term *liberation* was by liberation theologist **Gustavo Gutierrez. Karl Marx** in his *Economic and Philosophical Manuscripts* (1844) famously asserted that freedom means the end of necessity. In *Capital* (1864), he states: 'the realm of freedom actually begins only where labour which is determined by necessity and mundane considerations ceases'. Necessity is a hindrance produced by an unequal capitalist economy that is characterised by the exploitation of the proletariat and its labour by the bourgeoisie, which controls the means of production and extracts the surplus value of labour.

1. No one can enjoy liberty in an unequal society that is divided along class, where one class forever exploits the other. True liberty, said Marx, can only be realised in a classless society, and thus necessitates restructuring the entire capitalist system of economy.

2. While in liberalism, liberty of the individual is central, socialism and Marxism on the other hand emphasise collective human emancipation as being vital to liberty.
3. Marxists see freedom in much wider terms in terms of the removal of obstacles to human emancipation, which implies the manifold and all-round development of human capability and the bringing into being of a form of association and enterprise worthy of human nature.
4. Marxism underlines the formation of a collective enterprise which may be brought about by the imposition of human control over both nature and the social conditions of production. Social cooperation is essential in this enterprise.

CREATIVE LIBERTY

Neo-Marxists have advanced the idea of *creative liberty*. **Herbert Marcuse**, in *One Dimensional Man* (1964), his landmark critique of modern capitalist industrial society, asserted that the capitalist market hindered the realisation of the multi-dimensional, individual, creative self. By both encouraging and enforcing *mass consumption* and *mass consumerism*, capitalism has systematically and completely destroyed individual creative freedom and expression.

Eric Fromm, another neo-Marxist social theorist, in his works *The Fear of Freedom* (1942) and *Escape from Freedom* (1941), similarly contended that capitalist society is inherently unable to provide and ensure individual freedom as within the capitalist system human beings are turned into controllable machines of mass production.

FEMINIST CONCEPTION OF LIBERATION

Feminists around the world have advocated structural changes and complete social transformation of the gendered relations of production and gendered social spaces through their slogan: 'Personal is Political'.

Kate Millett emphasised how masculinity and femininity were not biologically given but created around the terms 'male' and 'female'**.** Socialisation was actively undertaken to make women and men conform to particular gender roles.

Sylvia Walby said that patriarchy results in the subjugation of both men and women to a structure of power where they have fixed social roles. Men are forced to become providers for the family and the perpetrators of violence. Women and men both need to be freed from patriarchy and rigid gender roles.

Germaine Greer, who famously said: 'You cannot liberate people by force', stresses that liberation for women does not and should not mean equality with men or the freedom to imitate what men have established, but to discover and to acknowledge for themselves what women think is important and worthwhile, and how to live, how to be, how to think for themselves. She also says that liberation, which requires challenging cultural norms, cannot be averse to change.

Important contemporary works on liberty:

Milton Friedman, *Capitalism and Freedom* (University of Chicago Press, 1962)

Isaiah Berlin, *Four Essays on Liberty* (Oxford University Press, 1969)

Joseph Raz, *The Morality of Freedom* (Oxford University Press, 1986)

Aung San Suu Kyi, *Freedom from Fear and Other Writings* (Penguin Books, 1991)

Nelson Mandela, *Long Walk to Freedom* (Abacus, 1995)

Amartya Sen, *Development as Freedom* (Oxford University Press, 1999)

2

EQUALITY

KEY CONCEPTS

Types of equality; equality of outcome; equality of opportunity; affirmative action; equality and difference; multicultural theory of rights; equality and socialism; equality and liberty

The concept of equality lies at the heart of normative political theory, and it is one of the most powerful social ideals. In simple words, equality is a relationship between two or more persons or groups regarding some aspect of their lives. However, there has been fierce debate as to the precise notion of equality, its principles, application, measures, material requirements, and the place and value of equality, especially in relation to justice. **Jean Jacques Rousseau** is considered to be the father of the modern concept of equality. In the twenty-first century, **Thomas Piketty** is considered to be the most important advocate of liberty, and whose works *The Economics of Inequality* (1997) and *A Brief History of Equality* (2021) have been most influential.

Inequality and difference in society have been based on privilege, power, hierarchy, race, class, caste, gender and division of labour among other things. The concept of equality can likewise be understood in many different ways depending on what aspects of human life, social and public or individual and private, are focused upon and accordingly, relevant attributes, applications, relationships and inter-linkages between them can be proposed.

KINDS OF EQUALITY

Foundational Equality

The earliest notion of equality which had an impact on political thought is often referred to as *foundational equality*, which advocates that all people are equal by the virtue of their shared human essence. Famous British economist and egalitarian **Richard H. Tawney** in his influential book *Equality* (1931) wrote a powerful critique of what he called 'The Religion of Inequality' in British society and argued that there was no rational justification for inequality and the gaping social and economic disparities in society, which existed simply because of prejudice and because they are accepted as inevitable when they are not. Tawney's other writings include: *The Acquisitive Society* (1920), *Education: The Socialist Policy* (1924), and *Religion and the Rise of Capitalism* (1926).

Foundational equality is closely linked to and sometimes used interchangeably with the notion of *formal equality*, which originated from the natural rights theories of the seventeenth and eighteenth centuries. The 'American Declaration of Independence' (1776), for example, simply states that: 'All men are created equal'. Likewise, the 'French Declaration of the Rights of Man and of Citizen' (1789) states that: 'Men are born and remain free and equal in rights'.

Formal Equality

Human beings are considered equal only in the sense that they are all born with equal, inalienable natural rights. *Formal equality* is based on the understanding that all members of society have equal status and possess equal rights regardless of their social background, and that by virtue of their common humanity, all are entitled to be treated equally by the rules of social practice.

In his renowned work *Politics*, **Aristotle** draws a correlation between justice and equality and asserts: 'justice is held to be equality, and it is, but for equals and not for all; and inequality is held to be just and is indeed, but for unequals and not for all.' Aristotle's statement emphasises treating like cases alike and unlike cases unlike. This also implies a defense and justification of natural inequality, and hence Aristotle's principle of formal equality is characteristically negative. Being confined to the task of eradicating special privileges of the upper classes, it also antagonised the aristocracy and the rich.

Critiques of Formal Equality

Karl Marx critiques formal equality and its corollaries in detail in his *Critique of the Gotha Programme* (1875). Marx sees formal equality as a 'market' or 'bourgeois' notion of equality, because within capitalist society it operates as little more than a façade, serving only to disguise the reality of class exploitation and economic inequality: '*equal right* here is still in principle—*bourgeois right*'. For Marx and Engels the real cause of inequality is the class structure of capitalist society; hence in order to abolish social and economic inequality it is this unequal, exploitative class structure itself that must be abolished, not inequality of wealth or resources or individuals. Emphasising that equality of labour must be the bedrock of socialist distribution, Marx is deeply critical of the idea of equality, whether conceptualised formally, in relation to rights, or substantively, as the normative foundation of socialist distribution. Because ultimately it is just an abstraction that masks what is really essential to human life, which is neither the formal rights that we may share in common with others nor how much of something we might have in comparison with others—but what people require as concrete individuals to 'develop their capabilities and powers in complete freedom.'

Radical feminists argue that the principle of formal equality is inadequate because it applies only to public life and ignores the fact that patriarchy—a social system in which men hold power and predominate in roles of political leadership, decision-making, moral authority, social and economic privilege and ownership and control of property—is rooted in the unequal structure of family and personal life. Feminists therefore gave the slogan 'Personal is Political'.

Legal Equality

The most important manifestation of formal equality is *legal equality* or 'equality before the law'. Legal equality is the cornerstone of the *rule of law* which holds that the law must treat each person equally, showing no regard or bias for the social and economic background, religion, race, colour, gender and so forth of any individual.

Political Equality

Political equality implies that all citizens should have equal access to the avenues of political authority, representation and democratic participation. It guarantees the enjoyment and exercise of the same political rights and capabilities to all citizens, including: to vote, assemble, speak freely, move about freely, hold office, and to petition the government. Universal adult franchise is one means of achieving political equality. **Jeremy Bentham** was the original proponent of the principle of one person, one vote. However, to be able to participate equally and freely in collective democratic decision-making, it is necessary that the ground conditions enabling such political equality must also be met; in other words, people must also be free, empowered, and have access to basic human needs like food, shelter, clothing, health and education.

Economic Equality

Economic equality is closely linked to political equality. **Harold J. Laski** asserted that, 'Political equality is…never real unless it is accompanied with virtual economic liberty; political power otherwise is bound to be the handmaid of economic power.' **Lord Bryce** declared that economic equality is 'the attempt to expunge all differences in wealth, allotting to every man and woman an equal share in worldly goods'. This is, however, a utopian notion which cannot be realised in actual practice.

The seventeenth-century movement for political and economic equality in Britain, during the English Civil Wars (1642–49), can be divided into two groups: the Levellers and the Diggers. The *Levellers*, including John Lilburne, Richard Overton and William Walwyn, demanded political equality and were committed to popular sovereignty, extended suffrage, equality before the law and religious tolerance. The *Diggers* (or the *True Levellers*), led by Gerrard Winstanley, William Everard and others, demanded economic equality and advocated agrarian socialism wherein land was held and farmed in common.

Moral Equality

The principle of *moral equality*, also known as *basic equality* or *human dignity*, is a principle of substantive and universal equality which asserts that all human beings, despite their differences, deserve to be treated with equal dignity and respect and to be considered one another's equals by virtue of their common status as human beings. Originating among the Greek **Stoics** who emphasised the natural equality of all rational beings, moral equality forms the basis of all modern political theories today.

Thomas Hobbes argued that in the state of nature, all individuals possess equal rights and capabilities and also an equal capacity to harm each other. He asserted in his famous work, *The Leviathan*: 'Nature hath made men so equal, in the faculties of body, and mind…'. **John Locke** said that all human beings have equal natural rights to both self-mastery and liberty. However, although it is fundamental to conceptions of justice, rights and liberty, the principle of moral equality is too abstract and needs to be defined and understood in more precise and concrete terms in order for it to function as a moral standard.

Complex Equality

Liberals considered the individual as a unit for political analysis, based on which they propounded the universal concept of equality. For Rawls the same basic primary goods are required in every society. But for *communitarians*, the unit for understanding the concept of equality is the *community*. And since there are various forms of community, no single yardstick can be used to define the concept of equality for all of them. For example, the notion of equality for a family is quite different from the notion of equality for a market; the family and the market are both forms of community.

Michael Walzer gave currency to the idea of *complex equality*. Walzer argues that focus needs to shift from distribution to the conception and creation of social goods. He insists that human beings are the ones who give meaning to social goods which ultimately determines their social value. Therefore, different social meanings are attached to the same goods in different social contexts. There is no single set of basic goods which could be universally conceived of and accorded the same value. Therefore in Walzer's words, 'All distributions are just and unjust relative to the social meanings of goods at stake.' Walzer contends that the same distributive standards do not prevail across different 'spheres' of social life. For instance, the market and the government/political power are distinct and separate spheres. The norms for distributing goods in each sphere are internal and specific to each, and cannot spill over.

EQUALITY OF OUTCOME

The idea of an equality of outcome is the most radical and controversial face of *egalitarianism*, or the doctrine of the equality of humankind characterised by belief in equal political, economic, social and civil rights for all people. A concern with 'outcomes' rather than 'opportunities' shifts attention away from the starting point of life to its end results, from chances and opportunities to rewards. This is a goal on which there is a clear and major ideological divide: socialists, communists and some anarchists regard a high level of social equality as a fundamental and necessary goal; conservatives and liberals on the other hand believe that aiming for such a goal is not only unnatural but also unethical and hence undesirable.

The demand for equality of outcomes is commonly associated with the ideals of material and social equality, the equality of social circumstances, living conditions and equal wages for equal work. Marxist support for the collectivisation of productive wealth reflects the Marxist desire to build a classless society that is founded on a unifying and common interest and that is free of exploitation.

To achieve equality of outcome in society at large would require a similarly extensive system of manipulation, which is often derided as 'social engineering'. The drive for equality therefore involves regimentation and coercion, which is typically associated with a powerful state apparatus.

From the radical viewpoint, however, there is also a strong and direct connection between equality of outcomes and equality of opportunity. It is not so much that equalising outcomes might be a necessary means to the equalisation of opportunities, but rather that the two kinds of equality essentially amount to the same thing. Radical equality of opportunity seeks to correct for all unchosen disadvantages—natural as well as socially imposed disadvantages. Where this is achieved, differences of outcome, it is argued, can only reflect genuine differences of ability, taste and choice. However, this conceptualisation has also been criticised. Marxist thinker Milovan Djilas, in his work *New Class* (1959) contended that an ideal Marxist society could succumb to bureaucratisation wherein there was no rule *of* the proletariat and instead there was rule *over* the proletariat.

EQUALITY OF OPPORTUNITY

When agents have a chance to achieve the same goals without being hindered by the same obstacles, they are said to have equality of opportunity. The notion of equal opportunities can be found in the writings of **Plato**, who proposed that social status should be based strictly on individual ability and effort. To ensure this, the educational system should offer all children equal opportunity to realise their talents and capabilities.

A limited or minimal conception of equality of opportunity could be understood as just a procedural conception to simply mean that a person's socio-cultural background should not affect their chances of getting a good education, of being selected for a job and so on. Securing this kind of equality of opportunity would involve careful monitoring and regulation of recruitment and promotion procedures in educational institutions and the labour market.

Seen from a radical viewpoint on the other hand, even the full-blooded pursuit of securing conventional equality of opportunity, by eliminating socio-economic disadvantage, would not be adequate. It could be argued that correcting for social and economic disadvantage does not really yield true equality of opportunity, because it leaves untouched natural or inborn disadvantage.

Ronald Dworkin argues in *Taking Rights Seriously* (1977) that each citizen of a state has a right to receive equal respect and concern of those who govern him/her, and that this is a fundamental political right. Social democrats and modern liberals believe that equal opportunity is the cornerstone of social justice. Eric Rakowaski and Elizabeth Anderson both support the idea equality of opportunity.

John Rawls: Harmful and Beneficial Inequality

One of the most influential political philosophers of the 20th century, a liberal, John Rawls believed that every form of inequality cannot and should not be eradicated. Inequality which is beneficial for the least advantaged sections of society should continue, he argued, but inequality which is harmful for the least advantaged should be abolished. According to Rawls, inequality in a democratic society is beneficial for the most disadvantaged because the government levies taxes on the rich, which are then distributed among the poor. Rawls held that liberty or rights cannot be compromised for the sake of maintaining equality. He supported a capitalist or market economy.

Rawls propounded a theory of social justice in his work *A Theory of Justice* (1980). He believes that the people behind the veil of ignorance would choose the following principles:

1. Each individual should have equal right to the most extensive system of total basic liberties compatible with a similar system of liberty for all.
2. Social and economic inequalities should be so arranged so that they are both:
   a) to the maximum benefit of the least advantaged; and
   b) attached to offices and positions open for all under conditions of fair equality of opportunity
3. ***Principle of lexical priority***
   a) Rawls prioritises the three different principles given by him in the following order, in case a conflict arises in their practice: (i) liberty principle, (ii) equality of opportunity principle, and (iii) difference (inequality) principle.
   b) In case of the equality principle, the principle of fair equality of opportunity shall take precedence over the principle of maximum benefit to the least advantaged in the situation of a conflict.
4. Equality of opportunity is concerned with the distribution of social primary goods. There are two types of primary goods:
   a) *Social primary goods*: these include liberty, wealth, opportunities which are available for the society to distribute.
   b) *Natural primary goods*: these include personal characteristics or natural talents. Society cannot influence the distribution of these goods.

Rawls said that primary goods shall be distributed in the initial condition and for the marginalised sections. Thus for Rawls, equality of opportunity points towards an egalitarian ideal, but a very specific one: that of a meritocratic society. The concept of *meritocracy*—a political system in which economic goods and/or political powers are vested in individuals on the basis of talent, effort and achievement, rather than wealth, social class or status—is an ancient one, dating back to the Greeks. But the term itself was coined by **Michael Dunlop Young** in his work *The Rise of the Meritocracy* (1958) to refer pejoratively to rule by an intellectual American elite. Meritocracy, in its wider sense, may be any government run by an elite, 'ruling or influential class of educated or able people'.

EQUALITY OF WHAT?

Attempts to address economic equality have traditionally focused on distributive issues. However, any attempt to apply the principle of equality between individuals must first come to terms with what exactly needs to be equalised. Therefore, the 'what' of equality has a distributional aspect to it.

Equality of Welfare

1. **Richard Anderson** defines welfare as 'preference satisfaction' and asserts that: 'According to equality of welfare, goods are distributed equally among a group of persons to the degree that the distribution brings it about that each person enjoys the same welfare'.
2. **Utilitarian** thinkers also argue that the project of distributional equality amounts to the distribution of welfare. **Jeremy Bentham** asserts that, welfare refers to the happiness which is understood as the net balance of pleasure over pain that the individual experiences.
3. A society that believes in distributing welfare equally is not concerned with the share of resources which are ultimately possessed by each person. Rather, it is concerned with how these resources are instrumental in securing for each individual a level of satisfaction or happiness which is equal to everyone else's.

Equality of Resources

Ronald Dworkin, who has dealt extensively with the equality of resources, holds the equality principle as being central to society and its sovereign virtue. Equality of resources for him implies that a distributional scheme treats people as equals 'when it distributes or transfers so that no further transfer would leave their shares of the total resources more equal'. Dworkin is an egalitarian who believes in a market economy along with a democratic government. He said liberalism is related to morality. All citizens must have a concern towards their fellow citizens in society. Dworkin suggests a two-stage process for the realisation of equality of resources:

1. ***The ambition-sensitive auction*:** Being a liberal, Dworkin said that efficiency and risk should be awarded. Individuals are free to choose their preferences according to their ambitions. Individuals are also responsible for outcomes of their choice. This is also known as *option luck*, implying that society is not responsible for the marginalisation of a person. Dworkin asks us to imagine that all of society's resources are up for sale in an auction in which everyone is a participant. Everyone starts with an equal amount of purchasing power and uses it to bid for these resources that best suit their plan for life.
2. ***The envy test*:** Equality requires the fair distribution of resources and equal opportunity and capacity for purchasing resources. Therefore nobody can complain about biases in the initial condition. A successful auction meets the envy test. This implies that if the auction works out, everyone will be satisfied with the result, in the sense that they do not prefer anyone else's bundle of goods to their own.
3. ***The insurance scheme*:** Dworkin is also aware that people may be deprived due to adverse economic and/or social conditions. One of the first scholars to recognise that physical disability is the worst kind of deprivation, for compensating physical disability he suggested the policy of insurance.
   a) Unfortunately, the auction can only meet the envy test if we assume that no one is disadvantaged in terms of natural assets, which is not possible in the real world. Therefore, the auction needs to be both *ambition-sensitive* and *endowment-sensitive*.
   b) Dworkin mentions two kinds of luck which can hinder an endowment-sensitive auction:
   Option luck: a result of deliberate and calculated gambles, e.g. a person who buys stocks in exchange and earns profit because of a sudden rise in the prices of his stocks.

Brute luck: a result of risks and not deliberately calculated, e.g. a person is hit by a meteorite whose course could not be predicted.

c) To resolve this, Dworkin suggests that compensation 'before' the auction would ensure that each person is equally able to choose and pursue a valuable life. This compensation will be in the form of an insurance scheme that would take care of natural, undeserved equalities.

Equality of Capabilities

Amartya Sen said that development should not be measured in terms of economic development alone, and held the Human Development Index (HDI) to be a central measure of development. He said equality cannot be understood as a universal concept. Sen held that democracy and freedom are co-related. Freedom is associated with the ability to choose from options which are available in a democracy. Access to resources is important for developing capability. External conditions like patriarchy are responsible for the lack of development of women's capability because women have internalised inequalities and deprivations due to patriarchy, which confines and restricts them in multiple ways. If an individual has a certain skill but is unable to make use of it due to externally imposed constraints, this shows lack of capability. Lack of opportunity is also responsible for non-development of functions. This is a view propounded by Amartya Sen to provide a better understanding of freedom in his work *Development as Freedom*. A person's capabilities consist of the sets of functioning s/he can achieve given the personal, material and social resources available to her/him.

A *capability* is the ability to achieve a certain sort of function. Capabilities do not measure actually achieved functioning, but a person's freedom to achieve valued functioning. For example, literacy is capability, while reading is a function. In a society where people are illiterate, a state should actively promote people's ability to read, thereby leading to enhancement of literacy. The more freedom a person enjoys, the greater the range of effectively accessible, significantly different opportunities s/he has for functioning or leading her/his life in ways s/he values most.

The question raised by Sen's approach is: what capabilities should society be obligated to equalise? This requires us to identify particular goods within the space of equality which are of egalitarian concern. Equality in the space of capabilities may therefore demand an unequal division of resources to accommodate the disabled. What citizens ultimately owe one another is the social conditions of the freedoms that people need to function as equal citizens.

Because of differences in their internal capacities and social situations, people are not equally able to convert resources into capabilities for functioning. They are therefore entitled to different amounts of resources so they can enjoy freedom as equals. The idea of human development became popular due to Sen's concept of capability. Martha Nussbaum also contributed to the development of the capability approach.

AFFIRMATIVE ACTION

One particularly difficult issue which the principle of equal opportunity leads to is that of 'reverse' or 'positive' discrimination. This is a policy associated with *affirmative action*, which discriminates in favour of disadvantaged groups in the hope of compensating and correcting for past injustices. Affirmative action is a formal effort to provide increased employment and educational opportunities for socially and economically disadvantaged groups. The following justifications were provided for the adoption of affirmative action policies:

1. ***Proportional equality***: The treatment of relevant persons or groups according to their due. This means that distribution will not be numerically equal but will be

governed in relation to persons' deemed rightful needs.

2. ***Compensation*:** The policies of affirmative action are often seen as compensation for past or historical injustices suffered by a particular social or cultural group.
3. ***Empowerment*:** Affirmative action policies are also seen as empowering measures for particular disadvantaged groups to enhance their capabilities and to provide a level playing field for all citizens.

Christopher Edley explores the potential forms that affirmative action could take in the future and presents three models:

1. ***The 'colour-blind' version*:** This model of affirmative action entails race-based measures as a remedy only for those people who can prove that they are direct victims of discrete or overt acts of discrimination.
2. ***The 'opportunity and anti-discrimination' version*:** This model seeks to provide equal opportunities, but does not require equal outcomes. It acknowledges the deep harm that racism creates in the form of social, economic and other disparities among races, and seeks to correct these harms.
3. ***The 'remediation plus inclusion' version*:** This version of affirmative action is Edley's 'preferred' approach and essentially it suggests that diversity constitutes 'a compelling state interest'.

These three models give insights into a neo-world order that is likely to accommodate plurality as an instrument of progression instead of exploitation.

POSITIVE EQUALITY AND AFFIRMATIVE ACTION

There are three key elements where affirmative action programmes have an edge over the traditional notion of positive equality.

1. Affirmative action programmes are pro-active, including policies and procedures for ensuring a diverse applicant pool. Affirmative action does not mean quotas for hiring and promotion, which are in fact illegal. Nor does it necessarily mean preferential hiring.
2. The most common feature of affirmative action programmes is the emphasis on recordkeeping and identification of accurate availability statistics so that organisations can accurately gauge their progress towards their diversity goals.
3. Affirmative action policies are outcome-based; issues of internationality are not central. Demonstrating intentionality, which is typically a major issue of concern for equal employment opportunity programmes, is problematic because of the contemporary form of bias.

EQUALITY AND DIFFERENCE

Communitarianism: Pluralism and Equality

The *communitarians* contend that the individual is not an abstract category akin to the conception of the liberal individualistic self. Instead, they assert that the individual self is a situated self that is deeply embedded in culture and tradition. **I. M. Young** advocated the principle of differential citizenship to ensure the accommodation of diversity. **Michael Walzer** in his work *Spheres of Justice: A Defense of Pluralism and Equality* (1983) asserted that pluralism and diversity are closely associated with the realisation of equality in society. The communitarians argue that a liberal politics aimed at ensuring equality through a regime of legal and political rights needs to be replaced with a 'politics for the common good'. Communitarians also criticise Marxism for its exclusive focus on economic equality and ignorance of cultural and civilisational diversity.

There are three kinds of rights inherent to the ***multicultural theory of rights*:**

1. First, there are rights related to governance. These include special representation rights as endorsed by **Will Kymlicka** in his work *Multicultural Citizenship: A Liberal Theory of Minority Rights* (1995). Kymlicka refers to them as *self-government rights.* They include various forms of federal provisions and representation rights.
2. The second family of multicultural rights seeks to accommodate a variety of cultural practices within large states. These are referred to as *poly-ethnic rights*. These might also seek to give special assistance to a disadvantaged minority. For example, the Bilingual Education Act (1978) which was designed to enable parallel instruction in non-English languages for children.
3. The third family of rights relates to the rights of recognition. These involve issues of collective dignity and of a group's attitude towards others and itself.

Bhikhu Parekh said that group rights or cultural rights are important for minorities to enable them to preserve their collective identity. **Kymlicka** perceives 'culture as a self-sufficient civilization with its own institutions and values' and asserts that cultures are valuable and distinct, and therefore no universalist conception of equality can be ethically imposed on them. Therefore, Kymlicka insists that regimes of group differentiated rights are necessary for the preservation of difference and diversity.

Feminism: Difference versus Equality

Difference feminism recognised that there are differences between men and women but asserts that no value judgment can be placed upon these differences and that members of both sexes have equal moral status as individuals. Difference feminism arose in the 1980s and 1990s, addressing the '**difference-versus-equality**' debate, and partly in reaction to popular *liberal feminism* which highlighted similarities between women and men in order to demand equal rights and treatment for women. Difference feminism by contrast aimed at equality between men and women, but emphasised their differences and argued that identicality or sameness are not necessary in order for men and women, and for masculine and feminine values, to be treated on par.

EQUALITY AND SOCIALISM

The most vehement supporters of economic equality are the Socialists and the Marxists. In the contemporary context, democracy has ensured political equality but failed to remove inequalities in other spheres. On the other hand, capitalism has worsened and further created inequalities of all kinds. Socialism seeks equality in the spheres of social, political as well as economic life. Socialists seek radical equality by devising comprehensive programmes that are geared towards reducing or completely removing inequalities among humans through collective action. Socialism defends the equal rights of liberty to all. It maintains that in the absence of equality, the liberty of some will be based upon the lack of liberty for others.

EQUALITY AND LIBERTY

The relationship between liberty and equality has always been fraught and deeply contested. Various approaches and theories have therefore been proposed by different people and political traditions at different periods of time. **Aristotle** said that inequality between humans is natural. Vilfredo Pareto, Gaetano Mosca and Robert Michel's are **elitists** and therefore oppose equality. **Crystal Bell** believes in the ideal of a just meritocracy. **Lord Acton** said that the very aspiration of equality destroys the idea of liberty. **Alexis de Tocqueville** said that the ideal of equality is responsible for the tyranny of the majority; liberty requires difference, disagreement and dissent, which is not possible in the presence of equality. **Classical liberals** and **libertarians** believe that trying to create greater equality leads to diminishing of liberty. **Robert Nozick** and **Tocqueville** are proponents of the idea of libertarianism which stands in sharp contrast to the idea of egalitarianism.

For **liberals** and **neoliberals**, the individual is more important than the collective, hence their focus is on the liberty and rights of the individual. For **neoliberals**, liberty and equality are antagonistic to each other. While neoliberalism in principle sees the neoliberal ideal of formal equality before law as being broadly compatible with the ideals of civil and political equality, it however rejects the redistributional imperatives that form the basis of both economic and social equality. Hence, neoliberalism in practice directly conflicts with and negates the realisation of economic and social liberties and rights.

Egalitarians like **John Rawls** and **Ronald Dworkin** however believe that liberty and equality are ideals complementary to and compatible with each other. Dworkin argues that individual liberties exist but that they derive from the right of the individual to receive equal concern and respect. Dworkin denies that there is any conflict between liberty and equality.

Jean Rousseau, in his book *Discourse on the Origin and Basis of Equality* (1755), said man was born free in the state of nature. But with the emergence of civilisation arrived progress, industrialisation and capitalism, which put the majority of humanity in shackles imposed on them by a small minority. Rousseau advocated an idea of equality wherein all citizens would be forced to participate in the democratic process on an equal basis. However, the word 'citizen' itself was not inclusive of everyone in society, but excluded groups like women and slaves from participation in the democratic process. When Rousseau talks about the importance of political participation and free debate, he also propounded the idea of 'equality of all opinions within the sphere of representation'.

Socialists emphasise equality and in order that the interests and welfare of all, especially the poor and the disenfranchised, be protected, socialism advocates strengthening the powers of the state. In the socialist state, liberty is however suppressed in the name of equality.

According to **Steven Lukes**, author-editor of the influential book *Power: A Radical View* (1974), there may be broadly three ways of looking at the relationship between liberty and equality.

1. The first view is that liberty and equality are completely opposed to each other and in direct conflict. The rise of one inevitably leads to the diminishing of the other.
2. The second view is that liberty and equality may conflict but that they can be made to adjust and accommodate each other. Liberal egalitarians like **John Rawls** believe that while liberty is the core principle of the liberal state, equality is necessary to bring about the widespread exercise and enjoyment of freedom itself. **Harold Laski** asserted that 'Political liberty is a myth in the absence of economic equality'. In the idea of *reflective equilibrium*, Rawls says that in case of a conflict between the two exponents of the equality principle, the *equality of opportunity* shall prevail over *affirmative action*.
3. The third view is that liberty and equality are complementary to each other. **Marquis de Condorcet** and others believed that liberty and equality represent a chain of human values and ideals that are harmonious to each other.

While Lukes believes that the first and second set of views are more idealistic as they provide us with an understanding of thinkers committed to striving towards a more equal and free world, he advocates that the second and third views be followed as they are more practical.

In the name of liberty, the principle of survival of the fittest cannot be justified. The interests, wellbeing and freedom of the least empowered and least enfranchised must be protected in any civil society/state. At the same time the individual cannot be completely subordinated to and made a slave of the society or the state. Therefore liberty and equality are both necessary and both need to exist and to function complementarily and in coordination with each other, not antagonistically. Either one cannot prevail at the cost of the other.

3

JUSTICE

KEY CONCEPTS

Moral, legal, political and social justice; Marxist theory of justice; procedural theory of justice; distributive justice; Rawlsian theory; libertarian and communitarian view of justice; Dworkin's view, Amartya Sen's view; relationship between liberty, equality and justice

The concept of justice has undergone multiple theoretical changes and evolved with the passage of time. The significance of the ideal is self-evident from the fact that almost all noble virtues, ethical and political philosophies, ideologies and social, egalitarian as well as individualist claims are rationalised and justified with reference to the ideal of justice.

MORAL JUSTICE

The ancient Greek philosopher **Plato** believed that the ideal of justice can only be achieved by securing a harmonious cooperation in society between the three elements of the human soul: wisdom, courage and temperance. He advocated a distinct social organisation based on a rigorous system of education and intellectual training, regulated by strict norms of social conduct. Plato insisted that the creation of an ethical, virtuous, well-educated and balanced human being is crucial to the establishment of a just society. A just society cannot be brought about through state repression or legal obligations alone. John Locke, Adam Smith, Herbert Spencer and Jeremy Bentham are the major thinkers within this tradition.

LEGAL AND POLITICAL JUSTICE

John Locke in his work *Two Treatises on Civil Government* (1689) saw the government as a trust whose only function was to preserve and protect the natural rights of citizens, i.e., their rights to life, liberty and property. All claims to justice relied on these fundamental entitlements.

Adam Smith in his treatise *The Wealth of Nations* (1776) emphasised the natural attribute of trade and commerce which characterises human nature. He propounded the *theory of the invisible hand* of the market, asserting that if individuals are allowed to freely pursue their commercial interests in a free-market society, it would automatically lead to the realisation of collective interests. Smith assigned three main roles to the state:

1. Granting security to citizens
2. Arbitrating justice between rival claims
3. Taking broader policy decisions other than economic ones

Jeremy Bentham in his work *Introduction to the Principles of Morals and Legislation* (1789) insisted that the most important goal of any political order was securing the 'greatest happiness of the greatest number'. Anything which goes against this ideal would be unjust and unfair, he said.

SOCIAL JUSTICE

The concept of social justice is a broad and comprehensive concept which includes social, economic and political justice, and is often traced to the ideas of **Plato** in his seminal work, the *Republic.* However, it disappeared from the terrain of political theory, until the advent of the Industrial Revolution in the eighteenth and nineteenth centuries. There was an increased focus on social justice with the ideas of **J. S. Mill** and **T. H. Green** regarding *positive freedom.* The *welfare state* emerged in response to the policy recommendations of theorists like **J. M. Keynes** and to cater to the demands of the newly emerging civil society. **Karl Popper** defines justice as 'piecemeal social engineering' which is different from 'utopian social engineering'. For an overview of social justice, see *Why Social Justice Matters* (2005) by **Brian Barry**.

MARXIST THEORY OF REMEDIAL JUSTICE

The Marxist ideology is committed to the realisation of social justice. Marxism asserts that capitalist society is based on the exploitation of the proletariat by the bourgeoisie. This exploitation is rooted in the private ownership of the means of production by the bourgeoisie. Marxists therefore reject the liberal conception of individual justice, which they perceive to be an instrument of the bourgeoisie and which would not lead to any change in the unequal and unjust social relations between the bourgeoisie and the proletariat.

For Marxists capitalism is the basic reason behind inequality and injustice in society. Therefore, an equitable distribution of goods alone is not sufficient for social justice, but must necessarily be accompanied by the total destruction of capitalism and a radical restructuring of society. In the words of Karl Marx, 'Justice is achieved with the elimination of class society and the establishment of a classless society.' This classless society would be characterised by the common ownership of means of production and fair and equal social relations. This just redistribution of resources would be guided by the principle: 'from each according to his ability and to each according to his need.' The Marxist theory of justice is therefore based on complete social restructuring and redistribution of resources. As it seeks to remedy existing conditions of exploitation, inequality and injustice under capitalism, it is also referred to as the *remedial* or *redistributive theory of justice.*

PROCEDURAL THEORY OF JUSTICE

For libertarians, 'just outcomes' are those arrived at by the 'just actions' of individuals, and a specific distributive system is not essential for justice. Classical liberals and neo-liberals believe in the *procedural theory of justice*, which involves the idea that the procedures which allocate resources and resolve disputes must be fair and just, and must also be seen to be fair by people. It is also founded on the belief that the market, if not interfered with, would make the best and most efficient use of available resources and information. Procedural theories of justice are thus based on a close association with the workings of the free market economy.

Entitlement Theory of Justice

For the neo-liberal **Robert Nozick**, justice is not about agreeing to fair principles, but about respecting individual rights to *self-ownership* and to own property. His concept of justice, known as the *entitlement theory of justice*, argues for the institution of a *laissez-faire*, 'night-watchman state' which leaves citizens free to decide what they want to do with what is theirs. In his work *Anarchy, State and Utopia* (1974), Nozick contends that John Rawls fails to see people as individuals and criticises Rawls' conception of distributive justice. As a neo-liberal, Nozick believes in the following principles of ownership and entitlement:

1. Initially everything in the world was un-owned.

2. Individuals own themselves.
3. Property ownership is the result of individual labour following just actions and outcomes.
4. An individual is entitled to own anything and transfer any property as long as this does not negatively impact or harm anyone else.
5. Just acquisition and transfer of property does not permit the use of coercion, violence, fraud, stealing etc.
6. Once property has been justly acquired, a free market becomes necessary.

Friedrich. W. Hayek in his works *Law, Legislation and Liberty* (1973) and *The Mirage of Social Justice* (1976) holds that the very conceptualisation of social justice is meaningless. He asserts that individuals differ in their talents and skills, and therefore, equality before law is bound to create inequality in terms of their actual material status. Like for Robert Nozick, justice for Hayek too implies the non-interference of the state.

DISTRIBUTIVE JUSTICE

In his classic treatise *Nicomachean Ethics*, **Aristotle** speaks of *narrow justice* and *broad justice*. Narrow justice implies a sense of equality and *proportionality*. According to him, proportionality may be of three kinds:

1. *Distributive proportionality*: Different individuals in the same condition or state should receive the same or equal treatment.
2. *Corrective proportionality*: Punishment should be proportionate or equal to the crime.
3. *Reciprocal proportionality*: The price of something should be proportionate or equal to the value of that thing.

Within the Aristotelian framework, a just and equitable distribution implies a distribution of resources proportionate to the capabilities of individuals and their contributions to society. Therefore, it is also known as *proportionate justice*, as contrasted with *arithmetic justice* wherein everyone is treated equally. Capitalists and neo-liberals like Nozick believe that resources should be distributed on the basis of individual capability and efficiency, while egalitarians like John Rawls support distribution based on need, although Rawls combines both capability and need to explain the liberal concept of justice.

The Criteria of Distribution

The criteria employed for distribution of goods and services are desert, merit and need:

1. *Desert*: According to **Adam Swift**'s concept of just desert, the rewards or punishments that a person receives or is subjected to are a consequence of individual efforts and actions.
2. *Merit*: Liberals and neo-liberals believe in the distribution of resources according to merit and that the meritorious should be rewarded.
3. *Need*: Need as a criterion suggests that people might differ in their capabilities as well as their needs. Therefore, justice implies not only responding to people's capabilities but also their needs. Socialists and Marxists support the principle of needs in distribution.

In the contemporary context, theories of distributive justice are translated into the affirmative action policies and inclusive policies of the welfare state.

JOHN RAWLS' THEORY OF JUSTICE

Centrality of the Individual

John Rawls was deeply influenced by the ideas of German philosopher Immanuel Kant who formulated the idea of abstract individualism by asserting that 'individuals are the kingdoms of ends and means'. Rawls also asserted that 'the self' is prior to its ends and that therefore, any relevant theory of justice should be based on individual human rationality emerging from human understanding. Thus, for Rawls justice is neither divine nor natural, but purely the result of individual human choice. He visualised society as a just and fair system of cooperation between free and equal citizens, and formulated his understanding of justice as a theory of *social contract* in which all are equal stakeholders and all have equal status.

Social Contract: The Original Position and the Veil of Ignorance

Rawls' theory of *social contract* is founded on what he calls the ***original position*** and the ***veil of ignorance***. The 'original position' is an impartial point of view which requires people to see themselves as free and equal entities who as a society agree upon and commit themselves to principles of social and political justice. The 'veil of ignorance' is an essential device to ensure this impartiality of judgment, to level everyone and make them stand on an equal footing. Removed from their social and historical circumstances, individuals behind the veil of ignorance will have no knowledge of their personal characteristics or endowments; they are only aware of certain basic common interests they all share, and general knowledge about biology, economics, geography and so on. Thus those behind the veil of ignorance do not know their entitlements or where the fault lines of social difference and discrimination lie, and have no specific ideas of what is a good life; but they will have a 'sense of justice'. If now given a list of the key ideas of justice drawn from social and political philosophy, and told to choose one that best enables them to pursue their interests and goals, Rawls argues that for those in the original position, the most rational choices would be two principles of justice.

1. *The first principle* guarantees to all the basic equal rights and freedoms needed to secure the fundamental interests of free and equal citizens and to pursue a broad range of what is considered 'good'.
2. *The second principle* guarantees to all a fair equality of educational and employment opportunities, enabling fair competition and securing the basic economic means and resources needed to pursue their goals and preserve their self-respect as equal and free individuals, and maximise benefit to the least advantaged.

According to Rawls these principles of justice, which he calls 'justice as fairness', are thus the result of a choice procedure in the original position intended to 'incorporate pure procedural justice at the highest level'.

Pure Procedural Justice

Rawls insists that justice must emerge as the result of a hypothetical social contract or agreement which in turn would be arrived at by people deprived of any knowledge that could make the agreement unfair. Rawls argues that his theory of the 'original position' is a conceptualisation of *pure procedural justice* which is devoid of any prejudices, preconceptions or prior arrangements.

Although he concedes people's welfare to be important, Rawls is critical of Jeremy Bentham's concept of justice and rejects the majority as the basis of any system of justice. Jeremy Bentham's notion of justice is *consequentialist*, i.e. one where the consequences or results are more important than the means or the processes to obtain them; he focuses on happiness that can be obtained without individual liberty and rights. As a liberal, for Rawls individual liberty and rights are always paramount for building a just society, and the procedure is more important than the result because Rawls believes that fair procedures are more likely to produce fair results.

A *deontological theory of ethics* suggests that the morality of an action should be based on whether or not that action itself is right or wrong under a given set of rules and principles, rather than on the consequences of that action.

Principle of Lexical Priority

In Rawls' theory of justice, individual liberty and rights come before public good and cannot be curtailed for the sake of people's welfare. He said justice is the first virtue of a society and no society can be sustained without it. Justice is also more important for Rawls than efficiency. Here Rawls is more akin to Plato for whom justice is the central value of a society, and different from the neo-liberals who favour efficiency as the most important. He believed in an inclusive justice that excluded neither the rich nor the poor and asserted that a market economy could also be a fair and just economy. But where socialist nations curtailed liberties and rights in the name of equality, Rawls held that liberty could be curtailed for the sake of liberty alone.

The Maximin and the Difference Principle

A central idea in John Rawls' influential work *A Theory of Justice* (1971) is the ***maximin principle*** of choice which helps us choose from given options when one is unsure of the outcome that will result from that choice. Also described as *risk and uncertainty averse*, it advises that in some circumstances, the right decision/choice is the one which maximises the least or minimum outcome, i.e. the one which makes the worst possible outcome as good and advantageous as can be. The maximin principle asks us to evaluate each available option in terms of the worst possible outcome that could result from choosing that option, and to pick the option that offers us the best worst outcome, i.e. the 'maximum minimum' or the '*maximin*'.

It becomes necessary here to mention the ***difference principle***, which is at the heart of Rawl's conception of 'justice as fairness'. The difference principle states that social and economic inequalities and differences should be rearranged so as to ensure the maximum benefit to the least advantaged members of society. Because it requires maximising the share of goods that go to those with the smallest share, the difference principle is also called a 'maximin principle of justice'; Rawls rejected that name precisely because it could be and was often confused with the 'maximin principle of choice'. The *difference* in his difference principle stands for protective discrimination against the rich and well-endowed, who shall provide compensation for the most disadvantaged in the form of progressive taxation. It ensures that basic primary goods are available to the least advantaged sections.

The wellbeing of members of a society is assessed by their allocation of primary goods, which are of two types:

1. *Social primary goods* for e.g. liberty, wealth, income, self-respect, education, opportunities which are available for the society to distribute.
2. *Natural primary goods* for e.g. individual characteristics and natural talents, the distribution of which cannot be influenced by society.

Institutional Framework for Distributive Justice

Rawls formulates a comprehensive institutional framework for the realisation of social and distributive justice in society. This framework would comprise the following four branches with different functions:

1. The *allocation branch* keeps the price system competitive by preventing the formation of a unreasonable market power and changes property rights through taxes and subsidies.
2. The *stabilisation branch* takes care of employment opportunities.
3. The *transfer branch* is responsible for maintaining a social minimum by way of unemployment and family allowances.

4. The *distribution branch* preserves an approximate fairness in the distribution of shares by means of taxation.

LIBERTARIAN THEORY OF JUSTICE

The **libertarian** conception of justice views human beings as individuals who possess free will and agency, are creative, and must be able to guide their own lives as they know best in order to achieve their potential and to flourish. Libertarians hold that the decisive factor of justice as a guiding social principle must be human nature and its need for autonomy. Libertarianism thus greatly values individual freedom and argues for justice that protects individual liberty and private property, as against justice that ensures fairness, order, harmony and welfare. For this reason, libertarians are also against the idea of distributive justice.

COMMUNITARIAN THEORY OF JUSTICE

Communitarians assert that individuals can only be identified as members of pre-existing social groups and organisations. This means that the interests, needs and opinions of individuals are shaped and defined by the societies and communities they belong to. Hence, their notions of distributive justice and its criteria emerge out of this theoretical context of social diversity. Communitarians therefore reject John Rawls' idea of 'the original position' and contend that individuals removed from their social, economic, historical and cultural contexts and denied that knowledge will not be able to make choices, informed or otherwise.

In *Liberalism and the Limits of Justice* (1983), **Michael Sandel** argues that the Rawlsian conception of justice is artificial because it is arrived at by atomistic individuals who are 'stripped' of all socio-historical context and identity, which effectively renders their understanding, choices and 'social contracts' meaningless and irrelevant.

Alasdair MacIntyre, who wrote *Whose Justice? Which Rationality?* (1988), focuses on the prior necessity and importance of morality over and above that of rationality in his work *After Virtue* (1981). **Michael Walzer** argues in *The Spheres of Justice* (1983) that no system of justice can be evaluated as being inherently just or unjust and that evaluation of justness or fairness is possible only on the basis of the social meanings attached to the goods at stake. Amartya Sen in his work *The Idea of Justice* (2009) comprehensively critiques Rawls' theory of 'procedural justice', asserting that justice itself is more important than the procedures through which it is obtained.

RAWLS' RESPONSE TO THE COMMUNITARIAN CRITIQUE

In response to the communitarian critique which emerged in the 1980s of his theory of justice, Rawls modified his position in his work *Political Liberalism* (1993). He acknowledged the significance of social diversity and conceded that a socio-political theory of justice should be formulated bearing in mind the diversity and plurality of society. He also argued that the concept of social justice is distinct from the people's moral aspirations and implies the formation of a liberal democratic system which can accommodate the cultural diversity of the society in question. Rawls conceptualised the idea of a 'basic structure' geared towards the creation of a shared political culture through the mechanism of constitutional democracy, and further proposed the concept of an *overlapping consensus* in which people are in broad agreement about what the *basic structure* of their society and state should be, despite existing socio-cultural differences. Rawls also strongly supports the formation of international cooperative organisations. In his work *The Law of Peoples* (1993), Rawls proposes eight principles to which, he argues, all well-organised peoples across all nations would largely agree:

1. People are free and independent; their freedom and independence must be respected.
2. People must observe all international treaties and undertakings.

3. People are equal.
4. People have the right to self-defense.
5. People must observe non-intervention.
6. People must honour human rights.
7. People must observe certain specified restrictions in the conduct of war.
8. People have a duty to assist other peoples living under unfavourable conditions that prevent their having a just or decent political regime.

THE FEMINIST CHALLENGE TO RAWLS

In arguing that justice is the first virtue of all social institutions, Rawls recognises that the family is part of the sphere of justice since injustice also occurs within the family. However, he insists that this injustice is necessary since the family is also a sphere of love and sacrifice, which are 'higher ideals', and that therefore all concerns of injustice within the family are irrelevant.

In doing so, as Susan Moller Okin observes in her criticism of Rawls, he ignores the socialisation of women which forces them to be the only ones to sacrifice their interests for the family. Okin, who wrote *Justice, Gender and the Family* (1989), argues that any theory of justice which is silent about the inequalities within the family is an incomplete one. On Rawls' theory of 'social contract', she asserts that it is made by men for men and does not represent the voices of women.

Rawls is also criticised for ignoring gender identities while conceptualising his 'veil of ignorance'. Some feminists also argue that the model of a self-interested, autonomous and rational individualist is a typically male conception, leaving little scope for values like nurture and care, and hence it needs to be replaced.

RONALD DWORKIN'S VIEW OF JUSTICE

Ronald Dworkin's view of justice is guided by the belief that the moral task of citizens and public officials is to make their society a more faithful realisation of liberal democratic ideals. He gives more importance to individual choices and luck for obtaining justice than to the fair distribution of primary goods. He argues that people with equal resources could end up with unequal benefits due to their choices, and distinguishes between *option luck* and *brute luck*. If someone goes blind due to a genetic problem, Dworkin attributes it to bad brute luck, but he credits buying a lottery ticket and winning to good option luck. In other words, option luck is a calculated and deliberate choice made by individuals while brute luck means unforeseen problems, and the inequality arising out of human choices should be part of any conception of justice. Dworkin feels that differences in wealth generated by differences 'traceable to genetic luck' are unfair.

AMARTYA SEN'S THEORY OF JUSTICE

To the question of what metric egalitarians should use to determine the degree to which a society could realise its ideal of equality, Nobel laureate and economist **Amartya Sen** proposes two metrics: *welfare* (utility); and Rawlsian primary goods. Sen introduced the concept of ***capability equality*** between these two extremes where *capability* means what various goods can do for people, apart from their welfare. Rawls believed that just institutions distribute primary goods justly such that the worst off are as well off as possible according to the primary social goods measure. Sen disagrees and argues that persons born with different physical and psychological propensities will be unequally efficient transformers of resources such as primary social goods into the goals they seek. Due to genetic, age or other factors people have varying capabilities to convert resources into effective freedoms. These variations enable people differently to build freedom in their lives, despite having the same primary resources.

Sen considers two individuals who are allotted the same primary goods; but one is fit, hardy and quick-witted while the other is lame, illness-prone, slow-witted and lacks physical coordination. Despite such obvious differences, the primary social goods metric will not show this disparity. Sen thus believes that given these glaring individual disparities, for a real and holistic theory of justice, we must look beyond the distribution of opportunities, income and other primary goods. A measure of people's real freedom to achieve the kind of *functioning* they have reason to value should be the basis of interpersonal comparisons. Sen's notion of capability thus represents effective freedom, whereas Rawlsian primary goods are just a means to this freedom.

RELATIONSHIP BETWEEN LIBERTY, EQUALITY AND JUSTICE

The notion of justice is fundamentally linked to the notions of liberty and equality, and cannot exist in isolation from them. Liberty, the freedom to choose, is vital for ensuring human dignity and capability. Equality implies equal opportunity, but also to be equal in the eyes of law, regardless of individual differences. Justice stands for fairness and equal opportunity for all in order to maintain a level playing field and ensure balance and harmony in society. Liberty and equality are thus both necessary for maintaining balance in society.

Justice involves freedom and choice for everyone, and basic social security for the underprivileged. Liberty without equality results in the survival of the fittest and the rule of the strongest. Equality without liberty results in suppression of human expression and creativity and individuals become slaves of the state. Fairness implies lack of discrimination and equal opportunity for everyone. For libertarians, justice implies the presence of liberty. For socialists, only equality makes justice fruitful, while egalitarians like John Rawls hold that liberty and equality are both necessary in equal measure for justice to be obtained.

4

RIGHTS

KEY CONCEPTS

Negative and positive rights; legal rights; moral rights; natural rights; utilitarian, libertarian, and communitarian theories of rights; three generations of rights; human rights

The concept of rights is a relatively modern concept which evolved with the rise of the modern industrial nation-state and the emergence of the ideas of liberal individualism. T. H. Green and W. N. Hohfield said that rights are a form of *claim*. Changing social, economic and political conditions give rise to the demand for new civil and political rights. Rights are neither static nor fixed in time and place but dynamic. What was only a claim in the past can become a right in the future, and vice versa. The 'divine right theory' of the Medieval Ages, which arbitrarily vested absolute powers in the ruler to be answerable to no earthly authority but only to God, is no longer recognised.

The rise of the existing liberal doctrines of individual rights is attributed to three major historical processes of radical socio-political transformation, namely:

The Glorious Revolution of 1688 in England: It was a bloodless revolution driven by the rich business classes who wanted more recognition within the monarchical absolutist regime. It led to the emergence of the idea of 'King in Parliament'.

The American Declaration of Independence, 1776: This was the first formal statement by the people of a nation asserting their right to choose their own government.

The French Revolution, 1789: The most important contributions of this revolution were the Declaration of the Rights of Man and Citizen, and the ideals of Liberty, Equality and Fraternity.

NEGATIVE AND POSITIVE RIGHTS

Rights may be divided into two broad categories.

***Negative rights*:** These are rights that entail non-interference from the state and society at large, for example, the basic inalienable human rights to life, liberty, privacy, self-respect. Negative rights grant holders the right to freedom from something.

***Positive rights*:** These are rights that impose obligations on others, the society or the state, which is required to take some action to ensure the fuller enjoyment of rights by the bearers. Social and economic rights are positive rights, for example, the right to education and the right to earn a livelihood.

LEGAL RIGHTS

The four basic components of rights are known as *Hohfeldian incidents* after the American legal theorist, **Wesley Newcomb Hohfeld**, who discovered them. According to Hohfeld, a *right* is something that expresses a certain relationship between two parties: the holder and the observer of the right. Rights may be characterised by four basic elements:

1. ***Privilege*:** Privilege rights mark out what their bearer has no duty *not* to do. For example, if I find a shell on a beach, I can pick it up. I am not bound by any duty to not pick it up.
2. ***Claim*:** Claim rights create duties for others. For instance, if an employee is working for an employer, she can claim her wages. This claim implies that it is the employer's duty to pay the employee her due wages.
3. ***Power*:** Power rights imply the ability to change one's own or another's claim as well as privilege rights and duties. For example, a ship's captain has the power right to order the cabin boy to clean the deck.
4. ***Immunity*:** Immunity rights imply protection against the encroachment of one's privileges or claim rights by another. For example, civil servants have an immunity right to not be dismissed when a new government comes into power.

MORAL RIGHTS

In his work *Taking Rights Seriously* (1977), **Ronald Dworkin** asserts that the concept of rights imposes a sense of moral responsibility on others. Therefore, the bearers of rights uphold a strong sense of rights, while those at the receiving end or those upon whom the claim is made represent a weaker sense of rights. This means that the rights of individuals cannot be sacrificed for the collective goals or common interests of others. Dworkin uses the metaphor of rights as 'trumps', which implies that rights permit their holders to act in certain ways even if some social aim would be served by doing otherwise. Dworkin also emphasises that rights as claims impose a duty upon others to protect the rights of the rights-bearer.

Dworkin's theory identifies only two moral rights as inalienable, namely: 1) the right of citizens to be treated equally; and 2) their right to have their human dignity respected. This claim is not based on any general philosophy of politics or any historical tradition, and hence it must be regarded as a speculative claim based upon individual reason. Therefore, it is an *a priori* claim which takes precedence upon all other kinds of claims granted by historical tradition or political philosophy or otherwise. Another aspect of Dworkin's theory is its emphasis on absolute individualism.

THEORY OF NATURAL RIGHTS

The first and the most influential statement on natural human rights were given by **John Locke** in his work *The Second Treatise on Civil Government* in 1690. In his *doctrine of natural rights* Locke speaks of man as being born with a natural entitlement to perfect freedom and uninhibited enjoyment of all the rights and freedoms granted by nature. Since the state of nature precedes any kind of social or political organisation, therefore the rights granted by nature are also not subject to any human authority or the approval of any social or political order.

Locke's doctrine of natural rights greatly influenced the founders of the American Constitution. **Thomas Paine**, a founding figure of the American movement for independence, defended the doctrine of natural rights in his work *Rights of Man* (1971). **Thomas Jefferson** and **James Madison**, founding figures of the American Constitution also gave primacy to the Lockean doctrine. It is widely believed that the Charter of Fundamental Rights in the American Constitution—the first written constitution in the world to include a declaration on fundamental human rights—is a legal representation of Locke's theory of natural rights. The American 'Declaration of Independence' states that: 'We hold these truths to be self-evident, that all men are created equal, that they are endowed by their Creator with certain unalienable Rights, that among these are Life, Liberty and the pursuit of Happiness.'

Critique of the Doctrine of Natural Rights

Karl Marx in his work *On the Jewish Question* (1844) asserted that the doctrine of natural rights is self-contradictory because these are rights of the egoistical and acquisitive individual, and are enjoyed only by the capitalist class at the expense of others and through the exploitation of others.

Edmund Burke criticised the idea of 'natural' rights and insisted that rights originate from customs and traditions. He rejected the atomistic conception of the individual propounded by Locke and said that the individual is a communitarian self located in society and its customs and traditions. Locke's theory of natural rights was also strongly criticised by utilitarians like Jeremy Bentham.

UTILITARIAN THEORY OF RIGHTS

The utilitarian theory of rights originated with the ideas of the English philosopher **Jeremy Bentham**, who believed that the proper aim of any kind of social, political or moral theory should be to secure the 'greatest happiness of the greatest number'. Bentham contended that the concept of natural rights is very similar to the medieval notion of divine rights, which he dismissed as 'nonsense on stilts' as it was too abstract and hypothetical to be taken seriously. He said the idea of inalienable natural rights which precede the state was philosophically absurd and historically fallacious, and that in the absence of the state, the doctrine of natural rights is effectively rendered 'aimless' and 'unscientific'. He asserted that all people have a natural right to happiness—which he defined and quantified within the utilitarian theory as *utility*—and argued that the objective of any social or moral theory or legal doctrine must be to maximise *aggregate social utility*. Bentham therefore formulates a legal conception of rights wherein rights serve as the means to an end, i.e. happiness, wherein the state or existing political order acts as the guarantor of this happiness.

LIBERTARIAN THEORY OF RIGHTS

Robert Nozick bases his theory of rights on the historical conception of justice. He calls it the 'entitlement theory of justice', which is based on a defense of the free market and capitalist system and consists of three principles:

1. *Principle of just initial acquisition*: A person who acquires a holding in accordance with the principles of justice in acquisition is entitled to that holding.
2. *Principle of just initial transfer*: A person who acquires a holding in accordance with the principle of justice in transfer from someone entitled to that holding is entitled to that holding.
3. *Principle of rectification*: This provides for the redressal of past injustices.

COMMUNITARIAN THEORY OF RIGHTS

Communitarians take the 'individual' as the unit for the distribution of resources. However they contend that the individual is not an abstract universal category like the liberalist conception of the individualistic self, but instead is a 'situated self' deeply embedded in community, culture and tradition. Communitarians argue that the liberal politics of rights needs to be replaced with a 'politics for the common good'. In his work *Liberalism and the Limits of Justice* (1982), Michael Sandel criticises the universalism of the liberal conception of rights and justice as being metaphysical and meta-ethical, and hence unreal and impractical. Communitarians thus insist that any relevant and practicable theory of rights must emerge from the existing traditions and customs of living communities, conditioned by their particular historical experiences.

THE FEMINIST CHALLENGE

Feminists contend that most social and political systems based on individualism are based on male dominance and subjugation of women. Therefore, all theories of rights and justice are rendered irrelevant unless the sources of this patriarchal subjugation, exclusion and oppression of women and other marginalised groups are acknowledged, identified and questioned. **Susan Moller Okin**, in her work *Justice, Gender and the Family*, contends that the family, which is a site of great injustices and inequalities, is excluded from the entire discourse on rights and social justice.

I. M. Young shows that different cultural groups have different histories and historical experiences, both as individuals and groups. Accordingly, as opposed to the idea of a universal citizenship, she propounds the idea of *differential citizenship*, which consists of the following values: equal participation in public life; focus on the common good; and equal treatment of all.

THREE GENERATIONS OF RIGHTS

The history of struggles and claims for rights in general has been broadly divided into three phases which led to the emergence of three generations of rights.

Civil and Political Rights

The claims for which the American Civil Rights Movement fought for in the 1950s and 1960s belong to the first generation of civil rights claims. The foundations of civil and political rights lie in the ideology of John Locke and Jeremy Bentham.

***Civil rights*:** These are the basic legal rights that a person must possess in order to secure the status of equal citizenship in a liberal democratic state, for example, the right to own property, the right to make and enforce contracts, the right to freedom of speech and expression etc.

***Political rights*:** These include the rights necessary to ensure political participation and representation, for example, the right to vote, the right to stand in elections etc.

Socio-economic Rights

The claims for socio-economic rights emerged with the rise of welfare functions of the liberal democratic state. The rise of the feminist movement and communism also contributed to the assertion of these demands. Tracing the relationship between civil rights and socio-economic rights, **Harold J. Laski** asserted that, like the rights to freedom of speech, the realisation of civil and political rights must also be accompanied by the availability of and access to basic education and healthcare facilities; otherwise, these rights are meaningless.

T. H. Green stressed that social and economic rights are essential for the moral development of an individual. Liberal theorists like **John Rawls** and developmental economists like **Amartya Sen** have also emphasised the importance of socio-economic rights in securing a level playing field for all individuals in a market-dominated society. Rights like equal wages for equal work, basic healthcare facilities, right to primary education, abolition of discrimination on the grounds of class, caste, sex or race also became the central focus of many socialist movements emerging across the globe.

Rights of Cultural Membership

There are three kinds of rights inherent to the *multicultural theory of rights*. First, there are *rights related to governance*, which include special representation rights as endorsed by Will Kymlicka in his work *Multicultural Citizenship*. The second category of multicultural rights seeks to accommodate a variety of cultural practices within large states. These might also seek to give special assistance to a disadvantaged minority, e.g. the Bilingual Education Act (1978) designed to enable parallel instruction in non-English languages for children. The third category relates to *rights of recognition*. These involve issues of collective dignity and of a group's attitude towards others and itself.

Bhikhu Parekh said that cultural rights are important for the minorities to enable them to preserve their collective group identity. **Will Kymlicka** perceives culture as a self-sufficient civilisation with its own institutions and values. He asserts that cultures are unique, valuable and distinct, and so any universalist conception of rights cannot be ethically imposed on them. Therefore, Kymlicka insists that regimes of group differentiated rights are necessary for the preservation of difference and diversity.

The third generation of rights, which may be broadly termed the *rights of cultural membership*, has received considerable attention in recent years. Will Kymlicka and Bhikhu Parekh are the propounders of cultural rights. Cultural rights demand the right of equal respect and the right of equal dignity. Cultural rights are different from socio-economic rights. These include linguistic rights for members of cultural minorities and the rights of indigenous people to preserve their cultural institutions and practices and to exercise some measure of political autonomy. These rights are related to the emerging theoretical perspectives of multiculturalism, feminism and communitarianism.

Postmodernist Rights

These are new kinds of rights related to individual identity which have been facilitated particularly by the *postmodernist discourse* on constructions of identity, history and society. The most prominent of these has been the demand for the rights of those who identify as lesbian, gay, bisexual, transgender, queer, intersex, asexual and pansexual (LGBTQIAP+). Members of the Queer Community comprising various sexual orientations and self-defined gender identities who have sought to gain recognition as well as acceptance in the eyes of law which criminalises specific kinds of sexual behaviour and also in the wider society which regards them as taboo.

HUMAN RIGHTS

Human rights are rights inherent to all human beings regardless of their race, sex, nationality, ethnicity, language, religion or any other status. The term is all-encompassing of various kinds of universal and moral rights including the right to life and liberty, freedom from slavery and exploitation, freedom of opinion and expression.

Natural rights are considered to be moral, and not historical rights. They are natural because, as argued by T. H. Green, they are essential for the development of individual personality. The discourse of natural rights is a classical political philosophy discourse as compared to the newness of the human rights discourse. They are in the nature of claims placed upon the society, state, community as well as other individuals. Human rights, on the other hand, are claims placed also on the international order and global community. Green says that natural rights are moral claims which are recognised by the society and protected by the state.

L. J. MacFarlane has underlined the distinguishing characteristics of human rights as compared to other moral and legal rights. These include: universality; individuality; practicability and enforceability.

The ***philosophical and moral justifications*** of human rights include: human dignity; reason; autonomy; equality; capability; and consensus.

HUMAN RIGHTS ARE RELATIVE

John Locke propounded the concept of human rights in the form of natural rights. Liberals like Locke claim that human rights are available for each and everyone across the world, and that hence, human rights are universal. But Marxists demonstrated that the concept of human rights is not universal but only meant for the rich and propertied, and hence advocated for social and economic rights for all. **Maurice Cranston** said human rights cannot be applied universally due to differences in social and economic conditions of citizens, but they may be applied in the form of civil and political rights.

Liberals conceived of human beings as atomistic, secular and rational. However, feminists have argued that human rights are inherently patriarchal because the liberal conception of human beings is itself only of men and not women. Communitarians hold that the liberal concept of individual human rights is detached from the community, and therefore meaningless. Multi-culturists advocated for cultural rights of difference, which was denied by the liberals. From the above, it may be said that morally and philosophically, human rights may be considered universal, but politically and culturally, human rights are relative and specific.

5

DEMOCRACY

KEY CONCEPTS

Procedural and substantive democracy; direct democracy; representative democracy; liberal democracy; types of liberal democracy; deliberative democracy; illiberal democracy; neo-Marxist perspective; consociational democracy

The term *democracy* is derived from the Greek words *demos*, meaning people, and *kratos* or *kratia*, meaning power. Democracy may broadly be said to denote a system or process of collective decision-making that is characterised by a kind of equality among the participants at a critical stage of the decision-making process. A democracy is a government by the people in which political power is vested in the people and exercised directly by them or by their elected representatives under a free and fair electoral system.

WHY DEMOCRACY?

There are two basic justifications given for why democracy is essential to human society: intrinsic and instrumental. We assert the *intrinsic* value of democracy, that is, we argue that democracy is valuable for its own sake because it is the fairest and most just way of giving expression to equality among citizens. Democracy may also be justified as a way of minimising the abuse of political power by distributing it equally among citizens. Thus its intrinsic value derives from its moral superiority as a way of giving effect to political equality.

The other justification for democracy is its *instrumental* role in human development, to the extent that it encourages people to take responsibility for their political lives. Thus democracy may also be valued instrumentally, that is, as a means to other ends.

PROCEDURAL AND SUBSTANTIVE DEMOCRACY

Modern democracy works through a *representative government* and its institutions, that is, people elect their representatives to a legislature or assembly, and these representatives are authorised to take decisions on behalf of those who elected them. Ultimate sovereignty, however, remains with the people, who can hold their representatives accountable, and refuse to re-elect them when the next election comes round. This form of democracy is often termed *procedural democracy*, because it emphasises the procedures and institutions of democracy.

However, democracy should not be seen merely as a set of procedures and institutions, for e.g., free and fair elections, legislative assemblies, and the constitutional governments arising out of these. The wide existing social and economic inequalities make it difficult, even impossible, for any formal participation in democracy to be meaningful or effective. These inequities are only aggravated under capitalism and hence must be checked by the state. This is why social theorists emphasise the importance of *substantive democracy*. Socialists seek to transform society in egalitarian directions via the regulatory policies directed by the democratic processes of the state. The development and functioning of a welfare state is an instance of the social democratic theories of the state.

CLASSICAL MODELS: DIRECT DEMOCRACY

The birthplace of classical democracy is ancient Greece. The Greek philosopher Cleon claimed that Greek democracy, also known as *direct democracy*, stood for a model of government which was 'of the people, by the people and for the people'—a slogan that was later famously echoed by Abraham Lincoln in his historic speech, 'The Gettysburg Address'.

Direct democracy is characterised by the direct participation of all adult constituent citizens in the day-to-day administrative processes of government. French revolutionary thinker Jean Jacques Rousseau was highly influenced by the Greek model of direct democracy, which implied an organic conception of democracy, wherein the city state was conceptualised as a dynamic living organism, and the citizens or polity as its organs. It was also known as the *plebiscitarian* model of democracy.

All major decisions were made by the *Ecclesia* or Assembly and all propertied adult male citizens were members of the Ecclesia, which met at least forty times a year. Public officials were chosen on the basis of a lots system. A system of payment for administrators was also introduced. A council comprising 500 citizens acted as an executive of the committee. The presiding officer of the Ecclesia could only hold office for the period of a single meeting of the Ecclesia. This kind of democracy was practicable only in small city states with manageable populations.

However, as critics have noted, Greek democracy was also based on the active exclusion of women, slaves and children who were labeled 'passive citizens', and hence is far from an ideal model.

REPRESENTATIVE DEMOCRACY

Limited and Indirect: Representative democracy is a limited and indirect form of democracy. It is limited in the sense that participation in government is infrequent and brief, being restricted to the act of voting in elections held every few years. It is indirect in the sense that the public does not exercise power by itself but elects those who will rule on its behalf. The strength and advantage of representative democracy is that it offers a practicable form of democracy through which even large populations can participate in the governmental process.

Electoral: The central idea in representative democracy is the idea of *popular consent*, expressed through the act of voting. Representative democracy is, thus, synonymous with and a form of electoral democracy in that popular election is seen as the only legitimate source of political authority. Thus the essence of representative democracy lies in two key concepts: *political pluralism*; and *open competition* between political philosophies, movements and parties. However, although these features may be necessary preconditions for representative democracy, they should not be mistaken for democracy itself.

LIBERAL DEMOCRACY

The main features that characterise a representative democracy under liberalism are its institutions and its values.

Institutions: There are certain primary institutions without which a liberal democratic government cannot function. The first is an *electoral system based on universal adult franchise* which guarantees every citizen one vote. The second is a *parliamentary government characterised by the separation of powers*. In his influential work *The Spirit of Laws* (1750), French philosopher **Montesquieu** propounded the principle of separation of powers, arguing that the legislative, executive and judicial functions of the government must necessarily be divided among separate and independent bodies of the government in order to prevent and limit the abuse of power and to safeguard liberty.

Values: A liberal democracy upholds liberal values and is based on the principle of *equal moral worth* of every individual citizen. **Jeremy Bentham** insisted that this principle was manifested in the adoption of universal adult franchise. He also upheld *equality* as an important value of any liberal democracy since democracy does not discriminate between people on the basis of their socio-cultural backgrounds or physical attributes.

Jean-Jacques Rousseau emphasised the importance of *popular sovereignty* as a fundamental liberal democratic value as it underlines that the authority and power of a state are created by the unanimous consent of its people, through their elected representatives. The people are the ultimate source of all political power and legitimacy of the government. **John Locke** saw the liberal democratic government as the guarantor and *protector of the natural rights* of all individuals.

J. S. Mill held that a liberal democratic government was the only acceptable way in which people's liberties could be reasonably and fairly constrained based on their democratically obtained rational consent and agreement. In his essay, *On Liberty* (1859), Mill saw democracy in the form of the tyranny of the majority as presenting new threats to individual liberty. But he supported the ideal of *deliberative* democracy as it would lead to the 'highest and harmonious' development of individual potential and enable the people to achieve a higher level of self-realisation and moral development. Thus, for Mill, democracy is essentially an educational and emancipatory experience.

CONTEMPORARY DEMOCRACY

Contemporary representative democracy is practised through the proportional representation system and voting systems like first-past-the-post. The inclusion of civil society and social movements is equally important in decision-making. While there are several different models of representative democracy that are attributed to specific thinkers broadly within the utilitarian and liberal traditions, such as James Mill, John Locke and John Stuart Mill, **C. B. Macpherson** in his work *The Life and Times of Liberal Democracy* (1977) propounded four liberal models, namely: protective, developmental, equilibrium, and participatory democracy.

Protective Model

The protective model was based on the principle of protecting and guaranteeing certain basic rights of the people against the tyranny of the state, such as natural rights, the right to individual liberty, and the rights to property and universal adult suffrage. John Locke, believed to be the original proponent of this model, asserted that 'Government is a trust held on the behalf of the people', which implies minimum government to ensure maximum individual freedom. Following the American and the French Revolutions, democracy became associated with the protective model, which argued that democracy alone could protect the governed from oppression by those who govern.

Developmental Model

This model is often traced to the ideas of **Jean Jacques Rousseau** and **J. S. Mill**, who insisted that democracy was essentially an educational experience which should aid the moral and intellectual development of society and the self-realisation of the individual. For Mill, democracy stands for the fundamental commitment to the self-development, participation and growth of all individuals, equally.

C. B. Macpherson said the individual has two types of capacity: a creative and an exploitative capacity. Capitalism promotes acquisitiveness, aggression, consumerism, competitiveness, mechanistic mass production and the exploitative capacity of individuals; it also suppresses their innate desire to be creative. Mill's critique of capitalism led to the emergence of the developmental model of democracy, based on the intrinsic values of democracy.

Equilibrium or Elitist Model

The equilibrium model of democracy was developed by **Joseph Schumpeter** in his work *Capitalism, Socialism and Democracy* (1942). Schumpeter defined liberal democracy as the political institution and process by which parties and individuals compete for the people's mandate and for political power. He compares political behaviour with market behaviour. Electoral competition creates a market in which politicians act as entrepreneurs who pursue power by forming government, and individual voters behave like consumers, voting for the party/candidate with the policies that most closely reflect their own preferences. Schumpeter rejected the relevance of values and morality in democracy and argued that democracy is not an end in itself, but rather, an institutional arrangement for arriving at political decisions wherein some people govern for the realisation of other people's goals.

Anthony Downs also referred to this model as the *elitist* model of democracy as it implies rule by the political elite. **C. Wright Mills** in his work *The Power Elite* (1956) recognised three groups of elites who hold and control political power in American society, namely politicians of the federal government, defense personnel and industrialists. The equilibrium/elitist model is a *procedural* model of democracy, where the emphasis is on procedures that aim to provide a practical framework and mechanism for democracy to function. There is also emphasis on protection of rights and entitlements.

Pluralist Model

Pluralists essentially believe that democracy has nothing to do with values but is simply a procedural mechanism for choosing the political leadership who will represent the polity and establish government. The main proponents of the pluralist model include **Karl Mannheim**, **Raymond Aron**, **Robert Dahl** and **Charles Lindblom**. Dahl and Lindblom proposed the concept of *polyarchy* or the rule of many, a term coined by Dahl to describe modern-day American democracy. They argued that although the economically powerful and privileged exert more political influence than ordinary citizens, no individual elite or single group of elites can permanently dominate the political process and system, and that active electoral competition and *political bargaining* is intrinsic to a polyarchy.

Robert Dahl holds that in a pluralist democracy, multiple diverse groups express their ideas and are able to develop a certain understanding of political representation. However, he later modified his theory, insisting that there are only a limited number of groups which have actual access to and control of power. Dahl specifies the exact nature of pluralist democracies and argues that:

1. If competitive electoral systems are characterised by multiple unequal interest groups with strong views on different issues, then democratic rights will be protected and extreme political inequalities, other than those guaranteed by law and constitutions, will be largely avoided.
2. *Competitive equilibrium*: Empirical evidence suggests that at least certain polities, like the USA and UK, fulfill these conditions. Dahl is convinced that power is shared by many groups in a society representing diverse interests where each group defends its particular interests through government, thus creating a proclivity towards what he calls a 'competitive equilibrium' that benefits all citizens in the long run. Democracy is the process by which ordinary citizens exert a relatively high degree of control over their political representatives, in two ways: through *regular*

elections and through political competition among parties, groups and individuals. Dahl dismisses concerns about the 'tyranny of the majority', expressed by Madison, Mill and Tocqueville, and argues that it is impossible because elections express the preferences of multiple, divergent and competing groups, rather than the wishes of a single strong majority.

3. *Neo-Pluralism*: Related to their pluralist model of democracy, Robert Dahl and Charles Lindblom founded the concept of *neo-pluralism*, which argues that business associations are more important than other groups present in society. Neo-pluralism could refer to any one of several models of political power, including pluralism, elitism, or consociationism; but more specifically, it now usually refers to Dahl's pluralist theory of political power as elaborated in his work *Who Governs* (1961).

Participatory Model

The active participation of citizens and a responsive government are two important fundamentals of a participatory democracy, as emphasised in the writings of Nicos Poulantzas, Carole Pateman and C. B. Macpherson. These proponents derive diverse insights from the Marxist, feminist and liberal perspectives, that seek to make democracy more emancipatory, inclusive, accountable and self-regulatory, while also reframing it within the ideas of pluralism and deliberative democracy. Participatory democracy is a normative theory. Theories which support participatory models of democracy try to bring in mechanisms of direct democracy by adapting them to modern conditions.

Rejection of electoral democracy: The participatory model rejects the electoral or procedural models of representative democracy. Instead, it emphasises popular control of political and civil society institutions in which, rather than electing representatives to take decisions on their behalf, citizens play a direct and active role in making decisions that affect their lives and society. Participatory democracy thus seeks to democratise not just the electoral process but also academic institutions and the workplace, and emphasises the importance of transparency, accountability and inclusiveness in the decision-making process.

Some basic features of participatory democracy include:

1. Decisions are by consensus rather than by majority.
2. Members feel on par with one another.
3. Citizens propose policy reforms and vote directly on policy decisions, rather than through elected representatives.
4. Citizens engage in structured dialogue and deliberation through citizen assemblies and councils to arrive at informed decisions rather than through political representation.

C. B. Macpherson argued that participation has a developmental aspect that transforms the participant, fosters personal growth, makes citizens better informed and naturally oriented towards the common good. His emphasis was on equality, freedom, critical thinking and civility. He was influenced by J. S. Mill's critique of *possessive individualism*, and believed that a democratic society should accommodate market competition, while also embracing the liberal value of right to equal self-development.

Carole Pateman, in *Participation and Democratic Theory* (1970), criticised Robert Dahl and Giovanni Sartori. Sartori's book *Democratic Theory* (1962) claimed that democracy is not for the common man but rather a rule for politicians. Pateman exposed the differences between social contract theories and democracy with regard to participation and showed how representative democracy, a liberal democratic theory, is associated with patriarchy. In her famous work, *The Sexual Contract* (1997), she argued that the 'sexual contract' presupposes the 'social contract', and an equal social contract does not exist since it does not take into account gender-based inequalities.

Pateman supported the idea of *self-management* through participatory democracy models. She asserted that citizens must be actively involved in decision-making processes regarding their daily lives, and that this would lead to more open and flexible political institutions at both the local and national levels. This increased participation would further enable experimentation with new political structures which would lead to wider institutional reform.

Jane Mansbridge in her work *Beyond Adversary Democracy* (1980) distinguished between two forms of participatory democracy: unitary and adversary democracy. *Unitary democracy* is based on common interests, shared goals and friendship, and implies a strong faith in mutually shared democratic values. *Adversary democracy* is based on conflicting interests and derives from the possessive individualism of Locke and Hobbes wherein the quest for political power and its institutionalisation is based on self-interest rather than common goals. Adversary democracy is thus antagonistic to the very ideals of participatory democracy.

Nico Poulantzas advocated for a participatory democracy founded on *socialist pluralism*. Socialist pluralism recognises that the state is not a homogenous, unified entity, but a complex and dynamic structure comprising multiple competing and overlapping structures, each with its own interests and power dynamics. Poulantzas' idea of participatory democracy involves the direct participation of the working class in decision-making through popular, self-governing assemblies and councils, thereby challenging capitalist domination and the power of the ruling class, and creating a more democratic society. This implies greater accountability of parliaments, bureaucracy and political parties towards the public, and also a well-organised and politically aware working class and strong people's movements.

DELIBERATIVE DEMOCRACY

Deliberative democracy, also known as *discursive* democracy, derives from the thought of J. S. Mill. Coined by Joseph M. Bessette in his work *Deliberative Democracy: The Majority Principle in Republican Government* (1980), it holds deliberation, structured dialogue, debates and discussion to be the essence of democracy and central to political decision-making. Supporters of deliberative democracy argue that parliamentary democracy is the better model. They also reject representative democracy or the vote-centric model, and favour the rights of minorities because they believe representative democracy may turn into majoritarianism and the 'tyranny of the majority'. However, it adopts elements of both consensus-based decision-making and majority rule, and is broadly compatible with both representative and direct democracy. Deliberative democracy emphasises the importance of establishing an egalitarian ethos and institutional rules and practices of democracy based on principles of formal equality.

Deliberative democracy criticises the procedural or electoral model of democracy and argues that democratic decision-making is not only about aggregating preferences through voting but must also be preceded by authentic deliberation. Robert Goodin talks about deliberative democracy from 'within', emphasising on legitimacy, simplicity and easiness.

James Fishkin highlighted the following features of deliberative democracy:

1. *Information*: Access to accurate and balanced information so that participants can take informed decisions on any given issue.
2. *Random selection*: Participants must be randomly selected to ensure a balanced representation of diverse perspectives, interest groups and stakeholders.
3. *Inclusive*: The deliberation process must ensure that marginal and underrepresented

groups are included, have an equal voice and get equal consideration.

4. *Dialogue*: Participants must engage in respectful and open dialogue with the aim of seeking mutual understanding and common ground.
5. *Consensus*: Decisions must be arrived at by consensus.
6. *Feedback*: Participants must know how their inputs were used in the decision-making and how the decision was arrived at.

Joshua Cohen identified the following features of deliberative democracy:

1. Deliberative democracy is an ongoing and autonomous process whose participants expect it to continue into the indefinite future.
2. Citizens are a part of the democratic structure as constituents of different institutions that are built and formed through deliberations.
3. Commitment to a pluralism of values and shared common aims within the polity.
4. Citizens prefer to know the *causal history* of each legislation, how it came to be created and then legitimised, i.e. for each law to be traceable to a deliberative process.
5. Members recognise and respect each other's deliberative capacities, which implies the existence of free speech.
6. Cohen also emphasises the concept of *reasonable pluralism*, which implies the acceptance of different and incompatible worldviews and the importance of good faith.

ILLIBERAL DEMOCRACY

An illiberal democracy is one in which elections and other democratic institutions exist, but where individual rights and civil liberties are often curtailed and where the rule of law and independent institutions such as the judiciary and the media may be weakened or co-opted to serve the interests of the ruling party or leader. Illiberal democracy is often associated with leaders or parties that are nationalist, anti-immigrant and opposed to liberal values such as free speech, minority rights, and protection of individual liberties. Such leaders or parties often use the language of democracy to legitimise their rule, but use repressive tactics such as media censorship, voter suppression, and the harassment of political opponents to maintain power. Illiberal democracy has been on the rise in recent years, with leaders such as Viktor Orban in Hungary, Recep Tayyip Erdogan in Turkey, and Jair Bolsonaro in Brazil being seen as examples of this phenomenon. Illiberal democracy represents a direct threat to democratic values and institutions, and leads to the erosion of civil liberties and the concentration of power in the hands of a few.

MARXIST THEORY OF DEMOCRACY

The Marxist theory of democracy derives from the ideas of Karl Marx and the social democrats. It is a radical theory based on a critique of the liberal models of democracy.

Critique of Liberal Democracy: Marx said that liberal democracy is a step ahead from feudalism since it leads to the creation of a structure that guarantees formal freedoms, but that the ethic of equality within the liberal model of democracy is fallacious.

Dictatorship of the Proletariat: Marx propounded the idea of 'dictatorship of the proletariat' to substitute for liberal capitalist democracies, whereby the proletariat will take power and control over the means of production from the bourgeoisie, and ultimately bring about the socialisation of the means of production.

Communism: The Marxist theory of higher communism implies the abolition of the state and the establishment of a classless, stateless society. This is a radical understanding of the notions of people's participation, statehood and democracy. For Marx, democracy is not only a form of government but a form of society where the community owns the means of production. There is thus no class division. The realisation of the ideals of equality and fraternity implies the actualisation of real democracy. People will be liberated from exploitation and they shall work according to their capacity and receive according to their need. Communist countries advocated a model of people's democracy through the dominance of a single party, that is the Communist Party. Lenin exemplified the prominence of the party within this system through his model of '*democratic centralism*'.

Neo-Marxist Perspective

Chantel Mouffe and **Ernesto Laclau** criticised the model of one-party rule within the Leninist system, and advocated a return to classical Marxism. They advocated socialist anarchism and focused on bringing about greater cooperation among people in society to ensure the establishment of a genuine communist society. They asserted that democratic justice and practices must be extended to the family, workplace and community. They also advocated decentralisation of political power in the hands of local governments.

Michael Hardt and **Antonio Negri** focused on the *ethic of revolution*, a philosophical and political framework that emphasises the importance of collective action, solidarity and the common struggle for social and economic justice. They sought to develop autonomous, self-governing communities that can resist and overthrow the global capitalist hierarchical structures of power and relations. Such a revolution they argue must be based on a shared vision of a new, more egalitarian and just society that is built up through the collective struggles of ordinary people, transformative action and decentralised networks of cooperation.

CONSOCIATIONAL DEMOCRACY

In a *consociational* democracy, different social groups or communities share power and participate in decision-making processes. This model is often used in societies that are deeply divided along ethnic, religious or linguistic lines, where there is a need to balance competing interests and ensure that minority groups are adequately represented in the political process. Power is shared between a coalition of political parties representing different groups or communities, and decision-making is based on consensus rather than majority rule. Belgium, Switzerland and the Netherlands are consociational democracies.

Arend Lijphart propounded the theory of consociational democracy wherein he suggested various measures, such as a grand coalition, proportional representation, mutual veto and segmental autonomy, to ensure the inclusion of diversity and avoid majoritarian domination by any one group in government. He argues that it is better than the Westminster model of parliamentary democracy followed in the United Kingdom and elsewhere, and believes India, Belgium, Australia and Switzerland to be the best examples of consociational democracy.

Democracy and Difference: Highlighting the ever-growing diversity of democratic political systems, cultural groups and liberal societies, **I. M. Young** asserts that the representation of this diversity, i.e. of each and every cultural group, is essential within any prescribed model of democracy. Similarly, in *Democracy and Difference* (1996), **Seyla Benhabib** explores the relationship between democracy, identity politics, difference and recognition, and argues that democratic societies must find ways to address the concerns and needs of diverse social groups, including those based on ethnicity, culture, gender and religion, rather than seeking to ignore or erase them.

Democracy and Development: The 'Lee Thesis', propounded by former Singapore premier Lee Kuan Yew, sees democracy as an obstacle to economic development, and controversially argues that dictatorships and authoritarian regimes are more conducive to rapid growth in the context of Asian economies. Amartya Sen and others have strongly critiqued the Lee Thesis, contending that democratic governments are accountable, responsible and sensitive to people's needs, and open to their criticism, which dictatorships are not. Ruchir Sharma asserted that other South East Asian nations may show greater economic advancement, but the Indian democracy provides better welfare facilities to its people.

Jürgen Habermas said capitalism is an obstacle to the freedom and development of the individual. Capitalism promotes an unthinking mass culture where media is a tool controlled by big industry and business for protecting capitalist and state interests, rather than a tool for public discourse. Public space for genuine and meaningful dialogue, debate and discussion is shrinking rapidly in capitalist economies as people are reduced to being passive spectators watching the spectacle. This is completely destructive for any democracy, which demands continuous, active and informed participation of the polity in the political system.

Cosmopolitan Democracy: In his book *Models of Democracy* (1987), **David Held** propounded the idea of cosmopolitan democracy which advocates for the creation of democratic institutions beyond the nation-state, and the democratisation of transnational actors like the International Monetary Fund, World Bank, United Nations Security Council and World Trade Organization. It is based on the idea that global issues like poverty, climate change and terrorism need solutions that can only be achieved through global cooperation and decision-making. However, Held does not stress upon the responsiveness of non-state actors to anyone.

Neo-Liberal Democracy: This is a fusion of neoliberal economic policies, such as free-market economics, privatisation, and individual rights and freedoms, coupled with representative democratic institutions and procedures. Liberals like **Samuel Brittan** contend that democracy is under overload and that electoral politics has become self-defeating for economic growth, while British political theorist **David Marquand**, who propounded the theory of 'Democratic Deficit', argue that, 'Democracy is to adults what chocolate is to children: tempting, harmless in small doses and dangerous in excess.'

Select further readings on democracy:

Robert A. Dahl, *A Preface to Democratic Theory* (1956)
Robert A. Dahl, *Polyarchy: Participation and Opposition* (1972)
Robert A. Dahl, *Democracy and Its Critics* (1989)
Anthony Downs, *An Economic Theory of Democracy* (1957)
Jurgen Habermas, *Theory of Communicative Action* (1981)
A. D. Lindsay, *The Essentials of Democracy* (1940)
Joshua Cohen and Joel Rogers, *Associations and Democracy* (1995)
Christian Fuchs, *Digital Democracy and the Digital Public Sphere* (2023)
C. B. Macpherson, *The Real World of Democracy* (1992)
C. B. Macpherson, *The Political Theory of Possessive Individualism* (1962)

6

POWER

KEY CONCEPTS

Definitions of power; dimensions of power; institutionalisation of power; Marxist view, feminist view, elitist theory of power, pluralist theory of power; power as consent; postmodern view of power; power as authority; bureaucracy

WHAT IS POWER?

Power is the ability to influence or control the behaviour of others, to shape the course of events or decision-making processes in ways that benefit oneself or one's interests. Power can be exercised in many different forms and contexts, including physical force, economic resources, social status, knowledge, or the ability to mobilise people and resources towards a particular goal.

Power can be both *formal*, that is, associated with institutionalised authority and backed by laws and regulations, and *informal*, that is, deriving from personal relationships, social networks or other sources of influence. The exercise of power is often contested as different individuals or groups have competing and conflicting interests and goals. This is why the study of power is a central concern in political science as well as other fields.

Politics as Power

The focus on power within modern political thought is often traced to the ideas of **Niccolo Machiavelli** and his influential work *The Prince*, according to which the ruler, 'The Prince must be strong as a lion and cunning as a fox'. Many scholars also credit **Kautilya** and his *Arthasastra* for providing an original perspective and focus to the power view of politics. Kautilya insisted that power or *bal* was crucial for maintaining royal authority or *danda* and ensuring discipline and organisation, but that power must also be exercised in accordance with the principles of *dharma*. **Thomas Hobbes** advocated power politics and legitimised the power of the king through the *monist* principle of sovereignty, which envisions a single sovereign ruler in a state who exercises absolute power. The church and all other institutions are subordinate to the king, who is the centre of power.

Power and Politics

Power is inseparable from politics. **Robert A. Dahl** asserts that the government of a state wields power over its citizens specifically because it can impose punishment, imprisonment, death or exile on them in case of non-compliance of law, and even otherwise. Therefore, citizens are obliged to comply with the government's commands. **Harold Lasswell**, in his work *Politics: Who Gets What, When and How* (1936), says politics is about conflicts over scarce resources, and power is the means through which this struggle is conducted.

Max Weber situates both power and politics squarely within the state: 'State is the form of human community that lays claim to the monopoly of legitimate use of physical violence within a particular territory.' Politics is thus about the territoriality and punitive power of the state. **Adrian Leftwich** said, 'Politics is not a separate realm of public life and activity. It is at the heart of all collective social activity,' and asserts that power is what distinguishes politics from other spheres of human activity. Leftwich defined power as the ability to achieve a desired result, by whatever means. Politics, he insists, is in essence power. **Talcott Parsons** asserted that power is central to politics in the same way that money is central to economics.

DIMENSIONS OF POWER

Power is applicable to all aspects of human life and hence it has multiple dimensions, which may be more or less relevant in different contexts, often interrelated and mutually reinforcing. Common dimensions of power include: political power, economic power, coercive power, social power, ideological power and symbolic power.

Power as Decision-Making

Robert A. Dahl, in *Who Governs? Democracy and Power in an American City* (1961), asserts that the one who takes decisions in the administrative system and in society is the one who yields power. In *Modern Political Analysis* (1963), Dahl explains how the concept of power is different from other forms of influence, such as inducement, force, authority, coercion, legitimacy and hegemony, and elucidates these concepts in the form of a relationship between A (Alliance) and B (Bill) in which A exercises some form of influence over B. He says, 'A is said to have power over B if A makes B do something that B wouldn't have otherwise done.' So, when A exercises power over B, B does what A wants, or else A will deprive B of something that B values.

Kenneth Boulding, in his work *The Three Faces of Power* (1989), enumerates three forms of power through which most decision-making usually takes place: stick, deal and kiss. *Stick* symbolises coercion, the threat of or actual use of physical violence that is deployed to bring about compliance to certain decisions. *Deal* refers to the process of influencing decision-making through mutual agreement such that all concerned parties benefit from the decisions. *Kiss* refers to influencing decision-making through sentimental or emotional appeals.

Power as Agenda-Setting

Exercising power to plan or to set a particular agenda about which decisions should be taken or not taken and determining which issues are worth considering and should take precedence over others is the power of setting agenda. In their 1962 essay, 'Two Faces of Power', **Peter Bachrach** and **Morton Bartaz** focus on two forms of agenda-setting in politics:

1. The *overt agenda*, which is known and visible to the public and is announced through mechanisms like party manifestos.
2. The *covert agenda*, which is not revealed to the public and refers to the underlying, hidden diplomacy and manoeuvring aimed at the exclusion of specific issues and concerns from the agenda.

Power as Thought-Control

Steven Lukes, in *Power: A Radical View* (1974), suggests that power is a fundamentally contested concept and describes three dimensions that are relevant in different contexts:

1. *Power as decision-making*: Situations where power is exercised to ensure that certain kinds of interests and agendas prevail over others.
2. *Power as non-decision-making*: Situations where power is exercised to ensure that

certain kinds of interests are not considered for decision-making at all.

3. *Power as thought-control*: Lukes argues that this is the most radical view of power: the power to influence and shape people's perceptions and opinions. Here, power is structural, invisible and works in subtle ways such that people perceive certain views and interests to be their own. Lukes asserts that this kind of exercise of power is more durable and efficient because it derives its legitimacy from the people's consent. Lukes' radical view of power is considered to be closely associated with the neo-Marxist idea of power.

INSTITUTIONALISATION OF POWER

Institutionalisation of power refers to the processes by which power relations become embedded in formal organisations and institutions, like governments, corporations, or other large systems. This can be beneficial, for e.g. it can provide stability, predictability and order in political systems and efficiency in functioning. But it can also have harmful consequences as it can lead to the entrenchment of power imbalances and inequity, especially if institutions are resistant to change, autocratic, unjust and oppressive.

Theory of Social Contract

Thomas Hobbes, revered as the first and greatest of all social contract theorists, believed that humans beings are fundamentally selfish and that the natural state of humanity was a 'state of war' characterised by constant struggle for power and resources. In the state of nature there is no authority to arbitrate in this mad scramble for power. As a result, human life is 'solitary, nasty, poor, brutish and short'. To escape and survive this perpetual state of violence and chaos, Hobbes argued that individuals must enter into a 'social contract' and agree by mutual, rational consent to surrender all their rights and freedoms and submit to the authority of a single sovereign power: the 'Leviathan' or the Absolute State. The state as Leviathan is all-powerful, maintains order, protects the common good, and wields absolute power to impose punishment.

Constitutional Power

Absolute state power is a dire threat to individual liberties and rights. **John Locke** is the first among liberal thinkers who tried to limit the power of the state through *constitutionalism*, i.e. by advocating a limited and constitutional government. Locke also propounded a theory of social contract, in his work *Two Treatises on Civil Government* (1884). He believes that in the state of nature, all men are free 'to order their actions, and dispose of their possessions and persons as they deem fit'. The state of nature is governed by a law of nature, which, Locke says, is the law of reason.

Unlike Hobbes, Locke's conceptualisation of the state of nature is not characterised by conflict and chaos. Likewise, Locke's theory of social contract does not entail the total surrender of individual rights and liberties to the state. People retain their natural rights, i.e. the rights to life, liberty and property, which Locke calls '*properties*'. Citizens have the right to oppose and abolish the state if it threatens their properties, which cannot be taken away without their consent. The state is responsible only for ensuring that one person does not impinge on the rights of another. Locke advocates minimal government and asserts that the government which governs the least is the best.

Locke's theory of social contract has been influential in shaping modern political thought and has contributed to debates around individual rights, the role of government, and the nature of political power.

People's Power

Jean-Jacques Rousseau propounded the concept of *popular sovereignty*, which is based on the idea that the people as a collective whole are the legitimate source of all political power. He believed that the general will is always focused on the common good, and that a truly democratic society is one in which the general will of the people can express itself freely. But Rousseau also acknowledged that it can be difficult to determine what the general will actually is.

MARXIST THEORY OF POWER

Power, hegemony and exploitation are closely interlinked concepts. The Marxist view of power is rooted in the idea that all power is primarily economic in nature. In *Das Kapital*, the foundational text of Marxism, **Karl Marx** shows that power is not just control over political institutions but control of the means of production and the material resources necessary for human survival. Classes in Marxist theory exist only in relation to each other, and that relation becomes exploitative when one section of the populace produces a surplus whose use is controlled by another section. It is also this exploitation which gives rise to class conflict.

The ownership and control of the means of production give the ruling class (the *bourgeoisie*) the power to exploit the working class (the *proletariat*) and maintain their dominance or hegemony. Marxism sees the capitalist mode of production as inherently exploitative as it relies on extracting surplus value from the labour of workers, who are paid far less than the value they produce. Marxism also emphasises the role of ideology and culture in maintaining the power of the ruling class.

Power as Hegemony

The modern concept of *hegemony*, or the dominance of one group over others, is credited to Marxist thinker **Antonio Gramsci**, and is central to any understanding of the dynamics of power. In his famous *Prison Notebooks*, Gramsci saw hegemony as the cultural and ideological means through which the state controlled its citizens. Drawing upon the Marxist concept of *base* and *superstructure*, Gramsci divided the superstructure into two parts, namely:

1. *Structures of coercion*: These include organs of the state such as the army and police, which use force or the threat of force to ensure compliance and the dominance of the bourgeoisie.
2. *Structures of legitimation*: These include civil society organisations, social, cultural and religious groups, family, mass media and educational institutions.

Civil society generates a web of social relations and ideas which reaffirm the hegemony of the dominant class. It controls and influences public behaviour in multiple ways, ultimately justifying capitalist rule and upholding capitalist values as universal. Gramsci believes that Marxism must therefore aim not only to overthrow the capitalist class but also to destroy the value system that sustains and supports capitalist rule.

Louis Althusser distinguishes between *repressive state apparatuses* (RSAs) and *ideological state apparatuses* (ISAs). RSAs are the military, police and courts, which use methods of direct repression and violence or threat of violence to ensure compliance. ISAs include religious and cultural organisations, traditions, customs, media, schools, universities and civil society. They shape people's beliefs and values so as to reproduce and reinforce the dominant ideology and social order of the ruling class in subtle but powerful ways, making it difficult for individuals to challenge or resist it.

FEMINIST THEORY OF POWER

Feminist theory examines how power operates within gender relations and how gender inequality is reproduced and reinforced through power structures. Feminists criticise traditional conceptions of power, which often focus on formal political institutions and ignore how power is embedded in everyday life. The feminist critique of power focuses on patriarchy. **Sylvia Walby** in *Theorizing Patriarchy* (1990) argues that patriarchy is not just about controlling women but about subjugating both men and women to structures of power, within which they must comply with established gender norms, roles and responsibilities. Under patriarchy, even if women have power, it is used only to reinforce and perpetuate the existing patriarchal social order.

Kate Millett, in her book *Sexual Politics* (1970), argued that the unequal relations between men and women in society are in fact nothing but power relations. Radical feminists transformed the concept of gender parity into a political theory and reinterpreted concepts like 'power' and 'domination' as modes of oppression that justified men's 'superiority' and women's unequal status, powerlessness and subordination vis-à-vis men. Thus, women's issues were no longer seen as just their personal problems but as part of the larger politics of gender relations and roles as defined by patriarchy.

Importantly, feminist theorists also point out that gender is not the only axis of power in society, and that gender intersects other forms of inequality such as race, class and sexuality. *Intersectionality*, or the idea that multiple forms of oppression interact and compound each other, is a key concept in the feminist critique of power.

ELITIST THEORY OF POWER

The elitist theory is rooted in the belief that society is fundamentally unequal and that some individuals or groups are inherently better suited to govern than others. It argues that power is concentrated in the hands of a small, privileged group of individuals or institutions who control the political, economic and social systems. This group, called the *power elite*, includes wealthy business leaders, high-level politicians, and members of the military and intelligence communities. The power elite maintain their dominance over society by controlling the media, influencing public opinion, and controlling access to resources and opportunities.

Classical elite theorists like **Vilfredo Pareto** and **G. Mosca** reject both democracy or the people's power and Marxism, and argue that elites must rule society because the masses are either too disorganised, stupid and incapable or too disinterested to rule. The elites are, they believe, the superior minority in any aspect of governance, and power circulates between the masses and the *governing* elite and the *non-governing* elite. Pareto, who wrote *The Mind and Society* (1916), said 'history is the graveyard of aristocracies'.

Modern elite theorists argue that while elite power may or may not be necessary to achieve order and stability in society, it is a reality of governance today. C. Wright Mills asserts in his book *The Power Elite* (1956) that American democracy is a sham, and the US is in fact ruled by three elite groups: the president and his clique, big corporate houses, and the arms industry. President D. Eisenhower described the American military-industrial complex as the most powerful elite group in America.

Elitist theory is criticised for being far too pessimistic about the potential for democratic participation and because it fails to acknowledge the power of ordinary people to challenge the status quo, topple governments and bring about radical social and political transformation.

Ruling Class versus Ruling Elite

The terms 'ruling class' and 'ruling elite' are often used interchangeably to refer to the group of individuals or institutions that hold power in a society, but while 'ruling class' emphasises the economic dimension of power, 'ruling elite' includes other domains of power as well.

While elitist theory emphasises the concentration of power in the hands of a small, privileged group of individuals or institutions, Marxist theory argues that power is fundamentally shaped by the economic relations between classes. In Marxist theory, the *ruling class* refers specifically to the economic class that owns and controls the means of production and thus also controls the distribution of wealth in society and maintains its dominance by exploiting the labour of the working class. In contrast, *ruling elite* can refer to any group of individuals or institutions that hold power in a society regardless of their economic status, for e.g. political leaders, military and intelligence officials, the judiciary, the media and other influential groups that shape and create public opinion.

Elitist theory highlights the role of formal political institutions, such as government and the judiciary, in maintaining the power of the elite. Marxist theory asserts that economic relations are the primary determinant of power and that formal political institutions are shaped by the economic interests of the ruling capitalist class.

PLURALIST THEORY OF POWER

In direct opposition to the elitist theory, the pluralist theory argues that power is distributed among a diverse set of groups and actors who compete for power and control over resources, rather than being concentrated in the hands of a few. Pluralists believe that different groups have different interests, and that power is balanced through a system of checks and balances in which many groups compete for influence and no single group can dominate others completely. They assert that power is not only held and exercised by formal political institutions, like governments and political parties, but also by social interest groups, movements, labour unions and other organisations. In his work *Who Governs? Democracy and Power in an American City* (1961), Robert Dahl observed based on his research in New Haven that there is no single elite group controlling power but rather, multiple competing groups.

POWER AS CONSENT

The concept of *power as consent* refers to the idea that power relations in society are not solely based on coercion or force, but also on the acceptance or consent of those who are subject to that power. Individuals and groups in society may accept the power of those in authority either willingly or passively, rather than being forced or coerced to obey. Power as consent is often associated with French philosopher **Michel Foucault**, who argued that power operates not only through direct force, but also through the production and dissemination of knowledge, norms and values that shape individual behaviour and people's perceptions of themselves and their world.

Hannah Arendt regards power as something that arises from collective action and shared agreement among people. For Arendt, power 'corresponds to the human ability not just to act but to act in concert. Power is never the property of an individual; it belongs to a group and remains in existence only so long as the group keeps together.' She clarifies that power should not be confused with force and violence. Similar thoughts underlie **Talcott Parsons**' idea that power is a medium of mobilising commitment or obligation for effective collective action, and that power rests on socially accepted forms of legitimacy. Parsons saw power as a means of preserving social order and stability and for achieving social integration and cooperation. He believed it is necessary for society to function effectively, and is unwilling to treat power as anything connected with compliance or coercion.

In critique, scholars have argued that power as consent downplays the role of coercion and force in maintaining power relations and that it assumes a greater degree of agency and autonomy on the part of individuals and groups than may be realistic in many social contexts.

POSTMODERN VIEW OF POWER

Traditionally power is understood in terms of political power, or in economic and ideological terms, as in Marxist theory. Rejecting the traditional view, **Michel Foucault** argues that power is not something possessed or exercised by individuals, governments or institutions, but permeates all social relations and is constantly being negotiated and contested. Foucault's conception of power is closely linked to his ideas about knowledge and discourse. Power is pervasive and operates in complex and subtle ways through social norms, cultural values and *discourses*, which are systems of meaning that shape our understanding of the world and how we think, act, and relate to one another. Power comes from knowledge and knowledge is determined by society. As societies change, power also changes. In the modern world, states exercise power through information technology and systems of visible and invisible public surveillance.

POWER AS AUTHORITY

Power that is backed by legitimacy is known as authority. Power as authority is often associated with formal institutions, such as governments or courts, that are recognised as having the right to make and enforce rules and regulations and to exercise control over people based on their perceived right to do so. Charles E. Lindblom asserted that all politics is a struggle for authority between competing actors. Robert Dahl observed that authority is at work when there's 'an automatic pattern of obedience', and 'When B tends to do A's bidding automatically, unthinkingly and unreflectively.' German sociologist **Max Weber**, in his work *Protestant Ethic and the Spirit of Capitalism* (1904), classified three types of power as authority:

1. *Rational-legal authority*: Those who wield this kind of authority are usually anonymous and exercise power neutrally within formal political structures. Their authority stems from written laws and procedures and they follow established rules. The bureaucracy is an example.
2. *Traditional authority*: This kind of authority is vested in those who wield power or hold powerful positions because of historical or cultural reasons, for example, the religious authority of the Pope in Vatican City.
3. *Charismatic authority*: This derives from the charisma and unique personality traits possessed by certain individuals who thereby command the respect and authority of multitudes, which enables them to exercise authority over them, for e.g. the spiritual, moral and intellectual authority that leaders like Gandhi, Ambedkar and Netaji command over Indians.

THE BUREAUCRACY AS A POWER BLOC

Bureaucratic institutions like government agencies or large corporations can wield power and influence over society because they control access to resources and take decisions that affect the lives of citizens. Bureaucracies can be seen as power blocs because they have the authority, ability and the resources to make and enforce social and economic policies, and maintain status quo. Bureaucratic systems may promote consistency, efficiency and accountability, but they can also be rigid, inflexible, even regressive.

The idea of bureaucracy as a power bloc has been criticised for its tendency to prioritise efficiency and stability over innovation and responding to social needs. **Max Weber** saw the bureaucracy as a rational, efficient and predictable system of organisation. But he also recognised its drawbacks and argued that it was important to balance efficiency with transparency and responsiveness to change.

Class Biases in the Bureaucracy

The bureaucracy is not a neutral institution. The analysis of class biases entrenched in the state bureaucracy is extended by neo-Marxists like **Ralph Miliband**, who highlight the role of senior civil servants in acting as a conservative veto group that actively dilutes, even blocks the radical progressive initiatives of socialist ministers and governments. Miliband argues that top civil servants are conservative in that they are either consciously or unconsciously aligned with the existing socio-economic elites within their sphere of influence. This may be for several reasons. Firstly, despite formal requirements of political neutrality, top civil servants often share similar educational and social backgrounds with leading industrialists and business managers, and are thus likely to share their prejudices and general outlook. Secondly, recruitment and promotion procedures are designed to ensure the ideological suitability of rising civil servants, and to rule out anyone who may harbour radical or socialist sympathies.

Table 1.6.1: Weberian View versus Marxist View

Max Weber's Bureaucratic Model	*Marxist Model of Power as Exploitation*
1. Power is exercised by the rational institution of bureaucracy.	Power is exercised by the state which is an instrument of the bourgeoisie.
2. The bureaucratic model is hierarchical to ensure the efficient and effective exercise of power over subordinates.	Marxists repudiate hierarchy. They see it as a form of oppression and argue for the overthrow of the hierarchical order by the proletariat.
3. Bureaucracy is a permanent institution. It is essential for managing the society.	The bureaucracy is composed of the elite who parasitically exploit the working class to sustain themselves.
4. Bureaucracy is a neutral institution. It functions on the basis of established rules and procedures.	Both bureaucracy and the state are instruments of coercion and power to ensure the material and ideological dominance of the bourgeoisie and preserve the capitalist order of society.

LEGITIMATION CRISIS

The concept of legitimation crisis was introduced by the German sociologist and philosopher Jurgen Habermas in the 1970s. It refers to a situation in which the ruling power or government is no longer able to garner the consent and support of the population owing to a decline in confidence in its leadership and administration, thus leading to a crisis of legitimacy. Habermas argued that the capitalist order is always prone to such crisis because of the inherent tensions between the logic of the market and the democratic principles of political legitimacy.

1. Democratic process and socio-economic rights demand higher spending on public welfare and social security, while capitalists seek to maximise profits at the expense of public welfare.
2. Higher taxation is necessary for budgeting for social security and welfare rights, which is opposed by the capitalist mode of production.
3. Democracy demands greater accountability, transparency, democratic participation, and decisions for the common good, while capitalists seek to increase their own advantage.
4. These opposing tendencies lead to multiple crises within the economy and social order which cause acute public distress (e.g. unemployment, inflation), which ultimately results in a crisis of legitimacy wherein the state's authority is challenged.

Anthony King and **Richard Rose** propounded the '*overload thesis*', which argues that political parties always set unattainable objectives in their exaggerated manifestos and make promises which neither can be, nor are intended to be, fulfilled with the available resources. The burden of these unfulfilled promises results in increased expectations and demands, ultimately resulting in a democratic overload.

State Action During Legitimation Crisis

Habermas and **Claus Offe** demonstrate how in such a crisis, the capitalist order deploys various methods of legitimising and retaining its power, including elections, minimal welfare state policies and social reform politics, to show that it is committed to the welfare of all citizens, and not just the wealthy and powerful. Frequently, however, the capitalist state also uses the mass media to project a one-sided and favourable view of its policies to influence public opinion, and to counter and muzzle popular dissent.

The modern state, according to Habermas, takes recourse to '*system steering*' and ideological measures to legitimise and stabilise existing power structures. System steering refers to the use of technical means to control systems like the economy, the legal or the political system. This involves an 'uncoupling' or dissociation of the *economic sphere*, i.e. wage labour and capital relations, from the *political sphere*, i.e. institutions of governance. This means that the exploitative relationship between wage labour and capital is no longer part of the political sphere, which in turn becomes less democratic, less participatory and more impersonal, bureaucratised and distanced from the ruled. Such a system is, however, held together ideologically by 'universalist' legitimising discourses of rights, justice and citizenship by which the rulers give themselves the moral claim to rule.

7

CITIZENSHIP

KEY CONCEPTS

Origins of citizenship; kinds of citizenship; perspectives on citizenship

The concept of citizenship has evolved over time, and different societies and political systems have different definitions and expectations of what it means to be a citizen. However, essentially, citizenship implies a set of legal and social relationships between individuals and the state or community to which they belong. It can be acquired in multiple ways, including by birth, descent, naturalisation, or by marriage. Citizenship is usually granted by a state or a country and implies a sense of belonging to a particular community or nation.

Modern citizenship is a legal status that confers broad rights, privileges and responsibilities upon individuals, such as:

1. right to vote and participate in the political process;
2. right to receive protection and services from the state;
3. right to work and reside in the country;
4. right to access public services such as healthcare and education;
5. the obligation to pay taxes;
6. the duty to serve in the armed forces (in some countries)

HISTORICAL ORIGINS

For Greek philosopher **Aristotle**, citizenship meant active participation in the political community, to help govern and be governed in turn, and to contribute to the common good. Citizenship thus entailed both rights and duties. Aristotle distinguished between two types of citizens: those entitled to participate in the highest levels of decision-making, and those who are not. But he firmly believed that all citizens must play an active role in the political process and take part in public debates.

Jean Bodin and **Thomas Hobbes** both saw citizenship as closely linked to the state and the exercise of political power. While for Bodin citizenship was closely linked to loyalty and obedience to the state, Hobbes saw it as a social contract between citizens and the state in which individuals surrendered their rights and freedoms to the state in exchange for stability and security. For **Niccolo Machiavelli**, an ideal citizen must be willing to defend the country against external and internal threats and sacrifice personal interests for the common good. **Jean-Jacques Rousseau** believed civic virtue and participation were necessary virtues of citizenship.

KINDS OF CITIZENSHIP

Passive Citizenship

Passive citizenship refers to a status in which individuals possess the legal rights and protections associated with citizenship, but do not actively exercise those rights or engage in the political life of the community. Passive citizenship may be the result of systemic barriers that prevent certain groups from fully accessing their rights as citizens. It could also be a deliberate choice of those who prefer to avoid politics or who are disillusioned with the political system. **Hobbes** and **Rousseau** have both been associated with the idea of passive citizenship.

Universal Citizenship

Universal citizenship refers to the idea that all human beings are entitled to the same rights and protections, regardless of their nationality or place of origin. The term is often used in discussions of global justice, human rights, and the responsibilities of states towards refugees and migrants. In the context of international law and politics, universal citizenship challenges the traditional notion of citizenship as a status conferred by a particular state or nation, and argues that basic human rights should be recognised and protected by all states.

Citizenship under Capitalism and Liberalism

With the development of capitalism and liberalism, two broad traditions of citizenship arose.

1. *Civic Republicanism*: Citizenship is not just a matter of legal and political status, but involves a commitment to the common good, emphasises civic virtues and active participation in the political community. The state actively works to promote the well-being of all citizens, and not just a privileged few.
2. *Liberal Individualism*: Citizenship is primarily defined by legal and political status, and individuals are free to pursue their own interests and aspirations within the framework of the law. The state's primary role is to protect individual rights and freedoms and maintain a stable legal and political order.

Equal Citizenship and Integration

Two essential features of modern citizenship can be summarised as:

1. *Equal or Horizontal citizenship*: All individuals have equal rights and obligations within the political community regardless of their social status, gender, race, religion etc. Equal citizenship underlines the idea of equal treatment and equal participation of all and non-discrimination, and recognises the importance of socio-economic equality in ensuring a just society. All members have equal voice and stake in the decision-making process, and the government's role is to represent and serve the interests of all citizens equally.
2. *Integration*: This is a two-way process by which new individuals and groups integrate or become members of a society and are able to participate fully in its political, social and economic life. For individuals, integration may include learning the language, understanding the laws, developing cultural competencies. For the receiving society, it involves creating conditions that allow immigrants and newcomers to participate fully in the society and hence become its complete citizens, for e.g. providing language skills and cultural training, promoting diversity and tolerance.

DIFFERENT VIEWS OF CITIZENSHIP

Derek Heater argues that citizenship can be understood in two ways: as a status and as a practice. As a *status*, it implies the legal and political rights and obligations that come with membership in a particular community or nation-state. As a *practice*, it implies the active participation of individuals in the socio-political life of their community. Heater also underlines the importance of historical context in shaping the meaning of citizenship, which has been redefined over time, reflecting changes in political, economic, and social structures.

T. H. Marshall in *Citizenship and Social Class* (1950) defines citizenship as the full and equal membership of a political community that entitles individuals to certain rights and privileges that are essential for social and political participation in modern societies. Marshall identified three main types of citizenship rights: civil, political, and social.

1. *Civil rights* are the basic legal rights that protect individuals from discrimination and arbitrary treatment by the state, such as the right to freedom of speech, freedom of assembly, and the right to a fair trial.
2. *Political rights* include the right to participate in the political process, such as the right to vote and stand for office.
3. *Social rights* are the rights to a minimum standard of living, such as access to education, healthcare, and social security.

Jens Hoffmann asserts that citizenship is not just about legal status, rights and privileges, but equally about the active involvement of citizens in shaping the political agenda and holding their representatives accountable.

The Marxist View

Marxism views citizenship as a product of class society where the rights and privileges associated with citizenship are tied to economic and social status, and determined by an individual's relationship to the means of production. Marxism asserts that the key feature of capitalist societies is the exploitation of the working class by the ruling class, which results in the alienation of workers from the products of their labour and from the political process. Marxists see citizenship as a form of legal recognition granted to individuals by the capitalist state in order to legitimise its rule and preserve existing power relations; it is a tool used by the ruling class to maintain control over the working class. The working class, however, lacks true citizenship because they do not have the same economic and social rights as the ruling class.

Marxists argue that workers and other oppressed groups can only achieve full citizenship through collective struggle against capitalist exploitation and the establishment of a socialist society in which the means of production are owned and controlled by the working class. In this sense, citizenship is not seen as a universal, static or fixed concept, but rather as a dynamic and contested arena of struggle over power and resources.

The Feminist View

Feminist theories of citizenship highlight the ways in which gender shapes citizenship, and how citizenship rights are often constructed in ways that disadvantage women and other marginalised groups. Feminist scholars like Rian Voet (*Feminism and Citizenship*, 1958), Carol Gilligan, Jean Bethke Elshtain ('Citizenship and Armed Civic Virtue', 1986), Mary G. Dietz ('Feminism and Theories of Citizenship', 1987) have critiqued traditional conceptions of citizenship as being too narrow and patriarchal, and argued for more inclusive definitions that recognise how gender intersects with other social identities such as race, class, and sexuality. Feminist theorists such as Sara Ruddick (*Maternal Thinking*, 1989) have also highlighted the importance of recognising care work and reproductive labour as important components of citizenship, as these are often devalued and invisible forms of labour that are disproportionately performed by women.

The Multicultural View

The multicultural theory of citizenship acknowledges that contemporary societies are made up of diverse cultural, ethnic and religious groups, and that citizenship too should be able to accommodate and respect these differences.

Differentiated citizenship: According to **Marion Young**, citizenship is not a uniform or homogeneous concept, but a complex, multifaceted one shaped by various social factors like class, culture, gender, and different groups have different experiences of citizenship. Young argues that therefore we need to adopt a differentiated approach to citizenship which recognises and values the diverse ways in which people experience and engage with political life. Promoting greater cultural diversity and inclusion, and group-specific rights are important.

Multicultural citizenship: **Will Kymlicka** argues that the increasingly multicultural fabric of modern societies has given rise to new issues and conflicts as ethnic and national minorities demand recognition and support for their cultural identity, which must be recognised. In his book *Multicultural Citizenship: A Liberal Theory of Minority Rights* (1995), he advocates for the special rights of minorities—for self-governance, representation, and polyethnicity. Contesting the equal and universal citizenship of liberal ideology, like Marion Young, Kymlicka also emphasises that no single formula can be applied to all groups, and that the needs and aspirations of immigrants are very different from those of indigenous peoples and national minorities.

Citizenship in a Globalised World

Yasemin Soysal, in her book *Limits of Citizenship* (1994), critiques the notion of citizenship as a fixed and exclusive status, and argues that in an increasingly globalised world it is important to recognise the multiple forms of belonging in modern societies. The increasing movement of people across borders challenges traditional notions of citizenship and demands new forms of political participation and representation, she asserts.

Chantal Mouffe asserts that traditional liberal conceptions of citizenship focused on a set of individual rights and legal status are inadequate to address the complexities of modern politics, and that citizenship must be an active, ongoing process of radical political engagement. She emphasises the importance of the public sphere, public debate, and collective identities in defining political identities and citizenship.

Michael Walzer underlines the importance of cultural diversity and pluralism, and argues that different communities should be allowed to express their unique identities and values within a larger framework of shared citizenship. He also stresses on active democratic participation, and is critical of radically disengaged or passive citizens of the state.

Selected further readings on theories of citizenship:

Pluralist theory of citizenship: David Held, *Political Theory and the Modern State* (1989); Engin F. Isin and Bryan S. Turner, *Handbook of Citizenship Studies* (2003).

Marxist theory of citizenship: Anthony Giddens, *A Contemporary Critique of Historical Materialism* (1981).

Liberal theory of citizenship: T. H. Marshal and Thomas Bottomore, *Citizenship and Social Class* (1950).

Republican theory of citizenship: Benjamin Barber, *The Conquest of Politics* (1988); Michael Walzer, *Spheres of Justice: A Defense of Pluralism and Equality* (2008); Patrick Watson and Benjamin Barber, *The Struggle for Democracy* (2000).

Part 2: Political Traditions

KEY CONCEPTS

Liberalism; Conservatism; Socialism; Marxism; Feminism; Ecologism; Multiculturalism; Postmodernism

8

LIBERALISM

KEY CONCEPTS

Historical context of liberalism; basic principles of liberalism; classical liberalism; modern liberalism; American versus British liberalism; neo-liberalism, libertarianism

Liberalism is a political, moral and economic philosophy that emphasises individual freedom, equality and the rule of law. It is based on the idea that people should have the freedom to pursue their own interests and goals as long as they do not harm others, and that the state should protect and promote this freedom through a system of rules, laws and institutions.

David G. Smith said 'Liberalism is the belief in and commitment to a set of methods and policies that have as their common aim greater freedom for individual men.'

Walter B. Gallie said that all political concepts are essentially contested and that the political concerns of liberals have changed greatly over past three centuries, which has led to many variants of liberalism.

CONTEXT OF EMERGENCE OF LIBERALISM

The Enlightenment, the Industrial Revolution, the growth of democracy all played a role in shaping the emergence of liberalism as a dominant modern political and economic ideology. Liberalism rose to prominence in the nineteenth and twentieth centuries in response and opposition to the following socio-economic conditions:

1. *Mercantilism*: This was a kind of protectionism which believes that state control is good for the economy, that a nation's wealth and power depended on its ability to increase its exports and limit imports, and that the state can shield the economy from collapse through the use of protective tariffs.
2. *Domination of the church*: Post Enlightenment, thinkers challenged the infallibility and power of the church, arguing for the separation of the church and the state and a secular, democratic society. They also emphasised upon religious tolerance, individual rights, rationality, a scientific temper and liberty, all of which laid the foundations for liberalism.
3. *Conservatism*: The belief that traditional political and social institutions can curb the inherently selfish and destructive instincts of humans. Conservatism seeks to preserve established social norms, order and hierarchy, including those related to religion, family and authority. It represented the interests of the aristocracy and the church. However, it also advocated for the rule of law, individual rights, and

private property, which were important values of liberalism.

BASIC PRINCIPLES OF LIBERALISM

Some of the core values of liberalism include: individualism, equality, liberty, rationality, tolerance for diversity, secularism, limited government, capitalism, democracy and human rights.

1. *Individualism*: Liberalism is best understood as a theory of the good life and the social, economic and political arrangements, rules, rights and freedoms within which individuals may lead that life.
2. *Liberty*: Individuals must have complete liberty of self-ownership and self-determination of their life and goals, and the means with which to achieve those goals.
3. *Rationality*: Liberalists assert the importance of human rationality, or the prowess of observation, analysis and decision-making, as being central to the creation of social and political institutions. Rationality is what enables individuals to rule themselves as well as to enjoy their freedom.
4. *Toleration and respect for diversity*: The emphasis on individual liberty implies a tolerance of views which may not be compatible with one's own. It also underlines a respect for diversity and differences.
5. *Limited constitutional government*: Liberalism avoids absolute and arbitrary power and advocates a government whose powers are restricted by a constitution, which serves as a higher law and outlines the fundamental rights and liberties of the people. The concept of limited government also implies a separation of powers, where the legislative, executive and judicial branches of government are kept separate in order to prevent any one branch from gaining too much power. Liberals reject the divine rights theory, the racial superiority theory of Nazism and Fascism as well as the Marxist theory of class struggle.
6. *Secularism*: John Locke argued that 'True religion can make no demands on the state' and propounded the modern doctrine of religious toleration. In the European context, secularism essentially implied the separation between the Church and the State.
7. *Capitalist market economy*: A free capitalist market economy ensures freedom of competition between individuals, which would ensure, in the words of John Locke, that people are free to dispose of the fruits of their labour in ways that they themselves deem fit. Libertarians have even argued that the market can be entrusted with the protection of life and liberty of individuals through private contracts.

CLASSICAL LIBERALISM

Classical liberalism emphasises individual freedom, personal responsibility, and limited government. It advocates a free market and laissez-faire economics, civil liberties under the rule of law, including the right to free speech, freedom of religion, and the right to own property. Works that have been influential in shaping classical liberalism include:

John Locke: *Two Treatises on Civil Government*
Adam Smith: *The Wealth of Nations*
Alexis De Tocqueville: *Democracy in America*
Montesquieu: *The Spirit of Laws*
Jeremy Bentham: *Utilitarianism*
Herbert Spencer: *Man versus State*

Features of Classical Liberalism

1. *Individualism*: **Thomas Hobbes** and **John Locke** are regarded as the original proponents of the doctrine of individualism which places the individual at the centre of all political discourse. Individuals are seen

as an end in themselves, and political and social institutions as the means to achieve that end. Individualists regard the state as a necessary evil and aim to limit its role to providing security to its citizens. They also believe that individuals enjoy certain pre-political a priori freedoms in the form of natural rights.

While Hobbes cannot be considered a liberal philosopher because he supported the idea of absolute government, his ideas laid down the philosophical foundation of liberalism. Hobbes believed that the individual is the fundamental unit of society, state and government, and argued that individuals are rational beings who seek to protect their self-interest.

2. *Night watchman state*: John Locke, considered as a father of liberalism, believed in a limited state, also called a *police state*, a *negative state*, or a *night watchman state*, that performs essential functions such as maintaining public order through police and protecting against external threats through an army. He advocated for the freedom of contract and a minimal government, and believed that the best government is one that governs the least.
3. *Natural rights*: **John Locke** was the original proponent of the theory of individual natural rights, which he called *properties*. The Lockean doctrine included three inalienable rights granted to every individual at birth: the rights to life, liberty and property. These rights serve as claims against government authority and seek to limit state power.
4. *Laissez faire state*: French for 'leave alone', *laissez-faire* stands for non-intervention in economic activities by the state. It is central to liberal theory as it regards individual property rights as a necessary precondition for liberty. It regards the state as a necessary evil because its existence implies restrictions on individual freedom. However, state authority also guarantees protection of individual rights and freedoms against encroachment by others.
5. *Utilitarianism*: It is a form of liberalism advocated by **Jeremy Bentham** which aims to maximise pleasure and minimise pain. Bentham is a materialist who rejected the concept of natural rights and social contract, and defended individual liberty on the basis of pleasure and pain. He believed that the state is a utilitarian institution created by individuals who seek to increase their pleasure. Utilitarianism holds that the aim of politics should be the 'Greatest Happiness of the Greatest Number', and proposes a method called the 'Felicific Calculus' to aggregate individual pleasures in society.
6. *Society as a collection of individuals*: Individualism and utilitarianism view individuals as distinct, atomistic entities existing independently and in isolation from one another. They view society as a collection of such individuals who come together to achieve common objectives.
7. *Capitalism*: **Adam Smith** in his influential work *An Inquiry into the Nature and Causes of the Wealth of Nations* presents an economic argument for laissez-faire individualism, and says that economic growth relies on the exploitation of nature, division of labour, expansion of markets, free trade, capital accumulation, and free and fair competition.

MODERN LIBERALISM

Modern liberalism, also known as *positive liberalism*, emerged in response to political and social changes such as the growth of socialism, increasing poverty, and the rise of mass movements. It rejected the idea of a laissez-faire state and instead advocated for a welfare state. Originally propounded by **John**

Stuart Mill, other important scholars within the tradition are **L.T. Hobhouse**, **T. H. Green** and **Harold J. Laski**.

Features of Modern Liberalism

1. *Welfare state*: A system of government responsible for the social and economic well-being of its citizens, it aims to provide equal opportunities, equitable wealth distribution, and assistance for those unable to access basic amenities. In *The Beveridge Report* (1942), **William Beveridge** outlined the vision to battle against what he called the 'five giants': idleness, ignorance, disease, squalor and want. This became the basis for the welfare state in Britain. **T. H. Green** said the main role of the welfare state was to 'hinder the hindrances'.
2. *Social liberalism*: It is a form of liberalism that advocates a regulated market economy and the expansion of civil and political rights. Its emergence was marked by social security measures announced by several American presidents, which aimed to benefit the marginalised sections including widows, the old and unemployed. For example, the New Deal Policy by Franklin D. Roosevelt, the New Frontier Program by John F. Kennedy, and the Great Society Program by Lynden B. Johnson. **T. H. Green** noted that the idea of the 'community' as a distinct socio-political unit had begun to replace the centrality of individualism in liberal political philosophy during this time.
3. *Keynesianism*: In his book *The General Theory of Employment, Interest and Money*, **John Maynard Keynes** advocated active government intervention in the economy, emphasised upon public works programmes and supported social welfare expenditure. Keynesianism thus marks a radical departure from classical laissez-faire liberalism.
4. *Positive freedom*: As conceptualised by thinkers like **Leonard Hobhouse** and **J. A. Hobson**, positive freedom emphasised the ability to act according to one's own will as a necessary condition for realising the full potential of the human self. This was in contrast to *negative freedom*, which was defined as absence of external constraints. **J. S. Mill** and others in this tradition also underlined the importance of possessing one's own will in achieving positive freedom, which was linked to ideals of social and cultural progress.

Problems of the Welfare State

The welfare state gained popularity in Europe and in the USA after 1945, and is often called the 'Nanny State' because it advocates public expenditure on social security. However, in the 1980s, it became clear that the welfare state economy was on the brink of collapse. This was acknowledged by British Prime Minister Margaret Thatcher in 1979 and US President Ronald Reagan in the 1980s. While the welfare state advocates the distribution of social goods, efficient production of goods is essential to ensure better distribution.

British versus American Liberalism

British and American liberalism both share a commitment to individual rights and civil liberties, democracy, the rule of law, and both promote free market and capitalism. But they differ in their emphasis on the role of the state, the promotion of social welfare and healthcare policy, and in their historical contexts. American liberalism is also influenced by Robert Dahl's theory of *pluralism* which argues that there are multiple competing centres of power in American politics, each of which has some degree of influence over government policy.

State's role: British liberalism places greater emphasis on the state's role in ensuring social welfare and reducing economic inequality, while American liberalism is more focused on individualism and promoting economic growth through free-market policies.

Healthcare: British liberalism generally supports universal nationalised state healthcare, while American liberalism advocates a more market-based approach.

Social welfare: British liberalism has historically been more supportive of social welfare programmes like unemployment benefits and housing assistance, while American liberalism has been more skeptical of such policies.

NEO-LIBERALISM OR LIBERTARIANISM

Neo-liberalism is an extreme form of laissez-faire individualism that advocates for free-market capitalism, competition, private enterprise, deregulation and reduced government intervention in the economy. It emerged in the twentieth century in response to the perceived failures of the welfare state and Keynesianism. The writings of Robert Nozick, Milton Friedman and F. W. Hayek have been influential in shaping neo-liberalism.

Features of Neo-liberalism

1. *Minimal and neutral state*: Neo-liberals argue that individual liberty and choice are of utmost importance, and thus the state should have minimal involvement in society. The state's functions should be limited to maintaining public order and protecting the nation's territorial integrity. Neo-liberals believe in the rationality and autonomy of individuals, and thus view the state's role as similar to that of an umpire who mediates disputes between various conflicting groups.
2. *Criticism of welfare state*: In *Road to Serfdom*, **F. W. Hayek** criticises the welfare state, arguing that expansion of the state would inevitably lead to totalitarianism. He views socialism, planning and collectivism as tools to curtail individual freedom and supports a free market economy.
3. *Rolling back of the state*: **Robert Nozick** argues that the state came into being to defend the property and rights of individuals. It has no legitimate function beyond providing security and arbitration for justice and defense. He therefore advocates the rolling back of the state in the form of a minimal 'Night-watchman state'.
4. *Repudiation of social justice*: Libertarians point out that the concepts of welfare and social justice are subjective and hence may vary according to individual needs and preferences. Therefore the best way to achieve true real social justice they say would be to allow individuals to freely make their own choices in a market economy, without state intervention.
5. *Individual freedom and market economy*: **Milton Friedman** criticises the welfare state, and argues that capitalism and the enjoyment of freedom are inherently linked. He supports limited state intervention only in spheres where the market is insufficient.

Reaganomics, the neo-liberal economic policies promoted by US President **Ronald Reagan** during the 1980s, were built upon four key concepts: reduced government spending; reduced taxes; deregulation; and controlling inflation by slowing the money supply.

Thatcherism was a brand of economic neo-liberalism propounded by the conservative British government of **Margaret Thatcher**, who supported the monetarist ideas of Reaganomics. Privatisation characterised by the sale of state-owned industries and services to the private sector was a key concept.

6. *Egalitarian Liberalism*: Libertarianism ignores the needs of the marginalised and weak and promotes the survival of the fittest, while the welfare state ignores the importance of liberty. **John Rawls** tried to find a pragmatic balance between the values of liberty and equality through his conception of egalitarian liberalism, which gives equal importance and recognition to the individual as well as to society.

Contemporary Challenges for Liberalism

Following the disintegration of the Soviet Union in 1991, Francis Fukuyama claimed that liberal democracy had won the battle of ideologies, referring to its global triumph. However, in the twenty-first century, communitarianism and multiculturalism, which emerged in England, Australia and USA during the 1980s, have presented new challenges to liberal ideologies. The extent to which they align with or diverge from liberal ideology nevertheless remains a matter of debate.

9

CONSERVATISM

KEY CONCEPTS

Origins of conservatism; definition of conservatism; types of conservatism

HISTORICAL ORIGINS

The historical origins of conservatism can be traced back to the late eighteenth century in Europe, particularly in reaction to the dramatic social and political changes brought about by the French Revolution of 1789. The conservative movement emerged in response to the radicalism of the French Revolution, which threatened to overturn the established social order, including the traditional monarchy, aristocracy, and the established church.

Conservatism is often associated with the works of British political philosopher **Edmund Burke**, who articulated many of its central themes in his writings. Burke was a strong critic of the French Revolution and, in his book *Reflections on the Revolution in France* (1790), saw it as a dangerous attempt to create a new social order based on abstract theories rather than practical experience and tradition. He believed that society is an organic entity that grows and changes over time and that institutions and traditions must be preserved and adapted to changing circumstances rather than destroyed in the name of progress.

Modern conservatism is associated with the **Tory Party** in Britain, also known as the Conservative Party.

Was Aristotle Conservative?

Many scholars consider **Aristotle** to be a conservative thinker because of his emphasis on preserving the traditional social and political order of ancient Greece. He also believed in the importance of preserving the institution of private property and the family as the foundation of society. Additionally, Aristotle believed that change should be gradual and incremental, rather than sudden and revolutionary. However, others argue that Aristotle's political thought is more nuanced than the simplistic label of 'conservative' can capture. They point to his emphasis on the common good and his recognition of the need for some degree of political participation and representation by the masses. They also note his recognition of the potential for the abuse of power by elites and the need for checks and balances on their authority.

Cicero is often considered a conservative thinker due to his emphasis on traditional Roman values and his defense of the Roman Republic and its institutions as vital to the well-being of the state. Cicero also believed in *natural law* that emphasises the importance of universal moral principles, and opposed the excesses of power by individuals or factions.

While Cicero's political views may not align with contemporary conservatism today, his emphasis on traditional values and institutions, mixed government, and natural law have influenced conservative thought.

WHAT IS CONSERVATISM?

Conservatism is a political and social philosophy that emphasises the importance of tradition, continuity, and stability. It seeks to preserve established institutions and values, and resist or minimise social change, in order to maintain stability and promote individual responsibility and self-reliance. Conservatism often emphasises the importance of limited government and free-market economics, and tends to oppose extensive government regulation and intervention in the economy. It also tends to prioritise individual freedom and rights, while maintaining a preference for traditional social norms and values.

Conservatism is a relative term as it depends on the political perspective; for e.g., liberals can be considered conservative in comparison to Marxists. But all conservatives are not necessarily opposed to liberty, rights, or reform.

General Principles

Principles of conservatism vary depending on the specific branch of conservatism and the historical context in which it emerges. However, there are some broad general principles that are commonly associated with conservatism.

1. *Tradition*: Conservatives often value the wisdom of the past and believe that traditions and customs provide a framework for a stable society.
2. *Order and authority*: Conservatives usually support a hierarchical social order and believe that authority and obedience are necessary for maintaining social stability.
3. *Property*: Conservatives tend to support the right to own and control property, and often view private property rights as fundamental to individual freedom.
4. *Limited government*: Conservatives generally advocate for a limited role of government in society, and support a free-market economy and individual initiative.
5. *Social stability*: Conservatives often prioritise social stability over social change, and are sceptical of radical social movements and experimentation.
6. *Human nature*: Conservatives generally hold a pessimistic view of human nature, believing that individuals are flawed and imperfect, and that societal structures are necessary to mitigate these flaws and maintain order.
7. *Community*: Conservatives prioritise the community and common good over the individual and believe that traditional social institutions, like the family and church, are crucial to the well-being of individuals and society.

It is important to note however that these principles are not fixed and there can be significant variation among different conservative movements and individuals.

TYPES OF CONSERVATISM

1. *Religious conservatism*: The Taliban in Afghanistan, the Islamic Republic of Iran, the Christian Right in the US which opposes abortion, and the Hindu Right in India which promotes religious intolerance are all examples of religious conservatism.
2. *Social conservatism*: Social conservatives wish to preserve social customs and traditions, and generally favour a free-market economy. Economists like **Adam Smith** and **David Ricardo** support the principle of a market economy.
3. *Libertarianism and the New Right*: Neo-liberals or Libertarians such as **Friedrich Hayek** and **Robert Nozick** are considered part of the New Right. Former British

prime minister Margaret Thatcher was heavily influenced by Hayek. Charles Murray believed that the welfare state is a major cause of the breakdown of the family. Libertarianism emphasises individual liberty, free markets, and limited government intervention in the economy and in people's lives. The New Right combines elements of conservatism, libertarianism, and populism. Ronald Reagan in the US and Margaret Thatcher in the UK are prominent figures.

4. *Nationalist conservatism*: **Benjamin Disraeli**, former UK prime minister, argued that it is everyone's social obligation and moral responsibility to empower the less well-off sections of society. This is also known as *one-nation conservatism*, and as *Tory democracy*. One-nation conservatives believe that social inequality is a threat to national unity and that the state has a responsibility to intervene in the economy and provide social welfare to the less privileged.
5. *Authoritarian conservatism*: It is associated with the belief that individuals must subordinate themselves to the interests of the community or the state, and advocates a strong, centralised and authoritarian government to maintain social order and uphold traditional values.

10

SOCIALISM

KEY CONCEPTS

Features of socialism; Utopian/early socialism; evolutionary socialism; collectivism; twenty-first century socialism

Socialism is a theory or system of social organisation that advocates ownership and control of the means of production and distribution, capital, land, etc., by the community as a whole, usually through a centralised government. In Marxist theory, socialism refers to the stage following capitalism in the transition of a society to communism, also known as the 'Dictatorship of the Proletariat'. In this phase, the proletariat takes control of the bourgeoisie state apparatus and works towards the establishment of 'Higher Communism', wherein all remnants of capitalism, including private property and the bourgeoisie state, will ultimately be destroyed. **Andrew Vincent** notes that the word *socialism* derives from the Latin root '*sociare*', meaning to combine or share. The term socialism was coined by **Henri de Saint-Simon**, one of the founders of utopian socialism.

BASIC FEATURES OF SOCIALISM

1. **Emphasis on Community:** The earliest socialists contrasted the ideology of socialism with liberal individualism. They criticised the notion of the atomistic self as it failed to address the concerns of the community. Socialists insist that man is a social animal, finding fulfillment in collective living.
2. **Fraternity and Cooperation:** Contrasted with the liberal competitive capitalist market, socialists emphasise cooperation and fraternity among humans who aid each other and co-exist in collectivities based on solidarity.
3. **Equality:** Defenses of inequality have existed in political thought since the times of Plato. It was believed that some kind of economic and political inequality was necessary to maintain social order and stability. However, following decolonisation, the abolition of slavery and racism, equality has become a necessary and cherished ideal. In modern times, democracy has ensured political equality but failed in removing inequalities in other spheres, while capitalism has worsened inequalities of all kinds. Socialism seeks complete and radical equality in social, political and economic life, through programmes based on affirmative and collective action. It defends equal rights of liberty and property for all and argues that in the absence of equality, the liberty of some will be based on the lack of liberty for others.
4. **Stratification of Society:** Socialism rejects traditional hierarchies based on divine rights

or custom. It emphasises human reason and progress, and aims for scientific objectivity in its theoretical ventures. Socialism believes that the only theoretically and politically relevant principle of stratification in the modern capitalist society is 'Class'.

5. **Anti-Capitalism and Common Ownership:** Capitalism has created and reaffirmed new inequalities of all kinds and further perpetuated hereditary inequities through the institution of private property. Socialism aims at human emancipation through an enlightened management of resources.
6. **Emancipation:** Liberal thought is centred on the liberty of the abstract individual, whereas, socialist thought emphasises total human emancipation. Marxists see freedom in much wider terms as the removal of obstacles to human emancipation, through the manifold development of human ability and power. It underlines the formation of a collective enterprise worthy of human nature, realised through human control over both nature and the social conditions of production. Social cooperation is essential in bringing this about.

Forms of Socialism

Cyril E. M. Joad said that socialism is like a hat which has lost its shape because so many have worn it, alluding to the various forms of socialism that emerged globally. Despite the diversity of socialist ideologies, the basic tenets for all remain the same: belief in the principle of common ownership of property, economic and social equality, and fraternity. While all socialist ideologies prioritise the collective over the individual, the mechanisms and methods for obtaining the goal of socialism differs in each.

UTOPIAN SOCIALISM OR EARLY SOCIALISM

Utopian socialism, also known as early socialism, was the first wave of modern socialist thought. Its aim was to create an ideal society based on cooperation and equality. These socialists were called 'utopian' because they believed in creating perfect societies that were free from poverty, inequality and other social ills. The term 'utopian' refers to the idea of the possibility of social transformation involving the elimination of individualism, competition, and private property. Utopian socialists believed that capitalism was inherently flawed and must be replaced with a new economic system based on cooperative ownership and control of the means of production. However, they did not recognise the need for class struggle or the revolutionary role of the proletariat. They also believed in the importance of social harmony and sought to create communities based on shared ownership and decision-making. They asserted that despite the fundamental morality and rationality of human nature, modern civilisation had corrupted human thinking and resulted in overriding selfishness.

Robert Owen is often considered the father of socialism in Britain, and his work *A New View of Society* (1813) was influential. A factory owner, Owen introduced multiple measures designed to transform factory workers into a self-supporting, self-educating, and self-governing community. He denounced private property. Other early thinkers who influenced utopian socialism include **Thomas More** and **James Harrington**. Famous utopian socialists include **Charles Fourier** and **Henri de Saint-Simon**, who proposed various models for creating ideal societies based on their own ideas and beliefs.

Henri de Saint Simon believed in the abolition of all privileges at birth, rewards determined according to the amount of labour contributed by the individual, and common ownership of land, capital and all instruments of labour. In his most important work, *The New Christianity*, he also envisioned an egalitarian revision of Christianity.

Charles Fourier believed that modern civilisation was fundamentally flawed, deceitful, hypocritical and parasitic. He founded an ideal community by organising people into small, self-contained 'intentional communities' called *phalanxes*, based on cooperation, shared tastes and interests, and shared labour.

While their specific visions differed, all utopian socialists shared a common goal of creating a more just and equitable world. Some significant works of authors associated with early utopianism or utopian socialism include: Thomas More, *Utopia* (1516); Tommaso Campanella, *The City of the Sun* (1602); James Harrington, *The Commonwealth of Oceana* (1656); and Gerrard Winstanley, *The Law of Freedom in a Platform* (1652).

EVOLUTIONARY SOCIALISM

Evolutionary socialism, which developed in the late nineteenth and early twentieth centuries, particularly in Germany and Britain, rejected the revolutionary approach of earlier socialists and instead advocated for the gradual, democratic transformation of society through reforms, rather than the violent overthrow of the existing order. **Eduard Bernstein**, a German socialist and close associate of Karl Marx, is often seen as the father of evolutionary socialism. Bernstein wrote a book titled *The Preconditions of Socialism and Task of Social Democracy* (1899), popularly known as *Evolutionary Socialism* (1909), in which he argued that the development of the capitalist economy had created a more complex and diverse society, and that socialist movements needed to adapt their strategies to this new reality. The emphasis was on achieving social and economic justice through the reform of existing institutions, rather than the establishment of a new, separate, socialist society.

Ferdinand Lassalle was a German socialist and labour leader who founded the German Workers' Association, which later became the Social Democratic Party of Germany. Lassalle was influenced by the ideas of French socialist thinkers like Saint Simon and Charles Fourier. Like Bernstein, he sought to achieve socialism through democratic political reform rather than revolution. Lassalle believed that the working class should form a political party and use their votes to gain power and implement social and economic reforms.

Forms of Evolutionary Socialism

Alternatively known as *Fabianism* and *democratic socialism*, evolutionary socialism is opposed to revolutionary socialism. The Fabian Society was founded in 1884. Many Fabians played a key role in the foundation of the British Labour Party in 1900. **George Bernard Shaw, Graham Wallas** and **Sydney Webb** were leading figures of the Fabian Society.

Evolutionary socialism includes some of the following different schools of thought: Fabianism, Revisionism, Democratic Socialism, and Socialist Democracy.

However, the ultimate goal of all forms of evolutionary socialism is one: to attain socialism through the use of democratic methods and constitutional government. The variations in names mainly reflect the specific different circumstances of their origins. Fabianism, for example, was developed by British socialist intellectuals. Revisionism was introduced by Eduard Bernstein of Germany, who revised Marxist ideas and rejected the notion of a revolution as the means to achieve socialism. In Germany, democratic socialism is known as socialist democracy because the socialist party in Germany emphasised the use of democratic processes to achieve socialism.

Features of Evolutionary Socialism

1. **The Moral Principle:** Socialists in Britain have been influenced by Christian morality, and believe that since human beings are the creation of God, individuals should be more sympathetic towards their fellow human beings. Poverty and inequality present in society go against the moral conscience of human beings. The purpose

of human life is not only to acquire more and more property, but fraternity and social service are primary aims to lead a better and moral life.

2. **Socialism by the State:** Evolutionary socialists see the state, and not the proletariat, as the primary agent of social transformation. Therefore, they argue for active state intervention in the society and economy, generally in the form of redistributive policies and affirmative action. They focus on a socialist reformation of the state rather than a complete restructuring or regime change. **Eduard Bernstein**, in his work *Evolutionary Socialism: A Criticism and Affirmation* (1899), sees the state as an instrument for bringing about socialist change and for ending class exploitation. So he opposes the abolition of the state.
3. **Piecemeal Reform:** Evolutionary socialists condemn the ideal of revolution within Marxist theory and perceive it as resulting in chaos, anarchy, instability and disorder. Instead, they insist on gradual, piecemeal changes in the nature of reform rather than complete change. They emphasise the importance of peaceful, consensual reform for stability, order and growth. Evolutionary socialists agree that changes are necessary in society, but believe in more gradual, incremental methods of realising those changes through existing political and democratic institutions.
4. **Social Diversity:** Evolutionary socialists criticise the Marxist conceptualisation of society as being composed of two antagonistic classes. They believe that this division ignores wider social and cultural realities. Therefore, they insist that society be composed of diverse groups with diverse social and cultural identities, all of which need to be recognised, and their needs and interests adequately addressed.
5. **Guild Socialism:** Guild socialism was originally proposed by **Arthur Joseph Penty** in his book *The Restoration of the Gild System* (1906), and later developed by **G. D. H. Cole**, who wrote *Guild Socialism: A Plan for Economic Democracy* (1920). **S. G. Hobson** also supported the idea of guilds as the basis of modern industrial production. Guild socialists advocated for functional representation instead of territorial representation, and called for the establishment of separate political and economic parliaments.
6. **Syndicalism:** Syndicalism advocates for the organisation of society around labour unions or *syndicates*, particularly in the industrial sector. It believes that workers' interests are best served by direct action such as strikes and boycotts, rather than through traditional forms of political action like voting or legislation. Syndicalists seek to abolish wage capitalism and replace it with a system of worker self-management and ownership of means of production. Their goal is to establish a socialist society based on workers' control of industry and society. Syndicalism was influenced by **Proudhon** and by the French social philosopher **Georges Sorel** who, in his book *Reflections on Violence* (1908), argued that violence is morally right and a necessary and positive force. Sorel believed that the working class could only achieve true liberation through a revolutionary strike to overthrow the capitalist system and establish a new order.
7. **Reform in Capitalism, and Market Socialism:** Evolutionary socialists believe in the possibility of, and thus advocate for, the humanisation of capitalism, through a mixed economy characterised by state control over major industries, centralised economic planning and progressive taxation. *Market socialism* conceives of an economic system in which the means of production (capital)

are publicly or collectively owned, and the allocation of resources follows market rules. It involves restructuring the ownership of the means of production, promoting political pluralism, and regulating capital and labour markets.

In the early 1950s, the Yugoslavian Communist Party attempted to apply the ideas of market socialism in practice. The initiation of Five-Year Plans in the Soviet Union was an implication of the adoption of Fabian socialist policies. However, the implementation of the Five-Year Plans was not a direct consequence of the adoption of market socialism, but rather a product of Soviet state planning.

8. **Reconciliation of Liberty and Equality:** Evolutionary socialists criticise the radical egalitarianism of the Marxists, and argue that liberty and equality are not contradictory but complementary ideals. Ensuring radical equality of the kind as promoted by revolutionary socialism would lead to restriction in terms of choice and denial of the fruits of their labour to the meritorious. Therefore, they assert that equality must be complimented by liberty of choice, expression and by constitutional democracy.
9. **Property is the Result of Community:** Democratic socialists do not agree with the view that property is created by labour, and instead assert that property is the result of community. Therefore, they argue that property should also be under the control of community. They are for state ownership of industries, and believe that progressive taxation is important for maintaining the goal of economic equality.

COLLECTIVISM AND SOCIALISM

Collectivism and socialism are related concepts, but not exactly the same. Collectivism refers to the idea that the group or community is more important than the individual, and that the individual should subordinate their interests to those of the group. Socialism, on the other hand, is a political and economic system that aims to create a classless society in which the means of production, distribution and exchange are owned and controlled by the community as a whole, rather than by individuals or corporations. Socialists argue that this is necessary to eliminate exploitation and inequality in society, and that the state should play a central role in managing the economy to ensure the well-being of all citizens.

While socialism is a form of collectivism, not all forms of collectivism are socialist. For example, some religious communities may practise collectivism without adhering to socialist principles. Additionally, some socialist ideologies, such as libertarian socialism, prioritise individual liberty and autonomy alongside collective ownership of the means of production.

SOCIALISM IN THE TWENTY-FIRST CENTURY

The Soviet Union, the torchbearer of socialism in the world, disintegrated in 1991. China, another important communist country, adopted market socialism and open economy policies in 1979. These huge changes led many to question the future of socialism and its possible extinction. **Francis Fukuyama**, in his work *The End of History and the Last Man* (1992), even went on to declare that the disintegration of Soviet Union marked the 'Triumph of Capitalism' and the end of political theory. Neo-liberal economic policies spread quickly thereafter throughout the world in the form of financial capitalism and globalisation, aided by international financial institutions like the IMF and World Bank.

The Third Way or Neo-Revisionism

Anthony Giddens' **Third Way**—developed in the 1990s as a response to the perceived weaknesses of both traditional Left-wing and Right-wing ideologies—tries to reconcile the principles of socialist democracy and neo-liberal capitalism. Also known as *neo-revisionism*, the Third Way advocates for a market economy and globalisation, but also emphasises the role of government in promoting social justice, economic security, and social inclusion. It argues that the state should intervene in the economy to create an environment in which people can take advantage of globalisation and technological progress, while also supporting the interests of those who are at risk of being left behind.

Features: Key features of the Third Way include the recognition that a market economy is dynamic and suitable, but also leads to the 'survival of the fittest'. Therefore, the competitive market model should be combined with a concern for the community and the moral responsibility of individuals towards the community.

While neo-revisionists emphasise the importance of self-reliance, liberty and individual autonomy, they also stress the need for basic welfare facilities for all. They coined the term '*Workfare State*', which implies the provision of basic facilities for life to all individuals, while also necessitating individual initiative and hard work. Giddens believed that imparting values, skills and knowledge is more important than the distribution of social goods. Therefore, while competition is essential for strengthening the economy, fraternity is equally important for stability in society.

The Third Way has been adopted by some centre-left political parties in Europe, such as the UK's New Labour under Tony Blair.

Table 1.10.1: Liberalism versus Marxism

Liberalism	*Marxism*
1. Centred around the importance of human dignity and rationality. The individual self is the most important political unit.	The situated self, rooted in community values and class context is the central focus. Class emancipation is equated to human emancipation.
2. Advocates a model of free-market capitalist economy as essential for achieving freedom.	Sees the capitalist economy as the source of all exploitation and un-freedom in society. Aims for the destruction of capitalism.
3. Conflict is caused by the presence of diverse and conflicting interests in society.	Conflict is caused because of conflicting relations of production wherein one class owns the means of production and dominates and exploits the other.
4. Supports status-quoism. Argues for piecemeal, incremental change in the nature of gradual reforms.	Supports revolutionary change based on comprehensive social and economic restructuring.
5. State and democracy are seen as the primary agents for social change.	The revolutionary masses of the proletariat are the primary agents of social change.
6. Advocates limited constitutional government.	Advocates dictatorship of the proletariat.

Table 1.10.2: Marxism versus Socialism

Marxism	*Socialism*
1. Advocates complete destruction of capitalism and comprehensive restructuring of social and economic relations.	Believes in humanistic reform of capitalism.
2. Ultimate goal is the abolition of the state and private property.	State is perceived as the primary agent for social change.
3. Society is conceptualised as a division between two antagonistic economic classes.	Society is composed of diverse groups with various political, socio-cultural and economic identities.

Marxism	*Socialism*
4. Argues for revolutionary change.	Argues for piecemeal reform and peaceful, gradual, constitutional change as a means for bringing socialism.
5. Economic mode of production is the sole focus of theory.	Morality, religion and culture are equally important factors in theorising about society and social change.
6. Democracy serves the interest of the bourgeoisie and needs to be abolished along with the capitalist state.	Democracy is essential for bringing in peaceful socialist transformation.

Table 1.10.3: Marxism versus Neo-Marxism

Marxism	*Neo-Marxism*
1. Theory centred on economic determinism of economic, social as well as political relations.	Focuses on the importance of civil society, religion and culture as contributing to the dominance of the bourgeoisie class in the form of hegemony.
2. Objective, positivistic and scientific approach.	Humanistic approach.
3. Advocates violent revolution and dictatorship of the proletariat for social change.	Advocates democratic reform and the development of counter-hegemonic cultures.
4. Focuses on the repressive and coercive functions of the state.	Focuses on the ideological dimensions of state administration and dominance.
5. Focuses on the economic impacts of capitalism.	Emphasises the psychological impacts of capitalism.

11

MARXISM

KEY CONCEPTS

Communism; key principles of Marxism; historical materialism; class struggle; alienation; Bolsheviks versus Mensheviks; Mao Zedong; neo-Marxism

REVOLUTIONARY OR SCIENTIFIC SOCIALISM-MARXISM

Karl Marx and Friedrich Engels formulated one of the most influential and radical versions of socialism, which they called 'Communism'. Unlike other socialists, they emphasised the importance of an empirical and scientific explanation of society and history. Marx and Engels rejected capitalism as an inherently flawed system and predicted its eventual destruction based on causal relations which they saw as scientific.

Marx and Engels aimed to create a systematic, scientific theory of socialism that could be put to practice, in contrast to the ethical form of socialism. They believed that an ideal community cannot be visualised and realised without knowledge of historical conditions. It can only emerge through revolutionary action that is historically appropriate. Socialism, in their view, is a stage of historical development. Their central thesis, known as 'Historical Materialism', explains the dynamics of historical development as the result of a class struggle between the ruling class and the working class.

KEY PRINCIPLES OF MARXISM

Economic Determinism

According to Marx, society is divided into two main components: *the base* and *the superstructure.* The base represents the economic mode of production. The superstructure consists of the legal, political, religious, aesthetic or philosophical aspects of life. Marx argues that the economic base determines and shapes the formation and functioning of the political, legal and cultural superstructure. Different economic modes of production, such as feudalism or capitalism, have corresponding political, legal, and social structures that sustain them.

Marx also argues that the dominant class, which owns and controls the means of production, also dominates the state and shapes social relations. This means that the bourgeoisie, who own the factories, land and other means of production in capitalist society, also control the government and use it to maintain their power and interests.

Materialism

Marx's philosophy centres around the idea that economic factors play a dominant role in shaping society, including its government, culture, and state. He believes that religion and ideology are shaped by economic factors rather than being a significant influence on society. *Historical materialism* is the term Marx used to describe his economic interpretation of history, which asserts that the progress of history and civilisation is determined by economic factors. Marx's view of the historical process is dialectical, and he calls it *dialectical materialism.*

According to Marx, history moves through a series of stages, each of which has a *thesis*, an *antithesis*, and a *synthesis*. The driving force of history is the development of productive forces, the most important of which is technology. Marx identifies six stages of human history in his account of historical materialism, each characterised by a different mode of production. Mode of production refers to the sum total of relations of production and means of production. The six modes of production under historical materialism are: Primitive Communism, Slave Society, Feudalism, Capitalism, Dictatorship of the Proletariat and Higher Communism.

Class Struggle

Marx says the individual is a part of society, and society comes into existence for fulfilling the physical needs of people. But due to the presence of private property and inequality, society is divided into opposing classes. In capitalist society, these two classes are the bourgeoisie and the proletariat. The bourgeoisie is the class of modern capitalists, owners of the means of production and employers of wage labour. The proletariat is the working class which sells its labour as a commodity and is exploited under capitalism. The relation between these two classes is paradoxical, cannot be reconciled and therefore needs to be restructured. In the opening lines of his famous work, *The Communist Manifesto*, Marx observes that the 'history of all existing societies is the history of class struggles.'

Human Nature

Human beings are good by nature but the capitalist system creates inequality and disparity in society. Marx argues that human nature is both dynamic and constant. It is rooted in its context and does not exist in the form of the liberal conception of the atomistic self. He uses the concept of *praxis* instead of the liberal focus on 'rationality'.

Praxis implies the creative action or activity through which humans change their world and themselves. This praxis contains the human essence and refers to the creative self of humans. This idea implies that even manual labour involves creativity, and it led to widespread criticism of the capitalist focus on the superiority of intellectual labour.

Revolutionary

Marx rejected **Hegel's** idea of dialectics, which conceptualised historical development in the terms of an evolution of ideas. He refuted Hegel's claim that the end of history was in sight with the formation of the bourgeois state. Instead, he asserted that the realm of freedom, which for Hegel was a distant possibility, could be realised here and now, through conscious change in the form of the socialist revolution.

Marx also criticised the possibility of piecemeal reform or gradual change, asserting that the change would be absolute, revolutionary and it would be bloody. He has been extensively criticised for his advocacy of violence in the form of 'bloody revolution'.

State

Marx envisages the establishment of a communist society which is classless and stateless. There is no private property and each will work according to their capacity and they will receive according their need. **Vladimir Lenin** in his book *The State and Revolution* explains the two stages of the dictatorship of the proletariat, one is socialism and the other is communism.

Bolsheviks vs Mensheviks

The Russian Social Democratic Labour Party witnessed a disagreement between Julius Martov and Lenin, with the former leading the minority group called Mensheviks. The Mensheviks argued that industrialisation must take place before a communist revolution. On the other hand, Lenin belonged to the Bolsheviks, who were the majority group. George Plekhanov was known as the father of socialism in Russia. Bukharin, a Russian Marxist, authored *Imperialism and World Economy*. He did not agree with the Bolshevik revolution and wrote *Socialism and Political Struggle*. Similarly, Trotsky and Rosa Luxemburg also opposed the Bolshevik method of revolution.

Lenin's Contribution

V. I. Lenin brought about the first communist revolution in Russia in October 1917, and is known for his contributions to the development of Marxist ideology, which is called Marxism-Leninism. Lenin claimed that he only executed the idea of Marx and considered Marx to be like a God. However, he brought about the following changes in Marx's ideas:

1. Lenin argued that the highest stage of capitalism is imperialism.
2. He emphasised the importance of the communist party as the vanguard of revolution and the need for communist ideology.
3. Lenin extended the meaning of the proletariat class to include peasants, propounding the concept of the weakest link, and claiming that revolution in Russia was possible.
4. He advocated for a model of bureaucratic centralisation known as 'democratic centralism.'
5. Lenin supported decolonisation struggles and criticised colonialism and neo-colonialism in underdeveloped countries.

Mao's Communism

Mao brought about communist revolution in China, a nation with an agrarian economy and feudal society. He made some changes in Marxist ideas to suit Chinese social and economic conditions. Mao emphasised the following points:

1. For Mao, peasants became the vanguard of the revolution, and labourers were considered secondary.
2. Villages, and not cities, became the centres of revolution. Capitalist nations were surrounded by Asian-African developing economies. Therefore, the communist revolution will demolish both capitalism and feudalism.
3. Mao supported guerilla warfare and said that power goes out of the barrel of the gun.
4. Mao believed that consciousness or ideas were more important than material conditions for obtaining the goal of communist revolution.

Drawbacks of Marxism

Critics of Marxism argue that it is an economic reductionist theory that ignores the importance of other factors in understanding society, history, state, religion, and culture. They claim that Marxism is not scientific and that Marx's interpretation of history is more of his own imagination than an explanation of then-existing history. Others argue that the concept of dictatorship of the proletariat turned into a dictatorship over the proletariat. The mismanagement of the socialist system led to the disintegration of the Soviet Union, and the Marxist emphasis on economic equality resulted in the suppression of liberty, rights, and democratic forms of government.

After World War II, the capitalist state became a welfare state and adopted ideological tools to strengthen capitalism, leading to the emergence of neo-Marxism or Western Marxism. Western Marxism is a distinct tradition that includes the ideas of scholars such as Rosa Luxemburg, Georg Lukacs, Antonio Gramsci, Theodor Adorno, Herbert Marcuse, Walter Benjamin, and Jurgen

Habermas. Neo-Marxists criticise capitalism and orthodox Marxism and emphasise the importance of democracy for social change.

The Emergence of Neo-Marxism

The context in which Neo-Marxism emerged can be traced back to the aftermath of World War II. As capitalist states transitioned into welfare states, they began to adopt ideological tools aimed at strengthening capitalism. This shift meant that the capitalist state was no longer solely a coercive entity. Meanwhile, in the Soviet Union, Stalin implemented a one-party dictatorship and dismantled all democratic and representative institutions.

Despite these developments, the working class in capitalist societies remained unprepared to bring about a communist revolution. It was in this context that Neo-Marxism, also known as Western Marxism, emerged. Neo-Marxist thought critiques both capitalism and Orthodox Marxism. Neo-Marxism comprises the ideas of the following groups:

1. Austro-Hungarian Marxism
2. Frankfurt School
3. Structural Marxism

Western Marxism / Neo-Marxism

The various strands of Neo-Marxism can be categorised under the umbrella of Western Marxism. Scholars have identified a distinct tradition of Western Marxism, with some of the most important figures including Rosa Luxemburg, Karl Liebknecht, Georg Lukacs, Karl Korsch, Antonio Gramsci, Jean-Paul Sartre, Theodor Adorno, Herbert Marcuse, Walter Benjamin, and Bertolt Brecht. In recent years, this tradition has also been continued by thinkers such as Louis Althusser, Michel Foucault, and Jurgen Habermas. Western Marxism has given rise to a number of distinct schools of thought, including Council Communism, Austro Marxism, the Frankfurt School, and Structural Marxism.

The fundamental assumptions of Western Marxism can be summarised as follows.

1. It identified alienation, fetishisation and commodification of social relations as important issues before the socialist movement.
2. It was deeply apprehensive of the loss and stunting of critical reason under the sway and machinations of capital.
3. It drew attention to the domain of superstructures, particularly culture, and argued for the need to resist and challenge dominance, suppression, repression and marginalisation manifest in this sphere. It drew attention to the presence of subaltern culture and the creative possibilities they hold out to resist dominance and pose radical alternatives.
4. It displayed a strong commitment to the promotion of socialist democracy and showed greater responsiveness to learn lessons from liberal democracy and rights. It was critical of some of the socialist regimes for disregarding democratic norms and the restrictions they placed on freedoms and rights.
5. It tried to face the predicament of the failure of revolutionary socialist movements in the West by advancing alternative explanations. The work of **Antonio Gramsci**, the Italian Marxist, has been pioneering in this regard. He explores the issues of the reproduction of hegemony of the dominant classes by invoking *consent* of the dominated. These alternative explanations have called attention to the interventions of socialists in civil society, ideology and popular cultures much more than earlier versions of Marxism suggested.
6. Western Marxism has tended to stress on mass movements and popular mobilisation for the purpose of political ascendancy of the proletariat. The stress on revolutionary violence that we find in Leninism and Maoism is less visible in this version.

Euro-Communism

Euro-communism believes in democratic methods and peaceful change. They rejected the idea of violent struggle for the objective of communism. **Palmiro Togliatti** who founded the idea of Euro-communism also advocated for a multi-party system and a pluralist society.

The Frankfurt School

It emerged in Germany in the 1920s and 1930s. It can be associated with an anti-Bolshevik radicalism and an open-ended or critical Neo-Marxism. The ideas of the thinkers of the Frankfurt School fall under the heading of 'critical theory'. Key figures within the Frankfurt School include: **Max Horkheimer, Freidrich Pollock, Theodore Adorno, Eric Fromm, Herbert Marcuse, Franz Neumann**, **Walter Benjamin** and **Otto Kirchheimer.**

They sought to engage with and synthesise aspects of the works of mainly Kant, Hegel, Marx, Weber, Lukacs and Freud. The critical theory of the Frankfurt School was concerned with comprehending the central features of contemporary society by understanding its historical and social development. It was largely an attempt to recover a critical and emancipatory potential that had been overrun by recent intellectual, social, cultural, political, economic and technological trends. **Kolakowski** identified the following features of Frankfurt school:

(i) It did not treat Marxism as sacrosanct but as a starting point and a helpful tool in analysing and criticising existing culture.
(ii) Its programme was strictly non-party in orientation. It never identified itself with any political movement either of communism or of social democracy.
(iii) It was profoundly influenced by the interpretation of Marxism developed by Lukacs and Korsch in the 1920s.
(iv) Though they were influenced by the concept of reification developed by Lukacs they opposed the concept of praxis to emphasise the independence and autonomy of theory.
(v) Despite their divergences with Lukacs they accepted the Marxist position on exploitation and alienation of the proletariat.
(vi) The Frankfurt School was a revisionist one in revising orthodox Marxism but remained a revolutionary intellectual movement.

Alienation

In Marx's sense, an action through which a person, a group, an institution or a society becomes an alien to:

1. The results or products of its own activity and thus to the activity itself;
2. To the environment in which it lives; and
3. To other human beings;
4. Loss of control over the self, and therefore human beings become like machines. This is an extreme form of alienation.

Therefore, alienation is always self-alienation, i.e., alienation of the man from himself (from his human possibilities), through himself (through his own activity). Self-alienation is not just a descriptive concept but also an appeal, a call for a revolutionary change (de-alienation) of the world.

Self-alienation has been perceived through many lenses. The Neo-Marxists insist that the de-alienation of economic life cannot be achieved only through abolition of private property. It is a psychological implication of capitalism which requires appropriate solution. **Herbert Marcuse** depicted the psychological problems of capitalism in his book *One Dimensional Man* (1964) with reference to alienation. He focuses on self-emancipation, decentralisation of movement and the reconciliation of alienated humanity with nature.

Jurgen Habermas observed that the liberal conceptualisation of the atomistic self was an extreme form of alienation. It was a consequence of the technological advancement of industrial capitalism which had turned men into cogs and screws in machines.

Democracy

Since his earliest writings, Marx was committed to the ideal of direct democracy. **Kautsky** and other Euro-communists envisaged the ultimate victory of socialism through the system of the ballot boxes and parliament. **Lenin**, on the other hand, rejected the views of Kautsky and others. He argued that the bourgeois democracy, like any other form of state, was a form of class rule and had to be demolished by the dictatorship of the proletariat.

Gramsci believed that there was a development of popular forces within bourgeois democracies because of political mobilisation and the development of a counter-hegemonic culture. These developments would ultimately lead to a socialist transformation. Neo-Marxists opposed the idea of a bloody revolution underlined by the doctrine of the dictatorship of the proletariat. They sought socialist transformation through models of holistic democracy.

Rejection of Class

Marxists advocate a pyramidal model of society as a model of social stratification. At the peak of the pyramid are a small number of elite bourgeoisie classes who control all means of production and wealth, while the wide base comprises the huge masses of the revolutionary proletariat.

Conversely, the Neo-Marxists advocate an elliptical model of social stratification to refer to the changes in social structure in the contemporary context. Herein, both the top and the base are narrow. The top consists of the elite bourgeoisie who control the means of productions. The base consists of the poorest of the poor proletariat who are preoccupied with trying to survive. The middle part is broad and is made up of the intermediate middle class who are engaged in bureaucratic administration and provide services to the bourgeoisie.

Neo-Marxists believe that in contemporary times, this intermediate middle class is the one capable of presenting a counter-hegemonic culture to oppose the dominance of the bourgeoisie. The middle class becomes the leader of the 'bourgeois democratic revolution' which precedes the socialist transformation.

Humanism

Humanism is a philosophical stance that emphasises the value, agency and dignity of human beings, individually and collectively, and supports the maximisation of individual liberty and opportunity. This maximisation is consistent with recognitions of social and planetary responsibility.

Hungarian Marxist **George Lucas** in his book *History and Class Consciousness* proposed the idea of Cultural Marxism. Neo-Marxists emphasise the significance of human consciousness in ensuring the perpetuation of the bourgeois regime. They assert that this consciousness needs to undergo a radical transformation under the spread of a socialist consciousness. **Louis Althusser** distinguishes between the repressive state apparatuses and ideological state apparatuses. The repressive state apparatuses are the military, police and courts which use methods of direct repression and violence to ensure compliance. The ideological state apparatuses are religion, culture, traditions, familial customs, civil society etc. which impact human psychology, shape public opinion and behaviour, function on the basis of ideological hegemony and concessions, and thus ensure the entrenchment of dominant modes of thought. The Neo-Marxists therefore insist that for the success of any kind of socialist transformation, only a change in economic mode of production will not suffice. A change must also be brought in through a counter-hegemonic socialist culture.

12

FEMINISM

KEY CONCEPTS

Development of feminist thought; three waves of feminism; liberal feminism; socialist and Marxist feminism; personal–political divide; eco-feminism; post-feminism

ORIGIN AND DEVELOPMENT

Feminism as a term denotes the investigation and understanding of discrimination against and oppression of women. It underlines attempts to abolish such domination and advocates the agency, autonomy and emancipation of women in all spheres.

Feminism as a political theory can be traced to the 1600s, to the writings of **Mary Astell**. In the 1700s, **Olympe de Gouges**, a French female revolutionary, wrote a pamphlet titled '*Declaration on the Rights of Women and Citizens*' that criticised the French Revolution, and demanded the inclusion of women as equals in the French Republic. *The Vindication of the Rights of Women* by **Mary Wollstonecraft**, published in 1792 in England, was another significant work that criticised the English state for ignoring women's rights, and demanded civil and political rights for women, including suffrage and education.

The feminist movement has been categorised into waves or phases as a political and social movement, with each wave focused on specific socio-political, economic, cultural and ideological goals. These waves emerged chronologically, encompassing both thought and action. In *Modern Political Ideologies*, Andrew Vincent notes that feminism refers to both an ideology and a movement.

FIRST WAVE

The first wave of feminism, spanning the eighteenth century to the early twentieth century, aimed to secure basic civil and political rights for women, such as education, suffrage, and employment rights. The metaphor of 'waves' representing the various surges of feminism dates to 1968 when **Martha Weinman Lear** published an article in the *New York Times Magazine* titled 'The Second Feminist Wave'. The first wave focused on achieving gender equality in public life, with many Black women in America also advocating against slavery and promoting feminist concerns through anti-slavery societies.

J. S. Mill's essay 'On Liberty' marked the emergence of feminism as a political theory. Mill advocated equal rights for men and women, including voting rights for women. He argued that women lived like slaves in their homes, and their goal in life was reduced to getting married. Mill believed that denying women the right to vote based on tradition was unjust as it was presumed that they were incapable of managing public and political affairs. Mill's views, co-authored with his spouse **Harriet Taylor** in *On Subjection of Women*, suggested that women seemed unequal because they had been socialised differently through cultural norms.

In 1848, **Lucretia Mott** and **Elizabeth Cady Stanton**, called the Seneca Falls Convention with the support of the Black abolitionist leader **Frederick Douglass** to demand women's rights. The convention supported women's rights to equality and citizenship.

In 1869, **Elizabeth Cady Stanton** and **Susan Anthony** formed the 'National Woman Suffrage Association' and launched a journal called *The Revolution*. By 1893, New Zealand became the first self-governing country to grant all women the right to vote. The American Constitution granted suffrage rights to women in 1920, and in UK all women over 21 years got the right to vote in 1928.

Liberalism and Feminism

Liberal feminists underlined the values of progress and rationality within liberalism. While criticising the democratic state, and demanding civil and political rights which they had been denied, they still viewed the state as the guarantor of freedoms. Liberal feminists remained sceptical of the state but believed in its capacity to bring about social change, aligning with the liberal principle that democracy was key to change and progress.

Table 1.12.1: Liberalism versus Feminism

Liberalism	*Feminism*
1. Advocated constitutional government and equality before law.	Women were recognised as equal before law. However, the state refrained from interfering within the unequal sphere of family.
2. One person, one vote. However, initially women were denied voting rights.	Women had to struggle for acquiring suffrage rights.
3. Repudiated discrimination on any grounds.	Women struggled to end wage discrimination in employment and for securing basic civil and political rights.
4. State was seen as the agent of change and guarantor of rights.	Various schools had different perspectives on the state. While liberal feminists viewed the state with optimism, radical feminists repudiated it as an agent of patriarchy.
5. Welfare state provides social basic goods.	Radical and socialist feminists sought to replace the welfare state with women's communes.
6. Advocated parliamentary democracy.	Radical feminists said the personal is political. They were skeptical of democracy since men claimed to represent women, while women themselves were relegated to the private sphere.

Socialism and Feminism

The socialist and Marxist feminists critiqued the ideas of the liberal feminists. They derived mainly from the ideas of **Friedrich Engels** and his book *The Origin of Family, Private Property and the State*, wherein Engels argued that the institution of private property, domestication of animals, and knowledge of impregnation made women the first proletariat. He claimed that prior to the emergence of industrialisation and urbanisation, matriarchal societies existed where women owned the means of production as the home was the centre of production. Men were subordinate to women and mainly engaged in grazing animals. However, the rise of capitalism made the city the centre of production controlled by men, leading to the historical defeat of women. Engels famously stated that thus in the institution of family, men are the bourgeoisie and women are the proletariat.

Socialist feminists asserted that it is not just relations of production but also the relations of reproduction that lead to the subordination of women. They focused on the sexual division of labour and demanded equal pay for women and also maternity benefits like community crèches at workplaces. Some also argued for communal mechanisms for child rearing and education. **Maria Myes** asserted that domestic work is often disregarded as 'shadow work'.

Table 1.12.2: Socialist versus Marxist Feminism

Socialism	Marxism
1. Advocated economic equality between the haves and have nots.	Broadened the horizons of economic equality to argue for wage equality between men and women.
2. Advocated the abolition of capitalism and common ownership.	Emphasised that the capitalist economy utilised the cheap labour of women and stressed on the *invisibilisation* of domestic labour.
3. Advocated communal ownership of means of production.	Advocated economic independence of women.
4. Advocated the abolition of discrimination.	It stressed upon the worth of women as possessing equal productive capacities as men.
5. Class was the primary unit of social stratification.	Gender was equally important as class as a factor causing inequality.

SECOND WAVE

The second wave of feminism emerged after the 1950s and it was a period of great political activity. The first wave had mainly focused on suffrage rights, legal obstacles to acquiring education rights and property rights etc. The second broadened the debate to include issues like sexuality, substantive equality and injustices within the family, and drew attention to issues like rape and domestic violence.

Betty Friedan was a leading figure in the feminist movement in the US. Her 1963 book, *The Feminine Mystique*, is often credited with sparking the second wave of feminism. Radical feminists, however, drew a line between individualistic conceptions of liberalism and the sisterhood-based solidarity which formed the basis of feminism. This was the era of the Radical Feminists. They were inspired to a great degree by the Marxist feminist discourse which distinguished between the relations of production, as being a part of the public sphere and the relations of reproduction as being a part of the private sphere. They advocated structural changes and complete social transformation of the gendered relations of production and gendered spaces through their slogan: 'Personal is Political'.

Patriarchy

The idea of patriarchy was developed by the socialist and the radical feminists. The liberal feminists made no reference to it. The word patriarchy comes from the word '*patriarchus*' meaning the male head of the family. It signifies the imposition of male authority on women in all spheres of society. Feminists however, do not question men; rather they question the masculinist order of society.

Betty Friedan illustrated the creation of a cultural myth within society wherein women were socialised in such a way that they sought fulfillment and security within the domestic sphere in their roles as mothers and wives. Women, she argued, are not valued as individuals, but as mothers, daughters and wives, for their social roles. However, women could never actually realise their true self, which resulted in a crisis of identity and disorder. Friedan also coined the term 'Problem with no name' to denote the implications of this identity crisis. Herein women were inseparably associated with their domestic roles and lost their own sense of identity and self-fulfillment.

Sylvia Walby said that patriarchy results in the subjugation of both men and women to a structure of power where they have fixed social roles. Men are forced to become providers for the family and the perpetrators of violence.

Kate Millett emphasised how masculinity and femininity were not biologically given, but were created around the terms 'male' and 'female'. Socialisation was actively undertaken to make women and men conform to particular gender roles.

Personal–Political Divide

From the times of Aristotle to Hannah Arendt, politics has been seen exclusively as an activity of the public sphere. Women, on the other hand, were seen as part of the personal sphere within the home, and only men had access to the public sphere. Radical feminists transformed the idea of reform into a political theory by redefining concepts like 'power' and 'domination' as oppressive ontologies like 'achievement' and 'superiority'. They defined women's unequal status using terms like subordination, powerlessness and oppression, effectively making women's issues a part of their political relationship with men. Personal problems were no longer seen as individual issues, but rather as universal to all women due to their gender-based oppression by men.

Women were regarded as a part of the personal sphere wherein their work was unpaid. Thus, they were seen as unemployed or as housewives. This was referred to as the '*invisibilisation* of women's labour'.

Simone de Beauvoir in *The Second Sex* asserts that 'one is not born a woman; rather, one becomes a woman', implying that one is socialised to become a gendered individual. She argues that the term 'personal' denotes the unequal domestic sphere wherein women are exploited and subjugated through the patriarchal family.

Radical feminists like **Simone de Beauvoir** and **Kate Millett** also hold that women are restricted by their own bodies. Thus, freedom for them implied greater control over their own bodies, sexuality and reproductive functions in the form of maternity care, abortion rights, contraceptives etc.

Private–Public Divide

Susan Moller Okin (1989) elaborates that 'the personal is political' argument comprises four separate claims.

1. First, it highlights the fact that the private sphere is a sphere of power. Due to patriarchy, the rights and duties, advantages and disadvantages are unequally distributed within the family.
2. Second, it is how the explicitly political sphere defines and infiltrates the personal sphere.
3. Third, the private sphere and particularly family life creates the psychological conditions that govern public life.
4. The fourth and final claim is that the gendered division of labour within the private sphere, with women taking on most or all the domestic and caring tasks, creates barriers for women in all other spheres and thus spills over into all other areas.

State

Radical feminists contend that the state is a social institution. Since society is patriarchal, the state cannot remain neutral or autonomous either. **Carol Pateman**, in *The Sexual Contract*, says that the state is not a welfare agency, but works only towards preserving the interests of the patriarchal social order. The state's welfare services are geared towards the preservation and glorification of motherhood, which effectively renders women's other identities, social roles, responsibilities and accomplishments irrelevant.

While Marxists sees capitalism as the root cause of exploitation, feminists blame the patriarchal order. In both scenarios, the state, by itself, cannot function as an independent and effective agent of social reform.

Justice and Ethics of Social Care

John Rawls, in *A Theory of Justice*, recognises that the family is a part of the sphere of justice since injustice occurs within the family. However, he insists that this injustice is necessary since the family is also a sphere of love and sacrifice, which are 'higher ideals'. Herein, all concerns of injustice are irrelevant. In doing so, as **Susan Moller Okin** observes in her criticism of Rawls, he ignores the socialisation of women which forces them to be the only ones to sacrifice their interests for the family. Rawls is also criticised for ignoring gender identities while conceptualising his 'veil of ignorance'.

Maternal Feminism

The maternal feminists differed from earlier feminists in their emphasis upon the differences between men and women. **Carol Gilligan**'s book *In a Different Voice* argues that justice and care are two distinct moral systems. While the moral thought concerning justice is centred on men, women's roles are evenly spread across both the spheres. Gilligan inferred that while men tend to be competitive and autonomous, women tend to think with concern for others. However, masculine characteristics are privileged over feminine ones. The masculinist sense of justice implies rationality and neutrality, whereas the feminine sense of justice implies an ethics of caring and sharing based on emotions, love and compassion. Gilligan contends that the masculinist sense of justice must be replaced by the feminine ethics of care.

Eco-Feminism

The term eco-feminism was coined by the feminist scholar **Francois d'Eaubonne** (1974). Other scholars associated with eco-feminism are **Susan Griffin, Mary Daly** and **Vandana Shiva**. Like maternal feminists, eco-feminists emphasised the differences between men and women, and also between nature and culture. Men were seen as representatives of culture, which was constructed and valued autonomy, rationality and neutrality. Women were associated with feminine ethics that valued emotions, love, caring and sharing, qualities believed to be more closely associated with nature.

Cultural feminism and *spiritual* feminism are both regarded as offshoots of eco-feminism. The cultural feminists emphasise the cultural and religious dimensions of patriarchy which legitimise violence against women through customs, traditions and social practices. They advocate comprehensive cultural reform along with political, economic and social change to improve the condition of women. Spiritual feminists believe in a close connection between the feminine spiritual essence and nature, and argue for women's equitable representation in all spheres of socio-economic and cultural life to ensure the transmission of this essence to all of society.

THIRD WAVE: POST-FEMINISM

The third wave of feminism was seen as a response to the failure of the first and second waves. It focused on the concept of *intersectionalities* and on looking beyond the binaries of male and female gender identities. It was during this wave that post-modern feminism, Black feminism and women-of-colour feminism emerged.

Post-modern Feminism

Judith Butler argued in *Gender Trouble* that earlier feminist ideas are bound to a heterosexual matrix, and it is important to question that. She held that both gender and biological sex were socially constructed. **Denis Kandiyoti** held that there are *multiple patriarchies* and that there must be continuous bargaining and negotiation with patriarchal structures.

Black Feminism and Intersectionalities

Black feminists included figures like **Rosa Park** and **Audre Lorde**, who famously said, 'Don't use my back as a bridge.' Lord claimed that the issues of black women and of women of colour are different from those of white feminists. Lord emphasised that black women face a double burden of both gender and racial discrimination at the hands of black men and white men as well as women.

Kimberley Crenshaw proposed the concept of *intersectionalities* and said that we need to look at various overlapping access points of discrimination like caste, class, gender. Intersectionality refers to the interconnected nature of social categories such as age, caste, class, gender, sexuality, ethnicity, and the ways in which they overlap and intersect to create experiences of oppression and privilege for individuals belonging to multiple marginalised groups and who face multiple forms of discrimination.

Lesbian feminism

Charlotte Bunch asserted that true feminists are lesbians. Lesbian feminists attempted to define lesbianism in a political sense, emphasised on severing their relations with men and on forging sexual, romantic as well as emotional bonds across communities of women. **Adrienne Rich** termed this the 'lesbian continuum'.

Post-colonial feminism

Gayatri Chakravarty Spivak said that women of the West do not consider Asian and African women as equal members of the feminist movement, and asserted that while talking about discrimination, it was important to move from the centre to the margins.

Table 1.12.3: Radical versus Liberal Feminism

Radical Feminism	*Liberal Feminism*
1. Focused on female emancipation from the patriarchal social order.	Focused on female empowerment through the granting of civil and political rights to ensure gender equality.
2. Emphasis on sisterhood-based solidarity.	Emphasis on individualism.
3. The Personal is Political.	Concentrated on inequality in and securing access for women to the political sphere.
4. Centred on sexual autonomy and rights to contraceptives etc.	Centred on civil and political freedoms.
5. Advocated revolutionary change and total restructuring of society.	Advocated gradual, constitutional reform.
6. Focus on creating social consciousness.	Focus on political activism.
7. Transformation of the private realm and familial relations.	The public–private divide was untouched.

Table 1.12.4: Egalitarian versus Difference Feminism

Egalitarian Feminism	*Difference Feminism*
1. Advocated human rights.	Advocated different kinds of rights of diverse women of different socio-cultural groups.
2. Focus on personhood.	Focus on alliance, community and sisterhood.
3. Advocated gender equality.	Advocated recognition of diversity, removal of all forms of discrimination including on the basis of race, caste, class, sexuality.
4. Men also seen as victims of patriarchy and as allies.	Men seen as perpetrators of violence.
5. Advocated abolition of differences.	Celebrated differences.
6. Pro-human.	Pro-women.
7. Engaged with men.	Separated from men.

13

ECOLOGISM

KEY CONCEPTS

Origins of ecologism; environmental ethics; environmental value system; types of ecology; post-materialism; eco-socialism; eco-anarchism; eco-feminism

ORIGINS

The term ecology was coined by German zoologist **Ernest Haeckel** and is derived from the Greek word *oikos* which means household or habitat. Ecology encompasses the idea that the non-human world is worthy of our moral consideration, known as *eco-centrism*. To support this concept, social, economic and political systems must be restructured to align with the needs of the ecology. While environmentalism aims for the survival of humanity, ecologism prioritises the protection of ecology, making it a wider, more comprehensive concept than environmentalism, which is anthropocentric. **David Ehranfeld** called this the 'Arrogance of Humanism'.

Rachel Carson's landmark book *Silent Spring* (1962) brought attention to the dangers of pesticides and their impact on human life, including a link to cancer. **Paul Ehrlich** and **Richard Harriman** wrote *How to be a Survivor* (1971). **Edward Goldsmith** wrote *Blueprint for Survival* (1972). In Germany, the slogan 'Neither left nor right but ahead' was adopted to stress the need for protecting the ecology. **E. F. Schumacher**'s book *Small is Beautiful* (1973) is critical of reliance on new sources of energy, and advocates a Buddhism-inspired economic philosophy that prioritises people's well-being over economic growth.

ENVIRONMENTAL ETHICS

In the modern world, both liberalism and Marxism emphasise material advancement, often neglecting the importance of the non-human world. However, it is argued that the moral standards that apply to human beings should also be applied to other species. **Peter Singer** is a philosopher who has defended the concept of animal rights, while in the US, **Tom Regan** wrote *The Case for Animal Rights* in 1983.

Post-materialism

People in the Western world have come to realise that material pleasure is not the ultimate objective of life, as noted by the sociologist **Inglehart.** Australian philosopher **Warwick Fox** has gone beyond deep ecology and laid down the principle of 'Transpersonal Ecology'. In his book *To Have or To Be* (1979), **Eric Fromm** said that self-realisation is the ultimate goal of life. Materialism is considered the most significant threat to the environment.

Eco-socialism

Eco-socialism combines elements of socialism with ecology and seeks to address both social and environmental issues by advocating a fundamental transformation of the economy. Eco-socialists believe that capitalism is inherently exploitative and unsustainable and argue that a socialist system is necessary for a sustainable society that prioritises social justice and ecological sustainability. They advocate protection of natural resources and the environment, and argue that these resources should be managed for the benefit of all people. Eco-socialism also seeks to promote a more equitable distribution of wealth and resources.

Marxists said capitalism is the root cause of environmental degradation. **Rudolph Bahro** said industrialisation is the basic reason behind environmental problems.

Eco-anarchism

Eco-anarchism, also known as green anarchism, combines anarchism with environmentalism to advocate for the dismantling of hierarchical power structures, including the state, and the establishment of a society based on decentralised, non-hierarchical decision-making and voluntary cooperation. Eco-anarchists view the domination and exploitation of nature as a direct result of the domination and exploitation of people, and seek to create a society that prioritises ecological sustainability and social justice. They often promote the use of direct action and mutual aid as means of achieving these goals, and oppose capitalism, industrialism, and other systems that they see as environmentally destructive and oppressive.

Anarchists reject human domination over the natural world, see the state and government as unnecessary, and advocate for a 'Social Ecology'. **Murray Bookchin**'s works, such as *Our Synthetic Environment*, *Ecology of Freedom* and *Remaking Society* further developed this idea. **Anna Bramwell** argued in the *Fading of the Greens* that sustainable development is possible with the support of electorate.

Environmental issues became urgent in the 1970s during the Cold War, but it wasn't until 1990 that nation states started uniting to protect the environment. The nature of environmental problems is complex because the rising temperature of the earth can turn Siberian land fertile, while the Sahara Desert can extend into other parts of the world. Although industrialised nations emit more greenhouse gases, their adverse impacts are more visible in developing nations. The initial debate for environmental protection was sparked by the Club of Rome's report titled *Limits to Growth* in 1972. Civil society organisations, such as Friends of the Earth and Greenpeace, have emerged to provide strong leadership and connectivity to environmental movements worldwide. They have also contributed significantly to academic research and theorisation concerning environmental issues. The first recognised Green political party was formed in New Zealand in 1972.

The Tragedy of the Commons

Garrett Hardin wrote *The Tragedy of the Commons* (1968). The Stockholm Conference of environment emphasised the protection of global commons. Resources known as global commons identified as the common heritage of mankind. The first effort for the preservation of environment is related to the protection of global commons. There are two types of global commons:

1. Those located within the sovereign territory of a state, like the Himalayan glaciers and the Amazon forests.
2. Global Commons which are not located within the territory of any particular states for e.g. Antarctica, the open seas and whales in addition to that open sea.

ENVIRONMENTAL VALUE SYSTEM (EVS)

An Environmental Value System (EVS) is a worldview that determines how individuals and, by extension, the societies they form, perceive and therefore evaluate environmental concerns.

The three environmental value systems are Technocentrism, Anthropocentrism and Ecocentrism.

1. **Technocentrism:** This system places trust in humans and technology as always having the capacity to provide solutions to scientific, political or environmental issues. A free market and economic growth are perceived as highly important factors.
2. **Anthropocentrism:** An approach premised on the idea that humans are the dominant species on earth. Humans can act as 'managers' of all aspects of the environment to fulfil our own requirements. In this view, nature exists for the welfare of humankind and non-human entities are resources that may be justifiably exploited for the benefit of humanity.
3. **Ecocentrism:** It is a philosophy of development based on a nature-centred and holistic worldview. This approach seeks to minimise resource use or the disruption of natural processes in order to operate within the carrying capacity of ecosystems. This emphasis is on a less materialistic approach to life, with greater self-sufficiency at the level of societies.

TYPES OF ECOLOGY

1. **Gaia Hypothesis:** Named after the ancient Greek goddess of Earth, it posits that the Earth and its biological system behaves like a huge single entity. It implies that the Earth is neither a material entity nor a mechanical system. It is an organic view of the earth and its processes.
2. **Ecosophy:** Ecosophy or ecophilosophy is a philosophy of ecological harmony or equilibrium. It was coined by **Felix Guattari** and **Arne Naess** who assert that the knowledge of nature is more important than the knowledge of the social world.
3. **Deep Ecology:** It is an environmental philosophy which promotes the inherent worth of all living beings regardless of their instrumental utility to human needs, plus the restructuring of modern human societies in accordance with such ideas. It was propounded originally by **Arne Naess**. In *The Ecology of Wisdom*, Naess asserts that gradual, incremental change is not sufficient for preserving the climate. The relations and interactions between human beings and ecology need to be revolutionised by a renewed consciousness enriched with this conceptualisation of universal solidarity and fraternity. The planet has an independent existence and is not dependent upon help from humans. Nature can heal itself if left alone.

Table 1.13.1: Deep Ecology versus Shallow Ecology

Deep Ecologist	*Shallow Ecologist*
Ecological	Environmental
Ecocentrism	Light anthropocentricism
Mysticism	Science
Radical holism	Reluctant holism
Value in nature	Instrumental value
Bio centric equality	Conserve non-human nature
Animal rights	Animal welfare
Anti-growth	Sustainable growth
Ecological consciousness	Personal development

The deep perspective completely rejects any lingering belief that the human species is in some way superior to, or more important than, any other species or indeed nature itself. It advances the more challenging idea that the purpose of human life is to help sustain nature, not the other way around.

1. *Inherent value*: The well-being and flourishing of human and nonhuman life on Earth have value in themselves or intrinsic and inherent value. These values are independent of the usefulness of the nonhuman world for human purposes.
2. *Diversity*: Richness and diversity of life forms contribute to the realisation of these values and are also values in themselves.

3. *Vital needs*: Humans have no right to reduce this richness and diversity except to satisfy vital needs.
4. *Population*: The flourishing of human life and cultures is compatible with a substantial decrease of the human population. The flourishing of nonhuman life requires such a decrease.
5. *Human interference*: The present human interference with the nonhuman world is excessive, and the situation is rapidly worsening.
6. *Policy change*: Policies must therefore be changed. These policies affect basic economic, technological, and ideological structures. The resulting state of affairs will be deeply different from the present.
7. *Quality of life*: The ideological change is mainly that of appreciating life quality (dwelling in situations of inherent value) rather than adhering to an increasingly higher standard of living. There will be a profound awareness of the difference between big and great.
8. *Obligation of action*: Those who subscribe to the foregoing points have an obligation directly or indirectly to try to implement the necessary changes.

ECO-FEMINISM

The idea that feminism offers a distinctive and valuable alternative to green issues has grown to such a point that ecofeminism has developed into one of the major schools of environmental philosophy. Its basic theme is that ecological destruction has its origins in patriarchy: nature is under threat not from humankind, but from men and institutions of male power.

Such a position is adopted, for instance, by **Mary Daly** in *Gyn/Ecology* (1979). Daly argued that women would liberate themselves from patriarchal culture if they aligned themselves with 'female nature'. The notion of an intrinsic link between women and nature is not new. Pre-Christian religions and primitive cultures often portrayed the Earth or nature forces as a Goddess, an idea resurrected in some respect in the Gaia hypothesis. **Susan Griffin** also supports the idea of ecological feminism.

Modern eco-feminists, however, highlight the biological basis for women's closeness to nature, in particular the fact that they bear children and suckle babies. The fact that women cannot live separate from natural rhythms and processes in turn structures their politico-cultural orientation. Traditional female values therefore include reciprocity, cooperation and nurturing.

In the male world intellect is ranked above intuition, materialism is valued over spirituality, and mechanical relationships are ranked over holistic ones. In politico-cultural terms this is reflected in a belief in self-serving, competition and hierarchy. The implications of this for the natural world are clear. Patriarchy in this view, establishes the supremacy of culture over nature, the latter being nothing more than a force to be subdued, exploited or risen above. Ecological destruction and gender inequality are therefore part of the same process in which 'cultured' men rule over 'natural' women.

14

MULTICULTURALISM

KEY CONCEPTS

Definition of multiculturalism; Will Kymlicka's theorisation; Bhikhu Parekh's view; liberalism and multiculturalism; feminism and multiculturalism

EMERGENCE OF MULTICULTURALISM

Multiculturalism can be defined as a state's capacity to effectively and efficiently deal with cultural plurality within its sovereign borders. As a political philosophy it includes a wide range of ideologies. Proponents of multiculturalism reject the ideal of the 'melting pot' in which minority groups are expected to assimilate into the dominant culture. Instead, they describe it as a 'salad bowl' and as a 'cultural mosaic'. Multiculturalism seeks the inclusion of the views and contributions of diverse members of society while maintaining respect for their differences. They also oppose the forced assimilation of diversity into one dominant mainstream culture.

The emergence of *communitarianism* in the 1980s had an impact on issues of cultural and social diversity, including multiculturalism. Communitarianism emphasises the importance of shared values, community ties and social responsibility, encourages individuals to balance their interests with the needs of the community. It also argues that minority cultures and identities should be respected and preserved, but not at the expense of the larger society. This approach is reflected in multiculturalism, which aims to promote cultural diversity and support minority rights while also upholding the shared values and norms of the broader society.

WILL KYMLICKA'S PERSPECTIVE

Multiculturalism, by very definition, opposes monoculture. Will Kymlicka asserted that while legal democracy recognises equality in the civil and political domains, cultural hierarchies persist in democratic nations. Multiculturalists prioritise the rights of minorities. Kymlicka identified three phases in the development of multiculturalism through history, namely:

1. Multiculturalism as a form of communitarianism
2. Multiculturalism in the context of liberalism
3. Multiculturalism in the form of nation building

Drawbacks of the Liberal Democratic State

In his book, *Multicultural Citizenship: A Liberal Theory of Minority Rights* (1995), **Will Kymlicka** asserts that group-specific rights are consistent with liberalism, and argues that if a culture is not respected, then the self-respect and dignity of its members is also threatened. In *Liberalism, Community and Culture* (1989), Kymlicka distinguishes between two types of communities:

1. *Political community*: This refers to the community created by the sovereign liberal

democratic state in which all are regarded as equals.
2. *Cultural community*: This is based on respect for the cultural identity of all individuals. No culture is to be regarded as superior or inferior to others.

Kymlicka perceives culture in two important ways: *(a)* Culture as providing a context for individual choices, and as essential for achieving individual autonomy; *(b)* Culture as the object of deep human bonds.

Multicultural theorists also see liberal democracy as perpetrating the cultural dominance of the majority by promoting a majoritarian democracy. They criticise the *first-past-the-post* electoral model, and instead argue for models based on the principle of *proportional representation.*

Welfare State and Human Rights

Kymlicka further argues that the doctrines of the welfare state and human rights also fail to address the question of cultural rights and diversity. The welfare state aims to provide social security to maintain national unity and integrity, and is apprehensive of the affirmation of particularistic identities. It thus advocates the creation of a national identity which is often the identity of the dominant cultural group. Traditional human rights doctrines, according to Kymlicka, likewise give no answer to questions of cultural identity and rights.

Politics of Recognition

Drawing on a range of well-established theories, the politics of recognition differs in its attitude towards the liberal notions of justice. **Charles Taylor** asserts that human identity is not formed in isolation but rather through active relationships with others. This is why recognition from others is essential for our own identity and sense of self. Taylor asserts that it can be particularly harmful to our self-respect and self-perception if others reflect to us a 'confining, demeaning or contemptible picture' of our identity. The struggle for recognition can only be resolved through 'a regime of reciprocal recognition among equals'.

In *Multiculturalism, Liberalism and Democracy* (1999), **Rajeev Bhargava** and others argue that this implies that every member of society must be recognised as an equal by that society. Within the community too, no individuals should be subordinated to others.

Radical multiculturalism is based on critical theory, adopts both socialist and feminist perspectives, and is critical of liberalism, which is seen as assimilationist with flawed notions of justice. A prominent philosopher in this tradition is **I. M. Young**.

Liberal multiculturalism, in contrast, advocates multiculturalism based on liberal values and retains the liberal emphasis on the individual by asserting that recognising cultural difference is essential for the individual and thus for human equality. Will Kymlicka's thoughts fall within this tradition.

Politics of Identity and Difference

Kymlicka talks about two broad patterns of cultural diversity.

1. *National minority or subnational groups*: Such groups arise from the incorporation of previously self-governing, territorially concentrated cultures into a larger state. They typically aspire to maintain themselves alongside the majority culture, and demand various forms of autonomy or self-government to ensure their survival as distinct societies.
2. *Ethnic groups or poly-ethnic minorities*: Here, cultural diversity arises from individual and familial migration. Such migrants often coalesce into loose associations or 'ethnic groups'. They typically wish to integrate into the larger society and expect legitimate acceptance from it. While they do seek recognition of their ethnic identity, their

aim is not to become a separate and self-governing nation, but to modify the institutions and laws of the mainstream society to make them more accommodating of cultural differences. Identifying members of the group based on some, or all, shared common attributes, like language, gender, religion, culture, ethnicity etc., helps in identity formation. Their mobilisation based on these markers is called *identity politics*.

Two Regimes of Rights

After making a distinction between subnational and poly-ethnic minorities, Kymlicka suggests two distinct regimes of group-differentiated rights to resolve their particular concerns regarding political recognition and representation.

1. *Self-government rights*: Kymlicka asserts that these are the most important rights, and links their provision to the federal principle. He notes, 'Where regional minorities are regionally concentrated, the boundaries of federal subunits can be drawn so that the national minority forms a majority in one of the subunits. Under these circumstances, federalism can provide extensive self-government for a national minority guaranteeing its ability to make decisions in certain areas without being outvoted by the larger society.'
2. *Polyethnic rights*: Kymlicka says these are rights to enable ethnic groups and religious minorities to express their cultural pride and particularity, in ways that do not hamper their participation in the economic and political institutions of the larger society.
3. *Special representation rights*: A form of political affirmative action to help particularly oppressed or disadvantaged socio-ethnic groups, these rights include measures like reservation of seats in the national and provincial legislatures, and adoption of proportional representation systems. Kymlicka argues that members of minority groups are uniquely disadvantaged in terms of access to their own cultures, and are therefore entitled to special protections. He views cultural identity as intrinsically valuable to individuals, and so supports group-differentiated rights to ensure equality among different cultural groups within a state.

BHIKHU PAREKH'S PERSPECTIVE

Bhikhu Parekh rejects Will Kymlicka's categorisation of cultural minorities, and contends that the right to cultural identity is a primary entitlement for all communities and that cultural diversity is an essential condition of human freedom; hence, there can be no hierarchy between them. In *Rethinking Multiculturalism: Cultural Diversity and Political Theory* (2002), Parekh advocates a *pluralist universalism* which holds that all of humankind is embedded in different and unique cultural communities, each of which deserve equal respect in their own right, and asserts that all cultures are beneficial to members of other cultures.

Parekh distinguishes between two dimensions of culture:

1. Culture denotes a cultural community. All communities are equally entitled to have rights to their cultures. All these rights need to be respected.
2. The degree of respect we have for a particular culture and its content depends upon our assessment of it.

In an extensive argument on the benefits of intercultural dialogue, Parekh asserts that in a culturally diverse context, people become more aware of the contingency and limitations of their own culture, which motivates them to engage in 'mutually beneficial dialogue' with other cultures. This dialogue leads to the development of a consensus as a response to disputed practices.

ACCOMMODATION OF MULTICULTURALISM BY LIBERALISM

Kymlicka believes that liberals do not inherently oppose multiculturalism, and he supports the 'good multiculturalist' who values individual freedom and choice while also protecting communities and cultural diversity. However, Kymlicka opposes the 'bad multiculturalist' who uses culture and tradition to justify suppressing individual freedom and choice. Kymlicka, therefore, broadly sees liberalism and multiculturalism as complementary to each other.

However, Brian Barry is critical of multiculturalism and, in *Culture and Equality* (2001), argues that while preserving cultural diversity is important, it should not be allowed to override or limit individual freedom and political equality. He criticises multiculturalism for placing too much emphasis on group rights and group identity, which he believes can lead to the oppression of individuals within those groups. Instead, he argues for a more liberal and universalist approach.

MULTICULTURALISM AND FEMINISM

In her book *Is Multiculturalism Bad for Women?* (1999), **Susan Moller Okin** asserts that certain aspects of multiculturalism can have negative consequences for women's rights, particularly in relation to practices that are justified on cultural or religious grounds but which violate basic principles of gender equality. Okin argues that cultural relativism should not be used to justify patriarchy and practices that harm women. Her book sparked a significant debate between cultural diversity and gender equality in liberal societies.

15

POSTMODERNISM

KEY CONCEPTS

Features of postmodernism; Foucault and postmodern theory; critique of postmodernism; end of ideology

The idea of the 'end of ideology' is a much contested one, and the emergence of post-modernism suggests that no ideology can claim to be perfect and universally applicable. Post-modernism is a movement which originated in France in the 1960s. The term 'postmodernism' was coined by **Jean-Francois Lyotard** in 1979. Major proponents of the tradition include **Gilles Deleuze, Jacques Derrida, Michel Foucault** and **Jean-Francois Lyotard.** The roots of post-modernism can be traced back to German philosopher **Friedrich Nietzsche** who famously declared that 'God is Dead' and is considered the father of *nihilism*. Nietzsche's works, such as *Beyond Good and Evil* (1886) and *On the Genealogy of Morals* (1887), have greatly influenced post-modern thought.

KEY FEATURES

Basic features of postmodernism include:

1. **Rejection of metanarratives:** Jean-Francois Lyotard rejected the concept of metanarratives, which are grand narratives that claim to be universal, objective an all-encompassing. Instead, he argued that knowledge is diverse, plural and multidimensional. In his book *The Post-modern Condition: A Report on Knowledge*, Lyotard embraced the idea of poly-narratives and introduced the concept of *language games*. He argued that universal truth is often established through the dominance of technical and scientific power.
2. **Anti-foundationalist:** *Anti-foundationalism*, also called *nonfoundationalism*, is any philosophy which rejects the idea that there is some fundamental belief or principle which forms the basic ground or foundation of inquiry and knowledge.

   Richard Rorty argues that knowledge is not objective, and therefore truth cannot be objective and universal. The understanding of knowledge and truth depends upon society, history and tradition. Lyotard likewise contended that metanarratives are a product of modernity. He believed that such grand narratives are speculative, and should remain so, and is critical of Marxism in particular.
3. **Deconstruction:** According to **Jacques Derrida**, the modern concept of truth is often binary, dividing knowledge into opposing categories such as rational or irrational, capitalist or Marxist. However, truth is relative and requires deconstruction, which means reconstructing it from

different perspectives. *Deconstruction* is a method of challenging the stability of concepts and oppositions that are commonly perceived as fixed. In his book *Of Grammatology*, Derrida famously declared the 'end of the book and the beginning of writing,' emphasising that context is more important than the text itself. Derrida argues that no knowledge can be entirely objective or universal.

Derrida's deconstruction method aims to disrupt the hierarchical structure of conceptual oppositions. He contends that the real world is similar to a text, and interpretation is crucial to understanding the constitution of the social world. Therefore, deconstruction radically challenges the stability and basis of language and meaning, revealing the inconsistencies and contradictions within it, leading to a reconstruction of meaning from different angles.

4. **Knowledge is power:** French philosopher and social theorist **Michel Foucault** argues that knowledge is not neutral, objective or fixed, but shaped by social context, power relations, and historical conditions. 'Knowledge is power' suggests that knowledge is a source of power and authority that can be used to shape and influence the social world. In other words, knowledge is not just a reflection of reality, but is also used to construct and shape reality.

   Archaeology of knowledge: Foucault demonstrates that power and knowledge are interrelated and mutually reinforcing. Power is not just held by individuals or institutions, but is also embedded in knowledge itself, as certain forms of knowledge are privileged over others. Knowledge can be used to create social norms, institutions, and practices that reinforce existing power structures and exclude marginalised groups. Thus, those who control knowledge also have the power to shape social reality. *Archaeology of knowledge* involves examining how discourses are constructed, how they shape our understanding of the world, and how they are used to exercise power.

MICHEL FOUCAULT

Michel Foucault, one of the most influential postmodern theorists, radically redefined the notion of power, positing that power was not just repressive, but also productive. He argues that power is *capillary* and is already present throughout the structure, providing identity and subjectivity to its constituents. Foucault does not see the state and government as the sole centres of power, but said that power is located everywhere, like capillaries in the body.

Governmentality: Foucault introduces the concept of *governmentality* to refer to the increasing homogenisation and organisation of society through a vast bureaucratic machine that evolves endless ways of classifying people. Foucault uses this term to describe how power operates in modern societies, the many ways in which individuals and institutions are governed and controlled, including through technologies of power, like surveillance, discipline and control. Foucault argues that *governmentality* extends beyond the formal structures of government to include a range of visible and invisible institutions, practices, and discourses that shape our behaviour and subjectivity. Thus, the state creates the identity of the people through governmentality, which becomes increasingly normalised and hence unquestionable. Foucault argues that knowledge is a function of all these power relations. Therefore, power is not always something negative but is also about the individual will, the understanding of freedom and, most importantly, the possibility of resistance.

Power and Resistance: Foucault believes that power relations always contain within them the possibility of resistance. In his work *Discipline and Punish*, he elaborates on the concept of the Panopticon Prison, originally proposed by Jeremy Bentham, to illustrate the extent of modern governmental power. The Panopticon is a spherical prison with a watchtower at its centre, and cells located around the periphery. Each cell has two windows, one facing the watchtower and the other facing outside. The prisoners are housed within these cells, and can never know if there is a guard in the watchtower or not. Therefore, they always behave in accordance with the prescribed rules, and power is exercised naturally without the use of actual force.

The Panopticon is a site for experimentation and reform. It does not seek to exterminate deviants who disobey rules. Rather, it seeks to reform them. Foucault employs this model to explain the exercise of power in institutions like the hospital, the school and the modern state. In his work, *The History of Sexuality*, he asserts that the knowledge of sexuality is created and promoted by society. Therefore, the truths based on this knowledge are not objective truths, and change in response to changes in socio-cultural contexts. Foucault further contends that power is also associated with resistance.

Famous books of Michel Foucault include:

1. *Madness and Civilization* (1961)
2. *The Order of Things* (1966)
3. *The Archaeology of Knowledge* (1969)
4. *Discipline and Punish* (1975)
5. *The History of Sexuality* (1976)
6. *Power* (2002)

CRITIQUE OF POSTMODERNISM

Judith Butler contends that the usage of the term 'postmodern theory' is itself problematic, because it encompasses too diverse a range of ideas that cannot be reduced to a single process of thought or ideology. As a result, the term *postmodernism* is often invoked by those who oppose it as much as by those who support it, making it a problematic and contested term. Butler's critique of postmodernism is mainly focused on its failure to address issues related to identity politics, particularly those related to gender and sexuality. She argues that postmodernism often assumes a universal subject that can easily deconstruct and critique existing social norms and structures, without fully accounting for the ways in which those norms and structures shape individual identities and experiences. Butler also critiques the emphasis on language and discourse in postmodernism, arguing that it can lead to a form of linguistic determinism which assumes that language constructs reality, rather than the other way around. She argues that this can lead to a neglect of material and embodied aspects of social experience, particularly in relation to gender and sexuality.

'THE END OF IDEOLOGY'

The 'End of Ideology' is a concept that originated in the mid-twentieth century, particularly in the 1950s and 1960s, during a period of political and ideological consensus in the Western world. It was a belief that the traditional political ideologies of liberalism, conservatism, and socialism were no longer relevant or useful in explaining or solving the problems of modern societies. This concept emerged from the belief that the major ideological conflicts of the past, particularly those of the nineteenth and early twentieth centuries, had been largely resolved, and that the societies of the Western world had achieved a level of stability and prosperity that made further ideological struggle unnecessary. According to this view, the main political and economic issues of the day could be solved through pragmatic and technocratic approaches, rather than through ideological conflict.

The concept of the 'End of Ideology' was popularised by American sociologist Daniel Bell in his 1960 book of the same name. However, the idea has been critiqued by scholars as being a naive and flawed assumption, as ideological conflict and struggle continued to play a major role in global politics, particularly in the decades following Bell's book.

Despite the ongoing debates on the end of ideology, various ideologies such as communitarianism, multiculturalism, environmentalism and postmodernism are gaining momentum in the contemporary era.

Unit II

POLITICAL THOUGHT

KEY THINKERS

Confucius, Plato, Aristotle, Niccolo Machiavelli, Thomas Hobbes, John Locke, Jean-Jacques Rousseau, Georg W. F. Hegel, Mary Wollstonecraft, John Stuart Mill, Karl Marx, Antonio Gramsci, Hannah Arendt, Frantz Fanon, Mao Zedong, John Rawls

1

CONFUCIUS (551–479 BCE)

KEY CONCEPTS

Confucianism; monarchical state; morality

Confucius, also known as Kong Qiu, was a great Chinese sage and philosopher born at Sang Ping in the State of Lu (modern-day Shandong province) in China. His clan name was Kong and his given name was Qiu. His disciples called him Master Kong, which later beccame Latinised as Confucius. Confucian philosophy is a major Chinese philosophy which encompasses a set of moral, social, political, and spiritual teachings that aim to guide individuals in living a harmonious and virtuous life. Confucianism believes that there is a basic natural order and balance which exists in this universe, and that this order and balance should be reflected in human life and relationships too. Because there is an order and balance in nature, balance in the human world is natural.

Confucianism, also known as Ruism or Ru Classicism, has evolved over time and had a profound influence on Chinese and East Asian culture, ethics, governance and social structure throughout history. Many elements of Confucian teachings still resonate in different aspects of East Asian societies even today.

RELATIONSHIPS

Confucius taught that **humaneness**, **reciprocity**, and **virtue** are the core of all human relationships. He also believed that all relationships are based on **hierarchy**, and not on the principle of equality. He saw the family as the primary unit of human relationships, and within the family there are five principle relationships:

1. Sovereign and subject
2. Husband and wife
3. Parent and child
4. Elder brother and younger brother
5. Friend and friend

MONARCHICAL STATE

Under Confucianism, the king was seen as the Son of Heaven, divinely ordained to rule, and as the father of the people. The relationship between the ruler and his subjects was the same as that of a father and son. The state was considered to be a welfare state and the moral guardian of the people; its role was to educate and transform the people for the better. Confucianism also believes in the perfectibility of human beings and that they are fundamentally good by nature.

TEACHING THROUGH DIALOGUES

The writings and teachings of Confucius are available to us in the form of collections of conversations, sayings and dialogues called ***Analects*** which are attributed to Confucius and his disciples. The ***Analects*** is one of the most important and foundational texts in Confucian philosophy, believed to have been compiled and written by Confucius' followers after his death. It consists of a series of brief passages, often as dialogues, that cover various aspects of life, moral conduct, social relationships, governance, education, and personal cultivation.

MORALITY

For Confucius an understanding of ethics and ethical and moral behaviour is central to his philosophy. Confucius teaches five principle virtues:

1. **Ren** (Altruism and humanity): Ren stresses the importance of cultivating compassion, empathy, respect, fairness and moral virtue for fostering harmonious relationships.
2. **Yi** (Righteousness): Yi involves the sense of doing what is right, just, and morally upright, both in one's personal conduct and in interactions with others.
3. **Li** (Good conduct): Li refers to proper conduct and etiquette in various aspects of life, including social interactions, ceremonies, and relationships.
4. **Zhi** (Knowledge): Zhi stresses on the importance of pursuing knowledge, education, self-cultivation and growth through learning, application of knowledge, self-reflection and insight.
5. **Xiao** (Filial piety): Xiao emphasises respect, obedience and care towards parents, elders, and ancestors. It places value on social harmony, hierarchical relationships and the well-being of the community as a whole.

Further, Confucian identified three methods of acquiring wisdom:

1. Reflection (this is termed the 'noblest' way)
2. Imitation (understood to be the easiest way)
3. Experience (the most bitter way)

BOOKS OF CONFUCIUS

1. Book of Documents
2. Book of Rites
3. Classics of Poetry
4. Analects of Confucius
5. Spring and Autumn Annals
6. Book of Changes
7. Book of Songs

2

PLATO (427–347 BCE)

KEY CONCEPTS

Athens; Deductive method; virtue; Plato's Republic; nature of society; social stratification; Plato's views on education; philosopher king; state as university, church, and family; Platonic vs modern communism; justice

The systematic study of ancient Greek philosophy begins with Plato, widely recognised as one of the most important and influential figures of Western philosophy. Plato propounded the theory of the ideal state and the ideal citizen, covering various aspects related to the harmonious and balanced relationship between citizens and the state.

Plato was born in 428/427 BCE in Athens, Greece. His real name was Aristocles. He was given the pseudonym 'Plato' derived from 'Platon', meaning broad, by his wrestling coach Ariston because of his broad and strong shoulders. Plato was a disciple of Socrates and the teacher of Aristotle. Sparta defeated Plato's home state Athens in the Peloponnesian War. This war and its aftermath, and the socio-political conditions of Athens during the early years of his life profoundly influenced and shaped Plato's thinking.

ATHENS IN PLATO'S TIME

Plato witnessed democracy at work in the city-state of Athens where all important decisions concerning the polity were made by the assembly of citizens or the Athenian Ecclesia, which was the principal democratic institution. Male citizens of Athens over the age of twenty who had completed military training could become members of the Ecclesia. They could participate in debates, propose laws, and vote on various matters. All major decisions regarding legislation, policies and the governance of the city-state were taken in mass meetings of the Ecclesia, which met at regular intervals. The Assembly Council consisted of 500 citizens who acted as its steering committee. The population of Athens was about 250,000 but only 50,000 were citizens of Athens. The rest of the people, including women and slaves, were denied citizenship.

Plato also saw the extremely cruel and tyrannical rule of the **Thirty Tyrants**, a pro-Spartan oligarchy installed in Athens after Athens was defeated by Sparta in the Peloponnesian War. The Thirty Tyrants are said to have executed 1,500 people without trial. Thereafter, when democracy was restored in Athens, Plato's teacher and mentor, the 70-year-old Socrates, was given the death penalty by the democratic government and forced to drink poison. There was constant fighting between various city states and corruption, ignorance and factionalism were rampant in Athens. All of these factors, especially Socrates' death sentence, deeply influenced Plato's thinking.

DEDUCTIVE METHOD

Plato recognised politics to be an integral part of ethics and considered political science and political thought to be a part of morality. He employed the *deductive method* to analyse ethics and politics. Also known as *dialectic* or the *Socratic method*, the deductive method involves deriving knowledge of an object from general principles to specific instances. It is a process of philosophical inquiry that involves a systematic approach to reasoning and analysis and follows a specific pattern of question-and-answer dialogue to arrive at logical conclusions. The Platonic method bears a resemblance to the systematic approach used in geometry.

In Plato's philosophy, the *idea of the good* is of supreme importance, akin to the concept of God for a religious individual. According to Plato, the material world is a mere reflection of this supreme idea of the good, much like shadows cast by the world of ideas. Central to Plato's philosophy is his concept of justice, which serves as a guiding principle for various aspects of society. Education, communal living, and the idea of a philosopher king are all ideas derived from the principle of justice. Plato's method is not empirical, relying instead on abstract reasoning and philosophical inquiry.

While **Chester C. Maxey** argued that Plato was the first utopian philosopher, **Ernest Barker** maintained that he was an idealist rather than a utopian thinker. Plato's Academy, established in 387 BC, marks a milestone in the evolution of higher education and is considered to be the precursor of the modern university.

Organic state: Plato and Aristotle both believed in the idea of the organic state and saw the state as analogous to a human body. Just as parts of the human body are considered less important than the body, they considered the state, or the whole body, to be more important than the individuals comprising the state. Neither Plato nor Aristotle made any distinction between community and state.

Idealism: Idealism is a philosophical approach that begins with abstract ideas as the foundation of thought. Idealists perceive the material world to be derived from these ideas, which may encompass concepts such as the soul or the idea of the good. They prioritise moral considerations and focus on *what ought to be* rather than *what currently exists.*

Rationalism: As a rationalist, Plato placed great emphasis on reason and logic, and was deeply critical of customs and traditions. He regarded laws to be part of the same framework of customs, and instead championed the knowledge-based reasoning of the philosopher king as a superior guiding force and the basis of justice.

'VIRTUE IS KNOWLEDGE'

Plato's teacher Socrates famously proclaimed, 'Virtue is knowledge,' a truth which Plato embraced. Virtue in essence signifies excellence. The virtue of ice is to cool, while the virtue of fire is to burn. Since every individual is unique and possesses unique qualities and abilities, acting in accordance with one's nature and capabilities constitutes virtue. Through education, one can acquire knowledge and right thinking that foster the cultivation of virtue. The Socratic notion of virtue is akin to the concept of *dharma* in Indian philosophy which represents a moral and ethical path.

The ultimate human goal is to cultivate virtues and ethical and good conduct. The king's virtue is to rule, the soldier's is to protect the state boundaries, the producer's is to strive for increased productivity. Plato holds that working as per one's abilities leads to the establishment of a just society. According to him, the amalgamation of wisdom, courage and patience fosters the growth of virtue within individuals and a sense of justice. A virtuous individual therefore also implies a just individual. Plato believes in the operation and regulation of society based on knowledge. Virtue, for him, is not only the acquisition or the knowledge of ideas but also leading moral and ethical life. For Plato the purpose of life is not obtaining power or wealth but leading a truthful and ethical life—that is the essence of being truly human.

THE REPUBLIC

By far one of Plato's most important and influential works is *The Republic*. Written in a dialogue form, it discusses a range of ideas including virtues, the ideal state, the ideal ruler, the philosopher ruler, the theory of justice, the education system, development and education of the individual, and communism. Scholars have said that Plato's *Republic* deals not only with political philosophy, education, psychology and metaphysics but with practically every aspect of human life. The great philosopher Rousseau said *The Republic* is the finest book ever written on education. Some of Plato's other important works, generally classified into dialogues and letters, include:

1. *Charmides*
2. *Lute* dialogues
3. *Gorgias*
4. *Meno*
5. *The Trial and Death of Socrates* (this includes the dialogues *Euthyphro*, *The Apology*, *Crito* and *Phaedo*)
6. *The Symposium*
7. *The Statesman*
8. *The Theaetetus*
9. *Philebus*
10. *Sophist*
11. *Timaeus*
12. *The Laws*
13. *Critias*
14. *Minos*

In *The Republic*, Plato formulates three key ideas or theories that describe reality, the human condition, knowledge and thought.

1. **The Allegory of the Cave:** This is a metaphorical story that depicts a group of prisoners who have been chained inside a dark cave since birth, facing a wall. They can only see the shadows of objects projected onto the wall by a fire behind them. Since the shadows are their only perception of reality, they believe them to be real. Plato uses this allegory to symbolise the human condition, suggesting that most people live their lives in a state of utter ignorance and illusion, perceiving only the shadows of reality which they mistake for reality. The allegory also represents the philosopher's journey to truth, knowledge and enlightenment, as one prisoner is freed, climbs out of the dark cave and discovers the true nature of reality, symbolised by the sun and the world as seen in the light of the sun.
2. **The Metaphor of the Divided Line:** Plato presents this metaphor to explain his theory of knowledge and levels of human understanding. The line is divided into two sections and further divided into four subsections. The lower section represents the *visible realm*, while the upper section represents the *intelligible realm*. The subsections represent different levels of cognition: imagination, belief, thought, and understanding. The metaphor of the divided line illustrates that true knowledge and understanding can only be attained through the rational apprehension of the Forms or Ideas, which exist in the intelligible realm.
3. **The Doctrine of Forms:** Also known as the Theory of Forms or Ideas, this is one of Plato's most important and influential philosophical concepts. According to this doctrine, the material world as perceived through the five senses is transient and imperfect, while true reality lies in the realm of Forms. *Forms* are eternal, unchanging, and perfect essences or archetypes that exist independently of physical objects.

They represent the ultimate reality behind all appearances and provide the basis for knowledge, truth and understanding. For example, there is a Form of Beauty, which is the ideal and perfect concept of beauty that exists separately from individual imperfectly beautiful objects in the physical world. The Doctrine of Forms emphasises the pursuit of knowledge and the attainment of truth by contemplating and understanding these abstract and timeless forms.

NATURE OF REALITY

Parmenides posited that reality is constant and unchanging while **Heraclitus** argued that everything is in a perpetual state of flux, famously stating that one cannot step into same river twice. Plato, however, sought to reconcile these opposing ideas in a synthesis by proposing that the realm of Ideas or Forms is permanent, while the physical world undergoes continuous change.

Plato used the allegory of the cave to illustrate his division of reality into the world of Ideas and the world of objects. For Plato, the entire material world is a reflection or a manifestation of these Ideas or Forms, of which the 'Idea of the Good' is supreme. While the material world is subject to transformation, he argued that ideas are immortal and unchanging. For instance, beauty as an idea is eternal and perfect, while physical objects of beauty undergo change and decay. Plato thus emphasised the study of Ideas rather than the material realm because for him Ideas are the ultimate and only reality.

Plato held that the ultimate purpose of education is to impart knowledge of the Idea of the soul. In Plato's view, an ideal state is the collective expression of all the virtues embodied by the individuals living in it. He thus proposed that a good individual and a good state are mutually interdependent and beneficial, and that the state does not emerge out of an oak or a rock, but is shaped by the character of the individuals who inhabit it.

Knowledge and Belief

Plato draws a clear distinction between knowledge and belief or opinion. For Plato, education is necessary to dispel ignorance, belief and opinion, and attain true knowledge. He challenged the blind acceptance of customs and traditions, also considering them forms of ignorance.

Knowledge (*episteme*) is a higher form of understanding that transcends mere opinion. Knowledge is grounded in the realm of Ideas or Forms, which are eternal, unchanging and universal, and represent the ultimate truth and reality behind the physical world. For Plato, true knowledge is obtained through rational contemplation and understanding of these Forms.

Opinion (*doxa*) or belief refers to the changing world of sensory perception. Opinions are subjective, influenced by personal biases, emotions, and the imperfect nature of the physical world. They are often based on incomplete information, appearances, and the fluctuating nature of the material world. Plato viewed opinion as a lower form of understanding as it lacks the stability, universality and certainty of knowledge.

STRATIFICATION OF SOCIETY

For Plato, the community is more important than the individual. He organised society into three distinct classes, to align and correspond with characteristics of the soul. Plato identified three key elements in the individual human soul: *wisdom*, *courage* and *appetite*. Those whose soul is dominated by wisdom/reason he deemed as fit to become 'philosopher king'. Souls dominated by courage will become warriors, and those dominated by appetite will form the producer class.

Classification of Souls

In *The Republic*, Plato presents the concept of a 'Noble Lie' through a tale. In this metaphorical representation of human souls as precious metals, Plato associates the *gold soul* with the philosopher, the *silver soul* with the warrior, and the *bronze soul* with the producer or labourer. This classification of souls into gold, silver, and bronze symbolises different levels of moral and intellectual qualities. The gold soul represents the highest level, characterised by wisdom, reason and a pursuit of knowledge. The silver and bronze souls represent lower levels of moral and intellectual development. Plato suggests that individuals who possess a higher level of understanding and wisdom (represented by the gold soul) are concerned less with accumulating material things, and more with the wellbeing of the soul, the pursuit of virtue and truth.Plato suggests that in order for society to function properly, such 'noble lies' are propagated by the social elite.

Plato outlined three stages of education. One who completes the first stage of education will be eligible to join the producer class. Completing the second stage of education will qualify one to join the warrior class. One who completes all three stages of education will be qualified to become philosopher king. But Plato observed that individuals possessing wisdom are in a minority and that majority of individuals do not undergo the formal education required to become philosopher kings.

Plato asserts that there is an organic relationship between the individual and the state. Society is comprised of all three classes, and each class fulfills the needs of the others. The *producer class* fulfills material needs; the *warrior class* ensures the safety and security of the state and its polity, and the philosopher king exercises control and governance over the other classes. Plato visualised that an ideal, civil and just society should be governed by individuals or philosopher kings endowed with virtue, ethics, knowledge and wisdom. Plato rejected the principle of inheritance as a criterion to determine an individual's status in society.

THE EDUCATION SYSTEM

Plato views the ideal state as an educational institution, rather than a political or a legal institution. He believed that all problems of the city-state stem from the mindset of its populace, and that therefore, they can be resolved by changing their minds. Such a transformation, Plato knew, is possible only through education.

Purpose of Education: Plato saw education as a means to shape and build character, hone individual abilities and faculties. Education is the medium through which the world of ideas like perfect justice and beauty could be accessed. The ultimate objective of education for Plato is to lead a virtuous and moral life. Plato's philosophy is centred around building an ideal state and ideal citizens, and the relationship between the two. In this context, he puts great emphasis on the importance of education. In his theory of education elucidated in *The Republic*, he assimilates the merits of the educational systems of both Athens and Sparta, while discarding their demerits.

Education in Athens: Education was imparted up to 20 years of age in Athens, where emphasis was given on subjects like literature and music. Law was taught through literature. According to Plato, Athens put greater emphasis on the intellectual development of its pupils. Education was the private affair of individuals and the Athenian state played no role in it. Plato believed that the state must provide education to its citizens. The ultimate objective of good education must be to foster the creation of good, virtuous citizens and a just society.

Education in Sparta: In Sparta, education was the state's responsibility. Children were handed over to state officials at the age of seven, and given rigorous physical education and training to make them into warriors who could defend safeguard Sparta. According to Plato, there were many demerits in the Spartan educational system: the syllabus was limited, narrow and lopsided. There was over-emphasis on physical and military education while subjects like literature, logic and mental ability were largely neglected.

Three Stages of Education

Adopting the best of both Sparta and Athens into his theory of education, Plato delineated the educational process into three broad stages, laying equal stress on the development of physical and mental abilities. The three stages were as follows.

1. *First stage*: The first stage of education covered ages 10 to 20 years. During this period, students received instruction in gymnastics, dieting, physical education, and music. Medical science was also taught to maintain bodily health, eliminating the need of doctors in the ideal state. Plato emphasises the moral development of children by instilling qualities of tolerance, courage and enthusiasm. Subjects like music, literature, poetry and other fine arts were included for harmonising the soul. Plato believed the knowledge of music would help children appreciate beauty, foster peace and harmony, thereby reducing unrest and minimising the need for laws and courts. Music was considered food for the soul, and gymnastics as nourishment for the physical self.
2. *Second stage*: The second stage of education, from 20 to 30 years, laid greater emphasis on subjects like mathematics and astrology to help pupils grasp and understand intangible and abstract concepts. Knowledge of mathematics was also considered helpful in strategising and organising the military during war.
3. *Third stage*: Upon completing the second stage, only those who passed the examination were eligible for the third stage of education, which lasted from 30 to 35 years. Philosophy held paramount importance at this stage, leading to the attainment of real knowledge and truth. After 35 years of education, Plato recommended 15 years of practical training. He believed that problems like factionalism and ignorance require a mental cure, which only education can provide.

Plato asserts that education imparts knowledge of the soul, rationality and inculcates the spirit of communal living. Education enables individuals to distinguish between knowledge and opinion. True knowledge cultivates virtues and morality within individuals, leading them to view the material world with less importance. Those who acquire knowledge of the supreme good ascend to become philosopher kings.

Many subsequent scholars have embraced Plato's ideas, recognising that long-term change and social reform is possible only through education.

THE PHILOSOPHER KING

Plato delineated five types of governments: Aristocracy, Timocracy, Oligarchy, Democracy and Tyranny. His concept of a 'philosopher king', propounded in *The Republic*, refers to a supremely wise and knowledgeable ruler skilled in the art of governing. Some important features of the philosopher ruler include:

1. The philosopher ruler emerges after acquiring extensive knowledge and profound wisdom through a philosophical education, which cultivates a love for wisdom, critical thinking, and the pursuit of truth. Plato emphasises that these qualities are more important than mere adherence to laws.
2. The philosopher ruler possesses a strong sense of justice and fairness, and understands its importance in governance.
3. Plato asserts that the philosophical education must instill a detachment from the material world and cares, and the philosopher king must neither need nor desire personal property or family. He must have no attachments. Being free of material and familial concerns, the ruler can rule based solely on the best interests of society.

4. Plato rejects the idea that cobblers, tailors or barbers could become kings, arguing that just as only doctors can treat physical ailments, only a philosopher king can heal societal diseases.

George Holland Sabine describes Plato's philosopher king as an example of 'enlightened despotism', because the philosopher king's rule is based on his individual wisdom and abilities rather than on adherence to laws or a constitution. Ruling is seen as an art, where 'enlightened' refers to rule by a philosopher and 'despotism' implies a total rejection of democracy as a form of government. Sabine argues that Plato's system of governance can be categorised as an absolute monarchy. According Plato, the administration of the state must be based on the wisdom of the ruler rather than in accordance with laws. The king is the ultimate and only source of knowledge and truth and is endowed with a strong sense of justice. Plato's conceptualisation of the philosopher king leads to a categorical rejection of democratic governance. In ancient Greece, Athens had a democracy while the Spartan state functioned as an oligarchy. Plato held that the rulers or kings in these systems were selfish, incompetent and ignorant.

THE STATE AS UNIVERSITY AND CHURCH

Plato seeks to maintain unity within the state, and sees property and family as major obstacles to achieving such unity. The state's highest objective in his view is to provide education. In ancient times, religious education was an integral part of overall education, encompassing the role of the church. Religious education was also the state's responsibility. Therefore the state was considered primarily as an educational institution. This is why the state can also be likened to a university. The Platonic Republic represents an ideal state where law and punishment do not exist. Plato posits that the institution of family hinders the unity of the state, which is why he forbids the guardian class from having their own families. According to Ernest Barker, Plato's concept of the ideal state envisages the state itself as family. Education and communism are considered essential for preserving this ideal Platonic state.

COMMUNISM AND THE STATE AS FAMILY

Plato advocated for communism as a means to establish a just society. He believed communism would serve as a tool to protect the guardian class from the negative influences of wealth and personal attachment, which he saw as the biggest human weaknesses and impediments to achieving his ideal state. Plato's theory of communism, presented in *The Republic*, addresses the divide between the rich and poor and aims to eliminate conflicts and rivalries among the small Greek city-states. The idea of communal ownership of property in Greek city-states is very old. In Athens, the state exercised a monopoly over forests and mines, while Sparta had a communal dining system.

Plato's communism implies that the guardian class will not have individual families or own private property. Instead, the entire state would function as one family for the guardian class, thus fostering unity within the Greek city-state. Communism promotes the notion of a *state-family*. The producer class will fulfill the physical and material needs of the guardian class. Plato advocated two types communism: communism of property, and communism of family.

1. The guardian class of Plato's ideal state comprised the philosopher king and soldiers, who must rule and protect the state. So that it governs neutrally, justly and in the best interests of the state, Plato barred the guardian class from owning private property or families.
2. Plato advocated for the prohibition of families within the ruling and warrior classes. Women were to be considered as common property, with every woman being

a wife of the state, and all children regarded as children of the state. Neither the children would know their biological parents nor will parents know who their children are. Plato believed that the institution of family instills selfishness and weakness in individuals, leading to narrow-mindedness and prejudice. He saw these emotions as impediments to the unity and integrity of society.

3. Plato saw the communism of the family as a way of producing a superior population for the state. He believed it was necessary for women to be liberated from their homes in order to achieve freedom and equality. By removing the constraints of traditional family structures, Plato aimed to create a society where the philosopher rulers could focus on their roles and responsibilities to the state rather than being influenced by personal attachments.

These ideas put forth by Plato regarding the guardian class, the abolition of families, and the communism of the family were seen as essential components for the formation of an ideal state and harmonious society, where the pursuit of common goals took precedence over individual interests.

CRITICISM OF PLATO'S COMMUNISM

Plato's communism has faced much criticism for its potential negation of individual growth and liberty. Ernest Barker argues that just as learning any art or skill requires specific tools and equipment, property plays an important role in the moral development of individuals. Abolishing private property could thus hinder the progress and growth of individuals.

Aristotle also criticised Plato's communism, advocating for the importance of the family as a foundation for the state and emphasising the cultivation of love and ethics through familial institutions. He considered eliminating the family for the sake of unifying the state to be unnecessary. Aristotle argued that love and morality, essential for an ideal state, can only be cultivated through the institution of the family.

Barker contrasts Plato's *abstract universalism*, where concepts are detached from concrete realities, with Aristotle's *concrete universalism*, emphasising the importance of understanding and appreciating particular circumstances and contexts of individuals and communities.

Despite the shortcomings of Plato's communism, it is worth noting that the ideas of communal family and communal property existed in certain societies of the time. Plato advocated for communism in order to establish a just society and create a unified state. While these ideas may be flawed, they demonstrate Plato's attempt to address societal challenges and strive for an ideal social order.

PLATO'S COMMUNISM VERSUS MODERN COMMUNISM

While Plato's communism and modern communism share some similarities in their pursuit of social transformation, they are different in their basis, goals, applicability, and the contexts in which they arose.

1. *Purpose*: Plato's communism aimed to create an ideal unified state and virtuous society by abolishing private property and family. It focused on the guardian class and good governance. Modern communism emerged in the nineteenth century in response to capitalism. Its goal is to establish a stateless, classless society.
2. *Scope*: Plato's communism applies mainly to the guardian class, comprising philosopher kings and soldiers. It does not extend to the entire society but aims to eliminate material and familial distractions to ensure effective governance. Modern communism seeks to create a stateless, classless society for all members of society, based on social

ownership of the means of production and economic equality.

3. *Basis*: Plato's communism derives from his philosophy and is rooted in the idea that communal living, shared property and absence of familial attachments promote unity, virtue, justice, harmony and good governance. Modern communism is influenced by Marxist theories, emphasises scientific analysis of socioeconomic systems, and is mainly concerned with addressing economic disparities and advocating social justice.
4. *Historical context*: Plato's communism developed in ancient Greece and was influenced by the societal structures and philosophical ideas then prevalent. Modern communism emerged as a response to the industrialisation and social inequality of the nineteenth century, particularly in capitalist societies.

Table 2.2.1: Plato's Communism versus Modern Communism

Plato	*Marx*
1. Ideal, unified state	1. Stateless, classless society
2. Moral and spiritual	2. Economic and material
3. Education to build guardian class	3. Class struggle for revolution

THEORY OF JUSTICE

Plato presents his theory of justice in *The Republic*, with the subtitle 'Concerning Justice'. Plato's theory is grounded in his philosophy of education, and in his belief that 'knowledge is virtue', influenced by Socrates. He emphasises the importance of virtuous and knowledgeable citizens in freeing the state from problems like factionalism, infighting, ignorance and brute selfishness, making education a prerequisite for character development and building a moral, just and harmonious society.

Rejecting Sophist Justice

Plato engages in lengthy debates and dialogue (dialectics) with various characters in *The Republic* to challenge by way of logic and reason the individualistic, materialistic and utilitarian notions of justice put forth by the Sophists. According to Cephalous, performing one's duties and paying one's dues is justice. For Polemarchus, doing good to friends and bad to enemies is justice. Thrasymachus contends that justice is the interest of the stronger, while Glaucon believed that justice is the need of the weak, and results from mutual agreement among individuals. Glaucon's ideas are closer to those of Hobbes.

In contrast, Plato argues against the idea that justice is solely fulfilling one's self-interest or adhering to the principle of 'might is right'. Justice, according to him, is about performing one's moral duties and giving everyone their due, it concerns the welfare of all members of society, not just a select few. Importantly, Plato also believed that justice is an inherent quality of the human soul, that it is natural and not artificial, for man is naturally disposed to be just.

Meaning of Justice

Plato's vision of a just and virtuous society is characterised by reason, courage, wisdom, appetite and temperance. Justice is not something imposed from the outside but arises naturally from the harmony within oneself and society. Temperance, which involves balance, restraint and self-control, is crucial. Ethical, educated, fair-minded and virtuous individuals who live in accordance with the natural qualities of their souls are needed for a just society. Justice requires that each social class fulfil its duties and functions without interfering with the work of others. Harmony and a sense of proportion are therefore central to justice.

Basis of Justice

Plato's concept of justice is based on the idea of harmony between classes in society and within the elements of the soul. Two fundamental principles that form the basis of justice:

1. *Division of labour*: Each of the three classes in society—the guardians, the warriors and the producers—is assigned specific functions and work as per their capabilities.
2. *Specialisation of work*: Each class strives for excellence and perfection in their stipulated work.

Education, Plato argues, is the most powerful means of attaining justice. He envisages an ideal society divided into classes based on their education, and duties determined by capability and temperament, according to the classification of souls. Plato sees education as key to developing virtue, but he does not give importance to codified or institutionalised laws and rules in achieving justice. Plato also employs communism as a means of establishing justice, with the guardian class foregoing private property and families, while their material needs are met by the producer class. This establishes an organic relationship between the three classes, contributing to overall harmony and justice in society.

PLATO'S JUSTICE AND MODERN JUSTICE

Plato's theory of justice is based on the concept of duties, whereas the modern understanding of justice is based on the concept of freedom and rights. Plato's theory focuses on moral and philosophical principles, while modern justice relies on the framework of laws, crime and punishments. Plato sought to create an ideal and just society through education, whereas modern thinkers rely on law enforcement and punishment as the only means to secure justice. Plato's theory emphasises social unity and harmony, although his disciple Aristotle criticised his ideas of communism as extreme for neglecting the importance of the family and the village community in establishing social cohesion and unity.

Plato's theory of justice largely disregards individual rights and freedoms. The ideas presented in *The Republic* are idealistic and moral, with a strong emphasis on envisioning an ideal state and ideal rulers and citizens. However, Plato was well aware of the many inherent anomalies and complexities of nature and society. In an attempt to address these, he proposed the formation of an ideal state. Some scholars like Chester C. Maxey consider Plato to be the first 'utopian thinker.'

Rule of Law

During the later years of his life, Plato wrote the works *Statesman* and *Laws*, which focused on more practical aspects of the state and governance. In these books, departing from his earlier rejection of formal law, he emphasised the importance of the 'Rule of Law'. Unlike his earlier strong advocacy of communism, he also acknowledged the importance and value of family and private property. His recognition of the 'Rule of Law' reflected his understanding of the need for a just and orderly society governed by fair and impartial laws.

PLATO AND FASCISM

Richard Crossman in his book *Plato To-Day* (1937) contends that Plato was wrong both for his time and ours. Plato's endeavour was to construct a perfect society free of the three principle evils that confronted the Athens of his time: class wars, a tyrannical government and bad education. As Sparta was relatively free from social and political instability, it became for Plato an alternative model. Crossman observes that Plato had poor faith in the ability and intelligence of the common man. According to him, Plato was also mistaken in his belief that a just government could be established by a revolution, or that the ultimate truth could be realised by suppressing freedom of thought.

Arnold J. Toynbee saw Plato as being cynical, reactionary and inhumane, though highly intelligent, imaginative and deeply concerned with the welfare of his fellowmen. **Bertrand Russell** (1961) questioned the feasibility of finding a perfect set of 'wise' persons who could be entrusted with governing, and contended that since this was not feasible, democracy was the best bet. **Isaiah Berlin** (1969) pointed out that Plato did not grant the individual the freedom of choice, which was an inalienable human right. **Karl Popper** in his influential book *The Open Society and Its Enemies* characterised Plato as an enemy of liberty, rights and democracy, arguing that his ideas were inimical to the principles of an open and free society because of his overemphasis on duties and discipline while neglecting the importance of rights and individual freedom.

Plato is also said to have influenced fascist ideologies, such as those espoused by Hitler and Mussolini. Plato and fascist thinkers view the state as a moral institution capable of ensuring a better life for its citizens, with absolute obedience to the ruler being paramount. Fascism believes in a supreme and autocratic state that is not bound by any law or constitution. In *The Republic*, Plato places great faith in the wisdom of the philosopher king, and does not give importance to laws, which he saw as part of custom.

It is important to note, however, that these associations of Plato with fascism are subject to much debate and interpretation. Different scholars hold varying perspectives on the influence and implications of Plato's ideas in relation to fascist ideologies.

IN DEFENCE OF PLATO

Ronald B. Levinson and **Gilbert Ryle** argue against labelling Plato as a fascist and contend that it is wrong to evaluate his ideas solely through a modern lens and within the context of contemporary liberal democracy. Plato's philosophy should be examined within the specific historical, political and social context of ancient Greece in which it originated, they assert.

Critics who assess Plato's ideas through the framework of liberal democracy or other modern traditions may overlook the nuances of his philosophy. While there may be superficial similarities between some of Plato's concepts and fascist ideologies, there are also significant divergences between them. An important one is Plato's emphasis on wisdom and morality as the most crucial attribute of a human. Plato believed only ethical individuals possessing wisdom should be eligible to become philosopher kings, highlighting the importance of intellectual capacity. In contrast, fascists view humans primarily as emotional beings and vehemently opposed notions of equality, freedom, socialism, democracy and human rights. Further, in Plato's view women were eligible to hold positions within the guardian class, whereas fascists typically uphold traditional gender roles and hierarchies.

Plato's philosophy has been criticised as monarchical, totalitarian and as a precursor to fascist ideology. However, it is unreasonable to label him as an enemy of free society considering that ancient Greek society itself had communitarian tendencies. Plato advocated free and compulsory education for all without discrimination. Significantly, he also believed that women were eligible to become members of the guardian class, and, according to some readings, seems to have opposed slavery, all of which would position him as a progressive thinker in the context of ancient Greece. In *The Republic*, Plato presented his vision of an ideal state and the philosopher king as the foundation for a just society. But in his later work, *Laws*, he also showed partial acceptance of the principle of 'Rule of Law' and incorporated elements of democratic principles. This reveals an evolution in Plato's thinking and his willingness to consider alternative perspectives on governance.

John Herman Randall observed that Plato wrote *The Republic* to demonstrate that the Spartan model of government was in effect totally absurd and impractical. **Allan Bloom** (1968), agreeing with **Leo Strauss**, asserted that: 'Political idealism is the most destructive of human passions and the *Republic* is the greatest critique of political idealism ever written ... The *Republic* serves to moderate the extreme passion for justice by showing the limits of what can be demanded and expected of the city.'

Selected readings on Plato:

Ernest Barker, *Political Thought of Plato and Aristotle* (1906).

Ernest Barker, *Greek Political Theory: Plato and his Predecessors* (1918).

Bernard Bosanquet, *A Companion to Plato's Republic for English Readers* (1895).

Richard Lewis Nettleship, *Lectures on the Republic of Plato* (1922).

3

ARISTOTLE (384–322 BCE)

KEY CONCEPTS

Teleological method; inductive method; Aristotle and Plato; Aristotelian view of the state; moral development; pluralism and communism; the golden mean; master science; theory of family; views on slavery; rule of law; justice; revolution; citizenship

Aristotle, a renowned philosopher in the Western tradition with a prolific and hugely influential body of work, was both a disciple of Plato and a teacher to Alexander the Great. Born in 384 BCE in Stagira, Greece, he was deeply influenced by the culture and traditions of his homeland. He studied under Plato at Plato's Academy and later founded his own school, the Lyceum. Known for his pragmatism, Aristotle sought the balance between extremes, advocating the path of the golden mean or the middle path. Aristotle's teachings cover an incredibly wide range of subjects, including ethics, politics, logic, biology and metaphysics. He emphasised the importance of observation and empirical evidence in understanding the natural world. Following the death of Alexander the Great, Aristotle left Athens and sought refuge in Chalcis, 'preventing Athenians from committing a second crime against philosophy'. His ideas have had a lasting impact on philosophy, science, and across fields of knowledge throughout history.

TELEOLOGICAL METHOD

According to Aristotle, everything in the world has a purpose, goal, end or *telos*. He believed that the end of a thing is more natural than its beginning. Further, the essential 'form' of a thing is more natural than its matter. Matter is attracted towards evolving a coherent form, just like the development of a family is attracted towards the formation of a state. He adopted a *teleological method*, which means that everything in life is driven by some purpose. The purpose of a family is to become a state. The purpose of potential is to become actual. The purpose of human beings is to lead a good and virtuous life. Aristotle rejected the distinction between the world of matter and the world of ideas, asserting that ideas (or forms) are found within matter just as beauty lies in beautiful objects. The purpose of human life, for Aristotle, is not the acquisition of power or wealth but the pursuit of happiness through moral and virtuous living. His teleological method can be understood in the following terms, using the example of crafting a table:

1. Material cause: the wood used for making a table.
2. Efficient cause: the instruments used for making a table.
3. Formal cause: the idea of the table in the mind of the carpenter.
4. Final cause: the completed and furnished table.

INDUCTIVE METHOD

Aristotle's inductive method, also known as empirical induction, is a process of reasoning that involves drawing general conclusions based on specific observations or instances. It is a method of logical inquiry where he sought to establish universal principles by gathering and analysing data from the natural world. Instead of starting with preconceived ideas or theories, he emphasised the importance of careful observation and systematic collection of evidence. He would make generalisations and formulate hypotheses based on the patterns and regularities he observed in specific cases. Aristotle's inductive method played a significant role in his scientific and philosophical investigations, allowing him to derive knowledge and understand the natural world through empirical observation and logical inference.

Aristotle's contributions to both political science and biology are remarkable and distinct, and he is considered the father of both disciplines. He approached the study of politics through a teleological lens, focusing on the purpose and ultimate goals of political systems. In biology, his approach was empirical, emphasising careful observation and data collection. His inductive method, rooted in empiricism, involves drawing general conclusions based on specific examples or instances.

In his comparative approach, Aristotle conducted a comprehensive study of the constitutions of 158 different states, analysing and comparing their structures and functions, and studying the behaviour of individuals in these states. These unique approaches showcase Aristotle's extraordinary interdisciplinary thinking and his significant contributions to multiple fields of study.

COMPARING ARISTOTLE WITH PLATO

Aristotle, like Plato, believes in the concept of an organic state and sees the state as a natural institution rising from the fundamental needs of human beings. Like Plato, he also believes that the state is of greater importance than individuals. In ancient Greece, there was no clear distinction between society and the state, and the notion of sovereignty was absent. Aristotle considers the state to be a moral entity rather than a purely legal or political one.

Several differences also arise when comparing Aristotle with Plato. Aristotle is characterised as a pragmatic, scientific and empirical thinker, earning him the title of the 'first political scientist' by **Chester C. Maxey**. In contrast, Plato's ideas are often seen as romantic, idealistic and utopian, seemingly detached from worldly practical realities. Further,

1. Aristotle disagrees with Plato's concept of the 'communism of the family', asserting that family and property cannot be separated from the individual. He argues that the institution of the family is natural and essential for fulfilling human needs, and criticises Plato's extreme views on communal ownership and the state as family. Aristotle rejected Plato's contention of unifying Greek city-states through the communism of the family, emphasising the importance of recognising the strong bonds inherent between parents and children.
2. Aristotle dismisses Plato's notion of the philosopher king as 'imaginary' and 'utopian', finding it unrealistic to expect such intellectually and morally superior individuals to exist in reality.
3. Aristotle believes that Plato's idea of common ownership or communism of property is impractical as human beings have a natural emotional attachment to their possessions.
4. Aristotle emphasises the rule of law as opposed to the rule of an ideally just individual.

THE STATE

Aristotle posits that the family comes into existence for fulfilling human needs, and multiple families come together to form a village. The aggregation of villages then gives rise to the state. Aristotle believes in the concept of organic state, and asserts that the state takes precedence over individuals as the whole is more significant than its parts. Philosophically, the state is more important than individuals, but from an empirical or chronological perspective, individuals precede the state.

Aristotle suggests that human beings possess both animalistic and god-like characteristics. While humans share physical needs with animals, their moral capacity resembles that of gods. According to Aristotle, those who live outside of a state are either beasts or gods. The state is a moral institution, not required by animals because they have only physical needs, and it is irrelevant to gods who embody absolute perfection and morality and have no physical needs. Aristotle maintains that the state comes into being to sustain human life and to promote the good life. The good life implies a moral existence, while just existence pertains to the physical aspect.

Plato also contends that the state is a natural and organic institution that enables individuals to lead virtuous lives, a notion that Aristotle embraces. The ultimate objective of human life is to fulfill moral needs. But while Plato considers politics as a part of ethics, Aristotle treats politics as an independent discipline and as a 'master science' because it subsumes other sciences and disciplines, and involves the study of moral beings.

Functions of the State

Aristotle said, 'Man is by nature a political animal,' underlining the essentially social nature of humans. He considered the state to be a natural and organic institution that arose out of human needs. In his teleological approach he argues that the whole is more important than its parts. Thus, just as the body is more important than its organs, the existence of the state precedes that of the individuals in it. Underscoring the vital role of the state, and the social and political dimensions in human life, Aristotle famously contended that those who can live without a state are either beasts or gods, but they cannot be considered fully human.

According to Aristotle, the state assumes full responsibility for the all-round physical, intellectual and moral development and welfare of its citizens, and performs several functions, such as:

1. Production of food.
2. Providing education and training in the arts.
3. Providing military training.
4. Performing religious, legal and judicial functions.
5. Imparting morality, ethics and virtue through education.
6. Enabling citizens to achieve all-round physical, intellectual and moral excellence through education.
7. Safeguarding the security and general wellbeing of citizens.

MORAL DEVELOPMENT

According to Aristotle, individuals can attain moral development in three ways.

1. *Nature*: Aristotle believed that human beings are innately predisposed towards certain virtues and moral qualities, and that individuals are born with certain natural potentialities that can contribute to their moral growth. For example, some people may have a natural inclination towards courage or kindness, which may form their moral basis.
2. *Experience*: Individuals acquire moral virtues through experience and their interactions with the world and people around them. By trial and error and by observing the consequences of their acts, they gain a better understanding of what is morally right and wrong.
3. *Reasoning*: Aristotle considered reasoning or practical wisdom (*phronesis*) as crucial to moral development and believed

that individuals must engage in rational thinking and reflection to discern the right course of action in different situations. Reasoning involves considering ethical principles, evaluating consequences, and making sound judgments based on moral values.

PLURALISM AND COMMUNITARIANISM

Ernest Barker argues that Aristotle established the groundwork for pluralism by recognising that the state is composed of various associations. Modern communitarians, such as **Alasdair MacIntyre**, also find inspiration in Aristotle's ideas as they prioritise the collective life of the community over the individual's life. Aristotle considered the state the highest of all institutions and called it the 'association of associations', as it fulfills both physical and moral needs of its citizens. The state contributes to the moral development of citizens in the following ways:

1. *Education*: The state provides opportunities for education, which plays a crucial role in shaping the outlook, moral character and virtues of its citizens.
2. *Participation in legislative and judicial activities*: Aristotle believed citizens should actively participate in the state's decision-making processes, whereby they can contribute to the formulation and enforcement of laws that uphold moral standards and promote justice.
3. *Participation in other political activities*: By taking part in activities like public deliberation, advocacy and other public affairs, individuals have the opportunity to shape the moral and ethical direction of the state.

THE GOLDEN MEAN

Plato is often seen as being extreme for his rejection of the family and private property. But Aristotle, taking a more moderate stance, asserts the centrality of the family and the village in the development of the state. Plato argues that the very existence of the family goes against the unity of the state. However, Aristotle asserts that family and property are extensions of the individual's identity and personality in time and space, and crucial for a happy life, cultivating friendships, and for moral development.

While Plato believed in the philosopher king, Aristotle held that a polity is the best and most practical form of government. Plato rejected customs and traditions as products of ignorance, believed that women could become guardians, and was possibly critical of slavery. But Aristotle considered women inferior to men and accepted their subordination. He also advocated and justified slavery, saying that equality is unnatural. Aristotle has been labeled the first Whig by some commentators, drawing a parallel with the liberal political party in England. It is interesting to note that both Aristotle and the Whigs endorse a middle path, reflecting a moderate stance.

POLITICS, THE MASTER SCIENCE

Aristotle believed that 'Man is by nature a political animal' and regarded political life as the highest activity of human existence. Human beings have the ability to communicate, which enables them to engage in social life, and distinguishes human life from animal life. Aristotle distinguished between the 'natural animal' and the 'political animal', arguing that while they may have similarities in external form, the political animal possesses certain distinct and unique qualities, which include:

1. The capacity of thought and reasoning.
2. The capacity for language and communication.
3. The capacity for political organisation.
4. The capacity for moral and ethical judgement.

Aristotle considered political science the 'master science'. The ultimate goal of human existence for him is to live a moral and ethical life, and political science is the study of such a life. Aristotle called politics the master science and art because it subsumes and determines the order of other sciences and disciplines to be studied by every class of citizen in a state. Subjects like military science, economics and medicine, which focus on the general good of humans, all come within the ambit of politics according to him. He viewed economics as the art of household management. Aristotle equated the idea of 'good' with happiness or *eudaimonia*, which he believed could be attained through education—again an integral part of politics.

Kinds of Knowledge

While he recognised the independence of the different sciences, Aristotle saw the need for a system of classification, and divided knowledge into three broad categories: productive, practical, and theoretical knowledge.

1. *Productive knowledge*: This pertains to craftsmanship or any activity that involves creating or producing something and focuses on the skills and techniques required to bring about a tangible outcome; for example, carpentry, painting, masonry or any form of craftsmanship.
2. *Practical knowledge*: Also known as prudence or practical wisdom (*phronesis*) involves the application of ethical principles and moral judgment to make decisions and act virtuously in everyday practical matters. It includes knowledge of human behaviour, social interactions, and the ability to navigate ethical dilemmas, which are crucial for leading a good and virtuous life.
3. *Theoretical knowledge*: Also known as speculative knowledge or contemplation (*theoria*) is concerned with understanding the nature of reality, seeking truth, and contemplating abstract ideas. It involves intellectual inquiry and the pursuit of knowledge for its own sake, rather than for any practical or productive purpose. Theoretical knowledge encompasses fields such as philosophy, mathematics, physics, and metaphysics.

Aristotle considered theoretical knowledge the highest and most noble form of knowledge, as it seeks to grasp the universal principles and causes that govern the world. But he argued that a well-rounded, wise individual must possess all three types of knowledge, with theoretical knowledge serving as the foundation for practical and productive pursuits.

HAPPINESS

Aristotle believes that the ultimate human goal is happiness or *eudaimonia*—not mere pleasure or material possessions, but happiness that is attained by living a moral, virtuous life, by exercising the ability to think and to reason. Aristotle also believed that true happiness comes from living in society for humans are essentially social beings. And so he placed great importance on friendship and considered it an end in itself for the attainment of happiness. He emphasised that genuine friendship and cordial relationships hold greater value than the acquisition of material wealth. In his work *Politics*, Aristotle acknowledged the principle of property ownership, but saw it as a means to a virtuous life. The ultimate happiness, in his view, can only be achieved by developing one's reasoning and logical capacities.

Aristotle regarded human beings as nature's finest creations, distinct from both animals and gods. While animals are driven by physical needs alone, and gods do not have any, humans have both physical and moral dimensions. While physical needs are essential for humans, their ultimate goal is a virtuous life. Aristotle thus believed that human beings are half animal and half god. Gods represent the epitome of moral perfection. While humans share basic physical needs with animals, their ability to think, reason, self-reflect, and their moral capacity aligns humans more closely with the divine.

THEORY OF FAMILY

Ernest Barker argues that according to Aristotle, the study of economics is a part of the study of politics, including domestic institutions such as *family*, *slavery* and *property*. Aristotle recognises the importance of the family as a social institution crucial for the moral development of individuals and the cultivation of nobility, and sees economics as the art and skills of family and household management. For Aristotle, a family comprises a husband, wife, children, and slaves, with the master and husband possessing the most wisdom, and the woman being less wise than man. In children wisdom is still nascent.

William A. Dunning highlights Aristotle's arguments regarding the importance of the family. The family educates children to become good citizens of the state. It imparts the head of the family with the skills of managing and directing, thus serving the interests of the state. The family also teaches slaves to be virtuous.

While Plato advocates for the concept of a *state-family*, where the head of the family and the head of the state are one and the same, Aristotle acknowledges the family as a separate unit, distinguishing the head of the family from the head of the state. The primary objective of the family for Aristotle is to fulfill physical material needs, and that of the state is to fulfill moral needs. While the head of the family may treat different family members unequally, the head of the state treats all citizens equally.

THEORY OF SLAVERY

Ancient Greek and Roman society used slaves and their economies were dependent on slavery. Unlike Plato, who did not formally discuss the institution of slavery in his works, Aristotle strongly advocated slavery and, in *Politics*, provided grounds for its justification.

Aristotle classifies all human beings into two categories: the *superior* (non-slaves) and the *inferior* (slaves). The superior are characterised by wisdom, courage and knowledge, and deemed eligible to rule others, while the inferior lack the capacity for autonomy and leadership. Aristotle believed that slaves, though physically strong, lack intellect and reason, are incapable of self-rule, and so must be ruled by others. He also believed slavery is a natural institution, not manmade.

He argued that differences and inequality between individuals are based on what they are naturally endowed with at birth. Since everything in nature has a purpose (teleological method), those endowed with intellect/wisdom govern, while those lacking it serve as slaves. This division is based on their respective natural strengths and capacities. Aristotle excludes slaves from administrative duties.

Aristotle draws an analogy from biology to explain and justify the existence of slavery, and inequality, difference and hierarchy in human society. He argues that just like the brain controls the body and its constituents, the master controls slaves. Just as there is a hierarchy between the body parts, i.e. among the brain, heart, blood, stomach, each has a different value and function, similarly those who are physically stronger but low in intellect are better suited for physical labour, while those with superior intellect for non-physical labour.

The superior rule over the inferior in the natural world in a mutually beneficial relationship. By relieving masters from domestic chores, slaves provide them with the leisure to engage in the affairs of the state and fulfil their legislative and judicial functions for the wellbeing of all citizens. Aristotle thus believes that slavery is advantageous for both slaves and masters, and asserts that serving a virtuous master can help slaves develop morals and virtue.

A Comparison with Modern Slavery

Human societies have evolved and rejected slavery as fundamentally offensive to any notions of humanity, liberty, equality and justice. The very idea of owning another human being as property is a grave violation of the most basic principles of human life, human rights and dignity, and an affront to the inherent worth and autonomy of individuals. No form of slavery is justifiable today under any circumstances or pretext.

Aristotle's perspective on slavery, however, differs from the brutal and inhumane practices associated with modern slavery. Although slavery was an accepted practice in ancient Greece, it is important to note the distinctions between his views and the historical reality of slavery in more recent times, particularly during the eighteenth and nineteenth centuries in Africa.

1. *Prisoners of war*: Aristotle excluded prisoners of war from being categorised as slaves based on their captivity, recognising that they did not inherently lack in intellect or virtue.
2. *Children*: Aristotle argued against slavery based on inheritance and believed that the children of slaves should not automatically become slaves due to their parentage. This contrasts with the hereditary enslavement and perpetuation of bondage that has characterised many instances of modern slavery.
3. *Duties*: Aristotle said that the duties of slaves should be confined to domestic tasks within the households of their masters, rather than extensive/hard labour for production purposes.
4. *Liberation*: Aristotle recognised the potential for slaves to acquire intellect and wisdom through learning and, in such cases, advocated for their liberation from slavery.
5. *Humane treatment*: Aristotle advocated for the humane and compassionate treatment of slaves. In contrast, modern slavery has witnessed extreme dehumanisation, exploitation and commodification of individuals, treating them as objects to be bought, sold, and exploited for labour or other purposes.

LIBERAL OR CONSERVATIVE?

Aristotle's views on political and social matters encompasses elements that can be associated with both liberal and conservative perspectives, making it difficult to categorise him as one or the other. While he supports private property and endorses a form of government known as polity, which aligns with contemporary constitutionalism, he also holds conservative views on several aspects of society. Aristotle's support for private property aligns with liberal principles that emphasise individual rights and ownership. His belief in the middle path as the optimal approach to societal change reflects a pragmatic perspective that seeks to balance stability and progress. However, Aristotle's advocacy of slavery and his assertion of the inherent inferiority and subordination of women to men is conservative. These views are rooted in the prevailing conventions and thinking of his time, which he considered had endured for centuries. This aligns him with conservative thinkers like Edmund Burke, who emphasise the importance of tradition and gradual change.

FORMS OF GOVERNMENT

Aristotle has classified forms of government into six categories, which can be grouped under two broad headings: pure forms, and perverted forms of government.

Among the *pure forms*, monarchy and polity are considered ideal forms of governance that prioritise the people's interests. Monarchy is the rule of one individual, while aristocracy is the rule of a few who possess wealth, wisdom and virtue. Polity is the rule of many, with a moderate level of virtue. In contrast, the *perverted forms*, tyranny, oligarchy, and democracy, are driven by selfish and narrow interests. Tyranny is the rule of one individual based on power, while oligarchy is the rule of a few who prioritise their own wealth and property over all else. Democracy is the rule of the many, and its defining feature is liberty.

Aristotle considered monarchy to be the best form of government due to its concentration of power and potential for virtuous rule, but he regarded polity as the most practical and feasible form of government as it allows for the participation and representation of a broader section of society.

Polity, the Golden Mean

Aristotle believed that establishing a stable and well-functioning state required a practical and balanced approach. He highlighted two forms of government: oligarchy and democracy. He regarded democracy as the worst form of government among the best options, yet the best form of government among the worst choices available. Oligarchy is the rule of a few individuals driven by self-interest, while democracy is, for Aristotle, the rule of the ignorant and poor masses. Aristotle advocated for a 'golden mean' between these two extremes, which he believed could be achieved through *polity*, or the rule of the many.

Polity can be described as a mixed form of government that combines elements of wealth and influence from the rich, with the numerical strength and support of the wider population. Aristotle considered polity to be the best practicable option for protecting the state against possible revolution. A constitutional government was for him the best form of government because it harmonised the features of democracy and oligarchy. Such a government based on majority rule, he argued, would help reduce the number of enemies and conflicts within the state, thus contributing to its stability and cohesion.

The Constitution and State

Aristotle does not differentiate between the concepts of constitution and state. He highlights that the main purpose of the state is to cultivate virtue in citizens. In his work *Politics*, he rejects Plato's notion of a philosopher king, and endorses the 'rule of law' instead, reflecting a liberal commitment to a system where laws and regulations guide and govern the functioning of society. According to Aristotle, constitutions have several advantages including:

1. *Separation of powers*: A constitution helps to delineate and distribute powers among different branches of government, ensuring a system of checks and balances.
2. *Delegation of powers*: It defines the allocation of powers and responsibilities to various levels of government, ensuring effective governance.
3. *Determining objectives of the state*: It sets out the fundamental goals and principles that guide the functioning of the state, establishing its purpose and priorities.

IMPORTANCE OF THE MIDDLE CLASS

Aristotle classified society into three classes: the rich, the middle class, and the poor. The rich possess great wealth but are a minority, while the poor have little or none but are many. According to him, a well-functioning government should ensure equal participation of both the rich and the poor in governance. Aristotle believed that the best form of government could be established through the influence and mediation of the middle class. The rich are often contemptuous and hostile towards the poor, and their arrogance and tendency to disregard the law often lead to conflicts. The poor are envious of the rich, and may lack knowledge and maturity, making it challenging for them to understand and abide by the law. This creates a climate of discord and distrust between the two extremes.

In contrast, the middle class embodies a sense of justice and equality. They strive to achieve consensus and actively engage in constructive dialogue. Their engaged presence can contribute to building a virtuous society. Aristotle valued the reasonable and practical opinions that emerge from the middle class as they have a greater understanding of the needs and aspirations of the entire community. By ensuring the participation and influence of the middle class in governance, Aristotle believed that a more balanced and harmonious society could be achieved, fostering justice, equality, and the common good.

THE RULE OF LAW

Aristotle rejected Plato's idea of the just philosopher king and emphasised the primacy of community reason over individual reason. According to Aristotle, the law represents dispassionate reason, contrasting with Plato's view that customs, traditions and laws (as part of customs) are rooted in ignorance and unreason. Aristotle believed in the 'rule of law' and considered law as 'passionless reason'. In his work *Politics*, he stated that a just and lawful individual surpasses all beings, and that the law is objective and holds higher status than personal reason. Key elements of Aristotle's understanding of the rule of law include:

1. *Equality under the law*: The law applies equally to both rulers and subjects.
2. *Government bound by law*: Rulers rule in accordance with the law, not of their free will.
3. *Consent of the governed*: The government's legitimacy is derived from the consent of the subjects.

Aristotle advocated a realistic, moderate and pragmatic approach, acknowledging the significance of traditions, conventions, and precedents in society. In this he shared common ground with modern thinkers like Edmund Burke, who also recognised the importance of preserving established customs and conventions and valued the stability they provide. **David Miller** described Aristotle as a philosopher of natural law. **Hans Kelsen** claimed that the constitutionalism of Aristotle failed to adequately identify the distribution of power, wealth and citizenship within society.

THEORY OF REVOLUTION

Aristotle explores various aspects of the state, law, property, justice and revolution in his work *Politics*. He discusses how changes in the form of government, for instance, transition from monarchy to tyranny, can occur through revolution. He identifies the unequal treatment of equals and the equal treatment of unequals as a major cause of revolution.

Inequality as the Cause of Revolution

Aristotle distinguishes between two types of equality: *proportional equality* and *absolute equality*. The rich advocate for proportional equality, that is resources should be distributed not strictly equally or 'arithmetically', but in proportion to their merit. Whereas the poor demand absolute equality, desiring an equal distribution of resources regardless of merit. The rich may argue for defending inequality, while the poor strive for equality. This aspiration for equality is a fundamental cause of revolution in every form of government, he asserts. In a democracy, the rich may incite revolution because the poor desire arithmetic equality, while in an oligarchy, the poor may revolt against the misuse of public funds by the wealthy. Aristotle argues that polity, a form of government that balances the interests of different classes, minimises the likelihood of revolution.

Aristotle also identifies other causes of revolution, including:

1. Corruption within the ruling class.
2. The desire for respect and dignity.
3. The incompetence of rulers.
4. Rewarding the incompetent and punishing the competent.
5. Mistrust and conspiracy amongst different classes.

6. Usurpation of power by any one organ of government.

THEORY OF JUSTICE

Aristotle, like Plato, emphasised the importance of justice in the state. He viewed justice as 'virtue in action,' which involved the moral conduct of individuals performing their duties. He also propounded a specific meaning of justice based on the 'rule of law', which is regulatory in nature. He asserted that obeying the law and administering rewards as per individual capabilities and punishing those who violate the law is justice. According to Ernest Barker, Aristotle believed that law, justice and education are the foundations for a spiritual state. Aristotle's theory of justice can be divided into two parts.

Distributive justice: The state should distribute offices, rewards and resources according to each individual's capabilities and contribution towards society.

Corrective justice: The state should penalise and punish those who disobey the law.

Aristotle believed that a virtuous and just life are synonymous with each other. He held that there is an organic relationship between the state and the society, and that the virtue of justice in each individual is necessary to ensure harmony in society. Aristotle applied the teleological method to explain that everything is driven by a purpose, and that justice can be achieved by maintaining cordiality and harmony in society, which will bring happiness. Fulfilling one's duties and engaging in moral and virtuous activities are central to Aristotle's understanding of justice, which endorses Plato's concept of substantive justice.

THEORY OF CITIZENSHIP

Aristotle believes that only those who actively participate in the affairs of the state are eligible to become its citizens, and that residence within a state's boundaries should not be the sole criterion for getting citizenship status. Aristotle argued that a good human being is synonymous with a virtuous human being, which is universal and unchanging. But being a good citizen would vary depending on the form of government. A person can be a good citizen without necessarily embodying all the qualities of a good human being, while a good human being should inherently also make a good citizen. However, Aristotle acknowledged the possibility that all good human beings may not necessarily be good citizens.

Aristotle's notion of citizenship differs from the contemporary concept of being a mere taxpayer. Individuals residing in a state may vary in their abilities and capacities, but he believed that their common objective must be the holistic development of society. Ernest Barker compared Aristotle's concept of citizenship to shareholders who participate in the deliberative and judicial functions of the state.

Aristotle made no distinction between the qualities required to be a good ruler and a good citizen. According to him,

1. A good citizen may not possess all the qualities of a good human being, but a good ruler should definitely possess all those qualities.
2. A good ruler must have practical knowledge, experience and wisdom, whereas a citizen may not require them to the same extent.

Aristotle wrote on an astonishing range of subjects. His contributions cut across several fields—he is also known as the 'father of Biology', for instance. A few of his notable works, in chronological order, include:

1. *Nicomachean Ethics*
2. *Politics*
3. *Metaphysics*
4. *The Athenian Constitution*
5. *Eudemian Ethics*
6. *On Virtues and Vices*

7. *Rhetoric*
8. *Physics*
9. *On the Soul, and On Memory and Recollection*
10. *The Categories*
11. *Poetics*
12. *The Organon* (a collection of six works, including *Topics*, *Prior Analytics* and *Posterior Analytics*)
13. *Meteorology*
14. *Oeconomica* (Economics)
15. *Magna Moralia*
16. *Historia Animalium* (History of Animals, or Inquiries into Animals)
17. *On Dreams*
18. *On Divination in Sleep*
19. *On Youth, Old Age, Life and Death, and Respiration*

4

NICCOLO MACHIAVELLI (1469–1527)

KEY CONCEPTS

Modern statecraft; Italian nationalism; virtue and fortuna; power politics; Machiavelli on human nature; politics and religion; morality; republicanism; liberty

Niccolo Machiavelli, born in 1469 in Florence, Italy, lived during a transitional period from the Middle Ages to the dawn of the Modern Age. Italy at that time was a fragmented and vulnerable state, comprising small principalities and susceptible to foreign aggression. This greatly influenced Machiavelli's political thinking as his primary objective was to address the challenges faced by Italy and propose strategies for its unification and strength.

LITERARY CONTRIBUTION

Machiavelli's most famous and controversial political treatise is *The Prince*, in which he advises rulers on the art of governance. This influential text delves into the pragmatic and often ruthless aspects of statecraft, focusing on how rulers can maintain and consolidate their power in challenging circumstances. Machiavelli's insights in *The Prince* were shaped by his observations of contemporary politics and his desire to see Italy become a more cohesive and formidable nation.

In his second work, *Discourses on Livy*, he explores the benefits and challenges of a republican government and a political system based on the participation of citizens, highlighting the virtues of civic engagement and the potential for a more balanced distribution of power. His third book, *The Art of War*, discusses practical warfare, including military organisation, strategy and the importance of well-trained, disciplined forces. His fourth work, *History of Florence and of the Affairs of Italy*, is testament to his stature as the first great Italian historian.

A MODERN THINKER

Machiavelli is regarded as a modern thinker. According to **R. N. Berki**, many of his ideas laid the foundations of modern thought and a new era characterised by reason. The Age of Reason placed emphasis on rational thought, and witnessed major scientific inventions and discoveries. The emergence of nation-states was a defining feature of this modern age, which saw a significant shift in focus from religious, philosophical and metaphysical concerns to physical, material and economic ones, which led to the development of secular thought. Machiavelli's understanding of political dynamics and his ability to navigate the complexities of practical governance established his reputation as a key figure in political theory and practice. Notwithstanding his association with ruthless, amoral and unscrupulous politics and the fierce criticism his views have consistently drawn, Machiavelli's contributions to modern political thought are indisputably regarded as influential. **Hegel** in fact praised *The Prince* as a brilliant and genuine depiction of real political genius with the highest and noblest purpose.

Practical Politics

Machiavelli's approach to political thought marked a radical departure from the traditional methods of the Greek era and the dominance of religious doctrine in the medieval period. He embraced a more *pragmatic* and *realistic* methodology, rejecting conventional approaches. Instead of relying solely on philosophical knowledge, Machiavelli employed empirical methods by drawing on human psychology and historical examples to understand the politics around him. He recognised that the rise and fall of states could be observed throughout history, and emphasised that a powerful ruler was essential for building a strong state. These insights were derived from lessons found in historical accounts.

A PRODUCT OF HIS AGE

William A. Dunning believed that Machiavelli was a product of his age, profoundly influenced by the societal, political conditions of his time. **George H. Sabine** adds that had Machiavelli been born in a different time, his views would likely have been different. During his time, Europe and Italy were undergoing major social, political and internal transformations. Despotic monarchies were emerging in England and France, while Italy remained divided into multiple principalities, with the Church as its biggest internal obstacle against unity. External threats from powerful monarchies like France and Spain further exacerbated the situation. Meanwhile, important inventions, explorations and advancements in communications were also taking place in Europe. All these factors lead to the rise of the middle class.

According to **Sabine**, Machiavelli is the father of the school of *universal egoism*, which posits that every human being is driven by self-interest and greed and seeks to maximise their own security, wealth and wellbeing. This leads to conflict and struggle. Machiavelli recognised the creative intelligence of the people of Italy, but also acknowledged their corruption. Given these circumstances, he therefore supported the idea of a powerful ruler ('The Prince') who could unify and secure Italy.

Residing in Florence, Italy, which was part of the divided nation, Machiavelli witnessed the obstacles posed by the Church and the aggression of France and Spain. He believed that the strength of these countries stemmed from their powerful rulers who, through repeated attacks, sought to keep Italy divided. Only a really strong ruler, Machiavelli argued, could address the multiple internal and external challenges faced by Italy. His realistic approach advised the ruler to be cautious of external attacks from neighbours, and to enhance military capabilities.

Italy was the heart of the Renaissance, which emphasised the centrality of the human being. Breaking away from Platonic and medieval thought, Machiavelli sought to separate politics from ethics, and challenged the idea that the king must be bound by moral principles. Instead, he redefined morality, asserting that the ruler's greatest moral duty was to strengthen and secure the state. Thus he laid the foundations for both secular thinking as well as the idea of nationalism.

NATIONALISM

At a time when strong nation-states were emerging, such as neighbouring England and France, Italy—faced with both internal divisions and conflicts, and external aggression—remained fragmented and weak. Machiavelli therefore stressed the urgency of creating unity among the five principalities of Italy, and sought to generate a spirit of nationalism in its people. He argued that a powerful prince was necessary in order to unite Italy, curtail the inherent corruption of its populace, build a strong nation, and defend its sovereignty.

Machiavelli challenged the notion that the church was more powerful or more important than the state. He argued that the church neither had the capability nor the power to unify Italy, and, in fact, it only hindered other institutions from doing so. Machiavelli's infamous phrase, 'the end justifies the means' clearly conveys that he thought any means by which Italian unification could be achieved were both necessary and legitimate, and must be employed. **Michael B. Foster** supported Machiavelli's ideas, arguing that they were not driven by selfish or personal interests but aimed at the defense and consolidation of a strong state.

VIRTUE AND FORTUNA

According to Machiavelli, the virtue of a ruler/ prince lies in his ability to adapt to changing circumstances. He must seek power, and prioritise the creation of a citizens' army or *militia* to defend the state. While a prince may exhibit qualities of a good human being, he may also resort to cruelty and disregard moral principles in order to protect the interests of the state. Virtue, in the case of an individual, is distinct and should be guided by moral principles. However, for a prince, argued Machiavelli, virtue lies in strengthening the power of the state and defending it.

Machiavelli introduces the concept of *fortuna*, which refers to external social and political conditions that are beyond the prince's control. Just as a river becomes uncontrollable during floods, Machiavelli characterises fortuna as unpredictable and capricious. However, he asserts that a prince can exert control over fortuna and thereby enhance his virtue. Just as a mighty river can be tamed by building a dam to regulate its waters, a powerful and intelligent prince can also manipulate adverse political conditions in his favour.

Machiavelli distinguishes between two methods of fighting: one using law and the other using brute force. The first method belongs to humans, while the second belongs to beasts. When the first method proves inadequate to protect the interests of the state, the second method becomes necessary, Machiavelli argues. A prince must therefore possess the qualities of both a lion and a fox: the power and courage of a lion, and the cunning of a fox.

POWER POLITICS

The concept of *power politics* did not emerge during the Greek Age, which focused on idealism and metaphysics, or in the Medieval Age, which was heavily influenced by the dominance of the Church and religious doctrine. Departing from both, Machiavelli introduced a new realist perspective in political theory and practice that stressed the importance of building a strong autonomous state with a supreme ruler at its helm. Disregarding considerations of morality, idealism and traditions, he advocated for cultivating an all-powerful ruler.

Machiavelli argued that the rise and fall of states can only be understood within the context of power politics, asserting that weak states will not survive. Separating morality from politics, he saw power as a means to secure and strengthen the state. He recognised that human beings are inherently driven by self-interest and egoism, and asserted that states could be governed by the use of power, force and coercion. He therefore advised princes to acquire knowledge and skills in the management of power, the 'Art of War,' and the enhancement of military capabilities.

Machiavelli's ideas marked a shift towards a pragmatic approach to politics, focusing on power dynamics and the tactical means of securing and maintaining power. His views demonstrate that Machiavelli was not just a political scientist but also a political strategist.

HUMAN NATURE

In the Greek Age, humans were regarded as moral and virtuous, while in medieval times, they were seen as fallen beings. Influenced by the transitional age he lived in, Machiavelli presented a secular understanding of human nature, approaching it through an empirical lens rather than a metaphysical or theological one.

In the modern age, individuals were driven by materialistic pursuits rather than salvation or liberation. Machiavelli believed humans are basically selfish and driven by greed, with their ultimate goal being acquisition, expansion and protection of property. To effectively govern, the ruler must know how to manage and control these greedy, corrupt, selfish individuals. Machiavelli advocated the use of both *love and fear* in controlling humans. Love alone was insufficient as individuals act kindly only to serve their own interests; fear was a more reliable and lasting method of control, he held. However, he cautioned against the excessive use of fear to prevent any harm to the ruler. He also advised kings not to acquire or seize the property of their citizens, emphasising the importance of maintaining the trust and loyalty of the people. ('Citizens', in this context, referred exclusively to men, since at the time women were not seen as independent but rather as belonging to their families or husbands.) Machiavelli further advised that while the king could seek assistance from alliance partners, he should not become dependent on them, and must preserve his independence and autonomy in governing the state.

In portraying human beings realistically and pragmatically, Machiavelli laid the foundation for liberal and utilitarian ideas that resonated with later thinkers like Hobbes and Bentham.

STATECRAFT

Machiavelli's focus was not on abstract philosophical or theoretical questions on the nature and origin of the state, or issues of justice and citizenship. As **Andrew Hacker** suggests, he is concerned with the practical workings of politics rather than theoretical dimensions. His goal and concern was the unification of Italy, and the means necessary to achieve it. Machiavelli's analysis of politics was grounded in pragmatism and *realpolitik*, leading some to view him more as a strategic thinker rather than a traditional political theorist. Machiavelli believed that the use of deceit, coercion and violence were justified if they met the end goal, in this case, prevent the disintegration of Italy and secure its future.

In *The Prince*, Machiavelli discusses in detail how a ruler should be and how he should act. Princes must possess qualities of both a lion and a fox in order to maintain order and control over the state, he asserts. The lion represents brute power and raw courage and the ability to inspire fear and intimidate, while the fox symbolises shrewd cunning and the flexible agility to navigate political challenges. Machiavelli's ideal prince is modeled on the lord of Romagna, **Caesar Borgia**. Machiavelli believed that the use of force was essential to control chaos and unrest and maintain stability, as contended by **Sheldon Wolin** who describes *The Prince* as an 'economy of violence'. Machiavelli astutely advised that a prince should also exhibit virtuous and religious traits and appear duty-bound and ethical, but must not hesitate to employ deceit, unscrupulous tactics and violence when necessary. **Michael B. Foster** compares Machiavelli to a carpenter, since he taught the craft of politics.

POLITICS AND RELIGION

The Church held enormous power in medieval times and often challenged the authority of the state. Machiavelli was not opposed to religion itself, but believed that Christian virtues had no place in politics. He was especially against the interference of the Church in political affairs, seeing it as a major obstacle to the unification of Italy. He therefore strongly argued for the separation of the Church from the state and politics, laying the groundwork for secular political thinking.

Machiavelli believed that politics was not a domain of moral goodness, and emphasised that in order to rule effectively, a ruler must in fact learn how *not to be* 'good' and free himself from conventional morality. While he acknowledged the importance of compassion, humanity and religiosity in a ruler, he stressed that a ruler must not flinch from employing amoral and unscrupulous means whenever necessary for the safety of the state.

Machiavelli recognised the power of religion as a means of instilling fear, discipline and obedience in subjects. He saw God as an unknown power that inspires fear in people. He also acknowledged that for many, the fear of God is deeper and more enduring than the fear of the ruler. Machiavelli understood that religion could thus be a useful tool in serving the interests of the state and adopted a utilitarian approach towards religion, using it to bolster the state's power. However, critics argue that his manipulation of religion for political objectives should be seen as promoting communalism rather than secularism.

In Machiavelli's redefinition of politics as power politics, power is the only guarantee for the state's security. He stressed that the king must know the 'art of using religion' to acquire, expand and maintain power. The king must also create and maintain a strong, well-equipped citizens' army or militia as a regular force rather than relying on rented armies. Significantly, Machiavelli also advised the king that subjects must be made to believe that the state is providing them freedom—but, in fact, it should not.

STATE AND MORALITY

Machiavelli redefined the very understanding of morality. He argued that all actions taken by the king to empower, strengthen and secure the state against external attack are moral and justified. He freed the king from the obligation of adhering to moral principles, while expecting subjects to abide by them, arguing that if the ruler were to strictly follow moral norms, the state would never become powerful or attain unity, because human beings are inherently selfish and greedy. According to **Isaiah Berlin**, Machiavelli was not a lover of evil; he was 'amoral' rather than 'anti-moral' and believed that the ruler and state must remain neutral to moral principles. Machiavelli established two standards of morality: one for the ruler, and one for ordinary citizens. While citizens are bound by moral norms, the ruler's actions are exempt from moral judgment. Machiavelli's departure from the Greek traditions of Plato and Aristotle led to a significant shift in the understanding of politics and governance, which he redefined as an amoral vocation.

REPUBLICAN GOVERNMENT

In his *Discourses on Livy*, Machiavelli compared and analysed different forms of government to determine their suitability in different socio-political conditions. He averred that given the egoism, corruption and selfishness rampant in the Italian people, absolute monarchy may be the most appropriate for Italy. However, Machiavelli was convinced that the republican or democratic form of government was the best because it promoted the unity and integrity of the state. Machiavelli's views on the ideal republican form of government may be summarised as follows:

1. There is greater tolerance in the republican system as it provides some powers and rights even to minorities, and operates according to the rule of law.

2. It is citizen-centric and emphasises citizens' welfare, ensuring the unity and integrity of the state.
3. If an individual is deemed incapable or incompetent to rule a republic, citizens have the freedom to choose their own ruler. This also encourages their voluntary obedience to the ruler.
4. The collective wisdom of a group of people is more effective than the wisdom of one individual.
5. Machiavelli believes that a republican government is practicable only when citizens are moral and virtuous like in Switzerland. He said: 'Public affairs are easily managed in a city where the body of people is not corrupt; and where equality exists, there no principality can be established; nor can a republic be established where there is no equality.'

According to **George H. Sabine**, Machiavelli's views are contradictory because on the one hand he asserts that human nature is fundamentally and universally egoistic and selfish, and on the other hand, he claims that Swiss citizens are moral and virtuous, which is paradoxical. Other commentators have argued that Machiavelli was neither for nor against republican government and that he did not align himself with any particular political stance, unlike Rousseau's democratic ideals or John Locke's liberalism. For Machiavelli, ends had to justify the means. **Quentin Skinner** praised Machiavelli, arguing that he propounded the founding principle of Republican democratic modes of government.

LIBERTY

In *Discourses on Livy*, Machiavelli defends the republican system of government as a means of preserving liberty, highlighting that only free citizens can contribute their talents for the greater glory of the state. He emphasises that states can achieve greatness when civil liberty is upheld as it allows individuals to marry by their choice, have children who are born free rather than enslaved, and fosters the flourishing of art and industry.

Machiavelli defines liberty as two basic kinds of freedom.

1. *Liberty of possessions and family life*: Individuals should have the freedom to own property, and to have a family and lead their own family lives.
2. *Individual liberty*: Each individual must be able to do what they want, within the bounds of the law.

Quentin Skinner argues that civic virtue is essential for enjoying liberty, implying that citizens should be honest and moral as liberty cannot be cherished in a society plagued by corruption and selfishness. Machiavelli acknowledges the intelligence of Italians but bemoans their corruption and greed, leading him to conclude that a powerful monarchy, rather than a republican government, would be more suitable for Italy. Machiavelli sees liberty as a fundamental aspect of a flourishing society. However, it is important to note that Machiavelli's understanding of liberty is within the context of a well-ordered republic, where civic virtue and moral conduct are crucial for the enjoyment of liberty.

While **Leo Strauss** referred to him as a 'teacher of evil,' **R. N. Berki** suggests that his views should be seen in the context of his times and understood in perspective. **M. B. Foster** argues that *The Prince* can be seen as a book of advice to either become a cunning and powerful opportunist prince, or to protect oneself from such a prince.

However, according to **Hugo Albert Rennert**, 'No man has been more harshly judged than Machiavelli,' and that while '*The Prince* has been termed a manual for tyrants,' Rennert reminds us that: 'We must bear in mind the atmosphere of craft, hypocrisy, and poison in which he lived—his was the age of Caesar Borgia and of Popes like the monster Alexander VI and Julius II. Whatever his faults may have been, Machiavelli was always an ardent patriot and an earnest supporter of popular government.'

Machiavelli's realpolitik, focus on statecraft, power, pragmatic and realistic view of politics, and his separation of morality from politics continues to resonate in the modern world today. **Ernst Cassirer** calls Machiavelli a 'Galileo of politics' who created an empirical method for the study of politics and history.

WORKS OF MACHIAVELLI

1. *The Art of War* (1521)
2. *The Discourses on Livy* (1531)
3. *The Prince* (1532)
4. *Florentine Histories* (1532)

5

THOMAS HOBBES (1588–1679)

KEY CONCEPTS

Mechanical materialism; state of nature; natural law; the social contract; fear, reason, and power; absolute monarchy; individualism; secular state; Hobbes and democratic thought

Thomas Hobbes was born in 1588 in Malmesbury, England. It was a tumultuous period of political upheaval marked by confrontation between the monarchy and parliamentary government, ultimately leading to the English Civil War. The prevailing conditions of ceaseless chaos, fear and insecurity deeply influenced Hobbes' perspectives on the state of nature, human nature, sovereignty and social contract. Hobbes witnessed the division between those who favoured a monarchical system and those who supported a parliamentary form of government. His observations and experiences during this period shaped his ideas and theories on governance and the nature of society.

Hobbes' era was also marked by important scientific discoveries, explorations and the emergence new scientific theories. Newton's theory of gravity, in particular, exerted a profound influence across Europe, transforming the understanding of the natural world.

While Hobbes' most important and influential treatise is *Leviathan* (1651), some of his numerous other notable works include *The Elements of Law, Natural and Politic* (1650), *A Dialogue on the Civil Wars, Behemoth* (1681), *De Corpore* (The Body; 1655), *De Cive* (The Citizen; 1642), *De Homine* (The Man; 1658), which delve into aspects of the natural sciences, human nature, political philosophy, law and the foundations of social order.

MECHANICAL MATERIALISM

Hobbes rejected the scholastic method then prevalent in Oxford University, which sought to prove the existence of God through reason. His approach to studying political science differed from the philosophical methods of Plato and Aristotle and the historical approach of Machiavelli. Drawing inspiration from the scientific revolution taking place in Europe, Hobbes incorporated the study of physics, geometry and psychology to propose a new theory known as *mechanical materialism*, which posits that everything in the universe, including human beings, is composed of matter and operates according to mechanical principles of matter and motion.

Influenced by Galileo's Law of Motion and Euclid's geometry, Hobbes employed a deductive method rooted in geometry. He applied the principles of physics to argue that everything in the universe is composed of matter, which consists of particles in motion. Drawing upon psychology, he posited that individuals have unlimited desires and are attracted towards certain objects and repulsed by others. In *Leviathan*, Hobbes famously proclaimed that 'human desires come to an end only after his death'. Like Machiavelli, Hobbes believed that self-preservation is the most fundamental desire of human beings, leading them to acquire power and influence.

While Hobbes' logical and rational approach is difficult to deny, his justification for absolute monarchy as necessary for a stable, strong and secure state has been widely criticised. His hypothesis about human nature, akin to geometric reasoning, has also been debated. Despite this, scholars like Michael Oakeshott regard *Leviathan* as the greatest and perhaps only masterpiece of political philosophy written in the English language.

STRUCTURE OF THOUGHT

Human Nature: Hobbes said that the basic assumption about human nature is analogous to the geometric principle which states says that the sum of the three angles of a triangle is 180 degrees. Similarly, he argued that every human being harbours an ever-growing number of desires and an insatiable need for their fulfillment, which ends only with death. Humans have their preferences and aversions. Ultimately, each pursues their self-interest and security, which leads them to enter into a 'social contract' to escape the anarchy of the state of nature and ensure their self-preservation.

State of Nature: Hobbes describes the state of nature as being characterised by chaos and violence, where individuals are caught in ceaseless conflict for power and survival, resulting in lives that are impoverished, short, nasty, brutish and full of fear. Without any governing authority to control their actions, absolute anarchy and disorder prevails. According to Hobbes, the state of nature is identified by:

1. Absence of state and government.
2. Absence of morality and ethical norms.
3. Absence of private property and culture.
4. Absence of laws and justice.
5. Absence of civilised and organised society.

To escape the perils of this violent and fearful state, Hobbes argues, individuals exercise their reasoning and come together to form a state through the social contract. His conceptualisation of the state of nature underscores the necessity of a social contract and a powerful governing authority to end the anarchy inherent in the absence of organised society.

However, critics such as **Geoffrey M. Vaughan** have challenged Hobbes' assertion that human lives are endangered in the state of nature, and argue that under the state, individuals may become akin to slaves. According to **Rousseau**, 'individualism ends with the end of freedom.' **John P. Plamenatz** explains that for Hobbes, the state of nature was a 'state of war', since every man could interpret the laws of nature individually and compete against the other.

NATURAL LAW

Hobbes' theory of social contract is based on his concept of natural law. Hobbes believed that individuals possess endless desires, but they also possess the natural faculty of *reason*, which he referred to as the 'natural law' or 'the law of reason'. As a materialist thinker, Hobbes believes that reason prevents people from self-destruction. In *Leviathan*, he enumerates 19 types of natural laws which aim to make life more secure, peaceful and meaningful. Hobbes' natural law or the law of reason is essentially synonymous with prudence, and thus differs significantly from the universal religious laws of medieval times. It can be summed up as follows:

1. All individuals must strive for peace.
2. All individuals must willingly surrender some of their rights for the sake of greater peace and security.
3. All individuals must willingly enter into a social contract.

SOCIAL CONTRACT

Hobbes' social contract is a hypothetical rather than historical theory, built on the foundation of natural law and grounded in reason, rational self-interest, and utility. It posits that individuals must unite to form a state in their own best interests. In Hobbes' words: 'I authorise and give up my right of governing myself to this man, or to an assembly of men, on the condition that they give up their right to him, and authorise all his actions in like manner.' He argued that for self-preservation, people must willingly relinquish their natural rights and power to a supreme ruler, state or governing authority. Importantly, according to Hobbes, both the 'State' and the 'King' are the *outcomes* of the social contract, not *parties to* it.

The social contract is a voluntary agreement entered into by individuals who recognise the benefits of living under a central authority, and a means to establish a structured society governed by agreed-upon laws and institutions that ensure protection of individual interests, where the sovereign has the power to make and enforce laws for the wellbeing of all. Hobbes' theory of natural law and social contract emphasises the importance of rationality and self-interest in creating a harmonious social order, and serves as a foundation for his broader political philosophy and understanding of the role of government in securing a stable and peaceful society.

Artificial State: The state, society and government all come into existence through a single contract, with self-preservation as the common goal. The state, society and government are all thus artificially created utilitarian institutions. Unlike for Plato and Aristotle, the state is not a natural or organic institution for Hobbes, nor a divine one. Once the social contract is established, people will surrender all their rights and powers to the state/king, except the right of self-preservation. Upon dissolution of the social contract, people will revert to the state of nature.

Atomistic Society: Hobbes believed in the primacy of individuals, and regarded the state and society as artificial, mechanistic constructs created by individuals. Drawing an analogy from physics, Hobbes likened individuals to atoms, emphasising the idea that everything is composed of matter. He did not attach much significance to social institutions like family, church or university, traditionally regarded as integral components of society. Hobbes' concept of an atomistic society finds support among thinkers like **John Locke**, **Jeremy Bentham**, and **J. S. Mill**, all of whom identify as individualists and proponents of a liberal ideology.

FEAR, REASON AND POWER

All of Hobbesian thought can be understood through the lens of three key concepts: fear, reason and power. Hobbes, said to have been born prematurely when his mother heard of the impending invasion of the Spanish Armada, attributed a significant role to fear in his life, stating that his mother gave birth to twins: 'I and fear'.

In the state of nature, there is fear of a violent death. Formation of the state creates a new fear: the fear of an absolute king. The social contract, on the other hand, arises from reason which transforms self-interest into rational self-interest, he argues.

Hobbes believed that every individual, driven by their inherent selfishness and egoism, desires greater power and glory. In absence of a strong governing authority, there will be anarchy. The power of an absolute king is the only way to regulate the behaviour of selfish human beings and achieve order, stability and security within society.

ABSOLUTE MONARCH

Hobbes employs the social contract to legitimise the king's power, arguing that the king derives his authority from the people's consent, thus incorporating an element of democracy. The notion of a contract signifies collective consent, emphasising the voluntary agreement between individuals and the establishment of the state.

The king is not a party to the contract, but the result of it, despite which he holds absolute power. Hobbes elevates the king to the status of a mortal god possessing unlimited power, not bound by any constraints or norms, natural, moral, divine or otherwise. His departure from the views of **Jean Bodin**, who acknowledged the king's subjection to both natural and divine laws, is significant.

Hobbes' stance on democracy is complex. On one hand, he acknowledges the importance of people's consent and the social contract, which aligns with democratic principles. On the other hand, he strongly supports the power of an absolute monarch. While his justification may appear contradictory, it is rooted in his belief that an all-powerful monarch is necessary to maintain order and stability in society. Hobbes' theory thus incorporates elements of both democracy and support for an absolute monarchy.

ABSOLUTE STATE

The state in Hobbes' view holds absolute, indivisible and inalienable power. The commands of the state carry the force of law and are not limited by moral principles, customs or traditions. Hobbes contends that everyone, even dissenting minorities, must obey the state as any opposition to it is deemed unreasonable and threatens the security of entire society.

In advocating for an absolute state, Hobbes leans toward authoritarianism. In arguing that individuals forfeit all their rights to the state, having no recourse against state actions, implies that the state can legitimately resort to coercion. As the government and state derive their authority from the people's consent, any protest against government is seen as a protest against the people themselves. Hobbes' view aligns with **George H. Sabine**'s analogy of the state as a hypothetical corporation where the state's rights supersede those of its members.

Hobbes opposes the idea of separation of government powers and advocates for consolidating the three branches of government—legislative, executive, and judicial—under the state's authority. Echoing Machiavelli, Hobbes advocates for governance based on the fear of punishment. He also places the church entirely under the control of the state, diminishing the role of other institutions in enacting laws contrary to the state's interests. Hobbes' ideas lay the groundwork for the concept of legal sovereignty, further developed by **John Austin** into a more comprehensive framework.

INDIVIDUALISM

Hobbes' concept of government is based on his theory of consent and his strong belief in inherent human rationality. The seeds of liberal ideology can be found in his thought. He views the individual as a rational being and as the fundamental unit of society, forming the basis for the creation of the state and government. The ultimate objective of individuals he believed is self-preservation. If the state fails to ensure the self-preservation of its citizens, individuals have the right to reject its authority. Hobbes thus sees society largely as an aggregation of atomistic individuals.

According to **G. H. Sabine**, individualism is a means, and the absolute state is an end. Hobbes goes to the extent of saying that if the state fails to secure the self-preservation of its citizens, it does not deserve to be obeyed. Hobbes asserts that the state is an artificially created and utilitarian institution, not a divine or a natural one. Drawing from this line of thinking, **A. E. Taylor** argued that Hobbes was an individualist rather than an egoist, and posed a challenge to the church, state and parliament. Hobbes' thinking thus laid the foundation for **Jeremy Bentham**'s utilitarianism, which emphasises the pursuit of the greatest happiness for the greatest number of individuals.

LIBERALISM AND UTILITARIANISM

As a rationalist, Hobbes rejects the unquestioned acceptance of traditions, customs and culture. He asserts that as rational beings, individuals best know their own interests, and that everyone acts out of self-interest. This philosophical foundation laid by Hobbes establishes the basis of liberalism. Liberals also espouse rationalism, individualism, and question the authority of traditions.

Importantly, Hobbes does not oppose the right to property. He acknowledges that the state is a necessary instrument for self-preservation and, therefore, a purely utilitarian institution that emerges from the collective consent of individuals through social contract. However, despite these liberal aspects, Hobbes cannot be classified as a liberal due to his unqualified support for an absolute state.

SECULAR STATE

Hobbes challenges the notion of the Church as a divine institution and instead views it as a creation of the people. As a materialistic thinker, Hobbes rejects the theory of the divine origin of state, and considers the Church to be subordinate to the state. In this, he aligns with **Machiavelli**'s separation of the Church from the state on rational grounds. Hobbes believes that like other institutions, the Church is also created by individuals, but that all institutions are subordinate to the state, which has absolute power.

With respect to the state and religion, Hobbes contends that,

1. Everyone is free to choose their faith. The state does not dictate the faith of individuals.
2. Religious beliefs are subjective, not objective truths. The institution of state is necessary to contain conflicts arising over religious matters.
3. The Church is an institution like any other. The state holds supreme authority.

DEMOCRACY

Instead of a parliamentary form of government, Hobbes supported a despotic monarchy. Instead of citizens' rights, he supported unlimited powers for the king. He considered the king the embodiment of absolute power, freed from all restrictions, and the ultimate source of all laws. These ideas of Hobbes may seem anti-democratic. However, there are elements in his thought that can be associated with democracy.

1. Hobbes' theory of consent is based on a social contract among people, implying a democratic process of collective agreement.
2. He views the state as a utilitarian institution whose primary function is preserving the lives of its citizens, which aligns with democratic principles of people's welfare.
3. For Hobbes, the creation of the state, society and government are the result of a social contract, involving the consent and participation of the people.
4. If the state fails to protect people's lives and ensure their safety, it is not obligatory upon people to obey the state.
5. Hobbes was the first thinker to recognise the equality of physical and mental abilities among people, which challenges hierarchical systems and supports a democratic notion of equal worth and opportunity.

Therefore, while supporting an absolute state and seeming anti-democratic, Hobbes' ideas also contain elements that resonate with democratic principles such as consent, people's participation and welfare, dissent, and equality.

POLITICAL OBLIGATION

Hobbes' concept of the social contract is not intended to provide a historical account of the origin of the state, but rather a philosophical and hypothetical interpretation to justify the state's necessity and why its orders should be obeyed. Hobbes argues that a powerful state is preferable to anarchy and violent death. The social contract serves to justify the need for a state to ensure the security and wellbeing of individuals.

Hobbes' theory of the social contract is a philosophical exploration of political obligation. According to **Leo Strauss**, the basis of obligation in Hobbes is physical as the state holds absolute power. **A. E. Taylor**, on the other hand, suggests that Hobbes' political obligation is derived from the law of nature, which is synonymous with the law of prudence. **Michael Oakeshott** contends that Hobbes' notion of obligation is comprehensive, encompassing physical, rational and moral obligations. The contract is established for the rational self-preservation of individuals, and in transferring all power to the king, it becomes a moral obligation for people to obey the orders of the state. The state, being the most powerful institution, holds all authority in its hands.

LIBERTY

Hobbes believed that the absence of law is liberty. Law is the command of the all-powerful and despotic king. True liberty cannot be attained in the chaotic state of nature where life is constantly threatened. Liberty needs law, which is only possible under a state. Liberty, for Hobbes, does not imply a disregard or violation of law or harming others. The actions of individuals must be restricted and subject to limitations.

Hacker argues that the idea of liberty is present in Hobbes' philosophy, and he distinguishes the Hobbesian state as absolutist rather than totalitarian. A totalitarian state implies a fascist regime that controls every aspect of an individual's life. In contrast, individuals under the Hobbesian state are free to do as they please, except oppose the state. Challenging the state's authority would lead to a return to the state of nature, where true liberty cannot be enjoyed.

Vaughan criticised Hobbes' conception of liberty, arguing that while liberty is not attainable in a state of anarchy, it is equally lost under an all-powerful state, describing the situation as a choice between falling into the deep sea or into a deep gorge, signifying the loss of liberty in both conditions.

CAPITALIST OR INDIVIDUALIST

C. B. Macpherson, in his work *The Political Theory of Possessive Individualism*, characterises both Hobbes and Locke as proponents of *possessive individualism*. According to Macpherson, Hobbes can be seen as a capitalist thinker who supports market forces and commodifies labour. He criticises Hobbes' concept of the state of nature, arguing that it reflects the values and structures of a capitalist society and suggests that Hobbes constructs a hypothetical state of nature to legitimise and support capitalism.

Critiquing Hobbes' advocacy for absolute power in the hands of a monarch, Macpherson contends that Hobbes supports a despotic and powerful king to safeguard the interests of the capitalist class and maintain peace and stability. Without a strong sovereign, the property and security of the capitalist class would be threatened. However, **Sabine** disagrees with Macpherson, asserting that Hobbes laid the groundwork for individualism rather than solely serving the interests of capitalism.

Hobbes' ideas were shaped not only by the political and social context of his time but also by the scientific advancements and intellectual debates that characterised the era. His writings continue to be studied and debated, contributing to the development of political theory and our understanding of human nature and societal governance.

6

JOHN LOCKE (1632–1704)

KEY CONCEPTS

Moral, legal, political and social justice; Marxist theory of justice; procedural theory of justice; distributive justice; Rawlsian theory; libertarian and communitarian view of justice; Dworkin's view, Amartya Sen's view; relationship between liberty, equality and justice

John Locke, born in 1632 in Wrington, Somerset, England, is an English philosopher widely regarded as a founding father of modern philosophical empiricism and political liberalism. His works served as inspiration for both the European Enlightenment and the American Constitution. He lived during a time of conflict between the monarchy and parliamentary democracy. A staunch advocate of rights and liberty, Locke rejected the divine theory of state and strongly supported a limited constitutional government that would safeguard the people's rights and freedoms. Locke is recognised as an individualistic, liberal and empirical thinker.

Locke's philosophical ideas align closely with those of renowned figures in modern science, especially Robert Boyle and Sir Isaac Newton. His political thought was grounded in the idea of a social contract between citizens, and in the importance of tolerance, particularly in religious matters. Many of his political ideas gained acceptance in England following the Glorious Revolution of 1688–89, and in the United States after the country's Declaration of Independence in 1776.

LITERARY CONTRIBUTION

John Locke's most influential and famous works are *An Essay Concerning Human Understanding* (1689), in which he developed his theory of ideas and his account of the origins of human knowledge in experience; and *Two Treatises of Government* (1690), in which he discusses his views on the origins of the state and the social contract, and defends a theory of political authority based on natural individual rights and freedoms, and the consent of the governed. Another notable work is *Letters Concerning Toleration*, where Locke advocates religious tolerance and freedom.

Locke can be regarded as a philosopher of common sense, differing from **Thomas Hobbes** in terms of methodological purity. Locke believed all knowledge is derived from sensory experience. He draws inspiration from medieval traditions, particularly the ideas of **Richard Hooker** in Of the Laws of Ecclesiastical Polity (eight books, 1593–1662), while also embracing empiricism. Locke is a passionate defender of liberty and individual rights. According to **C. L. Wayper**, Locke represents both the culmination of a great tradition (the medieval tradition), and the beginning of another great tradition (liberalism). **Sabine** terms Locke a 'thinker of paradox'. Influenced by Richard Hooker's ideas, while religion and traditions are integral to Locke's thought, he also pioneered the empirical method of inquiry and knowledge. His philosophy reflects the common sense of the British people, who experienced a peaceful revolution.

HUMAN NATURE

Like Hobbes, Locke also supports the social contract theory, but their objectives differ. Locke employs a structure of thought similar to Hobbes. However, unlike Hobbes' pessimistic view of human nature, Locke believes that humans are inherently good and rational beings, even though individuals are pleasure-seeking. In contrast to Hobbes' chaotic, violent, fearful and anarchic view of the state of nature, Locke envisions a peaceful state of nature in which individuals enjoy natural rights, which he asserts inherently exist in the state of nature. For Locke, society itself exists within the state of nature. However, Locke admits that some inconveniences may arise in this state.

Natural Law

Locke's understanding of natural law differs from that of Hobbes, and is influenced by the ideas of the medieval scholar Richard Hooker. According to Locke, natural law is synonymous with divine law. Natural rights, derived from natural law, are seen as religious laws prevalent in the medieval period. Locke believes that natural law is a set of universal principles or moral rules that are inherent in human nature and derive from God's will. According to Locke, these principles are discoverable through reason and apply to all individuals equally.

For Locke, natural law serves as a standard by which human laws should be measured. Human laws should aim to protect natural individual rights such as right to life, liberty and property. If a manmade law contradicts natural law or infringes upon anyone's natural rights, Locke argues that it is illegitimate and one has the right to disobey it. Laws, according to Locke, are not contrary to freedom but a means to facilitate it.

Locke also emphasises the importance of consent in the establishment of political authority and the creation of laws. He asserts that legitimate political authority derives from the consent of the governed, and laws should be made by representatives who act in the best interests of the people. Locke's conception of law thus revolves around the idea of natural law as a moral standard that guides human laws and protects individuals' natural rights, and emphasises the importance of reason and consent.

SOCIAL CONTRACT

Hobbes justified the establishment of absolute monarchy based on the social contract, whereas Locke proposed a modified approach by advocating for a limited constitutional government through the social contract. In the state of nature, initially there was peace, Locke argues, but certain problems arose due to the absence of written laws, a law enforcing authority, and a dispute settlement body like a judiciary. Although the state and society existed in the state of nature, there was a lack of government, which posed a threat to natural rights, particularly the right to property.

To address these issues, the primary objective of the social contract, according to Locke, was to preserve and protect the right to property. However, Locke did not specify the exact number of social contracts, leading to different interpretations by scholars. **G. H. Sabine** suggests that Locke proposed two contracts, with the first establishing society and the second leading to the formation of government. **Ernest Barker** proposes that the first step involves the formation of a contract, while the second step involves the creation of a 'trusteeship'.

In Locke's social contract, only one key right is transferred to the government—the right to punishment. The concept of a *two-stage social contract* is significant for Locke, as according to him, it ensures that a revolution does not result in anarchy. Instead, it simply replaces the government while keeping the state intact.

RIGHT TO FREEDOM AND RELIGIOUS TOLERATION

The concept of law, argues Locke, is not contrary to liberty but a means to preserve liberty. He believed that law protects and enhances liberty, and strongly advocated for a limited constitutional government that would ensure maximum liberty, rejecting the idea of absolute state and despotic monarch proposed by Hobbes.

During the rule of the Stuart monarchy in 1661–1662, conflict arose between the Catholic-inclined monarchy and the majority of English people who were Anglicans. The English Parliament enacted the Clarendon Code, which enforced religious uniformity in worship. Locke, however, strongly opposed religious uniformity and advocated for religious toleration and freedom of worship. In, *A Letter Concerning Toleration*, Locke expressed his views on freedom and religious freedom. He championed religious tolerance, asserting that everyone is entitled to enjoy religious freedom, and argued that the faith of the king or the state cannot be imposed on the subjects.

As a follower of Christianity, he strongly opposed the control of religious sentiments by society or the state. He also believed that the role and functions of the church should not be restricted by coercive powers. The state, being created by the people through a contract, holds the power of punishment. Locke advocated for a secular state where the role of the state is limited, and emphasised the importance of providing individuals with full economic freedom.

NATURAL RIGHTS

Locke is regarded as the father of the theory of natural rights, that is, the right to life, liberty and property. Among these, Locke placed particular emphasis on the right to property, considering it an integral part of the right to life. He believed the acquisition of material property is a result of an individual's capacity and labour. Locke's ideas greatly influenced the framers of the American Constitution, such as **Thomas Jefferson** and **James Madison**. Jefferson, for instance, advocated for the people's right to life, liberty and the pursuit of happiness. The theory of natural rights was further supported by **Thomas Paine** in his work *The Rights of Man* (1792).

Natural rights are inherent and inalienable, or in other words, they can never be repealed or infringed upon. People must not be denied their natural rights, and the purpose of creating a state and government for Locke is to ensure the protection and preservation of these rights against any encroachment. They are moral rights that are not granted by any law or bestowed by the community or state. The state is in fact established to safeguard these rights. **James Tully** describes Locke as the father of constitutional government, highlighting the importance of an individual's sovereignty over their mind and body.

PHILOSOPHER OF REVOLUTION

Locke is often regarded as a 'philosopher of revolution' as his ideas played a significant role in shaping both the American Revolution and the Glorious Revolution of Britain in 1688. British historian **Peter Laslett** noted that Locke's *Two Treatises on Civil Government* was published in 1690, but it was actually written before the events of 1688. Its publication was delayed due to fear of repercussions from the king.

In the case of a revolution, only the government would change, Locke argued, and there would be no anarchy as the state itself would remain intact due to the two-stage social contract. Locke's views on revolution may be summarised as follows:

1. Locke outlined several conditions under which a revolution may be justified:
   i. The king acting in his own self-interest and against the rule of law.

ii. The king interfering with the independent functioning of the legislature.
iii. Changes in the mode of election without the people's consent.
iv. The king surrendering the people to a foreign power.
v. Neglect of legitimate duties by the executive branch.

2. Locke believed that citizens have a right to revolution when their natural rights are violated and their government fails to protect them, and when a government becomes tyrannical and oppressive.
3. The aim of a revolution he said is not to create anarchy but to restore and preserve the people's natural rights, and establish a new government that will better protect them.
4. Locke believed that a revolution should target the government rather than the entire state. He advocated for a limited constitutional government that would replace the oppressive regime while maintaining the continuity of the state.
5. Locke's concept of a *two-stage social contract* suggests that the people enter into a social contract with the government, granting it power to protect their rights. If the government fails to fulfill its obligations, the people have the right to dissolve that contract and establish a new government.

REJECTION OF DIVINE RIGHTS OF KING

Locke made a distinction between *parental authority* and *paternal authority*. Opposing the paternal authority of the state, which is considered natural like the authority of a father in a family, Locke criticised the idea of absolute monarchy and defended the foundation of limited constitutional government in his work *Two Treatises of Civil Government*. His critique was aimed mainly at **Robert Filmer**, the author of *Patriarcha* (1680), who defended the divine rights of the king and claimed that the king possessed a natural authority over his subjects, like a father's authority over his children. Locke disagreed, finding Filmer's theory absurd and indefensible, and asserted that while children are subject to the authority of their father and parent, adult subjects are not minors. Every individual is a child of God, inherently free and equal, and consent must be the only basis for obeying the orders of others, Locke asserted, challenging the authority of patriarchal rule and absolute or divine kingship.

RIGHT TO PROPERTY

Locke is a major proponent of the right to property, which he believes is the 'fruit of labour'. Every individual is the absolute and natural owner of their own mind and body, he asserts, and should have complete control over the property earned through their bodily and intellectual labour. Locke acknowledges that God has provided nature with abundant resources and everyone with equal capacity for labour. When individual labour is combined with natural resources, it becomes that individual's property. The state's main objective is to protect the life and property of individuals, he asserts. Locke's language often carries religious undertones, referring to property as a gift from God.

Locke's *labour theory of value*, which is rooted in these principles, grants individuals the freedom to acquire property. He argues that property is an integral part of individuality and the result of one's labour. Since individuals own their bodies, the property they acquire through their labour rightfully belongs to them. This has been called *possessive individualism*, and linked to the evolution of capitalism. Locke, however, believes that property earned by slaves and tenants would belong to their masters, as separate from the property earned through their own labour.

As discussed earlier, **C. B. Macpherson** argues that in such a framework, the majority of people may be denied their right to own or acquire material property. Characterising Locke as a staunch capitalist, Macpherson contends that Locke's main objective in advocating for the creation of the state and government is to justify the right to property. In Locke's view, people establish a government or a commonwealth in order to secure their property. Other scholars such as **John Dunn** and **Neal Wood** argue that Macpherson distorts history in his interpretation.

Limitations on the Right to Property

According to Locke's principles, no one is entitled to accumulate more than their fair share as everyone has the right to live a free and secure life. People have no right to destroy property or resources that are gifts from God. Locke acknowledges that acquiring property does not require consent from others since everyone has an equal capacity to labour or work, but he believes that individuals should only own a reasonable amount of land so that others are not deprived of their due share.

C. B. Macpherson terms Locke's philosophy of the individual ownership of body–labour–property as 'possessive individualism', and links it directly with capitalism. He argues that while Locke's limitations on the right to property are valid in an agricultural economy, they become meaningless in a capitalist economy. Macpherson suggests that the introduction of currency in modern times has paved the way for the acquisition of unlimited property. Locke's support for a limited and laissez-faire state based on contractual agreements serves the accumulation of capital and the promotion of free trade and business, suggesting his strong support for capitalism.

James Tully disagrees with **Macpherson**'s assessment, arguing that Locke's conception of property is comprehensive, and includes not just material possessions but also capacities of the human mind and body, which are according to Locke the most valuable possessions of individuals. Locke also supported taxation, which demonstrates that he was not solely a supporter of the property-owning class.

LIBERALISM AND CONSTITUTIONALISM

Locke's philosophy is centred on the individual and individual liberty, making him a key figure in the development of liberalism. While Hobbes saw no alternative to absolute government or anarchy, Locke sought a middle ground and advocated for a limited constitutional government. This is considered as Locke's key contribution to the philosophy of liberalism. Locke endorsed the concept of a laissez-faire state, which encompasses two elements:

1. Individuals have the freedom to enter into voluntary agreements and contracts.
2. The government should not act as a paternal figure, interfering excessively in the lives of individuals.

Limited Constitutional Government

Locke's concept of a limited constitutional government includes the following features:

1. Locke advocated for the separation of the three branches of government (legislative, executive and federative) to prevent the concentration of power and the potential for despotism. The legislative branch makes laws; the executive branch implements laws (including judicial functions); the federative branch handles the state's power in international treaties. **Montesquieu** later refined Locke's idea by explicitly defining the three branches of government as the legislature, executive and judiciary.
2. Individuals have the right to revolt against a government that violates their natural rights.
3. Locke believed the state is an artificial institution created by the people, and individuals inherently possess natural rights from birth. To maximise individual liberty, the functions of government must be limited.
4. Locke placed greater importance on reason rather than traditional and conventional beliefs.

5. Locke believed human beings are inherently rational and capable of understanding their best interests, striving to attain maximum pleasure.
6. Locke advocated for a limited role of the state, often referred to as the 'night watchman state'. The government's role should be minimal, and economic affairs should be governed by market forces, driven by the profit motive. He viewed the state as a necessary evil and confined its role to maintaining law and order, protecting citizens from external threats, and ensuring freedom of contract. This approach to governance is believed to benefit society as a whole.

The Paradox in Locke

There is a paradox in Locke's philosophy. While he is often regarded as a modern thinker and the father of liberalism, his ideas were influenced by medieval scholar Richard Hooker. Locke's notions of natural law and natural rights can be traced back to medieval thought. Despite liberalism's emphasis on rationality, Locke's beliefs are rooted in his belief in God. At the same time, he is also a proponent of empiricism, which holds that the existence of objects can be verified through our senses. However, the existence of God and natural law cannot be proven through our senses.

Another paradox lies in Locke's views on contract. He does not explicitly clarify whether there is one contract or two. Natural rights are derived from natural law, which is a metaphysical concept. On the other hand, Locke justifies the right to property based on the *labour theory of value*, which is an empirical idea. This inconsistency leaves the question of the number of contracts unresolved in Locke's philosophy.

Democrat or Capitalist?

Macpherson argued that Locke's ideas exemplify a form of protective democracy. Locke was against the paternal authority of the state and instead laid the groundwork for a constitutional government, where power is transferred to the majority community through the social contract, thus completing the *theory of consent* initiated by Hobbes. Locke's philosophy encompasses democratic values such as liberty and toleration.

However, Macpherson suggested that Locke cannot be strictly categorised as a democrat. One reason for this is that Locke supported the representation of the property-owning class, which implies a more capitalist inclination rather than a purely democratic one. Macpherson's analysis suggests that Locke's stance on property and its representation may overshadow his commitment to the principles of democracy.

COMPARING HOBBES AND LOCKE

Both Hobbes and Locke were influential thinkers of the seventeenth century who wrote during the turbulent period of the English Civil War. However, they held contrasting views on the form of government, the state of nature, and the social contract.

1. Hobbes favoured an all-powerful monarchy, seeing it as necessary to establish order and prevent constant conflict. In contrast, Locke supported a limited and constitutional government, emphasising the protection of individual rights and liberties.
2. Hobbes portrayed the state of nature as a state of perpetual conflict and war, while Locke depicted a state of nature where peace and coexistence were possible.
3. Hobbes believed the social contract was primarily for self-preservation, with individuals surrendering all their rights and powers to the king. Locke's social contract aimed at protecting the life and property of the people, with individuals surrendering only the power of punishment.
4. Both thinkers advocated for the theory of consent and rejected the divine theory of

the state. However, while Hobbes favoured an absolute monarchy, Locke advocated for a limited constitutional government.

5. Hobbes believed that in the aftermath of repudiating the social contract, people would revert to the chaotic state of nature, while Locke posited that the government would dissolve but the state and society would persist, with a new government emerging to replace the old one.

LOCKE'S RELEVANCE TODAY

Locke's ideas continue to be relevant in various aspects of modern society. He introduced the concept of natural rights, laying the foundation for human rights that are widely recognised today. Locke is often hailed as the father of liberalism due to his pioneering work in advocating for freedom and religious toleration. His ideas have had a significant impact on neoliberals like **Friedrich Hayek**. Locke's theories of consent and constitutional government have shaped the foundations of democratic societies around the world, while his contributions to empiricism have greatly influenced the field of philosophy and scientific inquiry.

Even 400 years after its inception, liberalism still remains relevant. Recognition of the right to property as a fundamental human and democratic right, as espoused by Locke, continues to be important. His ideas have garnered universal recognition, and figures like **Francis Fukuyama** argue that liberalism has emerged victorious in the historical ideological battle against communism.

Moreover, liberalism has evolved over time to incorporate new elements that address the changing needs and aspirations of people. It has adapted to fulfill the demands of contemporary society while upholding the core principles put forth by Locke. This adaptability has contributed to the ongoing relevance of Locke's thinking and the enduring influence of liberalism in shaping modern political, social, and economic systems.

Selected writings of Locke:

1. *Four Letters Concerning Toleration* (1689)
2. *A Letter Concerning Toleration* (1689)
3. *Two Treatises of Government* (1689)
4. *An Essay Concerning Human Understanding* (1690)
5. *Some Thoughts Concerning Education* (1693)
6. *The Reasonableness of Christianity* (1695)

7

JEAN-JACQUES ROUSSEAU (1712–1778)

KEY CONCEPTS

Rousseau and romanticism; equality; private property as a social evil; 'noble savage'; popular sovereignty; general will

Jean-Jacques Rousseau, a Swiss-born French philosopher, was born in Geneva in 1712. He is recognised as a prominent advocate of popular sovereignty and also as a theorist of nationalism. Rousseau introduced the concept of direct democracy in the context of modern society. French jurist **Léon Duguit** controversially attributed to Rousseau the role of being the father of Jacobin Despotism, as well as the inspiration behind the absolute doctrines of **Kant** and **Hegel**. His contributions to both political philosophy and moral psychology made him an enduring influence on modern thinkers across disciplines.

In 1749, in an essay competition sponsored by the Academy of Dijon on the topic: 'Has the progress of the sciences and arts contributed to the corruption or the purification of morals?' Rousseau's Discourse on the Sciences and Arts (known as the First Discourse) won first prize, with his theory that social development, including of the arts and sciences, corrodes both civic virtue and individual moral character. The First Discourse (published 1751) is an important work in which Rousseau introduced themes that he developed in his later work, such as the natural virtue of the ordinary person, and the moral corruption nurtured by the human urge to distinction and excellence.

Rousseau's most notable contributions to political philosophy include the *Discourse on the Origin and Basis of Inequality Among Men* (or *Discourse on Inequality*) (1754), the *Discourse on Political Economy* (1755), *The Social Contract* (1762), and *Considerations on the Government of Poland* (1772). Rousseau's central doctrine in politics—that only a state that is guided by the 'general will' of its members is legitimate—is discussed in *The Social Contract.* Another of his works, *An Essay on the Origin of Languages* was published in 1781, after Rousseau's death.

A ROMANTIC THINKER

Rousseau's romanticism is characterised by his emphasis on the individual's connection with nature, his celebration of emotions, his critique of rationalism, and of society. Rousseau rejected the prevailing Enlightenment ideals of reason and progress, instead embracing a more intuitive and emotional approach to understanding the world. Central to Rousseau's worldview is the idea that human beings are essentially and inherently good but are corrupted by society.

Nature: Rousseau saw nature as pure and untainted, an escape from the corrupting influences of civilisation. He celebrated the beauty and authenticity of the natural world and believed that individuals should strive to live in harmony with it. Rousseau believed that humans are inherently good and their corruption and unhappiness stem from the constraints imposed by society, and popularised the slogan 'Back to Nature,' advocating for a return to a more natural and organic way of life.

Emotions: Rousseau argued that reason alone is insufficient for understanding human nature and society, and that emotions, passions and intuition are vital aspects of human experience. He celebrated the expression of authentic emotions and valued individual freedom of thought and feeling.

Rousseau's romanticism encompassed a critique of what he saw as a surfeit of rationality and artificiality of society. He believed that civilisation had led to the erosion of inherent human goodness, freedom, emotions and authenticity. He rejected social conventions, institutions, and inequalities that he saw as constraining individuals and suppressing their natural inclinations, and advocated for a return to a simpler, more authentic way of life where individuals could express their true selves and live in harmony with nature. His ideas had a significant influence on the development of Romanticism as a broader cultural and intellectual movement in the late eighteenth and early nineteenth centuries.

Revolt against Reason

G. H. Sabine notes that despite the fact that Rousseau was writing at the height of the Age of Enlightenment, he held views that were strongly critical of reason, science, progress and intellectual advancement. His early work *Discourses on the Arts and Sciences* (1750) argues that the progress of civilisation has led to the corruption of human nature. Rousseau made a clear distinction between the Natural Man and the Rational Man, and believed that the problems of society stem from excessive emphasis on the rational aspect of human nature.

Rousseau's work *Emile, or On Education* (1762) presents his vision of an ideal education that focuses on nurturing the natural, emotional and moral development of individuals. He stresses the importance of nature, emotions, and hands-on experience in the education of a child, rejecting traditional methods that prioritise strict discipline and academic knowledge. It is worth noting that, unlike most thinkers of his time, Rousseau himself did not receive a formal education.

EQUALITY

Rousseau believed in the natural equality of all human beings, asserting that people are born free and equal, and inequalities arise from societal structures and external factors. In terms of natural or moral equality, Rousseau argued that all individuals possess inherent worth and emphasised the importance of recognising each person's fundamental humanity, dignity, and their shared capacity for reason and moral judgment.

Regarding social or political equality, Rousseau advocated for a form of egalitarianism within society. He believed that true freedom and justice could only be achieved through a *social contract* where individuals voluntarily submit to a *general will* that represents the common good. In this social contract, all citizens have an equal voice and contribute to the formation of laws and decisions that affect the community as a whole.

Rousseau distinguished between two types of inequality.

1. Rousseau acknowledged that physical and mental differences exist among individuals, such as varying strength or intellectual capabilities.
2. Rousseau argued that social and political inequality arises from the establishment of societal structures and becomes manifest with some individuals attaining wealth, respect and power, and others being subjected to subordination and exploitation.

Rousseau contends that the development of reason contributed to the institutionalisation of inequality. Rousseau opens *The Social Contract* with the profound statement: 'Man is born free, but is everywhere in chains.' He posits that initially people lived in harmonious communities, and advocates for a free and equal society where no one would be so wealthy as to buy others, and no one would be so impoverished as to be compelled to sell themselves.

Rousseau's vision of equality went beyond mere legal or formal equality, underlining the need for equal political participation and an equitable distribution of resources. His concept of equality was closely tied to his ideas of popular sovereignty and direct democracy. Rousseau argued that in a just society, all individuals should participate directly in decision-making processes, rather than delegating power to representatives.

However, while he championed equality, Rousseau also held views that are contradictory, such as his belief in the inherent differences between men and women, and that women were inherently inferior and artificial beings. Rousseau's commitment to the freedom and equality of *all* citizens is also limited by the fact that those citizens are exclusively male: women are subject to the authority of the state, and have no voice in the determination of the general will. This has been critiqued by feminist thinkers such as **Mary Wollstonecraft**, and others. Nonetheless, Rousseau's ideas on equality played a significant role in shaping subsequent discussions on social and political justice, challenged prevailing notions of inequality and advocated for a more egalitarian society.

PROPERTY AS A SOCIAL EVIL

Rousseau believed that the concept of private property was a key source of social inequality and the root cause of many social evils. He argued that in the state of nature, when humans lived in their original condition, there was no notion of private property and individuals collectively possessed and shared the resources of the earth. As society progressed and people became more civilised, the concept of private property emerged. The idea of 'mine and thine' led to individuals enclosing or fencing their land for the first time, thereby laying the foundation for the formation of the state.

In his *Discourse on Inequality*, Rousseau asserts that ownership of wealth and property led to social hierarchies and dominance as those who owned property also had the means to exert control over others who lacked property. This created division, conflict and exploitation, and the introduction of private property rights led to inequities in wealth, power and social status, as well as the emergence of social classes, he argued. Rousseau considers three types of inequality:

1. Economic inequality between the rich and the poor.
2. Social inequality between masters and slaves.
3. Political inequality between rulers and the ruled.

Rousseau criticised the unequal distribution of property and wealth, as it caused individuals to become dependent on others for their basic needs and subjected them to the authority and power of the property-owning class. He advocated for a more communal and egalitarian society, where property would be held collectively and resources would be shared to ensure the wellbeing of all members of society.

Rousseau's ideas on property have influenced socialist thinkers, who see private property as a source of social disparities and injustice. Some Marxist scholars, such as **Lucio Colletti**, consider Rousseau to be a precursor to **Marx**, highlighting the resonance between Rousseau's critiques of property and Marx's theories on capitalism and class struggle. Rousseau's views on property laid the groundwork for later debates on property rights, social justice, and the role of property in shaping societal dynamics.

HUMAN NATURE

Rousseau asserted the existence of a natural law governing human society. He believed that human beings possess an instinct for self-preservation and a natural aversion to causing harm to others unless their own survival is threatened. In the state of nature, humans were seen as *noble savages*, embodying a natural sense of compassion and self-love. This innate capacity for empathy allowed individuals to understand and sympathise with the pain and suffering of others.

However, this harmonious state of nature gradually transformed into a society marked by conflict. As people began to claim ownership over land and resources, inequalities emerged, leading to competition, envy, and ultimately, a departure from the harmony of nature. Rousseau viewed the emergence of property as a pivotal moment in human history, introducing division and conflict that distorted the natural inclinations of individuals. While humans possess an inherent capacity for self-love and sympathy, the introduction of property created a system where self-interest and the pursuit of personal gain took precedence over communal wellbeing.

Rousseau believed that humans are inherently good, but are corrupted by society, through the introduction of property, social hierarchies, and rationality. Rousseau viewed emotions and intuition as essential aspects of human nature, guiding human actions. He emphasised the importance of moral growth and believed that individuals must strive to cultivate their natural goodness through education, self-reflection, and a return to nature, simplicity and authenticity.

FREEDOM

Rousseau explores three distinct forms of freedom in *The Social Contract*: natural, civil, and moral freedom. He presents a framework that encompasses different levels of human will: private, general, and corporate will.

Private will refers to the selfish interests of individuals as natural beings.

General will is where individuals identify with the collective as citizens and prioritise the common good over personal interests, allowing for equal freedom under a set of laws.

Corporate will is where individuals identify with the interests of a particular subset of the population.

Further, according to Rousseau, human beings possess two kinds of wills: the *lower will* associated with physical desires and passions, and the *higher will* associated with moral choices. For Rousseau, freedom entails obedience to the *higher will*, which represents the notion of positive liberty and involves moral and virtuous actions. He argues that acting in accordance with the lower automatically compels individuals to also act according to their higher will.

Rousseau's concept of freedom has been described as paradoxical and forced, because individuals acting on their lower will are compelled to be free through their alignment with the higher will. This notion has led some, such as **Jacob Talmon** in his book *The Origins of Totalitarian Democracy* (1952), to argue that Rousseau's ideas laid the foundation for modern totalitarianism.

Rousseau's dominant concern is to find ways of preserving human freedom in a world where people are increasingly dependent on one another to satisfy their needs. These needs are material and psychological, of which the latter is more important. In modern society, individuals receive their identity and value from the opinion of others, which Rousseau sees as destructive of individual authenticity and corrosive of freedom.

He explores two means of attaining and preserving freedom: the first is political, aimed at building institutions that nurture the co-existence of free and equal citizens in a community where they themselves are sovereign; the second is a project for education that nurtures autonomy while avoiding the most destructive forms of self-interest. While Rousseau believes that the peaceful co-existence of individuals in relations of equality and freedom is possible, he is however pessimistic that humanity will escape from its dystopia of domination, alienation, and unfreedom.

POPULAR SOVEREIGNTY

Incorporating certain elements of sovereignty as discussed by **Thomas Hobbes**, Rousseau described sovereignty as an absolute, indivisible, supreme and inalienable power vested in the state. However, Rousseau's conception of the state differed from Hobbes' in that it had a moral dimension. According to Rousseau, citizens have a moral obligation to obey the laws and orders of the state. Unlike Hobbes, Rousseau believed that the power of sovereignty did not reside in any specific ruler or individual but was derived from the entire community. This view aligns more closely with **John Locke**'s ideas. Rousseau's concept of popular sovereignty can be seen as dismantling the concentrated absolute power of Hobbes' state as a Leviathan-like figure.

Rousseau was a strong proponent of direct democracy and criticised representative democracy as being ineffective. He emphasised the importance of nationalism and considered it a necessary element of civic religion, as discussed in his work *Considerations on the Government of Poland* (1772). He believed that the wellbeing of the community should take precedence over individual interests, highlighting the significance of collective welfare.

State as an Organism

George H. Sabine observed that Rousseau's ideas emphasise the value of community in the modern age. Rousseau perceives society and state as an organism, emphasising the importance of the state and society over the individual, and the interconnectedness and interdependence of individuals within a collective framework. Rousseau rejects the notion of an atomistic society, which prioritises individual autonomy and isolation.

It is also important to note, however, that Rousseau's notion of popular sovereignty did not impose restrictions on its exercise, which led some such as **Jacob Talmon** to interpret his ideas as precursors to *totalitarianism*. Talmon believed that Rousseau's emphasis on the *collective will* of the community and the subordination of individual interests to the *general will* could lead to the suppression of individual liberties and the dominance of a centralised state authority. Talmon viewed Rousseau's concept of freedom as a paradoxical notion, where individuals are compelled to act according to their higher will, which is determined by the collective. Talmon also criticised Rousseau's rejection of pluralism and his vision of a homogeneous society, arguing that it disregarded the diversity of individual interests and perspectives. He saw Rousseau's emphasis on the general will as a potential source of authoritarianism and the concentration of power in the hands of a few.

SOCIAL CONTRACT

In *The Social Contract*, Rousseau explored the concept of natural liberty and natural law, as it existed in the state of nature, which he believed represented a peaceful and harmonious state of existence. He described the state of nature as an evolutionary process, identifying two key revolutions that shaped human civilisation. The first revolution, characterised by communal life within families, was considered a golden age for humanity. It marked the advent of practices such as metallurgy and agriculture, which contributed to the progress of society. However, Rousseau argued that the second revolution, marked by the discovery of iron and the cultivation of crops, led to the emergence of private property and subsequent inequalities, ultimately disrupting the harmony of civilisation.

Recognising the need to address these inequalities, Rousseau proposed the *social contract* as a means to protect civil liberty. In this regard, his approach shares similarities with the ideas of **Hobbes**. However, Rousseau believed in a single social contract rather than multiple contracts among individuals. According to him, power is transferred to the entire community, not just the majority as advocated by **Locke**. The subject matter of the social contract in Rousseau's view aligns with Locke's perspective. It is important to note that while Rousseau and Locke shared some similarities in their ideas on the social contract and civil liberties, they also had significant differences in their views on the nature of power and the role of the community in governing.

GENERAL WILL

Rousseau's concept of the general will revolves around the idea of the common good. The general will represents the collective will of the people and encompasses the sum of their individual real wills. It is considered 'general' because it reflects the will of all and is directed towards the common good of society. It is important to note that the general will may not always align with the will of the majority. In fact, even the will of a single individual can be considered the general will if it is oriented towards the common good.

In *The Social Contract*, Rousseau discusses and defends at length his central political doctrine—that only a state that is guided by the general will of all its members can be considered legitimate. Rousseau thus equates the general will with sovereignty, freedom, and the state, and as a guiding principle for the governance and organisation of society. It is through the general will that the social contract is established, as individuals willingly come together to form a community governed by the principles of the common good.

However, Rousseau's concept of the general will is neither objective nor tangible; it is an abstract idea. As an idealist philosopher, Rousseau acknowledges that the general will exists as a conceptual notion rather than a concrete reality.

SEEDS OF REVOLUTION

Rousseau's ideas had a significant impact on the socio-political landscape of his time. His influence in shaping the ideological foundations of the French Revolution, and on **Maximilien Robespierre**, one of its most controversial figures, was profound and far-reaching. **Louis Auguste Blanqui**, a socialist and revolutionary thinker, was also inspired by Rousseau's ideas, finding resonance in his calls for social justice and transformation.

Rousseau's concepts of popular sovereignty, social contract and the general will, provided a powerful ideological basis for challenging the absolute monarchy and aristocratic rule that characterised pre-revolutionary France. His emphasis on the sovereignty of the people, and on a government founded on the consent and participation of the people, directly influenced the French revolutionaries' call for a democratic and participatory form of government.

However, it is important to note that Rousseau himself did not advocate for violent revolution, nor endorsed the reign of terror that accompanied the French Revolution. He believed in a peaceful transformation of society through the consensual establishment of a social contract.

Rousseau's thinking has had a profound influence on later philosophers and political theorists, although the tensions and ambiguities in his work have meant that his ideas have been interpreted and developed in radically incompatible and divergent ways. In modern political philosophy, it is possible to detect influences of Rousseau in liberal theories, communitarian ideas, civic republicanism, and in theories of deliberative and participatory democracy.

8

HEGEL (1770–1831)

KEY CONCEPTS

Civil society; philosophy of history; dialectics

Born in 1770 in Stuttgart, Germany, Georg Wilhelm Friedrich Hegel was a prominent philosopher and professor at Jena University. One of Hegel's notable statements is that the state represents the march of God on Earth. He views the state as a moral and supreme entity, a political community formed through the collective efforts of a group of individuals to lead a communal life. For Hegel, the state holds greater significance than the family or civil society, as it is not a natural institution like the family but rather a social construct. Hegel considers the state as a necessary precondition for the realisation of freedom within society.

Contrary to the tradition of the social contract, Hegel rejects the idea that the state arises from a voluntary agreement among individuals, and instead advocates for an organic conception of the state, emphasising its intrinsic nature and evolution. Hegel was influenced by the ideas of German poet **Johann Gottfried Herder**, who explored the idea of the nation and cultural identities. Hegel's philosophy encompasses various aspects of human existence, including the role of the state.

Some of Hegel's most important works include:

The German Constitution (1802), *The Phenomenology of Spirit* (1807), *Science of Logic* (1812), *The Encyclopedia of Philosophical Sciences* (1817), *Lectures on Aesthetics* (1818), *Elements of the Philosophy of Right* (1821), *Lectures on the Philosophy of Religion* (1827), and *Lectures on the Philosophy of History* (1857).

CIVIL SOCIETY

Hegel, as a Western philosopher, made a significant distinction between civil society and the state. According to him, the family is a natural institution, but in modern society, it is based on consent, mutual recognition and love. The family represents a particular domain of altruism, where love and care are directed towards one's family members. It is a sphere where individuals are willing to make sacrifices for the sake of their family.

In contrast, civil society exists as a separate entity, encompassing a broader concept characterised by universal egoism, where individuals pursue their self-interests. Hegel describes civil society as consisting of at least four different systems or institutions.

1. The first system is the system of *needs*, which involves the production and exchange of commodities.
2. The second system is the *administration of justice*, ensuring security and protecting property rights.

3. The third system is the *police*, which, in Hegel's understanding, refers to the welfare system aimed at promoting people's wellbeing.
4. The fourth system is the *corporation*, representing associations of workers and trade industries.

Significantly, Hegel uses the term 'police' to mean the welfare system within civil society. He believes a welfare state is necessary for individual freedom. The state, on the other hand, represents a domain of universal altruism, where the focus is on the wellbeing and welfare of everyone. Hegel also recognises bureaucracy, which he identifies as the *universal class*, to be an integral part of civil society.

FREEDOM

According to Hegel, freedom has a positive nature that goes beyond the mere fulfillment of desires. Hegel defines freedom as self-determination, the ability to make choices and act according to one's own will. Unlike **Hobbes**' understanding of freedom, for Hegel, freedom entails obedience to the order of the state.

Hegel argues that animals are not free because they are governed by drives and instincts and lack the capacity for self-determination. In contrast, human beings possess the faculty of *willing*, which is not separate from thinking but rather a particular mode of thinking. *Will*, in Hegel's view, is the translation of thought into action and existence. Further, human beings possess the faculty of consciousness, which distinguishes them from animals. Hegel emphasises that humans are primarily driven by their will rather than mere desires.

He defines freedom as the state of *being with oneself in an other*, suggesting that freedom involves self-control and self-acceptance. It is an attempt to categorise the events of the mind from the inside. It suggests that individuals are only truly free when they are able to recognise and reconcile their own subjective desires and needs with the objective reality of the world around them. This idea is closely related to Hegel's concept of *absolute spirit*, which posits that individuals can only truly understand themselves and their place in the world by understanding the larger social and historical context in which they exist.

Organic State: As an idealist, Hegel upholds the concept of the *organic state*. He asserts that the state holds greater importance than the individual and that it is not an artificial construct arising from a social contract. Hegel sees the state as an inherent and essential institution, embodying the collective spirit and functioning as an organic entity in society.

Real is Rational: Hegel's famous assertion 'real is rational and rational is real' encapsulates his belief that reality and reason are interconnected. According to Hegel, history represents the progressive development of reason or consciousness. The state, in particular, represents the pinnacle of this rational development. While Hegel acknowledges the supremacy of the state, he views it as a manifestation of reason itself, emphasising that true freedom can be found within the state.

Universal Spirit: Regarding human development, Hegel conceives of the universe as *Geist*, which can be understood as mind or spirit. Geist is not limited to the mind of an individual but encompasses a universal spirit. It is the concept of Being, with its opposite being Nothing. The synthesis of being and nothing leads to Becoming. The universal spirit then manifests itself in the material world, reflecting its own nature. This material reflection results in the evolution of various societal institutions such as the family, civil society, and ultimately the state. Hegel disagrees with **Locke**'s perspective that civil society is solely a sphere of personal freedom. Hegel also contests **Kant**'s notion that man is an end in itself.

PHILOSOPHY OF HISTORY

Hegel is a pioneering Western philosopher who introduced the concept of the evolution of history and formulated the dialectical method as a means to understand historical progression. *Dialectics* revolves around three key stages:

1. *Thesis*: The original idea or concept.
2. *Antithesis*: The contradiction or force opposing the original idea.
3. *Synthesis*: The combination of the positive aspects from both the thesis and antithesis.

Hegel believed that history unfolds as the evolution of human freedom, and the development of consciousness towards freedom progresses throughout human history. He identified distinct phases in the historical development of freedom.

1. *Oriental despotism*: This phase was characterised by regions such as China, India and Persia, where only a single individual or monarch held the status of being free.
2. *Greek city-state*: In this phase, some men within the Greek city-states experienced a certain degree of freedom.
3. *Roman Empire*: With the emergence of Christianity in the modern age, the concept of freedom expanded to encompass all human beings. Hegel observed that freedom is not innate or inborn but is gradually recognised and granted.
4. *German nation-state*: Hegel saw the true realisation of freedom occurring within the context of the state. The German nation-state represented for him an ideal embodiment of freedom.

Through these distinct phases, Hegel emphasised the progressive development of freedom throughout history, with each stage building upon the previous one. The culmination of this development is the establishment of a nation-state where he believed true freedom is attainable.

IMPACT OF HEGEL

Hegel's impact on political thought is complex and multifaceted. While he influenced thinkers across the ideological spectrum, his ideas have been subject to diverse interpretations and critiques, highlighting the ongoing debates surrounding his philosophy and its implications for contemporary political systems and individual freedoms.

One such thinker is **T. H. Green**, a liberal political theorist who was influenced by Hegel's ideas. Green is often associated with Neo-Hegelianism, as he incorporated Hegelian concepts into his own idealistic strand of liberalism, which emphasises the importance of ideas and values in shaping political systems. Another prominent figure influenced by Hegel is **Karl Marx**, who drew upon Hegel's dialectical method in his theory of historical materialism to develop his critique of capitalism and the concept of class struggle.

However, there are differing interpretations of Hegel's political implications. In his book *The Open Society and Its Enemies*, philosopher **Karl Popper** argued that Hegel's ideas were contrary to principles of liberty and democracy, and suggested that Hegel's philosophy laid the foundation for authoritarian ideologies such as fascism.

9

MARY WOLLSTONECRAFT (1759–1797)

KEY CONCEPTS

Critique of Burke; critique of Rousseau; feminism; equality of public domain

Mary Wollstonecraft was born in Spitalfields, London, in 1759. A passionate advocate for educational and social equality for women, she was one of the founding feminist philosophers who influenced and inspired generations of feminist scholars and activists. Wollstonecraft's works included a pamphlet titled *Thoughts on the Education of Daughters* (1786).

In *A Vindication of the Rights of Woman* (1792), one of the earliest and most influential works of feminist philosophy, Wollstonecraft responds to educational and political theorists of the eighteenth century who did not believe women should receive a rational education. Drawing inspiration from the ideals of the French and American Revolutions, she challenged societal norms and advocated for women's rights. In her association with **Gilbert Imlay**, and later her marriage with **William Godwin**, considered one of the forefathers of the anarchist movement, she delved further into progressive political thought.

CRITIQUE OF BURKE

In response to **Edmund Burke**'s *Reflections on the Revolution in France* (1790), which defended constitutional monarchy, aristocracy, and the Church of England, Wollstonecraft published *A Vindication of the Rights of Men, in a Letter to the Right Honourable Edmund Burke* (1790), attacking aristocracy and advocating for republicanism. Wollstonecraft not only targeted monarchy and hereditary privilege but also criticised the gendered language Burke used to uphold and glorify them. Burke associated the beautiful with weakness and femininity, and the sublime with strength and masculinity. Wollstonecraft turned these definitions against him, arguing that his dramatic portrayals transformed his readers—the citizens—into impressionable women easily swayed by appearances. *A Vindication of the Rights of Men* (1790) marked Wollstonecraft's first explicitly political and feminist work, in which she denounced Burke's defence of an unequal society that relied on the passivity of women, and also made her famous. According to **Claudia L. Johnson**, it was in the process of writing it that Wollstonecraft discovered the subject that would occupy her for the rest of her career.

CRITIQUE OF ROUSSEAU

In *A Vindication of the Rights of Woman, with Strictures on Political and Moral Subjects* (1792),

Wollstonecraft criticises writers like **James Fordyce**, **John Gregory** and **Jean-Jacques Rousseau**, who sought to deny women an education. In *Émile* (1762), Rousseau had famously said that women should be educated solely for the pleasure of men. Wollstonecraft's powerful rebuttal challenged these prevailing views and argues for women's right to an education that matches their social position—a position she then redefines. She asserts that women are crucial to society because they educate its children and because they can be companions to their husbands, rather than mere wives. Instead of viewing women as decorative objects or property to be traded in marriage, she insists that they are human beings deserving of the same fundamental rights and respect as men.

Rousseau did not support equal educational opportunities for women, contending that women are more emotional, and should prioritise the interests of their families over those of the nation. Wollstonecraft disagreed, arguing that the subordinate position of women contradicts principles of reason, liberty and self-determination. The marginalised status of women is not a natural order but a social construct, she asserted, arguing that education should promote personal growth and empowerment rather than reinforce subordination. She argued that reason and freedom were of utmost importance to women, who had been socially subjugated due to prevailing customs and mores, and strongly advocated for women to have equal access to education and opportunities for their intellectual and personal growth.

EQUALITY OF PUBLIC DOMAIN

Wollstonecraft did not challenge the institution of family or the traditional responsibilities associated with it. Instead, she emphasised the need for a more liberal outlook that would empower women within the family structure. She advocated for the recognition of women's dignity and self-worth, highlighting the importance of expanding their opportunities beyond menial occupations confined to the domestic sphere. Wollstonecraft believed that enabling women to pursue meaningful roles outside the family and in the public domain would ultimately enhance their contributions within the household. Her critique was not aimed at women's position in society per se, but rather at a society that treated women as mere property, denying them agency and equal rights.

SEEDS OF RADICAL FEMINISM

Wollstonecraft can be primarily classified as a liberal feminist who critically examines the subordination of women. However, some of her statements align closely with radical feminism. She expressed the view that marriage could be akin to legal prostitution, highlighting the unequal power dynamics and societal expectations placed upon women. Wollstonecraft also denounced the notion that women were mere convenient slaves, emphasising how the values of oppression and subjugation permeated institutions such as the monarchy, the church, and the military, recognising that without equal rights and opportunities for both men and women, any pursuit of justice would remain incomplete.

IMPACT

In the inaugural volume of their influential work, *History of Women's Suffrage* (1881), American feminists **Susan B. Anthony** and **Elizabeth Cady Stanton** included Mary Wollstonecraft's name on the dedication page alongside other notable figures in a gesture of respect and admiration. Wollstonecraft's profound impact on the feminist movement resonated with these trailblazing suffragettes, acknowledging her indelible contribution to the cause. **Virginia Woolf** referred to Wollstonecraft's life as an experimental journey, emphasising the pioneering nature of her ideas and actions.

Wollstonecraft's ideas continue to inspire contemporary feminist movements and contribute to ongoing discussions surrounding gender equality and the empowerment of women. Her critical examination of social norms and her call for equal rights remain significant contributions to the advancement of feminist thought.

In addition to her treatises, Wollstonecraft wrote two novels that demonstrated her political and feminist ideas: *Mary, A Fiction* (1788) and *Maria: Or, the Wrongs of Woman* (1798). She also wrote *Original Stories from Real Life* (1788), aimed at children.

10

JOHN STUART MILL (1806–1873)

KEY CONCEPTS

Utilitarianism; individualism and liberalism; freedom of speech and expression; liberty; harm principle; women's suffrage; Mill on democracy

John Stuart Mill was born in 1806 in London, England, during the era of the Industrial Revolution and the emergence of capitalism. He was educated by his father, Scottish philosopher, historian and economist **James Mill**, under the guidance of **Jeremy Bentham** and **Francis Place**, in pursuance of his father's aim of cultivating a genius intellect dedicated to advancing the cause of utilitarianism. Regarded as the most influential English-language philosopher of the nineteenth century, Mill was a naturalist, a utilitarian and liberal who combined the best of eighteenth-century Enlightenment thinking with emerging currents of nineteenth-century Romantic and historical philosophy.

LITERARY CONTRIBUTION

A member of the Liberal Party, Mill is a key figure in classical liberalism who contributed to social theory, political theory and political economy. He championed individual liberty and opposed unlimited state and social control. Following Jeremy Bentham as a proponent of utilitarianism, Mill explored scientific methodology through the works of others such as **William Whewell**, **John Herschel**, and **Auguste Comte**. Mill's transformative critique of Bentham's utilitarianism is one of his greatest contributions. He was also deeply influenced by moral and romantic writers like Samuel Taylor Coleridge and William Wordsworth, and sought to humanise and refine the principles of utilitarianism. Author of the early feminist work *The Subjection of Women*, Mill was also the second Member of Parliament to call for women's suffrage after **Henry Hunt** in 1832. His most important works include *System of Logic* (1843), *Principles of Political Economy* (1848), *On Liberty* (1859), *Considerations on Representative Government* (1861), *Utilitarianism* (1861), *An Examination of Sir William Hamilton's Philosophy* (1865), *The Subjection of Women* (1869) and *Three Essays on Religion* (1874).

UTILITARIANISM

Jeremy Bentham, a radical thinker, brought about a significant shift in the foundations of liberalism established by **John Locke**. He introduced the principle of pleasure and pain as the basis of defining liberalism, giving rise to utilitarianism as a variant of liberalism. Utilitarians, like other liberals, uphold the values of democracy, individual rights, and liberty. Additionally, they support a capitalist economy, aligning them with the liberal ideology. However, utilitarians differ from Locke in that they do not adhere to the principles of social contract and natural rights.

Mill, also a utilitarian, shares the belief in the principle of pleasure and pain. However, he is regarded as the last of the utilitarians and the first individualist because he prioritised moral development and liberty over mere pleasure. For Mill, moral development and the attainment of liberty hold greater importance than mere pleasure and welfare. He introduced the concept of three dimensions of human behaviour: the *aesthetic* dimension, the *sympathetic* dimension, and the *moral* dimension. By acknowledging these, Mill emphasised the significance of aesthetics, empathy, and morality in shaping human conduct.

INDIVIDUALISM AND LIBERALISM

Liberalism and utilitarianism both advocate for individual liberty and rights, as well as support constitutional democratic governments. They view the state as a mechanism or tool. However, Locke justifies liberalism based on the concept of natural rights, while utilitarians believe in the principle of pleasure and pain. Mill, building upon utilitarianism, provided a new foundation for liberalism. According to Mill, anything that increases pleasure has utility, and he extended this utilitarian argument to justify the existence of the state and government. Since the state and government can maximise the pleasure of individuals, they have utility. Mill can therefore be considered an individualist. However, he also recognises the importance of a limited and constitutional government in maximising pleasure, thus making him a liberal.

The idea of individualism can be traced back to Hobbes, but Mill became the first liberal philosopher to emphasise the moral and virtuous nature of human beings in the modern era. Mill asserts that societies are composed of individuals who possess moral and virtuous qualities, and believes that the development of a civilised society depends on the inherent goodness of individuals—a perspective that reveals the influence of Greek thought and philosophy on him. As a Member of Parliament, Mill viewed politics as a means for engaging in social service. He argued that the worth of a state (or society) is determined by the worth of its individuals. Unlike Bentham, who focused on the maximisation of personal pleasure, Mill was influenced by the Prussian philosopher **Wilhelm von Humboldt**'s belief that inner development holds greater importance than external progress.

ON LIBERTY

In his influential work 'On Liberty,' Mill provides a comprehensive analysis of the concept of liberty. According to Mill, any form of restraint is inherently negative, and true liberty is characterised by the absence of such restraints. He presents a compelling argument in favour of liberty, whose significance is considered to be on par with that of **John Milton**'s famous *Areopagitica* (1644), one of the most impassioned and enduring philosophical defences of the right to freedom of speech and expression, published at the height of the English Civil War.

In the nineteenth century, Mill asserts that liberty is crucial for moral, spiritual, intellectual, and human development. He defines liberty as the absence of restrictions and strongly opposes any limitations imposed on it. He identifies two types of liberty:

1. Freedom of speech and expression, where censorship is not permitted.
2. Freedom of action, which he further divides into two categories: *self-regarding actions*, that primarily affect oneself and do not infringe upon the rights or well-being of others; and *other-regarding actions*, that affect others and require consideration of their rights and wellbeing.

Mill's exploration of liberty thus highlights the importance of both individual autonomy and the ethical responsibilities individuals have towards one another.

FREEDOM OF SPEECH AND EXPRESSION

Mill's argument for freedom of speech and expression underscores the importance of individual autonomy, fallibility of individuals, societal development, and the need to guard against the tyranny of the majority in order to uphold liberty and foster progress in society.

1. **Individual Autonomy:** A liberal and an individualist, Mill asserts that individuals are sovereign owners and masters of their bodies and minds. Therefore, liberty is crucial for personal development. Freedom of speech and expression is a fundamental aspect of liberty, where everyone should have the right to express themselves freely. Liberty is an end in itself, not just a means to obtain pleasure. Liberty allows individuals to debate and to voice dissenting opinions, even against prevailing societal norms. A conflict of opinions is necessary to arrive at truth, Mill asserts.
2. **Truth is Multidimensional:** Mill opposes any restrictions on freedom of speech and expression because silencing others implies having a monopoly on truth, which is not tenable. There is nothing like perfect or absolute truth. Truth is always multidimensional and subjective. No one can claim that their opinion is perfect or infallible. Mill values the importance of a diversity of opinions and ideas, and the necessity for debates and dialogues to arrive at the truth. All ideas should be respected, he argues, as over time, the truth will prevail.
3. **Societal Progress:** Employing Charles Darwin's theory of *survival of the fittest* in his defence of freedom of speech and expression, Mill argues that truth emerges and survives after conflict between truth and falsehood. It weakens superstition, falsehood and conservative opinion, leading to progress and prosperity. Liberty of expression is thus vital for the moral development of individuals and equally important for the progress of society.
4. **Against Moral Policing:** Mill, however, highlights the dangers of moral policing as it poses a significant threat to liberty. The tyranny of the majority tends to suppress dissent and disagreement, often in the name of customs and traditions. Mill points out historical examples, such as the crucifixion of Jesus and the poisoning of Socrates, to illustrate how the tyranny of the majority can undermine liberty. He draws upon **Alexis de Tocqueville**, who emphasised that liberty can be absent even in democratic nations.

THE HARM PRINCIPLE

In addition to advocating for freedom of speech and expression, John Stuart Mill also upholds the importance of freedom of action, including the freedom to form unions and associations. However, unlike freedom of speech and expression, Mill recognises that freedom of action is not absolute. Actions that interfere with the lives of others are not permitted in the name of liberty. The *harm principle* highlights the balance between individual freedom and the need to prevent harm to others. While self-regarding actions should generally be free from interference, limitations can be justified when actions have a detrimental impact on the rights and wellbeing of others. Mill says: 'the only purpose for which power can be rightfully exercised over any member of a civilised community, against his will, is to prevent harm to others.' Meaning that an individual's action can be justifiably encroached upon if and only if that action might harm another individual. It may not however be prudent to intervene in all cases in which it is considered legitimate to do so. In this sense, the harm principle states the conditions under which interference is *permissible*—not the conditions under which interference is *desirable*.

Mill distinguishes between two types of individual actions:

1. **Self-Regarding Actions:** Individuals are free to engage in actions that pertain solely to their own lives, such as smoking or walking. This underscores Mill's individualist perspective, emphasising that nobody should interfere in the personal domain of others.
2. **Other-Regarding Actions:** Actions that have an impact on the actions of others are subject to restrictions. If an individual's actions harm others, the state has the authority to intervene, as everyone is entitled to the same amount of liberty. In addition to limitations imposed on other-regarding actions, various restrictions may be placed on individuals for the safety and security of the state and society. For instance, a police officer is prohibited from consuming alcohol while on duty. During emergencies, limitations on liberty can be imposed to ensure the wellbeing of the community.

MILL'S VERSION OF BENTHAM'S DEMOCRACY

Jeremy Bentham's concept of democracy is centred around the idea of equal representation, and the pursuit of the greatest happiness of the greatest number of people. He advocated for 'one person, one vote,' stressing the importance of counting everyone equally in a democratic society, with no one being given more weight than others. He opposed the idea of parliamentarians receiving salaries, believing it would help contain corruption and ensure that the focus remains on public welfare. Bentham endorsed the secret ballot system to enable individuals to express their choices without fear of coercion or influence.

Mill, however, criticised Bentham's version of democracy, considering it to be flawed, and in his work *Representative Government*, proposed modifications to it. In this, Mill was heavily influenced by **Alexis De Tocqueville**'s observations in *Democracy in America*, where he noted the presence of a 'Tyranny of the Majority' instead of true democracy. Mill's version of democracy incorporates the following features:

1. Mill believed that democracy should guarantee freedom of speech and expression. He opposed Bentham's 'one person, one vote' idea and instead favoured plural voting, where educated and affluent individuals were entitled to cast multiple votes.
2. Mill advocated for representative democracy, emphasising the need for fair representation of all sections of society, including minorities, rather than the dominance of the majority alone.
3. In his work *On the Subjection of Women*, Mill strongly supported women's voting rights, in contrast to Bentham, who remained silent on the issue.
4. Mill preferred an open and transparent ballot voting system, viewing voting as a public trust that should be subject to public scrutiny and criticism.
5. Mill opposed the provision of salaries and entitlements to parliamentarians as he believed that politics should be driven by selfless service rather than personal gain.
6. For Mill, democracy was not just a political system but a way of life. Drawing inspiration from Greek philosophers, he emphasised the importance of morality and virtues. Unlike materialistic thinkers from Hobbes to Bentham, Mill believed that genuine progress lay in moral development rather than focusing on physical and material advancements alone.

Mill argued that democracy is the best form of government as it encourages disagreement and dissent while promoting peaceful resolution of differences. Tolerance is a crucial aspect of democratic societies, and violent means should be avoided for settling disputes. Mill also saw democracy as a means of education, promoting the moral growth of individuals and fostering truthfulness and honesty. Hence, he supported the use of an open ballot. Mill believed that voting is not only a right but also a duty, with citizens acting as judges whose votes determine the future of civilisation. One of Mill's close associates, Lord Lothian, opined that democracy is not a cape that could be gifted by anyone; it is a habit that embodies a belief in aristocracy, giving more to life than merely taking from it.

VOTING RIGHTS FOR WOMEN

Mill is consider as an early supporter of Liberal Feminism. He was a strong advocate for women's voting rights and played a significant role in promoting gender equality. In *The Subjection of Women*, Mill recognised the inherent injustice in denying women the right solely based on gender. He believed women should have equal political rights and opportunities as men, and that political representation was essential for women's emancipation and ability to have a say in shaping the laws that govern society. Women's political participation would also contribute to a more just and progressive society, he asserted. Mill's arguments in defence of women's suffrage in *The Subjection of Women* were along the following lines:

1. The active participation of women in public and political life is crucial for the advancement of England's civilisation.
2. A truly developed civilisation cannot be achieved without achieving gender equality. The progress of Britain's civilisation remains incomplete without ensuring equal opportunities for both men and women.
3. While men may possess physical strength, one must recognise that legal strength should not be equated with muscular power. In an era of technological advancements, physical strength may not necessarily translate into power.
4. Liberty, comparable in importance to basic needs like food and water, must be granted alike to all individuals. Women continue to live under conditions akin to slavery within their families.
5. Women's marriages are often decided by their families, and they frequently become victims of domestic violence. The treatment of women as housebound slaves stems from the denial of their basic right to liberty.
6. Without providing women the opportunity to participate in public and political life, it is unjust to conclude that they are incapable of managing political affairs. Equality in political participation is necessary to evaluate women's potential in the political arena.

Mill's stance on women's voting rights aligned with his broader philosophy of individual liberty and the principle of equality, and was a significant departure from his predecessor Bentham, who did not explicitly address the issue. Mill's advocacy for women's suffrage was influential in the suffrage movement and contributed to the eventual enfranchisement of women in many countries around the world.

A RELUCTANT DEMOCRAT

According to **C. L. Wayper**, Mill's views on democracy have been characterised by critics as those of a 'reluctant democrat,' for a variety of reasons.

1. Mill did not endorse the principle of 'One person, one vote,' which suggests that he was not fully aligned with the core democratic principle of equal voting rights for all individuals.

2. Notwithstanding his views on equality, Mill excluded several groups of individuals from the eligibility to vote: the illiterate, the morally deviant and habitually drunk, legal bankrupts, those unable to pay taxes and dependent on public welfare.
3. Mill displayed more aristocratic tendencies than democratic ones, acknowledging that democracy may not be suitable for every society. He believed that Asian and African countries, in particular, were not yet ready for democracy, and instead recommended for them a form of 'benevolent despotism', which meant that the colonial ruler should not be utterly barbaric towards his subjects.
4. Mill's agreement with the idea of the 'White Man's Burden', as articulated by **Rudyard Kipling**, further confirms his conviction that democracy should be adopted based on the social, cultural development of the society in question. While Mill considered democracy suitable for Europe due to its advanced societal development, he viewed Asian societies as less developed, and therefore unsuited for democratic forms of government.

Mill's thinking was influenced by the ideas of **Auguste Comte**, particularly the concept of societal development occurring in stages. Mill's stance on democracy thus demonstrates a perspective that is shaped by his prejudices and beliefs on the readiness and development or otherwise of different societies in determining the appropriate form of government for them.

REVISION OF LIBERALISM

Mill's concept of liberalism underwent significant revisions as he grappled with the growing inequality brought about by industrialisation and urbanisation. While his idea of liberty was rooted in the principle of survival of the fittest, he was deeply concerned about the widening wealth disparities in society. Mill recognised the moral obligation to address these inequalities and introduced the concept of societal responsibility between the individual and the state. Influenced by the sociologist **Auguste Comte**, Mill rejected the notion that society is merely an aggregation of individuals.

Forerunner to English Socialism

In England, J. S. Mill is regarded as one of the founding figures of socialism, marking a departure from the traditional liberal ideology attributed to thinkers like **John Locke**, who advocated for a minimal state with a focus on law and order. According to the classical liberal view, the state's role was limited to being a regulatory authority, maintaining a laissez-faire approach to the economy where market forces governed economic activities. However, Mill recognised the deep economic disparities created by a capitalist economy, with the rich becoming richer and the poor becoming increasingly impoverished. This led to a situation where liberty was enjoyed mainly by the wealthy and the middle class, while the labourers lived and worked under terrible conditions.

In response to these issues, Mill proposed the idea of a *welfare state*, where the government's role extended beyond law enforcement to include the provision of healthcare, education, and social services. He advocated for regulated working hours, pensions for workers, and argued in favour of progressive taxation to promote public welfare. It is important to note, however, that Mill's revised liberalism did not reject capitalism outright, but rather sought to reform it and create a more equitable society. In doing so, he presented an alternative to the Marxist ideology that emerged during his time.

Mill's revision of liberalism transformed it from an ideology primarily benefiting the capitalist class into a necessity for the entire society. He advocated for the establishment of a welfare state and expanded the scope of liberty to encompass the wellbeing of the entire population. While Mill maintained his individualistic perspective when discussing liberty, he became known as one of the founding fathers of socialism in England due to his efforts to address economic disparities and promote social welfare, thereby offering a counterpoint to Marxist ideas.

REVISION OF BENTHAM'S UTILITARIANISM

1. **Distinction between higher and lower pleasures:** Mill agreed with Bentham that the ultimate goal of human life is to maximise happiness. However, he introduced the concept of higher pleasures, emphasising that true happiness lies in internal, mental forms of higher pleasure. Mill believed happiness involves the cultivation of moral virtues, the perfection of human nature, and controlling one's desires and appetites. In contrast, he viewed physical and external pleasures as lower forms of happiness.
2. **Qualitative differences of happiness:** Mill rejected Bentham's idea of quantitative happiness which believes in 'maximum happiness of the maximum numbers,' arguing that pleasure varies not just in quantity but also in quality. Disagreeing with Bentham's idea that all pleasures are equal, Mill asserted that there's a difference between what satisfies a human and what satisfies a pig, famously stating that, 'It is better to be Socrates dissatisfied than a fool satisfied.' Higher, spiritual and mental pleasures hold more value than lower, physical and material pleasures, he asserted.
3. **The objective of happiness is self-realisation:** Drawing inspiration from thinkers like **Humboldt** and **Coleridge**, Mill stressed the importance of spiritual and moral growth over material prosperity, and believed true happiness is achieved through inner growth and self-realisation. Mill shifted the focus from pleasure as the primary objective of utilitarianism to the moral and virtuous development of individuals. This shift in emphasis marked Mill as both the last utilitarian and the first individualist, as he placed the pursuit of moral development above the pursuit of pleasure.

CRITICISM OF MILL'S IDEA OF LIBERTY

Some of the key criticisms of John Stuart Mill question the completeness and practicality of his ideas on liberty, individualism, and the relationship between individuals and society.

1. *Negative vs. Positive Liberty*: **Isaiah Berlin** argues that Mill's concept of liberty is primarily negative in nature, focusing on the absence of external restraints. However, **Norman Barry** suggests that his notion of liberty emphasises the importance of self-realisation and moral development, which can be seen as a form of positive liberty involving self-moral control.
2. *Individual vs. Community*: Critics such as **Ernest Barker** argue that Mill portrays the individual as an isolated atom, detached from society and community, whereas in reality, every action of an individual has an impact on others, making it other-regarding and subject to interference. This challenges Mill's abstract view of the individual and his promotion of empty liberty and abstract individualism.
3. *Rights and Liberty*: **G. H. Sabine** points out that Mill does not fully align with **Locke**'s concept of natural rights or **Bentham**'s ideas of legal rights. Critics argue that without a strong foundation of rights, liberty becomes meaningless and empty.
4. *Self-Regarding vs. Other-Regarding Actions*: **Barker** critiques and rejects Mill's

distinction between self-regarding actions and other-regarding actions, arguing that Mill fails to acknowledge that individuals are part of a society. Mill's analogy of a broken bridge and the role of a policeman restricting someone from crossing is also seen as problematic. Critics argue that obeying the instructions of others goes against the essence of liberty and can be seen as a curtailment of freedom.

11

KARL MARX (1818–1883)

KEY CONCEPTS

Scientific socialism; historical materialism; class struggle; critique of capitalism; surplus value; revolution; dictatorship of the proletariat; dialectical materialism; economic determinism; Asiatic mode of production

Karl Marx was born in the city of Trier, Germany in 1818, to Jewish parents. He was baptised at six. Marx was educated from 1830 to 1835 at the high school in Trier. He pursued higher education at Berlin University. His early writings during this period reveal a spirit of Christian devotion and a longing for self-sacrifice on behalf of humanity. As a youth Marx was more influenced by the critical and radical social policies of the Enlightenment than by religion. His Jewish background exposed him to prejudice and discrimination that may have later led him to question the role of religion in society and ignited his desire for transformative social change. During his lifetime, Marx witnessed the height of capitalism and the dire conditions faced by the labouring class. Convinced that capitalism was evil and unjustifiable, he dedicated himself to build a better, more equal society which was not based on exploitation of one human by another. Marx's stature as one of the world's greatest humanists, and most influential political thinkers and social scientists of all time remains undisputed.

LITERARY CONTRIBUTION

In 1844, a young Marx authored the *Economic and Philosophic Manuscripts*, which provides insights into his early ideas. In 1848, he published *The Communist Manifesto*, voicing his concerns about the extreme exploitation endured by the working class. He called for the international solidarity of the working class and advocated for a revolution to overthrow capitalism. In 1867, Marx presented his theory of 'Surplus Value' in his monumental work *Das Kapital* (Volume I), in which he analysed in depth the capitalist mode of production and the exploitation inherent in it. In 1875, he wrote the *Critique of the Gotha Programme* (published posthumously in 1891), offering a detailed, phased plan of revolutionary strategy, including the 'dictatorship of the proletariat'. Besides these, Marx produced a phenomenal body of work together with **Friedrich Engels**, his lifelong friend and associate, of which a selective list is given below:

1. *Critique of Hegel's Philosophy of Right* (1843)
2. *The Holy Family* (1845)
3. *Theses on Feuerbach* (1845)
4. *The German Ideology* (1846)
5. *The Poverty of Philosophy* (1847)
6. *The Communist Manifesto* (1848)
7. *Wage, Labour and Capital* (1849)
8. *The Eighteenth Brumaire of Louis Bonaparte* (1852)
9. *The Grundrisse* (1857)

10. *A Contribution to the Critique of Political Economy* (1859)
11. *Value, Price and Profit* (1865)
12. *Capital, Volume I: A Critique of Political Economy* (1867) Capital, Volume II (1885)
13. *Capital, Volume III: The Process of Capitalist Production as a Whole* (1894)
14. *The Civil War in France* (1871)
15. *Critique of the Gotha Programme* (1875)
16. *Socialism: Utopian and Scientific* (1880)
17. *Ludwig Feuerbach and the End of Classical German Philosophy* (1886)
18. *The Economic and Philosophical Manuscript of 1844* (Paris manuscript), published in 1932

Influences on Marxist Theory

According to **Harold J. Laski**, Marx developed his theory of *scientific socialism* as a response to the chaotic socio-political landscape he encountered, and diverse intellectual, theoretical influences. Marxian methodology, influenced by German philosopher **Georg Wilhelm F. Hegel**, is *dialectical* and posits that matter evolves through the interplay of *thesis* and *antithesis*. Drawing inspiration from the French Revolution, Marx believed in the potential for revolutionary change, as evidenced in his early work, *The Civil War in France*. He was also influenced by the socialist movements in France. Marx's analysis of property was influenced by French socialist and economist **Pierre-Joseph Proudhon**'s book *The Philosophy of Poverty*, which argued that property is essentially theft. In response, Marx wrote *The Poverty of Philosophy*.

SCIENTIFIC SOCIALISM

Marx's theory of scientific socialism is a socio-political and economic theory that aims to analyse and transform capitalist societies. Key features of this theory are:

1. *Historical materialism*: Marx believed that social and historical development is primarily driven by material conditions, such as the means and the relations of production. Different stages of history are characterised by distinct economic systems, like feudalism and capitalism.
2. *Class struggle*: Marx viewed society as divided into two main classes: the bourgeoisie or capitalist class and the proletariat or working class. He argued that the inherent conflict of interest between the two leads to class struggle, as the bourgeoisie exploits the labour of the proletariat for economic gain.
3. *Dialectical materialism*: Marx's methodology, influenced by Hegelian *dialectics*, interprets social and historical change as a result of contradictions and conflicts between opposing forces (*thesis* and *antithesis*) that lead to a new *synthesis*.
4. *Critique of capitalism*: Marx critiqued capitalism as an inherently exploitative system that prioritises profit accumulation over the wellbeing of workers. He analysed the mechanisms of capitalism, such as surplus value extraction, alienation of labour, and crises of overproduction, which he argued perpetuate inequality and social injustices.
5. *Surplus value*: Marx's theory of surplus value, based on David Ricardo's *labour theory*, asserts that the value of any commodity is determined by the labour required to produce it. Marx modified classical economic thought by combining the concept of surplus value with his *subsistence theory*, which argued that labourers only received the wages necessary for their bare subsistence, while the capitalist class appropriated the surplus value in the form of surplus labour. Marx therefore advocated for the overthrow of capitalism by the working class or the *proletariat*. Marx was the first thinker to propose an economic interpretation of history and

to call for the replacement of the existing capitalist system. His critique of capitalism was comprehensive and detailed.

6. *Socialist revolution*: Marx advocated a revolutionary transformation of society where the proletariat would overthrow the bourgeoisie and establish a socialist system. He envisioned a classless society where the means of production are collectively owned and controlled by the working class, leading to a more equitable distribution of wealth and resources.
7. *Dictatorship of the proletariat*: During the transitional period between capitalism and full communism, a temporary 'dictatorship of the proletariat' would be necessary to consolidate power and overcome resistance from the ruling class. This dictatorship, Marx proposed, would aim to dismantle the capitalist state apparatus and establish the conditions for a truly egalitarian society.

Marx's theory has had enormous impact on social, political movements worldwide, inspiring various interpretations and adaptations. However, the implementation and outcomes of Marxist theories in practice have varied across countries and different political contexts.

CRITIQUE OF UTOPIAN SOCIALISM

Utopian socialists aimed to achieve economic equality in society driven by moral considerations. They rejected the existence of conflict in society and envisioned a world free from envy, inequality and hatred. They believed that the capitalist system in industrial society corrupted the inherently good nature of humans, leading them to oppose capitalism.

In his *Communist Manifesto*, Marx identified **Robert Owen**, **St. Simon**, and **Charles Fourier** as 'utopian socialists', criticising them for not addressing the systemic causes of exploitation and the elimination of disparities. He considered their ideas utopian because they did not provide a comprehensive analysis of the mechanisms of exploitation and social change.

Marx's approach to understanding society was grounded in his economic interpretation of history, and the modes and relations of production. Unlike Hegel's idealism, Marx adopted a scientific and empirical approach, examining how production was carried out under different economic systems. For example, feudalism relied on manual labour, while capitalism, post Industrial Revolution, employed machinery.

Marx's analysis of capitalist systems of the nineteenth century led him to believe that the inherent flaws of capitalism stemmed from the concept of private property, and contradiction between the means and relations of production. Workers were denied the full value of their labour and forced to subsist on the bare minimum as capitalists appropriated the surplus value they created, thus creating a situation of overproduction without sufficient buyers.

This provided the basis for a revolution to establish a classless and stateless society. As a materialist, Marx rejected the notion of divine power and viewed religion as a form of social control, and as an obstacle to the development of class consciousness, diverting attention from the material conditions and class struggles within society.

While Marx's understanding of socio-economic structures is based on empirical economic analysis and dialectical materialism, his emphasis on the goal of creating an egalitarian society free from exploitation based on social justice underline the moral dimension of his work.

ON THE HUMAN SPECIES

Marx viewed human nature as historically and socially constructed. He rejected the notion of a fixed, unchanging human nature, asserting that it evolves over time. He emphasised that human beings are inherently creative and productive. He saw labour as a fundamental aspect of human nature through which humans transform nature and produce the means of their existence. This creative activity is integral to human fulfillment and self-realisation. Marx also emphasised that humans are inherently social creatures who rely on cooperation and social relationships for their survival and development.

Vladimir I. Lenin once said that Marx's theory was a fusion of German philosophy, British political economy and French socialism. As a university student in Germany, Marx was part of a group called the Young Hegelians, who sought to push Hegel's philosophy to its radical limits. Marx endorsed Hegel's emphasis on the active nature of human beings, but rejected his idealism.

Embodied Consciousness

Marx rejected the idea of a purely abstract or idealist consciousness that exists apart from the physical world. For Marx, human consciousness is always an *embodied consciousness*, which means that in order to be able to think and feel, human beings must first be alive. Like other creatures, humans are part of the order of nature and dependent on nature for survival. However, unlike other natural creatures, human beings are 'universal' beings in that they can use all of nature for their sustenance instead of being limited instinctually to specific sources of nourishment. For Marx, the consciousness of human beings extends far beyond mere instinct. Human beings are active participants in the world, with their active nature being manifest not in thought alone, but also in 'sensuous human activity' as beings who live from nature. To live from nature, use natural resources, humans must engage in tangible, sensuous human activity.

For Marx, embodied consciousness refers to the understanding that human consciousness is inseparable from the physical, material existence of human beings and the material conditions in which they live. This active engagement with the material world is central to human existence and contributes to the formation of consciousness. Marx's concept of embodied consciousness aligns with his broader theory of historical materialism, which posits that social and economic structures shape human thought and consciousness over time.

DIALECTICAL MATERIALISM

Dialectics is an approach to understanding development and progress; *materialism* asserts that matter is the fundamental element of the universe. Society and history are in a constant state of motion and never static, argues Marx, which makes dialectics a suitable method for studying them. His understanding of social and historical change is rooted in the dialectical method.

Marxian materialism contends that motion is inherent within matter, as against **Hobbes**, who argued that motion is imposed on matter externally. In Marxist theory, *matter* pertains to economic factors that drive the progress of history and society, such as forces of production. Driven by inherent contradictions matter undergoes a dialectical process of change, until it reaches the highest stage of development. Dialectical development, which embraces contradiction, sees capitalism as the *thesis*, dictatorship of the proletariat as the *antithesis*, and communism as the *synthesis*.

While Marx uses Hegelian dialectics as an analytical tool, in works like *The Holy Family* and *Theses on Feuerbach*, he rejects Hegelian idealism. Unlike Hegel, who perceives the world as a manifestation of an absolute idea, Marx asserts that the world is fundamentally 'material' in nature and evolves in accordance with the laws of matter in motion. For Marx, 'matter' is an objective reality existing outside and independent of our minds, in contrast to the notion that only our minds truly exist. The central focus for Marx is not the history of philosophy but the history of economic production.

Key features of Marx's dialectical materialism include:

1. The dialectical process involving thesis, antithesis, and synthesis.
2. The synthesis combines the best of both the thesis and the antithesis.
3. The synthesis is the negation of negation.
4. Development is driven by contradiction as every object or thesis generates its opposite or antithesis.
5. Historical change is driven by material factors, not by God or any divine power.

CRITICISM OF FEUERBACH

In his *Thesis on Feuerbach*, Marx critiqued Feuerbach's 'contemplative' materialism for conceiving reality solely in the form of objects of contemplation, without recognising them as part of human activity from a subjective perspective. Feuerbach's contemplative materialism posits a separation between ideas and matter, and suggests that material life determines everything.

In contrast, Marx analyses materialism through the lens of historical and social conditions, considering the dialectical relationship between matter and consciousness. Marx contends that consciousness is embodied in human life, setting humans apart from animals whose lives primarily consist of sensory activities. Human consciousness and values find expression through human activity in the material world.

Human beings are natural creatures and rely on nature to fulfill their physical needs. However, they possess the ability to exert control over nature due to their consciousness. They have created an artificial world that is a product of their consciousness. Thus, the relationship between matter, material life and consciousness is not merely causal, as Feuerbach suggests, but rather a complex interplay, asserts Marx.

Marx argued that as human beings interact with nature and with each other, they shape a 'new world'—the outcome of their own sensuous human activity—which then becomes the object of their thought and actions. However, when this object—the externalised form of their own activity—starts to feel unfamiliar, when they struggle to comprehend and shape it according to their own purposes, human beings experience *alienation*.

Marxist materialism thus highlights the centrality of human agency and actions in shaping the world, as opposed to a passive contemplation of objects. Marx underscores the connection between material existence, consciousness, and the transformative power of human activity. It is through active engagement with the world that humans can overcome alienation and contribute to the creation of a more liberated and fulfilling society.

HISTORICAL MATERIALISM

Dialectical materialism is the philosophical framework that Marx adopted from Hegel. It is a method of understanding and analysing the world, underlining the dynamic nature of reality, the interconnectedness of contradictions, and the role of material conditions in shaping social development. Dialectical materialism recognises that change and progress occur through the resolution of contradictions and conflicts within society and nature.

Historical materialism is the Marxian theory that specifically focuses on the study of history and society, examining the ways in which material conditions, particularly modes of production and class struggles, shape the social, political and economic structures of different historical periods. Historical materialism emphasises the primary role of material factors, such as the productive forces and the relations of production, in driving historical change.

Dialectical materialism provides the philosophical foundation for understanding the dynamics of change and contradictions, while historical materialism applies this framework specifically to the analysis of historical processes and the development of human societies. They are interconnected and complementary aspects of Marxist theory that address different aspects of Marx's social analysis.

In *The Poverty of Philosophy*, Marx's critique of **Proudhon**'s *The Philosophy of Poverty*, Marx argued that Proudhon failed to provide a comprehensive explanation for the root causes of poverty and economic inequality. Marx believed that modern liberal thought disregarded the significance of tradition, history, culture and community. He embarked on an economic interpretation of history, pioneering the study of economic history. This approach, called *historical materialism*, complements his philosophical framework of dialectical materialism and forms the scientific basis of Marxism.

To grasp Marx's concept of historical materialism, we must first examine *modes of production*, which consists of two elements: the means of production (tools, equipment), and relations of production (class relationships). The conflict between the means of production and the relations of production shapes history, leading Marx to assert that 'the history of all existing society is the history of class struggle.'

Marx's understanding of historical materialism is progressive, suggesting that each stage of history represents an improvement over the previous one. For example, capitalism is considered superior to feudalism, even though exploitation persists in every phase of history. Capitalism, being the most advanced stage, institutionalises exploitation. Marx's interpretation of history is evolutionary and deterministic, culminating in communism as the final phase.

1. **Primitive communism:** The initial phase of societal development is characterised by primitive communism, in which the means of production were primitive, and economic resources were controlled by the community. There was no concept of economic inequality, private property, and no need for a state. Engels derived Marx's concept of primitive communism from **Lewis Morgan**'s work *Ancient Society*.
2. **Slavery:** As humans advanced in agricultural and domestication techniques, the notion of private property emerged. Slaves became the means of production. This phase marked the division of society into masters and slaves, establishing a class-based exploitation system. The state and government emerged as instruments of exploitation, with prisoners of war often becoming slaves rather than being killed.
3. **Feudalism:** Society was organised around the relationship between lords and peasants. The masters of the slavery system became feudal lords, and exploitation persisted through changes in the means of production. Land became the primary means of production, owned by feudal lords, and worked by serfs who had to surrender surplus production to the landlords. The kings appointed feudal chiefs to serve their economic and security interests. Society became divided between those who owned the means of production (haves) and those who did not (have-nots).
4. **Capitalism:** Capital emerged as the new means of production in this stage. This led to the rise of new social classes: the capitalist class (bourgeoisie) and the working class (proletariat). Marx believed that this transition was more progressive than the previous stages. Concepts of democracy, rights and liberty emerged, but the exploitation of the working class continued. New advanced means of transportation and communication accompanied the emergence of capitalism. The concepts of liberty and democracy under capitalism served the interests of the capitalist class alone, as did developments in the modes of production. Class consciousness would

eventually arise among the working class.

5. **Communist society:** Marx envisioned communism as the ultimate stage following the overthrow of capitalism by the working class. Communist society will be stateless, classless, just and egalitarian. People will work according to their capacity and receive according to their need. With the abolishing of private property, social classes and the need for a state would naturally wither away. Ideological divisions would become redundant. Division of labour would end, allowing individuals to engage in multiple roles and activities. The entire community would own the means of production, ensuring a collective responsibility. In this transformed society, individuals would transcend their class identities and become truly social beings. A sense of democratic fraternity would prevail, with economic equality as a fundamental principle, with emphasis on the welfare and cooperation of all members, creating a harmonious and egalitarian community.

CLASS STRUGGLE

Throughout history, societies have been divided into two classes: the 'haves' and the 'have-nots', for example, masters and slaves, patricians and plebeians, lords and serfs. Marx refers to this division as the principle of *social stratification*, which is not based on religion, caste, gender, language, ethnicity or nationality. The relationship between these classes is characterised by conflict and tension. This class conflict cannot be resolved through democratic or peaceful means, argues Marx.

In capitalist societies, the proletariat comprises those who sell their labour to sustain their lives, while the bourgeoisie owns the means of production. The relationship between the two is inherently exploitative, and no reconciliation between them is possible. Revolutionary change is the only way to bring about any meaningful transformation, asserts Marx. History progresses through the ongoing struggle between these classes.

Marx does not seek to merely describe the division of society into classes; his objective is to eliminate class divisions altogether and establish a society free from class-based exploitation and inequality.

REVOLUTION

Society was always divided into classes, but class consciousness emerged only during the capitalist era. Class consciousness is shaped by the material conditions of society and plays a crucial role in instigating revolution. Capitalism, with its creation of urban-industrial societies, served as a catalyst for the rise of class consciousness. Marx recognised that the seeds of capitalism's destruction lie within capitalism itself, and these seeds manifest in the form of the proletariat or working classes.

Living in urban centres, the proletariat experiences similar economic conditions, characterised by limited purchasing power and precarious employment. Capitalism prioritises production but restricts consumption due to the working class's reduced buying ability. Workers often face unemployment when production declines. As industries concentrate in large cities, the consciousness of the urban population grows, leading to a sense of shared oppression, misery, discontent, and purpose in overthrowing capitalism. The advancement of communication technology further amplifies awareness, transcending geographical boundaries and exposing workers to the exploitation prevalent worldwide.

This heightened consciousness and awareness among the working class eventually culminate in a revolution that aims to emancipate humanity by empowering the proletariat and placing all means of production under social ownership. Marx's rousing call to workers, 'Workers of the world, unite! You have nothing to lose but your chains,' reflects his belief in the unifying potential of the working class as agents of revolutionary change, as expressed in the *Communist Manifesto*.

ECONOMIC DETERMINISM

In his *Critique of Political Economy*, Marx delves into the philosophy of history and says that the anatomy of civil society can be understood by an examination of its political economy. He provides an economic interpretation of history, focusing on concepts like surplus value. In *Das Kapital*, regarded as a Bible by many, Marx explores the contradictions inherent within capitalism. He argues that the nature of the economy, which forms the *base* of society, determines the nature of the state, religion and ideology—the *superstructure*. The superstructure is fundamentally shaped by the economic base, i.e. the modes and relations of production.

To explain human progress, Marx and Engels developed a materialistic conception of history which posits that societal progress is driven by the dynamics of the material conditions and the class struggles arising from them. By emphasising the primacy of economic factors, Marx and Engels sought to unveil the underlying mechanisms that shape human history.

Critics often label Marx's theory of 'economic determinism' as 'economic reductionism'. Economic reductionism suggests that the economy is the sole factor that shapes society and the state. However, Marx did not neglect the influence of other factors, and it would be unfair to classify him as an economic reductionist. He can be better understood as an economic determinist who recognised the central role played by the economy in shaping social conditions.

RELIGION AND IDEOLOGY

Society is divided into opposing classes, and simultaneously, the world is divided between the material realm and heaven. Marx attributes the emergence of religion to social and economic inequality and the abiding need of the capitalist class to preserve that inequality in order to preserve their power and control. Religion is used by the capitalist class to distort class consciousness, and to function as a form of escapism or 'opium', under the influence of which the working classes are given to imagine a heavenly realm to momentarily forget their present misery and oppression in society. Similarly, ideology is employed by capitalists to sustain their exploitation and power. Marx thus characterised both religion and ideology as forms of *false consciousness*.

Religion and ideology both give rise to false consciousness, Marx argues. *Class consciousness*, on the other hand, is the opposite of this. Class consciousness makes workers realise that capitalism is the root cause of their exploitation and suffering. With the emergence of class consciousness, the class 'in itself' transforms into the class 'for itself'. Marx sees liberty, rights and democracy as mere ideologies. In a society divided by class and inequality, such false ideology and false consciousness is necessary to preserve status quo, he argues, but not in a classless, stateless society. Marx dismissed Hegelian ideas that consciousness determines social conditions, instead demonstrating that material, social and economic conditions shape human consciousness. Marx viewed the fulfillment of primary material or economic needs as the driving force behind human productive activities.

THE STATE

According to Marx, the capitalist state is an artificial institution, a machinery created by the capitalist class to serve its interests. The state is not a 'natural institution', an 'ethical institution', an 'organic' entity, nor is it the embodiment of divine purpose or the realisation of God's plan on earth, as Hegel believed.

In the natural primitive state, there was no state since there was no notion of private property, and society was not divided into classes. The capitalist class established the state to protect and preserve its control over the means of production, to perpetuate its exploitation of the working class, and to preserve inequality and status quo. Marx described the state as a mechanism of oppression and a manifestation of injustice. In a communist society, the means of production are collectively owned, resulting in a stateless and classless society.

DICTATORSHIP OF THE PROLETARIAT

Marx had earlier predicted the advent of communism, and a classless, stateless society, following the demise of capitalism. However, after observing the Paris Commune, he recognised the need for a transitional phase of history, which he termed the 'dictatorship of the proletariat', which acknowledges the existence of class and the state.

The 'dictatorship of the proletariat' represents the rule of the working class, under which a classless and stateless society would be established. Through his analysis of the French Revolution, Marx concluded that the bourgeoisie is inherently antagonistic towards the proletariat, and believed that the proletariat's rule was inevitable. Under the dictatorship of the proletariat, individuals would work according to their capacity and receive according to their need. To socialise the means of production, the state would perform several functions, including:

1. Abolition of private ownership of land and redirecting all land rents for public purposes.
2. Implementing a heavy progressive or graduated income tax.
3. Abolition of all rights of inheritance.
4. Confiscation of the property of emigrants and rebels.
5. Centralising credit through a national bank with state capital and exclusive control.
6. Centralising control over means of transport in the hands of the state.
7. Expanding state ownership of factories and production instruments, cultivating unused wastelands, and improving soil conditions according to a common plan.
8. Ensuring equal obligation to work for all individuals, and establishing industrial armies, especially for agriculture.
9. Integrating agriculture with industries; gradually eliminating the distinction between town and country by a more equitable distribution of the population.
10. Providing free education for all children in public schools and abolishing children's factory labour. Integrating education with industrial production.

These measures are part of Marx's vision for a transformed society that aims to eliminate exploitation and create a more equitable system for the wellbeing of all.

In his criticism of Marx, **Sabine** remarks that Marx is a better critic than a constructive thinker, because the 'best' of Marx's work can be seen in his criticism of capitalism, but the 'worst' of Marx is apparent in his idea of 'dictatorship of the proletariat' and communism. **Milovan Djilas** argued that any dictatorship *of* the proletariat soon becomes dictatorship *over* the proletariat, as political party and personality become more powerful than the rule of the working class.

MARXISM, SOCIALISM AND ANARCHISM

Marx distinguished Marxism from both democratic socialism and anarchism. Socialists advocated for a gradual, democratic transition towards socialism, whereas Marxism emphasised the necessity of revolutionary methods and dictatorship of the proletariat in a class-divided society. Anarchists, on the other hand, rejected the idea of the state altogether along with the dictatorship of the proletariat, including during the transitional phase.

In the *Critique of the Gotha Programme*, Marx's critique of the draft programme of the United Workers' Party of Germany, he addresses the dictatorship of the proletariat, the period of transition from capitalism to communism, the two phases of communist society, the production and distribution of the social goods, proletarian internationalism, and the workers' party.

ANALYSIS OF CAPITALISM

In *Das Kapital*, an in-depth analysis of capitalism, Marx criticised its effects, highlighting the ills of *commodity fetishism*. Under capitalism, commodities are assigned exchange values, leading to a sense of accomplishment that is detached from their utility. Human beings and human labour also become commodified, as slaves were. Marx distinguished between *use value* and *exchange value*, where use value refers to the practical utility of an object, while exchange value is determined by the market. Capitalism predominantly promotes exchange value, causing commodities to dominate human society. This leads to devaluing the contributions of those who produce the commodities. Paradoxically, human labour power itself becomes a commodity, further exacerbating commodity fetishism as the value of a commodity is detached from its utility. The growing consumerist pursuit and obsession with acquiring more commodities overshadow any human values. Under capitalism, machines and labour are crucial for production, but capitalists pay workers much less than the actual value of their labour and appropriate the surplus value as profit.

Marx's theory of surplus value builds upon **David Ricardo**'s labour theory, which holds that the actual value of a good (how much of another good or service it exchanges for in the market) is proportional to how much labour was required to produce it, including the labour required to produce the raw materials and machinery used in the process.

According to Marx and Engels, those who possess economic power also hold political power. Marx was one of the first thinkers to emphasise that economic factors like forces of production shape politics, and hence must be understood. Marx argued that the destruction of capitalism is inevitable as it fosters unlimited and unhealthy competition for profit, leading to the concentration of disproportionate wealth in the hands of a few, while the economic conditions of the proletariat progressively deteriorate, resulting in factory closures, unemployment, and misery.

ALIENATION AND FREEDOM

The concept of *alienation* encompasses the dual processes of *objectification* and *estrangement*. Objectification refers to the transformation of labour into a tangible product, where the labour becomes materialised in an object and is realised through its external manifestation.

Estrangement, on the other hand, encapsulates the sense of detachment and separation experienced by the labourer. In a capitalist system, workers sell their labour to capitalists, who own and control the means of production. As a result, the labourer becomes alienated from his/her own activity. Their labour is no longer a part of their being, but something external to them. The worker relates to their own labour as something foreign and disconnected from their personal life. This self-estrangement is a form of alienation.

Alienation implies a loss of freedom, where human beings are transformed into mere objects. It occurs when individuals are separated from society, productive activities and control over their own lives. Marx argued that in a capitalist economy, human beings become alienated from the very world they have created through their own labour. His early ideas on alienation, as found in the *Philosophical and Economic Manuscripts* of 1844 (known as the *Paris Manuscripts*), emphasise the unique qualities of human beings. He highlighted the capacity for labour as a distinct human characteristic which reflects their creativity.

Unlike animals that engage in activities solely for fulfilling their physical needs, human beings derive enjoyment and fulfillment from their work. Human actions are conscious and intentional. They do not merely work to satisfy their immediate physical needs. However, in a capitalist economy, labourers often find themselves working solely to meet their basic bodily needs. This leads to a loss of enjoyment and a sense of compulsion in their work, ultimately resulting in alienation from their own humanity.

Stages of Alienation

1. **Production:** The first stage of alienation is rooted in the process of production itself. In capitalist systems, the division of labour, intense competition and the imposition of compulsory labour contribute to the alienation of workers, reducing them to mere cogs in the productive machinery, and diminishing their role and autonomy.
2. **Society:** Capitalism creates an atomistic society where individuals become self-centred and focused on their own interests. The relentless pursuit of profit and cutthroat competition erode the sense of community and fraternity among people. Solidarity and cooperation are replaced by individualism and self-gain, exacerbating social alienation.
3. **Environment:** Marx, echoing Rousseau, stresses the need to reconnect with nature and advocates for a return to a more harmonious and authentic relationship between humans and nature. Marx argues that true social life should be characterised by enjoyment, creativity and a sustainable balance with the environment. By reclaiming a deeper connection with nature, the alienation from both the natural world and our own humanity can be alleviated, he asserts.
4. **Alienation from Self:** The most profound and extreme form of alienation occurs when an individual becomes estranged from their own self. A human being is thus reduced to the status of an object, a mere instrument or machine who operates mechanically, devoid of their true essence. It is a state of disconnection from one's own thoughts, emotions, beliefs and aspirations, leading to a loss of authenticity and a deep sense of inner emptiness. Marx saw alienation from oneself as a dehumanising consequence of the oppressive systems and conditions found in capitalist societies.

THE YOUNG AND THE MATURE MARX

While **David McLellan** argues that there is a continuity between the ideas of the young Marx and the old Marx, **Louis Althusser** disagrees, asserting that there is an epistemological break between the young and the old Marx. The writings of the young Marx reveal a more romantic and humanistic emphasis on freedom and democracy, in which the individual is more important than class and society. In contrast, the mature Marx is revolutionary, scientifically and historically materialist, dialectical, and positivistic.

While the young Marx delves into the psychological effects of capitalism, it is in his later years that he suggests ways of ending the alienation created by capitalist society. To overcome alienation, he asserts, individuals must liberate themselves not only from religion and God but also from the entire structure of alienation, namely capitalism, which is the root cause of human alienation. Capitalism destroys individual freedom and dehumanises people. Marx defines freedom as the elimination of material necessity, where individuals are free to choose their work according to their desire and inclination, rather than need.

A CRITIQUE OF MARXISM

There are diverse perspectives on the merits and limitations of Marxism. As interpretations and implementations of Marxist ideas vary widely, so do the specific criticisms levied against them. Some criticisms of Marxism are as follows.

1. Marxism's emphasis on collective ownership and class struggle has been criticised for disregarding individual freedom, autonomy

and suppressing personal initiative and creativity. However, mass-produced culture and consumerism under capitalism also stifle human expression and freedom, creating multiple levels of alienation and dehumanisation.

2. Marxist regimes have faced criticism for concentrating power in the hands of the state, leading to authoritarianism, repression of dissent, human rights violations, and economic inefficiency.
3. Marxism assumes a level of altruism, cooperation and ethicality that may not align with the realities of human behaviour.
4. Marxism places excessive emphasis on economic factors and class struggle, neglecting the influence of culture, ethnicity and religion in shaping society and impacting social dynamics in ways not solely reducible to economic relations.
5. Marxism's focus on eliminating class distinctions and redistributing wealth undermines motivation for productivity. Without the promise of individual rewards or the ability to accumulate wealth, the drive for innovation and progress may be stifled, argue critics.
6. Historical failures such as the Soviet Union are cited as evidence of the limitations of Marxist theory in practice. Capitalist economies are however no strangers to such failure, the Great Depression of 1929, and the Global Financial Crisis of 2007–08 being two.

Specific aspects of Marxism have also been cogently critiqued by liberation theologists, anarchists and feminists, among others, while they also embrace and adopt some tenets of Marxism.

ASIATIC MODE OF PRODUCTION

A significant drawback of Marxist theory is however posed by his limited understanding of Asiatic economies. Marx posited that the development of history and society is propelled by the material forces of production. However, he applied this method of development specifically to European societies, which raises a notable paradox. According to Marx, this developmental framework does not apply to Asiatic societies, which he regarded as stagnant, in contrast to the progressive nature of European societies. He argued that colonialism would act as an external force, driving Asiatic societies towards capitalism and initiating movement within them. Marxian analysis would therefore appear to be entirely Eurocentric in its perspective.

Critics such as **Dr Ambedkar** and **Ram Manohar Lohiya** have rejected Marx's analysis of Indian society, finding it inadequate and unsuitable for understanding the complexities of the Indian context. **Lenin**, too, did not fully embrace Marx's notion of Asiatic societies, maintaining that colonialism would not lead to the establishment of capitalism in these societies; rather, it would perpetuate exploitation and hinder the potential for communist revolution, even in Europe.

The critique of Marx's analysis of Asiatic societies raises questions about the universality and applicability of his theories. It highlights the limitations of a Eurocentric perspective and underscores the need for a more nuanced understanding of diverse social and historical contexts.

12

ANTONIO GRAMSCI (1891–1937)

KEY CONCEPTS

Realm of force vs realm of consent; hegemony; base and superstructure; relative autonomy of the state; Gramsci on civil society; traditional vs organism intellectuals

Antonio Francesco Gramsci was born in Ales, Sardinia, to a middle-class family of Albanian descent. A socialist activist, radical journalist, cultural commentator, and communist party leader in Italy, Gramsci has been hugely influential as a Marxist theorist of culture and politics in 'developed' capitalism. He was familiar with philosophical currents of the time, especially Italian neo-idealism, native intellectual and political traditions dating back to Machiavelli, and the main currents of Marxist thought. He was imprisoned by the Fascist regime, and wrote his most famous and philosophically rich texts in jail: the Prison Notebooks.

CIVIL SOCIETY

According to Gramsci, the strong influence of capitalism in Europe can be attributed to its ideological dominance. He argued that capitalist societies exercise ideological control through various institutions within civil society, such as the family, religious institutions, the Church, colleges, and the press. Despite the fear of communism spreading after the Russian Revolution in 1917, Italy saw the rise of fascism instead of communism. Gramsci viewed fascism as another form of capitalism, where brute force is employed by capitalists when they fail to maintain control through consent.

Lenin, on the other hand, believed that imperialism was the key factor behind the success of capitalism in capitalist countries. He asserted that capitalist nations were exploiting the natural resources of African countries, and once imperialism came to an end, the bourgeoisie in these countries would turn to exploit their own proletariat. Lenin predicted an inevitable communist revolution in Western European countries. While Gramsci admired the Russian Revolution of October 1917, he believed that such a revolution was not suitable for capitalist countries in Europe, where there was a clear distinction between civil society and the state. In contrast, in countries like Russia, this distinction was not as clear.

STATE

Marx famously argued that the state functions as an instrument of exploitation, representing repressive agencies such as the army and the police. Gramsci, however, presented a broader perspective, contending that the state is not solely a repressive institution but also an ideological organisation. In addition to its coercive functions, the state controls key aspects of society such as the media, press, schools and universities, influencing and shaping ideas and social norms. To maintain consent and support from the people, the state also adopts welfare measures, and is thus no longer recognised only as an agency of control or exploitation. Democracy, according to Gramsci, is utilised as a means to gain popular support.

Gramsci's theory of hegemony is closely connected to his understanding of the capitalist state. Rather than narrowly defining the state as merely the government, Gramsci argues that the 'capitalist state' rules through a combination of both *force* and *consent*: the state is both the instrument by which a ruling class maintained its dominance over society, and the medium through which it undertook a 'civilising activity', functioning as an 'ethical state' or 'educator' by promoting 'a certain way of life' for its citizens. The political society or the state represents the *realm of force*, while civil society represents the *realm of consent.*

Gramsci asserts that in capitalist society, the state does not represent the interests of everyone but rather serves as an institution of the bourgeoisie class. When the state fails to obtain the support of the people, it resorts to using force. The rise of a fascist state exemplifies a form of capitalist state where naked force is employed to control the population. The state possesses both the ideological apparatus and coercive instruments to exert control over society.

HEGEMONY

According to Gramsci, hegemony involves the ability of the leadership to create manufactured consent among citizens. He presents hegemony as the hypothesis that a social class aims to achieve *consensual domination* for its rule by progressively expanding its leadership across society. He distinguishes between two forms of domination: *coercive* and *ideological* domination. Unlike Lenin, who supported violent action against the state and government, Gramsci's concept of hegemony is not based on force. Instead, hegemony is achieved through the control of civil society, with the consent of the people. Gramsci emphasises cultural and ideological control over civil society, which includes institutions such as the family, schools, religious organisations, colleges, universities, and the press. Additionally, Gramsci argues that the welfare state, democracy, and the rule of law are means through which ideological control over the population can be established.

REJECTION OF POSITIVISM AND MATERIALISM

Gramsci strongly rejected the positivist and materialistic analysis of society proposed by Marx and Lenin. While **Marx** and **Lenin** emphasised the control of the means of production as the basis for capitalist hegemony, Gramsci argued against the principle of economic determinism. Instead, he believed that culture, ideology, and religion were more effective tools for understanding society. According to Gramsci, capitalists had already established their dominance within civil society by spreading their values throughout institutions such as the family, church and university. To challenge capitalist hegemony, Gramsci advocated for the development of a *counter-hegemony* that would promote communist values within civil society. He believed that the centre of dominance lay within civil society rather than solely in the forces of production. The ultimate goal of acquiring dominance, for Gramsci, was to establish communism and overthrow the hegemony of capitalists.

In Gramsci's framework, the task of acquiring dominance and leading the revolution fell upon organic intellectuals. He distinguished between *organic* and *traditional intellectuals*. Unlike traditional intellectuals, who supported the status quo and perpetuated exploitation, he saw organic intellectuals as agents of change who would play a crucial role in bringing about revolutionary transformation in society.

Base and Superstructure

Gramsci presented a new analysis of the *base* and *superstructure* model, which differs from that of Marx. While both Marx and Gramsci acknowledge the model, their interpretations of it vary. According to Marx, the economic structure, or the 'base', is the fundamental structure of society. The 'superstructure' is seen as a mere reflection of the base and lacks autonomy. Marx believed that by capturing the economic structure through revolution, the other structures would automatically change. He viewed the state as an instrument of exploitation and a medium for the capitalist class to exert dominance, a concept known as 'economic determinism'.

In contrast, in his analysis, Gramsci placed greater emphasis on the superstructure rather than the base. Although he agreed with Marx that the economic structure is the fundamental structure, Gramsci argued that Marx overlooked the significant role played by the superstructure. According to Gramsci, the structure consists of two components:

1. The state, government and police, which exercise coercive power.
2. Civil society, which operates through consent or 'manufactured consent'.

Gramsci's analysis highlights the central role of civil society. He rejects Marx's economic determinism and positivistic thinking, and is considered a proponent of Neo-Marxism or New-Marxism.

RELATIVE AUTONOMY OF STATE

Gramsci was influenced by the idealist Italian thinker **Benedetto Croce**, who said that economic factors alone are not sufficient to understand history or society. For Croce, culture, religion and consciousness are crucial for understanding the society and state.

While **Machiavelli** viewed the state as being completely autonomous from economic factors, **Marx** asserted that the state is entirely dependent on the economy (economic determinism). Gramsci, however, presented a nuanced perspective, suggesting that the state is partially autonomous from economic factors. While the economy does impact the state, non-economic factors such as culture and ideology play significant roles in shaping the state and government, he argued.

Gramsci modified Marx's economic interpretation by highlighting the importance of family, religion and ideology as crucial components that legitimise state power. According to Gramsci, capitalists are able to control states due to their hegemony in civil society. Contemporary Marxist thinkers, such as **Ralph Miliband** and **Nicos Poulantzas**, also support the theory of the relative autonomy of the state. While Marx argued that control over the means of production is equal to control over the state, Gramsci emphasised that gaining control over civil society is equally essential in order to capture the state.

CIVIL SOCIETY

Civil society holds a central position in Gramsci's ideas, deviating from Marx's perspective that primarily views civil society in economic terms, focusing on the mode of production and relations of production. Gramsci expands the concept of civil society to encompass institutions such as the family, school, church and media. These institutions serve to familiarise citizens with established behavioural norms and instill a natural respect for the authority of the ruling class. Gramsci argues that civil society was not fully developed in feudal countries like Russia during the 1917 Revolution, but it is more prominent in European capitalist and democratic nations. This development has allowed the capitalist class to acquire hegemony over civil society, thereby obtaining legitimacy in the eyes of the people. Gramsci contends that the establishment of communism requires an ideological and cultural revolution, often referred to as a 'passive revolution'.

Civil society is important for Gramsci because he sees it as the site where social and cultural dominance is established and maintained. Power is not exercised only through coercive state apparatuses but also through consent and ideological control. Civil society plays a crucial role in shaping and disseminating the dominant ideologies and values of the ruling class. Gramsci argues that the ruling class maintains its hegemony by controlling civil society as it is through these institutions that individuals internalise and reproduce the values, beliefs and norms that serve the interests of the ruling class. By exerting its influence over civil society, the ruling class can ensure the consent and compliance of the majority, even in the absence of direct coercion.

Civil society thus becomes a key battleground for challenging and transforming existing power relations. Gramsci believed that in order to challenge capitalist hegemony and establish a more equitable society, there needs to be a counter-hegemonic project that seeks to reshape civil society, challenge dominant ideologies, and promote alternative values and social structures. For Gramsci, the transformation of civil society is crucial for the success of revolutionary movements and the establishment of a socialist or communist society.

STRATEGY OF REVOLUTION

Gramsci highlighted the uniqueness of the 1917 Bolshevik Revolution, recognising its historical import, but also its inapplicability to European countries. Instead, he advocated for a strategy of ideological warfare in the realms of culture, art, literature and philosophical debates. Gramsci believed that revolutionaries should aim to attain dominance in autonomous civil society institutions and cultivate a new mass consciousness among the people. He acknowledged that transforming the ideas and minds of individuals in European countries would require a sustained effort over time. Gramsci employed a military analogy to outline two types of revolution:

1. *War of Position*: An ideological revolution, particularly relevant for industrialised nations, it involves a gradual process of building counter-hegemony and acquiring dominance within civil society institutions.
2. *War of Manoeuvres*: Direct action aimed at capturing the state and gaining control over the economic system, this approach is associated with immediate and forceful tactics.

Like Lenin, Gramsci too believed that the working class alone would not spontaneously develop revolutionary consciousness. He emphasised the role of the communist party and the need for working-class intellectuals to contribute to the development of a counter-hegemonic ideology. Gramsci recognised that the Russian Revolution was specific to a feudal and agrarian society, while European nations were industrialised and had democratic governments. He noted the strength of civil society in Europe and advocated for a *war of position*, focusing on achieving ideological hegemony within civil society institutions, rather than a direct and violent seizure of power like the Russian Revolution.

INTELLECTUALS

Gramsci stressed on the importance of achieving ideological hegemony within civil society. He viewed intellectuals as crucial agents in establishing this hegemony, and believed that a continuous movement for counter-hegemony was necessary. Capitalists had already established their dominance in civil society institutions, and Gramsci argued that intellectuals should replace this capitalist hegemony with alternative ideologies. He recognised that violent revolution was not relevant or applicable in developed and industrialised European nations, where civil society was stronger.

According to Gramsci, every individual is capable of being an intellectual since everyone possesses rationality and the capacity for critical thinking. However, he categorised intellectuals into two types:

Traditional intellectuals: Intellectuals belonging to the capitalist class and created and sustained by the ruling class. They often present themselves as neutral, but in reality they support the existing status quo and do not challenge it.

Organic intellectuals: Gramsci referred to the Communist Party of Italy as the organic intellectual, drawing from Machiavelli's concept of the 'New Prince'. Organic intellectuals aim to establish their own hegemony within civil society. Gramsci rejected the Marxian notion that society is strictly divided into two classes, and instead argued that there are different sections in society, namely:

1. The capitalist class
2. Those opposing capitalism, represented by organic intellectuals.
3. Individuals who are not directly involved in exploitation, but who also do not actively oppose capitalism. Gramsci believes they could be brought into the fold of organic intellectuals and contribute to the counter-hegemonic struggle.

GRAMSCI'S SELECT WORKS

1. *The Great and Terrible World* (1908)
2. *The Prison Notebooks* (1971)
3. *The Prison Letters* (1988)

13

HANNAH ARENDT (1906–1975)

KEY CONCEPTS

Theory of action; Arendt's view on freedom and liberty; purpose of politics; criticism of modernity; civic republicanism; theory of power; totalitarianism; republican revolution

One of the most important political philosophers of the twentieth century, Hannah Arendt was born in 1906 in Hanover, Germany, into a German-Jewish family. Forced to flee Germany in 1933 when Hitler rose to power, she lived in Paris for some years, before migrating to the US in 1941, where she became part of the intellectual circle in New York, and taught at various American universities, until her death in 1975.

Arendt is best known for two influential works. The first, *The Origins of Totalitarianism* (1951), was a study of the Nazi and Stalinist regimes that generated wide-ranging debate on the nature and historical origins of totalitarianism. The second, *The Human Condition* (1958), was a philosophical investigation of the elemental categories of the *vita activa* or active life. At the time of her death in 1975, Arendt had completed the first two volumes of her last major philosophical work, *The Life of the Mind*, which examined the three primary faculties of the *vita contemplativa* or contemplative life. She also published several influential essays on topics such as freedom, authority, tradition and the modern age. Her other works are *Between Past and Future* (1961), *On Revolution* (1963), and *On Violence* (1970).

A NEW PHILOSOPHICAL FRAMEWORK

Arendt engaged with the most crucial political events of her time, trying to grasp their historical and human import, and showing how they affected our categories of moral and political judgment. Through her writings, based on her own life experiences, she built a new framework through which one could come to terms with the twentieth-century horrors of Nazism and Stalinism, and went on to develop a set of philosophical lenses that could illuminate the human condition and provide a fresh perspective on the nature of political life.

Some of her works are considered classics of Western political thought. However, Arendt's political philosophy resists classification and cannot be characterised in terms of the traditional categories of conservatism, liberalism and socialism. A passionate advocate of fundamental human rights, including the right to action and opinion, she strongly supported constitutionalism and the rule of law. She was critical of forms of political community based on racial, ethnic and religious identity.

Neither Liberal nor Anti-Liberal

Arendt's political thought cannot, strictly speaking, be identified either with the liberal or with the anti-liberal tradition. Politics, for Arendt, is neither a means to satisfy individual preferences, nor a way of uniting people around a shared idea of the good. Politics for her is based on the Aristotelian idea of *active citizenship*, on the values of civic engagement and collective deliberation on everything that affects the political community. Arendt's philosophical antecedents thus derive from the tradition of *civic republicanism* originating in **Aristotle**, and continued in the works of Machiavelli, Montesquieu, Jefferson, and Tocqueville. For her, political activity is valuable because it empowers each citizen to exercise their agency, develop a capacity for judgment, and achieve some measure of political efficacy through collective action.

HUMAN ACTION

In her influential work *The Human Condition*, Arendt explores the significance of political participation and presents a 'theory of action'. Human actions, according to Arendt, encompass three practical dimensions: labour, work, and action.

1. **Labour:** The first dimension involves fulfilment of individuals' physical needs. Humans and animals share similarities as both engage in labour to meet their basic needs.
2. **Work:** The second dimension is where individuals create lasting objects and institutions. Unlike animals, humans possess the capacity for productive work that contributes to the development of society.
3. **Action:** The most crucial attribute of human activity, for Arendt, is action. This encompasses political participation and represents a moral act. Engaging in action involves working for betterment of the community, and it is this political dimension that sets humans apart from other species. Arendt's ideas align closely with Aristotle's belief in the superiority of human beings, despite their existence as part of nature. She emphasises that political participation, aimed at the welfare of the community, holds immense value in human life. Activities such as protests and civil disobedience can be considered forms of action and are vital aspects of human activity. While economic activity pertains to the private dimension of human life, political activity operates within the public sphere, taking precedence as the supreme domain in human affairs.

Further, she sees the two central dimensions of human action as freedom and plurality.

Freedom for Arendt does not mean the ability to choose among a set of possible alternatives or the freedom of choice, as valued by liberalism. By freedom, Arendt means the capacity to begin, to start something new, do something unexpected and unforeseen—a capacity, she asserts, that is inherent in all humans by virtue of being born. Action as the realisation of freedom is rooted in the fact that each birth is a new beginning, and the introduction of newness into the world. For Arendt, the birth of every individual holds the promise of a new beginning, and carries with it the capacity to perform miracles. To act for her means to be able to disclose one's self. Most of the examples of 'action' in the modern age that Arendt provides are, in keeping with her view of freedom, instances of revolutions and popular uprisings.

Plurality, the other central feature of action, implies that if to act means to take initiative, it also means that action is not something that can be done alone in isolation, i.e. independent of a plurality of actors who can judge what is being enacted. Action needs plurality in the same way that actors and performers need an audience; without the presence and acknowledgment of others, action would cease to be meaningful. Action, inasmuch that it needs one to make oneself known publicly through word and deed, and eliciting the consent of others, can thus exist only in a context defined by plurality, according to Arendt.

LIBERTY

Arendt's conception of liberty goes beyond the traditional understanding of individual rights and freedoms, and is closely tied to political participation and the ability to engage in collective decision-making within the public realm. Arendt emphasises the importance of political freedom, which she sees as the capacity to act and speak in the public sphere, to participate in the affairs of the community, and to exercise one's agency as a citizen. She believes that true liberty can only be realised through active engagement in public life and the expression of one's political concerns. Arendt also recognises that the realm of politics is subject to the influence of power and domination, and cautions against the potential for totalitarianism and the erosion of individual freedoms in modern societies.

Arendt was influenced by *existentialist* thinkers who emphasised the uniqueness of each individual. She rejected the idea that humans can be fully understood through scientific or positivistic methods, and believed that individuals are not mere reflections of abstract ideas. The true meaning of human existence can be only realised through lived experiences, and each person's experience is inherently unique—this understanding of human uniqueness is central to Arendt's conception of liberty.

Liberty for Arendt holds greater value in human life than material needs. She saw liberty as a fundamental aspect of human imperfection, signifying the capacity for individual agency and self-expression. Human action, she says, can be compared to a person striving to surpass their own previous records in a race, constantly pushing boundaries and seeking self-actualisation.

THE PURPOSE OF POLITICS

Arendt believed that the primary objective of political life should be the welfare and wellbeing of the community, not self-interest and economic prosperity. Arendt was influenced by existentialist thinkers like **Karl Jaspers**, who redefined the relationship between the individual and the state. She rejected the notion that obedience to the state is based on force and coercion, asserting that the state derives its legitimacy from the consent of the people. In her view, power resides in the people, not the state.

Arendt advocated for political action that involves the collective participation of the people, with the role of the state limited to endorsing the decisions made by the people. Rather than relying on coercion and punishment, she said the government should employ persuasion and consensus-building as means to convince the populace. Arendt saw political action and participation as an expression of freedom, reflecting the multilayered and unique nature of individuals, as highlighted by existentialist thinkers like Karl Jaspers.

She believed the ultimate source of political power lies with the people, and that the government is secondary. While elections and political parties are important components of democracy, Arendt emphasised that the power of the citizens themselves is the fundamental requirement for a democratic system to function effectively.

CRITICISM OF MODERNITY

In *The Human Condition*, and in some of her essays in *Between Past and Future*, Arendt articulated what is a largely bleak vision of modernity. However, she offers several suggestions regarding the resources that the modern age can still provide to address questions of meaning, identity and value.

For Arendt, modernity is characterised by the shrinkage or disappearance of the public sphere, which has been replaced by the private world of self-absorption and pursuit of economic interests. Modernity is the age of mass society, mass culture and the rise of the social, from a previous separation between the public and the private, of the victory of the working man over man as a political animal. Modernity is the age of bureaucracy and anonymous labour, the manipulation of public opinion and manufactured consent, rather than politics and informed action. It is the age when totalitarian forms of government like Nazism and Stalinism have risen as a result of the institutionalisation of terror and violence. Modernity for Arendt is where uniformity and conformity have replaced plurality and freedom, and where isolation and loneliness have eroded human solidarity and all spontaneous forms of living together. Modernity is where individuals, having lost their traditional norms and values, must now search for new grounds of human community.

1. **Loss of a common world:** The erosion of a shared common world, the fragmentation of society into specialised spheres and the loss of a unifying public space have contributed to a sense of alienation and the breakdown of meaningful connections between individuals, she argues.
2. **Loss of the public realm:** The erosion of the public sphere where individuals collect as political beings for meaningful dialogue, debate and collective decision-making. The public realm has been replaced by the dominance of the social and economic spheres, and the privatisation of human existence, the private world of self-absorption and pursuit of economic interests.
3. **Rise of individualism and atomisation:** Overemphasis on individualism, self-interest and personal gain has lead to the isolation and atomisation of individuals, and undermined the sense of community and shared responsibility vital for a vibrant public and political sphere.
4. **Loss of political agency:** Modernity has witnessed a decline in political agency and active civic participation in public affairs. The rise of bureaucracy and delegation of decision-making to experts and technocrats has diminished the direct involvement of individuals in shaping their own destinies and the life of their communities.
5. **Instrumentalisation of human life:** In modern society, individuals are valued primarily for their usefulness and productivity, as are personal relationships. This utilitarian perspective has reduced people to mere means for achieving social and economic ends, neglecting their inherent dignity, humanity and uniqueness.

Arendt's criticisms of modernity reflect her deep concern for the vitality of personal and political life, and the preservation of human agency and dignity in the face of the challenges posed by the modern world.

CIVIC REPUBLICANISM

Civic republicanism, as advocated by Hannah Arendt, emphasises that democracy extends beyond a mere focus on voting or electoral processes. The true essence of democracy lies in the power of the people. Arendt does not oppose representative institutions but underlines the need for democratisation and transparency within these institutions. She believes that an active citizenry is fundamental to the functioning of democracy.

Arendt identifies two dimensions of citizenship.

Space of appearance: This refers to active participation in political activities where individuals engage in public discourse, express opinions, and contribute to decision-making processes.

The common world: This signifies the presence of political institutions that provide a shared framework for collective governance. Arendt considers the space of appearance to be more significant than the common world.

According to Arendt, an active citizenry is the foundation of democracy. She views human beings as inherently moral and virtuous. Arendt introduces the concept of 'consensual democracy', which emphasises active civic participation in shaping collective decisions, and asserts that democracy should not be reduced to a simple rule of the majority. She redefines the relationship between citizens and the state, highlighting their interdependence. Laws created by the people are the result of collective consensus, aiming to secure common interests of society. The state itself becomes meaningless without the involvement of its citizens. Holding elections periodically is not sufficient to capture the true essence of democracy; active and ongoing citizen participation is essential, Arendt argues.

ARISTOTLE

Arendt was profoundly inspired and influenced by Aristotle, who considered participation in political life as the embodiment of 'virtue in action'. Arendt believed that true democracy existed in the ancient Greek era when citizens had the right to engage in political activities. However, while she deeply admired the democratic practices of the ancient Greek city-states, she also criticised the prevalence of slavery and the subordination of women and artisans in them.

As a political thinker, Arendt emphasised the significance of political life itself, considering it a means to achieve moral ends. She was influenced by existentialist philosophers like **Karl Jaspers** and **Martin Heidegger**, who explored questions of individuality, freedom, and the human experience. Arendt's work reflects her engagement with these existentialist ideas, as she sought to re-examine and revitalise political thought in the context of the modern world.

POWER

Arendt asserts that it is important to distinguish power from violence, as power is not synonymous with force or coercion. Power, she argues, is fundamentally based on consent and derives from the people. The collective action of individuals is essential for exercising and maintaining power. However, in situations where individuals live isolated lives, the potential for violence tends to increase.

For Arendt, politics is not merely a means to acquire power and influence but a platform to ensure justice and uphold human dignity. She strongly opposed the notion of defining human beings objectively. **Bhikhu Parekh** suggests that Arendt's political views align closely with those of **Gandhi**, **Lenin**, and **Mao**. Arendt emphasised the significance of community while also valuing individual freedom within the community. She believed that the legitimacy of government and state power stems from the people's consent, and hence, the government's role should be that of an initiator, with all its actions receiving the people's approval. This aligns with her vision of a *consensual democracy*.

Arendt stressed the importance of individuals, rather than political parties, emphasising active public participation in all aspects of community life as crucial. However, in the modern democratic era, the citizens' role has often been reduced to voting alone. Arendt believed that thinkers and intellectuals must play a vital role in influencing people by fulfilling several responsibilities, including imparting knowledge to citizens, encouraging criticism and dissent, promoting constructive engagement, and fostering dialogues among citizens on various issues.

ORIGINS OF TOTALITARIANISM

In her book *The Origins of Totalitarianism*, Arendt traces the roots of totalitarianism. While the ideas of **Plato** played a role in laying the basis for totalitarianism, modern industrial capitalist society also bears a responsibility, asserts Arendt. Totalitarianism is built upon terror and a false ideology or myth perpetuated by a ruling party that seeks unlimited power. Arendt classifies **Hitler**, **Mussolini** and **Stalin** as totalitarian leaders who used both terror and ideology to control all aspects of human activity, physical, psychological, emotional and spiritual, effectively suppressing individuality and freedom.

She traces the philosophical roots of totalitarianism back to Plato, who envisioned an ideal republic. Plato's analysis of human beings in *The Republic* aimed at creating the perfect state, ruler, citizen and polity—an ambition also shared by fascists. Plato's portrayed human beings objectively and instrumentally, devaluing their humanity and individuality. Hitler, too, sought to establish an ideal state, sacrificing human liberty, life and rights in the pursuit of this ideal. Arendt challenges the notion of an objective definition of the individual, asserting that human beings are fundamentally distinct from material objects.

Totalitarianism thrives in the context of industrial-urban mass societies, where individuals prioritise material needs at any cost, often undermining their own liberty and rights. Following the end of World War II, grappling with extreme economic hardship and unemployment, people often placed blind faith in totalitarian rulers as a means of escape. As a result, their role in society became confined to labour, while the crucial aspect of political participation, known as 'action,' was ignored.

In modern capitalist society, focused on work and profit, importance is given to wealth and material prosperity over individual liberty. In such atomistic societies, propaganda becomes a powerful tool for manipulating and controlling the masses. Arendt's analysis underscores the grave dangers of totalitarianism and its threat to humanity.

TOTALITARIAN REGIMES

Focusing on movements like Nazism and Stalinism, Arendt discusses the distinctive characteristics of totalitarian regimes which set them apart from other forms of non-democratic government.

1. **Total Control:** Totalitarianism extends beyond political control and encompasses every aspect of human life, including the economy, culture, politics, and society. The government regulates and dictates the lives of individuals in all these dimensions.
2. **Nation vs. State:** In totalitarian regimes, the concept of the nation takes precedence over the state. The nation is an emotional, psychological, and ethnic entity, often represented by the majority ethnic group, which can lead to the suppression of minorities under the guise of nationalism. The state refers to the administrative and legal apparatus of the government.
3. **State Domination:** Civil society is fully controlled by the state in a totalitarian system. Institutions such as the family, church and university are subject to state regulation. The state dictates the curriculum taught in universities and exercises control over media and the film industry. Dissent and criticism against the state are not tolerated, and the leadership and ruling party become the central sources of power.
4. **Suppression of Dissent:** Totalitarian regimes employ violence as a means to suppress dissent and opposition. The state promotes fear and terror among the populace to maintain control. Secret agencies are often employed to monitor and suppress any opposition from civil society.
5. **Brutal Use of Violence:** Both fascist and Stalinist regimes are notorious for their brutal use of violence, resulting in widespread terror, loss of lives, and the stifling of dissent and freedom of thought. Arendt critiqued the rise of communist ideologies, which led to the establishment of totalitarian states under the pretext of the dictatorship of the proletariat.

Arendt argues that in order to prevent the emergence of totalitarianism, people must exercise their collective power and actively participate in politics. Only by engaging in informed political action and ensuring the protection of freedom can the risk of totalitarianism be diminished and the erosion of humane and democratic values be halted.

REVOLUTION

Hannah Arendt was a fervent advocate of republican government and the preservation of human liberty. In her analysis of the American Revolution of 1776 and the French Revolution of 1789, she praised the former for establishing a limited constitutional government in America, which she believed was crucial in safeguarding individual liberty, and viewed the American Revolution as a successful example of political action leading to the attainment of its objectives.

In contrast, Arendt found the French Revolution to be less successful. Inspired by notions of necessity and want, the French Revolution aimed to bring social and economic transformation. Arendt drew a parallel between the French Revolution and communist revolutions, arguing that they were not genuine revolutions. According to Marxist ideology, the primary concern of individuals is their economic needs, with all other aspects being secondary. Arendt contested this perspective and asserted that revolutions driven solely by necessity often fall short of achieving their intended goals.

The French Revolution, in particular, failed to deliver on its aspirations for socio-economic transformation. Instead, it led to the establishment of a despotic rule in France after the revolution. Arendt identified this failure to be a consequence of the revolution's focus on necessity, rather than a broader understanding of the complexities of human values, and the importance of preserving individual liberties.

A HUMANIST

For Arendt, liberty was a fundamental aspect of human nature, and she rejected the notion that human beings are inherently egoistic and self-centred. While she recognised the significance of community, she also emphasised that the community should not suppress the liberty and individuality of its citizens. Arendt drew inspiration from the direct democracy of ancient Greece, but she did not outright reject representative democracy. Instead, she sought to reform representative democracy to ensure greater citizen involvement and participation.

Arendt did not align herself with liberalism or socialism, but she strongly criticised fascism and advocated for individual liberty. She also emphasised the importance of acting for the community and rejected the idea of an atomistic and individualistic society. Her goal was to make modern democracy more democratic by decentralising power from political parties and promoting active political participation by the people. Arendt believed that the state should govern its citizens through persuasion and education rather than relying on fear, coercion and punishment.

Arendt was critical of capitalism, which she saw as dehumanising, prioritising profit, competition and mass culture, but failing to preserve individual liberty and expression. She was also critical of Marxism. According to Arendt, both capitalism and Marxism posed dangers to liberty and democracy. Her ideas are rooted in humanism and transcend ideological divisions, making them relevant to the present age of postmodernism.

14

FRANTZ FANON (1925–1961)

KEY CONCEPTS

Confucianism; relationships; monarchical state; morality

Frantz Omar Fanon, also known as Ibrahim Fanon, was born in 1925 on the French island colony of Martinique in the West Indies. One of the most important writers in black Atlantic theory in an age of anti-colonial liberation struggle, his work draws on a wide range of psychology, philosophy and political theory, and its influence across the Global South has been deep and enduring.

Fanon engaged with the most urgent and vital issues of his day: language, sexuality, gender, race and racism, religion, social formation, among many others. He is most famous for two widely-studied and debated works: *Black Skin, White Masks* (1952). His two other works, *A Dying Colonialism* (1959), *The Wretched of the Earth* (1961), *Alienation and Freedom* (1961) and *Toward the African Revolution* (posthumously published in 1964) comprise short essays and analyses.

AGAINST COLONIALISM

Fanon was an immensely influential political leader who played a pivotal role in inspiring and shaping the national liberation movements that swept across Asia and Africa in the aftermath of the World War II. He recognised that peaceful means alone were insufficient to overthrow the oppressive yoke of colonial exploitation, advocating the use of violence as a necessary tool in this struggle. He was deeply influenced by figures such as **Jean-Paul Sartre** and **Patrice Lumumba**, whose ideas further shaped his own political ideology. For Fanon, colonialism is a 'total project', a project that does not leave any aspect, any dimension of the colonised human being and his or her reality untouched.

BLACK CONSCIOUSNESS

Fanon highlighted the inherent bias within European knowledge and ideas when it came to Asia and Africa. His critique extended to the French exploitation in Algeria, recognising that colonialism encompassed not only economic exploitation but also racial and ideological subjugation. In his seminal work *Black Skin, White Masks* (1952), he articulated the notion that the Black soul had become an artefact of the white man. European societies, driven by the notion of the 'white man's burden,' propagated the belief that Asian and African cultures were inherently inferior. Fanon vehemently contended that Europeans consistently projected themselves as superior and civilised while maintaining a biased perspective in their descriptions of Asia and Africa.

Black Skin, White Masks, Fanon's influential work on the subject of blackness, delves into the realms of consciousness and the social world to comprehend the roots of anti-Black racism. In the years following its publication, Fanon's focus evolves, encompassing a broader theory of oppression, colonialism, and resistance against the pervasive grip of coloniality as a system. This shift is perceivable when compared with Fanon's early contemplations on anti-Black racism. His profound insights into how anti-Black racism shapes and distorts the subjectivity of both white and Black individuals are pivotal in grasping the complex layers of colonial subjugation and the prerequisites for its ultimate emancipation.

NEO-MARXIST

As a Neo-Marxist thinker, Fanon expanded the understanding of societal disparities beyond the realm of class and emphasised the significance of racialism as a crucial factor in discrimination. Rejecting the principles of orthodox Marxism, he challenged the notion that the Western proletarian class was inherently revolutionary or sympathetic to the struggles of colonial peoples. Instead, Fanon asserted that Asian and African proletarians should not rely on the Western proletariat due to their privileged position.

Advocating for an alternative approach, Fanon proposes a combination of the peasantry, urban intellectuals, and rural dwellers as agents of social change. In his other well-known work, *The Wretched of the Earth* (1961), Fanon dissects the dynamics of power, characterising the Western bourgeoisie as both productive and parasitical, whereas the colonial bourgeoisie was merely parasitical. He argues that the colonial bourgeoisie served as a mere conduit for Western capitalism, lacking any creative role in the generation of wealth. He also dwells on violence as a necessary precondition for liberation. *The Wretched of the Earth* established Fanon as a profound and powerful thinker of anti-colonial struggle, revolutionary action and post-colonial statecraft and imagination.

LEGACY

Frantz Fanon was a heroic figure and a source of intellectual inspiration during his lifetime, and remains so years after his death. His ideas resonated deeply with those involved in anti-colonial and anti-racist struggles, shaping the work of thinkers and political activists from various parts of the Global South. Latin American activists drew on Fanon's insights, as did many in Africa and South Asia. His ideas continue to fuel discussions on race, nation, migration, language, and representation, among others. Fanon's wide-ranging impact stems from his capacity to engage with diverse perspectives and provide profound insights into the lived experiences of individuals oppressed by colonialism, as well as his ability to bridge different theoretical approaches and infuse analysis with vivid descriptions of the body and mind under colonial domination.

15

MAO ZEDONG (1893–1976)

KEY CONCEPTS

Chinese Communist Party; Contradiction; permanent revolution; guerilla warfare; democratic centralism; five year plan

Mao Zedong, also known as Chairman Mao, was a Chinese politician, poet, political theorist, and communist revolutionary. Born into a peasant family in Shaoshan, Hunan, Mao developed a strong sense of Chinese nationalism and anti-imperialism from an early age. The Xinhai Revolution in 1911 and the May Fourth Movement in 1919 left a deep influence on him. While working as a librarian at Peking University, Mao embraced Marxism-Leninism and became one of the founding members of the Chinese Communist Party (CCP). In 1927, he led the Autumn Harvest Uprising and participated in the Chinese Civil War between the Kuomintang (KMT) and the CCP.

Mao played a pivotal role in the establishment of the People's Republic of China (PRC) and served as the chairman of the Chinese Communist Party from 1949 until his death in 1976. Mao was an advocate of Marxist-Leninist ideology and his theories, military strategies, and political policies are collectively referred to as Maoism.

The Role of Consciousness: Marx emphasised the importance of material conditions, such as urbanisation and industrialisation, for a communist revolution to occur. However, Mao adapted communism to the realities of Asia and China, asserting that consciousness and ideas held greater significance in bringing about revolution than material conditions alone.

Peasants as the Vanguard of Revolution: Marx proposed that the proletariat or the working class had the capability to initiate revolutionary change, while peasants were seen as more conservative. Lenin broadening the definition of the working class to include peasants as well. Mao, however, presented a unique perspective by stating that peasants could serve as the vanguard of revolution. This view was expressed in his influential work, the *Report on the Peasant Movement in Hunan* (1925). While considering himself a Marxist-Leninist, Mao developed his own revolutionary strategy tailored to the specific conditions of Chinese society, which at the time was predominantly rural and lacking industrialisation.

ON CONTRADICTION

In his essay 'On Contradiction' (1937), Mao asserted that contradiction is an inherent aspect of existence, and that nothing can exist without it. He identified two types of contradiction:

1. **Antagonistic contradiction:** This exists between revolutionaries and their enemies. It encompasses the fundamental conflicts

and struggles that arise in the pursuit of social change.

2. **Non-antagonistic contradiction:** This occurs among the people themselves, within the working class, peasantry and intelligentsia. It refers to the tensions and conflicts that arise within a society even after a revolutionary transformation has taken place.

Recognising the presence of contradiction in socialist society, Mao advocated for the concept of permanent revolution. This means that even after a revolution has occurred, continuous efforts and vigilance are required to address contradictions and further advance the goals of the revolution. Mao believed that a dynamic and ongoing revolutionary process was necessary to navigate and resolve contradictions within society.

Mao disagreed with **Stalin**'s assertion that contradiction ceased to exist in socialist society following the abolition of capitalism. Mao believed that contradictions continue to exist in a communist society because no society can achieve absolute perfection. Mao also criticised the principle of peaceful coexistence put forth by **Khrushchev**, seeing it as inadequate or flawed in addressing the complexities and contradictions of the global political landscape.

PERMANENT REVOLUTION

The concept of permanent revolution was first propounded by **Marx** and **Engels**, and it was later endorsed by figures such as **Plekhanov** and **Trotsky**. While Lenin emphasised the importance of a politically trained leadership within the party, Mao placed significant emphasis on *mass mobilisation* as a driving force for revolutionary change. Several examples of mass mobilisation initiatives during Mao's leadership are outlined below:

1. Anti-Landlord Campaign (1949–52): This campaign aimed to redistribute land and eliminate feudal practices by mobilising the masses against oppressive landlords.
2. Hundred Flowers Bloom (1957): Encouraging open expression of opinions, this movement sought to gather diverse perspectives and promote intellectual freedom within society.
3. The Great Leap Forward (1958–60): This ambitious economic and social programme aimed to rapidly transform China into an industrialised nation through collective efforts and mobilisation of the masses, although its implementation led to significant challenges and setbacks.
4. The Great Cultural Revolution (1966–76): Launched to revive revolutionary fervour and combat perceived bourgeois influences within society, this movement involved massive mobilisation of students, workers, and peasants to challenge established authority and promote Maoist ideology.

Mao's emphasis on mass mobilisation reflected his belief in the power of the masses to bring about revolutionary change and shape the course of society.

GUERRILLA WARFARE

Mao believed that guerrilla warfare was a crucial strategy for revolutionary movements in countries with a predominantly rural population and underdeveloped military capabilities. He famously stated that political power grows out of the barrel of a gun, openly acknowledging his support for the use of violence as a means of achieving revolutionary goals. Diverging from traditional Marxist perspectives, Mao emphasised the significance of the village as the epicentre of revolution. He believed that just as cities are surrounded by rural areas, capitalist nations are surrounded by Asian and African countries. This perspective led him to assert that the communist revolution should be a global movement, extending its reach beyond individual nations. Mao's ideology reflected a shift from viewing revolution as confined to specific regions or countries and instead envisioned a worldwide revolution unfolding on a global scale. Mao stated in a lecture that 'politics is war without bloodshed while war is politics with bloodshed'.

Mao's strategic views on guerrilla warfare include the following:

1. *Protracted People's War*: Mao envisaged a prolonged struggle against the enemy. He believed the revolution should progress through three stages: strategic defence, strategic stalemate, and strategic offensive, gradually expanding the revolution's influence and strength.
2. *Mobilising the masses*: Mao emphasised the importance of organising the rural population, particularly peasants, to form a large revolutionary force. He believed the masses played a central role in guerrilla warfare and should actively participate in the revolutionary struggle.
3. *Guerrilla warfare*: Mao advocated for flexible and mobile guerrilla tactics, such as hit-and-run attacks, ambushes, and the use of small, highly mobile units. He believed in leveraging the advantage of surprise, agility, and knowledge of the local terrain to outmanoeuvre and weaken the enemy forces.
4. *Political warfare*: Mao stressed the need for effective political warfare alongside military actions. He believed in winning the hearts and minds of the people, gaining their support, and isolating the enemy by addressing their grievances and offering practical solutions to their problems.
5. *Base areas*: Mao advocated for establishing and consolidating base areas, which would serve as revolutionary strongholds and centres of governance, provide a safe haven for revolutionaries to regroup, train, and build popular support.

Mao's ideas on guerrilla warfare, as implemented during the Chinese Revolution, played a significant role in the ultimate success of the Communist Party in overthrowing the nationalist government and establishing the People's Republic of China.

DICTATORSHIP OF PROLETARIAT

Mao advocated for a 'United Front' comprising various groups, including the peasantry, the working class, the petty bourgeoisie, and the national bourgeoisie. He believed that this alliance was crucial for the success of the New Democratic Revolution, emphasising that dictatorship of the proletariat did not solely rest with one class but rather represented a coalition of multiple classes. Mao challenged the notion that the complete dismantling of state machinery was necessary, and presented a two-stage framework for revolution.

1. **Democratic Revolution**: This stage focused on addressing the issues of feudal landlords, bureaucratic capitalists, and foreign imperialists. The united front would work collectively to combat these forces and bring about democratic reforms.
2. **Socialist Revolution:** The success of the democratic revolution would lay the foundation for the subsequent socialist revolution. Mao envisioned that the new democratic society would naturally progress towards socialism and ultimately establish a communist society.

Mao's understanding of the united front and the two-stage revolution process aimed to create a path towards a more equitable and classless society.

DEMOCRATIC CENTRALISM

Democratic centralism is a guiding principle for the working of the communist party adopted by Mao, which finds its roots in Lenin's ideology. In his book *On the People's Democratic Dictatorship* (1949), Mao embraces this principle, acknowledging the significance of a single-party system in communist ideology. Centralism in this context pertains to fostering discipline and unity within the party. Democratic elements are also crucial, allowing for open debates and discussions before reaching decisions. Once a decision is made, it is binding on all party members, ensuring a cohesive and unified approach.

FIVE YEAR PLAN

Mao Zedong introduced the idea of the 'Five Year Plan' for the national economy (1953–57) to encourage the economic growth of China through heavy industry, agriculture, handicrafts, transportation and commerce.

SELECTED LIST OF WORKS

1. *On Practice and Contradiction* (1937)
2. *On Guerrilla Warfare* (1937)
3. *On Contradiction* (1937)
4. *On New Democracy* (1940)
5. *On People's Democratic Dictatorship* (1949)

16

JOHN RAWLS (1921–2002)

KEY CONCEPTS

Origins of citizenship; kinds of citizenship; perspectives on citizenship

John Rawls, an American political philosopher in the liberal tradition, was born in Baltimore, Maryland. He studied at Princeton and Cornell University, where he was influenced by the work of **Ludwig Wittgenstein**'s student **Norman Malcolm**, and at Oxford, where he worked with **H. L. A. Hart**, **Isaiah Berlin**, and **Stuart Hampshire**.

Rawls's adult life was academic. As a college student, Rawls wrote an intensely religious senior thesis and had considered studying for the priesthood. However, Rawls lost his Christian faith as an infantryman in World War II after witnessing death in combat at close quarters and learning of the horrors of the Holocaust. In the 1960s, he spoke out against the draft for the Vietnam War because it discriminated against black and poor Americans. The Vietnam War compelled him to critically study the flaws in the American political system that led it to prosecute so mercilessly what Rawls saw as an unjust war, and to consider how American citizens could ethically resist their government's aggressive policies.

Rawls's most significant contribution is his theory of *justice as fairness*, which outlines a vision for a just liberal society. His comprehensive exposition of justice as fairness can be found in his 1971 book, *A Theory of Justice* (1971). Throughout his life, he continued to refine and expand upon this theory, revisiting it in subsequent works such as *Political Liberalism* (1993), *The Law of Peoples* (1999), *Collected Papers* (1999), *Lectures on the History of Moral Philosophy* (2000) and *Justice as Fairness* (2001).

CENTRALITY OF INDIVIDUAL

Rawls was deeply influenced by the ideas of **Immanuel Kant** who formulated the liberal idea of abstract individualism by asserting that 'individuals are the kingdoms of ends and means'. Rawls also asserted that the self is prior to its ends, and that therefore, any relevant theory of justice should be based upon the centrality of individual rationality and must emerge from human understandings. Thus, Rawls rejected the idea of divine justice. He formulated his theory of the *social contract* based on two important conceptualisations: *the veil of ignorance* and the *original position.*

Rawls was critical of **Jeremy Bentham**'s concept of justice, particularly with regard to his emphasis on the majority. As a staunch liberal, Rawls does not compromise on individual liberties and rights, and individual dignity takes precedence when establishing a just society. Bentham's concept of justice is rooted in *consequentialism* where outcomes are more important, while Rawls argues that the fairness of the process is paramount, as a fair procedure is more likely to yield fair outcomes. Bentham puts strong emphasis on happiness, which can potentially be gained at the expense of liberty and rights. Rawls asserts that liberty and rights always come first, regardless of the pursuit of happiness.

SOCIAL CONTRACT AND JUSTICE AS FAIRNESS

Rawls posited that in a just society, no individual is excluded, and all individuals are considered equal partners in its creation. No one can exert influence or dictate terms to others when establishing a just society. Participants in the social contract imagine themselves in a future society where they could potentially occupy the least advantaged position. Consequently, everyone seeks to secure the basic primary goods within a just society, particularly if they belong to the least advantaged segment of society.

Justice is neither divine nor natural, but the result of deliberate choices made by individuals, Rawls argues. To establish principles of justice, he employs the social contract. In this contractual framework, all individuals are regarded as equal participants, holding an identical position. This equal standing is crucial for the creation of fairness within the concept of justice. It is important to note that Rawls' social contract is a philosophical construct rather than a historical account. By employing the social contract, Rawls aims to demonstrate the significance of justice and its role in creating a just society.

THE LAW OF PEOPLES

Rawls strongly supports the formation of international cooperative organisations. In his work *The Law of Peoples* (1993), Rawls proposes eight principles to which, he argues, all well-organised peoples across all nations would largely agree:

1. People are free and independent; their freedom and independence must be respected.
2. People must observe all international treaties and undertakings.
3. People are equal.
4. People have the right to self-defense.
5. People must observe non-intervention.
6. People must honour human rights.
7. People must observe certain specified restrictions in the conduct of war.
8. People have a duty to assist other peoples living under unfavourable conditions that prevent their having a just or decent political regime.

REFLECTIVE EQUILIBRIUM

The goal of political philosophy, for Rawls, is to arrive at justified conclusions regarding the direction of political life. According to Rawls, the degree of justification in one's political convictions depends on the extent to which one achieves *reflective equilibrium*. Reflective equilibrium occurs when all of an individual's beliefs, spanning various levels of generality, perfectly cohere with one another. In this state of reflective equilibrium, specific political judgments, such as condemning religious intolerance or racial discrimination, provide support for more general political convictions, such as recognising the basic rights of all citizens. These general convictions, in turn, support one's overarching abstract beliefs about the political realm, such as the belief in the freedom and equality of all citizens. Seen from the opposite perspective, in reflective equilibrium, one's abstract beliefs elucidate the rationale behind more general convictions, which then inform specific judgments. If one were to attain reflective equilibrium, the justification of each belief would stem from the interconnection and mutual reinforcement of all beliefs within these networks of support and explanation.

ROLE OF POLITICAL PHILOSOPHY

Rawls believes that political philosophy can fulfil some significant roles in public culture.

1. Philosophy can offer grounds for reasoned agreement when sharp political differences and divisions threaten to lead to violent conflict.
2. It can help citizens negotiate and orient themselves in their own world, understand what it means to be part of a certain society, and how people with that political status should relate to one another.
3. Political philosophy must offer real practical political possibilities that real citizens can support. It can also depict a utopian order that is ideal and to be wished and hoped for.
4. A fourth role is reconciliation: philosophy can show us that human life is not simply about corruption, cruelty, prejudice and power play, but that in some respects at least it is better as it is now than it was previously.

Rawls sees his own work as a practical contribution aimed at addressing the longstanding tension between liberty and equality in democratic thought. He seeks to outline the boundaries of civic and international tolerance. By presenting a framework, he offers citizens of democratic nations a means to perceive themselves as free and equal members of a society that upholds fairness for all. He presents an optimistic vision of a just and constitutional democracy that operates harmoniously within a peaceful global community. For individuals who may feel disheartened by the differing perspectives of their fellow citizens and humans, Rawls offers a reconciling perspective. He suggests that this diversity of worldviews is a product of, and can facilitate, a social order that promotes greater freedom for everyone.

Unit III

INDIAN POLITICAL THOUGHT

KEY TRADITIONS AND THINKERS

Dharmashastra, Kautilya, Arthashastra, Agganna Sutta, Barani, Kabir, Pandita Ramabai, Bal Gangadhar Tilak, Swami Vivekanadanda, Rabindranath Tagore, Mahatma Gandhi, Aurobindo, Periyar E. V. Ramasamy, Muhammad Iqbal, M. N. Roy, V. D. Savarkar, B. R. Ambedkar, Jawaharlal Nehru, Ram Manohar Lohia, Jayaprakash Narayan, Deendayal Upadhyaya

1

INDIAN POLITICAL THINKERS

KEY CONCEPTS

Matsynyaya; dharma; danda; features of Indian political thought

NATURE OF ANCIENT INDIAN POLITICAL THOUGHT

It is believed that any political thought in ancient India was a part of Hindu philosophy or the Hindu religion. In other words, the Hindu science of polity was not considered to have a separate identity of its own. But a closer look at the 'political' in various available sources makes it clear that ancient Indian thinkers did have a notion of the political, as distinct from either philosophy or religion. This erroneous conclusion of some scholars was a result of their fixed notions of politics and political science, derived mainly from the West.

Problem of Nomenclature

The confusion arises because of the large number of parallel terms used in ancient India for politics: *Rajadharma*, which means the duties of the ruler; *Kshatravidya*, the knowledge that the ruler should have; *Rajyashastra*, meaning statecraft or the science of state; *Dandaniti*, the art of awarding punishment; *Nitishastra*, the science of moral values or ethics regulating the lives of both the ruler and the ruled; and *Arthashastra*, an ancient Indian treatise on statecraft, political science, economic policy, and military strategy.

Concept of Matsyanyaya

Ancient India had a term equivalent to the Western concept of the state of nature: *Matsyanyaya*, which refers to the principle underlying the Law of Fish, that is, the proverb of big fish devouring the small. It recognised the strong devouring the weak. In ancient Indian political thought, Matsyanyaya explains the state of affairs in the absence of force or *danda*. Force is held to be the ultimate sanction behind the state. At the same time, it is recognised that force cannot be used arbitrarily, and various checks are introduced to ensure that the person entrusted with the authority to rule does use force at will.

Dharma and Danda

According to **Bhikhu Parekh**, Hindu political thinkers recognised political life in terms of two central concepts: *dharma* and *danda*, both of which are dependent on each other. Danda means discipline, force, restraint, constraint, or punishment. Dharma, derived from the Sanskrit root '*dhr*', meaning to hold, is the religious and moral law governing individual conduct and is one of the four ends of life. It is dharma which holds society together when each individual and group adheres to their specific duties, by following the *varnashrama dharma*.

SOURCES

As mentioned earlier, politics in India was not considered an independent and autonomous discipline. One has to unearth the notions of politics from a host of sources dealing with larger questions of human life, which are mainly religious and philosophical in nature. Important sources for studies of politics are:

1. Vedic literature
2. Dharmasutras and Smritis
3. Epics and Puranas
4. Arthashastras
5. Buddhist and Jain literature
6. Coins and Inscriptions
7. Greek and Chinese accounts
8. Other literature sources and Epigraphy

Several Indian nationalist historians, such as Bhagavan Lal, Inderjit Bhandarkar, R. L. Mitra, B. G. Tilak, and later, K. P. Jayaswal, R. K. Majumdar, and B. K. Sarkar, have offered their own interpretations of Indian history that counter imperialist ideology. They argued that what was prevalent in ancient India was not autocratic rule, but limited monarchy.

K. P. Jayaswal, in his *Hindu Polity* (1924), argued that ancient Indian polity had elements of both the Republics of ancient Greece and constitutional monarchies such as that of Great Britain. He concluded: 'The constitutional progress made by the Hindus has probably not been equaled, much less surpassed by any policy of antiquity.' While appreciating the attempt of nationalist scholars to inculcate self-confidence amongst the people during the nationalist movement, one must properly understand the limitations of this approach as well. R. S. Sharma, an eminent historian, has pointed out four important limitations of this nationalist and revivalist approach to the study of Indian political thought.

CHARACTERISTICS OF INDIAN POLITICAL THOUGHT

Political Life within the Framework of Dharma

One cannot find in ancient India any treatises dealing exclusively with political and social life, which can be comparable to Plato's *Republic* or Aristotle's *Politics*. A supernatural element pervades all writings; the divine is omnipotent and visible in the formation of society and government, the divine purpose is to be enforced by the king, and divine punishment reinforces earthly punishment, and sometimes supplants it.

Influence of Ethics

Social thought in ancient India not only assured certain fundamental principles of morality, but it also sought to direct material life as well. The king must consciously stimulate virtue and act as a guide to a moral life, in accordance with the morality stipulated in the Dharamshastras.

However, when it comes to international relations, one can see a confluence of ethics and hard reality. For example, Kautilya's discussion of diplomacy bears a marked resemblance to Machiavelli. One may notice a sudden fall from ethical abstraction to the rankest realism in the same writer.

Influence of Caste-based Social Structure on Politics

Caste occupied a prominent place in all social speculation during the later Vedic period, and had a direct bearing on the theory of government. The principle of *varnashrama dharma* in society was fixed on the basis of caste, with each varna assigned specific functions. It was the foremost duty of the king to see that every individual confined himself to performing the functions of the varna in which he was born. Caste was an ascribed status.

Government as Partnership with the Upper Varnas

In ancient India, the Kshatriyas, Brahmanas, and later, the Vaisyas, together formed the ruling class. The Shudras were the so-called serving class. 'Kshatra'—temporal power—derived its strength and authority from 'Brahma', the spiritual power. The Vaisya engaged in such occupations as agriculture and trade, and provided the economic basis of the state. The priest held the highest status. He was identified with the God 'Brihaspathy' instead of the temporal power, 'India', and his function was to interpret dharma and preside over the rituals.

No Clear Distinction between State and Society

Governmental and politics were viewed as part of the larger whole called society. In other words, society was at once religious, political, economic, and military. It was generally viewed in a comprehensive manner and not from an exclusively political angle. With no clear conception of either the state or government, the two terms were used interchangeably.

Monarchy: The Natural Outcome

Since the four-fold division of society entrusted the Kshatriya caste with the power to rule, monarchy was the natural outcome. There were non-monarchical forms of government as well; Kautilya's *Arthashastra*, for example, mentions '*dvairajya*' (rule by two kings), '*vyrajya*' (state without a king), etc. There were also '*ganasanghas*' which, according to K. P. Jayaswal, are comparable to modern republics. But these were more the exception than the rule, and monarchy usually prevailed.

Government was not Sovereign

The government in ancient India could not be regarded as sovereign in the Austinian sense of the term. It did not impart validity to the orders: rather, it shared in its validity. The government had no independent existence, its function being the sustenance of the social order. Sovereignty was, in fact, ultimately sourced in divine will. The individual, for his part, owed no unified allegiance or loyalty to anyone except society as a whole. It is only the pluralistic theory of sovereignty that can allow us to grasp the Indian phenomenon.

Other Distinguishing Features

Bhikhu Parekh mentions some other distinguishing features of the Hindu political tradition:

1. **First**, the Hindu tradition is basically inegalitarian. Although the idea of the moral equality of all men did develop later, it never developed the social, legal and political groups.
2. **Second**, the Hindu tradition of political thought is pluralistic in orientation. From the beginning, Hindu political writers had recognized the autonomy of social groups.
3. **Third**, political thought in early India was largely uncritical and apologetic of the established social order. Most Hindu writers justified the caste system from the perspective of the caste-based conception of dharma and the largely fatalistic concept which rationalised the degradation of the Shudras and slaves, as well as the extensive moral interference of the state. It ignored issues of social conflict.
4. **Fourth**, many Hindu writers wrote chiefly to attract the attention of rulers. Their works are largely manuals of ethics or administration, and hence are didactic and practical.

2

DHARMASHASTRA

KEY CONCEPTS

Divine origin of state; nature of the state; first codified law; justification of inequality

Dharmashastra, a genre of Sanskrit texts on law and conduct, is an important treatise on ancient Indian political thought. It was considered an embodiment of the complete knowledge given to Manu by Lord Brahma. The establishment of *Dharma*, or cosmic order, is the primary goal, with the powers and authority of king being only secondary. Its components include:

1. Dhrti (patience)
2. Ks'ama (forgiveness)
3. Dhama (self-control)
4. Asteya ('non-stealing'; honest behaviour)
5. Shaoca (cleanliness)
6. Indriya Nigraha (control of the senses)
7. Dhii (benevolent intellect)
8. Vidya (spiritual knowledge)
9. Satyam (benevolent truthfulness)
10. Akrodha (absence of anger)

The word 'dharma' implies one's conduct and social obligations in the cosmic order. The cosmic order and the social order established under the Dharmashastra are 'sacrosanct' and 'unalterable'. Politics came into existence to control individual and social conduct and maintain the cosmic order. Dharma is different from religion, and refers to the duty, morality, or virtue of a human being. Dharma donates the essence or quality of any object; the dharma of the sun, for instance, is to give light. Religion is a narrower term and includes three features:

1. Place of worship.
2. Religious scripture.
3. Faith in a metaphysical entity.

According to Manu, there are 10 virtues that individuals must adhere to if the principles of dharma are to be upheld—wisdom, patience, forbearance, purity, etc. But evil tendencies in human beings are the biggest obstacles to achieving the principles of Dharma, both letter and spirit. This creates a situation of **Matsyanyaya**, or might is right (see Chapter 1). In order to control this tendency in human being, *danda niti* is needed. Danda niti refers to punishment or use of force to control evil tendencies in human beings and persuade them to follow the dictates of 'Dharma'. Danda niti was synonymous with politics in ancient political thought, which concerned itself with both worldly pleasures and spiritual beliefs, in contrast to modern political thought, which seeks to provide materialistic and worldly pleasure. Ancient political thought also lays down the principles of **rajdharma,** which is a set of rules concerning the duties of a ruler. As per the rajdharma, the king was expected to govern the state in accordance with the dictates of the Vedas and Shastras.

DIVINE ORIGIN OF STATE

Manu believed in the divine origin of the state and that human beings possess a mixture of good and evil tendencies. When swayed by evil tendencies, individuals violate the principles of Dharma. This is what explains the emergence of Danda niti: according to Manu, the king is the divine symbol of Danda, created to save the world from anarchy. The king is said to possess unique qualities of all the major Gods—Indra, Vayu, Yama, Kuber, Agni, Varuna, and Chandra. As the embodiment of God on earth, any disobedience or betrayal of the king will be considered a betrayal of God. If the king refuses to obey the dictates of Dharma, he will, in his turn, be doomed along with his family, and be denied *moksha*.

In order to ensure social harmony and promote people's welfare, the state should be governed by a selfless and enlightened Yogi King who will uphold the principles of Dharma. The king is not allowed to create new rules or principles of Dharma; he is only to uphold and preserve them. Manu, who openly supported the monarchical form of kingship instead of democratic rule, believed that'not everyone possesses the qualities of a king. Here, his view of kingship departs from the Western view, where the monarch is considered the 'Agent of God' and the principle is that the 'king can do no wrong'.

NATURE OF THE STATE

The state is organic in nature and is comprised of seven parts, approximating the seven organs of the human body. The more powerful the component parts of the state, the stronger is the state itself.

Saptang Theory

The king is the head, the minister, the eyes, and its allies, the ears. The mouth signifies the treasury, the army its mind, and lastly, the capital and rashtra serve as the hands and feet. Dharamshastra believes in the organic theory of the state, where all seven elements of a state form its integral parts. These seven elements are as follows:

1. King (Swami)
2. Minister (Amatya)
3. Fort (Durg)
4. District (Janapad)
5. Treasury (Kosh)
6. Ally (Mitra)
7. Punishment (Danda)

Modern Western political theory identifies four elements of the state: population, territory, government, and sovereignty.

Welfare State

Rajdharma is the most important in dharamshastra and controls the entire state in government. The elements of state are also known as **Prakriti**. Chapter 7 of the Manusmriti defines the duties of king, which include income expenditure, maintenance, conduct of personnel, building of roads and forts, etc. Dharma occupies a central place in the Manusmriti. The king is also subject to Dharma, that is, the Rajdharma. He is to exercise danda and the wellbeing of the people is his main objective.

Principles of Government

The principles of government can be classified as:

1. Public security
2. Interstate relations.

Public security requires that the king detect two categories of thieves with the help of spies. The first category is known as **open thieves**, who make a living through fraudulent means and bribery. Gamblers and fortune tellers, and officials and physicians guilty of improper conduct are included in this category. The second class is that of **secret thieves**—burglars, robbers, and dacoits. Manu also mentions the six principles of diplomacy: (*i*) Peace, (*ii*) War, (*iii*) Neutrality, (*iv*) Mobilisation of army, (*v*) Seeking protection, and (*vi*) dual strategy.

Kautilya explained interstate relations through what is known as the Mandala theory. He proposed a six-fold policy for interacting with neighbours *arranged along the lines of a mandala system*, which comprised coexistence, neutrality, alliance, double policy, march, and war. To achieve this, he advised the king to resort to five tactics: conciliation, gift and bribery, dissention, deceit and pretence, and open attack or war.

Social Thought

Varna: In classical Indian thought, community or society is more important than the individual. Society is divided into four classes organically linked to one another.

1. **Brahmins**, who enjoyed the supreme position in the social hierarchy and followed intellectual and spiritual pursuits.
2. **Kshatriyas**, the warrior and ruling class.
3. **Vaisyas**, responsible for production. They were given educational rights.
4. **Shudras**, who had the lowest position in the social hierarchy and served the other varnas.

K. P. Jayaswal believed that the theory of divinity of the king had been advanced by the *Manusmriti* to support the Brahmin empire of Pusyamitra and counteract the Buddhist theory of the origin of the state by contract. V. R. Mehta is of the view that the Vaisya is the least preferred varna as Vaisyas always seek their own profit, rather than working for the well-being of others. He pointed to two contradictory features in the *Manusmriti:* on the one hand, varna is based on birth, but on the other, it is based on karma (deeds). According to *Dharamshastra*, a person who performs the Sradha without knowing the religious scriptures is bound for hell, proving that varna is based on deeds.

Gender justice: The *Dharamshastra* mentions that God resides wherever women are worshipped. Society was patriarchal, and women were not permitted a public role. Manu also ordered that women be kept under the regulation of men: in childhood, under the guidance of the father; as an adult, under the control of the husband, and in old age, under the care of the son.

Ashrams

1. **Brahmacharya:** This is the stage of acquiring education, training, and character building. The first 25 years are to be devoted to education.
2. **Grihastha:** In the next 25 years of life, a person fulfils his social and family obligations, like such as marriage, raising children, etc. It spans the period from 25–50 years.
3. **Vanapratha:** During this stage, a person detaches himself from worldly life. Vanapratha continues from 50–75 years.
4. **Sanyaas:** This stage is considered the stage of renunciation and spiritual emancipation. Sanyaas means stands for eschewing all material attachments, and loving towards humanity them above one's own family. Comprehensively Sanyaas stands for lifting attachment towards material world. Broadly Sanyaas refer to the attachment towards humanity. During Sanyaas, man donates control exerts domination over his own passions and desires, in order to attain moksha (liberation) from the cycle of birth and rebirth.

There are also the four **highest aims of life**, known as **Purusartha**. This term refers to **Dharma**, **Kam**, **Artha**, and **Moksha**. Dharma stands for duty, righteousness and moral values; the fulfilment of physical needs, and all worldly desires are encapsulated within Kam; Artha refers to prosperity and economic values; and Moksha, the highest aim among them all, denotes liberation, spiritual values, and self-actualisation. Sanyas, or asceticism, is a renunciation not of the world, but of material desires and prejudices. In this stage, a person is supposed to follow Selfless Action.

FIRST CODIFIED LAW

In the manuscript of *Vyavahara*, law was categorised under 18 heads.

1. Non-payment of debts
2. Deposit and pledges
3. Sale without ownership
4. Concerns among partners
5. Resumption of gifts
6. Non-payment of wages
7. Non-execution of agreements
8. Recession of sale and purchase
9. Dispute between owners and servants
10. Dispute regarding boundaries
11. Assault
12. Defamation
13. Theft
14. Robbery and violence
15. Adultery
16. Duties of man and wife
17. Separation of man and wife
18. Gambling and betting

Finance

Manu was a pragmatic thinker who understood that no state can run without the backing of strong finance. He propounded seven types of taxation, which included:

1. Land revenue
2. Fees
3. Fines
4. Taxes for use of river water and on boats
5. Taxes on animals
6. Taxes on artisans
7. Sales tax

JUSTIFICATION OF INEQUALITY

Dr B. R. Ambedkar (1891–1956), Indian jurist and social reformer who headed the committee that drafted the Constitution of India, argued that Dharmshastra provided a defence and justification of the Brahmanical system, and was the source of casteism and the varna system in India. Political scientist **Thomas Panthem** also stated that traditional Indian political thought is hierarchical, although **V. R. Mehta** disagrees with both of them, arguing instead that the varna system is based on a division of labour and is not determined by birth. He further stated that Brahmins who had no knowledge of the scriptures were not entitled to perform Sradha.

3

KAUTILYA AND THE *ARTHASHASTRA*

KEY CONCEPTS

Four branches of knowledge; secular thought; amoral politics; contract theory; welfare state; justice; king; principles of diplomacy; mandala theory; Machiavelli and Kautilya

Kautilya was an ancient Indian polymath who was a minister and royal advisor in the court of Chandragupta Maurya in the fourth century BCE. A more realistic thinker than Manu, his thoughts were a departure from the earlier traditions that espoused the supremacy of religion or Dharma. Kautilya gave precedence to economic prosperity above any other activity and wrote a book, the *Arthashastra*, which is a treatise on statecraft, polity, administration, and strategy. *Arthashastra* is divided into 15 Adhikaranas, 150 chapters, and 180 topics.

FOUR BRANCHES OF KNOWLEDGE

According to the *Arthashastra*, there are four necessary fields of knowledge.

1. Treyi: Three Vedas
2. Varta: Agriculture and commerce
3. Aanveekshiki: Philosophy and reflective science—samkhya, yoga
4. Danda niti: Politics and public administration

SECULAR THOUGHT

Kautilya gave primacy to artha over dharma. He believed that the state and king had come into being to control the economic activities of individuals. According to Kautilya, artha implies the livelihood of people and also refers to the virtue derived from acquiring wealth and material prosperity, that is, the acquisition of territory. Artha is an integral part of polity.

Arthashastra is considered a realistic book on statecraft because it rejects the concept of divine laws. Kautilya held the king as a sovereign institution, thus freeing him from all moral obligations of earlier ages, and viewed the law made by the king as supreme. The king's only duty was to ensure the welfare of his subjects and provide security for the state. Kautilya placed his faith in monarchical kingship rather than in any notion of democracy or aristocracy. His views echo that of the modern European thinker Machiavelli; in fact, Kautilya is also known as the Indian Machiavelli.

MORAL POLITICS?

Although *Arthashastra* deals primarily with statecraft and polity, it also makes clear that the king's main duty is towards his subjects. The king is not expected to be despotic or rule against the wishes of the people. He stated that *sham* (peace), *dam* (concession), *bheda* (divide and rule), and *danda* (punishment) were to be applied to maintain security of state, and that the end justifies the means. Morality is secondary to politics; moral principles are not applicable to the king. However, Kautilya was not expressly against moral principles, as he also stated that subjects should follow all moral principles, which were to be utilised when necessary to ensure the power and security of the state. For him, there are two parameters of morality—one for subjects, and another for the king. But he did accept a separation between politics and morality.

SOCIAL VIEWS

The social system as described in the *Arthashastra* is similar to that of the Dharmashastra. Kautilya believed in the four-fold varna system, the four highest aims of life—the **Purushartha**—and the four Ashramas. Thus, while his classification of the varnas is more liberal than that of Manu, he too believed in the supremacy of Brahmins and advocated a lower degree of punishment to Brahmins when compared to other castes, even for the same crime.

CONTRACT THEORY OF THE ORIGIN OF STATE

According to Kautilya, when the Matsyanyaya prevailed, the big fish consumed the smaller ones, thereby resulting in complete anarchy and instability. Kautilya took recourse to the theory of social contract to liberate people from anarchy; here, people pledged to pay one-sixth of their food grains and one-tenth of other goods as a tax to the king.

Like Aristotle, Kautilya also believed in the **organic theory of state**. Like the organs of a body, each element of state is inseparable from the others, and incapable of independent existence. There is harmony among the different organs of state, with each element being an integral part of the state. The state comprises of seven elements: Swami (king), Amatya (minister), Kosh (treasury), Janapad (district), Durga (fort), Mitra (allies), and Danda (punishment).

NATURE OF STATE

Like Manu, Kautilya believed that the state is organic in nature. The seven elements of state given above function like the seven organs of the human body, required for healthy functioning. A strong state requires strong elements of state. Even a single weak element will hamper the growth of the entire state.

WELFARE STATE (YOGAKSHEMA)

In the *Arthashastra*, Kautilya describes *Yogakshema* as the ultimate goal of any ruler. Referring to the protection and prosperity of all citizens, the objective of the state is seen as the happiness and prosperity (*Prajaranjan*) of the people. This is essential to the wellbeing of the state, as the king will get more taxes from wealthy subjects. Yogakshema refers to both the moral and material development of the people.

1. Yoga (addition to or furtherance of, and not the depletion of, all resources) and Kshema (balanced utilisation of resources) in all human pursuits.
2. Yoga and Kshema were considered the sources of exertion and peaceful possession, respectively. Material prosperity was never considered an end in itself; instead, it was believed that material provisions are essential, and it is the duty of the state to ensure this for all citizens.
3. A policy of minimum state welfare, while emphasising self-help for the individual. The state is to confine itself to helping the helpless, as it involves the well-being of the poorest of the poor.

The basic tenets of Yogakshema are:

1. To ensure the moral and material well-being of citizens.

2. The perfection, freedom, and self-realisation of all citizens.
3. The attainment of this perfection was to depend upon material, physical, moral, and spiritual welfare.
4. It is the combined duty of the individual, society, and the state to improve the lot of the citizens.
5. Yogakshema is to be attained through:
   (i) Dharma (Varnashramadharma, trivarga, svadharma, and morality)
   (ii) Danda
   (iii) Family.

JUSTICE

According to Kautilya, there are two types of law. Law courts that deal with the regulation of civil disputes are known as **Dharmasthiyas**, and law courts associated with criminal matters are known as **Kantakshodhana**.

KING

Kautilya has given high accordance to the position of the king, a position that he believes is analogous to that of the brain in the human body. The King, or Swami, is the head of the state. Kautilya stated that the King should have complete knowledge of the Vedas, the *Arthashastra*, and Danda niti, and should also have mastered techniques of statecraft. He should possess the highest quality of leadership as well as intellect and energy. A ruler should have the following qualities:

1. **Abhigamika:** The ability to win the hearts of people and inspire patience, or to promote the moral and material happiness of the citizens.
2. **Pragyaunas:** Intellectual abilities, such as the ability to learn, understand, and discuss.
3. **Utsahgun:** This includes acts of bravery and decision-making skills.

The king should be truthful, resolute, disciplined, and enthusiastic, and should possess lofty aims. He should be free from vices.

Amatya

- Amatya, or the Minister(s), comprise the second element of state. According to Kautilya, the Amatya and King are two wheels of the chariot. Arthashastra reminds us that the king can succeed only if he has competent councillors (Amatya) to guide him as his advisors. Kautilya believed that while the number of ministers should not be fixed, it should be determined by an elaborate system of recruitment. A minister should possess the following qualities:

(a) Born to a noble family
(b) Skillful
(c) Clever
(d) Influential
(e) Possessing dignity and endurance
(f) Displaying firm and loyal devotion
(g) Pure in character
(h) Endowed with excellent conduct, strength, health, and bravery
(i) Free from negative qualities like hatred, enmity, etc.

Kosh (Treasury)

Kosh is an extremely important element among the organs of state described by Kautilya. Kautilya believed that the power of the state was dependent upon the augmentation of Kosh (the treasury). A strong army can be raised only through the help of a strong treasury.

The foremost duty of a king is to keep the state treasury full and prosperous. The state should also maintain emergency funds to meet any emergency that might arise. Kautilya propounded three types of **taxation**.

1. **Theory of Maturity:** The state should not impose tax on any industry in its infancy.
2. **Theory of Rarity:** Those commodities that are extremely essential for the state should be made tax-free.
3. **Theory of Tax-Exemption:** According to Kautilya, certain activities, for example *yagnya*, should be exempt from taxation because of their importance in life.

Danda

Kautilya also stated that the existence of the state depends on a sound defence system with appropriate Danda. This also serves as an instrument to preserve and augment the wealth and power of the ruler. Kautilya prescribes different punishments for different crimes, calling for severe punishment for severe crime, including executions, economic sanctions, etc. However, so-called high-caste people committing the same crimes were to be given milder forms of punishment. In order to implement Danda niti, it was necessary to maintain a strong army.

Durg

Fortification is important to ensure the safety and security of the state. The Durg is the capital of the state. Kautilya's classification of forts is as follows:

1. Audak Fort (surrounded by water)
2. Parvat Fort (surrounded by mountains)
3. Danuk Fort (surrounded by deserts)
4. Van Fort (built in a dense forest)

Janapada

In *Arthashastra*, the word 'Janapada' implies both the territory and the population of the state. According to Kautilya, Gram is to be the smallest unit of the state, and will be headed by the Gramik. All disputes in the Gram will be resolved by the Gramik and boundary disputes shall be resolved by the **Panchgrami**, a group of 10 villages (sangrah). The Janapada should be prosperous and land should be fertile.

Mitra

Kautilya emphasised the necessity of having reliant Mitra (allies). According to him, an ideal ally has the following qualities:

1. Has been a friend of the family for a long time;
2. Constant in nature;
3. Amenable to control;
4. Powerful in his support;
5. Shares an interest;
6. Able to mobilise quickly when needed; and
7. Not a man who double-crosses his friends.

A comprehensive description of Danda and Mitra is available in Mandalla theory.

SIX PRINCIPLES OF DIPLOMACY

Being a realistic thinker, Kautilya believed that the state should maximise its strength and security. He offered six forms of diplomacy which a king should apply to strengthen the power of his state and defend its existing frontiers.

1. **Sandhi (peace):** Accommodation or convergence of interests on any issue among different states. This stands for a policy of peace.
2. **Vigraha (hostility):** Pursuing a hostile foreign policy towards states.
3. **Yana:** Mobilisation of an army.
4. **Aasana:** Remaining still and considering various options.
5. **Samsarya:** A policy of protection; weak states always seek the protection of strong states.
6. **Duaidhibhava:** Pursuing a dual strategy in its foreign policy—allying with one state while maintaining relations of animosity with another.

Figure 3.3.1: Kautilya's Six Principles of Diplomacy

Four Upayas (Strategies) of Diplomacy

1. **Sama (conciliation):** This is a policy of conciliation, which can be adopted when dealing with a stronger king.
2. **Dama (concession):** A policy of appeasing a stronger king.
3. **Danda (use of force):** This policy can be used against weaker states as a coercive measure against them.
4. **Bheda (divide and rule):** Promoting internal divisions and diversions within a state.

MANDALA THEORY

A Mandala refers to a group of states, and is a hypothetical concept which visualises circles of friends and foes. It describes circles of friendly and enemy states surrounding the king's state. Also known as the Mandala theory of foreign policy or simply Mandala theory, this theory is considered one of Kautilya's most important postulations regarding foreign policy. It is based on the geographical assumption that one's immediate neighbour is most likely to be an **enemy,** while the state next to the immediate neighbour is

Figure 3.3.2: Kautilya's Mandala Theory

Ari-mitra-mitra ⟸ Enemy's Friend's Friend

Friend's Friend ⟸ Mitra-mitra

Ari-Mitra ⟸ Enemy's Friend

Friend ⟸ Mitra

Ari ⟸ Enemy

Madhyama

Vijigishu ⟸ Conqueror

Parshinigra

Rear Enemy

Rear Friend ⟸ Akranda

Udasena ⟸ Neutral

Parashimgrahasara

Rear Enemy's Friend ⟸ Akrandasara ⟸ Rear Friend's Friend

likely to be friendly. The salient features of this theory are:

1. **Vijigishu:** The potential conqueror King, whom Kautilya calls Vijigishu. Thus, the king occupies central position in the circle.
2. **Ari:** The immediate neighbour of Vijigishu, who is his enemy.
3. **Mitra:** The immediate neighbour of the Ari or enemy. This state is the king's friend.
4. **Ari-Mitra:** The next state adjacent to the Mitra, who is seen as an enemy by the Vijigishu, but as a friend by the Ari.
5. **Mitra-Mitra:** The next state adjacent to Ari Mitra is viewed by Mitra as a friend, and is therefore the ally of the Vijigishu.
6. **Ari-Mitra-Mitra:** Friend to the Ari-Mitra, he is an ally of Ari and enemy of Vijigishu.
7. **Parshinigraha state**: The state that lies behind Vijigishu's state.
8. **Akranda:** The next kingdom, the ally to the rear, is called Akranda.
9. **Parashimgrahasara:** The friends of the enemy or the next kingdom in the rear are the Parashimgrahasara.
10. **Akarndasara:** The friend's friend in the rear.
11. **Madhyama (or intermediary):** This is more powerful than either Ari or Mitra. Madhyama, or intermediary, occupies a territory close to both the conqueror and his immediate enemy.
12. **Udasena:** While its geographical position is not defined, the Udasin is a most powerful state in the Mandala galaxy.

Mandala Theory and Kenneth Waltz

Kautilya explains international politics on the basis of an international structure. His analysis is not based on human nature. Similarly, American political scientist Kenneth Waltz believed in structural realism, that is, that the foreign policy of a state is shaped by the structure of international relations. There are interesting similarities between Kautilya and Waltz. In 1979, Waltz wrote *Theory of International Politics*, in which he discussed anarchy in international relations due to the absence of a higher authority that can adjudicate international disputes. Thus, states function as supreme institutions engaged in maximising their power. Kautilya also views international relations from the prism of Mandala theory, where the state, as the basic unit, is interlinked with other states. The capacity of each state varies, and there is a constant struggle among them to maximise their power and security.

ADMINISTRATION

Kautilya identifies five elements of good administration, *viz.*, the appropriate means to start undertakings; the excellence of men and materials; allocation of place and time; provision against failure; and the accomplishment of work. Fear, duty, and interest are among a number of motives that lie behind obedience to the orders of an administrator. Kautilya believed that good governance is only possible with the cooperation of both the people and the bureaucracy.

The **18 Tirthas** as elaborated by Kautilya are:

1. Minister
2. Priest
3. Commander of the Army
4. Prince
5. Chief of Palace Attendants
6. Chief of the King's Guards
7. Magistrate
8. Collector-General
9. Chief Treasurer
10. Commissioner
11. Town Guard
12. Chief of the Town
13. Superintendent of Mines
14. Chief of the Council of Ministers
15. Officer of the Army Department

16. Guardian of the Forts
17. Officer-in-charge, Boundaries
18. Officer-in-charge, Forests

Local Administration

A distinctive feature of the administrative system is its marked preference for a decentralised polity. There are indications that a Janapada was to contain 800 *gramas* with a *sthanika* at its centre. It is also mentioned that a Samaharta (chief Collector-General of revenue) should divide the Janapada into four divisions for revenue and administrative purposes. Under the sthanika, there are junior revenue officers called *gopas*, each in charge of 5–10 villages. With their help, the Samaharta maintains a record of all towns and villages. The gopa was responsible for maintaining a record of all agricultural and other holdings in the village and the census. He was to keep the accounts of 10 households, 20 households, or 40 households and would not only know the caste, gotra, the name, and occupation of both men and women in those households, but also ascertain their income and expenditure. To maintain order, the Samaharta relied on the *pradesta* or *pradesikas*, who were provincial officers in charge of the administration of a district, and were stationed at the headquarters along with the gopa and sthanikas. They operated both as revenue and police officers.

The next in the hierarchy was the village headman, who is referred to as the gramika. Power in the rural areas was to be centred in the hands of the Samaharta, with his subordinates spread all over the countryside. In the *Arthashastra*, decentralisation was for administrative convenience and efficiency alone. One should not deduce any notion of village democracy from a reading of the scheme.

Cities were to be kept neat and clean. The Kot-Palla was the officer-in-charge of the city and the Administrator was called the Nagaradhyaksha. Each city was divided into four parts and each part was headed by a Sthanika, assisted by a junior officer called the gopa, who looked after 20 households. Nagarakas, or city superintendents, were responsible for maintaining peace and law and order in the city, and kept an eye on the income and expenditure of both residents and foreigners. They were to take possession of unclaimed property and see that epidemics did not spread, maintain sanitary conditions, and keep a record of births and deaths. They could set up committees to take care of separate issues such as tax collection, maintaining market standards, the export and import of goods from cities, etc.

The affairs of the village were looked after by the Sangrahana (the headquarters of a sub-district). Two hundred villages constituted a Kharwatika, 400 constituted a Dronamukha, and 800 constituted a Sthania. Villages were run by gramiks and gopas, as stated earlier, and were given some measure of autonomy. Both gramiks and gopas were state employees posted in the village, and negotiated with the central government to get their development plans approved.

Kautilya states that the mining industry formed the source of the financial strength of the state, and the state could exercise power only because of its treasury. He provided an analysis of the functional specialisation and structural differentiation of the state, with 34 government departments and their respective heads, including ministers and a council of ministers.

Kautilya's *Arthashastra* is an excellent treatise on administration. He provides detailed descriptions of the entire administrative machinery of state, including requirements of officials, the number of departments, the auditing system, etc. There was a wide range of departments, including trade, weights and measures, agriculture, and mining. Officials were recruited on the basis of nobility.

The promulgation of laws and adjudication of justice were among the important functions of the state. The *Arthashastra* presents us with a full-fledged and developed idea of the judiciary. The king was regarded as the fountain of all justice and was expected to be strictly impartial in administering justice according to the law. He was responsible for protecting people from various forms of corruption. According to Kautilya, state functions included protecting the Dharma, administering justice, and promoting the interests of all people. Kautilya also places a number of restraints on the activities of the king.

SPY SYSTEM

Kautilya paid special attention to arranging a system of espionage, which would help to expose any form of discontentment against the state on the part of officials or citizens. The *Arthashastra* broadly describes two types of espionage: *sansthah* or stationary spies and *sancharah* or roaming spies. The former included false disciples (*kapatika*s), recluses (*udasthita*s), householders (*grihapatika*), merchants (*vaidehaka*s), and ascetics (*tapas*). The latter included students (*satri*s), desperados (*tikashna*s), and poisoners (*rasada*s). Women were recommended as spies in the second group, and were sent out disguised as wandering beggars (*bhikshuki*s), nuns (*parivrajika*s), shavelings (*munda*s), and courtesans (*vrishali*s).

MACHIAVELLI AND KAUTILYA

Both Machiavelli and Kautilya were realistic thinkers. One can find many similarities in their ideas.

1. **Statecraft:** Both *Prince* and *Arthashastra* are treatises devoted to statecraft, detailing how a King should rule over the people and the means by which the state can strengthen itself. While Machiavelli declared that every state is a potential enemy, Kautilya argued that the King should maintain four wings of the army.
2. **Secular State:** Since the state wants to maximise its power, security of state was a priority for Machiavelli. Kings should not believe in fortune alone. Kautilya also supported the policy of sam, dam, bheda, and danda, discussed above.
3. **Amoral Politics:** Machiavelli argued that the end justified the means. The Prince is entitled to adopt any means he chooses to strengthen the state. Kautliya, too, said that a King is not bound by the rules of Dharma.
4. **Realism:** Machiavelli always encouraged a Prince to know the **art of war**, and not rely solely on an army of mercenaries. Kautilya described a six-fold policy of diplomacy for a King, which are to be used on the right occasion: Peace (*sandhi*); War (*vigraha*); Neutrality (*asana*); Marching (*yaana*); Alliance (*saamarasya*); and Waging war with one and making peace with another (*dvaidhi bhaava*).

We can point out various differences between Machiavelli and Kautilya as well.

1. Kautilya's thought is more comprehensive, and includes political and economic diplomacy, as well as administration. However, Machiavelli's *Prince* focuses mostly on statecraft.
2. Machiavelli, who also wrote *Discourses*, believed that the republican form of government was the best, while Kautilya argued in favour of a monarchical form of government.
3. For Machiavelli, secularism was inspired by the strong and powerful Church of Rome. However, Kautilya sought a replacement of the Nand dynasty.

IMPORTANT FACTS

According to Kautilya:

1. There are 72 *prakriti*es of the Mandala Theory of State.
2. There are ***40 methods*** of ***embezzlement***, *as cited* in the *Arthashastra.*
3. The concept of **Rupadarshaka** refers to the Inspector of Coins.
4. There are 17 types of law described in the *Arthashastra.*

4

AGGANNA SUTTA

KEY CONCEPTS

Four noble truths; eight-fold path; Buddhist political thought; principle of righteousness

Aganna Sutta is the 27th *sutta* (dialogue) of the **Digha Nikaya** (long discourses) collection of dialogues attributed to the **Buddha**. The Agganna Sutta deals with moral and religious philosophy and describes a discourse imparted by the Buddha to two Brahmins, Bharadvaja and Vasettha, who left their family and varna to become monks. Political thought can be derived indirectly from these dialogues. Buddha was born in the sixth century BCE in Lumbini, Nepal. The earliest Buddhist sources state that the Buddha was born to an aristocratic Kshatriya family called Gotama (or Gautama), who were part of the Shakyas, a tribe of rice-farmers living near the modern border of India and Nepal. His father Śuddhodana was a chief of this clan, and their capital was Kapilavastu.

Legend and biographies also tell the story of how, when Gautama left his palace for the first time to see the outside world, he encountered human suffering in the persons of an old man, a diseased man, a decaying corpse, and an ascetic. Moved by these sights, he decided to leave his palace and live the life of a wandering ascetic himself. The Buddhist traditions present multiple paths towards liberation, as preached by the Buddha.

Early Buddhism was based on empirical evidence gained through the sense organs (*ayatana*). Buddha focused on practical questions related to bringing about an end to suffering, and did not engage in metaphysical debate or religious scriptures. He did not accept the four-fold division of **Varna** and held that there are four social classes:

1. Landed ruling class
2. Priestly class
3. Trading class
4. Hunters

BASIC RELIGIOUS TEACHINGS

Buddhism addresses the basic problems of human life and speaks about suffering, its causes, and possible solution. It does not concern itself with questions related to God or the soul; the aim of Buddhism is not the search for religious scriptures or orthodox practices. The teachings of Buddha aimed to liberate human beings from suffering, and include

(a) The four noble truths
(b) The eight-fold path.

Four Noble Truths

Buddha explored human suffering and offered the following theory:

(a) **Dukhha (suffering exists):** Suffering is real and universal. Suffering has many causes—loss, sickness, pain, failure, and the impermanence of pleasure.

(b) **Samudaya (cause of suffering):** Suffering is due to attachment, the desire for control over things. It can take many forms—craving for sensual pleasures, desire for fame, and the desire to avoid unpleasant sensations, like fear, anger, or jealousy.

(c) **Nirodha (end to suffering):** Attachment can be overcome. Suffering ceases with the final liberation (nirvana).

(d) **Magga:** In order to end suffering, you must follow the eight-fold path.

The Eight-Fold Path

The Buddha's eight-fold path consists of:

1. Right view
2. Right resolve
3. Right speech
4. Right conduct
5. Right livelihood
6. Right mindfulness
7. Right meditation
8. Right effort

POLITICAL IDEAS

According to professor **V. R. Mehta**, the Buddhist tradition lacks political thinking, as it is primarily a **religious tradition**. Nevertheless, we can infer some political thought from the *Buddha Charita*, written by Ashvaghosha, and some political teachings from the **Jataka stories**. The term '*sammat*' refers to contract and can be found in Pali literature—the Jataka tales, which mainly concern the previous births of the Buddha, in both animal and human form. Apart from this, the Sutta-Pitaka, the second of the three divisions of the *Tripitaka*, the definitive canonical collection of scripture of Theravada Buddhism, is also a source of a few political ideas.

Professor Mehta pointed out two paradoxical ideas mentioned in *Buddhachrita*:

1. Politics is similar to treachery, opportunism, and deceit. It is said that Buddhist monks should keep themselves away from kings and princes.
2. On the other hand, Buddhist tradition also holds politics as an important activity through which to manage society. Morality dominates thoughts in the Buddhist tradition.

SOCIAL CONTRACT

It is clear that the origin of the state lies in social contract. The state is not a divine institution, but an artificial institution one. Earlier, individual conduct was based on morality and people abided by the principle of Dharma. There was peace and harmony in society. Later, people became selfish and egotistic, which led to the emergence of anarchy in society. To maintain social order, the state became necessary. The state is the result of a contract among the people. The functions of state were similar to those laid out in the *Arthashastra* and *Dharmashastra*. Buddhist traditional thought subscribes to a **welfare state**, the primary objective of which is the wellbeing of the people.

Morality Centric

As in the *Dharmashastra*, morality occupies the highest position in the Buddhist tradition as well. The king is also subject to morality. If moral principles are neglected by the King, people too will not follow a moral path, thereby leading to the development of anger in nature. Subsequently, this disrespect of nature will result in no rain and no crops, and widespread hunger and starvation amongst the people. What this means is that any diversion from a moral path will result in the destruction of the community. Politics becomes secondary to morality as there is a cosmic moral order in the universe.

Form of Government

The state is a sovereign entity. There are **seven** symbols of sovereignty, and the Buddha, Dharma, and Sangha are the three basic elements of the Buddhist tradition. The Sangha is the Buddhist community, that is, the men, women, and children who follow the teachings of the Buddha. The Sangha is supposed to lead by example, and help others along their paths to enlightenment.

1. Buddha himself was a leader of the Sangha. He alone took decisions related to **initiation** in the Sangha, and there was no consultation with other monks. The Sangha was not based on any formal rules and regulations. Politically, it is considered akin to the **monarchical** form of government.
2. With the increase in the size of the Sangha, its functions were transferred to the monks (Bhikkus). The training and supervision of monks was the task of senior monks. The relation between senior and junior monks mimicked the relationship between a father and son. Politically, this form can be described as the **aristocratic** form of government.
3. Sangha became more organised, and issues such as the admission of monks and training became the prerogative of the entire community. The Sangha became synonymous with the community. In the first phase of evolution, decision-making power in the Sangha belonged solely to the Buddha. In the second stage, a few monks were given the power to take decisions. But in the third phase, the decision-making power was given to the entire community. This is very similar to the **republican** or **democratic** form of government.

The Principle of Righteousness

In Buddhist literature, danda does not play a central role. Dharma is to be upheld in more positive ways. This principle of righteousness differs from the Brahminical conception of dharma, and is closer to the Western conception of virtue. Brahminical literature lays out a different set of ethical principles for the king. What is *adharma* for ordinary people becomes dharma to the king when he is engaged in protecting the social order. This is called **Rajadharma**. Both the *Bhagavad Gita* and the Mahabharata provide detailed accounts of the concept of Rajadharma as dracticedom the dharma practised by ordinary citizens. Buddhists, too, consider the primary purpose of the state as being the safeguarding of the social order. However, this order is understood more in moral terms, and dharma must be the standard for all the king's activities. Righteousness is an ethical doctrine as well as a mental discipline. Buddhism advocates the application of the principle of righteousness in both internal and foreign polices.

5

BARANI (1283–1359)

KEY CONCEPTS
Statecraft; ideal king; law; armed forces, bureaucracy; justice

STATECRAFT

Ziauddin Barani hailed from Turkey and was the most important political philosopher of the **Delhi Sultanate**. He wrote *Fatawa-i-Jahandari*, a work containing the political ideals to be pursued by a Muslim ruler in order to earn religious merit and the gratitude of his subjects, in the fourteenth century. It is written as *nasihat* (a set of advice) to the Muslim kings. The founder of statecraft in Islamic theory, Barani hold a position similar to that of **Kautilaya** and **Machiavelli** in the history of Islamic rule.

Barani believed that the security of the state is the most important goal, in the ensuring of which any means can be adopted. Even the principle of **Shariat** can be compromised; according to Barani, the Shariat is a means to further a political objective. With regard to the Shariat, Barani stated that in the personal realm, the Sultan may choose to be lax in following it; however, he opposed the idea of laxity in the political sphere as it might lead to moral decay in the administration, for the ideal polity and the political person of the Sultan were closely interlinked.

IDEAL KING (SULTAN)

Barani made a distinction between the personal life of the Sultan and his political life. The Sultan was considered the agent of God where the welfare of his subjects was concerned, and was advised to reject five qualities:

1. Falsehood
2. Changeability
3. Deception
4. Wrathfulness
5. Injustice

However, it should also be noted that Barani was in favour of a king possessing the attribute of terror, as it is essential for enforcing justice. A Sultan should know both forgiveness and punishment. The Shariat formed the basis of justice.

Nobility

The Sultan was entitled to levy taxes, known as **Iqta**. He could select counselor to help him in this task, and this selection should be only from noble families who are loyal to the king. Counsellors should possess the following qualities:

1. Fear of God
2. Knowledge of history
3. Lack of greed

LAWS

Barani identifies two kinds of law:

1. Shariat
2. Zawabit

While the Shariat referred to the teaching and practices of the **Prophet Mohammad**, the term 'Zawabit' literally means 'state laws' in Persian. These were laws formulated by the king in consultation with his nobility, to cater to those situation which the Shariat was unable to fulfil. Zawabit should not be against the Shariat; ideally, the king, nobility, and administrative personnel should follow the Shariat, both in the personal domain and in public policies. The state laws, however, would be exercised in case of the inability to apply the Shariat.

ARMED FORCES

The Delhi Sultanate was the most powerful state, second only to the rule of the **Mauryas**. There was a four-fold division of the armed forces:

1. Infantry
2. Cavalry
3. War elephants
4. Auxiliary, like transporters and boats

The rank and file, such as the **Khan**, **Malik**, **Amir**, and **Sipahsalar**, were part of the cavalry.

BUREAUCRACY

The major task of the bureaucracy was to fix and collect the taxes. It operated at three levels:

1. At the Centre: the Wazir
2. At the Provinces: the Muqtis or Walis
3. At the level of the village: the Muqaddam

The **Diwan-i-Wazarat** was headed by the **Wazir**, who, as the prime minister, was the head of revenue. The **Naib, Musharif-i-Mamalik**, **Mustawfi-i-Mamalike**, and **Dabirs** were under the control of the Wazir. At the provincial level, the administration was headed by **Muqtis** or **Walis**, with the **Diwan** below him. At the local level, the **Muqaddam** was the head of the village.

JUSTICE

There were two types of courts:

1. Civil court
2. Criminal court

While dealing with religious cases, the King was assisted by the **Mufti** and **Sadr-us-Sadur**, or the pronvincial judge, and by the **Quazi-ul-Quzat,** or the chief judge, while dealing with secular issues.

6

KABIR (1398–1518)

KEY CONCEPTS
Utopia; Amar deshva; monotheism

UTOPIA

Kabir Das was a fifteenth-century Indian mystic poet and saint. He is respected by Hindus, Muslims and Sikhs; his writings influenced Hinduism's Bhakti movement, and his verses are found in Sikhism's scripture, the Guru Granth Sahib, the Satguru Granth Sahib of Saint Garib Das, and in the Kabir Sagar. He was born in Varansi and was brought up in a Muslim weaver family. He died in Maghar, close to Gorakhpur (in present-day Uttar Pradesh). He was a contemporary of Sikandar Lodi, Sultan of the Delhi Sultanate between 1489 and 1517. Kabir conceptualised an ideal village, **Begumpura,** where no private ownership of property, taxation, or injustice was permitted. **Monotheism** and **syncretism** existed without any presence of patriarchy and gender discrimination.

SUBALTERN APPROACH

Kabir stood against the caste system and represented the voices of the marginalised sections of society. He was against religious orthodoxy and the dominant class, and remained fiercely opposed to the Zamindari system. He devoted his life to fighting against caste, class, religion, and gender domination. One can find the seeds of socialism in the ideas propounded by Kabir.

Amar Deshva

Kabir visualised Amar Deshva as an **ideal society,** which would exist without any exploitation and discrimination. Society wouldbe based on democratic values and cultural plurality. There would be no injustice or hierarchy in Begumpura, which was considered an ideal polity, a kingdom of God.

Liberation

The ultimate purpose of human life is self-realisation. Kabir believed that there are three paths leading to the liberation of human beings:

1. Knowledge
2. Worship
3. Bhakti

A humanist and social reformer, Kabir sought to create an egalitarian society and opposed any discrimination based on caste and religion. He criticised both Hindu and Muslim society for their religious orthodoxy, and laid down the foundations of a **Bahujan Samaj**.

LITERARY WORKS

Kabir's spiritual master, **Ramanand Vaishnav Saint,** was a fourteenth-century Vaishnava devotional poet saint, who lived in the Gangetic basin of northern India. He is recognised as the founder of the Ramanandi Sampradaya, the largest monastic Hindu renunciant community in modern times. Both Ramanand Saint and Kabir exerted a deep influence on the great spiritual leaders and religious reformers, Dadu Dayal and Guru Nanak.

Several texts are attributed to Kabir, including *Kabir Bijak, Kabir Parachi, Sakhi Granth, Adi Granth* (Sikh), and *Kabir Granthawali* (Rajasthan). Bijak is comprised of three parts:

1. Sakhi
2. Sabad
3. Ramaini

MONOTHEISM

Strongly against idolatry, Kabir believed in **Nirguna bhakti.** Nirguna refers to the concept of a formless God, that is, that God does not exist in a particular form, neither does S/He have particular properties. In nirguna bhakti, God is worshipped in an unmanifested form. The human soul is deeply attached to God. He also explained that due to our attachment with the material world, we are unable to discover the unity that exists between **Soul** and **God.**

7

PANDITA RAMABAI (1858–1922)

KEY CONCEPTS

Feminism; educationist; nationalist; liberalism

Pandita Ramabai Sarasvati, social activitst and educationist, was born in Canara district of Karnataka in 1858 to a Marathi-speaking Chitpavan Brahmin family. She was the first woman to be awarded the titles of *Pandita* as a Sanskrit scholar and *Sarasvati* after being examined by the faculty of the University of Calcutta. In 1880 the University of Calcutta invited her to give a lecture after the news of her erudition in Sanskrit reached Calcutta. Her address at senate hall of Calcutta University was well-received and won her great acclaim.

FIRST FEMINIST

In 1882, Ramabai founded the Arya Mahila Sabha (1881). Influenced by the ideals of Jesus Christ, the Brahmo Samaj, and Hindu reformers, the purpose of the society was to promote the cause of women's education and deliverance from the oppression of child marriage. In an address before the Hunter Commission, she declared, 'In ninety-nine cases out of a hundred the educated men of this country are opposed to female education and the proper position of women. If they observe the slightest fault, they ... try to ruin the character of a woman.'

Her first book was in Marathi, titled *Stri Dharma-Niti* (*Morals for Women,* 1882). With the earnings from this book, she moved to Britain in 1883 to start her medical training; however, she could not continue her studies in medicine because of her progressive deafness. An ardent supporter of widow remarriage, Ramabai authored India's first feminist manifesto, *The High Caste Hindu Woman* (1887), which highlighted the darkest aspects of the lives of Hindu women, including child brides and child widows, and sought to expose the oppression of women in Hindu-dominated British India. She was against all caste and gender-based discrimination and opposed both child marriage and polygamy. Stating that the marginalised condition of women derived mostly from the *Manusmriti*, she set herself firmly against it.

EDUCATIONIST

Ignored the dictates of the caste system, Ramabai married Bipin Behari Medhavi, a lawyer and active member of the Brahmo Samaj. As theirs was an inter-caste and inter-regional marriage, it was considered deeply inappropriate for that age. After Medhavi's unfortunate death in 1882, only two years after their marriage, Ramabai, who was just twenty-three years old, moved to Pune and founded an organisation to promote women's education. During her stay in Britain (where, as stated earlier, she had gone in the hopes of pursuing medicine), Ramabai converted to Christianity. Among the reasons Ramabai gave for her conversion was her growing disillusionment with orthodox Hinduism and particularly what she saw as its ill regard of women. In 1886, she travelled from Britain to the United States at the invitation of Dr Rachel Bodley, Dean of the Women's Medical College of Pennsylvania. In the US, through speaking engagements and a wide network of supporters, Ramabai raised the equivalent of Rs 60,000 to launch a school in India for child widows.

In 1889, after she returned to India, she set up the **Sharda Sadan,** which had the support of many Hindu reformers. In 1919, her work in the field of education was recognized by the British government which awarded her the **Kaiser-i-Hind** medal.

NATIONALIST

While giving presentations in the US to seek support for her social activism in India, Ramabai met American suffragette and women's rights activist, Frances Willard, in July 1887. Willard invited Ramabai to speak at the national Woman's Christian Temperance Union convention in November 1887, where she gained the support of this large women's organisation. She said that the US is well-known for its liberal values like liberty, equality, and justice, and it is these same values that are needed for the fight against colonialism in India. Her work in the freedom struggle is also well-known, and she was one of the ten women delegates of the Congress session of 1889.

LIBERAL

Ramabi always spoke against the caste system and gender discrimination prevalent in society. Her school for child widows, Sharada Sadan, was moved to the the much quieter village of Kedgaon, and its name changed to Mukti Mission. In 1896, during a severe famine, Ramabai toured the villages of Maharashtra with a caravan of bullock carts and rescued thousands of outcast children, child widows, orphans, and other destitute women and brought them to the shelter of the Mukti Mission. By 1900, there were 1,500 residents and over 100 cattle in the Mukti Mission.

It is due to Ramabai's influence that women's participation in the national movement for India's freedom increased manifold. She was also in close contact with other feminist stalwarts and leaders like Tarabai Shinde and Anandibai Joshi. One of most influential women reformers of India, her Mukti Mission continues to function even today.

8

BAL GANGADHAR TILAK (1856–1920)

KEY CONCEPTS
Swadeshi movement; home rule; swarajya; conservatism

Bal Gangadhar Tilak, born Keshav Gangadhar Tilak, was a leader of the Indian independence movement, a nationalist, and a teacher. He was born in Ratnagiri, Maharashtra in 1856 to a Marathi Hindu Chitpavan Brahmin family. Among the first leaders of the movement for Indian independence, the British colonial authorities called Tilak 'The father of the Indian unrest', while Mahatma Gandhi termed him 'The Maker of Modern India'. Also an educationist, he was one of the founders of Fergusson College in Pune, and also founded the New English School (1880) and Deccan Education Society (1885).

NATIONALISM

Tilak joined the Indian National Congress in 1890 and was an active participant in all the annual conferences of the Congress. However, he opposed its moderate attitude, especially towards the fight for self-government, and was one of the most eminent radicals of the time. He moved a resolution on the Arms Act at the 1891 Conference of Congress and was elected as a member of the Bombay Legislative Council as well. He opposed the constitutional method adopted by Moderates in the Congress party like Gokhale and Ranade, stating that since there is no Constitution in India, a method of constitutional protest is illogical. He was instead in favour of direct political action.

Following the Partition of Bengal, which was a strategy set out by Lord Curzon to weaken the nationalist movement, Tilak encouraged the Swadeshi movement and the Boycott movement, which boycotted all foreign goods, law courts, and educational institutions run by the British government. Tilak's radical views were supported by Indian nationalists Bipin Chandra Pal in Bengal and Lala Lajpat Rai in Punjab. Together, they were referred to as the 'Lal-Bal-Pal triumvirate'.

As a journalist, Tilak brought out two newspapers, *Kesari* (in Marathi) and *Maratha* (in English), which he used to further the cause of Indian freedom against colonial policies. Quoting the *Bhagavad Gita*, Tilak stated that no blame could be attached to anyone who killed an oppressor without any thought of reward. Following this, on 22 June 1897, Commissioner Rand and another British officer, Lt. Ayerst, were shot and killed by the Chapekar brothers and other associates. Tilak was charged with incitement to murder and sentenced to eighteen months' imprisonment. When he emerged from prison in present-day Mumbai, he was revered as a martyr and a national hero.

Tilak was tried for sedition charges thrice by the British government—in 1897, 1909, and 1916. In 1909, he was charged for intensifying racial animosity between Indians and the British, and the judge, Dinshaw D. Davar, gave him a six-year jail sentence, to be served in Mandalay, Burma While in prison, he continued to read and write, further developing his ideas on the Indian nationalist movement, and wrote the *Gita Rahasya,* the analysis of *Karma Yoga* in the *Bhagavad Gita*. Upon his return to India, he started the Home Rule movement in 1916, and was a key player in settling the **Lucknow Pact** between the Congress and the Muslim League.

Tilak's conception of nationalism combined the spiritual philosophy of Vedanta with the Western notions of nationalism as propounded by Giuseppe Mazzini, Edmund Burke, and James Mill. Believing that historical legacy, and linguistic and religious unity were insufficient bases of nationalism, he called for political mobilisation under a nationalist economic ideology. To promote psychological unity amongst the people and bring them together, events such as the Ganapati festival and Shiv Jayanti were used by Tilak to build a national spirit that would go beyond the circle of the educated elite in their opposition to colonial rule. However, this emphasis on Hindu religious festivals alienated Muslims and exacerbated Hindu-Muslim differences.

HOME RULE

Tilak helped to found the All India Home Rule League in 1916–18 with G. S. Khaparde and Annie Besant. Tilak started his Home Rule League in Maharashtra, Central Provinces, and Karnataka and Berar region. After years of trying to reunite the moderate and radical factions, he gave up and focused on the Home Rule League, which sought self-rule. Tilak travelled from village to village, exhorting farmers and locals to join the movement towards self-rule. The league had 1,400 members in April 1916, and by 1917, membership had grown to approximately 32,000.

SWARAJYA

Tilak was one of the first and strongest advocates of Swaraj ('self-rule'). He is known for his quote in Marathi: 'Swaraj is my birthright and I shall have it!' He believed in the teachings of Vedanta and the *Bhagavad Gita*, which focuses on selfless action. In his *Gita Rahasya*, he stated that freedom is the soul of the home rule movement. While the duty of a king is to promote the welfare of the people, the people have the right to remove exploitative rulers.

For Tilak, Swarajya encompassed the following features:

1. The ruler and the people should belong to the same country, religion, and race.
2. Swaraj refers to a system of rule of law.
3. Swaraj should promoting the wellbeing of the people.
4. The government should be elected by and responsible to the people.

According to Tilak, Swarajya (self-government) is better than *surajya*, good government. For Tilak, swarajya is moral and spiritual, and teaches self-control and inner freedom. Swaraj was given its political form through home rule; Tilak firmly believed that no progress was possible without self-rule.

SOCIALLY CONSERVATIVE

However, Tilak was strongly opposed to the liberal trends emerging in Pune, such as women's rights and social reforms against untouchability. He was also opposed to inter-caste marriage, particularly of an upper-caste woman with a lower-caste man. Opposing the Sharda Act which aimed to increase the age of marriage of girls, he stated that was not against social reform in itself, but he was against the social reform espoused by the British government, believing that the British government only sought to divide Indian society on the pretext of social reform.

Tilak did not have a progressive view when it came to gender relations, and was not believe that

Hindu women should get a modern education. Rather, he had a more conservative view, believing that women were meant to be homemakers who had to subordinate themselves to the needs of their husbands and children.

BOOKS

1. *Shrimadh Bhagvad Gita Rahasya* (1915).
2. *The Arctic Home in the Vedas* (1903)
3. *The Orion* (1955)

9

SWAMI VIVEKANANDA (1863–1902)

KEY CONCEPTS

Spiritualsm vs materialism; cultural nationalism; empowering marginalised groups

Swami Vivekananda, whose birth name was Narendranath Datta, was born on 12 January 1863 in Kolkata to a traditional Bengali Kayastha family. He was a Hindu monk, philosopher, writer and the chief disciple of the mystic Ramakrishna Paramhansa. He was the founder of the **Ramakrishna Mission** (1897) and the **Belur Math** in Kolkata. Vivekananda was a major force in contemporary Hindu reform movements, and contributed to the concept of nationalism in colonial India. He also played an important role in introducing the frameworks of Vedanta and Yoga to the West, and in greater interfaith awareness, leading to greater recognition of Hinduism as a significant 'world religion'. **National Youth Day** is celebrated annually on 12 January to honour his birth anniversary.

RELIGIOUS AND SPIRITUAL LEADER

In 1880, Narendra joined Keshab Chandra Sen's *Nava Vidhan*. From 1881–84, he was also active in Sen's Band of Hope, which tried to discourage youths from smoking and drinking. His initial beliefs were shaped by the concepts of the Brahmo Samaj, which denounced polytheism and caste restrictions.

In 1881, Narendranath first met Ramakrishna. Although he did not initially accept Ramakrishna as his teacher and rebelled against his ideas, he was attracted by his personality and began to frequently visit him at Dakshineswar. Narendranath's father's sudden death in 1884 left the family bankrupt. He unsuccessfully tried to find work and began questioning God's existence, but found solace in Ramakrishna and his visits to Dakshineswar increased. Upon Ramakrishna's suggestion, he took to praying in the temple for knowledge and direction, gradually grew ready to renounce everything for the sake of realising God, and accepted Ramakrishna as his Guru. In 1886, Narendranath took formal monastic vows and took the name 'Swami Vivekananda'.

Vivekananda believed that religion is the essence and the soul of India. He believed in the philosophy of Advaita Vedanta and stood against the orthodoxy of Hinduism. He also opposed untouchability and the caste system. He was the first modern Indian who tried to define Hinduism for the world.

SPIRITUALISM MORE IMPORTANT THAN MATERIALISM

While acknowledging the scientific knowledge of the West, Vivekananda believed that spiritualism is the contribution of East to the world, and considered it superior to materialism, which he termed a lower from of development. Vivekananda reached Chicago in the US in 1893, where the 'Parliament of Religions' was to take place. There, Vivekananda gave a brief speech representing India and Hinduism. His speeches at the Parliament had the common theme of universality, emphasising religious tolerance, and he attracted widespread attention in the press, which called him the 'cyclonic monk from India'. Thereafter, he spent two years touring the US and parts of Europe, giving lectures, and his popularity expanded.

CULTURAL NATIONALISM

Vivekananda is considered the father of cultural nationalism in India. According to Sister Nivedita, while he was not a politician, he certainly was the greatest of nationalists. Despite never propounding any direct political ideas, he inspired nationalism in the youth. Nationalism was a prominent theme in Vivekananda's thought. He believed that a country's future depends on its people, and his teachings focused on human development. Stating that we should be proud to be Indian, he declared that the nation should be viewed as a mother, who should be protected at any cost. In 1918, the Sedition Committee Report accused Vivekananda of instigating young man and women to wage war against the British colonial government. His nationalistic ideas influenced many Indian thinkers and leaders. Sri Aurobindo regarded Vivekananda as the one who had awakened India spiritually.

For Vivekananda, 'Hindu' is a cultural term. The culture of India is the same throughout, and therefore a feeling of togetherness should bind the country. The word 'Hindu' covers Muslims, Christians, Jains, and every other group of people. He also claimed that the Vedas were the common scriptures for India and never accepted any distinction between Aryans and Dravidians.

EMPOWERING MARGINALISED SECTIONS

From 1888, Vivekananda travelled extensively in India for five years, visiting centres of learning and acquainting himself with diverse religious traditions and social patterns. He developed sympathy for the suffering and poverty of the people, and resolved to uplift the nation. He repeatedly addressed social issues: uplifting the people, eliminating the caste system, promoting science and industrialisation, addressing widespread poverty, and ending colonial rule. He believed that serving the weaker sections of society is the best medium for finding God (*Daridra Narayan*). Vivekananda felt that India was a civilisation, while the West was a set of nations; but in both the distance between the higher and lower classes is infinite. He sought to educate and raise the masses, as only through this would India emerge as a nation. In 1897 in Calcutta, he founded the Ramakrishna Mission, whose ideals are based on *Karma Yoga*, for the purpose of social service.

He believed in the principle of equality, as given in a Vedantic philosophy. He propagated the idea that 'the divine, the absolute, exists within all human beings regardless of social status'. No caste or gender discrimination is possible in true spiritualism, as according to Vedanta, the same soul lies in everyone. Vivekananda linked morality with control of the mind, seeing truth, purity, and unselfishness as traits which strengthened it.

Vivekananda's publications include:

1. *Raj Yoga* (1896)
2. *Karma Yoga* (1896)
3. *Bhakti Yoga* (published posthumously)
4. *Lectures from Colombo to Almora* (1897)
5. *Bartaman Bharat* (in Bengali; 1899)
6. *My Master* (1901)
7. *Vedanta Philosophy: Lectures on Jnana Yoga* (1902)
8. *Practical Vedanta* (1912; published posthumously)

10

RABINDRANATH TAGORE (1861–1941)

KEY CONCEPTS
Anti-imperialism; Indian nationalism; educational strategies; Gandhi and Tagore

Rabindranath Tagore was born on 7 May 1861 in the Jorasanko mansion in Kolkata. A Bengali polymath who worked as a poet, writer, playwright, composer, philosopher, social reformer, and painter, he reshaped Bengali literature and music, as also Indian art. In 1913, Tagore was awarded the Nobel Prize for Literature for his work *Gitanjali* (Song Offerings), his best-known collection of poetry. Tagore is the only person to have written the National Anthems of two countries: **Jana Gana Mana**, the National Anthem of India, which was composed as Bharat Bhagyo Bidhata and adopted as the National Anthem in 1950, and Amar Sonar Bangla, which became the National Anthem of Bangladesh.

AGAINST IMPERIALISM

Tagore was opposed to imperialism and colonial rule, and supported the nationalist movement.

Tagore believed in the principles of liberty, equality, and democracy. Imperialism, according to him, was based on exploitation and domination, which went against the values of liberty and equality.

Tagore was internationalist in his outlook and his views on various political systems are available. He praised nationalism in Japan, but was also critical of the tendency towards suppression displayed in Japanese policy. While the social and economic development achieved by the Socialists in Soviet Union was commendable, the corresponding suppression of liberty was painful to Tagore, and could never be suppported. Without freedom, there could be no human development, and he felt that the real development of human beings was spiritual and moral. Therefore, it appears that he was internationalist in his outlook.

Tagore was critical of European nationalism, stating that nationalism, as it existed in Europe at the time, was aggressive and expansionist. It had developed due to the strides made by modern science and technology, but was exploitative and based on war, arms, and violence. European imperialism had its origins in nationalism. While he was not against Western culture, he felt that freedom was necessary to even learn from other cultures.

INDIAN NATIONALISM

Tagore wrote songs in praise of the national movement, and two of his political compositions, 'Where the Mind is Without Fear' and 'Ekla Cholo Re (Walk Alone)' are the best-known, the second being a favourite of Mahatma Gandhi's. However,

Tagore was against the more extreme forms of Indian nationalism and believed that India had a right to be independent without denying the importance of what she could learn from abroad, a belief that led to severe criticism.

In 1919, as a reaction to the brutal Jallianwala Bagh massacre, Tagore renounced his knighthood, which the British Crown had bestowed upon him.

Tagore believed that liberty, equality, and fraternity ought to be at the base of Indian nationalism, along with humanism and cosmopolitanism. The development of spiritual and moral values was considered important, since scientific and technical development without a concomitant development of humanity could prove to be dangerous.

Nationalism in India is a political programme, and one associated with the consciousness of the community at a social level. Tagore was in support of India's freedom movement, and had declared it during the proposed Partition of Bengal in 1905. However, he felt that without the empowerment of society, nationalism would be reduced to a mere elitist concept. This had happened in Europe as well, and therefore he said that social equality and the removal of discrimination should be the first steps towards developing a strong nation.

EDUCATION WITH INDIAN CULTURE

Tagore believed that the primary purpose of education was to ensure the fullest development of the human personality. He set up a school, Sriniketan, and the university of Santiniketan, now known as Visva Bharati University, in 1918. Tagore had wanted to 'make Santiniketan the connecting thread between India and the world [and] a world centre for the study of humanity somewhere beyond the limits of nation and geography'.

Tagore employed a *brahmacharya* system of education in his institutions: gurus gave pupils personal guidance—emotional, intellectual, and spiritual, and teaching was often done under trees, in marked contrast to classroom teaching and the system of rote learning and emphasis on examinations that other educational institutions followed. He used the prize money from his Nobel Prize to set up and staff his schools, and himself took several classes.

GANDHI AND TAGORE

While Tagore was not in complete support of the non-cooperation movement launched by Mahatma Gandhi or with other aspects of Gandhian activism, the two great leaders had one central belief in common—the spiritual and moral development of human beings. There was also a lot of mutual respect and affection between them, with Tagore recognising Gandhi as the **Mahatma**, and Gandhi hailing Tagore as **Gurudev.** Tagore was also key in resolving a dispute between Gandhi and B. R. Ambedkar concerning separate electorates for those known as the 'untouchables' (now called Dalits), and was instrumental in ending one of Gandhi's 'fasts unto death'.

IMPORTANT WORKS

Known mostly for his poetry, Tagore wrote novels, essays, short stories, travelogues, dramas, and thousands of songs. Some of his published works are:

Gitanjali (*Song Offerings,* 1910)
Balaka (*The Flight of Cranes,* poetry, 1916)
Ghaire Baire (*The Home and the World*, fiction, 1916)
Nastanirh (*The Broken Nest*, fiction, 1901)
Gora (fiction, 1910)
Chitrangada (drama, 1892)
Dak Ghar (*The Post Office,* drama, 1912)
Creative Unity (translation, 1922)
Nationalism (translation, 1917)
The Spirit of Japan (translation, 1916)

11

MAHATAMA GANDHI (1869–1948)

KEY CONCEPTS

Non-violence; satyagraha; key influences on Gandhi; dharma; politics and religion; practical idealist; anti-industrialism; sarvodaya; Nai Talim; Ram Rajya; Gandhism

Mohandas Karamchand Gandhi, who is today venerated in India as the Father of the Nation, was born on 2 October 1869 in Porbundar, Gujarat. He was a lawyer, a freedom fighter and nationalist, and influential philosopher and thinker famous for his **non-violent resistance** against colonial rule. His leadership of India's freedom movement later inspired civil rights and freedom movement around the world. The honorific 'Mahatma' (great soul) was first applied to him in South Africa in 1914.

It was in South Africa, where he lived and worked for 21 years, that he first showed his leadership mettle, when he fought against apartheid (discrimination on the basis of race and skin colour) and led a civil rights movement against the injustice of colonial rulers. While he initially focused on the discrimination faced by Indians, he soon extended his movement to Africans as well, and by 1910, his newspaper *Indian Opinion* was publishing reports of colonial persecution of Africans in South Africa.

Gandhi's growing international reputation as a peaceful civil rights activist had reached India as well. In 1915, at the request of Gopal Krishna Gokhale, he returned to India, joined the Indian National Congress, and was introduced to the issues that Indian people were suffering under colonial rule. He exhibited his leadership first in Champaran, Bihar, in 1917, when he launched a non-violent protest in support of peasants who were being forced to grow indigo on plantations owned by Anglo-Indian plantation owners, This was followed by the 1918 agitations in Kheda, which had been hit by floods and famine, and where peasants were demanding relief from taxation. Through methods such as social boycott and public agitations, Gandhi's movement was successful, and the British suspended revenue collections.

Through his tools of Satyagraha and non-violence, he became the main architect of Indian nationalist movements such as the Non-cooperation Movement, Civil Disobedience Movement and Quit India Movement. To him goes the credit of transforming the national movement into a mass movement by reaching people all over the country and teaching people to be fearless, bold, and adopt non-violent methods for fighting against injustice.

He was opposed to industrialisation and materialism and believed in the *sarvodaya* economic model, which literally means 'welfare and upliftment of all'. He exhorted people to follow the Swadeshi path and called for an end to poverty through improved agriculture and small-scale rural cottage industries. While disagreeing with Nehru about the socialist economic model, Gandhi also critiqued capitalism, which was driven by endless wants and a materialistic view of man. He was in favour of a *grassroots democracy* with minimal state intervention.

KEY INFLUENCES

1. Gandhi published a Gujarati translation of **John Ruskin's** *Unto This Last* (1860), which reflects how greatly he was impacted by the essay. The Gujarati translation was titled *Sarvodaya* (1908). Ruskin's critique of the political economy emphasised dignity of labour, and he famously asserted that the labour of an advocate and a barber were both equally important in society. Gandhi incorporated this idea into his philosophy.
2. Gandhi was deeply influenced by Russian writer **Leo Tolstoy**. One of the three books that influenced him most was Tolstoy's *The Kingdom of God is Within You* (1894). He saw himself as a disciple of Tolstoy, for they both opposed state authority and colonialism; further, both hated violence and preached non-resistance.
3. Yet another book that influenced Gandhi was **Henry David Thoreau's** *On the Duty of Civil Disobedience* (1849). The notion of *Satyagraha* is influenced by Henry Thoreau, who had also propounded the ideas of civil disobedience and *passive resistance.*
4. Indian philosophy had a great impact on Gandhi. *Nishkam Karm Yoga* (self-less action) is a philosophy that Gandhi derived from the *Bhagavad Gita*. He was also influenced by the literature of the Bhakti saints, Advaita Vedanta—he based Satyagraha on the Vedantic ideal of self-realisation, ahimsa (non-violence), vegetarianism, and universal love—and the Upanishadic texts.

Gandhi never claimed **monopoly over truth**. He summarised his beliefs first when he said 'God is Truth', a statement he later changed to 'Truth is God'. Thus, *satya* (truth) in Gandhi's philosophy is 'God'. The only way to know the truth is through love or non-violence. Truth is absolute, but the knowledge of truth can only be partial and one-dimensional.

PURITY OF MEANS AND ENDS

For Gandhi, truth was the end, the means to which is non-violence. The essence of satyagraha is at the heart of Gandhi's political movement, that is, refusing to use brute force against the oppressor. While the abolition of colonialism was the end, satyagraha was the means to this end. This end usually implies a moral upliftment or progress of an individual or society.

Gandhi titled his autobiography *My Experiment with Truth*, which covers his life from early childhood till 1921. He believed that one does not need to be an ascetic to be moral; people should practice self-denial to become moral. Gandhiji believed in the 'purity of means as well as the purity of ends' and argued that only the right means can lead to the attainment of the right end. Gandhi based Satyagraha on the Vedantic ideal of self-realisation, ahimsa (nonviolence), vegetarianism, and universal love. Rejecting the belief that the end justifies the means, Gandhi compared ends and means with the seeds of a tree, stating that only the right kind of seed will lead to the growth of the right kind of tree.

Means and ends can be compared with action (*karma*) and its consequence (*phala*), which is also a famous teaching from the *Gita*, which explains that humans have control over their actions, but not over their consequences. Gandhi believed that ends and means are two sides of the same coin, and therefore he insisted on the path of satyagraha in his struggles for freedom in the national movement. His principle of means and end is also reflected in his theory of the relationship between politics and ethics. The principle of ethics Gandhi followed was based on the moral teaching of all religions, and he also expressed his firm faith on the 'spiritualisation of politics'.

DHARMA

For Gandhi, satyagraha was the truth. God was the absolute truth, omniscient and omnipresent, but the knowledge of truth is not absolute. Truth is multi-dimensional. Nobody can claim monopoly over truth. Love is the medium through which to obtain truth (that is, it is the path that leads to God). Love perforce means non-violence, and this non-violence should be mental and physical and through speech too. Truth, non-violence, non-possession, and celibacy are the basic elements of Dharma.

Based on Gandhian thought, the *seven sins* can be stated as:

1. Wealth without work is sin.
2. Pleasure without conscience.
3. Science without humanity.
4. Knowledge without character.
5. Politics without principles.
6. Commerce without morality.
7. Worship without sacrifice.

POLITICS AND RELIGION

Gandhi equated religion with morality and duty. Religion, to him, is not merely about worshipping the supreme power, but stands for welfare, for **Daridra-Narayan**. Gandhi always referred to the *Bhagavad Gita* as his spiritual guide, and his comparative studies of religions and interaction with scholars, led him to respect all religions. Politics is another word for *Lok Niti* (the wellbeing of the people). Politics should not be a means to gain power, but should be seen as a social service. Gandhi is considered a saint among politicians and as a politician among saints. Gandhi believed that *swaraj* can not only be attained with non-violence, but can also be run with non-violence.

According to Gandhi, politics cannot be divorced from religion. He believed that he could lead a truly religious life only when he participated in politics. As stated earlier, politics for him was a means to participate in public affairs for the sole purpose of serving the people, as the function of politics is integrally connected with the *welfare of people*. Gandhi said, 'Most religious men I have met, are politician in disguise. I, however, who wears the guise of a politician, am at heart, a religious man.' This remains the key to the value system of the political philosophy that he adhered to.

Gandhi believed that politics is the means by which to serve the cause of humanity, and this will eventually lead to a better understanding of truth. The 'Kingdom of God', Gandhi believed, lies within us. Therefore, individuals must engage in political activity to serve humanity. He stated: 'I could not live for a single second without religion. Many of my political friends despair of me because they say that even my politics are derived from religion. And they are right.'

Gandhi believed that power was merely a means to enable people, and not an end it inself. Political power was also a means to regulate public life in tune with the principles of ethics and morality.

SATYAGRAHA

Gandhi's idea of satyagraha was influenced in part by the writings of Henry David Thoureau, who propounded the idea of passive resistance. Satyagraha, however, is different from passive resistance. Passive resistance implies a peaceful opposition, with the possibility of taking recourse to violence when the need arises left open. Passive residence seeks victory for itself and defeat for its opponent. Satyagraha, on the other hand, refers to moral and communitarian ethics, and for the victory of truth. *Violence* is not to be applied in any condition; love towards one's opponent is the foundation of Satyagraha.

The essence of Satyagraha is 'soul force' as a political means, a refusal to use brute force against the oppressor. It seeks to eliminate antagonisms between the oppressor and the oppressed, aiming to transform or 'purify' the oppressor. It is not inaction, but determined passive resistance and non-cooperation.

For Gandhi, satyagraha is a method by which to secure rights through personal suffering, rather than opting for armed resistance. Satyagraha has the power to bring about a change of heart in one's opponent, persuading him to depart from the path of injustice. According to Bhikhu Parekh, Gandhi adopted this **'power of soul'** against various forms of brute force in South Africa, against British rule in India, and against unjust social practices prevailing in Indian society. The differences between Satyagraha and passive resistance can be stated as:

Table 3.11.1: Satyagraha versus Passive Resistance

Satyagraha	*Passive Resistance*
Moral Force	Peaceful Opposition
Power of Soul	Political Opposition
Victory of Truth	Defeat of opponent
Love towards opponent	Hate towards opponent
Violence cannot be accepted	Violence is possible

Gandhi was convinced that fighting evil through evil will only lead to greater evil. According to John Bondurant, Gandhi was in favour of fighting, but was firmly opposed to violence. Gandhi wrote: 'There must be no impatience, no barbarity, no insolence, no undue pressure. If we want to cultivate a true spirit of democracy, we cannot afford to be intolerant. Intolerance betrays want of faith in one's cause.' Satyagraha would lead to the moral upliftment of individuals, and enable them to control passions such as lust, anger, greed, and aggression. According to **R. R. Diwakar,** it is satyagraha which made Gandhi the Mahatma. It was the *satyagraha* formulation, as Dennis Dalton also stated, that deeply resonated with the beliefs and culture of his people, embedded him within the popular consciousness, and thereby transformed him into the Mahatma.

Through his non-violent movement and Satyagraha, Gandhi presented the world with an alternative method of conflict resolution and inspired many great civil rights activists, such as Martin Luther King and Nelson Mandela.

A person choosing the path of satyagraha includes embodies the following characteristics:

1. Love
2. Fearlessness
3. Non-violence
4. Truth

Everyone is a child of God, and thus a spiritual person will never fear anyone. However, it is interesting to note that Gandhi stood firmly against any form of cowardice. In a 1920 essay after World War I, Gandhi wrote, 'Where there is only a choice between cowardice and violence, I would advise violence.' Power, for him, is not merely physical or bodily power, but is primarily spiritual, reflecting the power of the soul. While anyone can choose passive resistance, satyagraha requires a person with a strong soul.

Apart from being a philosophy, satyagraha was a **political tool** in the fight against colonialism and imperialism. Gandhi is considered a practical idealist as he supported constitutionalism as a method of protest. However, support for satyagraha and Gandhian non-violence was not universal even in India, as the revolutionary factions within the Congress supported violent means of protest. It is undeniable, though, that Gandhi had discovered a new moral technique for fighting the British colonial government. Unity in both deed and action are the hallmarks of Gandhi.

PRACTICAL IDEALIST

In 1910, Gandhi established, with the help of his friend Hermann Kallenbach, an idealistic community they named Tolstoy Farm near Johannesburg in South Africa. It was here that he began practicing his ideals of non-violence and systematically trained his disciples in the philosophy of peaceful protests. Gandhi believed in absolute morality and practised every moral principle in his life. However, he was also willing to compromise during the nationalist movement for the good of the nation.

Gandhi was not materialistic as he believed that everthing in this universe has been created by God. His whole life was dedicated to the perpetual quest for truth. Non-violence for him is synonymous with love, which is the only medium through which to know God. While these principles appear idealistic, it is worthwhile to recall that Gandhi applied these ideals in his political life in form of satyagraha. In social life, Sarvodaya sought an end to unjust social practices and the upliftment of all. In religious life, he preached equal respect towards all religions.

URBANISATION AND INDUSTRIALISATION

Gandhi was against industrialisation and the use of heavy machinery, which carried within itself the threat to displace human labour. Gandhi challenged Nehru and the modernisers in the late 1930s who called for rapid industrialisation along the Soviet model, denouncing this as dehumanising. Writing in *Hind Swaraj*, he criticised modern civilisation and capitalism, which was driven by endless wants and a materialistic view of life. Gandhi's focus was always on moral and inner development.

Terming modern civilisation as materialistic, Gandhi declared that it presented an obstacle to the moral development of individuals. He appealed to people living in cities to effect a return to the villages. His views against industrialisation and urbanisation were similar to those of **John Ruskin** and **William Morris,** who believed that rapid industrialisation and modernisation would ultimately lead to a concentration of resources, which in turn will eventually lead to violence. The replacement of human labour with machines will lead to massive unemployment and widespread poverty and misery. He instead believed in production by the masses and called for ending poverty through improved agriculture and small-scale, rural cottage industries. Liberalism, socialism, and Marxism were also the product of modern civilisation, and thus Gandhism differs from all these ideologies.

SARVODAYA

As a young barrister in South Africa, Gandhi was presented with a copy of John Ruskin's *Unto This Last* (1860) by Henry Polak, a newspaper editor in Johannesburg who was also a close associate. The three lessons that Gandhi learnt from this book were:

1. The good of the individual is contained in the good of all.
2. All people have the same right to earn a livelihood through their work.
3. A life of labour, that is, the life of the tiller of soil and the handicraftsman, is a life worth living.

Inspired to build a Sarvodaya Society, he established the Phoenix Settlement in South Africa in 1904—a farm comprising 100 acres of land where everyone received the same wages, regardless of ethnicity or assigned tasks. The ideal village sarvodaya, according to Gandhi, ought to be self-sufficient in matters of food and clothing; their places of worship should be beautiful and clean; there should be a sewage system in every lane; it should have a public hall, a school, and a theatre hall; and there should be an efficient water supply system.

The term 'Sarvodaya' means 'uplift of all', or an awakening of all, and its goal is social reconstruction. While the ideal of Sarvodaya is concerned with the welfare of all, it reserves special concern for the downtrodden or the most disadvantaged. With social justice in mind, it states that while the upliftment of the poor is economic, there is a need for the moral upliftment of the rich.

Sarvodaya needs to be extended to society. Gandhi used the analogy of an *oceanic circle*: small waves lead to larger waves in the ocean. Similarly, the smaller units of society promote the wellbeing of larger units, and individuals seek the welfare of their families. Families together work for the happiness of the entire community.

Political Aspect

The state is a **soulless machine,** an organised form of violence. Gandhi was even against the parliamentary form of government, in which power resides in the hands of political parties. Gandhi's dream was to establish a **federation of villages** as according to him, India lived in its villages. The decentralised Panchayat Raj system (discussed in Unit 7) hews closely to the model of Gandhian democracy, which gives power in the hands of the people living at the grassroots. Power should not be concentrated at the top, but be from the bottom-up. In the Gandhian view of governance, there was no place for a political party.

Economic Aspect

Gandhi believed in the principle of *trusteeship*. The individual is merely a trustee of all property; the real owner of property is God. According to Gandhi, morality and economics cannot be divorced from each other. Through the principle of Sarvodaya, social justice will be ensured, and even the most depressed classes will be accorded their due share in society. Sarvodaya positions itself against utilitarianism, which believes in material welfare and the maximum happiness of maximum numbers. In contrast, sarvodaya seeks to secure the *spiritual and material welfare of humanity*.

Capitalism believes in the private ownership of property while socialists favour state ownership and control over all resources. For Gandhi, however, all property belonged to God and should be utilised for the wellbeing. People were urged to donate (*daan*) the property to ensure this well-being of the community, and to bring about economic equality for all. There can be various forms of daan, such as the donation of labour (*shram daan*), as well as the donation of material assets. Villages, too, can also be donated (*gram daan*), and thereby, social and economic change can be made possible though moral and spiritual means.

SARVODAYA, SOCIALISM, AND COMMUNISM

Socialism seeks the material welfare of people, and its chief goal to secure the emancipation of the working classes. Communism is based on the idea of class struggle, that is, overthrowing of the capitalist class by the working class through violent and revolutionary means. Sarvodaya, however, is different from both is many respects. While socialism sought to secure the welfare of the working classes, sarvodaya contemplates the material as well as spiritual welfare of all. To Gandhi, Bhikhu Parekh states, both communism and capitalism were wrong, in part because both focused exclusively on a materialistic view of humankind, and because the former deified the state with its unlimited power of violence, while the latter deified capital. Gandhi believed that a better economic system is one which does not impoverish one's culture and spiritual pursuits, and in that respect, he called for an emphasis on small-scale and rural cottage industries.

Instead of class conflict, sarvodaya seeks to bring about class cooperation. There is no scope for any violence; it insists on the spiritual emancipation of both the rich and the poor in order to restore harmony in society. Socialists believe in state-controlled economic production, but Gandhi believed in a decentralised economy. Manual labuor should be mandatory for everyone, handicrafts, small industries, and cottage industries should be the foundation of the economy. He argued that no human can degrade or brutalise the other without degrading and brutalising themselves, and that sustainable economic growth comes from service, not from exploitation. The Gandhian mode of economy is the most suitable for a populous country like India, where labour-intensive industries can be the most beneficial.

EDUCATION

Gandhi was opposed to the colonial Western system of education, stating that it led to a disdain for manual work and created an elite administrative bureaucracy. Gandhi favoured an education system that placed far greater emphasis on learning skills in practical and useful work, one that included physical, mental, and spiritual studies. His methodology sought to treat all professions equally and offer everyone equal pay. He proposed an **alternative educational system** that he called **Nai Talim** in his journal *Harijan*.

Nai Talim is a spiritual principle that focuses on the spiritual, ethical, moral, and practical development of children. Gandhi believed that Western education violated and destroyed indigenous cultures. Education should be indigenous and not imported from other countries, and it should be imparted in the mother tongue, be available in all villages, and teaching and learning practices must be woven through some sort of art and craft. Moreover, the Nai Talim philosophy called for free, universal basic education for all children. Gandhi wanted all students to learn crafts so they can develop an appreciation of the dignity of labour, and would lead to a holistic development of the mind, body, and soul.

SWARAJ

As previously stated, Gandhi believed that Swaraj could not only be attained through non-violence, but could also be run by non-violence. The political dimension of Swaraj is best exemplified through a decentralised, Panchayati system of government. Swaraj stands for freedom from colonial rule; however, Swaraj to Gandhi did not mean transferring the colonial-era British power-brokering system, and bureaucratic, exploitative class structure and mindset into Indian hands. There is no place for a Parliament and party in Swaraj.

S. M. Tewari states that Gandhi saw democracy as more than a system of government; it meant promoting both individuality and the self-discipline of the community. For Gandhi, democracy was a way of life.

Figure 3.11.1: Dimensions of Swaraj.

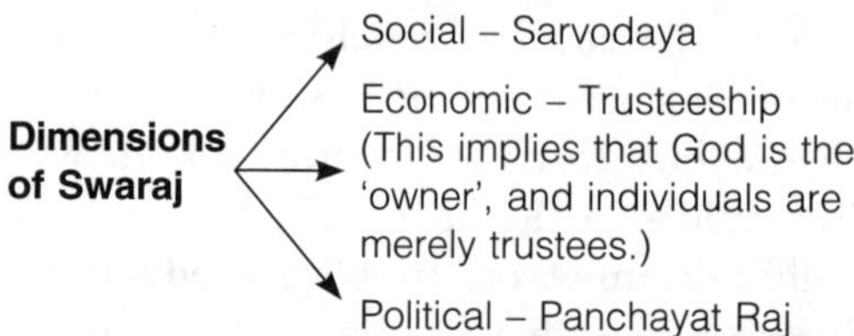

Gandhi criticised Western civilisation and modernity in his book *Hind Swaraj* (1909), where he severely critiqued the British form of Parliament. The word 'Swaraj' implies self-government or 'self-determination'. This term was used by leaders like **Tilak** and **Dadabhai Naoroji** as well. Gandhiji expanded the concept of Swaraj thus:

1. Swaraj is more than political independence from foreign rule. It implies moral and cultural independence against any form of coercion that inhibits an individual's potential.
2. It implies true democracy, in which people will not only elect its leaders but will also check their abuse of power.
3. The goal of Swaraj also implies 'moral regeneration', 'self-discipline', and 'self-purification', even after attaining independence.
4. The goal of Swaraj should be attained peacefully; Gandhi always emphasised on the purity of means as well as of the ends.

PHILOSOPHICAL ANARCHISM

Anarchism broadly means statelessness. Philosophical anarchism refers to a statelessness based on the moral nature of human beings. People who believes in the principles of truth and non-violence are not supposed to be regulated by others; rather, they are capable of self-regulation. Gandhi believed that the state is an organised form of violence and a soulless machine. The violence of the state is more dangerous than the violence of an individual.

Gandhi is also known as the pacifist anarchist. According to him, a non-violent state is like an 'ordered anarchy'. In a society of mostly non-violent individuals, those who are violent will sooner or later accept discipline or leave the community. He emphasised a society where individuals believed more in learning about their duties and responsibilities instead of demanding rights and privileges. Gandhi believed in a 'Ram Rajya', although he later accepted Panchayti Raj. He was in favour of a decentralised government, where the village is the centre of power. Thus, it would be a grassroots democracy without a political party.

DUTY AND RIGHTS

Gandhi stated that if each person followed their duty and their conscience, there would be no clash for rights. He believed in the primacy of the individual and his individual is one who is moral and works for the well-being of their family. While he was in favour of individualism, his individualism was not ranged against the community. Instead, the well-being of a community would automatically promote the well-being of the individual. For Gandhi, the duty of all lay in following the principles of truth and non-violence.

ENVIRONMENTALISM

The beauty of Gandhian thought lies in the centrality it accords to the principle of harmony. He believed in harmony among the people and was firmly against any conflict in society. Moreover, he emphasised harmony between human society and nature as well. He stated that while nature is bountiful enough to fulfil the needs of all people, nature can never fulfil the greed of even one person. Arraying himself against a consumerist way of life, Gandhi believed that some life forms are more capable of suffering, and non-violence to him meant the active effort to minimise hurt, injury, or suffering to all life forms. Therefore, he also explored food sources that reduced violence to various life forms in the food chain. He was also against heavy industrialisation, which would prove harmful to ecology.

NOT AN 'IDEOLOGY'

Gandhism designates the ideas and principles Gandhi promoted; of central importance is non-violent resistance. Gandhi himself did not approve of the notion of 'Gandhism', as he explained in 1936: 'There is no such thing as "Gandhism", and I do not want to leave any sect after me. I do not claim to have originated any new principle or doctrine. I have simply tried in my own way to apply the eternal truths to our daily life and problems.' He was only engaged in an experiment with truth; whatever he had said is neither absolute nor final as truth is dynamic and ever-changing.

He further stated that he had not discovered the principle of truth and non-violence because these have been present in Indian philosophy and culture since time immemorial.

Gandhi is considered a practical idealist who believed in the unity of deeds and actions. Therefore, K. G. Mashroowala stated that it is better to use the terms 'Sarvodayavaad' or 'Satyagraha Darshan', rather than Gandhism. Kriplani believes in a Gandhian viewpoint or Gandhian path, instead of Gandhism.

IMPORTANT WORKS ON AND BY GANDHI

Green Pamphlet (1896)
Indian Opinion (1904)
Young India (journal)
Navajivan (Gujarati monthly newspaper)
Harijan (journal)
The Story of My Experiments with Truth (autobiography)
Hind Swaraj
In Search of Gandhi, by Richard Attenborough.
Mahatma Gandhi, His Life and Ideas, by Charles Freer Andrews

The Life of Mahatma Gandhi, by Louis Fischer
Mahatma vs Gandhi, by Dinker Joshi
India After Gandhi: The History of World's Largest Democracy, by Ramchandra Guha
Political Philosophy of Mahatma Gandhi, by G. N. Dhawan
The Gandhian Way and *I Follow Mahatma Gandhi*, by J. B. Kripalani
Gandhi and Marx, by K. G. Mashruwala

12

AUROBINDO (1872–1950)

KEY CONCEPTS

Cultural–spiritual nationalism; sanatan dharma; passive resistance; human unity; spiritual and scientific development

Aurobindo Ghose was born in 1872 in Calcutta, Bengal. His father, Krishna Dhun Ghose, was a doctor and former member of the Brahmo Samaj religious reform movement. Aurobindo was an extremist nationalist leader, a political thinker, philosopher, and poet. He was also a journalist, editing newspapers such as the *Vande Mataram*. He was a freedom fighter associated with the revolutionary movement in Bengal called the Anushilan Samiti. He was arrested in the aftermath of a number of bombings linked to this organisation in a public trial where he faced charges of treason in the Alipore (bomb) Conspiracy case. However, Aurobindo could only be convicted and imprisoned for writing articles against British colonial rule in India, and was released when no evidence could be provided

During his imprisonment, he turned to spirituality and after his release, he retired from active politics and left for Pondicherry, where he immersed himself in spiritual work. A believer in human equality and universal oneness of all, he is particularly known for his contribution to spiritual thought.

According to Aurobindo Ghose, there is a fundamental unity between God, human beings, and the universe. He stated that the divine Brahma manifests itself in empirical reality through divine play. The central theme of his vision was the evolution of human life into a divine life in a divine body. He believed in a spiritual realisation that not only liberated but transformed human nature, enabling a divine life on earth.

Sri Aurobindo believed there was a need to awaken the Indian soul out of its slumber. The human soul could achieve its glory through the philosophy of Vedanta, which emphasises spirituality over the sciences. Carrying forward his ideas of Vedanta, he declared that the message of Vedanta was selfless action or Karma Yoga. In 1926, with the help of his spiritual collaborator, Mirra Alfassa (referred to as 'The Mother'), he founded the Sri Aurobindo Ashram in Pondicherry. Aurobino had started two weeklies, the **Karmayogin** and **Dharma.**

CULTURAL–SPIRITUAL NATIONALISM

Sri Aurobindo joined the state service in Baroda in 1893, after completing his education from England. It was here that he started taking an active interest in the politics of the Indian independence movement against British colonial rule, working behind the scenes as his position in the Baroda state administration barred him from an overt political activity. He believed that British rule was a denial of the creation of the Almighty and worked against the serving of God itself.

Aurobindo was influenced by studies on rebellion and revolutions against England in medieval France and the revolts in America and Italy. In Bengal, he established contacts and inspired revolutionaries such as Bagha Jatin or Jatin Mukherjee and Surendranath Tagore. His concept of nationalism was also deeply influenced by Bankim Chandra, the great Bengali novelist. However, after his imprisonment in the bombings by extremist revolutionaries following the partition of Bengal in 1905, Aurobindo's view of life changed radically because of certain spiritual experiences.

He claimed to have been visited by Vivekananda while in jail, and said that God had appeared to him in prison, placed the Gita in his hand, and helped him realise the simple truth of Sanatana Dharma. Aurobindo declared that nationalism in India is a gift of God. Since God is immortal, so too is the creation of God. Nationhood, he stated, cannot be confined to just a piece of land or a mass of human beings; it is greater than a geographical unit and people's imagination. India should therefore be viewed as a goddess, a mother.

According to Karan Singh, for Aurobindo, 'India was like incarnation of Goddess who for centuries has created and nourished her children and who, at the time was groaning under the yoke of [the] foreigner.' Sri Aurobindo Ghose advised his younger compatriots to unite and work for the liberation of their country. Nationalism is a faith and a creed, and akin to a religion.

LIBERATION OF INDIA

For Aurobindo, Swaraj was more than political freedom; it was a means to attain self-liberation and fulfillment of the Vedantic ideal. Through Swaraj, Aurobindo believed India could return to its 'old national individuality', free to play her role in the redemption of the whole world. National regeneration was thus not the final goal, but a stepping stone towards universal regeneration. Sri Aurobindo was the one to coin the slogan, **'no control, no cooperation'**.

SANATAN DHARMA AND WORLD RELIGION

Sanatan Dharma is not a dogma; it is a law of life. It alone can be the basis of world religions because it accepts all forms of religion—Christianity, Buddhism, Islam, etc.—and yet it is none of these. It alone combines science and faith. Aurobindo believed that there could be no freedom without religious and cultural regeneration. Nationalism, according to him, was not exclusive: it is inclusive, available for all classes and creeds. India would rise and achieve greatness only though following the path of Sanatan Dharma.

Sri Autobindo owed much of his philosophical beliefs to the *Rigveda*, the *Upanishads*, and the *Gita*. At the centre of his metaphysical system is the supermind, an intermediary power between the unmanifested Brahman and the manifested world. Taking inspiration for this idea from the Vedas, Aurobindo claimed that the supermind is not completely alien to us and can be realised within ourselves as well.

PASSIVE RESISTANCE

Sri Aurobindo used the following techniques and ideas during his participation in active politics:

1. **Poorna Swaraj:** He was critical of the moderate leaders of the Congress who adopted passive methods such as passing resolutions, holding prayers meetings, and petitioning, and those who raised a demand for self-government or dominion status within the British Empire. Like Bipin Chandra Pal, he was in favour of the inalienable status of Poorna Swaraj or complete sovereignty for the country, and was the first political leader in India to openly put forward, in his newspaper *Bande Mataram*, the idea of complete independence.
2. **Passive resistance:** The doctrine of passive resistance, articulated by Bipin Chandra

Pal, was a potent economic tool to fight against imperialism and colonialism. It was based on the notion of an organised refusal to participate in anything that would help the British administration. Inherent to the programme of passive resistance was a larger programme of 'Boycott', which was primarily economic. The concept of boycott was extended to include a four-fold practice of non-cooperation with the British government:

(a) Economic boycott
(b) Educational boycott
(c) Judicial boycott
(d) Boycott of the executive administration.

In his public activities, Sri Aurobindo favoured non-cooperation and passive resistance; however, in private he took up secret revolutionary activity as a preparation for open revolt, in case the passive revolt failed. In that, Aurobindo's form of passive resistance was different from that of Gandhi, who was completely opposed to any form of violence. Aurobindo's programme of passive resistance eventually embraced revolution completely, considering it the only path towards independence. Aurobindo began the newspapers *Yugantar* and *New Lamps for Old* to put forward his ideas of open revolt and the absolute denial of British rule.

HUMAN UNITY

During his stay in jail, Aurobindo moved away from politics and towards spiritualism. Consequently, his aim went far beyond the service and liberation of the country. In his spiritual teachings, he believed that Brahma (the Supreme reality) is the source of everything. The entire universe is a reflection of Brahma. The supermind, as discussed earlier, signified for him the fullest development of consciousness in human beings. His philosophy is based on *sat* (truth), *chit* (consciousness), and *anand* (bliss).

Real human unity, for Aurobindo, lies in the soul. It can be attained through yoga. In 1910, Sri Aurobindo reached Pondicherry, where he dedicated himself to his spiritual and philosophical pursuits. Aurobindo Ghose had consistently stressed the spiritual development of individuals, believing that it would lead to spiritual unity amongst the people. This would result in a harmonious relationship between all nations, and all of humanity. Freedom, equality, and justice can only be ensured in a spiritual society, where any chance of clashes or conflict on the basis of nationhood will be negated.

Aurobindo argued that human society has to pass through certain distinct stages in the course of its development. Political methods were incapable of leading to human integration, and economic integration is insufficient to invoke the unity of all people. While political and economic methods are external means by which to inculcate unity, real unity can only be achieved internally.

1. **Symbolic Society:** Closer to a tribal community, this is a stage of community formation and the growth of its traditions, customs, and institutions. People belonging to the same race or kinship groups follow the same symbols, which translates into religion for them. Thus, in this stage of development, natural instincts and religious symbols come together.
2. **Typal Society:** Here, moral ideals become more important. This is a stage of consciousness where people exercise their creative power and wisdom to think through their life and problems.
3. **Conventional Society:** Conventions, rules, and regulations become increasingly rigid. Social hierarchies become more fixed . This stage can be seen in all medieval societies.
4. **Rationalistic, Individualistic Society:** The growth of industrialisation and urbanisation leads to a development of materialism.

Individualism, a scientific spirit, and reason became the cornerstones of society. The ideologies of liberalism, socialism, and nationalism are the by-products of this modern society. However, this too is not the highest stage of development.

5. **Humanity:** While Sri Aurobindo did not reject scientific or materialist development, he stated that these form a lower stage of human development. The real and highest stage of development is spiritual in nature, and has to do with moral development. Unity lies in the human soul, and a spiritual person believes in universal brotherhood. Liberalism promotes political and economic unity, but has created more conflict than cooperation. The UN and WTO have failed to unite the world; socialism failed to empower humanity; and capitalism is unable to fulfil the aspirations of all people. Thus, it is moral and spiritual unity that is the need of the hour, and this can be achieved through yoga.

U. C. Dubey states, 'We are bound to determine the nature of reality as one or many, being or becoming. But Sri Aurobindo's Integral Advaitism reconciles all apparently different aspects of Existence in an all-embracing unity of the Absolute.' Dubey explains that for Sri Aurobindo, there is a higher reason, the 'logic of the infinite', in which his integralism is rooted.

SYNTHESIS OF SCIENTIFIC AND SPIRITUAL DEVELOPMENT

Aurobindo's belief that material and scientific development is of a lower order than spiritual development comes close to the beliefs and teachings of Vivekananda and Mahatma Gandhi. All development in the Western world is materialistic and scientific, but the apex stage belongs to spiritual and moral development, where India is supposed to play a leading role in the world. R. Puligandla said, 'He [Aurobindo] integrates in a unique fashion the great social, political and scientific achievements of the modern West with the ancient and profound spiritual insights of Hinduism.'

The supermind refers to the fullest **spiritual consciousness.** In *The Integral Yoga*, he stated: 'By the supermind is meant the full Truth—Consciousness of the Divine Nature—in which there can be no place for ... division and ignorance; it is always a full ... knowledge superior to all mental substance or mental movement.' Supermind is a bridge between Sachchidananda and the lower manifestation and it is only through the supramental that mind, life and body can be spiritually transformed

AN ALTERNATIVE TO LIBERALISM AND SOCIALISM

According to Aurobindo, socialism stands for economic equality but is artificial in nature. Socialism failed to lead to human unity because it attempted to build the ideal of human unity on the basis of economic equality. Liberalism, on the other hand, laid stress on liberty, but liberty without spiritual and moral development is hollow. For Aurobindo, real unity lies in the soul, which is internal and spiritual. That unity is possible only through Yoga.

Some of Sri Aurobindo's books are:

The Life Divine
Essaays on the Gita
The Synthesis of Yoga
The Ideal of Human Unity
The Renaissance in India with a Defence of Indian Culture
The Human Cycle
War and Self-Determination
Savitri: A legend and a Symbol
The Mother
Vedic and Philological Studies
Complete Works of Sri Aurobindo (published by the Aurobindo Ashram)

13

PERIYAR E. V. RAMASAMY (1879–1973)

KEY CONCEPTS

Anti-Brahmanical; Self-Respect Movement; Dravidian Movement; rationalism; abolition of caste; women's liberation; revolution and communism

Erode Venkatappa Ramasamy, popularly known as Periyar, was a social activist and politician who started the Self-Respect Movement and the Dravidar Kazhagam. He is known as the father of the Dravidian Movement and rebelled against caste and gender inequality in Tamil Nadu. Since 2021, his birth anniversary is celebrated as 'Social Justice Day' in Tamil Nadu.

Periyar promoted the principles of rationalism, self-respect, women's rights, and eradication of caste. He opposed the exploitation and marginalisation of the non-Brahmin Dravidian people of south India and the imposition of what he considered 'Indo-Aryan India'.

ANTI-BRAHMINICAL MOVEMENT

The term 'Periyar' means the 'Great One' or 'Respected One'. He joined the Indian National Congress in 1919 and held the chairmanship of Erode Municipality and undertook constructive programmes propagating the use of Khadi, picketing toddy shops, boycotting shops selling foreign cloth, and eradicating untouchability. In 1921, Ramasamy courted imprisonment for picketing toddy shops in Erode. He was the first non-Brahmin president of the Tamil Nadu Congress party. While he initially followed the teachings of Mahatma Gandhi, he later opposed the Congress and various facets of Hinduism and Brahmin domination.

Periyar led the famous Vaikom Satyagraha in 1924. In Vaikom, a small town in Kerala, then Travancore, there were strict laws of untouchability in and around the temple area. Dalits were not allowed even into the streets around and leading to the temple, let alone inside it. With anti-caste sentiment growing, in 1924, Vaikom was chosen as a suitable place for an organised Satyagraha. Under Periyar's guidance, a movement had already begun with the aim of giving all castes the right to enter the temples. Thus, agitations and demonstrations took place, and Periyar was even imprisoned for his participation. He received the title *Vaikom Veeran*, given by his followers who participated in the Satyagraha.

He founded the **Dravida Kazhagham** in 1944 and sought an independent Dravidian republic. He resigned from the Congress in 1925 because he felt that the party was only serving the interests of Brahmins.

SELF-RESPECT MOVEMENT

The Self-Respect Movement was a manifestation of the anti-Brahminical movement. From the beginning, it was described as bring 'dedicated to the goal of giving non-Brahmins a sense of pride based on their Dravidian past.' Ramasamy and his followers campaigned constantly to pressure the government to take measures to remove social inequality (abolish untouchability, the manual scavenging system, etc.), even while other nationalists focused on the struggle for political independence.

The propagation of the philosophy of *self respect* became Periyar's full-time activity from 1925. A Tamil weekly, *Kudi Arasu*, was started in 1925, while the English journal *Revolt* was started in 1928 to circulate these ideas. In May 1929, a conference of Self-Respect Volunteers was held at Pattukkotai, Thanjavur district. He also visited the Soviet Union and learned of their social order, which was based on the ideals of science and technology. The communist system there appealed to him as appropriately suited to deal with the social ills facing India.

RATIONALIST

The bedrock of Ramasamy's principles and the movements he started was rationalism. He believed that a an elite minority was exploiting and suppressing the majority. He wanted the exploited to reflect on their position and use their reason to realise that they were being exploited. Much like **Socrates** in classical Western philosophy, Periyar was a firm believer in **Rationalism** and **Humanism**. He was a champion of freedom and explained that wisdom lies in thinking and the basis of all thought is rationalism. He was inspired by **Buddha Thiruvalluvar**, as well as modern Western thinkers. Social justice on the basis of rationalism was Periyar's main objective. Ramasamy also blamed the capitalists for their control of machinery, which led the workers being exploited and their labour marginalised. He stated that simply acquiring titles or amassing wealth is useless if one has no self-respect or scientific knowledge.

ABOLITION OF CASTE

Ramasamy's philosophy did not differentiate between social and political service. He wanted the government, the political parties, and social workers to identify the evils in society and boldly adopt measures to remove them. The caste system had propagated the practices of purity and pollution, which grew endemic and led to the dehumanising of those considered lower-caste and the untouchables.

Ramasamy stated that the caste system in south India was linked with the arrival of Brahmins from the north of the country. The Vedas and Varnashram Dharma were thus seen as a mechanism for sustaining the caste system. He felt that a self-respecting rationalist would realise that the caste system stifled self-respect, and therefore would strive to get rid of this menace.

WOMEN'S LIBERATION

As a rationalist and social reformer, Ramasamy advocated forcefully that women should be given their legitimate position in society as the equals of men, be given good education, and have the right to property. He rejected all discrimination in society, whether based on caste or gender. He was keen that women should realise their rights and be fully-realised citizens of their country. Accordingly, he fought against orthodox traditions of marriage that led to the suppression of women, and evils like the dowry system and child marriage. Equality and freedom for women is essential, and husband and wife should be considered **companions** and **partners**. Ramasamy held that in matters of education and employment, there should be no difference between men and women.

URBANISATION AND INDUSTRIALISATION

One of the areas of Ramasamy's focus was on the upliftment of rural communities. In a booklet called *Village Uplift*, Ramasamy pleaded for rural reform. The distinction between rural and urban had meant an economic and social degradation for rural inhabitants and so he further advocated for the modernisation of villages by providing them with public facilities such as schools, libraries, radio stations, roads, bus transport, and police stations.

REVOLUTION AND COMMUNISM

The self-respect communist party was founded through a merger of the self-respect movement and communism. This Party emphasised the nationalisation of all industries, railways, banks, farming, etc. However, for Periyar, revolution was not to be achieved through violent means, but by revolutionising the thoughts and minds of the people.

HUMANIST

Ramasamy is regarded as a pragmatic propagandist who attacked the evils of religious influence on society, At a young age, he felt that some people used religion only as a mask to deceive innocent people, and regarded it as his life's mission to warn people against superstitions and priests. He was against any form of violence in human relations; rather, relations among people should be guided by the love of humanity and service.

Some of Periyar's well-known works are:

Why Were Women Enslaved?
Periyar on Buddhism
Thoughts of Periyar

14

MUHAMMAD IQBAL (1877–1938)

KEY CONCEPTS

Concept of Khudi; anti-imperialism; modernity and Islam; Islamic nationalism

Muhammad Iqbal was a poet, political philosopher, and scholar whose poetry in the Urdu language is considered among the greatest of the twentieth century. He is commonly referred to by the honorific Allama ('most learned'). He was born in Sialkot, Punjab in 1877 to a Kashmiri Muslim family. He considered Rumi his guide, and the philosophies of **Nietzsche** and **Bergson** also influenced Iqbal deeply, even though he later became extremely critical of Western civilisation.

Iqbal was knighted by the British in 1922. In 1930, he was made the President of the Muslim League. His statement during his presidential address, that the final destiny of Indian Muslim was to have a 'consolidated Northwest India Muslim state', is regarded as one of the earliest expressions of the impulse for **Pakistan**.

CONCEPT OF KHUDI (EGO)

Khudi refers to the self through which we can associate ourself with God. His first collection of poetry, the Asrar-i-Khudi, was published in 1915. The poems emphasise the spirit and self from a religious perspective. In Iqbal's use, the term 'Khudi' is synonymous with the word 'Rooh' used in the Quran to mean a divine spark which is present in every human being For him, the aim of life is self-realisation and self-knowledge. His teacher at Cambridge University, Nicholson, translated this volume it as *Secret of the Self.*

Iqbal founded three principles of Khudi:

1. The body and soul are equally important for the development of the human personality.
2. Self-control is essential.
3. The individual should recognise himself as an agent of God.

OPPOSITION OF IMPERIALISM

Iqbal believed that Hindu-Muslim unity was essential to oppose the colonial forces. After completing his B.A. from Trinity College, Cambridge, UK, in 1906, he earned a Doctor of Philosophy degree from the Ludwig Maximilian University of Munich in 1908. After his return to India, he began practising law at the Chief Court of Lahore, but soon quit law practice and devoted himself to literary works, becoming an active member of Anjuman-e-Himayat-e-Islam.

During his participation in the freedom movement, Iqbal remained active in the Muslim League. He did not support Indian involvement in World War I and stayed in close touch with Muslim political leaders such as Mohammad Ali

Jouhar and Muhammad Ali Jinnah. He was a critic of the mainstream Indian National Congress, which he regarded as dominated by Hindus. He was active in the Khilafat Movement as well. Ideologically separated from Congress Muslim leaders, Iqbal had also been disillusioned with the politicians of the Muslim League, owing to the factional conflict that plagued the League in the 1920s. He criticised Jinnah as well, but remained loyal to him, working constantly to encourage Muslim leaders and masses to support Jinnah and the League.

MODERNITY AND ISLAM

Iqbal's six English lectures were delivered at Madras, Hyderabad, and Aligarh, and dwell on the role of Islam as a religion and as a political and legal philosophy in the modern age. In these lectures, Iqbal firmly rejected the political attitudes and conduct of Muslim politicians, whom he saw as morally misguided and attached to power. He favoured reform in Islam along modern lines. However, he criticised Westernisation and the blind following of the materialist culture of the West.

ISLAMIC NATIONALISM

Iqbal was elected President of the Muslim League in 1930. In his presidential address on 29 December 1930, he outlined a vision of an independent state for Muslim-majority provinces in northwestern India:

> I would like to see the Punjab, North-West Frontier Province, Sind and Baluchistan amalgamated into a single state. Self-government within the British Empire, or without the British Empire, the formation of a consolidated Northwest Indian Muslim state appears to me to be the final destiny of the Muslims, at least of Northwest India.

Iqbal thus stressed both the need for the political unity of Muslim communities and also the undesirability of blending the Muslim population into a wider society not based on Islamic principles. He thus became the first politician to articulate what would become known as the Two-nation Theory—that Muslims are a distinct nation and thus deserve political independence from other regions and communities of India.

Iqbal is widely commemorated in Pakistan, where he is regarded as the ideological founder of the state. The Government of Madhya Pradesh in India awards the Iqbal Samman, named in honor of the poet, every year at the Bharat Bhavan to Indian writers for their contributions to Urdu literature and poetry.

Among the various publications of Iqbal are:

1. *The Development of Metaphysics in Persia* (1908)
2. *The Reconstruction of Religious Thought in Islam* (1930)
3. *The Call of the Marching Bell* (Urdu poetry, 1924)
4. Zabur-e-Ajam (*Persian Pslams*, 1927)
5. Asrar-i-Khudi (*The Secrets of the Self*, 1915)
6. *Javed Nama* (1932)

15

M. N. ROY (1887–1954)

KEY CONCEPTS

Communist Party of India; exploitative powers; class struggle in the Indian context; radical humanism

Manabendra Nath Roy was born in Bengal in 1887. He was a revolutionary, radical activist, and political theorist, as well as a noted philosopher of the twentieth century. He has the unique distinction of having worked with Lenin, Trotsky, and Stalin. Like Aurobindo Ghose, he began his political life as a militant nationalist.

Roy's career and thought passed thought three phases of development: In the first phase, which lasted up to 1919, he was a nationalist and revolutionary; in the second phase, Roy became a communist; and in the last and final phase, he moved away from orthodox Marxism and emerged as a radical humanist, attempting to chart a third course between liberalism and communism.

THE NATIONALIST PHASE

Support for revolutionary nationalism began to grow among the educated middle classes of Bengal by the end of the nineteenth century. Inspired by the writings of Bankim Chandra Chattopadhyay and Swami Vivekananda, M. N. Roy joined this movement against the exploitative colonial government. After the partition of Bengal was announced in 1905, a spontaneous mass movement against this was launched, giving radical nationalists like Roy and his co-thinkers an opportunity to build broader support for their ideas.

M. N. Roy, however, moved away from the moderate nationalists and he believed the only way to uproot the British government was through violence. Taking his cues from the Irish revolutionaries, he too believed in the politics of the bomb and pistol.

In this first stage of his life, he was a revolutionary and a member of an organisation named 'Yugantar', as well as of the Anushilan Samiti. On 6 December 1907, Roy successfully committed the first act of political theft to raise money for his secret society. He was accused of dacoity in Calcutta and was arrested, but released on bail because of this reputation as a student and social worker. His revolutionary ideals set him against the Indian National Congress and its peaceful constitutional means of protest.

Like many other revolutionary nationalists, Roy was convinced that only through an armed struggle against the British would they be able to gain independence from the British Empire. To further this end, he looked to a rival imperial power, that of the German Empire, as a potential source of funds and weapons. However, the British came to know of his plans and in an attempt to escape the British, Roy used a false French-Indian passport obtained for him by the Germans in China. Posing as a seminary student bound for Paris, he obtained an American visa and sailed for San Francisco.

ARDENT MARXIST

It was during his stay in the US that Roy began to develop his interest in Marxism. His socialist transition owed much to Bankimchandra's essays on communism and Vivekananda's message of serving the proletariat. In 1917, Roy fled to Mexico and the Socialist Party he founded in December 1917 was converted into the Communist Party of Mexico in 1919, the first Communist Party outside Russia. His inclination towards Communism began after he attended the second Congress of Communist International in Mexico in 1920.

1. Roy accepted all Marxist ideas and theories, like such as historical materialism, dialectical materialism, theory of surplus value, and class struggle. Moreover, he also accepted the Bolshevik method of revolution, which was propounded by Lenin. A few weeks before the 1920 World Congress of the Communist International, Vladimir Lenin personally received Roy with great warmth. At Lenin's behest, Roy formulated his own ideas as a supplement to Lenin's *Preliminary Draft Theses on the National and the Colonial Questions.* M. N. Roy is also a founder of the Communist Party in India.
2. Roy was also the first thinker to undertake a class analysis of Indian society. He believed in inevitability of class struggle and said that bringing about a communist revolution is the responsibility of the Communist Party of India (CPI), which represents the proletariat class.
3. In Roy's view, Communism could be achieved only through the methods of **Bolshevism**. He argued that the failure of the non-cooperation movement was due to the hesitant approach that the Congress adopted towards revolutionary means of struggle.

He believed that there are two exploitative powers: (*a*) an internal exploitative power, that is, the Congress, and (*b*) an external exploitative power, represented by British colonial rule. Elaborating this further, Roy accused the Congress of representing the bourgeois class, and of working in close communion with the British government.

Like Lenin, Roy did not accept any autonomous strategy of revolution for any particular nation. In his work *The Future of Mass Movement*, he had expressed his desire for a mass movement; however, he had also called for the Indian nationalist movement to be converted along the lines of class struggle.

According to M. N. Roy, the Congress and Swarajist leaders like Motilal Nehru represented the feudalistic class and were antagonistic to the interests of the proletariat class, which includes workers and peasants. In his work *Indian Problems and its Solutions* (1923), he called the Congress a bourgeois party, headed by bourgeois leaders like Nehru.

However, M. N. Roy's influence eventually began to fade. Bengal Krishan Party leader Saumendra Nath Tagore stated in a speech that the communist revolution cannot be brought to India because the few communists in India are insufficient in number to mobilise a mass movement. In 1929, he was expelled from the Communist International and he thereafter returned to India in 1930. In July 1931, he was arrested on a warrant issued in 1924, tried in Kanpur for conspiracy under Section 121-A of the Indian Penal Code, and imprisoned for six years.

NATIONAL AND COLONIAL QUESTION

Vladimir Lenin propounded a strategy for revolution that to his mind was applicable across the world. He believed that revolution in a capitalist nation depended upon revolution in the colonial nations. He divided the world into three groups:

1. Western Europe and the United States
2. Eastern Europe
3. Semi-colonies and Colonies

Lenin said that the possibility of a communist revolution had been suspended in capitalist nations due to their exploitation of colonial nations. Capitalist nations were exploiting the resources of **Africa** and **Asia**. Therefore, the proletariat of the capitalist nation were not marginalised; rather, they were receiving some profits due to the exploitation of colonies. This proved his argument that revolution in capitalist countries was inextricably linked with revolution in the colonies.

Lenin further stated that democratic and bourgeoisie forces were fighting against capitalist forces in India. It is important to note that he considered Congress the bourgeois force yet recognised its importance in the fight against colonial capitalist forces. He was in favour of a broad-based alliance between the bourgeoisie and the Communist Party, but was quick to state that this alliance would only be transitional. However, M. N. Roy disagreed, and said that Indian society would transform into a capitalist society economically since it is linked with the capitalist forces. But the proletariat is strong enough to bring about a revolution in India. He rejected an alliance with the Congress on the grounds of it being 'reactionary' and 'conservative' While Lenin considered Gandhi inspirational and the true leader of the mass movement in India, Roy believed that Gandhi was a cultural and religious revivalist. His popularity was due to the 'backwardness' of the Indian people.

To bring about a communist revolution in India, Lenin argued that an alliance was needed between the Communist Party and the Congress, even though the Communists should lead the revolution. This alliance is essential because both groups were fighting a common enemy, that is, the British government. After uprooting British colonialism, Communists would have to snatch power from the Congress. Roy, however, did not accept this strategy of allying with the Congress.

MARXIST ANALYSIS OF SOCIETY

As previously stated, M. N. Roy was the first thinker to analyse Indian society from a Marxist perspective. Indian Society was divided into the following classes:

1. Landed Aristocracy
2. Bourgeois and Intellectuals
3. Petty peasantry
4. Working class and landless peasants

Roy disagreed with B. R. Ambedkar's view that Indian society was divided on the basis of caste. He also did not believe that society could be analysed in terms of culture and religion, as Aurobindo had stated. Roy analysed social stratification on the grounds of economy. He said that Indian society had become capitalised because of the pervasive presence of British colonial forces, even though he also admitted that the social modernisation and economic development of India was not like that of Britain. Refusing to accept the Indian National Congress as representative of all of India, he felt that the Congress represented the interests of only the bourgeois and capitalist classes, going so far as to consider the Congress a junior partner in the exploitation of India, with Britain as the senior partner. To his mind, the withdrawal of the non-cooperation movement proved that the Congress was defending the interests of the bourgeoisie.

RADICAL HUMANISM

Disillusioned with both bourgeois democracy and communism, Roy devoted the last years of his life to the formulation of an alternative philosophy, which he called Radical Humanism. He wrote a detailed exposition on this in *Reason, Romanticism and Revolution*. Scientific or radical humanism owes its origin to the Renaissance. It is considered 'radical' because of its rejection of Marxism. Radical humanism is also known as 'new humanism' and propagated a scientific temperament, and is different from liberalism and the Vedantic philosophy. His new humanism was ranged against the following ideologies.

1. **Rejection of Marxism**

   Roy criticised Marxist thought and the theoretical basis of Marxism, which was based on economic determinism. He considered the principles of 'economic determination' and 'surplus value' meaningless.

2. **Reputation of Gandhi**

   M. N. Roy was critical of Gandhi and his moral and spiritualistic ideas, and found it impossible to collaborate with him. He believed that it was the ignorance of the masses and their traditional, irrational thinking that was responsible for Gandhi's popularity. Roy also criticised the Gandhian economic model, which was based on decentralisation, centred the village, and stressed on the importance of cottage and small-scale industries.

3. **Negation of Parliamentary Democracy**

   Roy was critical of parliamentary democracy, which he did not consider true democracy as it represented a political party and not the people. He said that the power of people is the essence of democracy, but this is suppressed under the power of the party and bureaucracy.

4. **Criticism of Vedantic Philosophy**

   Roy believed that Vedantic philosophy was merely the glorification of a medieval and conservative past. Dismissing the idea of a unique Indian spiritualism, he said that a similar spiritual though had been present in Europe during the medieval age as well.

5. **Against Fascism**

   With the declaration of World War II, Roy condemned the rising totalitarian regimes in Germany and Italy, instead supporting England and France in the fight against fascism. He believed that ultra-nationalism was dangerous for liberty. As a rationalist, he was critical towards the idea of fascism, which is based on anti-rationalism. According to Roy, a victory for Germany and the Axis powers would result in the end of democracy worldwide and India would never be independent as in his view, India could win her independence only in a free world.

BASIC ELEMENTS OF RADICAL HUMANISM

A. Liberty

1. Liberty is essential for the development of human life. Without liberty, no individual or society can develop fully.
2. Liberty is the supreme value which leads to the search for knowledge.
3. Roy's radical humanism proclaims man to be moral and spiritual. Roy opposed the coercive nature of the state, believing that this would curb human freedom. Therefore, he recommended a 'minimal state'.

B. Morality

1. Liberty and morality are the two essential principles of radical humanism.
2. For Roy, it is the individual that is supreme, greater than either class or the nation. Humans, he believed, were endowed with reason, and were the 'Measure of everything'.
3. He believed in a pluralistic society that ensures the peaceful co-existence of all castes, classes, and religions.

C. Scientific Temperament

1. Human beings possess a scientific temperament that enable them to question, inquire, and not take recourse to blind belief. He never accepted the centrality of religion and also refuted social customs and traditions. He believes that society can

only be changed through scientific tools. Therefore, he supported industrialisation and was epecially in favour of the industrialisation of agriculture.

D. Decentralised Government

1. Roy ranged himself against the traditional form of democracy in which power was concentrated in only a few hands. Instead, he proposed the decentralisation of democratic practices.
2. Roy was opposed to fascism because of it suppression of individual liberty in the name of ultra-nationalism.
3. Roy favoured the industrialisation of agriculture.
4. According to Roy, revolution should be brought about through education, and not by violent means.
5. He advocated a 'rationalisation of politics' through a party-less democracy, which is different from the traditional system of 'power politics'. His version of democracy would uphold the moral and ethical standards in politics.

E. Plural Society

1. Society, Roy believed, should not be defined in terms of class. Nationalism, in his view, is another monolithic way to define society. In contrast, he supported the presence of multiple groups and associations in society, which will enable the preserving of liberty for individuals and strengthen the democratic form of governance.

F. Party-less democracy

1. Roy was in favour of a radical democracy, where every citizen would be informed and consulted about the affairs of the state. In such a democracy, the danger of dictatorship—of any class, individual, or elite—would be reduced. People in this form of democracy would have the ways and means to exercise sovereign power effectively. In a party-less democracy, there would be maximum power at the grassroots level and minimum power at the apex.

Among the various works authored by M. N. Roy are:

India in Transition' (1922)
New Humanism: A Manifesto (1953)
The Problem of Freedom (1945)
Scientific Politics (1940)
One Year of Non-Cooperation from Ahmedabad to Gaya (1923)
Revolution and Counter-Revolution in China (1946)

16

V. D. SAVARKAR (1883–1966)

KEY CONCEPTS

Hindutva; revolutionary nationalism; Hindu identity

Vinayak Damodar Savarkar, born on 28 May 1883 in Nashik, was a politician, activist, and writer. His political activities started when he was young: in 1903, in Nashik, Savarkar and his older brother Ganesh Savarkar founded the Mitra Mela, an underground revolutionary organisation, which became the Abhinav Bharat Society in 1906. Its main objectives were to overthrow British rule and revive 'Hindu pride'. Savarkar continued his political activism as a student at Fergusson College in Pune, and was greatly influenced by the radical nationalist leader, Lokmanya Tilak.

While in London for higher studies, Savarkar was influenced by the life and thought of Italian nationalist leader, Giuseppe Mazzini. During his time in prison he wrote an ideological pamphlet known as *Hindutva: Who is a Hindu*?

REVOLUTIONARY NATIONALIST

Savarkar took part in nationalist movements such as the anti-partition movement of Bengal in 1905, as well as the Swadeshi movement. His brother, Ganesh Savarkar, had organised an armed revolt against the Morley-Minto reforms of 1909. V. D. Savarkar was accused of participating in a conspiracy to overthrow the British government in India by organising murders of various officials. Although he fled to France, he was arrested on 13 April 1910 in the case of the murder of Curzon Willie. He tried in India before a special tribunal. After being found guilty, he was sent to the Cellular Jail in the Andaman and Nicobar Islands. He wrote three clemency petitions to the British government starting a month after his arrival in the jail, in 1911, 1913, and 1917, and was moved to a jail in Ratnagiri in 1921, and released in 1924.

While in London, Savarkar involved himself with organisations such as India House and the Free India Society. He also published books advocating complete Indian independence by revolutionary means, one of which was *The Indian War of Independence* about the Indian Rebellion of 1857.

HINDUTVA

During his incarceration in Ratnagiri Jail in 1922, he wrote his *Essentials of Hindutva*, which formulated his theory of Hindutva. His views began turning increasingly towards Hindu cultural and political nationalism and in this period, he also wrote his ideological treatise, *Hindutva: Who is a Hindu?* For him, Hindutva encapsulated the glory of Hindu culture and is more a civilisational political and cultural category. He began working towards consolidating a Hindu state or Hindu *sangathan*. According to Savarkar, 'Hindu' does not refer to any particular religion, tradition, or race;

it is a nationality, referring to the people settling across the rivers Sindhu. Shatadru, Ravi, Chinav, Vitasta, Ganga, Yamuna, and Saraswati—the **Sapt Sindhu.** He began describing a 'Hindu' as a patriotic inhabitant of Bharatavarsha, venturing beyond a religious identity.

In contrast with Dayananda Saraswati, Swami Vivekananda, and Sri Aurobindo, who were religious men who introduced reforms in society and held Hinduism up before the world, Savarkar mixed politics and religion and started an extreme form of Hindu nationalism. The three essentials of Hindutva were: a common nation (*rashtra*); a common race (*jati*); and a common civilisation (*sanskriti*). He outlined his vision of a 'Hindu Rashtra' (Hindu nation) as 'Akhand Bharat' (United India), which would stretch across the entire Indian subcontinent.

A self-described atheist, Savarkar regarded being Hindu as a cultural and political identity. He preferred the word Hindutva over Hinduism**.** Hindutva incorporates the following features:

1. Those who have roots in this territory, which includes earlier generations.
2. Common race and shared blood relations.
3. Common culture.

He often stressed social and community unity between Hindus, Sikhs, Buddhists, and Jains, to the exclusion of Muslims and Christians. He defined Hindus as being neither Aryan nor Dravidian, but as 'People who live as children of a common motherland, adoring a common holyland'. However, he was an ardent critique of Hindu religious practices such as the caste system, which he viewed as irrational and as a hindrance to the material progress of Hindus.

REFORMER

As mentioned earlier, Savarkar opposed untouchability and the caste system. The caste system, according to him, was doing great harm to the cause of Hindutva. Social reform and political revolution should go hand-in-hand, he believed, and in his 1931 essay titled *Seven Shackles of the Hindu Society,* he wrote, 'One of the most important components of such injunctions of the past that we have blindly carried on and which deserves to be thrown in the dustbins of history is the rigid caste system.'

Among Savarkar's publications are:

1. *Hindu Pad-Padshahi* (1925)
2. *The Transportation* (1984)
3. *Moplah Rebellion*
4. *The Indian War of Independence, 1857* (1909)
5. *Hindutva: Who is a Hindu?*

17

B. R. AMBEDKAR (1891–1956)

KEY CONCEPTS

Anti-caste movement; Dalit rights; annihilation of caste; Brahmanical system; Buddhism vs Brahmanism; Ambedkar on democracy; Ambedkar on socialism; constitution; Gandhi and Ambedkar

Bhimrao Ramji Ambedkar, who is popularly seen as the architect of the Indian constitution and a pioneering anti-caste leader, was born in Maharashtra on 14 April 1891. He was an Indian jurist, economist, social reformer, and political leader who headed the committee drafting the Constitution of India from the Constituent Assembly debates, served as Law and Justice minister in the first Cabinet of Jawaharlal Nehru, and inspired the Dalit Buddhist movement after renouncing Hinduism.

Ambedkar was born to the Mahar caste, a historically marginalised Dalit community. As an untouchable, he suffered all kinds of social humiliation in his childhood. Although he attended school, Ambedkar and other untouchable children were discriminated against, not allowed inside the classroom, and received little attention or help from the teachers. After his family moved to Mumbai in 1897, he became the only untouchable enrolled at Elphinstone High School. Against all odds, he graduated from Elphinstone College, Bombay University, and went on to do his Masters and Ph.D. in Economics from Columbia University, New York, after receiving the Baroda State Scholarship. In October 1916, he enrolled for the Bar course at Gray's Inn, and at the same time enrolled at the London School of Economics where he started working on a doctoral thesis. In 1923, he completed a D.Sc. in Economics which was awarded from University of London, and the same year he was called to the Bar by Gray's Inn.

In defence of Dalit rights, Ambedkar went on to publish several periodicals, including *Mook Nayak* (1920), *Equality Janta*, and *Bahiskrit Bharat* (1927). As a Mahar, he was deeply concerned with untouchability and the caste system in India. He also studied the impact of colonialism on the Indian economy through his research, 'Administration and Finance of East India Company' and 'The Problem of the Rupee'.

ORIGIN OF SHUDRAS

Ambedkar offered a critical analysis of ancient Hindu religious texts in his work, *'Who are Shudras?'* His conclusion was that Shudras actually belonged to the Kshatriya varna, and were part of a Kshatriya clan who had challenged Brahmanical supremacy. This conflict with Brahmins led to the creation of a separate category in the varna system, termed the Shudras.

It was the Brahmins who excluded this group from all rituals and pushed them down to the position of fourth and lowest varna. Arguing that

Shudras, too, were part of the Aryan race, Ambedkar stated that the origin and current position of Shudras was not due to any incapacity on their part, but because of Brahmanical society.

BRAHMANICAL SYSTEM

The Brahmanical system is the root cause of all exploitation in Indian society. The caste system is hierarchical, and goes against the basic principles of human dignity. Shudras were denied equal opportunities of education, and were deprived of economic and social resources as well.

While Ambedkar admitted that a division of labour exists everywhere in the world, he pointed out that the division amongst labourers exists only in India. The inegalitarian Brahmanical system was legitimised and justified by various religious scriptures and texts. Freedom from British colonial rule, Ambedkar feared, may not be enough to free the depressed classes from the shackles of their slavery in the caste system.

ANNIHILATION OF CASTE

In his fight against the caste system, the annihilation or destruction of the Brahmanical system was a major objective. Those belonging to the depressed class need a new identity and occupations, and Ambedkar believed that citizenship in a democratic nation would provide that new identity for the people. Democratic identity is based on the dignity of individuals, which include practices such as inter-caste marriages and inter-caste dining. He also advocated separate electorates for the depressed classes, considering this essential for their empowerment. The representation of minorities is essential to aid the better functioning of a democracy. The provision of a separate electorate would ensure visibility and add value to these communities.

By 1927, Ambedkar had decided to launch an active movement against untouchability. He began with public movements and marches to open up public drinking-water resources, and also began a struggle for the right to enter Hindu temples. In a conference in 1927, Ambedkar publicly condemned the classic Hindu text, the *Manusmriti*, for ideologically justifying caste discrimination and untouchability.

In 1932, the British colonial government announced the formation of a separate electorate for 'Depressed Classes' in the Communal Award. Mahatma Gandhi fiercely opposed a separate electorate for untouchables, saying that such an arrangement would divide the Hindu community. On 25 September 1932, the agreement, known as the Poona Pact, was signed between Ambedkar (on behalf of the depressed classes) and Madan Mohan Malaviya (on behalf of the other Hindus), and it reserved seats for the depressed classes in the provisional legislatures within the general electorate.

EMANCIPATION OF DALITS

An ardent champion of all oppressed and depressed classes in India, Ambedkar lamented the injustice, humiliation, exploitation, and indignity which people from the depressed classes were subjected to in Indian society. He believed that social problems could only be resolved through the **constitutional method**; however, he was opposed to what he saw as the half-hearted and soft efforts of both Congress and Mahatma Gandhi towards the emancipation of Dalits. His opportunity to prove his leadership came in 1930, when he represented the Dalits at the Second Round Table Conference. It is here that differences between him and Gandhi were first observed, on the matter of separate electorates, discussed above.

Ambedkar also set up many organisations, such as the Bhahiskrit Hitkarni Sabha and the All India Scheduled Caste Federation to mobilise public opinion in his fight against the caste system. Through his journals and writings, he raised Dalit consciousness. Later, as Chairman of the drafting committee of the Constituent Assembly, he made elaborate provisions for the protection of Dalit interests.

Ambedkar was of the opinion that the state should play a positive role in emancipating the depressed classes. He also exhorted Dalits to work for their own salvation. Some of the methods prescribed by Ambedkar are:

1. The depressed classes of society should be given representation in legislative bodies.
2. Only a Dalit leader should represent the Dalit cause.
3. The state should take recourse to **affirmative action** to remove inequality in society by providing better educational and job opportunities at all levels of government.
4. The state should take coercive steps to prevent social practices that hamper the growth of Dalits and rob them of their dignity.
5. He was in favour of legal and constitutional safeguards to protect their rights and interests.
6. The annihilation of caste can itself eradicate untouchability, since the caste system is the root cause of untouchability.
7. He strongly recommended inter-caste dining, inter-caste marriage, and advocated a scientific and rational attitude towards religion.
8. He also recommended that the functions of a priest be performed by trained people under state supervision, rather than by Brahmins by virtue of their birth.
9. Dalits should discard their **traditional occupations** with which their untouchable status and the indignities they suffered were tied.
10. Dalits should also work to acquire the best possible education, become professionally qualified, and migrate to big cities.
11. Above all, Dalits should transform themselves by shedding their own inferiority complex attached to the ascribed status of caste, and instead acquire a professional status of their own.

BUDDHISM AS AN ALTERNATIVE

Initially, Ambedkar considered converting to Sikhism, which encouraged opposition to oppression and so appealed to leaders of the Scheduled Castes. However, after meeting with Sikh leaders, he felt that the Dalit community would not be completely accepted in Sikh society. Around 1950, he began devoting his attention to Buddhism, which he believed had posed the first challenge to Hinduism. Society, he said, was governed by the Brahmanical system when Buddhism came into being. In order to resist this new religion, Hinduism adopted new practices, such as preaching non-violence and vegetarianism. Those communities which refused to change their dietary practices were considered degrading and subjected to social boycott by the Brahmanical class. It is this community that institutionalised untouchability as an integral part of Indian society.

Ambedkar visited Burma twice during the time that his interest in Buddhism was ignited. After meeting with the Sri Lankan Buddhist monk Hammalawa Saddhatissa, Ambedkar organised a formal public ceremony for himself and his supporters in Nagpur on 14 October 1956. Accepting the Three Refuges and Five Precepts from a Buddhist monk in the traditional manner, Ambedkar completed his own conversion, along with his wife. He then proceeded to convert some 500,000 of his supporters as well.

Buddhism and Marxism is Ambedkar's last book. Ambedkar said that religion must relate to facts of life, and not merely to theories and speculation about God or the soul. Real religion lives in the heart of people, and not in religious scriptures. People and morality must be at the centre of religion; it is high ideals that are more important than noble works. Everything is subject to the laws of causation. Ambedkar said that

Buddhism is more scientific in its approach. It tries to reconstruct the world and make it happier, and does not seek to explain its origins or its end. He also said that Buddhism believes in a non-violent transformation of society.

CASTE AND DEMOCRACY

In a caste-based society, the upper castes automatically become the leaders of the community. Democratic ideals, however, are based on the principles of liberty, equality, and fraternity. Caste goes against each of these basic principles. Ambedkar believed that the national movement launched by the Congress was confined to only the country's freedom, and did not extend to the people's freedom. Democracy, he said, could be sustained in nations like Britain and the USA because of their social equality, while the social and economic inequality inherent in Germany and Italy led to the downfall of democracy in these countries. Therefore, democracy is not merely a form of government; it is for society and for an egalitarian economic system too. Ambedkar was never in favour of violent social change, like the Marxists were. He was influenced by John Dewey, who supported a democratic transformation of society. While speaking in the Constituent Assembly, he said that while bhakti in religion may be the road to salvation, in politics, bhakti or hero-worship leads to degradation and eventual dictatorship.

True democracy can only be achieved when political democracy is combined with social and economic democracy. Therefore, he was opposed to Brahmanical society, which oppressed Dalits and marginalised entire sections of society. According to Ambedkar, the Brahmanical system has the following characteristics:

(a) Denial of education to Shudras.
(b) Denial of property rights to Shudras.
(c) Suppression and subordination of women.
(d) The exclusion of untouchables from all positions of power.

MARXISM AND AMBEDKAR

According to Gail Omvedt, Ambedkar stated that class-based stratification of society is not a suitable description for India. Marxism believes in class and class struggle. However, according to Ambedkar, caste is the real problem of India. While class is determined by the economic status of a person, caste is based on birth in a Brahminical system. The Buddha, too, stood against caste and the Brahmin-centred caste system. Caste is a more important institution than class in India. He accepted the Marxist theory that the privileged section's exploitation of the masses perpetuated poverty and attendant issues. However, he did not see this exploitation as purely economic, stating instead that the cultural aspects of exploitation are as bad, or even worse, than economic exploitation.

Ambedkar was more influenced by Buddha than Marx. He united labourers, Dalits, and untouchables in their struggle against Brahmanical society. Although he supported the workers' cause, he was not a Marxist. He felt that Indian society was suffering from a double attack—that of a Brahmanical system and of a capitalist system. He also saw Communists as willing to resort to any means to achieve proletarian revolution, including violence, while he himself considered democratic and peaceful measures as the best option for change.

He rejected Marx's analysis of Indian society. Marx's view that there exist only two classes, the bourgeois (capitalist) class and the proletariat (working-class), and that capitalism is at the root of all exploitation ran counter to Ambedkar's, who saw the Brahmanical system as the root of all exploitation of Dalits. As stated above, while Ambedkar was in favour of overthrowing the caste system, he rejected Marx's belief in violent revolution, saying instead that social transformation and the emancipation of weaker sections of society can only occur through education, and not through revolution.

He refused to join the Communists in India because he believed that the group was dominated by upper castes, particularly Brahmins. He preferred Buddhism because he saw it as being based on principles of equality and justice, and seemed the only path to secure human emancipation.

SOCIAL JUSTICE

Ambedkar's ideas were not limited to the well-being of the depressed castes; he was in favour of gender equality and spoke for the welfare of the working classes too. The annihilation of caste and economic equality are essential conditions for strengthening legal justice. He supported liberty and fundamental rights for all; however, in the absence of social and economic equality, liberty will become the privilege of only a few.

Collective ownership of land was one of his important suggestions. Ambedkar was in support of **Fabian socialism,** that is, democratic socialism which works through a welfare state, which is the only instrument through which to end evils like poverty, starvation, and exploitation. Socialism is humanitarian and based on the moral values of equality and coexistence, regardless of caste or gender. Thus, he was in favour of state-controlled industries, which will ensure the well-being of every section of society.

He was also in favour of granting industry status to agriculture and advocated a **common ownership of land,** given that the major cause of inequality in India was the presence of land-based property. This will also automatically abolish the zamidari system in India.

Social change in India cannot be brought about through a class struggle. A peaceful democratic and constitutional mechanism is the most practical for bringing about change in our society. He rejected the **Gandhian** belief that society can be transformed through a collective change of heart. Ambedkar had immense faith in democracy, which he held necessary for human freedom and dignity. But as against the conventional form of democracy, he believed that political democracy should be combined with social and economic democracy. True democracy is not confined to mere freedom of expression, but will ensure basic minimum facilities to all sections of society, thereby developing their individuality and freeing them from exploitation. Thus, instead of class struggle, he supported democratic socialism.

He was not romantic like M. N. Roy, who supported a party-less democracy, and also rejected the Gandhian vision of Ram Rajya. Instead, he was in favour of a competitive multi-party system, fought through the political and constitutional method He called for All India Civil Services, and the prevention of 'tyranny of the majority' by safeguarding minority rights. In order to make constitutional democracy a success, citizens should adhere to c**onstitutional morality**. Liberty, equality, and fraternity are the three cornerstones of democracy; while fraternity it is not feasible without liberty and equality, the latter should not be suppressed in the name of fraternity.

IMPACT ON CONSTITUTION

Ambedkar was a Chairperson of the Drafting Committee of the Constituent Assembly, and was responsible for framing the Constitution of India. He had said that Article 32 is the heart and soul of the Constitution, which signifies the great import he placed on rights and liberty. He supported special rights for the minority sections of society, and special provisions have been made for the promotion of welfare and safeguarding the interests and rights of the Scheduled Castes and Scheduled Tribes. A strong federal government is essential for the empowerment of the depressed classes, though the implementation of the major provisions for minority welfare is the responsibility of the Union government.

A strong integrated judiciary, with the Supreme Court at its apex, is to safeguard the Constitution. Detailed provisions have been made for all organs of the government—the Executive, Legislature, and the Judiciary, as well as autonomous bodies like the UPSC, the Comptroller and Auditor General (CAG), Attorney General, etc., along with the powers and functions of each. Ambedkar was only too aware that Indian society is not democratic, and so he supported the presence of administrative bodies like the Election Commission of India and CAG, and included these in the Constitution.

Ambedkar was in favour of the concept of fundamental rights, with affirmative action (in the form of reservations) for the depressed and marginalised sections of society, in order to redress historical injustices done to them and improve their condition. Ambedkar was one of the ministers who argued for extensive economic and social rights for women, and won the Assembly's support for introducing a system of reservations of jobs in the civil services, schools, and colleges for members of SCs and STs, and Other Backward Classes (OBCs). India's lawmakers hoped to eradicate the socio-economic inequalities and lack of opportunities for India's depressed classes through these measures.

Ambedkar stated that securing seats for the SCs and STs in educational bodies, jobs, and legislative bodies is essential for the abolition of untouchability. He believed that the Directive Principles formed the basis to secure social and economic democracy, and tried to make it enforceable within the first ten years after the Constitution came into effect.

After India's independence, Ambedkar sought to secure the adequate representation of Dalits in the legislative bodies to ensure that the rights and interests of depressed classes are safeguarded. It is largely due to his efforts that Dalits have been mainstreamed to a considerable extent in Indian society.

GANDHI AND AMBEDKAR

(A) **Orientation:** Gandhi was a spiritual and moral philosopher. On the other hand, Ambedkar took a legal and political approach. Politics was secondary for Gandhi, who called for non-violence in the national movement for independence. Ambedkar, however, set up a political party and demanded separate representation for the Dalits.

(B) **Panchayat Raj:** Gandhi took a decentralised government as the model, as he was never in favour of the modern Parliamentary form of government taken from the West. But Ambedkar believed that the Parliamentary-federal form of government is the most suitable for India.

(C) **Social System:** Sarvodaya was the highest ideal for Gandhi. He opposed untouchability, yet accepted the importance of the varna system in Hinduism. Ambedkar believed in social justice and strongly felt that caste and varna were one and the same. Untouchability can be eradicated only by the Dalits This was in stark opposition to Gandhi, who believed that true change could only come with a change of heart. According to him, it is the upper castes who should lead the movement against untouchability.

(D) **Economy:** Ambedkar favoured industrialisation, and believed that urbanisation was essential for India. The state ought to control the major sources of economic production. Gandhi's utopia lay in small-scale or cottage industries, or a village-based economy. He was firmly against all heavy industrialisation, mechanisation, and industrial development.

Among Ambedkar's important publications are:

Waiting for a Visa (1935–1936; autobiography)

Castes in India: Their Mechanism, Genesis and Development and 11 Other Essays (May 1917)

Who Were the Shudras? (1946)

The Untouchables Who Were They And Why They Became Untouchables

Riddles in Hinduism
The Annihilation of Caste (1936)
Pakistan or the Partition of India
What Congress and Gandhi have done to the Untouchables; Mr. Gandhi and the Emancipation of the Untouchables
Philosophy of Hinduism; India and the Pre-requisites of Communism; Revolution and Counter-revolution; Buddha or Karl Marx

Ambedkar also set up the following important institutions:

1. Bahishkrit Hitakarini Sabha (1924)
2. Samta Sainik Dal (1927)
3. Independent Labour Party (1936)
4. All Indian Schedule Caste Federation (1942)
5. Republican Party of India (1957)

18

JAWAHARLAL NEHRU (1889–1964)

KEY CONCEPTS

Liberal nationalism; scientific humanism; democratic socialist; Non-Aligned Movement

Jawaharlal Nehru was born on 14 November 1889 in Allahabad. The first Prime Minister of independent India, he was an Indian nationalist, secular humanist, social democrat, statesman, and author. Nehru was one of the most prominent leaders of the Indian nationalist movement in the 1930s and 1940s. Nehru promoted parliamentary democracy, secularism, and science and technology during the 1950s, and had a powerful impact on India's journey as a modern nation.

The son of lawyer and nationalist Motilal Nehru, Jawaharlal Nehru was educated in England, at Harrow School and Trinity College, Cambridge, and trained in the law at the Inner Temple. Upon his return to India, he grew interested in national politics, and joined the Indian National Congress. He soon became the leader of a progressive faction of the party during the 1920s, and eventually of the Congress. Mahatma Gandhi (whom he first met in 1916) designated Nehru as his political heir. As Congress president in 1929, Nehru called for complete independence from the British Raj.

In 1920, Nehru organised first Kishan March in Pratapgarh (UP). His first big national involvement came at the onset of the non-cooperation movement in 1920, when he led the movement in the United Provinces (now Uttar Pradesh). Nehru was arrested on charges of anti-governmental activities in 1921 and released a few months later. He was elected as president of Lahore Session of the Indian National Congress in 1929, where the goal for the complete independence of the country was adopted.

LIBERAL NATIONALIST

Nehru believed that Indian nationalism was rooted in the universal values of liberalism. He played a leading role in the development of an internationalist outlook for the Indian independence struggle, seeking foreign allies for India and forging links with movements for independence and democracy around the world. Nehru saw the struggle for independence from British imperialism as a multinational effort by the various colonies and dominions of the Empire; it was not aggressive or expansionist, nor was it based on a notion of superiority over others. In 1927, largely due to Nehru's efforts, the Congress was invited to attend the Congress of Oppressed Ntionalities in Brussels, Belgium. The meeting was called to coordinate and plan a common struggle against imperialism. Nehru represented India and was elected to the Executive Council of the League against Imperialism

In 1929, Nehru drafted the policies of the Congress, which were to be applied to a future Indian nation as well. He declared that the aims of the Congress were:

1. Freedom of religion;
2. Right to form associations;
3. Freedom of expression of thought;
4. Equality before the law for every individual without distinction of caste, colour, creed, or religion;
5. Protection of regional languages and cultures,
6. Safeguarding the interests of the peasants and labour;
7. Abolition of untouchability;
8. Introduction of adult franchise;
9. Imposition of prohibition and nationalisation of industries;
10. Socialism; and
11. The establishment of a secular India.

These aims formed the core of the 'Fundamental Rights and Economic Policy' resolution drafted by Nehru in 1929–31, which were ratified in 1931 by the Congress Party session at Karachi

SCIENTIFIC HUMANIST

Nehru was a staunch believer in the humanity that vests within all and in social service, which to him was akin to a religion. He called for the combining of humanism and a scientific spirit, stating that the most important contribution of the Western world is their scientific temperament. It is only science that can improve the condition of the massesand remove the ills of society. For him, science was a state of mind, a thought process, and a way of life.

Under Nehru's leadership, the government attempted to develop India quickly by embarking on agrarian reform and rapid industrialisation. Agricultural production expanded until the early 1960s, as additional land was brought under cultivation and new irrigation projects began to have an effect. The establishment of agricultural universities, modelled after land-grant colleges in the US, contributed to the development of the economy. Nehru was also a passionate advocate of education, believing it essential for India's future progress. His government oversaw the establishment of many institutions of higher learning which are among the best even today, including the All India Institute of Medical Sciences (AIIMS), the Indian Institutes of Technology (IITs), the Indian Institutes of Management (IIMs), and the National Institutes of Technology. Nehru also outlined a commitment to guarantee free and compulsory primary education to all of India's children.

DEMOCRATIC SOCIALIST

While studying in Trinity College, Cambridge, Nehru was attracted to the ideas of **Fabianism.** He studied politics, economics, history, and literature with great interest, and the writings of Bernard Shaw, H. G. Wells, John Maynard Keynes, Bertrand Russell, Lowes Dickinson, and Meredith Townsend shaped much of his political and economic thinking. Their influence instilled in him a desire to realise equality in society through democratic means. He did not agree with the Marxist theory of class war and the dictatorship of Proletariat; his approach was more pragmatic than guided by any specific ideological commitment.

FOREIGN POLICY

On the international front, Nehru was opposed to military action and military alliances. He was a strong supporter of the United Nations. He was against the Cold War and ensured that India maintained a neutral position throughout this period. To this end, he pioneered the policy of non-alignment and co-founded the Non-Aligned Movement of nations, which professed neutrality between the rival blocs of nations led by the US and the USSR. Nehru was a key organiser of the Bandung Conference of April 1955, which brought twenty-nine newly independent nations together from Asia and Africa, and was designed to galvanise the non-alignment movement under Nehru's leadership.

Nehru believed that there should be a *world republic*, and not an empire that would exploit other countries for its own gains. The Directive Principles of State Policy, Part 4 of the constitution of India (Article 51), reflect this vision.

ECONOMIC DEVELOPMENT

Nehru advocated a mixed economy where the government-controlled public sector would co-exist with the private sector. He believed that the establishment of basic and heavy industry was fundamental to the development and modernisation of the Indian economy. The government therefore directed investment primarily into important public-sector industries—steel, iron, coal, and power—promoting their development with subsidies and protectionist policies. Nehru's preference for big state-controlled enterprises created a complex system of quantitative regulations, quotas, and tariffs, industrial licenses, and several other controls. This system was known in India as the Licence Raj.

As discussed earlier, under Nehru's agrarian reforms and industrialisation of agriculture also increased production, and led to the growth of the economy. The Green Revolution, an effort to diversify and increase crop production, began in the 1960s as part of these efforts.

Some important publications by Nehru are:

1. *The Discovery of India* (1946)
2. *An Autobiography* (1936)
3. *Letters from a Father to His Daughter*
4. *Glimpses of World History*
5. *The Unity of India*

19

RAM MANOHAR LOHIA (1910–1967)

KEY CONCEPTS

Caste and class; abolition of caste; non-violent means of social change; democratic socialism; four pillars of state; socialism and Gandhism

Ram Manohar Lohia was born in 1910 at Akbarpur, Uttar Pradesh. He was an activist in the Indian independence movement and a socialist political leader. He attended the Banaras Hindu University and then joined Vidyasagar College, University of Calcutta. For his higher studies, he attended Frederick William University (today's Humboldt University, Berlin, Germany). Lohia wrote his Ph.D. thesis on the topic of *Salt Taxation in India*, focusing on Gandhi's socioeconomic theory.

During the last phase of the nationalist movement, he worked with the Congress Radio, which was broadcast secretly from various palaces in Bombay until 1942.

REJECTION OF MARXISM

Lohia was one of the founders of the Congress Socialist Party (CSP) and editor of its mouthpiece, *Congress Socialist*. In 1936, Jawaharlal Nehru selected him for the post of secretary of the Foreign Department of the All India Congress Committee (AICC), the highest body of the Congress Party. By the time he gave up that responsibility in 1938, Lohia had begun to develop his own political standpoint, and had grown critical of positions held by the Gandhian leadership of the Congress and the Communists who had joined the CSP.

While ideologically opposed to capitalism, Lohia believed that Marxism cannot be applied to Indian society, as the Marxists believe that **class** is central to understanding society whereas for him, **caste** is the centrally important factor in Indian society. He disagreed with the historical interpretation of Marx as well, and differed from **Narendra Deva** and **J. P. Narayan** from his complete rejection of Marxism.

CASTE AND CLASS

In his work *Wheel of History* (1955), Lohia stated that caste and class are interchangeable in India. In India, exploitation does not exist solely in terms of either caste or class; rather, there are seven layers of exploitation, which need to be addressed, and/or redressed to bring about:

1. Equality between man and woman.
2. Against all political, economic, spiritual, and race-based inequalities.
3. Caste inequality, which should be eradicated.

4. Fight against imperialism and foreign domination.
5. for economic equality, planned production, and against private property.
6. Against unjust interference in the private lives of citizens.
7. Against all weapons and arms in society, and in favour of Satyagraha.

CASTE IN INDIAN SOCIETY

In his discussion on the caste system in India, Lohia went further to state that varna and caste are one and the same. To finally abolish the caste system, inter-dining among castes and inter-caste marriage are essential in society. Untouchability, too, needs to be completely removed from Hinduism. Since inequality was not only economic but also social, he was in favour of affirmative action targeted at the backward castes. He proposed **five reforms** which are necessary for the abolition of the caste system:

1. Change of heart among all citizens.
2. A rational interpretation of history.
3. Reform in politics.
4. A liberal language policy.
5. Religious efforts.

NON-VIOLENT MEANS FOR SOCIAL CHANGE

Lohia was part of the movement against English as an official language, and supported the proposal to make Hindi the national language. He proposed the Chouburja Rajneeti, that is, the four pillars of politics, in addition to socialism. According to this, the Centre, regions, districts, and villages would all be interconnected. Lohia also advocated for a socialist party that would include all other political parties.

He was also in favour of the peaceful Gandhian method to bring about social and political change.

DEMOCRATIC SOCIALIST

Lohia was one of the founders of the **Congress Socialist Party**. He remained a member of the Socialist Party when it fused in 1952 with the Kisan Majdoor Praja Party to form the Praja Socialist Party. Unhappy with this new party, Lohia led a split from it and re-formed the Socialist Party (Lohia) in 1956. In 1963, Lohia became a member of the Lok Sabha and in 1965, merged the Socialist Party (Lohia) into the Samyukta Socialist Party.

Lohia believed that democracy and socialism were two sides of the same coin. This again proves that he never endorsed the idea of a class struggle or any violent change in society. He further held the view that decentralisation is the essence of democracy, and, criticising the federal structure of the Indian Constitution, advocated for local self-government instead.

FOUR PILLARS OF STATE

Lohia stated that the **village, district, province, and the Centre** should be the four pillars of state. Each pillar is sovereign in itself, and will enjoy legislative as well as executive powers. In its election manifesto of 1962, the Socialist Party described the functions of the four pillars:

1. One-fourth of all planned expenditure of the government should be spent by the village, district, and city panchayat.
2. Police shall be under the control of the village, city, and district panchayat.
3. The post of collector should be abolished, and its functions distributed within the local government.
4. Agriculture and industry should be nationalised and brought under the control of the village, city, and district panchayat.
5. Economic decentralisation should be promoted by the utilisation of small machines.

Therefore, power should move from the bottom to the top, in contrast to parliamentary democracy, where power moves from the top to the bottom. Lohia's **Fifth Pillar** was the creation of a **World Government** and **Parliament of the World.**

COMBINING SOCIALISM WITH GANDHISM

One of Lohia's best-known works is *Marx, Gandhi and Socialism* (1963). As far as decentralisation is concerned, Lohia's ideas are very close to those of Gandhi, as both were seeking an alternative to the parliamentary form of government. Lohia also accepted the Gandhian method of satayagraha for mass mobilisation, as well as Gandhi's notion of simple living and the use of small machines as opposed to heavy industrial machinery. **Khadi**, he believed, could be an important tool in the generation of rural employment. However, he disagreed with Gandhi on the principle of trusteeship, and did not accept the idea of the **Charkha** (spinning wheel) and its dissemination either. Lohia was also in support of large-scale industries for railways, roadworks, and steel and iron.

Lohia's important works are:

1. *Aspects of Socialist Policy* (1952)
2. *Wheel of History* (1955)
3. *Marx, Gandhi and Socialism* (1963)
4. *Fragments of World Mind* (1949)
5. *The Caste System* (1964)
6. *Foreign Policy* (1963)
7. *Guilty Men of India's Partition* (1970)
8. *India, China and Northern Frontiers* (1963)
9. *Interval During Politics* (1965)

20

JAYAPRAKASH NARAYAN (1902–1979)

KEY CONCEPTS

Socialism; Gandhism; total revolution; partyless democracy

Jayaprakash Narayan, popularly referred to as JP or Lok Nayak, was an independence activist, socialist, and political leader. He was born in the village of Sitabdiara, in what is now Saran district, Bihar. He is remembered most for leading the mid-1970s opposition against Prime Minister Indira Gandhi, for whose overthrow he had called for a 'total revolution'. He was given the **Magsaysay Award** for public service in 1965 and in 1991, he was posthumously awarded the **Bharat Ratna**.

SOCIALIST

Jayaprakash Narayan went to the US for higher studies, first at Berkeley, then at the University of Iowa, and later at the University of Wisconsin. In Wisconsin, Jayaprakash was introduced to Karl Marx's *Das Kapital.* News of the success of the Bolsheviks in the Russian Civil War made him believe that Marxism was the way to alleviate the suffering of the masses in India as well. Marxism is against exploitation and capitalism, and he wanted to implement Marxist principles in Indian society. He joined the Indian National Congress in 1929 at the invitation of Jawaharlal Nehru, and was jailed in 1930 for civil disobedience against British rule. After his release, he formed the **Congress Socialist Party** (CSP) in 1934, which was a left-wing group within the Congress. Acharya Narendra Deva was the president of the party, and Ram Manohar Lohia was also among the members.

In his tract *Why Socialism?* (1936), he detailed the following objectives:

1. Transfer of all power to the producing masses.
2. A planned economy.
3. Socialisation of major industries.
4. Cooperative production.
5. Elimination of classes, princes, and landlords.
6. Distribution of land to the peasants.
7. Cooperative forming.
8. A secular state.
9. No discrimination on the basis of caste and gender.

GANDHISM

Jayaprakash Narayan was also deeply influenced by Gandhi's ideals. When Mahatma Gandhi launched the Quit India Movement in August 1942, Jayaprakash Narayan, along with other leaders like Suraj Narayan Singh, Gulab Chand Gupta, Pandit Ramnandan Mishra, etc., scaled the wall of Hazaribagh Central Jail with a goal to start an underground movement for freedom.

In 1952, he founded the **Praja Socialist Party**, which was merged into the **Krishak Mazdoor Praja Party**. In 1967, he became a part of the **Samyukata Socialist Party**.

Later in his life, he made an ideological shift towards Gandhian values, and sought to associate socialist ideals with the vision of decentralised governance that Gandhi had espoused. He advocated a politics of the people (*lokniti*) and the power of people (*lokshakti*) over power politics (*rajniti*) and state power (*rajyashakti*). He joined the Bhoodhan movement with Acharya Vinoba Bhave.

TOTAL REVOLUTION

Narayan returned to prominence in state politics in the late 1960s. The year 1974 saw high inflation, unemployment, and a lack of supplies and essential commodities. The Nav Nirman Andolan movement of Gujarat asked Jayaprakash to lead a peaceful agitation. However, the Bihar government used brutal force to suppress the movement and on 18 March 1974, police fired on unarmed demonstrators, killing eight people. On 5 June 1974, Jayaprakash addressed a large crowd at Gandhi Maidan in Patna, and declared, 'This is a revolution [*sampoorna kranti*], friends!'

Jayaprakash's vision of **Total Revolution** comprised **seven** changes:

1. Social
2. Economic
3. Political
4. Cultural
5. Ideological
6. Intellectual
7. Educational and Spiritual

PARTYLESS DEMOCRACY

Jayaprakash rejected the Western model of democracy, stating that party rivalry would give birth to demagoguery, depress political ethics, and increase manipulative tactics. He believed in a participatory model of democracy instead, where one party would not control power. Under his guidance, the Janata Party, a vehicle for the opposition to Indira Gandhi's government, was formed, and was voted into power and became the first non-Congress party to form a government at the Centre. Heeding JP's call, many youngsters also joined the JP movement.

JP's important works include:

1. *A Pleas for Reconstruction of Indian Polity* (1959).
2. *Prison Diary* (1976)
3. *Towards Total Revolution* (1978)
4. *Socialism, Sarvodaya and Democracy* (1964)

21

DEENDAYAL UPADHAYAYA (1916–1968)

KEY CONCEPTS

Integral humanism; antyodaya; alternative to capitalism and socialism; cultural nationalism

Deendayal Upadhayaya was born in Mathura district in 1916. He joined the Rashtriya Swayamsevak Sangh (RSS) in 1937 and was deeply influenced by **Nanaji Deshmukh** and **Bhau Jugade.** He was an Indian politician, proponent of the integral humanism ideology, and leader of the political party Bharatiya Jana Sangh (BJS), the forerunner of the Bharatiya Janata Party (BJP). In 1967, he became the General Secretary of the BJS.

INTEGRAL HUMANISM

Integral humanism was a set of concepts drafted by Upadhyaya as a political programme and adopted in 1965 as the official doctrine of the Jan Sangh. Humanism stands for reason, equality, and the supremacy of human beings, while integration denotes harmony and balance in society. The wellbeing of the marginalised section of society is particularly essential for integration, as society is akin to an organic unit. Every element of the societal unit is interdependent.

Upadhyaya also believed in the spiritual and humanistic philosophy of India, where integration is required at four levels:

1. Body
2. Mind
3. Intellect
4. Soul

Integration is crucial among the individual, society, nature, and god. Society should be free of conflict as harmony is indispensable in a healthy society. He first articulated the philosophy of integral humanism while participating in a lecture series in Mumbai. Integral humanism also stands against both individualism and communism, and comprises of two themes:

1. Morality in politics
2. Swadeshi and small-scale industries.

ANTYODAYA

The word Antyodaya signifies the rise of the last person and refers to the poorest of the poor. Upadhyaya stated that economic planning and growth should be evaluated on the basis of the empowerment of the poorest sections of society. Gandhi's vision of Sarvodaya is very similar to the theory of Antodaya.

Part of Antyodaya was also a welfare state, where the basic minimum necessities like free education and healthcare should be made available to all people. The Right to Food is a birthright of all. While material development of the people is necessary, equally important is the protection of the environment and the moral development of people.

ALTERNATIVE TO CAPITALISM AND SOCIALISM

Upadhyaya was against a blind copying of Western ideologies and systems, and believed that a 'Swaraj of Ideas' is more important in the reconstruction of any nation, and better suited to the development of India. An emphasis on Indian philosophy and culture is essential to ensure the holistic development of the country. While capitalism promotes increasing production accompanied by a widening disparity in society, socialism believes in the fulfillment of the material needs of all in society.

CULTURAL NATIONALISM

Upadhyaya turned to the ideals and teachings of Swani Vivekananda to propagate his idea of cultural nationalism. The following elements are essential for a nation to develop:

1. Land and its people
2. Collective will
3. A collection of principles, which exist in the form of a religion in India
4. Ideals of life

A nation is not merely a territorial concept, but is a result of the collective cultural values of the people. The nation is our motherland, and should be synonymous with the respect and love accorded to one's mother.

The state, according to Upadhyaya, merely reflects a territorial unit. A nation, on the other hand, is a cultural concept, based on certain eternal values and ideals which form its soul. He never believed in the ideology of ultra-nationalism, saying instead that the world is akin to a family (*Vasudhaiva kutumbakam*). The psychological attachment to one's nation is known as **Chiti**, and the energy received form this Chiti is referred to as **Virat**.

ECONOMIC IDEAS

Like Gandhi, Upadhyaya was in favour of a decentralised economy with focus on small-scale and cottage industries. It is essential that all people in a nation find worthwhile employment, but the principle of economics should be based on humanity. At the same time, attention must be paid to ensuring that the resources of nature are not over-exploited or destroyed.

ACTIVISM AND POLITICAL CAREER

Upadhyaya was a member of the RSS and worked full-time in the organisation from 1942. He started the monthly *Rashtra Dharma* publication from Lucknow in the 1940s, using it to spread the Hindutva ideology. Later, he started the weekly *Panchjanya* and the daily *Swadesh*.

In 1951, Upadhyaya joined the BJS and was appointed as General Secretary of its Uttar Pradesh branch, and later became the all-India general secretary. He also contested the by-poll elections for the Lok Sabha seat of Jaunpur from Uttar Pradesh in 1963, but failed to attract significant political traction and did not get elected.

Upadhyaya edited the *Panchjanya* (weekly) and *Swadesh* (daily) from Lucknow. In Hindi, he wrote a drama on Chandragupta Maurya, and later wrote a biography of Shankaracharya. He also translated a Marathi biography of Hedgewar.

UNIT IV

COMPARATIVE POLITICAL ANALYSIS

KEYWORDS

Approaches; Colonialism and decolonisation; Nationalism; State theory; Political regimes; Constitutions and constitutionalism; Democratisation; Development; Structures of power; Actors and processes

1

COMPARATIVE POLITICS

KEY CONCEPTS

Origin of comparative politics; traditional versus modern approaches; input-output approach; structural-functionalism; political sociology; political economy; modernisation theory; dependency perspective; New Political Economy; institutionalism

ORIGIN OF COMPARATIVE POLITICS

Ancient and Medieval Europe

Ancient Greek philosophers of classical Athens such as Plato and his well-known student, Aristotle (384–322 BCE), identified different kinds of political orders: for example, oligarchy (rule by the rich/elite) and democracy (rule by the masses, which Aristotle considered the least harmful derivative or indirect government). They tried to determine which form of government would be the best and most suitable to society.

Aristotle established six forms of government after a study of 158 constitutions. These include: monarchy, aristocracy, polity (a mixture of oligarchy and democracy), tyranny, oligarchy, democracy (direct and representative).

Aristotle established a *conceptual hierarchy* among these six forms. Herein, tyranny (one leader), oligarchy (a few leaders), and democracy (many leaders) are seen to work in the self-interest of those at the helm, and as the reverse of monarchy, aristocracy, and polity, which are viewed as being in public interest. Polity, according to Aristotle, is the 'Golden Mean' and the best form of government, while democracy is the worst.

Yet another early comparative research was undertaken by the French political philosopher **Montesquieu** (1689–1755) in his work *The Spirit of Laws* (1750), wherein he tried to uncover the relationship between geographical factors and particular forms of government. This book is considered one of the greatest works in the history of political theory and in the history of jurisprudence, and contained the seeds of the modern systems approach.

Montesquieu divided governments into three kinds: the Republic (a mixture of democracy and aristocracy, and based on virtue); the Monarchy (based on honour); and Despotism (based on fear). He also proposed the theory of the separation of powers—dividing political authority into the legislative, executive, and judicial powers. He stated that in the state that most effectively promotes liberty, these three powers must be the domains of different individuals or bodies, acting independently. He provided a structural-functional analysis of political systems.

In another of the best-known works on political systems, *Democracy in America* (1835), French sociologist and political theorist **Alexis de Tocqueville** (1805–1859), who believed that equality was the great political and social idea of his era, stated that the United States offered the most advanced example of equality in action. However, he warned that a society of individuals can easily become atomised and paradoxically uniform when 'every citizen, being assimilated to all the rest, is lost in the crowd', resulting in a democratic 'tyranny of the majority', in which individual rights could be compromised.

Modern India

Well-known Indian political scientist **Manoranjan Mohanty** had stated that comparative politics is not only about finding similarities or dissimilarities in different polities, but also about discovering relationships between them. He stated that comparative political studies has undergone three major phases:

1. Institutionalism, from the 1920s till the 1950s.
2. Behaviouralism and modernisation in the mid-1960s.
3. Emergence of the Third World Challenge from the 1970s.

TRADITIONAL APPROACHES

Legal Institutional Approach

1. This approach focused on the legal and constitutional framework within which the different organs of government have to function.
2. It studies the legal position, powers, and procedures which assign validity and legitimacy to governmental functions and institutions.
3. The major proponents of this approach are **Jean Bodin** (French jurist and political philosopher; 1530–1596), English philosopher and social reformer **Jeremy Bentham** (1748–1832), British jurist **A. V. Dicey** (1835–1922), and English philosopher **Thomas Hobbes** (1588–1679).
4. Among the major works in this field are:
   (a) James Bryce, *Modern Democracies* (1921)
   (b) Herman Finer, *Theory and Practice of Modern Government* (1949)
   (c) Karl J. Friedrich, *Constitutional Government and Democracy* (1941)

The traditional approach focuses on the study of government, and offers a comparative study of parliamentary form of government versus the presidential form of government, taking as examples the power of the US President and the political position of the British Prime Minister in a parliamentary democracy. The major proponents of this approach are the Italian political scientist **Giovanni Sartori** (1924–2017) and British journalist and economist **Walter Bagehot** (1826–1877).

DRAWBACKS OF TRADITIONAL APPROACHES

Eurocentric Studies

1. There have been demands to liberate comparative political theory from neocolonial domination, given that in the recent past, the developing countries of the erstwhile Third World have emerged as a significant political force in the international political climate.
2. The domination of the superpower states has also been challenged. The study of political activities has been confined to the government, viz., the functions of the legislature, executive, and judiciary.
3. In the 1960s, two other functions were added to this, namely welfare and administrative functions. However, this approach excludes the coercive function of government activity, and hence exempts countries that have experienced military rule.
4. Another sphere of organised society is associated with political parties. However,

the socioe-conomic dimensions of party support have not been studied adequately.

Universal-Particular Dilemma

1. This involves the question of whether comparative studies should involve universalist theories or particular explanations arising out of specific situations.
2. It is now generally argued that a confrontation between the general and the particular must lead to an enriched and refined general law, rather than settle for local explanations.
3. In 1955, Professor of Politics at Brandeis University, **Roy Macridis** (1918–1991), critiqued comparative political analysis, claiming that it functioned in a parochial manner as it focused only on the experiences of Western Europe. Further, it was descriptive rather than analytical in nature.
4. Comparative politics has been unable to achieve the status of a political philosophy as it lacks a foundation or a sacred core of concepts, definitions, or focus. It does not have any central body of literature or a grand theory.

MODERN APPROACH

Political Culture

Gabriel A. Almond and Sidney Verba, both renowned are among the most important political scientists, authored one of the most influential books on political culture, *The Civic Culture: Political Attitudes and Democracy in Five Nations* (1963). They defined three types of civic culture: parochial, subject, and participant. Their core idea was that democracy will prove most stable in societies where subject and parochial attitudes provide support to an essentially participant culture. This mix is known as *civic culture*. Almond and Verba conducted surveys in the USA, Britain, West Germany, Italy, and Mexico and identified three types of orientations on the basis of this study:

1. Allegiance: a positive attitude
2. Apathy: indifference
3. Alienation: a negative attitude

Almond and Verba propounded the concept of Civic Culture, which can be taken as an ideal type. According to them, civic culture is 'based on communication and persuasion, a culture of consensus and diversity, a culture that [permits] change but [moderates] it' (Almond and Verba 1963, 8). The following are the characteristics of a civic culture:

1. Orientation towards the political system in both the political and governmental senses;
2. Pride in one's nation;
3. Expectation of fair treatment from government authorities; and
4. Ability to talk freely and frequently about politics.

Culture is responsible for the participation of people in a political system. Almond and Verba listed three types of political cultures:

1. Participant cultures
2. Subject cultures
3. Parochial cultures.

Participant culture exists in nations like the US and Britain, where people are knowledgeable about the political system and their role within it. In subject cultures, while citizens are aware about the political system, they do not know the rights that accrue to them in this system. In parochial cultures, people neither know about the political system nor their role within it.

S. E. Finer, the author of *The Man on Horseback: The Role of the Military in Politics* (1962), stated that there are two reasons behind the instability of governments in developing countries:

1. Lack of legitimacy.
2. The presence of various associations.

Countries and their Political Cultures

Different countries have varied political cultures. Some of them are listed below.

1. **Britain** has a Homogeneous Culture.
2. **India** has an Elite Mass Culture.
3. **China** has a Subject Political Culture.
4. **Uganda** has a Parochial Culture.

Social Capital

American political scientist **Robert Putnam** authored the book *Bowling Alone: The Collapse and Revival of American Community* (2000). Best known for his theory of social capital, he stated that social capital refers to 'connections among individuals—social networks and the norms of reciprocity and trustworthiness that arise from them'. Social capital is the determining factor behind the participation of people in politics, and refers to family, church, social groups, etc., which influenced the participation of people. In *Bowling Alone*, he argued that there is a lack of participation in civic society due to the rise of individualist materialism; civic life is collapsing because Americans are no longer joining the groups and clubs that promote trust and cooperation, thereby undermining democracy. However, this theory has since been disputed by scholars.

MODERN APPROACHES TO COMPARATIVE POLITICS

The modern approach to the study of comparative politics was propounded in the following works:

1. *Study of Comparative Government* (1955) by Roy Macridis
2. *Comparative Politics: A Reader* (1963) by David Apter and Henry Eckstein (eds)
3. *Political Parties* (1915) by Robert Michels

David Easton, Gabriel Almond, G. C. Powell, Morton Kaplan, Karl Deutsch, and other behaviouralists were the pioneers in the application of Systems Theory—the *interdisciplinary study of systems,* that is, cohesive groups of interrelated, interdependent components that can be natural or human-made—in the analysis of political phenomena and theory-building in the discipline of Political Science during the late 1950s and 1960s.

While it is difficult to separate the political from the non-political, it is undeniable that all aspects of human life are affected by politics. David Easton propounded the theory of behaviouralism, which according to him sought to be 'analytic, not substantive, general rather than particular, and explanatory rather than ethical'. The eight characteristic features of behaviouralism are as follows:

1. Regularities
2. Verification
3. Techniques
4. Quantification
5. Values
6. Systematisation
7. Pure Science
8. Integration.

The General Systems Theory was coined in the 1940s by Austrian biologist **Ludwig Von Bertalanffy**, who sought a new approach to the study of living systems. The general systems theory is an interdisciplinary practice that describes systems with interacting components, and is applicable to biology, cybernetics, and other fields. It has been adopted in the social sciences, such as anthropology, sociology, psychology, and political science, as well.

From the perspective of political systems, society is not viewed as the sum total of compartmentalised units, each of which is entrusted with a definite function. There is an intimate relationship between social and political systems, and only the monopoly of force distinguishes political systems from other types of systems.

Characteristics of Political Systems

1. **Comprehensiveness.** The political system includes all political orientations and

interactions, legal and constitutional structures, and associational units such as parties or pressure groups

2. All parts of a political system are **interdependent.**
3. There are **identifiable points** in a political system, clearly demarcating where it begins and ends.

According to Gabriel Almond, there are five characteristics of political systems:

1. All political systems are fundamentally the same;
2. All political systems possess political structures;
3. There is a universality of political function;
4. All political institutions are multi-functional;
5. Political systems possess a culturally mixed character.

David Easton defines a political system as 'that system of interaction in any society through which binding or authoritative allocations are made'. And according to Gabriel Almond, a political system is 'that system of interactions to be found in all independent societies which performs the functions of integration and adaptation (both internally and vis-à-vis other societies) by means of employment or threat of employment of ... physical compulsion.'

TYPES OF MODERN APPROACHES

1. Input-Output Approach
2. Structural-Functional Approach
3. Political Economy Approach
4. Political Sociology Approach

INPUT-OUTPUT APPROACH

David Easton presented an analysis of the input-output approach in his article 'The Analysis of Political Systems', published in *World Politics* in 1957.

The key concepts of systems analysis are:

1. System
2. Environment
   (a) A system is distinguishable from the environment in which it exists, and is open to influences from it.
   (b) The environment of the political system is constituted of those aspects of a society that fall outside the boundaries of a political system. They consist of all other subsystems of a society.
   (c) The environment of the political system is composed of two different types of systems:
      (i) **Intra-societal environment:** That part of the social and physical environment that lies outside the boundaries of a political system and yet within the same society.
      (ii) **Extra-societal environment:** The systems that lie outside the society of which the political system is itself a social subsystem, and yet have important consequences for the persistence or change of a political system.
3. Inputs:
   (a) G. Almond and Sidney Verba assert that by the 'political' or 'input' process, we refer to the flow of demands from society to the polity, and the conversion of these demands into authoritative policies.
   (b) Some structures involved in the input process are political parties, interest groups, and the media of communication.
   (c) Inputs indicate the ways in which environmental processes and phenomena modify and affect the operations of the political system. The various kinds of inputs give a political system its dynamic character.

(d) The inputs that originate from within the system itself are identified as **'withinputs'**.

(e) There are two basic kinds of inputs:

(i) Demands:
This refers to the raw materials that the system is called upon to process.
These are the wants of persons or groups that are placed before the political system, and which require some special, organised effort on the part of the society to be settled authoritatively.

(ii) Support:
This refers to the energies that keep the system going.
This energy takes the form of actions or orientations, which are focused towards promoting or resisting a political system.

4. Output

(a) According to Almond and Verba, by 'administrative' or 'output' process, we refer to that process by which authoritative policies are applied or enforced.

(b) The structures predominantly involved in this process would include bureaucracies and courts.

(c) Outputs are those occurrences concerned with the authoritative allocation of values or binding decisions, and the actions implementing and related to them.

5. Feedback: The capacity of a system to persist in the face of stress is a function of the presence and the nature of the information and other influences that return to its actors and decision-makers.

6. Stress: A severe disturbance occurring in the environment of a political system that threatens to destroy it.

7. Demand Input Overload: Overstress may occur due to too many demands being made; or their variety and content may be such that they require an excessive amount of time to process.

8. Gate-keeping:

(a) All political systems have their own particular capacities and limitations. They cannot transform every input into an output. Gate-keeping protects the political system against being overstressed.

(b) Gate-keeping also prevents unwanted demands from entering the political system, and acts as a regulatory system.

(c) Political systems comprise the following sub-systems which carry out the function of gate-keeping:

(i) **Structural:** Political parties, pressure groups

(ii) **Cultural:** The belief and orientation of the people

(iii) **Communication channels**

STRUCTURAL-FUNCTIONAL APPROACH

Structural-functionalism is an application of the Political Systems Theory to the study of political life. This approach was initiated in the USA, in the 1950s and 1960s. The major scholars within this tradition are **G. Almond, G. B. Powell, Robert K. Merton,** and **Talcott Parsons**. Max Weber and Talcott Parsons are the two sociologists who influenced Gabriel Almond the most.

The **major works** that take the structural-functional approach to theory-building are:

1. *The Politics of Developing Areas* (1960), edited by Gabriel Almond and James Smoot Coleman
2. *Comparative Politics: A Developmental Approach* (1966) by Gabriel Almond and G. Bingham Powell

A. R. Ball defines structural-functionalism as 'a means of explaining what political structures perform what basic functions in the political system and it is a tool of investigation'. Structural-functionalism helps to measure the amount of change that a system can accommodate without seriously affecting its basic functional requisites.

- *Structure*
  1. Almond and Powell define structure as 'particular sets of roles which are related to one another'.
  2. Structures are those arrangements within a system which are concerned with the performance of functions or 'roles'. A particular structure may perform different functions; again, different sets of structures may perform similar functions.
- *Function*
  1. Robert K. Merton, Talcott Parsons, and Marion Levy were the first to use the concept of function in sociology. Gabriel A. Almond and his colleagues applied the concept to political science.
  2. Almond and Powell define function as: 'By function we mean the observable actions which make up the political systems.'
  3. Robert K. Merton defines function as: '... functions are those observed consequences which make for the adaptation and adjustment of a given system.'
- *Core Assumptions*
  1. Every political system has its structures, some of which may be more specialised and perform many functions, while others may be less specialised and perform fewer functions.
  2. Whatever the differences may be between the systems and their inherent structures, the same political functions are performed in all political systems.
  3. Political structures are multifunctional.
  4. All political structures perform their functions in a specific environment.

According to Almond, three basic types of functions are performed by all political systems for their continuance:

1. Functions related to a system's capabilities. These include five types of functions:
   (a) **Extractive:** To extract taxes and obedience from people
   (b) **Regulative:** How far the system is allowed to go to enforce law and order
   (c) **Distributive:** How goods and services are distributed
   (d) **Responsive:** How responsive the system is, as perceived by citizens
   (e) **Symbolic:** Whether the political system is in a position to gain legitimate support for its symbols, such as the national flag or the national anthem.
2. System maintenance and adaptation functions
   (a) Political socialisation:
      (i) Political orientations are acquired through a process of learning, known as political socialisation. This is the process through which a political culture becomes a part of one's personality.
      (ii) **Non-political agents** such as family, peer groups, and schools, as well as **political agents** like the mass media play important roles in the process of political socialisation.
      (iii) Sidney Verba emphasises the fact that there should be a continuity in the socialisation process, that is, what one learns in one's family must be complemented by 'what one learns from participation in politics'.
3. Conversion Functions
   (a) Input Functions:
      (i) **Interest Articulation.** This refers to the process by which different

and often conflicting interests are expressed by various sections of the population. There could be many avenues for expressing these interests, which can include institutions, political parties, and pressure groups.

(ii) **Interest Aggregation.** This refers to the process by which diverse interests are aggregated together, classified, and arranged into a hierarchy based on priorities, which take the form of agendas. Political parties are the main instruments for interest aggregation in democratic societies.

(iii) **Political Communication.** This refers to the process by which particular interests, attitudes, and policies are conveyed from the political system to the citizens and vice versa, or among the citizens themselves. Mass media is the instrument used in the modern system, while the family and community were the tools used in traditional contexts.

(b) Output Functions

The following output structures are responsible for performing these functions:

(i) **Rule-making:** This is performed by the Legislature.

(ii) **Rule application:** This is performed by the Executive.

(iii) **Rule adjudication.** This is performed by the Judiciary.

POLITICAL SOCIOLOGY APPROACH

The branch of learning which examines political institutions, processes, and ideologies in the light of corresponding social structures, processes, and modes of thought is called political sociology. It is an interdisciplinary field of study concerned with exploring how governance and society interact and influence one another at the micro to the macro levels of analysis, and examines the impact of political processes and decisions on social life. While it initially emerged as an approach, it later developed into a full-fledged discipline in itself.

The study of politics extends beyond formal procedures and institutions in the contemporary era. Therefore, the incorporation of sociology into political inquiry becomes essential, and political sociology grew into the study of power and the relationship between societies, states, and political conflict.

The roots of this approach can be traced back to the works of **Aristotle** and Italian statesman and philosopher **Niccolo Machiavelli.** Machiavelli's theory of revolution, which suggests that social and political conflict are not destabilising political factors, but are rather the grounding and animating force of free republics, and Aristotle's work on determining the best form of government pointed towards an interdisciplinary approach which combined methods and concepts from both political science and sociology.

Through their work and theories, German economist and philosopher **Karl Marx** and German sociologist **Max Weber** also provided a solid foundation to this approach. They turned to political analysis as a part of their social enquiry. While Marx focused on studying the basic structures of society, Weber delved into concepts such as authority, legitimacy, ideal type, rise of religion as a driving force in society, and forms of leadership.

Political sociology sought to achieve a synthesis between normative analysis and research. Since it focuses on the intersection between politics and society, political sociologists within this tradition use research methodologies that range from mathematical and statistical models to field questionnaires, which help in data collection and also provide analytical insights into the field of inquiry.

As stated earlier, political sociology is an interdisciplinary field of study and lies at the intersection of the disciplines of political science and sociology. Italian political scientist **Giovanni Sartori** had stated that there lay an ambiguity in the term 'political sociology', since it could alternatively be interpreted as a 'sociology of politics'. The discipline deals with the social circumstances of politics, that is, how politics is shaped by, and in turn shapes, other events in societies.

German-American sociologist **Reinhard Bendix** and American sociologist and political scientist **S. M. Lipset** stated that 'political sociology starts with society and examines how it affects the state'.

Nature of Political Sociology

1. Political sociology seeks to understand the process of interaction between government and society, decision-making authorities, and conflicting social forces and interests.
2. It aims to understand the sources and social bases of conflict, as well as the process of conflict management.

Scope of Political Sociology

1. According to **Greer** and **Orleans**, political sociology is concerned with the structure of the state, the nature and condition of legitimacy, and the nature of the monopoly of force and its use by the state.
2. Eminent sociologist **Andreu Effrat**, however, takes a broader view and states that political sociology is concerned with the causes, patterns, and consequences of the distribution and process of power and authority 'in all social systems'.
3. In their work *Political Sociology*, **R. E. Dowse** and **J. A. Hughes** state that one area of substantive concern for the political sociologist is the problem of social order and political obedience.
4. **Lipset** and **Bendix** describe the main areas of interest to political sociologists as: voting behaviour, concentration of economic power and political decision-making, ideologies of political movement and interest groups, political parties and bureaucracy.
5. Sociologist **Richard G. Braungart** has pointed out that political sociologists are concerned with the dynamic association among and between three things:
   (a) The social origin of politics
   (b) The structure of the political process
   (c) The effects of politics on the surrounding society and culture.

Political sociology should include four areas of study:

1. **Political structures** (for instance, social class, interest groups, elite bureaucracy, political parties)
2. **Political life** (such as electoral processes, political communication)
3. **Political leadership** (bases, types, and operation of the community power structure)
4. **Political development**

Critique of the Political Sociology Approach

1. Sartori asserted that political sociology is a part of political science. However, sociologists like Lewis Coser disagreed, and contended that political sociology is a branch of the discipline of sociology.
2. French jurist and sociologist **Maurice Duverger** was of the opinion that political sociology and political science are much the same, and the two can be used as interchangeable terminologies.
3. Political sociologists have traditionally focused more on the study of Western societies and Western political systems. Therefore, the discipline has tended to

ignore cross-national, cross-cultural, and cross-society study and research.

4. Marxists have also pointed out that political sociology holds neither relevance nor credibility without the accompanying study of political economy.

POLITICAL ECONOMY APPROACH

'Political economy' is a branch of social science that studies the relationship that forms between a nation's population and its government when public policy is enacted. It is, therefore, the result of the interaction between politics and the economy and forms the basis of the social science discipline. It refers to a specific way of understanding social and political phenomena whereby economics and politics are not viewed as separate domains.

Scottish economist **Adam Smith** considered political economy 'a branch of the science of a statesman or legislator'. German philosopher **Friedrich Engels** asserted that political economy studies 'the laws governing the production and exchange of the material means of subsistence'. In *Theories of Comparative Politics* (1994), political scientist **Ronald H. Chilcote** identified the following types of political economy:

1. **Mercantilism:** This was a form of economic nationalism that sought to increase the prosperity and power of a nation through restrictive trade practices. It refers to the economic theory that propounds that trade generates wealth and is stimulated by the accumulation of profitable balances, which a government should encourage by means of protectionism.
2. **Liberal-Capitalism:** Economic liberals tend to oppose government intervention and protectionism in the market economy when it hinders free trade and competition, but support government intervention where it protects property rights, opens new markets or funds market growth, and resolves market failures. The liberals argued for a capitalist market economy which would ensure the freedom of competition between individuals. This would ensure, in the words of English philosopher John Locke, who is commonly known as the 'father of liberalism', that people are free to dispose of the fruits of their labour in ways that they themselves deem fit.
3. **Marxism:** Marxism is a social, economic and political philosophy that analyses the impact of the ruling class on the labourers or working classes, leading to an uneven distribution of wealth and privileges in the society. It refers to a theory or system of social organisation that advocates the ownership and control of the means of production and distribution, such as capital, land, etc., by the community as a whole, usually through a centralised government. Marxists are critical of the capitalist economic system and see it as exploitative.

STAGES OF DEVELOPMENT

In 1960, American economist **W. W. Rostow** in his influential work, *Stages of Economic Growth*, attempted to provide a generalised view of the sweep of modern economic history and presented five steps through which all countries must pass in order to become 'developed'. Rostow's **stages of growth**, which is an important part of modernisation theory, are given below:

1. **The Traditional Society:** Here, the economy was dominated by subsistence activity, which evolved with limited production functions. This society lacked a systematic understanding of their physical environment which would have made them capable of regular inventions.
2. **The Preconditions for Take-off:** This stage was characterised by the gradual evolution of modern science and a modern scientific

attitude and the discovery of new lands, heightened by the extension of trade and the creation of colonies in newly discovered lands.
3. **The Takeoff:** This stage consists, in essence, of the achievement of rapid growth in a limited group of sectors, where modern industrial techniques were applied.
4. **The Drive to Maturity:** This is defined as a period when a society has effectively applied the range of modern technology to the bulk of its resources.
5. **The Age of High Mass Consumption:** The modern economy moved in three directions. It offered, through public measures, increased security, welfare, and leisure to the working force; it provided enlarged private consumption on a mass basis; and it sought enlarged power for the mature nation on the world scene.

Table 4.1.1: Differences between Traditional and Modern Societies

Traditional Society	*Modern Society*
1. Ascriptive, particularistic, diffuse, and affective patterns of action	A predominance of, and greater emphasis placed on, achievement
2. An extended kinship structure	A nuclear family structure
3. Little spatial and social mobility	High rates of spatial and social mobility
4. A deferential stratification system	Universalistic, specific, and neutral orientations of patterns of action
5. Mostly primary economic activities	Predominance of secondary economic activities
6. An undifferentiated political structure with traditional elitist and hierarchical sources of authority.	Highly differentiated political structures with rational-legal sources of authority

MODERNISATION THEORY

Modernisation theory is used to explain the process of modernisation within societies. It became prominent in the 1950s and 1960s, and favoured a capitalist-industrial model of development. It states that traditional societies will develop as they adopt more modern practices. The proponents of modernisation theory claim that modern states are wealthier and more powerful, and that their citizens are freer to enjoy a higher standard of living. The basic building blocks of the modernisation perspective are the presence of parallel tradition-modernity ideal types of social organisation and value systems.

In this theory, societies are understood as lying on an **evolutionary continuum,** wherein they are obligated to move from a position of tradition towards modernity. While Western nations are believed to have achieved the stage of modernity, 'Third World' countries are perceived to be below the threshold of modernity, as they have a preponderance of traditional features.

The primary sources of change take the form of innovations, that is, the rejection of procedures related to traditional institutions, together with the adoption of new ideas, techniques, values, and organisations. It is believed that through the process of modernisation, all societies would, by and large, undergo similar changes. Therefore, the history of the present-day modern nations is taken as the source of universally useful conceptualisations, which can be applied to all other coutries.

DEPENDENCY PERSPECTIVE

First proposed in the late 1950s by the Argentine economist and statesman Raúl Prebisch, dependency theory gained prominence in the 1960s and 1970s. According to this theory, underdevelopment is mainly caused by the peripheral position of affected countries (usually the erstwhile colonies and countries of the 'Third World') in the world economy. **Raul Prebisch** was a part of the United Nations Economic Commission for Latin America and the Caribbean.

The dependency perspective rejects the assumptions made by the modernisation theorists, and states that the development of a national or regional unit can only be understood in connection with its historical position within the worldwide political economic system, which emerged with the wave of European colonialism.

The global system is characterised by the unequal yet combined development of its different components. Dependency theory focused on individual nations, their role as suppliers of raw materials and cheap labour to 'developed' Western nations, and as markets for expensive manufactured goods from the industrialised countries. This unequal exchange relationship between developed and developing countries was viewed as contributing to the poor economic growth of the latter.

Dependency theory divides the world into two groups: the *centre*, made up of the developed nations of the West, is viewed as capable of dynamic development in response to their internal needs, and as the main beneficiary of the global links. On the other hand, the *periphery* is seen as having a reflex type of development, one that is both constrained by its incorporation into the global system and yet results from its adaptation to the expansionist requirements of the centre. The international division of labour did not lead to a parallel development through comparative advantage. Rather, the centre states gained at the expense of the periphery.

Andre Gunder Frank is a major thinker within the dependency approach tradition. Replacing the terms 'core/centre' and 'periphery' with '*metropolis*' and '*satellite*' nations, he declared that the people of less-developed countries are not to blame for the failure of their societies to develop. Instead, he suggested that Western nations deliberately failed to develop these countries. He put forward three important hypotheses related to the same:

1. In contrast to the development of the world metropolis (which is no one's satellite), the development of the national and other subordinate metropoles is limited by their satellite status.
2. The satellite nations experience their greatest economic development, and especially their most classically capitalist industrial development, only when their ties to their metropoles are weakest.

   A corollary to this second hypothesis is that all earlier development and industrialisation of these regions had been choked or channelled into different directions once the control of the metropoles had been re-established.
3. The regions which are the most underdeveloped and feudal today are the ones which had the closest ties to the metropolis in the past.

Brazilian economist **Theotonio dos Santos** coined a 'new dependency' theory, which expressed the idea of 'subordination', that is, the development of a country is directly linked to the development of other countries. This development is not brought upon by pre-capitalistic conditions, but rather by the patterns of capitalistic development of the countries together with their insertion into the capitalist system as given by imperialism. It further states that in order to overcome its underdevelopment, a country must break its dependency on other countries, and not merely modernise or industrialise its economy—this, in fact, could actually intensify its dependency on other countries. He provided a classification of dependency into: colonial dependency; financial-industrial dependency; and technological-industrial dependency.

NEW POLITICAL ECONOMY

The New Political Economy (NPE) is a relatively recent sub-school within the field of political economy. The aim of NPE scholars is to understand important issues that arise in economic spheres. A *neoliberal approach*, it has, in the context of globalisation, emerged as a dominant paradigm, providing explanations and prescribing remedies for underdevelopment in peripheral states. In its simplest definition, NPE is **the economic study of politics.** It is alternatively known as 'political economics', 'macro political economy', and 'positive political economy'.

This approach believes that less developed countries can develop and obtain a competitive advantage in an open world economy by rolling back state control. For instance, **P. Sainath's** work *Everybody Loves a Good Drought* (2002) points out clearly that the nexus of politicians, bureaucrats, and contractors is responsible for poverty and corruption in India.

At the heart of the neoliberal perspective lies the notion of 'separation' or dichotomy between the state and the market. This paradigm limits the role of the state to providing 'enabling' conditions of 'good governance', in which market forces can flourish unhindered. The NPE provides answers to a number of questions concerning the role of the state and public policy in economic development, and encompasses the perspectives of public choice, collective choice, and social choice theory.

Drawbacks of NPE

1. An exclusive focus on economic factors tends to undermine the significance of the 'political' in this approach. To be truly comparative, NPE needs to focus on a holistic and multidimensional approach to understanding the variables inherent in the relations between nations.
2. The conceptualisation of political economy is vague, abstract, and full of internal contradictions. While liberals strongly support an open and free capitalist world economy, Marxists vehemently oppose the same, viewing it as exploitative.
3. The political sociology approach also incorporates a focus on economic factors and modes of production. Therefore, the lines between the two approaches are blurred.

NEW INSTITUTIONALISM

The *Old Institutionalism* approach was popular in the late nineteenth and early twentieth centuries, and focused on **describing and mapping the formal institutions of government and the modern state.** In tandem with the constitutional approach, the emphasis was on charting the formal-legal and administrative arrangements of government and the public sectors. The main focus was on description, and not on providing an explanation or theory-building.

New Institutionalism amounts to 'bringing institutions back'. In political science, there have been a number of reasons for the renewed interest in institutions:

1. Social, political, and economic institutions have become larger, considerably more complex and resourceful, and more important to collective life.
2. There has been a renewed interest in the state in a number of schools of political analysis.
3. Institutional factors have figured prominently in explanations of why countries pursued such different responses to the common economic challenges of the 1970s and 1980s.

This approach was propounded by **James C. March** and **Mancur Olson,** who together authored *The New Institutionalism: Organizational Basis of Politics* (1984). All strands of new institutionalism share a common critique of atomistic accounts of social processes. The most important difference between behaviouralism and new institutionalism is that the focus on atomistic actors in the former is replaced by a focus on institutionally 'situated' actors in the latter.

Institutions are important as they provide actors with sets of behavioural incentives and disincentives, along with normative and ideational codes that shape not only behaviour, but also preferences, and with resources, including power resources. Many different schools of institutionalist analysis have emerged, which include:

1. Rational Choice Institutionalism
   (a) This approach borrows heavily from economics and adopts a 'deductive' methodology. **Mancur Olson** is a major proponent of this approach.
   (b) In comparative politics, rational choice institutionalism represents an attempt to apply micro-economic models of rationality to the analysis of the collective choices made in the political process.
   (c) Rational choice theory adheres to the principle of methodological individualism.
   (d) The rational choice approach assumes that actors are rational. Actors are also assumed to be selfish, intent on maximising utility.
   (e) Rational choice theorists argue that institutions are constructed by individual actors for rational purposes, and that individual actors engage in changing and shaping their institutional environments to suit their goals.
2. Historical and Sociological Institutionalism
   (a) The historical institutionalist approach is *inductive* and not deductive. It searches for empirical regularities through repeated observations, and not through deductive first principles.
   (b) Scholars of this approach argue that despite operating under conditions of constraint, actors remain interpretive subjects, capable of making choices.
   (c) The key question raised by this perspective is: What is the appropriate response to this situation, given my position and responsibilities? **March** and **Olsen** refer to this perspective as the 'logic of appropriateness'.
3. Cultural Institutionalism
   (a) From the perspective of cultural theory, individuals always make decisions in a manner that reflects the dominant ideas and beliefs widely shared by members of the communities of which they are a part.
   (b) The main assumptions are:
      (i) People define their interests according to the meanings, symbols, and traditional practices derived from their cultural environment.
      (ii) In order to act within society, people internalise cultural norms and practices without subjecting these to rational scrutiny.
      (iii) The manner in which people make their own decisions will be affected by the context of the cultural norms in which they are operating.
   (c) Institutions matter to cultural theorists because institutional practices are the embodiment of cultural values and beliefs.
4. Structural Institutionalism
   (a) Major assumptions:
      (i) Institutional structures determine the content of people's interests and beliefs.
      (ii) Action on the social stage is primarily a reflection of the relationships between the functional parts of institutional structures.
      (iii) Different institutional structures are governed by different 'laws of motion'.
   b) American sociologist **Theda Skocpol** provided an account of the factors that

led to large-scale political upheavals in France, Russia, and China. According to her, the revolutions that occurred in these societies were essentially revolutions 'without revolutionaries'. They were instead caused by structural conditions, such as the existence of strong community structures among peasants.

2

COLONIALISM AND DECOLONISATION

KEY CONCEPTS

Neo-colonialism; anti-colonial struggle; decolonisation

Colonialism is the policy or practice of acquiring full or partial political control over another country, occupying it with settlers, and exploiting it economically. It occurs when one nation subjugates another, conquering its population and exploiting it, often while forcing its own language and cultural values upon its people. The origins of the world can be traced back to the Latin word 'colonia', which means a place for agriculture. In modern times, the definition relates to 'a policy and practice of a power in extending control over weaker peoples or areas'.

Imperialism originated in the Latin term 'imperium', which means supreme power, 'sovereignty', or simply 'rule'. The dictionary definition of the word is: 'a policy of extending a country's power and influence through colonisation, use of military force, or other means'.

In his book *Imperialism* (2016), political scientist **J. A. Hobson** said that imperialism was an economic, political, and cultural practice common to nations with a capitalist economic system. However, he was critical of Western, specifically British, imperialism around the world. According to Hobson, colonialism is the process whereby a nation-state 'overflow(s) its natural banks and absorb(s) the near or distant territory of reluctant and unassimilable peoples'; its test lies in the power of colonies to transplant civilisations.

According to Professor **Manoranjan Mohanty**, colonialism refers to the historical process wherein an alien minority asserts racial and cultural superiority over another culture and territory, deemed inferior and/or economically weaker than itself.

FEATURES OF COLONIALISM

Hamza Alavi pointed out the following features of colonialism:

1. Integration and enmeshing of the colony with the world capitalist system in a subordinate position.
2. Hegemony of the capitalist nation due to unequal exchange between the coloniser and the colonised.
3. Drain of wealth (from the colonised nations).
4. Political domination (of the colonised nation by the colonising state).

NEO-COLONIALISM

In 1965, **Kwame Nkrumah**, who became Ghana's first president, coined the word neo-colonialism to describe the influence of the former imperial nations on the ex-colonies in the areas of economy, language, culture, and political philosophy. In his influential and radical book, *Neo-Colonialism: The*

Last Stage of Imperialism (1965), Nkrumah stated:

> I propose to analyse neo-colonialism, first, by examining the state of the African continent and showing how neo-colonialism at the moment keeps it artificially poor.... I propose to examine neo-colonialism generally, first historically and then by a consideration of the great international monopolies whose continued stranglehold on the neo-colonial sectors of the world ensures the continuation of the system. (ibid., xx)

The term 'neo-colonialism' came into use in the 1960s at a time when former European colonies in Africa were gaining their independence. It describes a continuing relationship between Western countries and former colonies that is said to offer the Western world many of the advantages of colonial rule without many of the costs.

Tanzanian anti-colonial activist and political **Julius Nyerere** proposed a concept of African socialism to combat neo-colonialism. Termed *Ujamaa* ('fraternity' in Swahili), this was a socialist ideology that formed the basis of Nyerere's social and economic development policies in Tanzania after it gained independence from Britain in 1961. This concept is based on three major tenets:

1. Work by everyone and exploitation by none
2. Equitable distribution of resources which are produced jointly
3. Equality and respect for human dignity.

ANTI-COLONIAL STRUGGLES

As a historical event, anti-colonialism refers to the struggle against imperial rule in colonised countries, mostly during the first half of the twentieth century. The end of World War II had sparked a multitude of anti-colonial movements, aimed at achieving self-determination. Anti-colonial movements such as the Indian nationalist movement led by the Indian National Congress, the movement led by the Association of Vietnamese Revolutionary Youth, and the United Gold Coast Convention took form in individual colonies.

British historian **Geoffrey Barraclough** has pointed out that there is no distinction between independence movements and liberation movements. These movements go through three distinct phases:

1. Proto-nationalism: When people demand reform in the colonial system
2. Rise of a new leadership
3. Mass movement.

THE UNITED NATIONS AND DECOLONISATION

Article 73 of the UN Charter states:

> Members of the United Nations which have or assume responsibilities for the administration of territories whose peoples have not yet attained a full measure of self-government recognize the principle that the interests of the inhabitants of these territories are paramount, and accept as a sacred trust the obligation to promote to the utmost, ... and, to this end:
>
> a. to ensure, with due respect for the culture of the peoples concerned, their political, economic, social, and educational advancement, their just treatment, and their protection against abuses;
>
> b. to develop self-government, to take due account of the political aspirations of the peoples, and to assist them in the progressive development of their free political institutions, according to the particular circumstances of each territory and its peoples and their varying stages of advancement; ....

The UNO adopted a declaration aimed at helping colonised nations and their people gain independence. Resolution 1514 (XV) proclaims the necessity of bringing colonialism in all its forms and manifestations to a speedy and unconditional end and declares that all people have a right to self-determination. The General Assembly set up a special committee on decolonisation in 1961. Termed The United Nations Special Committee on the Situation with Regard to the Implementation of the Declaration on the Granting of Independence to Colonial Countries and Peoples, or the Special Committee on Decolonization (C-24), it is exclusively devoted to the cause of decolonisation. The Committee originally comprised seventeen members, which was expanded to twenty-four. In 1962, India was elected as the first chair of the Decolonization Committee (Committee of 24).

3

NATIONALISM

KEY CONCEPTS

Defining nationalism; political community; social community; types of nationalism

The origins of the term 'nationalism' can be traced back to the Latin word *natio*, or 'something born', which was used by Romans to refer to a community of foreigners. It is commonly believed that in its modern sense of 'love for a particular nation', the term 'nationalism' was first used in the year 1798. The modern-day definition of nationalism is given as: 'identification with one's own nation and support for its interests, especially to the exclusion or detriment of the interests of other nations.'

'Nation' is defined as 'a large body of people united by common descent, history, culture, or language, inhabiting a particular country or territory'. The three major aspects that make up a nation are:

1. Sovereignty
2. Self-determination
3. Self-sufficiency.

A nation can be seen as comprising of two elements:

1. Objective: Language, race religion.
2. Subjective: Psychological, attachment, sentiment.

As an ideology, nationalism believes that **collective identity** is of greater importance than individual identity. It is based on the premise that the individual's loyalty and devotion to the nation-state surpass other individual or group interests. While the term 'nation' refers to a psychological attachment, 'state' refers to an administrative system. Government is a manifestation of the state. Without a state, a nation cannot survive. Translated into world politics, nationalism implies the identification of the state or nation with the people. There are broadly three types of nationalism:

1. Ethnic nationalism
2. Cultural nationalism
3. Civic nationalism

NATION AS POLITICAL COMMUNITY

One of the most significant nationalist thinkers is the Enlightenment philosopher **Jean-Jacques Rousseau**. He believed that nationalism was a vehicle for freedom and equality, realising the essence of humanity, and providing for government legitimacy. In *Nations and Nationalism since 1780* (1992), historian **Eric Hobsbawm** launched an enquiry into the question of nationalism. While stating that a nation is an invented tradition—for him, 'nation' is a changing, evolving, modern construct that is brought into being by nationalism, and not the other way around—he shows that events in the late twentieth century in Eastern Europe and the Soviet republics have only reinforced the central importance of nationalism in the history of the political evolution of the world.

In his influential work *Imagined Communities: Reflections on the Origin and Spread of Nationalism* (1983), **Benedict Anderson** coined the concept of nation as an 'imagined community'. He depicted a nation as a socially-constructed community, imagined by the people who perceive themselves as part of a group. Nationalism is universal, in that every individual belongs to a nation, yet each nation is supposedly completely distinct from every other nation. Anderson regarded national belonging as a central but underappreciated factor in the development of the state. He criticised both liberalism and Marxism for failing to account for the deep attachment that people have to their nations and for the profound historical impact that nationalism has had since the late eighteenth century.

Indian postcolonialist theorist **Partha Chatterjee** has discussed nationalism in general, and Indian nationalism in particular, in several of his books, including *Nationalist Thought and Colonial World: A Derivative Discourse* (1986). Stating that European colonialism had limited the imagination of the political community in Asia and Africa, he concludes that nationalism should be viewed as an ideology and not as a phenomenon. The most vocal critic of Benedict Anderson's thesis on nationalism, Chatterjee rejected Anderson's representation of nationalism as the creation of European pioneers and argued that nationalism was an ideology imposed by the colonising powers, such that 'even our imaginations must forever remain colonised'.

German historian **Friedrich Meinecke** made a distinction between 'cultural nation' and 'political nation'. His 1908 work, *Weltbürgertum und Nationalstaat* (*Cosmopolitanism and the National State*), traced the development of national feelings in the nineteenth century, and much of his work concerns the conflict between *Kratos* (power) and *Ethos* (morality) and how to achieve a balance between them.

Nationalism, to a large extent owes its existence to the presence of a common constitution; as the state and constitution are artificial institutions, it therefore means that nationalism, too, is an artificial construct. **Liberal nationalism** adheres to the values of freedom and equality. It is propagated by political philosophers who believe that there can be a non-xenophobic form of nationalism that is compatible with the liberal values of freedom, tolerance, equality, and individual rights. Nationalism and **Marxism**, however, are philosophically incompatible. Marxism identifies the nation as a socio-economic construction created after the collapse of the feudal system, which was then utilised to create the capitalist economic system. Karl Marx believed that nationalism was a temporary and unnatural phenomenon, and classical Marxists have claimed that nationalism is a bourgeois phenomenon.

NATION AS A CULTURAL COMMUNITY

Nationalism is not the creation of any individual, and hence, it cannot be seen as artificial. Rather, nationalism can even be considered a mystical and spiritual concept. German philosopher **Johann Gottfried Herder** propounded the concept of 'cultural nationalism' (*volksgeist*, or the unique spirit and character of a nation and its people), in which the nation is defined by a shared culture and a common language, rather than on the concepts of common ancestry or race. For **Ernest Gellner**, nationalism is the imposition of a high culture on society, replacing local, low cultures, and most multiculturalism. **Anthony Smith** stated that there is no link between modernisation and nationalism in his *The Ethnic Origins of Nations* (1986), and defined nationalism as 'an ideological movement for attaining and maintaining autonomy, unity and identity on behalf of a population deemed by some of its members to constitute an actual or potential "nation"'.

VARIETIES OF NATIONALISM

1. **Liberal Nationalism:** This combined liberal policies and issues with elements of nationalism. Liberal Nationalism stood for individual freedom, equality before the law, representative government, the constitution, as well as the inviolability of private property. Also known as 'civic nationalism', this theory developed in Europe around the eighteenth century. In the US, President Woodrow Wilson supported the principle of self-determination, which became the foundation of nationalism after World War I.
2. **Conservative Nationalism:** This is a nationalist variant of conservatism that concentrates on upholding national and cultural identity. National conservatives usually combine nationalism with conservative stances that promote traditional cultural values, family values, and opposition to immigration. **Disraeli** and **Enoch Powell** spoke in favour of conservative nationalism.
3. **Ultra-Nationalism:** An extreme form of nationalism, in this variant a country asserts or maintains detrimental hegemony, supremacy, or other forms of control over other nations (usually through violent coercion) to pursue its specific interests. The ideology of fascism owes allegiance to ultra-nationalism. A belief in the supremacy of one nation over another paves the way for the policies of expansionism and imperialism.
4. **Non-European or Anti-colonial Nationalism:** Nationalism in Asian and African nations emerged in movements against colonial and imperial exploitation, and their common historical suffering became a binding force against European imperialism. This form of nationalism seeks to reject the rule of colonial powers and gain independence, and refers to the first time that a group of people who had previously been treated as not part of a nation began to see themselves as equal members of a community.

In his classic text *The Breakup of Britain: Crisis and Neo-nationalism* (1977), Tom Nairn explains how nationalism emerges in colonial societies through his depiction of the 'slow foundering' of the United Kingdom, its fall from empire, and the gathering force of civic nationalism.

4

THEORIES OF STATE

KEY CONCEPTS

Features of the state; Weberian concept of state; government versus state; origin of the state; roles of the state; globalisation; developing nations; state and revolution; managerial theory of state; postcolonial state

Lasting from 1618–1648, the **Thirty Years War** was one of the longest and most destructive conflicts in European history. It aimed to establish freedom of religion, which seemed at times to be at stake. The leading cause was Emperor Ferdinand forcing Catholicism throughout the region, which made Protestants fear losing their rights to worship. It reached its climax with the Protestant Reformation after 1635, and pitted Protestant Sweden, Catholic France, and Germany's Protestant Princes against Catholic Hapsburg Austria, German Catholic Princes, and, towards the end, Catholic Spain.

The **Treaty of Westphalia**, signed in 1648, brought an end to the Thirty Years War. It was signed between the Holy Roman Emperor and the King of France and their respective allies. The Treaty recognised the sovereignty of the German Princes, and the scattered European States acquired territorial sovereignty. It laid the foundation for the formation of the modern State. The four main aspects of the Treaty of Westphalia are:

1. National self-determination;
2. Precedent for ending wars through diplomatic congresses;
3. Peaceful coexistence among sovereign states as the norm;
4. Maintained by a balance of power among sovereign states and acceptance of the principle of non-interference in the internal affairs of other sovereign states.

THE STATE

Core Features of the State

1. A State entails a territory that it considers its own.
2. A State entails a people. However, the numbers (that is, size of the population) are irrelevant.
3. A state is sovereign, that is, it holds the highest power and, in principle, can act with full freedom and independence. Sovereignty is the claim to the highest authority and power.

German sociologist **Max Weber** has studied the notion of sovereignty in States. He defined the State as a 'human community that (successfully) claims the monopoly of the legitimate use of physical force within a given territory'. This force had to be deployed in order for the State to exercise control and ensure obedience to its rules; only then could it qualify as the highest form of community. However, Weber asserted that this monopoly over the use of force should also be accompanied by legitimacy.

Weberian Conception of State

According to Max Weber:

1. A State possesses territory, people, and sovereignty.
2. This sovereignty can be explained by making a distinction between 'legal' and 'legitimate'. The use of physical force cannot just be based on legality or law; it should also be accepted as right or morally legitimate by citizens.
3. The use of physical force alone, however, cannot be the distinguishing factor between the State and other organisations.
4. Weber emphasises that some actor or institution should monopolise the legitimate use of physical force in order to prevent anarchy or lawlessness. This actor is the government.

DIFFERENCES BETWEEN GOVERNMENT AND STATE

1. The State is more extensive than government. It includes all institutions in the public domain and embraces all citizens who are part of the State community. Government is a part of the State.
2. The State is a continuing, permanent entity. A government is temporary.
3. Government is the means through which the authority of the State is brought under operation. It perpetuates the State's existence.
4. The State exercises an impersonal authority. The personnel of State bodies is recruited in a bureaucratic manner to ensure that they remain politically neutral, enabling State institutions to resist the ideological persuasions of the government.
5. The State represents the permanent interests of society or the general will.

According to the liberal ideology, the State is an artificial institution created to ensure the security of the people. The liberal theory of the functions, role, and nature of State power focuses on:

1. Ensuring, protecting, and enlarging individual freedom.
2. Limiting the role and functions of the State.
3. Allowing State interference only in circumstances where it leads to greater liberty and freedom for individuals.
4. Making individuals the source of State power.
5. Advocating a doctrine of limited political obligations.

Neoliberalism refers to market-oriented reform policies such as 'eliminating price controls, deregulating capital markets, lowering trade barriers', and reducing, especially through privatisation and austerity, State influence in the economy. Neoliberals believe in the concept of a *minimal State*. Swedish sociologist **Goran Therborn** stated that there are four instrument of State:

1. Instrument of government: the Executive and the Legislature.
2. Judiciary
3. Administrative
4. Coercive: the police and armed forces.

Norwegian political scientist **Stein Rokkan's** theory of nation-building is a significant liberal theory of State within comparative political analysis.

According to Rokkan, there are **four stages** in the development of the modern nation-state. The first two occur when political elites aim to consolidate their power and territorial independence. These four stages in nation-building are:

1. **State formation (Penetration).** It is the elites in society who initiated the unification of a given territory. Usually, elites groups in urban centres consolidated control over both the peripheral and urban areas. This was done through economic and military means.

   To exercise control and ensure compliance, institutions were created to provide order and see to the resolution of disputes (such as the police and courts), to provide external security (the army and diplomatic services), to extract resources (taxes and tolls), and to improve communications (roads and bridges).

2. **Nation-building (Standardisation).** The main concerns related to cultural issues such as a common language, religious differences, and compulsory education, and the focus was on creating a common identity and a common political allegiance.

   A common language was used to spread a standardised, compulsory education. Military conscription was used to strengthen the spirit of nationalism, and symbols such as the national flag, national anthem, etc., were emphasised to highlight a common history and common destiny.

3. **Mass Democracies (Equalisation).** The masses conquered the right to political decision-making, leading to the emergence of mass democracies. Political parties emerged to link citizens with the elites in Assemblies and Parliaments. Peaceful opposition to government was recognised as legitimate, as was a peaceful change in both parties and government. The introduction of universal adult franchise (UAF) came into being.

4. **Welfare States (Redistribution).** These States endorsed policies to strengthen economic solidarity between different segments of the population, and supported the creation of public welfare services for the marginalised. Progressive taxation and State contributions facilitated the transfer of resources from the wealthy to the less fortunate sections of the population. Welfare States are characterised by redistribution and equality of opportunity.

THEORETICAL APPROACHES TO THE ORIGIN OF THE STATE

1. Constitutional approach:
   (a) This approach emphasises the fact that the State is established through a contract between the citizens and the government, which defines the major functions of the State and the powers of the rulers. Social contract theory is an example.
   (b) Theories that follow this approach are concerned with the question of how the legitimacy of the State is established.
2. Ethical and moral approaches:
   (a) Here, the concern is with the ideal organisation of societies, so that individuals can live together as peacefully as possible.
   (b) Some take the view that individuals should have as much liberty as possible. Others view society as a collective entity concerned with the collective welfare of its citizens. Religious theorists believe that the State should establish the rule of God on Earth.
3. Conflict approaches:
   (a) These theories emphasise the conflictual nature of society and view the State as instrumental in resolving such conflicts. The **Marxist theory** is an example of this approach.
   (b) **Feminists** argue that States are established by men to control women, and that they should now become the battleground for women's liberation.

4. Pluralist approaches:
   (a) These approaches view the State as the main instrument for the resolution of conflicts and reconciliation of competing interests.
   (b) However, they do not view the State as an instrument of the dominant class and, unlike Marxists or feminists, see the State as a kind of referee, who uses its legitimate authority to ensure that all the interests of competing groups are treated fairly.
   (c) Thinkers within this tradition have also examined the grounds of political obligation.
5. Leviathan State:
   (a) This idea is associated with the **New Right Theory.** It is rooted in classical liberalism and in a radical commitment to individualism, which views the State as a self-serving monster intent on self-expansion and aggrandisement.
   (b) There is strong antipathy towards State intervention in economic and social life, and the State is viewed as a threat to individual liberty and economic security.

ROLES OF THE STATE

1. **Minimal State**
   (a) This conceptualisation has its origins in the ideas of the classical liberals, who aim for maximum individual freedom. It advances a negative view of the State and is rooted in social contract theory (which believes that people live together in society in accordance with an agreement that establishes moral and political rules of behaviour).
   (b) The State is only seen as instrumental in providing security and ensuring law and order, which in turn ensures that individuals do not encroach upon the liberties of others.
   (c) The minimal State exists to maintain domestic order and ensure that citizens do not break the contracts made with others in society.
   (d) Economic, social, cultural, and other responsibilities belong to the individual, and are a part of civil society. The New Right has proclaimed the need to 'roll back the frontiers of the state'.
2. **Developmental State**
   (a) This was a term coined by American political scientist Chalmers Johnson. Theorists in this tradition, who are mostly international political economy scholars, propound linkages between industrialisation and the development of the State.
   (b) This term is used to describe States which follow a particular model of economic planning and management. It was initially used to describe post-1945 Japan and its rapid modernisation and growth. The theorists stipulate that the later a country industrialises, the greater would be the State's economic role.
   (c) In both **Japan and Germany**, for instance, the State assumed a more 'developmental' role.
   (d) A developmental State intervenes in economic life to promote industrial development and economic growth.
   (e) This, however, does not amount to a socialist State; rather, it means that the State establishes a partnership with major economic interests due to its conservative and nationalist priorities.
3. **Social Democratic States**
   (a) The social democratic State belongs to one of the many socialist traditions. This State intervenes in society to bring

about broader social restructuring in accordance with the principles of fairness, social equality, and social justice.

(b) In countries like **Austria and Sweden**, for instance, the State has been guided by both developmental and social-democratic priorities.

(c) This marks a shift from the negative definition of the State, which views it as a necessary evil, towards a more positive view that sees the State as a means of enlarging liberty and social justice.

(d) The twin features of social democratic States are *Keynesianism* and *social welfare.* A social welfare system offers assistance to individuals and families in need, with such programmes as healthcare assistance, food stamps, and unemployment compensation.

(e) Keynesian economics aims to regulate capitalism in order to promote growth and to achieve full employment, which is possible through government planning and demand management through adjustments in fiscal policies, that is, in the levels of public spending and taxation. Keynesians believe that, because prices are somewhat rigid, fluctuations in any component of spending—consumption, investment, or government expenditures—cause output to change. If government spending increases, for example, and all other spending components remain constant, then the output will increase.

(f) This State is also an enabling entity, and is dedicated to individual empowerment.

4. **Collectivised States**

(a) These states are characterised by the principle of ownership by the State or the people of the means of production. They subscribe to the socialistic doctrine of ownership by the people collectively, and bring the entirety of economic life under State control. An important example is the former State of **USSR.**

(b) These States seek to abolish private enterprises altogether, establishing a centralised planned economy referred to as command economies.

(c) Their justification emanates from the socialist preference for collective ownership of private property.

(d) However, against popular expectations, the collectivised State in the USSR became permanent, and increasingly powerful and bureaucratic.

(e) Under **Premier Joseph Stalin**, socialism was effectively equated with statism.

5. **Totalitarian States**

(a) Totalitarianism is a form of government and a political system that outlaws all individual and group opposition to the State and its claims and exercises an extremely high, if not complete, degree of control and regulation over public and private life. The essence of totalitarianism is the creation of an all-embracing State that penetrates every aspect of human existence.

(b) It brings not only economy, but also education, culture, religion, and family life under State control. Examples are **Hitler's Germany, Stalin's USSR,** and **Saddam Hussein's Iraq.**

(c) Features of totalitarian States include the institution of a comprehensive process of surveillance and terroristic policing, and a pervasive system of ideological manipulation and control.

(d) These States eliminate civil society and the private sphere of life altogether.

(e) It is argued that Mussolini's notion of a totalitarian State was derived from the Hegelian notion of State as an 'ethical community', reflecting the altruism and mutual sympathy of its members.

STATE AND GLOBALISATION

States all over the world are influenced by globalisation. However, various conflicting perspectives exist on the dimensions and level of this influence. There are three major perspectives that predominate in our understanding of the impact of globalisation on the State. These are:

1. **Hyper-globalists**

   Hyper-globalists believe that we are living in a truly globalised world, that is, that all activities are in some way linked to globalisation. Our civilisation rests on a global economy and on global government institutions (such as the World Bank, the International Monetary Fund, and the United Nations). Japanese organisational therorist **Kenichi Ohmae** believed that the world is increasingly becoming borderless. Hyper-globalists believe that globalisation, which has grown ever more powerful and pervasive, signifies a new epoch in human history. It has replaced the State as a preeminent actor on the world stage.

   The market has also become a dominant force. According to **Daniel Yergin and Joseph Stanislaw**, the nation-state has lost its commanding heights to the market, and this is what marks the great difference between the twentieth and twenty-first centuries. In their *The Commanding Heights: The Battle for the World Economy* (2002), they state that across the globe, it has become an increasingly accepted dogma that economic activities should be dominated by market forces, and not by political concerns.

   While the importance of the nation-state has declined, this does not, however, mean either the end of the State or the end of the era of government.

2. **Skeptics**

   Paul Hirst and **Grahame Thomson**, in their *Globalization in Question: The International Economy and the Possibilities of Governance* (1996) do not agree with the globalist thesis and present five criticisms of the globalisation hypothesis:

   (a) This thesis does not provide a coherent concept of the world economy in which supranational forces and agents are decisive.

   (b) Pointing to evidence of the enhanced internationalisation of economic relationships since the 1970s is not in itself proof of the emergence of a distinctly *global* economic structure.

   (c) The international economy has been subject to major structural changes in the last century, and there have also been earlier periods of internationalisation of trade, capital flows, and the monetary system, especially from 1870–1914.

   (d) There are very few truly global transnational corporations (TNCs). Most so-called TNCs are really only multinational corporations that continue to operate from distinct national bases.

   (e) The prospects for regulation by international cooperation, the formation of trading blocs, and the development of new national strategies that take account of internationalisation are by no means exhausted.

Sceptics also believe that the State has reasserted itself in recent years and has become important as a key player on the world stage. Rapid technological development has resulted in the State acquiring greater insights into the lives of its citizens, which has enabled it to become more powerful and all-pervasive than earlier.

3. **Transformationlists**

Globalisation is a complex and controversial phenomenon, characteristic of today's society and highly influential in the lives of all the world's citizens. According to **Peter Dicken,** globalisation represents a more advanced and complex form of internationalisation that implies a degree of functional integration between internationally dispersed economic activities. Dicken and Held also said that the relation between globalisation and the State is a complex one. Sociologist **Ronald Robertson** recognised globalisation 'as a concept that refers both to the compression of the world and the intensification of consciousness of the world as a whole'. He stated that the rising global consciousness proves that we are living in a wider community. According to **Anthony Giddens,** while the role of the State has changed, it will not be diminished.

Transformationalists assert that the role of the State has neither been enhanced nor has it reduced due to globalisation. It has, in fact, *transformed.* They insist that sovereignty, which was earlier based on territory, is now more economic in nature. The role of regional economic organisations has become very important in this context.

In *The Retreat of the State: The Diffusion of Power in the World Economy* (1996), **Susan Strange** said that in the age of globalisation, the role of the State is changed. It is not only governments who are in charge of the world economy; big businesses, drug barons, and accountants, all encroach on the so-called sovereignty of the State. A new idea has emerged—that of *shared sovereignty.*

States now are also plagued by internal crisis. The number of civil wars has increased in contemporary times, as compared to inter-State wars. This era has also been marked by the rise of right-wing authoritarian governments in powerful countries across the globe. For instance, the **Chinese President Xi Jinping** has removed constitutional limits on the number of terms he can serve as President, opening up the possibility of him becoming a 'President for Life'. The rapidly growing connectivity in the form of social media networks has also begun to threaten the sovereignty and legitimacy of the State.

STATES AND DEVELOPING COUNTRIES

Despite the 'triumph of liberal democracy' after the end of the Cold War, nation-states across the developing world have adopted different forms of government. **North Korea** and **Iran** have been regarded as rogue States by international organisations due to their continued breaching of international laws and agreements, especially those concerned with nuclear deterrence. Iran has sought to enforce a mixed regime, which combines elements of theocratic government with parliamentary democracy.

Elsewhere, **Afghanistan** has been seen as a 'failed State' due to the government's failure to enforce law and order in society. **Saudi Arabia** and the **UAE** have sought to combine elements of theocracy with monarchical forms. **Sunil Khilnani**, Professor of Politics and History, has asserted that India has emerged as an ideal of democratic government among the developing countries.

STATE AND REVOLUTION

In his classic study *Revolutionary Change* (1966), Chalmers Johnson said that revolution occurs due to multiple disfunctions. In *Why Men Rebel* (1970), **Ted Gurr** stated that relative deprivation is the root cause of revolutions. 'Relative deprivation' is a term that Gurr uses to denote the tension that develops from what one 'ought' to have and what one 'does' have, which can lead people to violence. Gurr asserts that the deprivation does not have to be real for a revolutionary situation to occur; it just has to be seen as real by enough people.

Political scientist **James Davies**, in his *When Men Revolt and Why* (1971), states that rising expectations are the basic reason behind revolutions. When institutions inhibit rather than facilitate everyone's desire to live a full life, the result is likely to be violence. Yet he also maintains that we remain ignorant of the elemental forces that impel people and nations to resort to violence. We need to learn more about how humans respond to change so as to prepare ourselves for such responses to change. **Theda Skocpol** compared the French Revolution, Russian Revolution, and the Chinese Revolution and suggested that social and structural factors are responsible for revolution.

CORPORATE MODEL AND MANAGERIAL THEORY OF STATE

Marxists are always of the opinion that the State is a class instrument. Contemporary Marxist. **Alan Wolfe** says that capitalism in USA manifested in six forms of the State:

1. Accumulating State: Laissez-faire.
2. Harmony State: Bourgeoisie accepted the right and welfare of the people.
3. Expansionist State. The State increased its power after World War I.
4. Franchise State: This is also known as polyarchy.
5. Dual State: Parliamentary government exists along with the armed forces and a bureaucracy.
6. Transition State: Where the State supports multinational corporations.

POSTCOLONIAL STATE

Gunner Myrdal had said that the State in South Asia, and particularly in India, is an example of a *soft State*, and pointed to the presence of widespread corruption in India. In *State Directed Development: Political Power and Industrialization in Global Periphery* (2004), **Atul Kohli** analysed India, Nigeria, Brazil, and South Korea. On the basis of this study, Kohli offered three ideal models of the state:

1. Cohesive-capitalist State (mainly in Korea)
2. Neo-Patrimonial State (mainly in Nigeria)
3. Fragmented multiclass State (mainly in India)

It is argued that cohesive-capitalist States have been most effective in promoting industrialisation and neo-patrimonial States the least effective. The performance of fragmented-multiclass States falls somewhere in the middle.

Victor Azary and **Naomi Chazan,** in their 'Disengagement from the State in Africa: Reflections on the Experience of Ghana and Guinea' (from the book *Africa,* 1998), investigate how individuals and groups in two African countries, Ghana and Guinea, have attempted to cope with the State by distancing themselves from it as a protection against its instability and declining performance. Four major mechanisms of disengagement from the state, containing different combinations of social, economic, religious, political, and cultural elements, may be discerned in these two countries.

5

POLITICAL REGIMES

KEY CONCEPTS

Democratic regimes; electoral system; liberal democracy; majoritarianism; participatory democracy; non-democratic regimes; authoritarianism

DEMOCRATIC

Democracy means 'rule by the people'. The word comes from the ancient Greek words '*demos*' (the people) and '*kratos*' (to rule). A democratic country has a system of government in which the people have the power to participate in decision-making. Each democracy is unique and works in different ways. The five characteristics of democracy are:

1. Elected Representatives
2. Civil Liberties
3. Organised Opposition Party
4. Independent Judiciary, and
5. Rule of Law.

Democratic governance is regarded as the most refined type of government because it reflects the desires and goals of its citizens in society.

American sociologist and political scientist **Seymour Martin Lipset** was one of the first proponents of the 'theory of modernisation', which states that democracy is the direct result of economic growth. A democracy is based on the rule of law, founded on a spirit of constitutionalism, and has respect for the rights and liberty of citizens.

ELECTORAL SYSTEM

Electoral democracy is the type of representative democracy that is based on elections, on the electoral vote, as can be seen in modern Occidental or Western liberal democracies. Electoral democracy can also guarantee to protect personal freedoms. However, it is interesting to note that merely holding elections is no indicator of democratic regimes, as several non-democratic governments also hold elections. Therefore, while elections are a necessary condition of democracy, they are not a sufficient to ensure a democratic system. Rather, it is *constitutionalism* that is the essence of democracy.

LIBERAL DEMOCRACY

Liberal democracy or Western democracy is the combination of a liberal political ideology that operates under a representative democratic form of government. Liberal democracy emphasises the separation of powers of the government, an independent judiciary, and a system of checks and balances between branches of government. Multi-party systems with at least two persistent, viable political parties are characteristic of liberal democracies.

A liberal democracy will have the following features:

1. A democratic government
2. Constitutionalism
3. Competitive party system
4. Freedom of choice
5. Respect for the rights of the minority groups in society.

MAJORITARIANISM

Majoritarianism is often referred to as majority rule, which may refer to a majority class ruling over a minority class. Majoritarianism is a political philosophy or ideology, with the agenda asserting that a majority based on a religion, language, social class, or any other category of the population is entitled to a certain degree of primacy in society, and has the right to make decisions that affect the entire society.

In a majoritarian society,

1. The rights of minorities are ignored.
2. The electoral majority becomes the constitutional majority.
3. The majority may suppress the constitutional majority.
4. The elected government often goes against democratic institutions.

PARTICIPATORY DEMOCRACY

Participatory democracy, participant democracy, or participative democracy is a form of government in which citizens participate individually and directly in political decisions and policies that affect their lives, rather than through elected representatives. Participatory democracy happens when individual citizens of a democracy participate in the formation of policies and laws through consistent engagement. In a participatory democracy:

1. Election is one technique of participation.
2. The government supports the *active participation* of the citizens.
3. This form is the opposite of both majoritarianism and electoral democracy.
4. Recall: If necessary, the representatives of the people can be called back before completion of their term.
5. Initiative: The people themselves can take the initiative to make the laws.
6. Reference: Greater emphasis on learning the opinion of the people over the law enacted by Parliament.

NON-DEMOCRATIC REGIMES

Patriamonialism

The term 'patrimonial' is derived from the French patrimonial, 'inherited from an ancestor or ancestors', and directly from the Late Latin 'patrimonialis', from the Latin 'patrimonium', 'inheritance from a father'. Patrimonialism is a form of governance in which all power flows directly from the ruler, who claims the realm as their personal property and enjoys absolute power. There is no distinction between the public and private domains. These regimes are autocratic or oligarchic and exclude the lower, middle and upper classes from power.

Authoritarianism

Authoritarianism is a political system characterised by the rejection of political plurality, the use of a strong central power to preserve the political status quo, and reductions in the rule of law, separation of powers, and democratic voting. Spanish sociologist **Juan Jose Linz** defines authoritarianism as follows:

1. Limited political pluralism.
2. Political legitimacy based upon an emotional appeal for development
3. Minimal political mobilisation.
4. No defined executive power.

According to political scientist **Adam Przeworski**, authoritarian equilibrium rests mainly on lies, fear, and economic prosperity. However, economic growth may also weaken the authoritarian regime by making the economy too complex to be run by command.

American legal scholar **Mark Tushnet** developed the idea of *authoritarian constitutionalism*, and made a distinction between authoritarian constitutionalism and liberal constitutionalism. Authoritarian constitutionalism is a new category used by constitutional law scholars to refer to a distinct type of regime wherein there are faulty practices and a constitution with an authoritarian content. Citing **Singapore** as an example of authoritarian constitutionalism, he said that this represents an intermediate normative model between liberal constitutionalism and authoritarianism that has a moderately strong commitment to constitutionalism.

Bureaucratic-Military Authoritarianism

Bureaucratic-military authoritarianism refers to regimes that are governed by a coalition of military officers and technocrats. Political scientist **Mark J. Gasiorowski** suggests that it is best to distinguish 'simple military authoritarian regimes' from 'bureaucratic authoritarian regimes', in which 'a powerful group of technocrats uses the state apparatus to try to rationalize and develop the economy'.

Brian Lai and **Dan Slater** identify *strongman rule* as a form of authoritarian rule characterised by autocratic dictatorships depending on military enforcement, as distinct from three other categories of authoritarian rule, specifically:

1. Machine (Oligarchic Party Dictatorship)
2. Bossism (Autocratic Party Dictatorship)
3. Junta (Military Dictatorship)

6

CONSTITUTION AND CONSTITUTIONALISM

KEY CONCEPTS

Constitution; rule of law; forms of constitution; crisis of constitutionalism; classification of government; features of parliamentary government; prime ministerial government; presidential government

CONSTITUTION

The word 'Constitution' refers to the basic principles and laws of a nation, State, or social group that determine the powers and duties of the government and guarantee certain rights to the people in it. It is a written instrument containing the fundamental rules of a political or social organisation.

The features of a Constitution are:

1. The Constitution is the supreme law of the land.
2. The Constitution explains the power of the legislature, executive, and judiciary.
3. The Constitution places limitations over the power of the State.

CONSTITUTIONALISM

While every nation has a Constitution, the mere presence of a Constitution is no guarantee of constitutionalism. Constitutionalism refers to the rule of law; it is 'a compound of ideas, attitudes, and patterns of behavior elaborating the principle that the authority of government derives from and is limited by a body of fundamental law'. The difference between Constitution and constitutionalism is that the Constitution is created by the government, but the government itself is controlled by constitutionalism, which sets limitations on its powers and authorities.

While even non-democratic governments might have a Constitution, constitutionalism exists only in democratic nations. Opposed to the rule of men, constitutionalism means a limited government. Separation of power is essential for limiting the power of the State. Constitutionalism places restrictions over State power, and favours individual liberty and rights.

RULE OF LAW

Rule of law implies that every citizen is subject to the law. It stands in contrast to the idea that the ruler is above the law, for example by divine right. The rule of law is the political philosophy which states that all citizens and institutions within a country, State, or community are accountable to the same laws, including lawmakers and leaders. The three major elements of the rule of law are:

1. Supremacy of the law
2. Equality before the law

3. Predominance of the legal spirit, that is, the courts should be free from impartiality and external influence.

FORMS OF CONSTITUTION

A Constitution may either be unwritten, such as that in **Britain**, or may be written, like those of the **USA** and **India**. A Constitution may be both democratic and authoritarian in nature.

Table 4.6.1: Differences between Written and Unwritten Constitutions

Written Constitution	*Unwritten Constitution*
A written Constitution is one that is codified and written in a single document.	An unwritten Constitution is devoid of laws or provisions that are set in writing. However, it is documented, despite not being incorporated in a single book.
It is generally a feature of federal states.	It is generally a feature of unitary states.
In nations with a written Constitution, the Constitution is supreme.	In nations with an unwritten Constitution, Parliament is supreme.
Framed and compiled in a structured, step-by-step manner.	Evolves over a long period of time, with a new set of laws and guidelines being added as time progresses.
To ensure constitutional supremacy, the judiciary has more powers.	The judiciary has limited powers.
Examples: USA, India, France, Denmark, Australia, Japan	Examples: Britain, Israel, Saudi Arabia, New Zealand, Canada

CRISIS OF CONSTITUTIONALISM

In Political Science, a constitutional crisis is a problem or conflict in the function of a government that the political Constitution or other fundamental governing law is unable to resolve. A constitutional crisis takes place when:

1. Majoritarianism, or rule of the majority, places in jeopardy the supremacy of rule of law.
2. The spirit of the Constitution is violated in the name of electoral democracy.
3. Institutions become all-powerful and suppress the liberty and rights of the people.
4. Emergency provisions become a threat to constitutionalism.
5. The rise of great economic disparity also poses a challenge to constitutionalism.
6. Finally, the rise of authoritarian leadership directly harms the functioning of a constitutional order.

In the name of will of the people and mass mobilisation, rule of law is suppressed.

UNITARY AND FEDERAL GOVERNMENT

A government may be classified as either unitary or federal on the basis of the relationship between the Centre and the various units of State.

Table 4.6.2: Differences between a Unitary and a Federal Government

Unitary Government	*Federal Government*
Single government	Dual government (Centre and states)
Concentration of power in a single locus, that is, the Centre	Division of power between the Centre and the units.
The presence of either a written or unwritten Constitution	There is always a written Constitution
The Constitution can be either rigid or flexible	The Constitution is rigid.
Judiciary may or may not be independent	Independent judiciary
Constitution may or may not be supreme	The supremacy of the Constitution is a given
Legislature may be bicameral or unicameral	Bicameral legislature
Examples: France, Britain, Japan, China, Italy, Spain, Saudi Arabia, Sweden, and Norway.	Example: USA, India, Pakistan, Brazil, Switzerland, Australia, Canada, Russia

PARLIAMENTARY FORM OF GOVERNMENT

A democratic form of government can be classified into either a parliamentary or a presidential form of government. The Indian parliamentary system is derived from the British parliamentary system. Therefore, like the British Parliament, the Indian Parliament, too, comprises two houses. In Britain they are referred to as the House of Commons and the House of Lords, whereas in India, we call it the Lower House (Lok Sabha) and the Upper House (Rajya Sabha). As per Article 79 of the Constitution, the Parliament comprises the President, the Lok Sabha, and the Rajya Sabha.

A government has three organs: the **legislature**, the **executive,** and the **judiciary**. These organs derive their power from the Parliament. Thus, Parliament occupies a central position. Together, the Rajya Sabha and the Lok Sabha constitute the legislature. All the executive power is vested in the President; thus, Parliament combines within itself the legislature and the executive. This fusion is a significant feature of the parliamentary form of government.

Features of the Parliamentary Form of Government

1. **Responsibility of the executive.**
   The Lok Sabha is entitled to pass a no-confidence motion against the Council of Ministers (Article 75 [3]). The Executive or the Council of Ministers (CoM) does not enjoy the privilege of a fixed term, but continues in office for as long as it has the confidence of the Lok Sabha. For instance, the Atal Bihari Vajpayee government lasted only for thirteen days in 1996 because it did not have the confidence of the Lok Sabha.
2. **Cabinet Rule**
   The Parliamentary form of government is also known as a Cabinet government. This is because every decision is taken collectively by the cabinet of ministers. The Cabinet is headed by the Prime Minister.
3. **Collective responsibility**
   The Lok Sabha can pass a no-confidence motion against the entire Council of Ministers. Collectively they swim, collectively they sink—this is a well-known principle of parliamentary government. The complete Council of Ministers will defend the action of each minister, in instances where a particular minister fails to get through the demand for grants in the Lok Sabha, the Council of Ministers is expected to resign.
4. **Individual Responsibility**
   A minister shall hold office as per the pleasure of the President (Article 75 [2]). Thus, an individual minister is responsible to the President. In practice, ministers are responsible to the Parliament in general, and to the Lok Sabha in particular. The Prime Minister is also free to reshuffle his Cabinet when the need arises.
5. **Prime Position of the PM**
   The Prime Minister (PM) is considered the first among equals, often described by British constitutional experts as *primus inter pares* (the senior or representative member of the group, or first among equals). The PM heads the Cabinet meeting and decides the agenda; it is the PM who allocates the portfolios amongst ministers. However, the number of ministers has been limited to a maximum cap of 15 per cent as per the 91st Constitutional Amendment. The Prime Minister can reserve any ministry for himself, and any ministry that is not allocated to a minister shall remain in the control of the PM. As per the age-old parliamentary convention, The Ministry of Personnel, Public Grievances and Pension is headed

by the PM her/himself. S/he also heads the Department of Atomic Energy and Ocean Development.

6. **Nominal and Real Executive**

   The President is the nominal executive (*de jure*), whereas the Prime Minister is the real executive (*de facto*). All decisions are made in the name of the President; however, these decisions are exercised by the Prime Minister. The President shall appoint the Prime Minister, as per Article 75 (1).

7. **Fusion of Power**

   The Executive, or Council of Ministers, is drawn from the Parliament. Therefore, nobody can become a minister without first being a Member of Parliament (MP), except in a case where s/he acquires membership of the House within a time period of six months from the date of her/his appointment, failing which s/he ceases to be a minister.

PRIME MINISTERIAL GOVERNMENT

British lawyer and constitutional expert Sir Ivor Jennings has termed the parliamentary system the Cabinet System. In essence a cabinet system refers to a prime ministerial form of government. However, in India, neither parliamentary government nor prime ministerial government is mentioned in the Constitution. Features of the parliamentary form of government do exist in the Constitution, and the prime ministerial form of government is the practical form of parliamentary government, and denotes the following features.

1. **Prime Minister is the Nucleus of Power**

   Although all the executive decisions are taken in the name of the President, the real power is vested in the Prime Minister. Since the PM heads the Cabinet, all the executive decisions are exercised by her/him. The position of Prime Minister became even more pronounced in the 1970s, particularly during the tenure of Indira Gandhi (1966–1977; and again from 1980 till her assassination in 1984). In the late 1980s, during the tenure of Rajiv Gandhi (Prime Minister of India, 1984–1989), the Prime Minister's Office (PMO) was given primacy over the Cabinet Secretariat, and therefore the PMO became the periphery of power.

2. **Formation of Cabinet**

   The President appoints the ministers based on the recommendation of the Prime Minister. However, the allocation of portfolios is done by the Prime Minister, and ministers are chosen from both Houses of Parliament. There are four categories of ministers: the Union Cabinet Minister; Minister of State (MoS); Union Minister (Independent charge); and Deputy Minister. Together, the four categories are collectively known as the Council of Ministers. A Cabinet is the subset of the Council of Ministers as it consists of the Prime Minister and Union Cabinet Ministers alone.

3. **Election of PM**

   The Prime Minister is usually the leader of the majority party in the Lok Sabha. However, s/he may also be from the Rajya Sabha (as was the case with Dr Manmohan Singh, the thirteenth Prime Minister of India, from 2004–2014). The majority party chooses the leader of the House.

4. **Increasing Importance of the PMO**

   The Cabinet Secretariat plays a vital role in the parliamentary form of government, and maintains coordination between various ministries. As mentioned in point 1, the Prime Minister's Office has now virtually overshadowed the Cabinet Secretariat. The Principal Secretary to the PM is now more powerful than the Cabinet Secretary.

PRESIDENTIAL FORM OF GOVERNMENT

The presidential system is defined by the separation of the executive branch from other aspects of government. The head of government is elected to work alongside, but not as a part of, the legislature. The various features of this form of government are:

1. **President Occupies a Central Role**

   The President is elected directly by the people, and is thus responsible towards them. The President is the head of the Executive. Ministers are subordinate to the President, and the President can appoint anyone as minister and also fire a minister at any given time. The President also chairs the Cabinet meetings.

2. **Separation of Power**

   The United States of America is a classic model of the presidential form of government. The ministers are not part of Parliament, which is known as the Congress in the USA. Parliament cannot pass a no-confidence motion against the ministers, and the President cannot dissolve the Parliament either. Elections for the post of President is held every four years. However, elections for Congress are held separately, and their tenure is also separate from that of the President.

3. **Single Executive**

   The President is both the constitutional head and the administrative head. All power is vested in the President, with ministers being dependent on the President for their power. All decisions and policies are also taken by the president. The various ministers work according to the instructions given by the President.

4. **Fixed Term**

   A stable government is a unique feature of the presidential system. Due to the separation of power, Parliament cannot bring a no-confidence motion against the President. The presidential term is fixed for fours years and midterm elections are not held in the USA.

5. **Importance of Specialists**

   The President is choose his own ministers. In the USA, the Heads of Dpartments of State are appointed by the President and confirmed by the Senate. They are members of the Cabinet, and acting department heads also participate in Cabinet meetings, regardless of whether they have been officially nominated for Senate confirmation. The members of the Cabinet are often the closest confidants of the President.

Table 4.6.3: Comparison between Parliamentary and Presidential Forms of Government

	Parliamentary Government	*Presidential Government*
1.	President is the constitutional head	President is both the constitutional and administrative head
2.	There is collective responsibility between ministers in a government	No collective responsibility exists
3.	PM is administrative head or real head	No place for the office of the PM
4.	There is a Cabinet government, which takes all the decisions	President takes the decision, rather than the Cabinet
5.	Power lies in a group of ministers, for instance, the Cabinet	Power vests in the President
6.	Day-to-day responsibility	Responsibility is for a fixed term

Examples of countries that have a **parliamentary form of government:** UK, Germany, Italy, Japan, Canada, New Zealand, Netherlands, Australia, Portugal, and Israel.

Examples of countries that have a **presidential form of government:** USA, Brazil, South Korea, Afghanistan, Iran, Mexico, Indonesia, Chile, Turkey, Philippines, and Nigeria.

Examples of countries have a **semi-presidential form of government:** Russia, Egypt, France, Ukraine, Poland, Sri Lanka, Niger, Namibia, Mali, and Madagascar.

7

DEMOCRATISATION, TRANSITION, AND CONSOLIDATION

KEY CONCEPTS

Definitions of democracy; democratisation in East Europe, Africa, and Asia; state capitalist and authoritarian rule; guided democracy; Arab Spring

The word 'democracy' comes from the Greek words '*demos*', meaning people, and '*kratos*', meaning power; so democracy can be thought of as 'power of the people'. It is a way of governing which depends on the will of the people, and a form of government in which the people have the authority to deliberate and decide legislation, or to choose governing officials to do so.

DEFINITIONS OF DEMOCRACY

Political scientist **Raymond Gettell** defined democracy as the form of government in which the masses of the population possess the right to share in the exercise of sovereign power. **Bertrand Russell** was a consistent supporter of democracy and world government, and advocated the establishment of a democratic international government. According to him, democracy does not mean that one man's judgement is to be regarded as being as good as another's, but rather that there is to be an absence of discrimination between one man and another in political matters. **Chester Maxey** believed that democracy is a search for a way of life in which the free intelligence and activity of men can be harmonised and coordinated with the least possible coercion. **A. B. Hall** stated: 'Democracy is a popular government in the last analysis and ... that form of political organisation in which public opinion has control.'

According to **John Robert Seeley,** democracy is the government in which everyone has a share. As per **A. V. Dicey**, 'Democracy is a form of government in which the governing body is comparatively a large fraction of the entire nation.' **Robert MacIver** said that as a form of state, democracy is 'merely a mode of appointing, controlling and dismissing a government'. Its virtue lies in the fact that it 'has placed limits on the absoluteness of power'.

In *The Third Wave: Democratization in the Late Twentieth Century* (1991), Samuel P. Huntington analyses the causes and nature of democratic transitions, and describes three waves:

1. The first, 'slow' wave of the nineteenth century, 1828–1926: England, the USA, and France became democratic nations.
2. A second wave after World War II, 1943–1962: India and Israel became democratic nations.
3. A third wave beginning in the mid-1970s in Southern Europe (Spain, Portugal), followed by Latin America and Asia.

Political scientist **Renske Doorenspleet** stated that the fourth wave of democracy began with the disintegration of the erstwhile USSR.

DEMOCRATISATION IN EASTERN EUROPE

As President of the USSR, **Mikhail Gorbachev** sought to radically reform how the USSR was governed, how it operated, and how it cooperated with foreign countries. Therefore, he devised two initiatives:

1. Perestroika (restructuring)
2. Glasnost (openness)

He introduced these policies in an attempt to improve relations with the West as well as improve the state of the Soviet economy by introducing the processes of liberalisation and privatisation in the socialist economy of the Soviet Union. **Perestroika** refers to a series of political and economic reforms meant to kickstart the stagnant 1980s economy of the Soviet Union. This was the most fundamental change made to the nation's economic and political structure since the Russian Revolution of 1917. **Glasnost** was taken to mean increased openness and transparency in government institutions and activities in the Soviet Union. It reflected a commitment of the Gorbachev administration to allowing Soviet citizens to discuss publicly the problems of their system and potential solutions. However, the suddenness of these reforms, coupled with growing instability both inside and outside the Soviet Union, would contribute to the collapse of the USSR in 1991.

The dissolution of the Soviet Union resulted from a process of internal disintegration, which resulted in the end of the country and its federal government's existence as a sovereign state, and in its constituent republics gaining full independence on 26 December 1991. The Soviet Union had been experiencing internal stagnation and ethnic separatism for a long time. Although highly centralised until its final years, the country was made up of 15 top-level republics that served as homelands for different ethnicities. The most significant result of the breakup of the Soviet Union was the formation of several independent nations, among which are: Russia, the Ukraine, Estonia, Latvia, Lithuania, Georgia, and Armenia.

STATE CAPITALIST AND AUTHORITARIAN RULE

Authoritarianism is characterised by highly concentrated and centralised government power, maintained by political repression and the exclusion of potential challengers. It uses political parties and mass organisations to mobilise people around the goals of the regime and rejects political plurality while making use of a strong central power to preserve the status quo.

TRANSITION AND DEMOCRATISATION IN AFRICAN NATIONS

The State of **Kenya** is a presidential representative democratic republic, in which elected officials represent the people and the president is the head of State and government, while Nigerian politics takes place within a framework of a federal, presidential, representative democratic republic, in which executive power is exercised by the government. The States of **Gabon** and **Malawi** have experienced an authoritarian, presidential form of government, although in the 1990s, **Malawi** made a transition from authoritarianism to a democratic rule.

Namibia achieved independence from colonial rule in 1990 and **Nigeria** also adopted democracy in 1990. By 2006, **Ghana**, **Mali**, **Lesotho**, and **Senegal** had become democratic States. In **South Africa**, Apartheid (the Afrikaans name given by the white-ruled South Africa's Nationalist Party in 1948 to the country's harsh, institutionalised system of racial segregation) came to an end in the early 1990s in a series of steps that led to the formation of a democratic government in 1994.

GUIDED DEMOCRACY

Guided democracy, also called **managed democracy**, is a formally democratic government that functions as a *de facto* authoritarian government or, in some cases, as an autocratic government. Such hybrid regimes are legitimised by elections that are free and fair, but do not change the state's policies, motives, and goals. This was the political system in place in Indonesia from 1959 until the New Order began in 1966, and was the brainchild of President Sukarno, in an attempt to bring about political stability.

Authoritarian governments rule over the people in the name of the democracy. The Army becomes a key centre of power and Sukarno combined three ideas in his rule over the nation:

1. Nationalism
2. Religion
3. Communism

ARAB SPRING

The Arab Spring was a series of anti-government protests, uprisings, and armed rebellions that spread across much of the Arab world, including nations such as Tunisia, Morocco, Syria, Libya, Egypt, and Bahrain, in the early 2010s. The wave began when protests in Tunisia and Egypt toppled their regimes in quick succession, inspiring similar attempts in other Arab countries. Not every country saw success in the protest movement, however, and demonstrators expressing their political and economic grievances were often met with violent crackdowns by the security forces of their countries.

However, the Arab Spring could not succeed beyond a point because the democratic movement was suppressed in Egypt and Tunisia. Although the protest movements in 2011 were unique in their interconnected struggle for democracy across the region, the push to end corruption and improve citizens' quality of life did not end with the Arab Spring. Protests continued for years to come, and an additional wave of protests took place in the Arab world in the late 2010s and early 2020s.

STATES IN SOUTH AND SOUTHEAST ASIA

While initially founded as a socialist State with a centrally planned economy, **China** now has a mixed economy, described by its government as 'Socialism with Chinese characteristics'. China has enjoyed almost 30 boom years, with its GDP growing in double-digits, raising 500 million people out of poverty. The Chinese political system is authoritarian. There are no freely elected national leaders, political opposition is suppressed, all religious activity is controlled by the central CCP, dissent is not permitted, and civil rights are curtailed. Yet China's economy, driven by industrial production and manufacturing exports, has grown to become one of the largest and most powerful in the world over the past few decades.

'Junta' is a Spanish word that is used for military dictatorships. It refers to a council or committee meant for political or governmental purposes, especially a group of persons controlling a government usually after a revolutionary seizure of power. **Myanmar** has been ruled by a military junta for many of the years since it gained independence from British colonial rule in 1948. Here, the junta is a special form of military government where the hierarchy of the military is replicated in the structure of the government. Civilians are not allowed to participate in a junta government. The governments of Russia, China, India, Pakistan, Bangladesh, Vietnam, Laos, and Thailand are among those legitimising the junta by officially recognising them as the Government of Myanmar.

Politics in **The Philippines** is governed by a three-branch system of government. The Philippines has a representative democracy modelled on the US system. The 1987 Constitution, adopted during the Aquino administration, reestablished a presidential system of government with a bicameral legislature and an independent judiciary. The president is limited to one six-year term.

In his *Idea of India* (1997), **Sunil Khilnani** highlights the paradoxes and ironies that have surrounded the project of inventing **India** after its birth as an independent nation. India has managed to survive as a democracy even though a majority of its people live in dire poverty, possibly due to its political diversity.

8

MODERNISATION AND DEVELOPMENT

KEY CONCEPTS

Development; political decay; dependency theory; capability approach; postcolonial approach

DEFINTIONS OF MODERNISATION

Modernisation is a process of social change that is based on a scientific approach and logic. Theoretically, it began with the European Enlightenment, and in sociology, the term refers to the transformation from a traditional, rural, agrarian society to a secular, urban, and industrial one. It is a model of a progressive transition from a 'pre-modern' or 'traditional' to a 'modern' society. Sociologist **Shmuel N. Eisenstadt** emphasised that even among societies that followed the route taken by Western modernisation, there have been different ways of implementing the modern cultural programme; take, for example, the differences between European and American democracies. In his book *Modernization, Protest and Change* (1966), Eisenstadt summed up the following features of modernisation:

1. Social mobilisation
2. Social differences
3. Economic change
4. Political change

American political sociologist **Karl Deutsch** focused on the socio-demographic aspects of modernisation and defined political modernisation as 'the process by which there emerges mass political participation by the people and increased political decentralisation'. In *The Dynamics of Modernization* (1967), historian **C. E. Black** identified four phases:

1. Challenge to modernity
2. Consolidation of modernising leadership
3. Economic and social transformation
4. Integration of Society

Barrington Moore challenged modernisation theory and rejected the view that all modernising societies undergo essentially the same process, and argued that there are three paths to modernisation:

1. The emergence of a bourgeoisie can facilitate organic modernisation. This path leads to **liberal democracy**.
2. The second route is State-led. This path leads to fascism and totalitarianism.
3. Finally, peasant revolutions have brought about political transformations. These lead to **communism**.

American political scientist **Samuel Huntington** argues that changes in society are caused by tensions within the political and social system. He criticises modernisation theory, stating that its argument, that economic change and development are the prime factors responsible for the creation of stable, democratic political systems, is flawed. According to him, political modernisation consists of three basic elements:

1. The rationalisation of authority;
2. The differentiation of structure; and
3. The expansion of political participation.

Political development refers to the institutionalisation of political organisations and their activities. Development may not be linear, and political development can take the following forms:

1. Adaptation
2. Complexity
3. Autonomy
4. Coherence

DEVELOPMENT

After World War II, 'development' became the key are of focus for comparative politics. **James Smoot Coleman** was the leading theorist of his time in African political studies. His work fused liberal-democratic idealism and scientific realism. **Lucian Pye** was one of the pioneers in the 1950s and 1960s in developing theories about the political development and modernisation of Third World nations. His primary intellectual interest lay in exploring the cultural differences that help to explain why politics differs so greatly from one nation to another. He defined political culture as the composite of basic values, feelings, and knowledge that underlie the political process.

In *Political Culture and Political Development* (1965), Pye lists three elements of political development:

1. It involves a growing awareness of political activity, accompanied by greater participation, equality, and acceptance of universalistic laws.
2. It requires an increased governmental capacity to manage public affairs, control controversy, and cope with public demands.
3. It implies fundamental transformations in the machinery of government through greater structural differentiation, functional specificity, and integration of institutions.

Lucian Pye describes the following features of political development in societies:

1. Prerequisites of economic development
2. Politics of industrial society
3. Political modernisation
4. Operation of nation-states
5. Administrative legal development
6. Mass mobilisation and participation
7. Building democracy
8. Stability and orderly change
9. Mobilisation of power
10. Multidimensional social change

He laid out three characteristics that are generally related to certain aspects of political development:

1. Equality to the political culture
2. The problems of capacity to authoritative governmental structures; and
3. The question of differentiation to non-authoritative structures.

In his *Aspects of Political Development* (1966) pointed to six crises in the development of England:

1. Identity
2. Legitimacy
3. Penetration
4. Participation
5. Unification
6. Distribution

Sociologist **David Apter** made a study of different States, including Sri Lanka, Indonesia, and Myanmar. In *Politics of Modernization* (1965), Apter refers to three types of states: mobilisation systems; reconciliation systems; and modernising autocracy. He also described four stages of modernisation:

1. Stage of Contact and Control: Establishing Colonies
2. Stage of Reaction and Counter-action: Revolt against Colonial Rule
3. Stage of Contradiction and Emancipation: Widespread National Movements
4. Stage of Search for New Generative Solutions: Situation after Independence.

In *No Easy Choice: Political Participation in Developing Countries* (1976), a monograph on political participation in developing countries, Sanuel Huntington and Joan Nelson expands current theories of political participation and explores the social, economic, and political forces which influence participation in developing societies. They point to **five models** of political participation:

1. Liberal model
2. Bourgeoisie model
3. Autocratic model
4. Technocratic model
5. Populist model

According to **Edward A. Shils**, political democracy is 'a system of citizen government founded on representative institutions and public liberties'. He delineated three main types of political systems: totalitarian systems; oligarchic systems; and democratic systems. In his essay, 'Alternative Course of Political Development' he described five types of political systems:

1. Political democracy
2. Tutelary democracy
3. Modernising oligarchy
4. Totalitarian oligarchy
5. Traditional oligarchy

Shils believed that among these, traditional oligarchy is the worst form of political system.

John H. Kautsky, in his book *Political Change in Underdeveloped Countries* (1962), explores the influence of industrialisation on the politics of underdeveloped nations. He defined four kinds of political systems that have developed around the world:

1. Traditional aristocratic totalitarian
2. Aristocratic totalitarian
3. Intellectualistic totalitarian
4. Democracy

Norman Uphloff and **Warren Frederick Ilchman** believed that political science had failed in the past to meet its own standards of rigour and cogency. In their *The Political Economy of Change* (2017), they attempt to remedy these shortcomings by expanding the limits of social science analysis to deal with problems of allocation and productivity in all spheres of public choice, and not just in the economic sphere alone. They further define development as:

1. Increasing level of political solvency.
2. Increasing capacity to meet change.
3. Increasing capacity to generate demand.
4. Increasing capacity to increase the number of political entrepreneurs in society.

According to **Gabriel Almond**, a 'political system is the process of induction into the political culture. Its end product is a set of attitudes—cognitions, value standards and feelings—towards the political system, its various roles and role incumbents.' Almond and Powell defined political development as the 'increased differentiation and specialisation of political structures and the increased secularisation of political culture'. Its basic components are:

1. Secularisation of culture
2. Development of capacities
3. Differentiations in structures.

A. F. K. Organski sees the political development of nations as proceeding in a uniform order through four stages. In his *The Stages of Political Development* (1965), he describes development as passing through:

1. The politics of primitive unification—the development and growth of bureaucracies and political parties.
2. Politics of industrialisation—the political emphasis is on economic development.
3. Politics of national welfare.
4. Politics of abundance.

The third and the fourth stages are concerned with participation, integration, distribution, etc.

W. W. Rostow's take-off model (also called 'Rostow's Stages of Growth') is one of the major historical and structuralist models of economic growth. In *The Stages of Economy Growth: A Non-Communist Manifesto* (1960), he defined development as a sequence of stages through which all societies must pass. He postulated that economic modernisation occurs in five basic stages, of varying length.

1. Traditional Society
2. Pre-conditions for Take-off
3. Take-off
4. Drive To Maturity
5. Age of High Mass Consumption

Rostow asserted that countries go through each of these stages fairly linearly, and set out a number of conditions that were likely to occur in investment, consumption, and social trends at each state. Not all of the conditions were certain to occur at each stage, however, and the stages and transition periods may occur at varying lengths from country to country, and even from region to region.

Leonard Binder described the crises affecting political development in his book, *Crises and Sequences in Political Development* (2019) as:

1. Identity crises
2. Integration crises
3. Legitimacy crises
4. Resource mobilisation crises

POLITICAL DECAY

Political decay is a political theory, originally described by Samuel P. Huntington, which describes how chaos and disorder can arise from social modernisation, increasing more rapidly than political and institutional modernisation. Political development goes along with political decay. Huntington proposed a **Gap-hypothesis,** which means that a gap can occur between the expectations of people and their fulfilment of such expectations. Different social and economic factors contribute to both the political development as well as the political decay of nations. These are:

1. External forces, such as foreign governments, can affect the stability of established governments;
2. Social and economic forces that established political stability could change or disappear, leading to internal instability;
3. Economic development, such as shifts from an agriculture-based economy to a manufacturing-based one, as well as economic collapse, can also lead to political instability; and
4. Social developments, such as the proliferation of literacy, may lead to the rise and spread of new ideas.

DEPENDENCY THEORY

Dependency theory is the idea that resources flow from a 'periphery' formed by poor and underdeveloped states to a 'core' of wealthy states, enriching the latter at the expense of the former. This theory focused on individual nations, their role as suppliers of raw materials, cheap labour, and markets for expensive manufactured goods from industrialised countries. The unequal exchange relationship between developed and developing countries was viewed as contributing to poor economic growth among the latter nations. Dependency theory was introduced by Andre Gunder Frank, who argued that the developed West has 'underdeveloped' developing nations effectively by relegating them to a state of dependency.

The characteristics of dependency theory are:

1. Two sets of nations are involved, which includes an advanced and a poor nation.
2. Poor nations depend on rich nations.
3. Advanced nations actively cause dependence.
4. Advanced nations are interested in the resources of the poor nations.

For example, during the years 1650–1900, Britain and other European nations took over or colonialised other nations. They used their superior military technology and naval strength at the time to do so.

CAPABILITY APPROACH

In recent years, development is no longer limited to mere economic or political development. The real meaning of development lies in the growth of human capacities and skills. The capability approach (also referred to as the capabilities approach) is a normative approach to human welfare that concentrates on the actual capability of persons to achieve the lives they value, rather than merely having the right or freedom to do so.

Pakistani economist **Mahbubal Haq** is a pioneer in the field of human development. Economist and Nobel Laureate **Amartya Sen** believes in a capability approach to development. His capability theory approach is a theoretical framework that involves two core normative claims: first, the assumption that the freedom to achieve wellbeing is of primary moral importance; and second, that the freedom to achieve wellbeing must be understood in terms of people with capabilities.

Martha Nussbaum identified 10 capabilities, that is, real opportunities based on personal and social circumstances. She claims that a political order can only be considered as being decent if it secures at least a threshold level of these ten capabilities to all inhabitants. The core capabilities that she identified are:

1. Life
2. Bodily Health
3. Bodily Integrity
4. Senses, Imagination, and Thought
5. Emotions
6. Practical Reason
7. Affiliation
8. Other Species
9. Play
10. Control over one's Environment

POSTCOLONIAL APPROACH

Postcolonial theory holds that decolonised people develop a postcolonial identity that is based on cultural interactions between different identities (cultural, national, and ethnic, as well as gender and class-based), which are assigned varying degrees of social power. **Rajani Kothari** stated that political development is possible without modernisation, and conversely, modernisation may not bring political development. Kothari argued that freedom meant both the 'autonomy of man' as well as 'autonomy of states'. Embedded in Kothari's ideas of freedom was the idea of a strong, deep, and decentralised democratic structure, politics as a form of social transformation, and an indigenous, autonomous, self-reliant, and 'alternative' model of economic development.

9

STRUCTURE OF POWER

KEY CONCEPTS

Zero-sum principle; elitist theory of power; Pareto's theorisation; theory of democratic elitism; pluralism; ruling class

There is an unequal distribution of power and resources in society. The social distribution of power is based on the *Zero-Sum Principle*. Zero-sum is a situation, often cited in game theory, in which one person's gain is equivalent to another's loss, so the net change in wealth or benefit is zero. A zero-sum game is also called a strictly competitive game; it differs from non-zero-sum games, which allow for multiple parties to win or lose simultaneously. Examples of zero-sum games include poker, chess, and tennis in the entertainment world and future and options in the financial industry.

The **elitist** theory believes in the zero-sum concept of power. Elitism is the belief or notion that individuals who form an elite—a select group of people perceived as having an intrinsic quality, high intellect, wealth, power, notability, special skills, or experience—are more likely to be constructive to society as a whole, and therefore deserve greater influence or authority. Democratic elitism accepts the main premise of elite theory: 'no societies are governed by the people, by a majority; all societies, including societies called democratic, are ruled by a minority' (Burnham 1943, 184). Echoing this, **Schumpeter** stated that it is not the people, but the few who rule with the consent of the majority. The **circulation of the elite** is a theory of regime change described by Italian sociologist **Vilfredo Pareto** (1848–1923). He stated that changes of regime, revolutions, and so on occur not when rulers are overthrown from below, but when one elite replaces another.

Italian social theorist **Gaetano Mosca** believed that rule by a minority is an inevitable feature of social life. Elites are an organised minority while the masses are an unorganised majority. The ruling class is composed of the ruling elite and the sub-elites. He concluded that power is always in the hands of elites, and that the least bad government occurs when abuse of power is controlled by the rule of law. Sociologist **Robert Michels** contributed to elite theory by describing the political behavior of intellectual elites. He propounded the theory of the iron law of oligarchy in his 1911 book, *Political Parties*. He believed that all organisations were elitist and that elites have three basic principles that help in the bureaucratic structure of political organisation:

1. Need for leaders, specialised staff and facilities.
2. Utilisation of facilities by leaders within their organisations.
3. The importance of the psychological attributes of the leaders.

James Meisel stated that elitism grows largely due to three features:

1. Group cohesion
2. Consciousness
3. Conspiracy

In *The Managerial Revolution* (1941), philosopher **James Burnham** concentrated on the control of economic resources and said that the dominant class in a state-controlled economy will be managerial and not capitalist. The rulers of this new society will be the people who effectively control the means of production, that is, business executives, technicians, bureaucrats, etc.

In *The Rise and Fall of The Elites* (1991), Vilfredo Pareto states that the greater part of human actions owes its origins not in logical reasoning, but in sentiment. Elites rise to power, maintain dominance, and then fall; but only if another elite is struggling to take its place. Human actions are a combination of **residues**—those relatively unchanging and generally permanent elements, and motivating forces coming directly from sentiments—and **derivations.** According to Pareto, those factors which help in presenting logical explanations to activities on the basis of needs, nature, circumstances, and norms are known as derivations.

Pareto locates **six** residues:

1. **Residues of Combination:** These are the motivators which combine similar or opposites.
2. **Residues of Persistence of Aggregates:** These are the drives to maintain persistence or perseverance of man's relations to other men or places.
3. Residues **of Manifestation** of sentiments through external acts**:** Such residues impel us to express our sentiments by external acts.
4. **Residues of Sociability:** These residues enable communal living.
5. **Residues of the Integrity** of Personality**:** These are drives which helps us to integrate our personality and ward off injuries sentiments.
6. **Residues regarding Sexuality:** These are the residues concerning the sexual urges.

The first two residues are also known as **Innovators** and **Consolidators.** Pareto also described four categories of derivations:

1. Derivations of Assertion
2. Derivations of authority
3. Derivations in accord with sentiments or principles
4. Derivations of Verbal Proofs

Pareto further divided the elite class into two groups: **Speculator** (Class I) and **Rentier** (Class II). The speculator group is primarily responsible for change, for economic and social progress. The rentier group is a powerful element in stability, and in many cases counteracts the dangers attending the adventurous capers of the speculators. The first group is akin to the fox, and while the second can be compared to the lion.

Table 4.9.1: Pareto's Classification of the Political Elite

Dominant Residue	Economic Elite	Political Elite
Combination	Speculator (S)	Fox
Preservation	Rentier (R)	Lion

The history of humankind, according to Pareto, is the history of a continuous replacement of elites. Robert Michels studied the German Socialist Party and argued that democratic attempts to hold leadership positions accountable are likely to fail, since with power comes the ability to reward loyalty, the ability to control information about the organisation, and the ability to control what procedures the organisation follows when making decisions. He said: 'At the outset, leaders arise *spontaneously*; their functions are *accessory* and *gratuitous*. Soon, however, they become *professional* leaders, and in this second stage of development they are *stable* and *irremovable*'.

In his work, *The New Class: An Analysis of the Communist System*, **Milovan Djilas** proposed that in communist regimes, the party-state officials formed a class which 'uses, enjoys and disposes of nationalised property'. The Communist Party, too, is composed of elites. **Harold Lasswell** defined politics as 'who gets what, when and how'. This definition implies that. people are in conflict over values and society needs to have a set of procedures to resolve the questions of who gets what. He defined values as the desired goals and power as the ability to participate in decisions, and he explained political power as the ability to produce intended effects on other people. He listed the basic values as being those of difference, income, and safety, and stated that the elites in society accumulate most of these values. According to Lasswell, revolution implies a shift in the class composition of the elite.

Philosopher **John Plamenatz** states that in society, there is less restriction on freedom when the wishes of as many people as possible are given effect. Consent, rights, obligation are closely intertwined.

C. Wright Mills, in his *The Power Elite* (1956), defined the 'power elite' as the people in society who make all the decisions that matter. They head the military, the largest corporations, and the government. The decisions of other elites, such as the rich people and celebrities, do not really matter. Only the decisions of the few hundred people at the very top are of critical importance.

Carl Friedrich supported representative democracy and strongly opposed direct democracy, particularly the use and misuse of referendums, which he believed would lead to totalitarianism. He stressed the necessity for maintaining the rule of law, supplemented by a strong infrastructure of civil institutions, and was highly suspicious of popular grassroots movements.

THEORY OF DEMOCRATIC ELITISM

Democratic elitism accepts the main premise of elite theory: 'no societies are governed by the people, by a majority; all societies, including societies called democratic, are ruled by a minority' (Burnham 1943, 184). However, unlike the classical elitist theory, this approach does not consider democracy a myth.

Karl Mannheim, in *Ideology and Utopia* (1929), said that even if the elite takes the major decision on social policy, it does not mean that society is not democratic. Ideologies, according to him, are mental fictions whose function is to veil the true nature of a given society. They originate unconsciously in the minds of those who seek to stabilise a social order. **Joseph Schumpeter** defined democracy as the method by which people elect representatives in competitive elections to carry out their will. This definition has been described as simple, elegant, and parsimonious, making it clearer to distinguish political systems that either fulfil or fail these characteristics.

PLURALISM

Robert Dahl uses the term **polyarchy** (*poly*, 'many', and *arkhe*, 'rule') to describe a form of government in which power is invested in multiple people. It takes the form of neither a dictatorship nor a democracy. He established the pluralist theory of democracy—in which political outcomes are enacted through competitive, if unequal, interest groups.

RULING CLASS

In Marxist philosophy, the ruling class is the capitalist social class who owns the means of production and applies their cultural hegemony to determine and establish the dominant ideology (culture, mores, norms, traditions) of the society. According to Karl Marx, in all stratified societies there are two major social groups: a ruling class and a subject class. The ruling class derives its power from its ownership and control of the forces of production, and exploits and oppresses the subject class. This exploitation will only come to an end after the communist revolution.

IMPORTANT TEXTS ON STRUCTURES OF POWER

1. *Mind and Society*, Pareto
2. *The Rise and Fall of the Elites*, Pareto
3. *Political Parties*, Michels
4. *Psychopathology and Politics*, Lasswell
5. *Politics: Who Gets What, When And How*, Lasswell
6. *Democracy Through Public Opinion*, Lasswell
7. *Theory of Masses*, Gasset
8. *The Ruling Class*, Mosca
9. *Elite and Society*, Bottomore
10. *Power Elite*, C. Wright Mills

10

ELECTORAL METHOD

KEY CONCEPTS

Electoral models; single-member plurality system; second ballot system; alternative vote system; supplementary vote; proportional method of representation; additional member system; single-transferable vote system; types of political parties; interest/pressure groups; models of group politics; theory of social movement; new social movements

MODELS OF THE ELECTORAL METHOD

Trusteeship Model

The trustee model of representation is a model of a representative democracy. In this model, constituents elect their representatives as 'trustees' for their constituency. These 'trustees' have the autonomy to deliberate and act as they see fit in their own conscience, even if it means going against the explicit desires of their constituents; this is also called a free mandate. This model was formulated by **Edmund Burke** (1729–1797), an Irish MP and philosopher, who opposed the delegate model of representation. In the trustee model, Burke argued that his behaviour in Parliament should be informed by his knowledge and experience, allowing him to serve the public interest.

Delegate Model

The delegate model of representation is a model of a representative democracy. In this model, constituents elect their representatives as delegates for their constituency. In a delegate model, the elected official is there to be the voice of those who elected them and must act in accordance with their constituents' wishes, regardless of their personal opinion or view on the subject. This is most associated with **Thomas Paine**, who stated:

> The true . . . basis of representative government is equality of rights. Every man has a right to one vote, and no more in the choice of representatives. The rich have no more right to exclude the poor from the right of voting, or of electing and being elected, than the poor have to exclude the rich. . . .

Mandate Model

The mandate model views representatives as less independent actors. This came about after the emergence of modern political parties; now, constituents rarely vote for a representative based on their personal qualities, but more broadly, they vote for their party to be elected into government.

Resemblance Model

The Parliament becomes the microcosm that reflects the diversity of society. The resemblance model is less concerned about the way representatives are selected and more concerned about whether they resemble the group they claim to represent. It is similar to descriptive representation, that is, they argue that to represent a group of people such as the working class or women to its full potential, you must be a part of that social group yourself. Therefore, only people who have shared experiences and interests can fully identify with particular issues.

An electoral system or voting system is a set of rules that determine how elections and referendums are conducted and how their results are determined.

SINGLE-MEMBER PLURALITY SYSTEM (SMP)

Also known as the Majoritarian System or 'first past the post', this system of government is practised in the UK, the USA, Canada and India. Although several candidates may compete for the seat, the winner need only attract the largest number of votes cast. For this reason, this kind of electoral system is referred to as a 'single-member plurality'.

The features of this system are:

1. The nation is divided into single-member constituencies.
2. Voters select a single candidate, although multiple members can contest the election.
3. The winning candidate needs only to achieve the maximum number of votes.

The advantages of the SMP are as follows:

1. This system establishes a clear link between representatives and the people living in a constituency.
2. It offers the electorate a clear choice.
3. There is more probability of formation of governments with a clear mandate.
4. Smaller parties have less of a chance to form a government.
5. The stability of the government is almost certain, because this leads to the formation of a single-party government.
6. Stable governments are always better, in that single-party governments rarely collapse as a result of disunity or internal friction.

The disadvantages of the SMP are:

1. No relation can be established between the voting percentage and the seat percentage. The system 'wastes' many (perhaps most) votes. Only one candidate win the election, the one who gets the maximum votes, which is not the vote of the majority.
2. Small parties cannot form the government, and therefore third parties cannot share in the power.
3. It offers only limited choices.
4. There is a clear lack of representation of minority sections.
5. It discourages the selection of a socially broad spread of candidates and favours those who are attractive to a large body of voters.

SECOND BALLOT SYSTEM

An electoral system or voting system is a set of rules that determine how elections and referendums are conducted and how their results are determined. The two-round system (TRS), also known as *second ballot*, is a voting method used to elect a single candidate, where voters cast a single vote for their preferred candidate. Here, the election process usually proceeds to a second round only if in the first round no candidate receives a simple majority (more than 50 per cent) of votes cast. Usually only the two candidates who received the most votes in the first round, or only those candidates who received above a prescribed proportion of the votes, move to the second round. This system is prevalent in France, Egypt, Iran, and the Maldives. It is a part of the majoritarian electoral system.

The features of this system are:

1. There are single-candidate constituencies and single-choice voting, as in the first-past-the-post (FPTP) system.

2. A candidate needs an overall majority of the votes cast.
3. If no candidate gains a first-ballot majority, a second, run-off ballot is held between the leading two candidates.

This system has several advantages:

1. The system broadens electoral choice: voters can vote with their heart in the first ballot and with their minds in the second.
2. The candidate truly represents the majority because more than 50 per cent of the vote is required.
3. This also leads to a strong and stable government, as with the FPTP system.

The various disadvantages of this system are:

1. It is not suitable for the representation of minorities in society, and is also unfair to third parties.
2. Holding elections twice leads to greater expenditure.
3. A second ballot may strain the electorate's patience and interest in politics.

ALTERNATIVE VOTE SYSTEM (AV) AND SUPPLEMENTARY VOTE (SV)

The *alternative vote* (AV), also called *ranked-choice voting* or the *instant run-off*, is a method of election in which voters rank candidates in order of preference. If any single candidate receives a majority of first-preference votes, that candidate is deemed elected. If no candidate clears this hurdle, the last-place candidate is eliminated and her/his second preferences are reapportioned to others, and so on, until a candidate clears the threshold of 50 per cent of the vote plus one.

The *supplementary vote* (SV) is an electoral system used to elect a single winner, in which the voter ranks two of the candidates in order of preference. This method was used for electing Mayors and Police and Crime Commissioners in the UK. It is part of a broad group of 'preferential' voting systems, which include the AV used in Australia (House of Representatives) and the Contingent Vote used to elect the Sri Lankan President.

The features of these systems are:

1. There are single-member constituencies.
2. There is preferential voting. While the voter shall cast one vote, they will offer multiple preferences.
3. Winning candidates must gain 50 per cent of all the votes cast.
4. A quota is required to get elected. The candidate receiving the requisite quota in the first preference voting will be elected. If no one gets the quota in the first preferences vote, then a second preference vote will be taken into account.

The various advantages of these systems are:

1. There is a greater probability of forming a stable government.
2. Unlike the second-ballot system, the outcome cannot be influenced by deals made between candidates.
3. A single-party majority government is most likely to be formed.

These systems are not without their disadvantages:

1. It is more proportional than the FPTP system, but is still biased in favour of large parties.
2. The procedure of voting is complicated.
3. These systems, too, ignore the plurality and diversity in society.

PROPORTIONAL METHOD OF REPRESENTATION (PARTY-LIST SYSTEM)

Proportional Representation is a system used to elect a country's government in which parties gain seats in proportion to the number of votes cast for them. Here, subgroups of an electorate are reflected proportionately in the elected body. The concept applies mainly to political divisions (political parties) among voters. The essence of such systems is that all votes cast contribute to the result and are effectively used to help elect someone—not just a bare plurality, or (exclusively) the majority—and that the system produces a mixed, balanced representation reflecting how the votes have been cast.

British Member of Parliament **Thomas Hare** propounded the method of proportionate representation. The Hare quota may be given as: Total votes = the total valid poll; that is, the number of valid (unspoilt) votes cast in an election. Total seats = the total number of seats to be filled in the election. This method is used in Israel, Belgium, Germany, Luxembourg, and Switzerland, and the European Parliament.

This system has the following features:

1. The entire country is treated as a single constituency. Therefore, the nation is not divided into electoral constituencies.
2. Parties present lists of candidates before the electorate, in descending order of preference.
3. Electors vote for parties, not for specific candidates.
4. Parties get seats in direct proportion to the votes they receive in the election.
5. A 'threshold' may be imposed. For example, in Germany, a party that gets less than 5 per cent of the vote is not counted.

The many advantages of such a system are:

1. This is the only pure system of proportional representation due to the similarity between voting percentage and seat percentage.
2. It is the best for ensuring a representation of diversity.
3. It is easier for minority candidates to be elected.
4. There is no need to demarcate a separate constituency.
5. It is more democratic, since it ensures representation for even regional and smaller parties.

The disadvantages of this system are as follows:

1. No party will get a majority, which can lead to a weak and unstable government.
2. There is no link possible between representatives and constituencies.
3. The role of the party will become more important than that of the individual candidate.
4. This will further strengthen the role of political parties and centralisation of a political party.

ADDITIONAL MEMBER SYSTEM (AMS)

This combines two systems: first past the post and proportionate representation. In an election using the additional member system, each voter usually casts two votes: a vote for a candidate standing in their local constituency (with or without an affiliated party), and a vote for a party list standing in a wider region made up of multiple constituencies (or a single nationwide constituency). This method is used in New Zealand and Germany, where it is called Mixed Member Proportional (MMP), Nepal, Italy, Russia (State Duma), and the UK (Scottish Parliament and Welsh Assembly).

The various features of this system are:

1. There is a presence of two electoral methods. Therefore, the first past the post system can be adjusted with the list system.
2. Electors cast two votes, one for the party list and the other for the candidate of the major constituencies.

The advantages of this system are:

1. It strikes a balance in the concept of stability and accountability.
2. A representation of diversity is ensured while at the same time, the representation of the majority is kept intact.
3. This provides a voter with more alternatives It allows electors to choose a constituency representative from one party and yet

support another party to form the government.

However, the disadvantages of this system are:

1. This hybrid model may not be suitable for every nation. The instabilities faced by Nepal provide the best example of the drawbacks of this model.
2. The system creates two classes of representatives. The candidate chosen by the people may be more important than the one from the party list.
3. The size of representation increases automatically.
4. Parties become more centralised and powerful under this system.

SINGLE-TRANSFERABLE VOTE SYSTEM (STV)

The single-transferable vote (STV) is a multi-winner electoral system in which each voter casts a single vote in the form of a ranked-choice ballot. In an STV local government by-election, the number of stages is related to the number of candidates on the ballot paper, and will continue stage by stage until there are two candidates left. The one with the most votes transferred is elected. This system is in use in The Republic of Ireland and the UK (Northern Ireland Assembly), and is also part of the proportional method of representation.

Its features include:

1. There are multi-member constituencies.
2. Parties may put forward as many candidates as there are seats to fill.
3. Electors vote preferentially, as in the alternative vote system.
4. Candidates are elected if they receive a quota.

   The **Droop quota,** devised by British mathematician and lawyer **Henry Richmond Droop,** is the quota most commonly used in elections held under the single-transferable vote system. In an STV election, the quota is the minimum number of votes a candidate must receive in order to be elected. Any votes a candidate receives above the quota are transferred to another candidate. The Droop formula can be shown as:

$$\text{Quota} = \frac{\text{Total Number of Votes Cast}}{(\text{Number of Seats to be filled} + 1)} + 1$$

   That is, if 100,000 votes are cast in a constituency that elects four members, the quota is 100,000/(4+1) +1 = 20,001.
5. The votes are counted according to first preferences. If all the seats are not filled, the candidate at the bottom is eliminated, and her/his votes redistributed according to second preferences.

This system has certain advantages:

1. It is helpful to generate highly proportional electoral outcomes.
2. It ensures a better representation of minority groups.
3. There is greater choice available for the people.

The disadvantages of this system are:

1. Political parties become very important.
2. There is a greater probability of the formation of an unstable and coalition government.
3. There is no relation between the constituencies and members elected for Parliament.

POLITICAL PARTIES

Political parties are indispensable to any democratic system and play the most crucial role in the electoral process, in setting up candidates, and conducting election campaigns. In the 1770s, **Edmund Burke** defined political parties as 'a body of men united for promoting, by their joint endeavors, the national interest upon some particular principles in which they are all agreed'. Political parties function to link the legislature and the executive.

Joseph Schumpeter defined political parties as: 'A party is a group whose members propose to act in concert with the competitive struggle for political power.' He refuted Burke's conceptualisation of political party, stating that this definition referred to an ideological grouping. As stated in the previous chapter, **Robert Michels** propounded a theory known as the 'Iron Law of Oligarchy'. This law asserts that every party has a rigid form of oligarchy which exercises all the power. It provides a centralised organisation and imposes discipline. This is important because the rank and file of the party is usually too disinterested or apathetic to rule.

Otto Kirchheimer propounded the model of the 'catch-all party'. This is a political party that aims to attract people with diverse political viewpoints, and therefore appeals to a large section of the electorate. Kirchheimer employed this concept to explain how the social democratic consensus of 1950s Britain was causing the disappearance of what he called 'principled opposition' in political cultures. This means that he felt that politics was being robbed of all substance, conflict, and choice.

Political parties can be classified on the basis of two modes of classification: *(a)* the *structure* of parties and *(b)* the *party system.* On the basis of structure, **Maurice Duverger** organised political parties on the basis of two aspects: internal organisation and external organisation.

Organisational Structure

Maurice Duverger's classification of parties is generally accepted in political theory. The classification is as follows:

1. Elitist or Traditional Parties/Cadre Parties
   - (a) These parties have neither mass participation nor support from the masses. Membership is limited and selective.
   - (b) Political parties that emerged in the nineteenth century were mostly elitist.
   - (c) Selection is based on the fact that they seek quality rather than numbers.
   - (d) The **British Labour Party** and the **American Republican Party** are examples of elitist parties.

   Sigmund Neumann referred to these as 'Parties of Integration'. As he said: 'Modern parties have steadily enlarged their scope and power within the political community and have consequently changed their own functions and character. In place of a *party of individual representation*, our contemporary society increasingly shows a *party of social integration.*'
2. Mass parties
   - (a) These parties emerged in the twentieth century with the increase in the support of the citizenry for political parties.
   - (b) Membership was mass-based and the focus was on numbers.
   - (c) The newly independent 'Third World' countries have a large number of parties, which have been formed with the support of citizens.
   - (d) **Socialist and Communist parties** are examples of mass parties.

   Sigmund Neumann employed the alternative terminology of 'Parties of Representation' to refer to these political parties.
3. Intermediate parties

   An intermediate political party refers to any political party organised under the laws of the state whose candidate or nominees received less than 20 per cent, but not less than 10 per cent, of the total vote cast for the office in question at the most recent regular election. Although different from both elitist and mass parties, these parties are closer to mass parties.

Duverger also provided an alternative four-fold classification of political parties:

1. Caucus Parties
   (a) These are also called committee-type parties. The emphasis is on quality rather than quantity where membership is concerned.
   (b) They remain virtually inactive in the period between elections.
2. Branch Parties
   (a) This is a mass party with an open membership and a hierarchical structure, dominated by a centralised leadership.
   (b) The central leadership is the highest policy-making body.
   (c) Examples are: the German Social Democratic Party and the British Labour Party.
3. Cell Type
   (a) These parties stemmed from communism. They are smaller and more cohesive than the branch type of parties.
   (b) They are secretive and highly disciplined.
   (c) They have a wider political interest in social transformation.
4. Militia Type
   (a) These parties are modelled on the army command and control pattern.
   (b) Organisation is strictly hierarchical and based on sincere commitment and obedience towards the highest leader.
   (c) **Kufler's Storm Troopers** and the **Nazi party** are examples of militia-type parties.

On the Basis of Number

Italian political scientist **Giovanni Sartori** devised the most widely used classification method for party systems. He suggested that party systems should be classified by the number of relevant parties and the degree of fragmentation. Party systems can be distinguished on the basis of the number of relevant parties and degree of fragmentation.

1. One-Party System

   This implies the existence of only one party in a country. There could be two models of this system:

   (a) The first kind of one-party system is one in which only one party is allowed to exist. Opposition is legally prohibited and no other parties are allowed to exist. The **Chinese Communist Party** is an example of this system.
   (b) The second kind is the **Dominant Party System**. Within this system, opposition parties are allowed to exist. However, only one party retains electoral dominance. This party enjoys huge popularity among the masses and stays in governance for long periods of time. The dominant position that the Indian National Congress enjoyed in the decades following independence in India is an example of a Dominant Party System.
2. Two-Party system

   In two-party systems, there is constant competition between two dominant parties to secure a majority of the popular votes and seats in the **legislature.** One or more smaller parties may also exist within this system. However, they neither come to power, nor do they influence the outcome of elections. They may associate themselves with either of the major parties.

   A loose two-party system, as in the US, is characterised by flexible and minimal central control. Party members are not very committed to party ideologies. A tight bi-party system exists in Britain, characterised by strong, strictly organised parties with a committed and disciplined membership.

3. Multiparty system

   The existence of three or more dominant parties may be described as a multiparty system. Party systems in France, Italy, and Switzerland are examples of this type of system. In a multiparty system, three or more parties may come together at any point in time to form coalition governments. Such governments generally adopt a common minimum programme for governance, as they are not committed to any single ideology. Many of them may also bring together small parties with regional or sectarian interests. These may be of two types:

   (i) **Moderate Multiparty System**, is characterised by the presence of many parties. However, ideological differences are not very sharp and they do result in stable coalition governments.

   (ii) **Polarised Multiparty system,** characterised by sharp ideological differences and prolonged and unstable confrontations between competitive parties.

The multiparty system may be unable to provide the stability that is a feature of the two-party system, yet the competitive nature of several parties enables the efficient functioning of a democratic government.

ELECTORAL SYSTEM AND PARTY SYSTEM

As mentioned earlier, Maurice Duverger's Law points out the relation between the electoral system and the party system. This law holds that the simple majority electoral system, where the highest vote achiever is the winner (the first past the post system), tends to evolve into two-party systems. Accordingly, the electoral system of proportional representation would lead to the evolution of a multi-party system in the concerned country.

Joseph La Palombara and **Myron Weiner**, in their book *Political Parties and Political Development* (1966), traced the origins and development of political parties, explored their impact on the system in which they exist, and raised new questions about the potential role of parties. They stated that the political party emerges whenever the activities of a political system reach a certain degree of complexity, or whenever the notion of political power comes to include the idea that the mass public must participate or be controlled. They divided the non-competitive party system into:

1. One-party authoritarian
2. One-party pluralist
3. One-party totalitarian

Arendt Lijphart, in his work *Democracy in Plural Societies: A Comparative Exploration* (1977), explores the functioning of democracy in countries with deep religious, ideological, linguistic, cultural, and ethnic cleavages. He recommends consociational democracy—based on partnership—as the suitable model for pluralistic societies. This is characterised by:

1. A grand coalition government of segmental elites;
2. A mutual veto based on concurrent majority rule;
3. A proportionality in the allocation of public funds, parliamentary seats, and public service positions; and
4. A high degree of autonomy for all significant segments of plural society.

Lijphart examineds this practice in small European countries, and in Lebanon, Malaysia, Cyprus, Nigeria, and former Dutch and Belgian colonies. He further described three kinds of party-systems:

1. Consensual party system
2. Conflictual party system
3. Accommodative party system.

Giovanni Sartori, in *Parties and Party System: A Framework for Analysis*, devised the most widely used classification method for party systems. He suggested that party systems should be classified by the number of relevant parties and the degree of fragmentation. He proposed five kinds of parties:

1. Witness parties
2. Ideological parties
3. Responsible parties
4. Responsive parties
5. Purely demagogic

PARTY SYSTEM IN THE DEVELOPING WORLD

In his work *Politics in India*, **Rajni Kothari** argued that the Indian National Congress was a system, rather than a political party. He coined the term 'Congress System' to refer to the period of single party dominance in Indian politics, which ended after the elections of 1989. **Zoya Hasan** underlines the critical role political parties have played in establishing democratic politics in India. The existence of multiple social cleavages and variations across states have restrained a single type of political system from existing all across the country. According to Hasan, political parties display numerous contradictory features, which reveal the blending of different forms of modern organisation and participatory politics with indigenous practices and institutions. In *Parties and Party Politics in India* (2002), she referred to the Congress system as a 'Family Party System', and asserted that the same could be said of party systems of Bangladesh, Sri Lanka, and Pakistan.

However, many scholars have contested this conceptualisation and argued that the Indian party system is continuously changing, cannot be classified under a single label, and is therefore unstable. A great degree of factionalism exists in political parties in the developing world. However, the conflicting interests and ideas are not always accommodated within the political system. The party system in the developing world is also burdened with the responsibility of nation-building. It is often claimed that the available resources are inadequate to fulfil the economic and social aspirations of all the people.

INTEREST GROUPS/PRESSURE GROUPS

In every society, there is a process of presenting people's demands before the policy-makers. **G. A. Almond** and **G. B. Powell** stated, 'The process by which individuals and groups make demands upon the political decision-makers is referred to as interest articulation.' They further state:

> 'By "interest group" we mean a group of individuals who are linked by particular bonds of concern or advantage, and who have some awareness of these bonds. The structure of interest group may be organised to include continuing role performance by all members of the group, or it may reflect only occasional and intermittent awareness of the group interest. . . .'

Thus, an interest group is an association of people, set up to achieve certain specific objectives, for which purpose it may even pressurise the institutions of State. Those engaged in interest articulation may range from an unorganised mob to a systematic organisation.

Pressure groups are forms of organisations that exert pressure on the political or administrative system of a country in order to extract benefits out of it and advance their own interests. **David Truman** describes them thus: 'Pressure groups are attitude groups that make certain claims upon other groups in the society.' **Hitchner and Levine** assert that, 'An interest group is a collection of individuals who try to realize their common objectives by influencing public policy.' Therefore, 'The interest group is a part of both the general culture and social framework and the political structure of a particular state.'

Pressure groups have certain key features:

1. Based on certain interests: Each pressure group organises itself keeping in view certain interests, and thus tries to adopt the structure of power in the political systems.
2. Pressure groups are a part of the political process of a country, and use both modern and traditional means to put their demands forward.
3. They result out of increasing pressure and demands on resources. Scarcity of resources, claims, and counterclaims on resources from different and competing sections of society leads to the rise of pressure groups.
4. They attempt either to strengthen or change the direction of government policy, but do not seek to directly capture political power and run the government.
5. They represent a changing consciousness. For instance, the increase in food production or industrial goods does bring about a change in the way individuals and groups look at the world.

CLASSIFICATION OF INTEREST GROUPS

In a detailed analysis, Gabriel Almond classified interest groups into four types:

1. Institutional Interest Groups
   (a) These are closely connected with various institutions and even with political parties.
   (b) These groups also exist within the legislatures, bureaucracies, churches, corporations, and even armed forces.
   (c) They are formal organisations, very influential, and powerful.
2. Anomic Interest Groups
   (a) These groups often emerge when normal means of expressing dissatisfaction prove ineffective.
   (b) They may be concerned with religious, linguistic, or ethnic concerns.
   (c) They generally employ unconventional and usually violent means. They influence the political system in various unconventional ways.
   (d) These are more prevalent and influential in the developing world due to the particular nature of those societies, with their evident ethnic, communal, and racial cleavages.
3. Associational Interest Groups
   (a) These are closely associated with formally organised institutions.
   (b) These groups are functionally specialised and concerned with articulating the interests of specific groups, such as management, labour, business, and agriculture.
   (c) Institutional and associational pressure groups are predominant and exceptionally powerful in non-democratic and authoritarian forms of government.
   (d) These groups are generally concerned with economic interests. The Federation of Indian Chambers of Commerce and Industry (FICCI) is an example.
4. Non-Associational Interest Groups
   (a) Membership to these groups is based on ethnicity, kinship, status, and religion. They articulate their interests informally and irregularly.
   (b) They lack a permanent organisational structure, and predominate in the developing world as compared to developed countries.

ROLE OF INTEREST/PRESSURE GROUPS

Institutional Structures

The role of pressure groups depends to a large extent on the type of government that a country has. The role and significance of interest groups in a presidential system, such as in the USA, is more active than that in parliamentary democracies like Britain and India. Their role is minimum, or even non-existent, in one-party states.

Interest groups come to the political forefront when formal systems of representation prove inadequate in interest articulation. They are more successful in representing community values than political parties.

Lobbying

According to **Alfred de Grazia,** lobbyists are 'highly organized; they claim large membership lists; they have agents who are skilled in persuasion and public relations; they insist that their purposes are consonant with the public welfare.' Although lobbying is an American practice, it is also prevalent in many other democratic countries.

In the USA, the term 'lobbying' is used to indicate the technique of establishing contracts with the members of Congress and state legislatures, so as to influence them to vote for or against a measure. This is deployed to ensure the fulfillment of particular interests.

Party System and Pressure Groups

The type of party system present in a political system also determines the influence that pressure groups have on political processes. Pressure groups have a greater say in political decision-making in multi-party systems since they are often incorporated as factions. There is greater decentralisation of power within such systems, which creates more avenues for political participation.

On the other hand, two-party and one-party systems are more rigid, with less sharing of power. Consequentially, pressure groups either have very little say in political decision-making, or are not even allowed to exist, as is the case in authoritarian systems.

MODELS OF GROUP POLITICS

Pluralist Model

Political scientist **Robert Dahl's** work *Who Governs? Democracy and Power in an American City* (1961), is a case study of political power and representation in New Haven, Connecticut. He observed, after three months of research, that there is no elite controlling power. Rather, power is fragmented among plural groups, which compete with each other for more power and for control over scarce resources. Dahl asserted that the political system is essentially neutral and sufficiently fragmented to allow numerous points of access to various groups. He coined the term 'polyarchy' to refer to the democratic political system. However, Dahl changed his perspective on pluralism later, asserting that while power is distributed among various interest groups, some groups may be more powerful than others.

In *Community Power Structure: A Study of Decision Makers* (2017), sociologist Floyd Hunter studied the complex Regional City and stated that a small, stable group at the top of the social structure form the core group of power. Their decision-making activities are not known to the public, but they are responsible for whatever is done, or not done, in their community. Beneath this top policy group is a clearly marked social stratification, through which decisions sift down to the substructures chosen to put them into effect.

Arthur Bentley, in his work *The Process of Government* and **David Truman** in *The Governmental Process* argued that pressure groups ensure adequate decentralisation and separation of governmental powers, and therefore necessary to ensure the smooth functioning of a democratic government.

Corporatist Model

This model advocates the organisation of society into corporate groups, such as agricultural, labour, military, scientific, or guild associations, on the basis of their common interests. The corporatist model lays strong emphasis on a strict organisational hierarchy in pressure groups. They are often criticised for being anti-democratic, since they only cater to the interests of certain powerful groups.

New Right Model

This is a term employed by various right-wing political groups or policies in different countries. The New Right combines neoliberal economics (free market and minimal government intervention) with more traditional and conservative views on social issues. New Right theorists criticise pressure group politics, contending that it leads to instability and is inefficient in ensuring adequate representation. Instead, they emphasise the role of the market and open economy for the articulation of individual preferences.

POLITICAL PARTIES AND PRESSURE GROUPS

Maurice Duverger distinguished between political parties and pressure groups thus: 'Political parties strive to acquire power and exercise it.... Pressure groups, on the contrary, do not participate directly in the acquisition of power or in its exercise; they act to influence power.'

According to Almond and Powell, political parties and interest groups perform different functions. While interest groups are engaged in interest articulation, political parties perform the function of interest aggregation, that is, parties aggregate the competing and conflicting demands of interest groups, which are translated into coherent programmes and action plans. Thus perceived, political parties prevent interest groups from directly dominating the decision-making apparatus and process in a country.

However, while political parties are exclusive in their membership and have limited and rigid organisational structures, interest groups are more flexible and inclusive. This makes them more readily available as instruments of representation.

DEMOCRACY AND PRESSURE GROUPS

David Truman and Galbraith argued that pressure groups are essential for the proper functioning of a democratic government since they ensure an adequate division of power in society. On the other hand, the New Right Model of politics criticised the role of pressure groups, stating that they increase the democratic overload, which results in political instability.

The Corporatist Model theorists asserted that pressure groups only serve the interests of the most powerful sections of society. **Ralph Milliband** contended that interest groups are not legitimate centres of power since they are not accountable to any institution, while Robert Dahl believed that interest groups provide various avenues for political participation and contribute to keeping a check on power. Therefore, they play a positive role in democracy. **James Coleman**, however, makes no distinction between interest groups and pressure groups.

NEW SOCIAL MOVEMENT

Academic focus on social movements has been renewed in recent decades. The spread of the Black Civil Rights Movement in the USA in the 1950s and 1960s, students' movement in the 1960s and 1970s, the feminist movement, anti-nuclear protests, gay rights, animal rights, minority nationalism, and many other ethnic movements have contributed to this renewed emphasis. Before the 1950s, the Marxist and functionalist theories had provided a single explanation of social movements.

1. The term 'social movement' gained currency in Europe in the 19th nineteenth century,

in an atmosphere of political upheaval. The early growth of social movements was connected to broad economic and political changes in England in the mid-eighteenth century, including political representation, market capitalisation, and proletarianisation. This term was introduced in 1848 by the German sociologist Lorenz von Stein in his book, *Socialist and Communist Movements since the Third French Revolution* (1848). Various downtrodden groups organised agitations and made demands arguing for change in property relationships.

THEORY OF SOCIAL MOVEMENT

Jurgen Habermas propounded a comprehensive theory to explain New Social Movements. He argued that new social movements were products of a post-industrial social formation where the welfare State had made classic forms of exploitation and deprivation obsolete, and where modern society has created new forms of alienation.

Habermas asserted that our day-to-day lives are played out in two distinct spheres:

(a) The **social arena**, which comprises our interactions with the family and society at large, and
(b) The **professional and administrative sphere**, in which we work and interact with institutional authority.

He refers to the former as the 'Lifeworld' and to the latter as the 'System'. The lifeworld is the everyday world that we share with others. This includes all aspects of life, barring organised or institution-driven ones, and comprises shared meanings and understandings. The everyday actions performed in the lifeworld are generally communicative in nature. The system refers to common patterns of strategic action that serve the interests of institutions and organisations. System actions are essentially driven by money and power.

New social movements emerge at the seams of the lifeworld and the system to give expression to recurrent structural and cultural strains. These are not aimed towards revolutionary transformation; rather, they only seek piecemeal reforms. **Noam Chomski** and **Naomi Klein** point out that New Social Movements are anti-globalisation movements.

Ernesto Laclau and **Chantel Mouffe** assert that new social movements emerged in a post-industrial society where class antagonisms have ceased to exist. Therefore, Marxist analyses cannot be deployed to gain an understanding of these movements. In their work *Hegemony and Socialist Strategy: Towards a Radical Democratic Politics* (1985), they argued that social movements which attempt to create social and political change need a strategy that challenges neoliberal and neoconservative concepts of democracy. This strategy refers to the expansion of the liberal definition of democracy, based on freedom and equality, to include difference. Laclau and Moffe refer to this as **Radical Democracy**, which has its basis in a form of democratic pluralism.

NEW SOCIAL MOVEMENT IN DEVELOPING COUNTRIES

Ghanshyam Shah argues that 'objectives, ideology, programmes, leadership and organization' are the important constituents of social movements.

1. **Objectives:** The objectives of a social movement may vary, from narrow, particular, local issues to a broad agenda of social transformation.
2. **Ideology:** Also a dynamic concept, it provides direction to the evolution of common strategies and programmes. It ensures unity within the movement by inducing commitment and solidarity.
3. **Programmes:** These involve comprehensive strategies and action plans that are

important for realising the objectives of social movements.

4. **Leadership:** It gradually emerges during the growth of the social movement, and plays a crucial role in articulating ideology and aims, evolving strategies and programmes, and motivating the participants.
5. **Organisation:** A social movement may have an organisation that can range from a loose, informal or partial level to highly institutionalised and bureaucratised structures which take the form of corporate groups.

In post-Independence India, the main guiding ideologies have been varieties of socialism, which include various forms of democratic socialism (for example, Ram Manohar Lohia's socialism) as well as Communism. The Old Movements were most notably those of the left and national movements, which had class as the main basis for struggle.

Table 4.10.1: Differences between Old and New Movements

Old Social Movements	*New Social Movements*
1. These were primarily influenced by Marxist and Communist ideologies.	These were heavily influenced by the Critical Perspective of the Frankfurt School and post-materialist concerns.
2. They opposed economic inequality and exploitation.	They were centred on issues related to quality of life, identity concerns, and human dignity.
3. Examples include workers' movements and peasant movements.	Examples include feminist movements, environmental movements, and LGBTQIAP+ movements.
4. They engaged extensively with and criticised the role of the State in social and economic transformation.	They engage with the broader society and emphasise the democratisation of the State through wider political participation.
5. These movements focused on class antagonisms within society and were intrinsically ideological in nature.	These emphasised upon cultural, political, and identity issues.
6. These were the outcome of the inequalities and needs generated by an industrial society.	These movements emerged in a post-industrial society.

Gail Omvedt argues that the shift away from the earlier class-based movements towards more inclusive moments encompassing Dalits, farmers, women, and Adivasis should be understood as an attempt to redefine the sphere of economic production within which exploitation occurs. Ghanshyam Shah asserts that new social movements are related to the issues of a post-modern society, and described them as micro-movements. These movements are primarily concerned with protecting and enlarging the autonomy of civil society. They are not organised around economic issues or concerns of political power.

New social movements are not class-based and Stoicist, in the sense that they stand for humanity, cutting across all sectional interests and divisions. In that sense, these movements are social and not political. Rajni Kothari observed that such movements are based on a form of non-party politics, and asserted that not all efforts towards social change are aimed at the government. A change in government does not necessarily mean a change in politics.

New social movements, therefore, aim towards broader social transformation by engaging with society through alternative, non-political forms of organisation. In *Reinventing Revolution*, Omvedt distinguished four major movements as new Social Movements—the anti-caste movement, the women's movement, the environmental movement, and the farmers' movement.

Sunil Baviskar asserts that unlike the post-materialist concerns driving First-World environmentalism, Southern mobilisation is intrinsically linked to issues of material distributive justice. Struggles over natural resources are therefore perceived as combining shades of both 'green' ecological concerns and 'red' class politics. In the United States, environmental movements have predominantly emerged in a post-materialist or post-industrial society, where questions about 'quality of life' are not rooted in the politics of production, but in forms of consumption.

In contrast, Indian environmentalism links issues of ecology with questions of human rights, ethnicity, and distributive justice. This rootedness in issues of subsistence and survival has 'also prompted a thoroughgoing critique of consumerism and of uncontrolled economic development'.The need to assert a 'red' agenda for Indian environmentalism, and the anxiety to maintain a distance from First-World environmentalism, stems also from the desire to establish a link with Indian socialism.

The Chipko Movement

The Chipko movement, India's first celebrated environmental struggle, began in the early 1970s and pitted hill villagers who depended on forests for their livelihood against State forestry policies that prioritised commercial exploitation over subsistence use. Protest in the hills was marked by the large-scale involvement of women, leading some scholars to claim that the Chipko Movement was an 'eco-feminist' movement. A key element in Chipko ideology was opposition to commercial tree felling, on both ecological and social grounds. The movement ultimately led to the creation of the separate state of Uttarakhand.

It is interesting to note that the movement makes no mention of social disparities among hill people, nor did it make any effort to incorporate an environmentalist agenda into its programme.

New social movements in the developing world have also come to be known as grassroots movements since they represent the issues and concerns of the most socially and economically disadvantaged groups

UNIT V

INTERNATIONAL RELATIONS

KEYWORDS

Approaches to the study of International Relations; Theoretical concepts; Conflict and peace; United Nations; Political economy of international relations; Regional organisations; Contemporary challenges in the field

1

APPROACHES TO THE STUDY OF INTERNATIONAL RELATIONS

KEYWORDS

Idealism/Liberalism, Realism, Neoliberalism, Neorealism, Structural Marxism, Critical International Theory, Social Constructivism, Feminism, Postmodernism

LIBERALISM

Liberalism, also called *idealism*, in the context of international relations is an approach based on the belief that international cooperation and institutions can reduce conflict and promote peace among nation-states. Liberals do not believe in a state-centric approach; they believe that states are not the only actors in the international system and that international organisations, NGOs, and transnational corporations also play important roles. They see individual freedoms, democracy, trade and commerce, and the rule of law as key to promoting peace and stability in the international system by encouraging cooperation among states.

Basic Assumptions of Idealist Theory / Liberalism

1. Idealists believe that human beings are essentially good and democracy allows the unfettered expression of this goodness leading to a preference for peace.
2. Idealism seeks the causes of war not within anarchy but within the lack of democracy and morality and in the absence of international organisations and international law. These causes of war are considered by idealists to be by-products of international anarchy and seen as changeable conditions.
3. Idealism believes that war is transitional and temporary and not an inevitable possibility.
4. The main focus of idealism is on securing peace, justice and interdependence through the institutions of democracy, law, and order.
5. Idealism focuses on human nature and not on unitary states as prime actors within international politics.

The major conceptual implications of the extension of liberal thought to international relations include the following:

1. Democratic form of government
2. Peaceful resolution of conflict
3. Individual freedom and human rights
4. Independent judiciary
5. Ensuring peace and cooperation among nation-states

6. Abolition of aristocratic privileges
7. Equality before law
8. Free market and free trade under capitalism
9. Limited government

The Causes of War and Determinants of Peace

Causes of Conflict

1. Idealists assert that **arbitrary interventions by governments** in domestic and international affairs cause disturbances within the natural order through the violation of the natural rights of citizens of states and this leads to rebellion and conflict.
2. The **undemocratic nature of international politics** does not allow rational individuals to voice their concerns regarding international issues or matters of foreign policy of their own states, and this may cause conflict.
3. While the realists considered the **balance of power** necessary for survival of nation states, the idealists see it as a highly volatile and unstable and a possible ground for conflict. This, idealists believe, must be remedied through the institution of a world government.

Determinants of Peace

1. **Individual liberty coupled with national self-determination and democratisation** would lead to the institution of open governments which are responsive to public opinion thereby reducing the possibility of conflict as people would naturally choose peace, according to idealists.
2. **Global capitalism accompanied by free trade** would lead to economic and social prosperity of the states and this in turn would create interdependence among them, thereby leading to the states preferring diplomacy and negotiation over conflict.
3. **Collective security mechanisms** would prevent the states from taking arbitrary actions against one another, and the creation of a world government with powers to mediate in conflicts and enforce decisions on states would eventually lead to peace.

The Precursors to Liberalism or Classical Liberalism

1. **Immanuel Kant**
   (a) His work *Perpetual Peace: A Philosophical Sketch* is regarded as the origin of the Democratic Peace Theory.
   (b) Kant posited that individuals desire to be free and prosperous, and so democracy and trade are likely to expand. This expansion would naturally lead to the growth of international law and organisations which would facilitate these interactions and bring about peace.
   (c) He believed that war and conflict can be overcome, or mitigated, through concerted changes in both the domestic and international structures of governance.
2. **Jeremy Bentham**
   (a) Jeremy Bentham came up with the term 'international law'. In simple terms, international law is a collection of rules governing relations between states and other entities that are legally recognised as international actors.
   (b) He believed that constitutional states would benefit from adhering to international law in their foreign policies.
3. **John Locke**
   (a) Locke espoused the doctrine of natural rights of individuals. This is referred to as 'properties' in his book *Two Treatises of Government.* He is often regarded as the founding father of liberal theory.
   (b) His analysis of democratic governments and their ability to secure peace has been

extended to the sphere of international relations by liberal theorists.

THE DIFFERENT STRAINS OF LIBERALISM/IDEALISM

A. First Strain

For this strain of idealism, the focus is on the analysis and understanding of human nature.

1. The main proponent of this line of thought is **Richard Cobden** (1804–1865) who believed that the role of the state in the spread of peace and freedom in the world was minimal.
2. Cobden sought the answer in *objective general laws* based on human nature.
3. He also argued that *free trade* would ultimately lead to world peace. He was strongly influenced by Adam Smith and David Ricardo in his ideas.

B. Second Strain

Later, the focus shifted to an analysis of the state.

1. The main proponent within this line of thought is **Woodrow Wilson** (1856–1924), who espoused theories of liberal internationalism.
2. Wilson emphasised upon *self-determination of peoples* and advocated for the spread of democracy.
3. Wilsonian idealism was also focused on the spread of global capitalism, collective security regimes, multilateralism in international deliberations, open diplomacy in international negotiations as well as freedom of navigation and freedom of the seas.

Fourteen Points by Wilson

The fourteen points were declared by Wilson to negotiate the end of World War I in 1918, in his capacity as US President.

(1) Open covenants (agreements) of peace openly arrived at, with no secret agreements.
(2) Freedom of the seas outside territorial waters.
(3) Removal of all economic barriers to trade.
(4) Reduction of national armaments to the lowest level that is necessary for domestic safety.
(5) Free, open-minded and impartial adjustments of colonial claims.
(6) Evacuation of German troops from Russia and respect for Russian independence.
(7) Evacuation of German troops from Belgium.
(8) Evacuation of German troops from France, including the contested Alsace-Lorraine region.
(9) Readjustment of Italian borders along clearly recognised lines of nationality.
(10) Limited self-government for the people of Austria-Hungary.
(11) Evacuation of German troops from the Balkans and independence for the Balkan people.
(12) Independence for Turkey and limited self-government for other nationalities formerly living under the Ottoman empire.
(13) Independence for Poland.
(14) The formation of a general association of nations under specific covenants for the purpose of affording mutual guarantees of political independence and territorial integrity for large and small states alike.

C. Third Strain

For this strain of idealism, the main focus is on **the structure of the system.**

1. The main proponent of this line of thought, which is exemplified within theories of *neo-liberal institutionalism*, is **J. A. Hobson** (1858–1940).
2. While this line of thought bears strong resemblance to structural realism in its assertion of the anarchical nature of international system, it emphasises the role of institutions in securing peace and cooperation.

Types of Liberalism

Robert Jackson and Georg Sørensen divides liberal theories of international relations into four types:

1. Sociological Liberalism

For the proponents of sociological liberalism, the study of international relations is not only about the relations between governments but also about *transnational relations*, i.e., relations between peoples, groups and organisations belonging to different countries. The theoretical emphasis of this variant of liberalism is marked by a sense of *pluralism* and it *focuses on both the society and the state.*

Transnationalism can be defined as processes whereby international relations conducted by governments have been supplemented by relations among private individuals, groups and societies that can and do have important consequences for the course of events.

James Rosenau, who has worked extensively on foreign policy, focuses on transnational relations at the macro-level of human population in addition to those conducted at the micro-level by individuals. He points out that those individual micro-transactions have important implications and consequences for global affairs. He asserts that a new '*multi-centric world*' has emerged that is composed of diverse 'sovereignty-free collectivities which exist apart from and in competition with the state-centric world of "sovereignty bound" actors'. Multi-centric world here refers to transnational relations.

Cobweb Model versus Billiard Ball Model

John Burton in his book *World Society* proposes a *Cobweb Model* of transnational relationships. It is society-centric model where multiple channels of communication exist. Due to interdependence between states, the capacity of each state would decline. The Cobweb Model proposes a world that is driven by mutually beneficial cooperation rather than antagonistic conflict through increased interdependencies and inter-linkages, thus reducing the unpredictability of international anarchy.

The Cobweb Model is in contrast to the *Billiard Ball Model* of international politics that realists propose, where every state is autonomous and independent. It is a state-centric approach were communication passes through the state only and nations consistently collide with each other like the free-standing balls with hard shells in the game of billiards. **Arnold Wolfers** propounded this model based on the Westphalian world order. This is based on a principle of balance of power in an anarchic world.

Security Community

Karl W. Deutsch is another important proponent of the theory of sociological liberalism. He introduced the principle of regional integration and refuted hierarchical relations. He supported the idea of a world government. Two of his most important works are *The Nerves of Government* (1966) and *Political Community and the North Atlantic Area* (1957).

He said that social mobilisation leads to political development and economic transactions. He talks about the Transaction-Integration balance which proposes that integration is possible through transaction.

Deutsch coined the term '*Security Community*'. He said that a community of states can prevent the forcible settlement of conflict among its own members. A security community requires the community to have the ability to present a common military front collectively against an external state. The state and the security community must have common perceptions of threat, such as in a region where large-scale use of violence has become very unlikely or even unthinkable. It may refer to a group of states that enjoy dependable relations and have expectations of peaceful coexistence. People in a security community are also bound by the sense of community, mutual sympathy, trust and common interests.

Deutsch distinguished between two types of security community:

(i) **Amalgamated Community:** Such a community is created when two or more previously independent states form a common government, an example of which is the US federal system.

(ii) **Integrationist Community:** This is a pluralistic security community in which states retain their sovereignty, such as in the European Union.

2. Republican/Democratic Liberalism

Immanuel Kant is a key figure in Republican Liberalist thought. An important element of this line of thought is the Democratic Peace Theory. Key 'liberal' assumptions in Kant's framework include the belief in the rational qualities of individuals, faith in the feasibility of progress in social life, and the conviction that humans, despite their self-interest, are able to cooperate and construct a peaceful and harmonious society. Democratic states comprising of the independent voices of such individuals would never go to war with each other leading to '*perpetual peace*'.

In addition to democracy, republican liberals strongly believe in several other associated ideals like liberty, equality, fraternity and justice. The ideals of republican liberalism proved helpful in the making of the Pacific Union that Kant envisioned. It is not a common peace treaty, but rather, it is a zone of peace based on the common moral foundations of all democracies. A democratic government believes in pacific resolutions of domestic disputes. Similarly, international conflicts can also be solved through a pacific method. According to republican liberals, the basic reason behind war in this world is the lack of democratic government. A liberal state may get involved in a war with non-liberal states, but war between liberal states is a remote possibility. Liberal thinkers like **Francis Fukuyama** said that liberal democracy is expanding across the world and this is helpful for maintaining international peace. It is true that the number of democracies has gone up rapidly in recent years, indicating a movement towards a more peaceful world with international relations characterised by cooperation rather than conflict.

Another important contemporary thinker within this tradition is **Michael Doyle**. In his essay 'Kant, Liberal Legacy and Foreign Affairs', he asserts that democratic governments are controlled by their citizens who will not advocate or support wars with other democracies, and this will lead to a *zone of peace*. Another important work by Doyle is *Ways of War and Peace* (1997).

It must be noted that while many liberals agree that there is a **Democratic Peace Zone** among liberal democracies existing in Western Europe, North America and Japan, the Global South continues to face problems in this regard.

3. Interdependence Liberalism

Interdependence liberalism is a perspective in international relations that highlights the interconnectedness of states and the increasing importance of economic and social interdependence in shaping global politics. This approach emphasises the benefits of international cooperation and the role of international institutions in promoting peace and stability in the international system.

Interdependence liberals believe that the increasing interconnectedness of the world economy and society makes cooperation between states increasingly necessary and that international institutions can help to manage interdependence and promote common interests.

This perspective is often contrasted with (*a*) the realist approach which emphasises the role of power and self-interest in shaping international relations, and (*b*) the Marxist approach, which sees international relations as a reflection of economic inequalities.

However, interdependence liberalism recognises that power and self-interest are still important factors in international relations and that international cooperation is not always possible or beneficial.

Complex Interdependence

Joseph Nye and Robert Keohane differentiate between 'simple interdependence' and 'complex interdependence' in their books.

In basic terms, simple interdependence refers to the interdependence between nation-states while complex interdependence refers to the *interdependence among non-state actors* such as NGOs and transnational corporations.

Keohane and Nye, putting forth the idea of complex interdependence, posits that states and their fortunes are inextricably tied together in the contemporary era of increased connectivity and financial globalisation. This is further exemplified by the cobweb model discussed earlier. The complex relationships referred to in this concept can be observed in the international political economy. With increasing globalism, the political economies of the world grow interdependent. Keohane asserted that complex interdependence implies the participation of various and diverse actors other than states leading to a situation wherein there is no clear hierarchy of issues and deployment of force is thus rendered ineffective.

Complex interdependence constitutes relations on many different levels via many different actors and branches of government. There exist a host of transnational relations between individuals and groups outside the state.

In the book *After Hegemony: Cooperation and Discord in the World Political Economy* (1984), **Keohane** explores the challenges of cooperation in a world of complex interdependence. He argues that international organisations will play an increasingly important role in this world, as states pursue different goals simultaneously with transnational actors such as NGOs and transnational corporations who pursue their own separate goals free from state control.

In *Power and Governance in a Partially Globalized World* (2002), Keohane examines the changing nature of power and governance in a world where globalisation has created new challenges and opportunities. He highlights the importance of specific issue areas, where certain states or actors may command influence, but this influence may not translate to other issue areas. For example, Denmark and Norway command influence in international shipping because of their large merchant and tanker fleets. But this cannot easily translate to other issue areas.

Other notable books on this subject are *Transnational Relations and World Politics* (1971) *by Keohane and Power and Interdependence* (1977) by Keohane and Nye. They pointed out the following as important features of complex interdependence:

(a) Participation of non-state actors
(b) No hierarchy among the state
(c) Forces that are ineffective
(d) Distribution of resources is not related to military power

Complex interdependence is different from realist model in that realists believe in a state-centric world where force is an effective instrument of foreign policy and hierarchy exists in the world which is dominated by military capacity. Keohane and Nye posits complex interdependence as an alternative to the realist theory. They talk about how in realism, the '*high politics*' of security and survival get priority over the '*low politics*' of economics and social affairs. High politics here refers to military strength and military alliances associated with the state-centric world, whereas low politics refer to trade, commerce and mercantilist cooperation.

Joseph Nye explains the present world order as a **3D chess board** with the following features:

(a) The world is unipolar in a militaristic sense
(b) The world is multipolar in an economic sense
(c) There is no pole in cultural and/or social power

In his book *Soft Power: The Means to Success in World Politics* (2004), Nye talks about how complex interdependence conceptually belongs to the regime of **soft power**. Soft power implies the **ability to attract** and to **achieve goal through persuasion** rather than coercion.

Other notable works by Nye are *The Paradox of American Power* (2003) and *Understanding International Conflicts: An Introduction to Theory and History* (1997). Another major proponent of complex interdependence is **Richard Rosecrance**. In his book *The Rise of the Trading State* (1986), he says that the international system is characterised by the presence of two worlds: (*a*) the military political world and (*b*) the trading world. In the first half of the twentieth century, Japan emerged as the political military state, which resulted in the Second World War, but in the post-War period, Japan adopted a mercantilist policy and became a trading state. Rosecrance asserts that even the 'WW-II belligerent' states of Germany and Japan became trading states in the 1970s as they realised that war is a costlier method for fulfilling national interest in comparison to trade.

4. Institutional Liberalism

Institutional liberalism, also referred to as neoliberal institutionalism, is a strand of liberalism that believes international institutions can be beneficial. The following are the main tenets of institutional liberalism:

1. It focuses on the role of international institutions in obtaining international collective outcomes. Though the anarchic international environment impedes the realisation of collective goals, the structure of international institutions determines the extent to which collective goals may be realised. These institutions can be effectively reshaped or reformed to achieve collective interests.
2. Neoliberals assert that international institutions and organisations provide a platform for securing and maintaining peace and cooperation between nation-states because they impose rules and regulations or 'regimes'.
3. According to institutional liberals, an international institution can take the shape of an international organisation such as the European Union, or it can be a set of rules called a 'regime' (such as the NAFTA or North American Free Trade Agreement) that governs state action in particular areas.
4. Institutional liberals assert that there are two kinds of institutions:
   (1) *Formal Institutions*, which constitute (a) multilateral organisations with physical locations, buildings, staff, budgets, and resources at their disposal and (b) intergovernmental institutions such as the IMF and the World Bank
   (2) *Informal Institutions* which consist of, according to Stephen Krasner, 'sets of implicit or explicit principles, norms, rules, and decision-making procedures around which actors' expectations converge in a given area of international relations'.

Institutional liberals argue that institutions have made a significant difference in Western Europe after the end of the Cold War by acting as 'buffers' which helped absorb the 'shocks' sent out through Western Europe by the end of the Cold War and the reunification of Germany.

Major Scholars of Liberalism and their Notable Works

1. **Norman Angell**

   Patriotism Under Three Flags (1903), *The Great Illusion: A Study of the Relation of Military Power in Nations to Their Economic and Social Advantage* (1909), *The Foundations of International Polity* (1914).

2. **Charles Beitz**
   Justice and International Relations (1975), *Political Theory and International Relations* (1979).
3. **Michael Doyle**
   'Liberalism and World Politics' (1986), 'Thucydidean Realism' (1990).
4. **Francis Fukuyama**
   The End of History and The Last Man (1992).
5. **David Held**
   Models of Democracy (1987).
6. **John Hobson**
   Physiology of Industry (1889), *The Economics of Unemployment* (1922).
7. **Stanley Hoffmann**
   International Relations: The long Road to Theory (1959), *The State of War* (1965).
8. **Richard Rosecrance**
   The Rise of Trading State (1986).
9. **Woodrow Wilson**
   The State: Elements of Historical and Practical Politics (1889), *The History of the American People* (1902).
10. **Alfred Zimmern**
    The Third British Empire (1927).
11. **Kenneth Oye**
    Cooperation Under Anarchy (1986).
12. **Robert Keohane**
    Neorealism and Its Critics (1986).

REALISM

Precursors of Realist Theory

The origins of realist theory in the context of international relations can be found in the works of various philosophers within Western as well as Indian political thought. Some of these important thinkers are:

1. **Thucydides:** He was a Greek philosopher whose work *The History of the Peloponnesian War* is considered to be one of the origins of realism in international theory.
2. **Kautilya:** He dealt extensively with the concerns of international relations in various chapters of the *Arthashastra*. His major contributions include: elaboration of the theory of Matsya Nyaya and its extension to international relations, the theory of Mandala, the Saptanga theory of the state, the doctrine of Sarva Bhauma or world sovereign, and the Doctrine of Vijigisu.
3. **Machiavelli:** He is regarded as one of the most practical philosophers within Western political thought. He wrote in the context of the wars between Italian city-states and has been criticised extensively for his theories presented in the treatise *The Prince*.
4. **Thomas Hobbes:** He was an English philosopher who wrote about the significance of power and conflict in human relations and state operations and was criticised for the same. His theories are central to realism. His major work is *Leviathan*.

Basic Elements of Realism

The basic elements of realism are as follows:

(a) **National interest and national security:** National interest is defined in terms of power. A balance of power, alliances and military capability is essential to ensure the security of a nation. Preserving the unity and integrity of a nation is the core interest.
(b) **Power:** For realists, power primarily refers to military power, and economic power is a means to realise military ambitions.
(c) **Balance of power:** It is the main objective of states, apart from survival and self-help in an anarchic international system. States are fearful of the other states and know that they must operate in a way that serves

their national interest. The more powerful a state is in relation to its competitors, the less likely it is to be attacked. The states with greater power often attempt to tilt the balance of power in their favour.

(d) **Anarchy**: For realists, it is the ordering principle of international relations and it simply implies the absence of a regulatory world government.

CLASSICAL REALISM

One of the major proponents of classical realist thought in the twentieth century was the German–American IR theorist, Hans J. Morgenthau. He follows in the tradition of Thucydides, Machiavelli and Hobbes. His theories of international relations are encapsulated in the following six principles.

Six Principles of Morgenthau

1. **Politics is governed by objective laws that have their roots in human nature:** Morgenthau believes that human nature has not changed significantly since time immemorial. Therefore, it is necessary to develop a rational political theory that reflects these objective laws. Since human nature is permanent and unchanging, conflict of power too will exist forever.
2. **National interest is defined in terms of power:** This sets politics as an autonomous sphere of action apart from spheres such as economics (which is understood in terms of wealth) and others. The concept of power infuses rationality and comprehensiveness to the actions of actors in international relations.
3. **Interest is always dynamic:** While the idea of interest as the essence of politics is fixed, the kind of interest that determines state action in a particular space and time can vary. The way in which power is used is also determined by the particular political and cultural environment.
4. **Abstract moral principles cannot be applied to politics:** Realism recognises the moral significance of political action. However, it implies that universal moral principles cannot be applied to states; rather, they must be filtered through the concrete circumstances of time and place. Actions of states can change with the change in time and circumstances. No universal principle of morality can be applied over a state forever.
5. **Difference between moral aspirations of a nation and the universal moral principles:** Realism asserts that the moral principles of a nation cannot be equated with the moral laws that govern the universe. Realists however are not against morality. They do not favour morality but they are neutral towards it. They recognise that moral principles and power politics are distinct from each other. Actions of states thus cannot be judged on the basis of moral principles.
6. **Autonomy of international politics:** Politics is given preference over economics as political interest determines economic interest. In this, realists are different from Marxists. Politics is given more importance than ethics and morality. Since international politics is not governed by international law, power politics takes centre stage in international relations.

STRUCTURAL REALISM OR NEO-REALISM

Kenneth Waltz was a leading neo-realist thinker who provides a **more scientific** explanation of the international political system. His explanation of realism and conflict is comparatively more **objective** than Morgenthau's due to its focus on the structure of the international system. Waltz says that political structures are defined by their ordering principle, differentiation of functions and distribution of capabilities. Waltz employs the method of *deductive analysis* which implies moving from the macro, large-scale, more general explanations to micro, small-scale and particular phenomena. The opposite of this is inductive analysis, as seen in Morgenthau's principles, where he moves from an analysis of unitary human nature to a larger understanding of international politics.

Waltz's notable works are *Man, The State and War* (1959) and *Theory of International Politics* (1979).

Principles of Structural Realism

Waltz founded the branch of realism called structural realism, which comprises the following principles:

1. **Distribution of Capability:** According to Waltz, the capabilities of every state are not the same. The capability of a state comprises resources, technologies, demography, economy and military capacities. International politics is not based on the principle of equality because the capability of each state is different. Some states like USA are more powerful than states such as Russia. Due to the uneven distribution of capability, a security dilemma is bound to emerge. Therefore, structural realists believe that each and every state would want to maximise their capability.
2. **Anarchic Structure:** The structure of international politics determines the foreign policy of nation states. Waltz asserts that international politics is state-centric and anarchic in nature which means that there is no higher authority which sits above the great powers and the state is the Supreme Agency or the Supreme Actor. Conflict between states is thus inevitable and automatic. He alternatively calls it the '*Iron Cage Structure*'.
3. **Function of State:** Waltz said that the function of every state is same, i.e. every sovereign state is responsible for its own security. All states keep police and armed forces, irrespective of their size. Capability of states may be different but the function of the states is the same. Consequently, every state wants to maximise its stockpile of military hardware. Waltz talks about the *Black Box theory* which considers states as black boxes: they are assumed to be alike except for the fact that some states are more powerful than the others. He implies that states are 'similar functional units'.
4. **Bipolar World:** Waltz said that the bipolar world of the Cold War was more stable in comparison to the multi-polar world. He also stated that nuclear weapons are helpful for maintaining deterrence in international politics.
5. **Relative Gains:** Waltz rejects the liberal belief in the possibility of international cooperation by asserting that states cannot predict the benefits and harms of cooperation and this in turn hinders effective cooperation. States are concerned about other states gaining relatively more benefits than with what they themselves gain from cooperation and this leads to states focusing more on preventing other states from acquiring benefits.
6. **Problem of Cheating:** There is no way in which the states can predict the motives of other states so cheating becomes another major hindrance to cooperation.

OFFENSIVE AND DEFENSIVE REALISM

Waltz argues that his theory of international politics needs to be supplemented by a separate theory of foreign policy that can explain misguided state behaviour. Therefore, Waltz has to go beyond structural realism to explain how states act in the international system, and this has been termed *defensive realism* by theorists.

Table 5.1.1: Morgenthau versus Waltz

Morgenthau	*Waltz*
1. His analysis is based on human nature which he regards as selfish and egoist. 2. The nature of his analysis is more abstract and subjective and cannot be scientifically verified as it is based on human nature which can hardly be objective.	1. He employs a structural mode of analysis which bases its findings on a study of the architecture or structure of international politics which he believes to be anarchic. 2. His methodology is more objective and scientific, and therefore, can be verified.
3. His analysis is inductive (unitary analysis).	3. He utilises deductive reasoning.
4. According to him, the response of a state to a particular international situation depends solely upon the state's capability or power.	4. Since the major driving force for political action is the anarchical structure, the response of states to international situations would be similar.
5. Power is defined more or less in terms of military power.	5. Power consists of different elements and not just military power. Waltz introduces the concept of *Latent Power* which is based on the state's wealth and the size of its overall population. It refers to raw potential which can be tapped during conflict with rival states.
	6. According to Waltz, political structures are defined by their ordering principle, differentiation of functions and distribution of capabilities.

In contrast to Waltz's defensive realism, **John J. Mearsheimer** is a proponent of *offensive realism*. While the basic assumption of Waltz and Mearsheirmer is the same as they both consider the world to be anarchic, their approach is different.

Mearsheirmer's offensive realist theory states that the purpose of the state as a rational actor is to maximise its power because the international system always provides incentive for expansion. States always looks to establish hegemony over other states and consequently, the entire world. An offensive realist would argue that the recent aggressive policy of Russia proves that uncertain intentions are better than no intentions as a state can never be certain that another state will not use power against them. All great powers possess offensive military capabilities. The survival of the state is of supreme importance and therefore a state should be ready to take any action and must maximise power with the goal of establishing a hegemony. This is the tragedy of international politics in that a security-seeking state is often forced to engage in conflict and war as there is more utility in war than not going to war. Mearsheimer elaborates on this in his book *The Tragedy of Great Power Politics* (2001).

According to the defensive realist Waltz, the state is not a *power maximiser* but a *security maximiser*. Establishing a balance of power is better than trying to establish hegemony over the entire world. The central theoretical conclusion of structural realism (defensive realism) is that in anarchy, states 'balance' rather than 'bandwagon'. 'Bandwagons' attempt to increase their gains (or reduce their losses) by siding with the stronger party in hierarchic international orders. Waltz says that in an anarchic world, this is courting disaster as a state may end up strengthening another who may later turn on its ally. The power of others—especially the great powers—is always a threat when there is no international government to turn to for protection. 'Balancers' thus make an attempt to reduce this risk by opposing the stronger party.

Both defensive and offensive realists agree that nuclear weapons have little utility for offensive purposes, except where only one side in a conflict has them. If both sides have survival retaliatory capability, neither gains an advantage from striking first. The defensive realists argue that security should be the goal and not expansion because even if a state somehow manages to become the most powerful, balancing will occur wherein other states will team up to destroy/defeat the hegemon. Therefore, defensive realism champions security, which is about defending oneself, over expansion, which leads to wars and more defeat.

MAJOR SCHOLARS OF REALISM AND THEIR WORKS

1. **Raymond Aron**
   The Century of Total War (1954), *The Opium of the Intellectuals* (1955), *The Dawn of Universal History* (1961).
2. **Edward Hallett Carr**
   The Twenty Years' Crisis (1939), *The New Society* (1951).
3. **Robert Gilpin**
   War and Change in World Politics (1981), *The Political Economy of International Relations* (1987).
4. **John Herz**
   Idealist Internationalism and the Security Dilemma (1950), *Political Realism and Political Idealism* (1951).
5. **George Kennan**
   American Diplomacy (1951).
6. **Henry Kissinger**
   Nuclear Weapons & Foreign Policy (1957), *A World Restored* (1957), *World Order* (2014).
7. **Stephen Krasner**
   State Power and the Structure of International Trade (1976).
8. **Hans Morgenthau**
   Scientific Man versus Power Politics (1947), *Politics among Nations* (1948), *Politics in the Twentieth Century* (1948), *In Defense of the National Interest* (1951), *The Purpose of American Politics* (1960)
9. **Susan Strange**
   'International Economics and International Relations' (1970).
10. **Kenneth Waltz**
    Man, the State and War (1959), *Theory of International Politics* (1979)
11. **John J. Mearsheimer**
    The Tragedy of Great Power Politics (2001), *The Great Delusion: Liberal Dreams and International Realities* (2020).

Table 5.1.2: The Neo-Neo Debate, or Neo-Realism versus Neo-Liberalism

Neo-Realism	*Neo-Liberalism*
1. While both agree that the international system is anarchic, neo-realists say that anarchy puts more constraints on foreign policy and claim that neo-liberals minimise the importance of survival as the goal of each state.	1. Neo-liberals claim that neo-realists minimise the importance of international interdependence, globalisation and the regimes created to manage these interactions.
2. Neo-realists believe that international cooperation will not happen unless states make it happen. They feel that it is hard to achieve, difficult to maintain, and dependent on state power.	2. Neo-liberals believe that cooperation is easy to achieve in areas where states have mutual interest.
3. Neo-realists claim that neo-liberals overlook the importance of relative gains as they think actors with common with interest try to maximise absolute gains.	3. Neo-liberals want to maximise the total amount of gains for all parties involved, as opposed to neo-realists who believe that the fundamental goal of states in cooperative relationships is to prevent others from gaining more.

Neo-Realism	Neo-Liberalism
4. Neo-realists believe that anarchy requires states to be preoccupied with relative power, security and survival in a competitive international system.	4. Neo-liberals are more concerned with economic welfare, politico-economic issues and other non-military issues such as environmental concerns.
5. Neo-realists give more importance to the capabilities (power) of states over their intentions and interests. Capabilities are essential for security and independence. Neo-realists claim that uncertainty about the intentions of other states forces states to focus on their own capabilities.	5. Neo-liberals emphasise intentions and interests as opposed to capabilities and power.
6. Neo-realists state that neo-liberals exaggerate the impact of regimes and institutions on state behaviour. Neo-realists argue that the neo-liberal idea of facilitating cooperation does not mitigate the constraining effects of anarchy on cooperation.	6. Neo-liberals see institutions and regimes as significant forces in international relations.

ENGLISH SCHOOL

Hedley Bull and Martin Wight laid the foundation of the theory of international society. They presented an alternative to realism and liberalism. According to them, international relations can be described as a social arena. Member states compete for power and wealth, as realists have pointed out. But rights and democracy also exist alongside, which proves that liberals' claims are also partially true. There is no international organisation for regulating the behaviour of nation states but that does not imply it is anarchic because international society incorporates legal and moral restraints over the activities of nation states.

Bull, in his book *The Anarchical Society* (1977), makes an important distinction between International System and International Society. He states that unlike international systems, institutions of international society refer to the set of habits and practices that are necessary for realising common goals. Diplomacy and international law are two such institutions. Martin Wight, inspired by Kant, advocated *rationalist* traditions between realism and revolutionism. He wrote *Systems of States* (1977) and *Power Politics* (1978).

FUNCTIONALIST THEORY OF INTERNATIONAL RELATIONS

Functionalists consider the primary function of states to be welfare, and not merely regulation. With a *one-size-fits-all paradigm*, functionalism treats all states and international organisations alike as performing the same basic functions which include maintaining law and order, providing healthcare facilities, and ensuring education for all citizens.

After the Second World War, liberal democratic states became welfare states and there arose the need for cooperation among the states. The emphasis of functionalism is on the significance of cooperation in international interactions as opposed to realism's conceptualisation of the perpetuity of conflict.

A strong assumption underpinning functionalism is that the process of integration of nation-states takes place within a framework of human freedom. Therefore, cooperation and enhanced interaction are not to be undertaken solely or even primarily by the state or governmental institutions as there is a '*trust deficit*' among political actors which can be an impediment to the process. Rather, it is to be initiated and led on by *technicians* from the civil society like doctors, engineers, and scientists as no similar deficit exists among these technicians who can thus effectively cooperate with each other.

Appropriate international agencies are necessary to catalyse these interactions. According to functionalism, *international integration*, that is, the collective governance and material interdependence between states, fosters an internal dynamic among states that integrate in limited functional, technical and economic areas. The existence of functional international agencies would help in expanding the area of integration.

Spill-Over Effect

The functionalists assert that cooperation in non-political areas among technicians, economists and other functional actors would ultimately contribute to cooperation in the arena of politics and policy-making. This is because in the context of international relations cooperation in one domain influences and leads to cooperation in other arenas. Thus, attempts at building up scientific and economic cooperation are bound to spill over into the arena of political cooperation.

The spill-over effect can be seen in the economic and monetary policies of recent times and it explains how the euro as a currency came about after the integration of the European states from relatively unrelated policy areas.

The Working Peace System

David Mitrany in his book *A Working Peace System* (1943) challenged the political constitutional method of integration. He said that a constitutional federal arrangement is difficult to realise whereas a functional sociological approach is more practical as the basic functions of all states are the same.

Mitrany also rejected the protected model of collective security and instead supported a *functional arrangement* for transnational issues such as disease control. He said that the functional responsibilities of the states should be transferred to international agencies such as the World Health Organization (WHO) and Universal Postal Union (UPU).

He divided international organisation broadly into three categories:

(i) A general and fairly loose association (such as the UN and the League of Nations)
(ii) A federal system
(iii) Functional arrangements

Mitrany asserts that the League of Nations and the UN rest upon the ideals of national separateness and the member states are free to participate or not. This kind of arrangement is thus inadequate and uncertain in its working.

A federation is where a number of adjacent countries or groups of countries come together while maintaining their separateness, for a general purpose. Regarding the possibility of a world federation, Mitrany is of the opinion that it is restrictive and rigid since such a federation only forms to achieve a specific purpose.

Regarding the functional approach, Mitrany highlights the *common index of needs* that can cut across national boundaries. Functional arrangements enable *technical self-determination* as they can be concretely measured and adjusted according to changes in the scope and nature of the function as opposed to rigid political arrangements.

Mitrany visualises the integration of the social and economic functions of different states and non-state institutions, a vision he contrasts with the realist conceptualisation of conflicting states. According to him, this web of integration would provide the basis for a joint world government and political lines, he predicts, will be blurred in time.

Pre-requisites for Co-operation between States

1. Better infrastructure
2. Better facilities for communication
3. A democratic political system
4. A liberal economic model

Neo-Functionalism

Neo-functionalism is simultaneously a theory and a strategy of regional integration that evolved from the ideas of David Mitrany. An important theorist within this tradition is **Ernst Haas**, who in his extensive studies, analysed the European Union as an instance of large-scale regional economic integration. Neo-functionalism, as outlined by Haas in the mid-1950s, seeks to provide closer integration without forcing countries to integrate too quickly or with countries too far away.

The fathers of the European Coal and Steel Community, Jean Monnet and Robert Schuman, were French politicians who laid down the foundation of the European Union. Although Ernst Haas did not develop any general theory of regional integration, he focused on the development of cooperation within the European Union. According to Haas, cooperation and conflict both exist in regional organisation. Ernst Haas wrote a book *The Uniting of Europe* (1958).

Rejection of Political and Non-Political Separation

Neo-functionalists believe that separation between the political and the non-political is impossible. The European Union came into existence due to political initiative. The neo-functionalists assert that while initially, states integrate in limited functional or economic areas, later on these partially integrated states experience increasing need for further integration in related areas. This spillover leads to the blurring of boundaries between the spheres of economics and politics, according to neo-functionalist theory.

Importance of Conflict Resolution

Neo-functionalists say that conflict between states cannot be avoided, and therefore the European Union must incorporate some mechanisms of conflict resolution. Neo-functionalists acknowledge the reality of conflict in the process of regional economic integration and that it is a hindrance to cooperation. Nevertheless, integration is regarded as an inevitable process, rather than a desirable state of affairs that could be introduced by the political or technocratic elites of the involved states' societies. Neo-functionalism emphasises the importance of *conflict resolution* and the significance of the role of *dispute settlement* mechanisms in international politics.

Critique of Functionalism

1. Functionalist theory has been criticised for its inability to account for social change and the role of agency in political action.
2. The functional emphasis on the possibility of peace and considering peace and prosperity to be the dominant objective of nations completely ignores the reality of conflict in international relations. It also refuses to acknowledge the role of national interest in shaping and determining international interactions whether they take place at the inter-governmental or inter-societal levels.
3. By focusing exclusively on economic and social areas and placing a high importance of international institutions in securing cooperation in these areas, functionalism fails to understand the political realities of dominance, influence, coercion and negotiation and ignore their influence on social and economic issues. This affects the prioritisation of issues as well as the kind of decisions which are taken to resolve them.

MARXISM IN INTERNATIONAL RELATIONS

Marxism is a critical approach that questions both the mainstream, policy-driven approaches to IR theory as well as a classical approach, owing to the philosophical and sociological tradition propounded by **Karl Marx**.

Marx never overtly said anything regarding international relations. Indirectly, however, he referred to international politics and said that colonialism and imperialism will lead to the development of capitalism in Asian and African nations. According to his theory of the Asiatic Mode of Production, communist revolution would take place after the development of capitalism.

Vladimir Lenin builds on this and tries to associate class with the nation-state. He said that Asian and African nations belong to the proletariat or the working class, while capitalist states come under the category of bourgeois class.

Marxism in the context of international relations revolves around:

(a) A **class-based analysis**: In Marxism, class is more important than the nation state.
(b) A **holistic understanding of relations**: A study of social and economic conditions is crucial for understanding relations among nation-states.
(c) **Equality through the end of exploitation**: Economic differences and poverty should be abolished to obtain true equality.

Marxism is more than a theory of explaining world politics. It does not believe in maintaining status quo and hopes to bring about change and reform in international politics.

Some of Lenin's notable works are

1. *The Development of Capitalism in Russia* (1899)
2. *What is to be Done?* (1902)
3. *Imperialism, The Highest Stage of Capitalism* (1916)

Basic Tenets of Marxism in International Relations

1. Marxism fundamentally questions the notion of 'international' in IR. It sees classes and not sovereign nation-states as the major actors in international politics. Marxists contend that the questions of survival, reproduction, technologies and labour are of great importance and often influence foreign policies.
2. Instead of perceiving international institutions as inevitably fair and just, Marxists assert that the political superstructure is determined by the nature of the economic base which is made up of a particular historical mode of production, and hence caters to the interests of a particular class. This theory is known as *economic determinism*.
3. Marxists strongly oppose imperialism and colonialism. Lenin referred to imperialism as 'the highest stage of capitalism'.
4. If relations between nation states are dependent on production, this would lead to the exploitation of the proletariat through the appropriation of surplus value generated by production, as the bourgeoisie class has monopoly over the means of production. Marxists want to abolish this inequality between the classes.

Structural Marxism

Johan Galtung, the father of structural Marxism, pointed out the *structural violence* present in international politics. He said that there are four types of structural violence in global politics:

1. War, torture, or inhuman punishment
2. Lack of fundamental material needs such as shelter, food and water
3. Lack of freedom to choose one's belief, or deprival of human rights
4. Alienation or deprival of 'higher needs'

Except the first, all are examples of the kind of structural violence that occurs within and between states. He said that imperialism is not only economic domination but also political, cultural and military domination as well as domination in the field of communication. He said that the world can be divided into two: the *Core* or centre (highly developed) and the *Periphery* (less developed). This division exists within a nation too. Galtung said that structural imperialism is based on two mechanisms:

1. Vertical Interaction: The Core gets the financial reward through exploitation of the Periphery.
2. Feudal Interaction: This reinforces the inequalities produced by vertical interaction. The following are the features of feudal interaction:
   (a) Vertical interaction between the Core and the Periphery.
   (b) No interaction between Peripheries.

(c) No multilateral interaction.
(d) Interaction with the outside world controlled by the Core.

Dependency Theory

Dependency Theory was developed by the scholars Andre Gunder Frank and Samir Amin. They criticised the concept of the Stages of Economic Growth that Rostow proposed in 1960. In his book *World Accumulation, 1492–1789* (1978), Frank identified the three stages of capital accumulation:

1. Mercantilism (1500–1770)
2. Industrial Capitalism (1770–1870)
3. Imperialism (1870–1930)

He further said that since Asian and African nations have been subjected to exploitation, they are underdeveloping. He was the first to recognise and label the difference between the *un-developed* and the *underdeveloped.* All the nations belonging to Europe were earlier undeveloped. European states gradually became industrialised and urbanised, moving away from an agriculture-based economy. He uses the term underdevelopment to refer to the status of Asian and African countries which were under colonisation. According to Frank, underdeveloped nations cannot be developed as they are still under exploitation. Asian and African nations became politically independent, but economically and in many other ways they are under the control of developed nations, and this may be termed *New Colonisation.* International trade is more often than not against the interest of these underdeveloped Asian and African nations. These underdeveloped nations often have to negotiate *adverse terms of trade* as they export raw materials, as opposed to European and North American states who export manufactured goods. This is how the Core exploits the Periphery, and this exploitation will come to an end only after abolition of capitalism.

Dependency theory evolved from the ideas of Lenin, who divided nation states into two classes: he termed the European states the bourgeois class and the Asian and African states the proletariat. Similarly, dependency theorists divide the world into two categories of states: the core and the periphery.

The **core states** are the liberal-capitalist democracies of Western Europe and North America, who are the elite '*metropolis*' and who provide high wages and encourage high levels of investment and welfare services.

The periphery states are (often non-democratic) governments where workers can mostly expect wages below subsistence levels and where there are no welfare services, such as sub-Saharan and Central Africa, and parts of South Asia.

Since the resources and economic profits generated by the regional peripheries are diverted towards the core states located in Europe and North America, this kind of financial globalisation only contributes to enhancing the economic prowess of the countries of the Global North. He proposed the concept of 'Development of underdevelopment' to denote the deteriorating economic condition of the peripheral states as the result of their dependency on the core. Another notable book by Frank is *Dependent Accumulation and Underdevelopment* (1978).

New Dependency Theory

Theotonio Dos Santos, a Brazilian economist, propounded the concept of new dependency. According to him, Multinational Corporations (MNCs) are the new agents of exploitation, replacing nation-states. The rise of newly industrialised countries like South Korea, Taiwan and Singapore proved the inherent flaw in the dependency theory which saw the world as a binary of the core and the periphery. These newly industrialised nations were also subject to colonial exploitation but registered a high economic growth rate due to the adoption of a capitalist mode of economic development. It refutes the claim by dependency theorists who said that the Asian and African nations are underdeveloped and they will never register development. Disintegration of the Soviet Union further disproved the dependency theory.

The World-Systems Theory by Wallerstein

Wallerstein presented a modified version of the dependency theory in his famous book *The Modern World-System (1974)*. He introduced the idea of the *semi-periphery* to the binary of the core and the periphery. He also studied the rise and decline of core nations (dominant powers) in the world-system over time.

Core

Wallerstein pointed out three instances of hegemony: the **United Province of Netherlands** (also called the **Dutch Republic**) in the mid-seventeenth century, the **United Kingdom** in the mid-nineteenth century, and the **United States** in the mid-twentieth century. The core refers to these regions or these hegemonic powers that benefited most from changes in political power. In the initial period of expansion, the core included most of northwestern Europe (France, England and Holland).

Periphery

The periphery, in contrast, refers to the regions that lack a strong central government and that depend on coercive labour rather than fair wage-labour. These economies are most often dependent upon the export of raw materials to the core. Latin America and Eastern Europe were key peripheral zones in the sixteenth century.

Semi-Periphery

Wallerstein said that the semi-periphery comprised either regions that could be geographically located in the core but were undergoing a process of relative decline (such as Spain and Portugal) or regions that were rising economies located in the periphery. These regions too are exploited by the core. He argues that the semi-periphery is a crucial buffer between the core and the periphery.

Wallerstein also traces the geographical expansion of the world-systems over time. Two stages in particular mark the development of world-systems from the sixteenth to the late twentieth century. Based on this, he defined **two types of world-systems:** the earlier *world-empire* and the more recent *capitalist world-system.* He conjectures that the period of US hegemony may be coming to an end now that Japanese and Western European enterprises are challenging the American hegemony. Being a Marxist, Wallerstein recognises the fundamental contradiction in the capitalist world-system, which is that it is an exploitative system by its very nature.

Some of Wallerstein's notable works are *Geopolitics and Geoculture: Essay on the Changing World-System* (1991) and *The Decline of American Power: The US in a Chaotic World* (2003).

Figure 5.1.1: Features of Core, Periphery and Semi-Periphery

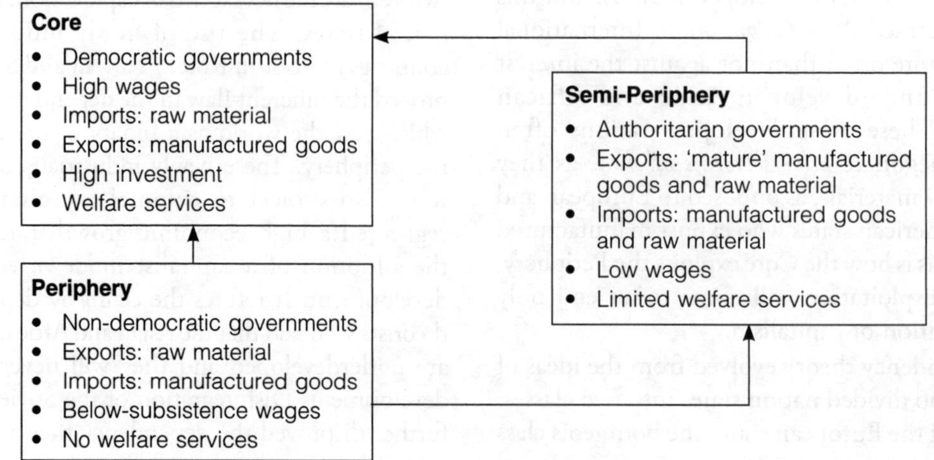

Critique of Marxist Theory: Economic Reductionism

Marxist theory has always been criticised due to its principle of economic reductionism. Marxists always analyse history, society, politics and international relations in terms of the modes of production and the relations of production, and neglect other factors. Therefore, Marxist analyses run the risk of being one-dimensional. Quincy Wright criticises the Marxist approach by saying that there cannot be a Marxist theory of international relations because Marxist theory is a political theory that revolves around capitalism, colonialism, and imperialism and is unable to explain concepts like national interest, security or diplomacy.

CRITICAL THEORY OF INTERNATIONAL RELATIONS OR NEO-MARXISM

According to Critical Theory, Marxism is not sacrosanct or absolute but a guiding principle. The **Frankfurt School** developed critical theory, which is not associated with any particular ideology or political party. Critical Theory challenges both the ideas of capitalism and Marxism. Classical Marxists emphasise economic factors, unlike neo-Marxists who believe that ideological and cultural factors are just as important as economic factors when it comes to understanding colonialism and imperialism. Neo-Marxists do not believe in economic determinism and scientific positivism. Instead, human factors and conscientiousness is more important for neo-Marxists.

Antonio Gramsci developed a theory of *hegemony*, where he described hegemony as a subtle form of political power which relied upon consent rather than coercion. In a hegemonic social situation, dominant groups (classes, class fractions, and their various allies) articulate a social vision which claims to serve the interests of all, and they use selective incentives to recruit junior partners into their coalition, in order to divide and disable opposition. Gramsci said that an atomised and depoliticised capitalist culture can be challenged by a counter-hegemonic political culture, and such a culture must be developed consciously by the communist movement.

Louis Althusser further developed Gramsci's theory and distinguished between ideological state apparatuses and repressive state apparatuses. The latter are a part of civil society and function through institutions like religion, education and other mechanisms by exercising hegemonic soft power. Neo-Marxists assert that this kind of power exhibits itself in the form of dominant ideology and culture, which represent the actual material interests of the dominant class and contribute to sustaining its practices of exploitation.

Robert Cox was a pioneer in using Gramscian conceptual vocabulary to make sense of historical structures of global power. In his book *Production, Power and World Order* (1987), Cox explicitly called into question the prevailing modes of theorising world politics, which were either positivist or had 'problem-solving' objectives. He said that globalisation is only beneficial for the capitalist nations and that is why the major powers facilitated the process of globalisation. Cox argues that counter-hegemonic social forces should engage in a *war of position* against the hegemonic powers.

He further said that globalisation from above must be counter with *globalisation from below*. The process of inter-state consensus take place within a common ideological framework, and the internal structure of state, which is hierarchical, is responsible for that consensus. According to him, the leadership of the state is more cultural and moral. Cox rejected the positivistic or scientific forms of inquiry and said that scientific theories cannot be applied in the social sciences. He said that each and every theory exists for some justification. He shows us an alternative perspective on the post-Cold War era, starkly different those most often discussed by realists and liberals. Changes in the balance of power between states and the alleged ascendancy of democracy over authoritarianism are subservient to what Cox calls '*global perestroika*'. Neo-Marxists thus agree that globalisation is a new tool of exploitation which functions as a mechanism for promoting imperialism and neo-colonialism under the guise of global capitalism.

Andrew Linklater is another important thinker who built on Gramsci's work on hegemony, and made major contributions to the neo-Marxist line of thought. He criticises realism, which champions struggle for power and considers the state as the most important institution, as well as capitalism, and instead proposes the idea of a democratic government without capitalist economy and emphasis on human security. In his book *Beyond Realism and Marxism: Critical Theory and International Relations (1989)*, he said that realists are not concerned about freedom and emancipation and Marxists failed to explain the sources of war. Linklater is also influenced by **Kantian ethics** in that he believes that nation states may transcend their borders without subordinating the liberty of the individual. He believes in supranational organisation and proposes *cosmopolitanism*, although he failed to explain how cosmopolitanism could be established. He also wrote *Men and Citizens in the Theory of International Relations* (1992).

Important Works

Johan Galtung: 'A Structural Theory of Imperialism' (1971), *Transarmament and the Cold War* (1988).

Robert Cox: *The Autonomy of Influence: Decision Making in International Organization* (1973), *Social Force, State and World Order: Beyond International Relations Theory* (1981), *Production, Power, and World Order* (1987), *Approaches to World Order* (1996).

Andrew Linklater: *The Achievements of Critical Theory* (1996).

Andre Gunder Frank: *Capitalism and Underdevelopment in Latin America: Historical Studies of Chile and Brazil* (1967)

Richard A. Falk: *Law, Morality and War in Contemporary World* (1963).

John Button: *International Relations: A General Theory* (1965).

The following sections give an overview of the **alternative theories of IR**, namely, social constructivism, feminism, and postmodernism.

SOCIAL CONSTRUCTIVISM

Constructivism is a structural theory of international relations that makes the following core claims:

(a) States are the principle unit of analysis for international political theory.
(b) States systems are created by human beings, therefore these systems are premised on 'ideas' rather than being material or empirical in nature.
(c) Identities and interests of states are the product of social structures.

The most important theorists within this tradition are **Peter Katzenstein**, who authored *The Culture of National Security* (1996), **Friedrich Kratochwil** who authored *Rules, Norms and Decisions* (1989), and **Alexander Wendt** who wrote the essay 'Anarchy is What States Make of It: The Social Construction of Power Politics' (1992). Wendt rejects the central thesis of neo-realism as propounded by Kenneth Waltz. He asserts that self-help and power politics are institutions, not essential features of anarchy. Anarchy is what states make of it. Therefore, the 'security dilemma' between sovereign states in situations of anarchy does not exist because any situation that states are in is a situation that they themselves have created. According to Wendt, the distribution of power may always affect states' estimation of a situation, but the extent of this effect depends on the inter-subjective understandings and expectations—on the 'distribution of knowledge'—that constitute their conceptions of self and other.

The Main Principles of Social Constructivism

The three main tenets of social constructivism are: (1) reality is not objective and scientific, (2) state is a social construct, and (3) the natural world is different from the social world.

1. Reality is not Objective and Scientific

Scientific and objective theories cannot be applied for the study of international relations because reality in social sciences is not material and external. Kenneth Waltz explains the theory of realism as objective facts which are not practical for studying the social life. Constructivists reject the notion of objective truth; social scientists cannot discover a 'final truth' about the world which is true across time and place.

Constructivists thus reject the strict positivism of the rationalist theories and assert that there is no external, objective social reality as argued, for instance, by realism (which focuses on the centrality of power in international relations). Constructivists talk about the social construction of reality. According to social constructivism, human relations, including international relations, consist of thought and ideas and not of material conditions or forces.

2. State is a Social Construct

Although the social world is in part constructed of physical entities, it is the ideas and beliefs concerning those entities which are the most important. In the ideational view held by social constructivists, what matters is what those entities signify in the minds of people, that is, the ideas. The core ideational element of constructivist focus is the *inter-subjective beliefs* (ideas, conceptions and assumptions) that are widely shared among people. The international system does not exist on its own like solar system. It exists only as an inter-subjective awareness among people. Thus, ideas must be widely shared for them to matter.

3. The Natural World is Different from the Social World

Since the socio-political world is a part of human consciousness, it cannot be conceptualised on the basis of any general, objective laws of nature. The *social world* is not a given, and does not exist independent of the thoughts and ideas of the people involved in it.

Constructivists perceive the realist theory of power as the core of *material reality* as reductionist—they claim that it overly simplifies the complex social, economic and cultural realities of international relations. The constructivists say that neo-realist uncertainty is closely connected to the fact that the theory is overly materialist. The constructivists pay close attention to the cultural, institutional and normative aspects of this complexity, and argue that a focus on thoughts and ideas leads to a better theory about anarchy and balance of power.

FEMINISM

It is important to note that in international relations, which deals with nation-states, gender is an important factor for understanding the behaviour of a state. Society is patriarchal and state is the product of society. In a patriarchal system, masculinity is often associated with rationality, power, independence and the public sphere, while femininity is associated with irrationality, the need for protection, domesticity and the private sphere. Feminist theory in IR developed originally in work on the politics of development and peace research.

Jean Bethke Elshtain wrote *Women and War* (1987), in which she says that there is no attempt to sort through the debate over the 'cause of war' in the international system and no appropriate policies to reduce the incidence of war. She is particularly concerned with how perceptions related to war are closely connected with the construction of gender roles in society. She also explores the reasons for the lack of attention paid to the relationship between gender and war in the Anglo-American tradition. She talks about the two dominant myths: 'Man as the Just Warrior' and 'Woman as the Beautiful Soul'. She also said that women are seen as **life-givers**, whereas men as *life-takers*. Elshtain suggests that we need to destabilise these myths that help to perpetuate war. She emphasises the need to develop 'alternative images of citizenship' and break away from the images traditionally associated with armed civic virtue. She also criticises realism which overlooks the social construction of state.

Cynthia Enloe wrote *Bananas, Beaches and Bases* (1989) in which she focuses on seven major arenas of gendered international politics: tourism, nationalism, military bases, diplomacy, agriculture, textiles and domestic service. She shows how women's participation and involvement facilitate tourism, colonialism and economically powerful states' exploitation of weak states. In turn, the creation of stable diplomatic military communities stationed abroad has been the responsibility of women as wives, girlfriends, prostitutes and hostesses. In her book *The Morning After: Sexual Politics at the End of the Cold War* (1993), she said that gender relations are important for understanding militarism, nationalism and the Cold War.

Another important proponent of feminism in IR theory is **V. Spike Peterson** who authored the book, *Global Gender Issues in the New Millennium* published in 1993. **Anne Sisson Runyan** is another notable feminist scholar in this area who wrote *Gender and Global Restructuring*.

J. Ann Tickner asserts that there are gendered perceptions in IR, hidden by purported 'gender neutrality' and 'objectivity'. She argues that the discipline of IR has connotations of maleness, based on a hegemonic masculinity which places masculinity in opposition to femininity that is less valued. Tickner targets Morgenthau's six principles of political realism as exemplary of the school of thought as a whole. She provides her own reformulation, a feminist critique of Morgenthau's principles, in the form of the following six principles:

1. 'Objective laws', on which politics is conceptualised, are based on a partial, masculine view of human nature. Tickner contends that human nature is both masculine and feminine.
2. National interest is multidimensional and uncertain, and hence it cannot be defined solely in terms of power. National interest demands cooperation rather than zero-sum solutions to a set of interdependent problems.
3. Power seen in terms of domination and control privileges masculinity and ignores the possibility of collective empowerment, which is another aspect of power associated with feminists.
4. We cannot separate morality from politics. All political action has moral significance.
5. The feminist perspective seeks to find common moral elements in human aspirations which could become the basis for de-escalating international conflict and building international community.
6. The feminist perspective denies autonomy of the political since this autonomy is associated with masculinity, especially in western culture. This demarcation presents a limited, partial and masculine worldview.

Feminist concerns have been widely deliberated upon and debated at the global level on multiple instances. These instances have seen the amalgamation of both state, non-state and inter-state actors at conferences representing concerns of various schools of thought encompassed by feminist concerns. Some of the important conferences include:

1. First World Conference on Women in 1975, in Nairobi.
2. World Conference on Women in 1980, in Copenhagen.
3. World Conference on Women in 1985, in Nairobi.
4. World Conference on Women in 1995, in Beijing.
5. World Conference of the International Women's Year by the UN in 1975, in Mexico.
6. Convention of the Elimination of All Forms of Discrimination against Women in 1979.

7. Declaration on Elimination of Violence against Women in 1993.

Feminism and Peace-Keeping: In October 2000, the UN Security Council adopted Resolution 1325. This resolution called for broad participation of women in peace-building post-conflict reconstruction. It advocates the inclusion of women in peace agreement, post-conflict decision-making, and the protection of women and girls in conflict.

POSTMODERNISM

Postmodernist provides an alternative to Marxism and realism. They reject overarching *meta narratives* and are against the idea of a single objective, scientific 'universal truth'. They proposed the *deconstruction* of established theories.

Postmodernism, as a theoretical idea, originated in France in the post-war era as a challenge to the philosophy of Existentialism. Existentialism is a form of rational philosophical theory which emphasises the existence of the individual person as a free and responsible agent determining their own development through acts of the will. Postmodernism as a theory thus rejects the concepts of rationality, objectivity and universal truth. It emphasises the diversity of human experience and multiplicity of perspectives.

Postmodernists also critique Marxism since it claims to provide an arbitrary meta-narrative of history. Post-modernist IR scholars consider themselves *de-constructivists*. The advent of postmodernism in IR theory has led to reflection on the interests and metaphysical suppositions which guide and frame knowledge. The entire paradigm of theory-building in the format of metanarratives is looked upon with skepticism. The postmodernists are also skeptical of neoliberal institutionalism which underlines the optimism that it is possible to fashion institutions that are fair and just for everyone. The notion of universal human progress is also systematically debunked by post-modernism.

Richard Ashley is one of the major proponents of postmodernist theory within IR. His major work titled 'The Achievements of Post-Structuralism' was published in 1996. Ashley says that technical reason robs theory of its critical role, and the role of social scientist is then the same as the role of a technician. He is against the positivist/scientific concept of theory and instead proposes a more 'reflective' perspective. He sees power as a network of disciplinary practices which help to constitute our identity-constructed selves. He said that power can be exercised from below as well as from above.

Rob Walker is another notable postmodernist who wrote *Inside/Outside: International Relations as Political Theory*. He criticises the principle of sovereignty. He speaks against the dichotomy that exists in IR theory, for instance, realism vs idealism, hierarchy vs anarchy, theory vs practice, and proposes a deconstruction of these binaries. Walker's postmodernist approach of IR can be summed as a *Discursive Practices Approach*.

Critique of Post-modernism: There is a common perception that postmodernism lacks in ethics and is self-annihilating because of its relativism, self-universalism and nihilism. Nihilism implies the belief that nothing in the world has real existence.

FOUR GREAT DEBATES OF INTERNATIONAL THEORY

A common way of narrating the divided history of IR is in terms of the Great Debates surrounding the key issues. The theory regarding the four great debates was propounded originally by I. J. Benneyworth. These include:

1. **Realism versus Liberalism**

   This was a debate between idealism and stoicism, between liberal scholars like Woodrow Wilson and realists represented chiefly by E. H. Carr. It is widely believed that the emergence of Nazism—Fascism and the beginning of the Second World War resulted in the triumph of realism in this debate because the biggest project of liberal idealism, the League of Nations, failed to achieve world peace.

2. **Traditionalism versus Behaviouralism**
   This was a methodological debate which emerged in the 1960s following the behavioural revolution in the social sciences and the emergence of positivism in the sciences. This debate took the rhetorical arguments about science and gave them methodological substance. For the proponents of the behavioral revolution, IR could move forward only if it consciously modeled itself on the natural sciences. The normativism and hypothesis-based theory construction of traditional IR scholars were rejected. The stress on observable data and measurement led the proponents of the new scientific model to engage in a series of sharp criticisms of the understanding of science adhered to by many realists and IR scholars.

3. **Neo-realism versus Neo-liberalism**
   Alternatively known as the neo-neo debate (discussed in detail earlier), the debate primarily took place with the critique of Kenneth Waltz brought forth by Robert Keohane and Joseph Nye in their book *Power and Interdependence* and the realist response delivered by Joseph Grieco.

4. **Rationalism versus Reflectivism**
   This is regarded as an inter-paradigm debate. Keohane takes the label of rationalism directly from the Rational Choice Theory, which has a methodology constructed from a commitment to positivism. These include all the mainstream theories including realism, liberalism, and to a lesser extent, radicalism. Keohane also noted the emergence of a series of theories sharply critical to the mainstream rationalist theories in his now infamous speech of 1988 (ISA Presidential address). He called these approaches reflectivist because while criticising mainstream rationality, they focussed on reflexivity and on the non-neutral nature of political explanation.

2

CONCEPTS IN INTERNATIONAL RELATIONS

KEYWORDS

State, state system and non-state actors, power, sovereignty, security: traditional and non-traditional.

STATE AND STATE SYSTEM

State can be defined in many ways but a simple definition is that a *state* is a centralised political organisation that imposes and enforces rules over a population within a territory as well as represents and protects that population in the international context.

The idea of states dates back to the Treaty of Westphalia (1648) that ended the Thirty Years' War.

The *state system* has four essential elements. These are:

(1) population
(2) territory
(3) government
(4) sovereignty (or independence)

In international relations, an *actor* is any entity that can influence global matters. Traditionally, states were considered to be the dominant actors on the international stage. A **state actor** is the ruling government that holds administrative and military power and can influence the state's foreign policy. Although state actors were earlier regarded as the sole and the most powerful actors in the international arena, technological developments, globalisation and social movements have gradually increased the capacity of the non-state actors over the state actors.

NON-STATE ACTORS, HUMAN RIGHTS AND SOVEREIGNTY

Even though the realists do not accept the importance of non-state actors, the liberal approach places a high importance on non-state actors. The influence of non-state actors has transformed international politics into global politics, according to liberals.

Wendy Pearlman and Kathleen Cunningham define *non-state actors* as 'organised political actors not directly connected to state but pursuing aims that affect vital state interests.' Non-state actors can be organisations or even influential individuals who have the political, economic or social ability to influence a national or international decision.

These are the different **categories of non-state actors**:

(a) Multinational Corporation (MNC)
(b) Inter-governmental Organisation, also known as Supra-national Organisation,

such as the UNO, the WTO, and the European Union.
(c) Non-Governmental Organisation (NGO)
(d) Terrorist organisations, like Al-Qaeda

The Question of Human Rights

Many international organisations have raised strong collective voices and have been working earnestly for the promotion and protection of universal human rights. Most prominent of these, the **Amnesty International Human Rights Watch** has been an active participant in human rights movements across the globe. The **World Social Forum** is another important international organisation that was created in 2005 with the intent of strengthening global civil society.

However, the world continues to be plagued by problems of civil wars, genocide, ethnic cleansing, transnational terrorism and proxy wars which have led to dramatic increases in the number of refugees. European countries, which have been the most immediate destinations of these refugees, have started closing their doors in the wake of rising protectionism and resurgent nationalism.

There has also been substantial increase in global poverty which has led some to argue that the discourse of universal human rights is not only about freedom from fear but equally about '*freedom from wants*' so as to lead to the preservation of human dignity.

Loss of Sovereignty

With rising globalisation and the increasing number of non-state actors like transnational corporations, the states suffer a loss of sovereignty due to their lack of control over financial flows, difficulty in regulation of triangular trade, and global companies taking advantage through regulatory arbitrage.

In 2008, among the 100 TNCs (Trans-National Corporations) with the highest levels of assets outside their home country, 57 were from Western European countries, 19 from the USA, 4 with dual headquarters in Western countries, 10 from Japan, 3 from South Korea and 1 each from Australia, Canada, China, Malayasia, Mexico, Singapore, and Hong Kong. The consequence of this extensive trans-nationalisation of major companies is profound. It is no longer possible to regard each country as having its own separate economy. Two of the most fundamental attributes of sovereignty, *control over currency and control over foreign trade*, have been diminished substantially.

As the logic of intra-firm trade is quite different from that of inter-country trade, it is not possible for governments to have clear expectations of the effects of their financial and fiscal policies on TNCs. As a response to higher tax rates imposed by a government, a company might change its transfer prices to reduce its tax bill. Several other motives might induce a company to distort transfer prices, including evasion of controls on the cross-border movements of profits or capital.

Governments have great difficulty regulating international transactions in case of triangulation of trade as well. It is difficult for governments to regulate the commercial activities of TNCs and MNCs because companies may choose to engage in regulatory arbitrage. If a company objects to one government's policy, it may choose to limit or close down its local production and increase production in another country.

Transnational companies generate clashes of sovereignty between different governments. If a company that has its headquarters in the USA and a subsidiary in the UK, the UK government can control the operations of the subsidiary but will have no control over the headquarters.

From Domestic De-regulation to Global Re-regulation

Domestic de-regulation and globalisation of economic activity means that regulation is now occurring at the global level rather than within individual countries.

According to John Baylis, Steve Smith, and Patricia Owens, there are three factors involved in the push towards globalisation of regulation: *First*, governments can reassert control only by acting collectively. *Second*, consumer pressures are leading to global codes of conduct being accepted by companies and implanted in collaboration with NGOs. *Third*, there is a necessity for global companies to submit to social and environmental auditing.

These factors have led to the collaboration between governments, NGOs and the UN Secretariat, who recruit the major TNCs as voluntary partners in the Global Compact to implement its ten principles of corporate social responsibility on human rights, labour standards, the environment and against corruption.

As a result of pressure primarily from American groups, the United Nations Charter contains Article 71, providing for the Economic and Social Council (ECOSOC) to *consult with NGOs*. In 1950, the Council formally codified this practice in a statute as NGOs are becoming an important means for *promotion of globalisation*. NGOs also provide additional funding for United Nations. **Greenpeace**, founded in Canada, is associated with other NGOs responsible for protecting the environment. Therefore, international politics, which earlier had the state as the main actor is now changing into a more globalised politics with the involvement of several types of non-state actors.

SECURITY

Security is the basic and the most fundamental need of the individual, according to Thomas Hobbes. The state comes into existence to ensure a secure life for its people. The state is thus treated as an instrument for providing security, or in narrower terms, for defence.

Traditional Threats

Realists want to increase the state's *military capability* and military alliances for maintaining security, while **liberals** believe in democracy and constitutionalism for maintaining security of a state.

Barry Buzan talks about the notion of '*security dilemma*'. To put it simply, a security dilemma exists when the actions of one state, in trying to increase its own security, causes a reaction in another state, which eventually decreases the first state's own security. It is a classical dilemma—the increase in the power of one state puts the other state under threat. States face a twin challenge as they have to increase their own power and convince other states that it is not a threat for them.

National security is closely related to international security when we look at the notion of security from the perspective of international society. International society is a *society of states* where peace, order and lawfulness exist. At the same time, a *balance of power* also exists along with internal law and international organisation. Military intervention, nuclear proliferation, and climate change are threats for international security. Threat to security is not necessarily *external*; it can also be *internal* in the form of terrorist attacks and insurgency. Non-state actors may also be the cause behind a threat. Totalitarian and authoritarian states can also create certain kind of threats.

Non-Traditional Threat of Security

It is also important to focus on the notion of *human security*, where security is considered from the perspective of the *individual*. Universal protection of human rights, humanitarian law and crimes against humanity fall under this category. Behind the philosophy of human security lies the idea of the *universal right of mankind*, as Kant defined it. This gives moral priority to the individual. Neo-Marxists and feminists too champion the idea of human security. *Humanitarian intervention* is often required in the international arena to ensure human security. The International Criminal Court (ICC) was established on 1 July 2002 for this purpose.

The United Nations Development Report (UNDP) published a human development report in 1994 which identified 7 **elements of human security**:

1. Economic
2. Food
3. Health
4. Environmental
5. Personal security
6. Community security
7. Political security

Debate about Human Security

The idea of human security is a contested concept in the sense that to ensure the security of human beings, the security of the state must be ensured.

Critics argue that the concept of human security is too broad to be analytically useful as a tool of policy-making. Secondly, it is more moralistic than real, and may cause more harm than good. It permits strong states to interfere in internal affairs of other nations who may not be as strong. It discounts the state as the provider of security. 'Freedom from fear' and 'freedom from want' comprise the fundamental scope of human security. Economists such as **Mahbub ul Haq** and **Amartya Sen** believe that an increase in freedom and an advancement of the richness of human life is the main objective of human development.

Instrumentalist versus Normative Approach

The liberal, Marxist and realist approaches to security are instrumentalist approaches, whereas the feminist, critical theory, and social constructivist approaches can be called normative.

The instrumentalist approach is a more materialist approach guided by power and interest of the state and/or the individual, while the normative approach focuses on ideas, norms and values while talking about security. Barry Buzan, who belongs to the Copenhagen school of thought, has a normative approach as according to him, security is not a narrow concept but a multidimensional one. State is an artificial institution created by individuals. Thus the security of state and the security of individual are complementary to each other. Buzan says security cannot be compartmentalised as human security and state security, national security and regional security, or ecological security and economic security as they are all interrelated.

SOFT POWER

Joseph Nye argues that successful states need both *hard power*, that is, the ability to coerce others, as well as *soft power*, that is, the ability to shape long-term attitudes and preferences. The USA promotes soft power with the help of its companies, universities, churches, foundations and other institutions of civil society. Culture, ideas and values of the USA thus become tools for promoting political power. Soft power refers winning of hearts and minds rather than winning wars. Nye popularised the term 'soft power' in his book *Bound to Lead: The Changing Nature of American Power* (1990) and *Soft Power: The Means to Success in World Politics* (2004). According to him, a country's soft power depended on these three resources:

1. Its *culture* (in places where it is attractive to others)
2. Its *political values* (when it lives up to them at home and abroad)
3. Its *foreign policy* (when others see them as legitimate and having moral authority)

To further elaborate moral authority, Nye says that seduction is always more attractive than coercion. While economic sanction is a kind of coercion, democratic values, human rights and individual opportunities can be considered seductive. In his book *The Future of Power* (2011), he says that soft power is a descriptive concept rather than a normative one.

Niall Ferguson and other neo-realists dismiss the concept of soft power. According to them, actors in international relations respond to only two things: economic incentives and force.

UKRAINE CRISIS

Ukraine crisis can be seen as an indication of the emergence of a **New Cold War** due to the following features:

1. Formation of *military alliance* like AUKUS and Finland and Sweden's desire to join NATO can be seen as a preparation for defence by states who feel threatened. Since the Second World War, Finland and Sweden have preferred the policy of *neutrality* in their foreign policy. It is thus a sea change in the foreign policy of Finland and Sweden, and this shows that Russia's aggression against Ukraine has threatened the security of other states.
2. An *arms race* is growing due to hostility between the USA and Russia. European states like Germany and France have increased their defence budgets.
3. Distrust and misperception have increased between the USA and Russia. The expansion of NATO has been resisted by Russia as well as China. Chinese expansionism has been opposed by the USA in the South China Sea. The US president has said that US is committed to protect the sovereignty of Taiwan.
4. The **QUAD,** re-established in 2017, has been strengthened further. China always objected to the formation of QUAD.
5. Changes in geo-politics have taken place in recent years. China wants control over South China Sea and Senkaku Island. The conflict between Russia and Ukraine is a result of these broader changes in geo-politics.

3

CONFLICT AND PEACE

KEYWORDS

Changing nature of warfare; weapons of mass destruction; deterrence; conflict resolution, conflict transformation.

CHANGING NATURE OF WARFARE

The nature of war and conflicts have changed considerably in the last century. While the first half of the twentieth century saw conflicts among the rich states of the First World, the latter half was dominated by conflicts among the developing nations. A high number of internal conflicts in the past few decades took place in Asia and Africa.

Some factors responsible for the changing nature of warfare are:

1. **Technological Progress:** Because of the advancement of technology, there has been rapid military innovation. High-tech arsenal has become more common and warfare has become more asymmetrical as it is difficult for technologically challenged nations to fight back.
2. **Political Changes:** The world politics in the modern world is cut-throat and it has become common to interfere in the domestic politics of other countries with the aim of destabilising the opponent government.
3. **Changing Strategy:** The strategy of traditional warfare, which had defeat as its objective, has changed. Newer strategies of warfare use the power to hurt to cause damage rather than defeat an opponent.
4. **Communication and Information Flow:** Globalised communication and easy flow of information around the world, the Internet, satellites, drones, phones, etc., are transforming both war and politics. These technologies make it easier for military forces as well as terrorists to attack targets with more precision.

CONFLICT AND RESOLUTION OF CONFLICT

There are various theories about conflict in international relations. **Konrad Lorenz** and **Ted Gurr** are two thinkers who have explored the psychological factors of violence and they state that human nature is the basic cause of conflict. Other political thinkers say that the internal characteristics of state, such as the form of government, ethnic diversity, and economic and military strength are the root causes of conflict. **Karl Deutsch**, however, says that conflict occurs due to the interdependence and interaction among nation-states. But it has been noted by many that conflict and its resolution have a cyclical nature in the international system, and as **Kenneth**

Boulding points out, the nature of international conflict as one marked by the alternation of peace and war.

Two major universities involved in study of peace and conflict are Michigan University and Uppsala University in Sweden.

Origin of Conflict Resolution

As discussed in earlier chapters, realists believe that balance of power is essential for security and peace, while liberals say that it is democracy and international organisational that can help a state become peaceful and secure.

The mathematician-biologist **Anatol Rapoport,** social psychologist **Herbert Kelman** and sociologist **Robert Cooley** are important scholars who have researched on conflict resolution. Cooley launched the *Journal of Conflict Resolution* in 1957 and established the Center for Research on Conflict Resolution in 1959.

Mechanisms for Resolution of Conflict

1. The UN is a *legal mechanism* to solve international disputes.
2. Reconciliation and unilateral concession may be tools for setting disputes, according to **Charles Osgood, Morton Deutsch** and **Amitai Etzioni**. The government can descale a conflict through *Confidence Building Measures* (CBM), which are measures that address, prevent, or resolve uncertainties among states.
3. *Negotiators or third-party officers* can reduce international conflicts, according to the American economist **Thomas Schelling**.
4. Cooperation among multiple political institutions can help solve a conflict. **Richard Barringer** talks about the early detection of conflict potential and resolution in his book *War: Patterns of Conflict.*

These mechanisms can also be categorised under two types: diplomatic methods and judicial methods.

Judicial Methods

There are several Articles in the UN Charter that pertain to conflict resolution.

Article 2 is about peaceful settlement of disputes. It says that members of the UN shall settle their international disputes by peaceful means in such a manner that international peace and security, and justice, are not endangered.

Articles 33 to 38 are also about pacific settlement of disputes. These discuss:

(a) Interpretation of treaties
(b) Questions of international law
(c) Existence of any fact related to breach of international obligations
(d) Extent of compensation in case of breach of international obligation

Articles 92 to 96 are about the International Court of Justice, which is a major judicial organ of the UN that plays a crucial role in resolution of international conflicts.

Diplomatic Methods

The diplomatic methods among these are the following:

(i) Negotiations
(ii) Good offices and mediation
(iii) Conciliation
(iv) Arbitration

The Hague Conventions of 1899 and 1907 led to the creation of a binding international court for compulsory arbitration to settle international disputes.

There are many non-violent procedures of conflict resolution that does not involve waging war. These may be pacific methods and yet also coercive. States turn to coercive but non-violent methods for the resolution of conflicts only when peaceful procedures are unsuccessful. Although these are diplomatic processes that do not involve violence or war, they still have a coercive effect. These non-violent coercive techniques are state actions such as: recall of diplomats; expulsion of diplomats, denial of recognition, rupture of diplomatic ties; suspension of treaties, etc.

Various Forms of Diplomacy

There are various types of diplomacies possible. Some of these are listed below.

1. **Multi-Track Diplomacy**

   Louise Diamond and **John M. Donald** wrote *Multi-Track Diplomacy: A Systems Approach to Peace.* The book has a systemic approach to peacemaking and conflict resolution, and identifies the players and activities that contribute to the peacemaking and peacebuilding process in a community. These are:

   Track I – Government or Peacemaking through Diplomacy

   Track II – Non-Governmental Professional or Peacemaking through Conflict Resolution

   Track III – Business, or Peacemaking through Commerce

   Track IV – Private Citizen, or Peacemaking through Personal Involvement

   Track V – Research, Training, and Education, or peacemaking through Learning (Thinktanks)

   Track VI – Activism or Peacemaking through Advocacy (NGOs)

   Track VII – Religion or Peacemaking through Faith in action

   Track VIII – Financial Activities or Peacemaking through Providing Resources

   Track IX – Media and Communication or Peacemaking through Information

2. **Gunboat Diplomacy**

   The basis of gunboat diplomacy is a full reorganisation of the legitimacy of using military force to achieve the goal of foreign policy.

3. **Dollar Diplomacy**

   This type of diplomacy involves the use of economic methods (for example, loans) to achieve the goals of the state.

4. **Public Diplomacy**

   Public diplomacy is different from traditional diplomacy, which is carried out through people with specialised professions.

5. **Shopkeeper Diplomacy**

   Shopkeeper diplomacy is a peaceful settlement of disputes between states through a series of negotiations.

6. **Ping-Pong Diplomacy**

   This special kind of diplomacy refers to the exchange of table tennis players between the USA and People's Republic of China in the early 1970s. On February 28, 1972 USA President Nixon visited Shanghai and the Shanghai Communiqué was issued between the US and the PRC.

Some important books on conflict resolution and peace-making are Kenneth Boulding's *Three Faces of Power* (1990) and *Stable Peace* (1978), and *The Underside of History: A View of Women through Time* (1977) by Elise Boulding

NUCLEAR PROLIFERATION

Weapons are nothing new in themselves: they are as old as the beginning of civilisation. But with the advancement of technology and modernisation, Weapons of Mass Destruction or WMD have been developed. These include nuclear weapons, biological weapons and chemical weapons. They are different from traditional weapons, which only cause harm to limited numbers, typically affecting defence personnel. WMD are capable of killing masses and therefore civilians also become the targets of WMD in modern warfare. The security of the entire world and its population is under threat due to presence of WMD.

Causes of Nuclear Proliferation

The international system is an anarchical system where every state is responsible for its own safety and thus their interactions with each other are laden with extreme unpredictability. Conflict of interests and consequentially war is a perpetual and imminent possibility. This is referred to as the *security dilemma*. Since the states are responsible for their own security, they want to surpass the capabilities of other states, and thus, all states seek to maximise their possession of weapons of mass destruction such as nuclear weapons.

The '**Atoms for Peace**' programme was announced by US President **Dwight D. Eisenhower** in 1953. The 'Atoms for Peace' program opened up nuclear research to civilians and countries that had not previously possessed nuclear technology. Eisenhower argued for a non-proliferation agreement throughout the world and argued for a stop of the spread of military use of nuclear weapons.

Since the inception of Non-Aligned Movement (NAM) in 1961, India has voiced its concerns strongly in the favour of a comprehensive nuclear disarmament which would eventually lead to a nuclear weapons-free world. However, this attitude transformed with the regime change in 1964 after Nehru's death and with the changing international context that caused heightened tensions in the subcontinent due to the Cold War. Additionally, the imposition of US sanctions in support of Pakistan during both the 1965 and 1971 wars and the 1962 Chinese aggression disturbed the balance of power in the subcontinent. To respond to this changing context, India conducted its first nuclear weapons test in 1974 and a second, more comprehensive one, in May 1998. The latter was immediately followed by nuclear tests by Pakistan in June 1998.

Various other nations of the world have been attempting to develop nuclear weapons and they have been dubbed 'irresponsible' by the P5 (the United States, China, France, Russia, and the United Kingdom, the five members of the Security Council) who were the earliest ones to acquire nuclear arsenals. A prominent example is Iran who wants to acquire nuclear advantage over its adversary, Israel.

The following are the main causes of nuclear proliferation:

(a) Lack of Collective Security

An important reason behind the continued proliferation of nuclear weapons is the lack of collective security regimes in the world. Contrary to popular expectation, the United Nations has been ineffective against countering US hegemony within the institution. A glaring instance is the 2001 Iraq invasion (on the grounds of preventing it from developing nuclear weapons) despite the fact that there was no consensus in UNSC regarding the operation due to strong opposition from Russia and China.

(b) Enhancing Status

An important driving motivation for the possession of nuclear weapons is also the accompanying socio-psychological impact associated with WMD. The nations who possess nuclear weapons are revered for their technological development as well as for their might. It enhances their say and status in the international arena. Pakistan and North Korea are important examples of nations who have enhanced their status through development and possession of nuclear weapons.

(c) Technological Advancement

Nuclear technology is an advanced dual-use technology due to its exceptional capacity for power generation. Therefore, it can be used for peaceful purposes such as scientific research and electricity production as well as a weapon for mass destruction. There has been strong advocacy of the use of nuclear technology solely for peaceful purposes at the global level but there are inherent complexities to this doctrine, because that would necessitate enhanced surveillance upon the nuclear reactors of the acting states which may impinge on their sovereignty.

Direction of Proliferation

In the post-Cold War world, the direction of proliferation moved from Europe to Asia. Earlier, the wave of proliferation was concentrated in Europe. But it gradually moved to Asia as India and Pakistan had nuclear weapons by 1998 and North Korea by 2006. North Korea withdrew itself from the Treaty on the Non-Proliferation of Nuclear Weapons (NPT) and tested nuclear weapons. This is why they are considered to be a rogue nuclear state which does not follow the international rules and norms. Iran is also in the race to get the nuclear weapons. It is believed that **Saudi Arabia** too has also been developing its nuclear programme because of its fraught relations with **Iran**.

New Cold War: China is one of the fastest growing economies and possibly soon to become the largest economy in the world. Its growth is based on technology, innovation and trade and challenges US military prowess. This has fueled a strategic rivalry between the two countries. In 2017, the US National Security Strategy called China as 'a revisionist power' seeking 'to erode American security and prosperity' and 'shape a world antithetical to US values and interests' as China has been proactive in undermining the US hegemony on multiple fronts.

EFFORTS TOWARDS NON-PROLIFERATION AND DISARMAMENT

Theories of Disarmament

- **Peace Theory**

  According to **John Burton** and **Inis Claude,** armament is one of the major causes of tension and fear among states. (Morgenthau however believed the opposite and he said that states do not fight because they have arms, but they have arms because they deem it necessary to fight.) Security dilemma occurs as a result of arms, and thus proponents of Peace Theory consider arms to be a cause behind wars. Disarmament thus can be an important step towards peace.

- **Economic Theory**

  Eisenhower in his **Atoms for Peace speech** argued for a non-proliferation agreement and advocated a stop of the spread of military use of nuclear weapons. **James Wolfe and Theodore Couloumbis** said that reduction in armament results in the release of funds and finances which can then be utilised for the well-being of the people. Therefore, disarmament can reduce expenditure of money and resources. (Hedley Bull however had an opposing view and he said that disarmament would prevent the development of new science and technology.)

- **Moral Theory**

  The moral argument against arms is that violence is morally wrong and arms are responsible for war. The concept of holy wars and just wars, even if they are can be morally justified, are not in line with the Gandhian concept of peace and non-violence, which support disarmament.

Treaties Associated with Arms Control

In the post-Cold War era, that is the 1990s, a new world order was established and several nuclear and conventional arms control agreements were implemented.

1. The **Treaty on Conventional Armed Forces in Europe (CFE Treaty)** was signed in 1990 (and entered into force in 1992) between the two great powers, the US and Russia (or erstwhile USSR). It imposed limits on the deployment of conventional military forces in Europe.

2. **Strategic Arms Reduction Treaty I (START I)** was signed in 1991 between USA and Russia and entered into force in 1994. START I is considered a successor to the expired SALT agreements (Strategic Arms Limitation Talks). START I expired in 2009. It enforced limitations on the deployment of strategic offensive arms.
3. **The Chemical Weapons Convention** was agreed upon in 1993 and entered into force in 1997. It imposed absolute prohibition on the production and stockpiling of chemical weapons all over the world.
4. **START II,** a successor to START I, was signed in 1993, and ratified in 1996 by the United States and in 2000 by Russia. It got automatically terminated following Russian withdrawal from the Treaty in 2002. START II provided for prohibition on the deployment of intercontinental ballistic missiles equipped with multiple independently targetable re-entry vehicles.
5. The **Treaty on Open Skies**, aimed towards unhindered aviation, was signed in 1992 and entered into force in 2002. Unarmed reconnaissance flights between NATO countries and Russia were permitted under the agreements constituting this treaty.
6. The **Ottawa Treaty** against the deployment of anti-personnel landmines was signed in 1997 and entered into force in 1999.
7. The **Strategic Offensive Reductions Treaty (SORT),** alternatively known as the **Treaty of Moscow,** was a strategic arms reduction treaty signed between the USA and Russia in 2002 and it entered into force in 2003. It expired in 2011.
8. The **International Code of Conduct against Ballistic Missile Proliferation**, also known as the Hague Code of Conduct, was signed in 2002 and it is the only normative instrument to check the proliferation of ballistic missiles.
9. **Convention on Cluster Munitions** is an international treaty that prohibits the use, transfer and stockpiling of cluster bombs. It was adopted in 2008 and entered into force in 2010.
10. The **New START Treaty** was signed between Russia and the United States in April 2010 and entered into force in February 2011. It aimed to reduce the number of strategic nuclear missiles by half.
11. **The Arms Trade Treaty** is a multilateral treaty that regulates international trade in conventional weapons. It was signed in 2013 and entered into force on 24 December 2014.
12. The **Comprehensive Nuclear-Test-Ban Treaty (CTBT)**, a multilateral treaty to ban nuclear weapons test explosions and any other nuclear explosions. This is discussed in more detail in the following section.

Some other treaties are:

- Partial Nuclear Test Ban Treaty (PTBT), signed in 1963.
- Strategic Arms Limitation Talks-I (SALT-I), signed in 1972.
- Strategic Arms Limitation Talks-II (SALT-II), signed in 1979.
- Intermediate-Range Nuclear Forces Treaty (INF), signed in 1987

The Comprehensive Nuclear-Test-Ban Treaty

The CTBT is one of the most important contemporary disarmament regimes which has been widely criticised for its discriminatory provision. It was signed in 1996, but has not yet entered into force. It prohibits the testing of nuclear weapons for both civil and military purposes and in all environments. As per the treaty, each state party undertakes the resolution not to carry out any nuclear weapon test explosion and to refrain from carrying out any nuclear tests.

Entry into force is an essential feature of CTBT, which means all the 44 states (as listed in Annexe 2) having nuclear research facilities will have to sign the CTBT for the treaty to enter into force. As of August 2011, 36 of these states have ratified the Treaty. Eight states still need to do so: China, North Korea, Egypt, India, Iran, Israel, Pakistan and the US. Ratification of the Treaty should be done within 180 days of its implementation. Thereafter it will come into force. A review of the Treaty can be done within 10 years of implementation of the treaty and a conference can be convened for this purpose.

The CTBT Organization promotes the Treaty so that it can enter into force. It has established a verification regime to monitor adherence to the Treaty. It is headquartered in Vienna. The *verification regimes* comprise the **International Monitoring System (IMS)** and the **International Data Centre (IDC)**.

Why India Refused to Sign the CTBT

India stressed on the importance of disarmament and *nuclear non-proliferation*, only the latter of which is incorporated within the CTBT. Therefore, the implementation of CTBT has to start with the disarmament of nuclear arsenals of the N5 (Nuclear Five), who are aiming towards vertical proliferation by developing computer-simulation techniques. Technologically, CTBT is flawed because it cannot prevent the nuclear development of P5 (Permanent Five) because they have already made progress using computer simulation techniques. This technique has enhanced their capability of conducting virtual tests and of modifying and developing their weapons with greater precision. Therefore, India has contended that CTBT is not aiming for a nuclear-free world and has thus refused to sign it. Rather CTBT is directed against Threshold Countries like India, Pakistan and Israel. The Entry into Force clause is also perceived as impinging on the sovereignty of nation-states.

The CTBT is also against the transfer of technology which will hamper the technological and scientific development of developing countries like India. It is for all these reasons that India has refused to sign the CTBT.

The Nuclear Non-Proliferation Treaty (NPT)

The Treaty on Non-Proliferation of Nuclear Weapons is an international treaty with an objective to limit the escalation of a nuclear arms race and the technology related to it. Further goals of the treaty include the promotion of cooperation among countries, encouraging the peaceful use of nuclear energy and achieving complete nuclear disarmament.

The Treaty was opened for signing in 1968 and came into effect in 1970. The NPT prohibits nations which do not have nuclear weapons from acquiring them, and at the same time, prohibs the nuclear states from helping others in acquiring nuclear weapons.

There are **five nuclear weapon states** under the NPT, namely the USA (acquired nuclear weapons in 1945), Russia (in 1949), China (in 1964), Britain (in 1952) and France (in 1960). These are nations that acquired nuclear weapons before 1 January 1967. Apart from the P5, four other states possess nuclear weapons, namely **India, Pakistan, Israel** and **North Korea.** They are perceived as violators and are not designated the status of nuclear weapon states.

The treaty stipulates that the N5 or Nuclear Five states are required to share nuclear technology and resources with the non-nuclear weapon states, but only for peaceful purposes. However, for the operationalisation of this transfer, the non-nuclear weapon states are required to sign the NPT.

According to the provision of the treaty, there will be periodical review of the NPT regime every five years. The NPT was extended indefinitely in 1995.

The NPT also provides for the *creation of a nuclear weapon-free zone*. As of 2016, there are five such regional treaties in place in populated areas of the world: Latin America and the Caribbean, Africa, Central Asia, Southeast Asia, and the South Pacific.

In addition, Mongolia has been given the status of a nuclear-free territory by the UNGA. Antarctica and outer-space are also considered as nuclear-free regions.

Criticism of NPT

Non-Nuclear Weapon States (NNWS) perceive the NPT as a **discriminatory treaty** as it focuses on preventing only horizontal proliferation while there is no limit on vertical proliferation. *Vertical proliferation* refers to the advancement or modernisation of a state's existing nuclear arsenal. *Horizontal proliferation* on the other hand refers to the direct or indirect transfer of nuclear weapons from one state to another. Therefore, although the NPT focuses on non-proliferation, it fails to include the objective of disarmament.

India too has always considered the NPT as discriminatory and has therefore refused to sign it. India has opposed the international treaties aimed at non-proliferation since they were selectively applicable to the non-nuclear powers. They also legitimised the monopoly of the five nuclear weapon states, which has in turn resulted in an exacerbation of the security dilemma of the NNWS.

India has strongly vocalised its demands for comprehensive nuclear disarmament instead of just non-proliferation. International law recognises all states as equal and sovereign in their own right. Therefore, India's position is that the NPT which compartmentalises states into NWS and NNWS and discriminates between them needs to be repealed.

India's Nuclear Explosions and Nuclear Policy

India's nuclear explosion of 1974, known as Pokhran-I, was India's first successful nuclear bomb test. It was seen as contradictory to India's support for a nuclear-weapons-free world. However, the then PM Indira Gandhi dubbed it as a 'Peaceful Nuclear Explosion' (PNE). The Indian nuclear programme had received technical and economic assistance initially from the US and Canada. But this assistance was withdrawn after Pokhran-I. In fact, India was strongly criticised by both the countries and they subsequently collaborated to ensure the imposition of economic and technological sanctions on India. India, however, received both diplomatic and technical support from the USSR in this context.

'No First Use' Doctrine

This is an important principle of India's nuclear policy. India has unilaterally declared that it will not be the first one to use nuclear weapons in the case of a conflict. It will however retaliate quickly and substantially to the use of nuclear weaponry by the antagonistic state. China too declared its adoption of NFU policy in 1964 and has retained its stand ever since.

However, the two major nuclear weapon states of the world, US and Russia, have not voiced their opinion regarding the No First Use Doctrine.

Multilateral Export Control Regime

A multilateral export control regime is an informal group of like-minded supplier countries who want to contribute to the non-proliferation of weapons of mass destruction through implementation of guidelines at the national level and control lists for exports. Some of these regimes are as follows:

A. **The Nuclear Suppliers Group**

The Nuclear Suppliers Group (NSG), popularly known as the London Club, is a transnational body comprising nuclear supplier countries that aim to control the proliferation of nuclear weapons by curbing the export of nuclear weapons development materials and related technology. It also seeks to improve the prevailing safeguards on existing nuclear materials.

The NSG was formed in the wake of India's nuclear tests in 1974 and it held its first meeting in 1975. There are 48 participating governments as of 2022.

B. **The Missile Technology Control Regime**

The 1980s saw the development of Inter-Continental Ballistic Missile Systems by many countries. US President Ronald Reagan, in a 1983 speech, announced the Strategic Defense Initiative, or 'Star Wars', as a defense against Inter-Continental Ballistic Missile attack. Fear like this led to the Missile Technology Control Regime, a multilateral export control regime whose members have an informal political understanding to limit the proliferation of missiles and missile technology. There are a total of 35 members within the MTCR, including Argentina, Australia, Austria, Belgium, Brazil, Bulgaria, Canada, Czech Republic, Denmark, Finland, France, Germany, Greece, Hungary, and Iceland. India became a member of the MTCR in 2016.

C. **The Fissile Material Cut-Off Treaty (FMCT)**

The FMCT is a proposed international agreement that would prohibit the production of the two main components of nuclear weapons: highly enriched uranium and plutonium. The negotiations on the treaty were initiated in 1992 by the US. India also remains committed to negotiations concerning the FMCT. The principle underlying the FMCT is that if the availability of raw materials (fissile materials) is restricted, it would subsequently contribute to non-proliferation of nuclear weapons.

D. **The Wassenaar Arrangement**

The Wassenaar Arrangement on Export Controls for Conventional Arms and Dual-Use Goods and Technologies is a comprehensive Multilateral Export Control Regime. It is a voluntary and non-binding agreement created by the major supplier countries that have agreed to cooperate in their effort to prevent and regulate the transfer of certain military and dual-use technologies. It was established in 1996 and has 42 participating countries as of 2017.

E. **The Australia Group**

Established in 1985 (after the use of chemical weapons by Iraq in 1984), the Australia Group is an informal group of countries formed to help member countries identify those exports which need to be controlled and making sure that they do not contribute to the spread of chemical and biological weapons. The group, initially consisting of 15 members, held its first meeting in Brussels, Belgium, in June 1985. With the incorporation of India in 2018, it now has 43 members.

Some Important Conventions

While a treaty refers to the bilateral or multilateral agreement signed between nation states, independent of the supervision of any organisation, conventions, on the other hand, are agreements reached by general consensus in the UN after they are ratified by all member states. Some important conventions are as follows:

1. The **Biological Weapons Convention** or the Convention on the Prohibition of the Development, Production and Stockpiling of Bacteriological (Biological) and Toxin Weapons and on their Destruction was adopted by the UNGA in 1971.
2. The **Chemical Weapons Convention** or the The Convention on the Prohibition of the Development, Production, Stockpiling and Use of Chemical Weapons and on their Destruction is an arms control treaty administered by the Organisation for the Prohibition of Chemical Weapons. It was

signed in 1993 and entered into force in 1997. It prohibits the large-scale use, development, production, stockpiling and transfer of chemical weapons.

Possibility of a Nuclear-Weapon-Free World

There are several treaties which have been instituted to establish nuclear-weapon-free zones in various parts of the world. These treaties have reinstated the hope that it would be possible to achieve a nuclear-weapon-free and peaceful world someday. Some of these treaties are:

1. The **Treaty for the Prohibition of Nuclear Weapons in Latin America and the Caribbean,** alternatively known as the Tlatelolco Treaty, prohibits Latin American states from acquiring, possessing, developing, testing or using nuclear weapons and prohibits other countries from storing and deploying nuclear weapons on their territories. It was signed in 1967.
2. The **South Pacific Nuclear Free Zone Treaty,** also known as the Treaty of Rarotonga, was signed in 1985. The treaty bans the use, testing, and possession of nuclear weapons within the borders of the South Pacific zone.
3. The **Treaty of Southeast Asia Nuclear-Weapon-Free Zone** was signed in 1995. The Treaty is also known as the Bangkok Treaty. It is a commitment to preserve the Southeast Asian region as a place free of nuclear and other weapons of mass destruction.
4. The **African Nuclear-Weapon-Free Zone Treaty** was signed in 1996. The Treaty is also known as the Pelindaba Treaty. It prohibits the research, development, manufacture, stockpiling, acquisition, testing, possession, control or stationing of nuclear explosive devices and the dumping of radioactive wastes in the African zone by the members.
5. The **Central Asian Nuclear-Weapon-Free Zone Treaty** was signed in 2006. It is a legally binding commitment by Kazakhstan, Kyrgyzstan, Tajikistan, Turkmenistan, and Uzbekistan not to manufacture, acquire, test, or possess nuclear weapons.

There have also been constant attempts on the part of the P5 superpowers to forcefully implement the NPT and the CTBT. For instance, strict economic sanctions were imposed on Iran for its arbitrary violation of the NPT.

Some Important Books on War

1. Michael Walzer: *Just and Unjust Wars*
2. Leo Tolstoy: *War and Peace*
3. A. J. Coates: *The Ethics of War*
4. Carl Von Clausewitz: *On War*
5. Mary Kaldor: *New and Old Wars*
6. Martin Van Creveld: *The Transformation of War*
7. Martin Wight: *Three Traditions of International Theory*

DETERRENCE THEORY

Deterrence is the idea that an inferior power (or a weak state), by virtue of the destructive power of its weapons (nuclear weapons in this case), could deter a more powerful adversary and preclude a surprise attack using the threat of reprisal or retaliation. Therefore, technically, deterrence operates on the principle of the capacity for retaliation or '*second strike capacity*'. Deterrence is also known as **Mutual Assured Destruction (MAD).**

Extended Deterrence: Alternatively known as a '*nuclear umbrella*', this is a strategy employed by the US. The US has extended its capacity for deterrence to its allies who share its security concerns, namely Japan and Korea, which are non-nuclear weapon states who are guaranteed American support in the case of a nuclear war. This has enhanced the security of both the US and its allies.

Complex Deterrence: The contemporary scenario, from the American and European perspective, has 'irresponsible states' like Pakistan and North Korea, who have acquired nuclear weapons and are also refusing to accede to the existing non-proliferation and disarmament regimes. This is conceptualised as a 'global threat' by American scholarship and complex deterrence is necessary to deter these 'rogue states' from using nuclear power.

Arguments in Favour of Deterrence

The prominent neo-realist **Kenneth Waltz** has acknowledged the relevance of deterrence in the prevention of an all-out military conflict between the major powers. Deterrence proved to be relevant in the Cold War which took place between 1945 and 1990 in a bipolar world dominated by major powers, the US and the USSR. However, despite moments of extreme tension like the Cuban Missile Crisis of 1962, the situation did not escalate into a full-fledged war or a direct confrontation with nuclear weapons, thanks to deterrence.

Waltz's Arguments: Nuclear weapons have vertically proliferated at a rapid rate as the nuclear weapon states have increased their arsenals. Horizontal proliferation of nuclear weapons among other states has happened very slowly. According to Waltz, this slow pace is fortunate as rapid changes in international conditions can be unsettling. He says that a gradual spread of nuclear weapons is better than no spread of rapid spread. The presence of new nuclear states will induce a sense of responsibility on the part of the existing possessors of nuclear power and these powers will develop a strong element of caution when it comes to using nuclear power. The likelihood of war would thus decrease as determent and defensive capabilities increase.

Arguments against Deterrence

The realist theory of deterrence as a mechanism for preventing large-scale conflict has been widely criticised. **Ward Wilson**, in his famous essay 'The Myth of Nuclear Deterrence' (2008) argues against the concept of deterrence.

Critics also contend that the principle of deterrence does not contribute significantly to the prevention of destruction since states, even if they restrain from using nuclear weapons, continue to use many other highly destructive weapons against each other. An instance is the 1999 **Kargil War** between India and Pakistan where the belligerents were both nuclear weapon states but chose conventional warfare. Deterrence is not applicable for limited wars such as this.

Scott Sagan argues against deterrence in his essay 'The Perils of Proliferation'.

Sagan's Argument: Professional military organisations, because of their common biases, inflexible routines, and parochial interests display organisational behaviours that are likely to lead to deterrence failures and result in accidental war.

One example of such a failure is the US attack on Iraq in 2003 in the name of self-defence. The US alleged that Iraq was involved in the making of nuclear weapons. Even though the allegation of US was not found to be correct, the US attacked Iraq and caused a *preventive war*.

CIVIL SOCIETY AND NON-PROLIFERATION

Recently, there has emerged strong voices of the civil society against the proliferation of nuclear weapons in the international arena owing to the harmful effects of radiation on human health and the environment. Civil rights movements have had a considerable influence in the politics and foreign policy in European and Scandinavian countries. Countries like Japan and Scandinavian societies consider nuclear weapons as a taboo and this is an example of how customs and traditions of a society can be helpful against proliferation.

The English School or the World Society approach of international relations too does not believe in the idea of a state-centric world. They believe that society can play a positive role towards abolition of weapons.

The **International Campaign to Abolish Nuclear Weapons** is a global civil society coalition working to promote adherence to and full implementation of the Treaty on the Prohibition of Nuclear Weapons. ICAN was launched in 2007 and has 541 partner organisations in 103 countries as of 2019. ICAN seeks to shift the disarmament debate to focus on the humanitarian threat posed by nuclear weapons, drawing attention to their unique destructive capacity, their catastrophic health and environmental consequences, their indiscriminate targeting, the debilitating impact of a detonation on medical infrastructure and relief measures, and the long-lasting effects of radiation on the surrounding area.

4

UNITED NATIONS

KEYWORDS

Aims, Objectives, Structure and Evolution of the UN; Peace and Development Perspectives; Humanitarian Intervention; International Law; International Criminal Court

FORMATION AND EVOLUTION OF THE UN

The idea for an organisation like the UN first appeared in the **Atlantic Charter,** a joint declaration released by US President Franklin D. Roosevelt and British Prime Minister Winston Churchill on **August 14, 1941.** Later, between 28 November and 1 December 1943, the **Tehran Conference** was organised to discuss the future course of action after Second World War, and it was the first Allied conference that featured the Big Three nations: the meeting was attended by US President Roosevelt, British PM Churchill and leader of the Soviet Union, Stalin. Roosevelt is considered to be the originator of the term 'United Nations Organisation'. The **Yalta Conference** was held in 1945 between all the three same leaders, which took forward the idea of the UN.

The Charter of the United Nations, which was signed on 26 June 1950, is the founding document of the United Nations. It was signed at the conclusion of the United Nations Conference on International Organization, which was attended by 50 nations. Later, Poland also joined which made 51 members the original founders of the UNO. The Charter of UNO was accepted on 24 October 1945 and therefore 24 October is celebrated as the United Nations Day. Presently the UN has **193 member states. South Sudan** is a latest member of the UN. The first session of the UN General Assembly was held on 10 February 1946 in the Westminster Hall of London. There are six official languages of the UN: Arabic, Chinese, English, French, Russian and Spanish.

AIMS AND OBJECTIVES OF THE UNITED NATIONS

The United Nations Organization (UNO) was established in the aftermath of the Second World War with the aim of peaceful resolution of the ongoing conflicts in the world. The objective of the establishment of the UN was to encourage the conduction of world politics on the basis of cooperation and co-existence. The following are some of the aims of the UN:

1. **Rules-Based World Order**

   A rules-based international order may be described as a shared commitment by all countries to conduct their activities in accordance with agreed rules that evolve over time, such as international law. The significance of some common values has been acknowledged by the entire humanity. Peaceful co-existence, freedom, equality and human rights are prominent among such values which have emerged from a universal human consciousness. International law is based on these values and the foundation of the UN lies in international law, which holds that all states are equally sovereign.

2. **Collective Security and Cooperative Security**

   The United Nations works for maintaining collective security. Every member state supports the Charter of the UN and UN in turn protects the security of member states. UN functions on the principle of '*One For All, All For One*'. Idealists and liberals strongly believe in the principle of collective security. According to **Charles** and **Clifford Kupchan**, under collective security, states agree to abide by certain norms and rules to maintain stability, and when necessary, band together to stop aggression. **Inis Claude** has argued that collective security depends on states entrusting 'their destinies' to a collective effort. **John Mearsheimer** has argued that collective security is inescapably flawed.

Cooperative security is also known as *collective defense*. Security maintained by NATO is an example of cooperative security. It is different from collective security because cooperative security is based on the principle of balance of power. It is only available for the member states which have founded the NATO. Therefore, in a way, it is helpful only for the powerful states. Cooperative security falls under the realist approach of International Relations.

The Main Objectives of the UN as Declared by the UN Charter

Article 1 of the UN Charter mentions the following purposes of the UN:

1. Promoting and protecting world peace and global security and making effective collective efforts towards the fulfillment of this objective so that threats to security can be abolished.
2. Developing friendly relations among nations on the basis of equality and self-determination.
3. Fostering worldwide cooperation in solving economic, social, cultural and humanitarian problems.
4. Functioning as an integrated mechanism for the fulfillment of these common objectives.

PRINCIPLES OF FUNCTIONING OF THE UN

In **Article 2** of the Charter, seven guiding principles for the UN have been mentioned:

1. The Organization is based on the principle of sovereign equality of all its Members.
2. All Members, in order to ensure to all of them the rights and benefits resulting from membership, shall fulfil in good faith the obligations assumed by them in accordance with the present Charter.
3. All Members shall settle their international disputes by peaceful means in such a manner that international peace and security, and justice, are not endangered.
4. All Members shall refrain in their international relations from the threat or use of force against the territorial integrity or political independence of any state, or in any other manner inconsistent with the Purposes of the United Nations.
5. All Members shall give the United Nations every assistance in any action it takes in accordance with the present Charter, and shall refrain from giving assistance to any state against which the United Nations is taking preventive or enforcement action.
6. The Organization shall ensure that states which are not Members of the United

Nations act in accordance with these Principles so far as may be necessary for the maintenance of international peace and security.

7. Nothing contained in the present Charter shall authorise the United Nations to intervene in matters which are essentially within the domestic jurisdiction of any state or shall require the Members to submit such matters to settlement under the present Charter; but this principle shall not prejudice the application of enforcement measures.

THE NATURE OF THE UN

The UN is an organisation based on nation-states. It is not a *world government*, but rather it is an *international organisation*. This can be substantiated by looking at the following examples:

1. The UN does not make laws for the world; rather the parliaments of the different nations make laws for their own nations.
2. The UN does not have a military arrangement of its own. Instead, it is based on the military cooperation between its member nation-states.
3. The UN does not have a financial source of its own. It is financed through contributions from its member states.

THE STRUCTURE OF THE UN

There are five principal organs established by the UN Charter: the General Assembly (UNGA), the Security Council (UNSC), the Economic and Social Council (ECOSOC), the International Court of Justice (ICJ) and the UN Secretariat.

General Assembly

This is a democratic organ because all states have equal representation within the General Assembly. The Assembly functions through various kinds of committees.

Committees of the General Assembly

1. Disarmament and International Security Committee
2. Economic and Financial Committee
3. Social, Humanitarian and Cultural Committee
4. Special Political and Decolonization Committee
5. Administrative and Income-Expenditure Related Committee
6. Legal Committee

Functions and Powers of the General Assembly

The UNGA meets in September every year. Various presidents and vice-presidents are elected during this annual meeting. In case of an emergency, a special session can be convened. The Assembly passed the Uniting for Peace resolution (UNGA Resolution 377) in 1950 during the Korean War. An 11th special session of the UNGA was held in 2022 during the Ukraine crisis.

According to **Article 18**, every Member shall have one vote and no state shall have more than 5 representatives in the Assembly. **Article 19** says that those states who fail to pay their share of financial contribution on time can be deprived of voting rights in the Assembly.

The powers of the UNGA have been mentioned between **Articles 10 to 17** of the UN Charter. Major decisions in the UNGA have to be taken by a two-thirds majority present and voting. Major decisions can pertain to the following subjects:

1. Maintenance of international peace and security.
2. Election of non-permanent members of the UNSC.
3. Election of members of the ECOSOC.
4. Entry of new members in to the UN.
5. Removal of members.

The resolutions of the UNGA are advisory in nature and these resolutions may vary for different states of the world. The Assembly does not legislate for nation-states. The election of the judges of the ICJ and the passage of budget for the UN is done by simple majority. In the year 1953, India's **Vijaya Lakshmi Pandit** became the first female president of the UNGA. Her Presidency is a reflection of the democratic nature of the UN where all states have equal voting rights in the UNGA.

Areas of Improvement

However, the role of the UNGA is gradually weakening and following **reforms** are needed:

1. The UNGA should receive adequate financial resources and be equipped with adequate working staff.
2. There should be clear determination of the programmes of the Assembly for the entire year.
3. The Assembly should be granted a special role in peacebuilding programmes and on issues related to human rights.
4. The strengthening of the UNGA is necessary to ensure control and balance in the Security Council.
5. Developing countries should play a decisive role in increasing the influence of the UNGA because they are in majority in the assembly.

Security Council

Functions of the Security Council

1. Maintaining international peace and security. This is the basic and most important function of the UNSC.
2. Attempting to prevent arms race.
3. Initiating military action against aggressor states.
4. Imposing economic sanctions on states in order to prevent or stop violence. For instance, the UNSC has imposed sanctions on Iran and Syria.

While other organs of the UN can only make 'recommendations' to member states, the Security Council has the power to make binding decisions that member states have agreed to carry out, under the terms of UN Charter.

Structure of the Security Council

Presently, there are 15 members within the UNSC, among which 10 are non-permanent and 5 are permanent members. In the year 1963, the Charter was amended and the number of non-permanent members was increased from 6 to 10. The Presidency of the Council is held by each of the members in turn for **one month** following the English alphabetical order of the member states' names. Non-permanent members are elected from various parts of the world and the prescribed proportions are as follows:

5 members from Africa and Asia
2 members from Latin America
2 members from Western countries
1 member from East Europe

The Security Council meets throughout the year. The UNSC requires a **9-member** quorum for the functioning of its proceedings. **Article 27** of the UN Charter allows the provision for voting. Permanent members of the UNSC have the power to **veto** a resolution, but the ten elected members, who serve two-year, nonconsecutive terms, are not afforded veto power**.** However, the absence of any permanent member is not considered as veto. There is also a provision for *double veto* in the UNSC.

Failures of the Security Council

The UN Security Council has more than once failed to fulfil its primary objective of maintaining international peace and security. Some of these instances are as follows:

1. The UNSC has failed to prevent the continuous testing of missiles and nuclear weapons by North Korea.
2. The UNSC could not protect Ukraine from Russian invasion.
3. The UNSC has failed to effectively control terrorist organisations in the world.

The UNSC passed **Resolution 1267** according to which no terrorist organisation affiliated to Al-Qaida would be granted financial or economic assistance of any type. **Resolution 1373** has also been passed according to which no state can grant any kind of aid or assistance to any terrorist organisation. However, this resolution has not yet been enforced. The use of veto by China on the issue related to Masood Azhar is a testimony to the fact that great powers want to use the UNSC for the fulfillment of their own interests and not with the intention of maintaining world peace.

The Economic and Social Council

The Economic and Social Council was founded in 1945 and it is one of the most important organs of the UN. It comprises **54 members** elected by the General Assembly for **three-year** terms. The ECOSOC coordinates the social and economic functions of the UN and its various agencies. It has fifteen specialised agencies, the eight functional commissions, and the five regional commissions under its jurisdiction, as well as various programmes and funds.

Functional Commissions

The following are the active functional commission of the ECOSOC:

1. Commission on Narcotic Drugs (CND)
2. Commission on Population and Development (CPD)
3. Commission on Science and Technology for Development (CSTD)
4. Commission on the Status of Women (CSW)
5. Statistical Commission
6. Commission for Social Development (CSocD)
7. Commission on Crime Prevention and Criminal Justice (CCPCJ)
8. Forum on Forests (UNFF)

Regional Commissions

The following are the active regional commissions of the Council:

1. UN Economic Commission for Europe (ECE)
2. UN Economic Commission for Africa (ECA)
3. UN Economic Commission for Latin America and the Caribbean (ECLAC)
4. UN Economic and Social Commission for Asia and the Pacific (ESCAP)
5. UN Economic and Social Commission for Western Asia (ESCWA)

Agencies

There are 15 specialised agencies of the ECOSOC. Some of the most important ones are Food and Agriculture Organization (FAO), International Labour Organization (ILO), International Monetary Fund (IMF), United Nations Educational, Scientific and Cultural Organization (UNESCO), World Bank Group (WBG), and the World Health Organization (WHO).

Ensuring the availability of adequate amounts of food for the rising populations of developing countries was a challenging task. So the FAO was constituted to end hunger in developing countries. It provided food grain assistance to developing countries. The FAO and WHO work in synchrony. Their cooperation is essential for taking effective action for the resolution of problems like food, hunger, malnutrition, healthcare and diseases which have common grounds.

UNESCO is aimed at promoting world peace and security through international cooperation in education, arts, science and culture. ILO deals with labour issues, particularly international labour standards, social protection and work opportunities for all.

Programmes

The UN is also a social unit which operates various kinds of development programmes. Under the UN Development Programme (UNDP), different kinds of initiatives are taken to alleviate poverty and support sustainabale economic growth in developing nations. The UN Environment

Programme (UNEP) works towards environmental conservation.

Funds

The UN has various funds that are either mainly or entirely maintained through voluntary contributions and have a governing body that reviews their activities. For instance, the United Nations Population Fund, formerly the United Nations Fund for Population Activities (UNFPA) provides aid and assistance which contributes to improving reproductive and maternal health worldwide. The United Nations International Children's Emergency Fund (UNICEF) was constituted for child welfare.

The International Court of Justice

According to **Article 92** of the UN Charter, the International Court of Justice is the principal judicial organ of the United Nations. The seat of the court is at the Peace Palace in the Hague (Netherlands). It is the only organ of the UN which is located outside of New York. It is comprised of **15 judges** who are elected to a **nine-year** term of office by the United Nations General Assembly. One nation cannot send more than one judge at a time. One-third of the judges are elected every third year.

Jurisdiction of the International Court of Justice is two-fold:

1. **Compulsory Jurisdiction:** This type of jurisdiction is related to legal disputes between the states. The disputes are settled according to international law. A citizen cannot approach the ICJ for any grievance.

   India approached the ICJ in the case of Kulbhushan Jadhav, who Pakistan arrested on the allegation of being an Indian spy, because Pakistan did not comply with the Vienna Convention on Consular Relations, an international treaty that defines a framework for consular relations between two sovereign states. The ICJ ordered Pakistan to give consular access to India and to review and reconsider the conviction as well as the sentence of Jadhav in an effective manner.
2. **Advisory Jurisdiction:** Any agency of the United Nations can seek advice from the ICJ. The ICJ can give advisory opinions on legal questions arising within its scope.

The official languages of working of the ICJ are **English** and **French**. Each member of the UN undertakes to comply with the decision of the ICJ. If any party to a case fails to comply with the decision of the ICJ, according to **Article 94**, the Security Council can pass a resolution against that state.

Indian Judge Dalveer Bhandari is one of the Judges in the ICJ.

Secretariat

The Secretariat is the executive arm of the UN whose function is to make administrative arrangements for the operations of the UN. The Secretary General of the UN is the *administrative head* of the UN and the Secretary General is appointed by the UNSC. However, prior to this, the Secretary General used to be elected by the UNGA through a special majority of two-third members present and voting. There is no provision for the tenure of the Secretary General in the UN Charter but on the basis of a resolution passed by the UNGA, the Secretary General is appointed for tenure of 5 years and they can also be re-elected in succession. The role of the UN Secretary General is both to be the head of the Secretariat as well as the primary diplomat in world diplomacy.

Many theorists and political scientists of the Global South are of the opinion that developing countries do not have adequate representation in the staff of the UN and thus reforms should be made to address this issue.

Trusteeship Council

The Trusteeship Council, one of the main organs of the UN, was established to supervise the administration of trust territories as they transitioned from colonies to sovereign nations. In the present, the **Trusteeship Council** is still part of the charter but the functioning of the council is suspended because all colonies which were under the jurisdiction of the UN have now become independent.

THE ROLE OF THE UN

Maintenance of International Peace and Security

According to **Article 1** of the UN Charter, the basic function of the UN is to prevent and bring an end to all kinds of challenges which could threaten world peace. Herein, a provision has been made regarding collective action against an aggressive state. According to **Articles 33 to 51** of the UN Charter, taking initiative for establishing world peace is the basic responsibility of the Security Council and for the fulfillment of this responsibility, the Security Council can deploy troops to ensure effective implementation of disarmament as well as encourage peaceful uses of nuclear energy. Under **Chapter VII**, the resolutions passed by the UNSC are binding on all members. The Security Council can also put economic sanction against a state. If economic sanctions fail, then Security Council can pass a resolution for military action against any state which is threating the security of the world. According to **Article 43**, it is the responsibility of all member states to ensure the availability of their military force in accordance with the resolutions passed by the UNSC. The Gulf War (1990) was the first instance where Chapter VII (Action with Respect to Threats to the Peace, Breaches of the Peace, and Acts of Aggression) was successfully implemented with the consensus of the permanent members.

However, due to the use of veto, that is, negative voting rights of the permanent members, it is often for possible for the UNSC to enforce military action for the resolution of disputes between states. For the passage of a resolution in the UNSC, the resolution should receive the support of at least 9 non-permanent members of the Council and should have no veto by any permanent member. Historically, the USSR and the USA have both used the veto in support of their allies during the Cold War. During the Ukraine crisis in 2022, the UN failed to maintain peace because Russia, as a permanent member of the Security Council, vetoed the resolution.

In case of misuse of veto by permanent members of the Security Council, it can adopt the provision mentioned in **Chapter VI** (Pacific Settlement of Disputes), which is non-binding, but encourages peace enforcement. In the year 1992, then UN Secretary General **Boutros Boutros-Ghali** in his report 'An Agenda for Peace' outlined peace-keeping and peace-building programmes.

Peace-keeping: The Post-Cold War world has seen an exponential rise in peace-keeping programmes conducted by the UN. Currently **12 peace-keeping operations** deployed by the Department of Peace Operations on three continents which include the operations in Serbia, South Sudan, Central African Republic, Mali, Cyprus, Lebanon, Israel, and Kashmir. Under these operations, the UN deploys and stations its peace-keeping forces to establish peace between conflict-ridden states or parties. These forces do not engage in combat. They may only engage in armed conflict for self-defense. Presently, doctors are also stationed along with peace-keeping forces. Due to their blue uniforms, they are popularly referred to as the '*blue helmets*'.

Peace-building: Preventive diplomacy ensures that diplomatic measures are taken before the emergence of conflict between two antagonistic parties in an effort to establish peace and prevent future violence. Peace-building programs are also aimed at assisting countries emerging from conflict, reducing the risk of relapsing into conflict and laying the foundation for sustainable peace and development.

Disarmament: The UNGA and other bodies of the United Nations also have as their objective the elimination of nuclear weapons and other weapons of mass destruction as well as the regulation of conventional arms. On 29 July 1957, the International Atomic Energy Agency **(IAEA)** was formed with the basic objective of exercising surveillance on the nuclear reactors of those countries who are signatories to the Nuclear Non-Proliferation Treaty.

Countering Terrorism: Global terrorism is a severe threat to the security of all states in the present world. After 9/11, many resolutions have been passed by the UN to restrain terrorism. The most important of these is Resolution 1373 which prohibits financial assistance to terrorist groups. It states that no nation can provide any kind of training or political support to any terrorist organisation. Emphasis is placed on mutual cooperation between states for restricting terrorist activities.

In the year 2005, the UN Secretary General constituted an anti-terrorist task force to encourage cooperation and harmony between states and control terrorism. A provision was also made regarding extending technical and other kinds of assistance to states to enable them to effectively combat terrorism. In 2021, the Security Council passed Resolution 2593, following the Taliban takeover in Afghanistan with the objective of tackling terrorism.

Protection of Human Rights

The Office of the High Commissioner for Human Rights has the lead responsibility in the UN for the promotion and protection of human rights. Although the Charter of the United Nations says that the UN shall never intervene in the internal affairs of any country, in some cases it has had to intervene in the domestic affairs of a nation for protection of human rights. The UN also has special advisers on the prevention of genocide.

Economic Role

The role of the UN is very crucial with respect to economic issues. **Article 1** of the UN Charter mentions that there is a need to foster mutual cooperation for the resolution of economic, social, cultural and humanitarian problems so that human rights and basic freedoms can be enhanced and encouraged. The UN is responsible for promoting economic welfare and cooperation in areas such as postwar reconstruction, technical assistance, and trade and development. The World Bank and its subsidiaries such as the International Finance Corporation and the International Development Association are primarily responsible for financing economic development. In 1964 the UN General Assembly set up the United Nations Conference on Trade and Development (UNCTAD) to address economic issues related to developing countries.

Social Role

United Nation is not only a political and legal entity, it also has social functions. The Preamble to the Constitution of UNESCO states that 'since wars begin in the minds of men, it is in the minds of men that the defences of peace must be constructed.' This highlights how important education and healthcare are for maintaining peace in the world. Issues like deprivation and rising global population have also been important areas of concern. Robert McNamara, the eighth United States Secretary of Defense, said that a rising population is more dangerous than the nuclear bomb. Various agencies, programmes and funds have been launched by the UN with the objective of eradicating poverty from the planet.

Millennium Development Goals (MDGs)

The Millennium Development Goals, announced in 2000, was a set of eight goals that the UN wanted to achieve by the year 2015. They were:

1. Eradicate extreme poverty and hunger.

2. Achieve universal primary education
3. Promote gender equality and empower women
4. Reduce child mortality
5. Improve maternal health
6. Combat HIV/AIDS, malaria and other diseases
7. Ensure environmental sustainability
8. Global partnership for development

Different states have seen varying levels of success with regards to the MDGs. While nations such as China and Brazil have registered a remarkable success in achieving these goals, African nations have had negligible progress in this regard. India has had average progress. However, the aim to achieve these goals by 2015 was impractical. The developed nations did not provide sufficient assistance to the developing countries to aid the achievement of these goals.

Sustainable Development Goals (SDGs)

In 2015, the UN announced a set of Sustainable Development Goals which are to be achieved by 2030, which replaced the Millennium Development Goals. These goals include social, economic and environmental goals. The abolition of all forms of poverty from everywhere, ensuring food security, adequate nutrition, bringing an end to world hunger, encouraging engagement in agriculture in accordance with the ideals of the SDGs and ensuring availability of overall inclusive education and proper healthcare facilities to everyone are some of the SDGs. SDGs shall also be the guiding force in bringing about gender equality, ensuring adequate sanitation facilities and water management. Ending economic inequalities existing between and within nations, conservation and preservation of the ecosystem, forestation and prevention of desertification, conservation of biodiversity also fall under SDGs. Last but not the least, promoting the development of the agencies and participatory mechanisms necessary for the achievement of these goals are also part of the SDGs.

REFORMS REQUIRED IN THE UN

Reforms in Peace-keeping

In the post-Cold War world, for effective peace-keeping and peace-building, the following reforms are needed with respect of peace-building programmes:

1. All member states should be committed to peace-building programmes. According to Article 43 of the UN Charter, all member states should make their troops available at the earliest when required for the maintenance of international peace and security.
2. When peace-building programmes are conducted in the Third World, the leadership should be handed over to countries of the Third World.
3. A peace-building commission must be instituted for the operationalisation of peace-building programmes.
4. More cooperation is required among the three stakeholders for successful implementation of peacekeeping operations. The three stakeholders are:
   (a) States which provide funds for the programme (the developed nations)
   (b) State(s) where the operation is carried out (the developing nations)
   (c) States that deploy the armed forces necessary for carrying out the operation

Financial Reforms

Presently, the UN is facing financial crises. Ensuring the availability of maximum financial resources is a challenge for the UN. However, the contribution of any country should not be more than a determined limit, because otherwise it would be impossible to ensure neutrality and impartiality in the functioning of the organisation. In the context of present times, the financial reform that is most crucial to ensure smooth functioning of the UN is that the determined contribution of every state must be paid within a fixed deadline. According to the Article 19 of the UN Charter, if a member of the UN is in arrears in the payments of its financial contribution to the organisation, it shall have no vote in General Assembly.

Structural Reforms: Reforms in the UNSC

In the post-Cold War world, world politics has undergone many radical transformations but the structure of the UNSC still reflects the balance of power established in the aftermath of the Second World War. This is why there is a need for structural change within the UNSC in the contemporary world. The inconsistencies of the UNSC are of two types: lack of transparency and lack of legitimacy.

The UNSC, although a very powerful organ, lacks transparency because the permanent members take decisions on the basis of behind-the-curtain deliberations. Thus, the process of voting is rendered irrelevant and remains ceremonial at best. An exception is when the president of the UNSC in 1994 took a new initiative where for the first time, particularly with regard to the formulation of peace-building programmes, non-member states were included within the discussions. Those states who were contributing to peace-building programmes were also consulted.

The most important structural reform required within the UN is the *democratisation of the UN Security Council*. The number of founding members of the UN were 51. However, now the number of members has increased to 193 (54 from Africa, 48 from Europe, 56 from Asia Pacific and 35 from Americas) and yet the number of permanent members of the UNSC is still 5. Africa and Latin America have no representation within the permanent membership. A huge emerging democratic nation like India still has not received permanent membership. Germany and Japan are considered to be the strongest contenders for permanent membership because both the states have made excessive financial contributions to the UN and also because these nations are two of the world's most powerful economies.

Proposals for Reform

Proposal of the Annan Plan (2005)

In March, 2005, the then UN Secretary General **Kofi Annan** recommended the extension of membership of the UNSC to **24 members**. He also asserted that this proposed increase would be done without granting veto powers to the new members. He proposed two models:

Plan A:

1. Addition of 6 new permanent members without the power of veto.
2. Addition of 3 new non-permanent members elected for a period of 2 years who could not be re-elected in succession.
3. The extension of membership would adequately and proportionately represent the various regions of the world. Two members each from Asia and Africa and one member each from America and Europe would be included.

Plan B:

1. No increase in the number of permanent members.
2. A total of 8 new semi-permanent members would be included who would remain members for a period of 4 years. However, they could be re-elected in succession.
3. One member would be non-permanent, who would be elected for a tenure of 2 years and could not be re-elected in succession.

Proposal of G4

The proposal of G4 was brought by **India, Brazil, Germany and Japan,** four countries which support each other's bids for permanent seats on the UNSC. The co-presenters of the resolution included Belgium, Bhutan, Czech Republic, Denmark, Fiji, France, Georgia, Greece, Haiti, Honduras, Iceland, Kiribati, Latvia, Lithuania,

Maldives, Palau, Poland, Paraguay, Solomon Island, Tuvalu, Ukraine and Nauru.

They proposed:

1. Addition of 6 new members without veto.
2. Addition of 2 new permanent members from Africa.
3. Addition of 4 new non-permanent members.
4. A total of 25 members.

Proposal of the Coffee Club

Uniting for Consensus (UfC), informally known as the Coffee Club, refers to the group of those countries who opposed the G4. This resolution was presented by Argentina, Canada, Costa Rica, Columbia, Malta, Mexico, Pakistan, Spain and Turkey, with the leadership of Italy.

They demanded:

1. There should be no change in the size of permanent membership.
2. Increasing the number of non-permanent members from 10 to 20, who would be elected for a 2-year term.
3. The total size of the UNSC should be 25 and decisions should be taken by a majority of 15 votes.

Some Important Facts about the UN

1. United Nations Conference on Trade and Development (UNCTAD), first held in 1964.

   Headquartered in Geneva, Switzerland.
2. United Nations Development Programme (UNDP), founded in 1965.

   Headquartered in New York, USA.
3. United Nations High Commissioner for Refugees (UNHCR), established in 1951.

   Headquartered in Geneva, Switzerland.
4. United Nations Children's Fund (UNICEF), established in 1946.

   Headquartered in New York, USA.
5. United Nations Educational, Scientific and Cultural Organization (UNESCO), founded in 1945.

   Headquartered in Paris, France.
6. Food and Agriculture Organization (FAO), founded in 1945.

   Headquartered in Rome, Italy.
7. World Health Organization (WHO), founded in 1948.

   Headquartered in Geneva, Switzerland.
8. International Labour Organization (ILO), created in 1919.

   Headquartered in Geneva, Switzerland.

HUMANITARIAN INTERVENTION

Intervention refers to actions undertaken by an organisation through interference in the domestic affairs of a nation state with the objective of alleviating human suffering. Humanitarian implies that the interference is for the protection of human rights. Article 1 of the UN Charter recognises the sovereignty of nation states, and therefore the interference in the affairs of a sovereign state is debatable.

Arguments in Favour of Humanitarian Intervention

1. The UN Charter commits to the protection of fundamental human rights. The promotion of human rights should be prioritised as much as international peace and security.
2. There exists a right of intervention on humanitarian grounds in customary international law.
3. The preservation of universal human rights is a moral obligation which is above any law or institution. Every person is entitled to and responsible for protecting the rights of others.
4. At the 2005 World Summit, all Heads of States and Governments affirmed the

responsibility to protect populations from genocide, war crimes, ethnic cleansing and crimes against humanity by employing measures that already exist to prevent atrocity crimes and to protect civilians from their occurrence.

Arguments against Humanitarian Intervention

1. Critics argue that the Article 2(4) of the UN Charter prohibits the use of force by one state against another and therefore, humanitarian intervention is illegal.
2. National interest gains higher precedence in international relations. In the wake of the US-launched Global War on Terror, humanitarian intervention has come to be seen with increased suspicion, particularly by the countries of the Third World and by powerful Second World countries like Russia and China.
3. No state wants to put the lives of their soldiers at risk. Realists argue that the entire discourse on humanitarian intervention is flawed since most states are not prepared to invest their manpower for restoring order in foreign states.
4. The right to humanitarian intervention gives the powerful states even more power to interfere in affairs of other nations and dominate the world.
5. There are no objective criteria which defines the grounds of intervention. For instance, during the Cold War period, India widely criticised the US for its intervention in Vietnam, but kept silent in case of Soviet intervention in Afghanistan.
6. Moral principle and human rights are not necessarily universal. Many allege that European morality underlies the discourse of universal human rights.

INTERNATIONAL LAW

The founding father of international law is **Hugo Grotius,** a Dutch humanist and diplomat. International law tells us about the relations between two nations. There are two parts of international law:

1. The subject of international law, which refers to a state or an international agency.
2. The object of international law, which may be the domain of human rights or maritime disputes.

The different *international legal personalities* are the states and international organisations. Individuals are not considered to be legal personalities.

The International Law Commission was set up by the General Assembly in 1947. In 1970, the United Nations General Assembly passed the Resolution 2625, 'The Declaration on Principles of International Law concerning Friendly Relations and Co-operation among States'.

Sources of International Law

Article 38(1) of the International Court of Justice lists the sources of international law. When international treaties or customary laws prove inadequate, then an International Court of Justice arbitration is required.

A. International Treaties

Treaties (sometimes called agreements or conventions) are one of the main sources of international law. The Vienna Convention on the Law of Treaties, 1969 defines a treaty and regulates treaties between states. Article 31 and Article 32 of the Convention are the most important. According to the Vienna Convention, treaties may be **bilateral** or **multi-lateral.** For instance, the Nuclear Non-Proliferation Treaty is a multi-lateral treaty whereas the Indus Waters Treaty between India and Pakistan is a bilateral treaty. The following are some of the most important treaties in history of international law:

I. Treaty of Westphalia (1648)
II. Treaty of Utrecht (1713)
III. Treaty of Versailles (1783, 1919)
IV. Treaty of Paris (1763, 1856)

V. Paris Peace Treaties (1947)
VI. Congress of Vienna (1814–1815)
VII. Brussels Conference (1890)

B. Customary Laws

International law is also derived from the customary practice of states. The general and consistent practices followed by states due to a sense of legal obligation, such as prohibition of slavery or genocide, are examples of customary law.

C. General Principles of Law

Some general principles of law as recognised by civilised nations are also sources of international law. For instance, a treaty that is signed between two nations must be followed by the nations. No state is allowed to make injury against other states. These general principles are principals that are recognised by the civil society.

D. Judicial Decisions and Work of Eminent Jurists

Article 38 refers to judicial decisions on national and international courts as a subsidiary means for the determination of rules of international law. **Hugo Grotius,** in his famous book *On the Law of War and Peace* (1625), formulated a doctrine of international law, that states:

I. All states are equally sovereign and independent.
II. The jurisdiction of the state is absolute over its entire area.

E. History of War and Diplomacy

International laws also have as their sources historical diplomatic decisions and declarations. Some of the important ones are the

1. The Atlantic Charter (1941)
2. Declaration by United Nations (1942)
3. Tehran Conference (1943)
4. Bretton Woods Conference (1944)
5. Yalta Conference (February 1945)
6. Potsdam Agreement (August 1945)
7. The Charter of the UN (June 1945)

It is important to note that **realists** do not believe in the principle of international law. National interest and power are the driving forces of international relations for realists. **Liberals** on the other hand support international law and international organisation.

Maritime Law

The United Nations Convention on the Law of the Sea (UNCLOS), 1982 is an international agreement that establishes the law for marine and maritime activities. It is also known as Law of the Sea.

Another example of maritime law is the **Antarctic Treaty** signed in 1959 among Belgium, Japan, South Africa, USA and former USSR.

INTERNATIONAL CRIMINAL COURT

The International Criminal Court (ICC) is the first and only permanent international court that investigates and tries individuals charged with the most serious crimes of concern to the international community, for instance, genocide, war crimes, crimes against humanity or the crime of aggression.

The Rome Statute established the ICC as a 'court of last resort' on July 1998 and it entered into force in July 2002. It is an intergovernmental organisation and international tribunal that has its headquarters in the Hague, Netherlands.

The ICC is intended to complement existing national judicial systems and not replace them. It may exercise its jurisdiction only when national courts are unwilling or unable to prosecute criminals. The ICC lacks universal territorial jurisdiction and may only investigate and prosecute crimes committed within its member states, crimes committed by nationals of member states, or crimes referred to the court by the United Nations Security Council.

There are four organs of the ICC:

1. Presidency
2. Judiciary (18 judges in 3 divisions)

3. Office of the Prosecutor
4. Registry

It is important to note that the ICC is not a UN organisation. It does not have its own police force or enforcement body.

As of November 2019, 123 states are parties to the Statute of the Court (those who have signed the Rome Statute), including all the countries of South America, nearly all of Europe, most of Oceania and half of Africa. India is not a member of the ICC and is critical of its functions.

5

POLITICAL ECONOMY OF IR

KEYWORDS

Globalisation; global governance and the Bretton Woods system, North–South Dialogue, WTO, G-20, BRICS.

GLOBALISATION

Globalisation is a slippery and elusive concept. It is a process brought about by policy changes of the state or government. It stands for the free flow of goods, services, and finances across the world. Globalisation refers to the integration of the economy of a country with the global economy. **Kenichi Ohmae** is one of the most influential proponents of the idea of a 'borderless world'. **Jan Aart Scholte** is another important thinker in the field of global studies who argued that globalisation is linked to the growth of 'supra-territorial' relations between people. **Marshall McLuhan** coined the term '*global village*' in his book *The Gutenberg Galaxy*.

The Origin of Globalisation

Regarding the origin of globalisation, there exists a diversity of views in international relations. **Amartya Sen** says globalisation is not new and in an earlier age, India and China were the centres of globalised trade. Now there are some new actors of globalisation such as the **WTO** and new aspects such as a global market, new means of transportation and advanced communication. Globalisation has today become a global phenomenon due to the advancement of digital technology. The following are some of the views on the origins of globalisation:

(a) **Modernisation:** According to **Anthony Giddens**, globalisation is simply a consequence of modernity. Urbanisation and industrialisation are processes of modernisation and so globalisation can be seen as a result of growing urbanisation and industrialisation.

(b) **Capitalism:** Marxists like **Immanuel Wallerstein** believed that the origin of globalisation lies in capitalism. He opined that capitalism is the prime mover in the process of globalisation.

(c) **Technology:** Liberals like **James Rosenau** held that technology is responsible for the origin of globalisation and called it the driving force behind the phenomenon.

(d) **Political:** Thinkers such as **Robert Gilpin** holds political factors to be solely responsible for the origin and intensification of globalisation.

(e) **Multi-Dimensional:** Many theorists believe that the origin of globalisation cannot be explained in terms of a single factor of causation as there are multiple factors behind globalisation. **Giddens** points out to four intersecting dimensions of globalisation, which are capitalism, the nation-state system, militarism and industrialism.

Globalisation and International Trade

There are two opposing schools of thought regarding global trade:

1. **Mercantilism and Protectionism**

   Mercantilism advocates governmental regulation of economy with the objective of increasing state power and security. The philosophy of mercantilism emerged in Europe as the leading political economic school of thought after the decline of feudalism. For mercantilist state control, the presence of army is necessary for maintaining the security of a nation. The state should also have control over economy in order to protect the domestic market. Mercantilists believe in the promotion of export and discourage imports by imposing a high tariff on importation. Mercantilism is a protectionist policy.

2. **Liberalism and Free Trade**

   Liberals believes in the principle of *comparative advantage*, according to which a global market economy with free trade is a beneficial for each and every nation. Every nation excels in the production of some items, which they should manufacture and export. For example, Japan has an advanced automobile industry and Scandinavian nations excel in shipbuilding. Hence, a free trade between these countries would be beneficial for both. The *neo-liberal economic policy* is the contemporary variety of liberalism which promotes free trade and a market economy.

Dimensions of Globalisation

Political

Political globalisation is also referred to as multilateralism. It refers to the creation and proliferation of multilateral international organisations such as the United Nations (UN), the World Bank, International Monetary Fund (IMF) and the World Trade Organization (WTO). A notable example of political globalisation is the Washington Consensus, which refers to a set of free-market economic policies supported by prominent financial institutions such as the International Monetary Fund, the World Bank, and the U.S. Treasury. The term *Washington Consensus* was coined by **John Williamson**, a British economist, in 1989. According to Williamson, the declining capacity of nation-states to organise economic and political life in a meaningful way allows power to be sucked downwards and as well as squeezed upwards.

Economic

Economic globalisation can be defined as the pervasive cross-border flow of goods, services, capital, technology, and labour. Globalisation is seen as the result of neo-liberal economic policy, which emphasises market economy or capitalist economy. Various institutions of global governance, like IMF, International Bank for Reconstruction and Development (IBRD) and WTO also promote neo-liberal economic policies. IMF focuses on the implementation of structural adjustment programmes. **Structural Adjustment Programmes (SAPs)** and **Structural Adjustment Loans (SALs)** are devices that the IMF and the World Bank have used to overcome what are viewed as structural inefficiencies that inhibit economic growth in the developing world. Used as the basis for the granting of loans during the 1980s and 1990s in particular, they showed a strong faith in economic liberalism and a desire to roll back regulation and government intervention in the name of free markets. SAPs mostly had similar aims and components for all countries in which they were applicable. They key reforms under SAPs included:

1. Reducing government spending, often through cutbacks in welfare provision, or

attempts to balance government budgets through increased government revenues (for example, through higher fees for government services).
2. Reducing or removing subsidies to domestic industries, which has often been part of import substitution strategies.
3. Reducing or removing tariffs, quotas and other restrictions on the import and export of goods.
4. Deregulating the economy generally as well as particularly removing restrictions on foreign investment to achieve capital market liberalisation.
5. Devaluing of the exchange rate in order to encourage exports and reduce imports.

Cultural

Cultural globalisation, as Thomas Friedman mentions in his book *The World is Flat* (2005), is the process whereby information, commodities and images that have been produced in one part of the world enter into a global flow that tends to 'flatten out' cultural differences between nations, regions and individuals. This has sometimes been portrayed as a process of McDonaldisation. Cultural globalisation is also fuelled by the so-called information revolution, the spread of satellite communication, telecommunication networks, information technology and the internet, and global media corporations.

Globalisation and the Global South

Initially, the idea of a Global South emerged in the form of a Third World movement or a Third World solidarity. The **Bandung Summit (1955)**, attended by representatives from twenty-nine governments of Asian and African nations, is an example of south-south cooperation. The **Non-Aligned Movement** was founded in 1961 to express the collective voice of the Global South. The Group of 77 or **G-77,** formed through a joint declaration at the United Nations Conference on Trade and Development in 1964. It is also an example of south-south cooperation which speaks for better terms of trade between the north and the south. Presently, G-77 is comprised of 134 developing countries. The demand for the **New International Economic Order (NIEO)**, a set of proposals advocated by developing countries to end economic colonialism and dependency through a new interdependent economy was also a result of south–south cooperation.

New Forums of Global South

In the age of liberalisation and globalisation, various forums of the Global South emerged. One such forum is that of India, Brazil, and South Africa **(IBSA)** Dialogue Forum which was formed in 2003. IBSA was created due to the failure of the Cancún Ministerial Conference of WTO in 2003. Around 2008, European nations and the US suffered a huge economic recession which affected the finalisation of the Doha Development Round. As a consequence, **BRICS** was formed in 2009. BRICS demanded reforms in global governance. It is also considered an alternative to the IMF as the BRICS Development Bank was set up in the year 2012. BRICS worked as a pressure group and succeeded in bringing about reforms in the IMF—it was decided that 2 out of 24 IMF directors shall be chosen from the Global South. This reform became possible in IMF only due to the lobbying of BRICS. Due to BRICS, China became the third largest member country in IMF alongside Brazil, India and Russia who are among the 10 largest stakeholders in the fund.

New Issues of the Global South

The Global South demanded reforms in IMF and spoke for an inclusive globalisation. The interests of the Global South must be protected while promoting sustainable development and thus reforms in the Security Council is also an important agenda. The international trade and financial institutions are still under control of the Global North while the Global South still lacks the requisite finance and technology that is necessary for ensuring their development. The dispute settlement mechanism of WTO should be reformed for serving the interest of the Global South. The on-going trade war between China and the US is harmful for the development of the countries of the Global South. Most prominent regional economic organisations like the European Union and NAFTA are located in the Global North which adversely affects regional economic cooperation in the Global South.

Paradox in the Global South

E. R. Wittkopf says that the notion of the Global South is a paradoxical concept. He said that the members belonging to the Global South can be classified as follows into three groups:

(a) **Newly Industrialised Countries:** South Korea has emerged as the industrial powerhouse of the world. Singapore and Taiwan too has emerged as new centres of economic growth. They are closely followed by Indonesia and Malaysia.

(b) **Oil-Exporting Countries:** Nations like Saudi Arabia, UAE, Mexico, Iraq, Kuwait, and Qatar are rich due to their huge resources of oil and natural gas.

(c) **Least Developing Countries (LDCs):** They are the most disadvantaged nations in the category of the Global South. Afghanistan, Bangladesh, Myanmar and Nepal are LDCs. Apart from these, some African nations such as Angola, Burundi, Chad, Rwanda, and Uganda also fall in this category. Some Latin American and Caribbean nations like Haiti and Madagascar, are also LDCs. A total of 47 nations qualify as LDC according to a report of the UNCTAD.

Consequences of Globalisation

Global Civil Society

It has been suggested that one of the consequences of globalisation has been the emergence of a *'transnational' or 'world' society*, as Barry Buzan discusses in his 2004 book *From International to World Society*. John Burton too talks about world society in his writings. However, the extent to which societal identities have been, or are in the process of being, established across the global population as a whole should not be overstated. Perhaps a fruitful way of thinking about the transitional dimension of society is the terms of what is called *'global civil society'*. An interest in the idea of a global civil society grew during the 1990s as a mosaic of new groups, organisations and movements started to appear, which both sought to challenge or resist what was seen as 'corporate' globalisation as well as articulate alternative models of social, economic and political development.

Cosmopolitanism

Global interconnectedness does not merely challenge us in terms of how we understand the world, but also in terms of our moral relationships. Widespread globalisation has undoubtedly had an ethical dimension in that it has renewed interest in forms of cosmopolitanism often expressed through growing interest in ideas that espouse *global justice or world ethics*. Nigel Dower talks about this in his book *World Ethics: The New Agenda* (1998) and Simon Caney explores these ideas in his essay 'Cosmopolitan Justice, Responsibility, and Global Climate Change' (2005). People thus have obligations (potentially) towards all the people in the world, regardless of nationality, religion, ethnicity and so forth, and constitute a single moral community. Such thinking is usually based on the doctrine of human rights. **Thomas Pogge** broke down rights-based cosmopolitanism into **three elements**:

1. Individualism, in that human beings or persons are the ultimate unit of moral concern.
2. Universality, in the sense that it believes that all individuals are of equal moral worth.

3. Generality, in that it implies that persons are objects of concern for everybody, not just their compatriots.

Other forms of moral cosmopolitanism have also been proposed by thinkers and political scientists. **Onora O'Neill** in her definition of cosmopolitanism used the Kantian notion, which says that we should act on principles that we would be willing to apply to all people in all circumstances, to argue that people have a commitment not to injure others and that this commitment has a universal scope. **Peter Singer** on the other hand, argued that the ethics of globalisation demand that we should act in a way that would reduce the overall levels of global suffering, thinking in terms of '*one world*' rather than a collection of discrete countries of people.

Globalisation and State Sovereignty

In the economic realm, there are forces that actually undermine the power and scope of the nation states. In the context of world markets, **David Held** identified five threats to the concept of state sovereignty:

(a) The role of multinational corporations, which have increased social and workforce mobility.
(b) Advanced technology and communication, often unregulated at a global level, undermines state sovereignty.
(c) The military power of nation states have been undermined with the emergence of NATO.
(d) The proliferation of international organisations like the European Union and the strengthening of international law that has control over individuals, governments and non-governmental organisations adversely affect state sovereignty.
(e) Security concerns results in domestic autonomy becoming limited and this threatens the state's position as the primary spokesperson of its citizens and its ability to determine domestic public policy and protect foreign interests.

Richard Falk argues that it is misleading to view the world as consisting of territorial units, each exerting supreme authority within its border and not elsewhere.

Susan Strange in her book *The Retreat of the State* (1996) rightly said that the present state is more like a medieval state where the power is decentralised. It is an example of shared sovereignty. According to Strange, the Hobbesian states no longer exist in the present age of globalisation.

Retreat of Globalisation

Walden Bello in his work, *Deglobalisation: Ideas for a New World Economy* (2002) said that 'de-globalisation' would bring about decentralised, distinctive, local economies and communities throughout the world. He calls for an 'anti-corporate globalisation' movement. He said that the Bretton Woods institutions fulfil only the interests of United States.

Joseph Stiglitz, in his work *Globalization and Its Discontents* (2002), say that the Western countries have forced the poor countries to remove trade barriers for selfish interests but they are keeping their own barriers intact. The US-controlled IMF with its SAPs puts an extra burden of high rates of interests on the developing countries. In the past, around 2008, the European Union and the United States of America went under the economic crisis, and presently COVID-19 has further escalated the economic issues faced by Europe and the United States of America. Former US President **Donald Trump** has also contributed to this growing deglobalisation through his use of policies like '**America First**'.

The question of retreat of globalisation is still a matter of debate. The **Regional Comprehensive Economic Partnership** (RCEP) was formed in the year 2020, a free trade agreement among the Asia-Pacific nations of Australia, Brunei,

Cambodia, China, Indonesia, Japan, South Korea, Laos, Malaysia, Myanmar, New Zealand, the Philippines, Singapore, Thailand, and Vietnam, which visualised the importance of globalisation and economic interdependence between nation states.

Some Important Books on the Topic of Globalisation

1. *Democracy and the Global Order* (1995), by David Held
2. *A Globalizing World? Culture, Economics, Politics* (2000), by David Held
3. *The Unseen Hand: An Introduction to the Conspirational View of History* (1985), by A. Ralph Epperson
4. *The New World Order* (1991), by Pat Robertson
5. *George Soros on Globalization* (2005), by George Soros
6. *Casino Capitalism* (1986), by Susan Strange
7. *Mad Money* (1997), by Susan Strange
8. *In Defense of Globalization* (2004), by Jagdish Natwarlal Bhagwati
9. *Only One Earth: The Care and Maintenance of a Small Planet* (1983), by Barbara Ward and René Dubos
10. *The End of the Nation State: The Rise of Regional Economies* (1996), by Kenichi Ohmae
11. *Another World is Possible, If...* (2004), by Susan George.
12. *End of Poverty: Economic Possibilities for our Time* (2005), *Common Wealth: Economics for a Crowded Planet* (2008), by Jeffrey Sachs

GLOBAL GOVERNANCE

Global Governance is a purposeful order that emerges from institutions, processes, norms, formal agreements and informal mechanisms that regulate action for a common good.

Global governance encompasses activity at the international, transnational and regional levels, and refers to activities in the public and private sectors that transcend national boundaries. It espouses cooperative action, which is based on rights and rules that are enforced through a combination of financial and moral incentives.

Precursor to the Idea of Global Governance: The Hegemonic Stability Theory

The Hegemonic Stability Theory is an approach prominent among many American political scientists which states that dominant military and economic power is necessary to ensure stability and prosperity in a liberal world economy. A hegemon is a state that has the capacity and the will to lead and overpower other states in the international system. Charles Kindleberger, Robert Gilpin and Stephen Krasner has presented explanations for international economic relations that are similar to this theory.

The theory has two main components:

1. It recognises that a liberal world economy is in constant danger of being subverted by rising nationalism and the spread of protectionism. This was clearly demonstrated by the so-called 'beggar-thy-neighbour' policies that resulted in the Great Depression of the 1930s.
2. A dominant or hegemonic power is likely to be both willing and able to establish and enforce rules. The hegemon is a state that is powerful enough to act in line with the objective of 'absolute gains' rather than 'relative gains'. By contrast, the smaller, less powerful states are forced to act more narrowly in line with their national self-interest.

Thus, to be a hegemon, a state must therefore

(1) have sufficient power to enforce the rules of the system.
(2) possess the will to use this power.
(3) be committed to a system that brings benefit to the mass of states.

Issues in Global Governance

Global governance is concerned with issues that have become too complex for a single state to address alone. Issues such as humanitarian crises, military conflicts between and within states, terrorism, pandemics, climate change and economic volatility pose serious threats to human security in all societies and thus require global cooperation.

In the absence of a single authoritative institution or a world government, global governance, comprised of elements and methods from both the public and private sectors, takes charge.

The goal of global governance, roughly defined, is to provide global public goods, particularly peace and security, justice and mediation systems for conflict, functioning markets and unified standards for trade and industry.

The report on 'Global Governance and Global Rules for Development in the Post-2015 Era' by the Committee for Development Policy, UN, asserted that effective global governance cannot be achieved without effective international cooperation.

Mechanisms of Global Governance

A *multitude of actors* define and shape the current structure of global governance. States, international organisations, NGOs, MNCs, scientific experts, civil society groups as well as transnational criminal and trafficking networks are all actors in world politics that take part in steering the political system.

There are **four general mechanisms or structures** in global governance: Intergovernmental Organisations (IGOs), Public–Private Partnerships (PPPs), private governance and tripartite governance.

IGOs such as the WTO and the UN are examples of existing state-centered governance mechanisms. The leading institution which carries the promise of being able to exercise global governance is the **United Nations**. It does not directly bring together the people of the world, but it brings together different sovereign nation-states. The UN's main mandate is to preserve global security. It can also settle international legal issues through the International Court of Justice and implement its key decisions through the Secretariat. The UN has added a range of areas to its core mandate since 1945. It works through a range of agencies and associated institutions to ensure greater shared prosperity and enhanced global stability.

The IGOs like UN have also worked towards expanding the capacity and access to resources by including private and non-governmental actors and institutions through **Public–Private Partnerships (PPPs)**. This has led to the creation of global collaborative networks wherein the IGOs shape and support the operations of NGOs and certain private enterprises. The **UN Global Compact** is one such example of an international PPP.

Beyond the UN, there are other institutions that play an important role in global governance. These include the **Bretton Woods institutions**, namely the IMF and the World Bank, which function to regulate the economy and credit markets.

Global governance is more generally affected through a wide range of organisations which act as intermediary bodies. These include those in charge of regional coordination such as **the EU and the ASEAN**, which operate to coordinate the policies of their members in a certain geographical zone.

Besides governments and international institutions, relevant actors in global governance also include civil society and businesses.

There are also *tripartite arrangements* established among state, private and civil society actors. These exemplify alternative, public-private or private governance arrangements. Two notable examples of this kind of an arrangement are instruments such as Publish What You Pay and the African Peer Review Mechanism.

THE BRETTON WOODS SYSTEM

The Bretton Woods Conference (officially known as the United Nations Monetary and Financial Conference) was held in 1944 in Bretton Woods, New Hampshire, to agree upon new rules for the post-WWII international monetary system. The Bretton Woods system of monetary management laid the rules for commercial and financial relations among the United States, Canada, Western European countries, Australia, and Japan after the 1944 Bretton Woods Agreement.

At the Bretton Woods Conference in 1944 it was agreed that all countries' currencies would be fixed at a certain value. They became fixed to the dollar, and the US Government promised to convert all dollars to gold at USD 35 per ounce. In other words, exchange rates were anchored to a *dollar-gold standard*. In August 1971, the US Government announced that it was suspending this convertibility of the dollar to gold. This removed gold from the dollar-gold standard and paved the way for major currencies to 'float' instead of staying at fixed values.

Bretton Woods Institutions

Bretton Woods institutions include the **International Monetary Fund** (IMF) and the **International Bank for Reconstruction and Development** (IBRD), popularly known as World Bank.

(a) **International Monetary Fund:** The IMF is a financial agency of the United Nations and an international financial institution, headquartered in Washington, D.C. The agency's major functions include providing economic assistance to secure financial stability and reduce poverty and manage balance of payments difficulties and international financial crises. The IMF now has a **membership of 190 countries** each of which contributes a **quota of resources** to the organisation (proportionate to the size of the member nation's economy) which also determines their percentage of voting rights and the amount of resources to which they can have automatic access.

Since the 1980s, the IMF has become an institution offering financial and technological assistant to developing and transition economies. The terms on which countries receive assistance include the government having to commit to undertake specific conditions of policy reform, called **'conditionality'**. Decision-making of the IMF is controlled by the members of G7. Economic assistance given by the IMF is also on the basis of political consideration.

(b) **World Bank:** The International Bank for Reconstruction and Development (IBRD) or the World Bank comprises 189 members and is headquartered in Washington, D.C. The World Bank provides long-term loans for development of economy and infrastructure. The IBRD began as an agency to foster reconstruction in war-torn Europe as well as development in the rest of the world. The World Bank is the world's largest source of development assistance, providing nearly USD 16 billion in loans annually to eligible members countries, working closely with the **International Development Association (IDA)**, the **International Finance Corporation (IFC)**, and the **Multilateral Investment Guarantee Agency (MIGA)**.

General Agreement on Tariffs and Trade

The movement towards free trade progressed in a series of steps. At the time of the Bretton Woods negotiations, the United States envisioned an international institution for the regulation of trade called the **International Trade Organization (ITO)**. The failure of negotiating governments to create the ITO later led to the General Agreement on Tariffs and Trade (GATT). The GATT was first discussed at the United Nations Conference on Trade and Employment, and signed in Geneva in October 1947 among 23 nations.

GATT was never intended to be a formal institution with enforcement powers. Instead, the emphasis was on negotiations and reaching a consensus to settle disputes among parties to the agreement, and it was thus first and foremost a commercial treaty. But as the trade systems changed and disputes multiplied, GATT evolved over time, and under pressure from the United States, increasingly became involved in disputes of trade settlement following increasingly legalistic procedures.

GATT operated on the principle of *decision-making by consensus.* It functioned on the principles of *non-discrimination and equal treatment.* The principle of the Most Favoured Nation (MFN) was an important instrument of functioning which was also later adapted by the World Trade Organization (WTO). In international economic relations and international politics, the most-favoured-nation treatment is one state according the most favourable tariff and regulatory treatment to another.

Trade Rounds

The primary objective of GATT was promotion of multilateral trade. With the changing international financial situation, the European economies began exhibiting protectionist tendencies by imposing high rates of tariff, and introducing quotas and subsidies. *Tariff* is imposed as a protective measure by a nation so that they can reduce import. *Quota* refers to a government-imposed trade restriction that limits the number or monetary value of goods imported or exported during a particular time period. Government *subsidies* help domestic industries by paying for part of the cost of production of a good or service by offering tax credits or by paying part of the cost a consumer would pay to purchase a good or service.

Since these policies became an obstacle in promotion of trade between nations, it was realised that reduction in tariff is necessary to encourage international trade. GATT tried to reduce tariff with the help of multilateral diplomacy. For this purpose, various round of talks and multilateral trade negotiations were organised. Given below are few of the important negotiations.

Kennedy Round (1964–1967)

The high point in the momentum towards a liberal trade regime in industrial products occurred with the mid-1960s Kennedy Round of negotiations. USD 40 billion in tariffs were eliminated or reduced.

Tokyo Round (1973–1979)

To cope with growing protectionist sentiments in the United States, the Nixon administration sought authority from Congress to negotiate lower tariff barriers with other countries. This congressional concession to the president laid the basis for the Tokyo Round of multilateral trade negotiations, concluded in 1979 after nearly six years of bargaining.

Uruguay Round (1986–1994)

In the Uruguay Round of negotiations, which began in 1986, barriers to trade in services (e.g., insurance), intellectual property rights (e.g., copyrights on computer software, music and movies), and investments (stocks and bonds) were put on the agenda as new issues and no state stood to gain as much from these provisions as the United States. The long-standing issues of world trade in agriculture had previously evolved outside of the main GATT framework. At the core of differences on agricultural trade were the enormous government subsidies that some leading producers paid farmers for competitive advantage in the international market. Whole new issues were included in the Uruguay Round such as:

(a) Trade in agriculture
(b) Trade in services
(c) Trade-Related Intellectual Property Rights (TRIPS)
(d) Trade-Related Investment Measures (TRIMS)
(e) Non-tariff barriers like subsidy and quota

Approach of the Global South towards GATT

GATT functioned on the principle of *equal treatment* of all the members. However, this principle was criticised and opposed to by the Third World countries which had recently gained independence after the wave of decolonisation that followed the end of WW-II and were impoverished and underdeveloped. The developed nations were industrialised and could sustain the requirements of free trade and low tariffs which the underdeveloped nations could not. Therefore, the Third World countries demanded *preferential treatment* and concessions in tariff. Developing nations also raised their voice against inclusion of agriculture and intellectual property rights under trade rules.

Conversely, the developed members from the First World asserted the principle of 'comparative advantage' which implied that the benefits from free trade and reduction in tariffs would ultimately reach the underdeveloped countries.

WORLD TRADE ORGANIZATION

The World Trade Organization (WTO) is the successor to the GATT. The Uruguay Round of GATT led to the creation of WTO and it began operations on 1 January 1995. The agreement that led to the establishment of the WTO is commonly known as the **Marrakesh Agreement** and it was signed in Marrakesh, Morocco in 1994.

The Formation of WTO: The 'Washington Consensus'

The formation of WTO is associated with the overall economic development in the world during the 1990s. The term 'Washington Consensus' was coined by economist John Williamson in 1989 and refers to a set of ten economic policy prescriptions considered to constitute the 'standard' reform package promoted for crisis-wracked developing countries by the international institutions based in Washington, D.C. The policy recommendations are as follows:

1. Fiscal discipline (cutting public spending)
2. Redirection of public spending from subsidies towards education, healthcare and infrastructure
3. Tax reform (broadening the tax base and cutting personal taxes)
4. Financial liberalisation (the deregulation of financial markets and capital controls)
5. Floating and competitive exchange rates
6. Trade liberalisation (free trade)
7. Openness to foreign investment
8. Privatisation of state enterprises
9. Legal security for property rights
10. Interest rates that are market determined

Structure of the WTO

The WTO is an institution with a well-organised structure. All decisions of the WTO are taken through voting wherein each member has one vote. The WTO also comprises a dispute settlement body that was lacking in GATT.

1. **Ministerial Conference**

   The WTO is comprised of **164 member governments and 25 observer nations** (such as Iran, Iraq, Bhutan and Libya). The **most important decision-making body** in WTO is the Ministerial Conference which meets once in every 2 years. Ministers of Commerce of the member states participate in the conference for promotion of multilateral trade.

2. **Trade Policy Review Body**

   This committee undertakes trade policy reviews of member states and considers the Director-General's regular reports on trade policy development. It reviews the export and import policies of the member state. In order to scrutinise the protectionist policies are adopted by the member's state against the principle of WTO.

3. **Dispute Settlement Body**

   The General Council convenes as the Dispute Settlement Body to deal with disputes between the WTO members. Such disputes may arise with regard to any agreement contained in the Final Act of the Uruguay Round.

4. **General Councils**

   The WTO deals with various issues of international trade such as goods, services and intellectual property rights. These issues are examined by three different councils:

   (a) The Council for Trade in Goods
   (b) The Council for Trade in Services
   (c) The Council for Trade-Related Aspects of Intellectual Property Rights (TRIPS Council)

Objectives of the WTO

(1) To set and enforce rules for international multilateral trade
(2) To provide a forum for negotiating and monitoring trade liberalisation
(3) To resolve trade disputes
(4) To increase the transparency of decision-making processes
(5) To collaborate with other international economic institutions
(6) To safeguard the interests of developing countries in the global trading system

Principles

The WTO has five important principles:

(1) **Non-discrimination:** The two major components of this principle are the most favoured nation (MFN) rule and the national treatment policy. The MFN rule postulates that a WTO member must apply the same conditions on all trade with other WTO members and national treatment means that imported goods should be treated as favourably as domestic goods.
(2) **Reciprocity:** It reflects both the desire to limit the scope of free-riding and the desire to gain better access to foreign markets.
(3) **Binding and enforceable commitments:** The tariff commitments made by WTO members are legally binding and enforceable.
(4) **Transparency:** The WTO members must be transparent. They should publish their trade regulations, allow reviews of trade decisions, respond to requests for information, and notify changes in trade policies.
(5) **Safety values:** The WTO permits its member states to take measures to protect the environment as well as public health.

Global South and the WTO

The WTO is headquartered in Switzerland which is at a great distance from the Third World. Also, the cost of litigation in the judicial procedure is very high which makes it difficult for developing countries to approach the Dispute Settlement Body in case of disputes. And sometimes, despite a verdict, various loopholes and the existing economic hegemony of the economic superpowers prevents the effective implementation of the DSB's decisions. All of these discourage the members of the Global South to speak against the discriminatory policies of the Global North.

Developed countries led by the US and the EU often seeks to find a way out of a deadlock at the WTO talks by forming large pressure groups on e-commerce, investment facilitation and MSMEs within the WTO with more than 70 members in each. Though the WTO is driven by consensus, the formation of these groups as an attempt to steer WTO away from its focus on multilateralism. This also renders the formal procedure of voting irrelevant. On the name of decision by consensus, the major powers end up taking every decision of the WTO. There are also Green Room meetings, which are small gatherings of representatives from up to 30 member countries, invited by the Director-General. The WTO has thus, in many ways, failed to respond to the needs of the Global South.

Ministerial Conferences of the WTO

Singapore Issues (WTO Ministerial Conference of 1996)

The first Ministerial Conference of the WTO took place in Singapore in 1996. The issues raised in the conference at Singapore are referred to as the Singapore Issues. These issues were pushed by the First World entities like the European Union, Japan and Korea, but were opposed by most developing countries.

(a) **Transparency in government procurement:** The Global North pushed for neo-liberal economic policies according to which governments are not permitted to give preferential treatment to their own companies for procurement by the government. Every stakeholder should have the same opportunity when it comes to government procurement.

(b) **Trade facilitation (customs issues):** No member of the WTO should be allowed to discriminate against other members in relation to the issue of customs.

(c) **Trade-related investment measures:** The member governments should not discriminate against foreign investors. Domestic industries cannot be allowed to be protected by the government.

(d) **Competition policies:** The government and the private sector should be given equal opportunity for the purchase of goods. No sector of economy should be reserved only for the government. The developed world pushed for the opening and liberalisation of the economies of developing countries.

(e) **Non-trade barriers:** For the first time, non-trade issues like labour and the environment was discussed in connection with trade.

Although these issues were discussed, disagreements between the developed and developing economies prevented a resolution of most of these issues.

Doha Development Round

The Seattle Conference (WTO Ministerial Conference of 1999) was opposed by various NGOs and civil society organisations through protests because the developing countries were resented being excluded from talks when the US and the EU were trying to sign a mutual deal on agriculture. The negotiations failed and the group later reconvened in Doha, Qatar, in November 2001 and this is what started the Doha Development Round.

Issues Discussed at the Doha Development Round:

(a) **Agriculture:** A mere 4 per cent of the population of the developed world is engaged in agriculture which is primarily commercial agriculture, whereas approximately 50 per cent of the population of developing countries is dependent on subsistence agriculture for their livelihood. WTO has raised the objection over the **Food Security Act** of India and they claim that India is providing agricultural subsidies which ignores the limits prescribed by WTO. According to the limit prescribed by WTO, a developed country can provide 5 per cent subsidy on their agriculture production according to the base year of 1986–1988. For a developing nation or a nation of the Global South, this limit is 10 per cent of their agriculture production. India argued that the base year of limit of subsidy should be changed because the price of agricultural products has risen faster in the Global South as compared to the developed world. Further, India argued that the Food Security Act aims for elimination of poverty, which is a goal set by the UN under its sustainable development programme. The Special Safeguard Mechanism (SSM) was thus included, which permitted developing nations to increase import taxes on agricultural goods in response to spikes in imports to protect one's own domestic agricultural market. The nations belonging to the Global North provides agricultural subsidies in various forms:

(i) **Green Box**: These are subsidies that do not distort trade, or at most cause minimal distortion. Usually, these subsidies are given for environmental conservation and research programmes and there is no limit on the government for giving this subsidy by WTO.

(ii) **Amber Box**: These subsidies distort production and trade (with some exceptions) and may be given on electricity, seeds and irrigation.

(iii) **Blue Box**: These subsidies are designed to reduce distortion. This comprise any support given by farmers to limit their production. There are no limits on spending on blue box subsidies.

(b) **Access to patented medicines:** This involves a discussion on Trade-Related Aspects of Intellectual Property Rights (TRIPS). The pharmaceutical companies in developed countries often hold patents on medicines and any barrier to this trade of patents can negatively impact public health needs in developing countries. The necessity for a waiver that allows easy export of pharmaceutical products made under compulsory licenses to least-developed countries was discussed.

(c) **Special or preferential treatment:** Earlier the Global North had made a commitment to ensure fewer tariffs on imported items from the Global South. But later they refused to comply and argued that since the Global South is not a homogeneous entity, only Least Developed Countries (LDCs) would be entitled to get the facility of preferential treatment in international trade negotiations. This commitment was reiterated in the Bali and Nairobi Conferences too. Preferential Treatment implies that all trading countries will levy zero tariffs on the exported items from LDCs.

(d) **Implementation issues:** The members of the Global South demanded discussion on implementation issues as the Global North was not willing to implement what they had earlier committed to regarding agriculture subsidies. Implementation issues were also found in the area of market access, especially of the **Non-Agricultural Market Access (NAMA)** agreement, which aims to reduce and eliminate tariffs with regard to industrial products.

Challenges Faced by the WTO

(a) **Rules undermined:** The unilateral tariffs being imposed by the US and China is not in concurrence with the established procedures within the WTO.

(b) **Nations going rogue:** The WTO is facing an increased influx of disputes from countries using concerns for national security as a justification for higher tariffs. These decisions are being taken by national governments in the name of national sovereignty.

(c) **Hearings paralysed:** Since August 2017, the US has blocked nominees to the WTO's appellate body, a key forum for mediating disputes, arguing that it has overstepped its mandate.

(d) **Market economy disputes:** China has contended that the US and the EU are violating WTO rules by continuing to treat China as a non-market economy in anti-dumping investigations.

(e) **Failed negotiations:** The countries of the Third World are pushing towards piecemeal accords centred on sectoral issues like e-commerce or investment facilitations. All of these issues bring to the fore the problem of disagreement over broad negotiation agendas of the WTO and the lack of consensus.

Table 5.5.1: Ministerial Conferences of the WTO

	Place	*Year*
1.	Singapore	1996
2.	Geneva	1998
3.	Seattle	1999
4.	Doha	2001
5.	Cancun	2003
6.	Hong Kong	2005
7.	Geneva	2009
8.	Geneva	2011
9.	Bali	2013
10.	Nairobi	2015
11.	Buenos Aires	2017
12.	Geneva	2022

NORTH–SOUTH DIALOGUE

The North–South Dialogue refers to the negotiations between the developing and newly independent nations of the Third World, that is, the nations in Asia, Africa, and Latin America, and the industrialised countries of North America and Western Europe over changes to the international economic system during the 1970s. The North–South Dialogue addressed issues related to trade and tariffs, international finance, foreign aid, and the governance of multinational companies and institutions. During the era of detente between the late 1960s and the late 1970s, the East–West tensions were less and the industrialised nations were willing to cooperate. Even later, the parties to the North–South Dialogue agreed to continue their discussions.

Global South

The Global South is generally understood to refer to the **less economically developed countries.** The term has been defined in various ways with reference to diverse socio-economic aspects characteristic of a particular group of nations. There are two prominent definitions of this term. First, the term has traditionally been used in the literature of intergovernmental development organisations—especially those which originated as a part of the Non-Aligned Movement—to refer to economically disadvantaged nation-states. It has been used as a post-Cold War alternative to the term Third World. Secondly, the Global South terminology is used in an extra-terrestrial sense, that is, to refer to the subjugated spaces and peoples lying at the periphery of wealthier and more developed capitalist countries and which are negatively impacted by contemporary capitalist globalisation.

The Global South comprises the regions of **Latin America, Asia, Africa and Oceania.** It basically denotes regions outside Europe and North America, mostly (though not all) low-income and often politically or culturally marginalised. The idea of a powerful Global North and a resistant Global South was promoted by the Zapatista Uprising in Mexico, the 'African Renaissance', and the World Social Forum launched in Brazil.

Drawing on post-colonial and subaltern studies, specifically the work of **Gayatri Spivak and Homi Bhabha**, scholars have embraced the term Global South to examine subaltern agency and oppression and to link localised struggles to dynamics of global power structures and dominant social groups.

Differences between the Global North and the Global South

The Global South is sometimes described today as a '*zone of turmoil*' because, in contrast with the Global North where '*peace, wealth, and democracy*' prevail, most people of the Global South live amidst 'poverty, war, tyranny, and anarchy'. According to Mohammed Ayoob, vast political, economic, and social differences separate the North and the South and the Global South is 'weak, vulnerable, and insecure, with these traits being the function of both domestic and external factors'.

Even though **democracy** has spread rapidly and widely since the end of the Cold War, becoming the preferred mode of governance throughout much of the Global South (China, Cuba, North Korea and Vietnam being obvious exceptions), the stable institutional arrangements that the mature democracies in the Global North have are rare in the Global South. Furthermore, many Global South countries lack well-developed domestic market economies based on entrepreneurship and private enterprise unlike the Global North.

Differences in **technological capabilities** also separate the Global North and South. Typically, Global South countries have been unable to evolve an indigenous technology appropriate to their own resources and are dependent on powerful multinational corporations (MNCs) of the Global North for the transfer of technical know-how. And in the information age, the most striking developments are taking place in the Global North. Information technology has not been distributed equally geographically; the highest density of computer connections to the global Internet is in the Global North, and the lowest is in Africa, in south of the Sahara, one of the poorest regions of the world.

Types of Countries in the Global South

A. **Least Developed Countries**

Forty-six countries have been classified by the International Monetary Fund as the least developed countries. More than two-thirds of these are in Africa, and most of the rest are in Asia. **Sudan, Togo, Uganda, Yemen, Afghanistan, Haiti, Rwanda, and Somalia** are the a few of these.

B. **Oil-Exporting Countries**

The poverty of the LDCs is in stark contrast with the comparative wealth of the Global South states that have fossil fuels to consume and export. The sixteen developing-country exporters of oil and other fuels, and especially the twelve members of the **Organization of the Petroleum Exporting Countries (OPEC)**, have escaped the LDCs' grim fate. Although many fall into the lower-middle or upper-middle income groups, some—notably the OPEC members like **Kuwait, Qatar** and the **United Arab Emirates**—have risen to the high-income group, with standards of living rivaling those of Global North countries.

C. **Newly Industrialised Countries**

The **newly industrialised countries (NICs) or newly industrialised economies (NIEs)** are countries that have experienced greater success than the oil-exporting countries. Their success lies in moving beyond the export of primary products—characteristic of both the LDCs and the oil exporters—to the export of manufactured goods. Today the NIEs are among the largest exporters of manufactured goods and the most prosperous members of the Global South.

Three states among the NIEs, the so-called Asian Tigers: **South Korea, Singapore, and Taiwan**—have, alongside Hong Kong prior to its 1997 reunification with China, taken extraordinary advantage of comparatively low wage rates to aggressively promote export-led economic growth.

D. **Countries in Transition**

The countries in transition, the twenty-eight remnants of the former Second World in Central and Eastern Europe, lie economically somewhere between the Global North and the Global South. Difficulties in placing a fair monetary value on the goods and services produced in centrally managed economies complicate their positioning.

Issues in North–South Dialogue

(a) **Inclusive Globalisation**: The Global South has accepted the model of liberal economy and globalisation, but the Global North wants the process of globalisation only for furthering their own interests. Globalisation should be inclusive and the advantage of global economy should be available both for the Global North as well as for the Global South.

(b) **Transfer of Technology**: The issue of transfer of technology has become more pertinent in the present world of liberalisation. The Global South needs eco-friendly technology in order to meet the goal of zero emission for preserving the environment. But the Global North does not want a transfer of the technology to the Global South.

(c) **Reforms in Bretton Woods Institutions:** Terms of international trade is not favourable for the Global South countries because they export the raw materials. Moreover, global financial institutions are still under the control of the Global North. All major financial decisions are taken by the Global North due to their dominance in the Bretton Woods Institutions, that is, the IMF and World Bank. Thus, reforms are necessary to ensure fair terms of trade for both the Global North and South.

(d) **Development and Environment:** In recent years, the preservation of environment has become a concern of the Global South but social economic development of the developing countries takes priority and is a pre-condition for protection of the environment. However, the Global North is trying to connect the non-trade issues like labour, environment and human rights with trade issues, which further disadvantages the Global South.

Eurocentricism and Neocolonialism of the Global North

Although IR is an interdisciplinary field with a huge thematic and contextual diversity and wide scope, it has historically been studied from a very **Eurocentric perspective.** Eurocentrism implies the dominance of the Westphalian discourse in tracing the history of the discipline of IR. This overlooks all political developments of a nation-state and its interactions with other nations if it is situated in a region other than Europe. Eurocentrism also implies the dominance of European and North American scholars and intelligentsia within the discipline of IR which not only ensures the preponderance of a particular perspective, but also shapes the way in which certain spaces and issues gain more importance than others.

J. Ann Tickner points out that issues of race and empire have been missing from mainstream IR theories despite the existence of solid scholarship in postcolonial and poststructuralist studies from the Global South. But the Eurocentric Global North ignores the scholarship of the Global South.

The Ghanaian leader **Kwame Nkrumah** in his book *Neo-Colonialism: The Last Stage of Imperialism (1965)* said that the developing world may have become independent politically, but technically and financially the Global South is still under the domination of the Global North. The financial institutions like the IMF and IBRD have become new tools for colonial exploitation and the Global South has been facing the problem of debt trap. Due to emergence of **new colonialism or neo-colonialism,** developing nations are now demanding a new international economic order.

South-South Cooperation

The term refers to the process of cooperation among the developing countries in the economic field and other areas. Presently, south–south cooperation is promoted as a viable strategy by developing countries for their development and progress. South–south cooperation was adopted by the **Non-Aligned Movement** as the basic principle of its economic approach to achieve its objective of collective self-reliance among developing countries. It is also a fundamental mechanism of India's economic diplomacy towards other developing countries and the LDCs.

In the present age of globalisation, south-south cooperation is also visible in the form of regional economic organisations like **ASEAN** and **Mercosur** (The Southern Common Market, comprising Argentina, Brazil, Paraguay and Uruguay). **BIMSTEC** (Bay of Bengal Initiative for Multi-Sectoral Technical and Economic Cooperation) is also a new forum for economic cooperation among South Asian countries. **BRICS** is a more recent and dominant voice in south-south cooperation.

North-South Cooperation

During the Cold War, the North-South Dialogue was initiated with the aim of a more egalitarian economic order in international politics. In post-Cold War era too this cooperation between the Global North and the Global South continued. G20 as well as APEC comprised of members of the Global North as well as members of the Global South.

Recently, the **Regional Comprehensive Economic Partnership (RCEP)** has been set up in 2020, which comprises member countries from both the North and the South. Members of RCEP include **China, Japan, Malaysia, Australia, New Zealand, Brunei, Cambodia, Indonesia, Myanmar, Singapore, South Korea, Philippines, Laos, Thailand and Vietnam**. Thus, south-south cooperation and north-south cooperation exist simultaneously in the arena of international politics.

G20

G20 or Group of 20 is an international forum for the governments and central bank governors from 19 countries and the European Union. It was founded in 1999 in response to several world economic crises to discuss policies related to financial stability.

The precursor to G20 was **G7** or Group of 7, which was formed in 1975 by the most developed nations, namely the **USA, Canada, France, Germany, Italy, Japan and United Kingdom**. It was set up for international financial management but the changing nature of global economy resulted into the eventual formation of G20. The importance of G20 was realised after the economic crisis of 2008 and now it is believed that G20 will likely replace the G7.

Members of G20 are Argentina, Australia, Brazil, Canada, China, France, Germany, India, Indonesia, Italy, Japan, Republic of Korea, Mexico, Russia, Saudi Arabia, South Africa, Turkey, The United States, the UK and the EU. G20 members account for more than 80 per cent of the world's GDP, 75 per cent of global trade and 60 per cent of the population. G20 does not have a permanent secretariat or staff. Spain is a permanent guest and always participates in the G20 summits. India is chairing the G20 in 2023.

G20 has two working tracks: the Finance track for finance ministers and central bank governors and the Sherpa track. The G20's proceedings are led by the Sherpas, who are appointed as personal envoys of the leaders of member nations. They oversee the negotiations that occur throughout the year and deliberate on the agenda for the summit. Since 2008, the G20 has convened at least once a year, with summits involving each member's head of government or state, finance minister, or foreign minister, and other diplomatic officials.

Table 5.5.2: List of G20 Summits

Summit	*Year*	*Host Country*	*Host City*
1st	2008	United States	Washington, D.C.
15th	2020	Saudi Arabia	Riyadh
16th	2021	Italy	Rome
17th	2022	Indonesia	Bali
18th	2023	India	New Delhi
19th	2024	Brazil	To be declared
20th	2025	South Africa	To be declared

BRICS

BRICS is comprised of Brazil, Russia, India, China and South Africa. The first four were initially grouped as BRIC in 2001 by the Goldman Sachs economist Jim O'Neill, who coined the term to describe fast-growing economies of the world. In 2011, South Africa joined the group and since then, it has been called BRICS.

The combined economy of BRICS is likely to become larger than the combined economic strength of G7. It together represents about 42 per cent of the world's population, 23 per cent of global GDP, 30 per cent of the total territory and 18 per cent of global trade. Formation of BRICS and G20 implies that the Global South is becoming the new centre of economy growth as the centre of power is moving from the Euro-Atlantic world to the Asia Pacific.

Rise of the Rest

Fareed Zakaria discusses the growth of new international players and America's place in the world in his 2009 book *The Post-American World and the Rise of the Rest*. In addition to highlighting the shift in the power balance of the global economy, with most of the growth in world output now coming from developing, transitional and emerging economies, the so-called 'rise of the rest' has a growing political dimension.

The main goals of the BRICS meeting have been to counterbalance the USA by ensuring better representation for the Global South and expanding the influence of the Global South, allowing the BRICS to be portrayed as the 'guardian of the interests of developing countries'. Some, therefore, view the rise of the BRICS as a major challenge to the US-dominated liberal Western order.

BRICS Development Bank

The New Development Bank, formerly called the BRICS Development Bank, was founded in 2014 for financing the project of development and the projects related to sustainable development in the Global South. BRICS Development Bank marks the beginning of a new international economic order based on equality.

It is also an alternative of the unequal International Monetary Fund (IMF), where decision-making is based on the quota which means the members holding more shares in the Fund will have greater voting rights. Since the members of the Global North have control over the IMF, every decision of the IMF is essentially taken by them. However, the decision-making of the BRICS Development Bank is based on the principle of equality. All members have the same voting rights and the share of members in the bank is also equal. While the IMF provides loans for the crisis of balance of payments, the BRICS Development Bank finances development projects.

The **BRICS Contingency Reserve Agreement (CRA)** was set up in 2015 to provide mutual financial support through additional liquidity during an economic crisis. It also functions as a global financial safety net.

BRICS Summits

The group has held annual summits since 2009, where member countries take turns to host. The first BRICS summit was held in 2009 with Russia as the host.

The 13th BRICS summit was held on 9 September 2021 through video conference with India as the chair. It was third time that India hosted the BRICS Summit after 2012 and 2016.

The 14th BRICS summit was held in 2022 under China's leadership. The 15th BRICS summit is scheduled to be held in South Africa's Durban in 2023.

Criticism against BRICS

According to critics, the significance of the rise of the BRICS may have been overstated.

1. **No concrete agenda for changing the global economic governance system**

has emerged from BRICS meetings, still less a vision of what a post-Western economic order might look like. Far from overthrowing the established order, the BRICS appears to be more intent on strengthening their position within it, enabling them to establish a partnership with the USA rather than indulging in 'hard' balancing.

2. The capacity of the BRICS to act as a single entity is severely restricted by the **political, ideological and economic differences amongst its members**. Brazil and India are democracies, while China and Russia are authoritarian, practising a form of state capitalism. Similarly, while Brazil and Russia are commodity exporters, specialising respectively in agriculture and natural resources, India, which specialises in manufacturing, is a commodity importer. Frictions from persistent Sino-Russian and Sino-Indian rivalry are likely to significantly impede the construction of an anti-US alliance.
3. The BRICS is a forum with highly **unequal members**. Although Russia may be its most assertive political voice, China is easily its dominant economic force. BRICS does not seem to reflect the common interests of 'the rest', but rather it is a device through which China can engage in 'soft' balancing with the USA without risking direct confrontation.

OTHER POLITICAL-ECONOMIC MOVEMENTS IN THE THIRD WORLD

1. **Non-Aligned Movement:** The Non-Aligned Movement (NAM) is a forum of 120 countries that are not formally aligned with or against any major power bloc. The movement began in 1955, when 29 Asian and African counties met in Bandung, Indonesia, to devise a strategy to combat colonialism. In 1961, leaders of these countries (which were mostly former colonies) met in Belgrade, Yugoslavia and formally founded the Non-Aligned Movement.
2. **A New International Economic Order**: The New International Economic Order (NIEO) is a set of proposals by developing countries to end economic colonialism and dependency through the establishment of a new interdependent economy.

   The emerging nations of the Global South were born into a political-economic order with rules they had no voice in creating. Beginning in the 1950s they began to seek the means to control their own economic futures. In the 1960s, 134 developing countries formed a coalition called the **Group of 77** (or G77). A decade later, in 1974, the G77 (now with more than 120 members) pushed for a **New International Economic Order** to counter the Liberal International Economic Order championed by the United States and the other capitalist powers since World War II.

   The main components of NIEO are:

   (a) Reforms in the Bretton Woods Institutions, namely the IMF, World Bank and WTO.
   (b) Transfer of technology from North to South.
   (c) Control over their own natural resources by the developing countries.
   (d) Regulation over the activities of MNCs.
   e. Demand for fair trade instead of economic aid.

6

REGIONAL ORGANISATIONS

KEYWORDS

Regionalism; European Union; African Union; Shanghai Cooperation Organisation; ASEAN.

REGIONALISM

Regionalism can be defined as the idea that political power is strengthened in specific geographic regions by the unity of nation-states known as 'blocks'. They are united by their common goals, incentives and interests. With rising globalisation, regionalism has become even more important as the world is more interconnected now. Regionalism takes different forms depending on the primary areas over which neighbouring states choose to cooperate.

Three types of regionalism can be identified:

1. **Economic regionalism:** Economic regionalism refers to the creation of greater economic opportunities through cooperation among states in the same geographical region. It is the primary form of regional integration, and it has become more so since the advent of so-called *'new' regionalism* in the early 1990s, which is manifested in the growth of regional trade blocks and the growing dependence on existing trade blocks. This surge has continued unabated, so much so that by 2005, all except one WTO member (Mongolia) was party to a regional trade agreement (RT).
2. **Security regionalism:** Security regionalism refers to forms of cooperation designed to protect states from their enemies, both neighbouring and distant ones. Regional integration may thus give rise what **Karl Deutsch** called a *'security community'*. Security regionalism can help build allies in order to prevent war and unite against a common enemy.
3. **Political regionalism:** Political regionalism focuses on the shared goals of the nation-states. It can be seen as a deeper form of regionalisation as the nation-states often share culture and values. Political regionalism usually has long-term plans to encourage greater integration between regional nation-states.

Theories of Regionalism

1. **Karl Deutsch**, a prominent thinker within the tradition of sociological liberalism, propounded an important theory of regional integration. He defined integration as 'the attainment within a territory, of a "sense of community" and of institutions and practices strong enough and widespread enough to assure for a long time, dependable

expectations of "peaceful change" among its population'.

2. The *functionalist theory* asserts that the proliferation of functional international organisations has occurred without adequate reorganisation and coordination due to the lack of global governance necessary to ensure accountability of such organisations. Therefore, there is an observable pattern of decentralisation in the international organisations of today. **David Mitrany** in his book *A Working Peace System* published in 1943 has observed that the process of economic integration is incremental and not absolute.
3. Scholars advocating federalism and the *federalist theory* strongly support regional integration as a counter measure to the monopolisation of power by a single state or hegemony and as a compensation for the lack of a central global governance. This is often referred to as *pooled sovereignty* which reinforced the federalist vision of 'unity' through diversity'.

New Regionalism

Unlike the older ideas of regionalism, which was geared more toward interactions between states, new regionalism refers to how a variety of state and non-state actors can be involved in a process of transformation of the world order.

Strategic regional organisations such as North Atlantic Treaty Organization (NATO), the Southeast Asia Treaty Organization (SEATO), and the Central Treaty Organization (CENTO), the Warsaw Pact and others which were a consequence of Cold War politics were aimed towards securing territorial dominance to ensure a strategic balance of power. However, this trend ended with the end of the Cold War and the disintegration of Soviet Union. The existing economic organisations were strengthened as they were freed of the direct influences of the two great powers. The European Union (EU), North American Free Trade Agreement (NAFTA) and The Association of Southeast Asian Nations (ASEAN) emerged as remarkable examples of regional economic integration under new regionalism.

EUROPEAN UNION

The European Union is a group of 27 countries that operate as a cohesive economic and political bloc. The population in the region covered by the EU is estimated at 444 million. The continent of Europe is considered to be one of the most highly industrialised and developed regions of the world. In 2018, the total GDP of the EU was estimated to be 18.8 trillion dollars which accounts for almost 22 per cent of global economy. This is a crude representation of the economic prowess of the EU.

Functions of the European Union

Economic Integration

The initiative to form the EU was strongly backed by the US which extended economic aid for reconstruction in post-War Europe in the form of the **Marshall Plan,** named after the then Secretary of State, George Marshall.

The foundation for regional integration was laid with the institution of **European Coal and Steel Community** in 1952. The ECSC comprised of West Germany, France, Italy, Belgium, Luxembourg and the Netherlands. The European Court of Justice was established in the same year.

The next step was the creation of the **European Atomic Energy Community** through the signing of the **Euratom Treaty** in 1957 and the creation of the **European Economic Community** in the same year by the **Treaty of Rome**. The latter laid the foundation for the establishment of a common market for all the member countries. The **Merger Treaty of 1965** merged all the three (ECSC, EAEC, EEC) leading to the creation of **European Communities** (ECs).

Later, the **Schengen Agreement** signed in 1985 paved the way for the creation of open borders without passport controls between most member states. The **Single European Act, 1986,** which was a revision of the 1957 Treaty of Rome, required the member countries to set a timetable for their economic merger and paved the way for monetary integration through the institution of a single currency.

The **Maastricht Treaty of 1992, alternatively called the Treaty on European Union**, received a great push with the end of the Cold War and concluded the process of regional integration. It laid the foundations for the European Union as we know it today. The ECs were incorporated within the EU, a European citizenship was created, and a common foreign and security policy was established through the foundation of the **European Central Bank** in 1998. It comes into existence by the **Amsterdam Treaty** and paved the road for the adoption of a single currency. Allowing a closer cooperation between the police and the judiciary in criminal matters was agreed upon.

The ECB is the central bank for the Euro and administers monetary policy within the Eurozone, which comprises 19 member states of the EU. It is located in Frankfurt, Germany. The ECB propounded the following criteria to be fulfilled for the inclusion of new member states in the Eurozone (EZ):

(a) Government deficit must not exceed 3 per cent of GDP.

(b) Gross government debt must not exceed 60 per cent of GDP.

(c) The member state must have achieved exchange-rate stability for at least two years according to the rules of European exchange-rate mechanism.

(d) The normal long-term interest rates of applicant nations must not have exceeded by more than 2 per cent the average of the interest rates in the three member states with the best record on price stability.

Political Integration

The European Coal and Steel Community initially comprised six European states. Three new members, namely Denmark, Ireland and UK, joined the ECSC on 1 January 1973. Greece became a member in 1981. Portugal and Spain joined the ECs in 1986.

Finland and Sweden joined the ranks of the EU in 1995. The Treaty of Nice signed in 2001 further expanded the membership of the EU. Ten new members joined the EU in 2004, namely, the Czech Republic, Cyprus, Estonia, Latvia, Lithuania, Hungary, Malta, Poland, Slovenia and Slovakia. Bulgaria and Romania joined the EU in 2007. Croatia is the newest member of the EU that joined in 2013.

The members of the EU have vocalised their support for the institution of **liberal political democracy** worldwide. Respect for democracy, human rights and individual liberty are the core **values** that have been incorporated as objectives as well as foundational principles within the EU. According to the **Copenhagen Criteria for EU membership** (1993), member countries must have stable, functioning democratic institutions which can ensure the protection of the EU's fundamental values. They must also have functioning market economies, with the ability to withstand competition in the single market.

Another political objective of the EU is to have a **common foreign policy**. The Maastricht Treaty which came into force in 1993 paved the way for common legislation, deliberation and decision-making concerning a common security and foreign policy. The office of the **High Representative of the EU** was created through the enforcement of the **Treaty of Lisbon** in 2009 (the treaty was signed in 2007). The High Representative was entrusted with representing the joint voice of the Union at all international forums. The Lisbon Treaty also provided for the creation of the office of the **President of EU** who would have a term of two and a half years.

The **EU has 10 strategic partnerships** with the following countries: Brazil, Canada, China, India, Mexico, Japan, the Republic of Korea (South Korea), Russia, South Africa, and the US. Even post Brexit, 21 members of the EU still retain the membership of NATO which makes US interference and influence always an imminent and inevitable possibility.

Social Integration

The EU is a **cosmopolitan collective** and an exemplary model of the benefits of financial globalisation. The free flow of goods, services and people across borders have enhanced connectivity and solidarity among the nations. The demographic composition of the EU is remarkable for its **diversity and pluralism** and their unity in spite of the differences among the nations is a result of sustained efforts towards peace, growth and inclusion.

The **Schengen Treaty** adopted in 1985 and enforced in 1995 led to the creation of Europe's Schengen Area. Originally five states, namely, **France, Germany, Luxembourg, the Netherlands, and Belgium** signed the treaty agreeing to abolish their internal border checks. This was the first step towards securing free movement.

Presently, with the exception of Ireland and Cyprus, all the member states of the EU are part of the Schengen Agreement. Four states which are not a part of the membership of the EU, namely Switzerland, Iceland, Liechtenstein and Norway, are a part of the Free Zone concurred in the Schengen Agreement.

Brexit: On 31 January 2020, the UK's 47-year EU membership came to an end as it withdrew from the EU. The **EU-UK Withdrawal Agreement** addresses several main issues in the UK's departure from the EU, including UK and EU citizens' rights and the UK's financial obligations to the EU. A key stumbling block in the withdrawal negotiations concerned arrangements for the border between Northern Ireland (part of the UK) and the Republic of Ireland (a member of the EU).

Structure of the EU: Inter-Governmental Organisations

The EU functions as a supranational body which makes it an exception among its contemporary regional organisations. It exercises various functions of governance through a multitude of intergovernmental mechanisms which include the following institutions:

1. **The European Council:** It is a collective body that defines the overall political direction and priorities of the EU. It is comprised of the heads of governments of the EU member states.
2. **The European Parliament:** It is the parliamentary institution of the EU whose members are directly elected by EU citizens aged 18 years or older. It exercises legislative functions for the EU and is composed of 705 members. It is headquartered in Strasbourg, France.
3. **The Council of the European Union**: It is an essential part of the bicameral EU legislature. It is composed of the Executive Governments of the EU's member states who meet to discuss, amend and adopt laws.
4. **The European Commission**: It is an executive body of the EU, responsible for proposing legislation, implementing decisions, upholding the EU treaties and managing the day-to-day business of the EU. It operates in the fashion of a cabinet government with 27 members, representing each of the 27 member states. The Commission President is proposed by the EC and elected by the European Parliament.
5. **The Court of Justice of the European Union (CJEU):** Headquartered in Luxembourg, the Court is entrusted with interpreting the EU law to make sure

it is applied in the same way in all EU countries. It also settles legal disputes between national governments and EU institutions. Its membership is constituted of one judge from each EU member state, accompanied by 11 advocates general and 2 additional judges, again from each EU member state.

AFRICAN UNION

The African Union is a continental union that consists of **55 countries of Africa**. The African union was launched as a successor to the Organisation of African Unity (OAU) in 2002. The AU was announced in the **Sirte Declaration** in Sirte, Libya in 1999. It was founded in 2001 in Addis Ababa, Ethiopia and launched in 2002 in Durban, South Africa.

AU member states are divided into five geographic regions:

1. Central Africa – 9 states
2. Eastern Africa – 14 states
3. Northern Africa – 7 states
4. Southern Africa – 10 states
5. Western Africa – 15 states

The African Union Commission (AUC), which is the AU's secretariat and undertakes the day-to-day activities of the Union, is based in Addis Ababa. In 2017, the AU admitted Morocco as a member state. India is a member of the African Union Partners Group (AUPG), which meets periodically in Addis Ababa.

The historical African Continental Free Trade Area (AFCFTA) agreement was adopted in March 2018 in Kigali and it entered into force in May 2019. The African Continental Free Trade Area is an ambitious trade pact to form the world's largest free trade area by developing a single market for goods and services for all of Africa and enhancing the economic integration of the continent.

34th Ordinary Session of the AU Assembly, held virtually on 6 and 7 February 2021, was organised by the African Union Commission (AUC) at Addis Ababa.

The Techno-Economic Approach for Africa–India Movement (TEAM–9) was launched in 2004 by India together with eight energy- and resource-rich West African countries (Burkina Faso, Chad, Cote d'Ivoire, Equatorial Guinea, Ghana, Guinea Bissau, Mali, and Senegal).

The India–Africa Forum Summit (IAFS) which is the official platform for African-Indian relations, is held once in every three years. The summit took place in 2008, 2011, and 2015.

SHANGHAI COOPERATION ORGANISATION (SCO)

After the disintegration of the Soviet Union, the USA emerged as the most influential power and Russia became the second most powerful nation. In order to limit the influence of USA over world politics, China and Central Asian states decided to cooperate with Russia. Thus, the Shanghai Cooperation Organisation was established in which China's role became primary. The SCO is the successor to the Shanghai Five, formed in 1996, between the People's Republic of China, Kazakhstan, Kyrgyzstan, Russia, and Tajikistan. At present, it has eight members:

1. China
2. India
3. Kazakhstan
4. Kyrgyzstan
5. Pakistan
6. Russia
7. Tajikistan

Afghanistan, Iran, Belarus and Mongolia have been included as observer nations. India and Pakistan were granted SCO membership much later, in 2017 and China claimed that relations between India and Pakistan will improve because of the Shanghai Cooperation Organisation. Critics however believe that Pakistan has been granted membership of the organisation to counterbalance India's position.

The basic objective of the establishment of Shanghai Cooperation Organisation is to **control**

separatism, **terrorism** and **fundamentalism** in the region. At present, the Shanghai Cooperation Organisation's aims are expanding to issues beyond security towards cooperation on economic fronts. Security experts have nicknamed the Shanghai Cooperation Organisation as the NATO of the East. Due to the China's rise in power, the role of SCO is fast growing as is China's desire to maintain its dominance in world politics.

India entered into a strategic partnership agreement with **Tajikistan** in 2012. Among the observer nations of the SCO, India's relations with Iran and Afghanistan are extremely cordial. The **Connect Central Asia Policy,** announced by India in 2012, focuses on India's strategic, trade and cultural relationships with the Central Asian countries.

Uzbekistan was the host country for the 2022 SCO Summit. The 2023 SCO Summit is scheduled to be held in India.

ASSOCIATION OF SOUTHEAST ASIAN NATIONS (ASEAN)

The Association of Southeast Asian Nations is a regional organisation which was established to promote political and social stability and cooperation amid rising tensions among the Asia-Pacific's post-colonial states. The motto of ASEAN is '*One Vision, One Identity, One Community*'.

ASEAN was established with the signing of the **ASEAN Declaration, alternatively known as the Bangkok Declaration** by five founding members: Singapore, Indonesia, Malaysia, the Philippines and Thailand. The membership expanded following the changes in regional context with the end of the Vietnam War in 1975 and the end of the Cold War in 1991. Brunei joined in 1984, Vietnam in 1995), Laos and Myanmar in 1997 and Cambodia in 1999. 8th August is observed as ASEAN Day as the organisation was established on 8 August 1967 in Bangkok, Thailand. The ASEAN Secretariat is located in Jakarta, Indonesia.

Reason behind the Success of ASEAN

According to Kishore Mahbubani, the co-author of *The ASEAN Miracle: A Catalyst for Peace*, there are several reasons behind the success of ASEAN.

1. **Strong leadership:** Among the founding members of the ASEAN were the remarkable personalities President Suharto of Indonesia, Prime Minister Lee Kuan Yew of Singapore and Mahatir Mohamad of Malaysia who possessed significant political influence and could thus provide a strong and able leadership to lead the venture for regional integration to success.
2. **Geo-political advantage:** The geo-political location of ASEAN at the juncture of major Asia-Pacific territorial and naval trade routes provides it enhanced strategic importance, and this helped in obtaining economic assistance from the US during the Cold War. Japan and the rapidly rising power China have also sought to increase the extent of their collaboration with ASEAN due to their competing interests and have also aided its development substantially in recent times.
3. **Market-oriented economy:** The adoption of free market economy by the ASEAN members has contributed greatly to the development of ASEAN. The ASEAN is the fifth largest economy in the world. It is also the fourth most popular investment destination globally.
4. **ASEAN-based regional network:** The ASEAN commands far greater influence on Asia-Pacific trade, political and security issues than its members could have wielded individually. The ASEAN member states have increasingly focused on enhanced connectivity to strengthen this regional network that benefits all members.

The ASEAN Model of Economic Development

The ASEAN is the third largest economy in Asia with a combined GDP of 3.3 trillion dollars as of 2021. It also has the third largest population of the world, comprising of 664 million people, and it has a significant advantage in demographic dividend as more than half of ASEAN's population is below 30 years of age.

The ASEAN Free Trade Area was created in 1992 to eliminate tariff barriers among the Southeast Asian countries. ASEAN has Free Trade Agreements (FTAs) with China, Japan, South Korea, India, Australia and New Zealand. Intra-ASEAN trade is almost 23 per cent of the entire trade of ASEAN.

The ASEAN also has various **multilateral forums** for enhancing its economic as well as diplomatic engagement with the other states. These include:

(a) The **ASEAN Regional Forum:** It is a 27-member multilateral grouping developed to facilitate cooperation on political and security issues. They signed the Treaty of Amity and Cooperation in Southeast Asia in 1976.

(b) **ASEAN Plus Three:** It is consultative group comprising ASEAN members and Japan, China and South Korea. It was created in 1997 following the global economic crisis. The three nations also provide much-needed economic assistance to the ASEAN countries.

(c) **East Asia Summit:** First held in 2005, this forum for strategic dialogue seeks to promote security and prosperity in the region and is usually attended by the heads of states from the ten ASEAN countries as well as Australia, China, India, New Zealand, Japan, South Korea, Russia and the US.

The ASEAN also established a common market called the ASEAN Economic Community (AEC) in 2015 which permits free and unhindered movement of goods and services, investment and skilled labour across international borders within the member states.

The territory of Southeast Asia comprising the members of the ASEAN was declared a nuclear-free zone in 1997 with the enforcement of the Southeast Asia Nuclear Weapon-Free Zone Treaty which has granted ASEAN a quintessential relief from security concerns and the global arms race, thereby contributing greatly to peace and development in the region.

ASEAN Community (ASEAN Concord II)

The **ASEAN Concord II** or **Bali Concord II** was signed in 2003 for the establishment of the ASEAN Community. The ASEAN Community however was finally launched in 2015. The ASEAN Vision 2020 (also called the Hanoi plan of action), declared in 1997, was also incorporated within the ASEAN Community which is comprised of three pillars:

(a) **ASEAN Political Security Community:** To build on what has been constructed over the years in the field of political and security cooperation, the ASEAN leaders have agreed to establish the ASEAN Political-Security Community (APSC).

(b) **ASEAN Economic Community:** The ASEAN Economic Community (AEC) had as its goal regional economic integration by 2015. AEC envisages (a) a single market and production base, (b) a highly competitive economic region, (c) a region of equitable economic development, and (d) a region fully integrated into the global economy.

(c) **ASEAN Socio-Cultural Community**: The ASEAN Socio-Cultural Community aims to contribute to realising an ASEAN Community that is people-oriented and socially responsible with a view to achieving enduring solidarity and unity among the peoples and the member states of ASEAN.

ASEAN's Relation with the Great Powers

ASEAN and EU: Statistically speaking, the EU is ASEAN's third largest trading partner, while

ASEAN is the EU's fifth largest trading partner. Total trade between the EU and ASEAN in goods and services amounted to USD 265 billion in 2011 wherein ASEAN achieved a surplus of USD 25 billion in its trade with the EU. The EU is also the largest source of Foreign Direct Investment into ASEAN which accounts for 24 per cent of the total FDI.

ASEAN and China: ASEAN emerged as China's largest trading partner in the first three months of 2020, surpassing both the EU and the United States. China's total imports and exports with the ASEAN member states increased by 2 per cent to a total of USD 297.8 billion. The bloc accounted for 14.7 per cent of China's overall trade for the period with a significant increase from 14 per cent in 2019.

ASEAN and Japan: The economic cooperation between the ASEAN member states and Japan has evolved considerably over the last few years. The total two-way trade value between the 10 ASEAN member states and Japan has increased to over 25 trillion yen in 2018, accounting for approximately 15 per cent of Japan's overall trade figures.

ASEAN's Relation with India

India's interaction with ASEAN began as a part of India's **Look East Policy** when India became a partner in the ASEAN Sectoral Dialogue in 1992. This was upgraded to a full dialogue partnership in 1995. In 1996, India became a member of the ASEAN Regional Forum and a summit level partner in 2002. The partnership was upgraded to a strategic partnership in 2012.

BIMSTEC, initially known as Bangladesh, India, Myanmar, Sri Lanka, and Thailand Economic Cooperation is a sub-regional initiative formed in 1997 in Bangkok. It started with four original members namely Bangladesh, Thailand, India and Sri Lanka. Myanmar, Nepal and Bhutan joined later. It was renamed the **Bay of Bengal Initiative for Multi-Sectoral Technical and Economic Cooperation**. It is seen as a reliable bridge between the SAARC and the ASEAN.

In recent times, the **Mekong-Ganga Cooperation** launched in 2000 marked a new phase in India's relationship with Myanmar, Cambodia, Laos, Thailand and Vietnam. It enhanced communication and transportation links to facilitate scientific and cultural cooperation between the nations.

In 2014, India announced **Act East Policy** with the intent to upscale its engagement with ASEAN member states.

India hosted the **ASEAN-India Commemorative Summit** in New Delhi on 26 January 2018 to mark the 25th anniversary of ASEAN-India Dialogue Relations. In the financial year 2017–18, Indo-ASEAN bilateral trade grew by almost 14 per cent to reach USD 81.3 billion. India's imports from ASEAN were valued at USD 47.13 billion while its exports to ASEAN stood at USD 34.2 billion.

The 19th ASEAN-India Summit was held in Phnom Penh, Kingdom of Cambodia, on 12 November 2022.

7

CONTEMPORARY CHALLENGES

KEYWORDS

International terrorism; climate change and environmental concern; human rights, migration and refugees; poverty and development; role of religion; culture and identity politics.

CLIMATE CHANGE AND ENVIRONMENTAL CONCERNS

Rachel Carson, a biologist and nature writer, in her book *Silent Spring* (1962) highlights the threat caused by pesticide to bird populations and human life and points out how pesticides are related to cancer. This and her other books have played a pivotal role in advancing the global environmental movement by putting the spotlight on environmental concerns. Environmental issues became an urgent matter from 1970s onwards and especially during the Cold War. But the different nation states came together with the goal of protecting the environment actively only from 1990 onwards.

The nature of environmental problems is complex. The complexities of climate change make it difficult for international governance to effectively deal with these issues. For instance, due to rise of temperature of the earth, the Siberian land can turn into fertile land, but the desert of Sahara can further extend to other parts of the world. The quantity of emission of greenhouse gases is higher in the industrial, developed nations but their adverse impact is more visible on the developing nations. It is difficult to bring these issues related to nature under the purview of international relations and yet it is essential that all nations work together unitedly to solve such environmental concerns.

E. F. Schumacher published a collection of essays titled *Small Is Beautiful: A Study of Economics as if People Mattered* in 1973. The book explores how the economic system impacts the way we live in the modern world and advocates for building our economies around the needs of communities instead of around corporations. He also discusses the issues of natural resources, pollution and the need for sustainable development. This book is also considered a seminal political work in the global environmental movement.

Zero-Growth Strategies

The initial debate for protection of the environment began when some environmentalists gave a call for the adoption of *zero-growth strategies*. Most important among them was the ecologist and economist **Herman Daly** who in his book *Towards a Steady-State Economy* discusses these strategies.

Zero growth or no growth may refer to:

1. **De-growth:** It is a political, economic and social movement based on ecological

economics, anti-consumerist and anti-capitalist ideas.

2. **Steady-state economy**: An economy consisting of a constant stock of physical wealth (capital) and constant population size. Daly's concept of a steady-state includes the ecological analysis of how the use of natural resources flow is related to the economy.
3. **Zero population growth**: A condition of demographic balance where the number of people in a specified population neither grows nor declines. Zero population growth is often a goal of environmentalists who believe that reducing population growth is necessary for the health of the ecosystem.

A Report titled **'Limits to Growth'** published by the Club of Rome in 1972 discusses how if growth trends in population, industrialisation, resource use and pollution continue at the present rate, we would overshoot the carrying capacity of the earth at some point in the next one hundred years.

Organisations and Programmes Dealing with Environmental Issues

Many organisations from the civil society have emerged which provide strong leadership and connectivity to environmental movements across the globe. They have also contributed significantly to academic research and theorisation concerning environmental issues. **Friends of the Earth International** and **Greenpeace** were established in 1969 and 1971 respectively. The first recognised green political party, **Green Party of Aotearoa**, was formed in New Zealand in 1972.

At the international level, concerted and organised efforts have been made under the aegis of the UN to forge consensus on environmental issues and on seeking permanent as well as feasible solutions. The **United Nations Environment Programme (UNEP)** is responsible for coordinating responses to environmental issues within the UN. The organisation also develops international environmental agreements, publishes and promotes environmental science, and helps national governments achieve environmental targets.

The Stockholm Conference

The UN Conference on the Human Environment, held in Stockholm, Sweden in 1972, was the UN's first major conference on international environmental issues. The Stockholm Conference led to the beginning of the UNEP and it became the first milestone in further international deliberation and diplomacy on environmental concerns. Additionally, it led to the establishment of global and regional environmental monitoring and surveillance networks. The meeting agreed upon the **Stockholm Declaration of 1972**, a Declaration containing 26 principles concerning the environment and development, an Action Plan with 109 recommendations, and a Resolution.

The conference also stimulated broader political and institutional changes to ensure the appropriate implementation of the agreed-upon principles. The role of environmentally active NGOs was also acknowledged and various measures were suggested to stimulate and organise their growth and efforts.

The Declaration, however, comprised some contradictory principles. For instance, on the one hand, Principle 21 acknowledged the states' sovereignty over their natural resources, which contradicts the international law which states that several resources including wetlands spanning across national borders are 'Common Heritage of Mankind' (global commons) which should be collectively managed, preserved and used for common benefit. State sovereignty can thus be regarded as a hindrance to effective and sustainable management of these resources.

Garrett Hardin published the essay 'The Tragedy of the Commons' in 1968 which popularised the theory of the tragedy of the commons. The theory refers to a situation in which individuals with access to a public resource ('a common') act in self-interest and, in doing so, ultimately overexploit and deplete the resource. The Stockholm Conference emphasised the protection of *global commons*. There are two types of global commons:

(a) Ones located within the sovereign territory of state like the glaciers of Himalayas and the forests of Amazon.
(b) Ones not located within the territory of any particular state, for example, Antarctica and the High Seas.

Environmental Philosophy

There are various strands of environmental philosophy:

(1) **Deep Ecology**

It is an environmental philosophy which promotes the inherent worth of all living beings regardless of their instrumental utility to human needs, in addition to the restructuring of modern human societies in accordance with such ideas. It was propounded originally by **Arne Næss** in a 1973 essay. In his book *The Ecology of Wisdom*, he asserts that gradual, incremental change is not sufficient for preserving the climate. The relations and interactions between human beings and ecology need to be revolutionised with a renewed consciousness enriched with this conceptualisation of universal solidarity and fraternity. The planet has independent existence and is not dependent upon aid from the humans. Nature can heal itself if left alone.

He distinguishes between deep and shallow ecological thinking. The table below lists the differences between deep ecology and shallow ecology.

The deep ecologist perspective completely rejects any lingering belief that the human species is in some way superior to or more important than any other species or indeed nature itself. It advances the more challenging idea that the purpose of human life is to help sustain nature, and not the other way around. The following are the basic principles of deep ecology:

(i) Human and non-human life on earth have intrinsic value in themselves. These values are independent of the usefulness of the non-human world for human purposes.
(ii) Richness and diversity of life forms contribute to the realisation of these values and are also values in themselves.
(iii) Humans have no right to reduce this richness and diversity except to satisfy vital needs.
(iv) The flourishing of human life and cultures is compatible with a substantial decrease of the human population. The flourishing of non-human life requires such a decrease.
(v) The present human interference with the non-human world is excessive, and the situation is rapidly worsening.
(vi) Policies must be changed, affecting basic economic, technological, and ideological structures. The resulting state of affairs will be very different from the present.
(vii) The ideological change is mainly that of appreciating quality of life (dwelling in situations of inherent value) rather than adhering to an increasingly higher standard of living. There must be a profound awareness of the difference between big and great.
(viii) Those who subscribe to the foregoing points have an obligation to implement the necessary changes directly or indirectly.

(2) **Gaia Hypothesis**

Named after the ancient Greek goddess of Earth, posits that Earth and its biological system behave as a single entity. It implies that the Earth is neither a material entity nor a mechanical system. It is an organic view of the earth and its processes. **James Lovelock** formulated this hypothesis and presented it in his book *Gaia: A New Look at Life on Earth*.

(3) **Ecosophy**

Ecosophy or ecophilosophy is a philosophy of ecological harmony or equilibrium. It was coined by Felix Guattari and Arne Næss. They assert that the knowledge of nature is more important than the knowledge of the social world.

Books:

How to be a Survivor (1975) – Paul R. Ehrlich, Richard L. Harriman

Blue Print for Survival (1972) – Goldsmith

Our Synthetic Environment (1962), *The Ecology of Freedom* (1982), *Remaking Society* (1989) – Murray Bookchin

Ecofeminism

The idea that feminism has a distinctive connection to green issues has grown prominence and developed into one of the major schools of environmental philosophical thought known as ecofeminism. It claims that ecological destruction has its origins in patriarchy and calls for an egalitarian, collaborative society in which there is no one dominant group.

Such a position is adopted, for instance, by **Mary Daly** in *Gyn/Ecology: The Metaethics of Radical Feminism* (1979). Daly argued that women would be able to liberate themselves from a patriarchal culture if they aligned themselves with 'female nature'. The notion of an intrinsic link between women and nature is not a new one. Pre-Christian religions and primitive cultures often portrayed the earth or nature forces as a goddess, an idea resurrected in some respect in the Gaia Hypothesis. **Susan Griffin** is also a proponent of the idea of ecological feminism. Her famous ecofeminist treatise is titled *Woman and Nature: The Roaring Inside Her*.

Modern eco-feminists, however, highlight the biological basis for women's closeness to nature, in particular the fact that they bear children. The fact that women cannot live separate from natural rhythms and processes in turn structures their politico-cultural orientation. Traditional female values therefore include reciprocity, cooperation and nurturing—values that have an ecological character.

In the patriarchal world, intellect is ranked above intuition, materialism is valued over spiritualism, and mechanical relationships are emphasised over holistic ones. In politico-cultural terms, this is reflected in a belief in self-serving acts, competitiveness and establishing and maintaining hierarchies and the implications of this for the natural world are clear. Patriarchy in this view, establishes the supremacy of culture over nature, the latter being nothing more than a force to be subdued, exploited or risen above. According to ecofeminism, cological destruction and gender inequality are therefore part of the same process in which 'cultured' men rule over 'natural' women.

Sustainable Development

Sustainable development can be defined as development that meets the needs of the present without compromising the ability of future generations to meet their own needs. The concept of sustainable development was crystallised and popularised in the **Brundtland Report of 1987**, issued by the **World Commission on Environment and Development** (the Brundtland Commission). This publication was in recognition of Gro Harlem Brundtland, the then Prime Minister of Norway. The conceptualisation of sustainable development in this report is rooted in earlier ideas about sustainable forest management and 20th century environmental concerns.

International Treaties and Conferences on Environmental Issues

Montreal Protocol

The Montreal Protocol on Substances that Deplete the Ozone Layer also known simply as the Montreal Protocol, is an international treaty designed to protect the ozone layer by phasing out the production of numerous substances that are responsible for ozone depletion. This multilateral environmental agreement was signed at an international conference held in Montreal, Canada in 1987.

The ozone is a protective layer of gas which is located in the stratosphere layer of the atmosphere situated at altitudes of 10–50 kilometers. It protects the earth's surface from the harmful ultraviolet rays of the sun which can cause a lot of harm. However, increased emissions of highly reactive chemical gases like bromine, fluorine, and chlorine, as well as their combinations such as chlorofluorocarbons are **Ozone Depleting Substances (ODSs)** which are extremely detrimental to the ozone layer and cause its rapid depletion. The stratospheric ozone levels over Europe and North America recently were observed to be about 10 per cent lower than in the 1970s. In some places, it was about 20–50 per cent lower. Rapid ozone depletion has also led to the visibility of an ozone hole over Antarctica.

The Montreal Protocol has provisions to reduce the production and consumption of ODSs to protect the ozone layer. It operates on the *principle of common but differentiated responsibilities* and assigns different timelines to developed and developing countries to meet the goal. The protocol has been ratified by 197 parties (196 members of the UN plus the EU) making it the first UN treaty to be ratified by every country in the world. The Multilateral Fund for the Implementation of the Montreal Protocol was set up in 1991 to help developing countries to comply with the provisions of the Protocol.

India became a signatory to the Montreal Protocol in 1992. India is an Article 5 country and is entitled to assistance from the Multilateral Fund in its efforts to phase out ODSs and switch over to non-ODS technologies. In India, the implementation of the Montreal Protocol comes within the ambit of the Ministry of Environment, Forest and Climate Change. The Ministry has established the Ozone Cell to implement the provisions of the Protocol.

In 1992, the phase-out timeline for developed states was preponed to 1995, and new controls were agreed upon to phase out HCFCs by 2030. The Kigali Amendment, an amendment to the Montreal Protocol has helped reduce HFC emission and decrease global temperature rise.

16 September is observed as World Ozone Day, officially called the International Day for the Preservation of the Ozone Layer. It is the day that marks the signing of the Montreal Protocol.

Earth Summit (Rio Conference)

The United Nations Conference on Environment and Development (UNCED) was organised in the Rio de Janeiro in Brazil in June 1992. It is popularly known as the **Earth Summit** or the **Rio Conference**. It was attended by political leaders, diplomats, scientists, representatives of the media and non-governmental organisations (NGOs) from 179 countries with the agenda to focus on the impact of human socio-economic activities on the environment. A 'Global Forum' of NGOs was also held in Rio de Janeiro at the same time which was attended by over 17000 people.

Agenda 21: It is an action plan concerning sustainable development but it is non-binding. It is a product of the Earth Summit. The plan has a social and economic dimension directed toward combating poverty and promoting health, especially in developing nations. It also covers a wide range of topics such as promoting sustainable urban development; combating deforestation; biotechnology management; managing fragile mountain ecosystems; and hazardous waste management. It focuses on strengthening the role of major groups including local authorities, trade unions, business and industry, scientist; women, indigenous peoples, youth, and farmers. The concluding section of the action plan deals with implementation issues, including financial mechanisms and institutional arrangements.

The Global Environment Facility was established on the eve of the 1992 Rio Earth Summit and one of its functions is to provide 'agreed incremental costs' to help developing countries implement aspects of the Agenda 21 programme.

The Rio Conventions

The Rio Conventions work closely together against challenges related to climate change, desertification and biodiversity loss. The following three sister conventions are the outcomes of the Earth Summit.

The UN Framework Convention on Climate Change (UNFCCC): It has been ratified by 198 parties as of 2022. The countries that have ratified the convention are unitedly called the Conference of the Parties (COP). It is the primary multilateral treaty governing actions to combat climate change through adaptation and mitigation efforts directed at control of emission of greenhouse gases that cause global warming.

The Convention on Biological Diversity (CBD): It is concerned with the preservation of the biological diversity of the earth through protection of species, ecosystems and habitats. 155 states are signatories to this convention, and it came into force on 29 December 1993.

UN Convention to Combat Desertification (UNCCD): It aims to promote coordinated international actions to address problems of land degradation in arid, semi-arid, and dry sub-humid areas resulting from various factors, including climatic variations and human activities.

Kyoto Protocol

The Kyoto Protocol is based on the principles and provisions of the UNFCCC. The protocol was adopted in Kyoto, Japan in 1997 and therefore, it is known as the Kyoto Protocol. It entered into force on 16 February 2005.

It is a legally binding international agreement to reduce greenhouse gas emissions. It applies to seven greenhouse gases: carbon dioxide, methane, nitrous oxide, hydrofluorocarbons, perfluorocarbons, sulfur hexafluoride and nitrogen trifluoride. The Protocol's first commitment period started in 2008 and ended in 2012. 36 countries had participated in the first commitment period. These included developed countries like the EU, USA and Japan who respectively committed themselves to reduce, during this period, their annual greenhouse gas emissions by 8 per cent, 7 per cent, and 6 per cent respectively as compared to the 1990 emission levels. The Protocol required the developed countries to make an average of a 5.2 per cent cut in their greenhouse gas emissions as compared to 1990.

Although the 36 developed countries had reduced their emissions during this period, global emissions still increased by 32 per cent between 1990 and 2010.

Flexibility Mechanisms: The Kyoto Protocol defines the following three mechanisms which are based on the trade of emissions permits. Under the Protocol, countries must meet their targets primarily through national measures but in case they are not able to, the Protocol offers an additional means to meet their targets by way of these mechanisms:

(i) **International Emissions Trading**: This envisages a system where a market in rights to pollute is created. For example, efficient power plants can sell their permits to emit carbon dioxide to others and a long-term reduction in the number of permits available will mean that the price of carbon rises, which in turn will lead to alternative power resources becoming more competitive and reduction in the overall amount of carbon dioxide emitted.

(ii) **Joint Implementation:** Under this mechanism, a developed country can receive credits against its own emissions reduction target by financing projects in another developed country.

(iii) **The Clean Development Mechanism (CDM):** This mechanism allows a country with an emission-reduction or emission-limitation commitment under the Kyoto Protocol to implement an emission-reduction project in developing countries.

Mitigation and Adaptation: Mitigation and adaptation are two strategies for addressing climate change. Mitigation is an intervention to reduce the emissions at source or enhance the greenhouse gas sinks. Adaptation is an adjustment in natural or human systems in response to actual or expected climatic stimuli or their effects, which moderates harm or exploits beneficial opportunities.

Rio+20 Summit

The United Nation Conference on Sustainable Development, also known as Rio+20, was held in Brazil in 2012. A non-binding 53-page document, '**The Future We Want**' was finalised which pledged commitment to sustainable development. Among the decisions taken, a particularly intense one focused on Sustainable Development Goals (SDGs) with the developing countries finally prevailing in setting up an intergovernmental process to develop these goals in a transparent and inclusive manner, consistent with the Rio Principles. The developed countries prevailed in restricting the scope of financial assistance and resources and technology transfer as aid to developing countries in their move towards sustainable development.

2015 United Nations Climate Change Conference (COP 21)

The COP 21 was held in Paris, France, from 30 November to 12 December 2015. Before the conference, countries were asked to submit Nationally Determined Contributions (NDCs) and this revealed a marked shift in the commitments from various countries. The conference negotiated the **Paris Agreement**, a global agreement on the reduction of climate change. It is a multilateral agreement within the UNFCCC signed to reduce and mitigate greenhouse gas emissions. Currently, the Paris Agreement has 195 UNFCCC members as signatories.

The agreement is based on the principle of common but differentiated responsibilities wherein different kinds of objectives are underlined for the developed and the developing countries. It is a sustainable and dynamic agreement with the goal of limiting global temperature increase to well below 2 degrees Celsius, while pursuing efforts to limit the increase to 1.5 degrees. The agreement also stipulates mechanisms for financial aid as it says that $100 billion in public and private resources will need to be raised each year from 2020 to finance projects that enable countries to adapt to the impacts of climate change.

The US withdrew from the Paris Agreement in November 2020. Monitoring and surveillance mechanisms prescribed by international agreements on climate change are often seen as impinging on national sovereignty. The withdrawal of the US from the Paris Agreement has strengthened this criticism.

The Global South's Needs

1. **Technology**: The Global South has increasingly demanded the transfer of clean technologies from the North at feasible costs to aid the achievement of the goals underlined by various international treaties and agreements.
2. **Capacity-Building:** The government institutions as well as citizens are increasingly in need of training and skill development to ensure effective participation in the global efforts towards environmental preservation.

3. **Finance:** The Global North has often assured the provision of economic aid and assistance to the Global South but the actual transfer of resources and funds has not happened sufficiently. The developing countries require more funds to work towards environmental conservation.
4. **Development:** The primary concern for the Global South is healthcare, nutrition, poverty alleviation, education and economic development and hence environmental concerns and issues generally take a backseat. Ongoing environmental movements in the Global South are also related to economic issues like displacement and loss of livelihood which ultimately supersede issues of conservation.
5. **Researchers:** Most of the scientists theorising on the environment belong to Europe and the USA. The interests of the Global South are often ignored in this Eurocentric environmental discourse. More research based in the Global South that addresses local concerns is the need of the hour.

Through an agreement in 2009, four newly industrialized countries—**Brazil, South Africa, India and China**—established the **BASIC** for fighting against the discriminatory policies adopted against the Global South by the Global North. The BASIC as a bloc works towards protecting the developmental needs of the Global South. But the differences among the BASIC countries is also apparent because China is already a leading economic power. Therefore, the interests of the countries within BASIC also vary.

Emissions by Different Countries

1. **Net Zero Emissions:** The United States is expected to commit to a net zero emission target for 2050 to reclaim global climate leadership. Other countries such as the United Kingdom and France are already committed to achieving net zero emission by 2050 while countries such as Canada, South Korea, Japan and Germany have expressed their intention to commit themselves to a net zero future. China is committed to achieving net zero emissions by the year 2060. India is also willing to commit to the target of net zero emissions by 2060, but it might be difficult as India, which is not yet as developed as China, is also looking to focus on economic growth in the next few decades.
2. **Overall Emission:** The top four emitters in 2017, which covered 58 per cent of global emissions, were China (27 per cent), the US (15 per cent), the European Union (10 per cent) and India (7 per cent), according to the projection by the Global Carbon Project. The rest of the world contributed 41 per cent to global emissions last year. The top 10 emitters were China, the US, the EU, India, Russia, Japan, Germany, Iran, Saudi Arabia and South Korea.

Table 5.7.1: Total CO2 Emissions by Country (in kT) as of 2019

1	China	10,291,926	10	Canada	537,193
2	United States	5,254,279	11	Brazil	529,808
3	India	2,238,377	12	South Africa	489,771
4	Russia	1,705,345	13	Mexico	480,270
5	Japan	1,214,048	14	Indonesia	464,176
6	Germany	719,883	15	United Kingdom	419,820
7	Iran	649,480	16	Australia	361,261
8	Saudi Arabia	601,046	17	Turkey	345,981
9	Republic of Korea	587,156	18	Italy	320,411

Figure 5.7.1: List of Nations with the Highest per Capita Carbon Dioxide Emissions

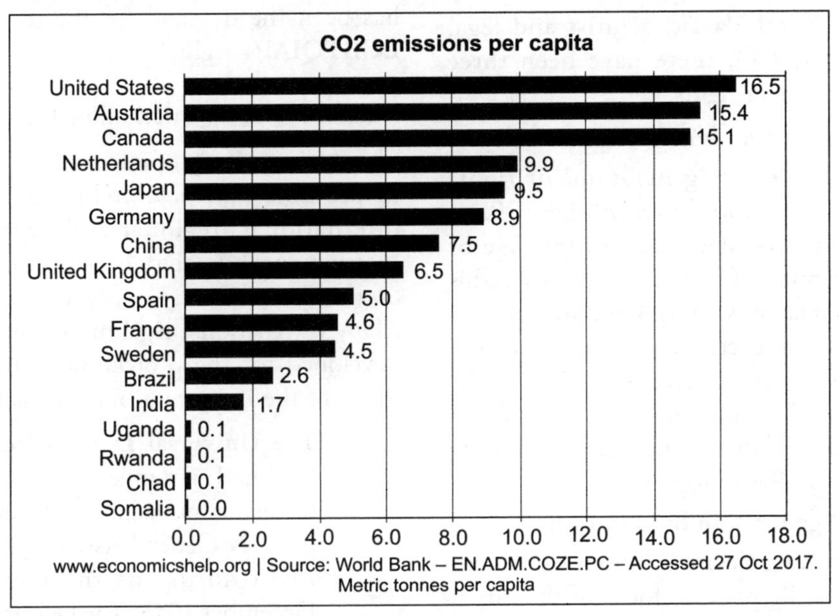

3. **Per Capita Emission:** India's per capita emissions were about 40 per cent of the global average and contributed 7 per cent to the global carbon dioxide burden. The United States, the largest emitter, was responsible for 14 per cent.

HUMAN RIGHTS

Human rights are rights inherent to all human beings, regardless of race, sex, nationality, ethnicity, language, religion or any other status. The term is all-encompassing and includes various kinds of universal and moral rights including the right to life and liberty, freedom from slavery and exploitation, and freedom of opinion and expression. **L. J. MacFarlane** has underlined the distinguishing characteristics of human rights as compared to other moral and legal rights in his book *The Theory and Practice of Human Rights*. These characteristics include: **universality, individuality, paramountcy, practicability and enforceability.**

T. H. Green argues that we are entitled to rights because this enables us to fulfil our moral agency, and thus, to contribute to the common good. **Wesley N. Hohfield** distinguishes between rights to do things (liberties or privileges) from rights to have things done for or to one (claim-rights). Rights, moreover, are not static but *dynamic*. What were or are claims at a point of time in the past or present becomes rights in the future. For instance, the claim of civil rights was made during monarchy and it became a right only after arrival of the democratic form of government. Earlier, women made claims for a better life and now these claims are recognised as rights by the society and the state.

There are many philosophical and moral foundations of human rights. Human rights are based on:

1. Human dignity
2. Reason
3. Autonomy
4. Equality
5. Needs
6. Capabilities
7. Consensus

Types of Human Rights

According to **Karel Vasak,** a jurist and legal advisor of UNESCO, there have been three generations of human rights.

1. **First-generation human rights**
   The first tier or 'generation' of rights consists of *civil and political rights*. These are rights that date back to the Age of Enlightenment (17th–18th century). This approach favours limiting the government by placing restrictions on state action. The rights set forth in Articles 2–21 of the Universal Declaration of Human Rights are a part of this grouping, alternatively known as Liberty Rights.
2. **Second-generation human rights**
   This second generation of rights broadens the primarily political focus of the earlier discourse to include various *rights of welfare* which are composed of different economic, social and cultural rights. These rights date back to the socialist tradition (19th century). These are rights that are conceived more in positive rather than negative terms and thus encourage the intervention of the state. Illustrative of these rights are the Articles 22–27 of the UDHR.
3. **Third-generation human rights**
   Contrasted to the earlier discourse of individualistic rights, these are *group rights or solidarity rights*. These rights are a product of the rise and decline of the nation-state in the last half of the twentieth century.

Apart from these three types of rights, there is a newer generation of rights and these are the *postmodernist rights*. These are new kinds of rights related to individual identity which have been facilitated particularly by the postmodernist discourse on constructions of identity, history and society. The most prominent of these contemporary discourses has been the demand for the identification of **LGBTQIAP+** rights.

Human Rights in International Law

There exists a body of international law designed to promote and protect human rights at the international, regional and domestic levels. International human rights law primarily consists of treaties and customary international law. Many international legal mechanisms have been developed for the protection of human rights. Some of the important ones are as follows:

(1) **The Universal Declaration of Human Rights:** It is a milestone document in the history of human rights. It was accepted by the UN General Assembly as Resolution 217A during its third session on 10 December 1948. The Declaration consists of 30 articles detailing an individual's 'basic rights and fundamental freedoms' and affirming their universal character as inherent, inalienable, and applicable to all human beings. The UDHR is widely recognised as having inspired the adoption of more than seventy human rights treaties, applied today on a permanent basis at global and regional levels.

(2) The International Covenant on Civil and Political Rights and the International Covenant on Economic, Social, and Cultural Rights adopted in 1966.

(3) The European Convention for the Protection of Human Rights and Fundamental Freedoms drafted in 1950.

(4) The American Convention on Human Rights adopted in 1969.

(5) The African Charter on Human and Peoples' Rights of 1981, alternatively known as the Banjul Charter.

(6) The Convention on the Prevention and Punishment of the Crime of Genocide of 1948.

(7) The International Convention on the Elimination of All Forms of Racial Discrimination adopted in 1965.

(8) The International Convention on the Elimination of Discrimination against Women adopted in 1979.

(9) **The Vienna Declaration and Programme of Action:** The major political upheaval following the disintegration of the USSR and the ongoing process of peace and security in Europe coincided with the reaffirmation of human rights as common international standard. At this juncture, the Vienna Declaration and Programme of Action (VDPA), adopted by consensus at the World Conference on Human Rights in June 1993 in Vienna, Austria, reconfirmed the Universal Declaration of Human Rights and the United Nations Charter earlier adopted by the UN.

Following are the main features of this historic convention:

(a) It proclaimed that all human rights are **universal, indivisible, interdependent and interrelated.** The 171 signatory states unequivocally stated that human rights had become a legitimate concern of the international community.

(b) For the first time, the significance of national and international particularities and various **historical, cultural and religious backgrounds** was recognised. It considered that the duty of states, regardless of their political, economic and cultural system, was to promote and protect all human rights and fundamental freedoms.

(c) It established a linkage between **democracy, development and respect for human rights** and fundamental freedoms.

(d) The **right to development** was affirmed as an important human right which should be attainable in a democracy. It proclaimed that the international community should promote an effective international cooperation for the realisation of the right to development and the elimination of obstacles to development.

(e) It focused on **women's rights and gender-based exploitation**, a topic which had never been debated with so much concern before this. It was stated that states would focus on the areas of domestic violence involving women and affirmed that it was a legitimate issue for the international community.

(f) It pledged to promote a special variety of education, that is, **human rights education**, through public policies.

Institutions for Protection of Human Rights

1. The **Office of the United Nations High Commissioner for Human Rights**, commonly known as the Office of the High Commissioner for Human Rights (OHCHR) or the UN Human Rights Office is a department of the Secretariat of the UN that works to promote and protect the human rights guaranteed under the UDHR. It was established by the UN General Assembly in the aftermath of the World Conference of Human Rights, 1993.
2. **The International Criminal Court of Justice** is the first and the only permanent international court with the authority to arbitrate in international issues of violations of human rights. The Court can prosecute individuals as well as states for international crimes concerning human rights abuses such as genocide, crimes against humanity, war crimes and ethnic crimes of aggression. It was established in 1998 and started functioning from 2002.

3. The **United Nations Human Rights Council (UNHRC)** is a United Nations body whose mission is to promote and protect human rights around the world. The UNHRC has 47 members elected for staggered three-year terms on a regional group basis. It was formed in 2006 by the UN General Assembly and is headquartered in Geneva, Switzerland.

Critique of Universal Human Rights

The discourse on universal moral human rights has been increasingly criticised since the emergence of the third generation of human rights, i.e., group rights. Theorists and movements from the Third World have contended that the entire conceptualisation of human rights is Eurocentric in nature as it is rooted in an atomistic, individualistic conception of the human self which is intrinsic to the materialism of Western thought.

Particularly, Saudi Arabia and the USSR, which have been the objects of extreme controversy and criticism in the contemporary era due to multiple alleged human rights violations have opposed the existing discourses of universal human rights and demanded more particularistic, indigenous rights which can be finalised, preserved and promoted by the national governments.

Mahathir Mohammad, a former Prime Minister of Malaysia and one of the founders of ASEAN, regarded the West as a 'morally decadent civilisation' and said that Asian society is different from the Western society as their values differ in terms of one's relation to family and authority and the idea of religion and spirituality.

MIGRANTS AND REFUGEES

According to the UNHCR Statute, *refugees* are persons who are outside their country of origin for reasons of feared persecution, conflict, generalised violence, or other circumstances that have seriously disturbed public order and, because of this, require international protection.

An international *migrant* can be defined as someone who changes their country of usual residence, irrespective of the reason for migration or legal status. Migration can be of two types: short-term or temporary migration, and long-term or permanent migration.

There are also *asylum seekers*. An asylum seeker is a person who has left their country and is seeking protection from persecution and serious human rights violations in another country, but they have not yet been legally recognised as a refugee. It must be noted that seeking asylum is a human right.

Migrants and refugees are very vulnerable to trafficking and exploitation, both on their journey as well as on their arrival in the destination country. They thus require **settlement** and **integration** into the culture and workforce of the country in which they have arrived.

United Nations High Commissioner for Refugees (UNHCR)

The Office of the United Nations High Commissioner for Refugees (UNHCR) was established on 14 December 1950. It protects and supports refugees at the request of a government or the UN. It also works towards providing durable solutions, such as return or resettlement of the refugees. The UNHCR is headquartered in Geneva, Switzerland.

UN Relief and Works Agency for Palestine Refugees (UNRWA)

The UN created the UN Relief and Works Agency for Palestine Refugees (UNRWA) in the aftermath of the Al-Nakba in 1948, which caused a major refugee crisis in the Arab region, resulting in the displacement of 700,000 Palestinian refugees.

Rohingya Refugees

The Rohingyaa are a stateless ethnic group who mostly follow Islam and reside in Rakhine State, Myanmar. Described by the media as one of the most persecuted minorities in the world, the Rohingya are denied citizenship under the 1982 Myanmar nationality law. There are also denied freedom of movement and access to education and jobs. The most recent mass displacement of Rohingya in 2017, when over 740,000 fled to Bangladesh, led the International Criminal Court to investigate crimes against humanity, and the International Court of Justice to investigate genocide.

POVERTY AND DEVELOPMENT

Poverty

Poverty is a state or condition in which one lacks the financial resources and essentials for a basic standard of living. Poverty can have many social, economic, and political causes and effects. Poverty and development are prime concerns of policy makers. Although poverty exists in all societies, the extent of poverty varies from region to region. The UN sees poverty as a denial of choices and opportunities and a violation of human dignity. Poverty is the lack of basic capacity to participate effectively in society.

Types of Poverty

There are two types of poverty:

1. **Absolute poverty:** It is also called 'extreme poverty' or 'abject poverty'. If there is severe deprivation of basic human needs, including food, safe drinking water, sanitation facilities, health, shelter, education and information, it is called absolute poverty.
2. **Relative poverty:** According to this theory, poverty is socially defined and dependent on social context. Definition of poverty should then vary depending upon time and place.

Causes of Poverty

Poverty can have various causes. Some of the common causes of poverty, especially in India, are:

1. Illiteracy or lack of access to education
2. Unemployment or no access to livelihoods
3. Unequal distribution of resources
4. Overpopulation
5. Limited or poor access to healthcare
6. Conflict and war
7. Poor governance or corruption

Ending Poverty

The 2030 Agenda for Sustainable Development recognises that ending poverty in all its forms everywhere is the greatest global challenge facing the world today and it is an indispensable requirement for global sustainable development. The General Assembly declared 17 October as the International Day for the Eradication of Poverty.

Development

Development is a process that creates growth and progress to improve the well-being of people. The purpose of development is a rise in the level and quality of life of the population and the creation or expansion of local regional income and employment opportunities. According to **A. P. Thirlwall**, development implies change and it may be used to describe the process of social and economic transformation.

The three basic components of development are life sustenance (fulfillment of basic needs), self-esteem (feeling of self-respect) and freedom.

Indicators of Development

1. Growth rate of National Income
2. Per Capita Income (PCI): The rise in PCI indicates economic welfare of the country.
3. Per Capita Consumption (PCC): An increase in PCC shows better quality of life of people and higher economic development of the country.
4. Physical Quality Life Index (PQLI): PQLI is the overall welfare of the people in life

expectancy, infant mortality rate, standard of living.

5. Human Development Index (HDI): HDI measures life expectancy, education and standard of living.
6. Industrial progress

TERRORISM

Terrorism, in a general sense, refers to the use of intentional violence and fear to achieve political or ideological objectives. It was first coined in the eighteenth century to refer to the terror used during the French revolution when the Jacobin leader **Robespierre** carried out terror activities, but the term became popular only in the late twentieth century.

Terrorism groups can be seen as a kind of *non-state actors* whose activities exacerbate international tension and undermine the state's authority and power. Terrorism appears to be intended to further *political objectives* through threat or use of *violence*, usually in opposition to a state government. Terrorist groups seek the political freedom, privilege, and property they think persecution has denied them. Terrorism differs from conventional warfare in the sense that it is a 'weapon of the weak'. It is embraced by those who have no realistic possibility of prevailing against their opponent in direct combat.

As a strategy, terrorism is practised by a diverse group of movements. Terrorist techniques are often deployed in the form of *guerilla or insurrectionary warfare tactics*. Ideologies like Marxism and Anarchism have on occasion justified the use of violence for obtaining equality in society. **Michael Ignatieff** says that this justification of the use of violence could lead to a form of *Nationalist Terrorism*, which aims to overthrow colonial rule or occupation, often with the goal of gaining independence for an ethnic, religious or national group. Examples are National Liberation Front (FLN) in Algeria and Liberation Tigers of Tamil Eelam (LTTE) in Sri Lanka.

Types of Terrorism

A. **Civil Disorder:** It is a type of collective violence that interferes with the peace, security, and normal functioning of the civil society.

B. **Political Terrorism:** This refers to violent criminal behaviour which is carried out with the intention of generating fear in the community for political purposes.

C. **Non-Political Terrorism:** The objective of this type of terrorism is something other than a political motive but it exhibits the same characteristics and employs the same tactics.

D. **State Terrorism:** The term state terrorism appears paradoxical because a state is responsible for the security of its people rather than their oppression, but human right activists allege that the state can also be responsible for terrorism. An example of state terrorism can be seen in Syria. The scale of state terrorism is often far greater than that of non-state terrorism.

E. **State-sponsored Terrorism:** Sometimes states try to harm interests of another state through terrorism as terrorism can be a less expensive means of harming the interest of the opponent. Terrorism by Pakistan against India is an example of **cross-border state-sponsored terrorism**. The action of the Israeli Government against the Palestinians in the occupied territories is also an example of state-sponsored terrorism.

F. **Narco-Terrorism:** It refers to the terrorism financed by the money drawn from illicit trade in narcotics. The region demarcated as the **Golden Crescent** (the areas lying in the tribal-populated terrains on the borders of Afghanistan, Iran and Pakistan) contributes a bulk of the opium and heroin that is traded to Europe and the United States through the Balkan route. Similarly, the largest opium-producing region, the

Golden Triangle comprising of the areas lying on the borders of Myanmar, Laos and Thailand, constitutes more than 65 per cent of the total opium trade in the world. Narco-terrorism is rampant in these two regions. The countries in Latin America facing the dangers of narco-terrorism include Peru, Colombia and Mexico. Peru, which produces almost two-third of the world's cocaine, is ravaged by one of the most notorious terrorist movements known as the **Shining Path** since the 1970s.

G. **Religious Terrorism:** It is a type of terrorism where violence is used as a strategy to achieve certain religious goals or which are influenced by a religious belief or identity. **Baylis, Smith and Owens** in their book *The Globalization of World Politics* say that *'new' terrorism* uses religion as a motivator and to provide the justification for killing noncombatants. This is a kind of postmodern terrorism. The theory of new terrorism is used by some authors to explain the underlying rationale of how *global jihadism* by militant Islamic groups is seen as a reaction to the perceived oppression of Muslims worldwide and the spiritual bankruptcy of the West. It is important to note however that terrorism is a political problem rather than a religious problem, and even in cases of religious terrorism, religion is merely a tool.

Terrorism is not new but the *international terrorism* or expansion of terrorism worldwide is a newer phenomenon. Modern means of technology and rising frequency of air services have contributed to making terrorism as a global phenomenon.

Countering Terrorism

Terrorism is a challenge that the international community must tackle together. Counterterrorism comprises the practices, military tactics, and strategies that governments, law enforcement bodies, businesses, and intelligence agencies use to combat or eliminate terrorism.

A. **War on Terror**

The war on terror, officially the Global War on Terrorism (GWOT), is a global counterterrorism military campaign that the United States initiated in the aftermath of the September 11 attacks. According to **Achin Vanaik**, the 9/11 attacks were distinct because outside of wartime, no single act by a non-state actor has been responsible for so many casualties and so much damage and the US homeland has not, in living memory, suffered so serious an assault of foreign origin.

Many have criticised the War on Terror for its breach of international law and Charter of the United Nations, and condemned it for reviving age-old imperialist notions. Since the end of the Cold War, several ideological banners have emerged which can be seen as covers for US imperial behaviour: 'humanitarian intervention', 'Weapons of Mass Destruction', 'Global War on Terror', 'regime change', 'defending democracy', 'failed states' and 'war on narcotics' can be seen as strategies of legitimisation employed by the US to justify their imperial aggression. The GWOT too can be considered a legitimising discourse. It is not some sort of 'clash of civilizations', but rather a clash between civilisation and those who destroy it. Critics have called the War on Terror the 21st century version of the 'civilizing mission' of colonial expansionism.

B. **International Treaties against Terrorism**

Liberals believe that collective effort is essential for containing terrorism. Financial resources and technology used in terrorism must be blocked by the United Nations. The following are a few international treaties concerning terrorism:

1. The Convention on Offences and Certain Other Acts Committed on Board Aircraft, also called the Tokyo Convention was adopted in Tokyo in 1963. It is considered to be the first international treaty concerning terrorism.
2. UN Security Council Resolution 1566 supports the idea that the crimes recognised by existing international treaties form a part of a code of terrorist offences.
3. International Convention on the Suppression of Acts of Nuclear Terrorism was adopted by the UNGA in 2005. It criminalises planning, threatening, or the execution of nuclear terrorism. Non-state actors, who are the main players of terrorism, are very much willing to utilise nuclear fuel or nuclear technology to attack their targets or even attack the nuclear power plant which will cause the same impact as a nuclear attack. The threat of nuclear terrorist attacks is rising in today's day and age.
4. International Convention for the Suppression of Financing of Terrorism was adopted in 1999. It proposes measures for the prevention of the financing of terrorism.

Double Standard: Good Terrorist and Bad Terrorist

Terrorism is a biggest threat for the entire world but the nations of the Global South are most threatened due to the lack of capability of the states to effectively counter terrorism. India in a UN Security Council meeting contended that the era of classifying terrorists as 'bad' or 'good' on the basis of political convenience must end immediately. The categorisation of terrorist acts by intent as religious or ideologically motivated may dilute the shared global commitment to combating terrorism.

Notable Terrorist Organisations

1. Boko Haram (Nigeria)
2. The Shining Path (Peru)
3. Harkat-ul-Jihad al-Islami (HUJI) (Pakistan and Bangladesh)
4. Hezbollah (Party of God) (Lebanon)
5. Abu Sayyaf Group (ASG) (Philippines)
6. Haqqani Network (Afganistan)
7. Kata'ib Hezbollah (Iraq)
8. Islamic State of Iraq and Syria (ISIS) (Iran, Libya and Syria)
9. Liberation Tigers of Tamil Eelam (LTTE) (Sri Lanka)
10. Jemaah Islamiyah (JI) (Indonesia)

CULTURE AND IDENTITY POLITICS

Clash of Civilizations

The Clash of Civilizations is a thesis which says that people's cultural and religious identities will be the primary source of conflict in the post-Cold War world. The American IR scholar **Samuel P. Huntington** is the original proponent of this theory. His theory marked a paradigm shift in the historical discourse of international relations from a focus on nation states and their alliances to a focus on conflicts between cultures. **Bernard Lewis** coined the concept of clash between civilisations in 1957, arguing that Islam and the West had irreconcilable values that could only be resolved through conflict. Huntington furthered Lewis's theory and adapted it to what he claimed to be a post-Cold War world.

According to Huntington's theory, nation states will remain the most powerful actors in world affairs, but the principal conflicts of global politics will occur between nations and groups of different civilisations. He wanted the 'clash of civilizations' to be a useful tool to policy makers and not just a theoretical concept. He claimed that his theory was not rooted in social science and therefore it could not be subjected to social scientific scrutiny. Instead, he proposed the theory as a framework of a paradigm.

Huntington's article 'The Clash of Civilizations?' was a response to his student Francis Fukuyama's 1992 book *The End of History and the Last Man* in which Fukuyama envisioned the end of the Cold War as the mark of the 'triumph of liberal democracy' which put an end to all major ideological conflict in the world and thus is also 'the end of political theory'.

Huntington defines a civilisation as 'the highest cultural grouping of people and the broadest level of cultural identity people have short of that which distinguishes humans from other species.' Huntington lists 'seven or eight major civilizations', which are the Western, the Sinic, the Japanese, the Islamic, the Hindu, the Slavic-Orthodox, the Latin American and possibly the African. He contends that the six powers that will dominate the twenty-first century, namely, America, China, Europe, Japan, Russia, and India are not merely different nation-states with conflicting interests, but they also belong to six different civilisations. The points where these civilisations meet are called 'fault lines' which would be, at the micro level, points of struggle and violence. At the macro level, states of different civilisations would compete for power, influence, and cultural and religious hegemony.

Huntington's theory was aimed towards guiding the US policy in maintaining its hegemony and furthering its interests throughout the world. He observes that the influence of the West is continually declining while that of Asian civilisations is expanding. The West with its 'universalist pretentions' in the form of its claims on universal morality as well as its attempts at securing hegemony is pitted against other civilisations that bear the brunt of westernisation and neo-colonialism in the guise of globalisation.

Conflict and the Muslim World

Huntington argues that the Islamic civilisation has experienced a massive population explosion which is fueling instability both on the borders of Islam and in its interior, where fundamentalist movements are becoming increasingly popular. Manifestations of what he terms the 'Islamic Resurgence' include the 1979 Iranian Revolution and the first Gulf War.

Huntington sees the Islamic civilisation as a potential ally to China, both having revisionist goals and sharing common conflicts with other civilisations such as the West. He identifies common Chinese and Islamic interests in the areas of weapons proliferation, human rights, and democracy that conflict those of the West, and feels that these are areas in which the two civilisations will cooperate.

Boris Yeltsin used the term 'cold peace' to describe future relations between Russia and the West. Russia, Japan and India are what Huntington terms 'swing civilizations' that may favor either side—the Western or the Islamic. Russia, for example, clashes with the many Muslim ethnic groups on its southern border (such as Chechnya) but, according to Huntington, cooperates with Iran to avoid further Muslim orthodox violence in southern Russia as well as to ensure continuation of the flow of oil.

Identity Politics

Identity politics is an approach in which people of a particular race, nationality, religion, gender, sexual orientation, social background, social class, or any other identifying factor develop political agendas that are based upon these identities. Identity politics is based on the idea that some groups and communities in society are oppressed and subjugated and a political movement is necessary to end that oppression.

The term 'identity politics' is used primarily to describe political movements concerning ideas of nationalism, multiculturalism, women's rights, civil rights, and LGBTQ+ rights. The term has been used in political discourse since at least the 1970s.

Criticism of Identity Politics: Those who criticise identity politics see it as inherently collectivist and prejudicial and often in contradiction to the ideals of classical liberalism. It has also been blamed for deepening political divisions.

Some notable examples include movements focusing on women's identity politics, caste identity politics, Black feminist identity politics, and Muslim identity politics.

Unit VI

INDIA'S FOREIGN POLICY

KEYWORDS

Postcolonial trajectory in the international arena; Non-Aligned Movement; India's nuclear policy and debates on disarmament; Multipolar world order; India's relations with major powers; India's relations with its neighbours; negotiating international regimes

1

PERSPECTIVES ON INDIA'S FOREIGN POLICY

KEYWORDS

India's postcolonial development; India as a rising power; India as an emerging political economy

There are many sovereign nation-states in the world, and the relationship between these sovereign nations is called international relations. International relations also include regional organisations, non-governmental organisations and international organisations, such as the United Nations and the World Trade Organization. A nation determines relations with other nations and organisations on the basis of certain policies and principles, which are centred on national interest. This set of policies and principles is referred to as foreign policy. The foreign policy of a country is thus its relationship with other countries and organisations, and the strategies it uses to protect its domestic and international interests.

POSTCOLONIAL DEVELOPMENT

Jawaharlal Nehru, who became the first Prime Minister of India upon India's independence in 1947, advocated peaceful coexistence, opposition to nuclear weapons and an effective United Nations. Nehru's foreign policy in this sense is *idealistic*. He emphasised peace over collection and protection of weapons. According to him, social and economic development was independent India's biggest priority. He supported the peaceful use of nuclear capability and tried to establish peace in Asia and all over the world, demanding the creation of a just world. Nehru refused to join the arms race as that would have affected India's economic development. This idealistic thinking of Nehru was based on the ideals of the national movement, which opposed imperialism and colonialism.

Under Nehru's leadership, India gradually rose as one of the leaders of the Third World. After independence, the **Asian Relations Conference** was held in New Delhi in April 1947 with the goal was to promote cultural, intellectual and social exchange between Asian countries. Later, the **Asian-African Conference** was held in **Bandung** in 1955, in which India played a central role.

Nehru's Idealistic Foreign Policy

1. **Autonomous Foreign Policy (Non-Aligned Movement):** Nehru tried to improve relations with other countries while keeping India apart from the military blocs. During the Cold War, Nehru and other leaders of newly independent countries of

the Third World devised the Non-Aligned Movement to protect their independence by not aligning with any major powers in case of international conflict like a war. This is how he designed a foreign policy that was autonomous and independent. The NAM is a movement against imperialism, colonialism and armaments. It stood for peaceful coexistence and it was the collective voice of the Third World, a platform to establish unity and a conference to end exploitation. Non-alignment was not the creation of a third bloc in the world, but a platform to eliminate all blocs. The intention of non-alignment was not the opposition of the US and the Soviet Union in particular, but rather, a general opposition to the idea of military blocs anywhere in the world. At present, this independent foreign policy is called strategic autonomy.

2. **Economic Development and Self-Reliancy:** Industrialisation of the country was given great importance by Nehru, and thanks to him, India's development towards a modern society was consistent. He did not give priority to increasing military power, but instead emphasised the economic development of the country. At the time of independence, India was economically backward and regional disparities existed, so India tried to obtain economic and technical assistance from both the US and the Soviet Union to meet domestic requirements. Pandit Nehru adopted a **mixed economic model** and gave priority to public enterprises to further the social and economic development of the country. He laid emphasis on education, health and social welfare of the people and wanted to build a self-reliant nation. His economic policy combined elements of both market economy and socialist economy.
3. **Afro-Asian Solidarity:** The Asian Relations Conference and the Bandung Conference were important steps towards building Afro-Asian solidarity. It was attended by **29** heads of state belonging to Asia and Africa. **Ten Principles** were accepted which eventually led to the foundation of NAM. According to Nehru, Asian and African countries newly independent and free from colonisation would have the same interests. He advocated for the creation of an equitable world through the unity of Asian and African countries.
4. **Friendly Relations with China:** Under Nehru's leadership, India tried to improve relations with China. Doing so was essential for establishing Asian unity. China was a neighbour of India but it was a member of the Communist military bloc. Plus, Pakistan's attitude after independence was unfavourable to India. Therefore, a friendly relationship with China was necessary for India because adverse relations with the two neighbouring countries was against India's interests.
5. **Strengthening the United Nations:** Nehru always pursued efforts to make the United Nations more effective. He stressed upon the fact that a peaceful coexistence of the world can be achieved through the United Nations. He gave great importance to the peaceful resolution of existing disputes in the world. The basic principles of Indian foreign policy were formulated in accordance with the ideals of the United Nations.

India was attacked by China in the year 1962, which was seen as a failure of Nehru's foreign policy. In the year 1964, nuclear tests were conducted by China which again posed a serious challenge to India's security. It was a matter of coincidence that Nehru died in 1964 and Lal Bahadur Shastri became the new Prime Minister of the country. In 1965, there was a war between India and Pakistan. Lal Bahadur Shastri died in 1966 during the **Tashkent Agreement** that was signed between India and Pakistan in Uzbekistan.

This resulted in Indira Gandhi becoming the new Prime Minister of India, which led to a qualitative change in Indian foreign policy.

During Indira Gandhi's tenure, there was an effective development of realism in Indian foreign policy, but in spite of this change, the idealistic elements remained. Indira Gandhi too maintained India's policy of non-alignment and continued to maintain an anti-imperialist and anti-colonialist stance. She strongly supported disarmament and opposed the intervention of major powers in the affairs of the Indian Ocean and South Asia.

Realism in India's Foreign Policy

A. **Military Modernisation:** Special emphasis was placed on security and storage of military goods because both Pakistan and China had become hostile neighbours of India. There was a huge increase in the size of the Indian Army and military modernisation was given priority. After 1965, arms export to India was banned by the US.

B. **Friendship with USSR:** Diplomatic relations were established between the US and China in the year 1971, and in the same year, on 9 August, there was a treaty of peace and friendship between India and the Soviet Union. **Sardar Swaran Singh**, then minister of external affairs, signed the treaty. Many said that India, instead of non-alignment, had through this treaty joined the military bloc, because the treaty clearly mentioned that if there was any kind of attack on either of the countries, they would help each other. Others did not consider it a violation of non-alignment, as the Soviet Union recognised India's non-alignment policy. The treaty was for peace and friendship, and not for military alliance.

C. **Defeating Pakistan:** In the year 1974, there was a peaceful nuclear explosion by India, which demonstrated that it was capable of making nuclear weapons. Pakistan was defeated by India in 1971 and neighbouring countries had acknowledged India's military capability. Sikkim merged with India in the year 1975. Security and military power was now given priority by India as it focused on procuring arms in large quantities from the Soviet Union. The West during this time adopted an anti-India policy.

India's Position in the Post-Cold War Era

In the 1980s, Indian economy was in crisis and India's economic growth rate was slowing down to as low as one per cent. Around the same time, there began a movement for temple construction led by Bharatiya Janata Party (BJP) who demanded construction of a Ram Temple in Ayodhya. The movement for an expanded system of reservation was also in progress. The country's economic credibility was at stake and in 1989, for the first time in the history of the country's democracy, a government of the National Front was formed which did not have an absolute majority in the Lok Sabha. The government was formed under the leadership of Vishwanath Pratap Singh, and it depended on the external support of the Bharatiya Janata Party and the communist parties.

This government proved to be unstable as it was dependent on the support of many parties. The Lok Sabha elections were held again in the year 1991 and P. V. Narasimha Rao's minority government was formed. India was unable to pay foreign exchange for the import of foreign goods and faced a crisis of Balance of Payments (BOP).

Global Changes Post 1991

The Soviet Union disintegrated in 1991 and Russia was formed. It marked the end of ideological conflict in global politics and the Cold War, and resulted in the establishment of better relations between the US and Russia. The increasing influence of globalisation and liberalisation led to the development of regional economic organisations. The Warsaw Treaty Organization (also known as the Warsaw Pact) which was a political and military alliance established in 1955 between the Soviet Union and Eastern European countries disintegrated in 1991. The world was now a **unipolar world**, and America became its controller, the single superpower. After the 1971 treaty, India became completely dependent on the Soviet Union for import of weapons. So following the disintegration of the Soviet Union, there was scepticism regarding the supply of arms. Since India's largest bilateral trade at that time was also with the Soviet Union, its disintegration and collapse of economy led to a crisis of import and export of goods, and India's exports to the Soviet Union almost came to an end.

Changes in Foreign Policy after the Cold War

In the year 1992, the **Look East policy** was adopted and this shifted the emphasis of Indian foreign policy towards strengthening the economic relations with the ASEAN countries as this region was emerging as a centre of economic development. Under this policy, India sought to strengthen relations with countries such as South Korea, Australia, New Zealand and Japan. India also established friendly relations with Myanmar's military regime. Economic development became the primary focus of Indian foreign policy and emphasis was placed on making the SAARC economically effective.

After the Cold War, Indian foreign policy became fiercely *realist*. In 1992, India also established diplomatic relations with Israel, which was a major change in foreign policy. Earlier, India had maintained friendly relations with the Palestinians and as Israel took over Palestinian land, diplomatic relations with Israel could not be established due to the antagonistic relationship between Palestine and Israel. But in 1992, diplomatic relations with Israel were established while retaining traditional relations with Palestine. This shows that emphasis was placed on *pragmatism* and middle path when it came to foreign policy. Further, the development of economic relations with the European Union was emphasised upon and investment, trade and exports were given central importance. Economic and trade relations with Africa and Latin America were also prioritised.

India faced a dilemma when USA began putting pressure on India to halt its nuclear programme. India was dependent on USA for economic assistance, but at the same time, it was necessary for India to focus on its security as, uniquely, India is surrounded by two hostile neighbours—China and Pakistan. China was a nuclear weapon state and Pakistan developed nuclear weapons covertly with assistance from China. Therefore, India had to take a decisive step towards strengthening her security. India conducted 3 nuclear tests (Pokhran-II, under the code name Operation Shakti) between 11 and 13 May 1998. India, while setting the objective of this nuclear test, said that it is for the development of *minimum nuclear deterrence*. This nuclear test was thus different from the nuclear test of 1974 (Pokhran-I). According to the theorists, the tests created one of the pre-requisites for India's aspiration to become a major power.

Changes in Foreign Policy in Recent Years (2014–Present)

Narendra Modi became the Prime Minister of India on May 2014. The era of coalition government ended in India and the Bharatiya Janata Party got an absolute majority in the House of the People. The BJP-led government focused on building a **dynamic and proactive foreign policy**. PM Modi has travelled to many countries on diplomatic trips and took the initiative to strengthen India's foreign relations.

Neighbourhood First Policy

For the first time, all members of the SAARC were invited by an Indian Prime Minister to the swearing-in ceremony. Further, the Prime

Minister's first foreign trip was scheduled to Bhutan, India's smallest neighbour. The PM also travelled to Nepal, Sri Lanka and Bangladesh in the very first year of his tenure. The very important issue of the exchange of enclaves and land parcels, pending since 1974, was discussed and an agreement was ratified with Bangladesh. This policy is influenced by the Gujral Doctrine, which was implemented in the year 1996 by then Foreign Minister Inder Kumar Gujral.

Cultural Diplomacy

Through cultural diplomacy, the government has tried to expand the ideological power of India and disseminate Indian culture across the world. PM Modi visited Kyoto, Japan and highlighted the cultural connections of Buddhism between Varanasi and Kyoto. During his visit to Myanmar, cultural and economic ties were strengthened. Yoga Day was publicised in India for the first time and Yoga Day programmes were held all over the world, which can be seen to contribute to increasing India's *soft power*. In 2007, leaders of sixteen member states of the East Asia Summit (EAS) had endorsed the proposal to re-establish Nalanda, the ancient seat of learning. Thus the **Nalanda University** was set up as another step towards strengthening cultural ties of India with other countries.

Act East Policy

The Look East policy was adopted by India in the year 1992, but there have been many hurdles in its implementation. The Act East policy seeks to focus on the implementation of Look East policy by strengthening relations with ASEAN countries through better development of infrastructure. The policy, although originally conceived as an economic initiative, has gained political, strategic and cultural dimensions.

Informal Diplomacy

Negotiations were held in Wuhan with Chinese President Xi Jinping as part of informal diplomatic visits by PM Modi. The emphasis of this discussion was on increasing trust and confidence and improving the relations between the two nations, so there was no specific issues decided upon for talks, nor was any declaration issued after the talks. Other instances of informal diplomacy include Japanese Prime Minister Shinzo Abe joining PM Modi in a kite-flying session in Ahmedabad and French President Emmanuel Macron being invited for sailing on the Ganges in Varanasi.

Connecting with the Indian Diaspora

While there has been no qualitative change in the foreign policy of the present government in this regard, there has been changes in the way the government connected with the diasporic population. India's policy of connecting with migrants started after 1998, but for the first time, the present government attempted to establish an emotional connection directly with the migrants living abroad. During the US visit of PM Modi, American people of Indian origin were publicly addressed by the Prime Minister. A public event for people of Indian origin was also organised during the Prime Minister's visit to Australia. The 'Make in India' programme, an initiative launched by Modi in September 2014, devised to transform India into a global design and manufacturing hub and it has seen considerable success, aided by a large amount of investment from the diasporic Indian populations.

Assertive Policy

India's foreign policy under PM Modi has changed from a policy of self-restraint to a much more assertive policy. Despite heavy pressure from China over Doklam, the Indian army refused to back down. China's Belt and Road Initiative (BRI) has also been assertively opposed by India. Further, India announced surgical strikes against Pakistan in more than one instance. In all these decisions, the change in India's attitude when it comes to foreign relations is noticeable.

INDIA AS A RISING POWER

India emerged from World War II as the world's fourth largest industrial power. Many suggest that India has the potential to become a global superpower. India's foreign policy has seen important changes with India's gradual rise in power.

Strengthening Partnership with USA

India and US relations grew decisively after 2001. The India and US **Civil Nuclear Agreement** of 2005 was an important landmark in India–America relations. Under this agreement, India agreed to separate its civil and military nuclear facilities and, in exchange, the US agreed to work toward full civil nuclear cooperation with India. This strengthened the strategic relations between the two countries as it gave India the status of a **responsible state**. This made India the only nuclear possessor state and non-NPT signatory permitted to engage in civil nuclear trade with other states.

India decided to go for a strategic partnership with USA partly due to China's aggressive behaviour. Since Russia has close relations to China and there is a power asymmetry between China and India, India needed a stronger partner in order to counterbalance China. India has been trying to further its partnership with Russia too. With respect to the ongoing Ukraine crisis, India has maintained a fine balance and is trying to maintain good relations with both the US and Russia. While many criticised Russia's invasion, India did not. However, as of now, India's partnership with the USA is its top priority for foreign policy.

Defence Relations and Arms Trade

India has developed cordial and friendly relations with countries like Iran after 2003. Defence relations with Israel too has strengthened steadily. Israel became the third largest supplier of hardware weapons to India. While India continues to buy arms from Russia, it is also buying large quantities of defence weapons from America and France.

From Non-Alignment to Multi-Alignment

While the Non-Alignment Movement (NAM) has been India's foreign policy for a long time, in the present changing world order, India is re-setting her foreign policy and cultivating strong strategic partnerships with several of the major powers at the same time. India is simultaneously in partnerships with USA, Russia and Japan through a multi-alignment foreign policy. India is a part of the Quadrilateral Security Dialogue, also known as QUAD, which comprises the USA, India, Japan, and Australia. India has also formed a trilateral partnership to work on a security structure for the Indo-Pacific region which PM Modi has titled JAI (Japan, USA, India). At the same time, India is also a part of the Shanghai Cooperation Organisation (SCO).

Therefore, it is clear that India's interests are very wide and diverse and all types of foreign relations have significance for India. It is noteworthy that after the 1997 economic crisis, the **Group of 20 (G20)** was established in 1999 to discuss issues related to global economy. This group includes developed countries like USA, Germany, Japan and also developing countries like India, China and Brazil. India has also been invited to participate in **G7** meetings, which comprise America, Canada, Germany, France, England, Italy, and Japan. India is also a member of the **G8 + 5** group, which includes the G8 nations as well as the emerging economies of China, India, Brazil, South Africa and Mexico.

INDIA AS AN EMERGING POLITICAL ECONOMY

In the past decades, there has been a qualitative change in Indian foreign policy in various areas including economy and trade. The foreign policy that Nehru set up favoured socialism and non-alignment but these were changed and national interests were given priority over ideology, thus giving birth to a more *pragmatic foreign policy*. In the 1990s, P. V. Narasimha Rao (then Prime Minister) and Dr. Manmohan Singh (then Finance Minister) drastically changed the existing economic policies and adopted the policy of *liberalisation*. The principle of prioritising of public enterprises was abandoned. Trade, investment and commerce were prioritised in the era of liberalisation and globalisation. Through building a relationship with the US, the only superpower in the world after the end of the Cold War, India could improve its economy. The support of United States ensured that India was financed in large amounts by the International Monetary Fund (IMF), which helped to end India's economic crisis. Therefore, maintaining good relations with the US was not an option for India but a necessary requirement.

While India has emerged as a major power in present times, it does not mean that India is no longer concerned with its relationship with the countries of the Third World. India is still placing emphasis on south-south unity and along with other developing countries, is opposing discriminatory policies run by developed countries. IBSA was established in the year 2003 with the objective of promoting international cooperation between India, Brazil and South Africa. The establishment of BRICS in the year 2009 is another testimony to India's multilateral diplomacy. Even today, India's interests with respect to the issues of the WTO negotiations (Doha Round) align with the interests of other developing countries.

PM Modi aims to make India the centre of manufacturing through the 'Make in India' programme. Make in India was launched by the government in 2014 and efforts were and are being made to develop India as an investment hub of the world. India is fast attracting foreign direct investment (FDI). In 2016, India attracted an investment of USD 60 billion. In 2019, India was the 9th largest FDI-recipient country with 51 billion dollars of inflows during the year. Through this programme, India is being projected as a convenient country for trade and a preferential place for investment.

GOVERNMENT AGENCIES RELATED TO FOREIGN POLICY

Ministry of Defence

Organisation of the Ministry of Defence (MOD)

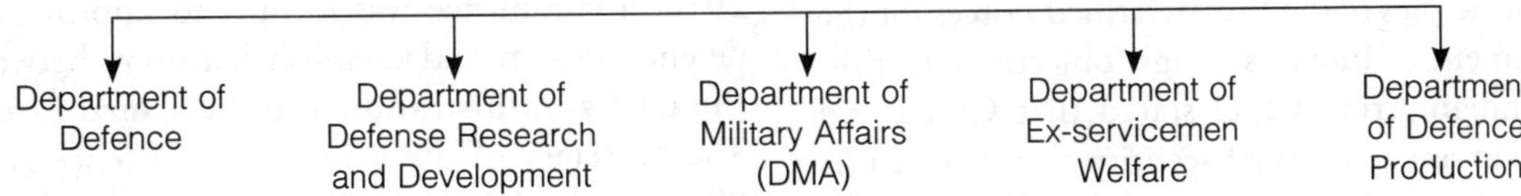

The MOD also has a **Chiefs of Staff Committee.** The Chiefs of Staff advise the Defence Minister and the Cabinet Committee on political affairs and on all military matters which require ministerial consideration. The Chiefs of Staff Committee is composed of:

(a) Chief of the Army Staff (COAS)
(b) Chief of the Naval Staff (CNS)
(c) Chief of the Air Staff (CAS)
(d) Chief of Defence Staff (CDS) (non-voting member).

Chief of Defence Staff

The appointment of the **Chief of Defence Staff** or the **CDS** is a new beginning in India's *strategic culture*. Critics have often argued that Indian foreign policy lacks a strategic culture, but this change shows that security is now a top priority of India's foreign policy.

The creation of the new Department of Military Affairs (DMA) in 2020 and the instituting of the post of Chief of Defence Staff (CDS) is momentous and a comprehensive reform that will help our country face the ever-changing challenges of modern warfare. The new DMA, with the CDS as its secretary, is staffed by senior military personnel and allows a direct involvement of the armed forces in the formal deliberative structure of the government. The DoD initially dealt with the three Armed Forces, a role that the DMA will now take over.

The CDS will manage **tri-service** organisations, agencies and commands. The Andaman and Nicobar Command is India's only tri-service theatre command. The role also involves being the Military Adviser to the Nuclear Command Authority, which controls India's nuclear arsenal and is headed by the Prime Minister. Separately, the CDS will be a member of the **Defence Acquisition Council** and the **Defence Planning Committee**.

Joint Doctrine of the Indian Armed Forces (2017)

A new military doctrine was announced in the year 2017 by the Indian Army Chief called the **Joint Doctrine of the Indian Armed Forces.** It is a strategic design that outlines the core philosophy and principles of the Indian Armed Forces for the attainment of India's strategic objectives. In this, the Indian Army Chief stated that China and Pakistan are traditional security threats of India and terrorism is a serious security challenge that needs special attention. He proposed that increased importance be given to India's **cyber security** and **space security**. Changing India's nuclear policy, the minimal deterrence was replaced with **credible minimum deterrence**. The formation of a unified military command in India was recommended.

Integrated Military Command: During the 1999 Kargil conflict, there was a lack of coordination among the three organs of the Indian armed forces. In the year 2001, a unified military command was formed in the Andaman and Nicobar Islands. The new military doctrine proposed that India should be divided into four integrated military commands to facilitate coordination between the three wings of the armed forces. While countries like America and China have already established integrated military command, a few problems exist when it comes to implementing it in India. First, an integrated command in India will increase rivalry among the three wings of the armed forces. The strength of the Army is the largest in terms of their number, while the Air Force is considered the most important wing. But due to the large strength of the Army, it is likely that the head of the integrated command would be chosen from the Army and not the Air Force. Secondly, there is no need of the Navy in North and West region, geographically speaking, as the deployment of Air Force in a short period of time is possible in these parts of the country. Because of these reasons, military modernisation is more necessary than an integrated command.

Defence Planning Committee

Cooperation between the various ministries is important for the effective formulation of foreign policy. Moreover, there is a need for better coordination between **administrative officers** and **officers of the armed forces**. In 2018, a committee was formed to improve the defence system and establish harmony between **the civil administration and the armed forces**. The Secretary of the Ministry of Defence is an officer of the Administrative Services who should coordinate with the Chiefs of the three armed forces. The chairman of the committee will be the National Security Adviser. The Chiefs of the armed forces will represent the armed forced and the Foreign Secretary, Defence Secretary and Finance Secretary will represent the administrative officers. The committee has the objective to create an integrated approach in relation to national security and efforts are to be made for self-reliance in the purchase of defence materials as well as production of defence materials.

Self-Sufficiency in Military Supplies

The principle of strategic partnership has been adopted by the present government to improve national security. Under this, private companies of India such as Reliance and Mahindra, and private companies of foreign countries such as Rafale and Lockheed Martin, will form a partnership in the defence production sector. Through this partnership, deadly weapons like fighter jets, tanks, and nuclear submarines will be built. Indian companies will have a 51 per cent share in the partnership and this will help India achieve self-sufficiency in defence equipment production. Currently about 60 per cent of the defence requirements are imported. The dismal and ineffective public-sector company operating under the Ministry of Defence led to the private sector taking up a bigger role in defence production.

Ministry of External Affairs

New Changes in the MEA

In 2020, the MEA's structure was changed considerably as seven new verticals and new divisions were introduced and a technology upgrade through New and Emerging Strategic Technologies (NEST) was done. Seven different Additional Secretaries were added and their tasks were reorganised along verticals like culture, and trade and development, amongst others. With this restructuring, **administrative tasks** have been separated from **diplomacy**. This new design will give more power to the Additional Secretaries and take off pressure on the Secretaries.

The seven verticals of the MEA are as follows:

- Cultural Diplomacy
- Economic and Trade Coordination
- Multinational Organisations and Global Summits
- Development Partnership
- West Asia and Africa
- Indian Ocean and Indo-Pacific
- Europe

The MEA wants to define the future of Indian diplomacy by introducing these new changes along with bringing in experts from the private sector and non-profit bodies. These new verticals will help the country fortify its soft power. This restructuring will also focus on neighbourhood-focused development, and give a boost to India's profile in multilateral groups and international summits. It is hoped that India's claim to a permanent seat at the United Nations Security Council will also get bolder.

The technology upgrade through NEST will help improve India's external technology policy and contribute towards meeting India's national security goals. It will foster technology diplomacy by encouraging collaboration with different partners in emerging fields such as artificial intelligence. International legal implications of new technologies can also be assessed more accurately and this will lead to more effective policymaking.

Figure 6.1.2: Organisation of the Ministry of External Affairs

External Affairs Minister
Dr. S. Jaishankar

Minister of State for External Affairs
V. Muraleedharan

Minister of State for External Affairs
Smt. Meenakashi Lekhi

Minister of State for External Affairs
Dr. Rajkumar Ranjan Singh

Secretary (CPV) & OIA
Dr. Ausaf Sayeed

Secretary (Economic Relations)
Dammu Ravi

Foreign Secretary
Vinay Kwatra

Secretary (East)
Saurabh Kumar

Secretary (West)
Sanjay Verma

Addl. Secretary & Financial Adviser
Manoj Sahay

Additional Secretary
(AD)
Sanjiv Ranjan

Finance
Dr. Satyanjal Pandey
Dir (Finance)

Pr. Chief Controller
of Accounts
S.S. Sagar

Secretary (CPV) & OIA

Division	Head of Division
Gulf	Vipul
WANA	Dr. Pradeep Rajpurohit
(OIA)-I	Anurag Bhushan (AS)
(OIA)-II	Manika Jain (AS)
OE & PGE	Bramha Kumar
CPV	Devesh Uttam
PSP	T. Armstrong Changsan

Secretary (Economic Relations)

Division	
Development Partnership Administration I	A. Ajay Kumar
Development Partnership Administration II	Abhilasha Joshi (AS)
Development Partnership Administration III	Satish Sivan
Development Partnership Administration IV	Abhilasha Joshi (AS)
ED Division	Md. Noor Rahman Sheikh
SCO	Yojna Patel
MER	Ninad S. Deshpande
East & Southern Africa	Puneet R. Kundal
Central and West Africa	Sevala Naik Mude
NEST	Mahaveer Singhvi

Foreign Secretary

Division	Head of Division
AMS	Vani Sarraju Rao (AS)
Bangladesh, Myanmar	Smita Pant
Centre for Contemporary China Studies Division	Srinivas Gotru
D&ISA	Muanpuii Saiawi
East Asia	Dr. Shilpak Ambule
Eurasia	Charanjeet Singh
Europe West	Sandeep Chakravorty
IOR Division	Puneet Agarwal
Northern	Anurag Srivastava
Pakistan, Afghanistan, Iran	J. P. Singh
Policy Planning & Research	Dr. Sumit Seth
External Publicity & Public Diplomacy	Arindam Bagchi (AS)
Gulf	Vipul
WANA	Dr. Pradeep Rajpurohit
Rapid Response Cell	Satish Kumar Sivan
Oceania	Paramita Tripathi

Additional Secretary (AD)

Division	Head of Division
Administration	B Vanlalvawna
Bureau of Security	Vijay Bhatia
Cypher, NGO & Vigilance & Inspection	Charanjeet Singh
EG & IT	Atul M. Gotsurve
CD Division	Muanpuii Saiawi
Establishment	Y.K. Sailas Thangal
GEM	D.C. Manjunath
SSIFS	Sanjiv Ranjan

Secretary (East)

Division	Head of Division
AMS	Vani Sarraju Rao (AS)
Archives & Record Managment	Manohar Ram
BIMSTEC, SAARC	Rudrendra Tandon (AS)
East Asia	Dr. Shilpak Ambule
Indo-Pacific Division	Geetika Srivastava
Latin America & Caribbean	G.V. Srinivas (AS)
Parliament & Coordination	Anil Kumar Rai
Right To Information	
RBB, I&T	Ravindra Prasad Jaiswal
Southern	Ravi Shankar (AS)
Oceania	Paramita Tripathi
States	C. Rajasekhar

Secretary (West)

Division	Head of Division
Central Europe	Arun Kumar Sahu
Eurasia	Charanjeet Singh
Europe West	Sandeep Chakravorty
Counter Terrorism	K. D. Dewal
Legal & Treaties	Uma Sekhar (AS)
Protocol	Anshuman Gaur
United Nations	Srinivas Gotru
United Nations Political	Prakash Gupta
Summits	L. Ramesh Babu

Note: Names given as of July 2023.
Source: Ministry of External Affairs website

2

CHANGE AND CONTINUITY IN INDIA'S FOREIGN POLICY

KEYWORDS

Determinants of foreign policy; Non-Aligned Movement, its historical background and relevance; India's nuclear policy

The basic aim of foreign policy is to preserve national interest. This is why foreign policy is not determined by political parties as national interest cannot change with the change of government. There are various elements in India's foreign policy that has changed since the Independence, while there are elements that have been retained as the old principles continued. This continuity in India's foreign policy can be seen in the *principle of peaceful coexistence* and the belief in the United Nations Organisation. India has also retained an *independent foreign policy*.

There have been several visible changes in India's foreign policy as well. India opted for a *liberal economy*, which is a marked difference from the earlier socialist model. India carried out nuclear testing and acquired nuclear weapons even though earlier, it was against nuclear weapons. As India grows to become a major power, it is cultivating strategic partnerships with other **major powers** and this is one of the main objectives of India's present-day foreign policy. While post-independence India emphasised more on building solidarity with Asian-African nations, with changing orientations India now wants to specifically develop economic partnerships with Asian-African nations, although the emphasis on solidarity still remains. While the Soviet Union was the most trusted ally of India during the Cold War, now a partnership with USA has become the top priority for India.

Thus, both change and continuity are characteristics of India's foreign policy. Many policies have evolved along with the evolving national interest, which also undergoes changes due to the changing world environment. Yet, some policies have remained the same, from the first Cabinet of Ministers to the present one.

DETERMINANTS OF FOREIGN POLICY

Geographically, India is a large country with a population of 135 crores, which is the second largest population in the world after China. India is also one of the oldest living civilisations in the world. It is the world's largest democracy. From a military point of view, India's Army is the third largest after China and America, its Air Force the fourth largest after America, Russia and China, and its Navy the sixth largest after the US, Russia, China, Japan, and Britain. In many ways, therefore, India is a major power and many factors determine its foreign policy.

The foreign policy of a country is determined by multiple factors, such as geographical size, geographical location and domestic condition. Policies are influenced by the natural resources, technical and financial capacity of the nation as well as the nature of the political system, and the history and culture of the country. In addition, regional and global factors are also important determinants of foreign policy.

Domestic Factors

1. *Geographical Factors*

Foreign policy is heavily influenced by geographical factors, and this has traditionally been termed *geo-politics*. Among geographical factors, the location, size, and topography of the country is very important. India is the 7th largest country in the world, with an area of 32,87,263 sq. km. The northern boundary of India is surrounded by the Himalayas. The role of this natural frontier is significant in the formulation of Indian foreign policy, especially policies related to national security. After 1962, China has established control over some important passes between Ladakh and Tibet, and the Sichuan–Tibet Highway has been built through Aksai Chin. In addition to that, China has taken over some important passes connecting Nepal, including the Kodari Pass, and is now claiming a large part of Arunachal Pradesh. These security threats affect Indian foreign policy, which places a special emphasis on building relations with the Himalayan nations, particularly **Nepal, Bhutan, and Myanmar**. China's position as a geographical neighbour thus has a significant influence on India's foreign policy.

India's location in the **Indian Ocean Region** also affects foreign policy. The Indian Ocean lies to the south of India and is the third largest ocean in the world spanning an area of 7.2 million square kilometres. India's central and dominant position in the Indian Ocean helps it to play a role of global importance. A **Far East Naval Command** was proposed for the **Andaman and Nicobar Islands** in 1998 to maintain its influence in the Indian Ocean. In 2001, the Andaman and Nicobar Command (ANC), the only tri-service theater command of the armed forces, was set up to safeguard India's strategic interests in Southeast Asia and the Strait of Malacca. It is important to note that Myanmar's Coco Islands, where China has developed a naval base, is only 40 km from India's eastern naval command. The US too has a military base in **Diego Garcia**, an island in the British Indian Ocean Territory. In the mid-2000s, India signed a military agreement with Indonesia for defence cooperation.

The Indian Ocean is important to India for both security and economic reasons. In 1997, the Indian Ocean Rim Association for Regional Cooperation **(IOR-ARC)** and the BIMSTEC were established. In the year 2000, the Ganga-Mekong project was set up to foster culture and commerce. China promoted the **String of Pearls** policy to maintain its influence in the Indian Ocean as it wants to control sea communication from Hong Kong to the port of Sudan, including the Malacca Strait and the Hormuz Strait. China has been supporting the development of ports in Pakistan (Gwadar), Bangladesh (Chittagong), Maldives, Sri Lanka (Hambantota) and Myanmar (Coco Islands). The 'String of Pearls' can be seen as the result of China's emerging geo-political influence, through which China seeks to improve its reach and control ports and air force bases.

2. *Political System*

A country's political system has a vital role in determining its foreign policy. Being the largest democratic country in the world, India always emphasised upon peaceful co-existence and supported the spread of democracy in the world in the post-Cold War world too. However, to maintain warm and harmonious relations with its neighbour Myanmar, India declined to react to the Burmese anti-government protests in 2007, maintaining a diplomatic stance that it does not believe that democracy can be imposed externally on any country.

The structure of Indian democracy has both a federal system as well as parliamentary governance. Therefore, the role of state governments in the formulation of foreign policy also becomes important. For example, the Tamil Nadu government attempted to pressurise the Union Government regarding the issue of Tamil conflict in Sri Lanka.

3. *Economic Development*

In the post-Cold War world, geo-economics has become as important, if not more, as geo-politics. India is the 5th largest economy in the world. It is an attractive market as well as an important investment destination. There is a huge potential for India's development, economic and otherwise. As a result, the economic elements in India's foreign policy must be given utmost importance.

It is necessary in the national interest that we do not depend on any one source for energy. India imports oil from Africa, Central Asia and Russia. It also has energy supply agreements with Latin American countries such as Venezuela. In foreign policy, energy security plays an important role and policies are formulated with support from the Ministry of Petroleum and Natural Gas, Ministry of Coal, Ministry of New and Renewable Energy (earlier known as Ministry of Non-Conventional Energy) and the Department of Atomic Energy. In the present era, controlling environmental pollution while maintaining economic development has become a basic challenge. Agreements have been signed with various countries on the issue of nuclear power generation.

4. *History and Tradition*

The history and tradition of a country too has a great influence in the formulation of foreign policy. Indian society has diverse cultures and traditions. Pacifist policies of Ashoka and realist policies of Kautilya have in many ways shaped India's present-day policies. Ashoka emphasised on peace, while Kautilya believed that ends justify the means. The early foreign policy of independent India however leaned more towards the tradition of peaceful coexistence adopted by Ashoka.

The following historical events of the recent past have had a great influence in determining India's foreign policy:

(i) Indo-China War of 1962
(ii) India-Pakistan War of 1965
(iii) India-Pakistan War of 1971
(iv) Indo-Soviet Treaty of Peace, Friendship and Cooperation, 1971

Critics have often said that India's tradition of idealism impacts its foreign policy as an overemphasis on peace and internationalism results in a lack of *strategic culture.* But foreign policies change according to changing circumstances, and in present times, strategic culture has become an important component of India's foreign policy. After coming to power, PM Modi announced new changes in the foreign policy based on five themes linked to Indian traditions: *Samman* (dignity), *Samvaad* (dialogue), *Samriddhi* (shared prosperity), *Suruksha* (regional and global security), and *Sanskriti* and *Sabhayata* (cultural and civilisational links). These can be seen as five *pillars of soft power* that can be used in a strategic sense, and are interlinked with greater political and economic goals of the country.

5. *Security*

A powerful army is essential for maintaining the security of a nation, and in that regard, India has strengthened its security policies considerably. India has the third largest defence force in the world and is moreover a nuclear-armed country. It uses its nuclear power as a deterrent against external threats, for instance, when its neighbours Pakistan and China engage in conflict with India. Therefore, maintaining a strong military power and working on its further development is important for India, and security is an important determinant of its foreign policy.

6. *Culture*

Cultural factors also influence foreign policy as cultural bonding can be one of the ways to prevent conflict and promote peace among nations. The pursuit of cultural diplomacy and soft power in India is carried out by MEA's iconic institutional structure, the **Indian Council for Cultural Relations** (ICCR) which was established in 1950 with the objective of reviving and strengthening India's cultural relations with the rest of the world. This was necessary to build warm relations with not just the nations in our neighbourhood but also with our strategic partners and new dialogue partners in Africa and Latin America.

Indian spirituality has a considerable global spread and one of its manifestations is the large number of Yoga centres spread across the world. On the suggestion of PM Modi, the UN General Assembly recognised 21 June as the International Day of Yoga. Another example is the 'Ramayana Circuit'. In May 2018, the Prime Minister and his Nepalese counterpart KP Sharma Oli jointly inaugurated a direct bus service between Janakpur in Nepal and Ayodhya in India. Under the Swadesh Darshan Scheme, 15 destinations have been identified for development.

Apart from these, there is intangible cultural heritage which includes traditions or living expressions inherited from ancestors, such as oral traditions, performing arts, religious and cultural festivals and traditional crafts. Multilaterally, UNESCO, through the World Heritage Committee and the Intergovernmental Committee for the Safeguarding of the Intangible Cultural Heritage, helps India promote an international, intercultural dialogue and in the long run, international peace and security.

7. *Diaspora*

The Indian diaspora plays a vital role in strengthening the relationship between India and USA. USA provided vaccines to India during COVID-19 due to the influence of diaspora and Indian ambassadors abroad. The Indian diaspora in the US works actively to protect the interests of India. **Civil Nuclear Agreement** between India and USA was signed in 2008 which was possible in part due to the lobbying of diasporic residents.

Aapravasi Ghat in Mauritius, which marks the entry point of more than two million indentured labour from India, a point of no return, was inscribed in July 2006 on UNESCO's World Heritage List.

The diasporic population can be seen as unofficial Indian ambassadors living abroad. The diaspora has a considerable contribution towards India's development in the following ways:

1. They enhance India's soft power.
2. India receives a large amount of remittance from diaspora across the world.
3. They contribute towards India's economy, especially its knowledge-based economy.

Regional Environment

A country's regional environment is also a major determinant of its foreign policy. In case of India, since its hostile neighbours China and Pakistan have entered into **Sino-Pakistan alliances,** there is a serious threat to India's security and thus the foreign policy needs to be strengthened accordingly to deal with the changing political environment.

As Russia and China are also strategic partners, India has focused on strengthening economic relations with other South-East Asian countries by adopting the Look East Policy (1992). To further boost trade and investments, India signed the South Asian Free Trade Area (SAFTA) agreement in 2004. The ASEAN-India Free Trade Agreement was also signed to promote trade between India and the ASEAN countries. In 2014, Prime Minister Narendra Modi stressed on the implementation of the Look East Policy through the Act East Policy, which was also welcomed by ASEAN member countries. Negotiations have been relaunched for an India-European Union Free Trade Agreement.

Global Order

The present era is the era of liberalisation and globalisation, and a nation's foreign policy has to undergo changes to reflect this changing global order. As a result of growing Indian-American relations following the Cold War, India has also been able to develop cordial and friendly relationships with Japan, Australia, and South Korea, resulting in the India-Australia Civil Nuclear Cooperation Agreement signed in 2014. Relations with Russia have always been strong and it has remained so in the post-Cold War world as well. But with recent changes in India's foreign policy, which are from a more realist approach, India is in agreement with not just Russia but many other countries including America, Israel, France and Britain for supply of military hardware, because relying on one country for the supply of weapons would not be wise for India's national security.

Global terrorism is one of the biggest security threats in the present world. India supported the democratic government in Afghanistan and attempted to put international pressure on Pakistan regarding the issue of cross-border terrorism as it believes that terrorism cannot be justified on any ground.

India has always supported sustainable development, but also raised the demand to preserve the interests of developing countries. It believes that the principle of *common but differentiated responsibility* should be used to solve environmental problems. A powerful United Nations (UN) is needed to address new security challenges or *non-traditional security threats* prevailing in the world such as climate, food and energy security issues. In this regard, India has stressed on the necessity of reforms in the United Nations and presented a claim for permanent membership in the Security Council.

NON-ALIGNED MOVEMENT (NAM)

The Non-Aligned Movement (NAM) is a forum consisting of 120 countries that are not formally aligned with or against any of the major power blocs. The Non-Aligned Movement originated during the Cold War as an organisation of states that did not want to align themselves with either the US or the Soviet Union, but sought to remain independent or neutral.

History of NAM

NAM was conceptualised through two summits: the **Asian Relations Conference** held in New Delhi in 1947 and the **Afro-Asian Bandung Conference** held in Indonesia in 1955.

Powerful visionaries from five newly independent countries—Jawaharlal **Nehru** (India), Gamal Abdel **Nasser** (Egypt), Kwame **Nkrumah** (Ghana), **Sukarno** (Indonesia), Josip Broz **Tito** (Yugoslavia)—were the founding fathers of NAM. The first summit of NAM was held in Belgrade, Yugoslavia in September 1961 and it was attended **by 25 countries.** During this conference, India's first prime minister, Nehru, laid great emphasis on the principles knows as **Panchsheel or the Five Principles of Peaceful Coexistence**. These were first mentioned in a 1954 Sino-Indian agreement where Jawaharlal Nehru and the then Premier of China, Zhou Enlai, issued a joint statement which included the five principles:

1. Mutual respect for each-others territorial integrity and sovereignty.
2. Mutual non-aggression.
3. Mutual non-interference in internal affairs of other nation-states.
4. Equality and cooperation for shared benefit.
5. Peaceful coexistence.

As of 2018, it has 120 members: 53 from Africa, 39 from Asia, 26 from Latin America and 2 from Europe (Belarus and Azerbaijan). In addition, 17 other countries and 10 international organisations hold observer status. The prerequisites to acquiring membership of NAM include: having an independent foreign policy; opposition to imperialism, colonialism and all forms of racism; not participating in any military blocs and not allowing one's territory to be used as a military base.

Non-Alignment in Foreign Policy

Non-Alignment is different from neutralism or isolationism. It refers to an active participation in international politics on the basis of the merits and demerits of an issue. It stands for the protection of sovereignty of every nation-state and opposes intervention and interference in a state's internal affairs. Non-aligned states oppose injustice and hegemony of the major powers and aims to establish a just democratic world. It believes in independence in foreign policy and encourages peaceful coexistence. Some are of the opinion that the objective of NAM is just staying away from military blocs or that NAM itself constitutes a separate third bloc, but that would be a reductive view as the main objective of NAM is to have a bloc-less world, a world without colonialism and imperialism. Opposing arms race and supporting peace and disarmament fall under the main aims of NAM. It also stood against racial apartheid in South Africa. It ensures both the economic and social upliftment of developing countries as well as constructive peace-building. NAM is in many ways thus a moral and idealistic movement.

NAM also served the national interest of India, because India in the Cold War era was looking for economic and technical assistance from all the major powers as post-independence, social economic development was India's main priority. After the Cold War ended in 1991, the movement shifted its focus to developing multilateral ties and connections as well as unity among the developing nations of the world, especially those in the Global South.

M. S. Rajan defines NAM as a *movement of the Third World*, calling it the collective voice of the Global South. NAM championed collective security as a principle for settling disputes. In its opposition to the domination and exploitation by the major powers, it stood against Pax Americana and Pax Sovietica. Rajan also defines NAM as a movement for *an independent and autonomous foreign* policy that helped establish an independent economic policy and adopt a form of government which considered the requirements of the Global South. He observes that in the Indian context, NAM was not merely an alliance or an organisation, but also an effective tool of pursuing a foreign policy aimed at achieving national interest which would not have been otherwise possible as a member of a great power-controlled military bloc. The NAM signified the assertion of newly-gained sovereignty in the form of an independent and autonomous foreign policy.

Principles of NAM

The principles of NAM are largely guided by the *Panchsheel* principles. In the **Afro-Asian Bandung Conference** held in 1955, the principles to promote peace and cooperation in the world was further developed as follows:

1. Respect for fundamental human rights and for the principles enshrined in the UN Charter and International Law. Many saw the NAM as a crucial factor to strengthening the power of the UN which had been rendered irrelevant by the bipolar dominance of the world by the two superpowers.
2. Respect for sovereignty, sovereign equality and territorial integrity of all states.
3. Peaceful settlement of international conflicts.
4. Respect for political, economic, social and cultural diversity of all countries, large and small, as well as their peoples.
5. Respect for inherent right of each nation to defend itself singly or collectively.
6. Abstention from the use of arrangements of collective defense to serve the particular interests of any of the big powers as well as abstention from exerting pressures on other countries.

7. Non-interference in the internal affairs of another state.
8. Promotion of mutual interests and cooperation through multilateralism in international politics.
9. Refraining from acts or threats of aggression against the territorial integrity or political independence of any country.
10. Respect for justice and international obligations.

Evolution of the Functions of NAM

The functions and objectives of NAM evolved with time from the time of its inception till the present day according to the changing international politics. The evolution of NAM can be traced across three different stages: the early Cold War era, later Cold War era (1970s and 1980s) and the post–Cold War era (since 1991).

Early Cold War Era

Against Apartheid: The prevalent practice of institutionalised racial segregation in Africa was known as the Apartheid. It was raised as an important issue in the first NAM conference, which called for the end of Apartheid. In the second conference at Cairo, the government of South Africa was warned against the continuation of the practice.

Disarmament: The NAM raised its voice on multiple occasions for the maintenance of peace, the cessation of arms race and the peaceful coexistence of all states. In the UNGA, India submitted a draft resolution saying that the use of nuclear weapons should be declared as a crime against humanity and should therefore be prohibited.

UNSC Reforms: NAM has, since its inception, argued for reforms of the UNSC and has opposed the domination of the US and the USSR in the Council. It contended for greater representation of the Third World countries to make the organisation more democratic.

Mediation between Belligerents Nations: NAM called for justice and peace and mediated among belligerents nations. An important instance is of India's intervention in the Korean Crisis where Nehru's role was regarded significant in re-establishment of peace in the region.

Later Cold War Era

By 1960, most of the nations belonging to the Global South became independent. Therefore, they became free politically and administratively. But economically, financially and technically, they were still dependent on the Global North. This technical, financial and economic subordination is referred to as neo-colonialism. NAM, in its second phase, fought against this neo-colonialism.

Economic issues gained primacy in this phase of NAM politics as opposed to the socio-political concerns characteristic of the period of its origin. At the **Algiers Summit in 1973**, the NAM members raised the issue of the creation of a **New International Economic Order (NIEO)**. The NIEO is a set of proposals advocated by developing countries to end economic colonialism and economic dependency through the establishment of a new interdependent economy. As part of the proposals, the NAM also demanded an international bank for developing countries as well as the construction of a 'New Information Order'. At the 1976 Colombo Conference, India proposed the creation of a Third World Bank to provide economic assistance to developing countries.

The US, however, criticised NAM for being biased towards the USSR since majority of the non-aligned countries had socialist governments. The US saw the NAM as an extension of the Socialist Bloc.

In 1977, the Janata Party government called for *genuine non-alignment*. According to the Janata Party, the Indian foreign policy leaned in favour of communism. Janata Party sought to have equal distance from the two superpowers and emphasised on improving relations with the US. A new arena of the Cold War emerged with the Soviet Union intervening in Afghanistan in 1979. The Indian government's attempt to have a better relationship with the US failed. The Janata Party government was the first non-Congress government in the Union rule to uphold the Non-Aligned Policy.

In the NAM summit held at Havana, Cuba in 1979, Cuba propounded the notion of a 'natural ally'. But India refused to accept this notion because it did not support the Soviet Union's intervention in Afghanistan. India supported the unity, integrity and sovereignty of Afghanistan. However, according to Cuba, the socialist bloc led by the Soviet Union is a natural ally of the Global South because the socialist bloc and the developing nations are fighting against the same problems like imperialism and colonialism.

The **7th NAM Summit**, in **New Delhi, 1983**, was the first to be held in India.. The Non-Aligned Conference was scheduled to be held in Baghdad in 1982, but it was instead held in New Delhi in 1983 due to the war between Iran and Iraq. India effectively supported the New International Economic Order at this conference.

Post-Cold War Era

After the end of the Cold War, the Non-Aligned Movement felt the necessity to redefine itself and reinvent its purpose and objectives in the new world order. Its original ideologies at the time of its foundation, namely national independence, territorial integrity, and the fight against colonialism and imperialism, were no longer as applicable in the post–Cold War world. NAM now emphasised on its principles of multilateralism, equality, and mutual non-aggression while continuing to remain a voice for the Global South. It also took up the responsibility to promote the requirements of the member-nations at the global arena and strengthen their political leverage so that they are not exploited by the developed nations. The Non-Aligned Movement has identified economic underdevelopment, poverty, and social injustices as the most common threats to peace and security that NAM must fight against.

The 18th NAM summit was held in Azerbaijan in 2019. The 19th summit is scheduled to take place in 2024 in Uganda.

Contribution of NAM

1. NAM de-escalated the conflict and distrust present during the Cold War between the USA and the USSR.
2. NAM strengthened the UN because the members of NAM supported the basic ideals of the UN, which is non-intervention, multilateralism and respecting the sovereignty of other states.
3. The members of NAM spoke against nuclear proliferation and opposed the arms race that existed during the Cold War.
4. NAM demanded economic equality in form of the New International Economic Order (NIEO).
5. A demand for a New International Information Order was also raised by NAM because the developed world has controlled almost all the means of information and spread their own propaganda.
6. During the Iran summit of NAM in 2012, NAM declared that each and every sovereign state has a peaceful right to develop nuclear energy and opposed the sanction imposed over Iran. According to them, since Iran is a signatory of the NPT, sanction over Iran is unjustified.
7. During the COVID-19 crisis, members of NAM collectively worked for coordination among the Global South to provide better healthcare facilities.

Relevance of NAM

Strategic Autonomy: A report titled 'Non Alignment 2.0: A Foreign and Strategic Policy for India in the 21st Century', authored by renowned analysts and policy makers like Sunil Khilnani,

Rajiv Kumar, Pratap Bhanu Mehta, Prakash Menon, Nandan Nilekani, Srinath Raghavan, Shyam Saran and Siddharth Varadarajan in 2012, re-emphasised the significance of NAM for India and its foreign policy for the next decade. In the report, the relevance of this grouping is proved on the basis of strategic autonomy. NAM emphasises on adopting independent and autonomous foreign policy. NAM as a movement may have become irrelevant, but the idea of autonomous foreign policy is still relevant. Strategic autonomy implies that a nation will not be subordinate to any of the major powers and instead adopt an independent foreign policy.

Strategic Influence: C. Raja Mohan on the other hand does not believe in the principle of strategic autonomy. He is of the opinion that if India is to become a major power, it would want to increase its influence across the world, in partnership with other major powers. India is now a part of **QUAD,** which is a quadrilateral cooperation over strategic security issues with the **United States of America, Japan, and Australia**. Raja Mohan believes that NAM has a limited the utility for India's foreign policy as India does not get the support it needs from the members of NAM when it comes to major issues such as cross-border terrorism.

Recently, the Indian PM hosted a video conference addressing a summit of the non-aligned nations. This shows India's efforts at promoting global cooperation to fight against emerging issues such as the COVID-19 pandemic. In the domain of foreign policy, this meeting holds great significance given the fact that the Indian PM had not attended the previous two NAM summits, held at Venezuela in 2016 and Azerbaijan in 2019 respectively.

INDIA'S NUCLEAR POLICY

The first prime minister of India, Jawaharlal Nehru, opposed the use of nuclear weapons and was in favour of a *nuclear weapons-free world*. The Indian Atomic Energy Commission was established in August 1948 with Homi Bhabha as the Secretary. Nehru wanted to build a peaceful nuclear energy programme for the economic and technical development of the nation. He also opposed nuclear proliferation and it was he who made one of the first calls for a ban on nuclear tests, in a speech in 1954, by proposing a 'standstill agreement' on nuclear testing. He submitted his proposal for a Comprehensive Nuclear-Test Ban Treaty (CTBT) to the United Nations Disarmament Commission in July 1954 as a step towards disarmament.

Although in the early years after Independence India envisioned a nuclear weapons-free world, *growing security concerns* because of India's hostile relations with its neighbours India and Pakistan led to changes in foreign policy. After the Sino-Indian War of 1962, when China conducted nuclear tests in 1964, India realised the need to strengthen its security. In 1974, India conducted a **peaceful nuclear explosion at Pokhran (Operation Smiling Buddha)**, and this proved India's capability of developing nuclear power. India rejected the Nuclear Non-Proliferation Treaty (NPT) in 1968 and till date has refused to sign it.

The Nuclear Non-Proliferation Treaty (NPT)

The Treaty on Non-Proliferation of Nuclear Weapons is an international treaty with an objective to limit the escalation of a nuclear arms race and the technology related to it. Further goals of the treaty include the promotion of cooperation among countries, encouraging the peaceful use of nuclear energy and achieving complete nuclear disarmament.

The Treaty was opened for signing in 1968 and came into effect in 1970. The NPT prohibits nations which do not have nuclear weapons from acquiring them, and at the same time, prohibs the nuclear states from helping others in acquiring nuclear weapons.

As stated earlier, there are five nuclear weapon states under the NPT, namely the USA, Russia,

China, Britain, and France. These are nations that acquired nuclear weapons before 1 January 1967. Apart from the P5, four other states possess nuclear weapons, namely India, Pakistan, Israel and North Korea. They are perceived as violators and are not designated the status of nuclear weapon states.

The treaty stipulates that the N5 or Nuclear Five states are required to share nuclear technology and resources with the non-nuclear weapon states, but only for peaceful purposes. However, for the operationalisation of this transfer, the non-nuclear weapon states are required to sign the NPT.

According to the provision of the treaty, there will be periodical review of the NPT regime every five years. The NPT was extended indefinitely in 1995.

The NPT also provides for the creation of a nuclear weapon-free zone. As of 2016, there are five such regional treaties in place in populated areas of the world: Latin America and the Caribbean, Africa, Central Asia, Southeast Asia, and the South Pacific.

In addition, Mongolia has been given the status of a nuclear-free territory by the UNGA. Antarctica and outer-space are also considered as nuclear-free regions.

Criticism of NPT and India's Objections

Non-Nuclear Weapon States (NNWS) perceive the NPT as a discriminatory treaty as it focuses on preventing only horizontal proliferation while there is no limit on vertical proliferation. Vertical proliferation refers to the advancement or modernisation of a state's existing nuclear arsenal. Horizontal proliferation on the other hand refers to the direct or indirect transfer of nuclear weapons from one state to another. Therefore, although the NPT focuses on non-proliferation, it fails to include the objective of disarmament.

India too has always considered the NPT as discriminatory and has therefore refused to sign it. The international treaties aimed at non-proliferation are opposed by India as they are only selectively applicable to the non-nuclear powers. These treaties also legitimise the monopoly of the five nuclear weapon states, resulting in an exacerbation of the security dilemma of the NNWS.

India has strongly vocalised its demands for comprehensive nuclear disarmament instead of just non-proliferation. International law recognises all states as equal and sovereign in their own right. Therefore, India's position is that the NPT which compartmentalises states into NWS and NNWS and discriminates between them needs to be repealed.

India's First Nuclear Test: A Peaceful Explosion

India's nuclear explosion of 1974, known as Pokhran-I, was India's first successful nuclear bomb test. It was seen as contradictory to India's support for a nuclear-weapons-free world. However, the then PM Indira Gandhi dubbed it as a 'Peaceful Nuclear Explosion' (PNE). The Indian nuclear programme had received technical and economic assistance initially from the US and Canada; however, as discussed earlier, their support was withdrawn after Pokhran I and sanctions imposed on India. However, India received both diplomatic and technical support from the USSR in this context.

India's Nuclear Policy in the Post–Cold War Era

The Soviet Union disintegrated in 1991, marking the end of the Cold War, and this had a considerable effect on India. India was heavily dependent on the Soviet Union for its security. USA thus became the leader of the post–Cold War unipolar world and insisted on nuclear non-proliferation. But India continued to face the same security threats from China and Pakistan, since China was a nuclear weapon state and Pakistan developed nuclear weapons covertly. It is because of these reasons that India refused to sign the NPT and CTBT and decided to continue conducting nuclear tests.

India initiated **Operation Shakti (Pokhran-II)** and **5** nuclear detonations were carried out between 11 and 13 May 1998. India, while setting the objective of this nuclear test, said that it was for the purpose of *minimum nuclear deterrence*. In this regard, this nuclear test was different from the nuclear test of 1974, which had as its goal the development of nuclear technology.

According to C. Raja Mohan, the nuclear testing in 1998 resulted in a leap forward in Indian foreign policy as India decided to adopt the principle of *credible minimum nuclear deterrence*. In spite of India possessing nuclear power, it is not recognised as a **Nuclear Weapons State** (NWS) according to NPT as only states which tested nuclear weapons before 1 January 1968 are recognised as nuclear weapon states. India is not willing to sign the NPT as in that case, the **International Atomic Energy Agency (IAEA)** would inspect the nuclear facilities of India and India will be under IAEA regulations. This might hamper India's nuclear research programme at put it at a disadvantage with regard to its neighbours, China and Pakistan. Raja Mohan is of the opinion that there is no harm in signing the NPT if India is declared a nuclear weapon state.

The Comprehensive Nuclear-Test Ban Treaty

The CTBT is one of the most important contemporary disarmament regimes which has been widely criticised for its discriminatory provision. It was signed in 1996, but has not yet entered into force. It prohibits the testing of nuclear weapons for both civil and military purposes and in all environments. As per the treaty, each state party undertakes the resolution not to carry out any nuclear weapon test explosion and to refrain from carrying out any nuclear tests.

Entry into force is an essential feature of CTBT, which means all the 44 states (as listed in Annexe 2 of the document) having nuclear research facilities will have to sign the CTBT for the treaty to enter into force. As of August 2011, 36 of these states have ratified the Treaty. Eight states still need to do so: China, North Korea, Egypt, India, Iran, Israel, Pakistan and the US. A review of the Treaty can be done within 10 years of implementation of the treaty and a conference can be convened for this purpose.

The CTBT Organization promotes the Treaty and has established a verification regime to monitor adherence to the Treaty. It is headquartered in Vienna. The verification regimes comprise the International Monitoring System (IMS) and the International Data Centre (IDC).

India's Objection to CTBT

India stressed on the importance of both disarmament and nuclear non-proliferation, only the latter of which is incorporated within the CTBT. According to India, the implementation of CTBT has to start with the disarmament of nuclear arsenals of the N5, who are aiming towards vertical proliferation by developing computer-simulation techniques. Technologically, CTBT is flawed because it cannot prevent the nuclear development of P5 (Permanent Five) as they have already made progress using computer simulation techniques. This technique has enhanced their capability of conducting virtual tests and of modifying and developing their weapons with greater precision. Moreover, compared to the few tests conducted by India, the major powers have conducted a large number of tests, for example, the USA has already conducted more than a thousand nuclear tests. According to UN data, the following are the number of tests that each of the major powers have conducted between 1945 and 1996, when the CTBT was opened for signature:

1. USA - 1032
2. Russia - 715
3. UK - 45
4. France - 210
5. China - 45

Moreover, the domain of CTBT was further extended to include limits on fissile materials and missile technology. This does not take into consideration the fact that nuclear tests may be essential in days to come for furthering *nuclear research* for reasons other than developing weapons. The CTBT is also against the transfer of technology which will hamper the technological and scientific development of developing countries like India.

India's stand on the nuclear issue is clear in that it proposes the complete abolition of nuclear weapons, also known as disarmament. But treaties like NPT and CTBT aim for nuclear non-proliferation and not complete disarmament. Therefore, India has contended that CTBT is not aiming for a nuclear-free world and has thus refused to sign it. Rather, CTBT is directed against Threshold Countries like India, Pakistan and Israel. The Entry into Force clause is also perceived as impinging on the sovereignty of nation-states.

India's Nuclear Doctrine

1. **No First Use Policy:** Soon after the nuclear tests of 1998, in August 1999, the National Security Advisory Board released a draft of the Indian Nuclear Doctrine. It declared a nuclear *No First Use policy*, meaning that India will not attack any non-nuclear-weapon state with nuclear weapons except for retaliation to a first strike. It was amended in 2003 to include a clause that in case of an attack of chemical or biological weapons, in retaliation India may use nuclear weapons. It acknowledges that a nuclear war between two nuclear powers can result in major and disastrous losses for both sides and so the No First Use policy is the most appropriate.
2. **Credible Minimum Deterrent:** The doctrine also proposed building and maintaining a **credible minimum deterrent**. This refers to the quantity of nuclear forces that India needs to possess to deter potential nuclear adversaries. The doctrine however does not quantify the minimum deterrent. It supports the development and maintenance of weapons for the purpose of deterrence and not attack. The doctrine says that India will continue with nuclear research as deterrence requires effective intelligence and early-warning capabilities. Nuclear forces must be operationally prepared at all time. To develop the capacity of deterrence, India must build a highly effective military system comprising of the three wings of the military (forming a *nuclear triad*): the Army, the Air Force and the Navy. Emphasis was also provided on missile development for the purpose of deterrence. Importance will be given to manufacture as well as storage of nuclear weapons, so that they are not lost, harmed or placed in the hands of an unauthorised body. Adequate arrangements will be made to avoid nuclear accidents and effective planning will be done for disaster management. In the year 2018, the term 'minimum' was removed from the new defence policy.
3. **Civilian Control**: A 3-tier Nuclear Command Authority was formed to manage the nation's nuclear weapons. The NCA comprises a Political Council and an Executive Council. The Political Council is chaired by the Prime Minister. It is the only body that can authorise the use of nuclear weapons. The Executive Council is chaired by the National Security Advisor and includes the chiefs of defence services as well as the Cabinet Committee on Security (CCS). It provides inputs for decision making by the NCA and executes the directives given to it by the Political Council. Thus, the control of nuclear weapons is put under civilian authority and not under the armed forces.

Global non-discriminatory nuclear disarmament is India's primary objective. India supports the idea of a *nuclear-free world*. While possession of nuclear weapons is considered essential for Indian security, in view of the lethal nature of nuclear weapons, confidence-building measures must be adopted so that potential danger of nuclear warfare can be minimised.

India's Nuclear Triad

India has a three-pronged military force structure consisting of land-launched nuclear missiles, nuclear-missile-armed submarines, and strategic aircraft with nuclear bombs and missiles. The tri-service theatre command called the **Strategic Forces Command (SFC)** is a part of India's Nuclear Command Authority (NCA). In India's nuclear arsenal, the 5,000-km range **Agni-V** intercontinental ballistic missile has been inducted, which brings the whole of Asia and China as well parts of Europe and Africa within its strike envelope. Similarly, the new **Rafale** jets have boosted the existing 'air vector' for delivery of nuclear gravity bombs. While India has robust land-based and air-launched weapons, its sea-based weapons are not as developed. India currently has only one Ballistic Missile Submarine (**SSBN**) that is **INS Arihant**, which has 750-km range K-15 nuclear missiles. In comparison, countries like the US, Russia and China have SSBNs with well over 5,000-km range missiles. India, however, has three more SSBNs under development.

Multilateral Export Control Regimes

A multilateral export control regime is an informal group of like-minded supplier countries who want to contribute to the non-proliferation of weapons of mass destruction through implementation of guidelines at the national level and control lists for exports. These regimes have a variety of provisions to prohibit nuclear non-proliferation as well as the proliferation of missiles and other arms. The following are some of the important regimes:

(1) **The Wassenaar Arrangement**

The agreement aims to and the spread of dual technology.

The Wassenaar Arrangement on Export Controls for Conventional Arms and Dual-Use Goods and Technologies is a comprehensive Multilateral Export Control Regime. It is a voluntary and non-binding agreement created by the major supplier countries that have agreed to cooperate in their effort to prevent and regulate the transfer of certain military and dual-use technologies and curb the export of conventional weapons. It was established in 1996 in Wassenaar, the Netherlands, and has 42 participating countries as of 2017. India was included in the Wassenaar Arrangement on December 2017. India is the 42nd country to be included in this arrangement.

(2) **The Missile Technology Control Regime (MTCR)**

The MTCR is an informal political agreement, with voluntary participation of 35 member countries, which is aimed at controlling the technological proliferation of missiles and unmanned aerial vehicles technology. It was founded in 1987, with the founding countries such as Canada, France, Germany, Italy, Japan, the UK and the United States.

India's membership: India gained membership of this group in June 2016. It was the first time since the 1998 nuclear tests that India became a member of a nuclear non-proliferation group. Following China's opposition to India's membership in the Nuclear Suppliers Group (NSG), India's MTCR membership can be seen as a significant event. It must be noted that China is not a member of MTCR. India, through its membership, gains access to better technology from the other countries of this group. However, in 1992, because of the opposition of the US, MTCR blocked the transfer of cryogenic engine technology meant for space rockets by Russia to India, fearing it could be used for missile technology. India thus was forced to develop its own cryogenic engines. Later in 2005, the US labelled India as a 'responsible state' with regards to nuclear behaviour. It must be noted that the MTCR is an informal understanding and not an official treaty so there is no legally binding clause that the members of the group will not transfer missile technology to other countries. Moreover, no distinction has been made between member countries and non-member countries in the MTCR. It is debatable whether India will actually benefit from the membership to this group.

(3) **The Australia Group**

In 1985, the Australian group was formed as a reaction to Iraq's use of chemical weapons in 1984. The aim of this group is to control the spread of chemical and biological weapons and identify the countries that export it. It currently has 43 members, including 27 members of the European Union. India became a member of the group in 2018.

(4) **Nuclear Suppliers Group**

The Nuclear Suppliers Group (NSG), popularly known as the London Club, is a transnational body comprising nuclear supplier countries that aim to control the proliferation of nuclear weapons by curbing the export of nuclear weapons development materials and related technology. It also seeks to improve the prevailing safeguards on existing nuclear materials. It was established in the year 1975 following India's nuclear test in 1974. As of 2023, NSG has 48 members. It must be noted that India is not a member of this group.

NSG provisions state that countries which have signed the NPT will be the only ones to be provided with nuclear fuel and technology. India has been given a special waiver in that it is the only country which, even without signing the NPT, trades in nuclear fuel from the NSG. This exemption was obtained after the Indo-American Civil Nuclear Agreement in 2008. While it may be beneficial for India to obtain membership of the NSG—this would end its isolation from the international nuclear trade as well as gain recognition as a responsible state—there are obstacles to its membership.

Obstacles in membership: The decision of NSG's membership is taken by consensus and China is a staunch opponent of India's membership. Apart from China, countries like Switzerland, Austria and Ireland are also opposed to India's membership as they believe that nuclear non-proliferation will be weakened if India becomes a member of the group.

3

INDIA'S RELATIONS WITH THE MAJOR POWERS

KEYWORDS

Relations with USA, USSR/Russia, and People's Republic of China

INDIA AND USA

The United States is a superpower that determines the world order in the contemporary world. It is considered to be the biggest economic as well as military power in present-day international politics.

The Cold War Period

Since the US is a democratic, liberal country like India, common democratic values strengthened the relations between the two countries. However, **Indo-American relations during the Cold War turned adverse** due to the following reasons:

1. India adopted principles and policies so that the public sector would occupy the 'commanding heights' of the economy, while America adopted the capitalist model of economic development.
2. America supported Pakistan on the Kashmir issue and not India.
3. America did not have a positive view of India's non-aligned foreign policy.
4. The US viewed India's improved relations with the Soviet Union with suspicion.
5. Further, when in 1961 India's campaign to liberate Goa from the Portuguese began, America supported Portugal which was a member of NATO and thus had friendly relations with the US.

Despite the above differences, there were some areas of *convergence of interests* between India and America for a brief period in the 1960s. In 1962, America provided full support to India in the Indo-China war including military assistance. But this cordial relationship did not prove to be very far-reaching as when the Indo-Pakistan War of 1965 began, America held both India and Pakistan to be equally responsible for the war and imposed restrictions on economic and military aid to India.

Indo-US **relations worsened once again in the 1970s**. Significant changes took place in world politics in the early 1970s and the relations between America and China improved. The Indo–Soviet Treaty of Peace, Friendship and Cooperation was signed between India and the Soviet Union in 1971 and due to this, relations between India and America became bitter. America, China and

Pakistan subsequently adopted an anti-India orientation and when in the same year, a war began between India and Pakistan, America assisted Pakistan by sending its seventh fleet to the Bay of Bengal against India.

In 1974, India conducted a peaceful nuclear test, which was strongly criticised by the US which then imposed sanctions on India in nuclear and technical fields. America used Pakistan's status as a frontline state to counter the Soviet Union. The US provided huge economic and military aid to Pakistan, which the latter covertly used against India. Due to India's friendship with the Soviet Union, Indo-American relations remained tense. Indira Gandhi's government in the early 1980s adopted an anti-America approach.

The Post–Cold War Period

In the post–Cold War period, India–USA relations improved due to various factors. India opted for a liberal economic model and consequently emerged as an attractive global market. The rise of China as a major power is USA's biggest threat. As China's neighbour, India shares the same threat. This shared threat coupled with common democratic values further strengthened the Indo-USA bond. America recognised India as a big market and considered it an important ally to counter the powerful rise of China. The presence of a large and powerful Indian **diaspora** in the USA also contributes to the maintenance of cordial relations between India and the USA. In **September 2001**, there was a major terrorist attack on the World Trade Center in America, and more than 2,000 people were killed. Post 9/11, terrorism too became a common security threat for both India and the US, which further deepened the **friendly relations** between the two nations. US foreign policy began the *war on terror* and India fully cooperated with America to counter terrorism. Following this, America began gradually lifting the sanctions imposed on India. US President Bill Clinton was supposed to visit India in 1998, but the visit was postponed due to the nuclear tests India conducted that year. Clinton finally visited India in 2000, resulting in a further improvement of Indo-US relations.

In 2003, the then Indian Prime Minister Atal Bihari Vajpayee, in a speech before the Asia Society, New York said that India and America are *natural allies*. The Bush administration considered the relationship between India and America to have taken a decisive turn in the post-Cold War world. According to America's Assistant Secretary of State for South Asia Affairs, Christina Roca, there had never been a more cordial relationship between India and America since India's Independence.

In September 2014, Prime Minister Narendra Modi paid a five-day visit to America. Following this visit, US President Barack Obama was appointed as the chief guest for the 66th Indian Republic Day as a reflection of the growing confidence in Indo-US ties.

Economic Cooperation between US and India

India is the fastest growing service sector in the world and is among the 10 largest markets. In the post–Cold War world, the Narasimha Rao government by adopting the policy of economic liberalisation laid the basis for a qualitative change in India–US relations.

There are several challenges however. Exports from developing countries like India are banned or restricted in various ways under US trade policies such as the Super-301, an amendment of section 301 of the Trade Act of 1974 intended to solve problems of the US bilateral trade deficits. It prohibits exports that promote unfair trade and harm US trade. Exports are also restricted on the basis of environmental standards as well as in cases where child labour or other illegal forms of labour have been used. There has also been a controversy regarding the implementation of a special safeguard mechanism against import of cheap American agricultural products. During the economic recession, the US administration also tried to restrict outsourcing businesses to India.

Indo-American Strategic Relations

Since 2004, Indo-US strategic relations have seen a steady development as the US began supplying defense equipment to India. The diplomatic initiative **Next Steps in Strategic Partnership** (NSSP) was jointly announced by the two countries in 2004. The **Civil Nuclear Cooperation Initiative** was signed between India and the US in the year 2005, as an example of a decisive change in the relationship between the two countries. This is not only an agreement in the field of energy between the two countries, but it is a testimony to the improving strategic relationship between them.

In 2005, a new **Defence Framework Agreement** was signed between India and America. Some of the important elements of this agreement are as follows:

(i) Defence Technology and Trade Initiative (DTTI)
(ii) Exchange of logistic support facilities
(iii) Joint development and manufacture of defense equipment and technology

Under this agreement, the Defense Procurement and Production Group was established and a Joint Working Group was instituted whose work was to be overseen by the Defense Policy Group and its subgroups (the Defense Procurement and Production Group, the Joint Technical Group, the Military Cooperation Group, and the Senior Technology Security Group).

India has one of the strongest defences in the world. As of 2022, India has a military spending of $76.6 billion which is the third highest in the world. A report published by SIPRI (Stockholm International Peace Research Institute) presents the military expenditure of different regions of the world between 1988 and 2021, as shown in the graph below.

Figure 6.3.1: World Military Expenditure, by Region, 1988–2021

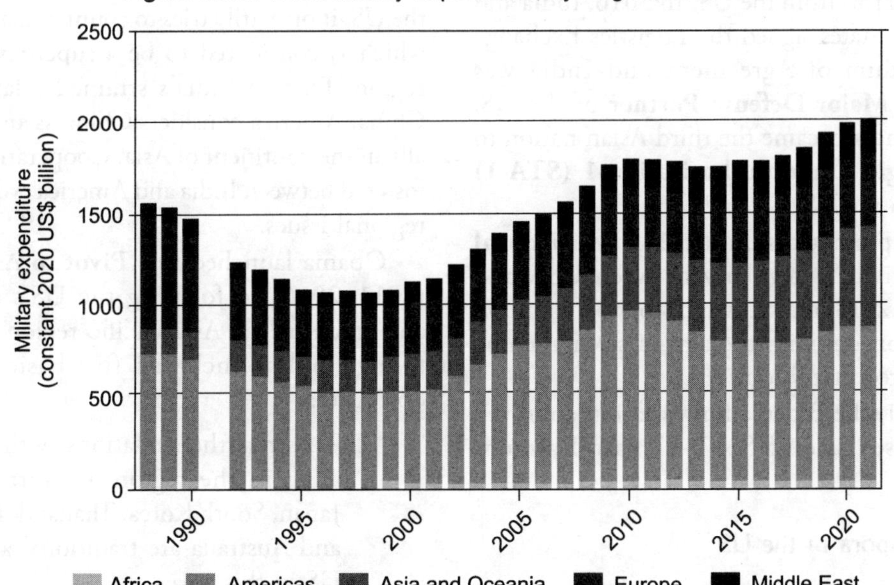

At present, India imports a considerable quantity of defense material from America, a nation with very developed defense technology. American aircraft such as Hercules, Globemaster, Romeo and Apache are bought by India for the purpose of strengthening its defence. In order to give priority to defence relations, an agreement was signed between the two countries in 2009 called the **End-Use Monitoring Agreement (EUMA)**. This allowed the US to periodically carry out an inspection and take inventory of all articles transferred to India, while allowing India to determine the place of inspection. It stipulates that defence equipment exported by the US will not be sold to any other country without prior permission of the US.

In 2015, during the second visit of US President Barack Obama to India, significant progress was made in the series of **Modi-Obama** talks where both countries agreed to renew the Defense Framework Agreement for another 10 years. This included a commitment to continue joint military exercises, exchange of intelligence and maritime security, and transfer of technology from the US for the production of defense equipment for India.

India, which is the world's third largest military spender after US and China, purchases most of its arms from the US. In 2016, India and the United States signed the Logistics Exchange Memorandum of Agreement and India was declared a **Major Defense Partner** of the US. In 2018, India became the third Asian nation to get **Strategic Trade Authorisation-1 (STA-1)** status from the US.

The diplomatic summit **2+2 Ministerial Dialogue** is held regularly between USA and India since 2018 to discuss and work on common issues of concern with the aim of strengthening India–United States relations.

In 2021, the Biden administration approved the proposed sale of Six P-8I Patrol aircraft to India.

Indian Diaspora in the US

People of Indian origin in the USA make a significant contribution towards deepening India–American relations. People-to-people ties are very important in strengthening diplomatic ties. According to the US embassy, in 2019, 15 million Indian visitors travelled to the United States, and Americans are now the second-largest group of foreign citizens visiting India. The people of Indian origin living in America (approximately 4.5 million) are highly educated and affluent, and roughly one-third of all immigrant-founded start-ups in the United States have founders who are of Indian origin. People of Indian origin thus have an enormous influence in US foreign policy. In 2019, a community summit called Howdy Modi was hosted by Texas India Forum (TIF), an Indian diasporic group in the US.

America, the world's oldest democracy, and India, the largest democracy, are thus *natural allies*. Since the two nations share common democratic values, the relations between them are friendly also on an ideological basis.

US Relations with the Asia-Pacific Region

The Asia-Pacific region is a priority in US foreign policy as it is an emerging economic region. While West Asia and South Asia are also important to the US, it primarily tries to counterbalance China, which is considered to be a superpower in this region. Due to India's strained relations with China, America considers China as an important ally in the continent of Asia. Cooperation is being fostered between India and America even on many regional issues.

Obama launched the **'Pivot to Asia' Policy** (2011–2016) to focusing the US's diplomacy and trade in the Asia-Pacific region. This new foreign policy included five basic pillars or objectives:

(i) To strengthen relations with America's allies in the region. Countries such as Japan, South Korea, Thailand, Philippines and Australia are traditional allies of the US in this area.

(ii) To strengthen relations with the newly emerging powers in the region. US designated India as an important emerging power and its relationship with India as the most defining partnership of the twenty-first century.

(iii) To build a constructive relationship with China. According to the US, it will welcome China, but will not hesitate to protect its own interests.

(iv) To strengthen the regional organisations of the region. One of the things the policy focused on was making ASEAN more dynamic.

(v) To promote economic relations with Asian countries and to improve relations with trans-Pacific countries so that a shared prosperity can be sustained. In this regard, the Pivot Asia Policy is not just a policy of military rebalancing.

Relations with the Indo-Pacific Region

India is a major power in the Asia-Pacific region, yet it was not allowed to join the Asia-Pacific Economic Cooperation or APEC. APEC is a major component in US ties with the Asia Pacific region but it excluded India for various reasons, including China's opposition and the fact that India does not border the Pacific Ocean, which all current members do.

According to Indrani Bagchi, a diplomatic editor, there are six interlocking layers to India's foreign policy regarding the Indo-Pacific region:

(i) Development of a blue economy that integrates and builds mutual prosperity. In 2015, PM Modi announced the policy called Security and Growth for All in the Region (SAGAR), which is India's doctrine of maritime cooperation in the Indian Ocean region.

(ii) Enhancing naval capabilities and building interoperable defense relationships

(iii) Building infrastructure and connectivity linkages

(iv) Informal alliances and grouping on security and humanitarian platforms

(v) Strengthening ASEAN

(vi) Reinforcing Indian cultural and religious links that form a common bond throughout the region.

Through this policy, India wants to expand its *strategic, economic and cultural reach* to the Red Sea and the Pacific.

Initially, the Modi government tried to balance India's relationship with both China and the USA by attempting to improve ties with China. For this reason, India organised informal summits with China such as the **Mamallapuram Summit** (2019) and participated in the **Wuhan Informal Summit** (2018). Although India tried to build a cordial relation with China, the Galwan clash in 2020–2021 changed India's approach as it decided to strengthen its partnership with the USA without taking note of China's concerns. To this end, India signed three foundational strategic agreements with the USA: LEMOA, BECA and COMCASA.

1. **Logistics Exchange Memorandum of Agreement (LEMOA)**

   LEMOA was the first of the three pacts signed in August 2016. LEMOA allows the American and Indian militaries to replenish each other's bases, and access supplies, spare parts and services from each other's land facilities, air bases, and ports, which can then be reimbursed. LEMOA is very useful for India–US **Navy-to-Navy cooperation**, since the two countries cooperate closely in the Indo-Pacific region.

2. **Basic Exchange and Cooperation Agreement (BECA)**

   BECA allows India to get real-time access to US geospatial intelligence that would help enhance the accuracy of automated systems and weapons like missiles and armed drones. Through the exchange of information on maps and satellite images, it allows India access to topographical and aeronautical data as well as advanced navigation and targeting products. Besides the sailing of ships, flying of aircraft, fighting of wars, and location of targets, geospatial intelligence is also critical to the response to natural disasters. The signing of BECA stemmed from the commitment in the joint statement during President Donald Trump's visit to India in February 2020.

3. **Communications Compatibility and Security Agreement (COMCASA)**
   COMCASA was signed in September 2018, after the first 2+2 dialogue during which then External Affairs Minister Sushma Swaraj and then Defence Minister Nirmala Sitharaman met the visiting Secretary of State Michael R. Pompeo and then Secretary of Defence James N. Mattis. The COMCASA allows the US to provide India with its encrypted communications equipment and systems so that Indian and US military commanders, and the aircraft and ships of the two countries, can communicate through secure networks during times of both peace and war. The signing of COMCASA paved the way for the transfer of communication security equipment from the US to India to facilitate 'interoperability' between their forces and potentially with other militaries that use US-origin systems for secure data links.

Relations with the South Asia Region

During the Cold War, Pakistan occupied a central position in the US's foreign policy. However, post Cold War, the USA changed its policy and made India a closer ally. Pakistan on the other hand has formed strategic ties with China. The US prefers India as an ally as it is a strong emerging market and an effective instrument to counter-balance China's power.

That the US prefers an allyship with India to one with Pakistan is evident from its foreign policies. The US signed the **Civil Nuclear Cooperation Initiative** with India, but not with Pakistan. The US now supports India in the Kashmir issue. It also backs India's claim for membership in the **Nuclear Suppliers Group** as well as its demand for permanent membership in the **Security Council**. The USA prefers a 'de-hyphenated policy', that is, a delinking of India and Pakistan in its foreign policy by building relations with India and relations with Pakistan separately rather than a singular India-Pakistan approach. For maintaining stability in Afghanistan, the role of Pakistan remains vital in US foreign policy.

Relations with the West Asia Region

The West Asia region is a major source of energy supply for the world. The US plays the role of a *net security provider* in West Asia due to regional conflicts and small sizes of the nation states in this region. The most important strategic allies of the USA in West Asia are **Israel, Saudi Arabia, UAE, Bahrain and Iraq**. Iran and Syria are the notable adversaries of the USA in the region. USA has supported the regime change in Syria by strengthening its sanctions over Iran.

China, on the other hand, wants to strengthen its strategic partnership with Iran. Russia is aligned with China and stands against any regime change in Syria. The withdrawal of United States troops from Afghanistan in 2021, marking the end of the war on Afghanistan, also put the USA in a challenging position with regard to West Asia.

India's policy towards West Asia is dynamic as of now. India has cultivated strong partnerships with **Israel, Saudi Arabia** and **UAE**. But Indo-Iran relations have been impacted due to the rising hostility between USA and Iran. India has stopped the import of oil from Iran but is unwilling to abandon its project in **Chahbahar**. As India needs US support for countering China, in return USA also expects India's support with respect to Iran. India always favours peaceful resolution of disputes in places such as Palestine, Syria and Iran. While US policies towards East Asia and South Asia are more favourable to India, in case of West Asia, American policies often become a challenge for India.

Difference of Interests in India–US Policies

1. **Threat to Democratic Values in the New World Order**

   The global support for liberal capitalist democracies seems to be declining with the frequency of economic crises. China, Russia and Turkey are adopting autocratic models in lieu of acquiring absolute sovereignty in political as well as international economic issues and for fulfilling their contested national interests. China's imperialist policy is against a rule-based normative world order.

   The theory of '*an uncertain world*' has been propounded by **S. Jaishankar** in his book *The India Way: Strategies for an Uncertain World* (2020). His theory attempts to understand how the global dynamics of diplomacy will evolve in a post-Cold War world characterised by multiple unprecedented developments. The USA, which once espoused an open and globalised liberal capitalist economy, is now adopting *protectionist policies*. US's disinterest has also led to a lack of progress in the negotiations of the Paris Agreement that deals with climate change. Thus India's position in relation to that of the US has also evolved and this is reflected in changes in foreign policy of both nations.

2. **America's Hegemony and Interventionist Policies**

   The US has repeatedly intervened in the Syrian Civil War and supported the movement to remove the **Assad government**. India on the other hand is a supporter of peaceful solutions to the Syrian crisis. Further, the US is trying to tighten sanctions against **Iran** by implementing the **Countering America's Adversaries Through Sanctions Act** (CAATSA), while India is keen to build friendly relations with Iran. On the issue of the Russian invasion of Ukraine, the US strongly opposed Russia whereas India did not. Instead, India adopted a middle path on the Ukraine issue by supporting the unity and integrity of Ukraine but at the same time not condemning Russia. These *interventionist policies* of America have posed a challenge in India-US relations.

3. **Differences on Multilateral Issues**

   There is a clear difference of opinion between the US and India with regard to multilateral issues. The US considers the Food Security Act introduced by India to be contrary to the rules of the World Trade Organization. But India considers it a necessity for poverty alleviation, which is of utmost importance to a developing nation like India. India views it as a social issue which should not be associated with business and trade, and this is opposed by the US.

INDIA AND RUSSIA

Russia is the largest country in the world in terms of area. According to the 2021 census, the population of Russia is about 144.7 million (excluding Crimea and Sevastopol). It is the successor of the former Soviet Union which expanded across both Europe and Asia. Russia has traditionally been a close friend of India. Soviet leader Joseph Stalin had a negative view of the Indian National Congress and Jawaharlal Nehru as he thought of them as supporters of capitalism and tools of the British. Therefore, during his rule from 1924–1953, the relations between India and the Soviet Union were not friendly.

Before and During the Cold War

In 1953, **Nikita Khrushchev** took over as the First Secretary of the Communist Party of the Soviet Union. He, unlike Stalin, did not view India as a supporter of capitalism and instead recognised the principle of *peaceful coexistence*. He approved of India's non-aligned foreign policy and supported India's approach on the Kashmir issue. Friendly relations grew between India and Russia during the period when Khrushchev was in power.

The Soviet Union did not support China during the 1962 Indo-China War, but nor did it support India. The Soviet Union saw this as a war not between socialism and capitalism, but between two independent countries. After the Indo-Pakistan War in 1965, the **Tashkent Agreement** was signed between India and Pakistan through the mediation of the Soviet Union.

In the Cold War period, the two countries grew strategically closer and India became Soviet's most trusted ally. During the Indo-Pakistan War of 1971, the Soviet Union provided India with crucial intelligence and also supported India's claim for permanent membership in the United Nations Security Council. In 1971, a strategic triangle was formed between the **US, China and Pakistan**, following which India entered into a treaty of peace with the Soviet Union to ensure security of the nation. After the 1971 Indo–Soviet Treaty of Peace, Friendship and Cooperation between India and the Soviet Union, there was a qualitative change in relations.

In the 1970s, the Soviet Union also became India's largest trading partner. Both countries strongly supported each other and trade through rupee and rouble flourished. The military intervention in Afghanistan by the Soviet Union in 1979 was not opposed by India. India gradually became dependent on the Soviet Union for the supply of weapons as Soviet weapons were cheap and they never imposed unfavourable conditions on weapons-supply.

The Post–Cold War Period

After the dissolution of the Soviet Union in 1991, India developed relations with the Soviet's successor, Russia. Post 1991, Russia placed significant emphasis on strengthening relations with European countries and America; however, it did not receive the economic aid that it required. Growing US influence led to the expansion of NATO into Eastern Europe. As a result of this as well as America's presence in Central Asia, Russia sought to counterbalance the US by improving relations with India and China. After 1995, Russian foreign policy once again emphasised its relations with India and other Asian countries, which led to a change in its foreign policy which till then had focussed more on the Euro-Atlantic regions.

A new era of strategic relations began when in the **Delhi Declaration of 2000 (Declaration on the India-Russia Strategic Partnership)** it was decided to further strengthen strategic relations between the two countries. Vladimir Putin laid great emphasis on improving relations with India and began an **annual strategic summit** between India and Russia, which has been held every year since 2000.

Friendly relations between Russia and India continue while relations between the US and Russia remain strained. The 2008 Russian attack on Georgia, a country backed by the US, shows that it wants to limit America's presence in the region. Russia has also shown opposition to Georgia and Ukraine's proposed NATO membership.

Military Relationship between India and Russia

In the post–Cold War period, Russia has provided sensitive weapons to India such as INS Vikramaditya, INS Arihant and the S-400 missile. As of 2022, about 70 per cent of India's military equipment is from Russia. The defense relationship between the India and Russia is not just limited to their roles are the buyer and the seller; joint production of weapons is also carried out by the two countries. One such example is the BrahMos missile, a supersonic cruise missile, which was a joint venture resulting from cooperation between India and Russia.

Table 6.3.1: Largest Exporters of Arms to India during 2018–2022

S. No.	*Country*	*Percentage of Total Arms Imported*
1.	Russia	45.1 per cent
2.	France	28.6 per cent
3.	United States	11.1 per cent

Source: Statista Research Department.

Table 6.3.2: World's Largest Arms Exporters during 2018–2022

S. No.	*Country*
1.	United States
2.	Russia
3.	France
4.	China

Source: Stockholm International Peace Research Institute.

Table 6.3.3: World's Largest Arms Importers during 2018–2022

S. No.	*Country*
1.	India
2.	Saudi Arabia
3.	Qatar
4.	Australia
5.	China

Source: Stockholm International Peace Research Institute.

Russia's Support on the Kashmir Issue

The former Soviet Union supported India on the Kashmir issue and considered Kashmir an integral part of India. The Soviet Union exercised its veto power in India's favour on the Kashmir issue in the Security Council, and Russia did the same in the post-Cold War period. Russia also opposed cross-border terrorism in Kashmir and categorically supported India on the Kargil issue in 1999. Russia views the revocation of Article 370 as an internal issue of India and not an international issue. According to Russia, all disputes between India and Pakistan should be resolved through bilateral negotiations such as the Shimla Agreement.

Allyship in the Fight against Terrorism

India and Russia are both countries that are prone to terrorism. For instance, Chechnya, an autonomous region within Russia, has been demanding separation from the state, and there have been terrorist attacks related to this issue. India too faces various kinds of terrorist attacks and has to deal with cases of cross-border terrorism. Russia strongly condemned the Mumbai terrorist attacks that occurred on 26 November 2008. Russia and India are cooperating to counter terrorism in Afghanistan as it affects both Russia (in regard to Chechnya) and India (in regard to Kashmir). In 2017, India and Russia signed an agreement to stop terrorism and to enhance bilateral cooperation in tackling various kinds of terrorism. Both countries oppose the double standards being used to combat terrorism by stating that there are no good or bad terrorists.

Nuclear Cooperation

India and Russia cooperate with each other for civil nuclear energy. The **Kudankulam Nuclear Project** was built in India with Russia's help and support and a proposal for setting up six new reactors with the help of Russia is being considered. Russia is also a major nuclear fuel supplier to India. Some apprehension has been expressed by Russia regarding the Civil Liability for Nuclear Damage Act, 2010 that was passed by the Indian parliament in spite of much debate and controversy. From Russia's viewpoint, the country providing the reactor should not be held liable in the event of a nuclear accident. The controversy over the Nuclear Liability Bill came to an end in 2015 when India announced the provision of an insurance pool for compensation.

Regarding the issue of India's membership in the NSG, while India's bid has been supported by major powers like America, Germany,

France and Japan, China has repeatedly blocked India's membership. China argues that for obtaining membership of the NSG, there must be separate criteria for countries that have not signed the Nuclear Non-Proliferation Treaty (NPT). But China indirectly supports Pakistan's engagement with the NSG, while Russia has supported India's bid for membership.

Bilateral Exchange for Energy Security

Russia is currently emerging as an energy superpower, being one of the largest exporters, while India is a nation dependent on oil imports—it imports 85 per cent of its oil—as it needs a large amount of energy to maintain economic growth. India and Russia are thus natural partners for energy collaboration. A bilateral strategy can help Russia gain access to new markets and at the same time help India meet its energy requirements. Such an arrangement can be a mutually beneficial collaboration between India and Russia.

People-to-People Contact between Russia and India

There have been several cultural initiatives to promote people-to-people contact between India and Russia. Jawaharlal Nehru Cultural Centre (JNCC) was opened as part of the Embassy of India in Moscow in 1989. In 2016, a Memorandum of Understanding and Cooperation was signed for Mahatma Gandhi Chair of Philosophy at the Institute of Philosophy of the Russian Academy of Sciences to encourage the study of Indian philosophy in Russia. Data from 2012 states that Hindi was taught to 1,500 Russian students in about 20 Russian institutions and Russian people have a great interest in Indian dance, music, yoga, and Ayurveda. In 2008, the Year of Russia was celebrated in India was held followed by the Year of India in Russia in 2009. In September 2011, a Festival of Indian Culture was organised in Russia, and several cultural events and academic conferences were organised to celebrate the 150th anniversary of Rabindranath Tagore. The Festival of Russian Culture in India was celebrated in 2012 to mark 65 years of the establishment of diplomatic relations between India and Russia. About 15,000 people of Indian origin reside in Russia and about 4,500 Indian students are studying in Russian medical and technical institutions.

Bilateral Trade between Russia and India

In the Cold War era, there was considerable exchange and trade between India and the Soviet Union, but in the post–Cold War world, bilateral trade between India and Russia has not really taken off. Although strategic ties between India and Russia are strong, bilateral trade is only US$10 billion as of 2019. The trade between the two countries is still limited to 'government-to-government' trade as Indian companies have not given priority to Russia when it comes to trade. India and Russia are aiming to reach US$30 billion in annual bilateral trade by 2025, and even then it is negligible compared to the trade between India and China, India and the US, and India and ASEAN.

India also encouraged the construction of an *international transportation corridor* to reduce the geographical distance between India and Russia. The North–South Transport Corridor is a ship, rail, and road route for moving freight between India, Russia, Iran, Europe and Central Asia.

Shared Visions on Global Issues

Both India and Russia have a similar international outlook as they both support the multipolar world order. The democratisation of the Security Council and India's request for permanent membership in the UN have also always been supported by Russia. Both countries oppose interference in the internal affairs of any state under the pretext of human rights. Both nations agree that terrorism cannot be justified on any grounds and that environmental problems must be solved through the principle of common but differentiated responsibility, that is, all states are responsible for addressing global environmental destruction but industrialised countries of the Global North bear greater responsibility.

Act Far East Policy

Prime Minister Narendra Modi launched the 'Act Far East' policy during his visit to Russia in 2019. As part of this policy, he announced a US$1 billion line of credit for the development of the resource-rich region. It was first visit by an Indian PM to Vladivostok in the Russian Far East region. He asserted that India will walk shoulder-to-shoulder with Russia in its development of the Far East. This allows Russia an opportunity to diversify from China since it is worried about the growing presence of China in its Far East.

Pragmatic Relations between the Major Powers

- **Russia-China**
  Relations between India and Russia are warm and friendly, but the basis of the relationship between the two countries is now mutual and realistic and is fully motivated by national interests. India is no longer dependent on Russia for weapons as it now purchases weapons also from America, France and Israel, because it is not in the national interest for any country to depend on a single source for the supply of arms. Similarly, weapons are being provided to China by Russia which was earlier provided only to India. China in turn provides these weapons to Pakistan. Russia has also indicated military aid to Pakistan in 2015. An agreement has also been signed between Russia and China to lay down an oil pipeline.
- **Russia–America**
  In 2017, the US Congress passed the Countering America's Adversaries Through Sanctions Act (CAATSA), which imposed new sanctions on Iran, Russia, and North Korea. USA–Russian relations have become more hostile now due to the Ukraine crisis. Differing viewpoints regarding democracy and human rights are also points of contention between the two nations. USA is a strong critic of Russian human rights violations. While USA supports liberal democratic values, Putin wants to become a life-long president. To this effect, he signed a law which may allow him to stay in power till 2036 as President of Russia. Putin also stated that he would not accept the values of Western countries. Due to these reasons, the conflict between Russia and America has grown manifold.

  In recent times, Russia has been adopting an independent approach on regional and global issues. It has strongly opposed US efforts to oust Bashar al-Assad from power in Syria. Russia annexed Crimea from Ukraine in 2014, beginning the ongoing Russo-Ukrainian War. Ukraine and Georgia want to join NATO, but Russia is against the expansion of NATO in Eastern Europe. In 2022, USA alleged that Russia is involved in a massive cyber-attack against USA. Russia also allegedly tried to interfere in the elections of USA.

  However, the conflict between Russia and America may not be permanent. In the G7 meeting held in Canada in June 2018, former US President Donald Trump took the initiative to invite Russia to offset the growing power of China. The present US President Joe Biden met with the Russian President Putin in 2021 to try and normalise the relation between the two countries, but no visible progress has been made.

The Ukraine Crisis

Even after the dissolution of the Soviet Union into 15 independent states, ethnic conflicts persisted among the various nations, and especially between

Russia and other states where people of Russian origin still reside. This has resulted in violent skirmishes primarily between Russia and Georgia and between Russia and Ukraine. The fourth Ukrainian President, Viktor Yanukovych, wanted to establish better relations with Russia but the people of Ukraine wanted to have better relations with Western countries. Yanukovych was removed from power in 2014 by the people of Ukraine and he took refuge in Russia. Consequently, there was military intervention by Russia in Crimea. Although in 1954, Crimea was ceded to Soviet Ukraine by Soviet Russia, in March 2014, the Crimea region of Ukraine was taken over by Russia and a plebiscite was held in Crimea in the presence of the Russian army. People of Russian origin are in the majority in Crimea, the region that was annexed by Russia.

In an attack against Ukrainian sovereignty, Russia sent troops into Ukraine on 24 February 2022. Russian forces attacked and tried to take over Mariupol and Melitopol in Ukraine. By taking over its ports, Russia wants to turn Ukraine into a landlocked nation and cut off its access to sea routes. Russia also wants to control eastern parts of Ukraine such as Luhansk and Donetsk which are near the Russian border. The ongoing Russo-Ukrainian War is being considered one of the biggest wars in Europe after the Second World War. The neutral nations like Sweden and Finland want to join NATO to protect themselves against Russia's aggression. All of Europe and USA are against the Russian invasion. Russia is now trying to build a close partnership with China.

This situation in global politics is now the biggest foreign policy challenge for India. India is trying to fend off China's aggression and is looking for USA's support in this regard. So, naturally, the USA is putting pressure on India to severe relations with Russia. But India is still dependent on Russia for its arms supply. India thus is walking a tightrope trying to maintain friendly relations with both USA and Russia.

INDIA AND CHINA

The most critical challenge for Indian foreign policy in the twenty-first century is India's relationship with China, which is rather complex. This is because there are long-standing conflicts between the two nations. It is difficult for India to choose which of the four C's should shape its strategic relations with China: cooperation, competition, containment, or conflict.

China calls itself the 'middle kingdom', that is, the state located between heaven and earth. It considers China to be the closest to heaven and China's civilisation to be the greatest. At present, China is the second-largest power in the world after the United States in terms of its economy and the military. Politically, China has a one-party government. The Communist Party has approved the removal of the two-term limit on the presidency, effectively allowing Chinese President Xi Jinping to remain in power for life.

'One country, two systems' proposal: In 1949, China emerged as a communist country when Chinese Communist leader Mao Zedong declared the creation of the People's Republic of China. The officials fleeing the communist takeover went to Taiwan, also known as the Republic of China. Unlike the communist economic system that was adopted in PRC, in ROC the liberal economic system continued. While one-party rule exists in China, there is multi-party democracy in Taiwan. Although Taiwan is part of China, Taiwan's economic and political systems are different. That is why PRC came up with the proposal of 'one country, two systems' to encourage Chinese unification. But Taiwan has refused this suggestion. In 1997 Hong Kong, formerly under British control, became part of China. Similar to Taiwan, Hong Kong too has a liberal economic system. China had assured that democracy would be established in Hong Kong and to fulfil this promise, in 2015, China announced the first election based on adult universal suffrage in Hong Kong in 2017.

Friendly Relations between India and China

Initially after India's Independence, friendly relations developed between India and China, the best example of which is the 1954 Sino-Indian agreement that included Panchsheel or the Five Principles of Peaceful Coexistence. The Panchsheel agreement was signed by then Indian Prime Minister Jawaharlal Nehru and Chinese Prime Minister Zhou Enlai. (Refer to Chapter 2 for more details.)

This was the golden period of friendship between the two countries and it continued through the 1955 Afro–Asian Conference, also known as the Bandung Conference.

Border Disputes between India and China

There have been territorial disputes along the borderlands between India and China for a long time, and these conflicts are still ongoing. These disputes stem from invasive policies and occupation of land near the borders. The 'Five Fingers of Tibet' is a Chinese foreign policy, now dormant, that although not stated in official documents, has been widely attributed to Mao's speeches. According to this construct, China is a hand of which Tibet is the palm and the *five fingers* are Ladakh, Sikkim, Bhutan, Nepal and Arunachal Pradesh, and it is the responsibility of China to 'liberate' these regions.

India–China War

During the 1950s, China built a 1,200 kilometres road connecting Xinjiang and western Tibet, of which 179 kilometres went through the Aksai Chin region claimed by India. China stated that there was no clear demarcation of the India–China border and rejected the McMahon Line as well. The McMahon Line (named after British negotiator, Sir Henry McMahon) divides the India–China border in the north-east of Bhutan. India has always considered this line as the official boundary line but China rejected it as an imperialist border determined in 1914 at the Shimla conference between British India and Tibet. China claims Arunachal Pradesh is the southern part of Tibet. In 1959, Tibetans revolted against China and amidst the crackdown that followed, millions of Tibetans including the Dalai Lama came to India who gave them refuge. This made China's approach towards India even more aggressive.

Subsequently, in September 1962, China launched a military invasion of India and took control of Aksai Chin, beginning the Sino-Indian War. Chinese forces entered Arunachal Pradesh and violent conflicts followed. The war ended when Chinese forces reached the claim line and subsequently declared a unilateral ceasefire and withdrew.

Since the 1962 war, China has controlled some very important parts of the Indian territory: there are several important passes between Ladakh and Tibet that are occupied by China. China has made a claim on Shipki La pass in Himachal Pradesh. It is noteworthy that some part of Pakistan Occupied Kashmir has been handed over to China by Pakistan.

Other Boundary Disputes

The border between India and China stretches 3,488 kilometres. The Line of Actual Control (LAC), in the context of the Sino-Indian border dispute, is the line of demarcation that separates Indian-controlled territory from Chinese-controlled territory. It is divided into three sectors. Arunachal in the eastern sector (which follows the McMahon Line), the western sector passes through Ladakh and the middle sector is adjacent to Himachal Pradesh and Uttarakhand. The India-China border dispute mainly concerns the McMahon Line in the north-east and Ladakh in the north-west.

Ladakh has always been a part of the state of Jammu and Kashmir. The state of Jammu and Kashmir was under the paramountcy of the British monarch before the independence of India. But after independence, it merged with India and became a part of the Indian territory.

China has made several claims over the last few decades such as under the Sino-Pakistan boundary agreement of 1963, Pakistan ceded 5,180 square kilometres of Indian territory in Pakistan Occupied Kashmir to China, which is considered illegal by India. In the eastern sector, China claims approximately 90,000 sq. km. of Indian territory in the state of Arunachal Pradesh and the area of Indian territory under the occupation of China in the Union Territory of Ladakh is approximately 38,000 sq km.

At present, there is a clear difference of opinion between India and China on the One Belt, One Road (OBOR) project. There is an ongoing dispute regarding the South China Sea too. As a result of the growing strategic ties between India and the US and India and Japan, China's approach towards border disputes with India is becoming more aggressive. At present, Japan gives a large amount of financial assistance to India for the development of infrastructure in the Northeastern states. The border disputes are thus largely the result of a power struggle between the major powers.

Delinking Policy

In 1979, Deng Xiaoping emphasised the goal of 'Four Modernizations' and placed a great emphasis on economic issues in Chinese foreign policy. An even greater emphasis was laid by him on the development of infrastructure in China. Socialist rule with state ownership was replaced by an open market economic policy. Foreign investment was attracted and a network of roads was laid in China. Xiaoping said that issues like border disputes should be left for the coming generation and therefore, an attempt was made to delink economic and political issues.

In the year 1988, Rajiv Gandhi visited China and announced that economic and trade relations with China will be increased and no longer suspended due to border disputes. Thus, the delinking policy was adopted by India too and an attempt was made to look at economic relations and border disputes separately. Since border dispute is a complex issue, it must be resolved separately and meanwhile, relations with China should be enhanced in other areas. This is unlike India's previous stance which was the belief that until the border dispute was resolved, relations with China could not be normal.

Galwan Clash and Change in India's Approach: India no longer believes in a delinking policy while dealing with China after the 2020–2021 Galwan skirmishes. All the measures that were adopted for maintaining peace and tranquility on the border was proved futile. The Chinese violence proved that the confidence-building measures have failed. The Galwan clash busted the myth that trade relations between two nations can be helpful for settling border disputes. It proved that China is a bigger threat to India than an opportunity and that India needs to opt for multiple approaches to contain China.

Steps Taken for Resolution of Border Disputes

In 1988, a Joint Working Group was established to resolve the border dispute. The Joint Working Group (JWG) was the first official bilateral mechanism formed after the 1962 Indo–China War to discuss the boundary question and find a solution. While border dispute resolution is a necessary condition for establishing better relations with China, it might not be sufficient.

Peace and Tranquillity on the Line of Actual Control (LAC)

Indian Prime Minister Narasimha Rao visited China in 1993 and met Chinese Premier Li Peng. They discussed ways to maintain peace and tranquility in the border area to resolve the border dispute. To reach this objective, they signed the Border Peace and Tranquility Agreement which aimed to promote friendly and peaceful consultations and stated that no country must use force against the other. Minimum deployment of troops along the Line of Actual Control must also be ensured. Friendly consultation in case of disagreements are also essential for the resolution of border disputes. The two countries should also not violate each other's airspace.

Confidence-Building Measures (CBM)

In 1996, a new initiative was taken to maintain peace along the Indo-China border. The Agreement on Military Confidence Building Measures was signed. The agreement reiterated some of the points of the 1993 agreement such as reduction of troops at the border. The agreement also proposed transaction of data in respect of deployment of soldiers as well as exchange of maps between the two countries. To build confidence, both sides must ensure that there are no major military exercises along the border. If a country wants to conduct military exercises of more than one brigade on either side of the border, then they would have to give prior notice.

Border Defense Cooperation Agreement (BDCA)

Border Defense Cooperation Agreement (BDCA) was an agreement signed between India and China in 2013 to foster border security cooperation between the two countries. A joint patrolling was proposed to prevent smuggling of drugs, weapons and wildlife articles across the borders. The agreement also stated that the armies of the two countries would not follow each other on the border. Disputes arising on the border would be resolved peacefully and through dialogue. Talks would be held between military officers on the border and this would enhance cultural exchanges between them.

Trade Relations between India and China

In 1988, India adopted the pragmatic delinking policy towards China, placing emphasis on trade relations while separate efforts were made to resolve the border dispute. Bilateral trade between India and China reached US$ 115.83 billion in 2021, making China India's largest trading partner, while India is China's 13th largest. Investments have also been made in India by many Chinese companies. Trade between India and China is growing much faster than other trading partners of China. But even after this enhancement in trade, China's stand on the issue of border disputes remains rigid. Cordial relations between the two in the Asian and South Asian region are at the core of the peace and security of the region.

Challenges in Economic Relations

India and China are competitive economies and they both export similar goods to the international market. A major threat to the Indian economy has been posed by imported goods from China. Due to the growing India–China bilateral trade, a 'dependency syndrome' has developed in the Indian economy and many of India's industries are on the verge of closure due to the widespread availability of cheap Chinese goods. As of 2021–22, India's trade deficit with China is around US$ 73.3 billion. India has not given China a Market Economy Status, a status conferred on the exporter country whose prices are not questioned.

Other Issues between India and China

Dams on the Brahmaputra River

India received the notification of the construction of a series of dams on the Brahmaputra river in Tibet by China in November 2010. China constructed the Zangmu Hydroelectric Project in Tibet, at a distance of 325 km from Lhasa. According to China, the flow of water through the dam will not be diverted in any way. And as per satellite imagery by India, the water of Brahmaputra river has indeed not been diverted. But in the future, this dam can be used for power generation, flood control and irrigation as well, which can affect the interests of India in a decisive way. It is important to note that when in 1997, the UN Convention on the Law of Non-Navigational Uses of International Watercourses was signed, China had vetoed the convention.

South China Sea Dispute

The South China Sea dispute exists between China and the ASEAN countries, which includes Vietnam, Brunei, the Philippines and Malaysia, and others. Spratly and Paracel are two archipelagos in the South China Sea that are disputed. At present, China has majority control over the islands.

China intends to expand its military strength by annexing disputed but mineral-rich islands. China has once again tried to show its dominance to the international community by creating its first Air Defense Identification Zone in the East China Sea in November 2013. It has imposed air traffic restrictions on the airspace around the area including the Japanese-controlled but disputed Senkaku Islands to the South Korean-claimed Socotra Rock.

Award of the International Tribunal: An application was filed by the Philippines to the Tribunal to settle the dispute over the South China Sea. The tribunal ruled in favour of the Philippines and rejected China's claim. China considers its territory up to the nine-dash line.

India champions freedom of navigation and supports keeping sea communication open. It also believes that a rules-based world order is the need of the hour. To balance China's aggressive policy in the South China Sea, Indian policies are becoming more assertive now.

Nuclear Issues

In 1964, China conducted nuclear tests. India then conducted a peaceful nuclear test in 1974 to maintain security. China considered this as nuclear blackmail. After India's nuclear test in the post-Cold War world in 1998, relations between India and China became very bitter. The United Nations Security Council resolution 1172 was adopted unanimously on 6 June 1998 after hearing of nuclear tests conducted by India and Pakistan in May 1998 and it demanded strict sanctions on nuclear tests.

China is the only superpower that does not negotiate with India on the nuclear issue because, according to China, this would legitimise India's nuclear power. China also opposed the India–US Civil Nuclear Agreement of 2005, calling it a major blow to non-proliferation. Since China always follows the policy of counterbalancing India, in 2010, there was a civil nuclear agreement between China and Pakistan. Through this agreement, China provides huge support to Pakistan in the nuclear field. Cooperation in the nuclear field between China and Pakistan poses a major threat to Indian security. According to China, Pakistan should also get an exemption in the nuclear field as India does. China indirectly opposes India membership in the Nuclear Suppliers Group (NSG).

Kashmir Issue

After the Indo-China War of 1962, China recognised Kashmir as a disputed territory and began supporting Pakistan's demand for a plebiscite in Kashmir. China's approach to the Kashmir issue has changed since 1990, a clear example of which was seen during the Kargil crisis in 1999 when China asked Pakistan to follow the Line of Control (LoC) and suggested resolving the Kashmir problem bilaterally. China thus has had an inconsistent policy on Kashmir, as it changes its position depending on its own interests. China now issues loose leaf stapled visas instead of properly stamped ones for residents of Kashmir and also banned travel of military officers stationed in Kashmir to China. But China has also raised an objection to the revocation of Article 370 in the context of Jammu and Kashmir.

Tibet Issue

Tibet and Xinjiang are two provinces which are considered to be matters of China's internal security. China has been settling ethnic Han-Chinese population in Tibet to ensure 'cultural unity' in Tibetan areas of China. China wants to remake Tibetan culture into mainstream Chinese culture by forcing Mandarin on people who speak Tibetan and Confucianism on Buddhists. China also wants to focus on economic development, while Tibetans demand cultural autonomy.

The Dalai Lama, the religious leader of Tibet, also used to be the head of state as the social system of Tibet was based on religious traditions. The British government accepted Tibet under Chinese suzerainty through a treaty signed with China in 1906. This Convention of Lhasa also dictated that a British agent would be appointed in Lhasa and India would establish a postal system for Tibet up to Gyantse as well as secure the trade routes to India in Tibet. India also got the right to deploy its troops in Tibet.

In 1950, the newly formed communist government of China announced that the People's Liberation Army must liberate Tibet. The Tibetans were severely repressed by China and this led to a sudden uprising in the Tibetan capital Lhasa in mid-March of 1959, resulting in a violent conflict between the Chinese and Tibetan peoples. China suppressed the rebellion so severely that the Dalai Lama had to flee to India through a secret route and thousands of Tibetans followed and took refuge in India. India granted asylum to Dalai Lama, but on the condition that he would not launch any movement against China from the territory of India.

Areas such as Tawang in Arunachal Pradesh and parts of Sikkim have a large number of Buddhists, and most of the Buddhist monasteries are influenced by Tibetans and the Dalai Lama. Due to this shared cultural history and the fact of providing asylum, India succeeds in putting pressure on China as there are followers of the Dalai Lama spread all over the world.

Cooperation between India and China

Despite occasional conflicts, there is cooperation between China and India on many areas. One such is on the issue of the BRICS Development Bank. India has also joined the Asian Infrastructure Investment Bank and is a member of the Shanghai Cooperation Organisation. China cannot ignore India's growing market. Since America and Europe are suffering from an economic slowdown, China–India cooperation can become the driver of world economy. China is the world's second largest and India is the world's third largest oil importer. So, there is a lot of potential for cooperation.

Track-2 Diplomacy: A new initiative was taken in 2013 to enhance cooperation between India and China, under which instead of government talks, dialogue between non-governmental agencies were promoted to improve government-to-government relations between the two countries. Through this Track-2 diplomacy, a friendly atmosphere can be fostered and the mistrust between the two countries can be reduced.

One Belt One Road Initiative

China plans to develop seaports and road connectivity in the form of the One Belt One Road project. It is also a way of developing China's soft power. China and Europe (through Italy) will be connected by road and rail through the OBOR project, which will pass through Russia, Central Asia, and West Asia. China plans to develop seaports in all the island countries of the Indian Ocean through the Maritime Silk Road project, which will connect China with Italy via Kenya.

Economic Importance

The OBOR project emphasises on enhancing trade relations with Southeast Asian countries, Central Asian countries, and the continent of Africa. It also seeks to take advantage of the natural resources of Central Asia and Africa, especially of Kenya. At present, China's internal consumption is on the decline and so, through this project, Chinese public enterprises would be getting investment opportunities in other countries.

Strategic Impact

The rise of China in the recent years have had a significant effect on global economy and geo-politics. China has established overseas military bases in Djibouti, Africa and Gwadar, Pakistan. Thus, her strategic ability has become powerful due to his increasing economic influence.

India's Objections

India primarily has two objections against the OBOR project. First, the issue of protecting the sovereignty of the nations through which the project passes has not been taken care of. The China–Pakistan Economic Corridor passes through Pakistan Occupied Kashmir, on which India asserts its claim, and this remains an unresolved issue.

Second, there is a general lack of transparency in this project. Since it is not clearly mentioned which countries and companies the project will invest in, there is no clarity regarding the terms of the agreements and the rates of interest.

India's Alternatives

India has several alternatives to the OBOR project that has enhanced the country's connectivity with other nations. For instance, the Chabahar port was developed by India for the first time in an overseas nation, and it is just 72 km away from the Gwadar port. Moreover, India and Japan, besides other countries, has supported the idea of an Asia–Africa Growth Corridor and many Asian and African countries have shown interest in cooperating for the development of its infrastructure. With the help of this growth corridor, Asia will be connected to Africa through the sea route. Jamnagar port in Gujarat will be connected with Djibouti in the Gulf of Aden. Apart from this, India will conduct capacity-building programmes in African countries and infrastructure will be developed by Japan.

As another alternative, India has emphasised on completing the Kaladan Multi-Modal Transit Transport Project, through which connectivity between Kolkata and Mizoram will be established via Myanmar.

India's Ambitions as a Major Power

India is a major power with growing influence in global politics. India has claimed a permanent seat in the UN Security Council, but China does not support India's candidature. India is recognised as a responsible nation with advanced nuclear technology, and thus India wants to be a part of the Nuclear Suppliers Group (NSG). But once again, China becomes an obstacle in the path of India's membership because of the rivalry between the two nations.

Rise of China as a Global Power

China's share in the GDP of the world economy, which was 1 per cent in 1945, has now increased to about 18 per cent in 2023, while America's share has reduced to only 22 per cent from 45 per cent in 1945. China is the largest bilateral trading partner of America, Japan, South Korea, Southeast Asia, Central Asia, Africa and India. China has set a goal to overtake the US economy by 2049.

Trust Deficit between India and China

Because of border disputes and other conflicts, there is serious mistrust between India and China. India's security concerns also increase with China's growing influence in South Asia and the Indian Ocean Region. Further, India's other rival Pakistan is supported by China. Moreover, relations are strained between China and India on the Tibet issue and China is unhappy with the Dalai Lama's presence in India. On the other hand, India does not support China on the One Belt One Road project, although most other countries of the world are in favour of it. China also considers the strategic relations established by India with the US and Japan as a threat, which has led to greater mistrust and disputes between the two countries.

In 2021–2022, India's trade deficit with China in bilateral trade was around US$ 73.3 billion, and it is estimated that it will cross US$ 100 billion in 2022–2023. To rectify this, self-reliance must play a key role in reducing China's influence in Indian markets and ensuring India's emergence as a superpower.

Sino-Pakistan Relations

As a result of the development of warm strategic relations between China and Russia in recent years, Pakistan has also received Russian weapons indirectly. So, China's influence over Pakistan has become an even greater threat to Indian security now. Pakistan's Gwadar port and the China–Pakistan Economic Corridor (CPEC) has strengthened Sino-Pakistan relations even further. Despite economic cooperation between India and China, China has always tried to reduce India's influence in South Asia. China employs a dual strategy to counterbalance India in South Asia through continued support of and military cooperation with Pakistan. It also attempts to counterbalance India through developing strong relations with India's smaller neighbours such as Nepal, Bangladesh and Sri Lanka.

4

INDIA'S ENGAGEMENT WITH THE MULTIPOLAR WORLD

KEYWORDS

India's relations with the European Union; BRICS; ASEAN; Shanghai Cooperation Organisation; African Union; Southern African Development Community; and Gulf Cooperation Council.

INDIA AND THE EUROPEAN UNION

The European Union is comprised of 27 member nations located in Europe. India and the EU cooperate on many areas, even though there are a few issues on which there are conflicts of interest.

Shared democratic values: Most of Europe has democratic nations. And India is the largest democracy in the world. Thus, democratic values are shared by both India and the EU and this has helped to build a strong, cooperative relationship between them.

Changed perception and flourishing economic relations: Earlier EU saw India as a spiritual nation with an ancient civilisation. Instead, the EU saw China as a key partner and larger market in Asia. But in recent times, EU has recognised the importance of India as a market in the age of liberalisation. EU is India's third largest trading partner (as of 2023), and India–EU trade in 2021–2022 was of US$ 116.37 billion (according to data published by the Department of Commerce, Government of India). Data by the Observer Research Foundation suggest that EU is one of the largest investors in India, and between April 2000–March 2020, there was a FDI (foreign direct investment) inflow worth US$ 109.55 billion.

Free trade agreement: Bilateral trade relations between India and EU is necessary for both the parties. Since India is not a part of RCEP (Regional Comprehensive Economic Partnership), a free trade agreement with EU would be very beneficial for India. EU nations too are looking an alternative to China, especially after the crisis of COVID-19, for diversification of supply chain and logistics. But there are a few issues that are proving to be obstacles in the signing of the free trade agreement:

(a) The EU has demanded lowering of tariffs on wines, spirits, dairy and automobiles. But India wants to protect its own domestic market by keeping these higher tariffs.

(b) India has demanded the lowering of non-tariff sanitary and phytosanitary barriers , which is especially relevant for food and agricultural trade.

(c) EU expects India to strengthen its intellectual property rights rules, which may have critical impact on India's vast pharmaceutical and generic drugs sector.

(d) EU promotes legally binding clauses related to human rights, social and environmental concerns, and labour standards which are difficult for a developing nation such as India to adhere to.

Developmental partner: European technology is essential for India for the development of smart cities, adapting clean energy sources and for national missions such as the Clean Ganga mission. Financial institutions of the EU invest in health sector and support sustainable urban development and mobility in India. The European Investment Bank has provided loans for three metro projects in India in Lucknow, Pune and Bengaluru.

Strategic partnership: EU is not a strategic entity, it depends on NATO for its own security. Moreover, differences exist among the EU members over issues of security and foreign policy. Therefore, strategic partnership is the weakest link between India and the EU. But in 2020, the 5th European Union—India Summit was held, which endorsed a common roadmap called the **Road Map 2025** to strengthen strategic partnership over the next five years. India and EU together want to focus on cyber security, maritime security, and development of 5G technology infrastructure in India. EU is a group of developed nations, so India would benefit from a collaboration on technical and research-related areas such as artificial intelligence and new technologies of communication. The India–EU strategic partnership also has on its agenda tasks like countering terrorism and radicalisation as well as combating money laundering. It also aims to strengthen military-to-military relations and deepen cooperation between naval forces of India and the EU.

Carbon tax: While the issue of climate change and carbon emissions are important, EU's proposed carbon border tax—a first for the world—might not be a suitable option for many countries of the Global South. Fundamental changes such as environmental protection cannot be brought about by forcing tariffs and the carbon tax may hit emerging economies like India very hard.

Future Prospects

India and the EU are natural allies but relations between the two need to be further strengthened. Presently, India focuses on relations with only a few members of the EU such as Germany, France, Belgium, the Netherlands and Italy. In recent years however, there has been a new focus on diversification of relations as India wants to strengthen its relations with all members of the EU. Eastern European members of the EU however are still sway from India's reach. India requires more experts specialising in European languages and more centres of European studies in international relations in Indian universities. Knowledge of European languages and cultures would in turn help in the promotion of India's soft power in Europe.

SHANGHAI COOPERATION ORGANISATION (SCO)

India's relations with Central Asian states improved considerably after the dissolution of the Soviet Union. Large reserves of natural gas and oil are available in Central Asian countries and thus it is essential for India to develop cooperative relations with the region. In this regard, Russia has been an important medium for entry into the Central Asian region. The Shanghai Cooperation Organisation, a political, economic, international security and defence organisation, was founded by Russia, China, and four Central Asian states (Kazakhstan, Kyrgyzstan, Tajikistan and Uzbekistan). India and Pakistan joined the SCO in 2017. The organisation's aim is to counter terrorism and separatism, ensure energy security, promote cooperation in cyber security, boost India's projects in Central and West Asia, maintain strategic autonomy, and combat fundamentalism in the region. India has strategic relations with Kazakhstan and Tajikistan. In Tajikistan, India has an air force base and there is also a proposal for a cooperative project of laying down a gas pipeline.

BRICS

BRICS was formed to facilitate multilateral cooperation between India, Brazil, Russia, China, and South Africa on economic and global issues. Financial assistance is provided by the BRICS Development Bank for the development of infrastructure in these developing countries. BRICS also aims to reform the international monetary system by keeping America's dominance in the global economy in check, and India supports Russia and China in this goal. India also has a role as a peacekeeper as it needs the BRICS alliance to be stable in order to ensure that trade among the member nations can carry on smoothly. India also ensures maritime security in the Indian Ocean region, which is an important region for BRICS. It is also an important forum for India to address its long-standing, complicated relationship with China.

The 13th BRICS Summit, with India as its Chair, was held on 9 September 2021. This was the third time that India hosted the summit, having previously done so in 2012 and 2016. The theme for the summit was 'BRICS at 15: Intra-BRICS Cooperation for Continuity, Consolidation and Consensus'. The 14th BRICS summit was hosted by China virtually in June 2022, and the 15th BRICS summit was held in August 2023 in South Africa.

ASEAN

ASEAN, a regional organisation comprising ten Southeast Asian nations, was established to promote political and social stability. India adopted a Look East policy soon after the economic liberalisation in 1991 to increase cooperation with countries in the East and Southeast Asia region. India became a Sectoral Dialogue Partner of ASEAN in 1992, a Dialogue Partner in 1995, an ASEAN-Regional Forum member in 1996, and a Summit-level Partner in 2002. This was upgraded to a strategic partnership in 2012. Indian subsequently announced its 'Act East' policy in 2014 with an intent to upscale its engagement with ASEAN member states.

Cooperation between India and ASEAN member countries is crucial to counter China's projection of power over the South China Sea islands. India's collaboration with ASEAN nations are necessary also for the development of the Northeast region, and especially to counter insurgency and terrorism among the Northeast states.

ASEAN is the one of the largest markets in the world and is comparable to the EU and North American markets. India signed a free trade agreement (FTA) for trade in goods in 2009 and another FTA in services and investments in 2014 with ASEAN. ASEAN was India's fourth largest trading partner in 2018. India has also signed Comprehensive Economic Cooperation Agreements (CECA) with various countries of the ASEAN region like Malaysia, Singapore, and Thailand. India also has defence ties with various ASEAN nations. For example, joint naval and military exercises are conducted between India and Indonesia (CORPAT), India and Singapore (SIMBEX and Bold Kurukshetra), and India, Singapore, and Thailand (SITMEX).

During a summit to commemorate 25 years of ASEAN–India relations in 2018, there was agreement that their strategic partnership should focus on building cooperation in the maritime domain. The 19th ASEAN–India summit was held in Phnom Penh, capital of the Kingdom of Cambodia in November 2022. The year marked the completion of 30 years of ASEAN–India relations.

AFRICAN UNION

The African Union is a continental body that consists of 55 countries of Africa. A successor to the Organisation of African Unity (OAU), the AU was founded in 2001 in Addis Ababa, Ethiopia and launched in 2002 in Durban, South Africa. India is a member of the AU Partners Group (AUPG), which meet periodically in Addis Ababa. Relations between India and the African Union (AU) have developed rapidly in recent years. India has had a long relationship with African countries since after Independence, India vocally supported decolonisation in Africa.

To extend its economic reach in Africa, in 2004, India began an initiative called Techno-Economic Approach for Africa–India Movement (TEAM–9), together with eight energy and resource-rich West African countries (Burkina Faso, Chad, Cote D'Ivoire, Equatorial Guinea, Ghana, Guinea Bissau, Mali, Senegal). The India–Africa Forum Summit (IAFS), which is the official platform for African-Indian relations, is held every three years. So far, it has taken place in 2008, 2011 and 2015. It is important to note that India is one of the five largest investors in the African continent. A pan-African e-Network project was proposed by India for development of information and communication technology in Africa. ITEC (Indian Technical and Economic Cooperation Programme) is also an important example of India's assistance to African nations. India is also a large contributor to UN-mandated peacekeeping efforts and other such operations in Africa.

SOUTHERN AFRICAN DEVELOPMENT COMMUNITY

The Southern African Development Community (SADC) is an inter-governmental organisation headquartered in Botswana. It was formed with the aim of furthering regional socio-economic cooperation and integration among 16 countries in southern Africa. It complements the role of the AU. India has bilateral trade relations with SADC. Broad areas of cooperation between India and SADC include: agriculture, water resources, human resources development, promotion of small and medium scale industries, non-conventional energy sources, communications, commerce, and banking. India accounted for around 7.3 per cent of SADC's total exports in 2017. There is also a considerable flow of FDI between India and the SADC region.

GULF COOPERATION COUNCIL

The Gulf region is in the immediate neighbourhood of India separated only by the Arabian Sea. The Gulf Cooperation Council is a political, and economic union comprising Bahrain, Kuwait, Oman, Qatar, Saudi Arabia, and the United Arab Emirates. The GCC countries are collectively host to a large Indian expatriate community. The common political and security concerns of India and GCC translate into efforts for peace, security and stability in the Gulf region and South Asia. The first GCC–India Industrial Conference was held in Mumbai in February 2004. India and GCC signed a **Framework Agreement** for enhancing and developing economic cooperation between the two parties in New Delhi in August 2004. The **India and GCC Free Trade Agreement** is under negotiation. India has traditionally enjoyed cordial relations and cooperation with the GCC. India's old, historical ties with GCC states coupled with increasing imports of oil and natural gas has led to a steady growth of trade and investment.

5

INDIA'S RELATIONS WITH ITS NEIGHBOURHOOD

KEYWORDS

SAARC; Gujaral doctrine; Look East/Act East policy; Look West policy; India and West Asia; India–Iran; India–Afghanistan; India–Pakistan; India and Central Asia; India–Nepal; India–Bangladesh; India–Sri Lanka; The QUAD; India and Bhutan; India–Maldives

INDIA AND SAARC: COOPERATION IN SOUTH ASIA

SAARC or the South Asian Association for Regional Cooperation was founded in 1985 in Dhaka through an initiative taken by then President of Bangladesh, Ziaur Rahman. Initially, both India and Pakistan expressed hesitation in joining SAARC due to the existing power rivalry in South Asia. India was reluctant because it viewed the formation of SAARC as an antagonistic union of the smaller nations of South Asia encircling India. On other hand, Pakistan was unwilling to join SAARC as it viewed the organisation as an India-centric body. Despite this mistrust, SAARC was formed with seven members: **Bangladesh, Bhutan, India, Maldives, Nepal, Pakistan and Sri Lanka**. **Afghanistan** joined SAARC later in 2007. There are nine nation states with observer status in SAARC, namely Australia, China, European Union, Iran, Japan, Mauritius, Myanmar, South Korea and the United States. Russia too has expressed its desire to become an observer.

Reasons for Regional Integration

In the present era of liberalisation and globalisation, politics is not a zero-sum game and cooperation can lead to a win-win situation for all cooperating states. In comparison to the West, South Asia is relatively less integrated as a region, even though it is the biggest market of the world due to its huge population. SAARC was formed from a need for regional integration among South Asian nations. The following are some of the reasons behind this regional integration:

1. **Geographical factors:** South Asian states are geographically interdependent. Nepal and Bhutan are landlocked states. Therefore, Pakistan requires a transit route through India in order to reach Nepal and Bhutan. Afghanistan is also a landlocked nation and India in turn needs a transit route through

Pakistan to gain access to Afghanistan. Cooperation is thus necessary to ensure smooth trade between the nations.

2. **Economic factors:** India and Pakistan are countries that need to import energy but Nepal and Bhutan have an abundance of hydropower. On the other hand, the economy of Nepal is dependent on tourism. Therefore, cooperation between these countries results in a win-win situation.
3. **Social factors:** South Asia, like other regions in the Global South, faces problems such as poverty, malnutrition and illiteracy. Bangladesh and Nepal are among the least developed nations and often have to depend on their neighbours for resources. Conflict among the neighbouring nations is thus harmful for the interest of each state, whereas cooperation can aid mutual development.
4. **Need for security:** Cross-border terrorism, illegal drug trafficking and human trafficking are *common security threats* faced by the entire South Asia region. Environmental degradation too is a new security threat for South Asia as it can promote river water disputes the among neighbouring states. Through regional cooperation, such disputes can be avoided.

Objectives of SAARC

According to the SAARC charter, the objectives of the association are:

1. To serve the people of South Asia and improve their standard of living.
2. To work for economic, social, and cultural development of the region, and to ensure dignity of life for every individual.
3. To create an atmosphere of unity and confidence among states in South Asia.
4. To solve common problems through mutual trust and cooperation.
5. To establish and improve mutual cooperation in economic, social, cultural, scientific and technological areas.
6. To enhance cooperation with other developing countries of the world that share similar goals.
7. To increase mutual cooperation among member states in order to protect the common interests of South Asia in different international platforms.
8. To seek increased levels of cooperation with other international and regional organisations.

Structure of SAARC

Like other regional organisations, the SAARC too has an elaborate institutional structure to ensure smooth functioning of the organisation:

1. **The SAARC Summit:** At the top of this structure is the meeting of the Heads of Government (HOGs) of the member states. Known as the SAARC Summit, this meeting of the HOGs is held once a year and it draw up the policies, programmes, and activities of the organisation.
2. **Council of Ministers:** The council consists of Foreign (External Affairs) Ministers of the member states, and it meets twice a year to formulate and devise methods of implementation of the policies and programmes of the organisation. The Charter of the SAARC has enlisted five major tasks for the Council of Ministers. These are: (*a*) to formulate policies for the organisation; (*b*) to determine levels of cooperation among member states; (*c*) to identify new areas of cooperation; (*d*) to create new infrastructures for the organisation as per requirements; and (*e*) to take decisions on matters of general interest to member states. The council is in effect the main decision-making body of the SAARC.
3. **Standing Committee:** The next in the administrative hierarchy is the Standing Committee. It is composed of foreign secretaries of every member state. This committee is also responsible for the

implementation of SAARC policies and programmes by analysing and supervising progress throughout the year. It sends an annual report to the Council of Ministers.

4. **Programming Committee:** This committee is made up of heads of SAARC divisions of member states. The main function of the Programming Committee is to assist the Standing Committee with selection of regional projects, mobilisation of external resources; and review of the activity calendar.
5. **Technical Committees:** The Technical Committees are made up of representatives of member states (who are professionals from sectoral fields). They are responsible for formulating the programs and projects in their respective fields and reporting them to the Standing Committee.
6. **Secretariat:** The charter has provided for a Secretariat of the organisation. This is the headquarters of the SAARC and is located in Kathmandu, the capital of Nepal. It is responsible for coordinating SAARC activities in the region. The Secretariat is headed by a Secretary-General appointed by the Council of Ministers.
7. **SAARC Regional Centres:** Since 1989, a number of Regional Centres have been set up with the aim to strengthen and promote regional cooperation. They implement programme activities and are managed by governing boards comprising representatives from all the member states, SAARC Secretary-General and the Ministry of Foreign/External Affairs of the host government.

   There are several Regional Centres across different SAARC capitals, some of which are:

   - SAARC Agriculture Centre or SAC in Dhaka (established in 1989)
   - SAARC Tuberculosis and HIV/AIDS Center or STAC in Kathmandu (established in 1992)
   - SAARC Disaster Management Centre or SDMC in New Delhi (established in 2006)
   - SAARC Meteorological Research Centre or SMRC in Dhaka (established in 1995)
   - SAARC Human Resource Development Centre or SHRDC in Islamabad (established in 1999)
   - SAARC Cultural Centre or SCC in Kandy, Sri Lanka (established in 2009)
   - SAARC Coastal Zone Management Centre or SCZMC in Male, Maldives (established in 2004)
   - SAARC Information Centre or SIC in Kathmandu (established in 2004).

Process of Decision-Making in SAARC

Since member states of the SAARC are unequal, decision-making by consensus is the rule of SAARC. The consent of every member is necessary for a decision to be considered final. Decision by consensus recognises the sovereign equality of the member states. Any member can block any decision or resolution from being passed by SAARC.

Achievements of SAARC

A. **Establishment of a Free Trade Area:** In the 1990s, SAARC member countries discussed the SAARC Preferential Trading Arrangement or the SAPTA to promote and sustain mutual trade and the economic cooperation. Later in 2004, a Free Trade Agreement was signed to create a free trade area among the SAARC nations, now known as the South Asian Free Trade Area (SAFTA). It came into force in 2006.

SAFTA includes provisions such as:

1. Removal of trade barriers and facilitation of free movement of goods among SAARC states.
2. Creation of an atmosphere of fair competition for free trade and providing equal opportunities to all member states.
3. Providing adequate and proper administrative infrastructure to make the SAFTA operational, and to sort out differences.
4. Providing appropriate machineries to extend to all member states the benefits of the agreement.

According to the SAFTA, member states are divided into 2 categories: *Least developed nations* which include Bangladesh, Nepal, Bhutan, Maldives and Afghanistan, and *developing nations* which include India, Pakistan and Sri Lanka.

Unlike SAARC, which has no dispute resolution mechanism, SAFTA incorporates a provision for dispute settlement.

B. **Strengthened Security and Social Development:** Since its inception, SAARC has signed various conventions and agreements to strengthen regional security and to realise social development. The following are some of the notable agreements: Regional Convention on Suppression of Terrorism, Regional Convention on Narcotic Drugs and Psychotropic Substances, SAARC Convention on Preventing and Combating Trafficking in Women and Children for Prostitution, and SAARC Convention on Regional Arrangements for the Promotion of Child Welfare in South Asia.

C. **The SAARC Food Bank:** The SAARC Food Bank was established to ensure food security at times at times of emergency (such as natural disaster, floods, earthquakes and others) which may cause major disruptions in food production, transportation, accessibility, and overall availability. The Agreement establishing the SAARC Food Bank was signed during the Fourteenth SAARC Summit in Islamabad.

D. **SAARC Development Fund:** When the South Asian Development Fund (SADF) was found to be inadequate, the SAARC Development Fund (SDF) was set up with the aim of industrial development, poverty alleviation, protection of environment, human resource development and promotion of social and infrastructure development projects in the SAARC region. The SDF was recognised by the eight SAARC members in 2010. Officially, SDF's objectives are "to promote the welfare for the people of the South Asian region; to improve their quality of life, and accelerate economic growth, social progress and poverty alleviation".

E. **South Asian University:** The South Asian University is another achievement of the SAARC. It is an international university established in 2010 by the eight SAARC member states. The university offers postgraduate and doctoral programs in several disciplines.

Challenges to SAARC

While there are many areas in which SAARC has seen success, there have also been disappointments and challenges in other areas.

1. **Trust Deficit:** The functionalist theory of regional integration believes that a minimum amount of trust is essential for proper economic integration. However, in case of SAARC, there lies a deep distrust between two of its major members, namely India and Pakistan.
2. **Difference in Security Threats:** Various members of SAARC treat each other as

security threats, and there is no common threat in South Asia. For India, China is a security threat, while for Pakistan, India is the threat. Again, for Afghanistan, Pakistan is a security threat. One cannot hope for a successful regional economic integration in such a threatened environment.

3. **Lack of Infrastructure:** Without better communication and transportation, regional economic integration is not feasible. In South Asia, Pakistan and Bangladesh refuse to cooperate with India with regard to allowing access to transit routes. The lack of telecommunication and proper banking facility further block the future of the free trade agreement and the SAFTA cannot be as successful as it could have.
4. **Balance of Power:** Regional economic integration is possible in an environment of peace and active cooperation. But due to the existing power rivalries in South Asia, the focus remains on attaining dominance than allowing the promotion of free trade. The issue of cross-border terrorism between Pakistan and India puts a further strain on the relationship between the two countries.
5. **Lack of Common Identity:** J. N. Dixit, a former national security advisor of India, says that the South Asian nations, although culturally and geographically similar and interlinked, try to maintain their own separate identity in the postcolonial world to legitimise their identity as separate nations. This is a hindrance to cooperation. Sri Lanka projects itself as closer to Southeast Asia than India. Pakistan always maintains its identity as an Islamic nation. Therefore, a common South Asian identity is missing, which is one of the challenges to regional cooperation.

The formation of BIMSTEC (Bay of Bengal Initiative for Multi-Sectoral Technical and Economic Cooperation) proves that India is not hopeful about the success of SAARC and is looking for an alternative. All members of SAARC are invited to the meetings of BIMSTEC except Pakistan. Moreover, the last Summit of SAARC was held way back in 2014 in Kathmandu. Pakistan was to host the summit in 2016, but it was postponed as India refused to participate. 38 years have passed since SAARC was established, but there has only been 18 summits—this itself tells the story of the failure of SAARC.

GUJRAL DOCTRINE

The Gujral Doctrine is named after Inder Kumar Gujral, an Indian diplomat who served as the 12th prime minister of India. In 1996, Gujral became the Foreign Minister and proposed a set of five principles to guide foreign relations with India's immediate neighbours. This doctrine was considered a landmark change in India's foreign policy as it changed the *principal of reciprocity.* It proposed that all neighbouring countries should not be treated equally and that India's stature and power are linked to the nature of its ties with its neighbours.

According to the Gujral Doctrine:

1. India should provide *unilateral concession* for smaller neighbouring countries, namely **Bangladesh, Sri Lanka, Nepal, Bhutan, and Maldives** instead of asking for reciprocity. India should give in good faith and trust.
2. *No South Asian nation should allow its territory to be used against the interest of another country of the region.* It is essential for generation of trust.
3. No country should interfere in the *internal affairs* of another, because each and every nation is sovereign.
4. All South Asian countries must respect each other's *territorial integrity* and sovereignty.
5. They should settle all their disputes through *peaceful bilateral negotiations.*

The unilateral concession for smaller neighbouring countries will have positive benefits for India as this will aid the economic development of these neighbours and the borders will remain peaceful. This might also prevent China's influence upon the neighbouring countries. India will also benefit financially because in the current era of liberalisation, bilateral trade with the smaller neighbouring countries will boost India's economy. Gujral doctrine also believes in peaceful resolution of dispute with neighbouring nations such as China and Pakistan.

The *Neighbourhood First Policy* by the present Modi government is in many ways similar to the Gujral Doctrine as both actively focus on improving ties with India's immediate neighbours instead of a tit-for-tat approach of reciprocity.

LOOK EAST POLICY

Soon after P. V. Narasimha Rao became Prime Minister, he launched the 'Look East' Policy (LEP) in 1992. Its implementation during the 1990s focused mostly on engagement with Southeast Asia and ASEAN. Besides wanting to capitalise on Southeast Asia's economic success, India wanted to have a politico-military engagement with the region, especially because its relation with the US had worsened and China on the other hand was rapidly forming links across Asia. Another objective of the LEP during the 1990s was thus to prevent Southeast Asia from falling under the influence of any one major power.

Factors that Led to the Adoption of LEP

1. ASEAN was gradually becoming the centre of economic growth and Asia Pacific an emerging region of economic prosperity.
2. Culturally and geographically, India was closely connected with ASEAN. The ASEAN nations such as Indonesia and Myanmar are geographically close to India and could act as the gateways for its entry into the East.
3. SAARC could not become a successful example of regional economic integration due to lack of trust among members and India's perpetual disputes with Pakistan. Therefore, India began looking east which led to the formation of BIMSTEC as a substitute of SAARC.
4. India had been attracting investment from ASEAN member nations as well as Japan and South Korea ever since India adopted the policy of liberalisation and privatisation in 1991.
5. The Northeast region of India became landlocked after the partition of India and the peripheral states of the Northeast faced many issues such as insurgency and continual violence. With the Look East policy, India hoped that Assam would become a centre of commerce and connectivity and the ensuing development would be a solution to the turmoil of Northeastern states.
6. The rising influence of China in Southeast Asia was a big challenge to India's ambition of becoming a major power.

Progress of the Look East Policy

India became a Sectoral Dialogue Partner of ASEAN in 1992, and subsequently a Dialogue Partner in 1996. It also became a member of the **ASEAN Regional Forum** or ARF, which comprises ten ASEAN members, ten dialogue partners and seven other countries including Pakistan and covers confidence-building measures or CBMs and preventive diplomacy. In 1996, India also participated in the Post-Ministerial Conference (PMC).

Since 2002, the two sides have established summit-level dialogue. In 2005, India also became a founding member of the **East Asia Summit** (EAS), a regional forum held at the level of heads of states/governments; its members include the ASEAN countries, and China, Japan, South Korea, Australia and New Zealand. A signal of the return or pivoting of the US to the South Asia region is its joining of the EAS mechanism in 2011, when Russia too became a member. The most recent development in the building of regional architecture by ASEAN is the **ADMM Plus Forum** (ASEAN Defence Ministers' Meeting Plus), which comprises ASEAN defence ministers plus defence ministers representing its 8 dialogue partners, namely China, Japan, South Korea, India, Australia, New Zealand, US and Russia. It was formed in October 2010.

Basic Components of the Look East Policy

1. **Trade and Commerce**

   The Look East policy was initially an economic strategy to boost India's trade and investment relations with the Southeast Asian region. India and ASEAN have witnessed accelerated trade and investment since the announcement of LEP in the 1990s with a lot of cross-investment between the members. For instance, exports rose from US$ 2.9 billion to US$ 19.1 billion in 2009 and Singapore has become the largest Asian investor in India, surpassing Japan and China.

   On 9 October 2003, **India and Thailand** signed a set of agreements to enhance cooperation in trade, agriculture and tourism: a Framework Agreement for establishing a bilateral Free Trade Area, an MOU on agricultural cooperation, and an agreement on tourism cooperation. With the improvement in economic ties between **India and Singapore**, the two countries signed a Comprehensive Economic Cooperation Agreement in 2005.

   Japanese trade and investment in India too have significantly increased in recent years. Indo-Japanese trade rose to US$ 10.91 billion in 2008–2009. Japanese FDI in India continues to expand. In 2007, Japanese automobile giant Honda announced its plan to set up its second car manufacturing unit in Rajasthan with an estimated investment of Rs 1,000 crore, while the Maruti-Suzuki partnership remains the leading car manufacturer in South Asia.

   South Korean investment in India was low in 1991 but it rose to equal that of Japan in later years. The South Korean automobile maker Hyundai created a wholly owned subsidiary in India for a total investment of US$ 700 million. Unlike most other foreign manufacturers, which established plants in India in order to gain access to the domestic market, South Korean firms have localised their production of components and parts using local labour, resulting in lower labour costs for global production and export. South Korea and India signed a Comprehensive Economic Partnership Agreement (CEPA) in August 2009, the first such economic agreement for India with a member of the Paris-based Organisation for Economic Cooperation and Development (OECD).

   India was **Australia**'s fourth largest merchandise export market and seventh largest merchandise trading partner in 2008–2009. Trade between the two countries has been rising at 30 per cent annually. However, Australia has an upper hand in this bilateral trade due to its abundant natural resources and high education. Like India's FDI in Australia, Australian FDI in India was as low as US$ 281.64 million in 2009. An Economic Cooperation and Trade Agreement was signed between India and Australia in 2022.

2. **Security**

   While the first phase of India's 'Look East' policy was ASEAN-centered and focused on trade and investment linkages, while the second phase of this policy announced in 2003 aimed to expand the definition of 'East', extending it from Australia to East Asia, keeping ASEAN at its core.

This marked a shift from trade to wider economic and security issues, including joint efforts to carry out coordinated counter-terrorism activities. Phase II of LEP saw more comprehensive defence cooperation, including arrangements for regular access to ports in Southeast Asia. Defence contracts have also been widened to include Japan and South Korea. Military contacts between India and Japan have also developed significantly and their navies and coast guards have engaged in joint exercises. India and Japan elevated their relationship to a Strategic and Global Partnership in August 2007. Air and land links to East and Southeast Asia have also been expanded, thus achieving greater physical connectively with Asian partners.

Since 1991, India has periodically had joint naval exercises with Singapore, Malaysia, and Indonesia in the Indian Ocean and later, also began similar exercises with Vietnam, Thailand, and the Philippines. India is particularly keen on deepening its military ties with Malaysia. A defence cooperation agreement was signed with Singapore in 2003 which made Singapore India's most important bilateral security partner in Southeast Asia.

3. **Political and Diplomatic Ties**

The second phase of LEP also advocated for closer political ties through more comprehensive dialogue across a wider range of issues as well as the development of regional groupings. India has successfully engaged the major powers such as the US, China and Russia in dialogue through the ASEAN summits and other forums.

In recent years, Delhi has openly indicated that the development of India's Northeast and the containment of insurgencies in the region are issues that the LEP should be able to ameliorate. The Northeast region, which is considered the gateway to the East and the Southeast Asia, has received a renewed focus with the Look East policy.

With regards to forming diplomatic ties, in 2004, India and Japan launched a joint bid to secure permanent seats on the United Nations Security Council, along with Germany and Brazil, as the Group of Four (G4).

4. **Regional Grouping and Forums**

Besides ASEAN, India has joined Asian countries in other regional groupings as well. One such grouping, launched in 1997, is the Bay of Bengal initiative for Multi-Sectoral Technical and Economic Cooperation **(BIMSTEC)**. Involving Bangladesh, Myanmar, Sri Lanka, Thailand, Bhutan, Nepal and India, BIMSTEC works to promote sub-regional cooperation in trade, investment and technological exchange. For India, the development and integration of its Northeast region has been an underlying motivation for its engagement with BIMSTEC. Another such grouping through which India engaged several Southeast Asian countries is the **Mekong Ganga Cooperation** (MGC) launched in 2000 which has as its members Myanmar, Thailand, Cambodia, Vietnam, Laos and India.

Most of the countries in Southeast Asia have unsettled maritime boundaries or have articulated claims to offshore assets, islands or seabed resources. Some of the world's busiest sea-lanes are located in the Indian Ocean. About 20 per cent of the world's oil supply passes through this region daily. These factors, combined with China's growing influence in the region, has led some of the ASEAN nations to regard India as a useful partner that can offset China.

5. **Soft Power**

Soft power or the intangible attraction of culture, ideology and shared values can enhance a nation's international credibility. India's soft-power potential lies mainly in its democracy, secularism, and pluralism as well as its considerable pool of skilled English-speaking professionals, diverse culture (Bollywood films being an important cultural export), food and handicrafts.

India has set up various cultural centres across Asia to enhance awareness of its rich and diverse cultural heritage and its local relevance. Each year the Indian Council for Cultural Relations (ICCR) sends performing arts groups to participate in festivals around Asia. To bolster cultural ties and increase soft power, various initiatives are taken such as the Japan-India Friendship Year 2007 which was to commemorate the 50th anniversary of the cultural agreement between Japan and India in 1957. Nearly 400 events were arranged in the two countries throughout that year.

6. **The Indian Diaspora in Southeast Asia**

   There is a considerably large Indian diaspora in Southeast Asia and the diasporic population is a crucial actor in increasing India's influence in Asia. Southeast Asia alone has an estimated 6.7 million people of Indian origin. The diaspora is an important force of India's LEP as it plays the role of a catalyst to bridge the gap between India and the South Asian countries to help improve bilateral relationships. The significant economic resource represented by the diasporic population and migrant labour remittances back to India has guided the government's efforts to engage this large community abroad.

ACT EAST POLICY

The Act East policy was announced in November 2014 by PM Modi at the 12th ASEAN-India Summit held in Myanmar. Announced as a diplomatic initiative to promote economic, strategic and cultural relations with the vast Asia-Pacific region at different levels, it is essentially an upgrade of the Look East policy. The elements of the two policies are largely the same. The Act East policy focuses more on strengthening and implementation of earlier commitments made in the Look East policy. PM Narendra Modi highlighted the 4 C's that the Act East Policy is based on: Culture, Commerce, Connectivity and Capacity Building. The new policy aims to address delivery deficit and work towards adopting transparency and good governance for improving India's rank in the 'Ease of Doing Business' index.

Focus of Act East Policy

1. **India's Northeast:** When the Look East Policy was launched in 1992, critics pointed out that a Look East policy is meaningless without looking at India's Northeast. Since 2014, with the announcement of the Act East policy, the government began to focus on the development of infrastructure in Northeastern states. The Pakyong airport has been built in Sikkim. The Rupsi airport in Assam has recently been inaugurated. The Agartala-Akhaura Rail Project has been announced. In 2019, the 110 MW Pare Hydroelectric Plant was inaugurated in Arunachal Pradesh.
2. **BIMSTEC:** When the Government of India realised that SAARC is a non-starter, it began to consider BIMSTEC as an alternative to SAARC. The grouping has developed cooperation in several areas such as trade and investment, transport and communication, energy, tourism, technology, fisheries, agriculture, public health, poverty alleviation, counterterrorism and transnational crime, environmental and natural resource management, and cultural and people-to people contacts. The member countries have also signed

a free trade area framework agreement in 2004 for free trade in goods, services and investment. The Act East policy places a strong importance of this regional grouping of BIMSTEC.

3. **Strategic Partnership:** There has been an active enhancement of strategic partnership under the Act East policy. While earlier strategic partnership with neighbours was limited to conducting military exercises like Milan and Bold Kurukshetra with ASEAN nations, in recent times India has furthered its strategic partnership to extend a 500-million-dollar line of credit to Bangladesh for purchasing military equipment. India has also been planning to sell its supersonic missile Brahmos to Vietnam. Indian Navy also signed a military logistics exchange agreement with Singapore Navy. India is gradually trying to strengthen its partnership with ASEAN without taking China into consideration. India and Australia decided to upgrade their 2+2 Ministerial Dialogue to a full 'comprehensive strategic partnership'.
4. **Indo-Pacific Region:** The Act East policy does not limit its focus to the Indian Ocean. As a growing power, India has been trying to extend its foothold beyond the Indian Ocean into the larger Indo-Pacific region. India is in favour of inclusive and open sea communication lanes as it supports freedom of navigation and a rule-based world order. ASEAN occupies a central position in India's strategy with regard to the Indo-Pacific. India, which holds annual naval drills called Malabar with the US and Japanese navies each year, agreed to invite Australia to join this military exercise. This further strengthens the grouping of Indo-Pacific nations called the QUAD.
5. **Addressing Deficit Delivery:** In the past, the failure to deliver on promises, that is, a severe delivery deficit, has negatively affected India's efforts to improve regional connectivity. With the Act East policy, India wants to focus on completing projects related to infrastructure in a time-bound manner. The Kaladan Multi-Modal Transit Transport Project initially launched in 2008 faced several delays in completion but now, a fresh deadline has been issued for completion of the project by 2023.
6. **CLMV Countries:** The CLMV countries are Cambodia, Laos, Myanmar and Vietnam. The Act East policy wants to focus on developing manufacturing hubs in CLMV countries, which are seeing the highest foreign direct investment growth, especially in manufacturing. In 2018, ASEAN was India's 4th largest trading partner accounting for 10.2 per cent of India's total trade while India was ASEAN'S 7th largest trading partner. The government has proposed the establishment of a Project Development Fund which will encourage Indian companies to develop manufacturing hub in CLMV countries as they are large potential markets for Indian products.
7. **Cultural Diplomacy:** Cultural diplomacy and spread of soft power is also a major focus of the Act East policy. India shares geographical, historical and civilisational links with ASEAN countries and it wants to strengthen these connections through cultural diplomacy. Nalanda University has been revived by the Government of India in Rajgir, Bihar. Myanmar and Thailand, which have a large Buddhist population, also share religious ties with the Buddhist culture in India. In 2018, the Indian Council for Cultural Relations (ICCR) announced the Ramayana Festival to celebrate 'shared heritage of the eastern world' in which cultural groups from various ASEAN member nations would participate.

Challenges to Act East Policy

There are several factors inhibiting the success of Act East Policy. Given below are some of these challenges:

1. **Opting out of RCEP:** The Regional Comprehensive Economic Partnership (RCEP), a new form of regional economic integration in the Asia Pacific region, was signed in 2020. It is led by China and includes all ten members of ASEAN as well as Japan, South Korea, Australia and New Zealand. India, however, opted out of the RCEP free trade agreement, as negotiations failed to address its core concerns. This has led to a disappointment in the region with India's economic policies.
2. **Growing power of China:** China's direct influence on the region has been steadily rising over the past decade. This makes India's position geopolitically difficult as relations between China and India remain strained. In 2020, ASEAN was China's largest trading partner while China has been ASEAN's largest trading partner for 12 years in a row.
3. **Poor trade with ASEAN:** The most robust of ASEAN's partnership groups, APT or ASEAN Plus Three, had a total trade of US$ 678.2 billion in 2011 which was 28.4 per cent of its global trade. In comparison, India's trade was US$ 74.9 billion or 2.9 per cent of ASEAN's overall trade, and its investment declined to US$ 1.8 billion in 2011 from US$ 3.4 billion in the previous year. This shows that India's leverage vis-à-vis ASEAN remains limited.
4. **Low ease of doing business:** India still occupies a low position (63rd rank as of 2020) in the Ease of Doing Business (EoDB) index. It is an improvement from 2014 when India occupied the 142nd rank. But labour laws and regulations continue to be very strict and complicated in India and the policy of land acquisition remains challenging. This makes it difficult for India to realise its trade potential with regard to the Act East policy but this can be tackled through reforms in laws and regulations.

INDIA AND WEST ASIA

India shares a long historical association with West Asia and India's relations with the region have evolved over the years.

Importance of West Asia

1. **Trade and Investment:** The Gulf Cooperation Council (GCC) is a political and economic alliance of Saudi Arabia, UAE, Bahrain, Qatar, Oman and Kuwait. India's trade with GCC nations is estimated to be valued at around US$ 100 billion as of 2023. PM Narendra Modi visited Saudi Arabia in April 2016 decided to transform the existing buyer-seller relationship into a more extensive partnership.

   As per data from India's commerce ministry, bilateral trade between India and the GCC has increased to US$ 154.73 billion in FY 2021–2022 from US$ 87.4 billion in 2020–2021. India's exports to the GCC saw a 58.26 per cent increase to about US$ 44 billion in FY 2021–2022, against US$ 27.8 billion in FY 2020–2021. Of the GCC countries, UAE is India's number one trade partner allowing trade in its many economic free zones across the constituent seven emirates: Abu Dhabi, Dubai, Sharjah, Ajman, Ras al-Khaimah, Umm al-Quwain and Fujairah.
2. **Food Security:** GCC states and India cooperate in the sensitive area of food security for mutual benefit. A new farm-to-port project has been proposed which will be similar to a special economic zone (SEZ) but in the style of a corporatised farming zone where crops would be grown for

the UAE market, with dedicated logistics infrastructure to transport the produce to the port. Agriculture research is also an area of cooperation between India and West Asia. Digitalisation of the economy is another area which will benefit from bilateral cooperation.

3. **Energy:** The GCC countries are accountable for over 60 per cent of India's energy imports and constitute the most convenient energy supply source needed to cater to India's ever-growing energy needs. India needs more energy to propel its projected GDP growth rate of 8–10 per cent per annum for the coming decade. The energy needs of India will continue to grow in tandem with the growing middle-class incomes and thus bilateral relations with GCC and West Asia is of utmost importance to India. In 2022, India has been ranked the third largest primary energy consumer in the world. Gulf nations want to take advantage of this vast Indian market and continue trade in energy.
4. **Diaspora of Expatriate Indians:** Presently, there are above seven million Indians living in the GCC countries, making them the largest expatriate group in the region. The Indian expatriate population accounts for a significant portion of the total population of each country. Indians are key to the UAE's construction, retail, financial services, healthcare, manufacturing and transport sectors.
5. **Civilisational Link:** India and the UAE region share a deep civilisational connection, with a recorded history of cultural exchange and historical linkages spanning centuries. In modern times both regions have shared a colonial past and struggles for independence. In the present day too, India and UAE enjoy a strong bilateral trade, commercial and cultural relationship.

Recent Changes in West Asia

1. **Changing Equations in West Asia**

   In the past, Palestine has been an issue affecting unity among the West Asian nations, and the recognition of Israel's claim continues to be a problem. In 2020, UAE and Bahrain established diplomatic relations with Israel under the Abraham Accords. It is worth noting that Jordan and Egypt already maintain diplomatic relations with Israel. In 2022, US declared that it will launch a new four-nation dialogue with India, Israel and the United Arab Emirates, calling it the West-Asian Quad.
2. **Diversification of Economy**

   The UAE has become a model of economic development in West Asia. More than 50 per cent of UAE's GDP comes from the service sector now whereas earlier it was dependent on export of petroleum and gas. Saudi Arabia and the rest of the West Asian nations are looking towards the model of UAE for diversification of their economies. Renewable sources of energy like solar power, wind power and hydropower are increasingly becoming popular and are in demand now. Introduction of these alternate sources are necessary as being merely dependent on petroleum exports is not sustainable in the long term.
3. **Terrorist Threat**

   Iran is considered a new threat of security for West Asian nations. In 2019, Saudi Arabia called Iran the 'world's chief sponsor of terrorism' accusing it of sponsoring terrorism. Israel too has always blamed Iran for sponsoring terrorism. Many West Asian nations in recent years have spoken against terrorism. UAE does not support Pakistan because of issues of terrorism, which is a sentiment shared by India as it is plagued by cross-border terrrorism.

Changes in India's Policy towards West Asia

1. **De-Hyphenation of Israel and Palestine**
   India has been following a de-hyphenation policy towards Israel and Palestine in the recent years as it wants to cultivate simultaneous friendly and cordial relations with both Israel and Palestine. Maintaining relations with Israel is in the interest of India for the long term, as is maintaining cordial relations with Palestine. India does not want to take sides in this age-old conflict over identity and land (Jerusalem) and supports the two-nation theory as a solution to this problem.
2. **UAE and Saudi Arabia as New Partners**
   India's foreign policy has become increasingly active towards the West Asia region in the recent years. In 2022–2023, the UAE with US$ 76.16 billion was the third largest trading partner of India. Saudi company Aramco is planning a multi-billion dollar investment in India's Reliance Industries to diversify its oil business. It wants to buy 20 per cent share of Reliance's refinery. Although earlier UAE and Saudi Arabia preferred Pakistan as a trade partner, now the Indian market has proved to be a greater attraction for the West Asian nations. India was invited as an observer nation to the conference of Organisation of Islamic Cooperation (OIC). Cyber security, maritime security and intelligence are some of the important areas of cooperation between India, Saudi Arabia and UAE.
3. **Attracting Investment through Free Trade**
   Due to the rising conflict between China and India, India has been looking for alternative sources of investment. On the other hand, West-Asian nations are cash-rich countries who are also interested in the Indian market as they want to diversify and no longer be dependent upon oil and gas. To allow greater access for UAE exports entering the Indian market, the two countries signed the landmark UAE-India Comprehensive Economic Partnership Agreement in 2022.
4. **Increasing Connectivity**
   In May 2016, India signed a tripartite agreement with Iran and Afghanistan to develop the Shahid Beheshti Terminal at Chabahar, Iran. India has stopped its oil import from Iran since 2019 due to sanctions imposed by USA on Iran, but it continues to develop the port for ensuring connectivity in Afghanistan and Central Asia. Increasing connectivity with West Asia is important to India as it is not a part of Belt and Road Initiative started by China. Being a major power, India wants to develop its own port in Iran.
5. **Being a Net Security Provider**
   India is a 'swing state', meaning it has a decisive influence on the outcome of global issues. While it is impacted by the changing political equations of West Asia, it is also in a position to play a major role as a net security provider in maintaining peace and stability in the region. India has never supported violence either by Palestinian Hamas or by Israel and plays a mediating role in solving West Asian crises.
6. **Vaccine Diplomacy**
   As part of Vaccine Diplomacy in the Wake of COVID-19, medical support and aid was exchanged globally between different nations. In 2020, at the request of the Kuwaiti government, an Indian rapid response team comprising 15 doctors and health professionals was sent to Kuwait. In the same year, India sent a team of 88 medical professionals to the UAE. In turn, India received 7 metric tons of medical supplies from them.

INDIA AND IRAN

Importance of Iran

There is a large scope for a beneficial relationship between India and Iran in diverse areas such as regional security and stability, transportation (connecting India with Central Asia, and connecting Iran with South and South East Asia), trade and investment, tourism, as well as cultural and academic exchanges based on historical civilisational links. As Iran has more than 15 per cent of the world's gas and 10 per cent of the world's oil, energy cooperation with Iran is also essential to India. Because of their geostrategic location the two countries can also play a significant role in ensuring peace and stability of the West Asia region.

Golden Phase in India-Iran Relations

After the end of the Iraq–Iran War in 1988 and the first Gulf War in 1991, it became easier for India to build ties with Iran. Prime Minister Narasimha Rao paid a successful visit to Iran in 1993, Vice President K. R. Narayanan visited the country in 1996 and Prime Minister Atal Bihari Vajpayee in 2001. From the Iranian side, President Rafsanjani visited India in 1995 and President Khatami in 2003 as the Chief Guest for the Republic Day parade.

The signing of the 'Delhi Declaration' and the 'Memorandum of Understanding on the Roadmap to Strategic Cooperation' during President Khatami's visit to Delhi is significant because these agreements envisaged a comprehensive deepening of ties. India and Iran agreed to work together for the finalisation of a Comprehensive Convention on International Terrorism at the United Nations. The agreements signed proposed cooperation in science and technology, as well as support in areas such as vocational training, urban water management and cultural exchange. Foreign Office consultations and institutional interaction between the National Security Councils of the two countries were also envisaged. The initiative for joint development of Chabahar Port in Iran and linking it by road to Afghanistan was welcomed for its potential for investments in infrastructure projects. For India, connectivity through Iran to Central Asia and Afghanistan is important for strategic reasons, and for this purpose, cooperation with Iran for the development of the Chabahar Port as well as surface transport network is essential.

Iran's Relations with Other Major Powers

The bilateral visit between India and Iran, although successful, could not escape the complications in Iran–US relations. Soon after PM Vajpayee's Iran visit in 2001 and President Khatami's India visit in 2003, the USA attacked Iraq. After removing Saddam Hussein from power, the US turned its attention to Iran and its nuclear programme, attributing motives of weaponisation to it. This affected the India–Iran relations, and difficulties continue due to the extraneous factors such as tensions between Iran and the US, the GCC countries and also Israel. India stopped its oil import from Iran due to sanctions by the USA. So unless the dynamics of Iran's relations with these countries changes, India can only manage and maintain basic bilateral relations, without being able to expand or deepen its ties.

On the other hand, rivalry between US and China has resulted in China wanting to contain US influence in West Asia. To this end, China in 2021 signed a comprehensive strategic cooperation agreement with Iran for 25 years. This has affected India's relations with Iran as soon after, Iran dropped India from the Chabahar rail project, citing funding delays, four years after India and Iran signed an agreement to construct a rail line from Chabahar port to Zahedan along the border with Afghanistan. China wants to maintain similar friendly relations with Saudi Arabia too and this rising influence of China in West Asia poses a further challenge for India's interests in the region.

Iran's Nuclear Programme

As of now, there is no credible evidence that Iran's nuclear programme has gone beyond the stage of peaceful uses of nuclear technology. According to reports, Iran has enriched uranium but only up to 20 per cent, which is permissible peaceful use of nuclear technology, whereas weapons-grade uranium requires 90 per cent enrichment.

Iran is a signatory to the NPT but it has the right under Article 9 of the treaty to opt out of it in supreme national interest as was done by North Korea. It is possible, as in Iran's neighbourhood, there are several nuclear powers including Israel. But as far as India is concerned, the countries whose possession of nuclear weapons may matters to India already have them, and Iran does not fall in that list. With Iran, India neither has a common border nor any serious bilateral problems. But even then, India's relations with Iran might be affected by the latter's position on the issue of nuclear power. India's stand, based on its national interest, would be to discourage nuclear proliferation and maintain friendly relations with Iran, US, GCC and Israel. It is thus a complex and multi-dimensional situation. India's view on this issue can be summed up as follows:

(i) Iran should abide by its commitments in terms of NPT and Additional Safeguards.
(ii) The International Atomic Energy Agency (IAEA) is the legitimate forum to decide the nature of Iran's nuclear programme and ensure whether it is abiding by its international commitments.
(iii) Iran has full right to develop nuclear technology for peaceful purposes.
(iv) Any attempt at a military solution to Iran's nuclear programme will have far-reaching consequences.

Iran and the P5+1 (China, France, Germany, Russia, the United Kingdom, and the United States) reached a historic nuclear deal on 14 July 2015 that limits Iran's nuclear programme and allows monitoring in exchange for relief from nuclear sanctions.

INDIA AND AFGHANISTAN

Afghanistan is an Islamic country located at the crossroads of Central Asia and South Asia. Afghanistan borders Pakistan in the east, Iran in the west, and Turkmenistan, Uzbekistan and Tajikistan in the north. In the northeast, Afghanistan borders China and Pakistan-occupied Gilgit Baltistan, which is a region claimed by India as its own part. The area of Afghanistan is 652,864 sq. km and the population officially estimated to be around 32.9 million. It is a landlocked state and is inhabited by ethnic groups such as Pashtuns, Uzbak, Tajik, Hazara and others.

Monarchy and Its Aftermath

When the policy of non-alignment was adopted in Indian foreign policy, the then ruler of Afghanistan, Zaheer Shah also agreed to the policy of non-alignment. As a result, friendly relations between India and Afghanistan continued on regional and global issues. Afghanistan was a peace-loving country during this period.

In 1973, the monarchy in Afghanistan ended when his regime was overthrown in a coup d'état by his cousin and former prime minister, Mohammad Daoud Khan. Daoud Khan took an aggressive view on the issue of the **Durand Line**. The Durand Line was the dividing border between India and Afghanistan during the British rule, but after the Partition of India, the line became the border between Pakistan and Afghanistan. According to Afghanistan, Pakistan is a new state, not a successor to the British Empire, and therefore, the border between Pakistan and Afghanistan should be redrawn.

In the 1970s, the USSR sent troops into Afghanistan in order to prevent the influence of Pakistan, which was an ally of the USA. Pakistan was used by the US as a front line state to counter the Soviet Union's military intervention in

Afghanistan. The then ruler of Pakistan, General Zia ul-Haq, received huge economic and military support from the US and was also supported by China and Saudi Arabia. The provisions of the 1988 Geneva Accords directed the Soviet Union's forces to withdraw from Afghanistan due to the failing economic condition of the Soviet Union, but even then peace in Afghanistan could not be achieved.

The Rise of Taliban

The Taliban is a militant political movement by Islamic fundamentalists who want to govern the state, economy and society in Afghanistan according to principles of Islam. The influence of Taliban also increased the influence of Pakistan in Afghanistan. Only three states in the world—Pakistan, Saudi Arabia and the United Arab Emirates—recognised the Taliban government when it first came to power. The Taliban government was not recognised by any other country, including India. During the rule of Taliban leader Mullah Omar in the late 1990s, India and Afghanistan had the most hostile relations. In the year 1999, Indian Airlines aircraft IC-814 was hijacked from Kathmandu and landed in Kandahar. Government of India released Masood Azhar in exchange for the passengers of the plane. Close ties were formed between Taliban leader Mullah Omar and Al Qaeda chief Osama bin Laden in Afghanistan during this period. On 11 September 2001, the US World Trade Centre was attacked by Al Qaeda.

War on Terror

Following the terrorist attack on the World Trade Centre in September 2001, the US launched Operation Enduring Freedom (OEF) against the Taliban, which was also supported by the Northern Alliance and India. The US attacked Afghanistan under the garb of the War on Terror. It was a complex situation for Pakistan because it supported the US attack against the Taliban, even though earlier Pakistan was the biggest supporter of the Taliban. Taliban government was overthrown by the US forces.

After the end of Taliban rule, India again developed close relations with Afghanistan. The first presidential election was held in Afghanistan in 2004 and Hamid Karzai was elected as the President. With the emergence of democratic Afghanistan, India–Afghanistan relations gained new strength. Afghanistan became a member of SAARC during the 14th annual summit. India played an active role in the development of infrastructure in Afghanistan. In fact, after 2001, the entire global community supported Afghanistan to aid socio-economic development. In 2012, through the Tokyo conference, the world community assured that by 2016, Afghanistan would be provided US$ 16 billion in financial aid to prevent it from sliding back into chaos when the US foreign troops leave.

Withdrawal of American Troops and the Return of the Taliban

The Taliban had been trying to re-group and re-establish their influence in Afghanistan for a long time. Taliban opposes America, which it considers to be imperialist, as well as the constitutional and democratic rule of Afghanistan.

US President Joe Biden announced on 14 April 2021 that it was time to end the war in Afghanistan. He said that the Afghans were responsible for their own future and the US was not providing any guarantees. This aligned with the long-held Indian position of supporting "an Afghan-led, Afghan-owned and Afghan-controlled" peace process. The US Armed Forces completed their withdrawal from Afghanistan on 30 August 2021, marking the end of the 2001–2021 war. With the end of the war, the Taliban reclaimed power over Afghanistan.

Relations between Pakistan and Afghanistan

Afghanistan is a landlocked country and is therefore dependent on Pakistan for trade. Pakistan does not provide any transit routes to India that would allow entry into Afghanistan. As a result, India is trying to enter Afghanistan via the Chabahar port of Iran. The possibility of India's presence in Afghanistan puts pressure on Pakistan as it is located between India and Afghanistan, and relations between Pakistan and Afghanistan are adverse. It has alleged that the Afghan government is promoting Baloch separatism in Pakistan and accused Afghanistan of supports Pashtun Islamic terrorists. Pakistan promotes Pakistani-backed rule in Afghanistan.

Relations between India and Afghanistan

India has supported Afghanistan in various ways. Till 2022, India invested more than US$ 3 billion for the welfare of the people of Afghanistan.

Development of Infrastructure

India has helped build various infrastructural projects in Afghanistan. India's most significant contribution to rebuilding of Afghanistan was the Parliament built at a cost of US$ 90 million. India also helped to restore the Stor Palace in Kabul. The Salma Dam or India-Afghanistan Friendship Dam is a 42-MW hydropower and irrigation project in Herat Province that completed by India in 2016. India also assisted the construction of the Zaranj Delaram Highway located close to the Afghanistan–Iran border. The 150-million highway is of great strategic importance to India. India also built the 220kV DC transmission line from Pul-e-Khumri which supplies electricity to Kabul. India also restored several telecommunications lines and infrastructure in several other provinces.

Capacity-Building

India restored the Indira Gandhi Institute for Child Health built with India's help in 1985. India has also delivered assistance to Habibia High School in Kabul. Significant cooperation was also done in the fields of training of personnel working in fields of agriculture, banking and computers. India is also pursuing an aid programme for the sustainable development of Afghanistan. In India, students from Afghanistan are given special scholarships in medical, engineering and management institutions. Indian Medical Missions holds free consultations camps in several areas. Healthcare centres were built with India's support in border provinces of Badakhshan, Balkh, Kandahar, and others.

Defence Relations

India helped to train Afghan army and police officers and cadets as part of nation-building efforts in Afghanistan after 2001. A strategic partnership between the two had also been reached before the Taliban takeover. In 2016, the Indian Prime Minister had visited Afghanistan. Two helicopters were given to Afghanistan by India and for the first time India had provided weapons to Afghanistan. India–Afghanistan relations are based on mutual interest, which may not change with the change of government.

India's Strategic Objectives

India has two strategic objectives in its engagement with the Taliban.

1. It wants to prevent Pakistan from using Afghanistan as strategic depth against India. The Taliban takeover of Afghanistan is likely to embolden Pakistan to use its Afghan proxies against India, with possible ramifications for Kashmir. It is possible that terrorism in Kashmir may be controlled through better relations between India and Afghanistan.
2. India has made substantial investments in Afghanistan—around $3 billion—that need to be protected.

INDIA AND PAKISTAN

India and Pakistan have a complex and hostile relationship that is rooted in historical and political events, the most important of which is the Partition of British India in August 1947. Due to this hostility, the India–Pakistan border is one of the most militarised international boundaries in the world. The root cause of the dispute between India and Pakistan is the **deep distrust** between the two countries. Pakistan has been waging a proxy war against India, which is a serious threat to Indian security. The Indus river water dispute, the Kashmir dispute as well as the Kulbhushan Jadhav dispute are the results of this distrust. The hostile relation between India and Pakistan has led to unrest in the South Asia region and is hampering the SAARC's effectiveness.

Post Independence

India and Pakistan established diplomatic ties after independence, but the relationship soon turned sour because of the effects of the partition and conflicts regarding territorial claims over various princely states, most notably that of Jammu and Kashmir. Kashmir was invaded by Pakistani paramilitary forces in October 1947 and they took under their control almost one-third of Kashmir, now known as Pakistan Occupied Kashmir.

Liaquat Ali Khan was the first Prime Minister of Pakistan. The constitution of Pakistan came into force in the year 1956 and Pakistan adopted a parliamentary democratic rule with Islam as the state religion. But democracy in Pakistan could not be sustained as in 1958, martial law was declared in Pakistan and Gen. Ayub Khan, the Commander-in-Chief of the Pakistan Army came into power. Ayub Khan became president and used his military power to try and take over Kashmir. War broke out between India and Pakistan in 1965 due to Pakistan's attack on India.

1965 War and the Tashkent Agreement (1966)

The 1965 war between India and Pakistan was the second conflict between the two countries over the status of the state of Jammu and Kashmir. While India was still recovering from the damages of Sino-India War of 1962, Pakistan wanted to use this opportunity to take over Jammu and Kashmir. The war began on 24 April 1965, when Pakistan Army attacked the Rann of Kutch region. The Pakistani Army later entered Kashmir with the launch of Operation Gibraltar. Although the war ended in a standoff, the conflict is seen as a strategic and political defeat for Pakistan as it did not succeed in acquiring Kashmir.

Peace negotiations, mediated by the Soviet Union, were hosted in Tashkent (now in Uzbekistan) to end the war, where Indian Prime Minister Lal Bahadur Shastri and Pakistani President Ayub Khan signed the Tashkent Agreement on 10 January 1966. The basic provisions of this agreement are as follows:

- India and Pakistan will try to establish relations as good neighbours in that they will never use force against each other and will settle disputes peacefully.
- Economic relations and trade between India and Pakistan as well as telecommunications and cultural exchanges will be re-established.
- Normal diplomatic relations will be restored between the two countries and the High Commissioners of the two countries will resume work in their respective posts again.
- War prisoners will be exchanged.
- A joint team will be set up to make recommendations on other matters related to both countries.

In 1969, Ayub Khan resigned from office and invited commander-in-chief of the army General Yahya Khan to take over control of the country. During his dictatorship, he began Operation Searchlight in order to suppress Bengali nationalism and stop Mujibur Rahman from becoming the Prime Minister of Pakistan, which triggered the Bangladesh Liberation War. Yahya Khan used violence in East Pakistan leading to a large number of refugees from East Pakistan migrating to the Northeastern states of India, which in turn affected India's security. Pakistan tried to suppress the movement of democracy in East Pakistan while India aided the Bangladeshi resistance army known as the Mukti Bahini. In December 1971, Pakistan attacked India by launching airstrikes. The strikes led to India declaring war on Pakistan, and Pakistan was ultimately defeated. Following this, East Pakistan became the independent state of Bangladesh. It was also a refutation of Pakistan's two-nation theory. Pakistani ambassador and writer Husain Haqqani in his book *Pakistan: Between Mosque and Military* has considered Zulfikar Ali Bhutto's ambition as the root cause of the partition of Pakistan. After the 1971 Indo-Pakistan war, the Shimla Agreement was signed in 1972 between the two countries.

Shimla Agreement (1972)

The Shimla Agreement was a peace treaty signed in Shimla, India between Zulfikar Ali Bhutto, the then President of Pakistan, and Indira Gandhi, then Prime Minister of India. The purpose of this agreement was to free the prisoners of war who were under the custody of the Indian army as well as allow Pakistan to formally and diplomatically recognise Bangladesh. The provisions of this agreement were as follows:

- Both countries will hold bilateral talks for peaceful resolution of all disputes and problems and will not take unilateral action or use force against each other. Neither country will violate territorial integrity nor will they interfere in each other's political independence.
- The following measures will be taken to normalise relations between the two countries:
  (i) All communication between the countries will be re-established.
  (ii) Transit routes will be provided, establishing close relations between the countries.
  (iii) There will be cooperation in business and economic sectors.
  (iv) Exchange of science and culture will be enhanced.
- The ceasefire line of 17 September 1971 will be recognised as the Line of Control (LOC) between India and Pakistan.

Zulfikar Ali Bhutto continued as the President and later as Prime Minister, until General Zia-ul-Haq seized power in a coup in 1977 and subsequently became the President in 1978. Martial law was established again in Pakistan under Zia-ul-Haq and the principle of Islamic solidarity was promoted.

Lahore Declaration (1999)

Following India's nuclear tests (Operation Shakti) in May 1998, Pakistan conducted its own series of atomic tests. This led to rising tensions and fear about a possible nuclear war in the region. Then Prime Minister Atal Bihari Vajpayee took a bus trip to Pakistan in the year 1999, raising a lot of positive expectations. Subsequently, the Lahore Declaration was signed between India and Pakistan which reiterated the points of the Shimla Agreement in spirit, stating that the two countries would resolve disputes through bilateral and peaceful settlement. Under the terms of the Lahore Declaration, a mutual understanding was reached regarding the development of nuclear weapons and it discussed ways to avoid a nuclear race and both non-conventional and conventional conflicts. The treaty included the following points:

- The two countries will work towards mutual peace and stability to ensure development and prosperity of the people.
- Permanent peace and good bilateral relations are essential for the future of both countries.
- Both countries will implement the Shimla Agreement in letter and spirit.
- Both countries committed to the principles and purposes of the Charter of the United Nations as well as the principles of peaceful co-existence.

In addition to these basic principles of the Lahore Declaration, a memorandum of understanding was also signed between the Foreign Secretaries on the following subjects:

- Both countries will initiate steps such as nuclear CBMs to prevent nuclear conflict and increase security and mutual credibility.
- The two countries will provide information to each other before testing missiles to prevent the possibility of sudden and unauthorised use of nuclear weapons.
- Both countries will try to ban further nuclear testing.

Kargil Conflict (1999)

The positive expectations that were raised by the Lahore Declaration soon died down as the very next year, in 1999, Kargil was infiltrated by the Pakistani Army, turning the relationship between the two countries highly hostile. In the same year, army chief Pervez Musharraf removed then Pakistani Prime Minister Nawaz Sharif from power and took over, declaring martial law once again. As a result, India ended negotiations with Pakistan altogether, refusing to negotiate with a military ruler. Due to the war between India and Pakistan, the conference of SAARC which was to be held in 1999 was postponed and later held in Kathmandu in the year 2002.

Ally to the War on Terror

Soon after the US initiated the War or Terror in 2001, the Indian armed forces were mobilised in December 2001, to thwart the active promotion of cross-border terrorism and posturing by Pakistan; this was called Operation Parakram. This was the largest deployment of Indian forces on the border after 1971. India also demanded that the United States declare Pakistan a terrorist state and also opposed the adoption of double standards in the war on terror. As Pakistan became a US ally in the fight against terrorism, India argued that the very state that sponsors terrorism cannot be an ally in the war on terror.

Restoration of Democracy

In the early 2000s, there was growing domestic and international pressure on Pakistan to end military rule. On 18 August 2008, Musharraf resigned as president under pressure from the coalition government ending the military rule. He was succeeded by Asif Ali Zardari, who became Pakistan's 11th President. However, the Pakistani army continues to be powerful and has significant influence on the civilian government.

Role of the Military

The political system in Pakistan has always been dominated by the military. The army plays an influential part in governance. The army took control of the state for the first time in 1958, when Marshal Ayub Khan came into power. After another coup in 1977, General Zia ul Haq became the new military ruler of Pakistan who ruled from 1978 to 1988. Once again in 1999, General Pervez Musharraf sacked Pakistan's elected Prime Minister Nawaz Sharif from the government and held power until 2008.

Pakistan currently has a democratic government, but the real control over government is that of the army and this has made it difficult for Pakistan to establish peace with India. The powerful military also has economic interests in the country because most of the business in Pakistan is controlled by retired military personnel.

Core Issues of Dispute

Although the partition of India was largely based on religious lines, nation-building in the name of religion does not remain feasible for Pakistan anymore. Bangladesh, also a Muslim-majority country, separated from Pakistan; the country also has to confront the growing threat from Pakistani Taliban, which demands an Islamic State. As a result, Pakistan is struggling with an internal crisis and has consequently adopted an anti-India policy for legitimising their position as a nation. Zulfikar Ali Bhutto had said in the UN Security

Council on 22 September 1965 that Pakistan 'will wage a war for a thousand years' against India. His doctrine of bleeding India by 'inflicting a thousand cuts' was pursued on many occasions, and especially in Jammu and Kashmir.

Kashmir Issue

After the partition of India, the princely state of Kashmir merged with India. But this merger was not accepted by Pakistan and in the year 1948, Pakistan indirectly attacked India. In 1965 and 1971, there were wars between the two countries and after being defeated in the traditional wars, Pakistan began promoting proxy wars through cross-border terrorism in Kashmir. Even today, Pakistan continues to sponsor terrorism in Kashmir and is constantly trying to destabilise the region.

Revocation of Article-370: In August 2019, India took a decisive step and a radical shift in policy by announcing the revocation of Article 370, which takes away the special status of Jammu and Kashmir. The government is taking steps to change how the region will be governed, a decision that will have major consequences for the state's people as well as the country's relationship with Pakistan. Through this, Jammu and Kashmir ceased to be a state and became two union territories: Jammu and Kashmir and Ladakh. The government further argued that Kashmir is no longer a disputed area and suggested India's claim over the Pakistan Occupied Kashmir (PoK).

Surgical Strike

Following the Uri terror attack on India in 2016, India started a surgical strike against Pakistan. Abandoning the principle of strategic restraint adopted by India, an aggressive policy was adopted and the Line of Control was also crossed by India. India claimed that this attack was not against Pakistan, but against terrorism and so Pakistan should also cooperate with India. This action of India was also supported by countries like USA.

A surgical strike involves penetrating deep into the territory of the enemy country to destroy certain targets. On 19 September 2016, the Indian Army attacked terrorist bases in Pakistan occupied Kashmir and destroyed some terrorist training centres. This action is an example of India's changing foreign policy which is more aggressive when it comes to protecting the unity and integrity of the nation.

Ways to Normalise Relations

Nuclear Confidence–Building Measures

The Lahore Declaration of 1999 can be considered as the basis of nuclear CBM between India and Pakistan. The following are the main elements of confidence-building measures adopted by the two countries:

- Mutual discussions between foreign secretaries regarding security and nuclear principles.
- Creating an environment of permanent security and peace between the two countries.
- Agreement regarding the issuance of prior notice and prior notification regarding the testing of missiles.
- Making a functional hotline between the Foreign Secretaries of both countries.
- To take measures to reduce the nuclear threat and to prevent accidents in nuclear sector (of nuclear plants or nuclear weapons).

CBM between India and Pakistan in the nuclear field is of great importance as Kashmir has been globally identified as a *nuclear flashpoint*, a zone where the risks of nuclear conflict are extraordinarily high.

Composite Dialogue

Several rounds of composite dialogue have taken place between India and Pakistan over the years. In 2004, a new round of dialogue started under which the two countries adopted a flexible approach, recognising that there are several issues of dispute between the two countries on which negotiations should be held simultaneously and institutionally. Some of the issues that were discussed are: Peace and security including CBMs, Jammu and Kashmir, Siachen, Sir Creek, Wullar barrage/Tulbul Navigation Project, terrorism and drug trafficking, economic and commercial cooperation, and promotion of friendly exchanges in various fields. The subsequent round of composite dialogue between India and Pakistan was postponed following the 2008 Mumbai terrorist attacks.

People-to-People Contact

On 24 October 2019, officials from the Indian and Pakistani governments met at the zero point on the international border to sign an agreement operationalising the Kartarpur Corridor. This corridor connects the Dera Baba Nanak shrine in India's Punjab with Gurdwara Darbar Sahib in Pakistan's Punjab, and the agreement guarantees Indian pilgrims visa-free access to this corridor to travel to the holy site in Pakistan.

China-Pakistan Economic Corridor (CPEC)

China and Pakistan share close ties with each other and this Sino-Pak axis presents a big challenge to India. Currently, the largest country to invest in Pakistan is China. With the One Belt, One Road (OBOR) project, China wants to connect Kashgar in Xinjiang province to Gwadar port of Balochistan in Pakistan. This route will make it easier for China to send oil and goods as well as enter the Indian Ocean directly through the Arabian Sea.

Indian Prime Minister's Initiatives to Improve Relations

PM Modi visited Pakistan in December 2015. This was an Indian Prime Minister's first visit to Pakistan after a gap of 12 years. This was a sudden unannounced visit and the Prime Minister travelled directly to Pakistan from Afghanistan in an attempt to improve bilateral relations. But following the Prime Minister's visit, there was a terrorist attack on the air force station located in Pathankot district of Punjab, India, in which Pakistan's terrorist organisation Jaish-e-Mohammed was involved.

INDIA AND CENTRAL ASIA

The Soviet Union was a federal union made up of 15 republics joined together by a shared socialist ideology. In the year 1991, the Union was dissolved and the constituent republics states that were previously part of the former Soviet Union (USSR) emerged as independent Central Asian countries, namely **Kazakhstan**, **Tajikistan**, **Uzbekistan**, **Turkmenistan** and **Kyrgyzstan**. These are all landlocked countries who are dependent on Russia and West Asian countries for trade. Russia and China are the two major powers located near them.

'Connect Central Asia' Policy

The 'Connect Central Asia' policy was announced in 2012 with the intent to improve connectivity with Central Asian countries. Transportation to the region is key for the connectivity, because Central Asian countries are landlocked and India does not share a border with these countries. A significant emphasis was placed on the 4Cs: Commerce, Connectivity, Consular and Community. A Track II diplomacy initiative has been taken by India to further deepen relations with the region. It is noteworthy that India has already succeeded in building strong cultural relations with these countries.

India's Foreign Trade Policy 2015–2020 placed great a priority on the completion of the International North–South Transport Corridor, a 7,200-km-longmulti-mode network of ship, rail, and road route for trade between India, Iran, Azerbaijan, Russia, Central Asia and Europe. India is connected by rail, road and air with Moscow via Iran. Emphasis is also being laid on strengthening water transportation connectivity so that India can trade directly with the East European countries. India is the third largest energy importing nation in the world and better connectivity with these countries will improve India's energy security for India. The Chabahar port in Iran is already being developed by India to make the North-South Corridor effective.

Growing Cooperation between India and Central Asia

India is carrying out *capacity-building and skill development programmes* in the Central Asia region, through which citizens of Central Asian countries are being trained in education, health and information technology sectors by a large number of English-speaking engineers and doctors from India.

India and Kazakhstan also share close relations and this is evident from the **civil nuclear agreement** between the two countries. Kazakhstan and India are also collaborating in the fields of energy, information technology and health. The role of both countries in the reconstruction of Kazakhstan is also notable. In view of the increasing importance of Kazakhstan, in 2009, the President of Kazakhstan was invited as the chief guest at India's Republic Day celebrations.

In July 2015, Indian Prime Minister Narendra Modi visited all the Central Asian countries and during his visit, the main emphasis was on improving **cooperation against terrorism**. The heads of states discussed this issue as the Central Asian region is as affected by terrorism as India. This is because for the creation of an Islamic state in West Asia, violence is perpetrated by ISIS in the region which also affects Central Asia.

Central Asia and America

When the previously socialist republics emerged as independent states with the dissolution of the USSR, America encouraged the establishment of democratic rule in these countries. China and Russia started to consider the growing influence of America in this region as a threat. In 2011, Kyrgyzstan became the first country in the Central Asian region where a democratic and peaceful transfer of power took place.

INDIA AND NEPAL

Nepal is a country in the foothills of the Himalayas to the north of India. The birthplace of Lord Buddha, Nepal is close to India religiously, culturally and linguistically. The population of Nepal is 2.9 crore as per the 2021 census and the area is 147,516 square km. Nepal is a buffer state between India and China. Nepal shares its northern border with Tibet, the eastern border with Sikkim, and the southern border with Bihar and Uttar Pradesh in India. Between India and Nepal, there is an open border of about 1,770 km, where there is free movement of people. The Indian rupee is legally recognised as a currency in Nepal. India accounts for about two-third of Nepal's merchandise trade, about one-third of trade in services, one-third of foreign direct investments.

The Principle of Equal Distance with India and China

In 1955, King Mahendra become new King of Nepal in place of King Tribhuvan. He tried to build better diplomatic relations with China in 1956. Around the same time, China built the Kathmandu and Kodari highways. The Nepalese Citizenship Act of 1952 granted Indians the right to immigrate to Nepal become Nepalese citizens easily, which caused resentment in Nepal and Nepal's royal family's dissatisfaction with India grew. As a result, Nepal began growing more friendly towards China as King Mahendra wanted to use the China card to balance India's influence and have equal diplomatic distance with both China and India.

Mass Movement for Democracy

After 1990, multi-party democracy was restored in Nepal for the first time and democratic elections were held. Common people supported this restoration of democracy and it was called Jana Andolan or People's Movement. India too supported democracy in Nepal. In this democratic system, the king became the constitutional head and the real powers of government were vested in the Parliament. However, democratic rule in Nepal failed to provide a stable government and the subsequent instability left the common people very disappointed.

In February 1996, the People's War was declared by the Maoist insurgents. In a highly significant political move, the Maoists decided to join mainstream politics in Nepal, ending rule of the monarchy. In November 2006, the ten-year civil war in Nepal formally ended with a peace agreement signed between the Maoists and seven major political parties. Monarchy was abolished in Nepal on 28 May 2008 and Nepal became a democratic, socialist, secular, and sovereign republic.

The second election of the Constituent Assembly was held in Nepal in 2013 and despite many differences, the new constitution of Nepal came into effect in 2015. In accordance with this constitution, a parliamentary, federal, and secular form of governance has been adopted in Nepal with the creation of seven different provinces for local governance.

The Madheshi Problem

In Nepal, the area between the hills and plains is called the Madheshi region. The Madhesh province was formed after the adoption of the Constitution of Nepal. The Madheshi region consists of 22 districts, which share borders with India. More than 40 per cent of the population of Nepal lives in the Madhesi region. Sixty-five per cent of Nepal's agricultural production and 76 per cent of Nepal's total revenue comes from this region. Madheshis speaks Maithili, Bhojpuri and Hindi languages. They have cultural and marital relations with Indians.

The Madheshis demanded better representation through the creation of two provinces for themselves, because out of the 75 districts of Nepal, about 20 districts have a large population of Madheshis and Madheshis are in absolute majority in five districts. The constitution gave equal representation to each state in the upper house, but Madheshis demanded representation on the basis of population which they deemed fairer.

Relations with India

The basis of friendly relations between India and Nepal is the **1950 Indo-Nepal Treaty of Peace and Friendship**, which exemplifies the special relationship between the two countries. Under the provisions of this Treaty, Nepalese citizens enjoy many advantages in India and can avail facilities and opportunities at par with the Indian citizens. It allows for free movement of people between India and Nepal and cooperatation between the two countries on the issue of security. It assures that citizens of both countries will be allowed to work across the border. The two nations will also collaborate on matters of defence and foreign policy and Nepal will consult India before purchasing arms from any other country.

Ever since India's independence, India has provided support for the economic development of Nepal. A lot of the basic infrastructure in Nepal was built with India's aid. Nepalese soldiers are also trained in India. Import of goods from Nepal to India is duty-free. India also provides a transit route for transport of goods between Nepal and the Kolkata port. The basis of trade between India and Nepal is the 1996 Treaty of Trade, which was later amended in 2009. There are provisions in this treaty regarding simplification of regulations and favourable customs duty. There is also a provision for the formation of a joint committee for trade-related issues.

India also provides economic assistance and other aid to Nepal during emergencies, one example of which was 'Operation Maitri' or 'Operation Friendship' during the 2015 Nepal earthquake. It was a rescue and relief operation in Nepal by the Government of India and Indian Armed Forces in the aftershock of the massive earthquake.

Cooperation in Power Projects

Nepal has large rivers like Mahakali, Karnali, Koshi and Gandak, which have high hydroelectric potential. Theoretically, Nepal has a hydropower generation capacity of 90,000 MW, of which 43,000 MW is economically feasible. Data from 2011 suggests that Nepal produces only 650 MW of hydropower. There is thus an immense scope of cooperation between India and Nepal in the field of hydroelectric power generation. Bhutan, for instance, has benefitted immensely from effective cooperation for hydroelectric power with India. Nepal on the other hand imports electricity from India.

The following are a few notable agreements on the issue of hydroelectric power projects between India and Nepal:

1. Kosi Agreement: An Agreement on Kosi Project was signed between India and Nepal in 1954 and amended in 1966, for building, operation and maintenance of Kosi barrage and associated structures.
2. Gandak Agreement: An agreement was signed on 4 December 1959 between the governments of Nepal and of India on the Gandak Irrigation and Power Project.
3. Mahakali Treaty: A treaty was signed in 1996 for the integrated development of the Mahakali River including the Sarada Barrage, Tanakpur Barrage and Pancheshwar Project.
4. Arun-III Project Development Agreement: In 2018, India and Nepal signed an agreement for the development of a 900-megawatt hydroelectric project on the Arun river in Nepal, which will boost economic cooperation and reduce the trade deficit of Nepal with India.

Cooperation to Increase Connectivity

The Motihari–Amlekhgunj pipeline is a 69 km long trans-border **petrolium pipeline** between Amlekhgunj Oil Depot in Nepal and Motihari, Bihar in India. It was developed to ensure cheaper supply of oil between India and Nepal.

Further, India announced the development of a new **rail project**, comprising an electric rail track linking Kathmandu with Raxaul (Bihar), during the visit of Nepali Prime Minister K. P. Sharma Oli to India in 2018. It also served as an effective response that would balance the growing influence of China on Nepal, as China had earlier announced a rail project connecting Kathmandu. The Indian government has also spent nearly Rs 550 crores to extend the Jaynagar-Bijalpura-Bardibas railway project with the aim of improving rail connectivity between India and Nepal. The project was developed by IRCON, and all rail engineering and infrastructure works are complete.

Border Dispute between India and Nepal

The source of the Kali River has for long been a point of dispute between India and Nepal. While the Indian stand is that Kalapani is in Pithoragarh district from where the river originates, Nepal alleges that the river originates either from Limpiyadhura which is around 15 km from Kalapani, or from Lipulekh, and considers both the locations along with Kalapani as part of Darchula district of Nepal's Sudurpaschim province. The recently-released map by Nepal included all these areas as part of its territory.

The disputed region shares a border on the north with the Tibet Autonomous Region of China and with Nepal in the east and south. The region is placed in between Limpiyadhura, Lipulekh, and Kalapani trijunction between Nepal, India and China (Tibet). The root cause of the Indo-Nepal dispute also has political dimensions because in the past, Nepali Marxist leader K. P. Sharma Oli has allegedly promoted 'anti-India sentiments' and adopted a neutral view on the Doklam dispute arising between India and China.

Recent Political Instability in Nepal and Its Effects

In 2021, Nepal faced a massive political crisis when the president of Nepal, Bidya Devi Bhandari, dissolved the parliament of Nepal twice within a span of six months on PM K. P. Sharma Oli's recommendation. Following this, Nepal's opposition parties approached the country's Supreme Court against the decision of the President. When PM Oli's party could not form a majority, the President ignored the constitutional provisions that allowed government formation from within the sitting Parliament and instead dissolved the country's House of Representatives. Facing this political crisis amidst COVID-19 has put even more pressure on the worsening economy of Nepal. Since the restoration of democracy in Nepal post 1990, there have been 24 governments in just 12 years. After the abolition of monarchy and rise of a new Nepal in 2008, there were 8 Prime Ministers in 8 years, resulting in a grave political crisis. Nepal's economic development has been badly affected by this political instability and the people are highly disappointed. These political factors have also affected Nepal's relations with its neighbours.

Nepal's former Prime Minister K. P. Sharma Oli stated that while India has great importance for Nepal, it also wants to strengthen relations with China. It is noteworthy that China provides a very high amount of economic aid for the development of infrastructure in Nepal. This is necessary especially for the promotion of tourism in Nepal. In 2021, K. P. Sharma Oli was replaced by Sher Bahadur Deuba of Nepali Congress. There has been a positive turn in Indo-Nepali relations after the arrival of Sher Bhadur Deuba, as the PM adopted an India-first policy. Prime Minister Modi visited Nepal in May 2022 to further cement relations between India and Nepal.

INDIA AND BANGLADESH

The country of Bangladesh lies on the eastern border of India. It is surrounded by India on all three sides. Its area is 1.48 lakh sq. km and its population is 16.9 crores as of 2021. For maintaining connectivity with Northeastern states, Bangladesh is a very important neighbour for India.

From East Pakistan to Bangladesh

The movement for freedom, the Bangladesh Liberation War, started in East Pakistan against the ongoing military rule and attempts of religious unification in Pakistan. As a result, in 1971, East Pakistan became the independent secular, democratic and socialist state of Bangladesh under the leadership of Sheikh Mujibur Rahman.

India's support in the creation of the independent nation of Bangladesh has been significant. Evidence of a cordial relationship with Bangladesh can be seen in the India–Bangladesh Treaty of Friendship, Cooperation and Peace, a 25-year treaty that was signed on 19 March 1972 with the aim of developing close bilateral relations between the two countries. The creation of Bangladesh as an independent nation gave India an enormous edge in the ideological and geo-political arena, as the principle of the two-nation theory was finally disproved.

Assassination of Democracy

When Sheikh Mujibur Rahman was assassinated in 1975, a dictatorial military government was established in Bangladesh instead of the democratic, secular, socialist system and the ban on Islamic parties was lifted. The new ruler of Bangladesh, the military officer Ziaur Rahman, attempted to build better relations with Islamic nations, revealing religious bigotry in foreign policy.

When the Soviet Union invaded Afghanistan in 1979, the tension between US and USSR rose and as a result, the US attempted to thwart Soviet intervention by training the Pakistani Mujahideen. This is how America used Islamic fundamentalism to counterbalance the Soviet Union, whose influence was growing in Afghanistan, Pakistan and Bangladesh. On the other hand, after the Islamic Revolution of Iran in 1978–1979, Islamic rule started to be seen as a possible option in the world. Religious fundamentalism and military rule in Bangladesh became more effective in the context of these incidents happening across the globe.

After the assassination of Ziaur Rahman in 1981, General Hussain Muhammad Ershad took over as the new ruler of Bangladesh. Ershad tried to run the country on the basis of Islamic principles and due to his policies, the country's relationship with India suffered. When there was an issue in water-sharing between India and Bangladesh, General Ershad said that even if all of Bangladesh became a desert, it will never bow down to India, and that Bangladeshis would survive with or without the water from Farakka because Islam was born in the desert. As is evident from this, Ershad's policies were steeped in religious fundamentalism. When Bangladesh declared Islam as the official religion in 1988, the country grew ideologically closer to Pakistan.

Restoration of Democracy

The military dictatorship in Bangladesh came to an end in 1990 and the multi-party democratic system was accepted. In this democratic system, the Awami League tried to revive the Constitution of 1972 and restore secularism. It is believed that the Awami League's approach has always been comparatively more favourable towards India, as opposed to the Bangladesh Nationalist Party (BNP). With the victory of the Bangladesh Nationalist Party in the Bangladesh elections, various issues come to the centre stage, such as border dispute, illegal migration, the Farakka dam issue, terrorism in the Northeastern states, problems of transit routes and trade imbalance. After the year 1990, Pakistan used Bangladesh to carry out a 'proxy war' against India. However, with the coming of Sheikh Hasina Wazed (of Awami League) to power in June 1996, India–Bangladesh relations saw significant improvement. The most important example of this progress is the agreement regarding the sharing of the waters of the Ganges river.

India and Bangladesh Relations

Connectivity

Bangladesh is geopolitically very important to India for connectivity among the Northeastern states. After the partition of India, the Northeastern region of India became a landlocked region. The region is connected to the rest of India only by the Siliguri corridor, which is about 40 km wide. Bangladesh has also allowed India to use Mongla and Chittagong ports, and the rail connectivity between Akhaura in Bangladesh and Agartala in India is almost ready. If Chittagong port is connected to Agartala by rail, the movement of goods from the Northeastern states to other regions of India will become much easier. In this era of liberalisation and globalisation, both countries would be able to benefit from mutual cooperation as Bangladesh is surrounded by Northeastern states on three sides, while the Northeastern province of Tripura is surrounded by Bangladesh on three sides. In 2015, a bus service between Kolkata and Agartala, Tripura was started, which goes through Dhaka. This agreement is a matter of decisive importance for India because even though there is currently the Siliguri corridor connecting Kolkata to Agartala, the distance is above 1,500 km, as opposed to the new route through Bangladesh which is just 500 km. Apart from this, a bus service was also started between Kolkata and Guwahati, which also goes via Dhaka.

The two Prime Ministers jointly inaugurated the newly restored railway link between Chilahati (Bangladesh) and Haldibari (India) on 17 December 2020. Dhaka-Siliguri-Gangtok-Dhaka and Dhaka-Siliguri-Darjeeling-Dhaka bus services were also introduced to enhance people-to-people contact between the countries. The Feni Bridge (Maitri Setu) connecting LCS Subroom (Tripura) and LCS Ramgarh (Bangladesh) has been jointly inaugurated by the two Prime Ministers on 9 March 2021.

Development Partnership

Bangladesh is the biggest development partner of India and its largest regional trade partner. India has extended three Lines of Credits (LOC) to Bangladesh in the last eight years amounting to US$ 8 billion for development of infrastructure in various sectors including roads, railways, shipping and ports. In addition to LOCs, the Government of India has also been providing grant assistance to Bangladesh for various infrastructure projects including the construction of the Akhaura–Agartala rail link, dredging of inland waterways in Bangladesh and construction of the India–Bangladesh Friendship Pipeline to transport high-speed diesel.

Border Disputes

India shares a 4,096-kilometre-long border with Bangladesh. The Indo-Bangladesh border passes through West Bengal, Assam, Meghalaya, Tripura and Mizoram. While earlier, there was frequent border disputes between the two countries because of ambiguous colonial boundaries and a complicated system of enclaves, these were resolved through a series of territorial exchanges finalised in 2015.

Exchange of Enclaves: Enclaves referred to the Indian territories situated in Bangladesh and Bangladeshi territories located in India. The main body of Bangladesh contained 102 Indian enclaves and the Indian mainland contained 71 Bangladeshi enclaves. The problem of enclaves rose during the integration of the princely states after the Partition of India, in which the princely states of Cooch Behar and Rangpur merged with India and Pakistan respectively. A Land Boundary Agreement was signed on 16 May 1974 between Indira Gandhi and Sheikh Mujibur Rahman for the exchange of enclaves and the surrender of adverse possessions. The Teen Bigha Corridor, a strip of land belonging to India on the West Bengal–Bangladesh border, was leased to Bangladesh in September 2011 to allow access to enclaves. The exchange of enclaves was eventually finalised during the visit of Indian Prime Minister Modi to Bangladesh in 2015.

Although the majority of the boundary has been demarcated, there remains the issue of the undemarcated land boundary of approximately 6.1 kilometres in three sectors—Daikhata in West Bengal, Muhuri River–Belonia in Tripura and Lathitila–Dumabari in Assam, and this is currently being negotiated. The dispute arose due to the changing course of the Muhuri river in this region.

Sharing of River Water

In 1972, an Indo-Bangladesh Joint Rivers Commission (JRC) was formed for river water sharing between India and Bangladesh. A major cause of the dispute between India and Bangladesh was the construction of Farakka dam. The purpose of its construction is to divert the water of the Ganges towards the Hooghly river, so that sufficient quantity of water is maintained for the Kolkata port to run. The second purpose of the construction of this dam is to supply water for drinking and industrial purposes to Kolkata. The problem of water sharing of the river Ganga arose mainly during the 'lean season' (which is the low flow period between January and May).

Farakka Agreement

A long-term solution to this water-sharing problem was reached in 1996, when a landmark 30-year agreement, the Ganges Water Sharing Treaty or the Farakka Agreement, was signed between Prime Minister Deve Gowda and Sheikh Hasina. Presently, Bangladesh is also apprehensive about the project of interlinking rivers that India has inititated, but India has assured Bangladesh that the waters of the Ganges and the Brahmaputra rivers will not be diverted from Bangladesh. The water division of the Monu, Khowai, Gumti, Muhuri, Dharla, Dudhkumar and Teesta rivers was also discussed but no final solution has been reached regarding the water-sharing of these rivers between the two countries.

Teesta River Water Dispute

India and Bangladesh first entered into an ad-hoc agreement in 1983 on the issue of sharing of the Teesta river. It was decided that 75 per cent of the water of Teesta would be divided between India and Bangladesh, of which 39 per cent was to be given to India and 36 per cent to Bangladesh and the remaining 25 per cent was to be kept for free flow. At present, a permanent agreement for Teesta river water sharing has been proposed, under which 42.5 per cent of the water will be allocated to India and 37.5 per cent to Bangladesh and 20 per cent will be left for free flow.

Tipaimukh Dam Issue

The Tipaimukh dam is being built at the confluence of the rivers Barak and Tuivai, but this is opposed by Bangladesh. According to Bangladesh, the construction of this dam will restrict the flow of water in two rivers of Bangladesh, Kushiyara and Surma. And since basic livelihood of the people of Bangladesh is based on agriculture, the construction of dam can be highly harmful for them. But according to India, this dam will help in food control, development of fisheries and also improve water transport. The issue of the Tipaimukh dam was raised in the Joint Rivers Commission in 1972, but remained unresolved and was thus again raised in 2005.

Cooperation for Internal Security

The border between India and Bangladesh is being fenced to control movement of illegal migrants and terrorists across the border.

Rohingya Refugees: India is not a signatory of the UN convention on refugees. Despite this, India has historically been welcoming towards refugees. For instance, refugees from Tibet were granted asylum in India and refugees from Sri Lanka are settled in Tamil Nadu. Several thousand Rohingya refugees are living in Jammu and Kashmir, even though India has categorically refused to take in Rohingya refugees. Although, adopting a humanitarian attitude towards the refugees, food grains were sent to Bangladesh as aid and assistance.

Defense Cooperation

High-level exchanges between the two countries in the area of defense include the second edition of the India–Bangladesh CORPAT called Exercise Bongosagar, which was held in October 2020. The Regional Commanders Level Meeting of Coast Guards was conducted virtually on 19 October 2020, and the third Annual Defense Dialogue on 2 November 2020. In the same month, the Indian Army also gifted trained horses and dogs to the Bangladesh Army. The Indian Air Chief visited Bangladesh on an official four-day goodwill visit in February 2021.

Economic Cooperation

Indo-Bangladesh bilateral relations have been mutually beneficial. Especially on the trade front, India and Bangladesh proposed the Comprehensive Economic Partnership Agreement (CEPA) which can further boost the trade between the two countries. In August 2010, India signed a US$ 1 billion credit agreement with Bangladesh to finance its infrastructure projects. Since 2011, India has provided duty free access to Bangladesh on all tariff lines except tobacco and alcohol under SAFTA. In 2011, Prime Minister Manmohan Singh announced duty-free import of 61 items from Bangladesh, that were earlier barred from entering India, a majority of which relate to textiles, particularly readymade garments. India also proposed a transit route from Bangladesh to Bhutan and Nepal that will boost trade. Negotiations on the free trade agreement between

India and Bangladesh are also going on and efforts are being made to implement it in the future. The total trade turnover between India and Bangladesh in 2021–2022 touched US$ 18.2 billion.

Demarcation of Maritime Boundary

According to the 1982 United Nations Convention on the Law of the Sea, territorial sea extends over 12 nautical miles from the nearest point to the baseline of a country. Beyond this, over 200 nautical miles is the Exclusive Economic Zone of the state. Beyond 200 nautical miles, it is open sea.

For a long time, since 1974, the Bangladesh–India maritime boundary demarcation remained pending and the waters were not delimited in the Bay of Bengal. In 2014, this problem of the maritime boundary of India and Bangladesh was resolved by the Permanent Court of Arbitration, headquartered in The Hague, Netherlands. This resolved India's maritime dispute with Bangladesh, Myanmar, and Thailand and further strengthened and improved India's relations with Bangladesh. The award of this tribunal has also accepted India's claim on the island of New Moore. India's authority has also been recognised over areas near the Haribhanga river located in the Bay of Bengal.

Following this decision, both countries can now search for natural resources in their respective regions. The Indian company Oil and Natural Gas Corporation Limited (ONGC) may be invited for oil and gas exploration in the Bangladeshi territory. The path of cooperation in the energy sector between the two countries has thus been cleared.

India's Most Friendly Neighbour

India's relationship with Bangladesh was further strengthened with Prime Minister Narendra Modi's two-day visit between 26 and 27 March 2021. The Indian PM visited Bangladesh on the invitation of his counterpart PM Sheikh Hasina to participate in the golden jubilee of the independence of Bangladesh and the birth centenary of Sheikh Mujibur Rahman, the eminent leader of Bangladesh's freedom struggle. This visit also commemorates 50 years of diplomatic relationship between India and Bangladesh. Three new border haats were inaugurated to promote people-to-people connectivity between the two countries. Increasing connectivity was a focus of the visit and to this end, a new train called "Mitali Express" connecting Dhaka and New Jalpaiguri was inaugurated.

Rise of a New Bangladesh

In December 2018, Sheikh Haseena became the prime minister of Bangladesh for the third consecutive term. Due to political stability of their government, Bangladesh is becoming an engine of economic growth in South Asia. In the fiscal year 2021–2022, Bangladesh registered a GDP growth rate of 7.2 per cent which shows a very positive transformation of Bangladesh. Pragmaticism in foreign policy is also one of the reasons for Bangladesh's economic growth as it is open to receive assistance from China as well as from India.

INDIA AND SRI LANKA

Sri Lanka is an island country in the Indian Ocean, southwest of the Bay of Bengal, and it is separated from the Indian peninsula by the Gulf of Mannar and the Palk Strait. Sri Lanka's strategic situation is very important as it is situated on the sea communication lane of the Indian Ocean. Sri Lanka has a population of 22 million, of which 75 per cent are Sinhalese and 15 per cent Tamil. The common religion among the Sinhalese is Buddhism and among the Tamil it is Hinduism. India and Sri Lanka have ancient cultural and religious ties. While India became independent in 1947, Sri Lanka gained independence from the British rule in 1948. The two countries, however, adopted different foreign policies.

The Issue of Ethnicity and the Sri Lankan Civil War

The prolonged conflict between the Sinhala majority and Tamil minority in Sri Lanka has had a serious effect on bilateral ties between the two countries. The Tamil population living in Sri Lanka is associated with India, but within this too there are two categories of Tamils:

(i) Those who settled in Sri Lanka from India centuries ago. This comprises a population of about 3 million and they originally resided in the Jaffna province of Sri Lanka.
(ii) Those Tamils who were taken to Sri Lanka by the British government to work in tea gardens. They are a population of about 8.5 lakhs and they mostly reside in the Batticaloa and Trincomalee regions.

Discrimination against Minorities

With the Ceylon Citizenship Act of 1948, a law hostile to Tamils of Indian origin, almost a million Tamil persons were deprived of citizenship. While only Tamilians of Indian origin were affected by this citizenship act, in the year 1956, the government declared Sinhalese as the only official language of the country. This was discriminatory to all Tamils, thus proving further that the policies of the Sri Lankan government were averse to the Tamil minorities.

Emergence of LTTE

The LTTE (Liberation Tigers of Tamil Eelam) was a Tamil militant organisation based in northeastern Sri Lanka. It was formed in 1976 as a reaction to the continuous discrimination against and violent persecution of Sri Lankan Tamils by the Sinhalese-dominated government.

The LTTE had the following demands:

(i) They wanted a separate state (eelam), not just autonomy.
(ii) They wanted to create this separate state through violent struggle and did not agree to any talks or discussions with the Sri Lanka government.

In 1983, an anti-Tamil pogrom was carried out by Sinhalese mobs and this was the catalyst which led to the LTTE's escalation of the intermittent conflicts to a full-scale nationalist insurgency. This is how the Sri Lankan Civil War began.

Indo–Sri Lanka Peace Accord

Ethnic strife in Sri Lanka had taken a new turn since the 1980s, as Tamils began resorting to violent activities to combat Sinhalese atrocities against them. Between 1983 and 1986, about 25,000 Tamil refugees arrived in India. In 1986, the Tamil areas of Jaffna peninsula were completely surrounded and blocked by the Sri Lankan army. As a result, India decided to provide aid to the Tamils there on humanitarian grounds. Operation Poomalai (Eagle Mission 4) was launched by the Indian Air Force to air-drop supplies over Jaffna in Sri Lanka. Since the persecution of Tamils in Sri Lanka also affected the Tamil population of South India and threatened India's unity, national interest and territorial integrity, India attempted to negotiate a political settlement with Sri Lanka. The Indo-Sri Lanka Peace Accord was signed between Rajiv Gandhi and J. R. Jayewardene in 1987 to resolve the problems of the civil war. Under the terms of this agreement, India decided to send its peace-keeping forces to Sri Lanka. The other provisions of this agreement were as follows:

(i) This agreement proposed, for the first time, the formation of 9 provincial governments under the unitary form of government rule in Sri Lanka so that Tamils could gain autonomy. Two separate provinces were proposed for the Tamils of the northern and eastern provinces.
(ii) Local subjects of governance, education, health, and transport would be entrusted to these provincial governments.
(iii) These provincial governments would also hold elections.

The Sri Lankan government made the Thirteenth Amendment to the Constitution of Sri Lanka to implement the provisions of this agreement. However, this constitutional amendment could not be implemented effectively in practice as there were several shortcomings. For instance, power over police and land were not given to the provincial governments. Since the Sri Lankan government was not supportive of handing over governance related to land and police to the provincial governments, Tamil autonomy could not be achieved and two-thirds of the Sri Lankan army remained stationed in the Tamil-majority Northern province. Sri Lankan government has also been accused of genocide during the civil war by the government of the Northern Province.

It must be noted that there was significant opposition to the peace accord. The presence of the Indian Peace Keeping Force was seen as going against the sovereignty of Sri Lanka and the LTTE had not been made party to the talks. So after a few months, the LTTE refused to give up arms and declared their intention to continue the armed struggle for an independent Tamil Eelam.

End of LTTE

In 2009, Velupillai Prabhakaran, founder and leader of LTTE, was killed by the Sri Lankan army while conducting an aggressive military operation. The Sri Lankan government headed by President Mahinda Rajapaksa argued that the terrorist problem in Sri Lanka has been resolved through the elimination of LTTE. But Tamils on the other hand, led by the Tamil National Alliance, argue that it is ethnic discrimination that led to terrorism, and hence the root of the problem has not been resolved by the abolition of LTTE. The formal civil war in Sri Lanka however ended with the end of LTTE, although the provisions for autonomy of the Tamils are yet to be implemented.

Fishing Disputes

The livelihood of local residents of the coastal areas of both countries is dependent on fishing. To avoid disputes, India–Sri Lanka maritime boundary agreements were signed in 1974 and 1976 respectively to define the international maritime boundary between the two countries. The width of the sea between India and Sri Lanka ranges from 10 miles to 30 miles. According to international maritime law, the sovereignty of the country extends up to 12 nautical miles from the territory of the country. Since the Palk Strait is very narrow, fishermen from both countries often end up violating each other's borders, and consequently disputes arise between the two countries.

Katchatheevu

Katchatheevu is a 163-acre uninhabited island administered by Sri Lanka. The island currently has no human habitation and is used only by fishermen. Situated in the middle of the Palk Strait, this region was the centre of dispute between the two countries for a long time and both countries claimed ownership citing history. The island of Katchatheevu is extremely important to the local fishermen as the fishing communities in both India and Sri Lanka rely on the catch from this region for their livelihood. Hence the issue of Katchatheevu was an emotional issue. Although it was a previously disputed territory between India and Sri Lanka, in 1974, PM Indira Gandhi handed over the island to Sri Lanka.

Strategic Relationship between India and Sri Lanka

Military Relations

India is the largest country that provides training to Sri Lankan troops. After LTTE was eliminated, India also provided supplies of military hardware to Sri Lanka. There is mutual cooperation between the two countries on the issue of maritime security. The International Maritime Security Conference Galle Dialogue 2014 was held on 1 and 2 December 2014 in the Sri Lankan port city Galle. To promote existing bilateral military relations, navies of the two countries participate in the SLINEX bilateral naval exercises. The Mitra Shakti bilateral exercises are also conducted between the two armies. Sri Lanka plays a major role in being the net security provider in the Indian Ocean Region.

Civil Nuclear Agreement

Sri Lanka's former President Maithripala Sirisena came to India in 2015 and the two countries concluded the civil nuclear agreement on 16 February 2015. It is notable that this is Sri Lanka's first civil nuclear agreement with any country. This nuclear pact would encourage cooperation in the exchange of knowledge, expertise and resources, capacity-building and training with regards to nuclear energy, and nuclear safety and security.

Economic Relations

India has been steadily strengthening its economic relations with Sri Lanka. In 2011, Indian Foreign Minister S. M. Krishna visited Sri Lanka and provided financial assistance to Sri Lanka for railway construction and rehabilitation works in the northern province. It must be noted that Tamils have a majority population in the northern and eastern provinces of Sri Lanka. The Indian foreign minister also signed an agreement to open two new consulates in northern Jaffna and southern Hambantota. There was an agreement between the two countries to restore ferry service between Colombo to Tuticorin and Talaimannar to Rameswaram, a service that had previously been banned in 1983. Thus it appears that the issue between India and Sri Lanka regarding the Tamil population is no longer a major obstacle.

India and Sri Lanka also signed a free trade agreement in 1998 which is considered a model of economic cooperation in South Asia. India is not security threat but an opportunity for smaller neighbouring countries who can benefit from trade with India. Indian tourists visit Sri Lanka in largest numbers and contribute majorly to the economy of the country.

When Sri Lanka faced the worst economic crisis in its history in May 2022, India provided economic assistance worth US$ 2.5 billion to help overcome the economic crises. When the economic crisis turn into a political crisis in Sri Lanka, India became the first neighbouring country who came forward to support. Since refugees from Sri Lanka also come to India, any crisis in neighbourhood has a direct impact on India.

Influence on India's Foreign Policy

India has a federal system where the union government has the right to formulate foreign policy, but that does not mean that the states have no importance or influence. In the era of the coalition government between 1996 and 2014, the influence of state governments on foreign policy issues was more visible as the union government depended on the support of regional parties. Since the union government was supported by the various parties from Tamil Nadu, the demand of the people from this state became even more effective as more than 50,000 Sri Lankan Tamil refugees resided in Tamil Nadu. Therefore, the challenge before Indian foreign policy was to assure the people of Tamil Nadu that India had the ability to contribute positively towards the cause of the autonomy and rehabilitation of Tamils. In the 16th Lok Sabha elections in India after May 2014, the Bharatiya Janata Party won an absolute majority in the Lok Sabha, and the Tamil cause was no longer a major factor in the formulation of Indian foreign policy.

PM Modi's visit to Maldives and Sri Lanka in 2019 demonstrated the priority that India attaches to the Security and Growth for All in the Region (SAGAR) doctrine in its foreign policy. His visit is considered a sign of India's affirmation of solidarity with Sri Lanka in the wake of the deadly Easter terror attacks in April 2019 in which over 250 people were killed.

China's Presence in the Indian Ocean

Sri Lanka is located in the Indian Ocean Sea Lane of Communication, which is considered very important for global trade. Trade between the east coast of India and the west coast also goes through Sri Lanka, because due to the Sethusamudram canal project, movement through the Palk Strait is not possible.

The Colombo Port City project is being built by China. The Mattala Rajapaksa International Airport has also been built with China's support, who has also expressed interest to build an oil refinery in Sri Lanka's Hambantota Port. This port can also be used for military purposes in the future, which would be a big challenge for Indian security. While China is constantly trying to increase its presence in the Indian Ocean, it is also promoting Pakistan's presence in Sri Lanka. Because of these reasons, India is intensifying its economic relations with Sri Lanka since the most effective way to control China's influence is to improve relations with the neighbouring countries.

THE QUADRILATERAL SECURITY DIALOGUE (QUAD)

The Quad or Quadrilateral Security Dialogue is a strategic security dialogue between Australia, India, Japan and the United States. It was started in 2007 by former PM of Japan Shinzo Abe although the informal foundation was laid down earlier in 2004 for cooperation during the December 2004 Indian Ocean earthquake and tsunami. It was re-established in 2017 after negotiations and a summit was held in March 2021. Quad is looking for cooperation in the following areas:

- **Covid and Global Health**
  Over US$ 1.2 billion Covid vaccine doses have been pledged globally. Japan offered to provide a US$ 3.3 billion loan for a Covid emergency support programme. Australia pledged to deliver US$ 431 million in grants for vaccines.
- **Cyber Security**
  Cyber security is considered as a new security threat. The rise of China is also a common threat for the Quad, and therefore group plans to coordinate between governments and industries for the adoption and implementation of shared cyber standards and the development of secure software. Moreover, creating a trusted digital infrastructure is also an objective of the Quad.
- **Infrastructure**
  China's Belt and Road Initiative has been criticised as debt-trap diplomacy, accusing China of plunging developing nations into massive debt. The economic crisis in Sri Lanka is one such example. To counter this, the Quad is committed to providing US$ 50 billion as economic grant for the development of infrastructure. The USA-led Indo-Pacific Economic Framework for Prosperity (IPEF), which has 14 countries as members, is a new initiative of Quad. This economic grouping is an alternative of the China-led Regional Comprehensive Economic Partnership (RCEP).
- **Space**
  Cooperation over and exchange of sensitive technology is an example of strategic cooperation among the Quad members. The group encourages exchanging satellite data for the purpose of monitoring climate change and disaster management. The Quad will also cooperate over long-term sustainability of the outer space environment.
- **Critical Technology**
  All the members of Quad except India are leading countries in terms of development of modern technology. China is a competitor of the USA in the field of technology development. Supply of semi-conductors, support for development of 5G, research on artificial intelligence and cooperation over innovation are included in the new agenda of the Quad.

- **Climate Change and People-to-People Exchange**
  Quad is aiming for cooperation over renewable, clean energy. The Quad members also want to cooperate on green shipping networks and hydrogen partnership. In order to strengthen relations through people-to-people contact, the Quad also encourages the exchange of students between the member countries.

The Quad's Role in Geo-Politics

The world today is divided into factions due to Ukraine crises and there is a growing possibility of a new cold war. All the European countries and the USA are against Russia but China supports Russia. China calls the Quad a new NATO. During the 2022 summit of Quad held in Tokyo, the President of USA said that in case of a Chinese attack over Taiwan, the USA is committed to protect Taiwan. China and Russia have a growing relationship in that they are both against USA.

A free and open Indo-Pacific region is the basic objective of Quad, which champions a rules-based world order. All its members share the same democratic values. In contrast, the rise of China and the aggression of Russia are being considered as new threats against the democratic liberal world order. In recent times, China has become the largest naval power in the world and its aggressive approach in the South China Sea has become a maritime security threat. Further, China's support of North Korea increases the security threat for the rest of the countries. So, indirectly, the Quad is looking to contain China's power.

India's Relation with the Quad

India shares its border with China, and so it is not willing to adopt a directly hostile stance against China. Because of the Ukraine crisis, European countries are more united than before and are looking towards USA for security although the ASEAN nations are not willing to take a side. Quad Plus, which constitutes the four Quad countries and New Zealand, South Korea and Vietnam, can become more powerful and effective with support of Europe and ASEAN. It must be noted that among the Quad members, Japan and Australia are also members of the China-led RCEP and thus have strong economic relations with China. Also, India is the only member of the Quad which did not take an anti-Russian stand during the Ukraine crisis. Further, the USA could not curtail Russia's aggression against Ukraine. Because of these various reasons, nation states are no longer depending on others but have to rely on themselves for their own security.

Multi-alignment diplomacy is the core strategy of India. While USA is India's strongest strategic ally, India cannot ignore the importance of Russia due to its dependency on Russian arms supply. This is especially because the India–USA defence partnership has still not begun the joint production of arms. For obtaining the goal of self-reliance in defense, India is searching for multiple options. India has alsp begun engaging with smaller countries for economic diplomacy. The India–UAE and India–Australia free trade agreements are examples worth noting.

INDIA–BHUTAN

Bhutan is a small, independent country in the eastern Himalayas. A sovereign nation, it is also a member of the United Nations. Bhutan has a Buddhist majority population of about 8 lakhs. Bhutan holds great significance for India as it shares borders with the Northeastern states of India as well as with China.

There were special political relations between British India and Bhutan, as was evident in the Sinchula Treaty of 1865. The British agreed that they would not interfere in Bhutan's internal affairs, but that Bhutan's foreign policy would be decided by England. Later in 1949, two years after India gained independence, the very important role of formulating Bhutan's foreign policy and defence policy was handed down to India. India is now responsible for external affairs and security of Bhutan.

India and Bhutan thus had cordial and friendly relations from the beginning. Bhutan is the only country in South Asia that does not have diplomatic relations with China. After the Indo-China War in 1962, Bhutan's importance increased further and formal diplomatic relations between India and Bhutan were established in 1968. In 1971, Bhutan became a member of the United Nations. Although an independent and sovereign state, Bhutan adopted constitutional monarchy in 2008, moving away from absolute monarchy. Bhutan's transition towards democracy was peaceful. The first multi-party democratic election in Bhutan was held in 2008, following which relations between India and Bhutan further intensified.

Military Relations

In 1949, Bhutan and India signed the Treaty of Friendship, calling for peace between the two nations and stating that Bhutan will conduct its foreign policy as per the instructions of India, but India will not interfere in Bhutan's internal affairs. The treaty also states that Bhutan will not purchase arms and weapons from other countries without India's permission. In practice, India holds the responsibility of protecting Bhutan, and to this end, Indian forces are commissioned to protect Bhutan.

The Treaty of Friendship of 1949 was amended after the restoration of democracy in Bhutan in 2007. While the original treaty mentioned that Bhutan's foreign policy would be determined by India, the amendment stated that India and Bhutan would formulate foreign policy through mutual aid. Through this amendment, Bhutan was now allowed to purchase arms from other countries as well.

Economic Cooperation and Energy Security

Bhutan is a nation endowed with hydroelectric potential, and India needs large amounts of energy to sustain its economic growth rate. The Chhukha and Tala hydropower projects are notable examples of cooperation between India and Bhutan in the field of hydroelectric energy. India has invested heavily in these projects with an energy buy-back agreement for 99 years. During the Indian Prime Minister Narendra Modi's visit to Bhutan in June 2014, the PM addressed a joint sitting of the Parliament in Bhutan and the two countries agreed to cooperate in the hydropower sector, laying the foundation stone for the 600 MW Kholongchhu hydropower project. During Prime Minister Modi's visit to Bhutan in 2019, both sides once again emphasised the importance of hydropower development as one of the most important areas of mutually beneficial bilateral cooperation. The two Prime Ministers formally inaugurated the recently completed 720 MW Mangdechhu Hydroelectric Plant. Both sides noted that with the coming on stream of this project, the jointly created generation capacity in Bhutan has crossed 2000 MW.

It is noteworthy that India's role in the social and economic development of Bhutan is highly decisive. The trade of services under SAFTA has been allowed at the Thimphu Conference of SAARC.

Cooperation against Terrorism

The Northeast states of India are affected by extremist violence, and several militant organisations operating in the area seek refuge in Bhutan. Since Bhutan is located near the Siliguri corridor of India, Bhutan's insecurity becomes India's security concern. In December 2003, Operation All Clear was launched by mutual cooperation between India and Bhutan against militants and Assam separatist insurgent groups in Bhutan. Through this operation, effective action was taken against the militant groups to prevent them from taking refuge in Bhutan.

Other Areas of Cooperation

India and Bhutan participated in the Asian Rhino Range States Meeting, hosted by the government of Indonesia, which had as its objective saving the rare species of living rhinos and maintaining their populations at specific sites. This is an example of cooperation in the environmental field.

As the existing Indo-Bhutan relations are mainly based on the cooperation of hydroelectric power projects, during his 2019 visit, Prime Minister Modi stressed over the need for diversification of relations. The two prime ministers formally launched a facility to allow the use of Indian-issued RuPay cards in Bhutan, which would greatly help Indian travellers to Bhutan by reducing the need to carry cash, while at the same time boosting the Bhutanese economy and further integrating the economies of the two countries. Both sides resolved to expedite work on the next phase of the project, that is, the issuance of RuPay cards by Bhutanese banks and allowing their full inter-operability in both countries. Along with the launch of RuPay, a study to analyse the feasibility of India's Bharat Interface for Money (BHIM) app in Bhutan was also proposed with the aim to promote cashless payments between the two countries.

The two Prime Ministers inaugurated the ground station of the South Asia Satellite in Thimphu, which was constructed with the support of the Indian Space Research Organisation (ISRO). The leaders also agreed to collaborate on the joint development of a small satellite for Bhutan.

Disputes and Conflicts

Border disputes between China and Bhutan: Like the China–India border, the 477-km Bhutan–China border is also disputed. The border dispute between China and Bhutan lies in the Chumbi Valley area, which is very close to the Siliguri Corridor in India (at a distance of five kilometres). The strategic location of the Chumbi Valley is extremely important, which is why dispute over this region becomes a security threat for India. China is trying to open its embassy in Bhutan and also considering a plan to lay a rail line in the Chumbi Valley. In 2017, there was a China–India border standoff, called the Doklam standoff, which was a military border standoff between the Indian Armed Forces and the Chinese army over Chinese construction of a road in Doklam, near a trijunction border area claimed by both Bhutan and China. Since according to the Indo-Bhutan Treaty of 1949, India has the responsibility of protecting Bhutan, the Indian army fights on behalf of Bhutan in case of disputes between China and Bhutan. Although India already has a very cordial relationship with Bhutan, the incursions by Chinese troops are a problem faced by both, which brings the two countries even closer.

Ethnic conflicts: Ethnic conflicts have led to the current Bhutanese refugee situation in Nepal. As many Nepalese people began migrating to southern Bhutan for employment, the Buddhist Drukpa community, who are a majority in Bhutan opposed and discriminated against the Nepali immigrants, driving them away. Even though there are no disputes between India and Bhutan, but due to the Nepalese refugees fleeing to India from Bhutan, India has also been affected by this conflict.

INDIA AND MALDIVES

The Maldives is a series of islands to the south of Lakshadweep, which is located in the Indian Ocean. The population of Maldives is 5.2 lakhs as of 2021, and Islam is the official religion. Many Indian expatriates reside in Maldives, who are mainly doctors, nurses, technicians, workers and teachers. Migrants residing in Maldives mainly belong to Kerala and Tamil Nadu. It has the highest number of people of Indian origin after Bangladeshi origin. The Maldives has ethnic, linguistic, cultural and trade relations with India. Important trade routes of the world pass through the Maldives. The US naval base 'Diego Garcia' in the Indian Ocean is also near the Maldives. India, Sri Lanka and Maldives have jointly established a mechanism for security in the Indian Ocean, covering trade, environment, ocean pollution and other issues.

In 1988, there was an attempt to overthrow the government in the island republic of Maldives. The coup d'état attempts against Maumoon Abdul Gayoom's presidency was started by rebels led by Abdullah Luthufi. The intervention by Indian armed forces codenamed 'Operation Cactus' helped save the government from being overthrown. Following this, in the 1990s, there was a strong emphasis on building economic relations between Maldives and India.

Beginning of Democracy

For the first time, a multi-party democratic election happened in Maldives in 2008, and democracy was restored in Maldives. Mohammad Nasheed won in the democratic elections, and he always supported strong ties with India. Since the Maldives' economy depends largely on tourism, Mohammad Nasheed tried to promote the tourism industry. During his tenure, many Indian companies and businessmen got the opportunity to work in Maldives, including the GMR group.

China and Maldives

After Abdulla Yameen came to power in the Maldives in 2013, the strategic relationship between China and Maldives has been growing rapidly and the amount of investment by China in the Maldives has multiplied. A large number of tourists coming to Maldives are now from China. The Maldives has also signed up for the Maritime Silk Road project proposed by China. Chinese President Xi Jinping visited the Maldives in 2014 to further strengthen China's relations with the Maldives. The China-Maldives Friendship Bridge has been constructed in Maldives by China to exemplify the close cooperation between the two nations.

6

INDIA'S NEGOTIATION STRATEGIES IN INTERNATIONAL REGIMES

KEYWORDS

The United Nations; World Trade Organization; International Monetary Fund; Intergovernmental Panel on Climate Change

INDIA AND THE UNITED NATIONS

India is a founding member of the United Nations Organisation. India participated in the Washington Conference organised between December 1941 and January 1942 and in the San Francisco Conference in 1945 which led to the establishment of UNO. The UN was officially established on 24 October 1945. Indian foreign policy has always abided by the fundamental commitments of the UN and the basic tenets of Indian foreign policy are compatible with the UN ideals. India has always vocalised its support in favour of a stronger UN since the UN is the most significant representative of humanity and peace in the world and international law is characteristic to its functioning.

Role in Security Council

In the post-Cold War world, India was elected as a temporary member of the UNSC in 1991. India held the temporary membership once again between 2010 and 2012. During that period, India expressed its support for UNSC Resolution 678. Iraq was instructed to retreat from Kuwait but it did not, so the resolution noted that despite all the United Nations efforts, Iraq continued to defy the UNSC. After Kuwait was successfully freed from Iraqi influence, the northern territory of Iraq was declared a No-Fly Zone. India consistently voiced its support for the unity, integrity and sovereignty of Iraq. However, when the UNSC declared a No-Fly Zone over Libya, India remained absent from the voting procedure on Resolution 1973 and instead expressed its support for the unity, integrity and sovereignty of Libya. India raised the issue of terrorism in the UNSC and when in 2001, after the 9/11 attacks, Resolution 1373 was proposed against terrorism, India its expressed full support. India has been elected eight times as a non-permanent member of Security Council (1950–1951, 1967–1968, 1972–1973, 1977–1978, 1984–1985, 1991–1992, 2011–2012 and 2021–2022).

Role in Ending Racism and Colonialism

In 1961, a special committee was instituted under the chairmanship of an Indian, C. H. Jha, called the 'Special Committee on the Situation with regard to the Implementation of the Declaration on the Granting of Independence to Colonial Countries and Peoples', also known as the Special Committee on Decolonisation, or C-24. The committee heard the appeals of all those countries and peoples where colonial regimes were still existent.

Role in Disarmament

In 1954, India was the first country to demand complete abolition of nuclear testing. This demand was raised by PM Jawaharlal Nehru in the UN. Subsequently, India played a leading role in the finalising of the Partial Test Ban Treaty in 1963. In 1978, then Indian Prime Minister Morarji Desai once again suggested a ban on nuclear weapons testing at the Special Session of the UNGA. In 1988, in his address to the special session of the UN, former Indian PM Rajiv Gandhi initiated the phased abolition of Weapons of Mass Destruction (WMD) by 2020. India co-sponsored the resolution for the Comprehensive Test Ban Treaty in 1996 but did not sign it because of its discriminatory character. Indian foreign policy still believes that comprehensive, universal and complete nuclear disarmament is a possibility and thus supported nuclear non-proliferation in the Iran issue.

Role in Development

Article 55 of the UN Charter mentions that the UN shall promote 'higher standards of living, full employment, and conditions of economic and social progress and development'. In the 60s, as a consequence of the joint effort of India and other developing countries, development was acknowledged as the primary goal within the UN agenda. Further, Indian professors D. R. Gadgil and V. K. R. V. Rao conducted research on the official development aid being granted to developing nations. According to former UN Secretary General Boutros Boutros-Ghali, in the post–Cold War world, the UN would take on the role of a development mechanism because poverty, illiteracy, unemployment and health problems are issues which are a threat to the security of all humanity. To ensure improvement in areas such as poverty, starvation, illiteracy and high mortality rates, the UN declared the Millennium Development Goals (MDGs), which are 8 goals that UN member states agreed to try to achieve by 2015. Further, in 2015, the UN laid out 17 Sustainable Development Goals (SDGs) to be achieved by 2023 to ensure dignity, peace, and prosperity for the planet and humankind.

Role in Peace-Building

With regard to fostering international peace and stability, India has performed a major role in peace missions conducted by the UN. India has not stationed its armies with any kind of strategic advantage in mind, in adherence to the UN's ideals. India also is one of the largest contributors of troops for peace-building missions. As of 2023, it has contributed approximately 2,75,000 troops to peacekeeping missions in various parts of the world, with around 5,900 troops currently deployed in 12 UN missions. In peace missions conducted by the UN, India have always had active participation and 159 Indian Army soldiers have laid down their lives so far. The professional excellence of Indian soldiers in the UN peacekeeping force operations has been praised all over the world.

After the Second World War, Cold War politics infiltrated Asia through the Korean War. About 6,000 Indian peacekeeping soldiers were sent as part of a Custodial Force to oversee the repatriation of about 20,000 prisoners of war (POWs), led by General K. S. Thimayya. The Indian peacekeeping force provided both military and healthcare aid in the Korean War. Between 1956 and 1967, 12,000 Indian soldiers worked as a part of the UN Emergency Force. In 1960, Indian soldiers played a decisive role in the resolution of the Congo crisis. 39 Indian soldiers lost their lives in this operation.

In the post–Cold War world, there was a notable increase in the peace missions conducted by the United Nations because in this era, conflicts took on new and more comprehensive forms. India's military contributions in Cambodia and Somalia were considered significant. Out of Somalia's total forces, one-third was comprised of Indian soldiers. Apart from the Somalia crisis, Indian military contributions in Mozambique, Liberia, Angola, Sierra Leone, Rwanda, Haiti and Lebanon were also of great importance.

In the contemporary era, UN peace missions are operational in Ethiopia and Eritrea and Indian peacekeeping soldiers are playing a notable role in these missions. Lieutenant-General Satish Nambiar was the first Force Commander and Head of Mission of UNPROFOR, the United Nations Protection Force in the former Yugoslavia during 1992–1993 under whose leadership forces of multiple nations were stationed in the crisis-affected area. In 2000, General Vijay Jaitley was appointed as the chief commander of the peace mission conducted in Sierra Leone.

In March 2000, former UN Secretary General Kofi Annan instituted a special panel under the chairmanship of Lakhdar Brahimi for the study of peace programs. According to the reports of the study, the capacity of an army to engage in a war of attrition and its courage to take risks plays a significant part in peace missions because armies usually find it difficult to maintain their stance in long-drawn conflicts. This correlates with what happened in 1992 when America ordered its soldiers to retreat from Somalia because American soldiers were massacred in Mogadishu. Indian army's capacity in this regard is significant because in 1993, Indian soldiers and three Indian doctors lost their lives but India still did not retreat from Somalia. India also successfully completed its role in peace missions in Egypt, Malaysia and Nigeria. However, in 2000 in Sierra Leone, India ordered the early return of its armies.

Role in General Assembly

UNGA is one of the most important organs of the UN because all member states have representation in the Assembly. In 1953, Vijaya Lakshmi Pandit was elected as the eighth president and first woman president of the UNGA. Presently, India is a member of Organizational Committee of the Peacebuilding Commission (PBC).

Role in the Human Rights Council

With the aim of ensuring the protection of Human Rights, the Human Rights Council was instituted in the year 2006 and India was elected as a member. India voted against a country in the Human Rights Council for the first time on the issue of Sri Lanka because India found the efforts of the Sri Lankan government inadequate with regard to ensuring the autonomy of Tamils and their rehabilitation in the aftermath of ethnic conflicts.

Role in International Court of Justice

The International Court of Justice is an important organ of the UN which is responsible for the peaceful resolution of global legal disputes. Many Indian judges have played significant roles in the ICJ. Presently, Dalveer Bhandari is the sole Indian judge elected to the ICJ. He has been a member of the Court since 2012 and was re-elected in 2018. In the initial phase of the elections, Bhandari received the support of the UNGA while a British judge received the support of the Security Council. Subsequently, a recommendation was made for the institution of a joint committee comprised of members from both the UNGA and the UNSC for the resolution of the deadlock. However, the British judge retracted their name during this period and Dalveer Bhandari was elected as a judge of the ICJ.

INDIA'S ROLE IN THE WTO

India has been a member of General Agreement on Traffics and Trade (GATT) since 1948 and a member of the World Trade Organisation (WTO) since 1995. Initially India reacted to globalisation and the WTO adversely as it felt threatened. So between 1996 and 2001 India was not very proactive in the conferences of WTO. However, after 2001, India proactively championed the causes of the Global South through forums and coalitions such as G20 and G33. India especially stands up for the protection of the interest of the Global South as far as the issue of agriculture is concerned. India's proposals negotiate issues like allowing developing countries to maintain the right level of tariffs as is necessary for the developmental needs without bowing to the pressures of the international market. India also wants to form a consensus with other developing countries to prevent entry of non-trade issues such as environment, sustainability and labour standards into the trade negotiations, as these disproportionately harm the economies of the developing nations.

India does not oppose the WTO but demands inclusive globalisation, which would allow a free flow of natural resources. Since the very beginning, India has always supported multilateralism in trade but it should benefit all, and not just a few rich nations.

INTERGOVERNMENTAL PANEL ON CLIMATE CHANGE (IPCC)

The IPCC is an intergovernmental body of the United Nations responsible for advancing knowledge on human-induced climate change. It was established in 1988 by the World Meteorological Organization (WMO) and the United Nations Environment Programme (UNEP). It is headquartered in Geneva, Switzerland. IPCC's main activities include preparing assessment reports, special reports and methodology reports assessing the state of knowledge about climate change. So far, six reports have been released (1990, 1995, 2001, 2007, 2015 and 2021). The latest report, for the first time, made an assessment of the regional and sectoral impacts of climate change. It has included risks to and vulnerabilities of mega-cities around the world. For the first time, the IPCC report has looked at the health impacts of climate change. The report identifies India as one of the most vulnerable hotspots with several regions facing very high risk of climate disasters such as flooding, sea-level rise (Mumbai) and heat waves (Ahmedabad). It has identified several cities, including Chennai, Bhubaneswar, Patna and Lucknow, that are approaching dangerous levels of heat and humidity. India is now looking for ways to limit climate change, although for a developing nation these changes are expensive and difficult to implement.

7

CONTEMPORARY SECURITY CHALLENGES

KEYWORDS

Maritime security; energy security; environmental security; migrants and refugees; water resources; international terrorism; cyber security

INDIA'S CONTEMPORARY SECURITY CHALLENGES

China–Pakistan Axis

In May 2020, Chinese forces suddenly occupied positions across the Line of Actual Control (LAC) in Eastern Ladakh. The military conflict on the Kailash Range lasted nine months, till January 2021. There was a large deployment of troops, tanks, heavy artillery and missiles at high altitudes. Disengagement did not lead to de-escalation, and the troops stepped back from the LAC but are still deployed in large numbers. India for the first time has to share unsettled borders with a superpower like China. India now faces security threats from unsettled borders with its two nuclear-armed neighbours, China and Pakistan, who are close allies.

Dependence on Import

India is the world's third-largest military spender after the US and China, but a manpower-intensive military means it has to set aside a large portion of its defence budget to pay salaries and pensions. It has been the world's second-largest arms importer for almost a decade now because it has been unable to develop a self-sufficient domestic defence industrial base. The lack of orders or encouragement for indigenous defence products has led to this external dependence. This, however, is risky as it makes national security vulnerable—external suppliers may not provide weapons or product support in a crisis. The lack of indigenous weapons also reduces India's defence exports, and so the diplomatic influence that India could have had with friendly nations is also curtailed.

With the Ministry of Defence's reforms (see Chapter 1) in 2020, new changes have been brought in. Whereas earlier the three defence services functioned as attached offices of the defence ministry, with the new restructuring, the military has been brought into the chain of decision-making. The government is also promoting an Aatmanirbhar Bharat programme to boost the indigenous Indian defence industry. It has already begun discussing orders to enhance defence exports.

Unmanned Aerial Vehicles or UAVs: In Azerbaijan, UAV strikes on Armenian soldiers created an overwhelming psychological impact and Armenia settled for peace on humiliating terms. This was the first time UAVs helped a country defeat conventional enemy armour. UAVs are dangerous especially because small nations can easily gain asymmetric advantage with low-cost UAVs and at a fraction of the cost of highly expensive fighter jets; cheap and expendable UAVs can pin down and destroy surface forces. India has had to import UAVs as its own Rustom-2 (medium-altitude long-endurance drone) is not ready yet. China, on the other hand, is a world leader in UAVs. Its UAVs have been used by many countries in actual operations. Pakistan too has an indigenous R&D and manufacturing base and has used its Burraq UAV to strike alleged terrorist targets on the Afghan border.

Chinese Threat in the Indo-Pacific Region

The Chinese navy has grown at a very fast pace and is now one of the largest navies in the world. According to a report by the CSIS (Center for Strategic and International Studies, Washington, D.C.), between 2014 and 2018, China launched more submarines, warships and amphibious vessels than the number of ships currently serving in the navies of Germany, India, Spain and the United Kingdom. The US Department of Defense's 2020 China Military Power Report shows that the US is concerned about China's military growth even though they themselves are a superpower with a larger budget, greater technological sophistication and a global and powerful navy.

In the western Pacific, the threat is against the US and its allies, mainly Japan. In the Indian Ocean Region too, China has stretched lines, but it is addressing these in naval terms, although China does have vulnerabilities along its sea lines of communication, which it is now trying to improve.

Economic Diplomacy

Economic diplomacy has been an important part of foreign policy since 1991. India adopted the policy of liberalisation and privatisation in the post-Cold War world. Economic diplomacy is a comprehensive term which includes:

(i) Promotion of trade and business
(ii) Strengthening regional economic integration
(iii) Protecting energy security
(iv) Defending the nation's interest in multilateral forums like the WTO
(v) Speeding up the process of economic reform

Trade and Business: With two-way trade between India and China at US naval base 'Diago Garcia 77.7 billion, China was India's largest trading partner in 2020. This shows the complex nature of the post–Cold War world politics. India has a 69-billion-dollar trade deficit with China as of 2022. USA is the second largest trading partner of India and UAE is the third. It has been estimated that India will become a US naval base 'Diago Garcia 5 trillion economy by 2025–2026 and US naval base 'Diago Garcia 7 trillion by 2030.

Regional Economic Integration: USA–China conflict is an indication of the beginning of a new cold war. But the formation of the Regional Comprehensive Economic Partnership (RCEP) shows that economic interdependence is the reality of present-day world politics. Since SAARC is highly unlikely to take off in the future, India has been pushing in favour of BIMSTEC. Since India is not a part of China-led RCEP, the finalisation of free trade agreements with the EU and the USA is a priority for the government of India.

Defending India's Interest in Global Forums: As of 2022, India is the fifth largest economy of the world, after USA, China, Japan and Germany. At the same time, India belongs to the Global South and eradication of poverty is the topmost objective of India. Although the WTO raised objection over the Food Security Act of India, India's position has been clear and consistent over the years on the topic of agriculture: India believes that agriculture is a matter of social security in India rather than of trade. India is not willing to commit to the target of net-zero emission of CO_2 since that will hamper India's developmental interest.

Economic Reform: Attracting Foreign Direct Investment (FDI) is necessary for the economic growth of India. But MNCs, which were willing to relocate their set-up from China, are not showing much interest in investing in India because of bureaucratic difficulties. The problem of red tape affects the economic prospect of India. Thus, there is an urgent need of reforms in labour laws and the process of land acquisition in India. The lack of consensus between the centre and the state governments escalates the problem further. So even though USA, Japan, South Korea, France, and Germany have developed strong strategic partnerships with India, it has not resulted in a strong economic partnership.

Pakistan's Proxy War Strategy

2008 Mumbai Attacks: The 2008 Mumbai attacks were a series of terrorist attacks that took place in November 2008, when ten members of Lashkar-e-Taiba, a militant Islamist organisation from Pakistan, carried out coordinated shooting and bombing attacks lasting four days across Mumbai. A Pakistani terrorist, Ajmal Kasab, was captured alive. For the first time, India had direct evidence of Pakistani terrorism on Indian lands, and later American terrorist David Headley also testified that in the years leading up to the Mumbai attacks the ISI, Pakistan's Intelligence, retained a close alliance with the LeT. According to India, Pakistan must take action against the people involved in the Mumbai terror attack. There is evidence also of the involvement of Hafiz Saeed, the co-founder of Lashkar-e-Taiba.

Siachen Conflict: The Siachen glacier is the highest battlefield in the world, and that is why it is strategically important. It is located in the Karakoram range and to its west are the Saltoro mountains. A military conflict between India and Pakistan started over the disputed 1,000-square-mile area of the Siachen glacier when in the year 1984, Pakistan tried to take control over the Siachen region. The Indian government started Operation Meghdoot in 1984 which evacuated the Pakistani troops and took control of the 70-kilometre-long Siachen glacier. China-controlled Shaksgam Valley can be monitored from Siachen. Earlier a part of Pakistan-occupied Kashmir, the Shaksgam Valley was handed over to China in 1963 by Pakistan. The Karakoram Pass is a part of Siachen. By controlling Siachen, the Kashmir–Ladakh highway can also be monitored effectively. The Nubra river that flows in Ladakh also originates from Siachen.

ENERGY SECURITY

According to the International Energy Agency (IEA), India will overtake the European Union as the world's third-largest energy consumer by 2030. In its India Energy Outlook 2021 Report, it says that India at present is the fourth largest global energy consumer, after China, USA and the European Union. As of now, India is excessively dependent on coal and oil for maintaining the country's energy supply. There is a pressure on India to reach the goal of economic development as well as meet the goal of sustainable development, which is difficult as it is a developing nation.

In 2015, India and France launched the International Solar Alliance (ISA) to boost solar energy in developing countries. India wants to diversify its energy consumption by developing alternate forms of energy such as nuclear energy and solar energy. India is still dependent on West Asia for maintaining its energy supply. African, Central Asian, and Latin American nations and Russia are also emerging as new suppliers of energy for India.

WATER SECURITY

The Indus Waters Treaty, a water-distribution treaty between India and Pakistan to use the water available in the Indus River and its tributaries, was signed in 1960. The treaty was finalised through the mediation of the World Bank. Through this agreement, the western rivers like Indus, Jhelum and Chenab were considered as rivers of Pakistan and Sutlej, Ravi and Beas—the eastern rivers—were identified as Indian rivers. India is allowed limited use of water (non-consumption use such as power generation) on Pakistan's rivers. This water treaty is a unique example of cooperation between India and Pakistan, because despite the two big wars (1965 and 1971) between the two countries, the treaty is still intact.

A new controversy emerged when Pakistan protested against India's construction of the Baglihar Dam on the Chenab river. Pakistan has also objected to India's construction of the Kishanganga project and the Salal and Dul Hasti projects in Doda district of Kashmir. Pakistan has alleged that India is using up Pakistan's share of water. However, Pakistan's argument may be based on its own domestic politics. Much of the water of the Indus river is used up by Punjab in Pakistan and therefore, provinces like Sindh and Baluchistan do not get enough water. It has been alleged that Pakistan stokes anti-India sentiments to divert the demands of these states. At present, the flow of water in the river is decreasing due to the reduced amount of snow on the glacier and decreased rainfall. The Indus Waters Treaty of 1960 also mentions how the dispute between the two countries may be resolved: Resolution can either be through a discussion by the governments of both countries or the dispute can be resolved by the International Court of Justice. It is noteworthy that in case of the Baglihar Project and the Kishanganga Hydropower Project, the International Court of Justice ruled in favour of India and against Pakistan.

The Indus Waters Treaty states that there should be cooperation between the two countries regarding the availability of river water. However, there is a need to increase the scope of this treaty. It also needs to include joint river water management and a provision prescribing that both countries improve their water management internally. There is an urgent need to adopt transparency in water data transactions. After the Pathankot airbase attack in September 2016, India called for a review of the Indus Waters Treaty to put pressure on Pakistan.

INTERNATIONAL CROSS-BORDER TERRORISM

According to Ministry of Home Affairs reports, Pakistan has repeatedly used terrorism and covert action as an instrument of state policy against India. It has recruited, trained, financed and armed militant terrorists. This cross-border terrorism is rampant and a constant threat to India's security. As of 2022, India has a list of 36 persons accused of involvement in terrorist activities in India and designated as terrorists under the Unlawful Activities (Prevention) Act, 1967 (UAPA), but Pakistan has not taken any action against them. Syed Salahuddin, who is the head of the United Jihad Council and Hizbul Mujahideen resides in Pakistan. Dawood Ibrahim, who is believed to be responsible for the 1993 Mumbai bombings, and Masood Azhar, who is related to Jaish-e-Mohammed, also live in Pakistan. Pakistan has also been accused of promoting the trade of counterfeit notes and drugs in India, especially on the Indo-Nepal border.

Since the years following Indian independence, the Indian military has had to deal with Pakistan repeatedly and the army has spent over three decades fighting counter-insurgency in Jammu and Kashmir. The cross-border commando raids of 2016 and the Balakot air strike of 2019 showed for that India is not deterred by Pakistan's nuclear weapons-enabled terrorism.

MARITIME SECURITY

One of India's biggest maritime security threats is also from its neighbour Pakistan. The **Sir Creek Dispute** arises from the difference in interpretation of the maritime boundary line between Kutch and Sindh. Before India's independence, the provincial region was a part of the Bombay Presidency of British India. But after India's independence in

1947, Sindh became a part of Pakistan while Kutch remained a part of India. Pakistan claims the entire creek as per paragraphs 9 and 10 of the Sindh Government Resolution of 1914 signed between the then Government of Sindh and Rao Maharaj of Kutch. The resolution demarcated the boundaries between the two territories and included the creek as part of Sindh, thus setting the boundary as the eastern flank of the creek popularly known as the Green Line. However, India claims that the boundary lies mid-channel as depicted in another map drawn in 1925, and this demarcation was made by the installation of mid-channel pillars back in 1924. According to India, the dispute should be resolved through The United Nations Convention on the Law of the Sea that was adopted in 1982. However, Pakistan claimed that area is not navigational and therefore the UN convention is not applicable for solving the dispute.

CHALLENGES IN FOREIGN POLICY

India is now developing a close strategic partnership with the United States of America. However, India also wants to retain friendly relations with Russia that it has traditionally had. But USA and Russia are rival powers. The rise of India's neighbour China as a superpower is also a threat to India and so this power asymmetry between China and India is forcing the latter to cultivate a strong partnership with USA to counterbalance China's hegemony. Thus, present-day Indian foreign policy can no longer adhere to the non-alignment policy that India earlier had.

Unit VII

POLITICAL INSTITUTIONS IN INDIA

KEYWORDS

The Indian Constitution; constitutional philosophy and ethos; fundamental rights and essential constitutional law; concept of basic structure; executive and legislature at central and state levels; federalism; electoral process and ECI; local governmental institutions; constitutional and statutory bodies

1

MAKING OF THE INDIAN CONSTITUTION

KEY CONCEPTS

Colonial heritage; contribution of the Indian national movement; Composition; ideological moorings; constitutional debates

THE CONSTITUENT ASSEMBLY

In 1934, the Indian National Congress (INC) made the demand for a Constituent Assembly part of its official policy. In March–April 1942, the British instituted the Cripps Mission in order to gather full Indian support for their efforts in World War II, through negotiations with the INC and the Muslim League. The Mission was headed by senior minister, Stafford Cripps, who had accepted the idea that an elected body of Indians should frame the Constitution. The Cripps Mission tried to reconcile the demands of the INC and the Muslim League and proposed that at the end of the War, India would be granted a dominion status and a Constituent Assembly would be set up to draft the Constitution of India, and the members of this Assembly would be elected based on proportional representation by the provincial assemblies and princely states. Further, the provinces not agreeing to the new Constitution could create their own separate Union, which would also be granted dominion status. Meanwhile, control of defence and external affairs would remain with the British central government. Provinces would be grouped geographically into three regions–

i. One region dominated by Hindus
ii. Another dominated by Muslims
iii. A third with equal population

INDIRECT ELECTION

Members of the Constituent Assembly were elected from the members of provincial legislative assemblies. Population ratio of representation in the Constituent Assembly would be one to one million. A total of 93 members were from the princely states. Members of princely states were to be nominated by the ruler of princely states. The Cabinet Mission Plan provided for an interim government. Nehru became vice-president of the interim government and by default, the Prime Minister. The first meeting of the Constituent Assembly was held on 9 December 1946, without the participation of the Muslim League. Rajendra Prasad was elected president of the assembly in its second sitting, held in January 1947, when the Objective Resolutions were accepted (these resolutions were to be the guiding principles which would help draft the Constitution).

NATURE OF THE CONSTITUENT ASSEMBLY: INDIA IN MICROCOSM

Granville Austin has referred to the Constituent Assembly as a 'microcosm in action' since the Constituent Assembly was dominated by one party, the Indian National Congress, in a society dominated by one party, again the Congress. Of the 296 seats allocated for the provinces, the Congress won 208 seats. The Congress was a *national front*. Representation of the minorities was adequate. In all, 88 seats were given to minorities among 235 seats allocated to provinces including Indian Christians, Anglo Indians and Parsis. **M. R. Jayakar** and **Shyama Prasad Mukherjee**, members of the **Hindu Mahasabha**, were also included. The socialist and communist parties decided not to join the Assembly.

Transitional Parliament/Union Government

The Constituent assembly played a dual role:

(i) Drafting the Constitution
(ii) Interim parliament

Fourteen members of the union government (cabinet ministers) were also part of the Constituent Assembly. President of the Constituent Assembly **Rajendra Prasad** and Speaker **G. V. Mavalankar** were exceptions who did not play a similar dual role. **B. M. Rau** was not a member of the Assembly but was an advisor to it.

Major Committees

The Constituent Assembly had 8 major committees:

1. Rules of Procedure Committee – 15 members + chairperson (15+1)
2. Steering Committee
3. Advisory Committee on Fundamental Rights, Minorities and Tribal and Excluded Areas
4. Drafting committee – 6 members + chairperson, Dr Ambedkar (6+1 members)
5. Union Power Commitee
6. Union Constitution Committee (14+1)
7. Provincial Constitution Committee (23+1)
8. States Committee (5+1)

Prominent non-Congress members were A. K. Ayyar, H. N. Kunzru, N. G. Ayyangar, Dr Ambedkar, K. Santhanam, M. R. Jayakar, Sachchidananda Sinha, K. M. Munshi, John Mathai and S. P. Mukherjee. The process of decision making was democratic as most of the decisions were taken by *consensus*. Four members of the Congress who played a vital role in the making of the Constitution include Jawaharlal Nehru, Maulana Azad, Rajendra Prasad and Vallabhbhai Patel, says **Granville Austin**.

Advisory committee was comprised of two sub-committees:

a. Fundamental Sub Committee
b. Minority Sub Committee

2

PHILOSOPHY OF THE INDIAN CONSTITUTION

KEY CONCEPTS

Preamble; Fundamental Rights; Directive Principles

PREAMBLE

The Preamble should begin in the name of God, Member of Constituent Assembly **H. V. Kamath** had argued. However, **M. Ananthasayanam Ayyangar** had felt that the Preamble should start with an invocation to Mahatma Gandhi. But **Dr Ambedkar** and **H. N. Kunzru** did not support either idea. Therefore, the Preamble begins with 'We, the people of India'.

The Preamble of the Indian Constitution is inspired by the constitution of the United States of America. The Preamble incorporates the fundamental objectives and ideals of the Constitution. It was approved by the Constituent Assembly on 22 January 1947 in the form of *objective resolution* which took resolve to bring about social, economic, and political justice in India. The Preamble sets the philosophy of the Constitution and it is also considered to be the 'horoscope' of the Constitution. **Nani Palkhivala,** an outstanding lawyer and defender of civil liberties, said that the Preamble is an introduction of the Constitution. **Friedrich** said that Preamble manifests the public opinion and the Constitution draws its power from the people. **Nehru** said that the Preamble synthesises the ideals of two great revolutions of the world—ideals of the **French Revolution,** namely liberty, equality and fraternity; and the ideals of social and economic justice which are drawn from the **Russian Revolution**.

Features of the Preamble

1. **Source of Power:** The Preamble begins with the phrase—'We, the People of India'. This phrase refers to **citizens** who have completed the age of **18 years**. The Constitution is the supreme law of the land but the people made the constitution; therefore, people are supreme. Thus, sovereignty lies in the people.
2. **Ideals:** The Preamble indicates the ideals of the Constitution. Dr Ambedkar said that political democracy began in India after Independence but social and economic democracy was yet to be attained. The Preamble visualises the goal of social and economic democracy. **Granville Austin** says that the Indian Constitution is a *social document* rather than a legal document and the Preamble fulfills social objectives in the following ways:

(a) **Justice:** The Preamble is looking at social, economic, and political justice. Social justice means just distribution of social good in society. Political justice ensures equal participation of the people in the political system. **Every citizen** is entitled to form unions, associations, and political parties.

(b) **Liberty:** The Preamble envisages the freedom of expression, thought, belief, faith and worship. Each and every citizen enjoys the liberty which is invested in the freedom of conscience, which is another name for religious freedom. This holds that the belief and worship is the personal choice of the individual and will never be dictated by the government. This is the *crux of secularism.*

(c) **Equality:** Equality of status and opportunity is an integral part of the Preamble. The Constitution provides equality for everyone.

(d) **Fraternity:** Fraternity means the feeling of brotherhood or belongingness. Fraternity denotes psychological unity among the people. Fraternity is essential for unity and integrity of the nation apart from protecting the dignity of the individual. The Preamble includes the phrase, 'unity and integrity of the nation'. The idea of nation reflects physical unity made possible through psychological integrity. Without unity and integrity of the nation, liberty, equality and justice cannot be realised. After Independence, India faced various security threats to this unity and fraternity:

(i) The accession of princely states.

(ii) Naga secessionist movement in the Northeast.

(iii) Communal partition of India.

(iv) Militia invasion into Jammu and Kashmir supported by Pakistan.

3. **Form of Government:**

(a) **Sovereignty:** The Preamble declares the form of government instated for realising the goals mentioned in the Preamble. 'Sovereign' denotes that the Government of India is supreme in the territory of India. The government is free to choose its economic, social and defence policies. The government cannot be dictated by any other state. Therefore, India pursued an autonomous foreign policy and was no longer subordinate to the British government.

(b) **Socialist:** The term 'socialism' was incorporated in the Preamble by 42nd Constitutional Amendment in 1976 by the Indira Gandhi government. The Avadi Session of Congress Party held in the year 1955 led to the Congress's declaration that the socialist structure of society was its goal. Indira Gandhi stated that socialism in this context was different from the Soviet Union.

Professor **K. T. Shah** in the Constituent Assembly had requested the inclusion of the term 'socialism' in the preamble. But Dr Ambedkar had not agreed with Shah because social and economic justice is the other name of socialism.

(c) **Secularism:** The term 'secularism' was also added in the Constitution by the 42nd Amendment although the spirit of secularism was inherent in the Constitution already; for example, the Preamble contains the freedom of speech and expression, belief, faith and worship.

(d) **Republic:** The literal meaning of 'republic' is that the head of state shall be elected. Head of state should not be hereditary like in Britain. Broader meaning of republic is, power lies in the people.

(e) **Adoption:** The Preamble was adopted by the Constituent Assembly on 26 November 1949. The 'Constituent Assembly' is mentioned for the first time in the Preamble in the last line. The Preamble does not mention date of enforcement of the Constitution but it carries the date of adoption.

In the **Berubari Union case** (1960), the Supreme Court held that the Preamble was not part of the Constitution. Berubari is the name of village which was located in West Bengal and the West Bengal government was reluctant to give any territory of Berubari to Pakistan. The case assessed whether the parliament has the power to grant any territory of the state to a foreign country under Article 3 of the Indian Constitution. Second, the case tried to determine whether legislative action is necessary for the implementation of the Nehru-Noon Agreement. The SC rejected the demand for referendum, and held that Article 3 does not apply on the transfer of land to any external state like Pakistan. The parliament can change the boundary of the state. Thus, Article 3 is applicable within the India. Article 368 is needed for the transfer of any piece of land to external state.

However, the Supreme Court observed in the **Kesavananda Bharti case** (1973) that the Preamble is an integral part of the Constitution. Thus, the dispute came to an end.

Interpretation of the Constitution

The Supreme Court stated that the Constitution is not merely a collection of articles, in the famous **Kesavananda Bharti case**. The Constitution incorporates various ideologies and theories, and the Court held that these ideologies are paramount while interpreting the Constitution. The Court propounded the *spirit of the Constitution* which is preserved in the Preamble. It also said that context is more important than written words or text of the Constitution. The Preamble is utilised in the interpretation of the Constitution. For example, the Supreme Court extended the meaning of right to life under Article 21. It said that 'right to life' means the right to life with dignity, which is written in the Preamble.

The Indira Gandhi government tried to override the Fundamental Rights in the name of implementation of Directive Principles of State Policy (DPSP). The Supreme Court said that there should be harmony and balance between Fundamental Rights and DPSP in the landmark **Minerva Mills's case** (1980). The Court ruled in the **S. R. Bommai case** (1994) that secularism is the basic structure of the Indian constitution, which is also written in the preamble. The Court had interpreted Article 356 in association with the Preamble, this Article does not include the term 'secularism'.

Basic Structure of the Constitution

The Supreme Court is of the view that the *heart and soul* of the Indian Constitution cannot be amended. The Constitution is like the body of a human being in which some organs are more important than other organs. The Principle of Basic Structure' has been made by the Supreme Court in 1973 in the **Kesavananda Bharti case**. Various elements of the basic structure propounded by Supreme Court are mentioned in the Preamble:

1. Democratic republic government
2. Secularism
3. Sovereignty
4. Unity and integrity
5. Harmony between liberty and equality

In the **Puttaswamy case** (2018), the Supreme Court ruled that the Right to Privacy is a Fundamental Right which is an extension of Right to Life and Dignity. The Preamble includes the term 'dignity'. This undescores the importance of the Preamble.

It appears that the basic structure and the Preamble are complementary to each other.

Non-Enforceable: Since the Preamble is the philosophy of the Constitution, therefore, it is moral in nature. Nobody can approach the Supreme Court for enforcement of any provision of the Preamble. No law enacted by the parliament can be challenged on the ground of violation of the provisions of the Preamble. It can only serve as a guide to interpreting the Constitution.

Soul of the Constitution

The Preamble is the *soul* of the Constitution, **Thakur Das Bhargav** had remarked in the Constituent Assembly. The Preamble is like a distillation of the Constitution. As we have discussed, the Preamble includes ideals and philosophy of the Constitution. It also contains the form of government. Aims and ideology of the Constitution are visible in the Preamble. It is also important to note that **Dr Ambedkar** said that Article 32 is heart and soul of the constitution. Preamble is moral in nature, which tells us about the goals of the Constitution and cannot be enforced in court of law.

Horoscope of the Constitution

K. M. Munshi said that the Preamble is the horoscope of the Constitution. The Preamble speaks of a democratic and republic government, which is why the Indian President is elected and Council of Ministers is responsible for the Lok Sabha. Fundamental Right contains the freedom of conscience which reflects secular value. The Preamble believes in socialism, Article 39 (b) (c) of Directive Principle of State Policy (DPSP) says that operation of economy should be carried out for the well-being of community. Economic resources should not be concentrated in few hands.

Philosophy of the Constitution

PM Nehru said, 'Democracy has been spoken of chiefly in the past, as political democracy, roughly represented by every person having a vote'. **Dr Radhakrishnan** has put it as, 'Poor people, who wander about, find no work, no wages and starve, whose lives are a continual round of sore affection and pinching poverty, cannot be proud of the Constitution or its law'. **Dr Ambedkar** in his concluding speech in the Constituent Assembly, held:

> Political democracy cannot last unless there lies at the base of it social democracy. What does social democracy mean? It means a way of life which recognises liberty, equality and fraternity *as* the principles of life. These principles of liberty, equality and fraternity are not to be treated as separate items in a trinity. They form of union of trinity in the sense that to divorce one from the other is to defeat the very purpose of democracy.

A fitting commentary on the foregoing contents of the Preamble to our Constitution can be best offered by paraphrasing a few lines from Prof. **Ernest Barker:** There must be a capacity and a passion for the enjoyment of liberty—there must be sense of personality in each, and this ought to be generally spread through the whole community.

Constitutional Morality

The Preamble introduces a new and modern constitutional morality. Liberty, equality, fraternity and justice are basic moral principles of the Constitution. Our society may not be democratic but our Constitution believes in democratic moral values. Social morality cannot be against constitutional morality. The Supreme Court in the **Sabrimala case** (2018) said that social morality should be subordinate to constitution morality. Therefore, restricting the entry of women into the temple was interpreted as being against constitutional morality. Constitutional morality is broader than the principles contained in the Preamble. The Supreme Court said in **Manoj Narula case** (2014) that entry of criminals in the Parliament is against constitutional morality.

FUNDAMENTAL RIGHTS

Rights refer to claims made by citizens and/or an individual against the state. However, rights are not gifts of the state or government but rather, a *gift of the Constitution*, which is made by the people of India. Fundamental Rights put limitations over the *powers* of the state. Fundamental Rights are supreme and and observes the primacy of citizens over the state. It guarantees constitutionalism and the rule of law. Fundamental Rights are incorporated in Part III of the Indian Constitution, and it was the most debated part in the Constituent Assembly. The **J. B. Kripalani Committee** was constituted for consideration over Fundamental Rights in the Constituent Assembly.

Meaning of State

Part III of the Constitution begins with Article 12, which incorporates the definition of state. Fundamental Rights are available against the state. According to Article 12, 'state' includes:

1. Government and Parliament of India
2. Government and legislature of every state
3. All local and other authorities
4. Within the territory of India or under control of Government of India

The Supreme Court interpreted the meaning of 'state' in various cases. For instance, it ruled that authorities funded by the state come within the domain of the state, which includes University of Delhi, All India Institute of Medical Sciences, and other agencies.

Policy of privatisation and liberalisation was initiated in India in 1991. Consequently, the functions of the state have minimised. Private players entered in education, health, transportation, and banking sectors. Fundamental Rights are not available against private actors. There is no provision of reservation in private companies. This means privatisation is shrinking the scope of Fundamental Rights.

Special Protection of Fundamental Rights

Article 13 provides protection of Fundamental Rights. Article 13 contains following kinds of law:

1. **Pre-constitutional laws**
   These are the laws which were made and have come into force before the commencement of this Constitution. Simply put, it means that the law existed before 26 January 1950. In case of a conflict between pre-constitutional laws and Fundamental Rights of Part III, Fundamental Rights shall eclipse the pre-constitutional laws. It is also known as the *doctrine of eclipse*. Pre-constitutional laws shall not become null and void but will become *inoperative*, says Article 13(1) of the Part III.
2. **Priority of Fundamental Rights**
   The state cannot make any law which takes away or violates Fundamental Rights included in Part III. Laws enacted by the state shall be declared null and void if they encroach upon Fundamental Rights. There may be various segments of a law, and if one part of a law goes against Fundamental Rights, the entire law shall not be declared *ultra vires* but only that part becomes null and void which is inconsistent with Fundamental Rights. This is known as the *principle of severability*. The Supreme Court makes separation between legal and illegal parts of the law and only the illegal part is declared null and void as per Article 13(2).
3. **Definition of Law**
   Article 13(3) of the Fundamental Rights defines law. Law includes ordinance, bylaws, regulation, custom and notification. Administrative offices are authorised to make supplementary law. It is known as delegated legislation. Bylaws are secondary legislation, made by the executive. Ordinance

is a law made by the President. **Bylaws** are a supplementary law. Regulation is essential for implementation of law. Notification implies the publication of law in a government gazette. And customs is a form of law that prevails in tribal societies.

4. **Difference between ordinary law and constitutional law**

   The Parliament can make a law over the Union List and the states can enact a law over the State List under Article 246. The Parliament needs simple majority for making a law. But the Parliament can amend the Constitution while exercising **Constituent Power** under Article 368. Amendment of the Constitution requires special majority. By applying its **Constituent Power,** the Parliament can amend Fundamental rights. Article 13 (4) was added in 1971 by the **24th Constitutional Amendment**, which gives this power to the Parliament: the amendment of Fundamental Rights. Thus, restrictions of article 13 (2) are not applicable on constitutional amendments. Fundamental Rights are not beyond the amending power of the Parliament.

I. RIGHT TO EQUALITY

Fundamental Rights begins with the Right to Equality. Article 14 says that each and every one is equal before the law and that there shall be equal protection of law. Article 14 contains two types of equality:

(a) Equality before law
(b) Equal protection of law

(a) **Equality before Law:** The notion of equality before law is taken from **British law**. It is propounded by the **British scholar Dicey**. This implies equal treatment for everyone. Same set of laws is applicable over everyone. This creates the rule of law or supremacy of law. Nobody is above the law. Individual office, status, property do not matter in the eyes of law. Similar punishment is prescribed for everyone. No discrimination is permitted between individuals while enforcing the law.

However, equal treatment for each and every one appears to be a *negative concept*. The social conditions and context is not identical for every individual. Thus, the same set of laws cannot maintain equality, instead sensitive treatment and focused help is required of the state for marginalised sections of society. Article 14 includes the *positive concept of equality* borrowed from the **US Constitution.**

(b) **Equal Protection of Law:** It means that the law will protect the underprivileged sections of society. Different laws are required for different people. For protection of Scheduled Castes and Scheduled Tribes, the Parliament has enacted separate laws. **Women and children** are also protected from negative equality. The same law should not be applicable for men and women because social conditions are adverse for women. The Parliament can make discrimination but it should be **rational and logical**. The grounds of discrimination are not mentioned in Article 14. The Supreme Court has declared the various grounds for discrimination in different cases (see below).

Table 7.2.1: Two Types of Equality

	Equality before law	*Equal Protection of law*
1.	Equal treatment	Differential treatment
2.	Negative	Positive
3.	Of British origin	Taken from the US Constitution.
4.	Same law for everyone	Protective law for deprived sections

The Base of Discrimination

Any law made by the Parliament or state legislatures becomes null and void if the law violates Article 14. The Supreme Court said that the following grounds may be reasonable:

1. **Geographical ground** may be a fit case for discrimination, for example same set of laws cannot be applied over the residents of Delhi and of the Northeast.
2. **Profession** may be a logical basis for discrimination, for example, armed personnel receive alcohol on duty but this is not available for doctors.
3. **Social and educational background** came to be considered as a basis of differentiation. Reservation is allowed for the marginalised sections of society. It is not available for the privileged groups.

However, the above-mentioned bases of discrimination are not absolute and the Supreme Court can propound other bases from time to time. The **Supreme Court** thus protects the Fundamental Rights.

No Discrimination by State

The state shall not discriminate against citizens **only** on the grounds of **religion, race, caste, sex** or **place of birth**. 'Only' indicates that discrimination is possible on the other grounds like physical fitness or educational qualifications. 'Citizen' means that this right is not applicable for aliens or foreigners. Equality does not mean absence of all discrimination but elimination of irrational discrimination according to Article 15(1).

Equality in Public Places

No **citizen** shall be subject to any **disability, liability, restriction** on **grounds only** of **religion, race, caste, sex, place of birth,** with regard to:

(a) Access to shops, public restaurant, hotels and places of public entertainment; or
(b) The use of wells, tanks, bathing ghats, roads and place of public resort; or
(c) Maintained wholly or partly out of state fund; or
(d) Dedicated to the use of general public, described in Article 15(2).

Each and every word connotes a *wider meaning*, like shop includes barber shops and clinics of doctor too. Use of 'general public' and 'state fund' is significant which means this is not available in the private domain. Nobody can demand equality in, for instance, a **private swimming pool**. The **British government** reserved some **hotels or restaurant** for the **British** only; they were not open for Indians. The Fundamental Rights forbids the state to carry out any discrimination in *public places*. Nor is a citizen entitled to practise discrimination in the public domain.

Balance Between Rights and Justice

Fundamental rights are *not absolute* but are kept under various *limitations*.

Special Provision for Women and Children

Article 15(3) is an exception of the Right to Equality and provides special protection for **women and children**. As we have just discussed, the state shall make some special provision for the empowerment of women and children. It is similar to the notion of social justice. Special provision includes better education facility, reservation and other welfare policies.

Special Provision for Socially and Educationally Backward Class

Article 15(4) says that the state will provide special provisions for the advancement of:

(a) Socially and educationally backward class of citizens
(b) Scheduled Castes and scheduled Tribes

Article 15(4) was inserted in the Constitution by the first Constitutional Amendment in 1951 due to ruling of the Supreme Court in **Champakam Dorairajan** case (1951). Supreme Court declared null and void the reservation given by the Madras government in **medical colleges**.

The Constitution does not explain the meaning of socially and educationally backward classes of citizens. According to **Article 340,** the President shall appoint a **Backward Classes Commission**. In **1953,** the **Kaka Kalelkar Commission** or the First Backward Classes Commission was appointed. **Bindheshwari Prasad (B. P.) Mandal Commission** was appointed in 1979 by the Janata Party government. Mandal Commission held that the socially and educationally backward classes means the **backward caste**. Therefore, caste and class are interrelated in India. Class denotes the economic and modern stratification of society. However, caste is a traditional parameter to stratify society. Technically, caste and class are different but practically, often it is similar in India. The terms Scheduled Caste and Scheduled Tribes are included for the first time in the Government of India Act 1935.

Reservation in Educational Institution

Human Resource Minister Arjun Singh announced for reservation in private educational institutions in the early 2000s. Consequently, the 93rd Constitutional Amendment was put forth in the Constitution and Clause (5) was inserted in Article 15 in Part III. According to Article 15 (5), reservation for socially and educationally backward classes of citizens and scheduled caste and scheduled tribes was granted in:

1. Central educational institutions;
2. Private educational institutions, aided or non-aided;
3. Reservation is not applicable in minority educational institution.

Central educational institutions included the IITs, the IIMs, and central universities. 'Private educational institutions' included institutes irrespective of whether they are receiving funds from the government or not. Minority educational institutions refers to institutions which are set up by the minority communities under Article 30.

Economically Backward Classes

Ten per cent reservation for the Economically Weaker Sections (EWS) in educational institutes and employment was introduced by the **103rd Constitutional Amendment** in 2019 which allowed the state to make:

(a) Any special provision for the advancement of economically weaker sections of citizens.
(b) Special provision includes admission in education institutions.
(c) Admission in private education institution, funded by government or not receiving funds from the government.
(d) Special provision is not applicable for minority educational institutions.
(e) Reservation in educational institutions should not exceed 10 per cent.

The Constitution does not define economic backwardness; the government is eligible to determine economic backwardness, under Article 15(6).

Equality in Public Employment and Appointment

Equality of opportunity is available for all citizens, relating to employment or appointment to any office under the state. *Employment* deals with the terms and condition of the job. *Appointment* means entry into the job. Promotions are related to employment. Equality of opportunity is not applicable in *private jobs*. There is a difference between *equality* and *equality of opportunity*. Equality reflects equal treatment but equality of opportunity provides equal opportunity to become unequal. Every citizen is given an equal opportunity to appear in civil services exams. However, the result of the exam cannot be same for every candidate. This right is available only for citizens (Article 16 [1]).

No Discrimination: Employment or appointment under state shall not be discriminated only on the grounds of **religion, race, caste, sex, descent, place of birth, residence, or any of these.** Article 16 incorporates new grounds of **descent and residence,** which are not mentioned in Article 15. **Descent** means origin or background of the person in terms of family or nationality. **Residence** refers to home or house of a person. The term **'only'** prescribes that discrimination is possible on other grounds like **marks** in **examination** or **physical fitness.**

Discrimination on the Basis of Residence: Residence may be criteria for employment and appointment under state, union territory, or local authority. Regarding the appointment on the basis of residence, **parliamentary law** is needed. **State legislature** is not empowered to make law. Appointment on the ground of residence can be made for any classes of employment. It is determined by parliamentary law. Article 16 (3) is the base of the regionalism in India, which has manifested itself in the **Sons of Soil** Movement too. Regional disparity exists in India therefore, residence as a ground can protect the interests of backward states.

Reservation in Appointment: The state can provide reservation of appointment or post in favour of any **backward class** of citizens. Reservation is allowed when the state feels that the backward class of citizens does not have **adequate representation** in services of state. Article 16(4) provides reservation which is very much debatable in the public domain. Reservation in appointment began in the year **1955** in the form of reservation for Scheduled Caste and Scheduled Tribes. These groups got 22 per cent reservation in appointment under the state. Further, the **V. P. Singh** government introduces 27 per cent reservation for the Other Backward Classes (OBCs) in the year 1990 for central and all-India services. Therefore, the quantum of reservation has gone up to 49.5 per cent. By **103rd Constitutional Amendment,** 10 per cent reservation is provided for economically weaker sections. Percentage of reservation has now reached up to 59.5 per cent. Ratio of reservation in terms of percentage under state differs from state to state. However, the ceiling of reservation is 69 per cent in Tamil Nadu and the reservation in Maharashtra has gone up to 78 per cent. Thus, debate is bound to emerge. And various issues regarding reservation can be described as follows:

1. **Meaning of Backwardness**

   The **Bindeshwari Prasad Mandal Commission (1979)** applied three criteria for identification of backwardness:

   1. social
   2. economic
   3. educational

   The Mandal Commission said that **backward caste** is also **backward class.** The Supreme Court said that backwardness means **social and educational backwardness** in the **Indra Sawhney case,** which is popularly known as the **Mandal case.** SCs and STs are also backward. Therefore, 'backward class' has been considered as Other Backward Classes (OBCs), where 'other' means other than Scheduled Caste and Scheduled Tribes. The Supreme Court ruled that **backward class** is not a homogenous category and introduced the notion of **creamy layer in the Mandal** case in 1992. Creamy layer is only applicable for OBCs and not for reservation of SC and ST. People belonging to creamy layer are not eligible for reservation. The notion of economic backwardness is also included in the Constitution by 103rd Constitutional Amendment, as noted earlier.

2. **Upper Limit of Reservation**

   The Supreme Court in the Mandal case said that the ceiling of reservation should not exceed to 50 per cent. Court said that more than 50 per cent reservation will hamper the concept of **equality of opportunity. Article 335** of the Constitution says that while providing reservation for SCs and

STs, efficiency of services should not be compromised. According to 103rd Constitutional Amendment, Article 16 (6) is inserted in the Constitution. It gives 10 per cent reservation for EWS, thus decision of the Mandal case was automatically overruled by the parliament. Ceiling of reservation has gone up to 59.5 per cent in central services and all India services. The 103rd Constitutional Amendment is being challenged by youth for equality in the Supreme Court.

3. **Reservation in Promotion**

   The candidates belonging to SCs and STs also avail of reservation in promotion. The Supreme Court in the **Mandal case** said that reservation is applicable for the initial appointment. Reservation in promotion is *ultra vires*, the Court observed. It is against **efficiency** and **equality of opportunity**. However, the government brought about the 77th Constitutional Amendment act in year 1995. It inserted article 16 (4A) which provides benefits of reservation to Scheduled Caste and Scheduled Tribes in jobs. They will get benefit of **consequential seniority.** Supreme Court again blocked reservation in promotion in **Nagaraja case** in the year 2006**.** Supreme Court ruled that reservation in promotion can be allowed, if it fulfills the following criteria:

   (a) The members of Scheduled Caste and Scheduled Tribes are still backward.

   (b) Their representation is still inadequate in services under the state.

   (c) The efficiency of services shall not be compromised.

   Therefore, the Supreme Court said that reservation in promotion is allowed with certain conditions. But debate rages on over the issue till this day. There are demands for the application of creamy layer for reservation of SC/ST based on the argument that the benefit of reservation is appropriated by the well-to-do sections of SC/ST.

4. **Reservation for Backlog Vacancies**

   The Supreme Court said that the *carry forward rule* is constitutional. The Court allowed the government to carry forward unfulfilled vacancies of the reserved category. Unfulfilled vacancies are known as backlog vacancies, which will be added in vacancies of next year. But the Court also said in the **Mandal case** that ceiling of reservation should not exceed 50 per cent. This means that 50 per cent limitation is applicable for backlog vacancies too. However, the 81st Amendment in the year 2000, inserted Article 16 (4B) in the Constitution which stipulates 100 per cent reservation for backlog vacancies. Ceiling of 50 per cent is not applicable for the backlog seats.

Equality in Religious Institutions

Article 16(5) authorised that any religious or denominational institution can appoint in their office, a person belonging to a particular religion or denomination. For example, management of a temple shall employ person(s) belonging to their own religious faith.

Abolition of Untouchability

Positive meaning of equality denotes equality of opportunity. Equality also refers the absence of *irrational discrimination*. Untouchability is the worst kind discrimination which believes that human beings are impure, or polluted. Article 17 said that untouchability is **abolished.** Its practice in any form is forbidden. Untouchability is a **punishable offence**, according to law. Generally fundamental rights are available against the state. But Article 17 is applicable against individuals too.

Untouchability is not defined in the Constitution. Generally, Fundamental Rights in the Indian Constitution are *not absolute*. Rights are subject to various limitations but Article 17 is an absolute right. Therefore, untouchability is not allowed in any condition or any ground. Fundamental Rights can be classified on the following grounds too:

(a) **Self-operative:** This means that parliamentary law is not needed for enforcing Fundamental Rights. Articles 14, 15 are self-operated Fundamental Rights.

(b) However, Article 17 requires a parliamentary act for enforcement of right against untouchability, since Article 17 envisages it as a punishable offence. The Parliament passed the **Untouchability (Offenses) Act 1955** for enforcement of Article 17. It is not a self-operative right. The Parliamentary Act of 1955 was renamed and amended in 1976 as the **Protection of Civil Rights Act, 1955.** The Act does not define the meaning of untouchability but it includes various examples such as:

   1. Denying entry in temples of public character;
   2. Any restriction in the entry of public places like shops and restaurants;
   3. Forbidding entry in hospitals;
   4. Discrimination over the use of pond, road or drinking water supply;
   5. Justifying untouchablity on philosophical grounds; and
   6. Disrespecting anyone on the basis of caste, amounts to untouchability.

SC/ST (Prevention of Atrocities) Act, 1989

This Act was passed by the Parliament for protecting the cause of Schedules Castes and Scheduled Tribes. The Act came under scrutiny due to decision of the Supreme Court in **Dr Subhash Kashinath Mahajan v. the State of Maharashtra (2018).** Initially, the Supreme Court said that the Act is misused, but later it overturned its own decision and admitted that the people belonging to SC/STs need special protection.

Separate Legal Procedure: Criminal law is based on the *presumption of innocence*. The Court presumes that a person against whom a chargesheet is filed by the police, is innocent. It is the responsibility of the police to prove that the person is guilty. Under the **SC/ST (Prevention of Atrocities) Act**, the judiciary does not follow the principle of presumption of innocence. **No anticipatory bail** is permitted under this Act. Person is arrested at once after the FIR. **Preliminary inquiry** is not required. However, in other cases preliminary inquiry is needed before the arrest.

Abolition of Titles

Titles are a privilege practised in undemocratic societies. The British government awarded titles like Rai Bahadur, Rai sahib, Taluqdar to create *hierarchy* in society. Title bestows privilege or nobility and are antithetical to the notion of equality. The British government had maintained an aristocratic class. The Constituent Assembly decided to abolish the title. **J. B. Kripalani** said that titles are against **socialist society**. **Article 18** seeks abolition of titles. It incorporates the following issues:

1. **Restriction over State**

   According to Article 18 (1), no title shall be conferred by the state. But military and educational titles shall be conferred by the state. Military titles like **Param Vishisht Seva Medal**, or educational titles like **Doctor** are permitted. Government of India introduced awards like the **Bharat Ratna, Padma Vibhushan, Padma Bhushan and Padma Shree** in **1954.** Supreme Court said that these are **awards not titles.** Therefore, the government can give awards the Court held in the **1996 Balaji Raghavan case**. The Court observed that equality does not mean equal treatment. **Equality and efficiency** are not against each other. Supreme Court also instructed that the award like **Bharat Ratna** should not be used as a prefix or suffix in the name of the person. Although no law exists, which prevents the person to use awards before or after his name.

2. **Restriction on Foreign Title**
   Citizens of India shall not accept any title from a **foreign state**. However, awards received by artist are not prohibited, says Article 18(2).
3. **Consent of the President**
   Article 18(3) holds that any person who is not a **citizen of India,** while holding any **office of profit** or **trust** under the state, shall not receive any titles from a foreign state, without the consent of the President.
4. **Restrictions on accepting present, emolument or office**
   A **person** holding **office of profit** or **trust under the state,** shall not accept any **present**, **emolument** or **office** from a **foreign** state without consent of the President.

II. RIGHT TO FREEDOM

Right to Freedom of Speech and Expression

Article 19 protects various rights regarding the freedom of speech and expression. It is available only for citizens. Article 19 covers the following rights:

(a) to freedom of speech and expression;
(b) to assemble peaceably and without arms;
(c) to form associations or unions; by the **97th Constitutional Amendment**, co-operative societies also included;
(d) to move freely throughout the territory of India;
(e) to reside and settle in any part of the territory of India;
(f) to acquire and dispose of property. (this provision was deleted from part III by 44th Constitutional Amendment in 1978 and no longer exists);
(g) To practise any **profession**, or to carry on any **occupation**, **trade**, or **business**.

Issues Related to Freedom of Speech and Expression

1. **Freedom of press:**
   Freedom of press is *inherent* in freedom of speech and expression. It is *not explicitly* written in the Constitution. Freedom of press includes both **print media** and **electronic media.** Freedom of speech and expression is not absolute in India. Freedom is subject to **sovereignty and integrity** of India, **security of the state**, **friendly relations** with **foreign state**, **public order, decency, morality, contempt, defamation** or **incitement to an offence.**
2. **Freedom to make films:**
   Speech simply means speaking but the media of expression are multiple. Press, films, writing books, social media are the various dimensions of expression.
3. **Defamation and Freedom:**
   Liberty is curtailed on the grounds of sedition. Section 499 of the Indian Penal Code (IPC) further states that defamation is a punishable offence.

Other Components of the Right to Freedom

1. **To Assemble Peaceably without Arms**
   This is the most important right in a democratic country like India. Citizens are entitled to organise and assemble for any common purpose. They have the right to organise **protest** against the government. In several instances however, the Supreme Court has held that the right to strike, or calling *bandhs,* is not a Fundamental Right. Assembly with arms is not permitted.
2. **To form Unions or Associations**
   This is not an absolute right brought about by the 16th Constitutional Amendment

1963. It is restricted on the grounds of **sovereignty** and **integrity** of India.

3. **To Move Freely**

   Every citizen is allowed to travel across India. Freedom of movement means *internal movement* within the territory of India. *External movement* is also a part of freedom of movement. Therefore, citizens are free to go abroad too. It is under the limitation of **sovereignty** and **integrity** of India, **public order** or **morality**. For example, during communal violence, freedom of movement can be curtailed.

4. **Freedom of Residence and Settlement**

   Residence denotes staying for short term. **Settlement** implies that the citizen is choosing their **permanent residence**. It can be curtailed in the interest of general public, or the protection of the interests of Scheduled Tribes. Nobody can be allowed to settle in Scheduled areas.

5. **Freedom of Profession, Occupation, Trade and Business**

   Every citizen is allowed to choose her profession. Profession is work, which indicates the expertise of a person. Occupation is associated with **livelihood**. **Business** is oriented towards appropriating profit. **Trade** is a term for the **exchange of goods.** Various limitations like professional or technical qualifications are essential for profession and occupation. The government can own any trade, business industry or services. It can be excluded partially and completely for citizens.

6. **Reasonable Restrictions**

   The various freedoms mentioned in Article 19 (1)(a)(g) are not absolute. The restrictions imposed must be for the particular purpose or object envisaged in the specific clauses—Articles 19 (2) to 19 (6). Grounds of restriction are written in the Constitution. The government can enact laws to restrict Fundamental Rights.

Protection against Conviction for Offences

Article 20 protects the people from any **criminal act**, and provides the **procedure** and **amount of punishment**. It states that nobody can be punished without the violation of law. It also forbids:

(a) ***Ex-Post-Facto* Law**

Article 20(1) states that a person can neither be convicted of any offence which was at the time of commission not charged as an offence nor be subjected to a penalty greater than that which might have been stipulated under the law in force at the time when the offence was committed. Hence, this is called an *ex-post facto* Law, that is, criminal law cannot be applied **in retrospect**, or after the fact (post facto). Civil law however, can be enforced retroactively.

(b) **Double Jeopardy Law**

In the Indian Constitution, the double jeopardy law has been inspired from the **United States**. No person can be prosecuted and punished **twice for** the same offence in **criminal law**. A person who has committed multiple crimes can be prosecuted multiple times. But the **same person** cannot be prosecuted and punished twice for the **same offence**. Administrative punishment is not counted in double jeopardy. It is applicable only for criminal offence in a court of law. Any **administrative officer** suspended from the department and later punished by a court of law is not protected under double jeopardy.

(c) **Right against self-incrimination/Freedom from Being Witness Against Himself**

No one is obliged to witness against his/her self. It is the responsibility of the **police** to show the **evidence of crime**.

Nobody can be **forced** to admit his guilt. Blood sample, fingerprint, or voice sample are not considered as being 'compelled to be witness against himself'. Therefore, Fundamental Rights are available in a court of law and after the punishment too.

Right to Life and Personal Liberty

Article 21 guarantees the Right to Life and Personal Liberty. It is not absolute right and can be violated through '**procedure established by law**'. Right to life and personal liberty has always been the subject of debates from 1950 till today. Interpretation of Right to Life is *dynamic*, that is, it is changing from time to time. The first landmark judgement regarding Right to Life and Personal Liberty was delivered in 1950.

Table 7.2.2: Established Legal Procedure and Due Process

Procedure established by law	Due process of law
1. Term mentioned in Article 21 of the Fundamental Rights	This term has been evolved by the judiciary, inspired by the US; it not written in the Indian Constitution.
2. Procedure written in law should be followed, while encroaching on the Right to Life and Personal Liberty under Article 21.	Procedure should be just, fair and reasonable; it should not be arbitrary.
3. Power of the Parliament is more important.	Power of judiciary becomes vital.
4. Procedure is enacted by the Parliament; the Judiciary cannot question the wisdom of the Parliament	Procedure should fulfill the norms of natural justice. Thus, judiciary can raise questions over reasoning of the Parliament

A Few Important Cases around Article 21

A. *Gopalan case (1950)*

A. K. Gopalan, leader of the Communist Party was arrested and detained under the Preventive Detention Act, 1950. This was challenged in the Supreme Court. Then Article 21 was explained by the Supreme Court as follows:

1. **Right to Life and Personal Liberty:** The Supreme Court said that the Right to Life and Personal Liberty means protecting the *organs and limbs* of an individual. It protects the individual from *arbitrary arrest.* However, Right to Life and Personal Liberty under **Article 21** and various freedoms in **Article 19** are **separate** from each other. It was a *narrower interpretation* of this Right.
2. **Procedure Established by Law:** The Court said that the Right to Life and Personal Liberty is available against the **executive** or the **police**. It is not available against the law made by the Parliament. Parliament makes laws which incorporate procedure too. Gopalan was arrested by the parliamentary act and **procedure** was followed too. Therefore, he was put behind bars legally. The Court said that it can protect the right of an individual when procedure prescribed in **law is violated**. Police cannot arrest anyone without the violation of any **law or procedure in law**.

B. *ADM Jabalpur v. Shivkant Shukla Case (1976)*

It is popularly known as the **habeas corpus case.** Through the **Emergency** to 1976, Fundamental Rights were suspended. It was *suspended by law* and prescribed procedure too. This controversial judgement of P. N. Bhagwati held that a person's right to not be unlawfully detained (i.e., *habeas corpus*) can be suspended in the interest of the state. The Supreme Court strictly followed the principle of procedure established by law and refused to protect Fundamental Rights. It was criticised as a **black day** for the Supreme Court.

C. *Maneka Gandhi Case (1978)*

1. **Liberal Interpretation of Right to Life:** In this landmark case, the Supreme Court

extended the meaning of Right to Life. The Court overruled its decision of the A. K. Gopalan case (1950), and held that the Right to Life and Personal Liberty should be combined with the rights invested in Article 19. **Article 19** and **Article 21** are *complementary* like two organs of a body. Therefore, the Right to Life includes the right to travel outside of India. The **seven judges bench** delivered a historical verdict because the Supreme Court said that various rights are **inherent** in the r Right to Life and Personal Liberty. The Court said that the **spirit of the Constitution** should be kept in mind while interpreting the letter or words of the Constitution.

2. **Due Process of Law:**

The **Maneka Gandhi** case is a historical one where the Supreme Court said that the Parliament is powerful enough to enact laws and decide on procedure established by law. But procedure must be **reasonable, fair and just.** Procedure should not be **arbitrary and unreasonable.** This is also known as **due process of law** (refer to the table earlier); which is a feature of the **American Constitution.** The Court said that procedure of **Passport Act 1967** is **unreasonable**, and thus,declared it null and void. The Court applied the principle of **reasonableness** in **Article 21** too. The term 'reasonable restrictions' is mentioned in **Article 19**. Reading **Article 19** and **Article 21** together means that the principle of **reasonableness** is applicable for **Article 21** as well.

Extended Meaning of Right to Life

Since the Maneka Gandhi case, the Supreme Court held that the Constitution is *not a static document*. It is *living document*. Therefore, the interpretation of the Constitution shall change according to changing circumstances. Expansion of the Right to Life should be visualised in light of **Public Interest Litigations (PIL)**. And the Supreme Court propounded the notion of the PIL in the 1980s. The broader meaning of the Right to Life includes:

1. Right to livelihood
2. Right to education
3. Right against sexual harassment
4. Pollution free environment
5. Right against arbitrary arrest and detention
6. Right against solitary confinement
7. Right to privacy
8. Right of reputation
9. Right of speedy trial

Triumph of Fundamental Rights

Fundamental Rights are the sign of a vibrant democracy. The Supreme Court propounded a landmark judgment in the **K. S. Puttaswamy case (2018)** and said that the Right to Privacy is an integral part of the Right to Life and Personal Liberty. The Court issued this decision while hearing the issue of the compulsory use of **Aadhaar.** The judiciary did not define meaning of privacy but said that privacy includes:

1. Choice of sexual relations
2. Marriage
3. Attire
4. Right to Privacy is also available in the public domain.
5. Nobody can be frisked publicly or openly.
6. Right to Privacy is **not an absolute** right.
7. Right to Privacy can be curtailed on the grounds of social justice and security of the country.

Right to Life is not Absolute

Right to Life is not an absolute right. Therefore, nobody is allowed to end his/her life. Nobody can waive Fundamental Rights; this is known as the *principle of waiver*. The Supreme Court had held in the **P. Rathinam case (1994)** that an individual can kill her/his self under the Right to Life and Personal Liberty in Article 21. But later in the **Gian Kaur case (1996)**, the Supreme Court overruled its earlier decision and said that Right to Life does not mean the **Right to Die**. In **2018**, the Supreme Court pronounced a landmark judgment as part of the 2011 verdict in the **Aruna Ramchandra Shanbaug** case. It said that **passive euthanasia**, is permitted under strict guidelines. Passive euthanasia implies the withdrawal of medical treatment from a terminally ill/vegetative state patient. The Court said that a person must be given the right to *die with dignity*. Right to Life is also subject to the procedure established by law. Therefore, the Parliament can penalise any person through procedure established by law.

Right to Protection Against Arrest and Detention

1. **Right Against Arbitrary Detention**
   Article 22(1) holds that no person shall be **arrested** and detained in **custody** without been **informed** of the **grounds of arrest.** Person can be arrested on the ground of violation of law. But **arbitrary detention** means arresting a person without information and without any valid reason. Arbitrary detention deprives an individual from the Right to Life and Personal Liberty.
2. **Consultation with Legal Practitioner**
   Everyone is allowed to consult a legal practitioner of his/her **own choice.** And the person shall be defended by legal practitioner (advocate). The Constitution has prescribed for **fair trails** because the **police** can frame charges against an innocent person too. And the accused is entitled to defend herself in a court of law with the help of lawyer, as per Article 22(2).
3. **Permission of Magistrate**
   Any person who is arrested and detained shall be produced before the **nearest Magistrate** within **24 hours**. It means that the police cannot detain anyone beyond 24 hours without permission of a Magistrate. These 24 hours does not include the **time of journey** from **place of arrest** to the **court of the Magistrate.** It guarantees rule of law and prohibits the possibility of a police state, according to Article 22(2).

Preventive Detention

Article 22(3) allows preventive detention. Preventive detention means detaining any person who has not committed a crime yet, in order to prevent the person against committing the crime in future. Therefore, it maintains an exception of *arbitrary detention*. An *enemy alien* is also deprived from the right against arbitrary detention. 'Alien' refers to a person who is not a citizen of India. Although the term enemy alien is not defined in the Constitution, the Parliament enacted the Enemy Property Act 1968 following the Indo-Pakistan War of 1965. The Act defines 'enemy' as a country which commits an act of aggression against India and its citizens. This automatically means **China and Pakistan** can be categorised as enemy states.

Table 7.2.3: Preventive versus Punitive Detention

Preventive Detention	*Punitive Detention*
1. Detaining anybody before the breach of law	Detaining anybody after violation of law
2. Detained by police	Detained by the order of a court of law
3. Detained merely on the basis of suspicion	Detained after a crime is committed
4. It promotes a police state	It is according to the rule of law
5. Police can detain beyond 24 hours, without the permission of a Magistrate	Police cannot detain after 24 hours, without the permission of a Magistrate

1. **Rights of Detainee**
   Article 22(4)(7) provides the right of a person under preventive detention. No person can be detained for a period longer than **three months** without a decision of the **advisory board**. Advisory board is comprised of persons who are either a judges of a high court, or a person qualified to be appointed as a judge of a high court.
2. **Representation Against Detention**
   The authority shall communicate the grounds of detention to the person being detained. The detainee shall be given the earliest opportunity to make their **representation** against the order. **Detention for More than Three Months.**
   Article 22 prescribe three types of detention:
   (a) Less than three months;
   (b) More than three months, which requires the permission of the advisory board;

The Parliament shall by law determine the period of detention for more than **three months.**

Grounds of Preventive Detention Law

Entry number 3 in the **Concurrent List** mentions preventive detention in the **Seventh Schedule**. Reasons behind preventive detention may be connected to security of the state. Maintenance of public order or the maintenance of supply and services to the community is the basis of preventive detention law. The **union government** and the **state government** are both entitled to make a law related to preventive detention. The origins of preventive detention law date back to the Bengal State Prisoners Regulation, III of 1818 enacted by the East India Company in the presidency of Bengal. Further, the British government had also enacted the Indian Defence Act 1939 which enacted martial law during World War II.

Preventive Detention Laws in Independent India

The first Preventive Detention Act was enacted by the Parliament on 26 February 1950. A. K. Gopalan, famous Communist leader was detained by the same Act.

Maintenance of Internal Security Act (MISA), 1971

The Parliament enacted MISA in 1971 during the prime minstership of Indira Gandhi. It was heavily misused by the Indira Gandhi government during the **Emergency** between 1975–1977. Leaders of Opposition were put behind bars. In the name of national security, opposition was suppressed. Thereafter it was repealed in 1978 by the **Janata Party government**, which was the first non-Congress government at the union after Independence.

Conservation of Foreign Exchange and Prevention of Smuggling Activities Act (COFEPOSA), 1974

It is aimed at prevention of money laundering and the smuggling of various articles. It was an economic adjunct to the controversial Maintenance of Internal Security Act (MISA) which was enacted in 1971. Though MISA was repealed in 1978, this law is still applicable at the present time in India.

National Security Act (NSA), 1980

The Indira Gandhi government enacted the NSA. The NSA was a revival of the MISA. The NSA is applied in India till today.

Terrorist and Disruptive Activities (Prevention) Act (TADA), 1985

The **Rajiv Gandhi** government brought about TADA for regulating militancy in **Punjab** but it was applied to the whole of India. It became the first act which defines **terrorism** in India. The National Human Rights Commission (NHRC) criticised the TADA which detained persons for **up to one year.** The Commission said that it was a draconian law; thereafter it was repealed in the year 1995. The famous actor Sanjay Dutt was detained under this Act for his role in the 1993 Mumbai serial blasts.

Prevention of Terrorism Act (POTA), 2002

The Parliament was targeted in an attack in December 2001. Subsequently, the National Democratic Alliance (NDA) government enacted the POTA in 2002. United Progressive Alliance (UPA) government came in to power in 2004 and repealed the Act in 2004.

Unlawful Activities (Prevention) Act (UAPA) 2008

The UAPA, also known as the Anti-Terror law, was enacted way back in 1967. Later various amendments were incorporated in the Act. The most recent amendment was brought about in **2019**. For the first time, this has made it possible for the union government to designate individuals as terrorists without following any formal judicial process. This Act also strengthens the reach and actions of the **National Investigation Agency (NIA)**. United Nations special rapporteurs have stated that the provisions of the UAPA 2019 contravene several articles of the Universal Declaration of Human Rights and the International Covenant on Civil and Political Rights.

III. RIGHT AGAINST EXPLOITATION

Right to Life means right to life with dignity. Exploitation means the unfair treatment of the potential and strength of a person for unscrupulous gains. Article 23 recognises the following forms of exploitation:

(a) Human trafficking;
(b) Forced begging;
(c) Similar forms of forced labour

According to Article 23(1), trafficking of human beings, forced begging, and other similar forms of forced labour are prohibited and any contravention of this provision shall be an offence punishable in accordance with law. This means that **trade of** human organs **is not allowed** and trafficking of child **is a part of human trafficking**.

Broader Meaning of Exploitation

The Supreme Court said in the **case** of **People's Union for Democratic Rights** (PUDR) **1982** that paying below minimum wages to workers amounts to exploitation. It was observed that some basic rights can be enforced against private people, contrary to the belief that Fundamental Rights can only be enforced against the state. The Supreme Court in this judgment expanded the interpretation of Article 21 of the Constitution (Right to Life) to include the **Right to a Livelihood as well as the Right to Live with Fundamental Human Dignity**. The Supreme Court also passed an order that every State Government should add construction industry in Section 3(3) of the Employment of Children Act, 1938 by the powers conferred to it under Section 3-A so as to prevent children below the age of 14 years to be employed under such hazardous work like construction site.

1. **Sexual Harassment**

   The Supreme Court expanded the meaning of exploitation in the famous **Vishakha case** in **1997**. The Court said that sexual harassment is more dangerous than physical assault. Sexual harassment is violation of Right to Life with Dignity. The Court also gave guidelines for **prevention of sexual harassment** at **workplace.**

2. **Compulsory Service**

   Article 23(2) holds that the state can impose compulsory service for **public purposes**. It will not be considered as **forced labour**. While imposing compulsory service, the state shall not make any discrimination on grounds only of **religion**, **race**, **caste** or **class**.

Right of Child Against Exploitation

Article 24 prohibits of employment of children in:

(a) Factories
(b) Mines
(c) Hazardous employment

Articles 23 and 24 are not *self-operated*; a **Parliamentary Act** is needed to enforce the right. Article 24 prohibits the employment of children below the age of 14, in any hazardous industry or factories or mines, without exception. This implies that the children between ages of 14 to 18 can be employed in any occupation. This lacuna is removed in the new act— Child Labour (Prohibition & Regulation) Amendment Act, 2016. This Act completely forbids the employment of children below 14 years of age. It also bans the employment of people between the ages of 14 and 18 in hazardous occupations and processes. But it allows children to be employed in certain family occupations and also as artists.

***Relation Between Article 24 and Article 21 (A)*:** Article 24 prohibits the employment of children below the age of 14 therefore, it is negative in character. Article 21 (A) was inserted in the Constitution by the 86th Amendment in 2002. According to Article 21 (A), the state shall provide free and compulsory education to all children of age 6 to 14 years as a Fundamental Right. The state shall enact laws for free and compulsory education, and thus, the Right to Education Act was made by the in the year 2009.

IV. RIGHT TO FREEDOM OF RELIGION

These rights were a subject of debate in the Constituent Assembly. One of the prominent members of the Constituent Assembly, **Rajkumari Amrit Kaur** raised objection over the inclusion of religious rights as a fundamental right. Kaur said that religious rights would prove to be an obstacle in the path of **social reform.** She held that religious rights could give constitutional protection to various discriminatory practices such as the purdah, sati, devadasi system, and so on. But religious rights were incorporated in Part III, which shows that the Indian state is **secular**. Religious rights are protected in Articles 25 to 28.

1. **Freedom of Conscience**

   Clause 1 of Article 25 states that all persons are equally entitled to Freedom of Conscience and right freely to–

   i. profess,
   ii. practice, and
   iii. propagate religion.

   'Profess' is associated with **religious beliefs.** Every person is free to choose her belief because it is the **conscience** of a person. One example for 'Practice' is the wearing and carrying of *kirpans* (traditional Sikh daggers). 'Propagate' refers to educating others about religious teachings. Freedom of religion ensures the division between state and religion. Because the state shall not determine, profess or practise religion.

2. **Restrictions over Religious Rights:**

   i. **Public Order, Morality and Health**

   Religious rights are not absolute. Article 25 (1) says that Freedom of Conscience is subject to **public order, morality and health**. The state is allowed to interfere in religious rights on the grounds of public order, which is the basic **responsibility of the state**. Nobody is allowed to **practise obscenity** in the name of religious rights.

   ii. **Secular Activity**

   Article 25 (2) places additional limitations over religious rights. The state is allowed to make a law to regulate any **economic, financial, political or other secular activity**. It can be associated with religious practice. Therefore, the state is allowed to **intervene** in religious matters but religious priests or institutions are not permitted to interfere in **secular activities** run by the state.

3. ***Social Reform***

   The state is empowered to make a law for social welfare. It cannot be challenged in a court of law on the grounds of religious right. The state can make a law for social reform. Therefore, **child marriage** is prohibited and **instant triple divorce** is declared as unconstitutional.

Religious Conversion

The Constitution neither mentions religious conversion nor does it prohibit the same. Allegedly due to mass religious conversions, **Odisha** became the first state to enact a law to curb religious conversion by the use of force, inducement, or fraudulent means in 1967. Madhya Pradesh also made a law to prevent religious conversion in 1968. Arunachal Pradesh enacted a law in 1978, Chhattisgarh (2000), thereafter, Gujarat (2003), Himachal Pradesh (2007), Jharkhand (2017), Uttarakhand (2018), also enacted laws on the same. It is important to note that Tamil Nadu too had enacted a law in 2002 but it was repealed in the year 2004.

Essential Features of Religion

The Supreme Court ruled that **slaughtering animals** is not an essential feature of religion. Use of **loud speakers** is not an essential feature of religion. Banning entry of **women** in temple is not an essential feature either. Bursting **fire crackers** may not be an integral feature of religion. No essential feature can be regulated by the state.

Freedom to Manage Religious Affairs

Religious rights apply not only to individuals but also to **religious institutions**. **Article 26** incorporates religious freedom for religious institutions. Fundamental Rights of religious institutions are mentioned below:

(a) Establish and maintain institutions for religious and charitable purposes.

(b) To manage its own affairs in matters of religion.

(c) To own and acquire movable and immovable property.

(d) To administer such property according to law.

This right is also subject to restrictions of **public order, morality and health.** Thus, it is *not an absolute right*. It is interesting to note that right to property as a fundamental right, no longer exists as a fundamental right for citizens, because the 44th Amendment (1978) removed Right to Property from the list of Fundamental Rights and converted it into a simple legal right. However, **Article 26** still provides the **Right to Property** as a Fundamental Right for religious institutions.

Secular State

(a) **Freedom from Payment of Taxes:**

The Constitution is the supreme law of the land, which is enacted by human beings. India is not governed by religious or divine law. The state levies taxes for running the government and for the welfare of the people. But the state shall not impose taxation for promotion **of any particular religion or religious institutions or** for the maintenance of any particular religious place of worship, under **Article 27**.

b. **Freedoms from Religious Instruction or Worship:**

Indian state is secular because Article 25 provides persons the **Freedom of Conscience.** The state shall not promote any religion through educational institutions. **Article 28 contains** following verities of educational institutions:

(i) **Wholly Maintained by the state:**

Central universities and central schools are examples of educational institutions wholly maintained by the state. **No religious instruction** is allowed in these institutions. Teaching 'Buddhist Studies' for academic purposes is not considered as religious instruction.

(ii) **Institutions Established by Trust**
The DAV school, Saraswati Shishu Mandir and so on, are examples of educational institutions, established by a religious trust. They are free to impart religious instruction because religious right is a fundamental right. The state shall not prevent a trust from imparting religious instructions.

(iii) **Institutions Recognised by the State**
Education institution recognised by the union state means recognition of UGC and CBSE. Education institutions receiving aid out of state fund includes **private educational institutions**. It is partly associated with the state and partly related to private persons. Therefore, religious instructions is allowed in these institutions with consent of students. If student is a **minor** then **consent** of **guardian** is needed.

V. CULTURAL AND EDUCATIONAL RIGHTS: PROTECTION OF THE INTERESTS OF MINORITIES

Article 29

Article 29 says that **any section of citizens** residing in the territory of India are entitled to have their distinct

(i) language,
(ii) script,
(iii) or, culture

They shall have the right to conserve their own **language, script** and **culture**.

No Discrimination in Educational Institutions: Article 29 is available for **citizens** only. According to Article 29(2), the citizens shall not be denied admission to any educational institution **maintained** by the state, or **receiving aid** from the state fund. Also, the state shall not discriminate on grounds only of **religion, race, caste, language or any of them.** Rights of minorities are significant in the Constitution. Because democracy automatically promotes the **rule of majority,** minorities' rights protect minorities from undemocratic decisions of the majority. The majority cannot impose **language** and **culture** on **minority.**

Article 30

1. **Minorities Rights to Establish Education Institution:**
All **minorities** shall have the right to establish and administer education institutions of their **own choice. Article 30(1)** mentions two types of minorities:
(a) Religious
(b) Linguistic
However, Article 30 does not define 'minorities'.

2. **Definition of Minorities:**
The National Commission of Minorities Act, 1992 initially defined five communities—**Muslims, Christians, Sikhs, Buddhists,** and **Parsis** as minorities. But this parliamentary act does not mention the *basis of identification* of minorities. The President by notification can include other communities as minorities. The Supreme Court said that identification of minorities should be classified on the **basis of states.** The Court said that the states in India are reorganised on a **linguistic basis**, in **TMA Pai Foundation case (2002)**. Therefore, minorities cannot be recognised on an **all India** basis. However, the Supreme Court never propounded **any criteria** for identification of minorities. The most crucial question still exists India: Who are the minorities?

According to the Census of 2011, **Muslims** constitute 14.2 per cent of the national population, **Christians** 2.3 per cent, **Sikhs** 1.7 per cent, **Buddhists** 0.7 per cent, and **Jains** 0.4 per cent of the total population. However, Muslims are in majority in the union territories of **Lakshadweep, Jammu Kashmir** and **Ladakh.** Similarly, Christians constitute the majority majority in **Nagaland, Mizoram** and **Meghalaya**. Sikhs have the majority in **Punjab**. Hindus constitute the majority for the whole of India, but they are minorities in a few states and UTs. The problem still persists because the criteria of minorities is not clearly articulated by the Supreme Court.

Minorities may be defined from a **numerical point** of view, i.e., whosoever is less than **50 per cent is a minority**. Following such a rationale, we could have exact quantification of benchmarks like 5 per cent, 10 per cent or 15 per cent for identifying minorities. Apart from numerical strength, *economic status* may be a base for recognition of minorities. For example, people belonging to Jain religion are less in numerical strength but economically they are well-off.

3. Minority Educational Institutions:

The Constitution does not define minority educational institutions. The Supreme Court in 2002 said that minority education institution means the institution which is established by minority communities. Educational institution belonging to minority community may be non-aided by the government. Even if the institution is funded by the government, it does not lose its minority status. Article 30 (2) states that the state shall not, when granting aid to educational institutions, discriminate against any educational institution on the ground that it is under the management of a minority, whether based on religion or language.

4. Right to Establish and Manage Educational Institutions

In the **TMA Pai Foundation case**, the Supreme Court delivered a landmark judgment, and said that the right of minorities to establish and administer educational institutions of their choice includes the following rights:

(a) To determine fee structure: the government shall not determine the same;
(b) Appointment of teachers and staff of their own community
(c) To determine the percentage of admission for non-minority community

Since the job of the state is to maintain education standards, therefore, it shall have right to regulate education institutions:

(a) Donation is not allowed because education institutions are not profit-making institutions.
(b) They are bound to follow academic standards and adhere to prescribed academic qualifications of teachers.
(c) An academic session should be based on the regulation of the government.

Various cases related to minorities have been settled by the Supreme Court like the **Unni Krishnan case (1993), St. Stephen's case (1991)** earlier.

5. Right to Property for Educational Institutions

Educational institution established and administered by minorities still enjoy the right to property. Compulsory acquisition of any property belonging to minority education institutions is restricted by laws made by the state.

Right to Property in the Original Constitution

Originally, the Right to Property was incorporated as a Fundamental Right in Article 19 (1) (f) which said that any citizen can acquire and dispose of property. Article 31 (1) also provided the Right to Property. However, any person could be deprived from the Right to Property, according to **procedure established by the law**. The state was empowered to acquire the property of any person provided that:

1. The property is acquired for public purposes; and
2. the state shall give adequate compensation

In order to enforce **Directive Principles of State Policy (DPSP),** the government tried to curtail the Right to Property. The Indian state is a welfare state; it had therefore launched the programme of **land reform** after 1950. India is a **federal state** and land was a **state subject.** Thus, various state governments enacted laws for land reforms. The acts related to land reforms in states were challenged in the **Supreme Court** on account of violation of Right to Property.

1. **The First Amendment**

   The **Bihar government** became one of the earliest states in India which enacted the land reform act. The Land Reform Act (1950) of the Bihar government was for the first time challenged in the Supreme Court in the **Kameshwar Singh case**. The Supreme Court nullified the Land Reform Act. For protecting the Land Reform Act, the Parliament brought about the **First Constitutional Amendment in 1951**. Article 31 (A) was inserted in the Constitution, which restricted the Right to Property in these ways:

   i. the acquisition by the state of any estate or of any rights therein, or the extinguishment or modification of any such rights
   ii. the taking over of the management of any property by the state for a limited period either in public interest, or in order to secure its proper management
   iii. the amalgamation of two or more corporations either in the public interest, or in order to secure the proper management of any of the corporations
   iv. the extinguishment or modification of any rights of managing agents, etc., or of any voting rights of shareholders thereof, or
   v. the extinguishment or modification of any rights accruing by virtue of any agreement, lease or licence for the purpose of searching for, or winning, any mineral or mineral oil. In a nutshell, Article 31 (A) established the foundation of the welfare state. It was an attempt to **promote socialism** in India. Before Independence, ***Jagir, Inam, Ryotwari*** were various types of estates. All of this was curtailed by the **First Constitutional Amendment**.

2. **The Ninth Schedule**

   The Schedule is needed for the extension of an Article. Article 31 (B) was incorporated in the Constitution, which resulted in the inclusion of the Ninth Schedule. This means the original Constitution had only **8 Schedules**; the Ninth schedule was added by the **First Constitutional Amendment**. It is created exclusively for the protection of the Land Reform Acts, which were kept away from **judicial review**. This is because any Act included in the Ninth Schedule shall not be challenged in a court of law on the basis of violation of Fundamental Rights of part III.

3. **Issue of Compensation**

   After the First Amendment, Right to Property was limited by Article 31(A) and Article 31(B). But Article 31 also provides for **compensation** payable to affected parties when a property has been acquired by the government**.** The Supreme Court in the **Bela Banerjee case (1953)** said that compensation should be adequate. Therefore, the **4th Constitutional Amendment** (1955) was added in the Constitution. According to the 4th Constitutional Amendment, the judiciary cannot inquire about the sufficiency of the compensation.

4. **Repealing of Compensation**

   Indira Gandhi brought about the **26th Constitution Amendment (1971)** and abolished the '**privy purses**' (compensation being paid by the government to princely state rulers). Compensation would be according to market rate, held the Supreme Court in the **R. C. Cooper case,** which is popularly known as **bank nationalisation case** (1970). Consequently, the **25th Constitutional Amendment Act (1971)** was passed by the Parliament; the term **'compensation'** was repealed and **'amount'** was inserted in Article 31 (2). Compensation denotes the payment due to damages to the person by the government. But amount does not indicate any harm to an individual. It depends upon the government to pay amount to the person. The 25th Constitutional Amendment rendered the Supreme Court unable to choose the amount of compensation for taking over such property for public use.

5. **Abolishing the Right to Property**

   As mentioned briefly earlier, the Janata Party government in 1978 passed the **44th Constitutional Amendment**. Therefore Article 19 (1) (f) and Article 31 (1) (2) were deleted from Part III of the Constitution. It means that the Fundamental Right to Property is no longer available for citizens. **Consequently, Article 32** cannot be utilised for protection of Right to Property. Today, the Right to Property is a **legal right** under **Article 300 (A)**, which says that no person shall be deprived of his property save by authority of law. Any person can approach the **High Court** under **Article 226** for protection of the right to property.

6. **Remaining Elements of Right to Property**

   Although the Right to Property has been deleted from Part III by the 44th Constitutional Amendment (1978), ironically Article 31 (A) and Article 31 (B) still exist in Part III of the Constitution. Therefore, some exceptional elements of the right to property are left out in the Constitution:

   i. If the government wanted to acquire property of any minority educational institution, the government shall provide amount to the institution at **market rates.**

   ii. If the government is acquiring agriculture land within the limitation of ceiling, then the government is bound to pay the amount at **market rate**.

VI. RIGHT TO CONSTITUTIONAL REMEDIES

Article 32 is a Fundamental Right in itself, and in addition to that **Article 32 enforces** other Fundamental Rights too. Without Article 32, other Fundamental Rights become meaningless. Because Article 32 allows the Supreme Court to issue direction order or writs for enforcement of Fundamental Rights. The Supreme Court exercises the following writs:

1. *Habeas corpus*
2. *Mandamus*
3. *Prohibition*
4. *Quo Warranto*
5. *Certiorari*

The Parliament by law can empower any **other court to** exercise writs mentioned above without limiting powers of the Supreme Court. Rights guaranteed in this Article shall **not be suspended.**

1. *Habeas Corpus*

   It is a **Latin term,** which literally means 'to have the body'. Article 21 gives the Right to Life and Personal Liberty. A person can approach the Supreme Court in case of arbitrary arrest and detention. The Court examines the reason behind the arrest. The Court can release the person in case of arbitrary arrest. *Habeas corpus* is available against the state and it can be utilised against any person too. For search of missing persons, we can approach the Supreme Court. It is the obligation of the police to search for the person. *Habeas corpus* is not available in the following matters:

(i) Person is under arrest due to conviction by judiciary.
(ii) Person is arrested because of contempt of court.
(iii) Person is arrested under laws allowing preventive detention.

2. *Mandamus*

It is also a **Latin term** which literally means 'we command'. It is an order issuesd by the Supreme Court to any *subordinate authority*. It can be issued by the Court against a public official, public corporation, tribunal, inferior court or the government to perform the legal duties which it has not or refused to perform. Therefore, a person heading a *public office* is bound to fulfill his *duty*. The police commissioner is responsible for maintaining public order. Any person can approach Supreme Court against police officer. *Mandamus* cannot be utilised against any **private person**. There are two public offices, who are given immunity from *mandamus*:

(i) President
(ii) Governor

The President and the Governor act according to the aid and advice of the Council of Ministers. Therefore, they are kept away from the domain of *Mandamus*.

3. **Prohibition**

A writ of prohibition is issued primarily to prevent/prohibit a subordinate court or tribunal from exceeding its jurisdiction in cases pending before it or acting contrary to the rules of natural justice. Article 21 says that Right to Life and Personal Liberty shall be deprived according to procedure established by law. **District court** is bound to **follow procedure** while adjudicating any case. The **Supreme Court** can stay the matter pending before the subordinate court. Popularly it is known as a **stay order**. Prohibition is exercised in the first stage of case, when it is **pending before** the subordinate court. Logically it is not available against **private persons**.

4. *Quo Warranto*

A **Latin term** which means 'by what warrant'. Through this writ, the Court calls upon a person holding a public office to show under what authority he holds that office. Fundamental right includes Right to Equality in employment and appointment under the state. Therefore, any unauthorised person is not eligible for appointment in **public office**. For example, the junior police officer is not entitled to hold the office of Director General of Police. *Quo warranto* is not applicable against any **private office**. For example, the appointment of Chief Executive Officer (CEO) of TATA Company is not fit for use of *quo warranto*.

5. *Certiorari*

This is a Latin term which denotes certification. This writ is issued by a court higher in authority to a lower court or tribunal ordering them either to transfer a case pending with them to itself, or to quash their order in a case. Criminal and civil matters originate from **district courts** or subordinate courts. But subordinate courts shall act according to **procedure established by law**. In case of violation of procedure, the **Supreme Court** issues *certiorari*. The Supreme Court also examines, whether subordinate courts have **exceeded their jurisdiction**. *Certiorari* is issued in **later stage** of any case, when a subordinate court has already delivered its decision.

Restrictions on Fundamental Rights

Article 33

As we have seen, Fundamental Rights are **not absolute** in the Constitution. Certain limitations are imposed on every Article. Apart from that, **Articles 33** and **34** impose further restrictions over Fundamental Rights. **Article 33** maintains a balance between Fundamental Rights and discipline for members of several classes of services. Article 33 empowers the **Parliament** to enact laws for curtailing the Fundamental Rights of following persons serving under the state:

(i) Members of **armed forces** like army, navy, air force.
(ii) Members of forces charged with the maintenance of **public order**, such as, the police and central armed forces like BSF, CISF.
(iii) Persons employed in any **bureau** or other **organisation** established by the state for purposes of **intelligence** or **counter intelligence**. Various intelligence agencies operate in India like the Intelligence Bureau (IB), Research and Analysis Wing (RAW), and military intelligence.
(iv) Persons employed in connection with **telecommunication** systems for the purpose of any force, bureau or organisation mention above.

This means that Freedom of Speech and Expression is restricted for members of armed forces. Religious freedom is also curtailed and the Parliament has enacted the **Army Act (1950)**, the **Air Force Act (1950)** and the **Navy Act (1950).** The Parliament also passed the **Police Forces (Restriction of Rights) Act, 1966** and the **Border Security Force Act, 1968**.

Martial Law

Article 34 suspends Fundamental Rights in a particular *geographical area*. Law related to martial law is enacted by the Parliament. Martial law is imposed for maintenance or restoration of order in any area within the **territory of India.** Persons responsible for maintaining martial law shall be given exemption. The Parliament can **validate any sentence** or punishment given by the person employed for maintaining law and order.

Parliament passed **Armed Forces (Special Powers) Act 1958,** which is known as the AFSPA. It was enforced for the first time in Assam and Manipur in 1958. It was also implemented in Jammu and Kashmir in 1988. It has also come into operation in Arunachal Pradesh, Meghalaya, Mizoram and Nagaland. The AFSPA can be imposed by notification from the **Home Ministry**.

Amendment of Fundamental Rights

1. Primacy of the Parliament

The Parliament is given the task of **social justice**. The Nehru government tried to amend Fundamental Rights for social justice. Fundamental Rights are the **only part** of the Constitution which is protected by a **special Clause**. Article 13 (2) states that if any **law** enacted by the state violates Fundamental Rights, it shall be declared null and void. The Parliament passed the First Constitutional Amendment Act in 1951. The Parliament amended Fundamental Rights and inserted the Article 15 (4) and Article 31 (A) and (B). In doing so, the Parliament encroached upon the Fundamental Rights, which was heard by the Supreme Court in the **Shankari Prasad case (1951)**.

A. *Shankari Prasad Case v. Union of India (1951)*

This case is referred to as a landmark judgment as it was the very first case that challenged the First Constitutional Amendment Act of 1951. The petition questioned the constitutionality of the Act based on the grounds that it was totally in violation of Part III of the Indian Constitution and thus, claimed that it should be proclaimed invalid. The Supreme Court said that First Constitutional Amendment Act is valid because:

(i) Law included in Article 13 (2) is not referring to **constitutional law**.
(ii) 'Law' in Article 13 (2) refers to **ordinary** law made by the Parliament or state legislature.
(iii) The restriction mentioned in Article 13 (2) does not apply to Constitutional Amendment Act. It is applicable for an ordinary law.
(iv) Thus, Fundamental Rights included in Part III cannot be amended by an **ordinary law**.
(v) However, Fundamental Rights can be amended by a Constitutional Amendment Act.
(vi) The Supreme Court admitted the **differences** between ordinary law of Parliament enacted in **Article 246** and the Constitutional Amendment Act enacted under the **Article 368.**
(vii) The Parliament plays a **dual role** as it enacts an ordinary law by **simple** majority, and it also amends the Constitution with **special majority**.

2. Triumph of Fundamental Rights

A. *Golaknath v. State of Punjab (1967)*

In this case, the Supreme Court overruled the decision of the **Shankari Prasad** case. The Court interpreted Article 13 (2) again.

(i) The Court observed that the law mentioned in Article 13 (2) also includes Constitutional Amendment Act.
(ii) It means Fundamental Rights cannot be amended either by ordinary law or by Constitutional Amendment Act.
(iii) thus implies that Fundamental Rights are beyond the amendment power of the Parliament.
(iv) The Supreme Court said that there is **no difference** between ordinary law and Constitutional Amendment Act.
(v) The Court observed that **Article 246 the source of power** both for ordinary law-making and for Constitutional Amendment Act.
(vi) Interestingly. the Court said that **Article 368** only outlines the procedure of Constitutional Amendment, not the power of the Constitutional Amendment Act.
(vii) For the Supreme Court, Fundamental Rights are **sacrosanct** and most important part of the Constitution. Therefore, they **cannot be amended.**

The Golaknath case created numerous problems before the Indira Gandhi government since they tried to amend Fundamental Rights for the implementation of **DPSP**. Thus, the Parliament brought about **24th Constitutional Amendment** for overruling the decision of Supreme Court in the **Golaknath case.** The Parliament was committed to restore its previous powers when it had been entitled to amend The Fundamental Rights. **Article 13 (4)** was **inserted** in the Constitution, which held that Fundamental Rights could be amended by Constitutional Amendments. The 24th Constitutional Amendment also restores the difference between ordinary law and Constitutional Amendment Act. This amendment was again challenged in the Supreme Court in the **Keshavanand Bharti case.**

3. Harmonious Relations between the Parliament and the Judiciary:

A. *Kesavananda Bharati v. State of Kerala and Anr (1973)*

The Supreme Court overruled the decision of the **Golaknath** Case but validated 24th Constitutional Amendment. The Supreme Court again restored the pre-1967 scenario. Therefore, the Court said that,

(i) Law included in Article 13 (2) is not referring to constitutional law.

(ii) Law in Article 13 (2) is **an ordinary law** made by the Parliament or state legislature.

(iii) The restriction mentioned in Article 13 (2) does not apply over Constitutional Amendment Act. It is applicable for an ordinary law.

(iv) Thus, **Fundamental Rights** included in Part III cannot be amended by an ordinary law.

(v) But Fundamental Rights can be amended by the Constitutional Amendment Act.

(vi) The Supreme Court admitted the differences between **ordinary law** of Parliament under **Article 246** and **Constitutional Amendment Act** under **Article 368**.

4. *Basic Structure and Fundamental Rights*

The basic structure doctrine is a legal doctrine, according to which, the constitution of a sovereign state has certain characteristics that cannot be erased by its legislature. In India, the Parliament plays a **dual role**—it enacts an ordinary law by **simple majority,** and it also amends the Constitution with a **special majority**. The Supreme Court stated that Fundamental Rights can be **amended** but the **basic structure** of the Constitution cannot be amended. However, what comprises the basic structure of the constitution shall be determined by the Supreme Court.

The Court said that Right to Privacy is basic structure of the Constitution. Therefore, **Article 21** is basic structure of the Constitution which shall not be amended. **Article 21** and **Article 19** are complementary to each other. Therefore, **Article 19** also appears as a basic structure of the Constitution.

For the Supreme Court, secularism is the basic structure of the Constitution and thus, **Article 25** is also part of the basic structure. **Article 14** is the soul of Right to Equality and rule of law, therefore, it is also part of basic structure. The Supreme Court has also maintained that **Article 32** is the basic structure of the Constitution because it is the base of judicial review, which is again basic structure.

FUNDAMENTAL DUTIES

Fundamental Duties were incorporated in Part IVA of the Constitution by the 42nd Constitutional Amendment (1976). Indira Gandhi appointed the Swaran Singh Committee for reviewing the original Constitution, which did not mention Fundamental Duties. Duty and Rights are two faces of the same coin. Fundamental Rights were already incorporated in the original Constitution. Inherent limitations over the Fundamental Rights necessitated the demand of Fundamental Duties.

Fundamental Duties were not included in the original Constitution, due to it being a liberal democratic constitution. Fundamental Rights are considered primary in the democratic political system. However, Fundamental Duties are professed in socialist countries. Fundamental Duties does not find any place in the Constitution of democratic countries like the **US, or the UK**. Apart from India, **Japan** is the only liberal democratic country which elucidates Fundamental Duty. Socialist constitutions like that of **China** contain Fundamental Duties.

Mahatma Gandhi had said that there is no need for rights if everyone follows his/her duties. A citizen's duties lie towards her family, educational institution, religious denomination, and so on.

Nature

Fundamental Duties are applicable *for citizens only*. They are moral in nature. It is **not enforceable in the court of law**. Nobody can take the help of the court and compel others to obey Fundamental Duties. No law can be challenged in the court of law on the grounds of violation of Fundamental Duties.

Fundamental Duties and the Power of State

Fundamental Duties enhance the power of the state. It is a citizen's duty towards the state. State becomes more important due to Fundamental Duties, and they manifest no limitations over the power of state.

DIRECTIVE PRINCIPLES OF STATE POLICY (DPSP)

Various committees were formed for making the Constitution. Fundamental Rights Sub-Committee was set up for enacting the list of Fundamental Rights. The Committee, headed by **J. B. Kripalani**, presented extensive and detailed documents of Fundamental Rights. Later, the advisor of the Constituent Assembly, **B. N. Rau** suggested the bifurcation of Fundamental Rights into two parts—the first part being justifiable rights, and the second segment categorised as Directive Principles of State Policy, or the DPSP. Since Fundamental Rights are available against the state, therefore, the government requires huge financial resources to apply Fundamental Rights. Thus, some Fundamental Rights were kept in Part IV of the Constitution, which is known as the DPSP. It is an extension of Fundamental Rights.

The DPSP are taken from the **instrument of instructions** of **Government of India Act 1935**. Part of DPSP is also influenced by the **Constitution of Ireland**. The Irish Constitution in turn, borrowed the DPSP from the **Spanish Constitution**.

Features

1. **Fundamentals of Governance: Article 37** of the Constitution states that the DPSP is not enforceable in a court of law. It is fundamental to governance in this country. It shall be the duty of the state to apply these principles while making laws. Therefore, the DPSP is not seen as being against the state. Application of the DPSP depends upon the will of the state.
2. **Welfare State:** The DPSP is the only part of the Constitution, which includes the notion of welfare state under **Article 38**. The state shall promote social order based on social, economic and political justice. The state strives to minimise the inequality in income, and endeavours to eliminate inequalities in status, facilities, and opportunities.
3. **Basis of a Socialist State:** The Indian Constitution combines the features of liberal democracy with socialist principles. Although the term 'socialism' was included in the Preamble by the 42nd Amendment in 1976, the spirit of socialism is inherent in Part IV of the Constitution, that is, in the DPSP.

   Article 39 (b) describes that ownership and control of the material resources of the community shall be distributed for the promotion of common good. **Article 39 (c)** holds that the economic system does not result in the concentration of wealth and means of production against the interest of common good.
4. **Social and Economic Rights:** The DPSP ensures rights of groups. **Article 41** provides right to work and right to education. States shall also provide public assistance in case of unemployment, old age, and sickness. It shall also give help in case of disability and other cases of 'undeserved want'. The state shall endeavour to provide early childhood care and education for all children until they complete the **age of 14 years**, under **Article 45**. State shall promote the educational and economic interest of the weaker sections of society. The DPSP is also for protection of Scheduled Castes and Scheduled Tribes from social injustice and all forms of exploitation.
5. **Gandhian Principles:** The DPSP envisions the tenets of liberal principles. States

shall take steps to separate the judiciary from the executive in **Article 50**. To reiterate, the DPSP also subscribes to the features of socialism.

Apart from these, DPSP includes Gandhian futures too. **Article 47** mentions that the state shall strive for the raising of the level of nutrition and standard of living of its people. Improvement of public health is the primary duty of the state. The state shall also endeavour to bring about prohibition of the consumption of intoxicating drinks and drugs injurious to health. State shall endeavour to organise agriculture and animal husbandry on modern and scientific lines. It shall also take steps for and preserving and improving breeds, prohibiting the slaughter of cows and calves, and other milch and drought cattle, under **Article 48**. **Article 40** says that the state shall take steps to organise village panchayats and endow them with such power and authority as may be necessary to enable them to function as units of self-government.

6. **International Peace: Article 51** of the DPSP holds that the state shall endeavour to:
   (i) Promote international peace and security.
   (ii) Maintain just and honourable relations between nations.
   (iii) Foster respect for international law and treaty obligation in the dealings organised people with one another.
   (iv) Encourage settlement of international disputes by arbitration.

   Therefore, Indian foreign policy is guided by the principles of peaceful co-existence. India stands against all forms of exploitation and hegemony.

Non-Enforceable and Non-Justiciable

The DPSP is not enforceable in a court of law unlike Fundamental Rights of Part III of the Constitution. Article 37 states that it is the duty of the state to enforce the DPSP. Nobody is allowed to approach the Supreme Court for enforcement of DPSP. Any law made by the state cannot be challenged in the Supreme Court on the grounds of violation of DPSP. Critics have said that the DPSP is like a cheque on a bank payable when able.

Due to non-enforceability of the DPSP, it was criticised by various members of the Constituent Assembly. **T. T. Krishnamachari** said that DPSP is a veritable *dustbin of sentiment*. **H. N. Kunzru** did not attach any value to **Directive Principles**. Scholars like **Sir Ivor Jennings** said that it was *pious aspiration*, and that Directive Principles denote Fabian socialism without the socialism.

On the other hand Directive Principles is defended by the various members of Constituent Assembly. **Panikkar** says that it is socialism in an economic sphere. It is different from political democracy. It stands for economic democracy, said **Dr Ambedkar**. **Granville Austin** said that by establishing these positive obligations of the state, the members of the Constituent Assembly made it the responsibility of future **Indian governments** to find a middle way between individual liberty and the public good, between preserving the property and the privilege of the few and bestowing benefits on the many, in order to liberate the powers of all men equally for contribution to the common good.

Enforcement of the DPSP

The DPSP is not enforceable in a court of law, according to **Article 37** of the Constitution. It is the conscience-keeper of future governments working in India. But **D. D. Basu** held that the DPSP can be enforced under **Article 356,** which says that when the state government fails to comply with the direction of the union government, it deems it fit to apply Article 356, because the governance is not being carried out in accordance with the Constitution. Disobeying instruction of the union government implies that the state government is not running according to **constitutional machinery**. Practically, **Article 356** has never been applied.

Relations Between Fundamental Rights and the DPSP

1. **Harmony:** Fundamental Rights are enforceable in a court of law under **Article 32**. Thus, the Supreme Court is bound to protect Fundamental Rights. The first case related to the dispute between Fundamental Rights and the DPSP came in the **Champkam Dorairajan case (1951)** in the Supreme Court. The Court struck down the act of then Madras government related to reservations in medical college. The Nehru government brought about the First Constitutional Amendment Act (1951), which restored the implementation of the DPSP and nullified the decision of the Supreme Court.
2. **Supremacy of Fundamental Rights:** In 1967, the Supreme Court said that Fundamental Rights are supreme and sacrosanct. Fundamental Rights cannot be amended by the Parliament. The Court gave this decision in the landmark **Golaknath v. Punjab State** case.
3. **Primacy of the DPSP:** The Indira Gandhi government was willing to overrule the verdict of the Supreme Court. The Parliament passed the **25th Constitutional Amendment**. It was the first occasion in constitutional history, when DPSP were given primacy over Fundamental Rights. **Article 39 (b), (c)** of the DPSP was given superior position to **Articles 14, 19, 31 of Fundamental Rights**, that is, for implementation of the former the latter may be violated. By the **42nd Constitutional Amendment Act**, position of DPSP was further strengthened. It provided that any Article of DPSP, not only Article 39 (b) (c), is superior to Articles 14, 19, 31 of Fundamental Rights. Therefore, the entire DPSP could be implemented, and could supersede Articles 14, 19, 31 of Fundamental Rights.
4. **Harmonious Construction:** The Supreme Court settles the dispute in the historical **Minerva Mills Case** (1980). The Court said that Fundamental Rights shall not be undermined in the name of welfare of the people. It held that the Indian Constitution is founded on the bedrock of the balance between the Fundamental Rights and the Directive Principles, and that they together stand for the commitment to social revolution. Relations between Fundamental Rights and DPSP must be harmonious.
5. **Active role of Judiciary and DPSP:** The Supreme Court introduced **Public Interest Litigation** (PIL) in the 1980s, and expanded the meaning of Right to Life and Personal Liberty under **Article 21**. The Court said that the Right to Life includes the right to free and compulsory education. Right to Life also includes pollution-free environment. It also incorporates the right to minimum livelihood.

   Liberal interpretation of Right to Life includes major components of DPSP. Thus DPSP is an extension of Fundamental Rights (FR). Thus, dispute between FRand DPSP becomes meaningless, today they are **complementary** to each other.

Conscience of the Constitution

Granville Austin says that the Indian Constitution is not a legal document; rather, it is a *social document*. It is an instrument for a bringing about *social revolution* in India. Structure of the Indian Constitution is taken from the **Government of India Act, 1935**. A parliamentary form of government, a federal government is instrument to fulfilling the goal of social justice.

Uniform Civil Code (UCC)

The Uniform Civil Code (UCC) calls for the formulation of one law for India, which would be applicable to all religious communities in matters such as marriage, divorce, inheritance, adoption. This is discussed under Article 44 of the DPSP, which lays down that the state shall endeavour to secure a Uniform Civil Code for citizens throughout the country. It was incorporated in the Constitution with the thought that it would be enacted at a later date when a national consensus emerged for it.

The UCC is meant to replace different laws currently applicable to various respective communities, and which are inconsistent with each other. These laws include the Hindu Marriage Act, Hindu Succession Act, Indian Christian Marriages Act, Indian Divorce Act, Parsi Marriage and Divorce Act. Although criminal law is the same for every citizen, civil law is not uniform, and in fact differs for different religious faiths. **Hindu Marriage Act 1955** is applicable for Hindus, Sikhs, Jains, Buddhists. **Muslim Personal Law 1937** is applicable for Muslims, and a separate set of laws also exists for Christians and Paris. Marriage and divorce laws are different for all religious communities.

A. **Equality before Law:** The Supreme Court in a landmark case ruled that Uniform Civil Code is essential for upholding the rule of law. In the **Shah Bano Case (1986),** the Supreme Court had invoked Section 125 of Code of Criminal Procedure, which applies to everyone regardless of caste, creed, or religion. The Court had also regretted that Article 44 of the Constitution of India regarding the Uniform Civil Code in India remained a dead letter, and observed that a common civil code would help the cause of national integration by removing disparate loyalties to laws which have conflicting ideologies.

B. **Constitutional Provision:** Since DPSP is non-justiciable and non-binding, it is the duty of state to enforce the same. Here, 'state' includes both the union government as well as the state government. **Goa** is the **only state** of the Indian union which has already **implemented the UCC**, although some amount of variation persists in Goa's civil laws. Till today, no union government has prepared a draft of proposed UCC. In the year 2018, the Supreme Court, declared the provision of instant **Triple Talaq** (Talaq-e-Biddat), which is regulated by Muslim Personal Law, as null and void **(Shayara Bano case, 2017)**. It true that the Supreme Court is in favour of the UCC but politically, it remains a debatable issue.

Comparison between Fundamental Rights and DPSP

1. Fundamental Rights are justiciable under **Article 32**. But the DPSP are not binding under **Article 37.** The Supreme Court can issue various writs for enforcement of Fundamental Rights. But same writs are not applicable for DPSP.
2. Fundamental Rights are civil rights, such as freedom of speech and expression, freedom of conscience and right to life. On the other hand, DPSP incorporates social rights and economic rights. For example, right to education, work and better working conditions for workers.
3. Fundamental Rights restrict the activities of state and therefore are negative. The state is not permitted to curtail the liberty of citizens on unreasonable grounds. DPSP directs the state to do something. Thus DPSP is positive in nature.
4. Fundamental Rights can be suspended during a national emergency but DPSP is

suspended, until and unless it is enforced.

5. State refers to union government, state government and district-level government under Fundamental Rights. DPSP denotes nation of welfare state.
6. Part of Fundamental Rights indicates towards liberal democratic ideology but DPSP synthesis, the liberal, socialist and Gandhian ideology.

3

CONSTITUTIONALISM IN INDIA

KEY CONCEPTS

Democracy; Social Change; National Unity; Checks and Balances; Basic Structure Debate; Constitutional Amendments

THE BASIC STRUCTURE DEBATE

The Constitution is a dynamic document which can be amended as per society's needs. However, the basic features of the Constitution of India should not be altered to an extent that the soul and identity of the Constitution is totally lost in the process. The basic structure doctrine is a legal doctrine that holds that the constitution of a sovereign state has certain characteristics that cannot be erased by its legislature. It is a judicial innovation to ensure that the power of amendment is not misused by the Parliament; in India, it was developed by the Supreme Court in a series of constitutional law cases in the 1960s and 1970s.

The parliament is the highest law-making authority, which is also entitled to amend the Constitution under Article 368. No limitation is placed over the amendment power of the parliament in Article 368; only Part III (Fundamental Rights) of the Constitution is given special protection under Article 13. It states that any law made by the states shall not violate the Fundamental Rights mentioned in Part III. Therefore, the basic structure debate starts with the amendment of Fundamental Rights.

A. **Shankari Prasad Case (1951):** The First Constitutional Amendment Act (which had made several changes to the Fundamental Rights provisions of the Indian Constitution) was challenged in the Supreme Court in the Shankari Prasad case. The Court observed that the parliament under **Article 368** can amend any part of the Constitution, including Fundamental Rights. Therefore, there is no limitation over the amendment powers of the parliament.

B. **Golaknath case (1967):** The **17th Constitutional Amendment Act** was challenged in the Supreme Court in 1967. The Supreme Court overruled its previous decision in the **Shankari Prasad case**. The Court pronounced that Fundamental Rights comprise the most important part of the Constitution. It is beyond the amendment power of the parliament. Under Article 368, the parliament can amend any part of the Constitution, except Part III of Fundamental Rights.

However, the parliament passed the **24th Constitutional Amendment** in 1971. It allowed the parliament to amend the Constitution, including Fundamental Rights. Clause (1) and (3) of Article 368 were inserted in the Constitution.

Article 368 (1) says that, while exercising its amendment power, the parliament shall change, add or repeal any part of the Constitution. Article 368 (3) includes that the Constitutional Amendment Act is not considered as an *ordinary law*. An ordinary law of the parliament shall not violate Fundamental Rights. But Fundamental Rights can be amended by *constituent power* of the parliament under Article 368. Parliament also passed the 25th, 26th and 29th Amendments. These Amendments were challenged in the **Kesavananda Bharati Case** (1973).

C. **Kesavananda Bharati Case (1973):** It is popularly known as the Fundamental Rights case, which was led by a **13 judges' bench**, significant in the constitutional history of India. The Supreme Court has overruled various decisions from time to time but the Kesavananda Bharati case verdict is still protected by the Supreme Court. Various issues associated with the case are as follows:

1. **Procedure and Power of Parliament:** The Court said that Article 368 includes procedure of the amendment of Constitution, which means:
   (a) Motion for amendment in the Constitution can be introduced in either house.
   (b) Needs special majority, that is, 2/3rd in both Houses.
   (c) President shall not exercise veto over Constitutional Amendment Act.
   (d) Joint sitting is not allowed.

Article 368 also incorporates the *power of amendment of the Constitution*. Power of parliament means it is empowered to amend any part of the constitutional referendum or any other mechanism is not written change in the constitution.

2. **Constituent power and ordinary law-making power of parliament:** The Supreme Court accepted that ordinary law is different from the Constitutional Amendment Act. Features of ordinary law can summarised as:
   (a) Parliament derives the power from Article 246.
   (b) It requires simple majority.
   (c) Therefore, a joint sitting of both Houses is permitted.

However constituent power of parliament can be described in following ways:
   (a) Parliament derives power from Article 368.
   (b) Special majority is needed for amending the Constitution.
   (c) Joint sitting is not allowed.

The Court ruled that the 24th Constitutional Amendment is constitutional. It means the parliament can amend any part of the Constitution including fundamental rights. Thus clauses (1) and (3) of Article 368 are valid.

3. **Amendment of Fundamental Rights:** The Supreme Court again overruled the decision of the **Golaknath Case** and said that the parliament is entitled to amend any part of the Constitution. Article 31(C) was considered as constitutional, which said that Article 39 (b) (c) of DPSP is more important than Articles 14, 19, 31 of the Fundamental Rights. It means Article 14, 19 and 31 can be superseded for implementation of Article 39 (b) (c).

Evolved Theory of Basic Structure

Principles of basic structure are mentioned nowhere in the Constitution. The concept of basic structure was first observed by the judiciary in the **Kesavananda Bharati Case** (1973). Issues related to basic structure are as follows:

1. **Limitation of Amendment Power of Parliament:** The Supreme Court said that an inherent and implied limitation is imposed over the power of parliament under Article 368. Therefore, power of amendment of parliament is not absolute. For the first time in independent India, Supreme Court struck down one element of the 25th Constitutional Amendment Act.
2. **Differences between Amendment and Total Change:** The Supreme Court also observed that amendment of the Constitution is constituent power of the parliament. But parliament cannot bring about total change in the Constitution. Amendment should not tinker with basic structure of the Constitution.
3. **Ideas and ideology of the Constitution:** According to the Supreme Court, the Constitution is not merely a legal document nor is it just a collection of articles. The Constitution is comprised of various ideologies and theories. Therefore, a list of basic structure pronounced by the Court is considered as following:
   - (i) Supremacy of the Constitution
   - (ii) Democratic-republic form of government
   - (iii) Secular state
   - (iv) Separation of power
   - (v) Federal form of government
   - (vi) Integrity and sovereignty
   - (vii) Amendment power of the parliament
   - (viii) Judicial review
   - (ix) Parliamentary form of Government
   - (x) Article 32, judicial independence
   - (xi) Essential features of individual freedoms secured to the citizen.
   - (xii) Equality of status and opportunity
   - (xiii) Liberty of thought, expression, belief, faith and worship.
   - (xiv) Mandate to build a welfare state.
   - (xv) The provision for social, economic, and political justice.

   It is worth noting that most of these terms are not mentioned in the Constitution.
4. **Soul and Spirit of Constitution:** Till today, the Supreme Court has not defined the basic structure, but the Court observed that context is more important than text while interpreting the Constitution.
5. **Amendment Power of Parliament:** Dr Ambedkar once said that whosoever is dissatisfied with our Constitution, needs 2/3rd majority to amend the Constitution. But **Kesavananda Bharati case** nullified this statement. For deleting basic structure of the Constitution, the parliament passed the 42nd Amendment (which granted power to the President, in consultation with the Election Commission, to disqualify members of State Legislatures), and inserted clause (4) (5) of Article 368 in the Constitution. Article 368 (4) (5) states that the parliament can amend any part of the Constitution, and that the Constitutional Amendment Act is not subject to judicial review. Supreme Court nullified Article 368 (4) (5) in the **Minerva Mills case (1980)** and said that judicial review is the basic structure of the Constitution.
6. **Ninth Schedule and Basic Structure:** Ninth Schedule is incorporated in the Constitution through the First Constitutional Amendment Act. Objective of the 9th Schedule was to protect land reform act of state government from judicial review. Any entry included in the 9th Schedule cannot be declared null and void on the basis of violation of Fundamental Rights. But after **Kesavananda Bharati case** in 1973, the 9th Schedule was utilised as a shield against judicial review. Various subjects were included in the 9th Schedule

unrelated to land reform. Reservations in the state of Tamil Nadu are included in 9th Schedule by the 76th Constitutional Amendment. **COFEPOSA** (Conservation of Foreign Exchange and Prevention of Smuggling Activities Act) is included in the 9th Schedule which is related to smuggling. Monopolies Restrictive Trade Practices Act (MRTP) is now part of the 9th Schedule.

In 2007, the Supreme Court said in the famous **I. R. Coelho** case that Court is of the view that 9th Schedule is also subject to judicial review with two conditions:

(i) It violates the basic structure.
(ii) It is included the in the 9th Schedule after 1973.

Therefore, basic structure becomes the cardinal principle for interpreting the Constitution.

4

UNION EXECUTIVE

KEY CONCEPTS

President; Prime Minister and Council of Ministers

THE PRESIDENT

The parliamentary form of government in India is borrowed from the British parliamentary system. But in Britain, the monarch is the nominated head of the government and succession is based on hereditary lineage. In India, the President is the head of state of the Republic of India. S/he is the nominal head of the executive, the first citizen of the country as well as the commander-in-chief of the Indian Armed Forces.

Indirect Election

Indirect election of the President is based on the Electoral College. Citizens are not allowed to vote directly for the President. Rather, the President is elected through indirect elections on the basis of a vote by members of the Parliament (MPs) and elected members of the legislative assemblies (MLAs). The President shall be elected by proportional representation by means of single transferable vote, according to Article 55. In fact, the method of election is linked with the function of election and power of the office. The President is elected indirectly due to reasons explained below.

Manner of Election

Although the size of the electorate for the election of the President is merely 4,896, the President is elected by all the states including the Union Territories of Delhi and Puducherry.

(a) **Uniformity among the states:** The number of elected Members of Legislative Assembly (MLAs) comes up to 4,120, including elected legislative members of Delhi and Puducherry. Each MLA is entitled to one vote but every MLA does not represent an equal section of the population. Therefore, the value of the vote of each MLA is different. An MLA of Goa represents a smaller population than an MLA of UP. For maintaining uniformity among states, **Article 55** mentions the following formulae:

$$\text{Value of an MLA Vote} = \frac{\text{Total Population of the state or Union Territory}}{\text{Total number of elected members of Legislative Assembly} \times 1000}$$

whereas, the vote of a Member of Parliament (MP) is calculated as follows:

$$\text{Value of an MP Vote} = \frac{\text{The sum of votes of elected members of all the Legislative Assemblies}}{\text{The sum of elected members of both the Houses of Parliament}}$$

(b) **Base of Census:** It is notable that 1971 is taken as a census base of the population of the state. Population growth rate was almost similar across India. After 1971, population growth rate became stable in South India. But the steep growth rate continued in North India. Accepting the latest census for the presidential election will marginalise the importance of Kerala and Tamil Nadu, and at the same time it shall be advantageous for UP and Bihar.

(c) **Uniformity between state as whole and Union:** Strength of elected Members of Parliament (MPs) stands upto 776. MPs include elected members of the House of the People (Lok Sabha) and elected members of the Council of States (Rajya Sabha). One MP represents threefold population than an MLA does. MPs and MLAs are given equal voting rights. But the value of the vote of an MP and the value of the vote of an MLA must be different in order to make parity between value of votes, given above in the formulae.

Cumulated vote value of MPs and MLAs in the 2012 presidential election was 10,98,882. The vote of one MP is 708. Total value of MP votes stands at 5,49,408. *Value of vote of each MP is the same.*

(d) **Proportionate Representation:** Article 55 provides for proportionate representation. Here, proportionate means uniformity among the states and uniformity between union and states as whole.

(e) **Quota:** Actual practice of proportionate representation is described in the Presidential Election Act 1951. According to an act made by parliament, candidates are supposed to get requisite quota. Quota is described in the above Act. Quota is mandatory in the proportional representation method of election.

Requisite quota for winning the presidential election = **5,49,442.**

(f) **Voting:** The MP or the MLA casts one vote but they give their preferences. They are free to mark their preference for every candidate in form like 1, 2, 3, etc. Even if one preference is valid, they can mark only 1. Voting pattern is incorporated in the **Presidential and Vice-Presidential Elections Act, 1952.**

(g) **Counting:** Getting maximum votes is not a guarantee of winning the election in proportionate representation. First and foremost votes of first preference are counted. Somebody receives a requisite quota in the counting of first preferences.

A dramatic scenario emerged in 1969, when no candidate got the requisite quota in the counting of first preferences.

(h) **Non-Participation:** Nominated members of the Rajya Sabha are not permitted to take part in the elections of the President because nominated members are themselves nominated by Presidents. Nominated members of Legislative Assemblies are not permitted to participate in the elections. Members of the Legislative Council are prohibited from participation in the elections of the President since the Legislative Council does not exist in every state of India.

(i) **Proposers and Seconders:** According to the Presidential Election Act 1952, there is a need of 50 members of the electoral college as proposers and other 50 members should second the proposal. It means support and significance of 100 MPs/MLAs was necessary. Apart from that Rs 1,500 should be deposited in the Reserve Bank of India for contesting the elections of the President. If a candidate receives less than 1/6th part of valid votes cast during elections, deposit amount is lapsed or forfeit.

(j) **Dispute:** According to the Presidential Act 1952, disputes regarding the election of the President can be settled only by the Supreme Court. Candidates participating in the election can challenge the validity of the elections of the President.

(k) **Anomalies:** Representation of citizens is not equal in the presidential election. Residents of UP are represented by a member of the House of the People, member of the Council of States and an MLA. However, residents of UTs except Delhi and Puducherry are only represented by the members of the House of People. Proportional representation for election of one seat also appears paradoxical.

Term of the President

The President shall hold office for a term of 5 years. Five years shall be counted from the date on which s/he enters her/his office, according to Article 56. President shall continue to hold office until her successor enters upon her office. The President is eligible to be re-elected for the office of the President, once, twice, or more times.

Qualifications of the President

No person shall be eligible for election as President unless s/he:

(a) is a citizen of India;

(b) has completed the age of 35 years; (The running age of 35 is not permitted; 35 has to be completed and running, for example 36 is eligible. Neelam Sanjeeva Reddy was the youngest President of India at the age of 64 years till our current President Droupadi Murmu took office in 2022. Venkat Raman was the oldest. He was 76 years, 7 months and 21 days when he became President.)

(c) and is qualified for election as a member of the House of the People. (This automatically means a person must fulfil the terms of the Representation of the People Act, 1951.)

(d) A person shall not be eligible for election as President of India if s/he holds any office of profit under the Government of India or Government of any state.

Conditions

The president shall not be a member of either house of the Parliament or of the House of Legislature of any state. And if a member of either house of the Parliament or a house of legislature of any state is elected as the President, he/she shall be deemed to have vacated his seat in the house on the date on which he enters upon his office as President.

The President shall be entitled without payment of rent to the use of an official residence. According to the second schedule of the constitution, the President shall receive Rs 10,000 per month. Parliament by law shall determine his emoluments, allowances, and privileges. Parliament made the Presidential emolument and Pension Act in 1951. As of now, the President receives Rs 5 lakhs per month as emolument according to the amendment in parliamentary act. No need for amendment in the constitution is required for hiking the salary of the President. The emoluments and allowances of the President shall not be diminished during his term of office.

Oath or Affirmation

For every President and every person acting as President or discharging the functions of the President, oath-taking is necessary before entering upon his office. The President takes oath in the presence of the Chief Justice of India, or in his absence, the seniormost Judge of Supreme Court solemnises the oath.

The President takes the oath to preserve, protect, and defend the constitution of India. The President will devote himself or herself to the service and will of the people of India under Article 60. Provision of oath of the

President is not provided in the 3rd Schedule of the constitution.

Procedure for Impeachment

Office of President may become vacant in a few situations. Zakir Hussain and Fakhruddin Ali Ahmad both died, while they were in office. Zakir Hussain became the President in May 1967 and died in May 1969, while in office. Fakhruddin Ali Ahmed became President in August 1974 and died in February 1977, while serving the nation as President.

The President may resign his office by writing to the Vice-President. The President may be removed from office by impeachment, according to the procedure described in Article 61. No President has been impeached in India till date. Violation of the constitution is the ground for impeachment of the President.

(a) The process of impeachment may be initiated in either house of the parliament.
(b) Resolution regarding the impeachment should be given by not less than one-fourth of the total members of that house. At least 14 days' notice in writing should be submitted to either house.
(c) Charge can be framed by either house and the other house shall investigate the charge.
(d) The President shall have the right to appear and to be presented such investigation.
(e) Thereafter, if the resolution is passed by a majority of not less than 2/3rd of total membership of the house, the President is removed from his office on a date, when resolution is passed.

Eventually the President is removed by the parliament. Speaker or chairperson presides over the house during the impeachment motion. Thus, it is known as a *quasi-judicial process.* Act done by President before impeachment shall not be invalidated due to removal of the President.

Vacancy in Office

An election to fill vacancy, caused by the expiration of the term of office of the President shall be completed before the expiration of the term.

According to **Article 62**, there may be following reasons of vacancy in the office of the President:

(i) Death
(ii) Resignation
(iii) Removal
(iv) Otherwise

The term 'otherwise' indicates that illness may be a reason. Person entering into office due to vacancy is entitled to hold office for the full term of 5 years.

Presidential Succession Act 1969

A curious and critical situation emerged due to the death of the President Zakir Hussain in 1969. Thereafter, the Vice-President V. V. Giri was appointed as the President for discharging the functions of the President. In an interesting development of events, V. V. Giri resigned from the office of the acting President. The Office of the President and the Vice-President both became vacant. Therefore, **Justice Hidayatullah** was appointed as the President in 1969 because of vacancy in both the office of the President and the Vice-President.

Protection for President and Vice-President

(a) The President or the Governor of a state shall not be answerable to any Court for the exercise and performance of the powers and the duties of his office. Although, a person is free to approach the court against the government of India, or the government of a state. If the president issues an ordinance, s/he is not answerable to any Court.

(b) **No Criminal Proceeding:** No criminal proceeding whatsoever shall be instituted or continued against the president in any court during her/his term of office. It implies no fresh case is permitted in the court of law after appointment of the President. If any case is pending against the person, it will also be suspended after assuring the office. But after assuming from office, he/she is not exempted from any proceeding in a criminal case.

(c) **Freedom from Arrest:** No process for the arrest or imprisonment of the President or the Governor of a state shall issue from any court during his term of office. Again, this immunity is available for the president during the term of office.

Under Article 361, the President enjoys these immunities in official capacity. S/he gets absolute immunity while functioning in official capacity. But exemption in personal capacity is limited to his term of office.

(d) **No Relief in Civil Proceeding:** Civil proceeding can be instituted against the President during his term of office for any act done by him in personal capacity. But a person who is willing to start proceeding against the President shall give notice before two months. Notice includes name, description and residence of the person, and relief he wants.

Executive Powers of the President

All the executive actions of the Government of India shall be expressed to be taken in the name of the President, according to Article 77. Orders and other instruments made and executed in the name of the President shall not be called in question. It shall be considered as valid and authenticated.

The President shall make rules for the more convenient transaction of the business of India. The President shall also allocate the business among the ministers, under Article 77. The major executive power of the President is the appointment of various authorities. Most important executive action of the President is to appoint the PM and the council of Ministers. President also appoints government of various states, CAG, CEC and Chairperson of UPSC to name a few.

Office Held during pleasure of President

President appoints various authorities but the method of their removal is different. The Prime Minister, Council of Ministers, and Governors hold office, during the pleasure of the President', which implies that they can be removed from their office without stating any reason.

Tenure of these authorities are not fixed, but it depends upon the wish of the President. No ground is mentioned in the constitution for their removal.

Approval of the Supreme Court

Chairperson of UPSC and members do not hold office during the pleasure of President. Chairperson of some statutory bodies like chairperson and members of NHRC, CIC can be removed by the President only on the recommendation of the Supreme Court. It is interesting to note that chairperson and members of the state public service commission are appointed by the Governor, but they are removed by the President on the recommendation of the Supreme Court. These offices are autonomous and not subordinated to the Executive. The Supreme Court is an independent and impartial institution and so the recommendation of the Supreme Court is mandatory.

Resolution of Parliament

Some authorities are removed by the President on the recommendation of the parliament. Judges of high courts, CAG, CEC can be removed from their office, with the resolution of parliament. Here, legislature exerts control over executive for the removal of these officers. Judges and CAG act as a kind of *watchdog* which keeps constant vigilance over Executive. The Executive is held accountable to the parliament. All authorities do not the same weight, thus their removal process is also different.

Legislative Powers

1. ***Summon/Prorogue***

   President is a part of the parliament. A close interdependence between legislative and the president is a unique feature of the parliamentary form of government. The President shall summon, prorogue and dissolve the House of People. It should be remembered that adjournment and adjournment *sine die* is the responsibility of the speaker.

2. ***Send Message***

   The President also addresses and sends messages to the House. President may send a message to either house of parliament for considering a bill pending in the house.

3. ***Nomination***

   President shall nominate 12 members in the council of states belonging to art, science, literature and social service.

4. ***Prior recommendation***

   Some bills require prior recommendation before their introduction to the house. These bills include:
   (a) Money Bill
   (b) Bill related to change in interstate trade and commerce
   (c) Any bill, which affects the power of taxation of parliament.
   (d) Bill concerned with changing the name, boundary and territory of the state.

5. ***Assent to bill***

   When a bill is passed by both houses of the parliament, it is presented to the President. President shall adopt one of the following courses of action:
   (a) Assent to the bill
   (b) Withhold the assent
   (c) Return the bill for reconsideration of the House. President can send a message for reconsideration of specific provision of the bill.

1. ***Money Bill***

   President's option regarding money bill is limited. The President can either assent the bill or withhold the assent. Money bills cannot be sent back to the House for reconsideration.

2. ***Time Limit***

   Constitution does not prescribe any time limit for giving assent over the bill. The President can exercise check and balance over the parliament against the hasty legislation. No bill becomes an act without the signature of the President. The President can keep any bill pending for indefinite time. It is popularly known as *Pocket Veto*.

   In 1986 president Gyani Zail Singh exercised Pocket Veto over Indian Postal Amendment bill. Since Independence, it was the first example of exercising Pocket Veto.

   Limitation over Reconsideration: The President is entitled to send a bill for consideration under Article 111. But the President cannot send a bill **twice** for reconsideration. Whenever the President takes time for consideration on a bill, that bill is suspended for the time being. It is popularly known as suspensive veto. President Abdul Kalam sent the **Office of Profit (Amendment) Bill** for reconsideration.

   Withhold Assent: Veto is a Latin term, it means *to forbid.* Although the term Veto is not written anywhere in the constitution, Veto refers to refusing the permission on a plan of action. Withholding means rejection of a bill by the President, it leads to finishing of the bill. Therefore it is popularly known as absolute Veto. First absolute veto was exercised by the First President of India, Dr Rajendra Prasad on the **PEPSU Appropriation Bill, 1954**. President R. Vennkataraman also exercised absolute veto in 1991. He refused to give assent to **salaries and allowances of M.P. Bill.**

3. *Assent the Bill*

Normally the president gives his/her assent to the bill. Bill becomes an Act after receiving assent from the President. The President acts according to aid and advice of the council of ministers. In fact, the Council of Ministers plays a vital role in passage of any bill.

4. *Ordinance making power of President*

Article 123 empowers President to issue an ordinance during:

(a) Recess of parliament, means parliament is not in session.
(b) President is satisfied that circumstances exist, which requires immediate action by parliament.
(c) Either House of parliament is in session or during a recess of parliament. Provision of ordinance is borrowed from the Government of India Act 1935.

1. *Impact*

Ordinance promulgated by the President shall have the same force and effect as an act of parliament. Power of issuing an ordinance is extended to the law-making power of parliament. Obviously parliament cannot enact a law over the state list. Thus the President cannot issue an ordinance over subjects of state list. Constitutional amendment is not permissible by an ordinance.

2. *Expiration*

Ordinance can be withdrawn by the President at any time. Parliament is entitled to disapprove the ordinance.

3. *Term*

Ordinance shall cease to operate at the expiration of six weeks or one and half month from reassembly from later date if two houses are assembling from different dates.

4. *Act and Ordinance*

Normally ordinance is considered as temporary law for addressing the urgent situation. Ordinance is law made by the President or executive. The Constitution states that an ordinance shall expire after 6 weeks, without approval of parliament, thus it is temporary. But we can point out various anomalies in the ordinance making.

(a) Ordinance goes against the basic spirit of the separation of power. Law making is the basic function of the legislature and not the job of the executive.
(b) Law should be made by the representative of the people. Debate and discussion are held in parliament before passage of the bill. Ordinance does not provide an opportunity to parliament to scrutinise the laws.
(c) Ordinances bypass the role of the parliament and the role of the opposition too. Drawback of the law is never highlighted.

5. *Judicial Review of Ordinance*

The Supreme Court nullified an ordinance promulgated by Indira Gandhi in 1969, which was aiming for nationalisation of 14 private banks in India. Court ruled that no urgent conditions exist for privatisation of Banks in **R. C. Copper Case (1970),** popularly known as 'nationalisation of bank' case. Thus, the President's satisfaction is subject to judicial reviews.

Indira Gandhi tried to change the judgement of the Court, and brought about 38th constitutional amendment. Clause (4) of Article

123 was inserted in the constitution, which prohibited the Judicial review of satisfaction of the President under article 123. Although Clause (4) article 123 was omitted from the constitution by 44th Constitutional amendment in 1978. Consequently, satisfaction of the President is subject to Judicial review. The Supreme Court said that repeated promulgation of an ordinance is unconstitutional in the **D.C. Wadhwa case (1987)**. Although practice repetition of an ordinance continues.

Judicial Power (Pardon)

The power of pardon is constitutional and moral too. To err is human, thus a punishment awarded by judges may need course correction in some instances. A sensitive approach towards justice and reform is necessary for the welfare and future of the country. Many are driven to crime due to situational pressures. Thus, it is noble to grant human beings an opportunity to reform.

President exercises numerous kinds of pardon under Article 72. The term pardon connotes multiple forms of lessening the punishment.

(a) **Pardon:** Person becomes free from all kinds of conviction. Therefore, punishment is automatically abolished. Person lives like a normal person who never committed a crime.

(b) **Commutation:** Changing the nature of punishment is also a variety of pardon. Commuting the sentence of a person from death penalty to life imprisonment is commutation. There is qualitative difference between death penalty and life imprisonment.

(c) **Remission:** Awarding lesser punishment instead of a harsher one is known as Remission. A person awarded 10-year punishment and the sentence is reduced to 5 years is an example of Remission. Here only the quantum of punishment is reduced. The quality of sentence remains the same.

(d) **Respite:** Reducing the punishment due to some extra-ordinary conditions: for example, a pregnant woman who has received life imprisonment can be set free. A person infected from incurable disease may receive respite.

(e) **Reprieve:** Suspension of the execution of sentence is reprieve. Naturally it applies in case of death penalty when execution is suspended due to decision of the President.

(f) **Scope of Pardon:** President can pardon a person received death penalty. Power of pardon of the President extends up to the executive power of the union government. The President is also empowered to pardon a person sentenced by Court Martial.

(g) **Grounds for pardon:** Constitution does not describe the grounds for pardon. Thus, it was settled by the Supreme Court in a landmark case of Maru Ram (1981) and Kehar Singh Case (1988). Pardon power of the president is a constitutional power rather than power in personal capacity. Arbitrary practice of pardon is unconstitutional. Pardon power is discretionary, it means the decision of the President may be contrary to the Judgement. It can overrule the Judgement of Supreme Court in case the President depends upon the aid and advice by the Council of Ministers. Here the Council of Ministers implies the ministry of Home Affairs. Oral hearing of the convict is not permitted. Person is not supposed to be present before the President. But mercy petitions in the written form must be communicated to the president. Nobody can be pardoned on the ground of caste, religion or regional consideration.

(h) **Time Limit:** Article 72 does not describe a time limit, in which the president shall communicate his/her decision regarding the pardon. Due to lack of time limitations, the President at one point had not disposed the mercy petitions regarding death penalty for more than decades. Thus a new twist came in the entire process of pardon, and the Supreme Court stepped into the matter.

(i) **Judicial Intervention:** Due to unexplained, unreasonable delay in disposing the mercy petitions related to death penalty, Supreme Court committed death penalty into life imprisonment. Interestingly, Supreme Court awards death penalty and Supreme Court exercises pardon too, even though pardoning power belongs to the executive. Death penalty of Murugan Santhan and Pervivalen has been commuted to life imprisonment.

Diplomatic and Military Powers

President appoints ambassadors in various diplomatic missions across the world. President also receives the introduction of diplomats appointed in India. Various international treatises are also signed in the name of the President. President also pays visits to various overseas nations for strengthening diplomatic relations with India.

Can the President Act Alone?

Article 53 says that the Executive powers vest in the president. At the same time, Article 74 states that the President shall act according to aid and advice of the Council of Minister, which is headed by the PM. Thus the President cannot act alone in the absence of the council of ministers.

Supreme Court unanimously opined in the **Ram Jawaya Case (1955)** that President is only the constitutional head and PM is the administrative head of the government. Article 53 and article 74 must be read out together. Interestingly, the council of ministers is responsible to the Lok Sabha. The President is not responsible to the House of people or to the people. Our constitution cannot be imagined to function, without the aid and advice of the Council of Ministers.

Scope of Presidential Discretion:

In fact, the constitution does not permit any discretionary powers to the President. And Article 74(1) inserts the world 'shall act' by 42nd Amendment. Thus, it appears that aid and advice of the Council of ministers is binding on the President. Practically, the President apply discretionary powers in the following ways:

(a) **Appointment of PM:** President shall appoint the PM according to Article 75(1). During a hung Lok Sabha when no single political party manages to get a majority in the Lok Sabha, the President applies his own discretion. Dr Shankar Dayal Sharma appointed Atal Bihari Bajpai as PM in the year 1996. Atal Bihari Vajpayee was the leader of the single largest party in the House of People. Although he could not get the support of the majority in the House of People.

(b) **Absence of Council of Ministers:** It is true that the President shall act according to aid and advice of CoM. But CoM was automatically dissolved due to the death of PM Gyani Zail Singh, appointed Rajiv Gandhi the PM of India after the death of Indira Gandhi on October 31 1984. Therefore, the President uses his/her discretion in the absence of the council of ministers.

(c) **Reconsideration over advice of CoM:** Article 74(1) empowers the president to ask the council of ministers to reconsider the advice rendered. For example, the Council of ministers advised the then president **K. R. Narayanan,** to impose Emergency under Article 356 in Bihar in 1998. But the President Narayanan sent the advice for reconsideration. CoM became the subject of criticism of people, thus it was withdrawn by the CoM. It proves that the President exercises real power too.

(d) **Disqualification of a Member of Parliament:** While deciding about disqualification, the President seeks advice from the Election Commission of India under Article 103. The President is not supposed to act on the advice of CoM always.

(e) **Veto:** President takes oath of preserving, protecting and defending the constitution. The President can use his power of check and balance, against CoM. President Zail Singh exercised Pocket Veto for the first time in 1986. President can put pressure on the government in the good faith of the constitution.

(f) **Caretaker Government:** The Constitution does make a distinction between the government and the caretaker government. A Caretaker Government runs only day-to-day administration. It cannot take away policy decisions. The caretaker government works between announcements of election and the formation of a new government. In 1979, Chaudhary Charan Singh lost the confidence of the house, but was instructed to be the PM of the caretaker government till fresh elections. The President is not bound to act on the advice of the caretaker government because the concerned CoM has lost the confidence of the house of people. The V. P. Singh government lost the confidence and advised for dissolution of House of People. On the other hand, the President appointed Chandra Shekhar as the Prime Minister.

(g) **Duty of PM:** Article 78 spells out the duty of PM:
   1. To communicate to the President all decisions of CoM related to the administration of the affairs of the Union and proposals for legislation.
   2. To furnish such information relating to the administration of the affairs of Union and proposals for legislation as the President may call for.

(h) **Permission for inquiry:** Governor grants permission for any inquiry against the Chief Minister related to corruption. Similarly, the president shall grant the permission against any inquiry against the Prime Minister. For instance, Ram Jethmalani, a distinguished lawyer, approached the Supreme Court for granting permission against PM Rajiv Gandhi in 1987, but the President refused to grant permission.

PARLIAMENTARY FORM OF GOVERNMENT

A democratic form of government can be classified into a parliamentary and a presidential form of government. The Indian parliamentary system has been sourced from the British parliamentary system. Therefore, like the British parliament, the Indian parliament also comprises two houses. In Britain these are, the House of Commons and the House of Lords, whereas we call them the Lower House (Lok Sabha) and the Upper House (Rajya Sabha). As per **Article 79**, the parliament consists of the President, the Lok Sabha and the Rajya Sabha.

A government has three organs: the legislature, the executive, and the judiciary. These organs derive their power from the Parliament. Thus, the Parliament occupies a central position. Rajya Sabha and Lok Sabha together constitute legislature. All the executive power is vested in the President thus, the Parliament is the combination of the legislature and the executive. This fusion of legislature and executive is the significant feature of parliamentary form of government.

Features

1. **Responsibility of the Executive:**
   It emphasises the responsibility over stability. Lok Sabha is entitled to pass a no-confidence motion against the Council of Ministers [**Article 75 (3)**]. Executive or Council of Ministers (CoM) do not

enjoy the privilege of a fixed term. CoM continues in office till it receives the confidence of the Lok Sabha. The Atal Bihari Vajpayee government lasted only for 13 days in 1996, because it could not get the confidence of Lok Sabha.

2. **Cabinet Rule:**
   Parliamentary form of government is also known as 'Cabinet government'. Each and every decision is taken by the Cabinet, collectively. The Cabinet is headed by the Prime Minister.
3. **Collective Responsibility:**
   Lok Sabha can pass a no-confidence motion against the entire CoM. Collectively they swim, collectively they sink is a well-known principle of parliamentary government. The whole CoM shall defend the action of each minister. In case, when any minister fails to get through the demand for grants in the Lok Sabha, the Council is bound to resign.
4. **Individual Responsibility:**
   A minister shall hold office during pleasure of the President [**Article 75 (2)**]. Thus the individual minister is answerable to the President. In practice, ministers are responsible to the Parliament in general and Lok Sabha in particular. The Prime Minister is free to reshuffle his Cabinet.
5. **Prime Position of the PM:**
   The Prime Minister is considered as the first among equals, often described by the British constitutional experts as *primus inter pares* (a first among equals, Latin). The PM heads the Cabinet meeting and decides the agenda. The PM allocates the portfolios amongst the ministers. However, the number of ministers has been limited to a maximum cap of 15 per cent of the total strength of Lok Sabha, as per the 91st Constitutional Amendment. The Prime Minister can reserve any ministry for himself. Ministry not allocated to any minister shall be under the control of the PM. As per the age-old parliamentary convention, the ministry of personnel, public grievances and pension is headed by the Prime Minister himself. He also heads the department of atomic energy and ocean development.
6. **Nominal and Real Executive:**
   The President is the nominal executive (*de jure*), whereas the Prime Minister is the real executive (*de facto*). All the decisions are made in the name of the President; however, these decisions are exercised by the Prime Minister. Thus, the Prime Minister is the real executive. The President shall appoint the Prime Minister as per **Article 75 (1)**.
7. **Fusion of Power:**
   Executive or Council of Ministers is drawn from the parliament. Therefore, nobody can become minister without being a Member of Parliament (MP) except in the case where he/she acquires the membership of either House within a time period of 6 months from the date of his/her appointment else he/she ceases to be a minister.

Prime Ministerial Government

Ivor Jennings has called the parliamentary system a Cabinet system. A Cabinet system essentially means the prime ministerial form of government. The terms parliamentary government or prime ministerial government are not mentioned in the Indian Constitution. Features of parliamentary government exist in the Constitution and prime ministerial government is the practical form of parliamentary government, which denotes the following features.

1. **Prime Minister is the Nucleus of Power:**
   Though all the executive decisions are taken in the name of the President, the real power

is vested with the Prime Minister. Since the PM is the head of the Cabinet thus, all the executive decisions are exercised by him. The position of Prime Minister became more pronounced in the 1970s, particularly during the tenure of Smt. Indira Gandhi on account of an overwhelming majority. In the late 1980s during the tenure of Late Shri Rajeev Gandhi, Prime Minister's Office (PMO) got primacy over the Cabinet Secretariat, therefore the office of PMO became the arena of power.

2. **Formation of Cabinet**

   The President appoints the ministers based on the recommendation of the Prime Minister. However, the allocation of portfolios is done by the Prime Minister himself. The ministers are chosen from both the Houses of the parliament. There are four categories of ministers:

   (i) the union Cabinet minister,
   (ii) Minister of State (MoS),
   (iii) union minister (Independent charge),
   (iv) deputy minister.

   All four are collectively called Council of Ministers. However, a Cabinet is the subset of the Council of Ministers as it consists of the Prime Minister and union Cabinet ministers alone.

3. **Election of PM**

   The Prime Minister is usually the leader of the majority party in Lok Sabha. However, he/she may also be from the Rajya Sabha (as in the case of Dr Manmohan Singh). The majority party chooses the leader of the House.

4. **Rising Role of PMO**

   Cabinet Secretariat plays a vital role in the parliamentary form of government. It maintains coordination among various ministries. The PMO has now virtually overshadowed the Cabinet Secretariat. It has become a super secretariat. Principal secretary to the PM is more powerful than the Cabinet secretary.

Conclusion

The prime ministerial government emerges due to command of one party majority in Lok Sabha. Prime ministerial government is more similar to the presidential form of government. Concentration of power is not better for democracy, but ultimately *the will of the people* is supreme in democracy.

PRESIDENTIAL FORM OF GOVERNMENT

In a presidential form of government, the following features apply:

1. **President Occupies Central Role**

   President is directly elected by the people, thus responsible towards the people. President is the head of the executive. Ministers are subordinate to the President. The President can appoint anyone as minister and sack the minister at any time. President chairs the Cabinet meeting.

2. **Separation of Power**

   The United States of America is a classical model of presidential form of government. Ministers should not be part of the Parliament. Parliament is known as Congress in the USA. Parliament cannot pass no-confidence motion against the ministers. President cannot dissolve the Parliament. Election for President is held separately every four years. However, elections for Congress are held separately and their tenure is also separate.

3. **Single Executive:**

   The President is the constitutional head as well as administrative head. All the power is vested in the President. Ministers are dependent on the President for their power. All decisions or policies are taken by the President. Ministers work according to the instructions of the President.

4. **Fixed Term Responsibility**

   Stability of the government is the unique feature of the presidential form of government. Due to separation of powers, Parliament cannot bring a no-confidence motion against the President. Similarly, the President cannot dissolve the Congress (Parliament). Thus presidential term is fixed and midterm elections not held in the USA.

5. **Importance of Specialist:**

   The President is allowed to choose the ministers according to his own wish. Ministers must not be members of parliament. Ministers are responsible towards the President. They are not accountable towards Parliament. Ministers do not sit in Parliament. Members of Parliament can not ask questions to the minister. Therefore, popularity and election is not the basis of choice of ministers.

Table 7.4.1: Parliamentary versus Presidential Government

Parliamentary Government	*Presidential Government*
1. President is the constitutional head	President is both constitutional and administrative head
2. Collective responsibility	Nothing like collective responsibility exists
3. PM is administrative head or real head	No peace for office of PM
4. Cabinet government, the Cabinet takes decisions	President takes the decision, rather than the Cabinet.
5. Power lies in groups like the Cabinet	Power vested in the President.
6. Day to day responsibility	Fixed term responsibility

REASONS BEHIND PARLIAMENTARY FORM OF GOVERNMENT

1. **Flexibility**

   The Council of Ministers (CoM) is a part of parliament. Thus the probability of conflict between the executive and the parliament is minimised. Separation of power in the US leads to dispute between executive and parliament. The founders of the Indian Constitution tried to avoid clashes between two organs of the government.

2. **Responsibility**

   The Indian Constitution makers held that responsibility is a more important feature of democracy than stability. Parliament can replace the Council of Ministers at any time.

3. **Useful for Diverse Society**

   Power is vested in a group and not in an individual in the parliamentary form of government. The Cabinet is the centre of power. The Cabinet can accommodate the diversity of region, religion and language. Members of Cabinet belong to all parts of India; they also comprise people from different religious groups, and so on. However, power is concentrated in the hands of an individual in the presidential form of government.

4. **Historical Experience**

   Parliamentary government was introduced in India by the British government. India has been practising the parliamentary government since 1935.

5

PARLIAMENT

KEY CONCEPTS

Structure; Role and Functioning; Parliamentary Committees

The second chapter of Part V of the Constitution begins with the constitution of parliament. According to this, there shall be a Parliament of the union government which shall consist of the President and two houses of Parliament. These are the Rajya Sabha (Council of States) and Lok Sabha (House of the People), as mentioned in Article 79. The Article also talks about the composition of the Council of States. popularly known as the Upper House (but such a phrase is not written in the Constitution).

THE COUNCIL OF STATES

Composition

According to **Article 80,** the strength of the Council of States is 250. Not more than 238 representatives come from states and union territories, in the Council of States. In addition to that 12 members are nominated by the President. The Fourth Schedule is complementary to Article 80. It describes the number of seats allocated for states and UTs.

A total of 225 seats are given to the states and 8 seats are allocated for UTs, according to the Fourth Schedule. 233 seats are filled up in the elections. 12 members are nominated by the President.

Nomination

Twelve members of Council of States are nominated by the President. They are persons having special knowledge or practical experience in:

1. Literature
2. Science
3. Art, and/or
4. Social Service

The idea of nominated members is drawn from England. The House of Lords in England is a non-elected body. Democracy is not a game of numbers only. Some people may not be popular leaders who participate in electorial politics, but their experience in social life may be beneficial for the entire nation. Sachin Tendulkar was nominated in Rajya Sabha on the grounds of art and social service. Scientists, poets, persons belonging to film and theatre may be nominated in the Rajya Sabha.

All 12 members do not retire at the same time. Thus, nomination shall not be held at one point of time.

Allocation of Seats

The allocation of seats was made on the basis of the population of each state, as per census data available at the time of passage of the Constitution. In case of a state having a population of over 5 million, one seat was given on the basis of per million for the first five million. An additional seat was given for every additional two million or part thereof exceeding one million.

Lack of Delimitation

Members in the Council of States represent the state, not any particular constituency. Thus, seats allocated for Council of State, does not change according to changing population of state. For example, 16 members have represented the West Bengal Council of State since 1950.

The first Council of States was constituted in April 1952. Actual members of the Council of States were 204, when it was constituted for the first time in 1952. By 1956, strength of The Council of States had gone up to 220.

Seats of Council of States were raised due to reorganisation of states in 1956. Again various new states were formed in 1960, 1964, 1966, 1972, therefore strength of Council of States grew to 231 by 1972. Seats of Council of States went up to 233 in 1987, due to the formation of Goa as new states' share of state in Council of States, but the seats reduced to 229 after JK was made a Union Territory in 2019.

Election

Members of the Council of States are elected by elected members of the State Legislative Assembly, under Article 80. Thus, members of the Council of States are not directly elected by the people. It is an indirect election under Article 80, which incorporates a system of proportional representation by means of single transferable vote. Representation of Union Territories in the Council of States is determined by the law enacted by Parliament.

Proportional Representation

Proportional representation refers to each political party being given representation in the Council of States, according to their strength in the Legislative Assembies.

Parliament enacted the **Representation of the People Act, 1951** for conducting the elections of Council of States. For maintaining proportional representation RPA 1951, incorporates a formula mentioned below

(a) Election of 1 seat = Total valid votes/Seats to be fulfilled + 1.
   Total valid votes refers to the elected members of the Council of States.

(b) Election for more than 1 seats

Ensuring proportional representation, formula changes for more than 1 seats:

$$\frac{\text{Total Valid votes} \times 100}{\text{Seats to be fulfilled} + 1}$$

Mode of Voting

Elected Members of Legislative Assemblies cast a single vote but record their preferences. Member of legislative assembly put and preferences, if 4 seats are to be fulfilled in the Council of States. Any person can cast single preference too.

Quota and Single Transferable

In proportional method of representation, quota is determined. Whosoever obtains the quota gets elected. Quota is derived according to the formula for election of more than one seat.

Suppose that elected members of Legislative Assembly are 100. And 4 seats to be fulfilled, then quota is 2001.

Open Ballot

Representation of the People Act (RPA) 1951 was amended in 2003, providing an open ballot in the voting of the Council of States. During voting for election of Council of States, each political party appoints its agent. Members of Legislative Assembly show their vote only to the agent of his political party. MLA is not permitted to show his/

her vote to any other person, otherwise his vote becomes invalid.

The Honourable Supreme Court in the **Kuldip Nayar case (2006)** said that provision of open ballot is constitutional. Court argued that since MLAs vote in the election of Council of States, it is an indirect election. Secret voting is applicable in a direct election, where citizens directly participate. From 2003, onwards election for Council of States was held on the basis of open ballot.

Residence

The Council of States represents the state; it does not represent the people.

Thus under the RPA 1951, initially only residents of that state were allowed to represent the state in Council of States. But RPA 1951 was amended in 2003, and now any citizen residing in the territory of India is entitled to represent the state in the Council of States. The Supreme Court observed that amendment in RPA is constitutional and valid in the Kuldeep Nayar case (2006).

Nomination

RPA was passed by the Parliament for complementing Article 80. The RPA outlined the comprehensive provision of election of Council of States, including the process of nomination. Rs 10,000 must be deposited for contesting the election of Council of States. In addition to that 10 per cent of elected members of Legislative Assembly, or 10 members of the Legislative Assembly, whichever is less, are required. It is applicable for the person belonging to the national party and regional party. An independent candidate requires 10 elected members of Legislative Assembly, as proposers. One proposer can propose the name of more than one candidate.

Invalid Votes

Invalid vote is also determined according to RPA 1951. If an MLA puts the same preference for two candidates, vote becomes invalid. MLA showing his/her votes to someone other than an agent of a particular political party, stands invalid. If a voter is not using the pen prescribed by the Election Commission of India, his/her vote is treated as invalid by by the ECI.

NOTA

NOTA refers to the 'none of the above' options in the elections. It was implemented by the Supreme Court in the **PUCL (People's Union of Civil Liberties) case, 1996**. But provision of NOTA is not applicable in the elections of Council of States since ordinary citizens do not take part in these elections. Elected MLAs participate in the elections, thus NOTA is not applicable in the indirect elections of the Council of States.

Tenure

Council of States is a permanent house. It never dissolves. Tenure of a member is 6 years. One third members of the Council of States retires every two years. After the constitution of Council of States, a lottery was held in 1954 and 1956 for retiring members of the Council. They could not complete their full tenure for 6 years.

In case any member resigns from the Council of States before 6 years, a new member is elected for the remaining period.

Anti-Defection Act

Anti-defection act is not applicable over election of Council of States. Members of Legislative Assembly of states participate in the election of Council of States. Thus, it becomes the internal procedure of the legislative Assembly. Horse-trading is a persistent problem of elections of the Council of States.

Principle of Equality of States

The US federal system is based on the principle of equality of states. Equal 2 seats are allocated for every 50 states. But the Council of States in India does not follow the principle of equality of states. The Council of States in India represents the state on the basis of population.

Each state enjoys equal power in the **Seventh Schedule**, over the State List. But unequal representation favours a bigger state. Under **Article 312**, a new All India Services can be created by 2/3 members of majority of present and voting Council of States. The smaller states are automatically marginalised. UP (31) Maharashtra (19) Tamil Nadu (10) are large states. Both Bihar and WB are alloted 16 seats each. Smaller states like Nagaland, Manipur, Tripura, Meghalaya, Sikkim, Mizoram represent one seat each only.

Council of States and UTs

Council of States also includes representation of J & K (4), Delhi (3) and Puducherry (1). Union territories are different from states.

Nomination of Specialists

12 members nominated by the President in the Council of States, do not represent any state. They are nominated to the Council of States based on the principle of functional representation.

HOUSE OF THE PEOPLE

Composition

1. House of the People shall consist of not more than 530 members. They are chosen directly by the people from the territorial constitution in the states according to **Article 81**.
2. Not more than 20 members representing the UTs can be chosen in such a manner.

Parliament passed representation of people Act 1951 (RPA). Parliament provided the method of first-past-the-post electoral system, both for states and Union Territories.

First-Past-the-Post

The entire nation is divided in territorial constituencies of equal size in terms of population. Multiple parties or persons can contest the election from any constituency. But only one person wins the election. Whosoever gets the maximum votes is declared as the winner. It is worth noting that a majority of votes is not required. Thus, it is a drawback of first-past-the-post system, it neglects the representation of minorities: the winner may get less votes than the losers put together.

Principle of Allocation of Seats

Readjustment implies two features:

1. Allocation of seats for states in the House of the People changes after each and every census (held once every decade).
2. Size of territorial constituencies also had undergone the change, after every census.

Strength of the first House of People was 489. It was based on the Census of 1951. Strength of the House of People has gone up to 484 after the Census of 1961. Finally seats in the House of People went up to 543, after the Census of 1971. Due to the increase in the seats of the House of People, seats allocated for states also changed. If the number of seats changes for states, territorial constitution is automatically altered.

Allocation of Seats

Article 82 speaks for readjustment of seats after every census. 2011 is the year of the last census. Population of India according to the Census of 2011 stands at 121 crores. But the strength of the House of People is based on the Census of 1971.

Strength of the House of the People remained intact after 1971. The Indira Gandhi government brought about the **42nd Constitutional Amendment** and seats of the House of People were frozen upto year 2000.

Again the **84th Constitutional Amendment** was incorporated in 2002, which says that seats for the House of People shall change after the Census of 2026. Size of the total population of India became double from 1971. But the strength of the House of People remains the same.

Changing Size of Constituency

Strength of the House of People shall remain unchanged before the Census of 2031. Size of the constituency within the state, however, have become unbalanced. Justice Kuldip Singh Commission was appointed for redrawing the boundary of the constituencies within the state commission appointed in 2002.

Delimitation of Seats

Delimitation literally means the act or process of fixing limits or boundaries of territorial constituencies in a country or a province having a legislative body. Delimitation implies the change in allocation of seats for states, and changing the boundary of a constituency. According to the mandate of **Article 82**, four delimitation commissions have been set up so far. First delimitation commission was set up in 1952. The commission was also set up in 1962, 1972 and 2002. Commission was established in 2002, and was unique. It did not change the composition of the House of People. It merely changed the boundaries of the constituencies. This gave rise to a peculiar situation. The strength of the House of People is based on the Census of 1971. But the boundary of the constituency is based on the Census of 2001.

Delimitation Commission

Article 82 authorises the parliament to make an authority to complete the task of readjustment of the boundary of the House of the Parliament passed the RPA 1950 and the Delimitation Commission Act.

Delimitation Commission Act incorporates following structure:

1. One member who shall be a person who is or has been a judge of the Supreme Court as chairperson appointed by the Central Government.
2. Chief Election Commissioner or an election commissioner nominated by the Chief Electoral Officer (CEO).
3. State Election Commission of that state.
4. A total of 5 members of Lok Sabha of that state and 5 members of Legislative Assembly of the concerned state. For states having less than 5 members of Lok Sabha, all members will become associate members.

Reservation of Seats

Article 80 talks about the composition of the House of the People. At the same time, Article 330 incorporates reservation of Scheduled Castes and Scheduled Tribes in proportion to the population of SC/ST. According to the delimitation of 2002, reserved seats for SCs (increased) to (84) and for STs has gone up to 47 in the House of the people.

Provision of nomination of Anglo-Indian persons has been abolished in 2020. By the same Constitutional Amendment, Article 334 is also changed, now reservation shall be continued upto 80 years from the commencement of the constitution.

Qualifications

Article 84 prescribed about qualification for membership of parliament. Membership of parliament implies membership of both Council of States and House of the People.

CONSTITUTIONAL PROVISIONS

Citizenship and Oath

Citizens of India are entitled to become an MP if they should make and subscribe to an oath and affirmation according to the format provided in the Third Schedule of the Constitution. Merely winning an election does not qualify a person to become a Member of Parliament. After oath, a person is considered a member of parliament. Following format is available in the Third Scchedule:

1. Will bear true faith and allegiance to the Constitution of India.
2. Uphold sovereignty and integrity of India.
3. Will faithfully discharge his/her duties.

Age

For membership of the Council of States, a person shall not be less than 30 years of age. In the case of Lok Sabha, a person shall not be less than 25 years of age. Thus, the Council of States is also considered as the House of elders.

Statutory Provisions

Citizenship, oath and age is constitutional for membership qualifications prescribed for membership of parliament in Article 84.

In addition, Article 84 also authorises the parliament to prescribe some more qualifications for membership of parliament. Thus, the Parliament enacted the **Representation of the People Act 1951 (RPA)**.

Registration

For membership of Parliament, an elector should be registered in any constituency across India. A voter is entitled to vote only in a constituency, where he/she is registered as a voter. For instance, PM Narendra Modi is registered as an elector in Vadodara constituency of Gujarat; though he contested constituency from Varanasi voted in Vadodara.

Not More Than Two Seats

Total number of seats of the House of the People stands up to 543. According to RPA 1951, no person is allowed to contest the election from more than two Constituencies.

Proposers

A member of a national or regional party reognised by the Election Commission of India, requires one voter as a proposer from the same constituency. An independent candidate needs 10 proposers who are voters in the same constituency. Rs 25,000 should be deposited according to RPA 1951. However, candidates belonging to SC/ST community shall deposit Rs 12,000.

DURATION OF HOUSES OF PARLIAMENT

Tenure

As we have just studied, one-third members retire every second year in the Council of States, which never dissolves. However, the House of the People shall continue for 5 years from the date of appointment for its first meeting. But the House of the People is subject to dissolution before 5 years by the President. The 11th Lok Sabha was dissolved on 4 December 1997, however, it had been elected on 7 May 1996. The 12th Lok Sabha was dissolved within one year. It was elected in March 1998 and dissolved in April 1999. This is known as premature dissolution of the Lok Sabha.

42nd Constitutional Amendment

Tenure of the House of the People had been extended up to 6 years from 5 years stipulated in **Article 83**. The 42nd Constitutional Amendment was brought about by the Indira Gandhi government in 1976. The five-year tenure was restored in 1978 by the 44th Constitutional Amendment by the Janata Party government.

Extension of Duration

Duration of the House of the People can be extended while proclamation of emergency is in operation for a period not exceeding one year at a time. Emergency announced on 25 June 1975 was withdrawn on 21 March 1977. The had Emergency continued for 21 months. Therefore, one year is not the maximum duration. It can be extended for many years. At a time, it shall not be extended for more than one year. When the proclamation ceases to operate, it shall not be extended for more than six months.

PARLIAMENTARY FUNCTIONARIES

Pro-Tem Speaker

Every Member of Parliament takes an oath and affirmation before the president or some person appointed by the President. After the election in the new House of the People, the President appoints the Speaker for the time being. The President appoints the seniormost member as **pro-tem Speaker** for a short time. Pro-tem Speaker is not chosen by the members of the House.

Pro-tem Speaker performs the following functions:

1. Subscribes oath and affirmation for newly elected members of the House.
2. Chooses the Speaker of the House.

Pro-tem Speaker is not appointed to the Council of States. Instead there, the chairperson of the Council subscribes to oaths and affirmation on behalf of the President.

Speaker

The President fixes the date for the election of the Speaker on the advice of the Ministry of Parliamentary Affairs. Normally, Speakers belong to the ruling party. For the election of the Speaker, one member proposes the name and others second the name. Deputy Speaker is also chosen by the members of the House in the same manner. The office of the Deputy Speaker is given to the principal opposition party. That convention was begun in 1977 by the Janata Party government. From 1980 onwards, the tradition was discontinued by the Congress Party. No fixed time limit is prescribed for choosing the Deputy Speaker. Nobody was chosen as Deputy Speaker in 16th Lok Sabha for 9 months. This could be because the NDA did not want to give concession to the Congress Party.

Panel of Chairperson

For smooth functioning of the Parliament, ten members are nominated by the Speaker. According to convention, the Speaker nominates one woman and one male from the opposition party. In absence of the Speaker and Deputy Speaker, the panel of chairpersons preside over the sitting of the House. Provision of panel of chairpersons is mentioned in the rules of Lok Sabha.

Leader of the House

The Prime Minister is considered as Leader of the House in the Lok Sabha. During the Prime Ministership of Dr Manmohan Singh, the PM was not the leader of the Lok Sabha, because Dr Singh was the member of the Council of States.

Leader of the House in the Council of States is nominated by the PM who happens to be the seniormost member of the Council of Ministers. If the PM is not a member of either House, any other member of the Council of Ministers may be nominated as Leader of the House. Narsimha Rao (1991) and Deve Gowda (1996) were not a members of either House, while being appointed as the PM.

Leader of Opposition

Democracy promotes disagreement and dissent thus the opposition stands for an alternate view. Constructive criticism is the responsibility of the opposition. It also offers alternative policy options. Constitution does not speak of a leader of the opposition.

The Parliament enacted the **Salary And Allowances of Leaders of Opposition in Parliament Act 1977**. For getting recognition as opposition party, one-tenth members of the strength of the House are needed. According to rules of the Lok Sabha, the opposition party stands for the second largest party in the House from a numerical point of view, according to the above-mentioned parliamentary act of 1977. Thus, 1/10 number is not mandatory in act of parliament. It is reason behind the dispute over recognition of opposition party.

Ram Subhag Singh became the first Leader of Opposition in the House of People in November 1969. After the split of the Congress Party, Congress (R) led by Indira Gandhi and Congress (O) was led by Ram Subhag Singh.

Recognition of the Leader of Opposition is beneficial due to the following facilities attached to office:

(a) Allotment of block of seats in the House.
(b) Allotment of room in parliament.
(c) Allotment of committee rooms for holding party meetings.
(d) Supply of official documents.
(e) Nomination to any parliamentary committee.
(f) Consultation for fixing the business of the House or any important matter before the House.

The Leader of Opposition occupies an important role in the appointment of Central Vigilance Commission (CUC), Central Bureau of Investigation (CBI), Central Information Commission (CIC) and Lokpal.

In the initial decades of parliamentary democracy, lack of opposition was visible due to domination of the Congress Party. In the 15th and 16th Lok Sabha, nobody was appointed as Leader of the Opposition, because of domination of the NDA alliance.

The Whip

Whip is a member of the House, who ensures the presence of the party members in the House. The Whip maintains discipline in the house, members vote according to instruction of the Whip. Chief Whip in the House of the People is the Minister of Parliamentary Affairs.

Chief Whip is associated by one or two ministers of state. An MP who disobeys party whip may lose the membership.

According to Anti-defection Act, the provision of the Whip is mentioned in the rules of the House of the People and the Council of States. It is written nowhere in the Constitution.

Secretary General

The Secretary General is not a constitutional office. It includes rules of the House of People and Council of States. Separate secretariat exists for both Houses. Many officers are required for running the House smoothly. Secretary General is the top administrative officer of this secretariat.

Proceedings of the House is conducted by the Secretary General (SG) in the name of Speaker. From summoning of the Parliament to functioning of the parliamentary committee, the entire work of the Parliament is managed by the SG.

SG is a civil servant appointed by the Speaker. SG performs parliamentary functions and administrative tasks too. Administrative tasks include recruitment of staff for the secretariat.

Role of the Speaker

Conduct of Business

Entire proceedings of the Parliament are carried out in the name of the Speaker. For raising any issue or introduction of the bill in the House of the People, permission of Speaker is mandatory. Speaker maintains parliament and decorum in parliament. Speaker constitutes parliamentary communities.

Umpire for House

Role of Speaker is not bound to party affiliation. Speaker regulates the proceedings of the House, but does not participate in the proceedings. He/she is not permitted to vote in the House, over any bill or resolution. In case a deadlock occurs in the House, then the Speaker is allowed to vote; it is popularly known as 'casting vote'.

Till today, no Speaker has exercised voting in the history of the Indian parliament. When resolution for removal of the Speaker is under consideration, Speaker shall cast vote as a member, it is known as voting in first instance.

Quasi-Judicial Power

The Speaker is entitled to disqualify an MP on the ground of defection according to Anti-Defection Act. Speaker Somnath Chatterjee had expelled 11 MPs on change of corruption in the year 2006. It was a landmark and historical decision because that was the first time members were expelled from the House.

Administrative Power

Speaker is the unique office and most important one in the parliamentary system. Speaker is the head of secretariat of House of People. The Secretary General assists the Speaker in disposing the administration functions of the secretariat. The Speaker is the only member of parliament who holds the office after dissolution of the House of the people. Speaker continues as the administrative head unless the new Speaker enters his/her office.

Removal of Speaker

Speaker vacates his/her office, if he/she ceases to be a Member of Parliament. Speaker can resign from his/her office in writing by his/her hand, addressed to the Deputy Speaker. Speaker may be removed from his office by resolution of the House of the People. Such a resolution should be passed by the majority of members present in the House. 14 days' notice is necessary for removal of the Speaker from his/her office. Deputy Speaker tenders his/her resignation to the Speaker.

Disqualification for Membership

Provision of disqualification for the Speaker is mentioned in **Article 102** of the Constitution. Same provision is applicable for a member of both Houses of the Parliament.

PROVISIONS OF DISQUALIFICATION OF MEMBERSHIP

1. **Office of Profit:**

   An MP may be disqualified if he/she holds any office of profit under state. Parliament is authorised to declare any office outside of ambit of office of profit under article 102.

   Parliament enacted the **Parliament (Prevention of Disqualification) Act 1959.** The Legislative Assembly of a state is permitted to enact its own law regarding disqualification.

2. **Statutory Provisions:**

   Neither the Constitution nor any statute of Parliament defines the office of profit. Act of Parliament includes those offices, which are exempted from the list of offices of profit. Offices which are not included in the Act are deemed to be offices of profit. A minister, minister of the union or state is not considered as an office of profit, because these offices are listed in the Act.

3. **Judicial Intervention:**

   Since any Act cannot include each and every office, thus, dispute is bound to emerge regarding the office of profit. The offices which are not included in the Act shall be considered as office of profit on the following grounds:

   (a) Whether the government is appointing the authority;

   (b) Government has power to terminate the authority;

   (c) The government determines remuneration;

   (d) Source of remuneration;

   (e) Power that comes from position.

These parameters are propounded by the judiciary. Receiving remuneration may not be the sole ground for deciding about the office of profit, observed the Supreme

Court in the **Jaya Bachchan case (2006)**. Power comes from authority and is also a significant criterion. Parliament amended the Act of 1959 retrospectively and included various offices within the Act.

4. **Unsound Mind:**
   Another disqualification is described in Article 102, which states that an MP may be disqualified if he/she is of an unsound mind and stands so declared by a competent court on the basis of a medical report.
5. **Undischarged Insolvent:**
   An insolvent is a person who is unable to pay his/her debt to the bank. Person may be discharged by the bank, when the bank recovers loan through seizing the entire property of that person. In case the bank fails to recover loan by seizing the property of the person, then the bank recognises a person as an undischarged insolvent. An MP who is an undischarged insolvent is likely to be disqualified.
6. **Not a Citizen of India:**
   In case an MP is not a citizen of India or has voluntarily acquired the citizenship of a foreign state, and he/she is under acknowledgement of allegiance or adherence to a foreign state, then he/she may be disqualified. Disqualification is decided by the President on the advice of the Election Commission of India.
7. **Law Made by the Parliament:**
   Article 102 enumerates four grounds of disqualification. In addition to that some articles empower parliament to enact a law for determining the disqualifications. Parliament enacted the **Representation of the People Act (RPA) 1951**. A person may disqualified as MP on the grounds of corrupt practices mentioned in the RPA 1951. When Indira Gandhi was an MP from Raebareli in UP, she was disqualified by the Allahabad High Court in the year 1975 on the grounds of corrupt practices.
8. **Vacation of Seats:**
   Member of Parliament can resign from the Parliament. Member of the House of the People may hand in his/her resignation to Speaker and Member of the Council of States shall present his/her resignation to the Chairperson of the Council of States. **Article 101** contains guidelines for vacation of seats and authorises the Parliament to enact a law for determining about vacations of seats. Parliament enacted the RPA in 1951.

Other important rules to note:

(i) **Simultaneous Election for Both Houses:**
In case a person is elected for both Houses at the same time, she/he may retain either the seat of the House of the People or of the Council of States. Person shall inform his/her decision within 10 days from the later of dates on which he is chosen. In case the person is unable to inform the Election Commission of India within 10 days, the seat of the Council of State falls vacant (RPA-1951). In case a person is elected for House of the People and a State Legislative Assembly, he/she must resign his/her membership of the State legislature within 14 days, or his/her seat in the House of the People will automatically fall vacant.

(ii) **Absence of Member:**
If a member of either House of Prliament is absent for a period 60 days, without permission of the House, his/her seat may be declared as vacant. Counting of 60 days excludes prorogation or adjournment of the House for more than 4 consecutive days. Suppose that the winter session of the Parliament continued for 20 days,

thereafter the Parliament was prorogued for 40 days. These 40 days will not be counted in 60 days. When the Budget session starts, again counting starts from 20 days onwards. Adjournment for one, two or three days shall be consented in 60 days. Normally adjournment for 5 days onwards happens in budget sessions, which is counted in these 60 days.

POWER AND PRIVILEGES OF MPs

The Parliament maintains control over the Executive or the Council of Ministers. Privilege, power and immunity is granted for Parliament due its special role and responsibility. Members of Parliament ask questions to the members of the Council of Ministers. Parliament is entitled to bring about censure motion against the government. Thus, special power is needed, which is incorporated in Article 105.

Privilege is available for:

1. **Parliament:** When a member is detained by an executive order, or arrested on a criminal charge, the Speaker should be intimated immediately. Each House has the power to punish its members for disorderly conduct. The House is empowered to control publication of proceedings. The House can prohibit the publication of any proceedings of Parliament. House is the sole authority in the matter of examining the validity of proceedings. The House can exclude strangers from the House. House shall determine the nature and quantum of punishment.
2. **Member of Parliament:** Freedom of speech is available for MPs within the House. Restrictions are not imposed over their freedom of speech. Members are given immunity that they shall not be arrested in any civil cases. However, this privilege is not extended for criminal cases. Members are not liable before any court of law, for whatever they have said or voted on in parliament. Members shall not be called as witness in the court of law. For example, an ordinary citizen speaking against the sovereignty of India can be prosecuted in court of law. But MPs are given immunity.
3. **Parliamentary Committee:** Parliamentary Committee is composed of the Members of Parliament. Thus, all privilege and immunity given for parliament is extended for communities too, under Article 105. Any evidence or person summoned by the Committee, also receives the benefits of privilege. Person or officers who refuse the direction of the Committee are considered to be in breach of privilege.
4. **Privilege is not Absolute:** Privilege of Parliament is essential for community conduct of business of House. Article 105 points out restrictions over the privilege like:
   (i) Subject to provisions of this consultation, privilege is available. It clearly indicates that the Constitution incorporates Fundamental Rights and equality before law.
   (ii) Judicial review is an extension of the principle of protection of Fundamental Rights.
   (iii) Rules, regulation, decorum of Parliament cannot be violated in the name of privilege.
5. **Lack of Codification:**
   Article 105 gives a brief description of privileges, which includes:
   (i) Freedom of speech
   (ii) Not liable to court for said and vote in parliament

   Comprehensive list of privileges is not written in the Constitution. Article 105(3) says that parliament shall define privilege from time to time.

Members and House shall enjoy those privileges, which were available before commencement of the Constitution. It is added in the Constitution by the 42nd Amendment. 42nd Amendment deleted the sentence of Article 105, which stated that parliament shall enjoy similar privileges like the British parliament (House of Commons).

How Breach of Privilege is Decided

Due to lack of a written list of privilege, ultimately Parliament decides about issues related to breach of privilege. Any member can raise the issue on the floor of the House. Speakers in the Lok Sabha or Chairperson in the Council of States refer this matter before the Privilege Committee. Committees exist in the both houses. Decision of the Committee is formal about the breach of privilege. Same Committee is authorised to punish the person.

DEBATE RELATED TO PRIVILEGE

Contempt and Privilege

Privilege is helpful for smooth functioning of parliament. Members cannot attend the session of Parliament in case of arrest. Obstructing the functioning of Parliament or committees refers to breach of privilege. But using unparliamentary language against other members, should be taken as contempt. Parliament never made a distinction between privilege and contempt.

Judicial Review

Proceeding of Parliament is not subject to judicial review. But the Constitution incorporates Fundamental Rights, and judicial review. In case of conflict between Fundamental Rights and parliamentary privilege, one needs to refer to the Supreme Court's landmark judgement in the **Keshav Singh case (1964).**

Parliamentary privilege is more important than a citizen's right of freedom of speech and expression. Thus, the Parliament can prohibit the publication of proceedings of Parliament. Judiciary is bound to protect the Right to life and personal liberty of citizens, under Article 21. Parliament cannot punish anyone arbitrarily, said the Supreme Court in the Keshav Singh case. But the fact of the matter is that the Parliament is not willing to accept any judgement of the Supreme Court.

Expulsion of Members

Speaker of the Lok Sabha Somnath Chatterjee expelled 11 members of the house in 2006 over charges of corruption, as we just discussed. Decision of the Speaker was validated by the Supreme Court in **Raja Ram Pal case (2007)**. It is worth noting that provision of expulsion is not mentioned in the Constitution or anywhere in statutes of Parliament.

Corruption and Privilege

No-confidence motion was brought about against Narsimha Rao in 1993. Members of Jharkhand Mukta Morcha (JMM) supported the government during the motion. It is alleged that members of JMM received bribery in exchange for voting. A case was lodged against them in the Prevention of Corruption Act 1988.

Codification

Codification of privilege will minimise the likelihood of emergence of dispute. Australia codified privilege and prescribed that contempt is different from privilege. Inflammatory speech against the Parliament is considered as contempt not breach of privilege. Penalty for violating the privilege is also fixed. Thus, it can be codified in India too.

SESSIONS OF PARLIAMENT

The President shall from time to time summon each House of Parliament to meet at such time and place as he/she thinks fit, according to Article 85. In practice, the President summons each House according to aid and advice of the Council of Ministers. According to Article 85, the gap should not be more than six months between the last sitting of the session and first sitting of next session. Put simply, the interval between Budget session and Monsoon Session should not be more than 6 months. Parliament made rules according to this provision of the Constitution. Rules made by House of the People provide that three sessions of parliament are commenced, namely:

(i) Budget session, which commences in February and March. It is the lengthiest and most important session of parliament.
(ii) Monsoon Session: It is held in the month of July-August.
(iii) Winter sessions are normally organised in the month of November.

Fixed Number of Sittings

Neither Constitution nor rules of the House of the People prescribe the beginning of parliamentary session from a fixed date. 3 January is the fixed date for the beginning of House in the US. We can increase the number of sitting days of Parliament by introducing fixed dates. Sessions are often postponed due to fear of criticism by the opposition party.

However, a fixed date of beginning of the session may create some problems. For example, Budget session of parliament of year 2020 was out short due to the Corona virus. Flexibility of date appears better than fixed beginning dates. Budget session of 2019 commenced in June due to the General Elections.

Special Session

Apart from the normal sessions of Parliament, Special sessions can also be summoned. For instance, a special session was convened in the year 2000 on completion of 50 years of enforcement of the Constitution. Special session was also held during the introduction of GST in 2016.

Prorogation

President is also entitled to prorogue the House. 'Prorogue' means discontinuation of a session or interval between two sessions. Prorogation of the House is done on the aid and advice of the Council of Ministers.

Dissolution

Article 85 also authorises the President to dissolve the Lok Sabha. Former Prime Minister V. P. Singh failed to get the confidence of the Lok Sabha in 1990. Subsequently he had to resign from the office of PM. He also recommended dissolution of the Lok Sabha. President R. Venkat Raman refused to dissolve the House of the People. Changing of the government has nothing to do with dissolution of the House of the People. Normally after completion of 5 years, which is tenure of the House of the People, it is automatically dissolved by the President.

Election results for 17th Lok Sabha were declared on 23 May 2019. Thereafter the 16th Lok Sabha was dissolved on 25 May 2019. The 17th Lok Sabha was constituted on 24 May, after a list of newly elected members of Lok Sabha was presented to the president by Election Commission of India. First session of Parliament began on 16 June 2019.

FUNCTIONS OF PARLIAMENT

Law Making

Conduct of business is not written in the Constitution, Parliament is entitled to frame its own rules and regulations under **Article 118**. The House of the People enacted its own rules and procedure for conduct of business in 1952. However, the Council of States framed its own rules in the year 1964.

Informal Beginning

Council of Ministers play a crucial role in the making of laws. First the Cabinet decides on making a law, then the Cabinet passes a resolution in that regard. Subsequently, the concerned ministry prepares a draft for enacting a law. If law is related to internal security, then law is drafted by the Minister of Home Affairs.

Each draft related to making of law, shall be presented before the Ministry of Law and Justice Ministry shall examine the legal dimension of law, whether the proposed law shall be sustained in a court of law. After approval of Ministries of Law and Justice, it is sent to the Ministry of Parliamentary Affairs. Minister of Parliamentary Affairs consults with Speaker or Chairperson for introduction of bill in the House. Speaker or Chairperson finalises date and time with consultation of Secretary General of the House.

First Reading

First reading means introduction of bill in the House. Copies of the bill are printed in two lots and circulated to members at least two days before the date of introduction. Date of introduction and date of information is also printed on the bill. Bill is printed both in English and in Hindi language.

Although bill is published after introduction in house, in special cases Speaker may order the publication of bill in Gazette before introduction of bill in the House. The **Code of Criminal Procedure (Amendment) Bill, 1953** was permitted to be published, before introduction.

A minister who desires to introduce a bill has to give 7 days, notice in writing of his intention to move for leave to introduce the Bill. After circulation of printed copies, bill is included in the list of business. On the day appointed for introduction of the bill, Speaker calls the minister-in-charge, who moves the motion for leave to an introduce the bill. Bill related to reorganisation of Jammu and Kashmir was not listed in the business of Parliament on that day. Bill was introduced in House without availability of printed copy. This became an issue of dispute.

Normally bill is not opposed at introduction level in the first reading. MP willing to oppose the bill can give notice to by 10 am. on the day it is listed for introduction. Bill can be opposed on the ground that it falls outside of jurisdiction of Parliament. The **Prevention of Communal Violence Bill 2014** was opposed on the ground of legislative competency. Then decision to introduce the bill was deferred. In case, when minister is adamant on introduction of bill, then it is put for voting.

A new practice was started in 1993 in the history of Indian Parliament. Departmentally related standing committees were constituted in order to strengthen parliamentary security over executive function. After the introduction of the Bill, it is now sent to the departmentally related standing committee. Report of the committee is advisory in nature.

Second Reading

It is the longest and most important stage of passage of any bill in parliament. It includes the following levels:

1. Committee
2. Report
3. Consideration

Second stage begins with discussion over the principles of the bill. The Constitution of the committee is not viable on every bill.

For minute scrutiny it is presented before a parliamentary committee.

Committee Stage

Due to the large strength of the House, Parliament finds less time to scrutinise over the Bill. Thus, bills are given to committees. Bill can be passed to two types of parliamentary committees.

1. **Select Committee:** It consists of members belonging to only one house. If a bill is introduced in the House of the People, members of committees are drawn only from the House of the People. Number of members is not fixed; it depends upon the House.

2. **Joint Committee:** Joint committee implies the member of committee is taken from both houses. Ratio of the House of the People and the Council of States is 2:1. Joint committee is better, since it takes the opinion of both houses. It saves time too. No time limit exists for the presentation of the report of the parliament committee.
3. **Report Stage:** Committee presents its report to parliament. Meanwhile Parliament can take opinion of the people on Bill. For eliciting the opinion of people, Speakers or chairpersons give instructions for printing the news in various newspapers across India. Speakers of various states also ensure the publication of issues. A report of public opinion is also tabled before parliament.
4. **Consideration:** Second Reading begins with consideration (discussion) on principles of bill. After receiving a report of committee and public opinion, clause by clause consideration begins. Members of each political party are allocated certain time in discussion according to their strength in Parliament.

During consideration, amendments to the bill may be proposed. Acceptance of amendment is decided by voice vote in the House. Critics oppose the provision of voice vote.

Third Reading

Third stage is the simplest, where Houses pass the bill with simple majority. Voice vote is commenced for rejection or acceptance of the whole bill. Voting does not take place for discussion or amendment in bill. Normally bills are never blocked in third reading.

Bill Transmitted to the Next House

Once a bill is passed from one House, say, House of the People, then it is transmitted to the next House (Council of States). If the next house passes the bill as it is, without any amendment; it is considered passed by both Houses. Other options are also available for the next House. It can suggest an amendment in Bill. Consequently, the bill is again sent to the first house (where bill was introduced). If first House agrees on amendment suggested by the next House, Bill is supposed to be passed from both houses.

Deadlock

It is interesting to note that the procedure for passage of a bill in not written in the Constitution. But provision of deadlock is incorporated in **Article 108** of the Constitution. If a bill is passed by first house and transmitted to next house, the bill is considered to be in deadlock if:

(i) The bill is rejected by the next house;
(ii) First house disagrees with amendment proposed by next house;
(iii) More than 6 months, lapsed from the date of reception of the bill, but next House did not pass the bill.

Due to deadlock, bill may be lapsed or President may summon joint sitting of parliament, under Article 108.

JOINT SITTING

The President may notify about his/her intention of summoning a joint sitting. The President's call for joint sitting is possible with the aid and advice of the Council of Ministers. Joint sitting shall be chaired by the Speaker. Deputy Speaker shall chair the sitting in the absence of the Speaker. In the absence of the Deputy Speaker, the sitting shall be presided over by the Deputy Chairperson of Council of States. Sequence of chairperson in joint sitting is not mentioned in **Article 108**, but it is incorporated in the rules of the House of People. If present members of the House of the People is 300 and present members of the Council of States is 200 then majority mark of 251 is require for the passage of bill. Majority of each separate house is not needed. Joint sitting of Houses is an exceptional provision. The following were passed through joint sitting:

1. **Dowry Prohibition Act 1961:**
   Both Houses were disagreed over the practice and definition of dowry. Congress commanded majority in the both Houses, even then disagreement occurred. Deadlock between two Houses indicated that freedom of speech and expressions were valued in the house.
2. **Banking Services Commission Act 1978:**
   Congress was no longer in power in the union government. Janata Party commanded majority in the House of the People but Congress enjoyed the majority in the Council of States. Deadlock between two houses resulted due to political revelry.
3. **Prevention of Terrorism Act (POTA) 2002:**
   A coalition government of the National Democratic Alliance (NDA) was headed by Atal Bihari Vajpayee. POTA was brought about for regulating and controlling terrorist activities. However, Congress was in a stronger position in Council of States, the Rajya Sabha. For resolving the deadlock, joint sitting was summoned.

OPPOSITION OF JOINT SITTING

Cumulative majority is needed for passage of any bill during Joint Sitting. It undermines the role of the Council of States. Strength of the Council of States is almost half the strength of the House of the People. Voice and objections of the Council of States are thus overruled. It is important to remember the relevance of the Council of States.

REPRESENTING THE STATE IN FEDERAL STRUCTURE

Law made by parliament is applicable across India. Council of States reflects the perspective of the states, which should not be overlooked. Parliament must work with a federal spirit.

House of Elders

Members of the Council of States are always senior and experts in various fields. Council of States is composed of senior lawyers, scientists and famous sports personalities too. Counting the numbers is a partial meaning of democracy. Wisdom and expertise is equally important.

House of Revision

House of the People represents the will of the people. Laws enacted by one house need revision. Even the House of the People can enact laws in haste. Council of States utilises more minute and comprehensive observation. Thus, the opinion of the Council of States does matter.

Integration

The Council of States and House of the People should not be segregated strictly against each other. Both houses play complementary roles. For instance, Chairperson of Council of States is elected by the members of both Houses. Moreover, departmental parliamentary committees are comprised of both Houses. Members of both Houses are given due representation in Joint Parliamentary Committee.

House of Obstruction

Criticism is the primary role of opposition. Opposition also suggests alternative policies. However, some argue that the Council of States has been obstructing each and every act of the House of the People in order to protect interests of party politics. When different parties command majority in two Houses, such dispute becomes visible. Thus, joint sitting is a constitutional provision, which may be utilised for breaking down deadlock.

Private Member Bill

Bill introduced by a Member of Parliament other than a minister, is a private member bill. Both an elected member as well as a nominated member can move such a bill. Members may be from the ruling party or the opposition party. Private members bill appears as a healthy practice, through which any MP can participate in law-making and challenge the monopoly of ministers in law-making, a monopoly which undermines the power of the Parliament.

Procedure:

Procedure is different for private member bill. The period of notice of a motion for leave to introduce a private member bill (PMB) is **one month**. Speaker may allow motion for leave to introduce PMB for less than one month. A member can give notice of not more than four bills during a session. Drafting the bill is the responsibility of the member himself/herself.

Two and half hours of Friday are allocated for private member bills. Member who introduces the bill becomes the member in charge of the bill.

Problems and Prospects:

In the last 70 years of functioning of Parliament, only 14 private member bills have been passed by the Parliament and become Acts. Interestingly 328 private member bills were introduced in parliament during the 14th Lok Sabha. Most of the private member bills were unable to travel beyond the first reading. Only 14 bills were discussed in all 328 bills introduced in the House, and none were passed by the house. All bills were lapsed.

For strengthening the private members bill, the day of introduction of the bill should be changed. Friday is the last working day of Parliament, when most of the members rush towards their constituency. More absence is visible on Friday in parliament. There is need for stringent regulation over the private member bill.

Nevertheless, privy purses were abolished by Private Members Bill through the **26th Constitutional Amendment**. Voting age was reduced from 21 to 18 by the **61st Constitutional Amendment Bill** with help of Private Member Bill. Apart from ordinary law, Private Member Bills can be utilised for constitutional amendments too.

Delegated Legislation

Laws made by executive or bureaucracy are known as delegated legislation. Parliament delegate the law-making power to the executive.

Parliament enacted the **Disaster Management Act 2006,** Section 6 to delegate power to the executive and accordingly, national authority shall have the responsibility for laying down policies, plans and guidelines. Delegated legislation is also known as subordinate legislation. Executive is subordinate to legislative by law. Rules, regulation notification made by the executive is subordinate legislation. Bylaws are supplementary laws for **Essential Commodities Act 1955** does not specify the number of essential commodities. It is quantified by the government through bylaws. Government can arrest hoarders of essential commodities by referring to the publication of rules in the official Gazette of Government of India.

Need for Delegated Legislation

Parliament makes the broad outlines of any law, while the rest of the things are left out for the executive to fill in the blanks. Parliament cannot enact each and every element of a law due to following reasons:

1. Lack of time
2. Technicality in making of law
3. Absence of expertise
4. Difficulty in operationalisation

Law is executed by the executive. The age of information technology and nuclear technology is also a challenge for lawmakers, which requires expert assistance from bureaucrats, in law making.

Criticism

Lord Hewart said that the power of bureaucracy thrives in the name of the executive responsibility towards Parliament. Laws made by the executive go against the spirit of division of power inherent in the Constitution. Power of bureaucracy increases manifold on the behest of delegated legislation. Parliament is responsible towards the people. Bureaucracy is an unelected body, which must not override an elected body like the Parliament. Rising speed of delegated legislation shows the decline of parliament.

Parliamentary Control

Parliament exercises control over the executive through parliamentary committee and subordinate legislation. Committees exist in the both Houses separately. They scrutinise the rules, regulations or bylaws made by parliament.

Therefore, the bureaucracy can violate the mandate of the Parliament. Moreover, three organs of the government are complementary to each other. Strict division of power is impractical. Government running becomes difficult in the absence of delegated legislation.

Lapse of Bill

Interestingly procedure for passage of bill is not mentioned in the Constitution. But procedure for lapse is incorporated in the Constitution under Article 107.

Prorogation

A bill pending in Parliament shall not lapse by reason of prorogation of the House, under Article 107. Normally passage of bill takes more than 6 months, thus discontinuation of House does not endanger the bill.

Bill Pending in Council of States

Bill pending in Council of States, which has not been passed by the House of the People shall not lapse on the dissolution of the House of the People.

Thirty-four bills that originated in Council of States are still pending, for example the **Delhi Rent Amendment Bill, 2013**. Two other bills are pending in the Council of States, which were introduced between 1998 to 2004. Then chairperson of Council of States, Venkiah Naidu had said that bills pending in Council of States for last 5 years should be lapsed. This requires amendment in the Constitution.

Bill Pending in the House of the People

Any bill pending in the House of the People shall lapse due to dissolution of the House, irrespective of whether it originated in the House of the People or in the Council of States. Any Bill passed by the Council of States pending before the Lok Sabha is bound to lapse.

A total of 22 bills were lapsed due to dissolution of the 16th Lok Sabha, because bills were blocked by the Council of States.

Joint Sitting

If the President has notified the holding of joint sitting before dissolution of Lok Sabha, the bill does not lapse. Joint sitting shall be commenced over the bill after reconstitution of new Lok Sabha, after election.

Bill Pending for Presidential Assent

Any bill passed by the both Houses and pending before the President for assent shall not lapse. Bills which the President has returned to the Council of States for reconstruction shall not lapse.

CONTROL OVER FINANCE

'Budget' is a popular French term, which implies a leather bag, filled with papers. Our Constitution does not incorporate the term 'budget', although it is widely used in the rules of Lok Sabha. **Article 112** of the Constitution uses the phrase 'annual financial statement', which is popularly known as budget. Parliament controls the financial expenditure of the executive through budget.

Procedure

Procedure for passage of budget is not mentioned in the Constitution. It is written in the rules of Lok Sabha.

Presentation

President causes to be laid before both the Houses of Parliament an annual financial statement, or estimated receipts and expenditure of the Government of India. The budget is presented to the Lok Sabha on such day as President directs. No fixed date is prescribed for presentation of budget. Earlier budget would be presented in last week of February, and now it is presented in the first week of February. There is no question hour on the day of presentation of the General Budget.

Budget Speech

General Budget is presented to Lok Sabha by Minister of Finance. The budget speech of the minister consists of two parts. Part A, dealing with general economic survey of the country, and Part B, containing the taxation proposals for the ensuing financial year.

Sets of the budget papers for circulation to members are supplied to the secretariat of the both Houses of parliament by the Finance Minister.

Discussion

No discussion of the budget takes place on the day it is presented to the House. Normally discussion is taken up after a week after the presentation of general budget. The House is at liberty to discuss budget as a whole, or any question of principle in the budget. The Minister of Finance shall reply at the end of the Budget General Discussion, which includes launching of various schemes and taxation.

Departmental Committee

History was created in the Parliament of India with introduction of departmental committees. Since 1993, departmental committees have examined the demand for grants minutely.

Discussion on Demand for Grants

Demands for grants are not generally moved in the House by the minister concerned. The Speaker fixes day and timing for each ministry to move their demands for grants before the House. Budget must be passed within a definite time schedule. Whenever discussion is commenced over demands for grants, members of each political party are given time according to their strength in the parliament.

Cut Motion

Members of opposition party may bring about cut motion. It is only a form of initiating discussion on the demand. If opposition successfully passes the cut motion in the Lok Sabha, it means that the Council of Ministers lose the confidence in the Lok Sabha. Normally Council of Ministers enjoy this confidence. There are three variations of cut motion.

1. **Policy Cut:** Object of motion is to disapprove the policy of ministry. This one is the most serious cut. According to this, amount of the demand may be reduced to Rs 1. Suppose that a ministry is asking for 500 crores, and Parliament wants to give merely one rupee. Member can suggest an alternative policy, because expenditure is correlated with policies.
2. **Economy Cut:** It refers to that amount of demand which is to be reduced. Amount shall be determined by the Lok Sabha. Opposition can raise the matter of reduction in the demand.
3. **Token Cut:** This is where a motion refers to the amount of the demand being reduced by Rs 100. If the Ministry is asking for 500 crores, then Parliament will deduct Rs. 100 in the 500 crores. It reflects specific grievances, which is the responsibility of the government. Members can give notice one day before the demand is likely to be discussed.

Guillotine

Few demands on grants may not be discussed in parliament due to frequent disruptions or of scarcity of time. Thus demand for grants, which are put for voting without time are known as guillotine. It is a French term which implies speedy execution of death. Increasing guillotine is a sign of decline of parliament.

Charged Expenditure on Consolidated Fund of India

Ministry tables its demands for grants under two heads:

1. Charge expenditure on consolidated fund of India.
2. Other expenditure proposed to be made from consolidated fund of India.

Charge expenditure on consolidated fund of India is discussed in both houses. But it is not submitted to vote in Lok Sabha, consequently cut motion is not applied on charged expeditions consolidated fund of India. Article 112 includes the following expenditure as charge expenditure on consolidated fund of India.

1. Emoluments and allowance of the President and other expenditure related to his office.
2. The salaries and allowances of chairperson and deputy chairperson of Council of States and the speaker and deputy speaker of Lok Sabha.
3. Debt charges for which the government of India is liable.
4. Salaries, allowance and pension payable to or in respect of Judges of the Supreme Court.
5. Pension payable to or is respect of the Judge of any High Court.
6. Salaries allowance and pension to or in respect of CAG.
7. Any sum required to satisfy any Judgement, decree or award of any court or orbital tribunal.
8. Any other expenditure declared by this Constitution or by parliament to be so charged.

Appropriation Bill

After passage of demand for grants. Parliament allows the council of ministers to withdraw money from the consolidated fund of India. Demand for grants is presented by each ministry separately but an appropriation bill is passed by parliament collectively.

Finance Bill

Till now all stages of budget discussed are about expenditure, but the finance bill is also related to receipts of money. Proposal of taxation for next financial year is tabled in Lok Sabha in form of finance bill. With passage of finance bill, budget is deemed to be passed by Parliament.

Power of Council of States in Budget

Council of States occupies a lower position in the making of budget. Demand for grants can be discussed in the Council of States, but it is not entitled to vote. Cut motion cannot be brought about in the Council of States. Appropriation bill and finance bill are money bill under article 110. Council of States suggest the amendment in money bill. But acceptance or rejection depends upon House of people. Council of States is merely a delaying house as for as money bill is concerned. Council of States can block the money bill for 14 days, thereafter it deems to be passed by the both houses.

Residuary Part of Budget

Since budget is an estimated expenditure and estimated income, thus money allotted for particular head may not be sufficient, or new services may emerge in due course of time which is not mentioned in the budget. Later parliament approves this expenditure.

1. **Supplementary Grant:** Entire procedure of budget is not mentioned in the Constitution. But supplementary and other grants are mentioned in Article 115 and apply when the a. Amount allotted for

particular services in the current financial year is found to be insufficient.

Suppose that if a project on high speed trains got budgeting support of 1000 crore, meanwhile amount may not be sufficient. Then again Finance Minister comes up with supplementary demand for each and every ministry collectively. Supplementary demand may be presented twice or thrice in a financial year.

2. **Additional Grant:** Due to enactment of new service in current financial year. Which is not part of the budgetary estimate. Minister of finance came up with additional demand after the formation of two new union territories namely Jammu and Kashmir.
3. **Excess Grant:** Supplementary additional and excess grants are incorporated in Article 115. Money has been spent on any service during a financial year in excess of the amount granted for that service is not new but expenditure has actually been incurred. It is presented to the parliament after the end of the financial year, in which the expenses were made. While legislative sanction is obtained before incurring expenditure under budgetary and supplementary grants. The demand for excess grant is presented to the legislature after expenditure has been incurred. However, upon scrutiny of the accounts at the end of the financial year, the audit may find some expenditure has been in excess of the grant. The Constitution provides for their regulations by legislature. Although this excess expenditure is examined by the public account committee.
4. **Votes on Account:** The financial year is from 1 April to 31 March. Money allocated by the budget of the previous year gets lapses by 31 March. Vote on account is a permission to withdraw money from the consolidated fund of India. It is interim permission of parliament to spend the money. Earlier it became a custom to take vote on account for 2 months, because the budget was passed by the end of May. As of now practice of vote of account abolished, due to passage of budget by the 31st March.
5. **Vote of Credit:** Article 116 includes votes on account, vote of credit and exceptional grant. Vote of credit is a grant meeting an unexpected demand upon the resources of India. Character of service is indefinite, which cannot state in detail in budget. It is a kind of blank cheque given by parliament to council of Minister.
6. **Exceptional Grants:** Exceptional grants simply means it is not stated in the budget. It does not include in the current services of any financial year.

MONEY BILL

Article 110 contains the provisions of the money bill. Although the decision of the speaker is final, whether a bill is a money bill or not. Money bill is related to three funds described in the Constitution that are consolidated, contingency fund and public account. Taxation and borrowing naturally comes within the domain of the money bill. Let's see the definition of Article 110.

(a) **Taxation:** Imposition, abolition remission (reduction) alteration or regulation of any tax. Thus finance bill seeks for imposition of taxation or alternation. Therefore it comes within the domain of the money bill.

(b) **Borrowing:** Regulation of borrowing of money or giving any guarantee by the Government of India, or any amendment respect to any financial obligation of India.

(c) **Custody:** The custody of the consolidated fund of India or contingency fund of India. Payment of money into or the withdrawal of money from any such fund. Money received by taxation and borrowing becomes the part of a consolidated fund. No money can be withdrawn from consolidated funds except with permission of parliament. Contingency fund is under control of the president. Amount of the contingency fund is fixed by parliamentary act.

(d) **Appropriation:** Appropriation of money out of consolidated fund of India. Therefore, appropriation bill is considered as money bill.

(e) **Charged Expenditure:** Declaring of any expenditure to be expenditure changed or consolidated fund of India or increasing the amount of any such expenditure.

(f) **Receipt of Money:** Receipt of money on account of consolidated fund of India or the public account of India or the custody or issue of such money on the audit and accounts of union or of a state. Any matter related to above mentioned classes.

Procedure for Money Bill

Procedure for passage of the money bill is different from an ordinary bill. Money bill is presented in the Lok Sabha, with previous recommendation of the President. Council of States can recommend an amendment in a money bill, but acceptance of amendment is the privilege of the House of people. No provision of joint sitting is permitted in the money bill. President shall not send the money bill for reconsideration of the parliament.

Nevertheless, the President shall either give assent or withhold the assent, on money bill.

FINANCIAL BILL (I)

Article 117 incorporates the financial bill.

Financial bill includes one element of a money bill described in Article 110; in addition to that it also incorporates administrative dimensions. Financial bill thus combines the elements of money bill and a partly ordinary bill. Financial bills may include taxation plus administrative subjects.

Procedure

It can only be tabled in House of People. Financial bill shall be presented in House of People with previous consent of the President. Barring these two points, other procedures resemble those that apply to an ordinary bill. The Council of States may introduce amendments for the bill. If needed, a joint sitting of both Houses is permitted.

FINANCIAL BILL (II)

This category of financial bill does not include any element of money bill described in Article 110 from the Consolidated Fund of India; it is worth noting that it deals with expenditure, not appropriation, from the Consolidated Fund of India. Article 110 contains appropriation from the consolidated fund of India.

Procedure

The second category of financial bill contains only one procedure of financial bill. President shall recommend the consideration of the bill. This recommendation is not mandatory; the rest of the procedures mirror those of ordinary bills. It can be introduced in either House. Council of States has equal authority to bring about amendment in the bill. Thus joint sitting is permissible.

ANTI-DEFECTION ACT

Defection is a major problem of parliamentary democracy in India. Instability occurs frequently due to defection and it shakes the faith of people in democracy. Defection applies to both MPs and MLAs. Defection is popularly known as Aya Ram, Gaya Ram, due to defection of a particular MLA from Haryana on multiple occasions.

Constitutional Provisions

The Tenth Schedule was added to the Constitution through the **52nd Constitutional Amendment** by the Rajiv Gandhi government. It creates a new ground for disqualification of Member of Parliament under Article 102 and disqualification of MLA under Article 191. Although popularly known as an Act, in reality it is not Act, instead a constitutional provision.

Meaning of Defection

1. **Elected Member:** MP or MLA has voluntarily given up his membership of a political party. Voluntarily giving up refers to resignation from the party, and leads to disqualification of members from the party.
2. **Independent Member:** A member of the House abstains from voting, or votes against the direction of the party. If the party has not accepted action of member within 15 days, he/she is disqualified from the house. A person not belonging to a political party, elected as an independent candidate shall be disqualified, if he/she joins any political party.
3. **Nominated Member:** Nominated member is disqualified, if the person joins any political party after expiry of 6 months. Thus anti-defection is applied for both elected and non-elected members of political parties and independent candidates too.

Merger

Split is recognised as defection, split refers to some members of a party who are willing to leave the party. Merger is not considered as defection, but 2/3 elected members of such party agree for merger. In smaller states, where the number of political parties is less, merger becomes frequent. Merger allows a kind of wholesale defection said by critics. Merger can form a new party too.

Exception

Anti-defection act is not applicable to the Speaker, Deputy Speaker of the House of the People or to Chairperson or Deputy Chairperson of Council of States. This is also true for the Speaker and deputy speaker of any legislative assembly of state.

Speaker can voluntarily resign from his/her party. He/she is free to join any other political party after ceasing the office of speaker.

AUTHORITY FOR ADJUDICATION OF DISQUALIFICATION

Speaker or chairperson is given the authority to pronounce the decision whether any member of house is subject to disqualification. Moreover no court shall have any jurisdiction in respect of or any matter connected the disqualification of a member. Speaker is considered as impartial and neutral while running the house, but role and decision of speaker is highly disputed.

Judicial Intervention

Constitution says that decision of speaker is final, which cannot be challenged in any Court of law. Further, Article 122 prescribe that validity of any proceeding in the parliament shall not be called in question on ground to any alleged irregularity of procedure. No member or office of parliament is liable before Court for any conduct of business or maintaining order in parliament. But now office of speaker is subject to judicial review. Decision of speaker may not be final said Supreme Court in **Kihoto Hollohan case (1993)**.

Judgment of speaker in connection of with disqualification does not come within the domain of procedure of house. Disqualifying the members is a quasi-Judicial act, which is subject to judicial review. It is true that speaker shall determine the procedure but procedure should not be invalid. Disqualification of member is not a procedural issue. There is different between irregular procedure and illegal procedure.

Changing the time of question hour in parliament is an example of irregular procedure. Running the house in absence of quorum is illegal procedure.

Functioning of Parliament

The primary objective of anti-defection Act is to maintain stability in the parliamentary forum of government. On the contrary, anti-defection laws undermine the freedom of speech of MP/MLA in the house, which is protected in Articles 105 and 194. Anti-defection Act is doing more harm than advantage for the functioning of parliamentary form of government. Voting against the instructions of party means losing the membership of party, which means losing the membership of house. Therefore level and quality of discussion and debate declined automatically. Anti-defection Act is constitutional according to the Supreme Court in Kuldeep Nayyar Case (2006).

PARLIAMENTARY COMMITTEE

1. **Meaning:** Parliamentary committee are comprised of members of parliament, elected or nominated. Committees are microcosm of parliament, which ensure the representation of members from each and every political party in house according to their strength in house. A parliamentary committee is appointed by speaker. It functions under the direction of speaker/chairperson of house. Present the report to speaker, committees receives secretariat assistance by the parliament. Decision of speaker is final, whether any committee is qualified to be a parliamentary committee.
2. **Utility:** Parliament transacts a great deal of its business through committees. Committees are permanent; however parliament sits in three sessions. Thus parliament always faces a shortage of time. Parliament is divided on party lines, committee work as a unit. Communities' functions behind the camera, division on party lines becomes invisible. Committees provide a hand of expertise to parliament. Rules of prorogation are not applied for committees. Parliamentary committees can summon anybody for security and the investigation function of parliamentary committees is the same like the function of parliament. Committees unified the members of Council of States and House of People.
3. **Sitting and Quorum:** Sittings of parliamentary committees are held in private. No outsiders or strangers are allowed to be present in the sitting of committees. Meetings of parliamentary committees are not held outside of parliament. Although informal meeting is permitted during study tour, quorum for Parliamentary Committee is 1/3 members of the committee. Committee is capable of summoning any person before the sitting committee.
4. **Ministers and Committees:** Parliamentary committees are small prototypes of parliament. According to the principle of division of power, minister belongs to the executive. Thus minister should not become member of parliamentary committees. If a member of a committee on petition on public account, estimate, public undertakings, or subordinate legislation, Government assurance or welfare of SC/ST, empowerment of women, departmentally related committees is appointed as minister, ceases to be a member of committee. But minister may become part of other committees. Above mentioned communities play significant role in controlling the Council of Ministers.
5. **Terms of Office:**
   (i) **Not Exceeding One Year:** A parliamentary committees nominated by speaker, hold office for a period not exceeding one year. This includes committee on private members bills, committee on papers laid on table, committee on government

assurances, committee on subordinate legislation, committee on empowerment of women, committee on absence of members from sitting of house, committee on welfare of SC/ST, library committee and House committee. It is worth noting these are standing (permanent) committees, which work throughout the year but members of committee change after one year. Some argue that the term and tenure of committees. Term and tenure of committees should be increased.

(ii) **Till Restructuring :** The business advisory committee, Rules Committee on petitions, committee of privilege do not exist for one year. Committees are nominated by speaker.

(iii) **Elected Not Exceeding One year:** Members of the committee on Public accounts, committee on Estimate, committee on public undertaking, committee on welfare of SC/ST are elected by the House. Terms should not exceed one year. Elections for committee shall be held according to proportionate representation with single transferable votes. Normally members of parliamentary committee are elected in the month of April and joint committee of office of profit is also elected by the house. Term of office of profit committee varies according to tenure of House of People.

(iv) **Ad hoc Committee:** Standing committees are permanent committees although members of committee may retire after one year. Whenever a bill is tabled in parliament, the Houses can constitute a committee for consideration over bill. Term of these committees are not fixed. They are ad hoc.. Railway convention committee is only ad hoc committee which is set up from time to time to evaluate the progress of dividend for railway. Otherwise ad hoc committees.

DEPARTMENTALLY RELATED STANDING COMMITTEE

1. **Evolution:** Council of Ministers should be accountable towards parliament. Parliamentary committees are brain of parliament which keeps tight control over functioning of executive. In 1989 only three ministers' demand for grants were discussed and demands in respect as many as 34 ministries were guillotined. For strengthening administrative and financial accountability, rules committee proposed to set up three subject committees in 1989 during 8th Lok Sabha. Finally, departmentally related standing committees were set up on 31 March, 1993. Thus there subject committees ceased to exist. A total of 17 departmentally related standing committees (DRSC) were set up in 1993. Moreover in 2004 the number of DRSC was increased from 17 to 24. Among 24 DRSC, 18 committees are subject to control of Lok Sabha and 8 are under control of Council of States.
2. **Composition:** From 2004 onwards membership in DRSC was reduced from 45 to 31 memebrs. 21 members are drawn from Lok Sabha and 10 members are taken from Council of States. Chairperson and speaker appoint the chairperson of committee. A minister cannot be nominated as a member of DRSC.
3. **Term:** Term of each DRSC is fixed one year from the date of its inception.
4. **Functions:** The function of each of the standing committee are:

(a) To consider the demand for grants of each minister and table a report be in parliament, although the report of DRSC is persuasive in nature. It does not censure the government. Thus DRSC strengthened financial accountability and reduced the problem of guillotine.
(b) To examine such bills related to concerned ministers as are referred to committee by chairperson or speaker. Thus setting up ad hoc committees on each and every bill is not mandatory. Because the DRSC ensures a permanent (standing) committee to examine the bill.
(c) Every ministry prepares an annual report, which is tabled in the house. Annual report describes the functioning of the ministry. DRSC considers the annual report of the ministries and makes a report for parliament.
(d) To consider long-term policy documents, although they do not consider the matters of day to day administration of ministries.

Role of Parliamentary Committee

(a) **Financial Accountability:** Council of Ministers should be accountable towards parliament; this is the basic feature of parliamentary form of government. Financial accountability is the most important, which is impossible without a public account committee, estimate committee and committee on public undertaking.
   1. **Public Account Committee:** It comprises 22 members, 15 are drawn from Lok Sabha and 7 are taken from Council of Statess. PAC is chaired by a member of the opposition party. PAC receives assistance from CAG. It checks unwise methods of expenditure and financial irregularity. It also examines the reason behind excess expenditure, money shown in account legally granted by parliament to the ministry. Expenditure items approved by parliament cannot be spent on other items. Committee never questions the policy made by the government.
   2. **Estimate Committee:** Estimate committee is composed of members of the Lok Sabha. The fundamental objective of examination by the committee are economy and efficiency in administration. It also ensures that money is laid out within the limits of policy implied in the estimate. Although the committee never comments on policies, it recommends whether a particular policy is not producing the desired result. Committee is entitled to suggest any alternative policies for improving efficiency and economy in administration.
   3. **Committee on Public Undertaking:** It was formed in 1964. Composition of this committee is similar to the composition of the public account committee. 15 members are drawn from the House of People and 7 members come from the Council of States. Committee examines the reports and account of select PSUs. It also scrutinises reports of CAG regarding PSUs. Autonomy and efficiency of PSU are other issues looked into by committee, in fact it performs the role of public account committee and estimate related to functioning of PSUs.

(b) **Conduct of Business:** Smooth functioning of parliament becomes impossible without help of parliamentary committees. Business advisory committee allocates date and timing for discussion over the bill. It also allots timing for discussing motions and resolutions. Rules Committee recommends change in the procedure of conduct of business in parliament, for example change in the timing of question hour is the responsibility of the rules committee. Thus the ex-officio chairperson of both committees is speaker. Any new issue emerges before parliament which cannot be given to any existing committees. Then it is allotted to the General purpose committee. General purpose committee considers and advises the speaker on the matter concerning the affairs of the House.

(c) **Inquiry:** Committee on petitions examines petitions presented by members of house with consent of speaker. It addresses the grievances of members. Committee on petitions also compiles various suggestions and letters regarding bills presented in the parliament. Committee on privilege examines breach of privilege cases.

(d) **Scrutiny:** Whenever a minister assures parliament about some policies, action, while speaking on motions and resolutions ministers assures the house, whether these assurances were fulfilled is examined by committee on Government assurances. Committee on subordinate legislation scrutinise rules, regulations made by executive.

(e) **Facility of Members:** House committee ensure facility of accommodation for members of Parliament. Responsibility of Library committee is to provide books in library and sitting facilities for Members of Parliament.

(f) **Welfare Functions:** Parliament committee on the welfare of scheduled caste and schedules tribes was constituted in 1988. Committee is comprised of 30 members including 20 from Lok Sabha and 10 from Council of States. Term for member cannot exceed one year. Committee considers the report of national commission for scheduled caste and national commission for scheduled tribes. Committee also examines measures taken by Union Government and State Government for wellbeing of the community. It also keeps an eye on implementation of constitutional provisions for wellbeing of SC/ST communities. Committee on the empowerment of woman is constituted in 1997 during 8th Lok Sabha. Committee is comprised of 30 members (20 + 10). The term of committee does not exceed one year. It considers the report of National Commission for Women. Action of Union Government initiated for empowerment of woman is also looked into by committee.

Joint Parliamentary Committee (JPC)

According to rules of the House of People, various standing committees are Joint Committee like Public Account Committees and departmentally related standing committees. Some joint committees are also set up for examining bill tabled in the House.

But a new tradition began in the history of parliament in 1987, when a Joint Parliamentary Committee (JPC) was established a case of corruption. This can be seen as going against statutory procedures of Parliament.

Terms and conditions of JPC shall be determined by the House. Members of the Committee are also decided by the JPC. The first JPC was formed in 1987 for investigating the matter of corruption related to purchase of Bofors weapons.

Again JPC was reconstituted for inquiring about a scam in the share market in year 1992. Recently, demand for sitting up JPC was raised in the year 2018 for inquiring about allegation of corruption in the purchase of Rafale Fighter Jets from France. Speaker did not conceded the demand, thus JPC was not constituted.

Public Account Committee is a standing committee which looks into the matter of financial irregularity, so the. demand of JPC is questioned. But scope of inquiry of JPC may be broader than PAC. Some expenditure are beyond the scrutiny of PAC, but ambit of inquiry of JPC shall be determined by the parliament.

Exclusive Committees of Council of States

1. Business advisory
2. Committee on Petition
3. General purpose committee
4. Committee on subordinate legislation
5. Committee on Privileges
6. Committee on Government assurance
7. Rules Committee
8. Ethics Committee

Drawback of Parliamentary Committee

1. **Absenteeism:** Most of the members of parliamentary committee do not attend the meetings of parliamentary committee regularly; chairpersons of committee are also absent frequently. Venkiah Naidu suggested that if members of committees are absent from two consecutive meetings of the committee they should be replaced from committee.
2. **Lack of Fixed Numbers of Meetings:** No fixed time limitation is enacted for the committee to present its report. Number of meetings is not decided either. Thus it depends upon the committee of meetings to fix meetings and make them more effective.
3. **Lack of Expertise:** Committees are created for increasing expertise and effectiveness. But members are not interested in reading and research. Without knowledge, the committee becomes ineffective.
4. **Term is too short:** Term of most committes is limited to a year. Thus, by the time members acquire experience and expertise, the committee has to be dissolved. Therefore terms of the committees should be increased at least for 3 years or more.
5. **Advisory:** The recommendation of committee is not binding on the government, but it is merely advisory. Therefore nobody takes the report of committee seriously.
6. **Party Division:** Every political party is given due representation in the parliamentary committee. But committees are still affected by party loyalty and direction of the party. During 15th Lok Sabha, chairperson of PAC, Dr Murali Manohar Joshi was removed from the chair of the committee.

Parliamentary Forums

Parliamentary committee are result of rules made by these of people and Council of States. Thus committee have statutory sanctions. However forums are informal mechanism of consultation of members of parliament with ministers and experts. Forum does not have any statutory basis. Committee present their report before parliament but forum is a kind of training programme for MPs. Committee enjoys the privilege of parliament, but forum does not enjoy any such privilege.

1. **Meaning:** It is seminar organised for enhancement of the knowledge of Member of Parliament. A forum gives an opportunity to MPs to interact with subject experts and officers of ministry, in order to develop deeper insight on subjects. Members becomes more informed with help of experts, ministers and members of NGOs. This ensures better understanding of critical national issues present before the parliament.

RESOLUTION

Conduct of business in Parliament is carried out in form of resolution. Resolution is an opinion of the house. Resolution may be expressed in form of will or action of house. It is one of the procedural devices to raise discussion in Lok Sabha on a matter of general public interest.

(a) **Categories of Resolution:**

1. Resolution may an expression of opinion of the house. These are not binding on the Government.
2. Resolution may be in form of statute, for example tabling a bill in parliament is an example of resolution. Private members bill, or bill regarding the reorganisation of J&K is a resolution.
3. Parliament can control its own proceeding through resolution.

(b) **Types of Resolution:**

There are three types of resolutions:

1. **Private Member Resolution:** Private members bill is an example of private members resolution.
2. **Government Resolution:** Resolution approving international treaty, convention or agreement where union government is a part. Resolution regarding the approval of certain policies of the government like National Rural Health Mission is approved by parliament. Recommendation of certain committees also comes within the ambit of resolution.
3. **Resolution Under the Constitution:** Under article 61, resolution is required to (impeach) president from his/her office. Removal of chairperson and deputy chairperson of the Council of States needs to be moved in the form of a resolution. Speaker and deputy speaker are also removed from their office through resolution. The term resolution is mentioned in the Constitution repeatedly. Council of States passes a resolution for enacting any law by parliament in state list under Article 249. Similarly the Council of States passes a resolution for creation of an all India service under article 312. Approval of proclamation of emergency under article 356 is approved by parliament in form of resolution.

To conclude, resolution is required to make an act, pass constitutional amendment in parliament, but at the same time impact of resolution may be not statutory or constitutional. It may be in the form of expressing the will of the people too.

MOTION

Motion refers to proposal submitted to the House for knowing its decision. For example, motion is required for choosing the Speaker of House. Member's initiation of any action is motion.

A. **Types of Motion:**

According to rules of the House, motion can be categories in three varieties:

1. Substantive Motion
2. Substitute Motion
3. Subsidiary Motion

B. **Substantive Motion**

It is an independent and self-continued motion, capable of expressing a decision of House. Substantive motion must be put to vote of the house. Substantive motion is needed for impeachment of president removal of Judges of Supreme Court and High Court.

C. **Comparison of Motion and Resolution:**

It is pertinent to note that every self contained or substantive motion is resolution. Any decision of parliament begins in form of motion and concludes in form of resolution. A motion is requisite to remove judge from his/her office, when judge is removed by the special majority of House it becomes resolution. Motion is the first stage of removal of judge and resolution is the final on last stage of removal of judge. Therefore difference between motion and resolution is of procedure than of substance. However, one must note that every resolution begins as motion but each motion may not be concluded in resolution due to rejection by the vote of the House.

D. **Subsidiary Motion:**
Motion which depends upon other motion or relates to other motion is considered as subsidiary motion. When members of house move a motion that the bill be taken into consideration, for example.

Bill should be referred to the Select or Joint Committee, and comes within the domain of subsidiary motion. Motion for amendment in a bill is an example of subsidiary or secondary motion.

E. **Substitute Motion:**
Subsidiary motion or substitute motion are different from substantive motion. Substitute refers to replacement of original motion. However, subsidiaries come in the form of support of original motion. It is a related policy statement or situation.

Kinds of Motion

President is part of the Parliament but not a member of parliament under Article 87 President addresses both house assembly together. It is worth noting that the two Houses assembled together is not a joint sitting of parliament.

Assembling together is not considered as sitting of parliament since it is not presided by the Speaker. Both houses assemble together after the commencement of the first session after every general election to the House of people. First session of each year is also addressed by the President.

(a) **Motion of Thanks:** Few days after the president's address, a motion is proposed by a member and seconded by another member. Members of every political party take part in discussion. Subsequently voting takes place. PM replies the debate before voting. If the council of ministers lose in voting, then it will be assumed that CoM has lost confidence in the house. But the government does not fall automatically due to this. Government is given a chance to prove confidence in the house. Voting in Council of States does not impact the prospects of the government.

(b) **Adjournment Motion Matter of Urgent Public Importance:** Speaker prepares a list of business of each for transacting the function of house. Adjournment implies disruption or interruption of normal routine business of parliament.

Such a motion is often aimed at criticising the government and pointing out instances where it has failed in performing its duties. It is understood as a form of censure. The matter thus raised in the Lok Sabha:

1. Must be definite; matter should be specific and factual.
2. Must be urgent.
3. Must of public importance; it should not be related to individual grievances.

Adjournment motion is not normally allowed during budget discussion or during the discussion on the motion of thanks. Issues related to state government, where union government is not responsible cannot be raised through adjournment motion. Normally adjournment motion is taken up at 4.00 pm. It is not permitted in the Council of States because it censures the government.

(c) **Censure Motion:** Certain policies and action of the minister on council of ministers can be criticised by the House of the People Censure motion must set out the grounds or charge on which it is based.

(d) **No Confidence Motion:** Collective responsibility is the basic element of parliamentary form of government. Article 75(3) states the Council of Ministers shall be collectively responsible towards House of People. Rule 198 of Lok Sabha details the no-confidence motion (motions are governed by rules, and are not mentioned in the constitution).

A. **Conditions**

1. No less than 50 members of the House of the People should support the motion.
2. After receiving leave from the house, it must be taken up within 10 days.
3. No groundds are needed for bringing about motion.
4. Decision taken with simple majority, therefore we should take note of that council of minister requires confidence of house rather than majority of House.
5. No-confidence motion cannot be brought about twice in same session but no limitation is imposed on numbers of motion during term of Lok Sabha. A maximum number of six motions of no-confidence each was debated the 3rd and 4th Lok Sabha.

B. **Motion and Dissolution of House of People:**

Passage of no-confidence motion does not result in the dissolution of House of People. It only signifies the change of Council of Ministers. After passage of motion, all ministers are bound to resign immediately. No-confidence motion was passed against the V.P. Singh Government in 1990, thereafter Chandra Shekhar became the new PM. House of People remained intact.

C. **Political Goal:** First no-confidence motion was brought about against the Nehru government in 1963, although Congress commanded complete majority in the House of the People. But popularity of government was due to Indo-China War of 1962. Warning motion was introduced for influencing the will of the people. Again non-confidence motion granted in the House of people during 16th Lok Sabha. PM Narendra Modi's government enjoyed a comfortable majority and was unlikely to lose the vote. Thus primary purpose of motion was to influence the public opinion. Non-confidence motion consumes at least 2 or 3 days of House. A maximum of 15 no-confidence motion were encountered by the Indira Gandhi government.

D. **Confidence Motion:** Confidence motion is nowhere mentioned in the constitution, or in rules of House of People. It began due to emergence of minority government or coalition government. No-confidence motion is introduced by the opposition. But confidence motion is presented PM himself/herself, on instruction of the President. Then President Neelam Sanjeev Reddy asked PM Choudhary Charan Singh to prove confidence in the House in 1979. PM resigned rather than willing to face House of People. He was the first PM of India who never went entered the House. Similarly Narsimha Rao was asked to show confidence in the house although Congress had 244 members in the House of people, due to support of some other parties and absence of parties. Confidence is proved with simple majority. Thus government has less than 272 members in the house can prove confidence in the house. Council of States has nothing to do with these motions.

E. **Calling Attention on Matter of Urgent Public Importance:** Members of the House of the People give a notice to the Secretary General at 10.00 A.M. Members may call attention of concerned ministers. Thereafter minister give their response. Others members are also allowed to raise questions.

Calling attention motion is more frequently utilised than adjournment motion. Adjournment motion censures the government, but calling attention motion does not censure or criticize the government. Both kinds of motions raise matters of urgent public importance. Calling attention motion regarding misuse of social media and fake news, for example.

F. **Discussion on Matters of Urgent Public Importance for Short Duration:** Since adjournment motion amounts to criticism or censuring the government, Thus for discussing matters of urgent public importance, short duration discussion was introduced in 1953. There is no formal motion before the house, nor is there any voting. Members of the house can give a notice, and this has to be supported by the signature of at least two other members. It is utilised both in Council of States and House of People. Situation of law and order in Delhi was raised through short duration discussion. Time duration allotted for discussion is 2.30 hours. Concerned ministers reply to the debate last.

Notice for short duration discussion falls under rule 193 or 184. These are provisions of voting under rule 184 and voting is not permitted in rule 193. Thus the government avoids organising discussion under rule 184.

Short duration discussion is equally applicable in the Council of States and House of People.

G. **Questions:** Government becomes accountable through questions in parliament. Questions hour give an opportunity to know about administrative functioning of the Union Government.

(a) **Timing:** Question hour begins in the Lok Sabha between 11.00 am to 12.00 noon. Now the timing of question hour has changed in the Council of States. Question hour begins from 12.00 noon to 1.00 pm. in the Council of States.

(b) **Period for Notice:** 15 days advance notice is required for asking a question in parliament. Members give notice to the secretary-general and secretary forwards questions to concerned ministers. Ministry again send the answer to secretary, who includes the questions in the list of business.

(c) **Number of Questions:** 20 oral or starred questions and 230 written (unstarred) question can be asked in the House of People. 15 oral or starred questions can be asked in the Council of States and 175 written or unstarred questions are permitted in a day. No members can have more than 5 question both for oral and written answers. In case secretary general receives more notices for oral question than the prescribed limit, a lottery is used to finalised the questions. The Speaker calls the name of members one by one, they ask the question from concerned ministry. List of questions for oral answer is printed on green paper and that for written on white paper.

(d) **Supplementary Questions:** Supplementary questions can be asked only on oral (starred questions). A member who asked the question is entitled to ask two supplementary questions. Speaker may allow other members to ask one supplementary question.

(e) **Short Notice Questions:** A question related to matters of urgent public importance may be asked by a member on shorter than 15 days notice. Provision of oral answers is the rule for short notice questions. Although it is an exceptional provision, only one question is allowed in a day for short notice questions. Speaker takes consent of the concerned minister, whether the minister is capable of replying to the answer in a short time.

(f) **Division of Ministry:** Ministries of Government of India have been divided into 5 groups. These groups have been allotted Mondays, Tuesday and Wednesday, Thursday and Friday respectively. The grouping is done in such a way that each minister has one day fixed in the week for the answering questions in both Houses.

Half-An-Hour Discussion: It commences in the last 30 minutes of sitting and thus is known as half-an-hour discussion. Members may ask more clarification or information on starred questions and unstarred questions. Discussions are normally held there in three sittings in a week, namely Monday, Wednesday and Friday. The Speaker or Chairperson accepts the notice due to sufficient public importance granted to this discussion.

6

JUDICIARY

KEY CONCEPTS

Supreme Court; High Court; Judicial Review; Judicial Activism; Judicial Reform

The legislature, the executive and the judiciary are the three organs of government. Legislature makes laws; the executive is responsible for implementing the laws enacted by the legislature. Formulation of policies is also the task of the Executive. However, the judiciary is a dispute settlement mechanism. Peaceful resolution of disputes is an essential feature of democracy.

The judiciary is not associated with party politics. It is an *impartial, neutral institution*. Apart from impartiality of judiciary, it is an independent organisation of the government. Judiciary is not subordinate to the legislature or executive. The judiciary keeps in check the functioning of the legislature and the executive. Judiciary protects the principle of rule of law. The function of any agency of government should not encroach upon the fundamental law of the land, that is the Constitution. The Supreme Court is the guardian of the Constitution too.

Indian Constitution prescribes **three tiers of the judiciary:**

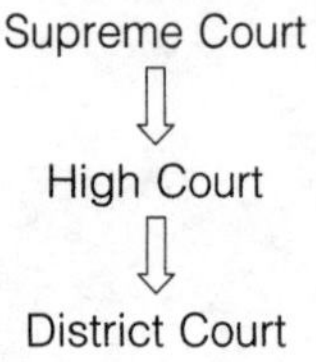

Provision of administrative tribunals was also incorporated in the Constitution by the **42nd Constitutional Amendment**. Now the tribunal has become a mandatory feature of Indian democracy. In the present age of technological advancement, numerous types of alternative dispute settlement mechanisms are put into place.

THE SUPREME COURT

A. **Constitution:** There shall be a Supreme Court of India, consisting of a Chief Justice of India (CJI) and not more than seven other Judges, under **Article 124**. The Constitution of India mentions 8 judges including CJI. But Article 124 authorises parliament to increase the number of Judges in the Supreme Court. Parliament enacted the **Supreme Court (Number of Judges) Act, 1956** to raise the number of Judges in the Supreme Court. According to this Act, the number of Judges can be increased up to 10 Judges excluding Chief Justice of India.

B. **Increase in Number of Judges does not need Constitutional Amendment:** After 70 years of the republic of India, Constitution still mentions number of

Judges as 7 excluding CJI. For the increase in the number of Judges, the Constitution need not to be amended. Amendment in parliamentary act is required. Parliament brought about amendment in 1960, and the number of Judges has gone up to 13, in 1977 again the number was raised up to 17. Number of Judges went up to 26 in 1988.

Parliamentary Act 1956 was amended in 2009; consequently the number of Judges became 31. Latest amendment in the Parliamentary Act was incorporated in 2019; hence the present strength of Judges of the Supreme Court stands at 34.

The number of judges is increased with the growing workload of the Supreme Court. Presently about 58,000 cases are pending before the Supreme Court.

Seat of Supreme Court

The Supreme Court shall have its seat in Delhi, according to **Article 130**. The Supreme Court may sit in other places. Thus, benches of the Supreme Court can be set up at one place in any part of India. More than one bench can also be created, provided that the Chief Justice of India goes ahead with the approval of the President.

Law Commission has recommended for setting up other benches of the Supreme Court in other parts of India. But the Chief Justice of India has not agreed with the proposal. Multiple benches are helpful for better access to justice but CJI shall maintain administrative control over the benches.

APPOINTMENT OF JUDGES

The President shall appoint a judge to the Supreme Court by warrant, under her/his hand and seal. The President shall appoint Judges on the recommendation of the National Judicial Appointments Commission (NJAC). NJAC was created by the **99th Constitutional Amendment** in 2014 by the NDA government. In practice, however, are not appointed by NJAC but by collegiums till today. Collegiums are not mentioned in the Constitution. The system evolved due to a conflict between the executive and judiciary on the issue of appointment.

Original Scheme

As per the original Constitution, before the 99th Amendment, **Article 124(2)** stated that, while appointing a Judge of the Supreme Court, President shall consult the Judges of Supreme Court and High Court as he deems fit. For appointment of Judges other than CJI, consultation with CJI is necessary. Seniormost judge of the Supreme Court would become the Chief Justice India, according to evolved convention.

Appointment of Judges became disputed in 1973, which involved government intervention. A. N. Ray, who occupied the fourth position in the seniority list of Judges of Supreme Court, was appointed as CJI. This appointment superseded the seniormost judges of Court, namely Justice Jaishanker Manilal Shelat, Justice A. N. Grover, K. S. Hegde. This invited widespread protests by bar associations and legal groups across the country. There was conjecture that the seniormost Judges were penalised by the Government, because they had supported the principle of basic structure in **Kesavananda Bharati case (1973).** Although the government defended this appointment on the grounds of merit; it is worth noting that A. N. Ray always supported the stand of the government in various cases in the Supreme Court, including Kesavananda Bharati.

Primacy of President

Consultation of President with Judges in mandatory for appointment of Judges to the Supreme Court. The opinion of the President ultimately prevails in case of conflict between President and Judges of Supreme Court in the appointment. This is the verdict of the Supreme

Court in **S. P. Gupta case (1982)**, which is popularly known as the **First Judges case**.

Importance to Judges in Collegiums

Supreme Court overruled the First Judges case (1982) in ***Advocates on Record Association v. Union of India (*1993**), popularly known as the **Second Judges case**. Now the Supreme Court said that appointment is related to independence of judiciary. This is a landmark case in the constitutional history of India, due to evolution of collegium. Collegiums comprise the seniormost judges of the Supreme Court including CJI. India became the first democratic nation where judges were appointed by judges themselves. Collegiums are an innovation of the Supreme Court in the Second Judges case. Although CJI became most powerful in collegiums, in practice consultation does not mean consultation with CJI only.

Reform in Collegium, 1999

Supreme Court expanded the collegium, which comprised the Chief Justice of India and four other seniormost Judges of Supreme Court. Supreme Court reformed the collegium in 1999 with the **Third Judges case**. Primary of judiciary remained intact in the appointment of Judges. Now the President acts as a 'post office' in the appointment of Judges. Decisions of the collegium must be unanimous. If two judges have adverse opinions about any appointment, recommendation shall not be sent to the President. But the opinion of CJI is mandatory in any decision of collegiums.

Drawback of Collegiums

All the appointments in the Supreme Court are done by collegiums till today. But judiciary itself pronounced that *separation of power is the basic structure of the Constitution*. Executive is given the task to appoint, according to the principle of separation of power. Judges appointed by Judges themselves goes against the basic norms of separation of power. Appointment of Judges by Judges amounts to encroachment of power of the executive by judiciary. This may be called judicial overreach.

Collegium works under the veil of secrecy. No transparency exists in the entire process of appointment. There is a lack of any objective parameter for appointment of judges, like the number of qualitative decisions delivered by a judge. Research paper or attendance of seminars is an example of objective criteria. Collegium never explains why some names are left out for appointment and others considered.

Executive is responsible towards the people. Judiciary on the other hand is a non-elected body, which cannot override the powers of the executive. Appointment process by collegiums may arguably be termed a *tyranny of the unelected*. Appointment is an administrative job, which needs a full secretariat and intelligence report too.

Judiciary cannot handle this complicated process easily. Regional representation and social equation is also kept in mind by the executive while conducting appointments. But the judiciary often neglects these factors.

NATIONAL JUDICIAL APPOINTMENTS COMMISSION (NJAC)

Appointment by collegium began in 1993. The executive was never satisfied with this procedure. The general elections in 2014 resulted in a historic win for the BJP, which got the majority on its own. A clear majority emerged for the first time since the 1984 election of the 8th Lok Sabha, when Congress had got landslide victory and 426 seats in the Lok Sabha. After a span of almost 30 years, a party had succeeded in getting a majority in Lok Sabha.

The government was determined to change the collegium process of appointment. The NJAC is also looking for an appointment process that is socially inclusive. Thus, the government brought about the **99th Amendment**, and inserted **Articles 124(A), 124(B) and 124(C)** in the Constitution.

Structure of NJAC:

A. **Ex-officio**

NJAC comprises of:

1. Chairperson—CJI (Ex-officio)
2. Two senior judges of the Supreme Court next to CJI, as members (ex-officio).
3. The Union Minister in charge of Law and Justice is also a member (ex-officio).

B. **Eminent Members:**

NJAC includes two eminent persons, nominated by a committee. Committee **comprises of:**

1. Prime Minister
2. Chief Justice of India
3. Leader of Opposition in the House of the People or leader of the single largest opposition party in the House of the People.

Tenure of nominated person shall be for a period of three years. They are not eligible for re-nomination. Among two persons, one of the eminent persons should belong to:

1. Scheduled Caste
2. Scheduled Tribe
3. Other Backward Classes
4. Minorities
5. Women

Above-mentioned structure displays a broad-based appointment. However, collegiums include only judges. Social inclusion is not a feature of Collegiums. NJAC fulfils representation of each section of community, specially marginalised sections of community under Article 124(A).

Function of NJAC

Commission shall recommend to President for **appointment of:**

1. Chief Justice of India
2. Judges of Supreme Court
3. Chief Justice of High Court
4. Other Judges of High Court
5. Recommend transfer of Chief Justice and other Judges of High Courts from one High Court to another High Court.
6. Ensure that the person recommended is of ability and integrity under **Article 124(B).**

NJAC looks for integrated method of appointment. NJAC shall work for the appointment of both Supreme Court as well as High Court.

Power of Parliament to Make Laws

Function of NJAC does not include the procedure of appointment of Judges. Seniority or merit may be a parameter, which is not outlined in the NJAC. Parliament is empowered to enact a law for delineating procedure of appointment. Regulating the procedure for the discharge of its function, parliament shall make law. Constitution does not clearly spell out the quorum of decision making. Decision of NJAC shall be based on majority or by consensus. It is left out for parliament to determine under Article 124(C).

NJAC *Ultra Vires*

Supreme Court said that NJAC violates the principles of basic structure. Judicial independence is the basic structure of the Constitution. Court is of the view that appointment of Judges is not merely an administrative issue, but it is related to judicial independence. In the past too, appointment and transfer of judges has been utilised against independence of judiciary.

Composition of NJAC is also objectionable, including Minister of Law and Justice. Presence of political member undermines independence of judiciary to be a full-fledged watchdog. Appointment of judges or lawyers appears an example of *quid pro quo*, or a favour or advantage granted in return for something. It simply means that Ministry of Law appoints judges, thereafter Law Minister practises under same judges.

No special qualification is attached with two eminent persons. Although they should have been associated with law and justice. Eventually Parliament shall lay down the procedure for appointment of judges. Thus, Parliament can count seniority or merit, as a parameter for appointment of judges. This will undermine the judicial independence, and pave the way for political interference and pave the way for political interference in judicial appointment. Practically no appointment is done by NJAC; consequently, judges are still appointed by collegiums.

Reform in Collegiums

The Supreme Court declared that appointment through NJAC stands null and void. At the same time, the Supreme Court admitted that appointment by collegiums is not perfect since various anomalies exist in the collegium. The court agreed for reform in Collegiums in 2015. But dispute exists over the following issues:

(a) **National Security:** Collegiums sends its recommendation to the Ministry of Law and Justice. The Ministry receives the intelligence report about the person recommended by collegiums. The Ministry does not share the intelligence report with collegiums. The Executive (Ministry) is entitled to withhold the appointment of any person on the ground to adverse intelligence report. The judiciary agreed that the Ministry can block any recommendation in the name of adverse intelligence report. The judiciary demanded the sharing of intelligence reports with collegiums.

(b) **Merit/Seniority:** Government always supports the appointment on the basis of merit. But the judiciary has the opposite view, merit is a subjective notion. Judges who pronounced an adverse decision against the government, may not be considered meritorious. Members of Bar Council of India belonging to the opposition party shall get labelled as not being as meritorious by the government. Judiciary is in favour of seniority. For maintaining regional representation and social inclusion, seniority may not be the sole factor.

(c) **Bench/Bar:** More than 95 per cent of Judges Appointment in the Supreme Court are drawn from the Chief Justices of High Court or a judges of High Court. They are popularly known as members of benches (Judge). Executive has emphasised that a certain percentage of Bar (advocate) members should be fixed for appointment as Judges in Supreme Court. Members of bar are affiliated with political parties too.

(d) **Transparency:** Government seeks transparency in the functioning of collegiums. Written explanation is needed as to why and on what ground any Judge is chosen. Reason should be stated behind the dropping of a particular person. Although the judiciary said that the judiciary `is a sensitive organism of the government and that principle of transparency may work against the independence of judiciary. How collegiums can give written explanations about not picking up about a sitting Judge of High Court.

(e) **Screening Committee:** Screening Committee needs to be constituted for minute examination of names of persons, suitable for appointment. Committee should be composed of retired Judges. Thereafter committee shall forward the name of candidates to collegiums. Screening Committee shall function under the supervision of the Ministry of Law and Justice. Judiciary is not willing to accept the proposal because it is an attempt to sideline the judiciary in the appointment of Judges.

Deadlock is not resolved yet over the appointment of Judges. Former Law Minister Ravi Shankar Prasad said that the government will not act merely as a post office. Executive should have a say in the appointment of Judges. But independence of judiciary is inevitable for democracy, which cannot be compromised at any cost.

Qualification for Judge of Supreme Court

Person shall not be qualified for appointment of Judge unless he/she is (a) Citizen of India; (b) has been a member of Bench for at least 5 years as a Judge of High Court, or two or more such courts in succession. A Judge of the High Court is promoted to the Supreme Court. Currently 25 High Courts exist in India. Normally the Chief Justice of the High Court is elevated as Judge of the Supreme Court. Apart from constitutional eligibility, some other factors are kept in mind. Each High Court is given due representation. Representation of women, minorities is also given priority.

Member of Bar

According to Article 124(2), a practising advocate of the High Court can be appointed as judges of the Supreme Court, if he/she has been practicing for at least 10 years as an advocate of the High Court, or two or more such courts in succession.

Practising lawyer of Delhi High Court, Indu Malhotra was appointed as Judge of Supreme Court in 2018. Santosh Hegde was appointed as Judge of the Supreme Court from the Bar. R. F. Nariman was also appointed as Judge of the Supreme Court directly from the Bar in 2014. Drawing members from the Bar raises the quality of judiciary. But only a handful of lawyers were enthusiastic about the office of Judge. It is surprising, but true, that successful lawyers may not want to become judges.

Place for Professor

A person can become a Judge, if the person is a distinguished jurist in the opinion of the President. The term 'distinguished Jurist' is wider, which includes both Judges as well as lawyers. Renowned scholars of university may be included in the category of distinguished Jurist. Till today teachers of the university have not been appointed as judges.

The Chief Justice of India

The Constitution does not provide any separate qualification for appointment of Chief Justice of India. The Constitution incorporates the qualification of Judges. But seniormost Judges are appointed as Chief Justice, according to convention.

The Indira Gandhi government neglected this convention twice. At first, as we discussed, A. N. Roy was appointed as Chief Justice when he occupied fourth place in seniority. Again Justice Mohammad Hidayatullah was appointed as Chief Justice in 1977 though Justice H. R. Khanna was the seniormost Judge of the Supreme Court at the time. Justice H. R. Khanna was penalised for his dissenting Judgement in ***ADM Jabalpur v. Shivkant Shukla case*** **(1976)**, more famously known as ***Habeas corpus*** **case**. Principle of seniority was again restored strongly by the collegiums. It is worth noting that the seniority of a Judge is decided according to the date of appointment in the Supreme Court. Seniority list of every High Court is counted separately. Appointment date of a Judge in the High Court is not considered a factor behind counting of seniority in the Supreme Court. Person may join the High Court earlier, but reach the Supreme Court later. For instance, Justice Jasti Chelameswar was appointed Judge of High Court before the appointment of Justice Dipak Misra, Justice T. S. Thakur. But Justice Jasti Chelameswar was appointed as Judge in the Supreme Court after the appointment of Justice Misra and Thakur, in Supreme Court.

Administrative Power

The term 'Chief' denotes administrative capacity. Value of the Judgement of Chief occupies the same weight like other Judges.

Chief Justice is responsible for **following administrative functions:**

1. CJI is master of roster; he is entitled to constitute benches of the Supreme Court. CJI nominates the Judges in benches.
2. Role of CJI is primary in the functioning of collegiums too. Opinion of CJI must be counted before recommendation for any appointment.
3. CJI also appoints various employees in the Supreme Court for running the registry of SC.
4. CJI applies various factors while constituting the benches. Seniority may not be the sole factor. Judges are specialised in different fields like civil matters, criminal cases or issues related to service. Allocation of Benches is decided on the basis of expertise too.
5. Role of CJI is also to head in matters of administrative reform, like the question of Implementation of E-government in the court.

Tenure of CJI

The Constitution provides that Judges of the Supreme Court shall hold office, until he attains the age of 65 years. Retirement age is prescribed in the Constitution, but age of entry is not mentioned in the Constitution. Due to convention of seniority in the appointment of Chief Justice, Justice G. B. Patnaik held the office for only 41 days. Justice S. Rajendra Babu became Chief only for 30 days. Chief Justice is administrative head of the Supreme Court, thus there are arguments for a fixed tenure of CJI. At least two years should be given to the Chief Justice to carry out some important administrative reforms. The convention of seniority is an obstacle in that path. Raising the retirement age to 70 years can also enhance the tenure of Chief Justice.

Removal of Judges

Article 124(4) empowers the Parliament to remove Judges. Parliament requires a special majority to remove Judges. Special incorporates **two features:**

1. Majority of total membership of that house, which implies a majority of 543 members of Lok Sabha and 245 members of Council of States respectively.
2. In addition to that, each House of Parliament needs not less than two-thirds of the members of the House present and voting there, 2/3rd of 543 (strength of Lok Sabha) and 245 are needed.

Resolutions for removal of Judges should be passed in each House separately in the same session of parliament. The President shall remove the Judge by an order, after resolution has passed in the Parliament.

Article 124(4) also mentions the ground of **removal of Judges:**

1. Proven misbehaviour, thus merely an allegation is not sufficient to remove the Judge. Misbehaviour is a broader term, which includes charge of corruption, sexual harassment, and so on.
2. Incapacity: it is typically physical in nature, due to illness.

Article124(4) mentions a brief provision for removal of Judges. Thus, the same Article empowers parliament to make a law for investigation and proof of the misbehaviour or incapacity. Parliament is entitled to regulate the procedure for removal by enacting law. Parliament enacted **Judges (Inquiry Act) 1968**, which provides detailed procedure for removal of Judges

Judges (Inquiry) Act 1968

A. **Resolution in House:** Resolution for removal of Judge can be introduced in either House of Parliament. Resolutions tabled in Lok Sabha require 100 members of Lok Sabha. If the resolution is tabled in (Rajya Sabha), signature of 50 members are essential. Resolution can be presented either before the Speaker, or Chairperson of the Rajya Sabh, but it should be addressed to the President. Speaker or Chairperson is entitled to reject the resolution. A resolution was presented to Chairperson of Rajya Sabha, Venkaiah Naidu in 2018. Venkaiah Naidu rejected the resolution outright. In case of acceptance of resolution, the Speaker or Chairperson shall constitute the committee. Committee is comprised of the **following members:**

B. **Constitution of Committee:** (1) CJI or other Judges of the Supreme Court, (2) Chief Justice of any High Court, (3) Distinguished Jurist.

The committee shall inquire about the allegation or charges against the Judge. If charges are inappropriate, the resolution automatically lapses. But in case charges are found to be correct, then further proceeding will continue. Committee will submit its report within 3 months. The Quorum of the committee consists of two members.

After approval of committee, resolution shall be discussed and voted on in each House of Parliament. Judges are given an opportunity to defend himself/herself on the floor of the House. Judge can send a lawyer before the House to defend him. Acceptance of defence of the Judge is the discretion of the parliament.

Passage of Resolution

Resolution should be passed by each House of Parliament separately, which **includes two conditions:**

1. Majority of strength of House
2. And 2/3 majority of present and voting.

Removal of Justice Ramaswamy, was the first instance of removal of a Judge of the Supreme Court in 1993. Resolution was introduced in Lok Sabha but it could not be passed by the House, due to lack of majority. Congress boycotted voting during resolution.

Committee instituted by the Chairperson found Soumitra Sen, Judge of Kolkata High Court, guilty in 2011. P. D. Dinakaran, former Judge of Karnataka high court resigned after the committee found him guilty. Till today Parliament has not passed a resolution of removal of the Judge.

Oath of Judge

The President shall administer oaths and affirmation to Judges of the Supreme Court. The President can appoint anyone for administering the oath. Format of oath is described in the Third Schedule of the Constitution. The Judge takes an oath to bear true faith and allegiance to the Constitution of India as established by law, and uphold the sovereignty and integrity of India.

> ... I will duly and faithfully and to the best of my ability, knowledge and judgment perform the duties of my office without fear or favour, affection or ill will and that I will uphold the Constitution and the laws.

Independence of the Judicary

The Supreme Court is the guardian of the Constitution. It preserves and protects the rule of law. Judiciary examines the validity of law made by parliament. The judiciary also scrutinises the function of the executive. Thus, judiciary must be independent from parliament or the executive. Judiciary is not subordinate to parliament or executive.

Removal

Judges of the Supreme Court do not hold their office, during the pleasure of the President. Parliament is entitled to remove the Judges from his office. Judges also enjoy fixed tenure of 65 years.

Bar of Practice

Article 124(7) stipulates that a retired Judge shall not plead or act in any court or before any authority within the territory of India. But Chief

Justice Sathashivam was appointed as Governor of Kerala, immediately after retirement. Justice Ranjan Gogoi was offered the membership of the Rajya Sabha, just after his retirement. It implies that falling in line with the government results in an award. Independence of the judiciary can be influenced through the offer of post-retirement jobs. Normally Judges are appointed as Chairperson and members of the National Human Rights Commission too although it is a quasi-judicial appointment. Debatable issue is whether appointment should be prohibited entirely or a cooling period of say 2 years should be applied.

Salaries

The Chief Justice of the Supreme Court shall receive Rs 10,000 per month, as specified in the Second Schedule of the Constitution. Other Judges shall get Rs 9,000 per month, as prescribed in the Second Schedule of the Constitution. **Article 125** of the Constitution allows parliament to determine salaries of Judges from time to time. The parliament-enacted **Supreme Court Judges (Salaries and Condition of Service) 1958 Act** sees amendment from time to time with the latest amendment being brought about in 2018. The Chief Justice of India gets Rs 2,80,000 per month. However, other Judges of Supreme Court receive Rs 2,50,000 per month; salaries of Judges do not require constitutional amendment but parliamentary act is sufficient.

Charged Expenditure

Moreover, salaries of Judges shall not be varied to his disadvantage after his appointment, says **Article 125**. Salaries, allowances, and pension payable to respect of Judges of Supreme Court shall be charged on consolidated fund of India. Thus, the Parliament cannot propose cuts on salaries of Judges.

The administrative expenses of the Supreme Court, including all salaries, allowances and pensions payable to or in respect shall be charged and servants of the court shall be charged upon on the consolidated fund of India.

Restriction on the Discussion in Parliament

Under **Article 121** no discussion shall take place in the parliament with respect to the conduct of any Judge of the Supreme Court or of the High Court while discharging his duties. If a resolution is pending before Parliament for removal of a Judge, discussion may be over the conduct of the Judge. However, Parliament discussed the conduct of then Chief Justice Dipak Misra without any process of removal in 2018.

Supreme Court's control over officers

All officers and servants of the Supreme Court are appointed by Chief Justice of India. Conditions of services of officers and servants shall be prescribed by Chief Justice and other Judges. Although it is subjected to any law made by Parliament.

The Supreme Court is an independent organisation which keeps check on the functioning of the legislature and executive.

Types of Judges

Constitution describes about the **following types of Judges:**

(a) Acting Chief Justice
(b) Ad Hoc Judges
(c) Retired Judge

Acting Judge: If the Chief Justice is unable to perform his duty due to absence for a reason categorised as 'otherwise', it refers to illness, then the President may appoint a Judge of the Supreme Court for the time being as an acting Chief Justice.

Ad Hoc Judges: President appoints ad hoc judges due to lack of Quorum, in the Supreme Court. A Judge of the High Court who is qualified to be appointed as Judge of the Supreme Court shall be requested to attend sitting of the Supreme Court.

Time for attendance in the sitting of the Supreme Court shall be decided by the Chief Justice of India. The Chief Justice of the Supreme Court shall consult the Chief Justice of the High Court, before requesting a particular Judge to participate in sitting on the Supreme Court.

Ad hoc Judge shall enjoy jurisdiction, power and privilege of Judge of the Supreme Court, while discharging his duties.

It is important to note that an ad hoc Judge is not appointed. He only attends the sitting of the Supreme Court. Quorum is not defined in the Constitution or rules of the Supreme Court. But there is a lack of Judges in various benches set up by the Supreme Court. Now the strength of the Supreme Court is 34 including CJI, for the first time in a long time, the Supreme Court got its full strength in 2019. Thus ad hoc Judges have never been appointed to the Supreme Court so far.

Retired Judge: The NJAC with previous consent of the President, requests to sit as Judge of the Supreme Court; such a person is eligible to sit as Judge if he/she fulfils the **following conditions:**

1. Held the office of the Supreme Court
2. Has held the office of a Judge of the High Court;
3. Duly qualified for appointment as a Judge of the Supreme Court.

While acting as a Judge, the President may by order determine power and privilege of Judge. Consent of that person is essential before he sits as Judge of the Supreme Court. Retired Judge shall deem to be a Judge of that Court. Permitting the sitting of retired Judges may be beneficial for disposing of the pending cases before the Supreme Court. Till today ad hoc and retired Judges are not given an opportunity to act in the Supreme Court.

Contempt of Court

Article 129 says that the Supreme Court shall be a court of record. Which decision of the Supreme Court shall be considered as evidence for other courts existing in India? Decision of the Supreme Court is accepted as a model for other courts present in the territory of India.

Verdict of the Supreme Court is binding on other organs of the government. If anybody or any organisation refuses to enforce or execute the decision of the Supreme Court, the Court can punish that person for contempt of court, under Article-129. Contempt of court is not defined in the Constitution but the Parliament has enacted Contempt of Court Act 1971.

A. **Contempt according to Parliamentary Act:** Parliament Act defines **two types of contempt:**
   1. **Civil Contempt** means willful disobedience of any judgement, decree, order, writ of a court, willful breach of an undertaking given to a Court.
   2. **Criminal Contempt** means the publication (by words, spoken or written) of any matter or the doing of any Court which;
      (a) Scandalises, or tends to scandalise, or lowers, or tends to lower the authority of any Court
      (b) Interferes or tends to interfere with due course of any judicial proceeding
      (c) Obstructs the administration of justice.
B. **Power to Punish:** The Supreme Court can punish anyone under contempt of court. Members of executive and legislative are punished from time to time. For instance, Judge of Kolkata High Court, C. S. Karnan was penalised in 2018, with the charge of Contempt of Court. Chief of Bar Council of India, V. C. Mishra received 3 years' imprisonment by Allahabad High Court in 1995. Only the Supreme Court and High Court are empowered to exercise the power of contempt. District Court or subordinate

courts are not given the power to punish the person. The High Court exercises the power of contempt on behalf of the District Court too. Because the Supreme Court and High Court is not a court of record.

C. **Fundamental Rights and power of Contempt:** Freedom of speech and expression is the fundamentals among Fundamental Rights. Article 19(1) allows citizens to speak against the legislative, executive and judiciary too. Institutions and organisations are merely a means for protecting the Fundamental Rights. Power under Contempt of Court discourages and undermines Fundamental Rights.

Nevertheless, Fundamental Rights enshrined in the Part III of the Constitution is not absolute. It is under various limitations and Contempt of Court is one of them. People tend to criticise the Election Commission to suit their political goals. These institutions are unable to exercise he power of contempt. Power of contempt seems important, which protects the judiciary. This is necessary to preserve the rule of law, people do not disobey the decision of the Supreme Court due to fear of contempt. Fair and reasonable criticism of decisions of the Supreme Court does not amount to Contempt of Court.

Democracy and Contempt

Basic feature of democracy lies in debate and dissent. Anybody can criticise members of the executive and legislature. judiciary should not be kept away from criticism. Criticising will minimize the problem of corruption. It is helpful in promoting transparency. There is a need to redefine the contempt power of the court. Contempt should only be limited to obstruction in the administration of judiciary. Nobody is allowed to interfere in the activities of court. But criticism of court must be permitted.

It is true that democracy enhances the spirit of freedom of speech and expression. But the judiciary is a sensitive organisation; which cannot be compared with other organisations. Decisions of the judiciary cannot satisfy each and everyone. Whosoever is disagreeing with the decision of the Supreme Court raises baseless criticism. Freedom of speech and expression is not an instrument to fulfil his own interest. It is a medium of promotion of wellbeing of the entire community. People tend to scandalise judiciary on political grounds and their own ideological ambitions. This proves the necessity of power of contempt.

Jurisdiction/Powers of Supreme Court

A. **Original Jurisdiction:** Federalism is the basic structure of the Constitution. Division of powers is the basic feature of federal form of government. The Seventh Schedule of the Constitution maintains division of power. Division of power automatically leads to dispute between Union and state. The Supreme Court is the dispute settlement mechanism. Disputes between centre and state or between states, can only be resolved by the Supreme Court.

Resolving the federal dispute is known as original Jurisdiction. Because the State government or Union Government shall directly approach the Supreme Court. No other court is empowered to settle the federal dispute. **Article 131** of the Constitution described **original jurisdiction of Supreme Court as:**

1. Between the Government of India and one or more states;
2. Between the Government of India and any states on one side and one or more other states on the other;
3. Between two or more states.

Citizenship Amendment Act 1955 was passed by the Union. However, various states together approached the Supreme Court against the act passed by parliament. Federalism is the structure of the

Constitution said by the Supreme Court in **S. R. Bommai case** in **1994.** There is one exception to the original jurisdiction of the Supreme Court under **Article 131**. Any treaty, agreement, instrument which is executed or entered into force before commencement of this Constitution means that the agreement was executed before 26 January 1950.

B. **Appellate Jurisdiction in Constitutional Issue:** Supreme Court is the highest court of appeal. Appellate power implies that a person shall not approach the Supreme Court directly. Entering into the Supreme Court against the decision of the High Court is appellate power. A certificate of High Court is essential for going to the Supreme Court. Criminal or civil matters (case) pending before High Court involves a substantial question of law as to the interpretation of this Constitution.

   Substantial question means interpretation related to the Constitution of various High Courts are conflicting with each other. Thus, the Supreme Court gives a final verdict.

C. **Appeal in Civil Matter:** Without certificate of High Court, no appeals lie before the Supreme Court. Appeal shall lie to the Supreme Court from any Judgement of the High Court. High Court certificate is essential:

   1. The case involves a substantial question of law of general importance.
   2. In the opinion of the High Court, the said question needs to be decided by the Supreme Court.
   3. Substantial question of law as to the interpretation of the Constitution wrongly decided.

D. **Appeal in Criminal Cases:** Suppose the District Court has acquitted any person. The High Court has then reserved the decision of the District Court and sentenced him to death. Appeal lies before the Supreme Court from the High Court. No certificate is needed from the High Court. The High Court has withdrawn any case for trial before itself, from District Court. Accused person is awarded death sentence by the High Court. Again, a person can appeal in Supreme Court without any certificate of High Court.

   Apart from appeal in Supreme Court without certificate of High Court. But in some cases an appeal is possible with a certificate of High Court. If the High Court certifies that case is fit for appeal. More than 90 per cent cases of the Supreme Court come in the form of appellate power.

E. **Special Leave Petition (SLP):** It is the discretionary power of the Supreme Court, which grants appeal from Judgement passed by any court or tribunal in the territory of India. Leave demotes permission, by Supreme Court for appeal in extraordinary matters under Article136. One limitation is imposed over SLP in Article 136, because the Supreme Court can entertain or allow any SLP against a decision passed by the Armed Forces Tribunal.

   It is worth noting that **Article 32** is open for members of the armed forces too; a person can approach the Supreme Court against Judgement of armed forces tribunal under Article 32.

   Article 136 is an exceptional or extraordinary power of the Supreme Court. A two-judge bench asked a Constitutional bench to decide the kinds of cases in which discretion should be exercised in 2010. The bench listed the following grounds for permitting the cases of SLP **under Article-136:**

   1. Cases with a substantial question law
   2. Matters of public or national importance.

3. Validity of central or state laws
4. Validity of Constitutional amendments
5. Difference of opinion between two High Courts.
6. If there has been a miscarriage of Justice
7. Violation of Fundamental Rights.

Admission of SLP is creating immense work load for the Supreme Court. According to an estimate 34,500 SLPs were filed in 2014 and nearly all of them were admitted for hearing by the Court. Thus it is no more an extraordinary power. It looks like a regular power of the Supreme Court. The Supreme Court refused to provide any guideline for exercise of SLP. The Constitution Bench of Supreme Court said in 2016, that there are still discretionary powers of the Supreme Court, which cannot be written, cannot be written or limited on any ground.

Innovation of the Supreme Court

Article 142 of the Constitution empowers the Supreme Court to pass an order for completion of justice. The Supreme Court may pass any order related to matters pending before it. Various cases were disposed of by the Supreme Court, while exercising the power under Article-142. This Article has become the major instrument of judicial activism in recent days. Supreme Court gave an order for paying the compensation to the victims of Bhopal Gas Tragedy, and cancelled the allocation of coal block in 2014. There should be no sale of liquor on the highways, the Court had ordered. Court allocated 2.77 acres of land to the trust for building of Ram Temple in Ayodhya, thus power of court is wider and comprehensive under Article 142.

Protection of Fundamental Rights

Article 32 allows a person to move to the Supreme Court. Article 32 is part of fundamental rights; it is an Article which enforces other fundamental rights too. Article-139 empowers Supreme Court, **to issue following writs:**

1. Habeas Corpus
2. Mandamus
3. Prohibition
4. Quo Warranto
5. Certiorari

Only the Supreme Court is the guardian of the Constitution. Fundamental rights are part of the Constitution. People can directly approach the Supreme Court for protection of fundamental rights. It is different from original jurisdiction. Writ jurisdiction is involved with conflict between individual and the state. However original Jurisdiction is related to the dispute between two agencies of states. Individual is not a part of original jurisdiction.

Power of President to Consult Supreme Court or Advisory Power

This Article speaks for the power of the President rather than Jurisdiction of the Supreme Court under Article 143, President can get opinion from the Supreme Court. The President can obtain questions of Law or fact, which is having public importance. President shall also seek options about treaties and agreements between states before 1950.

It is considered as the opinion of the Supreme Court, rather than Judgement of Supreme Court. The opinion of the Supreme Court is binding over the government. It is not the adjudicative power of the Supreme Court. It is the persuasive or conciliatory power of the Supreme Court.

A. **Not Binding:** Opinion of the Supreme Court is not binding, upon government. Supreme Court is not bound to give opinion on each and every issue, said by Supreme Court in **Ismael Faruqui case (1995)**. The Supreme Court refused to tender her opinion on whether a temple or mosque existed at the disputed site.

B. **Importance:** Opinion given by the Supreme Court is not binding on government.

But–

1. It is binding on High Courts and other courts in India, because the Supreme Court is a court of record.
2. Judgement of the Supreme Court inculcates public opinion too. No elected government wants to lose in the Supreme Court in a legal battle. Thus government can seek legal opinion of Supreme Court in advance, before they enact any law or making an order.
3. From the constitutional viewpoint, opinion of the Supreme Court, carries persuasive value. Collegiums' system of appointment in judiciary is an outcome of the opinion of the Supreme Court in Judges 3rd case in 1998. It becomes the permanent practice of judiciary.

C. **History:** While giving an opinion to the President, not less than 5 judges should be on the bench;

1. The first reference under 143 was made in Delhi Laws cases (1951).
2. Kerala Education Bill (1958)
3. Berubari Case (1960)
4. Special court reference case (1978)
5. President Bill (1974) was related to certain doubts related to election of President:
6. Keshav Singh Case (1965)
7. Cauvery Water Dispute Act (1991)
8. Ismael Faruqui Case (1995)
9. Judges–III case Advocate on Record
10. Jammu and Kashmir Resettlement Act (1982)
11. Election in Gujarat Legislative Assembly (2002)
12. Punjab Termination of Agreement Act (2004)
13. Allocation 2-G spectrum

D. **Classification:** Power of President to consult Supreme Court can be categorised as:

1. Important question of public importance where the Supreme Court is entitled to refuse to give advice to the President. Supreme Court said this in Kerala Education Bill (1958).
2. Second clause of Article-143 is related to agreement, treaty, concluded between union and state before commencement of the Constitution.

The Supreme Court is bound to give its opinion over these issues. But in the last 70 years, no reference came before the Supreme Court related to the second part of the **Article 143**.

Guardian of Constitution

Power of interpretation of this Constitution belongs to the Supreme Court, under Article 145. While interpreting the Constitution, the Bench should be composed of not less than 5 judges. The Constitution cannot incorporate each and every fact. Thus the Supreme Court fills in the blanks. The Constitution is a living document and changes according to changing circumstances. Meaning of words changes in the changing context of time and space. Therefore the Supreme Court involved the doctrine of Basic structure for protecting the Constitution. The Supreme Court protects fundamental rights. Ensure division of power and preserve the autonomy of the Supreme Court, election commission too.

Miscellaneous Powers

Electoral disputes related to the President and vice-president shall be settled only by the Supreme Court. The Chief Justice of the Supreme Court or senior most judges of the Supreme Court can also act as acting President. Chairperson and members of UPSC shall be removed from their office only after recommendation of the Supreme Court.

Conclusion

The Supreme Court is Supreme in terms of power and scope. The Supreme Court plays multiple roles from protection of fundamental rights to being guardian of the Constitution.

THE HIGH COURT

Union of India comprises of 28 states; there shall be a High Court for each state under **Article 214**. Presently these are 25 High Courts in India, which means a High Court is not established in each state. Because **Article 213** of the Constitution provides that by **parliament law:**

A. **Common High Court for two states**
   1. Common High Court for two states like Punjab and Haryana High Court is meant for both Punjab and Haryana.
   2. Bombay High Court exercises jurisdiction over Maharashtra and Goa.

B. **More than States:** Guwahati High Court has jurisdiction over Assam, Nagaland, Mizoram and Arunachal Pradesh.

C. **Extension of Jurisdiction of High Court to Union Territory**
   Parliament by law shall extend jurisdiction of the High Court over Union territory too. Jurisdiction of Punjab and Haryana High Court exercises jurisdiction over Chandigarh. Bombay High Court has jurisdiction over Dadra and Nagar Haveli, Daman *and* Diu. Now Dadra and Nagar Haveli, Daman and Diu are integrated as one Union Territory.

Benches and Circuit Benches

There shall be a High Court for each state, according to Article-214. But larger state Uttar Pradesh, Maharashtra and Madhya Pradesh have established their benches to. With the permission of the principal bench; a new bench can be set up in the state, which requires consent of the state including the governor.

Circuit Bench is set up at smaller places. It is not a permanent bench but it works only for a few months in the calendar year. Circuit bench is set up in Port Blair, which comes under jurisdiction of Kolkata High Court. It also ensures Justice at doorsteps of the people.

It is interesting to be noted that Mumbai High Court has **three** benches in Aurangabad, Nagpur and Panaji. Population of Maharashtra is 11 crore. Madhya Pradesh population stands up to 7 crores. Madhya Pradesh has two benches in Indore, Gwalior. However Uttar Pradesh keeps only one bench in Lucknow, although the population of Uttar Pradesh nearing 22 crore. Long pending demand for a new bench in Meerut exists.

High Court in Union Territory

Article 214 says that jurisdiction of High Court can be extended on Union territory. Same time Article-241 permits parliament to form High Court for Union Territory Delhi is union territory which keeps its own High Court Newly created Union Territory Jammu & Kashmir and Ladakh share a common High Court.

Constitution of High Court

The High Court shall consist of Chief Justice and such other judges as the President may from time to time deem it necessary to appoint, under Article-216. Strength of Allahabad High Court is 160, and strength of Sikkim High Court is merely 3. No parliamentary act is needed for raising the strength of the High Court. But notification of the President is necessary. After working out a new state, The High Court shall be constituted by the notification of the President, after request from the new state. New High Court is set up in Telangana.

Appointment of Judges

Every Judge of the High Court shall be appointed by the President by warrant under his hand and seal. Recommendation of NJAC is needed before appointment by the President. Practically it should be considered as a recommendation of collegiums. Collegium comprises Chief Justice of India plus 2 seniormost judges of the High Court.

Conditions of Services

A Judge of the High Court will act unless he/she attains 62 years of age. Retirement age of Judges should be increased to at least 65 years of age.

A Judge of the High Court can resign to the president by writing under his hand the office of Judges shall also be vacated, when a Judge of High Court is appointed as Judge of Supreme Court. Judges shall also be transferred from one High Court to other High Courts. According to evolved convention before the transfer is Judge, consent of the Judge is required. Process of removal of Judges of the High Court is similar to that of Judges of the Supreme Court.

Qualification of Judges

1. Only citizens of India are qualified to become a Judge.
2. Held the Judicial office in the territory of India for at least ten years. Thus district judges are promoted as Judge of the High Court as Judge.
3. Or has been an advocate of the High Court or two or more such court in succession for at least ten years. Members of the bar are also suitable for appointment as Judge.

Oath and Affirmation

The Governor administers the oath and affirmation for Judges of the High Court. Governor or a person appointed shall provide an affirmation in the format of oath as described in the Third Schedule, exactly like the Judge of the Supreme Court.

Restriction and Practice

Permanent Judge holding office, shall not plead or act in any court or before any authority in India. But he/she is allowed to plead before the Supreme Court and other courts, where he has not acted as Judge.

Salaries of Judges

Salaries of Judges of the High Court are prescribed in the 2nd Schedule. Salary of the Chief Justice of the High Court is fixed as Rs 9,000 per month. It shall be Rs 8,000 per month for other Judges.

Article 221, also empowers parliament to enact a law for determining salaries and pension of Judges of the High Court. Parliament enacted the **High Court Judges (Salaries and Conditions of Service) Act, 1954**. The Act has been amended various times. Recently it was amended in 2018. Now Chief Justice of the High Court receives 2.50 lakhs per month and other Judges get 2.25 lakhs per month.

Allowances, pension or lease of judges shall not be varied to his disadvantage after his appointment. A Judge shall also receive compensatory allowance, may be determined by Parliament.

Transfer of Judges

President shall transfer a judge of High Court on the recommendation of NJAC. Practically which means recommendation of collegiums? The Constitution does not prescribe the ground of transfer of Judges. Collegiums justified transfer on the bases;

1. Better administration of Justice.
2. Presentation of Local nexus between Judges and advocates.

Transfer of Judges of High Court first time came in limelight during national emergency between 1975–77. A total of 16 judges were transferred during the emergency. Transfer of Judges became a tool for demoralising a Judge went against the stand of the government. After the evolution of collegiums in1993, misuse of transfer of Judges almost came to an end. Former Judge of Karnataka High Court P. D. Dinkaran was transferred to Sikkim High Court, on the charge of corruption. Thus, transfer is not the solution.

Although transfer of Judges can improve or reduce the prospect to become Chief Justice of the High Court or elevation of Judges is determined according to seniority of Judges.

Collegiums for transfer of Judge

Collegiums for transfer of Judges are constituted of Chief Justice of India and four senior most judges of Supreme Court. In addition to that 2 Chief Justice of High Court, Chief Justice of High Court, from where he/she is transferred and Chief Justice of receiving High Court.

Types of Judges in High Court

(a) **Acting Chief Justice:** When the office of Chief Justice is vacant or Chief Justice is unable to perform duties of his office or office of Chief Justice is vacant then the president may appoint other judges as acting Chief Justice. Here acting denotes Judge for time being. The Office of Chief Justice may be vacant due to resignation or elevation for the Supreme Court as Judge. Judges may be unable to perform duties due some physical reason like illness. Swearing in ceremony is not needed for acting Chief Justice.

(b) **Additional Judge:** Additional Judges are appointed by the President of India, with consultation with NJAC. Whenever business of the High Court increases due to arrears of work additional judges are appointed for 2 years. Person must be qualified to be appointed as Judge. According to evolved convention Additional Judges are appointed as permanent Judges. Most surprising fact is there are 403 vacancies of Judges in the High Court. Strength of all 25 of High Courts in India is 1079. The High Court announced that they will not appoint additional Judges unless vacancies are fulfilled.

(c) **Acting Judge**: When a Judge of High Court other than Chief Justice is unable to perform his duties or office of Judge is vacant. The President with consultation of NJAC may appoint a person as Judge. Until a permanent Judge resumes his/her office. Duly qualified person appointment as Judge of High Court.

(d) **Retired Judges**: Retired Judges are not appointed but they are requested to sit and act as Judge in the High Court. A person held the office of Judge in that High Court or other High Court to set and act as Judge. Allowances of the Judge shall be decided by the President. Person shall have all jurisdiction and power of Judge. But a person shall not be deemed to be a Judge of the high court. Till today retired Judges are not requested to sit and act as Judge. Reason is not explained in the Constitution behind the request to Judge sit and act as Judge.

Jurisdiction of High Court:
Original Jurisdiction

High Courts are primarily a court of appeal. But few exceptions exist: Calcutta, Bombay and Madras High Court still exercise their original powers in civil cases too. It is worth noting that other High Courts of India do not have the original jurisdiction in civil cases. Original refers that a person can approach the High Court directly.

Elections dispute comes under the original jurisdiction of High Court. But the High Court has nothing to do with federal disputes.

Writ Jurisdiction

The High Court issues the writ under **Article 226**. High Court **issues the following writs:**

1. Habeas Corpus
2. Mandamus
3. Prohibition
4. Quo Warranto
5. Certiorari

The High Court issues the writs for protections of Fundamental Rights. In addition to that Article-226 is also utilised for other purposes too. Because Fundamental Rights Article-226 can be used for election disputes or for rights of property too. However the Supreme Court issues the same writs but only for protection of fundamental rights. Thus scope of 226 is wider than Article 32. Like the Supreme Court, the High Court also issues PIL. The Writ power of the High Court is restricted to the territory of a particular state. The High Court cannot issue writs for the residents of other states. But the Supreme Court is entitled to issue writ for the entire territory of India.

Primarily Court of Appeal

The High Court is primarily a court of appeal. Appeal in High Court comes against the Judgement of District Court. Appeal may be on the issue of fact as well on the basis of law.

Appeal may be over civil cases and on criminal cases too. No High Court has original jurisdiction criminal cases. Criminal cases in the High Court come only through appeal. If a person gets 7 years of imprisonment in a case by District Court, appeal in criminal cases permitted.

Letters Patent Appeal

Normally appeal means approaching higher courts from lower courts. But there may be appeal within a court too. Judgement of a single judge may be appealed to a division bench (two Judges) in the same High Court.

Power of Supervision

High Court is court of record. Thus Judgement of the High Court is considered as evidence for district court and other subordinate courts. The High Court is also having the power to punish on the basis of contempt.

The High Court also exercises administrative control over the district court, another subordinate Court. The High Court also controls administrative tribunals too. The High Court shall not have administrative control over armed forces tribunals. Administration control implies:

1. Appointment and transfer of Judges.
2. Disciplinary action against any Judges.
3. The District Judge is not removed from office.
4. District judge is appointed by the governor with consultation of the High Court.
5. After formation of Telangana state, district Judges were divided by High Court.

It is worth noting that the Supreme Court does not have any administrative control of our High Court. But the High Court exercises administrative control over district and subordinate court.

Central Laws and High Court

The Constitution provides a federal form of government which is based on division of power. But the judiciary is not divided between union and state. Integrated judiciary is the uniqueness of the Constitution; the Representation of People Act-1951 (RPA-1951) is enacted by parliament. Allahabad High Court ruled Indira Gandhi adopted corrupted practices for winning the Lok Sabha election from Raebareli (U.P.). Allahabad High Court said that Indira Gandhi violated RPA-1951, thus nullifying her elections.

Subsequently the 42nd Constitutional amendment was brought about and limited the power of the High Court. The High Court shall not examine the validity of Central Law (Law enacted by parliament). This provision was replaced by the 43rd Constitutional amendment, thus no longer valid today. Similarly, laws state government can be challenged in Supreme Court.

Integrated judiciary also implies that judges of the Supreme Court and High Court are appointed by the President; their removal process is also the same. Judgement of the High Court is appealed in the Supreme Court. Judges of the High Court are transferred in any state.

Independence of High Court

The High Court is established in every state. But the High Court is not subordinate to the legislature of the state. Legislature of the state cannot enact a law which minimises the jurisdiction of the High Court. Judges of the High Court are appointed by collegiums. Judge of High Court enjoy fixed tenure in office, he/she acts as Judge till again the age of 62 years salaries of Judges and their administrative officers is charged on consolidated fund of state. However, pension of Judge is charged on consolidated fund of India. Parliament and legislature of state cannot start debate over conduct of Judge.

Summing Up

The High Court is not capable of exercising to settle the federal dispute. The High Court does not enjoy power of consultation too like the Supreme Court. But the High Court protects Fundamental Rights. It is a court of appeal in civil as well as in criminal cases too. The High Court is not a guardian of the Constitution but gives judgement over Constitution but gives judgement over cases related to Constitution too, according to the standards fixed by the Supreme Court.

JUDICIAL REVIEW

The term 'judicial review' is not mentioned in the Constitution. Since the Constitution is written and every organ of the government is written in the Constitution, it is the supreme law of the land. Thus, law enacted by the parliament and the legislature of the state cannot encroach on the supremacy of the Constitution. The Supreme Court is given the task to examine the validity of laws enacted by the state. Thus, judicial review simply means reviewing the functions of legislature and Executive.

Division of Power

Federal form of government is the **basic structure** of the Constitution. The Seventh Schedule ensures division of power between union and state. No unit of government can encroach its limitation prescribed in the Constitution. Judiciary examines the act made by parliament and the legislature of the state.

Fundamental Rights

Article 13(2) of the Part III of Constitution Constitution confer the power of judicial review to Judiciary. Law made by parliament goes against the fundamental rights of the Constitution. It shall be declared null and void, by the Supreme Court or High Court. Power of judicial review is exercised by both the Supreme Court as well as by the High Court.

Limitation over organs of Government

The Constitution is supreme in India; each organ of the government is under various limitations. Legislature, executive and judiciary are subject to numerous restrictions, scope and quantity of these restrictions is reviewed by Judiciary. Act of the speaker is immune from the preview of Judiciary.

Rational Principles of Judicial Review

Judicial review simply means examining the functions of the legislature and executive by Judiciary. The Supreme Court is given the responsibility of interpreting the Constitution; initially the Supreme Court was committed to the following principles:

(a) **Text is important**

The Supreme Court relied over the text or words incorporated in the Constitution. Court supported the principle of procedure established by law in **Gopalan Case (1951),** because it is written in the Constitution. Therefore the Supreme Court protected the right to property in the **Bela Banerjee Case (1954)**, and said compensation means compensation at market rate.

(b) **Priority of Parliament**

The Constitution subscribes that no organ of government is Supreme in Indian Constitution. But parliament represents the will of the people, which is most important in democracy. Parliament is entitled to amend the Constitution and determine power of other organs of the government. Supreme Court in priority of the parliament.

Therefore, it accepted that parliament can amend the Fundamental Rights too, the court acknowledged this in the famous **Shankari Prasad case (1950)**.

(c) **Narrower Meaning of Right to life**

The Supreme Court relied over text in the interpretation of the Constitution. Supreme said the freedom of speech and expression under Article-19 and right to life and personal liberty during emergency. The Supreme Court said that a person can be deprived from his life and personal liberty, if the government enacted a law, the Supreme Court pronounced that view in ***ADM. Jabalpur v. Shiv Kant Shukla Case* (1976)**.

(d) **Limited Scope**

The Supreme Court admitted that the act of Governor is not subject to judicial review. Thus the Court refused to entertain cases related to misuse of Article 356. Ordinances were kept away from judicial review. Court never tried to encroach on the amendment power of parliament. First constitutional rights, yet court approved the amendment in the Shankari Prasad case (1951)(see: 9th ambit of judicial review).

JUDICIAL ACTIVISM, OR THE EVOLVING NEW PARAMETER OF JUDICIAL REVIEW

(a) **Context Became Important**

A kind of harmonious relation existed between the executive and judiciary during the premiership of Nehru. But conflict between executive and judiciary was visible when Indira Gandhi became Prime Minister. The Supreme Court and High Courts became proactive post the Emergency of Indian Democracy.

The Supreme Court said that the spirit of the Constitution is more important than words written in the Constitution. That view was advanced by the Supreme Court in the landmark **Kesavananda Bharati case (1973)**.

Court is of the view that implied limitation is inherent in the amendment power of parliament under article-368. Spirit of the Constitution includes philosophy and the soul of the Constitution. Philosophy and soul makes context of the mind of the person who framed Indian Constitution. Context is ever changing with time and space.

Liberal interpretation of Fundamental Rights

Right to life is not merely living like animals. A right to life implies life with dignity that was said by the Supreme Court in the historical **Maneka Gandhi case (1978)**. Court observed that Article 19 and Article-21 are complementary legal provisions. This is the beginning of progressive approach of the Supreme Court. Liberal and progressive approach of the Supreme Court is visible in the **Puttaswamy case (2017)** recently in which the **right to privacy** is considered as an element of right to life.

Supremacy of Judiciary

The Supreme Court has been applying the principles of due process of law. Earlier courts relied over the principle of procedure established by law. Nation of due process automatically enhances the power of the judiciary.

Procedure of law must be reasonable, which is examined by the judiciary. Any law enacted by parliament or amendment of Constitution can be struck down by Judiciary on the name of Basic structure of the Constitution.

Judiciary of India now became the most powerful Judiciary in the democratic nations across the world. Judges are appointed by Judges in India through collegiums.

Expanding the scope of Judicial Review

Imposition of Article 356 is subject to judicial review said by the Supreme Court in S. R. Bommai Case (1994). The Judiciary has also been examining the validity of constitutional amendment Kesavananda Bharati case (1973). The Ninth Schedule is no longer away from the scope of judicial review, according to the Supreme Court in I.R. Coelho Case (2006). In short each and every part, schedule and article of the Constitution is under judicial scrutiny now.

This new evolving role of judiciary is branded as judicial activism by critics. Generally judicial activism refers judicial intervention in the functions of legislature and executive. But the Judiciary never expressed an intent to undermine the role of other organs of the government. Thus the term judicial activism is debatable and disputed.

NEW FORMS OF JUDICIAL ACTIVISM

Judicial Legislation

According to the principles of separation of power, law making is the primary responsibility of the legislature. Thus the term judicial legislation appears paradoxical. Now the judiciary becomes the law making agency. For example, Representation of the People Act, 1951 (RPA) is enacted by parliament. Clause (4) of Section-(8) of the RPA provides that a sitting MP/MLA convicted by court for 2 years or more than two years shall not be disqualified. Person shall have an opportunity to appeal in the higher court. It is declared *ultra vires* by the judiciary.

Moreover Representation of the People Act (RPA) does not include the provision of NOTA; Supreme Court directed for incorporation of NOTA in Representation of the People Act (RPA) in the **People's Union *of* Civil Liberties (PUCL) case** in 2013. Further Supreme Court amended the SC/ST act of 1989 in the **Dr Subhash Kashinath Mahajan case**. Supreme Court also banned liquor shops within 500 meter of highways; till now state legislature makes law for distribution of liquor. Various examples prove that judiciary is playing the role of legislature. Thus it is also an example of judicial activism.

Judiciary in Role of Executive (Judicial Overreach)

Policy making is the major function of the executive. Executive also executes the law enacted by the parliament. But the judiciary plays the role of executive. The Supreme Court said the CBI should directly report to the Supreme Court in the **Vineet Narain Case (1997)**, popularly known as the **Hawala Case**. Nevertheless CBI comes under the jurisdiction of PM.

The Supreme Court directed the government for carrying out reforms in civil services, **T.S.R. Subramaniam Case (2013)**.

Similarly in 2006 Supreme Court gave direction for police reform in the famous Prakash Singh Case. The Supreme Court also took a hard step to reform BCCI and appointed Sunil Gavaskar as Chairperson of BCCI. Court cancelled the allocation of 2-G too.

Right from cleaning of Ganga and Yamuna, Court also intervened for cleaning of Taj Mahal. Court suggested the government conduct free testing for Covid-19 in private hospitals. However policy making is the exclusive domain of the executive. Therefore, it is categorised as harmful judicial activism. Intervention in the issues related to policy making is judicial overreach or excessive activism.

An Instrument of Social Revolution

Origin

During the national emergency between 1975-77 Judiciary was under heavy criticism. Critics argued that the judiciary could not protect the rights of citizens. Thus the judiciary said it is also committed for social justice. Adjudication is not only a task of the judiciary in democracy. Addressing common grievances, first time visible in case of Mumbai Kamgar Sabha (1976). Justice V. R. Krishna Iyer tried to protect the interest of unregistered workers.

First reported case of Public Interest Litigation (PIL) is ***Hussainara Khatoon vs. Home Secretary, State of Bihar* (1979).** An advocate filed PIL pointing out the thousands of under trial prisoners in various jails of ***Bihar PUDR vs. Delhi Government Case (1982)*** popularly known as the **Asiad workers case**. The Supreme Court said that getting less than minimum wages amount to violation of right to life.

Significance

Public Interest Litigation refers to concern of public. Simply, litigation is related to adjudication between the two parties. However, public implies the well being of the entire community, especially the welfare of marginalised sections of society. First time Supreme Court defines the scope of PIL in **S. P. Gupta case, or the Judges Transfer case (1981)**. Supreme Court changed traditional concept of locus standing (Procedure), which believes that only aggrieved person can approach standing and any third person is permitted to reach the court for protection of common cause. Thus, it also known as social interest litigation. It is recognition of group rights, like rights of workers, children, women, etc. Court can take *suo motu* action for protection of the interests of deprived sections of society. It is visualisation of Article 39(A) of Constitution, which seeks to attain the notion offer legal aid.

Justice is more important than procedure thus court changed adversarial public spirited person, NGOs can approach Supreme Court for a common cause. Report of newspapers is also considered as written by the Supreme Court. Now the door of the Supreme Court is open for marginalised sections of society. Both Supreme Court and High Courts can issue PIL.

Expanding Scope of PIL

First stage of PIL deals with issues related to underprivileged sections of society for example., the Asiad workers case, **Bandhua Mukti Morcha case (1984).**The latter case is related to liberation of bonded labourers. Primarily PIL was introduced for deprived sections of society.

The second stage of evolution of PIL is associated with issues of environmental degradation. Supreme Court M. C. Mehta Case. The Supreme Court also instructed the Delhi Government to ply CNG fitted buses in Delhi.

Later in the third phase of development of PIL, issues of corruption flooded in Supreme Court Vineet Narayan Case became very popular. PIL were filed for electoral reforms, police reform, administrative reforms and numerous other cases too. The Supreme Court said persons contesting the elections should disclose their criminal history, financial liability and educational background. Judgement came in PUCL case 2002; citizens have the right to know about the candidates.

PIL and Judicial Overreach

Due to widening scope of PIL conflict between executive and Judiciary further came in limelight. Court issues various orders related to administration, which is an exclusive domain of the Executive. It became an example of judicial overreach. Judiciary had crossed the proverbial Lakshman Rekha.

Judiciary Legislation came due to PIL Judiciary Started playing the role of Executive, because Judiciary set up a special investigation team (SIT) for unearthing the black money. Rafale deal also became the matter of PIL.

Criticism

Judgement of the Supreme Court is ultimately executed by the Executive. Thus conflict between judiciary and executive hampers the working of administration. Critics have raised concerns of possible misuse of PILs to armtwist the government. It was termed publicity interest litigation too. Some of the advocates are affiliated with political parties, and file PIL for setting political scores.

When lakhs of cases are pending before Supreme Court speedy Justice is not possible through PIL. Thus the real objective of the PIL is missed out, providing access to marginalised sections of society was the real motive of PIL.

Conclusion

Now the Supreme Court and High Courts are very vigilant about prevention of miscues of PIL. Reputed and authentic person are allowed to file PIL. Some people receive penalty by courts in charge of misuse of PIL. A specific guideline is the need of the hour.

RELATION BETWEEN THE EXECUTIVE AND THE JUDICIARY

Although three organs of the government are interrelated with each other, but relation between various agencies of the government is determined by various factors. We can classify changing relations in the following time framework.

HARMONY BETWEEN EXECUTIVE AND JUDICIARY

Separation of powers is an inherent feature of the Constitution. Parliament is empowered to amend the Constitution. Parliament brought about the first constitutional amendment for limiting the Fundamental Rights. Executive paid respect towards the judiciary. Judicial review never became an obstacle for obtaining the goal of social justice, during the premiership of Nehru. The judiciary reviewed ordinary law, but never touched the validity of constitutional amendment.

DOMINANCE OF EXECUTIVE

From 1967 onwards conflict became a regular feature between Parliament (executive) and judiciary. The **Golaknath case** was a turning point, when the first time the Supreme Court restricted the parliament to amend the Fundamental Rights. Then the Indira Gandhi government brought about the 25th Constitutional Amendment. It was the first attempt to limit the power of judicial review. Senior Judges were superseded in appointment in the Supreme Court. But finally the Supreme Court defended its power in form of principle of basic feature in **Kesavananda Bharati Case (1973).**

Dominance of Judiciary

Political system underwent tremendous changes after 1989. It was the beginning of coalition government or minority government at Union level. No party could have a majority in parliament resulting in the emergence of weak Prime Ministers. Apart from political instability, corruption and criminalisation of politics eroded the legitimacy of the political system. The Judiciary emerged as saviour of interest to the people. Judiciary became the primary centre of the faith of the people. Thus the judiciary propounded PIL. It became more proactive for protecting the rights of citizens. Debate of judicial activism and overreach also came into picture.

Turning Tide: Pre-emergence of Strong Executive

The spell of coalition goverment came to an end in May 2014. After three decades, a political party had managed to get majority in Lok Sabha. Narendra Modi emerged as strong PM just like Indira Gandhi was in the 1970s. Therefore, the government tried to overhaul the collegium system of appointment of Judges. NJAC was put into place, instead of collegiums. Minister of Law and Justice Ravi Shankar Prasad said the government shall not act like a post-office in appointment of Judges.

Summed up

The Constitution believes in harmony and cooperation among three organs of government. Independent and autonomous judiciary is the basic structure of the Constitution. But supremacy of Judiciary is unwarranted.

Issues of Conflict

Disagreement and dissent is the crux of democracy. But paralysis of government due to conflict is not a healthy feature of democracy. We can witness several issues of dispute between Executive and Judiciary.

Will of the People

Although it is an undeniable fact that no organ of the government is Supreme. But will of importance in a democratic form of government. Will of the people is represented by the parliament. Supremacy of Parliament is essence of democracy, which responsible towards the people.

Members of parliament and Executive blamed that Judiciary is disrupting separation of power. Former minister Arun Jaitley said that declaring NJAC as *ultra vires* amounted to tyranny of the unelected.

Judiciary is limiting the amending power of parliament. The Judiciary never accepted that it is active.

Judiciary is of the view that it is guardian of the Constitution. The Constitution is the manifestation of the highest will of the people. Majority in parliament does not empower any political party to destroy the basic structure of the Constitution.

Social Justice

Judiciary becomes an instrument of social justice, therefore discovering the PIL. Judiciary said that preamble incorporates an ideal of social justice. Justice does not mean adjudicating the dispute between two parties only. Social justice is the responsibility of the executive. Government knows the technical, financial dimension of any decision. Judiciary unnecessarily intervenes in administrative issues, like instructing the government for setting up open Jails.

Basic Structure

Parliament is given the power of amending the Constitution under **Article 368**. But the Judiciary deprived the parliament from amending the Constitution. Judiciary can strike down any law or Constitution of power. The judiciary argued that the Constitution is a living document. Thus interpretation of the Constitution automatically changes after changing time and circumstances. Judiciary does not belong to any political party. It is a neutral agency of settling disputes. For maintaining rule of law and protecting the fundamental rights, active judiciary is positive for democracy.

Conclusion

Unique features of the Constitution ensure, check and control by the judiciary over the Executive. Parliament is associated with political parties, thus the interest of a particular party is projected as national interest. But judicial intervention in every administrative matter must be avoided. Justice J. S. Verma rightly said that the Judiciary should act like an alarm clock. It should not act like a watch.

Subordinate Judiciary

Below the Supreme Court and High Court is the subordinate Court. Subordinate court is also known as district court. Subordinate court is considered a trial court. When a person is charged by state due to violation of law, every citizen is entitled to defend himself in court of law, though an advocate of his/her choice. Thus government or police frame the charge against the person. Judge ultimately decides about the validity of charges, under a complex procedure. Witnesses appear and they are examined by advocates; evidence is also submitted against the individual. Therefore it is called a trial court.

Appointment

District Judges are appointed by the Governor, with consultation of the High Court of that state. An advocate practisaing in a court of law for 7 years or engaged in judicial function or pleader for 7 years is eligible Judge is promoted and transfer of Judge is the capacity of Governor with consultation of the High Court.

Judge is also removed by the Governor from his/her in consultation with the High Court. Their removal is not like removal of a Judge of Supreme Court or High Court.

Appointment of other Judges

Appointment other than district judges is also done by the Governor. But the Governor gets the consultation of the High Court and state public service commission too. Exams for the appointment of other Judges conducted by the state public service commission, under supervision of the High Court subordinate judiciary, is under control of the state government.

Jurisdiction

District Court is located in each and every district of India. Dealing with Civil Cases people is known as District Judge. Civil Cases means cases related property and matrimonial disputes. While dealing with criminal cases the same person acts like a session judge. Criminal cases are related with murder, etc. which affects entire community. District courts can award the highest penalty to people who say death sentences. But the district does not deal with the fundamental rights. District court is empowered to entertain PIL. District court only deals with the issues of Indian penal code and civil procedure code.

Fast Track Court

Procedure of trial of district court is complex, consequently before district court, across India. Pending of criminal cases in against the right to life and personal liberty. It also encroaches human rights. The Supreme Court said speedy trial is a part of the right to life in Hussain Ara Case. Fast track Court was set up in India in 2002 after recommendation of the 11th Finance Commission.

Fast track court is district court in nature, but it only deals with criminal cases. Judge and procedure are the same but no adjournment is permitted in case. Case in heard on a daily basis, thus it becomes fast. By passing the procedure may result in injustice in criminal cases. Therefore delay is not allowed in Fast Track Court.

Tribunals

Indian Judiciary comprises the Supreme Court, High Court and district courts in the Constitution. District court or subordinate courts is composed of district judges and other civil judges.

Motion of tribunal was first incorporated in the Constitution by the **42nd Constitutional Amendment** in 1976. New Part 14(A) was added in the Constitution and Articles 323(A) and 323(B) provides for the tribunals. Amendment is passed after the recommendation of Swaran Singh Committee.

Meaning

Tribunals are not courts. Tribunal is composed of both administrative as well as judicial members. Tribunals are specialised in various fields like National Green Tribunal (NGT), which only deals with issues related to the environment. Central Administrative Tribunal (CAT), which adjudicates the cases related to administrative personnel. Tribunal are a combination of judiciary and other expert members. It is quasi-judicial bodies, because it shares some features of judiciary tribunals and incorporates the tenets of administrative bodies too.

Utility

Pending tens of thousands of cases in Judiciary is the biggest challenge for the Indian judicial system. Complex procedure is one of the major reasons behind delayed justice. Tribunals work on the principles of natural justice than civil procedure code or evidence act. Timely disposal of cases is uniqueness of tribunals. Justice is more important than procedure. Tribunals do not prefer complexity of procedure. Tribunals are cost saving too. It saves the traditional judicial system from unnecessary workload. Now society became complex without inclusion of expert Judges and cannot deliver Justice.

Beginning of Tribunals

Provision of administrative tribunals incorporated in **Article 323(A)**. Administrative tribunals include Central Administrative Tribunals (CAT) and State Administrative Tribunal (SAT). Parliament made an act in 1985 for executive tribunals.

Structure

Parliamentary act provides the structure of CAT, Tribunal is composed of at least one judicial member and one administrative member Head Quarter of tribunal is Delhi. 17 regular benches and 21 circuit benches consist of 7 members plus chairperson. However, Ahmedabad benches consisted of 2 people, including chairperson. Thus minimum strength must not be less than two. Entire strength of all benches. The Chairperson of Principal Bench is head of CAT, across India. Other 16 benches are headed by Vice-Chairpersons. They are appointed by the President with Consultation of C.J.I.

Term of Conditions

The Judicial member of CAT is or has been qualified to be appointed as Judge of the High Court. However administrative members should hold the office of rank of secretary for 2 years.

They hold office for 5 years age of chairperson shall 68 years or 5 years whichever comes earlier, vice chairperson and members shall hold the office for 65 years, Chairperson and members shall be removed in the ground of misbehaviour or incapacity **President** shall remove than on the recommendation of Supreme Court. Their salaries shall not be reduced, after appointment.

Jurisdiction

CAT settles the dispute related to terms and conditions of **services of following;**

1. Members of Indian Administrative Service.
2. Indian Police Service.
3. Personnel belonging to Central Service.
4. Civil Servants working in the Ministry of Defence.

Issues of Suspension, promotion or arbitrary transfer can be challenged before CAT for example Amitabh Thakur, IPS officer of UP Cadre was suspended by the UP Government. A member of Indian Revenue Service (IRS) was forcibly retired by the Government of India. He challenged the decision before CAT. Although aggrieved people should first approach their own department according to services rules. Thereafter they are allowed to approach the CAT.

CAT works on the principles of natural justice. Thus it does adopt a law enacted by parliament appealing against the decision of the court shall lie to the High Court. The Supreme Court changed the act of parliament. The Supreme Court said the decision of CAT shall lie before the High Court under Article 226. Subsequently an appeal for the Supreme Court is also open.

Limitation of Jurisdiction of CAT

(a) Members belonging to armed forces are part of the central government. But matters related to terms and conditions of their services do not fall under CAT. Since the Parliament passed **Armed Forces Tribunal Act, 2007**, now matters related to armed forces lie before the Armed Forces Tribunal Act.

(b) Members serving under Lok Sabha Secretariat and Rajya Sabha Secretariat do not come within the Jurisdiction of CAT because of Privilege of Parliament. The Speaker is the sole authority to maintain control over their members serving the parliament.

(c) Personnel associated with the Supreme Court and high belong to Central services. But they are away from Jurisdiction of CAT.

Chief Justice exercises the administrative control over the member working to Supreme Court. It ensures independence of the Supreme Court.

Drawback

Almost half of the vacancies of CAT are unfulfilled. CAT is working with half capacity. Nearly 50,000 cases are pending before CAT. It defeats the very purpose of establishment of CAT. Age of members and chairperson should possibly be raised up to 70 years.

Varieties of Tribunals

Article 323(B) is also incorporated in the Constitution by 42nd Amendment. It establishes the various **tribunals like–**

1. Taxation.
2. Foreign Exchange, import-export across custom frontiers.
3. Industrial and labour disputes.
4. Ceiling on urban property.
5. Land reform.
6. Election to parliament and legislation of the state.
7. Production, procurement or distribution of foodstuff.
8. Rent regulation.

These tribunals can be set up by parliamentary Act. All the tribunals are set up gradually, but tribunals for settling the elections dispute is yet to be set up gradually. The Armed Forces Tribunal was established in 2007. NGT was set up in 2010 for adjudicating environmental matters. The Cyber appellate tribunal also came into existence in 2010. Tribunal related to real estate also came into practice after 217. Now we are witnessing the benches of tribunals in India, in every field of life.

National Green Tribunal (NGT)

Context

Conservation of Environment received the constitutional states by 42nd constitutional amendment. Article-48(A) is inserted in the ConstitutionConstitutionwhich mandates that the state shall endeavour to protect and improve the environment and to safeguard the forest and wildlife of the country. Part of Fundamental duties also includes, protecting and improving the natural environment including forests, lakes, rivers and wildlife. And to have compassion for living creators under Article-51(A) etc.

Parliament passed various legislation for protecting and improving the environment. Wild life (protection) Act, 1972, Water (presentation and central pollution) Act, 1974, the Forest (Conservation) Act, 1989 etc.

The Supreme Court also expanded the meaning of right to life. Clean environment became an integral component of the right to life said by the Supreme Court in M. C. Mehta Case (1986). Subsequently numerous cases reached the Supreme Court related to environmental rights. In this context, the purpose of setting up **NGT is the following:**

1. Reducing overdependence on the Supreme Court.
2. Speedy disposal related to environmental issues.
3. Removing obstacles in the path of development projects due to unnecessary delay in the Supreme Court.
4. Specialised agency to address the problems of environmental degradation.
5. Ensuring easy access for citizens in tribunal to protect the environment.

Structure

NGT is a statutory body, set up by parliamentary act in 2010. **It is comprised of:**

1. Chairperson
2. Minimum strength of a judicial member should not be less than 10, but should not be more than 20.
3. Minimum strength of expert members should not be less than 10 and maximum strength should not be more than.

Principal Bench of NGT is located in New Delhi while regional benches are located in Pune, Bhopal, Chennai and Kolkata.

Terms and Conditions

Chairperson shall not be qualified for appointment unless he/she is or has been a judge of the Supreme Court of India or Chief Justice of the High Court. Judicial member is or has been a Judge of the High Court.

Expert members must have a degree in Master of Science with Doctorate or master of Engineering and have 15 years of experience in relevant fields. Chairperson or members shall not hold any other office during their tenure they shall not be eligible to get any employment or office within two years of ceasing the office.

The Chairperson shall be appointed by the Central Government with consultation of Chief Justice of India. Members shall be appointment by committee set up by Union government.

Chairperson and members shall hold their office for 5 years from the date on which they enter upon their office. But eligible for re-appointment Judge of Supreme Court shall not hold the office after he attained the age of 70 years. Chief Justice of High Court of Judge of High Court shall not hold the office after he attained the age of Sixty-Seven years.

Autonomy of NGT

Chairperson and members of NGT shall be removed central government, after an inquiry conducted by Judge of Supreme Court. Salaries of Chairperson and members and members shall not be reduced during their tenure in office.

Nature

NGT is not bounded by Civil Procedure Code. Evidence act is not applied in the proceeding of NGT. It operates on the principle of natural Justice.

Jurisdiction

NGT hears cases related to conservation of forest and environment. A person affected from environmental degradation may approach NGT. But third person is also entitled to approach NGT for protection of the environment. NGT can order the government to pay compensation to the victim due environmental hazards. Party or institution damaged by the environment is supposed to pay the compensation within 30 days. NGT banned the playing of 10 years old vehicles on the roads of Delhi. NGT also fined an art of living festival held on the bank of Yamuna NGT has the power of a Civil Court any person by depositing rupees 1000/- can reach in NGT.

Appeal in Supreme Court

1. According to act minimum strength should not be less than 20. But NGT is working with less than 10 members. Regional benches almost cease to operate.
2. Governments do not want to recruit real specialized members instead looking for bureaucracies as a member. It minimizes the importance of environment issues.
3. NGT is not capable of exercising the power of contempt. Nobody wants to pay compensation.
4. NGT do not have their own buildings. There is a lack of staff and finances too. It makes NGT less effective.

Tribunalisation and Court

Now tribunals are working in each domain of life, but critics said that tribunals are undermining the importance of Judiciary.

Separation of Power

Separation of power is the basic structure of Indian Constitution. Check and balance is the supplementary features of separation of power. Tribunals go against the principles of separation of power. The Judiciary is supposed to exercise check over the activities of the executive. But tribunals made then partners of each other.

Autonomy of Judiciary

Interestingly independent Judiciary is also counted as an important element of Basic structure. Major functions of Judiciary are now transferred to tribunals. Tribunals are not autonomous like Judiciary. Appointment is tribunals controlled by the ministries. Tribunals do not have control over their administrative staff. Members and chairperson can also be removed easily from their office. Their salaries are not charged on consolidated funds of India. All tribunals do not enjoy power of contempt too.

Necessity of Tribunals

No system can be foolproof. We can count numerous defects in tribunals. But without tribunals governance becomes problematic. Advantage of tribunals can be summed up as follows:

Harmony

Separation of power does not mean the lack of cooperation among two organs of the government. Two branches of government are like two organs of a body. Thus organs of a government is complementary with each other. Tribunal combines executive with Judiciary strict separation makes government dysfunctional.

Expertise

Justice becomes complex in the present age of the nuclear and cyber world. Judges are having knowledge in a particular branch of law; inclusion of experts in Tribunals makes Justice speedy and effective. Judges are not proficient in Environment or issues related to taxation.

Autonomy is Intact

Any Bench of tribunals is always chaired by judicial members of the tribunals. Moreover any decision delivered by tribunals is subject to appeal before the Supreme Court. Thus ultimately the judiciary keeps control over tribunals.

Lok Adalat

Judiciary is an independent and autonomous mechanism to settle the dispute. But the judiciary is too costly, beyond the reach of an ordinary citizen. But Judiciary is too costly, beyond the reach of an ordinary citizen. Procedure became more important than justice. Delayed Justice has been shaking the faith of the people in the entire judicial process.

For making Justice people centric rather than Court Centric. Article 39(A) was inserted in the part of DPSP by 42nd Amendment which promises about equal Justice and free legal aid. Justice is not denied to any citizen due to economic or other disabilities. The Supreme Court stressed upon that Articles 14, 21 and Article 39(A) is complementary with each other. Equality before law becomes meaningless in absence of equal access to court. Without equal reach in the Judiciary right to life becomes empty.

Justice P. M. Bhagwati and V. R. Krishna Iyer was the pioneer of Lok Adalat. First experiment began from Una Village of district Junagadh in Gujarat from 1982.

Statutory Status

1987 Lok Adalat were granted the legal states, Parliament enacted the Legal services Authority Act. It came into force from 1995. The Legal Services authority Act incorporates the following features:

Legal Aid

A. **Legal Aid:** For implementation of parliamentary act, National legal services authority (NALSA) is set up. NALSA is headed by the Chief Justice of India and other members. Every state shall set up state legal services authority. The District Legal Services authority is also established. It provides free legal assistance to SC/ST, ministries and people living below poverty. Legal aid is available in any court throughout territory of India in Civil or Criminal cases.

B. **Legal Literacy:** NALSA and SALSA provide awareness about various laws enacted by parliament about well being of the marginalized sections of society. Laws related to a dowry, sexual harassment communicated to the people.

C. **Lok Adalat:** Lok Adalat is the third component of Legal services authority act, 1987. Lok refers to people, court becomes people's court due to the **following factors;**
   1. Free of cost adjudication.
   2. It works on the principle of natural justice.
   3. Civil procedure code and Evidence Act is not allowed in Lok Adalat.
   4. Focus is over disposable of dispute.
   5. Dispute is settled on the basis of persuasion negotiations and informal concession.
   6. No appeal is allowed against the decision of Lok Adalat. It is final and binding over the parties.

Levels of Lok Adalat

Lok Adalats are organised in Supreme Court, High Court and District Courts too. Same court and the same Judge are part of Lok Adalat. But procedures are kept away so it becomes a people's Court. NALSA and SALSA organize Lok Adalat in various Courts.

Permanent Lok Adalat

Initially Lok Adalat wares ad hoc, because it sits once in a week. But legal services authority act, 1987 was amended in 2002. It provided information about permanent Lok Adalat. Its income court is fully devoted to Lok Adalat 6 days in a week. Permanent Lok Adalat are set up at district level, and cannot set up at higher level. This is because two High Courts or Supreme Court is beyond imagination.

National Lok Adalat

Lok Adalat is held in each and every court across India. Dates of National Lok Adalat is finalised by NALSA. Generally, three or four times in a year, national Lok Adalat is commenced.

Jurisdiction

By and large Lok Adalat settles civil cases dispute related to rent, insurance, and electricity bills are solved by Lok Adalat. But some minor criminal cases, which can be compounded in nature, are also settled by the Lok Adalat. Procedure cannot be passed in criminal cases. Thus criminal cases are adverse by the fast track court. Civil cases pending before courts can be transferred to Lok Adalat with consent of both parties. Any matter at the pre-litigation stage can be settled by Lok Adalat. Judge or retired Judge sits in Lok Adalat. Apart from that, social activists are also members of Lok Adalat. Dispute should be perceived through social dimension, rather than from legalistic point of view.

Drawback

Property cases worth more than 10 lacs cannot be brought before Lok Adalat. Consent of both parties is essential. Nobody can compel to change an unreasonable stand of a person. Settling disputes through compromise, negotiation suits the rich section of society. Pendency of cases before Lok Adalat is also an issue. Lawyers have their own interest. It hampers the functioning of Lok Adalat.

Arbitration and Conciliation

Lok Adalat and arbitration conciliation are two important components of Alternative refer to a different mode of dispute settlement. Traditional dispute settlement comprises the Supreme Court High Court and District Court. We can point out the drawbacks of traditional methods of **dispute resolution:**

1. Delayed Justice
2. Complex procedure
3. Costly
4. Technical Formal

It normally takes 25 years, when a case starts from district court and reaches up to apex court (Supreme Court). Civil procedure code, criminal procedure code, evidence act are an example of complex procedures. Freedom of advocate in court is not regulated yet. Top lawyer of the Supreme Court charges up to 50 lakhs for a case. It may go up manifold depending up to situation; courts adopt technical and formal rules, which causes delay of cases. Although speedy justice is an essential element of Good Governance. Without a speedy Justice environment of investment also discouraged.

In the post-liberalisation phase parliament passed Arbitration and Conciliation Act in 1996. For promoting alternative dispute settlement, parliament further amended the act in 2015 and 2019. Let's sum up the core elements of Act.

Arbitration Council of India

Arbitration simply means out of court settlement, by amendment of 2019, first time an institution shall be set up in India for promotion of arbitration. Arbitration council of India **comprised of:**

1. A Chairperson who is either a judge of Supreme Court or Judge of High Court or Chief Justice of High Court or an eminent person with expert knowledge in conduct of arbitration. It means a person not belonging to the Judiciary may be qualified to be appointed as Chairperson.
2. Practitioners or arbitration.
3. One member as professor with experience in arbitration.
4. One member is appointed by the Government.

Functions of Council

It is an independent body, for promoting arbitration. It is not made for resolving the disputes. But it will play the role of a think tank like UGC in the field of higher education.

Functions of council include

1. Framing policies for grading arbitral institutions are acceding arbitrators.
2. Making policies for the establishment, operation and maintenance of uniform professional standards for A.D.R.
3. To make India a robust centre for domestic and international arbitration.
4. Conduct examination and training.
5. Hold training, workshops and courses in the area of arbitration in collaboration with Law firms, Law universities and arbitral institutions.

Appointment of Arbitrators

The Supreme Court and High Courts are given the responsibilities to appoint the arbitrators. The Supreme Court will appoint arbitrators in international commercial disputes. The High Court will appoint arbitrators in domestic commercial disputes.

Confidentiality

Arbitrator is supposed to resolve commercial disputes between reliance and facebook. Thus confidentiality will be maintained by the parties. Disclosure of information may harm the business prospects of a company.

Time Limit

A statement of claim and defence will need to be completed within a period of six months. Arbitral awards should come within a period of 12 months after compilation of pleading. International commercial disputes should be resolved as expeditiously as possible. Matter should be disposed within 12 months from the date of completion of pleadings.

Conclusion

Appointment of arbitrators by the Supreme Court in Ayodhya Case shows the importance of arbitration. It promotes speedy Justice. Hope fully Justice will prevail instead of procedures.

73rd Amendment of the Constitution, decentralised the administration similarly Gram Nyayalaya the judicial system at grass root. Justice should be available to the doorsteps of the villagers. Parliament passed the act in 2008 for setting up Gram Nyayalaya. 25,000 village courts are supposed to be established, but till today merely 208 Gram Nyayalaya (Village Court) one functioning in India.

Structure

The state government shall appoint a Judicial Magistrate (*Nyaya Dilkari*) with consultation of the High Court. One or more Gram Nyayalaya shall be established for every Panchayat at intermediate hence. Where the intermediate level of Panchayat is absent a group of villages may be considered for establishment of Gram Nyayalaya. The State Government with consultation High Court will notify the Jurisdiction of village court. Panchayat at intermediate level is head quarter of Gram Panchayat.

Mobile Court

Judicial Magistrate sits in the intermediate level (block) of Panchayat. But the Magistrate can hold a mobile court outside of headquarters. Thus Gram Nyayalaya is popularly known as a mobile court too.

Working

Gram Nyayalaya proceedings are not bound by **Code of Civil Procedure** (1908) or **Indian Evidence Act (1872)**. It shall apply the principle of Natural Justice. Focus is to dispose of the matter immediately, without sticking to complex procedures. It permits conciliation and compromises and the Court also promotes plea bargaining. Plea bargaining refers to the fact that a person admits his/her guilt they will receive less punishment.

Jurisdiction

Jurisdiction of Gram Nyayalaya extends both in civil as well as in criminal domain too. Criminal cases in which imprisonment may be more than 2 years is not included in the Jurisdiction of Gram Nyayalaya.

Appeal

Appeal is open against the decisions of Gram Nyayalaya. Appeals lie in district court in criminal and civil cases. Thus Gram Nyayalaya is different from Lok Adalat.

Drawback

Nature of offence is not well defined in schedule I of act like theft, concealment receiving and disposal of stolen property.

Right to appeal against the decision of Gram Nyayalaya is self-defeating. Appeal allows the dispute to go on further. It is not serving the purpose of Justice at the doorstep of the people.

Administration of justice is included in the Concurrent List of the Seventh Schedule. It means it is the responsibility of both the union and state government. State government lacks the resources for implementation of Gram Nyayalaya.

State governments are unable to fulfil the vacancies of Judges pending for a long time. Then how they can establish a separate Gram Nyayalaya. Thus the vision of Gram Nyayalaya is yet to be realised.

ALL INDIA JUDICIAL SERVICES

The Constitution allows the parliament to create one or more All India Services. Provided that the council of state should be pass a resolution to that effect. Resolution should be passed by 2/3 of the members present and voting in council of state, under article-312. All India services shall be created for fulfilling the national interest.

Constitutional Provision

Motion of All India Judicial Service was incorporated by 42nd constitutional amendment under article-312. All India Judicial Service shall not be created inferior to post of district Judge. But the 42nd constitutional amendment is yet to be implemented. Report of Various Law Commission also supported the creation of a new All India Judicial Service.

Advantage

Till today a person who belongs to the Bar or has held a judicial office for 7 years, is appointed as district Judge. Creation of All India Judicial Services attracts more competent and efficient law graduates to join the district court.

Apart from drawing in young talent, the selection process will become more transparent and uniform across the nation. More than two crores cases are pending before the district courts. Creation of all India Services will be helpful for disposing pending cases too.

Examination shall be conducted by Union Public Service Commission. Person appointed as district Judge will be promoted in High Court onwards. It will further improve the quality of Judiciary for realising the dream of All India Judicial Services following action is needed.

Constitution Amendment

At present district Judge is appointed by the Governor with consultation of the High Court. Post inferior then district judge shall be appointed by the Governor with consultation of the High Court and state public service commission under article-233 and article-234. Appointment will be done by UPSC in All India Judicial Services. Thus the power of the state service commission and High Court is about to decline.

Committee

Since appointment of Judges is different from appointment.

Federal Government

District court and courts below that are managed by the state government. All India Judicial Services reduce the power of the state government of administration and police personnel. Since the Judiciary must be independent, it should not be subordinate to the executive. A committee is required to give advice to UPSC. Committee shall be composed of Judges of the High Court and other eminent persons. Committee will determine the pattern of syllabus of examinations.

Language

Task of Judges is extremely important. District court is a trial court, which records statements, the witness and record the evidence too. Therefore knowledge of language is inevitable for running the court. Regional language should be counted, while holding the All India Judicial Services.

Conclusion

Present method of appointment of district judges lacks transparency. But judicial administration except the Supreme Court and High Court belong to the Concurrent List. Cooperation between union and state is essential for realising the dream of All India Judicial Services.

7

EXECUTIVE AND LEGISLATURE IN THE STATES

KEY CONCEPTS

Governor, Chief Minister, State Legislature

GOVERNOR

Though India has a federal form of government, there is no separate constitution for the states in India. The Constitution of India incorporates the provisions of power of state governments in Part VI. Articles 152 to 213 discusses the power and formation of state governments. The Indian Constitution combines a *federal* form of government with a *parliamentary* government. The Governor is the *constitutional head* of the state government, according to parliamentary form of government. The Governor is also the representative of federal government in the states.

Constitutional Provisions

There shall be a governor for *each state*, according to Article 153. However, the same person may be appointed as Governor for *two or more states*, as incorporated by the **7th Constitutional Amendment** in 1956. The Governor is head of all executive powers of the state government. Any other functions can be transferred to the Governor by other authorities. Parliament or legislative assembly of states shall confer any function subordinate to Governor.

Appointment of Governor

The Governor of a state shall be appointed by the President. The Governor is appointed by **warrant** under the President's hand and seal, that is, appointment letter of the Governor is signed by the President. When **Nehru** was Prime Minister, the concerned Chief Minister (CM) of the state was consulted before appointment of the Governor. Later this convention was discontinued. The **Sarkaria Commission** had also recommended **consulting** with the CM of the state before appointment of the Governor. This is because the CM of the state is **elected** by the people, but the Governor is **not elected**. Consultations with the CM acknowledge the importance of the **federal structure.**

Convention

Governor appointed in a particular state, should not be a *resident of that state*. This convention is continued till today.

Reason behind Appointment

The Indian Constitution signifies strong powers of the central government. Appointment of Governor by the President is helpful for maintaining control over the states by the union government. The Governor is a representative of the union government in the states, and is regulated and controlled by the **Home Ministry.**

According to the convention of parliamentary form of government, the Governor is a constitutional head. Thus, the Governor is appointed and not elected. Had the Governor been elected then conflict between the Governor and the Chief Minister would have been inevitable, since the CM is the administrative and the real head of the state chosen by elected members of the state **Legislative Assembly**. Election of the Governor means more expenses too. Therefore, the Constituent Assembly discouraged the election of the Governor.

Term of Office

The term of Governor is specified in the Constitution in the following ways:

1. The Governor shall hold office during the *pleasure* of the president under Article 156. (The *term of pleasure* is not defined in the Constitution.)
2. Governor may resign from his office. Governor shall address the President in resignation, by writing under her/his hand.
3. Governor shall hold office for a term of **5 years** from the **date** on which he enters upon his office. It means he shall continue to hold office, notwithstanding the expiration of his term until his successor enters upon his office and takes oath.

Pleasure of the President and B. P. Singhal Case

The President may remove the Governor without citing *any reason*, without granting an *opportunity to be heard.* The Constitution does not prescribe any *grounds for removal* of the Governor. The Constitution does not mention the **transfer of** Governor but it is usual. The President removed Governors of UP, Gujarat, Haryana and Goa in July 2004, after the 14th Lok Sabha elections. Removal of Governors was challenged in the Supreme Court. The Supreme Court gave its verdict in 2010 in the **B. P. Singhal case**. The Supreme Court held the following:

1. The Court accepted the idea of the pleasure of the President, that is, the President has the *power to remove a Governor at any time*, without giving any reason. The Governor is not given any opportunity to be heard.
2. The President cannot exercise his power in an *unreasonable and arbitrary manner.* The Governor should be removed rarely and only if there are valid and compelling reasons.
3. *Change in the ruling party of the union government* is not a valid and compelling reason to remove the Governor. She/he should not be removed because ideology of the Governor is different that of the union government.
4. The Governor is a *constitutional office*, and is not a servant of the central government. She/he is also not an employee of the union government. Thus, she/he cannot be removed on unreasonable grounds.
5. Decision of removal of the Governor can be challenged in a **court of law**. The Court can ask for materials, processes and compelling reasons behind the removal of the Governor.

Despite the Supreme Court judgment, there have been allegations of the misuse of the office of the Governor. After the **B. P. Singhal Case**, the central government does not remove the Governor. However, Governors are **transferred** arbitrarily from one state to another. For example, former Governor of Gujarat, Kamla Beniwal was transferred to Mizoram in 2014. Similarly in 2020, Satya Pal Malik, Governor of Goa was transferred to Meghalaya. In such instances, often the Governors resign.

The Supreme Court's Intervention

As of now, removal of Governor is under **judicial review**. Decision of the Supreme Court is based on recommendations of various commissions appointed by the Court. The **Sarkaria Commission** suggested that the Governor should not be removed before 5 years. However, as mentioned earlier, the Governor can be removed with compelling reasons before end of term. Report of removal of Governor should be tabled before the parliament. The **M. M. Punchhi Commission** recommended that the Governor should be impeached like the President. Thus intervention of the Supreme Court appears justified.

Qualifications of a Governor

The Constitution refers to a brief **qualification** of Governor under Article 157. Any **citizen of India** who has completed the **age of 35 years** is eligible to become Governor. Practically, Governor is generally appointed after the completion of 60 years, or more than 60 years of age. Sarkaria Commission recommended that the Governor should be an **eminent person**. Person appointed as a Governor should not be associated with **local party polities**. Punchhi Commission also recommended that appointed person should have stayed away from active politics for 2 years before his/her appointment.

Composite Method Appointment

Despite such recommendations, politicians have served as Governor. Politicians are accommodated in the **Raj Bhavan,** the seat of the Governor. Politicians defeated in elections were also awarded the office of Governor. **Punchhi Commission** had recommended a **Talking report** of removal of Governor should be tabled before the parliament. method of appointment committee comprising of following members:

1. Prime Minister;
2. Home Ministers of Union Government;
3. Speaker of Lok Sabha;
4. Chief Minister of concerned state; and
5. The Vice-President.

Till today, recommendations of the Punchhi Commission have not been implemented. Thus, Governor is appointed by the President without any consultation.

Eligibility for the Role of Governor

1. The Governor shall not be **member of either** House of Parliament, or of state legislature.
2. If Members of Parliament (MPs) or state legislature are appointed as Governor, she/he shall be deemed to have **vacated** his seat in the House on the **date** on which he enters upon his office as Governor.
3. The Governor shall not hold any **office of profit**. Office of profit is not defined in the Constitution. Meaning of office of profit is similar, which is enacted by the Parliament in the Office of Profit Act, 1959.
4. The Governor shall be entitled to use his/her official residence without payment of rent. Emolument of Governor is prescribed in **Second Schedule** of the Constitution. Governor shall receive Rs 5,500 per month, according to the **Second Schedule**. Since then, the Parliament has enacted a law known as **Governors (Emoluments, Allowances and Privileges) Act 1982**. The Act is amended many times and the latest amendment was brought about in the year 2016. According to that Amendment, emolument of Governor has gone up to Rs 3.50 lakhs per months.
5. One further condition is incorporated in **1956** by the **7th Constitutional Amendment**. If the same person is

appointed as Governor of two or more than two states, emolument and allowance payable to the Governor shall be **allocated** among states. Proportion of allocation shall be determined by **President by order**.

6. Emoluments and allowance of the Governor shall not be diminished during his/her term of office.

The Governor does not **receive pension**. The Constitution is silent about pension nor did Parliament enact any law for the pension of the Governor. A bill was introduced in this regard in the **year 2012** in Lok Sabha. Bill could not pass since the debate over which government shall pay the pension to the Governor could not be resolved. Union government said it is responsibility of state government and state government refused to accept the obligation.

Oath

The **Third Schedule** of the Constitution includes the provision of the oath of the Governor. Article 159 prescribes oath and affirmation of governor.

Oath and affirmation is mandatory for the Governor before entering upon his office. Discharging of functions is permitted after oath. Chief Justice of High Court or seniormost Judge of High Court available initiate the process of oath-taking.

Format of Governor's Oath

The oath is uttered in the following form:

I, A.B., do swear in the name of God/solemnly affirm that I will faithfully execute the office of Governor (or discharge the functions of the Governor) of .... (*name of State*) and will to the best of my ability preserve, protect and defend the Constitution and the law and that I will devote myself to the service and well-being of the people of .... (*name of the State*).

Executive Powers of the Governor

The Governor is invested with executive, legislative and judicial powers parallel to that of the President.

1. **Appointment of Chief Minister:** One of the most important executive powers of the Governor is to appoint the Chief Minister, according to Article 164(1). Appointment of CM becomes easier when one political party commands majority in the state Legislative Assembly. But in case of a hung Assembly, appointment of CM becomes crucial and disputed too. Since the Governor is constitutional head of the state government, the role of the Governor should be *neutral and impartial* to party politics. The Governor should act according to following sequence. If no single party gets majority in state assembly, the **Sarkaria Commission** recommends any of the following to be appointed as the CM:
   (i) Leader of the largest pre-poll alliance.
   (ii) Leader of single largest party in Assembly, supported by other parties.
   (iii) Leader of largest post-poll alliance.

Punchhi Commission recommended the following sequence, in appointment of CM:

(i) A pre-poll alliance is to be regarded as one political party. Pre-poll alliance with largest number shall be invited first.
(ii) Single largest party with support of others.
(iii) Post-poll alliance with a few parties joining the government.

Recommendations of Sarkaria Commission and Punchhi Commission are more or less same. These guidelines are not followed by the Governor yet. The Supreme Court said that the Governor is entitled to appoint a Chief Minister but majority of the government shall be decided on the floor of the house.

2. Apart from the CM, other ministers are also appointed by the Governor, on her/his advice. The Governor can nominate members, corresponding to similar powers of the President. So, the Governor can nominate 1/6th of the total numbers of the Legislative Council under Article 171(5).
3. Chairperson and members of the State Public Service Commission (PSC), and the Advocate General are also appointed by the Governor. They hold office during the pleasure of the Governors but **cannot be removed by the Governor**. President shall remove Chairperson and members of State PSC, on the recommendation of the **Supreme Court,** should the need arise.
4. The Governor also appoints:
   (i) Head of State Finance Commission
   (ii) Advocate General of State
   (iii) Chairperson of State Election Commission
   (iv) Vice Chancellor of state universities
   (v) State Human Rights Commission
   (vi) State Information Commission
5. The Governor is consulted by the President in the matter of appointment of judges of the state High Court under Article 217 (1).

Legislative Powers of the Governor

1. **Summoning House**
   (i) Each House of state legislature meets at such time and place as the Governor thinks fits; there should not be gap of more than 6 months between the two sessions. Governor is also entitled to prorogue the House. The Governor shall also dissolve the **State Legislative Assembly**.
   (ii) In 2015, the Governor of Assam had **preponed** the summoning of the Legislative Assembly, without aid and advice of the Council of Ministers. In the **Nabam Rebia case (2016),** the Supreme Court held that the Governor shall not summon the State Legislative Assembly without aid and advice of the Council of Ministers and with the CM as its head.
   (iii) The Governor also addresses the State Legislative Assembly. Governor may send a message to the House for considering a bill pending in the House.
   (iv) At the commencement of the first session after each general election, the Governor shall address the State Legislative Assembly. It is also known as *special address* by the Governor.
2. **Bill Reserved for Consideration:**
   When State Legislative Assembly or legislature of the state passes a bill, it shall be presented to the Governor. The Governor shall exercise the following options under Article 200:
   (i) Assent over the bill
   (ii) Return the bill for reconsideration to house
   (iii) Money bill shall not be returned for reconsideration
   (iv) Withholding assent
   (v) Reserve the bill for the consideration of the President.
3. **Power of the President:**
   The President may direct the Governor to **return** the bill for reconsideration. Legislative Assembly must deliberate over the bill within 6 months. It shall be presented with amendment or without amendment again to the President for his reconsideration. The President is not bound to give his/her assent over the bill again, under Article 200. The President shall reserve the bill passed by state

legislature, if it violates the powers of the High Court.

4. **Time Limit for Assent:**

   No time limit is prescribed for not giving assent over the bill. The President did not give assent over the bill or reject the bill for decades. The **Sarkaria Commission** recommended for fixing of **4 month** time limit for the assent on Bill. The **Punchhi Commission** recommended the same.

5. **Ordinance Making Power:**

   Governor is entitled to exercise her/his power to make ordinances under **Article 213**. Governor is satisfied that circumstances exist, which render it necessary for him to take immediate action. Governor shall exercise the power in following circumstances under Article 213.

   (i) State Legislative Assembly of state is not in session.

   (ii) Both houses of the State Legislature are not in session; this is applicable where the State Legislative Council also exists apart from Legislative Assembly of state.

   (iii) One of the houses is not in session.

   The following points summarise the ordinance-making powers of Governor:

   (a) **Scope**

   Governor shall issue an ordinance on subjects belonging **to the state** list in the **7th schedule**. Governor is also capable to issue an ordinance on subjects included in the **concurrent list**.

   (b) **Tenure**

   Ordinance issued by the Governor means **law-making** by executive. However, law-making power of the state is given to legislative assembly of the state. Approval of the Legislative assembly is required **within 6 weeks** or one and half month. In case of rejection by the **State Legislative Assembly**, ordinances automatically **lapse.** Ordinance may be **withdrawn** by Governor at any time. If two houses of Legislature of the state are summoned on two different dates, six weeks shall be counted from **later** date.

   (c) **Re-Promulgation of Ordinance**

   Constitution does not mention the issue of **re-promulgation** of an ordinance. Practically, ordinances re-promulgate numerous times. Ordinances were extended up to 10 years. Thus 6 weeks time limit becomes meaningless. It is against separation of power. Re-promulgation of ordinance undermine the importance of Legislature of the state too.

   (d) **Satisfaction of Governor**

   Satisfaction of Governor is not described in the constitution. It is subjective that the governor can hold any ordinance. While issuing an ordinance, the Governor may not act on the aid and advice of the Council of Minister. This does not mean satisfaction of the council of Minister, which is headed by the Chief Minister.

   (e) **Limitation over Ordinance**

   Limitation over law-making power of the state government applies to ordinances too. Some bills cannot be introduced in the legislative assembly of state, without previous sanction of the President. For example:

   1. Bill related to change in the provision of inter-state trade and commerce under article 304.
   2. Bill related to inter-state river, water regulation under Article 288.

Governor shall not issue an ordinance, over above-mentioned subjects. Apart from that, several other limitation are also applied on ordinances like:

1. Bills reserved for consideration of the President. It shall not be subject for issuing an ordinance.
2. **Satisfaction of Governor** also put restrictions over council of Minister for issuing an ordinance.

Pardoning Power

The governor of a state shall have the power to grant pardon under **Article 161**. Pardon refers to *removal of guilt or conviction*. The person stands free from all the charges. In addition to this, punishment is also abolished. The person leads a normal Life. All Criminal and Civil Disqualification becomes null and void.

Various other lighter forms of pardon are also included in **Article 161**, like:

1. **Reprieve:** Suspension of execution of penalty or punishment.
2. **Respite:** Awarding lesser punishment due to some special circumstances like illness, or pregnancy in the case of women.
3. **Remission:** Awarding lesser punishment, reduction in quantity of punishment.
4. **Commutation:** *Qualitative reduction* in punishment, commuting death penalty in Life Imprisonment.

This power is exercised under the following frameworks:

(a) **Scope:**

Power of Governor extends over any law relating to a matter of executive power of state. Governor cannot pardon or commute a person convicted by the **Court Martial**. Governor cannot pardon a person who has received **Death Penalty**. Nevertheless, Governor can commute the sentence into life imprisonment from death penalty. Executive power of state covers both state list as well as concurrent list in 7th Schedule.

Governors shall exercise power of pardon by the **aid and advice of the Council of Minister**. Since power of Pardon is a **constitutional** power, thus application should be **reasonable**. It is subject to Judicial Review.

b. **Conduct of Business**

All executive action of the Government of state shall be expressed to be taken in the name of the **Governor**, under Article 166. Orders and other **instruments** are also made and executed in the name of Governor. Validity of these orders and instruments shall not be called in question. Governor shall make rules for more convenient transaction of the business of the government of the state. Governor shall also allocate business among ministers, according to the rule made by him/her.

ROLE OF GOVERNOR

1. **Constitutional Head**

According to Article 163 of the constitution, there shall be a **Council of Ministers** headed by the CM to give aid and advice to Governor. Constitution requires that Governor should act according to the aid and advice of the Council of Ministers. The Council of Ministers is elected by the People. The CM is the **Administrative Head of the Government**. Exercise of Pardon power and all the appointments made by Governor is done on the basis of aid and advice by council of ministers. Governor merely signs the bill, which is passed by legislature of the state, due to the effort of the Council of Minister.

But Article 163 explicitly gives *discretionary* power to Governor. The aid and advice of the Council Minister are *not binding* on Governor. Governor can take any decision contrary to the advice of CoM. Following issues are worth noting, where Governor applies discretion:

(a) Reserving a bill passed by Legislature of the state under Article 200.
(b) Governor also ensures that the government shall be carried on in accordance with the provision of this constitution under article 356.
(c) Withholding the assent over the bill passed by Legislature of state.
(d) Appointment of CM in case of hung state Legislative Assembly.

Discretionary powers of Governor are the bone of contention. Critics are of the view that the Governor becomes *an agent of the Union Government*. If the Governor applies his discretionary power on the basis of instruction of the union government, he undermines the autonomy of the state and federal structure of the Constitution.

2. **Representative of Union in State**

The Governor plays a *dual role* as the constitutional head of the state and also as the representative of the state in Union. Governors send regular report about the working of state to home ministry of Union Government. Article 371, is incorporated in the constitution by 7th Constitutional Amendment in 1956, Governor of Maharashtra, Gujarat, Nagaland, Assam, Mizoram, Arunachal Pradesh, Goa and Karnataka are given special responsibility.

3. **Special Responsibility**

(i) **Maharashtra and Gujarat:** Governor is entrusted of special responsibility to establish **development board** for **Vidarbha and Marathawada** under Article 371. Governor of Gujarat shall set up development board of **Saurashtra and Kutch**.

(ii) **Nagaland**: No act of parliament is applicable over religious, social practices of Nagas, unless Legislative Assembly of Nagaland approves under **Article 371(A)**. Governor shall ensure peace and progress of the state. Regional council shall also be set up by Governor in Nagaland.

(iii) **Assam:** Special protection is given for Tribal areas of Assam under Article 371B.

(iv) **Manipur**: Governor is given special responsibility for the development of **hilly areas of state**, under article 371(C).

(v) **Andhra Pradesh/Telangana:** Public employment and education is the special responsibility of Governor under **Article 371D.** Central University of Andhra Pradesh is also established by Article 371 (E).

(vi) Members of State Legislative Assembly of Sikkim shall consist of not less than 30 members (371) F.

(vii) **Mizoram:** Mizoram enjoys the same amount of autonomy as Nagaland. No parliamentary act shall applicable over Mizoram, unless State Legislative assembly by resolution so decides. Parliamentary act is not applicable over religious and social practices of Mizos, under Article 371(G).

(viii) **Arunachal Pradesh:** Maintaining law and order is special responsibility of Governor under Article 371(H).

(ix) **Goa:** Legislative assembly of the Goa shall consist of not less than 30 members under Article 371 (I).

(x) **Karnataka:** Governor of Karnataka shall ensure the establishment of a separate development board for Hyderabad–Karnataka region.

Governors of 12 states are given special responsibility in the constitution. Governor can get aid and advice of council of ministers, but advice is not binding upon governor.

4. **Administrative Head**
   During imposition of President's Rule (356) in the state, the governor acts as its administrative head. Council of Ministers is automatically dissolved during President Rule. Thus council of minister does not exist to give aid and advice to Governor. **Governor** is supposed to act alone without council of Ministers during President's Rule.
5. **Connecting Link between Union and State**
   Union government issues various directions and advisory to state governments through governor under **Article 256**. Executive power of state government shall not be exercised against a law made by Parliament. Parliament amended the Citizenship Act of 1955, consequently state shall not refuse to enforce the the law. The Governor must also report to union government about activities of insurgency in states like Manipur and Nagaland.

Supreme Court on Article 356

President's rule was imposed in Karnataka in 1989. Then CM of Karnataka, S. R. Bommai challenged the act of governor in Supreme Court. Meanwhile President's rule was also imposed in **Meghalaya (1991)**. The same was also executed in U.P., M.P. and Rajasthan, after demolition of Babri Mosque in U.P. Supreme Court heard all issues collectively in S. R. Bommai Case (1994). Various issues were involved in **S. R. Bommai** case:

1. **Federalism is Basic Structure:** Supreme Court said that misuse of Article 356 violates the spirit of federalism. Federalism is not an issue of *administrative efficiency*. It is the basic structure of the Constitution. State government is not subordinate to union government.
2. **356 is subjected to judicial review:** It is worth noting that **Article 361** says that President and Governor shall not be **answerable** to any Court for the exercise and performance of the powers and duties of his office. Consequently, the Court refused to examine the misuse of Article 356. But Court overruled its previous decision in **Bommai Case**. Court shall review the misuse of Article 356. It is **relative power** of President rather than absolute power. Since Bommai Case, Supreme Court ruled that **unreasonable** use of Article 356 shall be declared null and void.
3. **Meaning of Failure of Constitutional Machinery:** The term Failure of Constitutional machinery is not defined in Article 356. In a landmark judgement, Court said that failure of Constitutional machinery means that the legislative assembly of state is not summoned within 6 months. Else, Council of Ministers has lost the confidence of State Legislative Assembly, but still run the government. CoM failed to pass the appropriation bill in the house.

   Corruption, maladministration, is an example of **administrative failure**. Article 356 shall not be imposed on the ground of failure of **administrative machinery**.
4. **Suspension and Dissolution of House:** Court also said that imposition of president rule does not mean **dissolution of Legislative Assembly** of state. Dissolution refers to the **end of tenure** of Legislative Assembly. The Legislative assembly cannot be summoned and salary and privilege of MLA abolished altogether. Suspension denotes postponement of sitting of Legislative assembly of state. It can be summoned later. MLA also receives salaries with continuation of privilege. Suspension

of legislative assembly automatically suspend the council of Minister Court said that State Legislature Assembly shall be dissolved after approval of Parliament. Court went to the extent of saying that misuse of Article 356 is fraud with the Constitution. Even decisions to dissolve Legislative Assembly can be revoked in case of arbitrary misuse of Article 356.

5. **Secularism:** Communal violence may be a valid ground for imposition of Article 356. Therefore President's rule in U.P., M.P., and Rajasthan is upheld by Court. Secularism is the basic structure of the Constitution.
6. **Aid and Advice of CoM to President:** Article 74(2) puts restriction over judicial review of the aid and advice tendered by Council of Ministers to President, who shall not be inquired into any court. But court said that court is entitled to examine the **material facts** presented before President by the Council of Ministers.
7. **Floor Test:** Proving confidence in House is not the privilege of **Governor or President** Confidence/or majority of Council of Ministers shall be decided on the floor of the house.
8. **Summing Up:** Bommai case remains a landmark decision in the constitutional history of India. Court reiterated the decision in **Rameshwar Prasad case** (2006) case. This one put a check over misuse of Article 356. Crux of the problem is understood to be political, and not constitutional or legal.

8

FEDERALISM IN INDIA

KEY CONCEPTS

Strong Centre Framework, Asymmetrical Federal Provisions and Adaption, Role of Intergovernmental Coordination Mechanisms, Inter-State Council, Emerging Trends

DIFFERENT FORMS OF GOVERNMENT

Democratic government can be classified as **parliamentary** and **presidential** on the basis of relation between the legislature and the executive. Government may be **unitary** or **federal** on the basis of *geographical division of power*.

I. Federal Form of Government, Basic Features

1. **Division of Power:** Under the federal system, power is divided into **two sets of** government. The union government and the state government both draw their powers from the Constitution. The Seventh Schedule of the Indian Constitution ensures the division and allocation of powers and functions between the Union and the State legislatures.
2. **Decentralisation of Power:** Division of power promotes decentralisation of power. The federal government establishes multiple and autonomous units, which draw theirpowers from the Constitution. For example, the federal government of the United States of America (US) is comprised of 50 states, whereas 28 states exist in the Indian federation.
3. **Equal Partner:** The federal government and the state government complement each other. It is important to note that the state government does not receive their power from the central government, but rather, from the **constitution**.
4. **Written and supreme Constitution:** Division of power is maintained through the written Constitution. Neither the Centre nor the state government can alter the division of power.
5. **Bicameral House:** Two houses are mandatory for federal government—one house **represents the state** and the other, the people. **Rajya Sabha** represents the state in the Indian Constitution, whereas the **Lok Sabha** reflects the will of the people.
6. **Independent Judiciary:** Division of power can result in disputes. Hence the judiciary provides an *independent and neutral* dispute settlement mechanism. Neither the federal government nor the state government is entitled to settle the dispute.
7. **Protecting Diversity: Prof. Rashiduddin Khan** says that Indian society is federal

therefore, India opted for a federal form of government. The same view is held by **Prof. M. P. Singh** who said that the Indian federal system accommodates diversity of ethnicity. The federal government is a democratic method to accommodate the diversity of society. Formation of various states fulfills the need for cultural diversity. The state can adopt their own language as an official language. It protects **regional aspirations**. Therefore in a large and democratic nation like **India**, federal government is helpful to maintain **unity in diversity.**

II. Unitary Form of Government

1. **Single Constitution:** The Constitution recognises *one centre of power* in unitary government. Smaller states in size like Britain and Sri Lanka have adopted unitary government. Unitary government means one capital, single citizenship and centralised administration.
2. **Units are subordinate:** Other provinces or units can be established for administrative efficiency. But units are **subordinate** to the central government. Units or provinces are not **autonomous.**
3. **Centralisation of Power:** Provinces do not receive their power from the Constitution. Provinces are **dependent** on the central government for exercising their power. **Delegation of power** is the discretion of the central government.

THE US MODEL OF FEDERATION

1. **Federation is a Result of Contract:** The US is a *classical* model of federal government. Formation of federal government in the US is a result of **contract** among the independent and severing states. Independent states decided to form a **common government**, which is also known as the federal government. In the US, since the states formed the federation, power of the federal government is decided by the states. Therefore, the state government is powerful in the US federation.
2. **Power Sharing:** The US federation is comprised of **50 states**. Each state keeps its **own constitution**. The Governor of each state **is elected by** the people of the state. State services are also divided. Dual citizenship is a feature of the US federal system, that is, in the federal state, a person is not only the citizen of the country but also of the particular state where the person is born or belongs to.
3. **Powerful State:** The US Constitution only contains the **Federal List**. **Residuary** powers, that is, unwritten powers of the constitution, belong to the state governments.
4. **Indestructible Federation and the Indestructible State:** The state cannot **secede** from federation. And federal government cannot change the name, boundary of state, without the **consent** of the state.
5. **Equality among the States:** Equal power is **shared** between the federal government and the state government. In addition, the states are **also equal**. Each state sends **two representatives** to the senate, the upper house of the US Congress. Size and population of the 50 states is not same but their **representation is equal**.

STRONG CENTRAL FRAMEWORK/ UNIONIST MODEL OF FEDERATION

Confederation marked the start of Canadian federalism. It refers to the process of federal union in which the British North American colonies of Nova Scotia, New Brunswick and the Province of Canada joined together to form the Dominion of Canada. The term Confederation also stands for 1 July 1867, the date of the creation of the Dominion. Beginning in 1864, colonial politicians (now known as the Fathers of Confederation) met and negotiated the terms of Confederation, and their work resulted in the *British North America Act*, Canada's constitution. **The Canadian federation** is not a result of **contract among** the states, like that of the US federation. The states were carved out from the federation. There is a **common (single)** constitution for the centre and the states. Residuary powers belong to the central government. The central government appoints the governor in the states. The central government enacts a law over **state list,** in favour of **national interest**. The Canadian supported strong federal government. Thus, they prefer the term **union** rather than federation. Representation of every state is ensured in the upper house according to their population. Equal representation of a state is not adopted in Canada. Union in Canadian constitution denotes two features:

1. Federation is not result of a contract among the states.
2. It is an indication of strong federal government.

FEDERATION AND UNION

The distinction between 'federation' and 'union' is technical in nature. It only reflects the historical differences of different nations during formation of the federal government. Federation and union share common features, such as:

1. Division of power
2. Federal government and states are coordinate, that is, equal in rank and importance.
3. States drive their powers from the constitution.
4. There is a written and supreme constitution.
5. There is an independent and autonomous judiciary.
6. An upper house is present.

NATURE OF THE INDIAN FEDERATION

After the Partition of India, tendency of disintegration existed in India. Insurgency of **Naga groups** in the Northeast, and the hostile approach of Pakistan towards Kashmir necessitated the formation of *strong union* government. **Vallabhbhai Patel** supported strong federal government for *unity and integrity* of India. **Dr Ambedkar** also recommended that a strong federal government is essential for the welfare of Scheduled Castes and Scheduled Tribes.

Indian society is comprised of various languages, religions, regions and culture. Therefore, federal government was seen as the best option for accommodating the diversity of India. Therefore, the Constituent Assembly prefers a strong federal government.

Article 1 of the Indian Constitution says: India, that is **Bharat,** shall be a **Union of States.** The Indian Constitution contains all features of federal government like:

1. Division of Power
2. Written Constitution
3. Independent Judiciary
4. Rajya Sabha as the Upper House

But the term 'union' is inserted in the Constitution; 'federal' is not written anywhere in the Constitution. 'Union' indicates a strong federal government. The Supreme Court in the **S. R. Bommai case** (1994) said that federalism is the basic structure of the Constitution, and that federal government is not merely an administrative tool to run the government.

Quasi-Federal System

K. C. Wheare describes the Indian federal system as quasi-federal and sees the strong union government as going against the federal spirit. For him, the United States of America is the classical model of federation. However, the Indian parliament is entitled to enact laws over the State List. Emergency provision has further centralised the power of the union. In the initial decades, the functions of the Indian federation, the Planning Commission and the dominating role of the Congress Party made the union government more powerful.

Federation with National Interest

Alexandrowicz says that the Indian Constitution is federal, where national interest is primary. Article 249 refers to national interests. The very term 'national interest' shows that division of power is less important than serving the interest of the nation.

Cooperative Federation

Granville Austin is of the view that the Indian Constitution promotes cooperative federalism. The presence of Concurrent List in the Seventh Schedule indicates cooperation. **Article 263** also speaks about cooperation. Financial and administrative cooperation is inevitable due to the constitutional provision of cooperation.

Federal with Strong Union Government

Ivor Jennings says that the Indian Constitution is federal with strong centralising tendencies. The Constitution combines the feature of centralisation and de-centralisation. **Paul R. Brass** also remarked that the emergency provisions are a result of the fear of disorder, which results into formation of a strong union government. **Alfred Stepan** is of the view that Indian federalism is an example of '*holding together*' federation, whereas the US federation is a model of '*coming together*' federation. This view is more appropriate for describing the nature of Indian federation.

Centralising Features

'Union' implies a strong federal government,which includes the following features:

1. **State can be destroyed:** Union cannot be destroyed but name, boundary and size of a state is subject to **alteration**, under **Article 3**. Consent of state is not binding upon the union government.
2. **Division of power favours the strong union:** The Seventh Schedule maintains division of power. But the **Concurrent List** strengthens the union government. Union and state governments are capable of framing a law over the Concurrent List. In case of **conflict** between union and state, union law prevails over state laws. Entry 97, List I, mentioned in the Seventh Schedule is known as **residuary powers**, which lies in the hands of the union government.
3. **Command of union over administration:** Governors of state are appointed by the union government. All India services also centralise the power of the union. Union government is authorised to give instructions to the states.
4. **Lack of financial autonomy:** Revenue of state is not sufficient for the welfare programmes of states. Hence **states depend** upon the **grant** of the union government under **Article 275**.
5. **Nature of state is unified:** Federal government comprises of division of power. But the **judiciary** is not divided between the union and the state. **Citizenship** is single. **Integrated auditing** and **common Election Commission** exist in India for the union and the states.
6. **Common Constitution:** States do not have their **own constitution**. There is a common constitution for the union and the state. Power of union is enhanced due to **single constitution** because the parliament is empowered to amend the Constitution with few exceptions.

Unitary During Emergency

Indian Constitution is federal during normalcy. But it becomes unitary during emergency period. **National emergency** is mentioned in **Article 352**.

Provision of **financial emergency** is incorporated in **Article 360.**

Critical Evaluation

Due to the above-mentioned centralising tendency, critics observed that the Indian federation is *quasi-federal* in nature. Some went to the extent of saying that India has a **unitary government** with **few federal features. Sarkaria Commission** rightly pointed out a strong federal government is not antithetical to the autonomy of state. National interest may be primary in federation of India, according to critics like Austin, however, it is a cooperative federation.

CENTRE–STATE RELATIONS

Centre–state relations in the Constitution is drawn from the **Government of India Act 1935**. The Act enumerated three lists namely Centre, State and Concurrent Lists. However, residuary powers were allocated to the Governor General under this Act.

Law Making Power of the Parliament

Under **Article 245,** the parliament is entitled to make a law for the whole territory of India. Territory is comprised of-

(i) States
(ii) Union Territories
(iii) Any acquired territory

Extra-Territorial Power of Parliament

The Parliament is capable of making laws for Indians, who are residing in a **foreign country**. This known as extra-territorial power. Parliament can grant voting rights to **non-resident Indians** too under **Article 245**.

Law-Making Power of State Legislature

State legislature is empowered to make laws for the **state only**. Haryana state legislature can enact a law for Haryana only. Law-making power of state legislature is limited geographically under **Article 245**.

Division of Power in the Seventh Schedule

The Parliament shall enact laws over the **Union List.** The state legislature shall make law for **State List.** The **Concurrent List** is available for both, union and the states, according to **Article 246**. The Seventh Schedule is inserted for complementing Article 246. **Union List** contains **97 entries**, including the issues of **national importance** like defence, foreign affairs, banking and aviation. The **State List** incorporates 66 entries including police, public order, health, prison, agriculture. **Concurrent List** (47 entries) is comprised of social economic planning, electricity, newspaper, labour welfare, education, forest, civil and criminal procedure code. **Residuary powers** belong to the parliament.

Amendment in the List

Parliament is entitled to amend the list, although transferring any entry from **State List** to **Concurrent List** increases the power of the union government. Entries like education, forest, population control were shifted from State List to Concurrent List by the 42nd Amendment in 1976 by the Indira Gandhi government.

Interpretation of List

The Seventh Schedule ensures division of power between union and state. But division leads to dispute too, which is settled by the Supreme Court. The Court propounded the following principles while interpreting the list:

1. **Pith and Substance:** Content of law is more important than **title of law**. While interpreting the list, the Court examines the content of enacted law. Title is not the parameter for determining the entry.
2. **Colourable Legislation:** Union and state government cannot encroach on the entries mentioned in the Seventh Schedule through indirect machinations.

3. **Harmonious Construction:** Three lists are incorporated in the Seventh Schedule. They should be interpreted in a harmonious manner. AIIMS belong to the Union List; health comes under the State List. However, population control is mentioned in Concurrent List. All are interrelated with each other. Thus, they should be seen in light of harmony.

Autonomy of State

Federal form of government gives autonomous power to states. State Legislative Assembly is **directly elected** by the people. A council of ministers is drawn from the Assembly, headed by the Chief Minister. State Legislative Assembly is entitled to make laws over the State List, and the state government administers the subjects of the State List. State government can levy the taxes, collect and appropriate over the State List described in the Seventh Schedule. Thus, the **Chief Minister** is not subordinate to **Prime Minister** but they are **equal partners**.

A. Tendency of Centralisation in Legislative Domain

1. **Residuary power of legislation:** Article 248 gives the parliament **exclusive powers** for enacting a law over the Union List. The entries or subjects which are not mentioned in the Seventh Schedule are considered as residuary powers. Residuary powers are given to the states in federal system of the US. Residuary powers belong to union in India.
2. **Primacy of union over Concurrent List:** Indian Constitution incorporates the term 'union'. India is union of states. And union indicates towards *centralisation* of power and *national interest*. The Seventh Schedule ensures division of power and the union government and the state government both are entitled to enact a law over Concurrent List. For example, Concurrent List includes **criminal law**. So for example if the union government and state government each enacted a law for punishment in case of rape, in case of conflict between union law and state law, union law shall prevail (Article 254) over the law made by the states.
3. **Governor's right to reserve the bill**: The Governor is entitled to reserve any bill passed by the state legislature for the consideration of the President, under **Article 200**. Governor shall reserve the bill of state which undermines the power of the **High Court.** Practically, the Governor reserves the state bill of various kinds, for example, the religious conversion bill of the Rajasthan government (the Rajasthan Dharma Swatantrya Bill, 2006) was reserved by the Governor for the consideration of The President.

   The bill passed by the state legislature over Concurrent List becomes **primary** if it receives assent of the **President**, as per **Article 201**. State bill is given primacy over union bill. But Parliament has the capacity to later enact a new law to amend or repeal the law made by legislative assembly of the state over Concurrent List.
4. **National interest and power of parliament:** *Division of power* is the basic character of the federal government. But Indian Constitution promotes *national interest* which cannot be divided between union and states. The notion of national interest strengthens the power of union government. As we have discussed, parliament can enact a law over State List for **whole** or **any part** of the territory of India under **Article 249**. Parliament can enact a law after the resolution is supported by not less than **2/3rd** of the members present and voting in the Rajya Sabha (or the Council of States).

   Council of States supports the resolution because it is necessary in national interest.

Law enacted by the parliament shall remain in force for *not more than one year*. Further it can be extended for **one year** with approval of the **Rajya Sabha**. After expiry of resolution, the law shall be valid for **six months**.

5. **Parliamentary legislation with consent of states:** Two or more than two states can request the parliament to make a law over the State List under **Article 252**. Parliamentary act is applicable only for **those states that** passed resolution in that regard. Other states can **also request** for extension of act over them by passing such a resolution. Repealing or amendment in Act is not permitted by State Legislative Assembly. Parliament can repealing or amend the act. **Time limitation** is not mentioned in Article 252. Thus, an Act made by parliament is applicable over state until or unless parliament brings about change in law.
6. **International agreement:** Foreign affairs belong to Union List. The union government participates in international organisations. **Article 253** allows parliament to make any law for the implementation of any **treaty, agreement** or **convention**. Law made by the parliament is applicable for whole or any part of territory of India. Parliament shall also make a law related to application of any decision made at any international conference, association or other body.
7. **Federal government becomes unitary during emergency:** As we have noted, the Indian Constitution is federal in nature during normal times. However, it becomes unitary during a formally-declared **Emergency**, that is, division of power is *suspended* during national emergency. Although State Legislative Assembly and **Council of Ministers exist during national emergency**, yet the parliament is entitled to make laws over the **State List**. In other words, the **State List** becomes **Concurrent List**.

   Also, in case of **failure of constitutional machinery**, State Legislative Assembly dissolves and Council of Ministers and Chief Minister, no longer hold their office. It is popularly known as **president's rule**. Due to dissolution of state assembly, division of power is suspended automatically. Therefore, the parliament is capable to enact law over State List. That is reason Indian constitution combines federal features as well as unitary character.

B. Centralisation in Administrative Relations

Administrative or executive division of power follows the legislative division of power. This means entries mentioned in the Union List are administered by the union government, and subjects of State List are administered by the state government. Personnel of state government are responsible for the administration of the state. But tendency of centralisation exists in administrative relations.

1. **Appointment of Governor: President** is constitutional head of the union government. President is *elected* by an electoral college comprised of elected MPs and elected members of state assembly and Union Territories. Similarly, **Governor** is the constitutional head of the state government; however, s/he appointed by the union government. Governor is elected by the people of the state in the US. The role of Chief Minister of state is limited in the appointment and removal of Governor. Governor acts as a *representative* of union government. Therefore, the Governor acts according to **direction** of the union government, which can come into conflict with the power of elected Chief Minister.
2. **Instructions from union government:** State governments are considered as an

equal partner in federal government. State government derives their power from the Constitution. Under **Article 257,** union government is empowered to given directions for the state government in the field of:

(a) Construction of and maintenance of means of communication of **national** or **military importance**.

(b) Protection of railway within the state.

(c) Apart from **Article 257**, President shall issue instructions for education to children belonging to linguistic minorities in the mother tongue at the primary stage. Under **Article 350 (A)**, President shall appoint officers for linguistic minorities. And report of officer for linguistic minorities is sent for the state government under **Article 350 (B).** It shall be the duty of the union government to promote the spread of Hindi language under **Article 351**.

Union government's power of giving directions to the state government appears antithetical to the **autonomy of the state**. It is taken from the **Government of India Act, 1935**. Under the Act, the **Governor General** gave special instructions for state governments. This further enhanced the power of union government in the federal government.

Deployment of Central Armed Forces: Union government shall deploy the **armed forces** or other forces for the assistance of the state government. This provision is included in the Constitution by the **42nd Constitutional Amendment** in **1976**. However, the Janata Party government repealed the provision by the 44th Constitutional Amendment with 1978 because public order belongs to State List in the Seventh Schedule. Police is also the subject of state governments, therefore deployment of armed forces seems inappropriate according to federal spirit. Recently West Bengal government opposed the decision of the central government for deployment of Central Reserve Police Force (CRPF) in West Bengal during the 2021 state elections.

3. **All India Services:** Federal governments allow two sets of the government. Therefore, two types of services exist in the **US**. Federal services for the federal government and state services for the state government operate in the US. Indian Constitution incorporates **all India services** apart from union and state services. All India service is not divided between union and state. Because all India services are controlled by the union government. For example, the all-India **Indian Administrative Services (IAS)**, **Indian Police Services (IPS)** and **Indian Forest Services (IFS)** are subject to control of the union government. The IAS is under control of **Ministry of Personnel;** IPS works under the purview of **Home Ministry** of union government; IFS is subject to control of **Ministry of Environment, Forest and Climate Change** of union government.

Union governments provide training for members of all India services. Promotion and sacking of officers is also the responsibility of union government. Members of all India services are deployed in states. **Chief Secretary** is administrative head of state government but he belongs to the all India services. **Director General of Police (DGP)** is head of the police of state government associated with all India services. Therefore, all India services undermine the importance of state services. It challenges the federal form of government. **Deputation** of members of all India services is also determined by the union government. For instance, IPS officers of West Bengal can be deputed in Central Bureau of Investigation (CBI) for some time.

According to critics, all India services are against the *regional diversity* of India. It undermines linguistic diversity as well. Division of power demands division of personnel too, although all India services are helpful for maintaining unity and integrity of state. **Article 312** promotes *cooperative federalism* between union and state, and maintains a link between the two.

C. Financial Relations (Fiscal Federalism)

The financial division of power is influenced by the **Government of India Act 1935**. Union and state are autonomous and equal with each other. Therefore, **the Seventh Schedule** is the base of financial relations between union and state. Union government shall **levy and collect the taxes** mentioned in the Union List. Union governments also utilise the taxes appropriated (collected) by union government. The **concurrent powers of taxation** also belong to the union government. Union List incorporates entries like income tax, corporate tax and custom duty.

State government is entitled to levy, collect, and appropriate taxes on subjects in the State List. State list includes taxes on profession and trade, taxes on consumption of sale of electricity, alcohol for human consumption and taxes on agriculture and petroleum product. *Financial division of power* follows the *legislative division* of power. Therefore, union and state are independent in terms of levying taxation and collection of taxes.

Apart from the taxation, the union government runs various public sector industries. Union government receives income from Public Sector Undertakings (PSU) like Oil and Natural Gas Corporation (ONGC). Similarly, the state governments also runs small-scale industries and handicraft industries. State government receives the income from these industries.

Stronger Financial Power of the Union Government

The union government is capable of levying taxes on important subjects like income tax, corporate tax and customs. Union government can also borrow the money from foreign nations and from international organisations under **Article 292**. State government is not entitled to borrow money from foreign countries and international organizations. Minerals and mines are also subject of the Union List and state government only receives royalty from the union government.

State Governments are like Municipalities

Due to the weak financial position of state government, critics have said that state government are not autonomous financially. State governments are *dependent* on the union government for financial assistance; just like how the municipality does not have an autonomous financial power and are dependent on the state government for financial assistance. Legislative and administrative powers without financial autonomy are meaningless. It is worth noting that responsibility of the state is associated with **welfare activities.** Health is a major responsibility of the state government. Although education belongs to the Concurrent List, imparting education is a most important job of the state government. But resources of state government are not sufficient.

Financial Resources of State Government

1. **Revenue from taxation:** State governments levy taxes and collect and appropriate the taxes on the entries of State List in the Seventh Schedule. It is insufficient for carrying out welfare programmes of the state. But **Northeastern states** are heavily dependent on grants from the union government. **Ninety per cent** of revenue of Nagaland is funded by the union government. States like **Bihar** are unable to generate sufficient revenue for the expenditure of welfare. **West Bengal**

government is under a debt crisis therefore financial autonomy of the state is still lacking.

2. **Grant from the union government:** According to **Article 275,** the union government provides grants for the states on the recommendation of the Finance Commission. However, dependence of the state on the union for grant is opposite to the idea of equality and autonomy of states.
3. **Centrally Sponsored Scheme:** Union government launched various **centrally sponsored schemes (CSS)** like Mid-Day Meal Scheme and Ujjwala Yojana. States have raised their resentment against CSS, because the **priority of CSS** may be different from the preference of states. For example, Delhi government runs its own health scheme and therefore, it refuses to accept the Ayushman Bharat scheme run by the **union government**. CSS also imposes terms and conditions on the state government, which is against the autonomy of states. Welfare function is a task of the state government—CSS launched by central government thus encroach upon the power of states. However, it can also be argued that the basic cause of conflict between union and state over CSS remains political.
4. **Division of central taxes:** It is interesting to note that the central taxes levied by the union government and collected by the union government is divided between union and state, under **Article 270**. Central tax means income tax, corporate tax, and custom, as mentioned in the Union List in the Seventh Schedule. By the **80th Constitutional Amendment (2000),** all central taxes are divided between union and states. But **surcharge** and **cess** are not divided between union and state.
5. **Control of Mines:** State government receives the royalty from mining. Because mining is a part of the Union List Jharkhand is a rich state in terms of mines, it is still an economically backward state.

Financial Relation during Emergency

Under **Article 360** financial emergencies can be imposed in India by the President. Legislative Assembly, Council of Ministers and Chief Minister continue to exist during financial emergency. But **division of financial power** between union and state is **suspended.** Apart from that the power of union government increases in the following ways:

1. Grant received by state government can be suspended.
2. Union government can issue **instructions** to states regarding the financial expenditure.
3. Money bill passed by State Legislative Assembly can be reserved for the consideration of the President.
4. During financial emergency, state government will have to dependent on their own resources for expenditure because union government is unable to support the state government.

Financial relation in the age of liberalisation

Federal form of government is based on the principle of *equality and autonomy* between **union** and **state**. At the same time, it promotes *equality among states* too, because all the states derive same power from the Seventh Schedule. But states are not equal in terms of economic strength, population and area. Kerala, Maharashtra, Gujarat, Goa and Punjab are rich states. Oidsha, Bihar and Uttar Pradesh are considered as backward states in terms of per capita income.

In the present age of privatisation and market economy, investors are preferring investment in **rich states**. Therefore, *economic disparity* increases day by day between the states. This led to rising demand of **special status** by the Bihar government.

Social and ethnic conflict is also visible among the states due to migration of people.

Disparity is also growing **within the state**, for example **Marathwada** region is not getting enough investment in Maharashtra. However, **Mumbai** is attracting investment. Therefore, demands for **separate state hood** and **regionalism** are bound to emerge. This places a strain on the federal system in India. In the post-liberalisation age, subjects like **irrigation, agriculture, electricity and transportation** need urgent reform. However, irrigation, transportation are included in the State List. Without cooperation between union and state, economic reform and ease of doing business is not possible. Better **fiscal management** is also required by the state government. State governments are adopting **populist** programmes like making water and electricity free of cost. Some observers contend that this creates further burden on the exchequer.

The **Make in India** programme is incomplete without proper cooperation between union and state. Strengthening state economy is needed for a strong federation. Therefore, the state cannot rely only on the grants given by union government. **Good governance** is needed for the better fiscal management of the states. Conflict between union and state or between states is detrimental to economic development of India.

FINANCE COMMISSION

A. **Constitutional provisions:** The Supreme Court is entitled to settle **disputes** between union and states. But division of taxes is not the job of **judiciary**. Under **Article 280,** the Finance Commission is instituted for maintaining **fiscal federalism**. The President shall constitute a Finance Commission, comprised of a **chairperson** and **four other members**, under Article 280, within **two years** of the commencement of the Constitution. The First Finance Commission was set up in **1951** under chairpersonship of K. C. Niyogi. President shall constitute Finance Commission every **fifth year** or at such earlier time.

B. **Eligibility** and **terms and conditions** of chairperson and members are not specified in Article 280. This article authorised the parliament to determine the qualification of members by law. Therefore, the parliament enacted a law in 1951 for determining the qualifications of chairperson and members:
   - (i) Chairperson who has had experience in **public affairs.**
   - (ii) One member has been or is qualified to be **appointed as judge of high court**.
   - (iii) Members should have special knowledge of the **finances** and **accounts** of **union government**.
   - (iv) They should have a wide experience in **administration** or **financial matters**.
   - (v) They should have special knowledge of **economics.**

C. **Duties of the Finance Commission**
   1. All central taxes are divided between union and states under Article 270. Therefore, Article 280 talks about distribution of net proceeds of taxes between union and states, and of the allocation of taxes between various states.
   2. Principle which should govern the **grant-in-aid** from consolidated fund of India, to states.
   3. Measures needed to augment the **consolidated funds** of the state to supplement the resources of the **panchayat** on the basis of the recommendation made by Finance Commission of the state. It is added by the **73rd Constitutional Amendment Act (1992)**.

4. Similarly, measures needed to augment the consolidated funds of state to supplement the resources of the **municipalities** in the state on the basis of the recommendation made by Finance Commission of the state. This is included in the Constitution by the **74th Amendment (1992)**.
5. Any other matter referred to the Commission by the President in the interest of sound finance. It is popularly known as **terms of reference**. Ease in doing business, better implementation of central sponsored schemes, and debt crises of state government were terms of reference in the **15th Finance Commission**. President always asks for **new terms of reference** in every Finance Commission.

The report of the Finance Commission is tabled before each house of the parliament by the President, along with an explanatory memorandum as to the action taken on the report of finance commission. Parliament by law authorises the Commission to determine procedure and powers for their functioning.

D. **Nature of Finance Commission**

Finance commission is a *quasi-judicial* body because it performs a *partial judicial* role. Division of taxes is a *partial administrative* role. Therefore, the Commission includes a member qualified to be appointed as judge of High Court. The Constitution does not allow the Supreme Court to settle disputes related to Finance Commission and distribution of taxes.

Working of Finance Commission

A. **Vertical Division of Taxes**

Role of the Finance Commission is crucial in *fiscal federalism* in India. The Commission maintains **equality** among the various states and addresses the problem of regional disparity. The 15th Finance Commission allocated **41 per cent** share in total central taxes to states. Earlier the share of states was 42 per cent. Centrally sponsored schemes were **downsized** and share of states in central taxes increased. This is better for the financial autonomy of states, because centrally-sponsored schemes bypass the power of state government, with the local government receiving direct funding from union government.

B. **Horizontal division of taxes**

Finance Commission allocates more shares of central taxes to the backward states. In other words, **Odisha and Bihar** receive a greater share of central taxes. Although rich states like **Punjab** and **Maharashtra** contribute more in terms of central taxes. It proves that a strong federal government is beneficial for the poorer states. The 15th Finance Commission for the first time introduced the population base of year to be 2011. North Indian states like Uttar Pradesh and Bihar registered huge population growth after 1971 whereas that of of South Indian states became stable after 1971. The population base of year 2011 is seen as 'benefiting' the Northern states. Therefore, the decision has been opposed by the Southern states.

Table 7.8.1: Weightage for Various Indicators

Indicators	*Weight*
Demographic performance	12.
Population	15
Income distance	45.0
Area	15.0
Forest and Ecology	10.0
Tax Effort	2.5

C. **Population Base**

The year 2011 has been accepted as the base year for allocation of central taxes among the states. Populated states should not be penalised for their population growth. But the concern of Southern states also needs to be addressed. Therefore, fiscal management, good governance and development of infrastructure should be given equal importance for the distribution of taxes among the states.

The Finance Commission works to fulfill three principles:

1. **Equality** refers to the attempt to bridge regional disparity among the states.
2. **Need** is the second principle where poor states receive more assistance.
3. **Efficiency** is equally important for distribution of central taxes. Thus, tax effort should be considered to reward the Southern states for their better fiscal management.

D. **Asymmetric Federalism**

Louis Tillin said that the Indian federation is asymmetric because various states enjoy some special powers which are not available for others. Federation of the US is symmetric where each state enjoys equal power from the constitution. According to the Indian Constitution, Northeastern states are given **special autonomy** under **Article 371** and in the **Sixth Schedule**. The states dominated by tribal population are also accorded unique powers under the **Fifth Schedule**. Therefore, division of taxes also demands special attention to the backward states. Maintaining **equality** is the responsibility of the Finance Commission.

SPECIAL STATUS STATES

The idea of special status states is propounded by the **5th Planning Commission**. Constitution does not recognise the concept of special status states. The **5th Planning Commission** suggested special economic assistance to the states, which are identified by the following parameters:

(i) Hilly and have tough terrain;
(ii) Low population density and dominant tribal population;
(iii) Strategic location on international boundary;
(iv) Weak financial position; and
(v) Lack of development in economy and infrastructure.

In the beginning, three states, **Assam, Meghalaya, and Jammu and Kashmir** were included under special status states. Subsequently **Arunachal Pradesh**, **Himachal Pradesh**, **Manipur**, **Mizoram**, **Tripura, Sikkim** were also recognised as special status states. **Uttarakhand** was also included in this category in **2003**. (Uttarakhand was carved out as a separate state from Uttar Pradesh in 2000.)

States belonging to special status receive **90 per cent** as grant and **10 per cent** as a loan. However other states receive 70 per cent in form of grant and 30 per cent as loan. The union government often writes off their loan. Special status states also enjoy the provision of tax holiday and exemption from taxation. Therefore, it is easier for these states to attract investment.

The former governor of Reserve Bank of India (RBI), **Raghuram Rajan** suggested applying multiple indicators to identify special status states. It is also highlighted by the government in the budget speech of 2013. Special status of states should fulfill the new parameters like:

(i) State income in comparison to Average national income
(ii) Per capita income
(iii) Literacy rate
(iv) Human development indictors

Now **Odisha** and **Bihar** are less developed states still they have not been given the advantage of special status of states. Special status is not a panacea for all problems of backward states. Grant provided by the union government is not sufficient because backward states like Bihar and Uttar Pradesh are unable to **attract foreign direct investment (FDI)**. In the present age of privatisation and liberalisation, states should focus on good governance for economic development.

COOPERATIVE FEDERALISM

Federal form of government stands on the principle of *division of power* and *sharing of power*. These two concepts appear antithetical with each other. But cooperation does not negate the division of power. It shall not change the division of power envisaged in the Seventh Schedule. Cooperative means cooperation in **administrative domain** and over **financial issues.** The **Concurrent List** in the Seventh Schedule laid down the base of **cooperation.**

Practically, union government and state government both run for the welfare of the people. And economic development requires cooperation between union and state. For example, railways belongs to Union List and land is part of State List. Therefore, cooperation is needed for the successful operation of railways.

A. CONSTITUTIONAL PROVISIONS: INTER-STATE COUNCIL

Cooperative federalism developed in the US due to practical exigencies, but the Indian Constitution incorporates the features of cooperative federalism under **Article 263**. The President shall establish a council for serving the public interest under Article 263. This article speaks of the duty of the Inter-State Council:

(a) enquiring into and advising upon disputes which may have arisen between states,
(b) Investigating subjects related to common interest of
    - Some states or
    - All states
    - Union and one state
    - Union and more than one state
    - And discussing the subject itself
(c) Council shall recommend better coordination of policy and action associated with above mentioned subjects.

The President established the Inter-State Council in **1990**. As per Article 263, the President shall also define the nature and duties of the Council, as well as organisation and procedure. The **V. P. Singh government** for the first time established the Inter-State Council. Lok Sabha elections of the year 1989 are significant because no party commanded majority in Lok Sabha for the first time in the history of Indian elections. Regional parties were becoming stronger and they demanded autonomy of states. It is equally important to note that Sarkaria Commission recommended the setting up of the Inter-State Council to promote cooperation between union and states.

The Council considered recommendations of the Punchhi Commission. Common interest refers to standards of education, problems of internal security and terrorism. These problems can be solved through cooperation between union and states. The Council is a dispute settlement mechanism too. River water disputes can be addressed with the help of the Council. Maoist insurgency can be rooted out with the help of various states because public order and police belong to State List.

(a) **Structure**

The Inter-State Council is a **constitutional body**, but structure of the Council is not written in the Constitution. Structure was set up by the order of the President in 1990. Council is comprised of:

(i) The prime minister, who is the chairperson
(ii) Six cabinet ministers of union government, nominated by the PM

(iii) Chief Ministers of all states

(iv) Chief Ministers of all Union Territories (UT) having State Legislative Assembly

(v) Administrators of UTs not having state assembly.

(b) **Standing Committee**

Since the Council is a large body in terms of members, therefore the standing committee is set up for the smooth functioning of the Council. The standing committee is headed by home minister, nominated by the Prime Minister. Four cabinet ministers of union government are members of the standing committee. Apart from cabinet ministers, nine Chief Ministers of states are members of the standing committee.

(c) **Drawback**

It should be restructured on the lines of the GST Council where votes of states are equally important in comparison to the union. The Inter-State Council was set up in year 1990 but only 11 meetings have been held till now. The meeting of the committee was held in 2016 after a gap of 10 years. Absence of regular meetings is the basic drawback of the Council. Now the secretariat of council is located in the home ministry. Therefore, the union government has become more powerful. Importance of states should also be considered in the decision-making process.

B. STATUTORY PROVISIONS: ZONAL COUNCIL

Indian federation was reorganised in 1956 on the recommendation of the **Fazal Ali Commission**. Linguistic homogeneity was the strong base for reorganisation of states. For promotion of **coordination** and **cooperation** among the states, Zonal Councils were set up by a **parliamentary act** in **1956**. The Council aims to discourage the tendency of regionalism, separatism and looks to strengthen **unity** and **integrity** of India.

Structure

(a) **Members**

The Council for each zone is chaired by the **home minister** of the union government. Chairperson is not entitled to vote but exercise casting vote. Chief minister of states in the zone are members, and they act as deputy chairperson for one year in rotation. Zone is also comprised of two ministers from every zone are also included and they are nominated by the Governor of state. Two members of Union Territory are also drawn into the council, if the UT is part of the zone. Timing and date of meetings of zone shall be decided by the chairperson. The secretariat of zones is located in the **ministry of home** of the union government.

(b) **Advisory members**

Advisory members are not entitled to vote in the meeting. They do not participate in meetings. **Chief Secretary** of every state is a member of zone. **Development commissioner** of every state participates in meetings. One member is also nominated by the **NITI Aayog.**

(c) **Standing committee**

Standing committee of zone is comprised of **Chief Secretary** of every state included in the zone. Members of the **NITI Aayog** and ministers of union government can also be invited for meeting.

(d) **Various zones**

Zonal council is a *statutory body* enacted by a parliamentary act. According to the Act, **5 zones** exist:

1. Northern zone

- States – Haryana, Himachal Pradesh, Punjab, Rajasthan,

- UT – Jammu & Kashmir, National Capital Territory of Delhi, Union Territory of Chandigarh, Ladakh.

2. **Central Zone**

   Chhattisgarh, Uttarakhand, Uttar Pradesh and Madhya Pradesh.

3. **Eastern zone**

   Bihar, Jharkhand, Odisha and West Bengal.

4. **Western zone**
   - States – Goa, Gujarat, Maharashtra
   - UT – Daman and Diu, Dadara and Nagar Haveli

5. **Southern zone**
   - States – Andhra Pradesh, Telangana, Karnataka, Kerala, Tamil Nadu.
   - UT – Puducherry

The Northeastern states are not included in the zonal councils as the **North Eastern Council Act, 1972** mandates the creation of a separate council for these states.

Role

(a) **Socio-economic planning**

Various states are divided on a geographical basis. States are also created on the basis of **linguistic homogeneity**. But creation of separate state does not address the common social economic problems that exist in the region. Zonal Council promotes **cooperation** among the state over issues of women's empowerment and welfare of tribal community. Providing **education** and **health** are common objectives of all the states.

(b) **Inter-state Transportation**

For making of national highways, cooperation among the states is essential. For example, launching high speed trains between Mumbai and Ahmedabad requires cooperation between Maharashtra and Gujarat. River bridge is needed for maintaining connectivity between Uttar Pradesh and Madhya Pradesh.

(c) **Border Dispute**

Creation of smaller states results in border disputes between various states. Border dispute still exists between **Karnataka** and **Maharashtra** because **Belagavi** or **Belgaum** is part of Karnataka but dominated by Marathi-language speaking people. **River-water sharing dispute** between **Punjab** and **Haryana** is a longstanding problem. Zonal council can be utilised for solving these political problems.

(d) **Issues Related to Minorities**

Various groups coexist in any state/region. For example, we cannot assume that one state has only one language. Therefore, linguistic minorities exist in various states. And cooperation between states is necessary for addressing this issue of linguistic minorities.

(e) **Drawback of Zonal Councils**

It appears that the functions of the Inter-State Council and Zonal Council are overlapping with each other. Fixed date and schedule of meeting is not followed in either Council. Meeting depends upon the discretion of the **chairperson**. The secretariat of council is located in the Home Ministry which strengths the power of the union government.

NORTHEASTERN COUNCIL

The States Reorganization Committee headed by Justice Fazal Ali was constituted in 1953 to recommend the reorganisation of state boundaries. However, reorganisation of Northeastern states is not based on the recommendations of the **Fazal Ali Commission**. **Nagaland** was carved out of Assam in 1963 due to insurgency in the Northeast. In 1972, **Meghalaya**, **Manipur** and **Tripura** were also recognised as states. **Manipur** and **Tripura** were earlier UTs. **Meghalaya** was carved out from Assam due to the demands of **Khasi and Jaintia** tribes. In the year 1987, Mizoram was created as a separate state from Assam to provide autonomy of **Mizo tribes. North East Frontier Agency (NEFA)** was also accorded the status of state, namely Arunachal Pradesh in 1987.

Due to *ethnic reorganisation* of states in the Northeast, the parliament set up a **North Eastern Council** (NEC) for promotion of cooperation among states. Parliament passed the **North-Eastern Council Act in 1972**, which was further amended in the year 2002. Council was set up in the year 1972 and includes **Assam, Manipur, Meghalaya, Nagaland, Mizoram, Tripura, Arunachal Pradesh. Sikkim** was also included in **2002.**

Structure

The North East Council is chaired by a person nominated by the President of India, according to a parliamentary act. As of now, the President nominates the home minister of the union government as chairperson of the Council. The union minister responsible for the development of the Northeastern region is nominated as deputy chairperson. President also appoints three members associated with planning and economic development. The Governors and Chief Ministers of all **eight states** are members of the Council. Secretariat of the Council is located in **Shillong.**

Role

1. **Socio-Economic Planning:** The Council plays a vital role in the planning of development of the Northeastern region. The Ministry of Development of North Eastern Region receives advice for economic planning of the entire region. This ministry is unique because it combines all ministries together for the development of the Northeast. Due to formation of smaller states, **coordination** and **cooperation** of states is essential.
2. **Interstate Transportation:** Since the Northeast region is a hilly area **connectivity** is necessary. Efforts are underway to improve railway connectivity in the entire region. The Northeastern region is a gateway for **Act East** policy. **Bogibeel Bridge**, the longest rail-cum-road bridge in India, measuring 4.94 kilometres over the Brahmaputra river, is a major project of infrastructure. **Project UDAN** from Imphal to Shillong is strengthening aerial connectivity in the Northeast.
3. **Flood Control:** The Northeastern region has a vast potential of generation of hydroelectric power. The Council is promoting **tourism** and **development.** Power projects are helpful for flood control too.

The Northeastern region is still affected by the problem of insurgency. In the absence of security, development is incomplete. Political instability also affects the development of the region. States are smaller and therefore, prone to become unstable. Ethnic conflict also affects the pace of development.

NATIONAL INSTITUTION FOR TRANSFORMING INDIA (NITI AAYOG)

The NITI Aayog was established in India on 1 January 2015 by the resolution of the **cabinet** of the union government. It replaced the **Planning Commission** set up in the year 1950 for the development of human and physical resources of India. India adopted a socialist economic policy in 1950. Market economy was preferred in 1991 which was a major change in economy of India. Therefore, India opted for a privatised and liberal economic model. States demanded greater roles in making a plan for the development of India. It is worth noting that socio-economic planning is incorporated in the Concurrent List of the Seventh Schedule.

Nature

It is an expert body for making long-term plans for economic development of India. It is specialised institution which works as a think tank for planning. It is advisory in nature. Civil servants or bureaucrats are not included in the NITI Aayog.

Structure

NITI Aayog is headed by the **Prime Minister**. **Vice chairperson** is also nominated by the PM. An economist is usually appointed in the role. It is comprised of two full-time members. In addition, four cabinet ministers of union government are ex officio members of the aayog. Three other specialists can be invited from time to time. However, the **Chief Executive Officer (CEO)** of the Aayog is an **IAS officer**. The **governing council** of the Aayog in unique and is comprised of the Chief Ministers of all states and Union Territories, and administrators of UTs without Legislative Assembly. **Regional Councils** will also be set up from time to time.

Cooperative Federalism

States are autonomous and equal in the federal set-up of India. This is why the governing council of the Aayog is comprised of all states. For example, the Committee for Poverty Alleviation and the Clean India Mission (Swachh Bharat Abhiyan) are headed by **Chief Ministers** of the states. Therefore, states are given an *equal share* in the formulation of planning since every state has different needs. Therefore, *one size does not fit all.*

To explain this, **Rajasthan** is facing drought; however, **Odisha** is looking for better connectivity. Thus, decentralised planning is promoted by the governing council which is complementary to the basic feature of federal system. The Aayog also provides for the Regional Council. All the states of the **Himalayan region** are included in the **Regional Council**. For the Southern states also, such councils may be set up for addressing their problems.

Competitive Federalism

Competitive federalism means the promotion of competition for **economic development** and **investment** among various states. The NITI Aayog becomes catalyst for the promotion of **good governance** in states. The Aayog publishes various indicators for states, related to the development of infrastructure. It also highlights the progress of **human development index** of various states. In the present age of liberal and privatised economy, there is a stiff competition among the states for attracting tourists. However, competition is not antithetical to cooperation. Both exist side by side in the federal system of India.

GOODS AND SERVICES TAX (GST)

Federalism is a dynamic concept, which keeps changing according to changing political and economic environment. The economic policy of liberalisation and privatisation was adopted in India in 1991. It impacted the relation between the central government and the states. Although the Indian Constitution incorporates the base of liberal economy, **Article 301** tells us about the **trade, commerce and intercourse** throughout the territory of India. The Goods and Services Tax (GST) is included in the Indian Constitution by the **101st Constitutional Amendment**. GST is applicable over **indirect taxes** like **excise tax**, **service tax** and **taxation** over toll and entertainment tax. GST is not applied over **direct taxes** like income tax and corporate tax. GST promotes the idea of one nation one taxation, since the state taxes over State List like entertainment, toll tax, shall be uniform throughout the territory of India.

1. **Law-making power**

   The 101st Constitutional Amendment is a new scheme of division of power included in the Constitution. And **Article 246 (A)** was added to the constitution. Parliament is entitled to make a law regarding GST on the subjects of Union List. And every state legislature is given the power to enact a law related to GST over State List. Union government and state government are given **equal power** for making a law on GST because federal government is run on the principle of **equal power sharing.** Parliament can exercise exclusive power to making a law regarding GST over **interstate trade** or commerce.

2. **Interstate GST (IGST)**

   Union government shall levy and collect IGST on **interstate trade** or commerce according to **Article 269 (A)**. The division of IGST is ensured by the recommendation of **GST council** and is enacted by the Parliament as a law.

3. **GST Council**

   A. **Structure:** GST Council indicates cooperative federalism because the Council includes the representation of both the union government as well as the state government. According to **Article 279 (A),** the Council includes:

      (i) The **union finance minister** as a chairperson of the Council;

      (ii) **Union minister of state** in charge of revenue or finance;

      (iii) The minister in charge of finance or taxation or any other minister nominated by each **state government** are members.

   The members of the Council shall choose one of the members amongst themselves as **vice chairperson.**

   B. **Functioning of GST Council**

   Every decision of the GST Council shall be taken at a meeting by majority of not **less than 3/4th votes. Weightage voting** is applied in voting of GST council. Weightage voting means:

      (i) The vote of the central government shall have a weightage of **1/3rd** of total votes cast. It means union government is given **33 per cent vote share.**

      (ii) The vote of all the states putting together shall have a weightage of **2/3rd of total votes** cast. Therefore all 28 states are entitled to cast **67 per cent** vote. However, 75 per cent vote is require for any decision which is **3/4th majority**. And without **cooperation** between union and state, decision is impossible. Therefore, it promotes cooperative federalism.

   Article 279 (A) talks of the **quorum of GST** council which is **one half of the total number of members**. Council shall also determine its procedure and function. No act or proceeding of the GST council shall be invalid due to **any vacancy**, any defect in the appointment of the member. Decision of Council shall not be invalid due to any procedural fault.

   C. **Role of GST**

   Council shall make recommendations to the union and the states on the following subjects:

   1. The taxes, cess, surcharge levied by union government and states and local bodies, which may be subsumed in the GST.
   2. Goods and services exempted from GST or the goods and services subjected to GST.
   3. Model GST laws for IGST.
   4. **Threshold** limit of turnover below which GST may be exempted.
   5. Floor rates of GST.
   6. Any **special rate for** a specific period to rate additional resources during any natural calamity or disaster.

7. Special provision with respect to the states of **Arunachal Pradesh, Assam, Jammu & Kashmir, Manipur, Meghalaya, Mizoram, Nagaland, Sikkim, Tripura, Himachal Pradesh and Uttarakhand**.
8. Any other matter related to GST.

D. **GST over petroleum products**

Alcohol is exempted from GST due to opposition of state governments because alcohol is a **major source of earning** for **state governments**. **Article 279 (A)** includes GST levied on petroleum crude, high speed diesel, motor spirit (popularly known as petrol), natural gas and aviation turbine fuel. GST over these subjects depends upon the **decision of the GST council**. No constitutional amendment is needed for imposition of GST over above-mentioned items. Till today GST is not imposed over **petroleum products** due to concern of states. It again proves that without cooperation between the union and the states, economic development shall not be sustainable.

E. **Dispute settlement mechanism**

The Supreme Court is responsible for settling disputes between the union and the states. However, the dispute related to **financial matters** is kept away from the purview of the **Supreme Court**. However, **Article 279 (A)** discusses an **alternative dispute settlement mechanism** through the GST council. It says that dispute related to:

(i) GST between the Government of India and one or more states.
(ii) Between the Government of India and any states on one side and one or more other states on the other side.
(iii) Between two or more states.

Conclusion

GST marks a new beginning in the history of the Indian federation. GST reflects cooperative federalism between union and states. It is equally beneficial for both. Initially, GST was **opposed** by the rich and industrial states like **Gujarat** and **Tamil Nadu**. GST is a **destination-based tax**, and industrial states produce more goods, which are consumed in populated states like **Uttar Pradesh** and **Bihar**. Thus, GST is advantageous for the consuming states than the rich, producing states. In reality, it is better for the whole of India, since it has been smoothening the transportation of goods across India. **National interest** is more important than the interest of any particular state.

DISPUTE OF FEDERAL SYSTEMS

Interstate River Water Dispute

1. **Constitutional Provisions**

In a federal form of government, the Supreme Court is responsible for settling dispute related to union and state and between states. But **Article 262** authorises the Parliament to make laws regarding the use, distribution or control of the water of any interstate river or river valley. Article 262 also empowers the Parliament to keep away water disputes beyond the jurisdiction of the **Supreme Court** or any other court. According to the Seventh Schedule of the Indian Constitution, water, water supply, irrigation, canal, drainage and water storage belong to the State List, even though interstate rivers and river valleys are mentioned in the **Union List**.

2. **Statutory Provisions**

Due to reorganisation of states in 1956, various river water disputes emerged in India. Therefore, the Parliament passed the Interstate River Water Dispute **Act 1956**. This Act was further amended in the year 2019 to settle the interstate river water dispute in a more effective manner. Basic tenets of this Act are as follows:

(a) **Dispute Resolution Committee (DRC)**

Water disputes are more technical and political in nature and disputes can be resolved on the basis of a give-and-take principle. It shall not be produced before **tribunal** in first instance but it will be given to the DRC. The DRC comprises a Chairperson and expert members. It will settle the dispute within one year. In case of necessity, a six-month extension can be considered.

(b) **Permanent Tribunal**

Disputes shall be forwarded to the tribunal in case of any failure on the part of the DRC. Various tribunals were set up for adjudicating different water disputes. According to a recent amendment, there shall be only one permanent **tribunal** for resolving all existing water disputes. All existing tribunals will be dissolved. Water disputes pending before such existing tribunals will be transferred to the new tribunal. There may be multiple benches in one permanent tribunal.

(c) **Structure of Tribunal**

The tribunal will consist of a Chairperson and a Vice Chairperson. In addition to that, three judicial members and three experts will serve as a member of the tribunal. Every bench will have a Chairperson and a Vice Chairperson with a judicial member and an expert member.

(d) **Time-Bound Resolution**

The tribunal must decide on the dispute within the time-frame of two years. If needed, the time period can be extended by one year. Thus, it should be settled within a maximum period of three years.

(e) **Decision of the Tribunal**

Decisions of the tribunal will have the same validity as an order of the **Supreme Court**. Therefore, it is final and binding on the parties included in dispute. Publication of decision is not required in the official gazette. The decisions of the tribunal come into force without the publication of the decision in the Official Gazette.

(f) **Data Collection Bank**

The Union government will create an office or agency to maintain the data of every river basin at national level.

Judiciary and Water Dispute

A parliamentary Act provided that water disputes be kept away from the purview of the Supreme Court. Recent amendments to the Act also highlighted that the decision of the tribunal shall have the same force as the decision of the **Supreme Court**. However, water dispute are inspired by political interests. No separate authority exists for the enforcement of this decision. Therefore, problems are likely to emerge in the future.

The Supreme Court can grant special leave petition (SLP) under **Article 136**. The Supreme Court can grant the permission to make an appeal about the decision of the tribunal. It is also worth noting that the Supreme Court exercises a special power for the completion of justice under **Article 142**. Thus, the Court can entertain petitions regarding water disputes under Article 142. Hence, the doors of the Supreme Court are still open for resolving water disputes.

Water Dispute and Interstate Council

Water disputes are not legal disputes; therefore, the rule of the Supreme Court is limited in resolving such disputes. Interstate council was set up in the year 1990 for resolving water disputes.

Zonal councils have also been working in India since 1956. The very purpose of this council is to promote *cooperative federalism*, apart from resolving the disputes. The growing number of water disputes shows that cooperative federalism is yet to be strengthened in India.

POLITICAL PARTY SYSTEM AND FEDERAL DISPUTES (FEDERAL DYNAMICS)

The Indian Constitution specifies the division of power in the Seventh Schedule. The **Supreme Court** is given the task of settling disputes related to the federal system. But actual relations between union and state and between various states can be fully understood in the context of political relations. Relationship between union and state is bound to become cooperative if the same party rules in both union and state. But if the union government is run by one party and the state government is controlled by an opposition party, then a dispute is bound to emerge.

After Independence, the Congress formed government in both union and the states. It was an example of Unitary Party System. The Indian Constitution is federal but the federal party system emerged in India after 1989, that is, the system of coalition government. It comprises various political groups which therefore represent multiple centres of power. The new federal system emerged in India after 1989. State governments became stronger. Misuse of the following has arguably became rare:

1. Article 356
2. Office of Governor
3. Article 200
4. Deployment of central armed forces in states
5. All India Services

Coalition government represents various political parties in power, which is more suitable for a federal form of government. The dominance of one party in central and state governments strengthens the power of union government. But coalition government enhances the power of Chief Ministers of states. Same party in the union and states promotes cooperative federalism, as the relationship between the Centre and the state is then expected to be more stable.

Autonomy of State

A federal form of government gives autonomous power to states. Members of the state Legislative Assembly are directly elected by the people. The council of Ministers is drawn from the Assembly, headed by the Chief Minister. The State Legislative Assembly is entitled to make laws over the State List. The state government administers the subjects of State List. The state government can levy taxes according to the State List as described in the Seventh Schedule. Thus, the Chief Ministers are not subordinate to the Prime Minister but are equal partners.

The Demand for Autonomy of States

States are autonomous political entities because they derive their powers from the Constitution. Sometimes, the union government tries to encroach upon the power of the states and the states try to preserve their Constitutional powers. Autonomy of states is associated with the following issues:

1. The Governor of a state should act as a Constitutional head of the state government. The Governor's role as an agent of union government is against the autonomy of states.
2. Misuse of Article 356.
3. Misuse of Article 200.
4. Discrimination with state in allocating financial grant.
5. Misuse of Central Bureau of Investigation (CBI).
6. Transferring any subject from State List to Concurrent List.

The demand for autonomy of states was raised after 1967 because various regional parties got an opportunity to form the government in states.

However, the Congress Party was presiding over the union government. It was the Tamil Nadu government led by Dravida Munetra Kazhagam (DMK) that first raised the demand for autonomy. The Chief Minister of Tamil Nadu, Karunanidhi, appointed the Rajamannar Commission to examine relations between centre and state.

Radical Demand for Autonomy

The Rajmannar Commission suggested major changes in centre-state relations. It demanded for repealing **Article 356, Article 357** and **Article 365** related to the President's rule. It suggested that residuary powers should be given to the state government. It also recommended for abolition of planning commission. The Anandpur Sahib Resolution passed in **1973** by Akali Dal of Punjab said that the union government should keep only three subjects in Union List mainly Foreign Affairs, Defence and Communication. Rest of the subjects should be transferred to the state government. Therefore, it appears as though the state governments were demanding for **a** weaker union government. The West Bengal Government in 1977 also presented a memorandum for restructuring centre-state relations. It said that all provisions related to President's rule should be abolished. The union government rejected the demand for autonomy and said that it was a secessionist demand.

Restructuring of Central-State Relations

For the first time, the union government realised that demand for autonomy is genuine. Union government appointed the Justice Ranjeet Singh Sarkaria Commission on 9 June 1983. B. Shiv Raman and Dr S. R. Sen were the two other members of this commission. It submitted its report in January 1988. The commission maintained the spirit of the Indian Constitution. A powerful union government is an essential feature of the Indian Constitution, but autonomy of states is equally important. Issues related to federal restructuring are as follows:

1. **Governor:** The appointed Governor should be an eminent person and should not be associated with local party politics. The term of service of the Governor should be fixed at five years. The Governor shall not be removed before five years except under exceptional conditions. A verbal report regarding the removal of the Governor should be tabled before **Parliament**.
2. **Interstate Council:** The commission recommended for the implementation of Article 263, which provides for interstate council. Therefore, the commission suggested the promotion of **Cooperative Federalism**.
3. **Article 356:** The commission supported the utility of **Article 356**. The commission insisted that Article 356 must be used in exceptional conditions. Before the imposition of Article 356, all possibilities of formation of a government must be explored. The State Assembly should not be dissolved unless it is approved by the **Parliament**.
4. **Appointment of Chief Minister:** In case of hung assembly, the Governor should ask the leader of pre-poll alliance to form the government. Thereafter the Governor shall make various options—in sequence, the largest parties in assembly with the support of other parties can be called for the formation of a government. The leader of post-poll alliance should be given the chance for the formation of government.
5. **Article 200:** State bill is reserved by the Governor for the consideration of the President. The Governor should give his decision within four months.
6. **All India Services:** The commission said that a strong union government is the need of the hour. New **All India Services** should be created for furthering the national interest. It means that All India Services are not against the autonomy of states. The

commission also supported the centralised planning for development of India.

7. **Central Armed Forces:** Union government is permitted to send central armed forces in the states. Consent of state is not mandatory.
8. **Financial Autonomy:** The commission stressed the importance of Article 356, Article 357 and Article 360. But it also suggested that state governments should give more financial powers. Union government should not impose surcharge because surcharge is not divisible between union and state. Residuary powers belonging to taxation should be in the hands of the union government, but rest of the residuary powers should be transferred to the **Concurrent List**.

Conclusion

The commission emphasised cooperation between union and state. It said that a powerful union does not negate the autonomy of states. A powerful union and autonomous states are complementary to each other. Any political misuse of Constitutional provisions must be prevented. There is no need of radical restructuring of centre–state relations.

Punchhi Commission

During coalition government centre-state relations changed drastically. Union government constituted Punchhi Commission in 2007. Justice Madan Mohan Punchhi, former Chief Justice of India, was Chairperson of the Commission and submitted its report in 2010. Dhirendre Singh, Vinod Kumar Duggal, Madhava Menon, Vijay Shankar and Amarish Bagchi were members of this commission. The following issues were examined by the commission:

1. **Appointment of Governor:** The commission said that a Governor should be appointed by the recommendation of the committee. The committee shall consist of the Prime Minister, the Home Minister, Speakers of Lok Sabha and the Chief Minister of concerned states. The Vice-President of India can also be associated when required.
2. **Doctrine of Pleasure of President:** According to the Indian Constitution, the Governor shall hold office for five years or as long as the President pleases. The commission recommended that this provision should be deleted from the Constitution and that the Governor should be removed by impeachment of the Legislative Assembly of State. Therefore, the office of the Governor should not be taken lightly.
3. **Appointment of Chief Ministers:** The commission recommended that in case of hung assembly, the Governor should follow the following sequence for appointment of Chief Ministers.
   - (i) The leader of pre poll alliance should be appointed as the Chief Minister. The pre-poll alliance should be considered as a united party.
   - (ii) Leader of largest political party with support of other parties in State Legislative Assembly.
   - (iii) Leader of post-poll alliance.
4. **Bill Reserve by President: The** Governor is entitled to reserve any bill under Article 200 for the consideration of the President. The Governor should take a decision within six months.
5. **Autonomy of State:** Consultation with Interstate Council is mandatory before the enactment of any law over **Concurrent List**. The Parliament is entitled to make a law over State List for the protection of national interests. Consultation with interstate council is needed for making a law over State List associated with national interest. State government should be associated

before entering into any international agreement or treaties. Governor of state should not be appointed as Chancellor of Universities.

6. **Local Emergency:** In case of communal violence or social conflict the President's rule should not only be imposed in the entire state. It should be used in a few districts. Tenure of President's rule should not be extended for more than three months.
7. **National Unity and Integrity:** Central armed forces can be deployed for some time without consent of state government. There is need to create national centre for counter-terrorism, for strengthening internal security. National Integration Council should be made stronger and at least one meeting should be convened once in a year.

Conclusion

Demand of autonomy of state is a political issue. It can be addressed politically. The Prime Minister has emphasised 'Team India', therefore cooperation between union and state is essential. Autonomy of state is logical in a federal form of government in India.

REORGANISATION OF STATES

Types of States during British Government

British government categorised Indian states in following administrative units.

1. **British India States:** Eleven provinces were set up by the British government for administering India. These provinces included Mumbai, Madras, etc. These states were subject to administrative control of the British government. The British Government also controlled their defense and foreign matters. It means states were under the sovereign control of the British government. The British government introduced a democratic element for the ruling of these states. For example, members of State Assembly and premier (Chief Minister) were elected by the people according to the **Government of India Act 1935.**
2. **Princely States:** Administrative control over the princely states was subject to the ruler of princely states. But foreign affairs, defense and communication were controlled by the British government. Thus, the British government was sovereign over the princely states. Princely states were partially controlled by British government and partially regulated by rulers of princely states. The number of princely states was approximately 562. Jammu & Kashmir, Hyderabad and Junagarh were larger princely states. A democratic element of governance could not be incorporated in the princely states.
3. **Provinces of Chief Commissioners:** Chief Commissioner Provinces were totally subject to the British government. Geographically, these provinces were located strategically like the Andaman & Nicobar Islands. Culturally, these states were often dominated by a tribal population, for example, Ajmer, and Coorg.

Reorganisation of Princely States

The biggest challenge for Indian democracy after Independence was the accession of the princely states and reorganisation of 562 princely states. Sardar Vallabhbhai Patel adopted three-stage processes for the reorganisation of princely states.

(1) **216** princely states were acceded in their adjoining states. Adjoining states are put under **Part A** states.

(2) 275 princely states were merged with each other and therefore five new states were created. They are included in **Part B** states.

(3) 61 princely states were included and merged under **Part C** states.

Types of States in India's original Constitution

The Constitution of India which came into force on 26 January 1950 incorporates four types of states in the First Schedule of the Constitution.

1. **State of Part A:** Larger states controlled by the British government were included in the first part. These states included Assam, Bihar, Madhya Pradesh, United Provinces (Today known as Uttar Pradesh).
2. **State of Part B:** Part B states include the larger princely states like Jammu & Kashmir, Hyderabad, Junagarh, Mysore, Punjab and East Patiala States Union (PEPSU).
3. **State of Part C:** Part C states comprise smaller princely states like Ajmer, Bhopal, Bilaspur, Coorg.
4. **State of Part D and Other acquired territory:** Part D states include the Andaman and Nicobar Islands and other acquired territory shall also be the part of **Part D** states.

Table 7.8.2: Categories of States in Original Constitution

S. No.	Part (A)	Part (B)	Part (C)	Part (D)
1.	Assam	Hyderabad	Ajmer	Andaman & Nicobar
2.	Bihar	Jammu & Kashmir	Bhopal	Any other acquired territory
3.	Bombay		Bilaspur	
4.	Central province	Mysore	Cooch Bihar	
5.	Madras	Patiala and East Punjab State Union	Kodagu	
6.	Orissa	Rajasthan	Delhi	
7.	Punjab	Saurashtra	Himachal Pradesh	
8.	United Province	Travancore cochin	Kutch	
9.	West Bengal	Vindhya Pradesh	Manipur	
10.			Tripura	

Constitutional Basis of Reorganisation of States

According to Article 1, **First Schedule** is included in the Constitution. First Schedule mentions the name of various states of union and union territories.

1. **Territory of India:** Article 1 define the territory of India which includes
   (a) The territory of states
   (b) Union territories
   (c) Such other territories as may be acquired
2. **Federal Territory:** Article 1 discusses the **territory of India**. It is different from the federation of India. India federation includes **all states.** Federation does not include **union territories** and acquired territory. Because union territory is **subordinate** to the union government. Federation is comprised of states only. Because **power is shared** between union and states not between **Union and Union Territory.**

Establishment of New States

Parliament by law can admit new state into the union. Parliament can also determine terms and conditions of new states. For example Goa was admitted in Indian union by parliament in 1962.

Sikkim is only the state of India which is given the status of associate state by 35th Constitutional Amendment in 1974. Article 2(A) was specially created for Sikkim as associate state. But associate status of Sikkim state was deleted by 36th amendment. Therefore Article 2 (A) also deleted from the constitution, and Sikkim became like other states in India.

Formation of New States

Article 3 allows the parliament by law to:

1. Form a **new state** by separation of territory from any state or by **uniting** two or more states or parts of states or by uniting any **territory** to a part of any states. For example, **Uttarakhand** was created by separation of territory from Uttar Pradesh in year 2000. Various princely states were merged with each other thereby creating new states by merger of two or more than two states. Presently Belagavi, formerly known as Belgaum is a district of Karnataka but it can be united with Maharashtra by parliament. Any union territory can be made a state, for instance Arunachal Pradesh was union territory and later it was formed into a state.
2. **Increase the area of state:** It is not for the formation of new state but Parliament can increase the area of an existing state.
3. Parliament is also entitled to **diminish area of state** without forming a new state.
4. Parliament can also **alter boundary of any states**. It is important to be noted that area is measured of the extent of the surface. It is measured in square units. Boundary is dividing line or location between two areas.
5. Alter the **name of any state**, therefore state legislative assembly is not capable to change the name of any state. State can **suggest** for the change of name but it is authority of parliament to decide about changing of name.

Formation of New State and the President

The recommendation of the president is necessary before the **introduction of bill** related to formation of new state, alteration of area, boundaries or name of existing states. President shall refer the bill to legislative assembly of that state. President can specify a period in which legislative assembly express its opinion. Therefore Article 3 clearly indicates that the **consent** of state is not necessary for changing the name of boundary of state.

Formation of New State and Constitutional Amendment

Formation of new state requires an ordinary law of parliament. Parliament shall pass state reorganisation act with **simple majority**. Therefore, **constitutional amendment** is not needed for changing the name or boundary of state.

Indestructible Union with Destructible State

Indian union is **intact** but state can be **destroyed**, which means boundary and area of a state is subject to alteration. **US federation** is known as indestructible federation with indestructible states. The name, boundary or area of state cannot be changed without **consent of state** in the US. But the consent of state is not required in Indian union. Due to that feature critics observe that the existence of state depends upon the *will of union*. It is against the *spirit of federal government*. **Article 3** further enhances the power of union government. It is against the *equal and autonomous* status of states.

Indian federation should not be compared with USA because the demand for new states still exists in India. Article 3 is helpful for formation of new states smoothly. Indian society is still in a *transitional phase*. Federalism is a political concept; parliament cannot diminish or increase area of state, arbitrarily. To give one example, **Chandigarh** is recognised as a union territory due to competing claims of **Punjab** and **Haryana**. Parliament could not change the status of Chandigarh due to political compulsion. Any new state derives its power from the Seventh Schedule. They are not dependent over union government. **Article 3** is thus a **unique feature** of India federation. It is not against the federal system.

POLITICAL DEMAND OF REORGANISATION OF STATES

Indian society is federal because it is comprised of various groups classified by religion, language and race. Every group wants to protect and preserve their identity. Therefore *regional inspirations* are bound to emerge. Demands for new states are obvious for fulfillment of their *regional identity*. Indian national congress itself recognised the need of *linguistic reorganisation* of states in **1920 Nagpur session**. After independence, Justice **S. K. Dar** commission was appointed for consideration of demand of linguistic reorganisation of states. Commission did not accept the feasibility of linguistic reorganisation of states. Indian National Congress itself appointed a committee for consideration of linguistic reorganisation of states. **Jawaharlal Nehru, Vallabhbhai Patel and Pattabhi Sitaramya** were the members of the committee. Thus committee was popularly known as the **JVP Committee**. Committee refused to accept the formation of state on linguistic grounds.

Vishal Andhra Movement

Madras state incorporated the speakers of **three major languages**—Tamil, Malayalam and Telugu. Telugu language was second largest after Hindi in terms of population. And the first demand of linguistic states was raised by **Telugu language** speakers. **Potti Shree Rumallu** was a Gandhian leader who held an indefinite hunger strike. Subsequently he died and this triggered violence. Therefore, then home minister **K. N. Katju** announced the formation of Andhra Pradesh as the first state organised on linguistic basis (comprising Telugu speakers) in 1953. Thereafter for consideration of holistic demand of reorganisation of states, **Fazal Ali Commission** was appointed by union government in 1953.

State Reorganisation Commission

State Reorganisation Commission (SRC) was appointed under the chairpersonship of **Justice Fazal Ali. H. N. Kunzru** and **K. M. Pannikar** were other members of state reorganisation commission. State were reorganised in 1956 on the basis of recommendation of SRC. **First schedule of the constitution** was reorganised in the following way:

(a) **States**
(b) **Union Territory**.

Basis of State Reorganisation

SRC utilised the following parameters for the reorganisation of states:

1. Larger states were divided for **administrative efficiency** and better management of economy and finance.
2. Maintaining linguistic and **cultural homogeneity**.
3. Strengthening **unity and integrity** of India.
4. Better implementation of **economic planning**.
5. One language one state formula could not accepted because no state was comprised of **only one linguistic group. Mumbai** province was not divided in 1956. The demand of division of Punjab was not fulfilled. Thus, language was not the **only base** of reorganisation of states. Although Mumbai was divided in **Maharashtra and Gujarat** in **1960**. **Punjab** was also reorganised on the **bases** of language in year 1966. Punjab, Haryana were made as two separate states. With the reorganisation of Punjab first phase of reorganisation of state was completed. According to SRC

14 states and **three union territories** were established in India.

LINGUISTIC REORGANISATION AND UNITY AND INTEGRITY OF NATION

Earlier linguistic reorganisation was considered to be against unity and integrity of India. After communal division of India, linguistic demands of state were considered harmful for unity and integrity of India. But new demands of statehood were the result of **regional aspirations**. India is **plural** and **diverse** nation, therefore regional aspirations are natural. Formation of new state fulfilled the regional demands. Regional language became the **official language of state** which protected the **identity** of every regional group. **Political participation** of regional leaders resulted in democratisation of India. Therefore it appears that federation of India became more **stable** after the linguistic reorganization of states. Imposition of **one language** over entire India could have been more dangerous. Suppression of **minority language** can create the problem of disintegration. Thus unity is not **homogeneity** but unity of India means **unity in diversity**. **Regionalism** is different from **separatism** and demand of new state is an example of **regionalism**.

Formation of Nagaland

Nagaland was created in **1963 from Assam**. Formation of Nagaland was not based on the recommendation of **Fazal Ali Commission**. It was not created on the **basis of language**. Fazal Ali commission supported the reorganisation of larger state; however, Assam was **small state**. Nagaland is formed due to the following regions-

1. Naga region is a first area which witnessed insurgency after independence. **Angemi Phizo** was a leader of Naga movement. He demanded a sovereign state from India. It was the first **secessionist** demand in India. Nagaland was created to quell the **separatist** movement.
2. Nagaland is strategically located on the border of China.
3. Insurgency and **ethnic identity** is fundamental cause behind the formation of Nagaland. Northeastern states are different from other states of India. Thus the reorganisation of north-eastern state is not similar to the other parts of India.

It is worth noting that most of the Northeastern states are not financially autonomous. They are **dependent** on financial grants of union government. They continuously demand more financial assistance from the union government. These states are unable to manage their own financial resources. Constitutional autonomy is meaningless, suggest critics, without **financial self-sufficiency.**

REORGANISATION OF STATES IN AGE OF LIBERALISATION

The first phase of reorganisation of state was based on **linguistic identity**. But liberal and private economy **created disparity** between the states and within the states. Post liberalisation phase of 1991 benefitted **industrial states** more in comparison to the **backward states**. Three more states, namely **Chhattisgarh, Uttarakhand and Jharkhand** were formed in the year 2000. Following criteria was adopted for creation of these states:

1. Three states were carved out from **larger states** like Madhya Pradesh, Uttar Pradesh and Bihar.
2. Chhattisgarh, Uttarakhand and Jharkhand were comparatively **backward** regions in their states.
3. These were rich in terms of natural resources but local residents did not get advantage of their natural resources.
4. All the three regions had their separate geographical identity.
5. All three states had also **uniform** social and cultural identity too.

Telangana was formed in 2014 as a separate state of India through the bifurcation of Andhra Pradesh. The formation of smaller states in India is a debatable issue. And demand of Gorkhaland, Bundelkhand and Bodoland is still ongoing.

Argument in Favour of Smaller States

1. **Democratisation:** Smaller states means smaller size of **constituency** of state assembly. People are more nearer to their **representatives**. The size of district is small which create **efficient administration**. Access to high court is also easier in smaller states. Therefore people are more empowered in smaller states.
2. **Administrative Efficiency: Goa, Haryana, Punjab, Gujarat** are more developed states of India. They are smaller in size. However the larger states like **Uttar Pradesh** and **Bihar** are most backward states in India. It proves that smaller states are better for economic growth and development.
3. **Geographical Homogeneity:** Since India is diverse in terms of climate and topography. **Hilly states** required separate parameter of development. It needs autonomous mode of economic development. **Coastal region** requires different norms of development. Therefore states should be reorganised according to unique geographical features. Smaller states also fulfill the **cultural needs** of various regional groups.
4. **Identity Politics:** India is still a developing country, and society is dominated by caste, religious identity. For protecting their **unique cultural identity**, Gorkhas are demanding separate state. The people speaking **Bodo language** are demanding a separate state from Assam.

Challenges in Formation of Smaller States

1. **Political:** The demand for smaller state is an **endless political demand**. Creation of one state inspire the demand of next state. various states are carved out from **Assam**. Still the demand of Bodoland is going on. Smaller states are more prone to **political instability** due to smaller number of state legislative assembly.
2. **Economic–Administrative:** There is no co-relation between the size of state and their development. All Northeastern states are smaller in size, yet still lacking the economic development. **Haryana** is developed due to its **location** and better **infrastructure**, not merely due to its size. **Maharashtra** is larger state still counted in the category of developed state. Therefore **good governance** is requires for the development of states.
3. **Financial Burden:** Creation of new state need a separate **high court** and its own **secretariat**. New capital is necessary for running the state. Thus heavy financial expenditure is required for creation of new state. It is against the principle of better **fiscal management**. Government should spend more on social economic **welfare** rather than maintaining the administrative machinery.
4. **Strengthening Local Self Government:** The demand of smaller state cannot be satisfied. **Decentralisation** is better answer than formation of state. **Local self-government directly** empowers the people. Demand of new state is inspired by new political leaders. New state is not formed for the sake of better administration. Creation of smaller state created more problems for north-eastern states. However, local self-government discourages the concentration of power in the hand of political parties.
5. **Dispute between the States:** Water dispute is result of formation of new states. Maharashtra is still demanding the Belgaum from Karnataka. It means new state also creates **land boundary** dispute between the states.

Conclusion

Demand of smaller state is sign of **dynamic federal** system of India. But second state reorganization **commission** is need of hour for settling reorganisation of states. The formation of state should not be carried out on **ad hoc basis.** State reorganisation is required according to comprehensive outlook rather than **regional perspective**.

ASYMMETRIC FEDERALISM (ETHNIC FEDERALISM)

Indian constitution incorporates the ethnic diversity of India. Northeastern states are unique in terms of cultural and ethnic diversity. Constitution provides special provisions for marginalised sections of society. The members of Scheduled Castes and Scheduled Tribes are given special protection in the Constitution. The term scheduled caste is for the first time mentioned in the Constitution by Government of India Act 1935. According to Article 341 of the constitution, the president shall determines the list of schedule caste. President can take the consultation from the Governor, before making the list of scheduled castes. Scheduled Tribes are also marginalised sections of society. They are distinct from the mainstream of society. Their culture is unique and many tribal communities have traditionally lived in remote areas.

Scheduled Areas

Scheduled areas are incorporated in Article 244 and Fifth Schedule of the Constitution. President of India can identify any area of state as scheduled area. Scheduled area is based on the population of scheduled tribes. The president can identify an entire state as a scheduled area or any part of state as one. Scheduled areas are located in Andhra Pradesh, Chhattisgarh, Gujarat, Himachal Pradesh Jharkhand, Madhya Pradesh, Maharashtra, Odisha, Rajasthan and Telangana. The provision for drawing up scheduled areas is drawn from the Government of India Act 1935. It included excluded areas and partially excluded areas.

Article 164 of the Indian Constitution includes special provisions for Chhattisgarh, Jharkhand, Madhya Pradesh and Odisha. There shall be a minister in charge of tribal welfare. Minister can be given the additional charge of welfare of schedule caste and backward classes.

Administration of Scheduled Areas

1. **Tribal Advisory Council:** Tribal advisory council consists of not more than 20 members. Three-fourth members of the council shall be the representative of the scheduled tribes in legislative assemblies of the states. Governor shall make the rules for the appointment of chairperson of council and number of members of council. Procedure and meeting of council shall be determine by the governor.
2. **Functions of Council:** Governor shall make regulations for good governance in scheduled areas. The council can prohibit the transfer of land or restrict it to members of scheduled tribes. It can also regulate the allotment of land to the people belonging to scheduled tribes.
3. **Special Role of Governor:** Governor by public notification may direct that any particular act of parliament or the legislature of state shall not apply to scheduled areas. It is essential for preserving culture and rights of tribal communities. Governor shall send an annual report to the president.

Tribal Areas (Sixth Schedule)

Federal system of India combines the diversity of language, culture and ethnicity. Assam, Meghalaya, Tripura and Mizoram are the part of Sixth Schedule of the Constitution. District autonomous councils and regional autonomous councils are mentioned in the Sixth Schedule.

Function of District Council

District Council is an example of decentralised local government. It is Constitution within Constitution which protects the rights of land, water and forest of the tribal population. It also protects the cultural diversity of tribal communities. They are free to decide their social customs, marriage, divorce and inheritance of property. District Council is also entitled to appoint or to decide the succession of Chief of Tribal Community. Practice of shifting cultivation shall be regulated by the Council. Public health sanitation and matters related to village, town administration is in hands of the Council. Management of forest and use of any canal or water resources are under the purview of the council.

Power of District Council

The district council is given the legislative power over the above-mentioned subjects. It also incorporates executive power for administering the subjects included in the sixth schedule. Councils also set up their own judicial system which is headed by the chief of tribal community to settle disputes related to customs, marriage and divorce among the tribal community. Council is also entitled to levy taxes over the people.

Composition of District Council

District Council is comprised of 30 members. Members of the council are elected directly by the people. Councils work like a mini-states legislative council. One member is appointed as chairperson of the council. Other Members assist the chairperson, similar to how the council of ministers assists the CM. Voting rights of the person in the election of district of council is determined according to local customs and traditions.

Limitation of Parliament and State Legislative Assembly: District Council is autonomous and any law made by parliament and legislative assembly of state is applied to a council with permission of Governor of the State. Governor can place restrictions over implementation of any law passed by Parliament or Legislative Assembly of the state in the District Council.

Special Provision for Nagaland

Nagaland was created as a separate state in the year 1963. It is not part of the Sixth Schedule but all autonomy available for the Sixth Schedule is given to Nagaland and no act of parliament is required:

(a) Religious or social practices of the Nagas,
(b) Naga customary law and procedure,
(c) Administration of civil and criminal justice involving decisions according to Naga customary law,
(d) Ownership and transfer of land and its resources, shall apply to the State of Nagaland unless the Legislative Assembly of Nagaland by a resolution so decides.

EMERGENCY

The Indian federation has displayed strong unitary tendencies. The Constitution incorporates the provision of emergency in Part XVIII, from Article 352 to Article 360.

Emergency provisions show that maintaining unity and integrity of India was the primary objective of the makers of our Constitution. They tried to maintain balance between democratic rights and protecting order in society. The Constitution explains three kinds of emergency:

1. National Emergency
2. State Emergency on account of failure of constitutional machinery
3. Financial Emergency

I. National Emergency:

Presidential Proclamation of Emergency: The President can proclaim emergency, when s/he is satisfied that grave emergency exists, whereby the security of India or any part of territory is threatened by:

(i) War
(ii) External aggression
(iii) Armed rebellion

(a) **Whole country:** National emergency can be imposed across the territory of India. For example—Radhakrishnan, the then President, proclaimed **national emergency** on the grounds of external aggression from 26 October 1962 to 10 January 1968.

(b) **Any Part:** The term 'ntional emergency' is **nowhere** mentioned in the Constitution. Thus, emergency can be proclaimed in any part or territory of India. It implies that emergency can be imposed in one state too.

(c) **Actual Occurrence:** Actual occurrence of war is a criteria for proclamation of emergency. Emergency can be proclaimed on the probability of emergency threat in days to come as well.

(d) **Role of Cabinet:** Term **Cabinet** was incorporated in the constitution by the **44th Constitutional Amendment in 1978**. Otherwise, the term 'Council of Ministers' is preferred in the Constitution. Since 1978, the president cannot not proclaim emergency without **written communication of Cabinet** to the President. It is worth noting that Indira Gandhi advised President Fakhruddin Ali Ahmad for proclamation of emergency without consultation of the Council of Ministers.

(e) **Armed Rebellion:** Armed Rebellion was included in the Constitution by 44th Constitutional Amendment 1978 under Article 352. It is an important point to be remembered that Indira Gandhi proclaimed emergency on 25 June 1975 on the basis of **internal disturbance.** Internal disturbance is *vague and subjective*, and therefore, prone to misuse. Keeping that misuse in mind, the term internal disturbance was replaced with armed rebellion. It implicitly implies violent struggle by any group, such as insurgent groups, against the government.

(f) **Duration:** Thrice there has been an imposition of emergency.

1. 26 October 1962 – 10 January 1968: External Aggression
2. 3 December, 1971 – 21 March, 1977: External Aggression
3. 25 June, 1975 – 21 March, 1977: Internal Disturbance

First and second proclamation of emergency continued for almost six years. However, the third proclamation of emergency continued for two years. Thus, no maximum duration of emergency is described in the Constitution of India. Ultimately, the duration of emergency is decided by parliament.

(g) **Parliamentary Control over Executive:** Executive is accountable and responsible towards Parliament, consequently, each and every action of executive is controlled by the Parliament. If the Parliament does not approve the proclamation of emergency, within 30 days, the emergency automatically expires. Resolutions regarding the approval of parliament must be passed by both houses with a special majority. Here special majority requires:

(i) Majority of strength of House and
(ii) Support of 2/3rd members of each house present and voting.

Special majority implies that the ruling party must seek support of the opposition party too. Role of the council of states is equal in terms of approval and extension of emergency. After approval by both houses, the emergency continues for six month. The House can again pass resolution with special majority for extension of emergency for 6 months. Emergency must be extended for every 6 months.

(h) **Special Role of Council of States:** After proclamation of the emergency by the President, House of the People would dissolve within 30 days. Therefore, the Council of States must approve the resolution regarding the extension of emergency within 30 days with a special majority.

Meanwhile the newly elected House of the People must approve the resolution within 30 days, from its first sitting. Once the resolution is approved, the emergency is extended for 6 months.

(i) **Special Role of House of the People:** Emergency can be revoked in the following ways:
   (a) With presidential proclamation
   (b) Non-approval of parliament.
   (c) The House of the People can pass a resolution.

By 44th Constitutional Amendment for the first time, the House of People is given special power for revoking the emergency. It can be revoked, if 1/10th members of the strength of the House of the People request either the President or the Speaker to do so. (Speaker if House is in session; President if House is not in session.) Emergency can be revoked by a resolution with a simple majority of the House of the People.

(j) **Parallel Emergency/Dual Emergency:** Provision of **dual emergency** was incorporated in the Constitution by 38th Constitutional Amendment. When the third emergency was proclaimed on 25 June 1971, the second emergency proclaimed was also going on; the latter was imposed on the grounds of external aggression; whereas the former was imposed on the basis of internal disturbance. Simultaneous emergencies place restrictions on Fundamental Rights.

(k) **Extension of Tenure of House of the People:** Duration of emergency is extended by 6 months by a resolution of parliament, however the duration of the House of the People shall be extended for 1 year at a time. Similarly, tenure of legislative assemblies of state shall be extended for 1 year at a time. The election of the House of the People and state Legislative Assembly commenced in 1967, when the first proclamation of emergency was continued but the tenure of the Lok Sabha and the State Legislative Assembly of state were extended during the imposition of emergency in June 1975. Duration of House of the People was extended for two consecutive times.

(l) **Federation becomes Unitary:** Legislative Assemblies exist during national emergency under **Article 352**, but division of power gets suspended. Consequently, the union parliament is empowered to legislate over the subjects of State List. In other words, the State List enumerated in the Seventh Schedule becomes a Concurrent List. The President can promulgate an ordinance over State List too.

Legislative assemblies are also entitled to make laws over subjects of State List.

The union government shall extend its executive power and give direction to any state, on any issue. If an emergency is imposed or any particular territory, direction can be issued for other states too. Distribution of revenue under Aarticle 268 and Article 269 shall also be suspended, during emergency.

(m) **Undemocratic Tendency:** Fundamental Rights are considered as conscience of the Constitution. Citizens should be more powerful in democracy. When states suppress the rights and liberties of the people, it becomes autocratic and non-democratic. Three articles of the Constitution suppress rights of citizens when put together—Article 22, Article 34 and Article 352.

1. **Freedom of Speech:** Article 19 is automatically suspended. Emergency when proclaimed on the grounds of war or external aggression, results in suspension of Fundamental Rights under Article 358. Article 358 states the impact of proclamation of emergency under Article 352. The Supreme Court refused to protect the rights of citizens during Emergency in the famous ***ADM Jabalpur Vs Shivkant Shukla Case (1976)***. No person can approach the Supreme Court for protection of his/her rights. Case is properly known as Habeas Corpus case. No petition pending before Court shall be entertained.
2. **Suspension of Enforcement:** In addition to that, the President can give an order for suspension of enforcement of Fundamental Rights under Article 359. Thus Articles 32 and 226 shall not be available for persons during emergency. President can proclaim the list of Fundamental Rights to be suspended during emergency. This was the reason why PM Indira Gandhi imposed a dual emergency in June 1975.
3. **Rights beyond Suspension:** Some Fundamental Rights are beyond suspension, particularly Articles 20 and Article 21. The Janata Party government introduced the 44th Constitutional Amendment in 1978. As a result, Articles 20 and 21 remain in operation even on the imposition of emergency.

(n) Probability of Misuse of Emergency in Future:

1. **Constitutional:** Janata Party incorporated various provisions in Article 352 which minimise the probability of misuse of the emergency. No special majority required for approval and extension of emergency. Commanding 2/3rd majority in both houses appears a remote possibility.
2. **Judicial Review:** Since the 44th Constitutional Amendment proclamation of emergency is subject to **judicial review**, therefore, misuse of emergency becomes a tough task now.
3. **Political:** Indira Gandhi lost the general elections of 1977 due to imposition of emergency and misuse of provisions of emergency. Even today, the Congress becomes a subject of criticism due to imposition of emergency. Thus, no political party is willing to harm its prospects in future. Now the media

is also vibrant and alert, which can generate enormous pressure of public opinion on government.

State Emergency

Failure of Constitutional Machinery

Article 356 is included in Part XVIII of the Constitution, which is not categorised as the provisions of emergency. Article 356 begins with the title of failure of constitutional machinery. If the President is satisfied that the government of a state cannot be carried in accordance with the provisions of this constitution, she/he can proclaim an emergency based on the report of the Governor or otherwise too.

1. **Impact of Proclamation:** All or any powers exercised by the state government are automatically assumed by the President. The President can give these powers to any authority other than the legislature of the state. Therefore, this is popularly known as President's rule.
   (a) President also declares that powers of the legislature of state shall be exercised by parliament or under authority of parliament.
   (b) But the President cannot assume the power of the High Court or suspend the operation of the High Court.
2. **Revoking President's Rule:** President is authorised to revoke the presidential rule by subsequent proclamation. President's rule shall also come to an end if parliament fails to approve the resolution within 2 months after imposition of President rule.
3. **Duration of President Rule:** President's proclamation cannot continue for more than 3 years. But President's rule imposed in Punjab on the date of 11 May 1987, continued for 5 years due to the militancy in Punjab. The 59th Constitutional Amendment was brought about for validating the President's rule in Punjab.
4. **Extension:** Once both houses of parliament approve the President rule by simple majority, it can be extended for six months. For extending the duration of President rule beyond 6 months, again an approval of Parliament is required with a simple majority.
5. **Emergency and President's Rule:** For extending President's rule beyond more than one year, parliamentary approval is subject to the following conditions:
   (a) Proclamation of emergency is in operation in whole of India or in whole or any part of state, and
   (b) Election Commission certifies that holding elections in the legislative assembly of state is difficult. Normally president's rule continues for one year because these two conditions are difficult to be met.
6. **Special Role of Council of State:** After the proclamation of President rule, approval of both houses of parliament is needed with simple majority. During the imposition of President rule, if the House of People dissolves, President's rule must be approved by the council of state within two months with simple majority. After the constitution of the newly elected House of People, proclamation must be approved within 30 days, from the first sitting of the House of People.
7. **Federation becomes Unitary:** Federation becomes unitary during imposition of Article 356. Legislative assembly of state and council of ministers no longer exist in the state. Parliament can legislate over the subjects included in the state list. The President shall issue an ordinance for the concerned state. Parliament shall pass the appropriation bill of state. State becomes like a municipality, autonomy and co-ordinate power of state gets automatically destroyed.

8. **Fundamental rights impact:** Fundamental Rights are not affected by the proclamation of emergency on the grounds of failure of constitutional machinery because it is not considered an emergency.

Financial Emergency

Emergency denotes extraordinary or urgent situation, which demands immediate action. Article 360 provides for financial emergency.

1. **Proclamation:** Emergency is proclaimed by the President. Here, satisfaction of the President automatically means satisfaction of the Council of Ministers.
2. **Ground:** Financial emergency can be imposed on the ground of financial instability or credit, which threatens any part of the territory or of India.
3. **Duration:** Financial emergency can be imposed for an indefinite period. No maximum duration is incorporated in the Constitution of India. Although the President can revoke the emergency at any time. Interestingly till today no financial emergency has been proclaimed in India so far.
4. **Parliamentary Control:** Proclamation of emergency must be approved by parliament within two months, by simple majority. If the parliament fails to approve the resolution, it naturally lapses.
5. **Special role of council of states:** If the House of the People is dissolved during proclamation of emergency, proclamation must be approved by the Council of States within two months with a simple majority. After the constitution of the new House of the People, House must approve the proclamation within 30 days, from the first date of meeting of House of People. It also requires a simple majority.
6. **No need for repeated extension:** Once a financial emergency is proclaimed by the President and approved by parliament, it continues for an indefinite period unless it is revoked by the President. Approval of parliament every six months is not needed in a financial emergency.
7. **Impact on Federation:** Union shall extend to giving direction to any state to observe the financial propriety. Direction of union also includes money bill or other bill (financial bill) passed by the legislature of the state. The bill shall however be reserved for the consideration of the President.
8. **Reduction in Salaries:** President can also direct for reduction of salaries and allowance of all or any class of persons serving in connection with affairs of Union. Reduction of salaries also includes the salaries of Judges of the Supreme Court and High Court. Reduction of salaries and allowance of all or any class of persons serving in connection with the affairs of a state.
9. **Legislature of a state exists:** Legislative assembly of state does not get dissolved due to proclamation of financial emergency. The present Legislative assembly of the state as well as council of ministers also exist.
10. **No impact of Fundamental Rights:** Fundamental Rights are in effect during the financial emergency. Everyone is free to enjoy their Fundamental Rights. Economic crisis of 1999 is considered as severe in the economic history of India. But the emergency was not imposed.

Justification of Emergency

Emergency provisions are not key features of Indian Constitution. Emergency can be looked upon as an essential evil, which may be essential for preserving and protecting the unity and integrity of the state. Eminent freedom fighter and parliamentarian Mahabir Tyagi called emergency provisions a safety valve to uphold the Constitution in extraordinary situations.

Relevance of provision of emergency was shown in 1962 and 1975. It is a transitional provision of the Constitution and is exceptional in nature. For instance, financial emergency has never been applied till date. Fundamental Rights are not absolute, rather they are qualified. Unity and integrity of a nation is the primary condition for enjoying Fundamental Rights.

UNION TERRITORIES

Union Territory refers to territory specified in the First Schedule and other territories acquired by the union or not specified in the First Schedule.

Part VIII of the Constitution describes UTs. Presence of UTs appears paradoxical in the federal system of India. Union Territories were created due to various reasons.

(a) **Population:** Population of Andaman Nicobar Island, Dadra and Nagar Haveli, and Daman and Diu is less than 4 lakhs. Formation of state is not possible for such a small population.

(b) **Historical:** Puducherry was part of a French Colony. Dadra and Nagar Haveli, Daman and Diu were part of a Portuguese colony. Culturally these UTs were distinct and unwilling to merge their identities with the nearest state.

(c) **Strategic:** Apart from cultural uniqueness and less population, strategic and security factors may be the reason behind the formation of UTs. Andaman and Nicobar Islands are located approximately 1,400 kms in the Indian Ocean, away from Kolkata. Direct control of the central government is necessary for maintaining strategic control over the island. Recently J & K and Ladakh were created. They share borders with China and Pakistan, who are often hostile neighbours towards India and also put their false claim over several parts of the territory of India too.

(d) **Political:** Chandigarh is the Union Territory created due to political rivalry between Punjab and Haryana. After the formation of Punjab and Haryana in 1966, both states wanted to make Chandigarh as their capital. Subsequently Chandigarh became the capital of both Punjab and Haryana.

Features of Union Territories

1. **Constitutional Provisions:** The motion of Union Territory was incorporated in the Constitution of India in 1956 through the 7th Constitutional Amendment Act, after reorganisation of states.
2. **Administration:** According to Article 239, each and every UT shall be administered by the President. The President shall administer the UTs through administrators. Even the governor of an adjoining state may be appointed as administrator of state, who shall work independently from council of minister of that state for running the administration of the state.
3. **Legislature and Council of Minister:** Parliament by law may create a legislature for the UT and Council of Ministers for the same territory. No constitutional amendment is required for creation of the legislature and Council of Ministers in the UTs. Parliament passed the **Government of Union Territories Act 1963**. Similarly, the government of **National Capital Territory Act 1991** is passed by the parliament. Legislature was first created in Puducherry in 1963 and thereafter in Delhi in 1991. Jammu and Kashmir became the first state of India to be converted into Union Territory.
4. **From Union Territory to State:** Manipur, Tripura and Himachal Pradesh were UTs earlier. Later they were promoted as states. Goa, Mizoram and Arunachal Pradesh were granted full-fledged statehood.

5. **Difference between state and Union Territory:**
   (a) States are autonomous units of federal India. States draw their power from the 7th Schedule of the Constitution. Thus states are equal and coordinate to Union However Union territories receive their power from the Government of Union Territories Act 1963. Therefore, UTs are subordinate to the union.
   (b) Governor is the constitutional head of the state. The Governor acts upon the aid and advice of the Council of Ministers. However, the President administrates the UTs through an administrator appointed by him. The Administrator appointed by the President is not merely the constitutional head but administrative head too.
   (c) For changing the powers of the state we need a constitutional amendment. It requires 2/3rd majority; but power of UTs can be altered through a parliamentary act. It does not require a constitutional amendment.
   (d) States are not dependent on the union government for their power. The Seventh Schedule grants the power for states. But the power of UTs is decided by an Act of parliament. Even special provision with respect to Delhi, does not grant law and order, police and land to Delhi by 69th Constitutional Amendment Act 1991.
   (e) The Chief Minister is the administrative head of state, which is free to choose their administrative officers. In case of UTs, administrator becomes the administrative head than Chief Minister. Thus CM of UTs becomes dependent over the President for choosing the officers.
   (f) UTs are direct administration control of the President and union government. Thus the principle of division of power is not applicable for UTs. They are dependent upon the union government.
6. **Multiple ways of Administration:** Currently, UTs of J&K, Delhi, Puducherry have a legislative body. But other UTs do not have a legislature. Delhi and JK have their High Courts too. Rest of the UTs are deprived of their own High Courts. It is worth noting that the High Court of Punjab and Haryana is located in Chandigarh; it is not called the High Court of Chandigarh. Puducherry is given power over all subjects mentioned in the State List and Concurrent List. But land, police and law and order belonging to the state list rest with the union in the case of Delhi.

9

ELECTORAL PROCESS AND ELECTION COMMISSION OF INDIA

KEY CONCEPTS

Conduct of Elections, Rules, Electoral Reforms

ELECTION COMMISSION OF INDIA

The Constitution incorporates the provision of elections in Part XV. The entire structure, power and functions of the Election Commission are described from **Article 324 to Article 329**. An independent Election Commission is a mandatory pre-condition for holding free and fair elections. The Indian Constitution does not allow the Government of India or state governments to hold elections. Therefore, an autonomous body, that is, Election Commission of India is inserted in the Constitution.

Composition

According to Article 324, the Election Commission shall consist of the Chief Election Commissioner and such number of other Election Commissioners, if any, as the President may from time to time fix. Since 1993, the Election Commission has been a three member body headed by Chief Election Commission (CEC).

Terms and Conditions

Since the Election Commission is an independent body, therefore, terms and conditions of Election Commissioners are similar to terms and conditions of **Judges of the Supreme Court.** Parliament passed the **Election Commission (Conditions of Service of Election Commissioners and Transaction of Business) Act 1991.** Election Commissioner receives payment similarly as Judges of Supreme Court. Salary of Election Commissioner shall not vary adversely after his appointment. It is worth noting that the salary of Election Commissioner is not charged on consolidated fund of India. Tenure of Election Commissioner is 6 years or up to the age of 65 years, whichever comes earlier. The Chief Election Commissioner can be removed from his office like Judges of **Supreme Court** can be removed, and on the same grounds. It is interesting to note that the manner of removal of other commissioners is different from Chief Election Commissioner. Other commissioners are removed by the President with the **advice of Chief Election Commissioner**.

Reform in Structure

Reform in structure of Election Commission of India (ECI) is essential for carrying out electoral reforms. The Election Commissioner should be appointed by Committee instead of merely by the President. The procedure of removal of CEC and other commissioners should be the same. Constitution does not put any restriction on the post-retirement appointment of elections commissioners. However, there is a need to restrict the appointment of Election Commissioner after demitting the Office of ECI.

Administrative Wing of ECI

(a) **Chief Electoral Officer** – ECI in consultation with state government/Union Territory administration nominates or designates an Officer of the said State/UT as the Chief Electoral Officer to supervise the election work in the State/UT.
(b) **District Election Officer** – ECI in consultation with the state government/ Union Territory administration designates an officer of the said State/UT as the District Election Officer to supervise the election work of a district.
(c) **Returning Officer** – ECI in consultation with state government/Union Territory administration nominates or designates an officer of the Government or a local authority as the Returning Officer for each assembly and parliamentary constituency. Returning Officer is responsible for the conduct of elections in the parliamentary or assembly constituency and may be assisted by one or more Assistant Returning Officers (again appointed by ECI) in the performance of his functions.
(d) **Electoral Registration Officer** – ECI appoints the officer of state or local government as Electoral Registration Officer for the preparation of electoral rolls for a parliamentary/assembly constituency.

Role of the Election Commission

Election Commission plays a vital role in organising elections. The most critical challenge before the Election Commission of India is to implement norms and the Model Code of Conduct to ensure free and fair elections in the country. Its existence and independence are necessitated by history, which has revealed that self-governing elections are not free from disruption. Towards this end, it has been empowered to supervise political parties and candidates and take appropriate action in case of violations.

Functions

The functions of ECI are written very briefly in the Constitution of India. It only says that Election Commission shall hold election of:

(a) President
(b) Vice-President
(c) The members of Parliament
(d) The members of State Legislature

Detailed functions of Election Commission of India are described in The Representation of People Act, 1950 and The Representation of the People Act, 1951 (RPA). RPA 1950 details about the delimitation of the constituencies and increase in the seats of Lok Sabha and State Legislative Assembly. However, RPA 1951 deals with the entire process of election: recognition of political parties, nomination of papers in the election, and allocation of elections symbol are some of the functions of ECI. Furthermore, announcement of date for election and scrutiny of nomination papers, and declaration of result are also under the jurisdiction of ECI. ECI also depute observer in the elections and ensure that corrupt practices are not allowed in the elections.

Traditional Role of the ECI

Primarily ECI is responsible for holding free and fair elections. Initially, elections were held once in 5 years since Congress registered a landslide victory in the election of Lok Sabha and the election of State Legislative Assembly. Simultaneous elections to the House of People and State Legislative

Assembly were held till 1967. Many politicians were drawn from the National Movement, and therefore some sort of moral practices were present in the political scenario.

Changing Role of the ECI

Criminalisation of politics and politicisation of criminals became the permanent features of Indian politics since 1990s. The use of muscle power and money power became rampant in the election. Caste and religion were utilised frequently for winning elections. Moreover, elections were organised every year due to instability of coalition politics. It was matter of coincidence that T. N. Seshan became the election commissioner in 1990s who changed the entire functioning of ECI.

THE SUPREME COURT AND THE ELECTION COMMISSION (ECI)

The Supreme Court set-up fast track court for deciding criminal cases pending against the political leaders. According to existing laws, without conviction nobody is disqualified for participating in the elections. It is well-known fact that pending cases are a result of delayed decision in the court.

The ECI became powerful due to positive intervention of Supreme Court. Advice of ECI is not binding over the government but decision of Supreme Court is binding over the government. The ECI suggested implementation of various electoral reforms before the government but the government refused to implement these reforms. Consequently, Public Interest Litigation (PIL) are filed before Supreme Court for enforcement of electoral reforms. Now, candidates participating in the election declare their educational qualification, criminal background, and financial liability (2002). NOTA is also implemented with the instruction of Supreme Court of India. Several PILs are still pending in the Supreme Court for carrying out electoral reforms.

MODEL CODE OF CONDUCT

The idea of Model Code of Conduct came into existence for the first time in the general election of 1971. Kerala was the first state where the model code of conduct was applied during election of state legislative assembly in 1960. T. N. Seshan is responsible for strong enforcement of MCD across of India. Model Code of Conduct (MCD) is enacted by ECI in order to maintaining *level playing field* in the elections. The incumbent government should not receive any advantage to be in power. MCD is applied for:

(a) Candidates participating in the election
(b) Ministers
(c) Meeting and canvassing
(d) Political parties

A. **For Ruling Party:** Government shall not use resources of the state for the purposes of interest of party. Furthermore, government shall not instruct the officers in order to promote party interest. All the facilities available for the government, like guest house accommodations, are to remain accessible to all the political parties. MCD is applicable to ministers and officers. Ministers shall not use their official vehicles in the elections.

B. **For Political Party:** Members of political parties shall not use religious places for the furthering of political interests. They will not incite any religious sentiment for the gain of votes. Members of any political party will not engage in personal criticisms of the members of opposition parties. Parties are free to criticise the programmes and policies of the government.

C. **During Voting:** Political parties will not provide transportation facilities to the voters. Political parties or their members are not allowed to assemble near polling booths. No voter shall be threatened by any person. Agent of political parties cannot coerce any person for personal gains or interests.

Nature of the Model Code of Conduct

MCC is not a legal but it is moral in nature because it cannot be enforced in the court of law. MCC is deterrent to the probable misuse of power by the government. It is applicable to every stakeholder involved in the elections.

ELECTORAL REFORMS

Free and fair elections are a pre-condition for the successful functioning of democracy. Electoral reforms strengthen the probability of free and fair elections. Various commissions like Law Commission, Indrajeet Gupta Committee, Goswami Committee are suggested for numerous electoral reforms and other important reforms are mentioned below:

1. **Prevention of Criminalisation:** Politicisation of criminal and criminalisation of politics is the biggest challenge to Indian democracy presently. Therefore, some committees have argued that any person who is charge in the heinous crimes like murder or rape, should be disqualified for participating in the election. A person, who is convicted for two years for any crime should be disqualified for their entire life, rather than six years of the present provision. The person convicted in Court of Law shall not be eligible for holding any office in a recognised political party.
2. **Money Power:** Increasing use of money in elections is against the principle of level playing field. The ECI has fixed the upper limit of expenditure in the election of the House of the People and in the election of State Legislative Assembly. But upper limit is only applicable for the candidate, and expenditure of political party and other persons is not counted in upper limit. An MP is allowed to spend upto Rs 70 lakhs in the Lok Sabha elections but party can spend unlimited amounts.
3. **Transparency in Party:** Lack of internal democracy is the core problem of political parties. Apart from that, political parties never disclose the source of their funding. Information condition ruled that political parties are public authority therefore, they are subject to control of information commission. Political parties comes under the Right to Information Act but they are not agreed to tell about their source of funding. According to recent amendment of RPA 1951 no political party can receive cash donation more than Rs 2000, but a party can show each donation as below Rs 2000.
4. **Separate Secretariat:** According to Law Commission of India, Election Commission should have an autonomous secretariat like Supreme Court and CAG. As of now, ECI is dependent on the officers of union government, state government for holding the elections. During elections, ECI draws the administrative officer from various government departments. Therefore, ECI is unable to exercise their control over these administrative officers.

10

LOCAL GOVERNMENT INSTITUTIONS

KEY CONCEPTS

Functioning and reforms

LOCAL RURAL GOVERNMENT

Panchayati Raj

The practice of Panchayati Raj in India is realising the **Gandhian Dream.** Gandhi never supported the parliamentary form of government, which is based on **centralisation of power**. Sriman Narayan Agrawal was a staunch Gandhian in the Constituent Assembly. He said that model of democratic governance of Independent India should be based on Panchayati Raj. Literally Panchayati is made of **Panch + Aayat**, assembly of 5 respected and wise persons to serve the community. Vision of Panchayati Raj was in incorporated in the constitution in the part of **Directive Principles of State Policy (DPSP)**. The state shall take steps to organise village Panchayat and endow them with such powers and authority as may be necessary to enable them to function as unit of **self-government** under **Article-40.**

Nehru adopted a two-pronged strategy for **development** of Independent India. **Community Development Programme** was launched for the development of rural India in 1952. Heavy industrialisation was preferred for the development urban centres of India. National extension service is also implemented with help of Ford Foundation of USA in 1953. Community Development Programme could not succeeded in India. **Balwant Rai Mehta** Committee was in January 1957 for inquiring about causes of failure of community development programme. Balwant Rai Mehta was Chief Minister of Gujarat and belonged to Congress Party. Mehta submitted his report in November 1957. The committee pointed out that **Lack of Participation** of people was the major reason behind failure of community development programme. Civil Servants were given the responsibility for development of village, people were passive at the receiving end. For promoting participation of people, committee suggested implementation of decentralised government at local level in form of Panchayati Raj.

Recommendation of Balwant Rai Mehta Committee

1. There are three tiers of Panchayati Raj:
    - Panchayat at village – **Gram Panchayat. (bottom)**
    - Panchayat at block – **Panchayat samiti. (Intermediate)**
    - Panchayat at District – Zila Panchayat shall be established in India **(Top)**

2. Elections of Gram Panchayat shall be organised directly by the people. However, election of block and district Panchayat will be **held indirectly**. Elected numbers of village Panchayat shall choose the members of block Panchayat. Members of block Panchayat shall elect the members of district Panchayat.
3. All functions related to Planning and development shall be transferred to Panchayat.
4. Block Panchayat shall act as **executive agency** for implementation of Planning. District Panchayat will monitor, regulate and harmonise the functions of block Panchayat.
5. **District Magistrate** shall be chairperson of district Panchayat.

The Panchayats were inaugurated in Nagaur, Rajasthan on 2 October 1959 in Independent India. Andhra Pradesh became the next state to launch Panchayati Raj. Nevertheless 1960, was the dangerous decade for India, since it witnessed war in 1962 and 1965. On the other hand economic crisis was also at the doorstep of the nation. Thus potential of Panchayati Raj could not be fully realised.

For the first time, a non-Congress government had come into power in 1977 in the union of India. Gandhian Leader Jayaprakash Narayan was a key leader who opposed the Congress government. Janata Party Government tried to associate itself with Gandhian ideology. Government set up **Ashok Mehta Committee** for strengthening Panchayati Raj.

Recommendations of the Ashok Mehta Committee

1. Committee recommended for **two tiers for Panchayati Raj**. Mandal Panchayat and District Panchayat are two tiers of Panchayat. Mandal Panchayat refers Panchayat at Block level.
2. District Panchayat is responsible for implementation of planning. It is executive Committee for implementation of welfare schemes.
3. Committee also allowed participation of political parties in Panchayati Raj. Financial strengthening of Panchayat is also an objective of Ashok Mehta Committee. Panchayat should be given power to levying the taxes.
4. Committee recommended for reservation to community of SC and ST in Panchayat, according the ratio of population of the community.
5. **Nyaya Panchayat** should also be established for setting the dispute in village. Developmental function should keep away from adjudicative function.
6. There is a need to set up **state Finance Corporation,** and separate ministry of Panchayati Raj must be included in Council of Minister of State Government.

In 1985, GVK Rao Committee was appointed for revival of Panchayati Raj.

Constitutional Status

Rajiv Gandhi Government Constituted L. M. Singhvi Committee, for strengthening Panchayati Raj. First time **L. M. Singhvi Committee** recommended for the constitutional status of Panchayati Raj. Committee recommended for inclusion of **following features in Panchayati Raj:**

1. Three tiers of Panchayat should be constituted—Gram Panchayat (Village), Block Panchayat and District Panchayat.
2. Constitution of a **separate election commission** for holding elections of Panchayat.
3. **Finance Commission** is also required for strengthening the Panchayat.
4. **Political Parties** should not be allowed to participation in Panchayat elections.
5. **Nyaya Panchayat** is essential for settling the dispute at grass root level.

Political Initiative for Constitutional Status

Rajiv Gandhi government introduced **64th Constitutional Amendment, 1989** for giving constitutional status to Panchayati Raj. 64th constitutional amendment was passed in Lok Sabha but bill was stuck in the Council of State. Opposition claime that Rajiv Gandhi government tried to bypass the state government. Union government directly want to connect village and District Magistrate.

New Panchayati Raj (73rd Amendment)

Finally, Narsimha Rao Government brought about 73rd Constitutional Amendment in 1992. It gave constitutional status to Panchayati Raj. Part-9 in the constitution is allocated for Panchayati Raj. 11th schedule is incorporated in the constitution. Article-243(A) to 243(O) also became integral part of the constitution.

State Subject

It is included in the state list of the Seventh Schedule in a federal scheme of India. Panchayati institutions were already existant and functional in various states. Provisions of state Panchayats should not be inconsistent with 73rd Constitutional Amendment. States were given time period of **one year to amend** provisions of their Panchayati Raj, otherwise distinct feature state Panchayat shall expire. Due to this reason 73rd Constitutional Amendment is enforced from 1993. All state government are entitled to keep their own separate Panchayati Act. 73rd Amendment enumerates only **broad features** of Panchayati Raj, State Legislative Assembly, are capable to frame their own acts. Features which included from Article-243(A) to Article-243 in the constitution are known as compulsory features of Panchayati Raj.

Grassroots Democracy in form of Gram Sabha

Gram Sabha is the smallest unit of Panchayati Raj. Gram Sabha comprises of persons registered in the electoral rolls of a village. Article-243 mentions Gram Sabha, but legislature of state by Law, will give powers and functions to Gram Sabha. Power of Gram Sabha is determined by every state legislature. Gram Sabha is like a **parliament of village**; thus, it is the foundation of grassroots democracy. Gram Sabha is an example of **direct democracy.**

Lok Sabha exists at the top, Gram sabha is situated at grass root. Gram Sabha prepares **planning** for the development of village. Gram Sabha chooses about beneficiary of the various schemes directed for the welfare of villagers. All adult person registered in electoral rolls are the part of Gram Sabha. Thus, it is known as **rural self-government.**

Panchayat and Democratisation

Every state has **three tiers** Panchayat. Panchayat at village level—as known as Gram Panchayat. Article-243(B), mentions about Panchayat at grassroots. But it does not define the composition of Gram-Panchayat (Village–Panchayat). It is the responsibility of legislature of state to point out features of village Panchayat. Generally, village Panchayats in most states comprised of **Chairperson** and **5 ward members**. Members may be varying from state to state.

Elections of Panchayat are **non-party** politics in nature. It ensures true participation of the people. It realises Gandhian vision of decentralised swaraj where people are empowered.

Composition of Panchayat

According to **Article 243** of the constitution, composition of Panchayat is determined by the legislature of the state. Size of every Panchayat in terms of population should be equal across the entire state. Elections of members of Panchayat across the three tiers shall be held directly by the people.

Apart from the direct election legislature of a state may by law ensure **representation of the following:**

A. **Chairperson Level**

(i) Chairpersons of the Panchayat at the village level at the intermediate level.

(ii) In absence of **intermediate level representation of Chairperson at village level at the district level.**

B. **MP/MLA**

(iii) Representation MPs/MLAs, in Panchayat will only be ensured at an intermediate level or at a district level. MPs and MLAs are not considered for representation at the village level.

(iv) Representation of members of Council of States and representation of members of Legislative Council if they are registered as electors.

C. **Voting Rights**

(v) Right to vote of chairperson of Panchayat in the meeting of a Panchayat.

D. **Election of Chairperson of Village Panchayat**

(vi) Chairperson of Panchayat at the village level shall be elected in such a manner as the legislature of state may by law provide.

E. **Election of Chairperson of Block/ District**

(vii) Chairperson of Panchayat at the village level, be it at intermediate level or district level, shall be **elected indirectly**. Chairperson of intermediate Panchayat (Block) shall be elected by elected members of block/intermediate Panchayat elected members of District Panchayat shall elect the chairperson of District Panchayat.

Reservation/Social Justice and Gender Justice

Under Article-243, reservation is given to people belonging to **following categories in the** constitution under **compulsory provisions:**

1. The Schedule caste.
2. Scheduled Tribes.
3. Women.
4. Reservation for Other Backward Class citizens shall be determined by the legislature of state. Reservation for seats as well as chairperson, both is the responsibility of Legislature of state.

Reservation for SC/ST

Reservation is applicable for all three tiers of the Panchayat. It is applicable for a number of seats of Panchayat to be filled by direct election in the Panchayat. Quantum of reservation is fixed according to the ratio of SCs/STs in the Panchayat population. Reservation shall be in **rotation**. As for reservation of **Chairperson** is the ratio of in the Panchayat concerned. It shall be determined by legislature of the state. Nevertheless, quantity of reservation should be according to population of the state.

Reservation of Women

Seats under the reservation for women category are to be filled by direct election. Reservation at the level of **Chairperson** shall be determined by legislature of state. Not less than 33 per cent seats shall be reserved for women in **rotation**. Since Panchayat is the subject of State List, some states have increased the ratio of reservation for women up to 50 per cent.

Reservation for Backward Class

Legislature of state shall determine the **upper limit** of reservation in number of seats of Panchayat to be filled by direct election. Reservation for the seat of Chairperson shall also be determined by legislature of state.

Tenure of Reservation

Reservation for SC/ST in Panchayat shall be continued **up to 2030**, according to the **104th Constitutional Amendment**. **Article 334** is applicable for the reservation of Panchayat. This article ensures reservation of SC/ST in the Lok Sabha as well as in legislature of the state. But no time limit is applicable for the reservation of women and backward class of citizens.

Duration of Panchayat

Tenure of Panchayat is 5 years from the date appointed for its **first meeting**, under **Article (243) E**. In case of **dissolution** of Panchayat newly constituted Panchayat shall continue only for **remainder** of the period. If the existing Panchayat dissolves within 3 years, a new Panchayat shall be constituted for 2 years. If remainder period is less than **6 months**, election shall be held for full 5 years. **Ground** of dissolution is not mentioned in the constitution. It is for legislature of state to decide. Terms and condition for dissolution vary from state to state.

Disqualification for Membership

Process of disqualification from elections for state legislature of state is equally applicable for disqualification of members of Panchayat. Legislature of state is entitled to make any other rules for disqualification from elections of member of Panchayat. Andhra Pradesh enacted Law for disqualifying person from election of Panchayati Raj. Candidates having more than two kids are disqualified from contesting an election of Panchayat.

Eligibility of contesting in elections of Panchayat is **completion of 21 years.** Legislature of state shall be empowered to establish an authority or manner to **adjudicate** about disqualification.

Local Self Government/Third Tier of Panchayat–Devolution of Power

Objective

Article 243(G) of Panchayat points out the purpose and goal of **Panchayati Raj:**

1. Preparation of plans for economic development and social justice;
2. Implementation of schemes for economic development and social, justice, relating to matters listed in the Eleventh Schedule.

It is worth noting that the Panchayat are **not law-making bodies**. Planning economic development and social justice is the primary concern of Panchayat. The Eleventh Schedule includes **29 subjects**, which can be classified under the **following headings:**

A. **Agriculture:** Agriculture, minor irrigation, water management, fisheries, animal husbandry dairying and poultry etc.

B. **Industry:** Small scale industry including food processing, Khadi, village and cottage industry.

C. **Development:** Road, bridges, ferries, waterways, rural electrification, non-conventional source of energy, maintenance of community assets, public distribution system.

D. **Welfare:** Health, Sanitation, primary health centre, family welfare, women and child development, welfare of handicapped and mentally retarded, SC/ST etc.

Federal government runs on the principal of **power sharing**. Panchayat promotes self-government and as mentioned above, **29 subjects** were given for people at the grassroot. Now people in villages are not only **voters,** they take part in **decision-making**. Democracy is turning from representative to a **participative form. Self government** denotes, people are **masters** now; they will utilise local resources for local development, and they are not dependent upon their **representatives.**

The Seventh Schedule of the Constitution ensures power sharing. However, **the Eleventh Schedule** leads to **devolution of power**. This is real example of decentralisation, where power is transferred to **community**. Third tier **federation** is about directly empowering the people. Devolution of powers strengthens direct democracy.

Financial Devolution

29 Subject included does not point out any item related to **taxation**. Article-243(H) authorise the legislature of state to make a **law related to taxation;**

(a) **Levying Taxes:** Legislature of state authorise a Panchayat to levy, collect and appropriate taxes, duties, tolls and fees. Legislative assembly of Haryana authorise Panchayat to levy entailment tax. However, later, Haryana had withdrawn power of levying of taxation from Panchayat.

(b) **Levied and Collected by State, Assigned to Panchayat:** State can assign to a Panchayat such taxes, duties, tolls and fees levied and collected by state Government/this increases financial sources of Panchayat. Receiving and withdrawal of money by Panchayat from such fund.

(c) **Centrally Sponsored Scheme:** Constitution does not incorporate the provision of centrally sponsored scheme. But Panchayat receives grand from Central government from schemes like **MGNREGA** and **Ujjwala Yojana**.

State Finance Commission

The governor of state shall constitute state finance commission as soon as may be **within one year from the commencement** of the constitutional amendment act, 1992. There after state finance commission shall be constituted expiration of every 5th year. State finance commission shall make recommendation to governor for reviewing of financial position of Panchayat, under Article 243(H).

A. **Structure:** Constitution does not enumerate about **structure of state finance commission** structure implies for numbers of members and eligibility. Procedure and power of commission shall be defined by State Legislature.

B. **Function:** Article-243(H) spell about function of state finance commission, **which is mentioned below;**

1. Principle of distribution of taxes, duties, tolls and fees, levies by the state. Distribution of state taxes between state and Panchayat. Allocating shares among three level of Panchayat.
2. Determination of the taxes, duties, tolls and fees, which may be assigned to or appropriated by Panchayat.
3. The grant-in-aid to Panchayat from consolidated fund of state.
4. The measure needed to improve the financial position of the Panchayat.
5. Any other matter referred to the Finance commission by governor in the interest of sound finance of the Panchayat.

Governor shall present the recommendation of state finance commission before legislature of state. Governor shall also tell about action taken by government over recommendation of commission. Kerala appointed Principal Secretary as chairperson of state finance commission although state government does not implement the report the state finance commission.

State Election Commission (SEC)

Article-243(K) prescribes rules for the State Election Commission headed by a State Election Commissioner who shall be appointed by **Governor**.

Structure: the conditions of service and tenure of office of the state election commissioner shall be determined by Governor. But it is subject to law made by the Legislature of the state.

Function: The Superintendence, direction and control of the preparation of, electoral rolls of elections to Panchayat vest in State Election Commission.

It is worth noting that electoral rolls for election of Panchayat are different from **electoral of Lok Sabha, and legislative assembly of state**. There is need of **common electoral** rolls for election of MP/MLA and members of Panchayat. State Election Commission shall make request to Governor for availability of staff, necessary for discharge of functions.

Law for Election

The Representation of the People Act, 1950 and Representation of the People Act, 1951 made by parliament. It is not applicable for holding elections of Panchayat. Legislature of state can introduce right to recall in elections of Panchayat. Law for holding the elections of Panchayat shall be determined by the Legislative of the state.

Removal

Conditions of service of State Election Commission shall not be varied to his disadvantage after his appointed. State Election Commission shall be removed in like manner and like ground as judges of High Court. Critics said that State Election Commission is not independent body, because state government always chose a favourite person for appointment. Without reform in process of appointment, independent method of removal is incomplete.

Delimitation

Validity of any law related to delimitation of constituencies or allotment of seats shall not be called in question in **any court**. There is bar to court, which cannot interfere in delimitation of Panchayat.

Electoral Dispute

Legislature of state shall decide the manner in which **election petition** shall be presented. Legislature of state shall also decide about authority to decide the elections of Panchayat. Practically election petition related to dispute of elections of Panchayat, once election of Panchayat is over is presented before high court.

Application to Union Territory

Union territory without Legislative Assembly, **Administrator** of Union territory is entitled to apply provisions of Panchayati Raj. Union territory with Legislative assembly, the reference of Legislative assembly is essential. Thereafter President by Public notification direct for application of Panchayat in any part or entire Union territory.

Panchayat Not to Apply Certain Areas

1. **Scheduled Areas:** Areas dominated by tribal community, is categorized as scheduled areas, under Fifth Schedule of the Constitution. Scheduled areas are kept away from application of Panchayat. Although Article 243(M) allow **Parliament** to extend the Panchayat in Schedule areas. It shall not be considered as **constitutional amendment in 368**. Parliament extended Panchayat in Scheduled areas in **1996**. It is known as Panchayat Extension in Schedule Areas (PESA). Now Panchayat are enforced in Scheduled areas.
2. **Autonomous Areas and North Eastern States:** According to Article-243(M) of the constitution Panchayati Raj in not applicable for states of **Nagaland, Meghalaya and Mizoram.** Because Nagaland is given special autonomy in Article-371(A). Meghalaya and Mizoram are included in 6th Schedule. **District autonomous council** are set up in 6th schedule, which provides special autonomy for these states. The Hill areas of **Manipur** for which district council exists under any law for the time being in force.

   Darjeeling Gorkha Hill Council in West Bengal is also kept away Panchayat. Panchayat can be extended in states like Nagaland, Meghalaya and Mizoram. If

Legislative Assembly of that state passes a resolution to that effect. Resolution must be passed by **majority of total membership of that house**. In addition to that majority of not less than 2/3 members of that house present and voting. But Panchayat shall not be extended in **District Autonomous Council**.

3. **Arunachal Pradesh:** Provision of **Reservation** mention in Article-243(D) shall not apply to Arunachal Pradesh. Panchayat can be extended in Arunachal Pradesh but rules of Reservation are not applicable for Arunachal Pradesh.

Panchayats Extension to Scheduled Areas Act, 1996 or (PESA)

For the first time **Andhra Pradesh** government announced the extension of Panchayat in Schedule Area. However High Court of Andhra Pradesh declared it null and void. **Dileep Singh Bhuria Committee** has recommended about extension of Panchayat in Schedule Areas, in 1996. PESA is extended in 10 states, where tribal communities live. Panchayat is modified in order to apply local self government in scheduled areas, in **Andhra Pradesh, Chhattisgarh, Gujarat, Himachal Pradesh, Jharkhand, Madhya Pradesh, Maharashtra, Odisha, Rajasthan, Telengana.**

Structure

1. Reservation is mandated in ratio of population of ST/it should not less than half of seats of Panchayat shall be reserved for Scheduled Tribes.
2. Chairperson of each level of Panchayat shall be reserved for a member of scheduled tribes.
3. The Gram Panchayat shall be deemed to be executive committee of Gram Sabha. Gram Sabha will hold a meeting **at least once in two months.**
4. Person belonging to scheduled tribe will be selected as **chairperson** for the meeting of Gram Sabha.
5. The Quorum of the meeting of Gram Sabha shall be 1/5th of total members.
6. Gram Sabha may constitute Various Committee for the development and welfare of people belonging to tribal community.
7. If, person belonging to tribal community, is not represented in intermediate or district level of Panchayat. State Government should person belonging to ST than 10 per cent of total elected member of Panchayat.

Function

1. Gram Sabha shall ensure that **land** of tribal community is not transferred to non-scheduled tribe person.
2. Without approval of Gram Sabha land shall not be **acquired** of belonging to tribal community.
3. Management of natural resources agriculture, land, mines, minerals, minor forest reserve, and money lending, management of market is the mandatory function of Gram Sabha. No decision can be taken without involvement of Gram Sabha.
4. If legislation of state violates customary law, social and religious practices of tribal community. Gram Sabha will not permit this legislation in areas dominated by tribal community.
5. Gram Sabha will also make a mechanism for **dispute settlement.**

Earlier, the District Rural Development Agency (DRDA) was instrumental in the development of village. DRDA was comprised of administrative officers. Now **District Planning Committee (DPC)** becomes key, for making roadmaps of development of village/DPC is comprises of representative of people in Panchayat. Separate administrative officer is also created for the well being of people in rural areas, that is District Panchayat Raj Officer (DPRO).

Constitution makes a separate provision for maintenance of account by Panchayat. **Auditing** of same account is also responsibility of Panchayat under Article-243(K). Now it is known as **social auditing**, because members of Gram Sabha along with administrative officers of Panchayat sit together for examining of income and expenditure of Panchayat. This is helpful for making transparency in the financial administration of Panchayat. Right to information act is boon for promoting **transparency** in Panchayat.

Drawback and Recommendation

There may be numerous problems in Panchayati Raj. George Mathew summarises the problems in the **following three heads:**

1. Function
2. Finance
3. Functionary
4. Functionality

Panchayat are not getting, there all 29 subjects from state government. Panchayat got the constitutional status way back in 1992, but only 5 states transferred all 29 subjects to Panchayat, Haryana, Himachal Pradesh, Karnataka, Kerala and Sikkim are the five states.

Panchayat are still facing of the financial crunch. Administrative officers of Panchayat are under control of state government. But drawbacks of Panchayat cannot undermine it achievement. Need of hour is to strengthen the Panchayat, suggested by second administrative reform commission.

1. **Principle of Subsidiary**

   There is need of amendment of Article-243(G), which says that 29 subjects mention in 11th schedule shall be transferred by state government to Panchayat. Availability of 29 subjects must be mandatory for Panchayat. It should not be dependent over wish of state government.

2. **Financial Autonomy**

   Members of Parliament Local Area Development Scheme (MPLAD) provide 5 crore for each MP every year. 23 subjects are identified for the expenditure of MPLAD these all subjects are already part of 29 subjects of Panchayat. MPLAD should be scrapped/money of MPLAD should be spent through Panchayat. Recommendation of state Finance Communication must be implemented in letter and spirit. Panchayat should generate their financial resources **from non-governmental sources** too, like N.G.O. and corporate house can be the new source of funding of Panchayat.

3. **Administrative Control**

   Panchayat do not have any control over the transfer of administrative officer. Panchayat is not capable to take any disciplinary action against the administrative officers. Administrative officers are still under cadre control of union and state government. Officers belonging to Panchayat of Kerala are kept under control of Panchayat. It should be implemented across the states.

4. **Local Ombudsman**

   Corruption is major issue for non effectiveness of Panchayat. Nexus is visible between politician and administrative officers. ARC suggested for separate Local Ombudsman in order to tackling the problem of corruption.

5. **Autonomy of State Election Commission (SEC)**

   In 2018 Panchayat elections in West Bengal, majority of Chairperson at Local level of Panchayat were elected unopposed. Free and fair election is a major challenge of Panchayat. Therefore, appointment of state Election Commission should not be his privilege of Governor. State Election Commission should be appointed on the basis of recommendation of a committee. Thus state Election Commission shall act independently without fear or favour.

74TH CONSTITUTIONAL AMENDMENT, OR LOCAL URBAN SELF-GOVERNMENT

A. **Democratic Decentralisation:** 74th Constitution Amendment incorporates the provision of Municipalities. There shall be three types of Municipalities for three levels of cities.

(i) For smaller urban areas which are in transition from rural areas to urban areas, there shall be **Nagar Panchayat**.

(ii) For smaller urban areas **Municipal Council** shall be established.

(iii) For larger urban areas **Municipal Corporation** shall be instituted.

Every city shall be divided in the **wards** which will have equal size in terms of population. A city is divided in 50 wards or 30 wards depending upon the population of the cities. Wards means equal territorial constituencies located in a Municipal Area. All the seats in the municipal area shall be field by person chosen by **direct election**. Although election of the Chairperson of municipality shall be decided by legislature of the state. Since municipalities or the subject belong to the state list. Apart from the elected members of wards legislature of the states can insure the representation of:

(a) Person having special knowledge or experience in municipal administration.

(b) The Member of Parliament and member of state legislative council and state assemblies, which comprise wholly or partly the municipal area.

B. **Ward Committees:** Municipalities ensure the better representation of the people because the size of Lok Sabha Constituency and Constituency of state legislative assembly is bigger in terms of population. But a territorial area of municipality having of population of **3 lakhs** or more, ward committees shall be set up.

C. **Decentralise Planning:** Durga Das Basu said that the two unique features of 74th Constitution Amendment are described as follows:

(a) Autonomous political bodies in form of municipalities.

(b) Bodies that will decentralise the planning.

74th Constitution Amendment described about the District Planning Committee (DPC). Earlier District Rural Development Agency (DRDA) was responsible for poverty alleviation and developmental programmes. Now DPC is replacing DRDA. Basic function of DPC is-

(i) Matters of common interest between the Panchayats and the Municipalities including spatial planning.

(ii) Sharing of water and other physical and natural resources.

(iii) The integrated development of infrastructure and environmental conservation.

(iv) The extent and type of available resources whether financial or otherwise.

(v) Consultation with such institutions and organizations as the Governor may, by order.

Composition of DPC: The composition of DPC shall be determined by the legislature of state but seats in such committees shall be filled according to:

(a) 4/5th of the total members of such committee shall be elected and from amongst the elected members of panchayat at district level and the municipalities in district.

(b) Proportion to the ratio between population of rural areas and urban areas in district.

(c) Rest of the members shall be nominated by the legislature of the state. It is not mentioned in the constitution but rest of the 1/5th members of DPC are drawn from the administration, banking and the people having special experience in urban development. Elected members of parliament and the members of state legislative assembly can also be nominated but it depends upon the legislature of the state. It is not uniform in every state because municipalities belong to state list of 7th schedule. DPC send its reports to the state government.

The provision of DPC indicates about **decentralized planning.** Since independence central planning is preferred in India for Economic Development. In the present age of liberalisation and globalisation planning becomes indicated but decentralise planning is most effective for the diverse in plural nation like India. DPC makes plan for the entire district therefore, planning for village and urban areas is the common responsibilities of DPC and according to **74th Constitution Amendment**, 12th Schedule is incorporated in the Constitution. 18 subjects are included in the 12th Schedule, where DPC can make a plan for development of urban areas.

Committee for Metropolitan Planning: Every metropolitan planning committee shall prepare a draft regarding:

(i) The plans prepared by the Municipalities and the Panchayats in the metropolitan area.

(ii) Matters of common interest between the metropolitan and the panchayats

(iii) Co-ordinated spatial planning of areas.

(iv) Sharing of water and other physical and natural resources

(v) Integrated development of infrastructure and environmental conservations.

(vi) The overall objectives and priorities set by the Government of India and the Government of the State.

(vii) The extent and nature of investments likely to be made in the metropolitan areas by agencies of the Government of India and of the governments of the states and other available resources whether financial or otherwise.

(viii) Consult such institution of every Metropolitan Planning Committee shall forward the development plan.

Composition: Likewise DPC composition of metropolitan planning committee is not described in the constitution. However it is inserted in the constitution that not less than 2/3rd of members of such committee shall be elected. They shall be elected from the elected members of municipalities and chairpersons of panchayat in metropolitan areas. The proportion of ratio of members between municipalities and panchayat shall be decided according to the ratio of population. Other members shall be nominated by their legislature of the state. Members includes the officers of bank, engineer belong to department of electricity and elected members of parliament and the state legislative assembly. Although it is not mentioned in the constitution.

D. Common Features of 73rd and 74th Amendment:

Financial Devolution

18 Subject included does not point out any item related to taxation. Article-243(Y) authorise the legislature of state to make a law related to taxation;

(a) **Levying Taxes:** Legislature of state authorise a municipality to levy, collect and appropriate taxes, duties, tolls and fees. Legislative assembly of Haryana authorise municipalities to levy entailment tax However, later, Haryana had withdrawn power of levying taxes from municipalities.

(b) **Levied and Collected by State, Assigned to municipalities:** State can assign to a municipalities such taxes, duties, tolls and fees levied and collected by state Government/this increases financial sources of municipalities. Receiving and withdrawal of money by municipalities from such fund.

(c) **Centrally Sponsored Scheme:** Constitution does not incorporate the provision of centrally sponsored scheme. But municipalities receive grand from the Central Government.

State Finance Commission

The governor of state shall constitute state finance commission as soon as may be within one year from the commencement of the constitutional amendment act, 1992. There after state finance commission shall be constituted expiration of every 5th year. State finance commission shall make recommendation to governor for reviewing of financial position of municipalities, under Article-243(Y).

A. **Structure:** Constitution does not delineate the structure of state finance commission. Structure refers to the numbers of members and eligibility. Procedure and power of commission shall be defined by State Legislature.

B. **Function:** Article-243(Y) spell about function of state finance commission, which is mentioned below;

1. Principle of distribution of taxes, duties, tolls and fees, levies by the state. Distribution of state taxes between state and municipalities. Allocating shares among the three types of municipalities.
2. The determination of taxes, duties, tolls and fees, which may be assigned to or appropriated by municipalities.
3. The grant-in-aid to municipalities from consolidated fund of state.
4. The measure needed to improve financial position of municipalities.
5. Any other matter referred to the Finance Commission by governor in the interest of maintaining sound finance across the municipalities.

Governor shall present the recommendation of state finance commission before legislature of state. Governor shall also tell about action taken by government over recommendation of commission. Kerala appointed Principal Secretary as chairperson of state finance commission although state government does not implement the report the state finance commission.

STATE ELECTION COMMISSION (SEC)

Article 243(ZA) prescribes about State Election Commission headed by State Election Commissioner, shall be appointed by Governor.

Structure: The conditions of service and tenure of office of the State Election Commissioner shall be determined by Governor. But it is subject to law made by the Legislature of the state.

Function: The superintendence, direction, control and preparation of electoral rolls for elections to municipalities are vested in the State Election Commission.

It is worth noting that electoral rolls for election of municipalities are different from electoral rolla of Lok Sabha, and legislative assembly of state. There is a need of common electoral rolls for election of MP/MLA and members of municipalities. State Election Commission shall make request to Governor for availability of staff, necessary for timely execution of the functions.

Law for Election

The Representation of the People Act, 1950 and Representation of the People Act, 1951 made by the Parliament are is not applicable for holding elections of municipalities. Legislature of state can introduce the right to recall in elections of municipalities. Law for holding the elections of municipalities shall be determined by the Legislative of the state.

Removal

Conditions of service of State Election Commission shall not be changed to his disadvantage after he is appointed. State Election Commission shall be removed in like manner and like ground as judges of High Court. Critics said that State Election Commission is not an independent body, because state government has been biased with selection of a candidate for appointment. Without reform in process of appointment, independent method of removal is incomplete.

Delimitation

Validity of any law relating to delimitation of constituencies or allotment of seats shall not be called in question in any court. There is bar to court, which cannot interfere in delimitation of municipalities.

Electoral Dispute

Legislature of state shall decide the manner in which election petition shall be presented. Legislature of state shall also decide the elections of municipalities. Practically, post-municipality-elections, petition related to dispute of elections is presented before the High Court.

Reservation/Social Justice and Gender Justice

Under Article 243(T), reservation is given for persons belonging to following category in the Constitution under compulsory provisions:

1. The Schedule caste
2. Scheduled Tribes
3. Women
4. Reservation for Other Backward Class citizen shall be determined by the legislature of state. Reservation for seats as well as Chairperson, both is the responsibility of Legislature of state.

Reservation for SC/ST

Reservation is applicable for all three types of Municipalities. It is applicable for number of seats of Municipalities to be filled by direct election in the Municipalities. Quantum of reservation is fixed according to the ratio of population of SC/STs in the Municipalities. Reservation shall be in rotation. As for as reservation of Chairperson is the ratio of in the Municipalities concerned. It shall be determined by legislature of state. Nevertheless, quantity of reservation should be according to population of state.

Reservation of women

Reservation for women is applied for number of seats of Municipalities to be filled by direct election. Reservation at the level of Chairperson shall be determined by legislature of state. Not less than 33 per cent seats shall be reserved for women in rotation. Women reservation is ensured in the reservation of SC/ST available for women.

Reservation for Backward Class

Legislature of state shall determine the upper limit of reservation in number of seats of Municipalities to be filled by direct election. Reservation for level of Chairperson shall also be determined by legislature of state.

Tenure of Reservation

Reservation for SC/ST in Municipalities shall be continued up to 2030, according 104th Constitutional amendment. Article-334 is applicable for the reservation of Municipalities. This article ensures reservation of SC/ST in the Lok Sabha as well as in legislature of the state. But no time limit is applicable for the reservation of women and candidates belong to the OBC category.

Duration of Municipalities

Tenure of Municipalities is 5 years from the date appointed for its first meeting, according to Article-243(U). In case of dissolution of existing Municipalities, newly constituted Municipalities shall continue only for remainder of the period. If a Municipality dissolve within 3 years, a new Municipalityb shall be constituted but only for 2 years. If remainder period is less than 6 months,election shall be held for full 5 years. Ground of dissolution is not mentioned in the constitution. It is for the legislature of state to decide. Terms and condition for dissolution vary from state to state.

Disqualification for Membership

Disqualification for election of person for legislature of state is equally applicable for disqualification of member of Municipalities. Legislature of state is entitled to make any other disqualification for elections of member of Municipalities. Andhra Pradesh enacted Law for disqualifying person in election of Municipalities. Person having more than two kids are disqualified to contest an election of Municipalities.

Although eligibility of contesting in elections of Municipalities is completion of 21 years. Legislature of state shall empower to establish an authority or manner to adjudicate about disqualification.

RECOMMENDATION FOR REFORM

1. **Strengthening power of Mayor:** According to parliamentary form of government elected representative are given more power in comparison to the permanent executive which is the members of civil services, in Union and the State. Therefore, position of mayor in municipalities should be similar like PM in the Union Government and CM in the state government.
2. **Transfer of Power:** Public Order in an important subject for the administration of municipalities but it is still in the hand of state government. Municipal Government doesn't have any voice in maintaining public order, which weaken the position of municipalities.
3. **Ombudsman:** Corruption is a major problem in local self-government. And there is need of autonomous institution for the elimination of corruption, in the governance of municipalities.

Financial Resources: Union Government run the scheme for making smart cities. Municipalities are at liberty to adopt modern and sophisticated method for collecting the taxes. Now various municipalities are applying digital technology and e-governance for preventing the evasion of taxes. It is matter of surprise that some of the biggest municipalities of India like, Mumbai and Delhi are facing the financial crunch.

11

CONSTITUTIONAL AND STATUTORY BODIES

KEY CONCEPTS

Comptroller and Auditor General, National Commission for Scheduled Castes, National Commission for Scheduled Tribes, National Commission for Human Rights, National Commission for Women, National Commission for Minoritiess

NATIONAL COMMISSION FOR SCHEDULED CASTES

The 1931 Census, for the first time systematically categorised certain castes as 'depressed classes'. Thereafter, the **Government of India Act 1935**, for the first time, provided for notification of socially disadvantaged castes as 'Scheduled Castes', and a list of such castes was accordingly notified in the Government of India (Scheduled Castes) Order 1936. Scheduled Castes are defined in **Article 366[24]** of the Constitution of India, as 'Scheduled Castes means such castes, races or tribes or parts of or groups within such castes, races or tribes as are deemed under Article 341 to be Scheduled Castes for the purposes of this Constitution'.

The **Constitution (Sixty-eighth Amendment) Bill, 1990**, was passed unanimously by the Lok Sabha on 30 May 1990 and the Rajya Sabha on 31 May 1990. It received the President's assent on 7 June 1990 and was notified as the **Constitution (Sixty-fifth Amendment) Act, 1990** in the official Gazette on 8 June 1990.

Scheduled Castes and Scheduled Tribes came into being consequently, upon the passing of the above. The first Commission under the Constitution on 12 March 1992 replaced the Commissioner for Scheduled Castes and Scheduled Tribes and the commission set up under the Ministry of Welfare's Resolution on 1987.The first Commission consisted of Shri Ram Dhan as the Chairman. Consequent upon the **Constitution (Eighty-ninth Amendment) Act, 2003** coming into force on 19 February 2004. The erstwhile National Commission for Scheduled Castes and Scheduled Tribes has been replaced by

1. National Commission for Scheduled Castes; and
2. National Commission for Scheduled Tribes.

Structure

The Commission for Scheduled Tribes consists of:

- Chairperson
- Vice-Chairperson

Figure 7.11.1: Structure of the National Commission

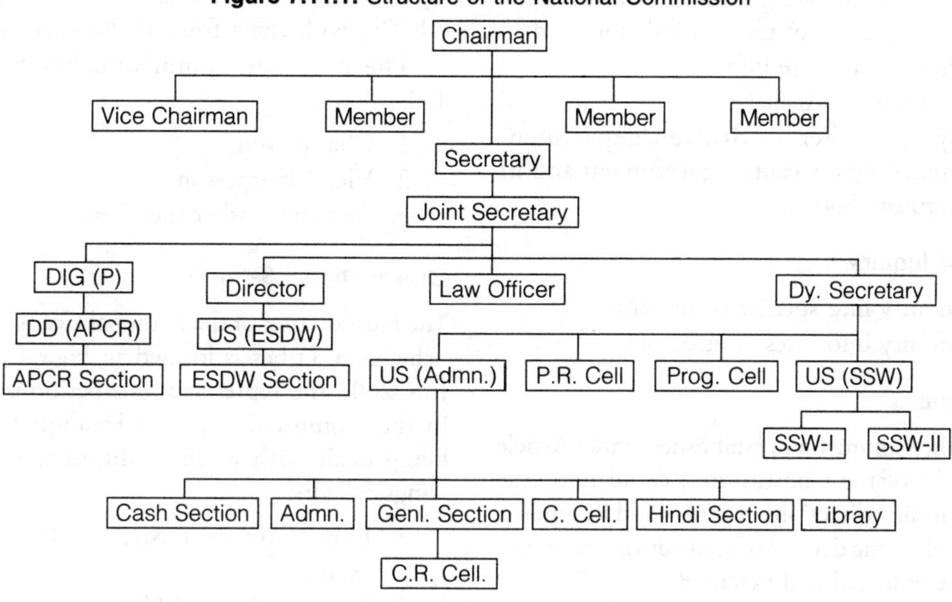

- Three other members
- They are appointed by the President by warrant under his hand and seal. The terms and condition of the offices of the Chairperson and members is determined by the President.

Functions

The functions of the National Commission for Scheduled Castes are enumerated in **Article 338[5]** of the Constitution which includes:

1. To **investigate** and monitor all matters relating to the safeguards provided for the Scheduled Castes under this **Constitution** or under any other law for the time being in force or under any order of the Government and to evaluate the working of such safeguards;
2. To **enquire** into specific **complaints** with respect to the deprivation of rights and safeguards of the Scheduled Castes;
3. To **participate** and **advise** on the planning process of socio-economic development of the Scheduled Castes and to evaluate the progress of their development under the union and any state;
4. To **present** to the **President**, annually and at such other times as the commission may deem file reports upon the working of those safeguards;
5. To make in such reports recommendations as to the measures that should be taken by the union or any sets for the effective implementation of those safeguards and other measures for the **protection, welfare and socio-economic development** of the Scheduled Castes; and
6. To discharge such other functions in relation to the protection, welfare, development and advancement of the Scheduled Castes as the President may, subject to the provisions of any law made by Parliament, by rule, specify.

Investigation by the Commission

Investigation by the Commission may happen in the following ways:

1. Investigation and inquiry by the Commission directly;

2. by an investigating team constituted at the Headquarters of the Commission; and
3. through its State Offices;
4. by the State Agencies;
5. by any other institution/departmenr funded by the central government and its statutory bodies.

Types of Inquiry

1. Inquiry into specific complaints
2. Inquiry into cases of atrocities

Limitations

1. The Commission, established under Article 338 of the Constitution, could not issue binding directions or orders and its reports, unlike the decrees of civil courts, could not be enforced and executed.
2. As the Commission is not an adjudicatory body that could issue binding directions or order therefore, it has no jurisdiction over service matters of an institution like the Indo-Tibetan Border Police (ITBP) [Refer to *Union of India & Anr vs. National Commission For Scheduled Castes*, 28 May 2014].
3. The Commission's reports are not an alternative to the hierarchical judicial system envisaged under the Constitution.

NATIONAL COMMISSION FOR SCHEDULED TRIBES

Creation and composition

The National Commission for Scheduled Tribes (NCST) is a constitutional body which was established by amending **Article 338** and inserting a new **Article 338A** in the Constitution through the **Constitution (Eighty-ninth Amendment) Act, 2003**. By this Amendment, the erstwhile National Commission for Scheduled Castes and Scheduled Tribes was replaced by two separate Commissions, namely (i) the National Commission for Scheduled Castes (NCSC), and (ii) the National Commission for Scheduled Tribes (NCST) with effect from 19 February 2004.

The National Commission for Scheduled Tribes has a:

1. Chairperson
2. Vice-Chairperson
3. And three other members.

Organisational Setup

The Headquarter of the National Commission for Scheduled Tribes is located in New Delhi. Till July 2006 the representations/petitions received in the Commission at the Headquarters were being dealt with in three different functional wings called:

1. Economic and Social Development Wing
2. Service Safeguard Wing
3. Atrocities Wing, and
4. Research Units

Regional Offices

The National Commission for Scheduled Tribes has **6 Regional Offices** located at Bhopal, Bhubaneswar, Jaipur, Raipur, Ranchi and Shillong.

Functions

The functions, duties and power of the National Commission for Scheduled Tribes have been laid down in **Clauses (5), (8) and (9)** of **Article 338A** of the Constitution, inserted by the Constitution (Eighty-ninth Amendment) Act 2003. Clause (5) states that it shall be the duty of the Commission:

1. to investigate and monitor all matters relating to the safeguards provided for the Scheduled Tribes under the Constitution or under any other law for the time being in force or under any order of the Government and to evaluate the working of such safeguards;

2. to inquire into specific complaints with respect to the deprivation of rights and safeguards of the Scheduled Tribes;
3. to participate and advise on the planning process of socio-economic development of the Scheduled Tribes and to evaluate the progress of their development under the Union and any State;
4. to present to the President, annually and at such other times as the Commission may deem fit, reports upon the working of those safeguards;
5. to make in such reports recommendations as to the measures that should be taken by the Union or any State for the effective implementation of those safeguards and other measures for the protection, welfare and socio-economic development of the Scheduled Tribes; and to discharge such other functions in relation to the protection, welfare and development and advancement of the Scheduled Tribes as the President may, subject to the provisions of any law made by Parliament, by rule, specify.

Procedural Autonomy

The NCST has autonomy over its procedures:

1. the procedure of investigation and enquiry by the Commission;
2. frequency of meetings of the Commission;
3. the duties of its Regional Offices;
4. the advisory role of the Commission; and
5. its monitoring functions.

Advisory Role of the Commission

Clause (9) of Article 338A provides that the union and every state government shall consult the Commission on all major policy matters affecting Scheduled Tribes. The policy matters referred to the Commission are discussed in detail in the meetings of the Commission on the basis of the views expressed by the members and the notes on the subject matter, indicating historical background, current status and relevant rules, and so on.

Functional Role

The Commission receives a large number of petitions from all parts of the country about the grievances relating to:

1. Alleged violation of service safeguards;
2. Matters relating to alienation of land, admission in professional and technical institutions particularly in medical, engineering, and so on;.,
3. Atrocities.

Issues Taken Up by the Commission

The Commission has divided the issues that come before it into the following categories:

1. Constitutional provisions for protection and development of STs
2. Socio-economic development of STs (land alienation, rights over MFP [minor forest produces], housing, education etc.)
3. Resettlement and rehabilitation of displaced tribals
4. Education
5. Service safeguards
6. The problem of authenticating ST certificates
7. Crimes and atrocities against STs

Representation in Court Cases

For proper implementation of the constitutional safeguards provided for the Scheduled Tribes and to advise the union and the state gGovernments on all major policy matters affecting the Scheduled Tribes, the Commission is on occasion required to file affidavits containing its views in cases relating to important issues concerning the STs filed in various courts by various parties, including the members of the ST community and/or by their associations, involving National Commission for Scheduled Tribes as one of the respondents.

NATIONAL COMMISSION FOR WOMEN

The National Commission for Women (NCW) was formed in **1992** under the **National Commission for Women Act 1990**. It is a Commission having the authority to review constitutional safeguards for women in the country. The main recommendation of the Commission is to facilitate redressal mechanisms and also take legislative measures to curb the disparity between the conditions of women and men. It provides the government with advice to make policies and laws that are more likely to protect and safeguard the rights of women. The Commission is also vested with the powers of a civil court. On 31 January 1992, the first Commission was constituted and was chaired by Jayanti Patnaik. The first male member in the NCW (National Commission for women) was Alok Rawat, IAS.

Composition

The Commission consists of a chairperson, a member secretary and five other members. The chairperson of the NCW is nominated by the central government. The central government also nominates the member secretary. The member secretary should be an expert in the field of management. He/she is an officer or organisation who is a member. The five members nominated by the central government should be individuals with **ability, standing** and **integrity**. They should have experience in **law, legislation, management, women's voluntary organisations, economic social development** and so on. Provided that at least **one member** each shall be from amongst persons belonging to the **Scheduled Castes** and **Scheduled Tribes** respectively;

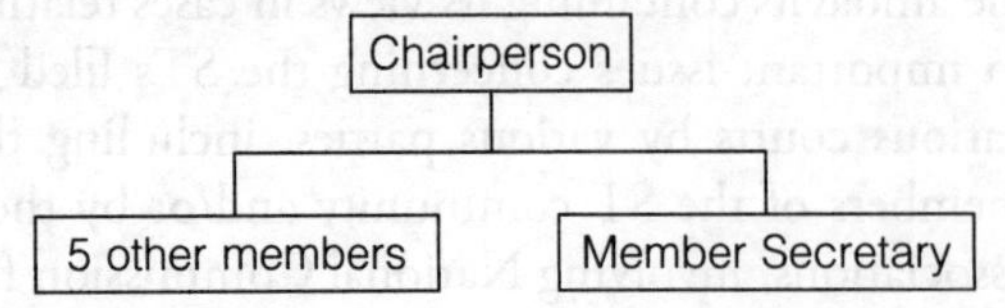

Term of office and conditions of service of Chairperson and Members:

(1) The Chairperson and every member shall hold office for such period, not exceeding **three years**, as may be specified by the central government.

(2) The Chairperson or a member (other than the member secretary who is a member of a civil service of the union or of an all-India service, or holds a civil post under the union) may, by writing and addressed to the central government, resign from the office of Chairperson or, as the case may be, of the member at any time; provided that no person shall be removed under this clause until that person has been given a **reasonable opportunity** of being heard in the matter.

Functions

The functions of the National Commission for Women are as follows:

1. **Presentation of reports:** To submit reports to the central government every year.
2. **Investigation and examination:** To investigate and examine laws under the Constitution, pertaining to the protection of the rights of women.
3. **Review:** To review and scrutinise all laws and make necessary amendments and alterations are made to meet the needs of the current world. This is to meet any break, incapacity or any inadequacies in the legislation.
4. **Cases of violation:** To ensure that there is no violation against women and taking due care of such cases.
5. ***Suo Motu* notice:** To take care of complaints and also *suo motu* matters about the deprivation of rights of women, and implement laws favouring the welfare of women.

6. **Evaluation:** To assess the development and the progress of women atthe centre and state level.
7. **Recommendation:** To recommend steps for the wellbeing of women and realising their rights.
8. **Special studies and investigation:** To understand the limitations in the system and curb them with strategic plans and mechanisms.
9. **Research:** To research and study the needs of women, such as healthcare and such related components. This is to make a proper support system to help the women in need.
10. **Participation in all spheres, particularly in planning:** To take measures to facilitate economic and social development and improvement of women by recognising their rights.
11. **Inspection:** To inspect the jail and remand homes to ensure that the women staying here are not exploited as they are vulnerable.
12. **Funding** To ensure there is a fund for litigation of matters relating to women rights.

Powers of NCW

1. Provide consultation on all major policy matters that affect women;
2. Issuing summons for the examination of documents and the witnesses;
3. Power to make any public record;
4. Receiving evidence on affidavits;
5. Discovery and production of documents; and
6. Summoning and enforcement of policy.

Annual report and audit report to be laid before Parliament: The central government shall cause the annual report together with a memorandum of action taken on the recommendations contained therein, insofar as they relate to the central government, and the reasons for the non-acceptance, if any, of any of such recommendations and the audit report, to be laid as soon as may be after the reports are received, before each House of Parliament.

NATIONAL HUMAN RIGHTS COMMISSION (NHRC)

Human Rights in Constitution

Fundamental Rights incorporated in Part III of the Indian Constitution describe about human rights. In fact, all Fundamental Rights are human rights. Although all human rights are not Fundamental Rights. Human rights refer the universal rights available for everyone across the world. But Fundamental Rights are available for citizens. Therefore, the scope of Fundamental Rights is limited. Human rights are moral however, Fundamental Rights are legal in their nature. Constitution also provides the autonomous and independent Supreme Court which protects Fundamental Rights.

Need of Autonomous Commission

The Supreme Court is already burdened with pendency of numerous cases. Approaching the Supreme Court is costly and time-taking. Hence, the National Human Rights Commission (NHRC) is set up exclusively for dealing issues related to violation of Human Rights. In the progression of India, formation of the NHRC is major step. The NHRC is an autonomous public body founded on 12 October 1993 under the Protection of Human Rights Ordinance of 28 September 1993. It was given a statutory base by the Protection of Human Rights Act, 1993.

Structure

The 2005 Paris Agreement at the UNFCCC (United Nations Framework Convention on Climate Change) which is also read as a human rights treaty, mentioned that a human rights commission should be an autonomous body. The

NHRC should not be under the subordination of a state or a government. The structure of the NHRC proves that it is an autonomous body.

According to the Protection of Human Rights (Amendment) Bill, 2019, a person who has been **Chief Justice of the Supreme Court** or a **Judge of the Supreme Court** will be the Chairperson of the NHRC.

The Act provides for two persons having knowledge of human rights to be appointed as members of the NHRC. The Act allows three members to be appointed, of which at least one will be a woman. Under the Act, chairpersons of various commissions such as the National Commission for Scheduled Castes, National Commission for Scheduled Tribes, and National Commission for Women are members of the NHRC. The chairpersons of the National Commission for Backward Classes, the National Commission for the Protection of Child Rights, and the Chief Commissioner for Persons with Disabilities as members of the NHRC.

The Act provides for a **Secretary General** of the NHRC and a Secretary of an SHRC (State Human Rights Commission), who exercise powers as may be delegated to them. The new amendment allows the Secretary General and Secretary to exercise all administrative and financial powers (except judicial functions), subject to the respective Chairperson's control.

Under the Act, and Chairperson of an SHRC is a person who has been a Chief Justice of a High Court. New amendment provides that a person who has been Chief Justice or Judge of a High Court will be chairperson of an SHRC.

Structure of NHRC

The chairpersons of the National Commission for Backward Classes, the National Commission for the Protection of Child Rights, and the Chief Commissioner for Persons with Disabilities are also members of the NHRC.

COMMITTEE FOR APPOINTMENT

Tenure

The Chairperson and the members of the NHRC have a tenure of five years. But if any member

Figure 7.11.2: The Structure of NHRC

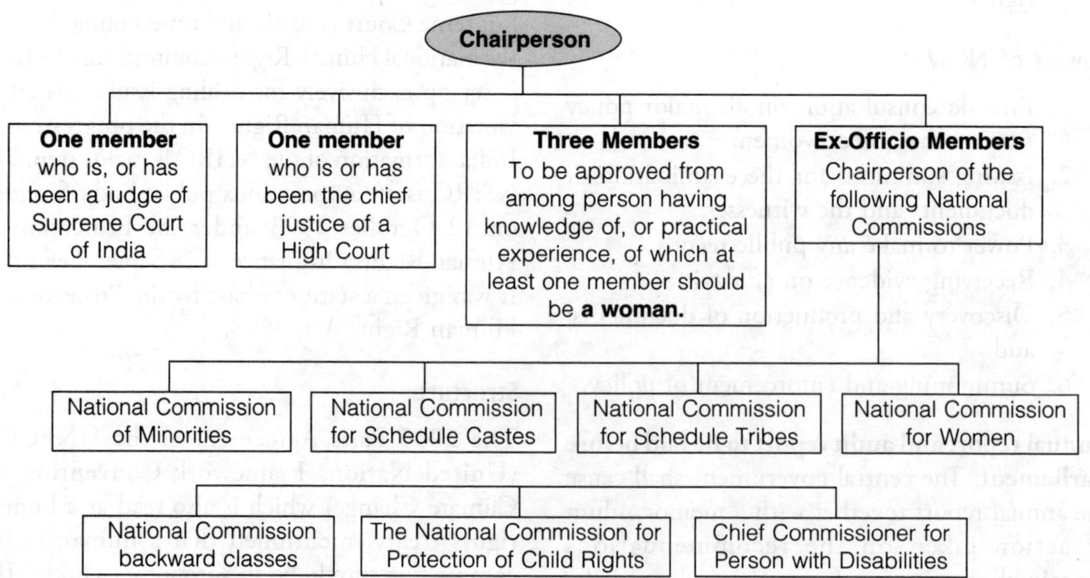

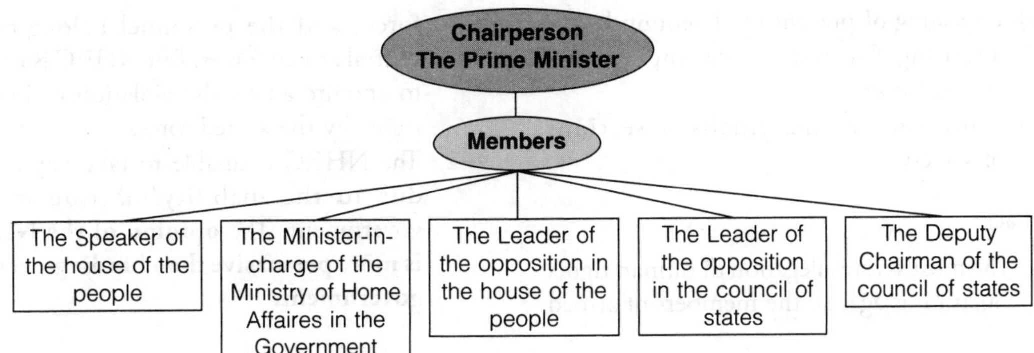

reaches the age of 70 years before the completion of his tenure, he or she has to retire from the membership. The new Amendment reduces the term of office to **3 years** or till the age of seventy years, whichever is earlier. However, the members shall hold the office for 5 years or the age of 70 years, whichever is earlier.

The Chairperson or any other member of this Commission can be removed by the President even before the expiry of their full term. They can be removed only on the charge of proved misbehaviour or incapacity or both, if it is proved by an inquiry conducted by a judge of the Supreme Court.

The headquarters of the Commission is at New Delhi. Though, with permission ofthe government, it can establish offices at other places in India.

Functions

Comprehensive powers and functions have been given to the Commission under Section 12 of the Act.

1. To investigate grievances regarding the violation of human rights either *suo moto* or after receiving a petition.
2. To scrutinise the failure of duties on the part of any public official in preventing the violation of human rights.
3. To interfere in any judicial proceedings involving any allegation of violation of human rights.
4. To visit any jail or any other institution under the control of the state government to see the living conditions of the inmates and to make recommendations thereon.
5. To review the safeguards provided under the Constitution or any law for the protection of the human rights and to recommend appropriate remedial measures.
6. To study treaties and other international instruments on human rights and to make recommendations for their effective implementation.
7. To undertake and promote research in the field of human rights.
8. To encourage the efforts of the non-governmental organisations (NGOs) working in the field of human rights.
9. To spread human rights literacy among various sections of society and to promote awareness of the safeguards available for the protection of these rights through publications, the media, seminars and other means.
10. To review all facts related to the activities of the terrorists which obstruct the way of the protection of human rights and to make recommendations for their effective implementation.

Role of Human Rights Commission

(a) Investigating custodial death
(b) Visiting factories

(c) Repealing of preventing detention laws
(d) Training for the police and central armed forces
(e) Protection of marginalised sections of society

Drawback

1. The most severe allegation of human rights violation is against the members of armed forces and the personnel belonging to central armed forces. But NHRC is unable to enquire about the violation of human rights by the armed forces.
2. The NHRC is unable to take any action due to the inability/inaction of the government. The **opinion of the NHRC is more persuasive than binding over the government.**

Unit VIII

POLITICAL PROCESSES IN INDIA

KEYWORDS

Nature of the Indian State; structural-functionalist perspective; Marxist perspective; neoliberalism; subaltern and cultural studies; Indian polity in the 1980s and 1990s

1

STATE, ECONOMY AND DEVELOPMENT

KEY CONCEPTS

Nature of Indian State; Development Planning model; New Economic Policy; Growth and Human Development

THEORETICAL DEBATES ON THE NATURE OF THE INDIAN STATE

There is no serious agreement on what constitutes the nature of the postcolonial state. But broadly speaking, there are two dominant approaches regarding the Indian state, that is, the liberal and the Marxist approaches. However, both these approaches are taken to be inadequate by emerging perspectives in postcolonial literature. This is because both liberal and Marxist theories focus on social determinants of the political process and the level of economic development and detract attention from the state, a significant agent in shaping and moulding political–social processes (Parekh, 1993).

Neo-liberal modernists, such as **Rajni Kothari**, **Atul Kohli**, **F. Frankel**, and **S. Rudolph**, focus on the different institutions and processes as the key elements to understand the state and political power in India. Marxist theorists, on the other hand, regard the political economy as the decisive factor and the principle of class analysis as the determining element in unpacking the idea of the state.

Neo-Marxists, such as **Sudipta Kaviraj**, **Achin Vanaik**, **Pranab Bardhan**, and **Partha Chatterjee** interpret the nature of the state from the perspective of orthodox Marxism, Gramscian and cultural terms. They argue that in the state, there are many different groups that try to surpass one another and sometimes they attempt to work in a coalitional arrangement so as to preserve their dominance. According to this view, the nature and autonomy thesis of the Indian state can be described in terms of changing balances in the ruling class coalition.

The early descriptions of the state concentrated on the functioning of political institutions and democratic processes. In India, the trend of analysing the state in terms of the state–society relationship began to emerge around the 1970s within the academic community. It started when the legal and institutional focus began to give way to a societal explanation under the impact of primarily two rival theoretical frameworks of analysis—*structural functionalism* and *Marxism*.

Structural functionalism is an approach built around the argument that despite social conflicts and tensions, the Indian state had the resilience to sustain itself. Following a structural functional framework, **Rajni Kothari** described the political system as working around a 'dynamic core' of institutions characterised by the dominance of the Congress 'system' (Chatterjee 2010). Similarly, **W. H. Morris-Jones** also stressed the capability of political institutions, especially one-party dominance, and more generally, representative institutions in bringing about social and economic changes (John-Morris, 1987). Rajni Kothari has attributed the existence of *pluralist tolerance* and the *culture of consensus* to the success of the Indian state, which was possible under the rule of the Congress system. However, Kothari's account of the consensual character of '*the Congress system*' was criticised with the onset of the democratic crisis, which culminated in the Emergency of 1975–1977, and the use of repressive state apparatus by the Congress, which broke down Kothari's consensus model.

In terms of the role of the state, **Gunnar Myrdal** discussed '*soft state*' as states that display 'various types of social indiscipline' and cannot act against vested interests of different powerful groups (Myrdal, 1968). Myrdal used the term 'soft state' to refer to newly emergent nations in the developing world, of which India is a classic example—India lacks the institutional capacity to enforce public policies to eradicate poverty and promote economic development. The observation of **Lloyd Rudolph** and **Susanne Hoeber Rudolph** also reiterate this view. They analyse the Indian political economy as possessing the dual characteristics of a '*weak–strong state*' and conceptualise two models to describe the autonomy of the Indian state: command polity and demand polity (Rudolph and Rudolph 1987). In '*demand polity*', societal demands—expressed as electoral pressure—dominate over the state. Here the citizens are sovereign where they try to represent their demands through representation by interests, classes, community and movements. In the '*command polity*', autonomous states are sovereign where state hegemony dominates over society (ibid). Here the argument rests on the state's role as the 'third actor', along with capital and labour, and by far the most powerful one, concerning both '*organised private capital*' and '*organised labour*' (Hassan, 2000). The Rudolphs maintained that the Indian democratic state is simultaneously weak and strong. It is strong because it controls the commanding heights of the economy but at the same time, it is weak as it fails to govern or provide equitable treatment to citizen demands. Therefore, the Rudolphs agreed that the autonomy of the Indian state has declined since Independence. The inability of the state to achieve its declared agenda has also been examined by **Atul Kohli**.

The inability of the Indian state to achieve its declared agenda in the 1980s, and the rising demands from the different groups of society that have not been responded to by the state, have led to an all-round 'crisis of governability' (Hassan 2001). To Kohli (2000), one underlying cause for this crisis can be the weakness of political institutions of the state, such as the decline and erosion of political parties.

F. Frankel, a social scientist, also commented on the Indian state and its democratic development. She raised an important argument in terms of the nature of the state. She observed that the Indian state apparatus was controlled by the dominant interests of the powerful and elite propertied class (Frankel, 2006). In their discussion, **Frankel** and **Rao** observe that the history of politics in independent India was one of the rising power of formerly low-status groups, such as the lower castes and the poorer classes in political institutions, and the attempt by upper-caste and middle-class groups to protect their privileges as public institutions (ibid.). Therefore, Frankel believes that policies of the government are being prepared through political compromises among political elites and leaders with accommodative politics, a kind of politics which jeopardises the state's agenda of radical social change in contemporary times. Therefore, as Frankel emphasised, the state is presently facing difficulties in confronting an accommodationist strategy of class conciliation in politics, and a commitment to transformative goals in society within a democratic framework (ibid.).

The position that was taken up by the structural functionalists was contested by the Marxists. It was argued that the Indian state was a class institution representing class oppression. For **Marxists,** the nature of the state can be understood in terms of both the long-term structural compulsions of Indian politics, which are determined by capitalism and the inclusion of the economy in the international capitalist system and its division of labour; and also in terms of the coalition arrangements and the changing balance in class coalitions dominating the state (Kaviraj, 1996).

Marxists also view the complexity of class formation, class conflict and class action as the major elements for understanding the limitations of state and capitalist transformation. **Prabhat Patnaik** has given three elements for ruling class coalition: monopoly bourgeoisie, land-owning elite, and bureaucratic managerial elite (Patnaik, 1972). The state structure is regulated and dominated by these three classes accordingly. But the imposition of Emergency in 1975 generated fresh controversy regarding the repressive powers of the state. After the imposition of Emergency, the discussion about the nature of the autonomy of the state has shifted to a discourse about the relative autonomy of the state.

The Marxist position was initially oriented towards the understanding of the **Indian State** from the *class perspective*. But the Gramscian intervention in the 1970s brought into focus several studies. **Achin Vanaik, K. N. Raj, Pranab Bardhan, Asok Sen, Sudipta Kaviraj,** and others viewed the state as *non-hegemonic*, and the role of the coalitional class as also important in terms of understanding the nature of the state. These coalitions of classes consist of the bourgeoisie, the rich and the middle peasantry, the landlords, the petty bourgeoisie, and the negation of these classes is rather fluid and complex (Gupta, 2013). According to a noted social class, proprietary class and professional class (Bardhan, 1984). During the first decade after Independence, the state elite in India enjoyed independent authority and enormous prestige, and were the main actors who redirected and restructured the nation's economy. Over time, however, with the strengthening of the main proprietary classes, the industrial and the agrarian bourgeoisie, the autonomous behavior of the state became restricted more to its 'regulatory' rather than its 'developmental' functions (ibid.). It is so because these class alliances have engaged in earning more profit for their sectional interest by reducing the state's role from development activities to the mere management of policies which favour the dominant proprietary classes.

After **Pranab Bardhan, Sudipta Kaviraj** has also commented about the dominant class model, in his essay 'A Critique of the Passive Revolution' following Antonio Gramsci's idea of passive revolution (Kaviraj, 1989). Kaviraj has given his observation regarding the process of class domination (industrial—capitalists, rural elites, and bureaucratic–managerial) in postcolonial India. Power has been shared by the dominant classes, as no particular class could exercise hegemony on its own. Thus, sharing of power became an endless struggle among the different dominant groups, with one class gaining ascendancy over another. Kaviraj provided a synoptic political history of the relative dominance and decline of the industrial capitalist, the ruling elites and the bureaucratic managerial elite within the framework of the passive revolution (Hassan 2000). Therefore, it can be said from Kaviraj's observation that nature and autonomy thesis of the Indian state can be described in terms of changing balances in the ruling class coalition.

Since the mid-1980s, under the influence of postcolonialism, postmodernism and *subaltern and cultural studies*, together with the decline of Marxism and the onset of globalisation and liberalisation, a major shift in the understanding of the social character of the Indian state has developed (Gupta, 2013). The principal trends in understanding the trajectory of the Indian state include the conceptualisation of the caste issue, following the rise of **Dalit** politics, politics of social justice, civil society, the rise of new social movements and the corporatisation of the Indian state in the wake of liberalisation.

There are certain primary considerations that involve an understanding of the social profile of the Indian state, which eventually impacted the trajectory of the state. First, the nature of India's participatory democracy has influenced the growth and awareness of different micro-identity groups, and it has also helped them in mobilising for their demands and further encouraged different movements for their identity assertion. This is reflected in the case of articulation of different demands and mobilisation of the marginalised sections such as **Dalits, Adivasis**, and ethnic groups, which were either suppressed or recognised by the state. Second, the rising voices of the marginalised sections and their assertions and mobilisations have contributed to the growth of different forces, which fuelled the growth of the non-Congress coalition at the centre and the states, which eventually led to the decline of the Congress party (Kothari, 1970). Third, corporatisation of the Indian state has led to a decline of the role of the state and opened up some major sectors of the economy to the market in the name of reforms, development or modernisation, and this has deprived sections that form the informal sector. Fourth, state–market negotiation also created a different sort of conflict. Protection of corporate capitalism by the state, in terms of promoting development, has led to the intensification of violence in many tribal-dominated areas. This has manifested in the form of '**Maoist**' violence in certain parts of the Indian state, and the rise of civil society, as the critique of state repression can be seen as one of the repercussions of state-led development. Again, the implementation of the state's poverty alleviation programmes, such as **Mahatma Gandhi National Rural Employment Guarantee Act** (MGNREGA) and its implementation, are done with the help of NGOs, bureaucrats and political parties, which opens up a new way of looking at the role of the state in the twenty-first century (Gupta, 2013). It can be said that the adoption of development programmes reinforces the state's role in development and legitimises the adoption of such programmes for a pre-capitalist sector, which continues to exist alongside the accumulation-based modern sector in the globalised world.

INDIA'S DEVELOPMENT PLANNING MODEL

Though planned economic development in India began in 1951 with the inception of First Five Year Plan, theoretical efforts had begun much earlier, even before Independence. The setting up of the **National Planning Committee** by Indian National Congress in 1938, the **Bombay Plan** (1944) by **J. R. D. Tata**, **G. D. Birla** and **Purushottamdas Thakurdas**, the **Gandhian Plan** by **Shriman Narayan Agarwal** in 1944, the **People's Plan** by **M. N. Roy** in 1945 (by Post-war Reconstruction Committee of Indian Federation of Labour), and the **Sarvodaya Plan** in 1950 by **Jayaprakash Narayan** were steps in this direction (*See* Ministry of Statistics and Programme Implementation website).

Five-Year Plans (FYPs) are centralised and integrated national economic programmes. Joseph Stalin implemented the first FYP in the Soviet Union in the late 1920s. Most communist states and several capitalist countries subsequently have adopted them.

Indian economy has been planned through these Five-Year Plans which were developed, executed and monitored by the Planning Commission till 2014. After the NDA government came to power in 2014, the Planning Commission was dissolved and instead a think tank called the NITI

Aayog (an acronym for National Institution for Transforming India) was instituted. Till 2015, India has had 12 Five-Year Plans; they were abolished by the NDA-ruled government.

NEW ECONOMIC POLICY

Under the leadership of the P. V. Narasimha Rao government, the **New Economic Policy** of India was launched in 1991. This entailed *economic liberalisation* or opening up of the hitherto protected Indian market to the global economy. This was accompanied by relaxation in import tariffs, opening the markets for private and foreign players, and reduction of taxes to expand the economic wings of the country. Former Prime Minister of India, **Manmohan Singh** is credited as being the father of the New Economic Policy sisnce he launched it as the Union Finance Minsiter in 1991. The NEP intended to bring down the rate of inflation, and also move towards higher economic growth rate and to build sufficient foreign exchange reserves.

SELECTED READINGS

1. *India's Emerging Economy: Performance and Prospects in the 1990s and Beyond* (2004), Kaushik Basu
2. *The Political Economy of Development in India* (1984), Pranab Bardhan
3. *State-Directed Development: Political Power and Industrialization in the Global Periphery* (2004), Atul Kohli
4. *Poverty and Plenty in the New India* (2012), Atul Kohli
5. *In Pursuit of Lakshmi: The Political Economy of The Indian State* (1987), Lloyd I. Rudolph and Susanne Rudolph
6. *India's Political Economy 1947–1977: The Gradual Revolution* (1980), Francine R. Frankel
7. *The Painful Transition: Bourgeois Democracy in India* (1990), Achin Vanaik
8. *Dominance and State Power in Modern India, Decline of a Social Order* (1990), Francine Frankel and M. S. A. Rao

UNIT IX

PUBLIC ADMINISTRATION

KEY CONCEPTS

The Indian constitution; Theories and concepts of public administration; Comparative public administration; Organisational theory; Managing organisations; organisational communication; conflict management; management by objectives

1

INTRODUCTION TO PUBLIC ADMINISTRATION

KEY CONCEPTS

Meaning and evolution; Public and private administration approaches: System Theory, Decision Making, Ecological Approach

PUBLIC ADMINISTRATION: MEANING

Administration refers to serving or to managing affairs of an organisation, and public administration refers to management of affairs of the government. Let us briefly look at a few popular descriptions of public administration:

Dimock and Dimock: The accomplishment of a politically determined objective is public administration.

Woodrow Wilson: Public administration indicates the detailed and systematic execution of public law.

L. D. White: Public administration is the composite of all laws, regulation, practice, relationship, codes and customs that prevail at any time in any jurisdiction for the fulfillment or execution of public policy.

Corson and Harris: It is the action part of the government that means by which the purposes and goals of the government is realised.

Pfiffner and Presthus: Public administration is mainly concerned with the means for implementing political values.

Luther Gulick: Public administration is that part of the science of administration which has to do with government.

Felix Nigro: A systematic definition of public administration is difficult but it includes the following features:

(i) Cooperative group effort in public setting;
(ii) Covers all three branches of the government—the executive, the legislative and the judiciary;
(iii) Part of political process in formulation of policy;
(iv) Different from private administration;
(v) Private groups and individuals providing services to the community.

Marshal E. Dimock:

Administration is concerned with the 'what' and 'how' of government.

For the first time in America, in 1788, Alexander Hamilton laid down the definition and aims of public administration in his collction of articles and essays called *The Federalist Papers* (in *Federalist No. 72*).

Minnowbrook (III) Conference (2008): In the Third Minnowbrook Conference held in 2008, it was observed that the nature of public administration is evolving. Public administration was reformulated and defined as—'a socially embedded process of collective relationship, dialogue, and action to promote human flourishing for all'.

From the above definition, two views emerged to define public administration—one is the broader view and the other the narrow view.

Broader view: This school of thought holds that public administration refers to activities of all three branches (executive, legislative and judicial) of the government. The broader view has been taken by Woodrow Wilson, Pfiffner, Marshal Dimock, and L. D. White, and so on.

Narrow view: According to this, public administration refers to only activities of executive branches of the government. Such views are held by Gullick, Simon, Willoughby, Fayol and Ordway Tead.

Nature of Public Administration

Integral View: According to this view, public administration encompasses all activities from clerical to managerial activity of the administration. This view constitutes the activity of all persons from top to bottom. L. D. White, Woodrow Wilson and Marshal Dimock are the main supporters of this view. This aligns with the broader view described above.

Managerial View: In the managerial view, public administration refers to only the managerial activities of the administration. In this view, constitute the activities of only the top person. Simon, Gullick, Fayol Smithburg and Thompson are the main supporters of the managerial view. This is akin to the narrow view described above.

PUBLIC ADMINISTRATION: EVOLUTION

A. Division between Politics and Administration

First phase of evolution of public administration is considered as *dichotomy in politics administration* (1887–1926). In 1887, father of public administration, Woodrow Wilson wrote an article 'The Study of Administration', which was published in *Political Science Quarterly*. He held that operationalisation of the government is more important than theory. Administration is separate from politics. The father of American public administration is Frank J. Goodnow (US), who wrote *Politics and Administration*. He says that politics is different from public administration. Goodnow says that politics expresses the will of the state, and administration is related to execution of policy.

The first textbook for public administration was written by Leonard D. White and was titled *Introduction to the Study of Public Administration* (1926). He said that administration is related to economy and efficiency and is a *value free science* (refers to an approach that aims to exclude a researcher's own values when conducting research with the aim of making observations and interpretations as unbiased as possible). Politics and administration are two separate functional areas.

B. Formation of Principles

Principles of Public Administration written by W. F. Willoughby is the second textbook of administration, which deals with principles and their application:

I. **Scientific Management** – Frederick Taylor discovered universal scientific principles for managing an organisation. The Taft Commission on economy and efficiency, undertook the comprehensive investigation of federal administration.

II. **POSDCORB** – Luther Gulick and Urwick coined the term POSDCORB which can be expanded as:

(a) Planning
(b) Organising
(c) Staffing
(d) Directing
(e) Coordination

(f) Reporting
(g) Budgeting

In their essay 'The Science of Administration', the dichotomy between politics and administration is reinforced, and value free science of management is accepted.

III. **Bureaucracy** – Wilson laid down the intellectual foundation of administration. Max Weber is the first theoretician who propounded ideal types of bureaucracy. Bureaucracy is associated with three different points of view.

1. Structural factors: include division of work and hierarchy.
2. Behavioural characteristics: refer to individuals becoming machines.
3. Achievement is the third purpose of bureaucracy. Weber founded the specific nature of bureaucracy and its special virtue.

Peter Blau suggested that bureaucracy refers to an organisation that maximises efficiency in administration or an institutionalised method of organising social conduct. Washington did not accept division between politics and administration.

Harney Fayol defines elements of administration in the term of POCCC:

1. Planning
2. Organisation
3. Commanding
4. Coordination
5. Controlling

C. Era of Challenge (1938–1947)

Human relations approach was applied to the study of public administration. And the idea of a dichotomy between politics and administration was rejected. Herbert Simon was a pioneer of behavioural approach; he received Nobel Prize in 1978. Human relations approach was developed by Elton Mayo. They challenged the classical approach of the study of public administration. Some of these seminal works have been mentioned below:

1. *The Function of the Executive* (1938) by Bernard.
2. *Elements of Public Administration* (1946) by F. M. Marx.
3. *Proverb of Public Administration* (1946) by H. Simon.
4. *Administrative Behavior* (1947) by H. Simon.
5. *The Science of Public Administration: Three Problems* (1947) by Robert Dahl.
6. *The Administrative State* (1948) by Dwight Waldo.

Dahl says that values of an individual, their personality and social framework are three factors.

D. Crisis of Identity (1948–1970)

There was debate over whether public administration is related to political science or to pure administration. Betweenn 1948 and 1970, Asian-African nations became independent and critical theory developed in the West. Following developments were significant:

1. Rise of a new human relations approach by Chris Argyris, Douglas McGregor, Renis Likert and Warren Bennis;
2. The evolution of comparative public administration;
3. Ecology approach developed by Riggs;
4. Administrative development by Riggs;
5. Emergence of new public administration;
6. Public choice approach developed by Vincent Ostrom;
7. Critical perspective.

The First Minnowbrook Conference held in 1968 which focused on relevance, values, social equality and changes led to the development of '*New Public Administration*'.

E. Public Policy Perspective (1971–1990)

Robert T. Golembiewski says that public policy approach involves two elements:

1. Interpretation of politics;
2. Programming of all administration.

PUBLIC ADMINISTRATION AND PRIVATE ADMINISTRATION APPROACHES

1. Differences between public and private administration:

Paul H. Appleby, John Gaus, Josia Stamp, Hebert A. Simon, and Peter Drucker argue that public administration and private administration are two different zones.

(i) Private administration works for **profit.** But public administration is oriented towards **service of the people.**

(ii) Public administration is controlled by law but private administration works on the principle of market economy.

(iii) Accountability is the soul of public administration and it must submit itself to public scrutiny, that is, it functions in a 'glass bowl'/'goldfish bowl'.

(iv) Public administration works under political control. Private administration is not subject to political control.

(v) Appleby stated that public administration has a wider scope than private.

Appleby's View: Public and private administration differ on the following grounds:

(i) Political character
(ii) Breadth of scope, impact and consideration
(iii) Public accountability.

Josia Stamp's View: According to Stamp, public and private administration differ on the following grounds:

(i) Principle of uniformity
(ii) Principle of external financial control
(iii) Principle of public responsibility
(iv) Principle of service motive.

Herbert Simon's View:

(i) Public administration is bureaucratic, whereas private administration is business-like.

(ii) Public administration is political, while private administration is non-political.

(iii) Public administration is characterised by red tape while private administration is free from it.

2. Similarities between public and private administration:

Henry Fayol, M. P. Follet, Luther Gulick and Lyndall Urwick believe that there is no difference between private administration and public administration. Both are organised on the basis of hierarchy. In the *New Public Management Model*, the public sector is learning the principles of efficiency economy and profitability form private sectors. The model of *Public–Private Partnership (PPP)* is a good example of cooperation between public and private administration.

APPROACHES TO PUBLIC ADMINISTRATION

1. System Approach

'System approach' is a new approach of public administration which is different from the classical approach. System refers to wholeness. System is comprised of various elements. Understanding the relation between various parts of the system is the core of system approach. Therefore, the internal mechanism of administration and the external environment are important for explaining the working of the system. **David Easton** developed the systems theory and **Chester Barnard** studied administration through system.

M. P. Follett observed that organisation is a social system. **Chester Barnard** remarked that organisation is a cooperative system. **Norbert**

Wiener propounded cybernetics and said that system is collection of input-output. This goes against the ideal theory of bureaucracy conceptualised by **Max Weber**. In Weberian theory, the ideal model of bureaucracy is a *closed system*, which works like a machine separated from the external environment.

2. Decision-Making Theory

Decision-making is the process. It is a culmination of an effort which moves towards a final decision. **Henri Fayol, Gullick,** belong to the *classical school*, that is, the *rationality model* of administration and held that decision-making is the result of the following steps:

(i) Identifying the problem
(ii) Conceptualisation of alternative
(iii) Choosing the best course of action
(iv) Implementing the decision
(v) Evaluating the effectiveness

Hebert Simon is best known for his analysis of decision-making. According to him, there are following steps in decision making:

(i) Intelligence activity
(ii) Design activity
(iii) Choice activity

Bounded Rationality: Hebert Simon has put forward an alternative model to the classical economic rationality model. Simon wrote a book *Administrative Behaviour a Study of Decision-Making Processes in Administrative Organization* in 1947. 'Bounded' refers to a limited rationality or understanding. In this, the administrative man is more important than the economic man. Simon belongs to the Behaviourist school which believes that there are three aspects of decision-making:

(i) Scheme of individual decision
(ii) Fact–value dichotomy
(iii) Bounded rationality

Further, Simon has presented six types of rationality in decision making:

(i) Subjective
(ii) Objective
(iii) Conscious
(iv) Deliberate
(v) Personal
(vi) Organisational

He said that **total rationality** is impossible in administrative behaviour. Even **maximising decisions** are not possible because human behaviour is characterised by **bounded rationality.** Following factors are responsible for bounded rationality:

(i) Dynamic nature of environment
(ii) Dynamic nature of objective
(iii) Inadequate information
(iv) Time and cost constraints
(v) Personal factors
(vi) Organisational factors
(vii) Alternative may not always work out

Criticism of Hebert Simon: Charles Lindblom founded the idea of **incrementalism** and said that change as a solution to a problem is not possible.

3. Ecological Approach

This approach evolved due to the emergence of newly independent Asian-African nations after 1945. Public administration and bureaucracy is a social fact. Therefore, economic, political, social, and cultural factors are essential for understanding bureaucracy. His study is value neutral and cross cultural. **F. W. Riggs** is a strong advocate of this approach, who wrote *Administration in Developing Countries: The Theory of Prismatic Society* (1964). It is the single most important contribution in the field of comparative public administration.

Riggs utilised three analytical tools to explain his administrative theories:

1. Ecological approach
2. Structural functional approach
3. Ideal models

Riggs developed the first model in 1956 by classifying society into

1. Agrarian society
2. Industrial society

He developed an equilibrium model named as *Transitia*, which is an indication of transforming the society. Riggs also developed a set of models for analysing administration in developing countries, these are:

1. Fused model
2. Prismatic model
3. Diffracted model

The Prismatic Model

The *transitional society* between the fused and diffracted societies is known as a prismatic society. Fused societies are 'primitive' and 'tribal'. The term *diffracted society* refers to industrialised and urbanised society. He pointed out the three important features of the prismatic model:

1. **Heterogeneity:** That is, a plural and diverse administrative approach in society. A traditional administrative setup exists in rural areas, and modern administration structure exists in cities.
2. **Formalism:** There is a difference between prescribed norms, rules and regulations, and practical behaviour.
3. **Overlapping:** There is a simultaneous presence of traditional society and modern structure of administration.

The Prismatic Sala Model

'Sala' refers to administrative sub-systems. Officers give preference to enhancement of power and wealth rather than welfare of the people. The officers of the government are more loyal to their own community rather than the government. Prismatic society is an unbalanced model of polity. Sala is characterised by nepotism in recruitment, institutionalised corruption and inefficiency. Bureaucracy becomes more powerful due to a weak political system.

Riggs pointed out five different aspects of the prismatic model:

(a) Nepotism and favouritism
(b) Poly-communalism
(c) Poly-normativism
(d) Bazaar, Canteen Model
(e) Authority versus control

Bazaar, Canteen Model

An economic subsystem proposed by Riggs is considered as the bazaar, canteen model. In this model, small sections of people may enjoy all benefits with control over economic institutions. Poverty, lack of social justice, and exploitation are the features of this model.

Criticism of Prismatic Sala Model

1. Complicated language
2. Lack of analysis of ecology
3. Status quo
4. Western bias
5. Negative orientation

Revision of the Prismatic Model: In his book, *Prismatic Society Revisited* (1973), Riggs revised his prismatic theory and he replaced the one-dimensional approach with a *two-dimensional approach*. Earlier he had focused on *differentiation* and later, he believed in *differentiation and integration*.

Books/Essays by Fred W. Riggs:

1. Frontiers of Development Administration (1970).
2. *Administration in Developing Countries—The Theory of Prismatic Society* (1964).
3. The Ecology of Public Administration (1961).

2

THEORIES AND CONCEPTS OF PUBLIC ADMINISTRATION

KEY CONCEPTS

Scientific Management Theory, Rational Choice Theory, New Public Administration, Development Administration

SCIENTIFIC MANAGEMENT THEORY

Frederick Taylor is considered the 'Father of management theory'. The term scientific management was coined by **Louise Brandeis** in 1910. He believes in the principle of the *economic man*, who is motivated by monetary benefits. Taylor said that *One Best Way* of doing a job. That consumes less *minute, motion and time.* Major writings by Taylor include:

1. *A Piece-Rate System* (1895)
2. *Shop Management* (1903)
3. *On the Art of Cutting Metals* (1906)
4. *The Principles of Management* (1911)

Principles of Scientific Management

Taylor believed that scientific management is a universal theory that can be applied all over the world. Therefore, socio-cultural factors are not important.

(i) **True Science of Work:** Taylor believed that there is a need to develop a 'science' of work. This can be achieved by systematic study of any work, organising knowledge and replacing the old thumb-rule method with a scientific method.

(ii) **Scientific Selection and Training:** He believed that the right person is needed for the right job. Workers' intellectual, psychological and physical qualities should be matched with the job's requirements.

(iii) **Coordination between Science and Men:** Taylor focused on getting best results by cooperation between science and work men, who are scientifically trained.

(iv) **Division of Work and Responsibility:** Taylor held thatworkers and managements had a joint responsibility.

Scientific management is not a single element but is comprised of the following:

(a) Science, not rule of thumb
(b) Harmony, not conflict
(c) Cooperation, not individualism
(d) Maximum output
(e) Greatest efficiency and prosperity

Techniques of Scientific Management

Taylorism includes *functional foremanship, motion study, time study, piece-rate plan* and *exceptional principles*. Better wages are important for harmony and productivity. These techniques are known as mental revolutions.

Followers of Taylor

H. L. Gantt emphasises on *habits of industry*. **Gilbreth** invented the *flow process chart. Emersion* focuses on productivity of correct organisation (**M. L. Cooke**).

Criticism of Taylor

Hebert Simon and **James March** termed Taylor's scientific management principles as a 'physiological organisation theory'. They refused to accept social and psychological principles of motivation and said that *economic reward* is sufficient for production.

RATIONAL CHOICE THEORY

Rational choice theory focuses on the *economic behaviour* of individuals. In this theory, every **individual** is considered rational. Therefore, individuals want to maximise on their own interests. Early reference to this theory is found in the writings of **Vincent Ostrom**. Other supporters of this approach are **James Buchanan, Gordon Tullock, William A. Niskanen**, and **William C. Mitchell.**

The choice of citizens is the basis for distribution of social goods. **Niskanen, Anthony Downs** and **Tullock** said that bureaucracy is only maximising individualistic and self-seeking activities. It is not a mechanism for public welfare. Bureaucracy wants to maintain monopoly over power. Niskanen suggested following steps for making bureaucracy *citizen-friendly*:

1. Strict control of executive and legislature over bureaucracy;
2. Promoting competition in delivery of public services;
3. Promoting privatisation and contractual jobs;
4. More information for public benefit.

Rational choice theory has been developed by economists. In this school of thought, it is held that capitalism and market economy are better for providing services to the people. *New Public Management (NPM)* is the product of rational choice theory.

NEW PUBLIC ADMINISTRATION (NPA)

The term 'New Public Administration' was first used by **Frank Marini** in his book *Toward a New Public Administration: The Minnowbrook Perspective* in 1971. New Public Administration originated in the First Minnowbrook Conference held in 1968 at Syracuse University under the patronage of **Dwight Waldo**. His article 'Public Administration in a Time of Turbulence' was published in 1968. NPA does not focus on science and objectivity but stresses on political values like equity, social justice, change and commitment. Relevance and client orientation form the focus of NPA. **Robert Golembiewski** delineated three features of New Public Administration:

1. Anti-positivist (a theoretical stance that proposes that the social realm cannot be studied with the investigation methods of the natural sciences, and that it different methods are required for the social sciences)
2. Anti-technical
3. Anti-bureaucratic

Origin

NPA is not against scientific methods but it wants to combine scientific method with values. The Vietnam crisis, cold war, and civil rights movement influenced the development of public administration. It is just like *post-behaviouralism* in political science. The following events led to the emergence of NPA:

1. The Honey report on Higher education for Public Services (1967), US.
2. Philadelphia Conference (1967) presided over by James C. Charlesworth.

3. Writings of Dwight Waldo—'Public Administration in a Time of Revolution' (1968).
4. First Minnowbrook Conference (1968)
5. Frank Marini's *Toward a New Public Administration* (1971).
6. *New Public Administration* written by H. George Frederickson (1918).

Themes

1. Relevance
2. Values
3. Social equality
4. Change
5. Client focus

Frederickson observed that new public administration is essentially **Second Generation Behaviourism.** He pointed out following features of NPA:

1. Less generic, more public
2. More prescriptive, less descriptive
3. Change-oriented
4. Committed to implement policy
5. More normative, less neutral
6. No less scientific

Robert T. Golembiewski identified five features of NPA:

1. The human being is potentially perfectible
2. The central role of personal and organisational ethics
3. Social equality
4. Relation list
5. Innovation and change

Dwight Waldo held that client-oriented bureaucracy, representative bureaucracy and people participation in administration is the result of NPA.

Criticism

It is *status quoist*, observed **Robert Golembiewski. Dunn** and **Fozouni** said that it is only an illusion of paradigm shift.

Important Books on the NPA

1. Principles of Public Administration – W. F. Willoughby (1927).
2. General and Industry Management – Henry Fayol (1949).
3. Papers in the Science of the Administration – Luther Gulick and L. F. Urwick (eds, 1937).
4. Creative Experience – M. P. Follett (1930).
5. Principle of Organization – Mooney and Riley (1931).
6. The Science of Public Administration: Three Problems – Robert A. Dahl (1947).
7. Philosophy of Administration – Marshal E. Dimock (1958).
8. The Functions of the Executive – Chester I. Barnard (1968).
9. The Proverbs of Administration – Hebert A. Simon (1946).

DEVELOPMENT ADMINISTRATION

Origin

The following reasons operate behind the origin of Development Administration:

1. Emergence of newly independent Asian-African nations;
2. US economic and technical assistance development;
3. Establishment of comparative administration.

Meaning

Martin Landau defines Development Administration as the engineering of social change**. Marle Fainsod** describes it as a path of modernisation and industrialisation. **Edward Weidner** defines development as a dynamic process of change or transformation. The main goal of development administration is *nation-building*. He defines Development Administration as an *action-oriented, goal-oriented* administrative system.

Riggs defines Development Administration as organised efforts to carry out programmes, which are projects thought by those involved to serve development objectives. **Donald C. Stone** defines that it is concerned with achieving national development. He identified **4 Ps**:

1. Plans
2. Policy
3. Programmes
4. Projects

The term 'Development Administration' was for the first time used by Indian civil servant **U. L. Goswami** in his article 'The Structure of Development Administration in India' (1955). The concept evolved in the context of community development programmes. Conceptual evolution of Development Administration was done by **George F. Gant, F. W. Riggs, Edward Weidner, Milton J. Esman, Han Bee Lee, John D. Montgomery,** and **Alfred Diamant.** They have realised that the *Western model of development* is not sustainable in *Asian-African* nations. A new kind of administration is needed for development of Asia and Africa.

Features:

George Gant felt that Development Administration is associated with *purposes, loyalties* and *attitudes.* Purposes refers to socio-economic progress. Loyalties should be towards people. Attitude must be positive. **V. A. Pai Panandiker** defined Development Administration as:

1. Change-oriented
2. Result-oriented
3. Citizen participation
4. Commitment to work

There are other features of Development Administration, including:

1. Time orientation
2. Client orientation
3. Ecological orientation
4. Innovation orientation

Administrative Development

Development administration is different form administrative development. However, **Riggs** said that administration of development and developmental administration are interrelated like the chicken and the egg.

Temporal and Spatial Dimension

Scholars like **Dwight Waldo, Peter Savage, Alfred Diamant** and **Hahn-Been Lee** believe in the temporal dimension of Development Administration, which means culture and society of India is different form the Western world.

Scholars like **James Heaphey, Henry C. Hart, Bertram M. Gross,** and **Stanley Hoffman** highlight the spatial evolution of Development Administration, which points out differences due to variations in religion, language and culture.

Criticism

It was *ideological* and *eurocentric*. Ideological refers to the conflict between capitalism and communism. **Riggs, Lucian Pye, and Shmuel N. Eisenstadt** said that Development Administration weakens political institutions.

3

COMPARATIVE PUBLIC ADMINISTRATION

KEY CONCEPTS

New public management, changing nature of public administration in the era of liberalisation and globalisation

Comparative public administration stands for *cross-cultural* and *cross-national* public administration. **Nicholas Henry** said that comparative administration is different from American or traditional public administration.

L. D. White observed that the public administration of **Russia** and **Iraq** are equally important as the administration of the **US**. **Robert Dahl** and **Dwight Waldo** said that *cultural factors* are important for understanding public administration. It is practice-oriented and wants to study the real world. **Riggs** said that American public administration is a subpart of the larger field of comparative public administration.

PURPOSE

Ferrel Heady identified *five purposes* of comparative administration:

1. Search for theory
2. Urge for practical application
3. Comparative analysis
4. Incidental contribution
5. Interest of researchers

Riggs described following *four purposes*:

1. To know about unique feature of a particular system.
2. Factors responsible for cross-national and cross-cultural differences.
3. Success and failures of administration in particular environment.
4. Strategy and reform

FEATURES

Riggs pointed out following trends in the study of comparative approach:

1. Shift from normative to empirical studies;
2. Changing individualist studies (Ideographic) to universal studies (Nomothetic);
3. Shift from institutional to ecological studies.

Further he said that comparative politics is a empirical, generalised, systematic and non-parochial field of study.

MODELS OF COMPARATIVE ADMINISTRATION

1. **Alfred Diamant, Robert Presthus, Ferrel Heady, Michel Crozier** and **Morroe**

Berger developed the *bureaucratic system approach*.

2. Riggs developed the *general system approach*. T. Dorsey developed the *information energy model.*
3. *Development Administration* was formulated by Riggs and Wiedner.
4. Martin Landau developed the *decision-making approach*.
5. Anthony Downs remarked about five types of bureaucrats—climbers, conservers, zealots, advocates, and statesmen.

FORMATION OF COMPARATIVE ADMINISTRATION GROUP

A comparative administration group was formed in 1961 under the committee of the American Society for Public Administration (ASPA, started in 1939). **Riggs** was the founder of this group. Others scholars associated with the group were **Alfred Diamant, Ferrel Heady, Dwight Waldo, Wallaca Sayre, Martin Landau, Willam Saffin, John Montgomary, Ralph Braibanti** and **Bertram Gross**. The ecological approach of Riggs formed the base of comparative public administration.

The comparative administrative group was dismantled in 1973 without contributing anything substantial. *The Journal of Comparative Administration* also ceased to publish in 1974.

NEW PUBLIC MANAGEMENT

David Osborne and Ted Gaebler wrote *Reinventing Government*, published in 1992, which gave birth to New Public Management. The emergence of market economy and liberalisation led to the evolution of NPM. The the Second Minnowbrook Conference, held in 1988, also led to its development.

New public management is the outcome of public administration in the age of liberalisation and globalisation. The market economy impacted the functioning of administration. Now citizens were no longer passive recipients but active customers with the freedom of choice. Therefore, administration is now driven by customers.

Christopher Hood is a leading exponent of new public management (NPM). It is different from the traditional management of Weber and Wilson. NPM focuses on three E's –

1. Efficiency
2. Economy
3. Effectiveness

Empowerment of citizens is the major objective of NPM. Hood said that NPM is a marriage of opposites. Minimum government intervention, de-bureaucratisation, decentralisation, market orientation of public services, privatisation and performance measurement are the features of NPM.

Origin

Following factors are important for the emergence of NPM:

1. Declining credibility of the state;
2. Emergence of the new right, that is, capitalism;
3. Emergence of the post-Weberian, post-Wilsonian bureaucracy;
4. Administrative changes in advanced Western countries.

The Third Minnowbrook Conference, held in 2008, focused on four specific areas:

1. Nature of public administration in a globalised world;
2. Complexity of the market economy and New Public Management;
3. Impact of interdisciplinary borrowing;
4. Public administration in changing environment.

Five major factors identified in the Third Conference were:

1. Relevance
2. Election of an African-American as the US president for the first time;

3. Western bias in the teaching of public administration in Asia;
4. Creating global discourse;
5. Retaining an independent identity.

The Conference also focused on a multi-theoretical approach and held that administration no longer refers to the government only. It also surmised that understanding non-Western experiences is equally important.

Mohit Bhattacharya pointed out the following aspects of NPM:

1. Flexible market-based form of public management;
2. Change in the role of the government;
3. Change in the citizen–government relationship.

Doctrine of NPM

Hood recognised the following components of NPM:

1. Professional management in the public sector;
2. Standard and measurement of performance;
3. Focus on output;
4. Shift to disaggregation of units in the public sector;
5. Greater competition in public sector;
6. Private-sector style management;
7. Discipline and parsimony in resources.

Nicolas Henry has identified 5 A's

1. Alertness – removing problems
2. Agility – open and communicative
3. Adaptability – improving quality
4. Alignment – NGO's and civil society's
5. Accountability – need of the people

Patrick Dunleavy propounded key components of NPM which are disaggregation, competition and incentives.

Administrative Megatrend: Hood identified four trends of NPM:

1. Slow down of public spending and staffing;
2. Privatisation and move away from core government institutions;
3. Digital governance in production and distribution of public services; and
4. International agenda to cooperate with other nations.

Contribution: Transparency in government and the Citizen Charter (a document of commitments made by a government organisation to the citizens or client groups) is the result of NPM.

4

THEORIES AND PRINCIPLES OF ORGANISATION

KEY CONCEPTS

Scientific management theory, bureaucratic theory, human relations theory

BUREAUCRATIC THEORY

German sociologist **Max Weber** is a pioneer who founded the concept of bureaucracy. For Max Weber, the following factors are important for the rise of bureaucracy:

1. Economy based on money;
2. Capitalist economy;
3. Emergence of democratic institutions;
4. Complex administration;
5. Modern means of communication; and
6. Growth of population and rationality

Weber held that bureaucracy is the most *universal, progressive modern form of organisation*; see *The Theory of Social and Economic Organization,* written by Max Weber and translated by Talcott Parsons (1947). The characteristics of bureaucracy can be summed up as following:

1. Hierarchy.
2. Formality: Official capacity is more important than the choice of person.
3. Every officer has a clearly defined sphere of competence.
4. Officers are appointed on the basis of a contract.
5. Personnel are selected on the basis of their professional qualifications.
6. They are given salaries.
7. Officers are freely selected on the basis of technical qualification.
8. The system offers careers with a system of promotion.
9. Discipline and control.
10. Official work is separated from structures of ownership.

Mohit Bhattacharya defines the features of bureaucracy thus:

(i) Division of work;
(ii) Hierarchy;
(iii) System of rules;
(iv) Role specificity;
(v) Rationality;
(vi) Impersonality;
(vii) Rule orientation;
(viii) Neutrality.

Albro Martin in his book *Bureaucracy* pointed out the five mechanisms of control:

1. Collegiality, which refers to control over collective decision-making;

2. Separation of power;
3. Amateur administration;
4. Direct democracy;
5. Representation

Criticism of Bureaucratic Theory

A. Instrumentalist Theory

Marxists believe that bureaucracy is the tool of exploitation. It is an instrument in the hands of capitalists for exploiting the people.

B. Functionalist Theory

Robert Merton in his article 'Bureaucracy Structure and Personality' said that *displacement of goals* is the trait of bureaucracy. *Dysfunctional consequences and trained incapacity* is the feature of bureaucracy. Their output is negligible.

Philip Selznick also said that goal displacement is the feature of bureaucracy, in his book *TVA and the Grass Roots* (1949). **Alvin Gouldner** in his book *Patterns of Industrial Bureaucracy (*1954) distinguishes between two types of bureaucracy:

a. Punishment-centered bureaucracy
b. Representative bureaucracy

C. Pathological Theory

Bureaucracy is considered riddled with red tape, inefficiency, secrecy and promoting self-interest. **Michel Crozier** said that the organisation of bureaucracy is rigid and that they cannot learn from their errors. **Veblen** also describes bureaucracy as trained incapacity. **Dewey** said that bureaucracy is *occupational psychosis,* which is also described as *professional deformation* by **Warnotte. Victor Thompson** spoke of the diseases of *bureaupathology* or *bureaupathic.* **Peter Principle** says that bureaucracy is any individual organisational behaviour, which is irrational and inefficient yet supported by the hierarchy. **Parkinson's Law** explains that bureaucracy is a self-maximising interest group. It works on the following principles:

1. Expansion of work
2. Rise of expenditure
3. Law of triviality – The bureaucratic system will try to project that expenditure is routine.

D. Developing Countries

Robert Presthus stated that bureaucracy is a product of Western culture. **Fred W. Riggs** observed that the system does not explain the environment in which it works, and therefore, it cannot be universal. **William Delaney** said that it is not useful for developing countries. **Joseph La Palombara** argued that the Chinese and Russian method of administration may be more effective.

E. Other Criticisms

Simon and **Barnard** said that bureaucracy reduces efficiency. **Simon** and **March** in their book *Organizations,* say that bureaucracy ignores human relations. **Warren Bennis** in his book *The Temporary Society* explains that the temporary work system is better. **Lloyd Rudolph** and **Susanne Rudolph** say that bureaucracy is inefficient.

Claus Offe says that there are two types of rationality—*organizational rationality* and *systemic rationality.* Systemic rationality changes according to changes in time and circumstances. **Peter M. Blau** wrote a seminal text on the subject, *Bureaucracy in Modern Society.* **Creel** and **Spitzer** said that bureaucracy is not a rational and modern concept.

Carl Friedrich idea and type are the paradoxical term **Reindhard Bendix—An Intellectual Portrait (1916), Higher Civil Servants in American Society.**

HUMAN RELATIONS THEORY

Organisation is a social system where *human behaviour* is the basic unit of analysis. Human relations theory is against the classical theory of scientific management propounded by **Taylor**. Happy workers are the secret to the success of an organisation. Human relations theory believes in the premise that the individual is a *social being*, and that it is wrong to perceive an individual as an *economic man*. **Roethlisberger** and **Dickson** wrote *Management and the Worker* (1966) where they summarise the features of the Hawthrone Studies:

(a) Organisation is social system; workers are not isolated and unrelated individuals.
(b) Workers have humanly attributes.
(c) Informal relations are more important. Division of labour may not be efficient.
(d) Social ethics is the foundation of an organisation.
(e) Psychological and social factors are more important than the physical condition of workplace.
(f) Non-economic rewards are more important.

Prof. George Elton Mayo, Harvard University, is recognised as father of human relations theory**.** Mayo came to be recognized as the leader in a series of experiments which became one of the great turning points in management thinking across the world. Major writings of Mayo include – *The Human Problems of an Industrial Civilization* (1945), *The Social Problems of an Industrial Civilization* (1945), and *The Political Problem of Industrial Civilization* (1947).

The Hawthorne Experiments

The origin of human relations theory dates back to the Hawthorne plant in the electrical company, Western Electric at Chicago. In these experiments, it was discovered that working cannot be enhanced merely by providing economic incentives, and that job satisfaction increased through employee participation in decisions rather than through short-term incentives. It was surmised that appreciation of the feelings and sentiment of the workers is more important for increasing production.

Some of the major phases of Hawthorne experiments are as follows:

1. Illumination Experiments;
2. Relay Assembly Test Room Experiments;
3. Mass Interviewing Programme;
4. Bank Wiring Observation Room Experiment.

1. *Great Illumination Experiments*

Human relations theory does not believe in the scientific management theory. Physical working conditions like the levels of illumination, room temperature, and so on are not important for enhancement of working.

2. *Relay Assembly Test Room Experiments (1927)*

Relay assembly test room experiments were designed to determine the effect of changes in various job conditions on group productivity as the illumination experiments could not establish relationship between intensity of illumination and production.

3. *Mass Interviewing Programme (1928–1931)*

About 20,000 interviews were conducted between 1928 and 1930 to determine employees' attitudes towards company, supervision, insurance plans, promotion and wages. Initially, these interviews were conducted by means of direct questioning such as 'Do you like your supervisor?' The interview programme gave valuable insights about human behaviour in the company.

4. *Bank Wiring Experiments*

This experiment was conducted to find out the impact of small groups on the individuals. Again, here Mayo found that man is not only an economic being but also a social being, that is, a member of a group, and that the management should try to understand group attitudes and group psychology. He used the key word *Rate Buster* for someone who does too much work. *Chiseler* refers to one who does too little. And the *Squealer* refers to the one who communicates negative feedback about others to supervisor.[1]

Three Features

Human relations theory is comprised of three basic features:

1. The individuals;
2. Informal organisation; and
3. Participated management

Critical Evaluation:

Alex Carey says that the experiments lacked scientific base because they were dependent on small samples. **Loren Baritz** argued that it has a pro-management stance, and workers describe them as *cow sociologists*. **Amitai Etzioni** says that it has too much focus on informal groups.

Peter F. Drucker is of the view that it ignores the economic dimension of human behavior. **Reinhard Bendix** says that **Mayo** is unable to define his ethics. **Daniel Sell** believes that the methodology was defective.

NOTE

1. For more information on the Hawthorne experiment stages, *see* https://www.yourarticlelibrary.com/management/4-phases-of-hawthorne-experiments-discussed-business-management/27888 (accessed May 2023).

5

MANAGING THE ORGANISATION

KEY CONCEPTS

Theories of leadership and motivation

Leadership is essential for running the organisation, and **Rensis Likert, Douglas McGregor, Chirs Aygyris** are the prominent scholars associated with leadership models.

A. QUALITY OF LEADERSHIP

Chester Barnard defined the four qualities of a leader:

1. Vitality
2. Endurance
3. Decisiveness
4. Persuasiveness

Paul H. Appleby says that good administrators should have the following qualities:

1. Willing to assume responsibility;
2. Continuing personal growth;
3. Action-oriented and good listener;
4. Works with everyone;
5. Seeks to obtain most able subordinates;
6. Self-confident and cares for power;
7. Respects subordinates and superiors;
8. Improves institutional performance.

Millet said that leadership quality includes good health, sense of mission, intelligence, integrity and persuasiveness. **Terry** said that emotional stability, human relations, personal motivation and technical competence are the qualities of leadership.

B. TYPES OF LEADERSHIP

Mary Parker Follet describes the three types of leadership –

1. Leadership of position (where the leader holds position of formal authority)
2. Leadership of personality (where the leader displays compelling personal qualities)
3. Leadership of function (where the leader displays both of the above traits)

C. FUNCTIONS OF LEADERSHIP

Follett pointed out the following functions of leadership:

1. Coordination
2. Definition of power
3. Anticipation
4. Organising the group
5. Developing leadership skills among the subordinates.

D. THEORIES OF LEADERSHIP:

1. **Trait theory**, popularly known as Great Man theory, is the idea that leaders are born with key characteristics and traits. **Bernard,**

Ordway Tead, Millet, Terry, Appleby and **Schell** are the major supporters of Trait theory.

2. **Behavioural theory**, which focuses on how leaders behave and what others can learn from them.
3. **Situational theory** states that leaders are influenced by their environment.

E. LEADERSHIP MODELS:

Rensis Likert has propounded the famous management system of *I-IV model.* The *Linking pin model* stems from the behvioural analysis of leadership also laid forth by Likert.

I-IV Model – consists of four systems of managements:

1. System – I: Exploitative Authoritative (where leaders have a low concern for employees and use methods such as threats and other fear-based methods to get their workers to conform; this may work well initially but later leads to demotivation among workers)
2. System – II: Benevolent Authoritative (where less control is exerted over employees, however, this system motivates employees through potential punishment and rewards. Even though lower-level employees are more involved in the decision-making processes, yet they are limited by upper management.)
3. System – III: Consultative Leadership (this is very closely related to the human relations theory. Subordinates gain motivation through rewards, occasional punishments, and some involvement in making decisions and setting goals)
4. System – IV: Participative System (promotes genuine participation in decision-making and goal setting in order to promote a workplace where all members equally share information; Likert holds this to be the most effective form of management)

Douglas McGregor wrote *The Human Side of Enterprise* (1960) and propounded that the nature of human beings determines the functioning of the organisation. His assumptions about two aspects of human behavior at work are popularly known as **Theory X** and **Theory Y.**

Theory X –The Coercive Compulsion – Average human beings do not want to work. They have little ambition and security. Essentially, Theory X assumes that the primary source of employee motivation is monetary, with security as a strong second.

Theory Y – Integration and Self-control – Human beings are enterprising in nature. Work is like play for them. There is self-direction and control in the service to which a human is committed. Achievement is a reward. On average, people learn under proper guidelines. Under these assumptions, there is an opportunity to align personal goals with organisational goals by using the employee's own need for fulfillment as the motivator.

Chris Argyris has written *Personality and Organization* (1957). He said that *self-realisation* is an innate capacity of human beings. The goals of the individual and that of the organisation are not contradictory with each other's. He held that sociology and psychology are complementary. He evolved the *T-group* or *Sensitivity Training*, a psychological technique in which group discussions are used to help group members increase awareness in themselves and others.

The writings of **Rensis Likert, Douglas McGregor, Chirs Aygyris** are known as the *Neo-Human Relations Movement.*

THEORIES OF MOTIVATION

A. Tradition Theory

Tradition theory of motivation comprises of:

1. Monistic theory
2. Economic theory
3. Carrot and stick theory

Classical or traditional theory believes that the worker is an *economic man*. This theory neglects sociological and psychological factor for analysing human beings.

B. Hierarchy of Needs

Abraham Maslow in his classic paper 'A Theory of Human Motivation' (1943) propounds the *hierarchy of needs*. He wrote *Motivation and Personality* (1954). He describes the hierarchy of needs in the following sequences:

1. Physiological needs
2. Security needs
3. Social needs
4. Esteem needs
5. Self-actualisation

The term *self-actualisation* was first coined by **Kurt Goldstein**. Self-actualisation, in Maslow's hierarchy of needs, is the highest level of psychological development, where personal potential is fully realised after basic bodily and ego needs have been fulfilled. It is 'the curative force in psychotherapy – *man's tendency to actualize himself, to become his potentialities* … to express and activate all the capacities of the organism' (Carl Rogers).

C. Herzberg's Two-Factor Theory

It is known as the *motivation maintenance* theory. The two-factor theory (also known as Herzberg's Motivation-Hygiene theory and dual-factor theory) states that there are certain factors in the workplace that cause job satisfaction while a separate set of factors cause dissatisfaction, all of which act independently of each other. *Motivation Hygiene* theory is a result of his empirical research. He identified five factors –

1. Achievement
2. Recognition
3. Work
4. Responsibility
5. Advancement

By *hygiene*, he indicates potential **dissatisfaction**. The **policy of the company, administration supervision, salary, interpersonal relations** and **working conditions** are the basic components of dissatisfaction. **Herzberg** described *unipolar traits*, which indicate that job satisfaction is separate from dissatisfaction.

6

ORGANISATIONAL COMMUNICATION

KEY CONCEPTS

Theories and principles, Chester Barnard, principles of communication, information management in the organisation

CHESTER BARNARD'S PRINCIPLES OF COMMUNICATION

Chester Barnard is another exponent of human relations theory, who worked as an executive in a telephone company. He wrote *The Functions of the Executive* (1938) and *Organization and Management* (1948). He pointed out the major features of organisations:

A. Features of Organisation

1. Organisation as a cooperative system
2. Formal and informal organisation
3. Consent theory of authority
4. Inducement–contribution balance
5. Moral responsibility
6. Communication

The *Acceptance theory of authority*, originally conceived by Mary Parker Follett, and popularised later by Chester Barnard through his 1938 book, *The Functions of the Executive*, holds that a manager's authority over his/her subordinates depends on the willingness of the subordinates to accept his/her right to give orders and comply with them. The psychological state of being obedient or disobedient is referred to as the *Zone of Indifference or Denial* by Barnard.

Informal organisation refers to the relationship between the people in an organisation based on personal attitudes, emotions, prejudices, likes and dislikes, and so on. They are created because of the operation of social and psychological forces operating at the work place. They performs *three functions*:

1. The communication of intangible facts, opinions;
2. Enhancing cohesiveness among employees;
3. Maintenance or the feeling of personal integrity.

He said that there are the following sources of satisfaction for employees:

1. Money or material inducement;
2. Non-material opportunity;
3. Physical condition of work; and
4. Pride of work.

Barnard is of the view that material rewards are ineffective beyond the subsistence level. He pointed out four types of general incentives:

1. Associated attractiveness;
2. Habitual method and attitudes;
3. Opportunity of participation;
4. Comfort in social relations.

B. Elements of Organisation

Barnard describe three elements of an organisation:

1. Communication;
2. Willingness to cooperate; and
3. Common purpose

C. Seven Principles of Communication

Since Barnard believes in human relations theory, he said that an organisation is not like a machine. Social relations and informal relations play a vital role. Barnard identified *seven principles of communication*:

1. The channel of communication should be definite.
2. Everyone should have a definite formal channel.
3. Line of communication should be direct and short.
4. Competence of persons.
5. Complete formal line of communication should be utilised.
6. The line of communication must not be interrupted.
7. It should be authentic.

D. Executive Functions

Barnard is the spiritual father of the social system school. He describes three essential functions of the executive:

1. Establishing and maintaining system of communication;
2. Securing essential efforts and services;
3. Formulation and defining of purposes.

E. Conditions for Better Communications:

Barnard pointed out four simultaneous conditions crucial for better communication:

1. Understanding communication
2. Communication is according to purpose of organisation.
3. Communication is compatible with his interest as whole
4. Physical and mental compliance with communication.

7

MANAGING CONFLICT IN THE ORGANISATION

Mary Parker Follett

Mary Parker Follett (1868–1933) is regarded as the *bridge* between classical approach and behavioural approach. She is considered as the forerunner of the *behavioural and human relations approach*. She does not agree with the classical theory of administration that is the scientific management theory. Her major works are:

(i) *The Speaker of the House of Representatives* (1896)
(ii) *The New State* (1918)
(iii) *Dynamic Administration* (1924)
(iv) *Creative Experience* (1924)

Follett stated that conflict is natural and not harmful for the organisation. She propounded the concept of *constructive conflict*. She discusses three methods for resolving the conflict in organisations:

1. Domination – victory of one party over the other.
2. Compromise – partial surrender of both concerned parties.
3. Integration – looking for a new solution which satisfies the needs of both. She observed that integration is the best method for resolving conflict.

MERITS OF INTEGRATION

1. It addresses the root cause of the problem and solves original conflict.
2. It makes use of better techniques and therefore saves time and resources.
3. It results in the emergence of new values and situations.

STEPS FOR INTEGRATION

1. Identifying core needs and bringing any differences out in the open;
2. Breaking down the whole demand into various constituent parts;
3. Examining the true meaning of symbol;
4. Preparation for response for others.

OBSTACLES TO INTEGRATION

1. High degree of intelligence, keen perception and worthy incentives are necessary, which are rare finds in administrators.
2. Domination is a habitual character.
3. Administrators believe more in theory than active steps.
4. Power-hungry managers.
5. Antagonistic language.
6. People are not trained for this kind of conflict resolution.

GIVING ORDERS IN ORGANISATION

Follett suggested four steps for giving orders in organisations:

1. A conscious attitude

2. A responsible attitude
3. An experimental attitude
4. A result-seeking attitude

Follett found out a *middle path* while giving orders because one must avoid both too much order and not giving orders at all. She believes in the *depersonalisation of orders*. She distinguishes between *power over* and *power with*. She argues that power with employees is more important than power over employees.

8

MANAGEMENT BY OBJECTIVES

Peter Drucker

Peter Drucker (1909–2005), who has been hailed as the 'founder of modern management', first introduced the term 'management by objectives' in his book *The Practice of Management* (1954). Management by Objectives is a dynamic system which integrates the company's need to achieve its goals for profit and growth with the manager's need to contribute and develop themselves. It has a results and goal-setting approach.

FEATURES OF MANAGEMENT BY OBJECTIVE (MBO)

1. Goal orientation
2. Participation
3. Key result areas
4. System approach
5. Optimisation of resources
6. Simplicity and dynamism
7. Operational
8. Accountability on multiple fronts
9. Comprehensive

BENEFITS OF MBO

1. Better managing
2. Clarifying
3. Encouraging personal commitment
4. Developing controls

PROCESS OF MBO

1. Defining organisational goals
2. Defining employees' objectives
3. Continuous monitoring of performance
4. Performance evaluation
5. Feedback
6. Performance oppression

PRINCIPLES OF MBO

1. Easy determination of responsibility
2. Saving time
3. Optimum utilisation of abilities
4. Increasing productivity
5. Enhancing research and development
6. Developing subordinates

CRITICISM OF MBO

1. **Halpern** and **Osofsky** maintain that Drucker critically fails to give specific and detailed protection to the subordinate in the MBO process against manipulation by superiors or their arbitrariness. Nor are the subordinates offered a recourse via any appeals procedure.
2. They also say that MBO takes the labour force as a homogenous entity and fails to respond to its variety and built-in resistances to manipulation.
3. MBO is pseudo-participative despite its claim that employee collaboration and their inputs in setting work objectives is crucial to the process.
4. MBO has also been criticised for encouraging short-sightedness among organisations,

wherein all resources of the company are only oriented towards achieving goals at the expense of other needs like nourishing human resources for the long run.

5. MBO overemphasises results and can compromise leadership since managers are focused only on achieving goals.

Unit X

GOVERNANCE AND PUBLIC POLICY IN INDIA

KEY CONCEPTS

Governance; Accountability and Control; Institutional Mechanisms for Good Governance; Planning and Development; Public Policy as an Instrument of Socio-economic Development

1

GOVERNANCE, GOOD GOVERNANCE AND DEMOCRATIC GOVERNANCE

KEY CONCEPTS

Dimensions of governance; Good governance; Role of civil services; Civil society

The concept of governance is as old as human civilisation. Governance refers to the ways in which a society or organisation is managed and directed, including the systems, processes and structures used to make and implement decisions, at any level, i.e. local, regional, national, international or corporate. It involves the exercise of authority, control, and direction over resources, policies, and activities, and encompasses both the formal and informal arrangements that shape how power is wielded and how decisions are made and executed. The government or state is a key actor in governance.

In his book *From Government to Governance: A Brief Survey of the Indian Experience* (2008), **Kuldeep Mathur** opines that governance is concerned with the changes taking place in the organisation of the state, and the changes in the state's relationship with the private sector and with civil society actors. The World Bank defines governance as the exercise of political authority and the use of institutional resources to manage society's problems and affairs. Governance is how power is exercised in the management of a country's economic and social resources for development.

DIMENSIONS OF GOVERNANCE

Governance encompasses the complex ways in which social institutions and social norms are organised and structured so as to exercise political authority in a manner that benefits everyone, and not just a select few, at all levels from the local to the global. There are several dimensions of governance, some of which include:

1. **Administrative:** Ability of the state to efficiently and effectively manage its human, financial and technological resources and to deliver basic services to the public.
2. **Economic:** This involves the regulation and management of economic activities, including employment, trade, investment, finance and industrial policies. It includes the state's ability to create jobs, and a conducive climate for business across sectors and ensure macro-economic stability.
3. **Social:** This includes ensuring social welfare, and providing basic essential services such as healthcare, education, and social security to citizens, taking care of the vulnerable sections of society.
4. **Political:** This refers to the mechanisms, processes and institutions that manage

power and authority in society, e.g. the government, political parties, electoral systems. The political dimension includes the nature of political contestation, the conduct of political players, and the use and abuse of political authority.

5. **Legal and judicial:** Ability of the state to maintain law and order, safeguard human rights, enable public access to justice and ensure timely delivery of justice. The legal dimension also includes the legal framework that governs society, laws, regulations, and judicial institutions, and their formation.
6. **Environmental:** Managing the impact of human activities on the environment and ensuring sustainable development.
7. **Ethical:** The ethical dimension involves promoting ethical standards and values in governance, such as transparency, accountability, equality and fairness.

GOOD GOVERNANCE

Good governance is characterised by transparency, accountability, participation, rule of law, and responsiveness to the needs and interests of all stakeholders. Good governance comprises the mechanisms, processes and institutions through which citizens and groups articulate their interests, exercise their constitutional and legal rights, meet their political obligations, and by which different stakeholders are able to mediate their differences to mutual satisfaction and agreement. Good governance means governance according to the rule of law, equality before the law, and equal protection of all under law. It is thus associated with efficient administration within a democratic framework, an administration that is seen and considered to be citizen-friendly, caring, responsive and accountable.

The **World Bank** used the term 'good governance', for the first time in 1989, with reference to action-oriented programmes to curb corruption in its client countries.

Features of Good Governance

The **Organisation for Economic Co-operation and Development (OCED)** delineated the key features of good governance in the following words: 'It is the promotion of democracy and open pluralistic societies, the strengthening of transparent, accountable, efficient and effective national and local government; the promotion of respect of human rights; the reinforcement of the rule of law, including fair and accessible legal and judicial system; the promotion of independent media and the dissemination of information; anti-corruption initiatives and efforts to reduce excessive military expenditure.'

Basic features of good governance include:

1. **Participation:** Active and informed civic participation is essential for good governance. Citizens must have a say in the decisions that affect their lives. This means there must be mechanisms in place for public participation and for people to voice their concerns and opinions.
2. **Accountability:** The government must be answerable and responsible to the people for its performance. This means it must be transparent in its actions and decisions, public officials must be accountable for their actions and decisions. This includes mechanisms for oversight, review, and punishment for wrongdoing.
3. **Transparency:** Information about the functioning, decision-making and actions of the government must be freely and easily accessible to citizens.
4. **Rule of law:** A clear and consistent framework of laws and regulations that are applied fairly and equally to everyone. This means that no one, including the government and its officials, is above the law.
5. **Efficiency and effectiveness:** Efficiency and effectiveness in public service dealings and in use of public funds. Government actions

must be effective in achieving intended goals, and efficient in using resources to do so.

6. **Equity and inclusiveness:** All citizens, regardless of gender, ethnicity or social status, must have equal access to opportunities and government benefits, and no one should be excluded or marginalised.
7. **Responsiveness:** Government institutions and processes must respond to citizens' needs and aspirations within a reasonable timeframe, which means effective and timely service delivery, and also responsiveness to feedback and complaints.
8. **Consensus-oriented:** Good governance requires deliberations between different interest groups in society to reach a broad consensus on what is good for the whole community and how this can be achieved.

SMART Governance

SMART is an acronym which, with reference to good and people-friendly governance, stands for:

Simple
Moral
Accountable
Responsive
Transparent

Simple: Simplification of the rules, regulations, systems and processes of government and its institutions through information communication technology (ICT) that is user-friendly and people-friendly.

Moral: Connoting the emergence of a new system of ethical values in the political and administrative machinery. Technology interventions improve the efficiency of anti-corruption agencies, police, judiciary etc.

Accountable: Facilitating design, development and implementation of effective management information systems and performance-measuring mechanisms, and thereby ensuring accountability of public service functionaries.

Responsive: Streamlining processes to speed up public service delivery and making the system more responsive.

Transparent: Bringing information that was hitherto confined to government offices to the public domain and making government processes and functions transparent, which in turn would bring accountability and equality before law in the responses of the government's administrating agencies.

Some important initiatives for smart and good governance in India include:

1. Right to Information (RTI)
2. E-Governance
3. Citizen's Charter
4. E-Choupal
5. E-Kranti
6. Capacity building and awareness programmes
7. Single window services
8. Public service bill

SMART governance can also refer to a framework for effective governance that focuses on achieving specific, measurable, achievable, relevant and time-bound goals, and emphasises the need for clear and specific objectives, measurable indicators, and a timeline for achieving those objectives.

Some Challenges for Good Governance

1. **Lack of transparency:** Lack of transparency in the functioning of government institutions and decision-making processes is a challenge to good governance in India.
2. **Corruption:** Corruption is a major challenge to good governance in India. It undermines public trust in the government and erodes the efficiency of public institutions at all levels.
3. **Inept legislators and criminalisation of politics:** Weak or corrupt and inept

legislators with criminal records, low levels of education, and no knowledge of development issues are damning for governance.

4. **Political interference:** Political interference in the functioning of government institutions can lead to decisions being made for political gain rather than in the public interest.
5. **Bureaucratic inefficiency:** The bureaucracy in India is often criticised for being inefficient, slow and corrupt, leading to endless delays and red tape in the implementation of policies and public services.
6. **Poorly empowered grassroots institutions:** Inadequate infrastructure, particularly in rural areas, and poorly empowered grassroots democratic institutions impede effective delivery of public services and programmes.
7. **Complex socio-cultural realities:** India is a large and diverse country with complex social and cultural realities that pose challenges to the formulation of public policies and programmes and their effective implementation.
8. **Weak implementation mechanisms:** This undermines the effectiveness of policies and programmes, particularly in key areas such as health, education and social welfare.
9. **Excessive centralisation of power:** This can be a serious challenge to good governance as it can lead to a lack of accountability, transparency, and limit civic participation in democratic processes, which are essential to governance. It can also result in unequal distribution of resources and opportunities, high corruption, inefficiency, and total disregard for the needs and concerns of all stakeholders, as power is concentrated in the hands of a few.
10. **Silencing dissent:** Violation of human rights by the government, silencing of dissent and criminalising dissenters, muzzling the media, and delays in delivery of judicial decisions, all pose serious threats to good governance.
11. **Poor coordination:** Lack of coordination and understanding between central, state and district-level/local institutions is leads to confusion, waste of resources and avoidable delays. Lack of proper consensus between the legislature, executive and judiciary is also detrimental to governance.
12. **Limited citizen participation:** A limited citizen participation, particularly of the disadvantaged and disempowered, and a passive or apathetic civil society which does not engage in the decision-making process on issues which directly affect the people undermines the government's accountability to citizens.

ROLE OF CIVIL SERVICES

1. **Constitutional Provisions:** Article 312 of the Indian Constitution says that new All India Services shall be established by the Parliament. There is provision of Public Services Commission for the union and the state under Article 315. The Constitution also provides autonomy for civil servants under Article 311(2). No civil servants shall be dismissed or removed or reduced in rank except after an enquiry in which he/she has been informed of the charges. He/she will also be given reasonable opportunity of being heard in respect of those charges. According to the Parliamentary Act, the Indian Administrative Service (IAS), Indian Police Service (IPS) and the Indian Forest Service (IFS) are the All India Services in the country.
2. **Autonomy and Neutrality:** Civil servants are supposed to work independently, neutrally and apolitically, and they are duty-bound to give their honest and unpartisan

advice and service to their political masters. The ultimate decision-making power rests with the political master (minister); it is the duty of civil servants to implement those decisions. Civil servants played a vital and autonomous role in nation building post-Independence during the prime ministership of Jawaharlal Nehru.

3. **A Committed Bureaucracy:** Indira Gandhi advocated for a committed bureaucracy, which implies that civil servants should be committed to the ideology of the political party in power.
4. **The Role of Bureaucracy in the Age of Liberalisation:** The role of the bureaucracy is closely associated with the functions of the state. After Independence, the bureaucracy was to function as an instrument for realising the national goal of socialism, and to formulate and implement policies and programmes of the welfare state.

   Since 1991, however, post-liberalisation and privatisation of the Indian economy, the role of the state has increasingly changed from being a controller and provider to that of a facilitator and middleman. The Indian bureaucracy underwent significant changes post-liberalisation, with the aim of making it more efficient, responsive and accountable to the public. Some of the major changes included:

   (i) **Reduction in size:** The size of the bureaucracy was reduced through voluntary retirement schemes and not filling vacancies.
   (ii) **Outsourcing:** Government departments started outsourcing certain services to private companies and NGOs to improve efficiency and reduce costs.
   (iii) **Introduction of technology:** Computerisation and the use of information technology were introduced to improve the efficiency of public services.
   (iv) **Decentralisation:** There was a shift towards decentralisation of decision-making, with more power given to the state governments and local bodies.
   (v) **Performance-based evaluation:** The performance of bureaucrats was evaluated based on specific targets and goals, rather than seniority or experience.
   (vi) **Privatisation:** The government started privatising several public sector enterprises to improve their performance and reduce the burden on the government. Public–private partnerships (PPPs) were also introduced, merging public and private sector undertakings.

5. **Lateral Entry:** Historically, bureaucrats in India were considered to be 'generalists', and expected to have a broad understanding of various aspects of governance, rather than specialised knowledge in a given field. However, in recent decades, experts with specialised skills have been admitted to the bureaucracy through *lateral entry*. Individuals with backgrounds in fields like software engineering, economics or informatics may now be appointed to positions in the government Secretariat, which was previously reserved only for Indian Administrative Service (IAS) officers. The idea is to bring in fresh perspectives and expertise to the bureaucracy to help improve the quality of governance.

CIVIL SOCIETY

The origins of the term 'civil society' can be traced back to the works of classical Greek and Roman philosophers like Aristotle and Cicero. Traditionally, the two terms 'state' and 'civil society' were often used interchangeably. However, Hegel was the first political philosopher who separated and differentiated civil society from the state. In the twentieth century, **Antonio**

Gramsci further analysed the concept of a civil society. **Jeffrey Alexander** holds that civil society is an inclusive, umbrella-like concept covering a plethora of institutions outside the state. According to **Niraja Gopal Jaya**, the civil society includes all forms of voluntary associations and social interactions not controlled by the state.

Everyone has the right to participate in public life. Civil society forms the backbone of a functional democracy. While it derives strength from the Gandhian tradition of volunteerism, Indian civil society today expresses itself in many diverse forms, encompassing formal as well as informal entities and activities, and includes the public sector, the media, NGOs, professional associations and informal groups of people from all walks of life.

The Role of Civil Society in Governance

Civil society plays a crucial and vital role in governance by providing a platform for citizens to participate in decision-making and holding the government accountable. The all-round active participation of civil society is essential to ensure that governance remains inclusive, participatory, and responsive to the needs of all. The many roles of civil society include:

1. Policy advocacy and formulation
2. Monitoring policy implementation, providing feedback
3. As an intermediary between government and citizens
4. Providing checks and balances to power
5. Ensuring accountability and transparency of government
6. Mobilising citizens and resources
7. As an active and engaged partner in development

Civil society organisations (CSOs) such as NGOs, community-based organisations (CBOs), and advocacy groups act as intermediaries between citizens and the government, representing the interests and concerns of the people. CSOs can influence policy-making by conducting research and providing evidence-based recommendations, engaging in advocacy and lobbying, and informing and mobilising citizens to take action. They can also monitor the implementation of policies and programmes and hold the government accountable for its actions. In addition to their advocacy and monitoring roles, civil society organisations can also contribute to the delivery of public services in partnership with the government. For example, NGOs may provide healthcare services in underserved areas or run literacy programmes for disadvantaged communities.

2

ACCOUNTABILITY AND CONTROL

KEY CONCEPTS

Internal and external accountability; legislative control; executive control; judicial control; administrative reforms; corruption; CBI; CVC

Accountability refers to the obligation of individuals or institutions to provide an account or justification of their actions and decisions to all relevant stakeholders, including the public. It is the mechanism that ensures that those who are entrusted with power and resources are answerable for their actions and decisions, and that they can be held responsible if they fail to meet their obligations.

Control refers to the process of regulating, directing, or managing the actions or behaviour of individuals or organisations to ensure that they align with the desired objectives or goals. Control can be exercised through various mechanisms such as rules, policies, procedures, feedback mechanisms, incentives, and sanctions or punishment. The purpose of control is to minimise risks and ensure that resources are used effectively and efficiently, and that the objectives of the organisation or society are achieved.

Accountability in governance may be enforced in several ways and through a combination of various mechanisms. For example, *political accountability* is enforced through the electoral process; elected officials are accountable to the citizens who vote for them, and can be removed from office if they do not perform their duties satisfactorily. *Administrative accountability* implies holding government officials accountable for their actions within the framework of the administrative system, through performance reviews, audits, and disciplinary actions. *Legal accountability* involves holding individuals or organisations responsible for their actions through legal mechanisms like fines, imprisonment or lawsuits.

INTERNAL AND EXTERNAL ACCOUNTABILITY AND CONTROL

Internal accountability and control refers to the mechanisms and processes within an organisation that ensure compliance with established policies, procedures and standards. It involves monitoring and evaluating the performance of employees and the organisation itself to identify areas of improvement and implement corrective measures as needed. Examples of internal accountability and control include internal audits, internal assessments, risk management, personnel management, efficiency survey, and performance management systems.

External accountability and control, on the other hand, refers to the oversight and regulation of an organisation by external entities, such as government agencies, the constitutional machinery i.e. the legislature, executive and judiciary, regulatory bodies and external auditors. It involves holding organisations accountable for their actions and ensuring compliance with laws, regulations and ethical standards. Public control through diverse interest groups including the media, voluntary organisations, civil society, citizens' charter, right to information and social audit are also a part of external controls. Examples include financial audits, regulatory compliance audits, and nonpartisan external reviews by independent experts or overseeing bodies. External accountability and control are particularly important for government and public organisations and those that provide essential services to the public as they are accountable to taxpayers and other stakeholders.

LEGISLATIVE CONTROL

The Parliament of India or the legislature exercises control over the executive branch of government through various mechanisms, including debates, questions, discussions, motions, and resolutions.

1. *Question hour*: Members of Parliament (MPs) can ask the ministers questions in Parliament, and the government has to respond. This is an important tool of legislative control as it holds the government accountable to the Parliament.
2. *Zero hour*: The period after the Question Hour when MPs can raise issues of urgent public importance.
3. *Adjournment motion*: This is a motion moved by an MP to draw the attention of the House to a matter of urgent public importance.
4. *No-confidence motion*: This is a motion moved by the Opposition to express lack of confidence in the government.
5. *Parliamentary committees*: These are committees of members of Parliament (MPs) who are appointed by the Speaker of the Lok Sabha or the Chairman of the Rajya Sabha to examine and report on various issues related to policy, administration, and finance.
6. *Discussion on budget*: The Parliament controls the country's budget. The government has to get its budget approved by the Parliament before it can be implemented.
7. *Debates on legislation*: Debates on proposed legislations in Parliament provide MPs the opportunity to discuss and deliberate on various issues related to policy, administration, and finance.
8. *Government audit report*: The central audit agency, the **Comptroller and Auditor General (CAG)** of India, reviews and examines the financial statements and activities of all government entities, including ministries, departments, public sector undertakings, and other government bodies and provides an independent, unbiased and comprehensive assessment of the government's financial performance and also its compliance with laws, regulations, and policies. The CAG reports any irregularities in the government's finances to the Parliament. The CAG report also identifies areas where improvements can be made and recommends measures to enhance transparency, accountability, and governance in the government's operations. The government audit report is thus a vital and important tool for ensuring good governance and preventing corruption in public institutions.

EXECUTIVE CONTROL

The Ministry of Home Affairs and the Prime Minister's Office (PMO) oversee the functioning of the ministries and other branches of the executive and ensure that they follow the laws and regulations. Ministers are individually and collectively responsible to their political bosses and to the Parliament for their actions and decisions.

The Comptroller and Auditor General (CAG) of India exercises financial and administrative controls on the executive by auditing the accounts of the government and reporting any irregularities to the Parliament. The Central Vigilance Commission (CVC) and State Vigilance Commissions (SVCs) likewise ensure that the executive acts in accordance with rules and regulations and are accountable for their actions.

The media and civil society also play a crucial role in monitoring the executive by raising public awareness about government actions and holding it accountable for its decisions and actions.

JUDICIAL CONTROL

Judicial control over the executive means the power of the courts to examine the legality of the actions of the government, its bodies and officials, and thereby to safeguard the rights and freedoms of citizens. The right of an aggrieved citizen to bring a civil or criminal suit in a court of law against a public servant for the wrong done to him or her in the course of discharge of public duty is also implied in judicial control. The Indian judiciary exercises control on the country's legislature and executive in several ways, some of which include:

1. *Judicial review*: The Supreme Court of India has the power to strike down any law passed by the legislature or action taken by the executive if it is found to be unconstitutional. This power is enshrined in the Constitution and is a crucial system of control that ensures the legislative and executive branches do not overstep their bounds.
2. *Writs*: The judiciary can issue writs, such as *habeas corpus*, *mandamus*, and *certiorari*, to ensure that the executive and legislature act within the confines of the law and the Constitution. For example, if a person is arrested without proper legal justification, the judiciary can issue a writ of habeas corpus to ensure their release.
3. *Public interest litigation*: The judiciary can take suo moto cognizance of issues that are of public importance and can initiate a public interest litigation (PIL) to ensure that the legislature and executive act in the best interests of the public.
4. *Contempt of court*: The judiciary can hold individuals or institutions, including the central and state governments and government bodies, in contempt if they fail to comply with court orders.
5. *Judicial activism*: The judiciary and the Supreme Court of India can also take an active role in policymaking and governance and use its powers to ensure that the legislature and executive act in the best interests of the public, and that the government does not abuse its powers.

ADMINISTRATIVE REFORMS

India's first prime minister **Jawaharlal Nehru** once said: 'Administration is meant to achieve something, and not to exist in some kind of an ivory tower following certain rules of procedure and, Narcissus-like, looking on itself with complete satisfaction. The test after all is human beings and their welfare.'

The Report of the Committee on Civil Service Reforms in India (2004), headed by P. C. Hota, observed that undertaking public service or administrative reforms in India in any sector at any level is a challenging exercise, given the logistics of its size, the diversity of its population, language, culture, available infrastructure and the diverse institutions of governance. India is the world's largest democracy. Any administrative reforms must therefore take into account the constitutional provisions governing the distribution of powers between the Union, the states and institutions of local government.

Reforms in British India

Before Independence, studies and reports undertaken by the colonial British government on reforms in the civil and administrative services in India included:

1. The Aitchison Commission or Public Service Commission (1886).

2. The Islington Commission or Royal Commission (1912–1915) on Public Service in India.
3. The Lee Commission or Royal Commission (1923–1924) on Superior Civil Service in India.
4. The Tottenham Report (1945–1946) on the Reorganisation of the Central Government.

Reforms after Independence

Reforms recommended in public services by various committees after Independence included:

1. The G. S. Bajpai Secretariat Reorganisation Committee Report (1947).
2. The Gopalaswami Aiyangar Committee on the Reorganisation of the Government of India (1949).
3. The A. D. Gorwala Committee Report on Public Administration (1951).
4. The R. N. Gopal Swami Report (1952).
5. The Paul H. Appleby Report (1953), recommending the establishment of an institute for public administration.
6. The A. Ramaswani Mudaliar Committee Report (1956), on qualifications for recruitment to the public services.
7. The V. T. Krishnamachari Committee Report (1962), on the Indian State Administrative Service and problems of district administration.
8. The First Administration Reforms Commission (ARC) Report (1966), on administrative reforms across sectors.
9. The D. S. Kothari Committee Report (1976), on recruitment policy and selection methods for the civil services (preliminary examinations were introduced).
10. The Satish Chandra Committee Report (1981) to review the civil service examination scheme (an essay paper was introduced and weightage for the personality test was increased.)
11. The Y. K. Alagh Committee Report (2001) to review the civil service examinations (introduced an objective paper in the preliminary examination).
12. The P. C. Hota Committee on Civil Service Reforms (2004).
13. The Second Administration Reforms Commission (2005), formed to revamp the public administration system.

Administrative Reforms Commissions (ARC)

The Administrative Reforms Commission (**ARC**) was set up by the Indian government for studying and recommending changes in the government's administrative and management practices from time to time. The ARC is composed of experts and professionals from diverse fields, and its reports and recommendations are meant to help the government improve its functioning and efficiency across sectors.

The **First Administrative Reforms Commission**, chaired by **Morarji Desai**, was set up in January 1966 as a commission of inquiry, to examine public administration in the country and recommend appropriate reform and reorganisation where necessary, involving the following aspects:

1. The Government of India machinery, its procedures and functions
2. The machinery for planning at all levels
3. Centre–state relationships
4. Financial administration
5. Personnel administration
6. Economic administration
7. Administration at state and district levels
8. Agricultural administration
9. Problems of redressal of citizens' grievances

In all, 20 reports containing 537 major recommendations, based on inputs from across central and state ministries, were compiled and placed before the Parliament in November 1977.

The **Second Administrative Reforms Commission**, constituted in August 2005 under the chairmanship of **Veerappa Moily**, was tasked with preparing a detailed blueprint for revamping the public administrative system. It had presented the following 15 reports to the GOI for consideration:

1. Right to information
2. Unlocking human capital
3. Crisis management
4. Ethics in governance
5. Public order: Justice and peace for all
6. Local governance
7. Capacity building for conflict resolution
8. Combating terrorism
9. Social capital: A shared destiny
10. Refurbishing of personnel administration
11. Promoting e-Governance as the smart way forward
12. Citizen-centric administration
13. Organisational structure of the Government of India
14. Strengthening the financial management system
15. State and district administration

CORRUPTION

In the words of Kautilya: 'Just as it is impossible not to taste the honey that finds itself on the tip of the tongue, so it is impossible for a minister of the government not to eat up at least a portion of the king's revenue.'

Transparency International defines corruption as 'The abuse of entrusted power for private gain'. Public servants in India can be penalised for corruption under The Indian Penal Code, 1860, and the Prevention of Corruption Act, 1988. Two amendments to the Prevention of Corruption Act, 1988, have been passed, in 2013 and in 2018. Highlights of the 2018 Amendment Act are:

1. Anyone taking bribes will face imprisonment for 3 to 7 years and will be levied a fine.
2. Anyone giving bribes can also be imprisoned for up to 7 years and be levied a fine.

The three main authorities involved in inquiring, investigating and prosecuting corruption cases in India are the Central Vigilance Commission (CVC), the Central Bureau of Investigation (CBI) and the State Anti-Corruption Bureau (ACB).

ANTI-CORRUPTION

The institutional framework to check corruption and redress citizens' grievances in India concerning corruption in government and public offices comprises the following:

1. Public Servants (Enquiries) Act, 1850.
2. Indian Penal Code, 1860.
3. Special Police Establishment, 1941.
4. Prevention of Corruption Act, 1988.
5. All India Services (Conduct) Rules, 1954.
6. Central Civil Services (Conduct) Rules, 1955.
7. Railway Services (Conduct) Rules, 1956.
8. Central Bureau of Investigation, 1963.
9. Central Vigilance Commission, 1964.
10. State Vigilance Commission, 1964.
11. Anti-Corruption Bureaus in different states
12. District vigilance officer
13. The Supreme Court of India and the different high courts
14. Administrative Tribunals
15. The Indian Parliament and its various committees.

CENTRAL BUREAU OF INVESTIGATION (CBI)

The Central Bureau of Investigation or CBI was set up in 1963 by a resolution of the Ministry of Home Affairs. Functioning under the jurisdiction of the Department of Personnel, Ministry of Personnel, Pension and Public Grievances, it is the premier investigating police agency in India and enjoys the status of an attached office. The CBI is not a statutory body and it was not established by an Act of the Parliament. It derives its legal power to investigate cases from the Delhi Special Police Establishment (DSPE) Act, 1946.

The CBI is an elite, autonomous central government body invested with wide-ranging powers, with the goal of checking crime, corruption and the abuse of power in high places, and bringing the guilty to justice. It is also the premier and nodal police agency in India which coordinates investigation on behalf of Interpol member countries. The extent of the CBI's power may be gauged from the fact that it is exempted from the Right to Information (RTI) Act.

The union government can authorise the CBI to investigate high-profile cases of crime or corruption in any state without prior consent or knowledge of the state government or parties concerned. The CBI also provides assistance to the Central Vigilance Commission (CVC).

The CBI has attracted controversies and criticism because it is invested with extraordinary and wide powers, but there are no checks and balances in place; reports of irregular practises, which are not subject to the RTI; excessive political influence; and a poor conviction rate.

CENTRAL VIGILANCE COMMISSION (CVC)

The Central Vigilance Commission (CVC) was initiated and established through a Government of India (GoI) Resolution in February 1964, on the recommendations of the K. Santhanam Committee on Prevention of Corruption (1962–1964). Following the Supreme Court directive of December 1997 to the GoI to confer statutory status upon the Commission, the CVC got statutory status in September 2003 through the Central Vigilance Commission Act of 2003.

The CVC was set up with the aim of exercising superintendence and vigilance over the administration of the various bodies and organisations which come under the executive powers of the Government of India. It was conceptualised as a fully autonomous institution, mandated to advise the authorities concerned on corrupt practices and improper conduct, along with the timely review and modification of procedures that may afford any scope for corruption.

The CVC is the main agency to check and prevent corruption in the central government and its bodies. It is authorised to receive written complaints from whistleblowers on any allegation of corruption or misuse of office by any employee of the central government or any corporation, company, society or organisation established by or owned or controlled by the central government.

The CVC is a multi-member body consisting of a chairperson and not more than two vigilance commissioners. They are appointed by the president of India on the recommendation of a three-member committee comprising the prime minister as its head, the home minister and the leader of the Opposition in the Lok Sabha. CVC members hold their office for a term of four years or until they attain the age of 65 years, whichever is earlier.

Functions and Powers of the CVC

Under the Central Vigilance Commission Act, 2003, some of the important functions and powers of the CVC include the following:

1. Oversee the functioning of and direct the Delhi Special Police Establishment (CBI) in the investigation of offences under the Prevention of Corruption Act, 1988; or offences under the Cr.PC for certain categories of public servants.
2. To inquire into or initiate inquiry on a reference by the central government, and review progress of such inquiries into offences alleged to have been committed under the Prevention of Corruption Act, 1988; or under the Cr.PC.
3. While conducting any inquiry, the CVC shall command all the powers of a civil court.

4. Exercise superintendence over the vigilance administrations of the various central government ministries, departments and organisations.
5. The government must consult the CVC before making any rules governing the vigilance of or disciplinary matters relating to persons appointed to the public services and the All India Services.

3

INSTITUTIONAL MECHANISMS FOR GOOD GOVERNANCE

KEY CONCEPTS

Right to Information; Central Information Commission; citizen's charter; Lokpal; Lokayukta; Consumer Protection Act

Institutional mechanisms provide the necessary framework and structure for ensuring good governance by establishing clear lines of authority, responsibility and functioning, and provide a framework for decision-making and accountability. Without such mechanisms, there would be a lack of consistency and coherence in government functions, leading to inefficiency, confusion and the potential for abuse of power.

Institutional mechanisms also help to promote transparency and accountability by providing a framework for public scrutiny of government actions. They help to ensure that decisions are made in a fair and impartial manner, and that there is a clear process for holding officials accountable when they fail to meet their obligations.

Importantly, institutional mechanisms also enable and encourage citizen participation in the governance process. By providing systems of public input and feedback, they ensure that the people's interests and concerns are taken on board in decisions that affect them. This helps build public trust in the government and promotes greater civic engagement in governance.

Some important initiatives for good governance in India include:

1. Right to Information (RTI)
2. E-Governance
3. Citizen's Charter
4. E-Choupal
5. E-Kranti
6. Capacity building and awareness programmes
7. Single-window services
8. Public service bill

RIGHT TO INFORMATION

Right to Information or RTI is a legal right given to citizens of India that empowers them to seek and obtain information from any public office and government authority. The Right to Information Act 2005 provides all Indians a means to access information hitherto restricted to public authorities. It is an essential tool for promoting transparency and accountability and for combating corruption in government institutions. The RTI is antithetical to secrecy in public administration and functioning. In 1992, the World Bank released a document entitled 'Government and Development' which enlisted seven aspects of good governance, one of them being transparency of and access to information.

The Right to Information is necessary for the following reasons:

1. It makes the government more accountable and responsive to the people's needs.
2. It reduces the gap between the administration and people.
3. It makes people aware of processes of administrative decision-making.
4. It facilitates informed, intelligent and constructive criticism of governance.
5. It increases people's participation in governance.
6. It promotes public interest by discouraging arbitrariness in administrative decision-making.
7. Greater transparency reduces the scope for corruption in public offices.
8. It discourages the abuse of power by public servants.

The History of RTI, Globally and in India

Sweden was the first country in the world to introduce as law the public right to information, conferring this right on its citizens through a direct constitutional provision way back in 1766. Other countries followed in its footsteps much later at various points in time.

Finland in 1951
The United States in 1966
Norway in 1970
Canada, Australia and New Zealand in 1982
Denmark in 1985
Greece in 1986
Austria in 1987
Italy in 1990
The United Kingdom in 2000
Pakistan in 2002
Bangladesh in 2008
Bhutan in 2014

The Supreme Court of India has been advocating since 1975 that the right to information is an intrinsic part of the right to freedom of speech and expression Article 19 (1) (a), which is guaranteed by the Constitution of India. However, several colonial-era laws favouring strict secrecy in administration and governance has restricted the disclosure of official and government information to the people. These include:

1. The Official Secrets Act, 1923
2. The Indian Evidence Act, 1872
3. The Commission of Enquiry Act, 1952
4. The All India Services (Conduct) Rules, 1954
5. The Central Civil Services (Conduct) Rules, 1955
6. The Railway Services (Conduct) Rules, 1956

The Fifth Day Commission (1994–1997) recommended the abolition of the Official Secrets Act and introduction of the Right to Information Act. In 2005, the Parliament enacted a new legislation: The Right to Information Act (2005), which replaced the old Freedom of Information Act, 2002.

Right to Information in States

Before the Government of India enacted and implemented the national RTI Act in 2005, several Indian states had already passed their own right to information laws.

1. Tamil Nadu was the first Indian state to pass the RTI as law in May 1997.
2. Goa followed close behind, in July 1997.
3. Rajasthan and Karnataka in 2000.
4. Maharashtra in 2000. Maharashtra repealed its earlier RTI Act of 2000 to introduce a stronger one in 2003.
5. Delhi in 2001.
6. Assam and Madhya Pradesh in 2002.
7. Jammu & Kashmir passed the RTI law in 2004.
8. Of these states, Madhya Pradesh had taken steps to enact a law on the RTI as early as

1997, but failed due to lack of consent by the Centre.

CENTRAL INFORMATION COMMISSION (CIC)

Established by the central government in 2015 under the provisions of the Right to Information Act 2005, the Central Information Commission (CIC) is not a constitutional body. It comprises one chief information commissioner and not more than 10 information commissioners. They are appointed by the president on the recommendation of a committee consisting of the prime minister as chairperson, the leader of the Opposition in the Lok Sabha and the union cabinet minister nominated by the prime minister. Officials of the CIC shall hold office for such term as prescribed by the central government or until they attain the age of 65 years, whichever is earlier. They are not eligible for reappointment.

Powers and Functions of the CIC

1. To receive and inquire into complaints from anyone regarding information requested under the RTI 2005.
2. The CIC can order an inquiry into any matter if it considers that there are reasonable grounds.
3. While investigating any complaint, the Commission shall have the powers of a civil court in respect of summoning of witnesses, asking for documents etc.
4. The jurisdiction of the CIC extends over all central public authorities.

State Information Commissions

The State Information Commission in each state is constituted by that state government. It has one state chief information commissioner (SCIC) and not more than 10 state information commissioners (SICs), who are appointed by the governor on the recommendation of the appointments committee headed by the chief minister.

CITIZEN'S CHARTER

The concept of a citizen's charter was initiated by former British Prime Minister **John Major** in 1991, and was started as a national programme intended to improve the overall quality of British public services. In 1998, the concept was renamed 'service first' in the UK. The Citizen's Charter is a document of commitments made by a government organisation to its citizens in respect of the services and schemes being provided or to be provided to them. Its objective is to streamline governance in tune with the needs of citizens and to build bridges between the public and the government.

Basic Principles of a Citizen's Charter

Quality: Improve quality of public services.

Choice: Wherever possible, give citizens the option to choose.

Standards: Clearly mention what to expect from a given service, and what to do if expected standards are not met.

Value: Provide value for the taxpayer's money.

Accountability: Be answerable to the public, at the level of the government official as well as the organisation.

Transparency: Maintain transparency in all rules, schemes, procedures and in redressal of grievances.

Participatory: Consult and involve citizens, invite feedback and inputs.

These principles were later elaborated as following the nine principles of 'Service Delivery' (1998), which were:

1. Set standards of service.
2. Be open and provide full information.
3. Consult and involve.
4. Encourage access and promote choice.
5. Treat all fairly.
6. Put things right when they go wrong.
7. Use resources effectively.

8. Innovate and improve.
9. Work with other service providers.

Citizen's Charter in India

In India the concept of a citizen's charter was first adopted at a conference of chief ministers of various states and union territories held in May 1997 in the national capital. The Indian model of the citizen's charter is an adaptation from the British model.

The tasks of formulating, coordinating, and operationalising citizen's charters are done by the Department of Administrative Reforms and Public Grievances (DARPG). The citizen's charter aims to secure citizens' rights and to create a mechanism to ensure timely delivery of goods and services and address their grievances. It requires every public authority to publish a citizen's charter within six months of the commencement of the Act and levies a penalty of up to Rs 50,000 for failure to render services.

OMBUDSMAN

An ombudsman is an independent official appointed by the government to investigate grievances raised by citizens regarding maladministration, corruption or other misconduct by public officials or government agencies. The ombudsman is a neutral and objective party who can mediate and resolve disputes between citizens and government bodies, and has the power to summon officials, examine documents, and recommend corrective actions. The ombudsman system provides an effective mechanism for citizens to seek justice and accountability from the government. It also helps to improve the quality of public services and increase transparency and accountability in government operations.

The concept of ombudsman first originated in Sweden in 1805. From the beginning of the twentieth century the system began to draw the attention of several other European states that followed suit; Finland in 1919, Denmark in 1955, Norway in 1961, and the Netherlands in 1981. New Zealand used the term 'parliamentary commission' for ombudsman in 1962. In 1966 the British government, in 1971 Israel, and in 1981 the Netherlands appointed a parliamentary commissioner. Australia, the US and Canada have an ombudsman at the state or provincial level. Also referred to as 'general surveillance of the functioning of the government', the ombudsman has powers to supervise general civil administration. Its main function is to protect the rights and freedoms of the people.

In India, the terms *lokpal* and *lokayukta* were coined by **Dr. L. M. Singhvi.**

LOKPAL

The First Administrative Reforms Commission (ARC), set up in January 1966 and headed by **Morarji Desai**, recommended the establishment of two special authorities designated as **Lokpal** and **Lokayukta** specifically for the redressal of citizen's grievances against public offices. These institutions were to be modeled on the pattern of the institution of the ombudsman in Scandinavian countries and the parliamentary commissioner for investigation in New Zealand.

Powers and Functions of the Lokpal

1. The Lokpal is empowered to investigate and address complaints against ministers and secretaries at the central and state levels.
2. The Lokpal Bill was first tabled in the Lok Sabha in 1968. The version enacted in 2013 was based on a draft of the Lokpal and Lokyuktas Bill, 2011. It came into force on 16 January 2014. It seeks to establish the institution of the Lokpal at the centre and the Lokayuktas at the state level.
3. The jurisdiction of the Lokpal includes the prime minister, his cabinet ministers, members of Parliament, and officers and officials of the central government of groups A, B, C and D.

4. The Lokpal consists of a chairperson and a maximum of 8 members, of which half shall be judicial members.
5. About 50 per cent of the Lokpal members shall come from amongst the SCs and STs, OBCs, minorities and women.
6. Selection of the Lokpal chairperson and members shall be through a selection committee comprising the PM, Lok Sabha Speaker, leader of the Opposition, the Chief Justice of India (CJI) or a sitting Supreme Court judge nominated by the CJI, and eminent persons nominated by the president of India. A search committee will assist the selection committee in the process of selection.
7. The PM has been brought under the purview of the Lokpal, although subject to exclusions under specific matters.
8. The Lokpal has the power of superintendence and direction over any investigative agency, including the CBI, for cases referred to by the Lokpal.
9. It enhanced maximum punishment under the Prevention of Corruption Act from one to 10 years.
10. The term of office for the Lokpal chairman and members is 5 years or till the age of 70 years, whichever is earlier.
11. The inquiry wing of the Lokpal has been vested with the powers of a civil court.
12. The Lokpal can recommend the transfer or suspension of public servants in connection with allegations of corruption or misconduct.
13. The Lokpal has the power to prevent or to order against the destruction of records during the preliminary inquiry.
14. While the Administrative Reforms Commission kept the judiciary outside the purview of the Lokpal and the Lokayuktas, as done in New Zealand, in Sweden the judiciary is also within the purview of the ombudsman.

LOKAYUKTA

Much before the enactment of the Lokpal and Lokayukta Act in 2013, many Indian states had already set up their own Lokayuktas. However, the structure, powers and functions of the Lokayukta are not the same in all the states.

1. The institution of Lokayukta was first established in **Maharashtra** in 1971.
2. Though Orissa passed an act in this regard in 1970, it only came into force in 1983.
3. Till date, 20 states and two union territories have implemented the Lokpal and Lokayukta Act, some of which include:
   Maharashtra – 1971
   Rajasthan – 1973
   Bihar – 1974
   Uttar Pradesh – 1975
   Madhya Pradesh – 1981
   Delhi – 1995
   Jammu & Kashmir – 2002
4. The appointment of the Lokayukta is by the governor of the state, in consultation with the chief justice of the state high court and the leader of the Opposition in the state Legislative Assembly.
5. Judicial qualifications are prescribed for the Lokayukta in the states of Uttar Pradesh, Himachal Pradesh, Andhra Pradesh, Gujarat, Orissa, Karnataka and Assam. But no specific qualifications are prescribed in the states of Bihar, Maharashtra and Rajasthan.
6. The term of office for the Lokayukta is 5 years or till the age of 65.
7. The Lokayukta is not eligible for reappointment.
8. In most states the Lokayukta can initiate inquiries based on a public complaint, but does not have the power to start investigations on his own initiative in the states of UP, Himachal Pradesh and Assam.
9. In Maharashtra, UP, Assam, Bihar and Karnataka, the Lokayukta can consider

cases of public grievance against maladministration as well as charges of corruption.

10. In Himachal Pradesh, Andhra Pradesh, Rajasthan and Gujarat, the Lokayukta can only investigate allegations of corruption, but not public grievances related to maladministration.

CONSUMER PROTECTION ACT, 2019

The new Consumer Protection Act was passed by the Parliament in 2019. It came into force in July 2020 and replaced the earlier Consumer Protection Act of 1986. It protects wide-ranging interests of consumers by providing them safeguards against defective and dangerous products, dissatisfactory services and unfair trade practices. It empowers consumers by establishing authorities for timely and effective redressal and settlement of consumer complaints and disputes.

Salient Provisions of the Consumer Protection Act, 2019

1. Definition of consumer: A person who avails of any services or buys any goods for self-use and not for resale or commercial purpose is considered to be a consumer.
2. The Act proposes the establishment of the Central Consumer Protection Authority (CCPA) as a regulatory authority.
3. The Act provides for the establishment of Consumer Disputes Redressal Commissions (CDRCs) at the national, state and district levels to address consumer complaints.
4. Consumers can now file complaints electronically and seek hearing through video conferencing.
5. The Act introduces the concept of product liability and penal consequences.
6. The CCPA may impose penalty on a manufacturer for a false or misleading advertisement.
7. There is provision for mediation as an alternate dispute resolution mechanism.
8. Authorities are empowered to take action against unfair trade practices.
9. The Act mandates the establishment of Consumer Protection Councils for promoting consumer awareness at the national, state and district levels.
10. To provide inexpensive, speedy and summary redressal of consumer disputes, quasi-judicial bodies called Consumer Disputes Redressal Commissions have been set up in each district and state, with the National Consumer Disputes Redressal Commission (NCDRC) at the apex. The pecuniary jurisdiction of commissions at each level is as follows:

    District commissions: Rs 20 lakh to Rs 1 crore

    State commissions: Rs 1 crore to Rs 10 crore

    NCDRC: Above Rs 10 crore
11. E-commerce transactions come under the provisions involving direct sales.

Consumer Rights

Under the Consumer Protection Act, consumers in India are entitled to several rights, which include:

1. Right to correct information on various aspects of goods and services.
2. Right to be protected from unfair or restrictive trade practices.
3. Right to protection against goods and services that can be potentially dangerous to life and property.
4. Right to be informed about the quality, quantity, potency, price and standard of goods or services.
5. Right to access a variety of goods and services at competitive prices.
6. Right to redressal of grievances and complaints.

4

PLANNING AND DEVELOPMENT

KEY CONCEPTS

Sustainable development; e-governance; Niti Aayog

Planning refers to the systematic process of analysing the current situation, identifying needs, priorities and resources, determining the best course of action to achieve desired outcomes, and formulating strategies and policies accordingly. Planning is done at national, state, district and local levels, and includes economic development, infrastructure and social welfare, and environmental conservation.

Development refers to the overall progress and improvement of societies, economies and individuals over time by way of implementing the strategies formulated during planning to bring about positive changes in society. Development includes economic, social and human development, and environmental sustainability, with the aim of enhancing the well-being and quality of life for individuals and communities.

Effective planning lays the foundation for successful development, and both are crucial for creating sustainable and inclusive societies. Both involve the participation of diverse stakeholders, including government, businesses, industry, non-government organisations, communities and the civil society, to ensure collective efforts towards achieving shared goals. By integrating social, economic and environmental considerations, planning and development aim to create balanced and equitable growth that benefits present and future generations.

SUSTAINABLE DEVELOPMENT

Development is that which meets the needs of the present without compromising the ability of future generations to meet their own needs. This most widely accepted definition of sustainable development was given by the Brundtland Commission in the *Report of the World Commission on Environment and Development: Our Common Future* (1987), also known as the *Brundtland Report.* Sustainable development calls for concerted global efforts towards building an inclusive, sustainable and resilient future for all people and the planet.

The three core elements of sustainable development are economic growth, social inclusion and environmental protection.

1. **Environmental Sustainability:** Nature is not inexhaustible and it must not be seen and used as an inexhaustible resource. Environmental sustainability involves making informed choices in daily life and following environmentally sustainable practices, conserving natural resources and using them rationally and responsibly to meet present needs without compromising

the ability of future generations to meet theirs. Key aspects of environmental sustainability include:

Waste management
Conservation of natural resources
Preservation of biodiversity
Conservation of ecosystems
Climate change mitigation
Sustainable agriculture

2. **Social Sustainability:** It focuses on creating and maintaining a just and equitable society that fosters social cohesion, inclusivity, gender equality, pluralism and diversity, development of communities and cultures to help achieve a reasonable, well-distributed and good quality of life, healthcare and education for everyone across the globe. Key aspects of social sustainability include:

   Equity and social justice
   Health and well-being
   Community engagement and participation
   Preservation of cultures and diversity
   Social cohesion and safety
   Responsible governance
   Education and lifelong learning
   Equal opportunities and rights for all

3. **Economic Sustainability:** It refers to an economy's ability to support long-term economic growth and development by the efficient management of resources, promoting efficiency and fostering economic stability to meet existing human needs without wasting or compromising the availability of resources for future generations. It focuses on equitable economic growth that generates wealth for all and equitable distribution of economic resources, without harming the environment. Key aspects of economic sustainability include:

   Sustainable economic growth
   Responsible consumption and production
   Resource efficiency and conservation
   Financial stability and economic resilience
   Social and economic equity
   International cooperation and trade

Economic sustainability aims to create prosperous and resilient economies that provide a high quality of life for all while safeguarding natural resources and minimising negative impacts of development on the environment and society. It works together with social and environmental sustainability to ensure a balanced and inclusive approach to development.

Sustainable Development Goals

Sustainable development goals or SDGs are a set of global goals established by the **United Nations** in 2015. They provide a comprehensive framework for addressing social, economic, and environmental challenges and promoting sustainable development worldwide. They provide a roadmap for all countries and stakeholders to work together towards a more sustainable and equitable future, balancing development with social progress and environmental protection. The SDGs cover a wide range of issues, are universal, applicable to all countries, and aim to be achieved by 2030. The 17 SDGs are as follows:

1. No poverty
2. Zero hunger
3. Good health and wellbeing
4. Quality education
5. Gender equality
6. Clean water and sanitation
7. Affordable and clean energy
8. Decent work and economic growth
9. Industry, innovation, and infrastructure
10. Reduced inequalities
11. Sustainable cities and communities

12. Responsible modes of consumption and production
13. Climate action
14. Life below water
15. Life on land
16. Peace, justice, and strong institutions
17. Partnerships for the goals

Global Initiatives on Sustainable Development

Individuals, organisations, partnerships and initiatives around the globe are working at local, national and international levels towards achieving a more sustainable future. Some examples of global initiatives focused on sustainable development are:

1. The Stockholm Conference on Human Environment, 1972
2. The Vienna Convention for the Protection of the Ozone Layer, 1985
3. The Basel Convention on the Control of Transboundary Movements of Hazardous Wastes and Their Disposal, 1989
4. The Convention on Biological Diversity, 1992
5. United Nations Convention to Combat Desertification, 1994
6. Kyoto Protocol, 1997
7. The Earth Summit (Rio+10), 2002
8. United Nations Sustainable Development Goals, 2015
9. Global Alliance for Circular Economy and Resource Efficiency
10. United Nations Environment Programme
11. Global Reporting Initiative
12. Green Climate Fund

E-GOVERNANCE

E-governance or electronic governance refers to the use of information and communication technologies (ICTs) to enhance the efficiency, effectiveness, transparency, and accessibility of government processes and services. It involves the application of digital technologies to transform traditional governance mechanisms and practices, streamline administrative processes, and improve interactions between the government and citizens. E-governance promotes citizen participation, and fosters a more inclusive and responsive government.

Types of government interaction in e-governance include:

G2G – Government to Government
G2C – Government to Citizen
G2B – Government to Business
G2E – Government to Employee

Advantages of E-governance

1. Fast, efficient, convenient and cost-effective service delivery to citizens.
2. Fosters transparency and accountability, and reduces corruption.
3. Empowers people through access to information.
4. Improves efficiency within government.
5. Improves interface with business and industry.
6. Expands the reach of governance.
7. Enhances accessibility to public services.
8. Saves costs and resources for government.
9. Enables data-driven, evidence-based and informed decision making.
10. Increased citizen engagement and inclusion through feedback mechanisms.
11. Environmental sustainability, reduced reliance on paper-based processes and reduced carbon footprint.

Disadvantages of E-governance

1. Creates a digital divide, where all those without access to internet, the necessary devices, technology or digital literacy are automatically excluded.
2. Raises concerns about privacy, data security, identity theft, misuse of personal

information, excessive state surveillance, and muzzling dissent.

3. Lack of infrastructure and technical capabilities poses a hindrance to effective implementation.
4. Exposes the populace and governance systems and sensitive data to cyber threats, data breaches, malware attacks and system vulnerabilities.
5. E-governance is totally dependent on technology, hence any failure in technology causes major disruptions in delivery of services or renders it useless.
6. E-governance lacks the personal human touch that traditional governance methods provide, which can lead to a sense of alienation in citizens.

E-governance Initiatives in India

The government has undertaken various e-governance initiatives nationwide, such as Digital India, Aadhaar, National e-Governance Plan, Goods and Services Tax Network (GSTN), MyGov, e-Ticketing and e-Passport, e-Courts, and DigiLocker.

Digital India, launched in 2015, aims to transform India into a digitally empowered society and knowledge economy. Some of its key initiatives include:

National Optical Fiber Network (NOFN)
BharatNet
State Data Centres (SDCs)
State Wide Area Networks (SWANs)
Common Services Centre (CSCs)
State E-Governance Service Delivery Gateways (SSDGs)
E-District
E-Hospital
E-Kranti
E-Sign
National Scholarship Portal
National Knowledge Network (NKN)

Recommendations of the Second Administrative Reforms Commission on E-governance

- Building a congenial environment.
- Business process re-engineering.
- Capacity building and creating awareness.
- Developing technological solutions.
- Monitoring and evaluation.
- Knowledge management.

NITI AAYOG

The NITI Aayog is a premiere policy think tank of the Government of India. It was established on 1 January 2015, by an executive resolution replacing the **Planning Commission of India,** with the aim of achieving sustainable development goals through the active involvement and participation of state governments in the planning process. The Prime Minister of India is the chairperson, and he appoints the vice chairperson; the governing council comprises the chief ministers of all the states and the lieutenant governors of the union territories.

Activities and concerns of the NITI Aayog can be broadly divided into four main heads:

1. Policy and programme framework
2. Cooperative federalism
3. Monitoring and evaluation
4. Think tank knowledge and innovation hub

OBJECTIVES OF NITI AAYOG

1. Fostering cooperative federalism and the active involvement of the states.
2. Formulation of plans at the village-level, and aggregation at higher levels.
3. Giving special attention to sections at risk of not benefitting adequately from economic progress.
4. Formulating economic policy that incorporates national security interests, with feedback for constant innovative improvements.

5. Forging partnerships with national and international think tanks.
6. Creating a knowledge, innovation and entrepreneurial support system.
7. Providing a platform for resolution of inter-sectorial and inter-departmental issues.
8. Building a state-of-the-art resource centre for research on good governance.
9. Focusing on technology upgradation and capacity-building across sectors.

5

PUBLIC POLICY AS AN INSTRUMENT OF SOCIO-ECONOMIC DEVELOPMENT

KEY CONCEPTS

Housing; drinking water; food security; National Rural Health Mission; MGNREGA; Right to Education; Jansunwai; social audit

India is committed to fulfilling by 2030 all the 17 sustainable development goals (SDGs) that have been identified by the United Nations in 2015.

HOUSING

SDG-11 aims to make all human settlements inclusive, safe, resilient and sustainable. The first national policy for housing was announced in 1988, and revised in 1994.

Atal Mission for Rejuvenation and Urban Transformation (AMRUT): Launched in June 2015 by PM Modi, AMRUT is an initiative to provide basic civic amenities and housing to the urban underserved areas, with a focus on the poor and the disadvantaged.

Housing for All Mission: 305 cities and towns have been identified under this Mission, also called the Pradhan Mantri Awas Yojana, which targeted building 2 crore homes for the urban poor by the year 2022.

Pradhan Mantri Awas Yojana (Urban): PMAY(U) was launched in 2015 to provide housing for all in urban areas by 2022. It provides central assistance to urban local bodies (ULBs) and other implementing agencies through the states, union territories (UTs) and Central Nodal Agencies (CNAs) for providing houses to all eligible families and beneficiaries against the validated demand for houses for about 1.12 crore. The size of a house for the economically weaker sections (EWS) can be up to 30 sq.mt. carpet area. However states/UTs may enhance the size of houses in consultation with and approval of the Ministry. PMAY(U) makes it mandatory for the female head of the family to be the owner or co-owner of the house under this mission.

DRINKING WATER

SDG-6 is a goal that aims to achieve universal and equitable access to safe and affordable drinking water for all.

The National Water Policy (NWP) was formulated to govern the planning and development of water resources and their optimum utilisation. The first NWP was adopted in September 1987. It was reviewed and updated in 2002 and later in 2012.

The National Rural Drinking Water Programme is a centrally-sponsored scheme aimed at providing everyone in rural India with adequate safe water for drinking, cooking and other domestic basic needs in a sustainable manner.

Swajal Yojana is a community-owned drinking water programme for sustainable piped drinking water supply powered by solar energy. It was launched in 115 districts of India.

Atal Bhujal Yojana is a central groundwater management programme that works through community participation in identified priority areas in seven states.

Jal Shakti was launched in May 2019 as an immediate response to the escalating water crisis in India. The **Nal Se Jal** scheme aims to provide piped water supply to every household by 2024.

Jal Jeevan Mission (JJM) aims to provide functional household tap connections to every rural household in India by 2024 and a supply of 55 litres of water per person per day.

FOOD SECURITY

The basic concept of food security globally is to ensure that all people at all times should have access to wholesome nourishing food for their active and healthy life, and it is characterised by availability of, access to, utilisation and stability of food resources.

The Mid-Day Meal Scheme was launched in 1995 to provide free meals to about 12 crore children studying in primary and upper primary classes. The objective behind the scheme was to address both hunger and basic education, improve the nutrient status and increase the attendance and retention rates among the children. The food calorie intake per meal by the children of primary classes was 450 calories with 12 gram proteins, while children in upper primary classes should get 700 calories with 20 gram proteins.

The National Food Security Act (NFSA), 2013 legally entitles up to 75 per cent of the rural population and 50 per cent of the urban population to receive subsidised food grains under the targeted public distribution system, with a uniform entitlement of 5 kg/person/month ration.

1. Pregnant women and lactating mothers (PWLM) are entitled to receive maternity benefits of not less than Rs 6,000.
2. PWLM and children in the age group of 6 months to 14 years are entitled to meals as per prescribed nutritional norms under ICDS, MDM (PM-Poshan).
3. It provides food security allowance to beneficiaries in the case of non-supply of entitled food grains or meals.

NATIONAL RURAL HEALTH MISSION (NRHM)

The national rural health mission (NRHM) was launched on 12 April 2005. It provides accessible, affordable and quality healthcare to the rural population, especially the most vulnerable groups. Special focus is given to the North Eastern states, Jammu & Kashmir, Himachal Pradesh, and the eight socio-economically backward states (Empowered Action Group or EAG states), which include Bihar, Chhattisgarh, Jharkhand, Madhya Pradesh, Orissa, Rajasthan, Uttaranchal, and Uttar Pradesh.

Objectives of NRHM

1. Reduction in infant morality rate and maternal mortality rate.
2. Ensuring population stabilisation.
3. Prevention and control of communicable and non-communicable diseases.
4. Upgrading and advocating AYUSH, Ayurveda, Yoga and Naturopathy, Unani, Siddha and Homoeopathy, for fostering a healthy lifestyle.

The National Health Mission (NHM) was launched by the government in 2013, subsuming the National Rural Health Mission (2005) and the National Urban Health Mission (2013).

Major Initiatives under NHM

- Janani Shishu Suraksha Karyakram (FSSK) 2011

- Rashtriya Bal Swasthya Karyakram (RBSK)
- Free drugs and free diagnostics service initiative
- PM National Dialysis Programme
- National Mobile Medical Units (NMMUs) and tele-consultation services
- Ayushman Bharat
- Pradhan Mantri Jan Arogya Yojana (PMJAY)
- Kayakalp, an initiative for awarding recognition to public health facilities
- National Quality Assurance Framework for health facilities
- National Ambulance Service (NAS)

MAHATMA GANDHI NATIONAL RURAL EMPLOYMENT GUARANTEE ACT

The National Rural Employment Guarantee Act (NREGA), 2005, is considered a milestone in the history of rural development in India. It was brought into force in 2006. The law was initially called NREGA but was renamed Mahatma Gandhi National Rural Employment Guarantee Act (MGNREGA) on 2 October 2009. The MNREGA was launched on 2 February 2006 from Anantapur in Andhra Pradesh, and initially covered 200 of the country's poorest districts. It covers 741 districts of India, barring only those with 100% urban populations. The Mahatma Gandhi National Rural Employment Guarantee Act (MGNREGA) is the foundation for the Mahatma Gandhi National Rural Employment Guarantee Scheme (MGNREGS) that provides guaranteed employment to the rural populace.

Objectives of MGNREGA

1. Providing not less than 100 days of unskilled manual work as a guaranteed employment in a financial year to every household in rural areas as per demand, resulting in the creation of productive assets of prescribed quality and durability.
2. Boost economic security, stability and productivity.
3. Help reduce mass migration of labour from rural to urban areas.
4. Eradicate poverty from large pockets of rural India.
5. Provide for additional 50 days of unskilled wage employment in drought/natural calamity notified rural areas.
6. Strengthening the livelihood resource base of the poor.
7. Proactively ensuring social inclusion.
8. Deepening democracy at the grassroots by strengthening Panchayati Raj Institutions.
9. Social protection and livelihood security for the most vulnerable people living in rural India by guaranteeing wage employment.
10. Rejuvenate the natural resource base of rural areas and create a durable and productive rural asset base.
11. Empower the socially disadvantaged, especially women, Scheduled Castes (SCs) and Scheduled Tribes (STs), through the processes of a rights-based legislation.
12. Strengthen decentralised, participatory planning through convergence of various anti-poverty and livelihoods initiatives.

RIGHT TO EDUCATION

The right to education serves as a building block to ensure that every child has the right to get a quality elementary education. The 86th Amendment to the Constitution of India in 2002 provides the Right to Education as a fundamental right in Part-III, Article 21A. The Right of Children to Free and Compulsory Education Act or the Right to Education Act (RTE) was enacted by the Parliament on 4 August 2009. India became one of 135 countries to make education a fundamental right of every child when the RTE Act came into force on 1 April 2010.

1. The RTE Act 2009 mandates the provision of primary education to all children

aged 6–14 years, reinforcing education as a fundamental right assured under Article 21A.
2. The Act specifies minimum norms in elementary schools, and mandates all private schools to reserve 25 per cent seats for children of disadvantaged sections (to be reimbursed by the state as part of the public-private partnership plan).
3. It describes the importance of free and compulsory education for all children between 6 and 14 in India under Article 21a of the Indian Constitution.
4. It prohibits all unrecognised schools, and makes provisions for no donation or capitation fees and no interview of the child or parent for admission.
5. It states that no child shall be held back, expelled, or required to pass a board examination until completion of elementary education.
6. It provides for special training of school drop-outs to bring them up to par with students of the same age.

The government also launched an integrated scheme for school education named **Samagra Shiksha Abhiyan** which combines three programmes of school education:

- Sarva Shiksha Abhiyan (SSA)
- Rashtriya Madhyamik Shiksha Abhiyan (RMSA)
- Centrally Sponsored Scheme on Teacher Education (CSSTE)

MONITORING AND EVALUATION OF PUBLIC POLICY: MECHANISMS OF MAKING THE GOVERNANCE PROCESS ACCOUNTABLE

Jansunwai

Jansunwai is a democratic way of familiarising the local people with government policies and the activities of the local public authorities so that they can understand what the government is doing towards the development of their communities. The practice of jansunwai as an instrument of grassroots social audit can be dated back to the pre-independence era and it has been widely appreciated as a democratic means of bolstering people's participation. It has evolved as a participatory practice of implementation of a scheme or programme, and as a method of social accountability that compels authorities to realise their public responsibility.

In the mid-1990s the Mazdoor Kisan Shakti Sangathan (MKSS) experimented with village-based Jan Sunwais (literally, public hearings) on development expenditure in a Jansunwai campaign, organised in five different development blocks of central Rajasthan. The local residents learnt a lot through public readings of informally accessed development records and documents. As the names were read out from the government labour lists, it had a dramatic effect and the responses were immediate and this exercise galvanised the people.

Social Audit

Social audit is a legally mandated process where potential and existing beneficiaries evaluate the social and ethical performance of a programme through a comparison of official records and actual ground realities. It aims to measure the impact of an entity's activities on society, including its stakeholders and the community at large. The primary objective of a social audit is to ensure accountability, transparency and responsible behaviour. During a social audit, various aspects of the entity's social performance are examined, such as labour practices, human rights, environmental impact, community development, and governance. The audit process involves collecting data, conducting interviews, engaging with stakeholders, and analysing the information to form an objective evaluation.

Benefits of Social Audit

1. Boosts participatory democracy.
2. Enhances transparency and accountability, promotes responsible and sustainable practices.
3. Deters corruption by bringing the guilty to law.
4. Aids recovery of misappropriated funds and resources and ensures their appropriate and targeted usage.
5. Ensures smooth implementation of social welfare programmes.
6. Enables identification of issues and potential risks, leading to better performance and reputation.
7. Helps identify areas where positive social contributions can be enhanced and aligned with the needs and expectations of stakeholders.
8. Creates a wider circle of beneficiaries.

Challenges to Social Audit

1. Lack of proper institutional mechanisms for implementation.
2. Social audits rely heavily on data, but gathering accurate and reliable data on social impacts can be challenging.
3. Lack of administrative and political will to act at the ground level.
4. Social impacts are difficult to quantify, and different stakeholders may have diverse perspectives on what constitutes positive or negative outcomes.
5. Unlike financial audits, social audits lack universally recognised frameworks and metrics.
6. Social audit units often lack access to official documents for verification.
7. Social audits can be resource-intensive in terms of time, expertise and finances.

Despite these challenges and disadvantages, social audits remain valuable and essential tools for promoting transparency and accountability. By continuously addressing these challenges, social audits can evolve to become more effective and influential in driving positive social change.

SELECT BIBLIOGRAPHY

Adams, Raymond, *Studies in Philology* (1945).

Amsden, Alice H., *The Rise of the 'Rest': Challenges to the West from Late-Industrializing Countries* (2001).

Arendt, Hannah, *The Origins of Totalitarianism* (1951).

———. *The Human Condition* (1958).

———. *On Violence* (1970).

Arneil, Barbara, *Politics and Feminism* (1999).

Arora, Balveer and Douglas V. Verney, *Multiple Identities in a Single State: Indian Federalism in Comparative Perspective.*

Austin, Granville S., *The Indian Constitution: Cornerstone of a Nation* (1996).

———. *The Supreme Court and the Struggle for Custody of the Constitution* (2004).

Bardhan, Pranab, *The Political Economy of Development In India* (1984).

Barry, Brian, *Theories of Justice,* (1989)

———. *Culture and Equality: An Egalitarian Critique of Multuiculturalism* (2001).

Baruah, Sanjib, *Durable Disorder: Understanding the Politics of North-East India* (2005).

Baxi, Upendra, *The Avatars of Indian Judicial Activism: Exploration in the Geographies of (In). Justice* (2003).

———. *Courage, Craft and Contention: The Indian Supreme Court in the Eighties* (1985).

———. *Taking Suffering Seriously: Social Action Litigation* (1987).

Bell, D., *A Communitarian Critique of Authoritarianism* (1995).

Bell, Denial, *The End of Ideology* (1960).

———. *The Coming of Post-Industrial Society* (1973).

———. *The Cultural Contradictions of Capitalism* (1976).

Berlin, Isaiah, *Four Essays on Liberty* (1969).

———. *Freedom and its Betrayal* (2002).

Bhagwati, P. N., *Social Action Litigation: The Indian Experience* (1987).

Bhargava, Rajeev, *What is Political Theory and Why Do We Need It?* (2010).

Bhatnagar, S. C., *E-governance: Opportunities and Challenges,* (1999).

Bhushan, Prashant, *Public Interest Litigation: Supreme Court in the Era of Liberalization* (2007).

Blechman, Barry & Stephen Kaplan, *Force without War* (1978).

Bottomore, T. B., *Elites and Society* (1964).

Braudel, Fernand, *The Identity of France* (1990).

Brecher, M., *Nehru: A Political Biography* (1959).

———. *Political Succession in India* (1966).

Buchanan, J. M., *The Limits of Liberty: Between Anarchy and Leviathan* (1975).

Calhoun, C., *Social Theory and the Political of Identity* (1994).

———. *New Social Movement of the Early Nineteenth Century,* (1993).

Caney, S., *Liberalism and Communitarianism: A Misconceived Debate* (1992).
Carson, Rachel, *Silent Spring* (1965),
Chopra, Vir K., *The Mirage of Good Governance* (1996).
Cohen, Elizabeth, *Semi-citizenship in Democratic Politics* (2009).
Cohen, Joshua, Howard Matthew, and Martha C. Nussbaum, *Is Multiculturalis Bad for Women?* (1999).
Dasgupta, P., *An Enquiry into Well-Being and Destitution* (1993).
de Beauvoir, Simone, *The Second Sex* (1949).
Derrida, J., *Writing and Difference* (1978).
Dhawan, Rajeev, *Governance by Judiciary: Into the Next Millennium* (2007).
Dobson, Andrew, *Ecological Politics in the Age of Risk* (1995)
———. *Green Political Thought* (1995).
———. *Justice and the Environment: Conceptions of Environmental Sustainability and Theories of Distributive Justice* (1998).
Douglas, Eugene Smith, *India as a Secular State* (1963).
Dreze, J., & Amartya K. Sen, *India: Economic Development and Social Opportunity* (2002).
Dunn, John, *Modern Revolutions: An Introduction to the Analysis of a Political Phenomenon* (1989).
Dworkin, Ronald, *Taking Rights Seriously* (1977)
———. *Sovereign Virtue: The Theory and Practice of Equality* (2000).
———. 'Equality, Luck and Hierarchy', *Philosophy and Public Affairs*, vol. 31, no. 2 (2003): 190–98.
Easton, David, *An Analysis of Political Structure* (1990).
Eulau, Heinz, *Behaviouralism in Political Science* (1969).
Evans, Tony. *Prospects for Democracy: North, South, East, West,* (1993).
Fernandes, *Leela, India's New Middle Class: Democratic Politics in an Era of Economic Reform* (2006).
Foucault, Michel, *The History of Sexuality: An Introduction* (1978).
Francis, Fukuyama, *Social Capital and Civil Society* (1999).
Frank, Andre Gunder, *Capitalism and Underdevelopment in Latin America: Historical Studies in Chile and Brazil* (1967).
Frazer, E., *The Problems of Communitarian Politics* (1999).
Friedman, T., *The Lexus and the Olive Tree* (1999).
Gallaher, Carolyn, et al., *Key Concepts in Political Geography* (2009).
Gandhi, M. K., *Hind Swaraj and Other Writings* (1909).
Ghali, Boutros, *An Agenda for Peace* (1992).
Gidden, Anthony, *A Contemporary Critique of Historical Materialism* (1981).
———. *Modernity and Self-identity: Self and Society in the Late Modern Age* (1991).
Gilpin, Robert, *U.S. Power and the Multinational Corporation: The Political Economy* (1975).
— —. *War and Change in World Politics*, (1981).
Goldmann, Kjell, *Transforming the European Nation-State: Dynamics of Internationalisation* (2001).
Goldsmith, Edward, *A Blueprint for Survival* (1972).
Goldstein, Joshua S., *Long Cycles: Prosperity and War in the Modern Age* (1988).
Goldstone, A. Jack, 'Theories of Revolution: The Third Generation', *World Politics* vol. 32, no. 3 (1980): 425–453.
———. *Revolution and Rebellion in the Early Modern World* (1991).
Goodwin, Jeff, 'Explaining Revolutions in the Contemporary Third World'. In *Social Revolutions in the Modern World*, edited by Theda Skocpol (1994).

Gordon, Lincoln, 'Libertarianism at Bay', *The American Economic Review*, vol. 39 no. 5 (1949): 976–978.
Gramsci, A. *Selections from the Prison Notebooks* (1971).
Green, T. H., *Lectures on Principle of Political Obligation* (1986).
Guha, Ramchandra, *India after Gandhi: The History of the World's Largest Democracy* (2007).
Hayek, F. A., *The Road to Serfdom* (1944).
Haywood, *Andrew, Political Theory* (2009).
Hekman, Susan J., *Gender and Knowledge: Elements of a Postmodern Feminism* (1990)
———. *Identity Crises: Identity, Identity Politics, and Beyond,* (1999).
Held, David, *Democracy and Global Order: From the Modern State to Cosmopolitan Governance,* (1995).
———. *Political Theory and the Modern State* (1998).
Held, David and A. McGrew, *Globalization/Anti-globalization* (2002).
Hobsbawm, Eric, *Globalization, Democracy and Terrorism* (2007).
———. *On Empire* (2008).
Hollinger, David, *Post-ethnic America: Beyond Multiculturalism* (1995).
Huntington, P. Samuel, *Political Order in Changing Societies* (1968).
Ikenberry, G. John, *What States Can Do Now,* (2003).
———. *Indian Federalism in a Comparative Perspective,* (1995).
———. *Indian Politics* (2003).
Jaffrelot, Christophe, *India's Silent Revolution: The Rise of Low Castes on North* (1957).
Jonathan Kirshner, *Currency and Coercion: The Political Economy of International Monetary Power* (1995).
Jones-Morris, W. H., *Politics Mainly Indian* (1964).
———. *Government and Politics of India* (1964).
Joseph, Sarah, *Political Theory and Power* (1988).
Jurgen, Habermas, *The Inclusion of the Other: Studies in Political Theory* (1998).
Kaplan, E. Ann & Michael Sprinker, *The Althusserian Legacy* (1993).
Keane, John, *Reflections on Violence* (1996).
Kennedy, Paul, *The Rise and Fall of the Great Powers: Economic Change and Military Conflict from 1500 to 2000* (1987).
Khan, Rasheeduddin, *Federal India: A Design for Change* (1992).
Kindleberger, Charles P., *The World in Depression* (1973).
Knorr, Klaus, *The War Potential of Nations* (1956).
Kochanek, Stanley, *The Congress Party of India: The Dynamics of One-Party Democracy* (1968).
Kohli, Atul, *The Success of India's Democracy* (2001).
Kothari, Rajni, 'Congress System in India', *Asian Survey*, vol. 4, no. 12 (1974): 1161–73.
Kuhn, Thomas S., *The Structure of Scientific Revolutions* (1970).
Kumar, Niraj, *The Role of the State in Development Process: A Study of the South Korean Experience* (2004).
Kymlicka, W., *Multicultural Citizenship: A Liberal Theory of Minority Rights* (1995).
Lasswell, Harold & Abraham Kaplan, *Power and Society* (1950).
Lazar, Harvey, Hamish Telford, and Ronald L. Watts. *The Impact of Global and Regional Integration on Federal Systems: A Comparative Analysis* (2003).
Levi-Strauss, Claude, *The Raw and the Cooked* (1969).
Lipset, Seymour Martin, *Political Man* (1963).
MacIntyre, A, *After Virtue* (1984).
———. *Whose Justice? Which Rationality?* (1988).

Majeed, Akhtar, *Federalism within the Union: Distribution of Responsibilities in the Indian System* (2004).

Malick, Rose, *Development Policy of a Communist Government: West Bengal since 1977* (1993).

Marshall, T. H., *Citizenship and Social Class and Other Essays* (1950).

———. *Sociology at a Crossroads and other Essays* (1963).

———. *The Right to Welfare and Other Essays*, (1981).

Mason, Andrew, *Ideals of Equality* (1998).

Mastanduno, Michael, *System Maker, Privilege Taker* (2009).

Matthew, Kramer, *Rights, Wrongs and Responsibilities* (2001).

Miller, Arthur, *Political Issues and Trust in Government: 1964–1970* (1974).

Miller, David and Micheal Walzer, *Pluralism, Justice, and Equality* (1995).

Miller, David, *The Blackwell Encyclopedia of Political Thought* (1987).

Millett, Kate, *Sexual Politics* (1970).

Mills, C. W., *The Power Elite* (1956).

Misra, B. B., *The Indian Middle Classes: Their Growth in Modern Time* (1961).

Nanda, B. R., *The Nehrus: Motilal and Jawaharlal* (1962).

Narayan, Jayaprakash, *Towards Total Revolution* (1978).

Norris, Christopher, *Deconstruction: Theory and Practice*, (1982).

———. *Deconstruction and the Interests of Theory* (1988).

Oakeshott, M., *Introduction to Hobbes* (1946).

Ole R. Holsti, Randolph M. Siverson, and Alexander L. George, *Change in the International System* (1980).

Otsuka, Michael, *Libertarianism without Inequality* (2003).

Palmer, Norman D., *Elections and Political Development: The South Asian Experience* (1975).

Pateman, Carole, *Participation and Democratic Theory*, (1976)

———. *The Problem of Political Obligation: A Critical Analysis of Liberal Theory* (1985)

———. *The Sexual Contract* (1988).

Poultantzas, N., *State, Power and Socialism* (1978).

Pyle, M. V., *Constitutional Amendment in India* (2003).

Quentin Skinner, *The Foundations of Modern Political Thought* (1978)

———. *Machiavelli on the Maintenance of Liberty* (1983).

———. *The Idea of Negative Liberty* (1984).

———. *The Paradoxes of Political Liberty* (1985).

———. *Thomas Hobbes on the Proper Signification of Liberty* (1990).

Raphael, D. D., *Problems in Political Philosophy* (1970).

Rawls, John, *A Theory of Justice* (1971).

———. *Political Liberalism* (1996).

Raz, Joseph, *The Authority of Law* (1979).

———. *The Morality of Freedom* (1986).

Robert Heilbroner, *An Inquiry into the Human Prospect* (1974).

Roche, M., *Rethinking Citizenship* (1992).

Rod, Aya, 'Theories of Revolution Reconsidered: Contrasting Models of Collective Violence', *Theory and Society*, vol. 8 (1979).

Sandel, Michael J. 'The Procedural Republic and the Unencumbered Self', *Political Theory*, vol. 12, no. 1 (1984): 81–96.

———. 'Moral Argument and Liberal Toleration: Abortion and Homosexuality', *California Law Review* (1989).
———. *Liberalism and the Limits of Justice* (1982).
———. *Democracy's Discontent: America in Search of a Public Philosophy* (1996).
———. 'Liberalism and Republicanism: Friends or Foes? A Reply to Richard Dagger' (1999).
Sartory, Giovanni, *Democratic Theory* (1965).
Savarkar, V. D., *Essentials of Hindutva,Samagra Savarkar Vangmaya* (1964).
———. *Indian Wars of Independence-1857* (1970)
———. *My Transportation for Life* (1984).
Schlesinger, Arthur, Jr., *The Disuniting of America* (1991).
Schwarzmantel, John, *Ideology and Politics* (2008).
Sen, Amartya K. *Liberty, Unanimity and Rights* (1982).
———. *Choice, Welfare and Measurement* (1982).
———. *Goals, Commitment, and Identity* (1985).
———. *Inequality Reexamined* (1992).
———. *Development as Freedom* (1999).
Sen, Anupam, *The State, Industrialization and Class Formation and Institutional Change* (1982).
Sen, Sarbani, *The Constitution of India: Popular Sovereignty and Democratic Transformation* (2011).
Sibley, M., *The Political Theories of Modern Pacifism: An Analysis and Criticism* (1944).
Siddiqa-Agha, A., *Pakistan's Arms Procurement and Military Buildup, 1979–99: In Search of a Policy* (2001).
Simmons, John A., *Justification and Legitimacy: Essay on Rights and Obligations* (2001).
Singh, Jasvir, *Regulation, Institutions and the Law* (2007).
Singh, M. P., and Rekha Saxena, *Indian Politics: Contemporary Issues and Concerns* (2008).
———. *Ideologies and Institutions in India Politics* (1998).
Somit, Albert and Tanenhaus Joseph, *The Development of American Political Science: From Burgess to Behaviouralism* (1968).
Spellman, W.M., *A Concise History of the World since 1945* (2007).
Spiro, Peter J., *Beyond Citizenship: American Identity after Globalization* (2008).
Stanford Levinson, *Wrestling with Diversity* (2003).
Stanley, John, *Equality of Opportunity as Philosophy and Ideology* (1977).
Sullivan, Noel, *Political Theory in Transition* (2000).
Suzumura, Kotaro, *Alternative Approaches to Libertarian Rights in the Theory of Social Choice* (1991).
Taylor, Charles, *Philosophy and the Human Science* (1985).
———. *Sources of the Self (*1989).
———. *The Politics of Recognition* (1992).
Theda, Skocpol, *Social Revolution and Mass Military Mobilization* (1988).
———. *State and Revolution* (1979).
Theodore, L. Putterman, *Berlin's Two Concept of Liberty* (2006).
Thoreau, Henry David, *The Writings of Henry David Thoreau* (1906).
———. *Walden; or, Life in the Woods* (1854)
———. *Walden and Civil Disobedience* (1986).
———. *Civil Disobedience and Other Essays* (1993).
———. *On Duty of Civil Disobedience* (2008).
UNDP, *Governance for Sustainable Human Development* (1997).

Verba, Sidney, Norman H. Nie, and Jae-On Kim, *Participation and Political Equality: A Cross-national Comparison* (1978).

Virmani, Arvind, *China's Socialist Market Economy: Lessons for Democratic Developing Countries* (2006).

Waltz, Kenneth N., *Theory of International Politics* (1979).

Walzer, Michael, *Obligations* (1970).

———. *The Communitarian Critique of Liberalism* (1990).

———. *On Toleration,* (1997).

———. *Spheres of Justice: A Defense of Pluralism and Equality* (1983).

Weiner, Myron, *Party Politics in India: The Development of a Multi-Party System* (1957).

———. *Party-Building in a New Nation: The Indian National Congress* (1967).

Weldon, T. D., *The Vocabulary of Politics* (1953).

Wheare, K. C., *Federal Government* (1964).

White, Harrison, *Identity and Control: A Structural Theory of Social Action* (1992).

William K. Carroll, *Organising Dissent* (1992).

Young, John W. and John Kent, *International Relations since 1945* (2004).